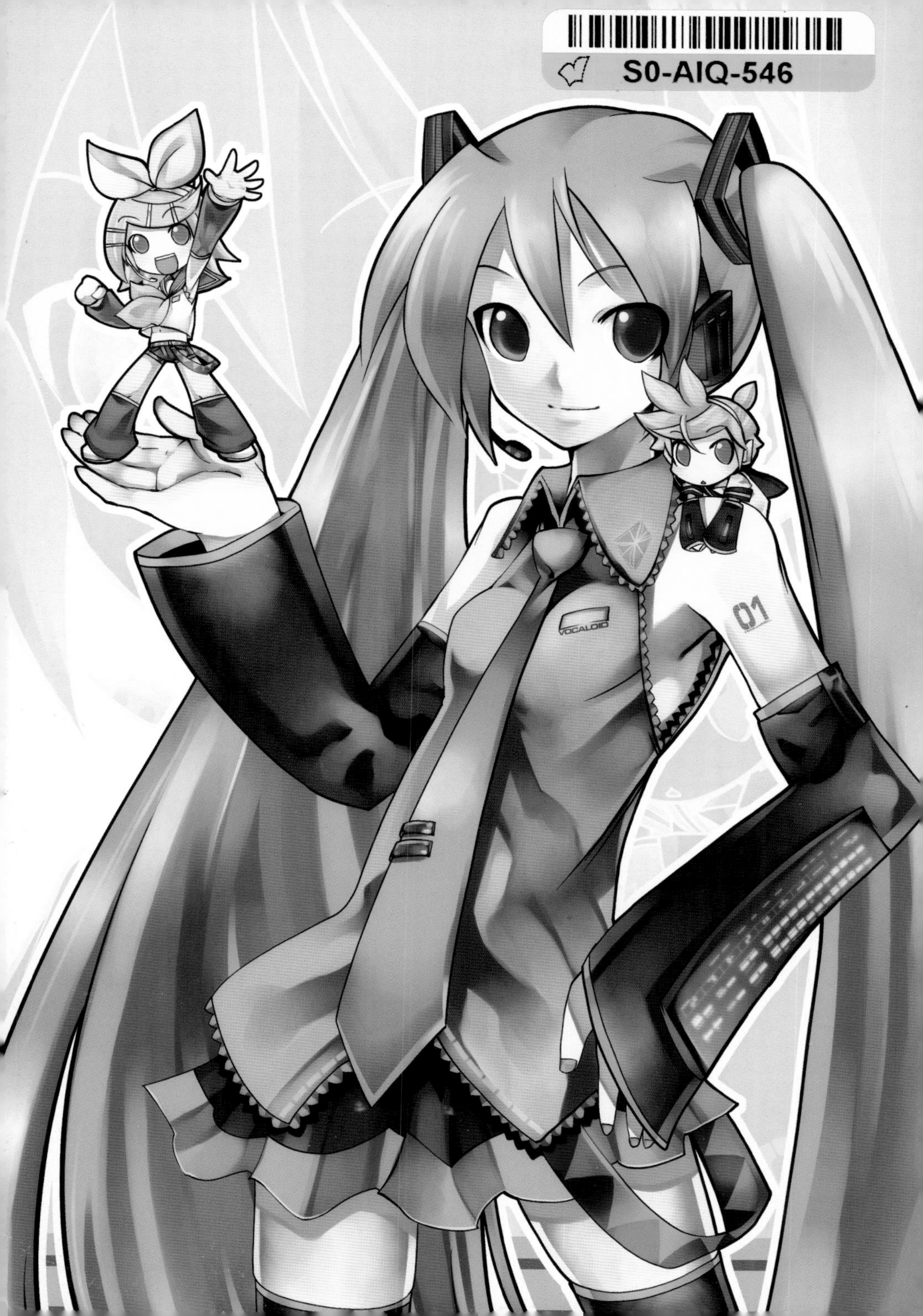

VOCALOID
01

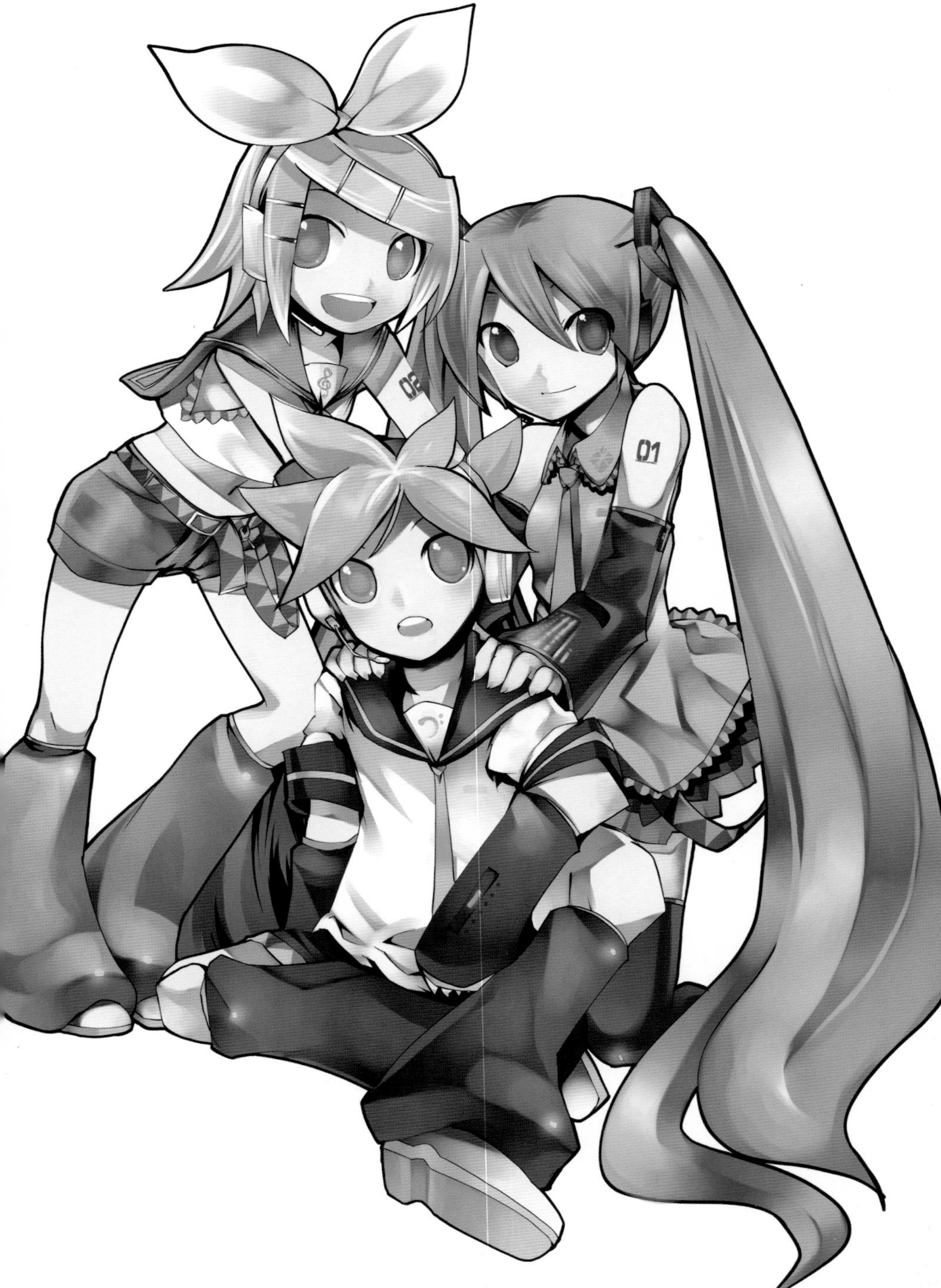
02
01

UNOFFICIAL HATSUNE MIX

STORY AND ART BY KEI

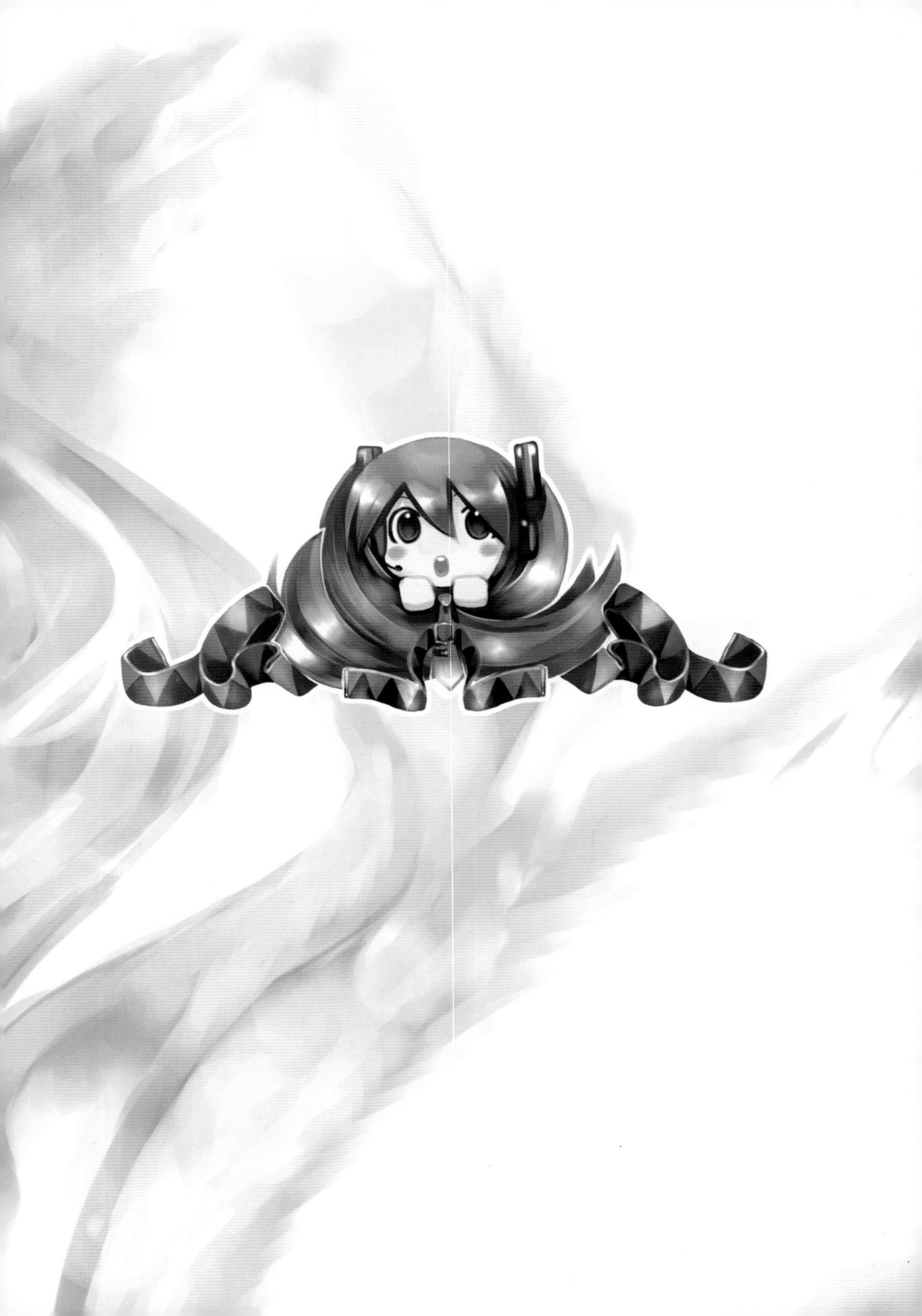

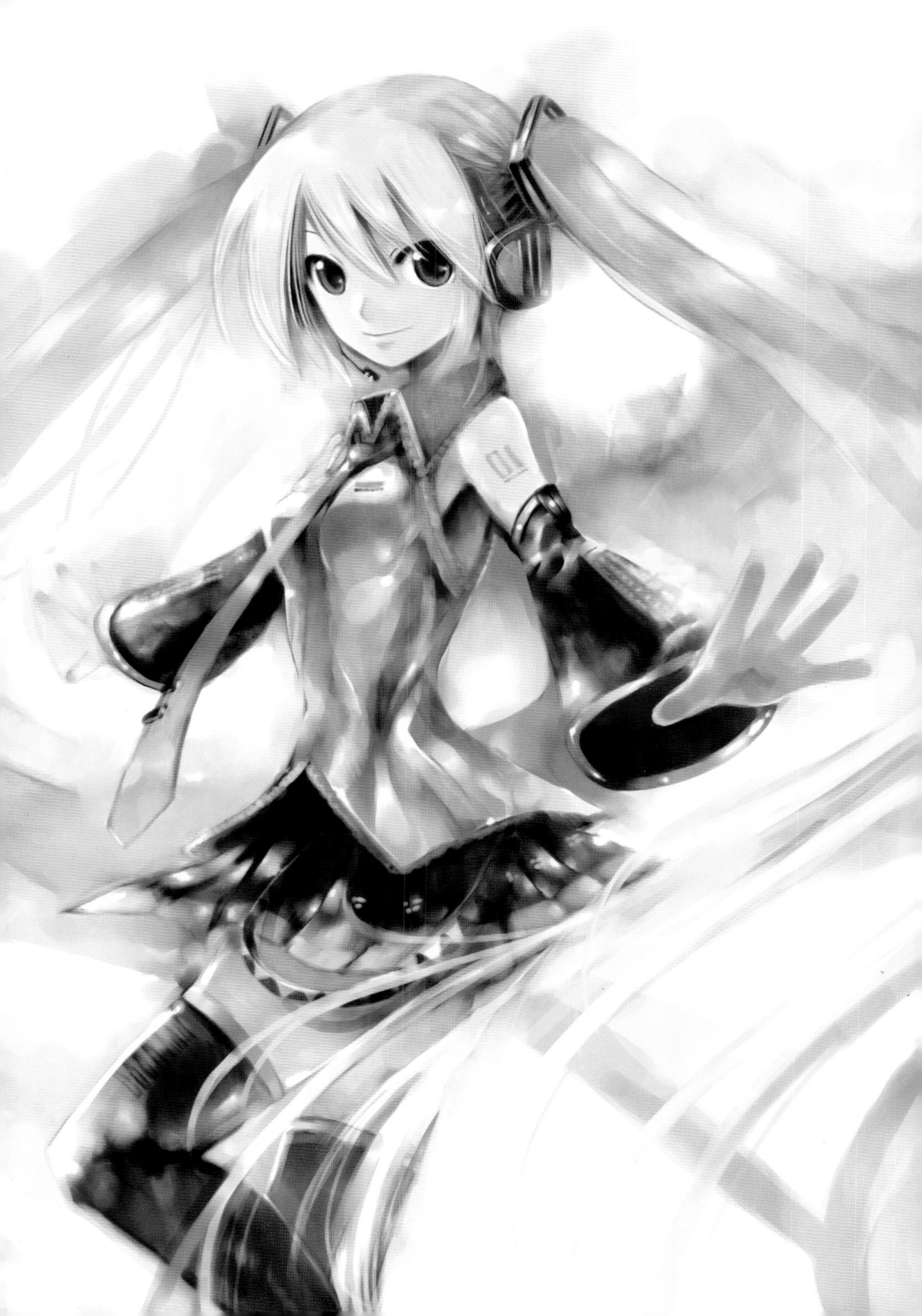

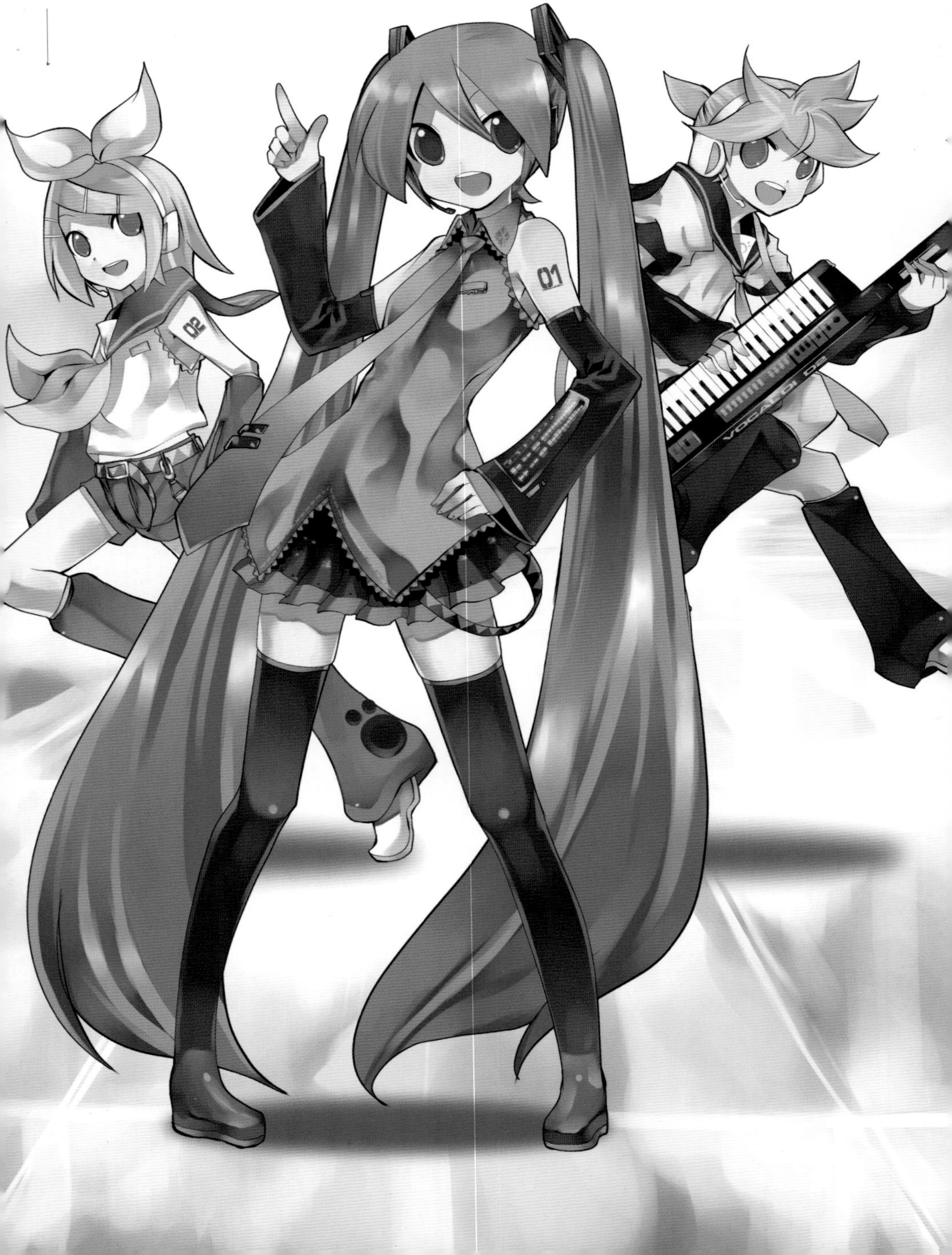
02
01

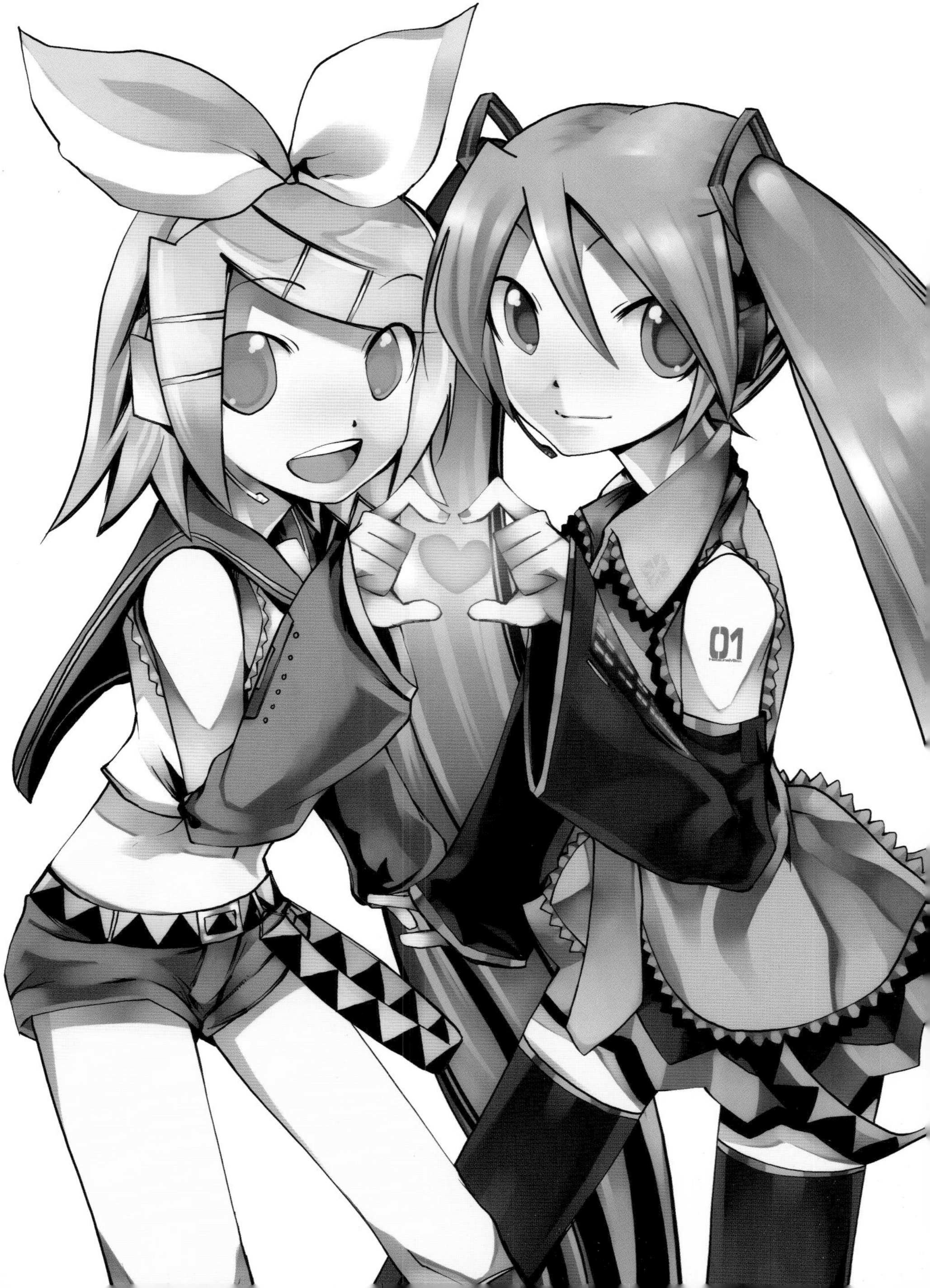
01

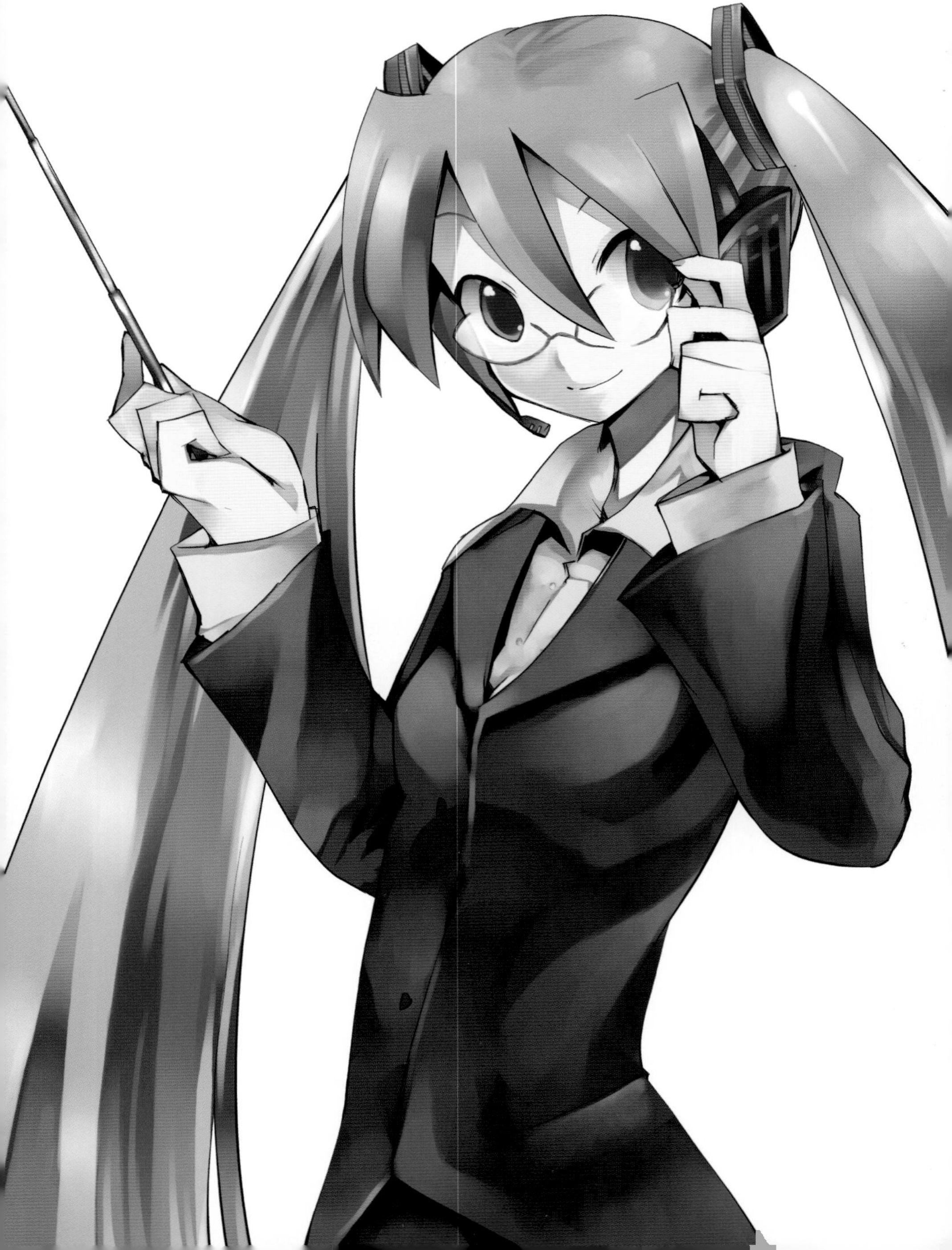

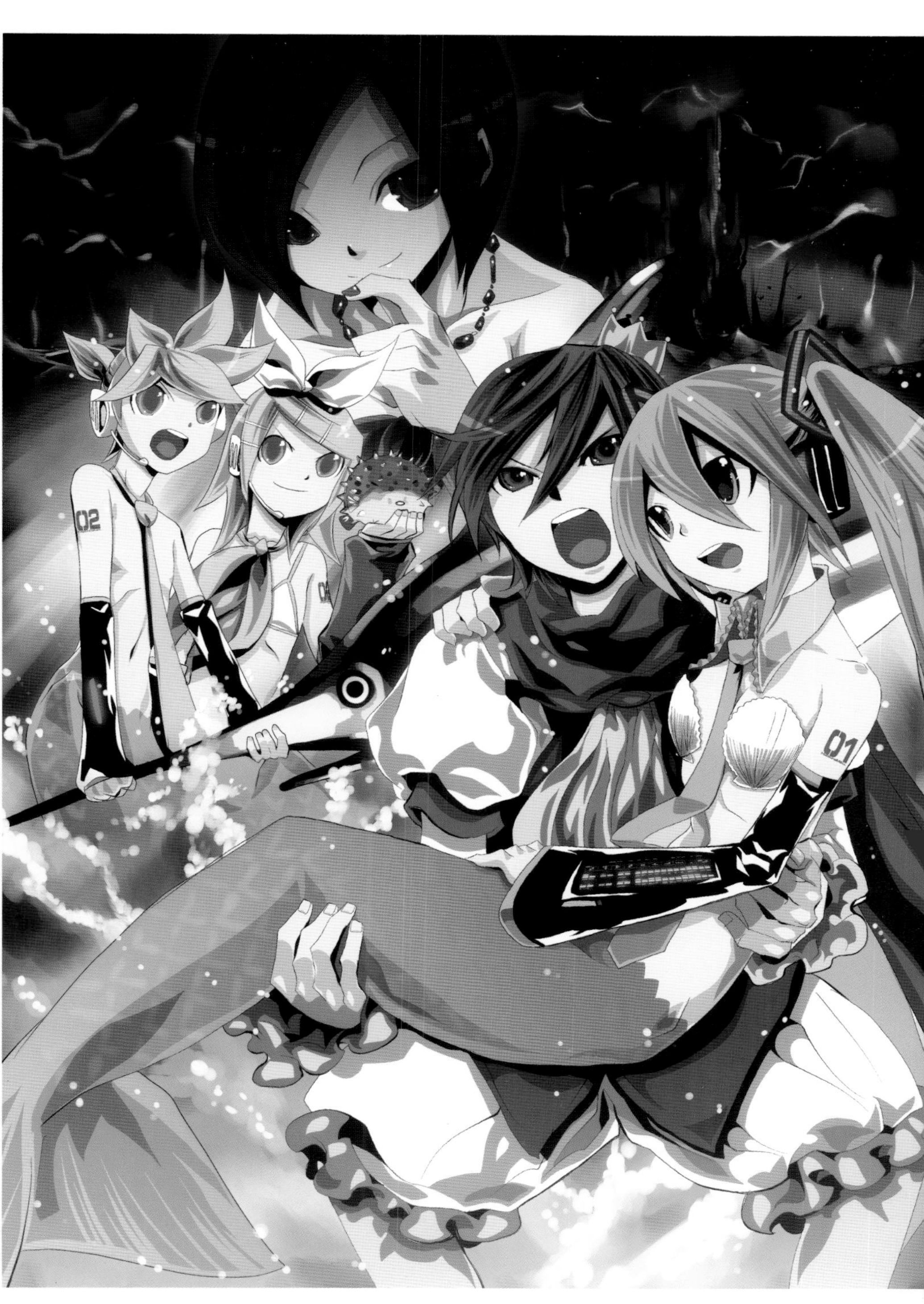
02
01

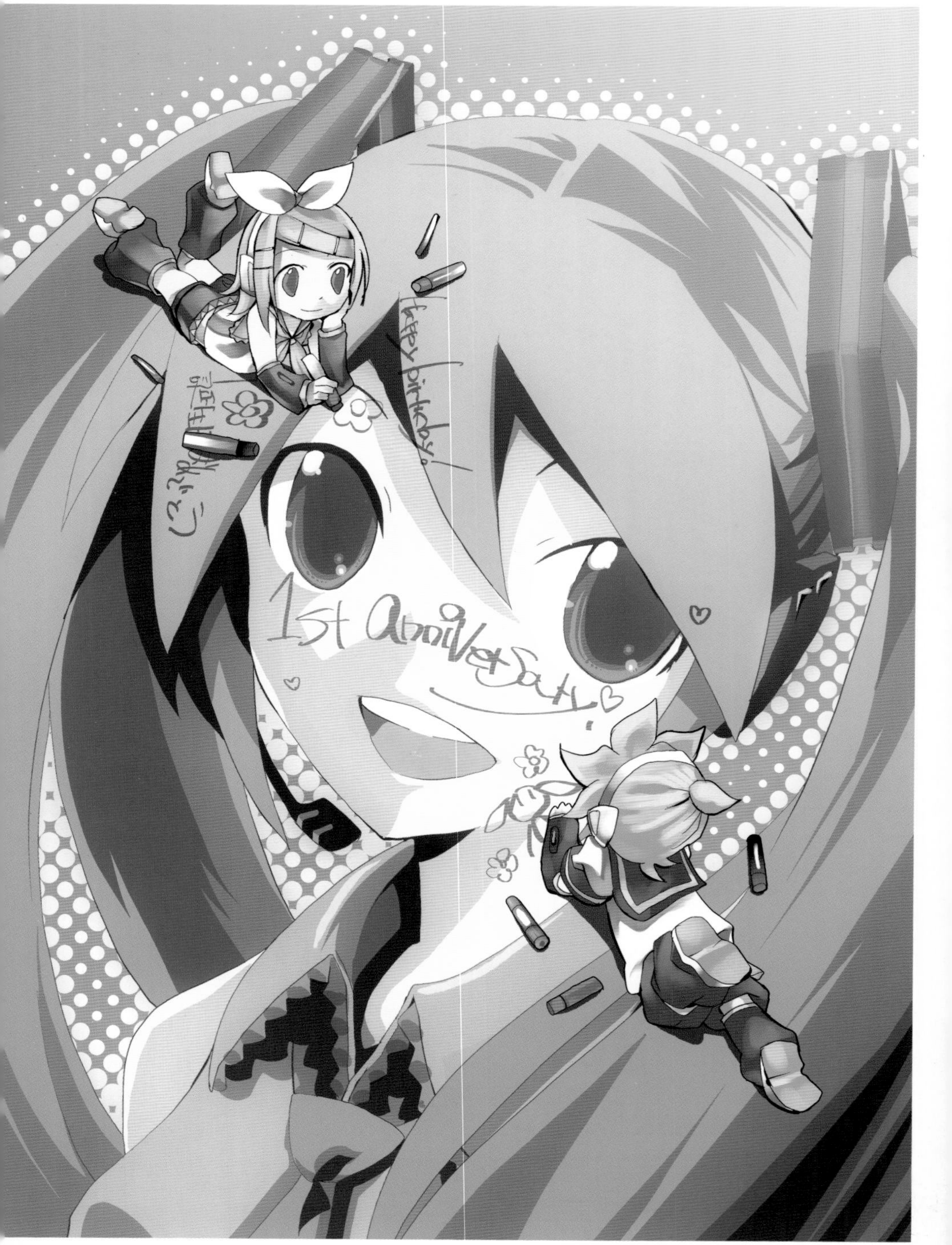
happy birthday!
1st anniversary

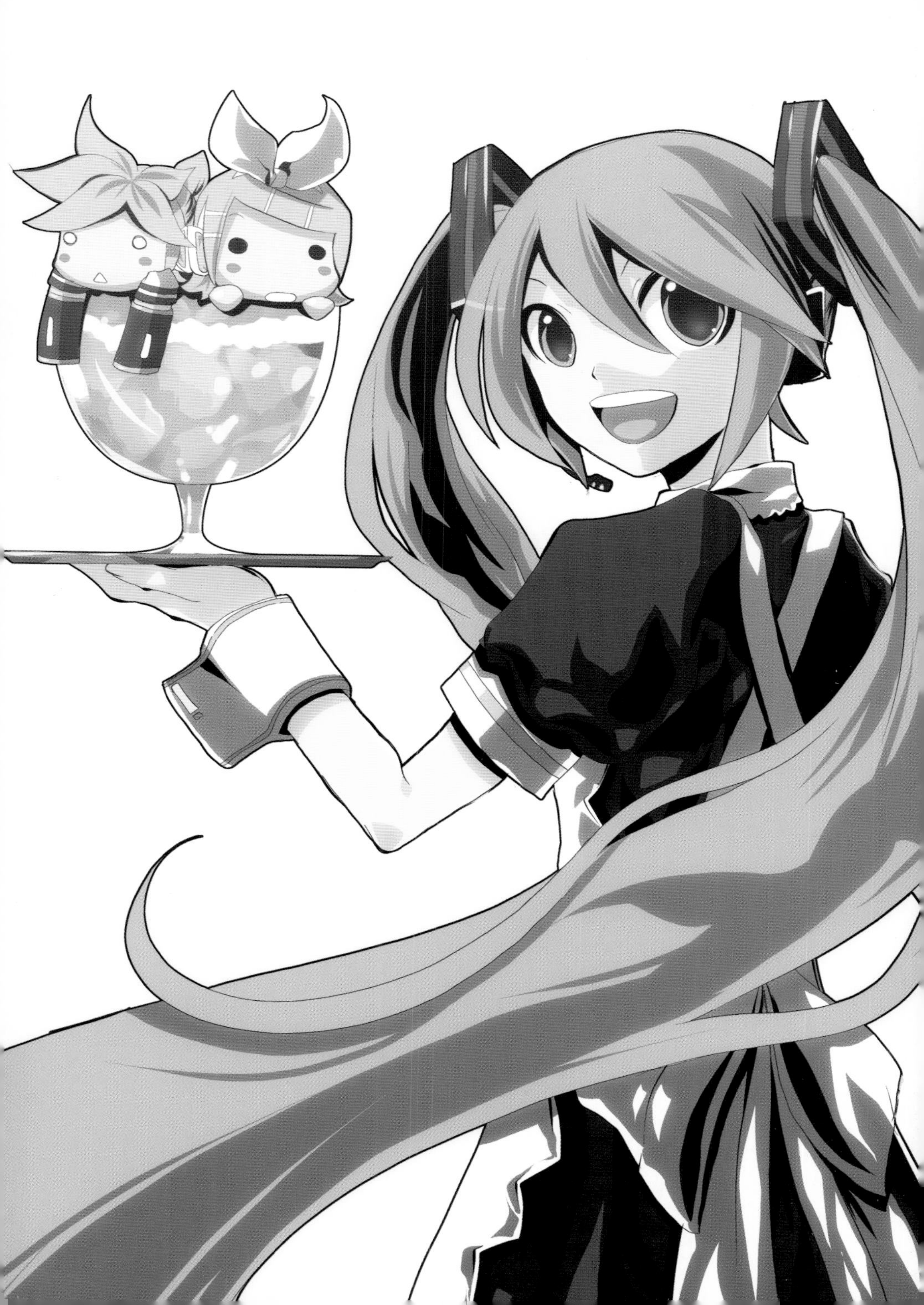

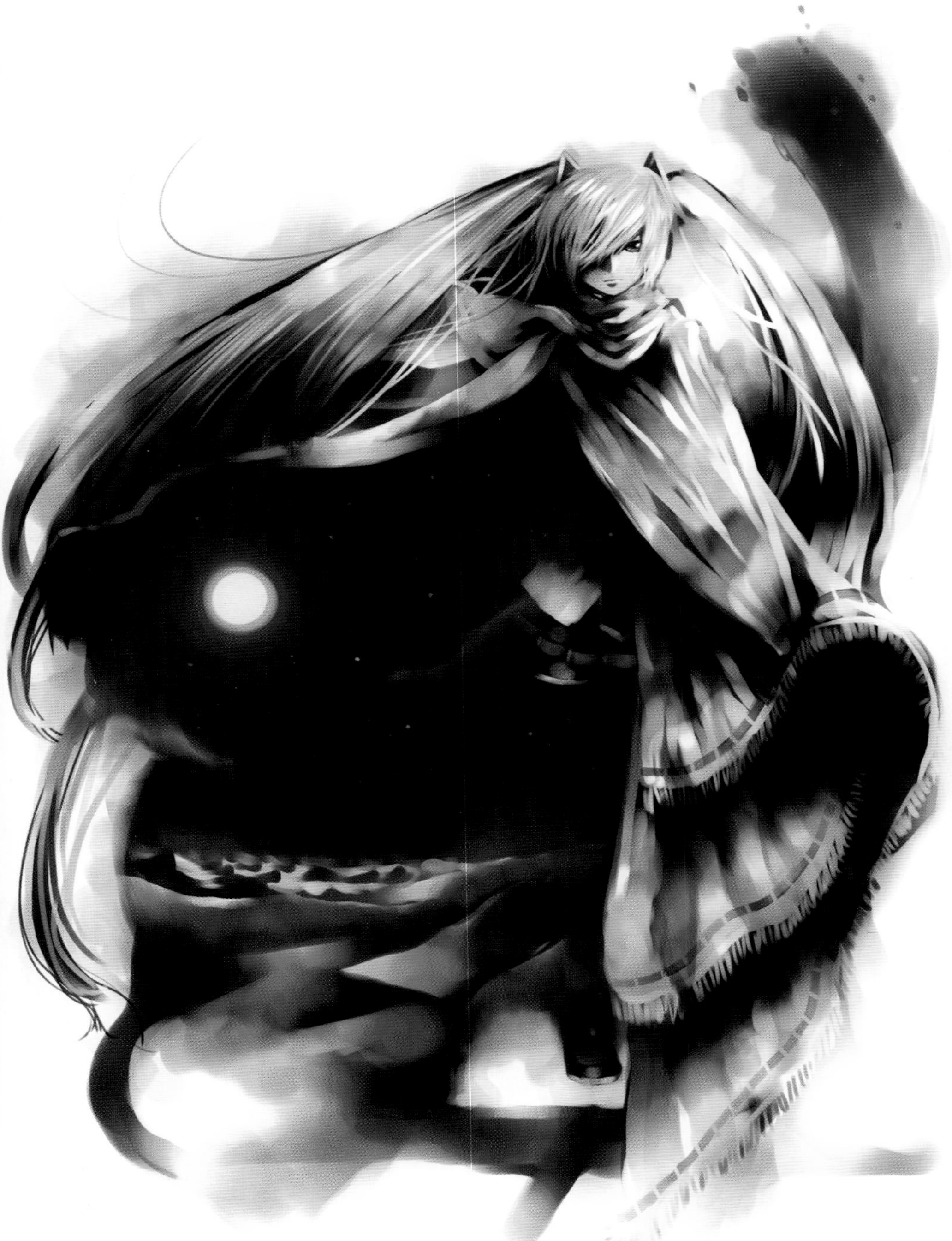

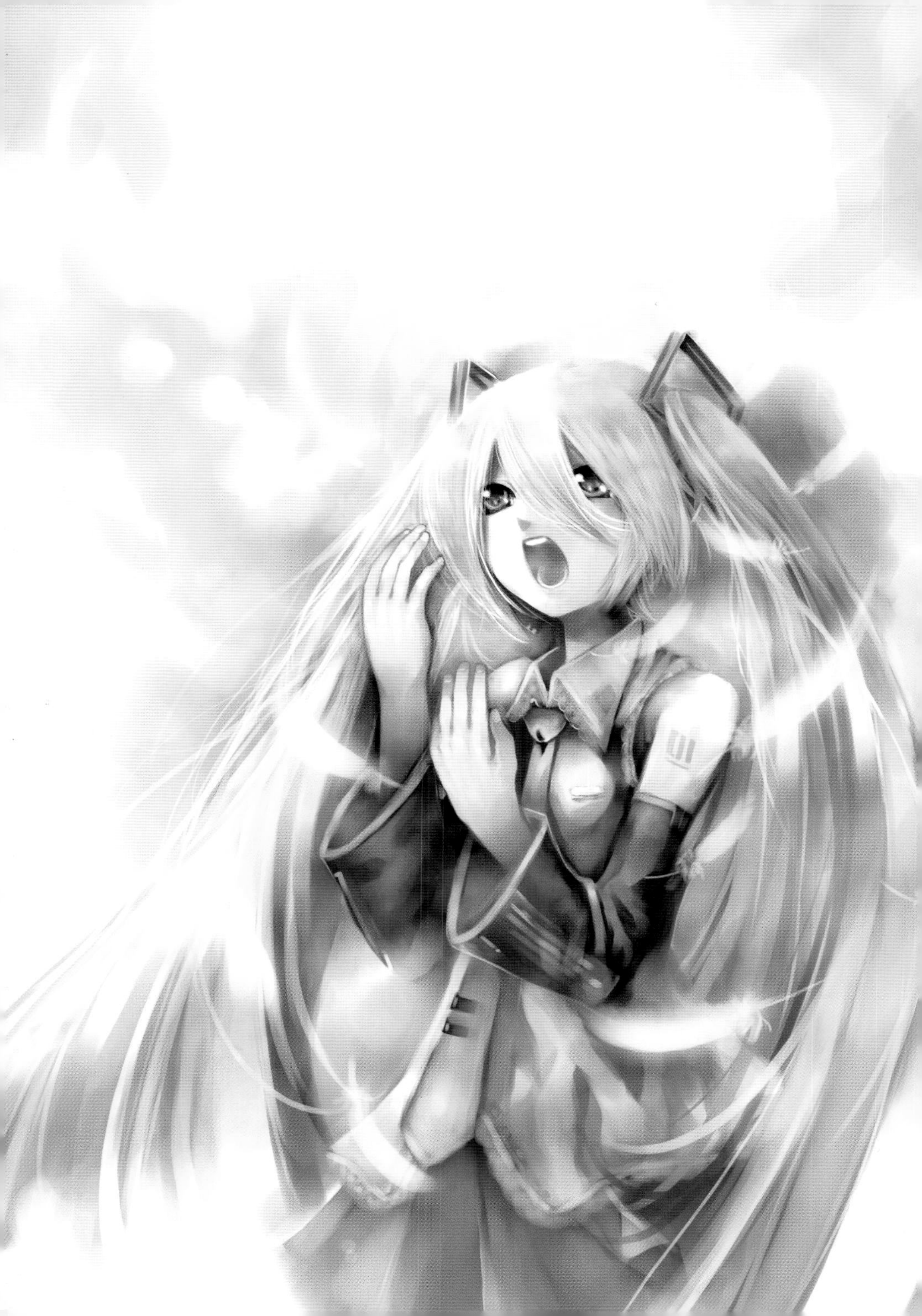

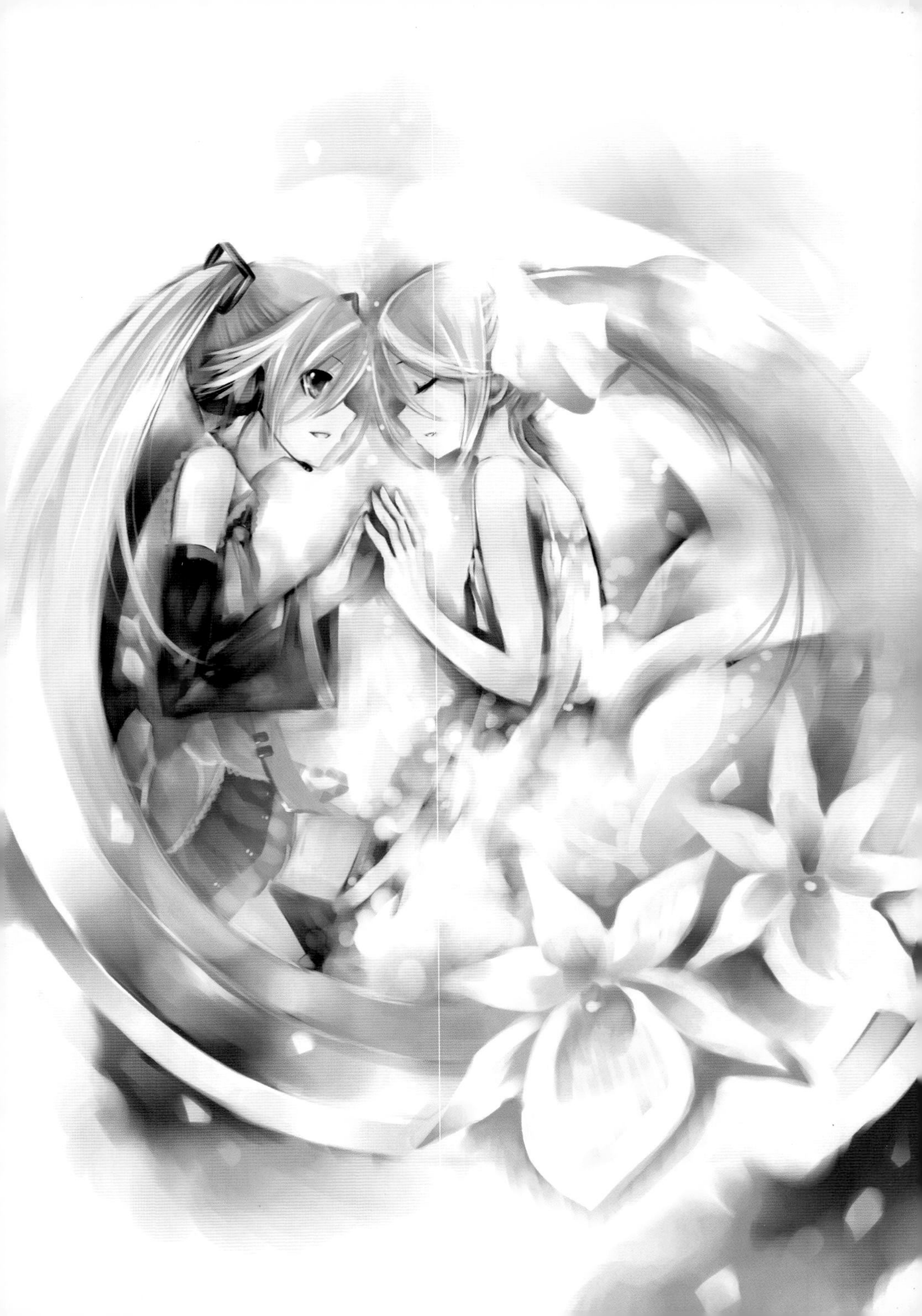

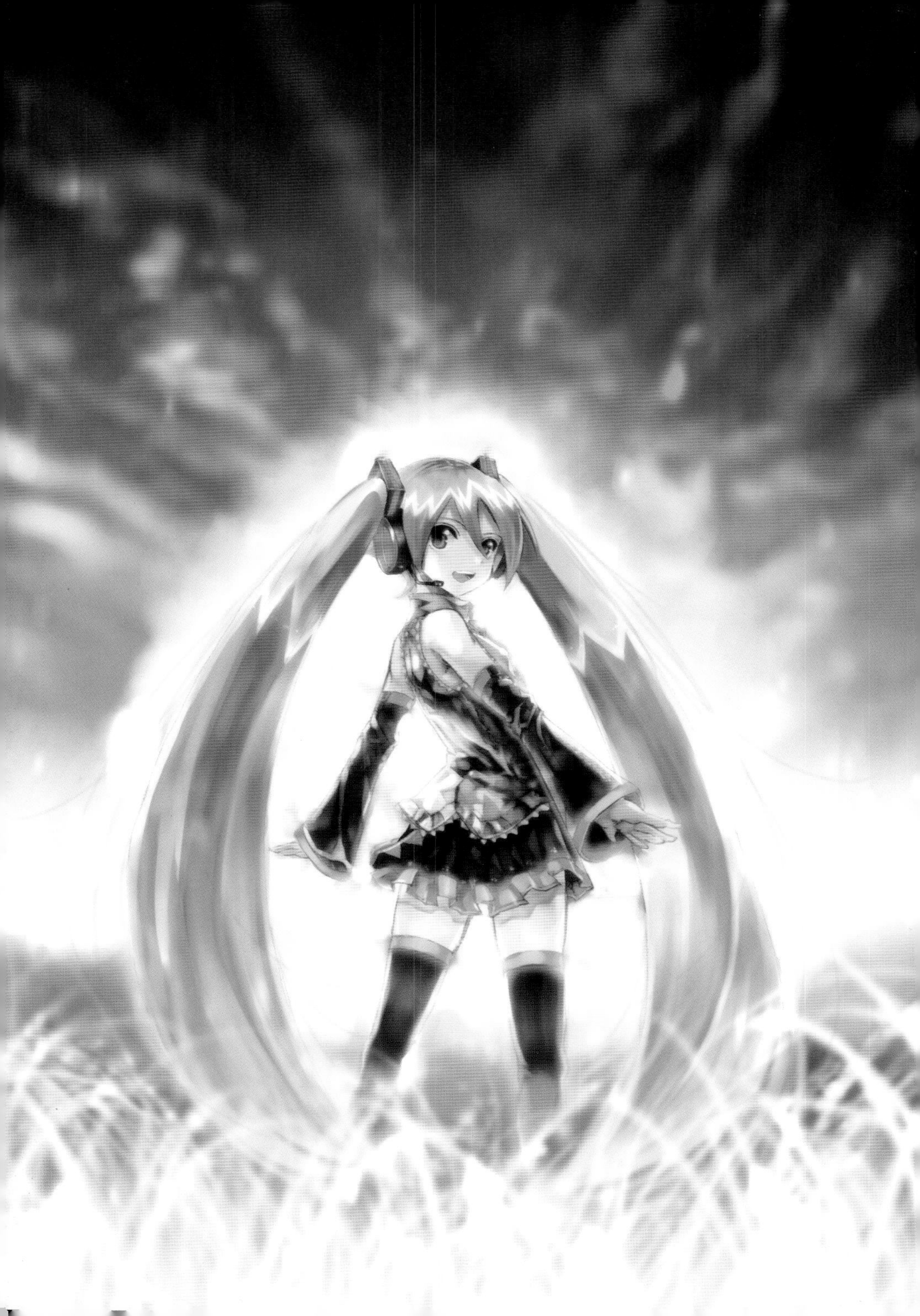

PART 1 TRACK LIST

NOTE: The terms "onee-chan" and "onee-san" get used a lot in this manga. They both mean "big sister," but don't necessarily mean the person is literally your sibling. Note too that even though Rin and Len are sometimes presented as twins, Rin gets to be the "older" one. ^_^

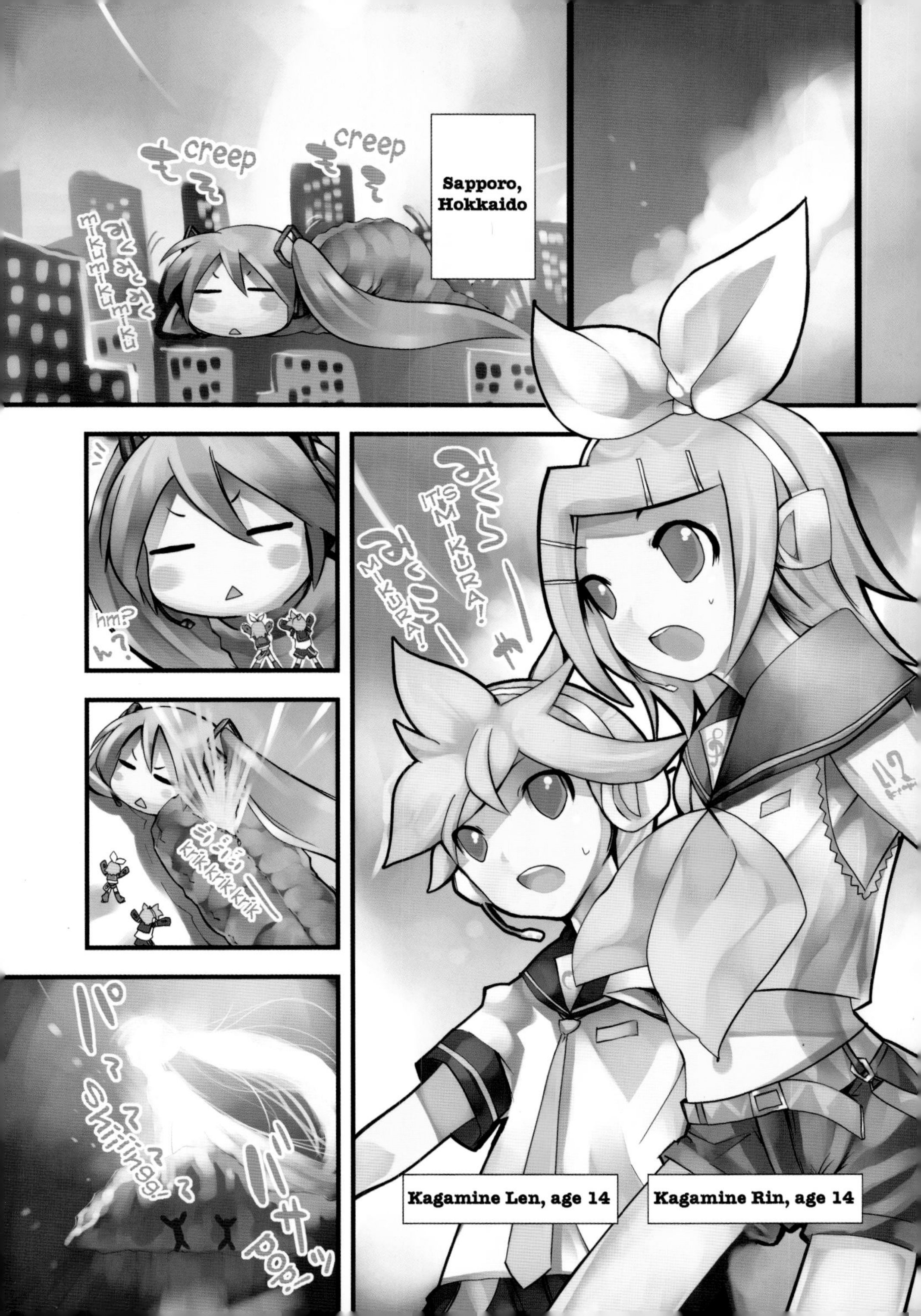
Sapporo, Hokkaido
creep
creep
mi-ku mi-ku mi-ku
IT'S MI-KU-RA!
MI-KU-RA!
Kagamine Rin, age 14
Kagamine Len, age 14
hm?
krik krik krik
pop!
shiiing!

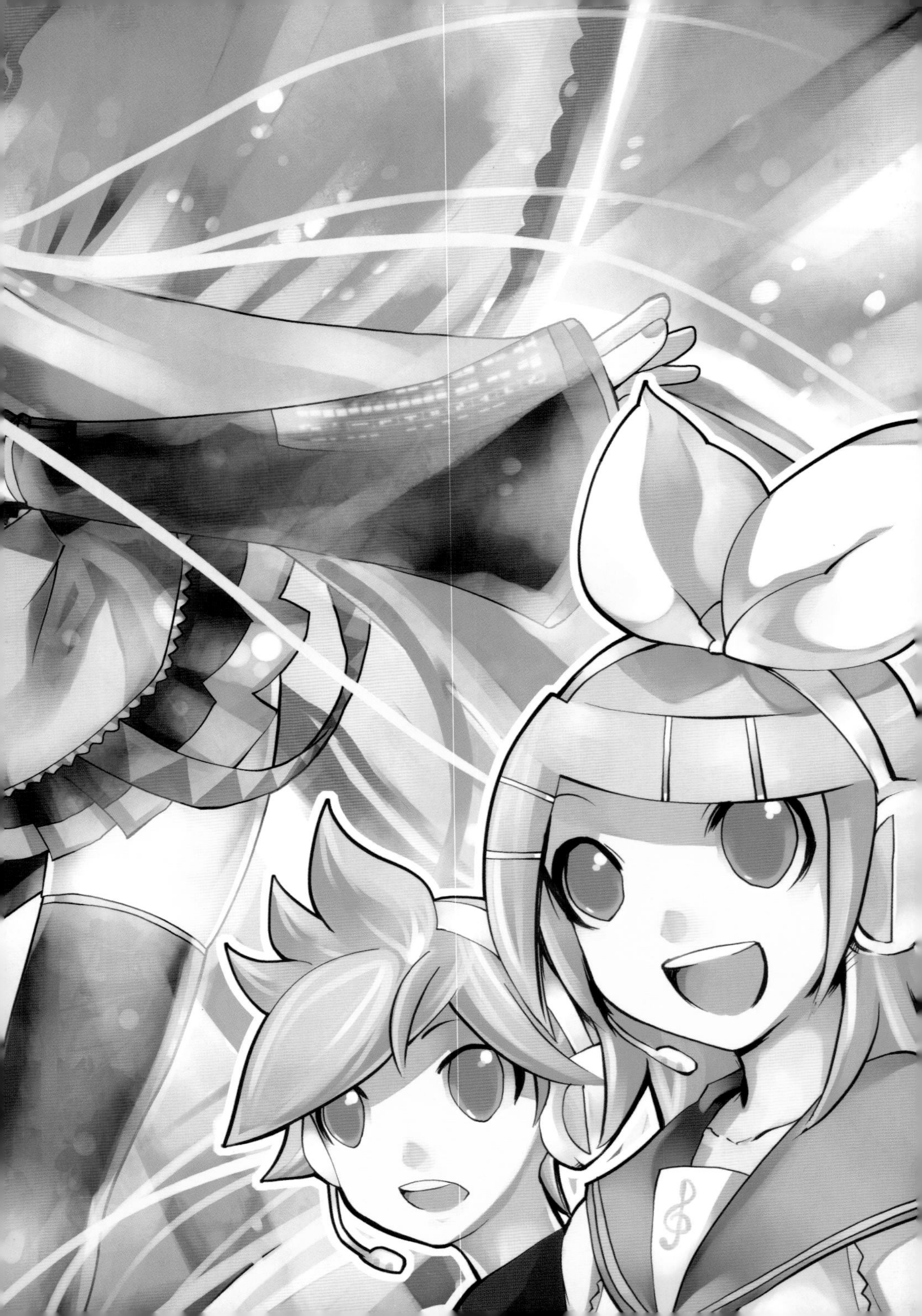

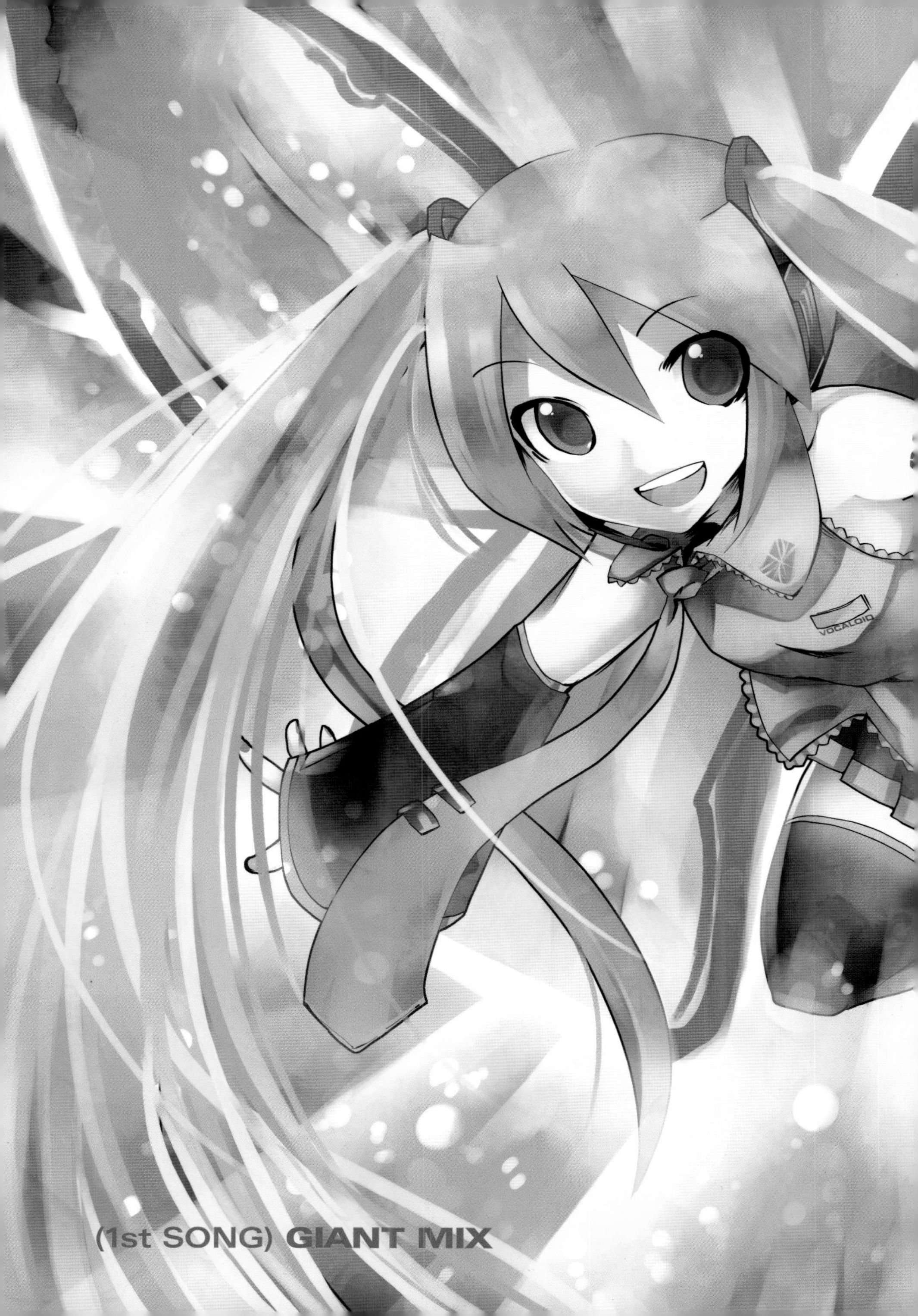
VOCALOID
(1st SONG) GIANT MIX

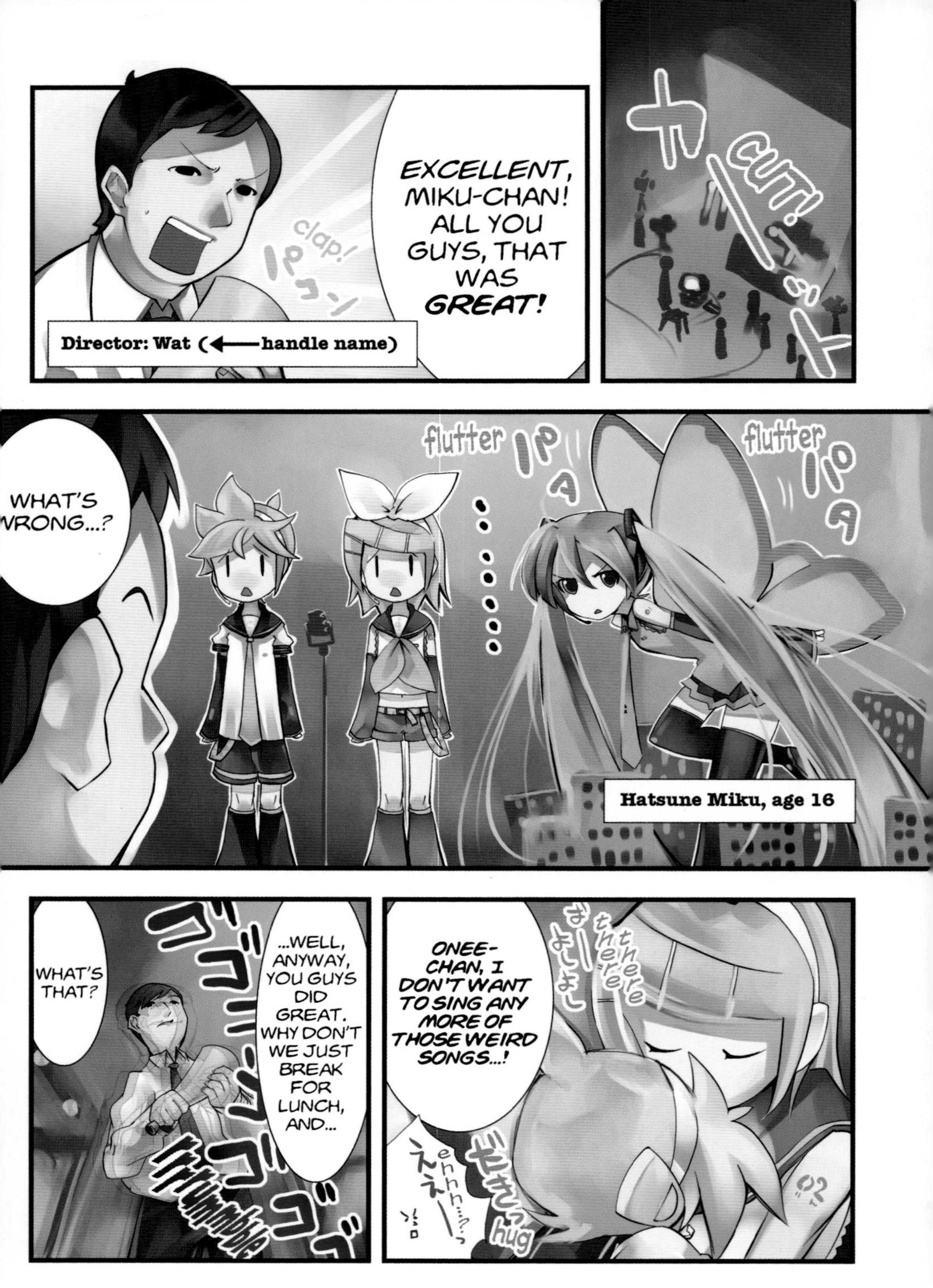
CUT!
EXCELLENT, MIKU-CHAN! ALL YOU GUYS, THAT WAS GREAT!
clap!
Director: Wat (← handle name)
flutter
flutter
......
WHAT'S WRONG...?
Hatsune Miku, age 16
ONEE-CHAN, I DON'T WANT TO SING ANY MORE OF THOSE WEIRD SONGS...!
there there
hug
ehhh...?
...WELL, ANYWAY, YOU GUYS DID GREAT. WHY DON'T WE JUST BREAK FOR LUNCH, AND...
WHAT'S THAT?
grumble

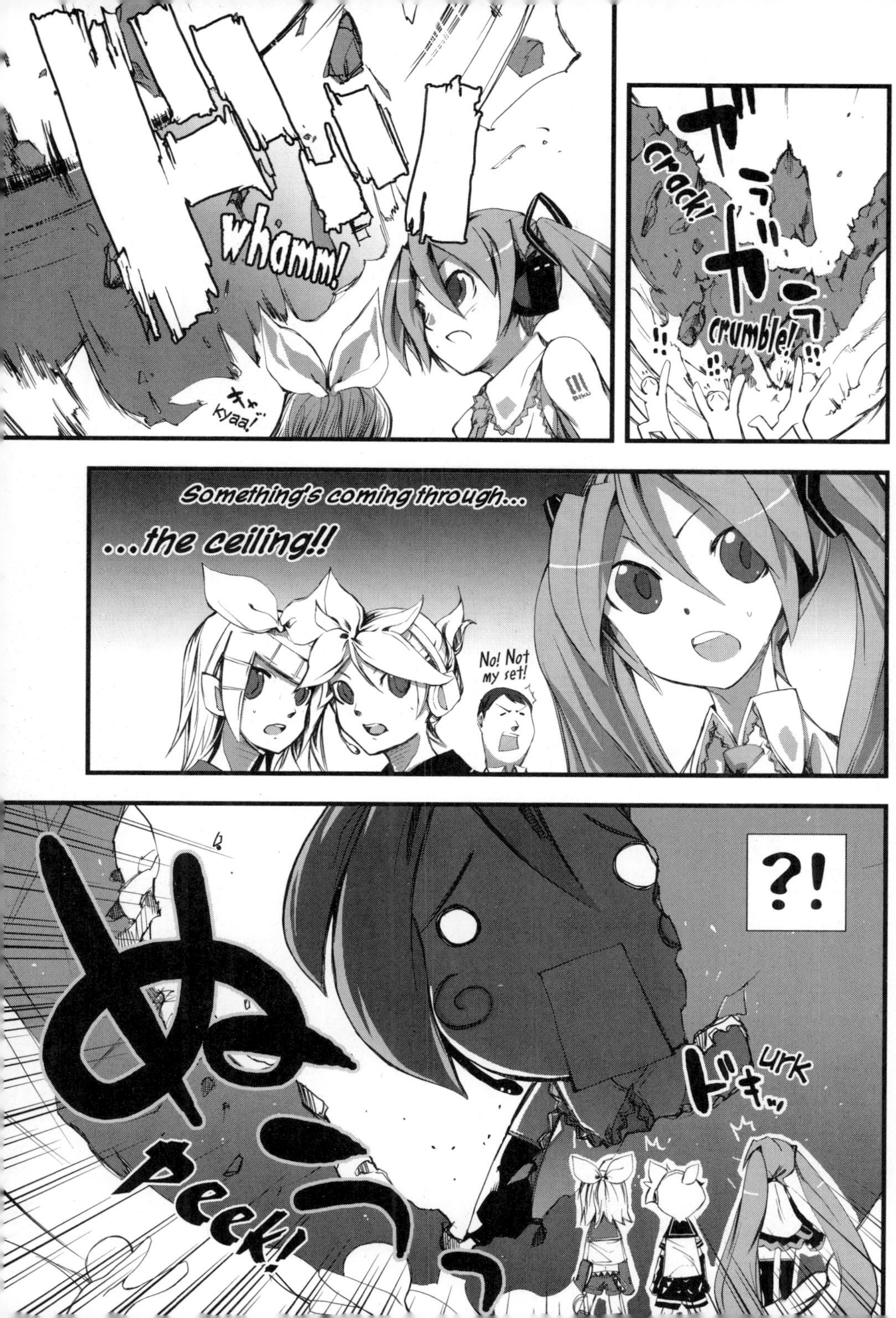
crack!
crumble!
!!
whamm!
kyaa!
Something's coming through...
...the ceiling!!
No! Not my set!
?!
urk
peek!

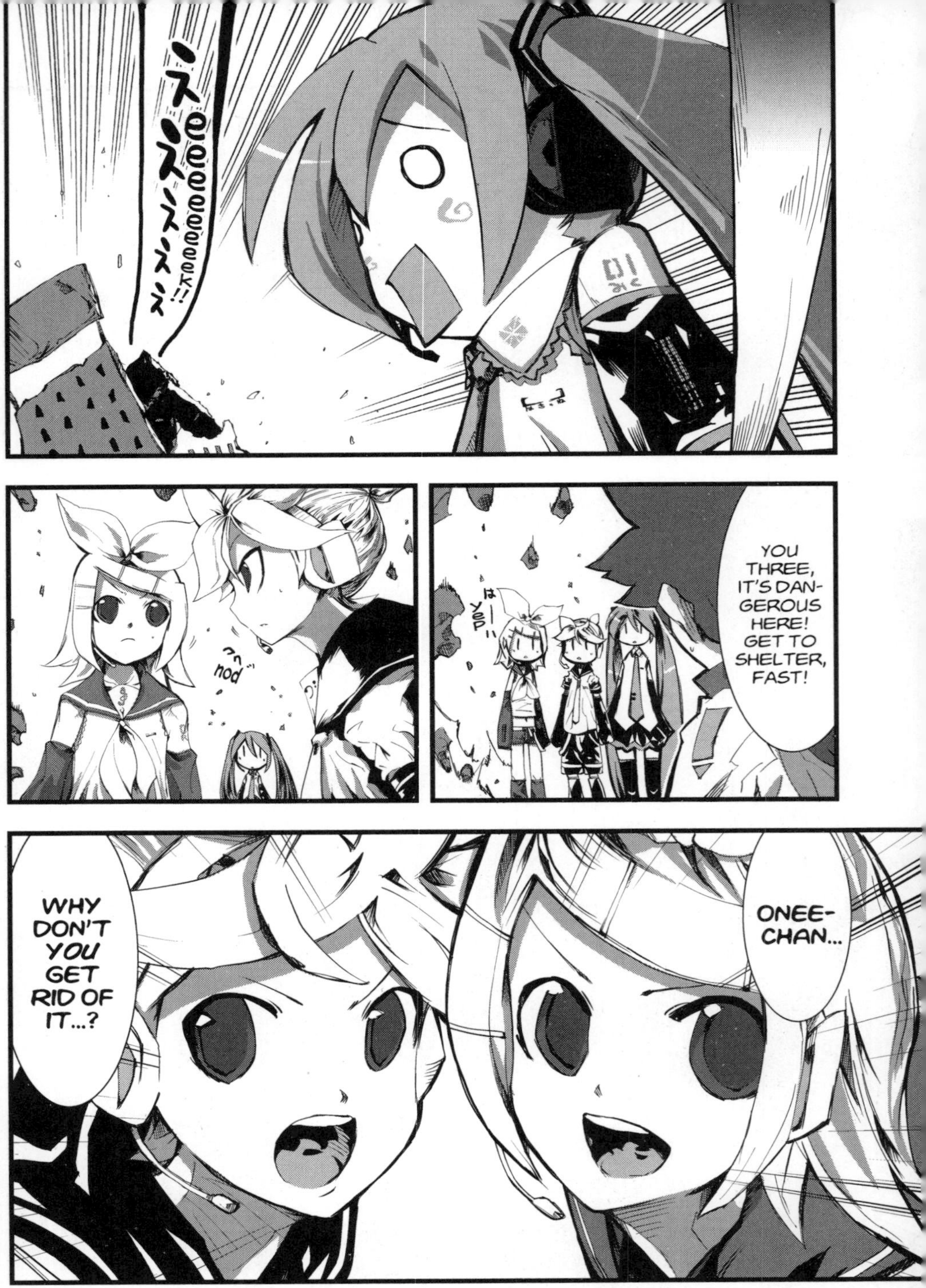
えええええええ
eeeeeeeek!!
YOU THREE, IT'S DAN-GEROUS HERE! GET TO SHELTER, FAST!
はーい
yep
こくっ
nod
ONEE-CHAN...
WHY DON'T YOU GET RID OF IT...?

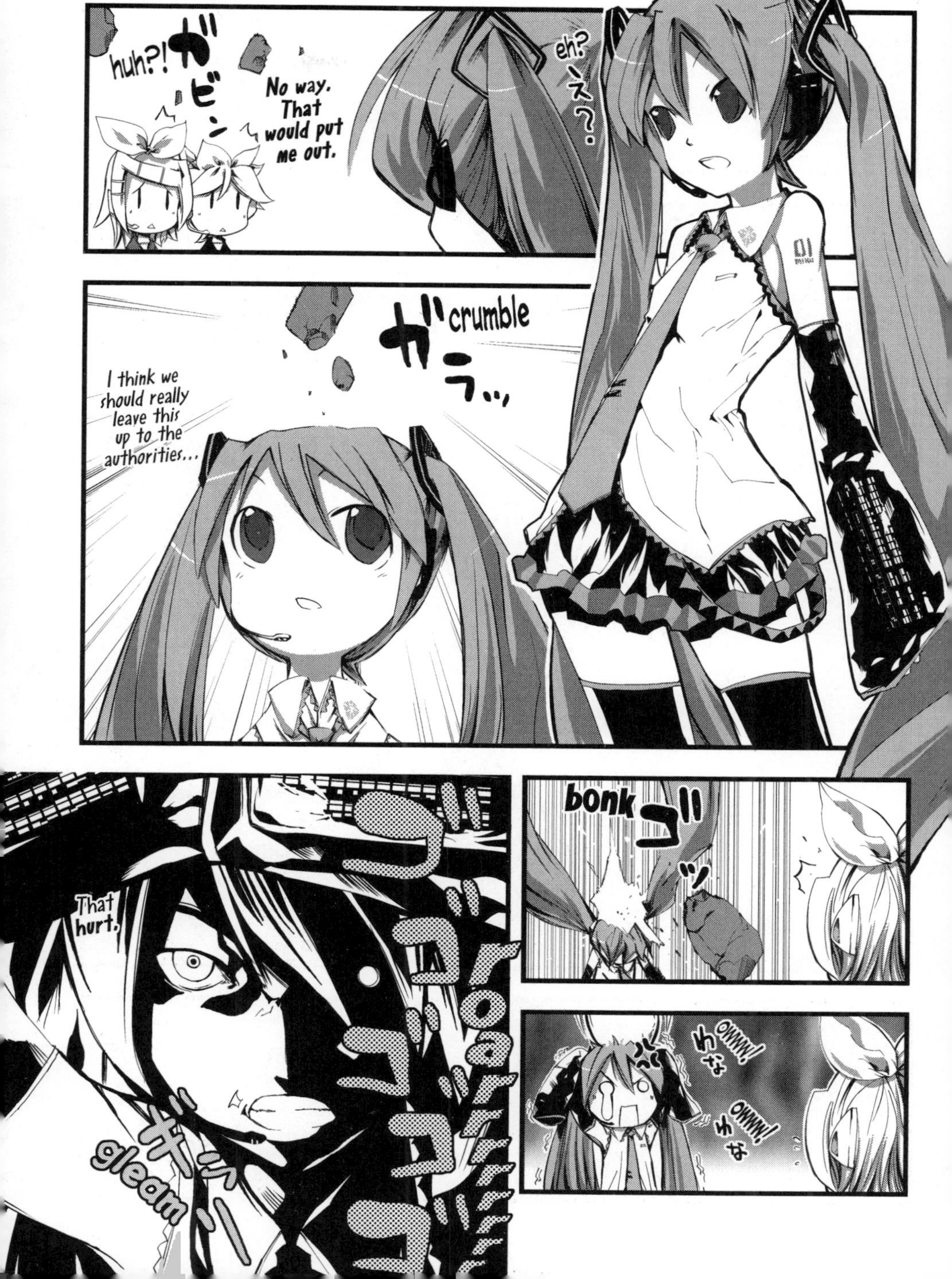
eh? え？
huh?! ガビン
No way. That would put me out.
crumble ガラッ
I think we should really leave this up to the authorities...
bonk ゴッ
OWWW!
OWWW!
That hurt.
roar ゴゴゴ
gleam

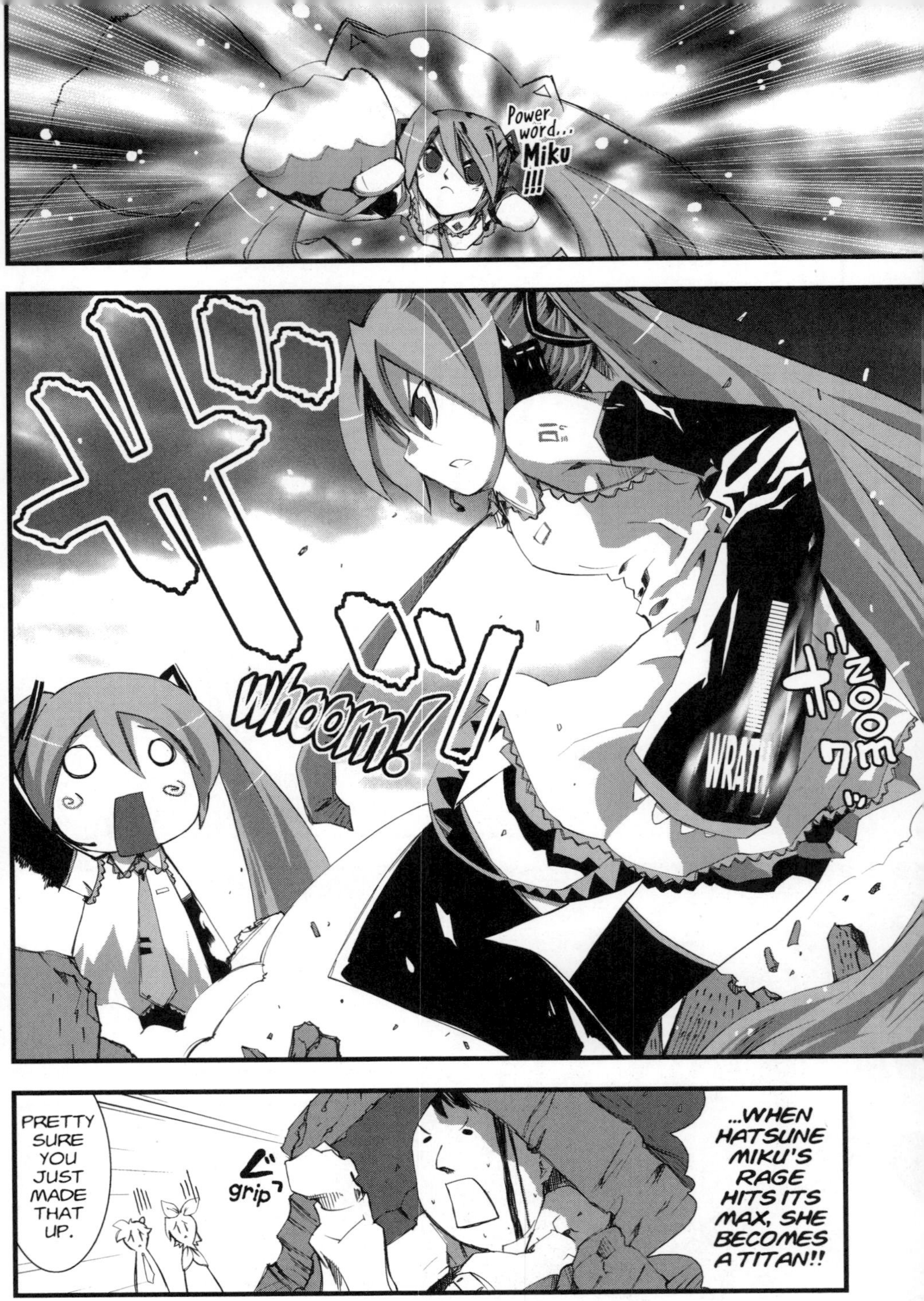
Power word... Miku !!!
WRATH
ZOOM
whoom!
...WHEN HATSUNE MIKU'S RAGE HITS ITS MAX, SHE BECOMES A TITAN!!
grip
PRETTY SURE YOU JUST MADE THAT UP.

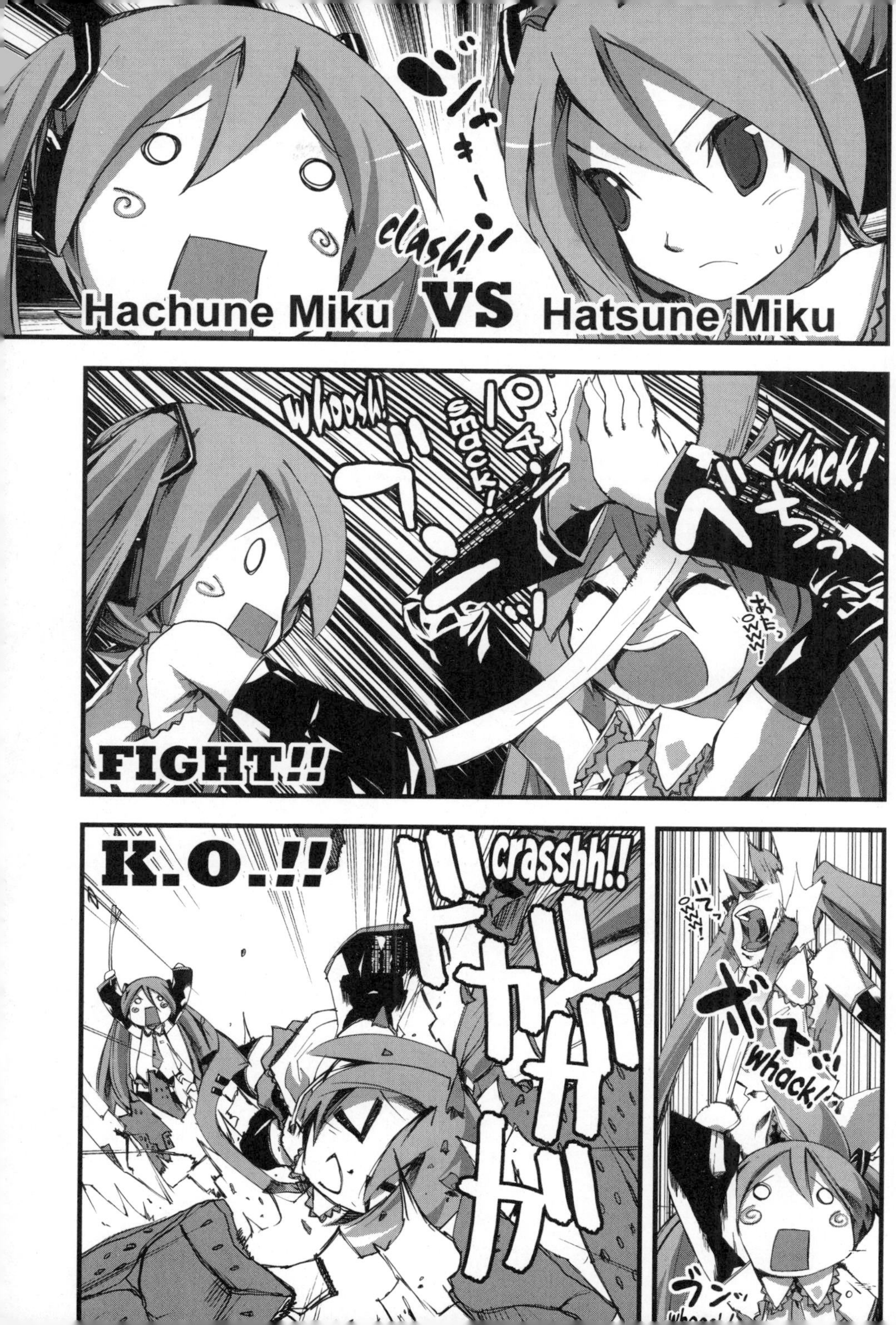

ジャキーン!!
clash!
Hachune Miku VS Hatsune Miku
whack!
べちっ
あたっ
owww!
パム!
smack!
whoosh!
FIGHT!!
ボス!!
whack!
てっ!!
owww!
ブン!!
K.O.!!
crasshh!!
ドガガガ

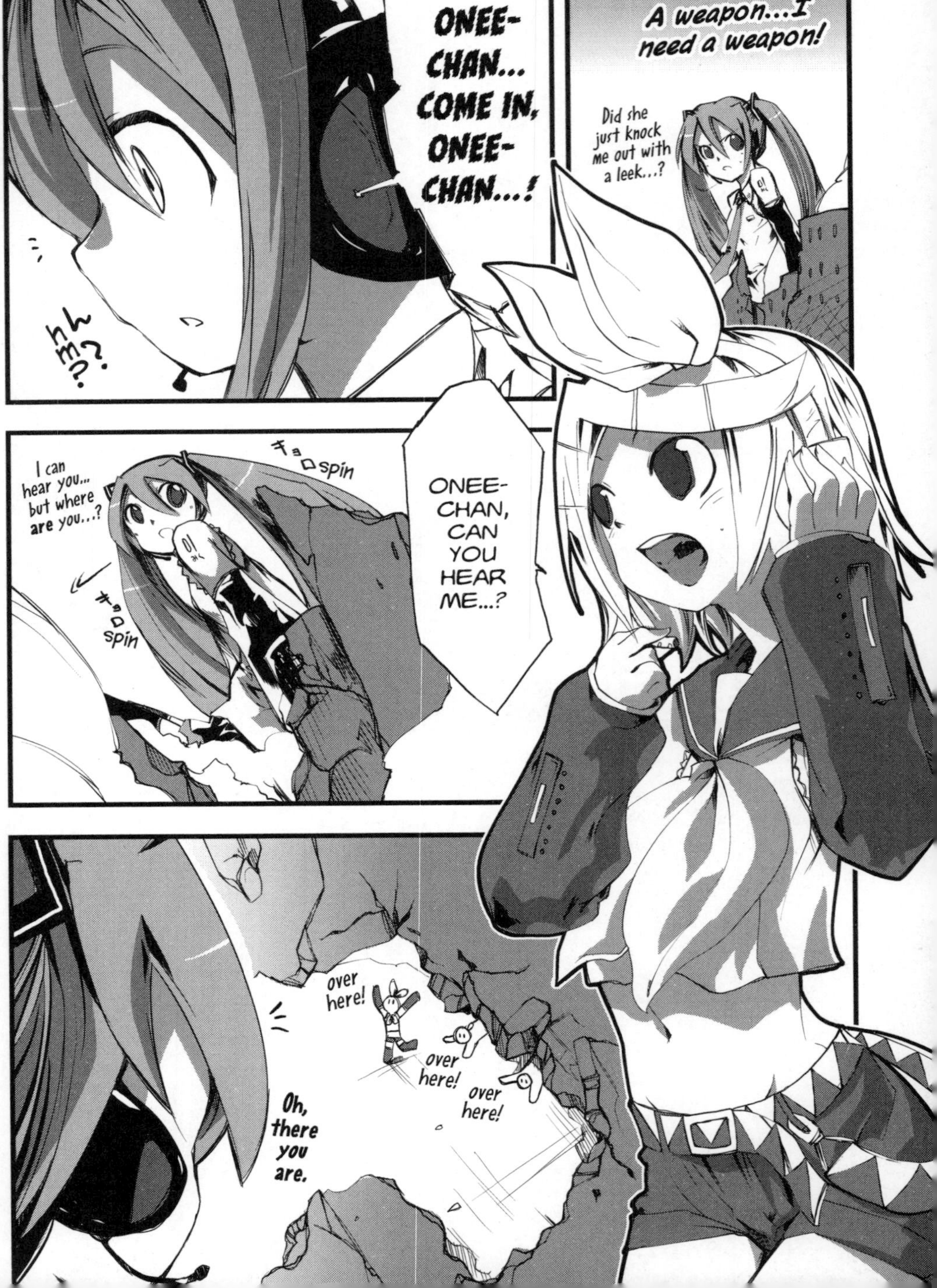
A weapon...I need a weapon!
Did she just knock me out with a leek...?
ONEE-CHAN... COME IN, ONEE-CHAN...!
hmm??
ONEE-CHAN, CAN YOU HEAR ME...?
I can hear you... but where are you...?
キョロ spin
キョロ spin
over here!
over here!
over here!
Oh, there you are.

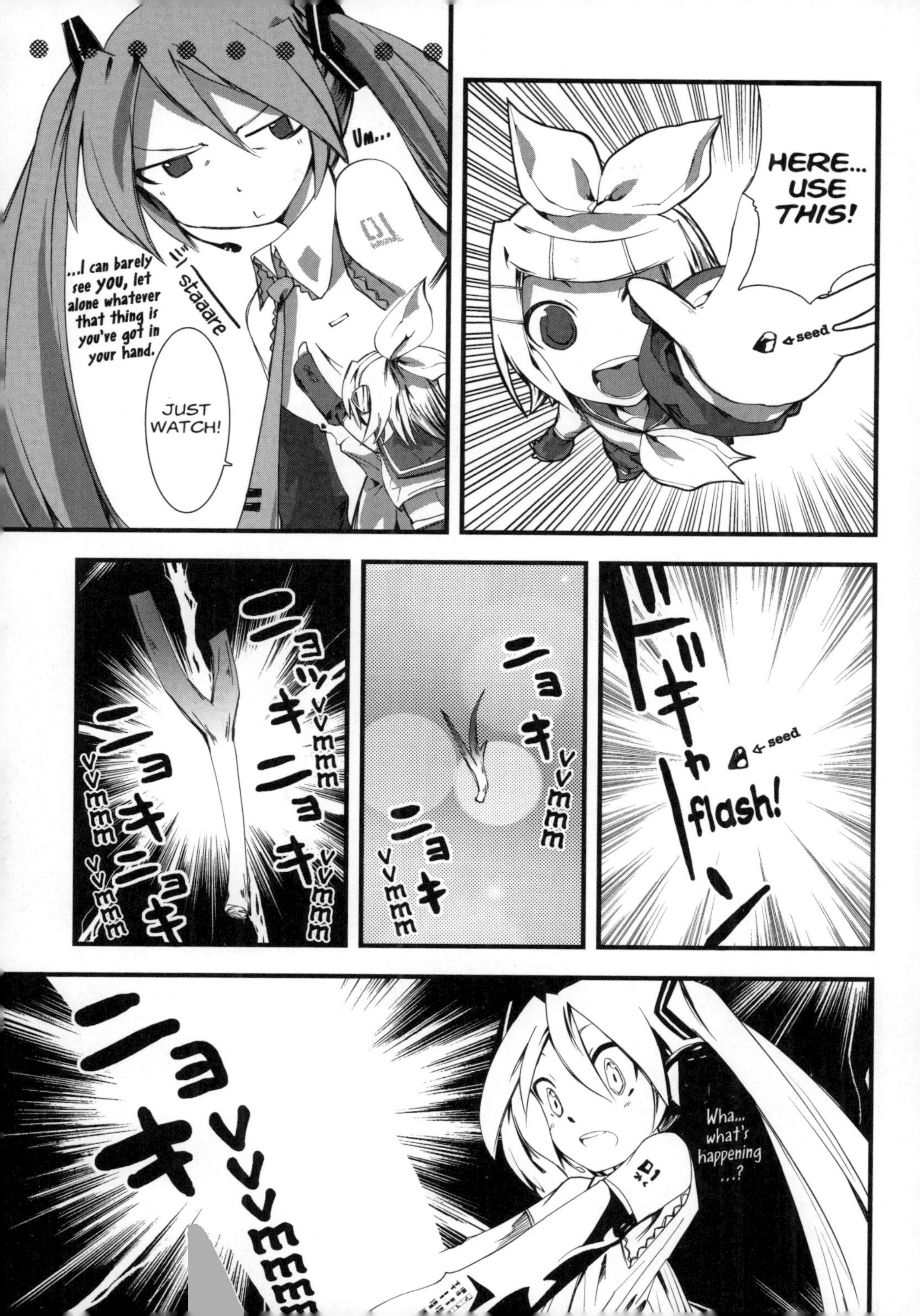
HERE... USE THIS!
seed
Um...
staaare
...I can barely see YOU, let alone whatever that thing is you've got in your hand.
JUST WATCH!
ドギャーン
flash!
seed
ニョキ
vvmmm
ニョキ
vvmmm
ニョッキ
vvmmm
ニョキ
vvmmm
ニョキ
vvmmm
ニョキ
vvmmm
ニョキ
vvvvmmmm
Wha... what's happening ...?

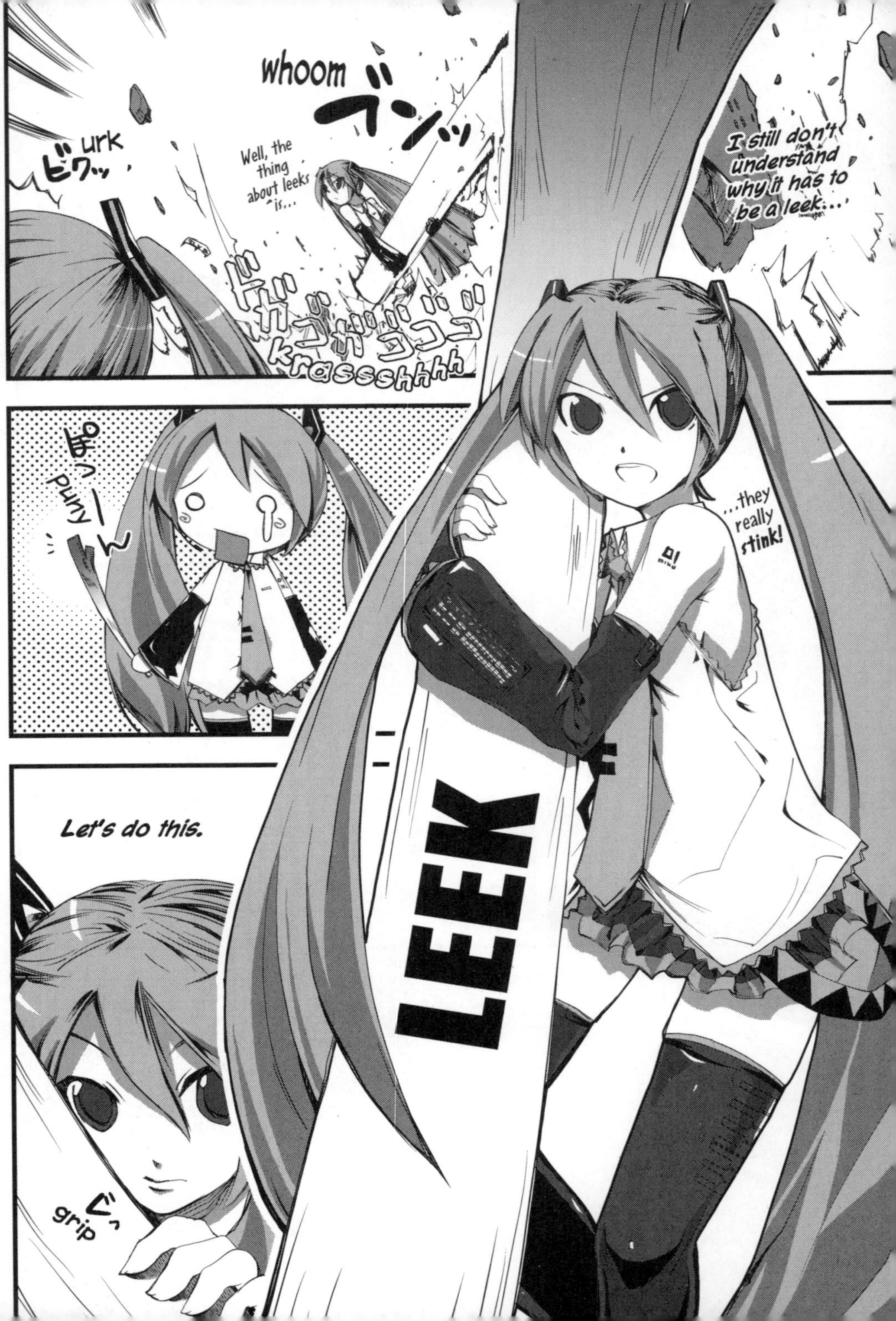
I still don't understand why it has to be a leek...
whoom
ブンッ
Well, the thing about leeks is...
ドガゴガゴゴゴ
krassshhhh
ビクッ
urk
...they really stink!
LEEK
ぽつーん
puny
Let's do this.
ぐっ
grip

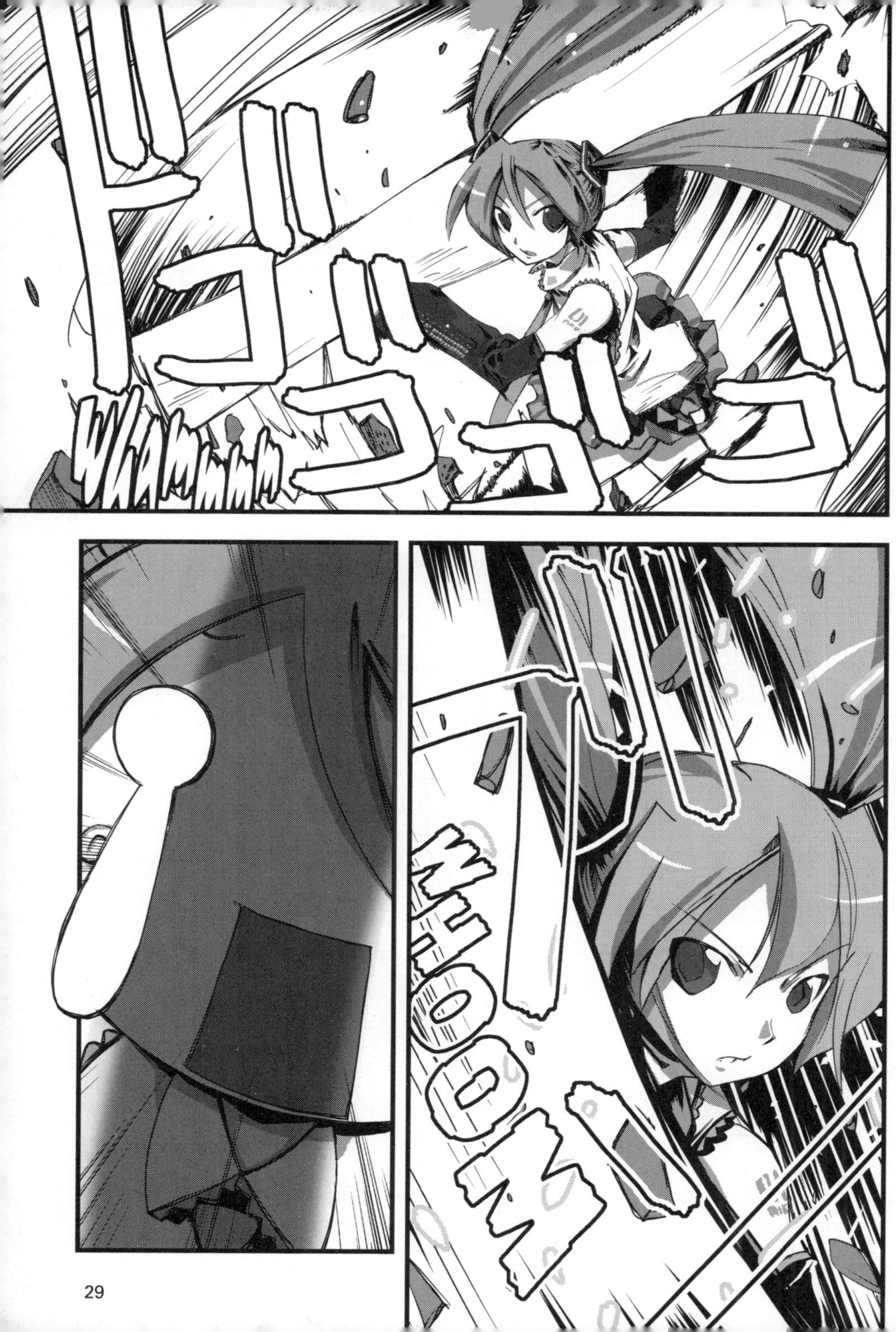
ドゴゴゴゴ
WHAMMMM
WHOOM!

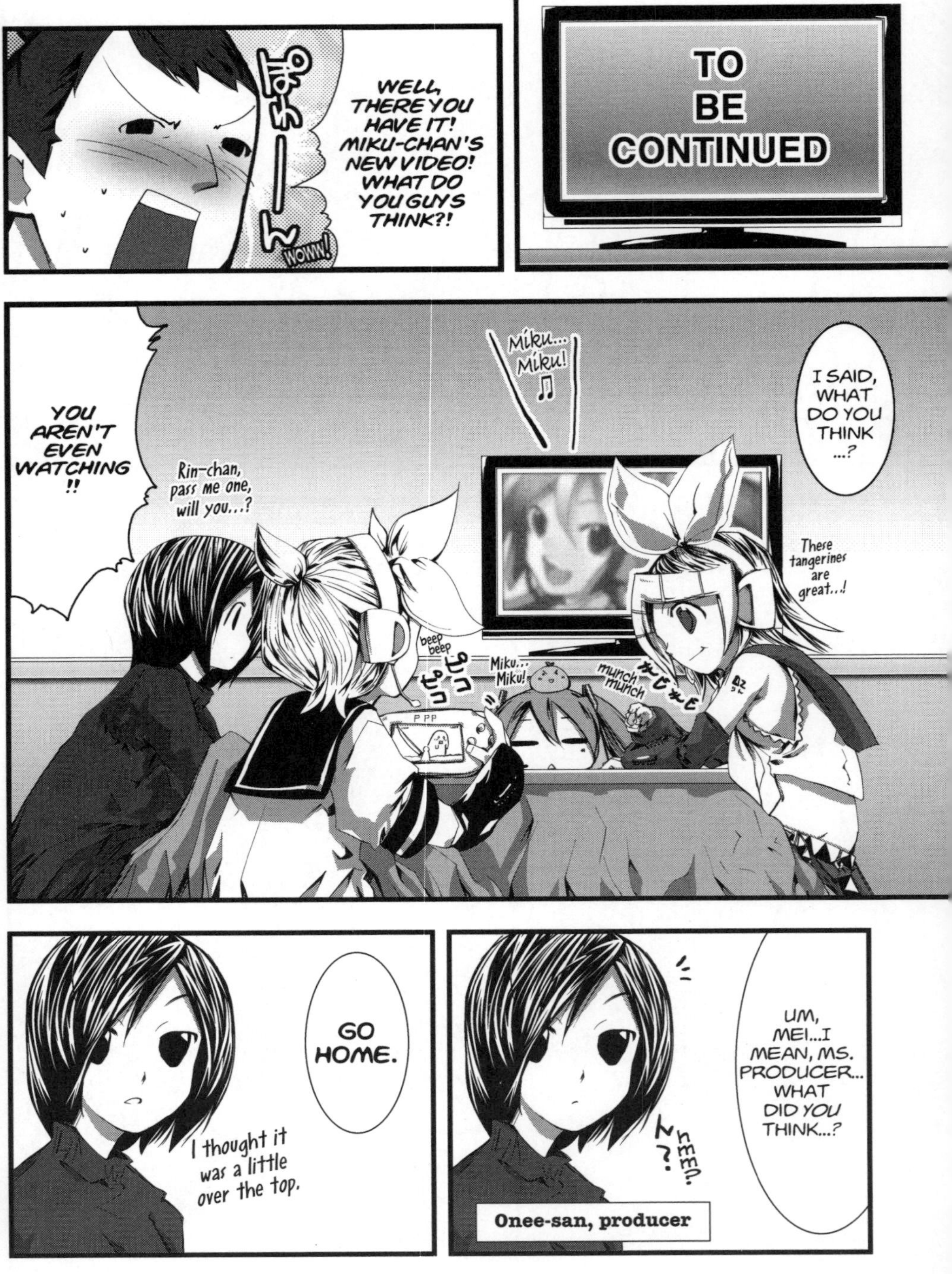
TO BE CONTINUED
WELL, THERE YOU HAVE IT! MIKU-CHAN'S NEW VIDEO! WHAT DO YOU GUYS THINK?!
WOWW!
I SAID, WHAT DO YOU THINK ...?
Miku... Miku! ♪
These tangerines are great...!
munch munch
Miku... Miku!
beep beep
Rin-chan, pass me one, will you...?
YOU AREN'T EVEN WATCHING !!
UM, MEI...I MEAN, MS. PRODUCER... WHAT DID YOU THINK...?
HMM?
Onee-san, producer
GO HOME.
I thought it was a little over the top.

(2nd SONG) CHOCOLATE MIX

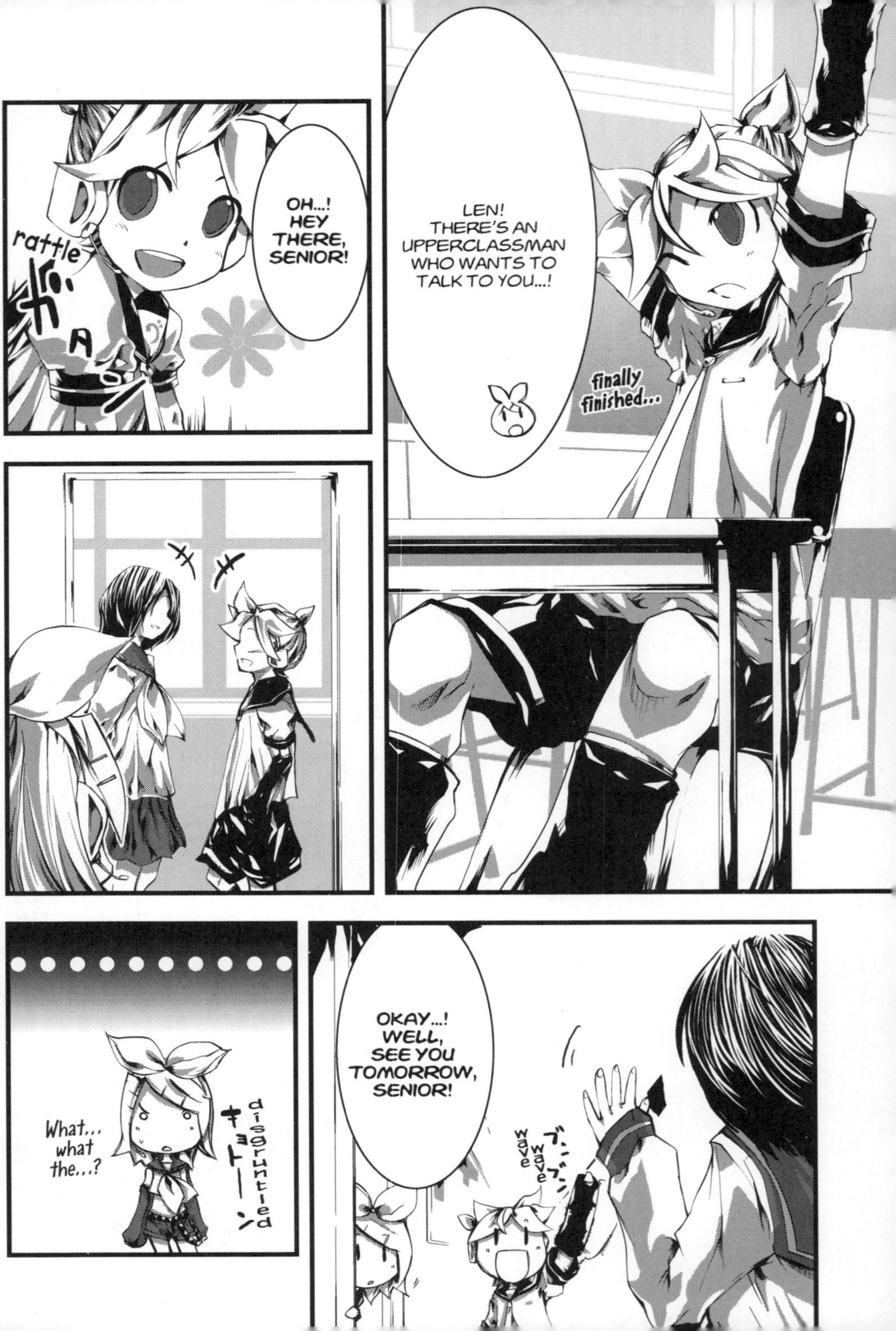
LEN! THERE'S AN UPPERCLASSMAN WHO WANTS TO TALK TO YOU...!
finally finished...
OH...! HEY THERE, SENIOR!
rattle
OKAY...! WELL, SEE YOU TOMORROW, SENIOR!
wave wave
disgruntled
What... what the...?

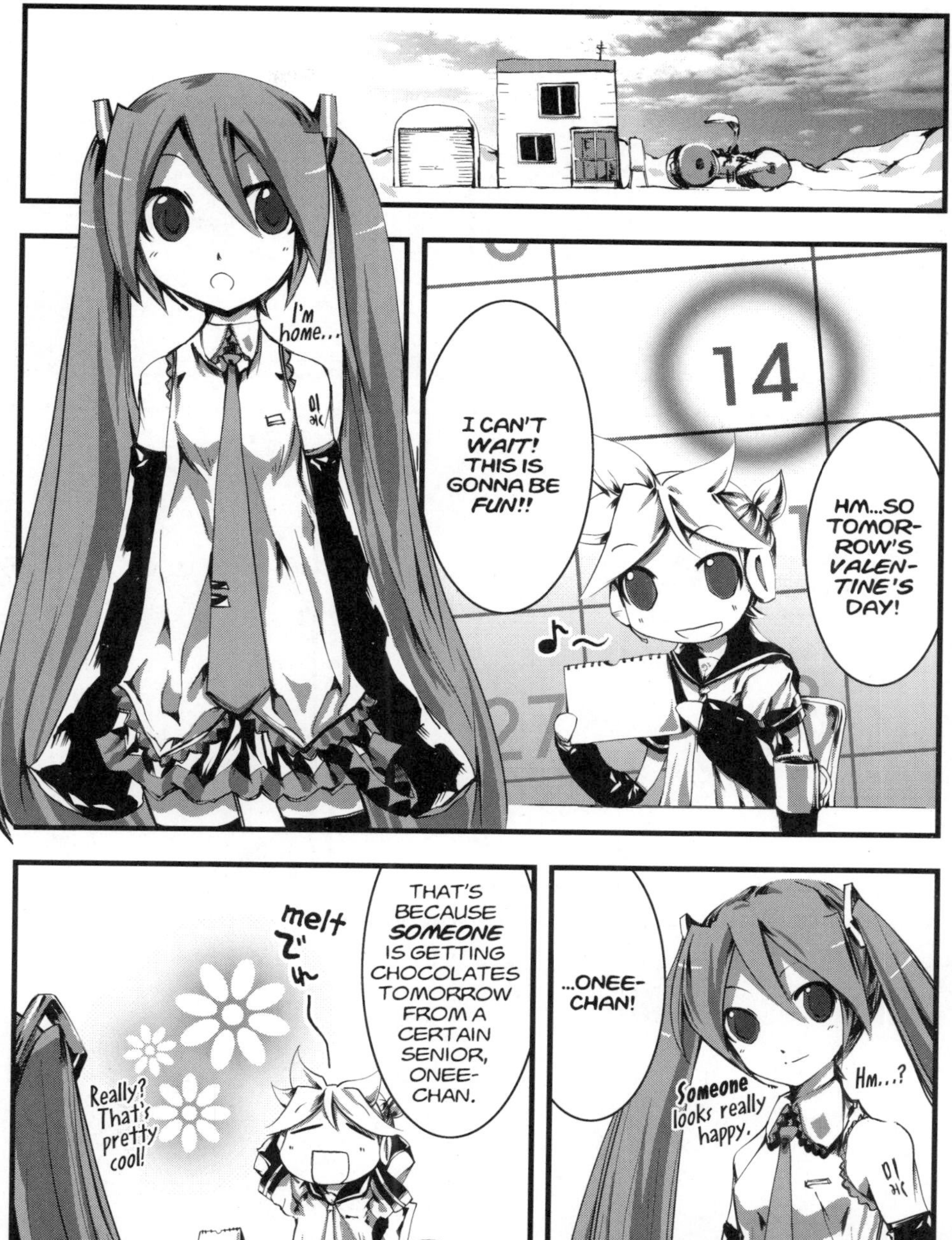
HM...SO TOMORROW'S VALENTINE'S DAY!
I CAN'T WAIT! THIS IS GONNA BE FUN!!
♪~
I'm home...
...ONEE-CHAN!
Hm...?
Someone looks really happy.
THAT'S BECAUSE SOMEONE IS GETTING CHOCOLATES TOMORROW FROM A CERTAIN SENIOR, ONEE-CHAN.
melt
Really? That's pretty cool!

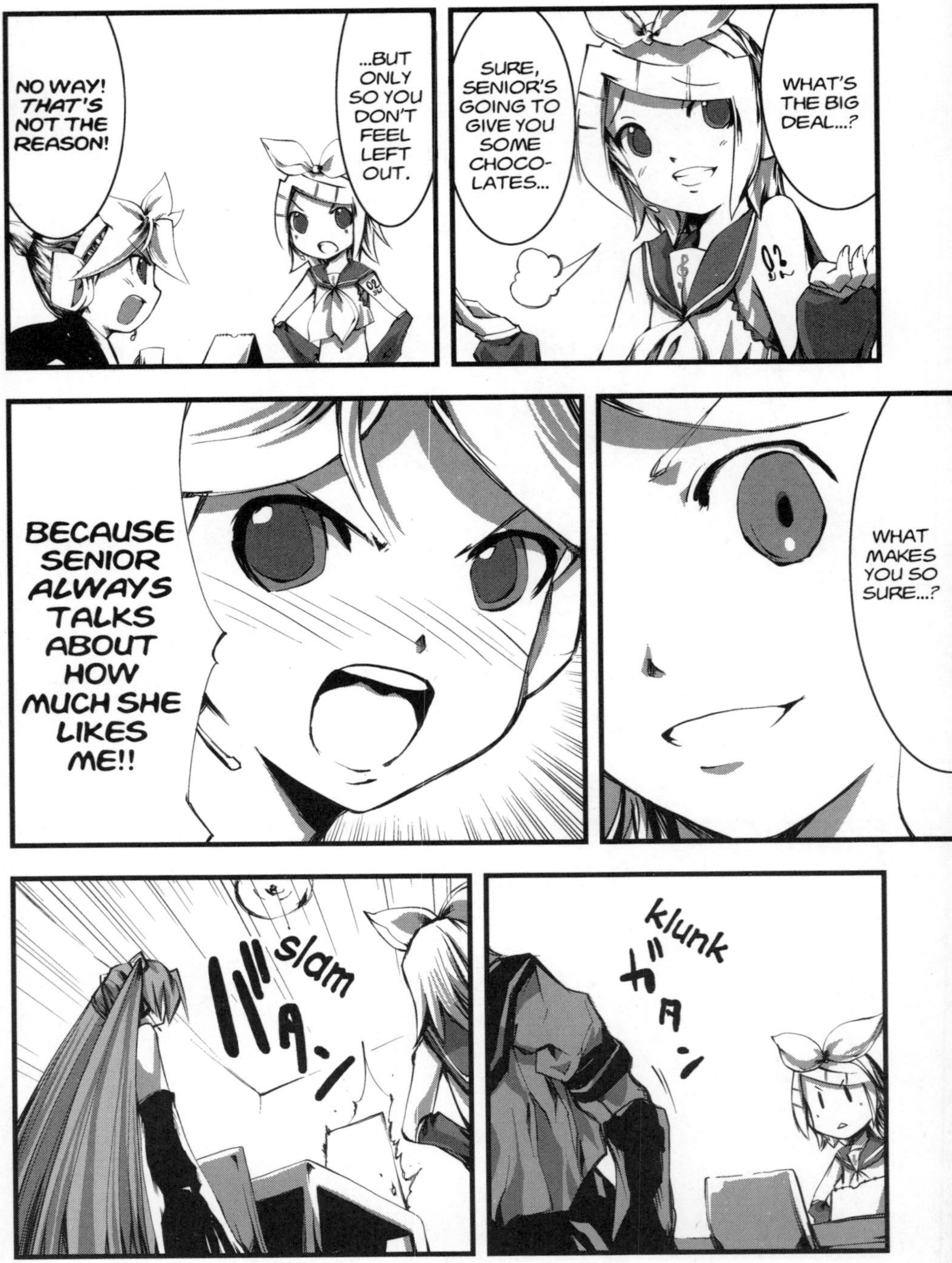
WHAT'S THE BIG DEAL...?
SURE, SENIOR'S GOING TO GIVE YOU SOME CHOCOLATES...
...BUT ONLY SO YOU DON'T FEEL LEFT OUT.
NO WAY! *THAT'S* NOT THE REASON!
WHAT MAKES YOU SO SURE...?
BECAUSE SENIOR *ALWAYS* TALKS ABOUT HOW MUCH SHE LIKES ME!!
klunk
slam

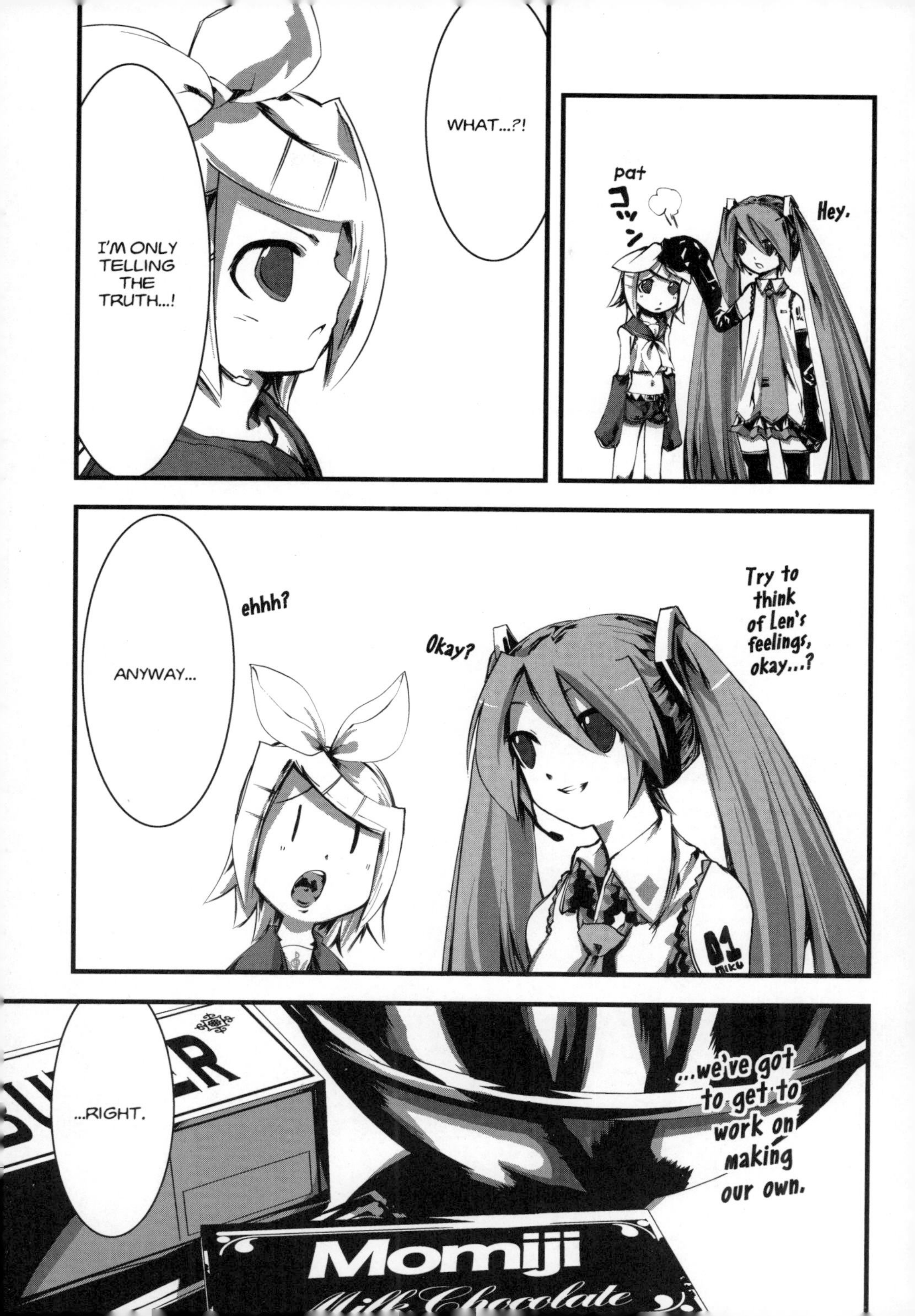

Hey.
pat
コッン
WHAT...?!
I'M ONLY TELLING THE TRUTH...!
Try to think of Len's feelings, okay...?
Okay?
ehhh?
ANYWAY...
...we've got to get to work on making our own.
...RIGHT.
Momiji
Milk Chocolate

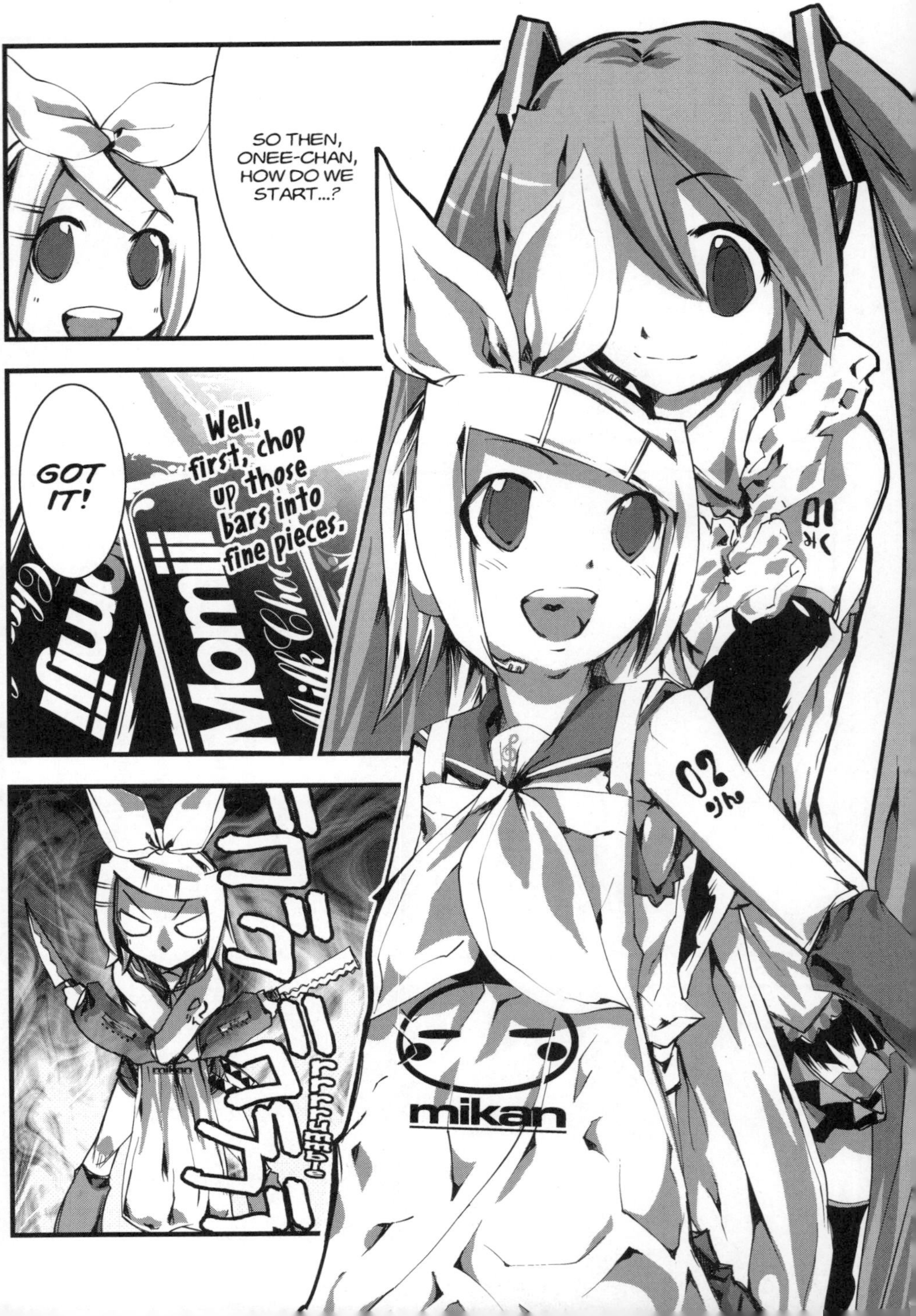

mikan
SO THEN, ONEE-CHAN, HOW DO WE START...?
Well, first, chop up those bars into fine pieces.
GOT IT!

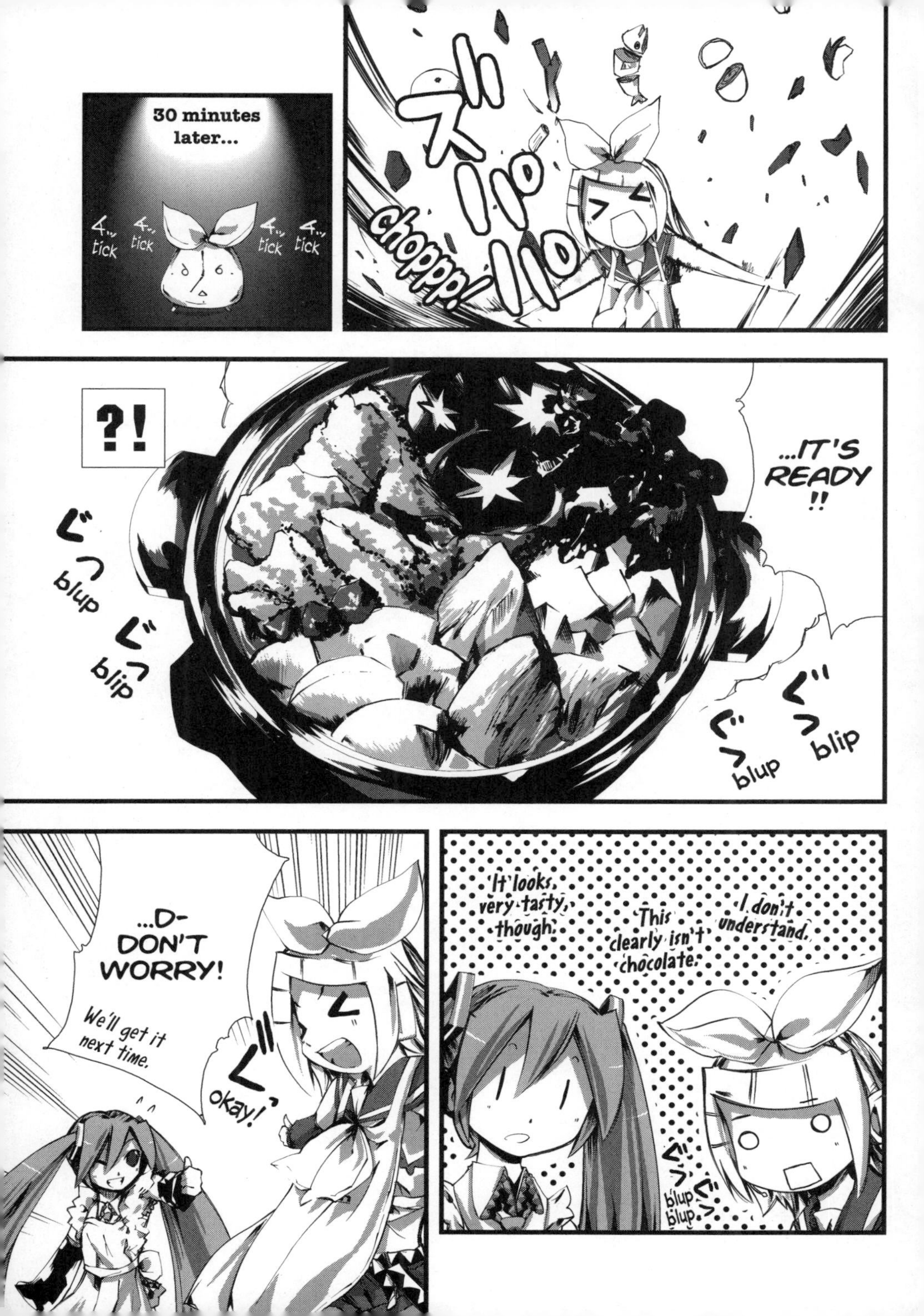
chopp!
30 minutes later...
tick
tick
tick
tick
?!
...IT'S READY!!
blup
blip
blip
blup
I don't understand.
This clearly isn't chocolate.
It looks very tasty, though.
blup
blup
...D-DON'T WORRY!
We'll get it next time.
okay!

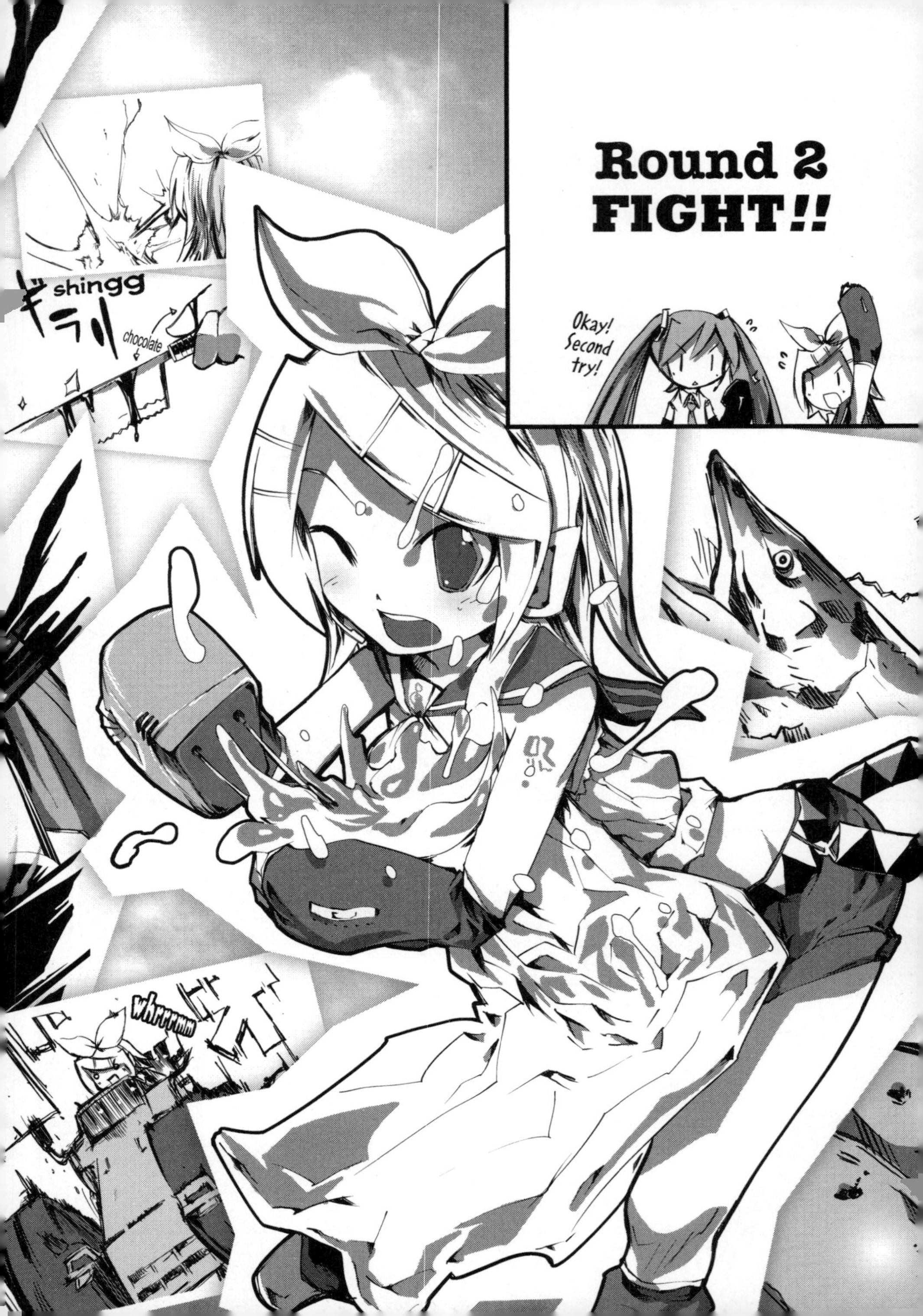
Round 2
FIGHT!!
Okay! Second try!
ギラリ
shingg
chocolate
whrrrmm

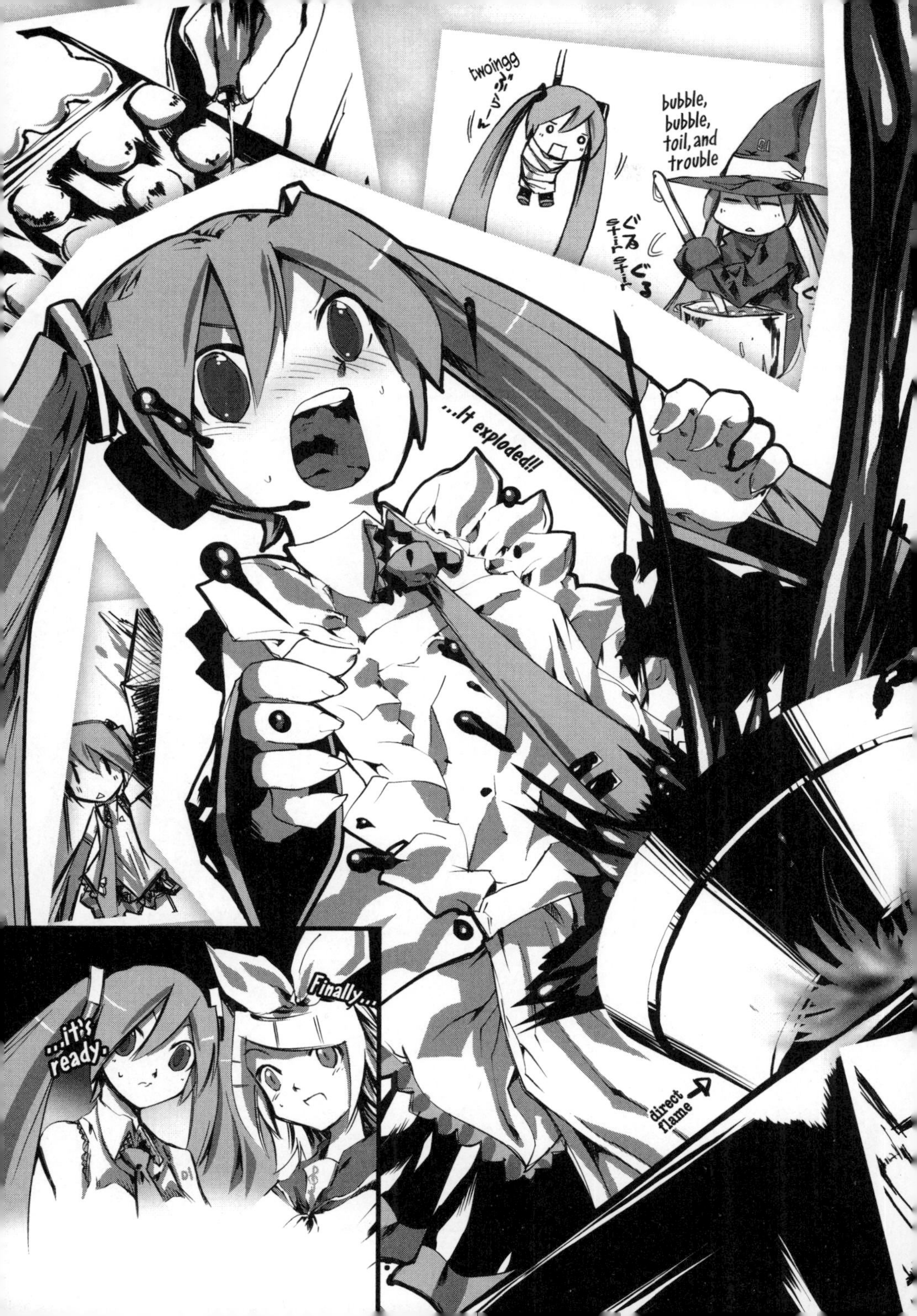
bubble, bubble, toil, and trouble
ぐる stir ぐる stir
twoingg
...It exploded!!
direct flame
Finally...
...it's ready.

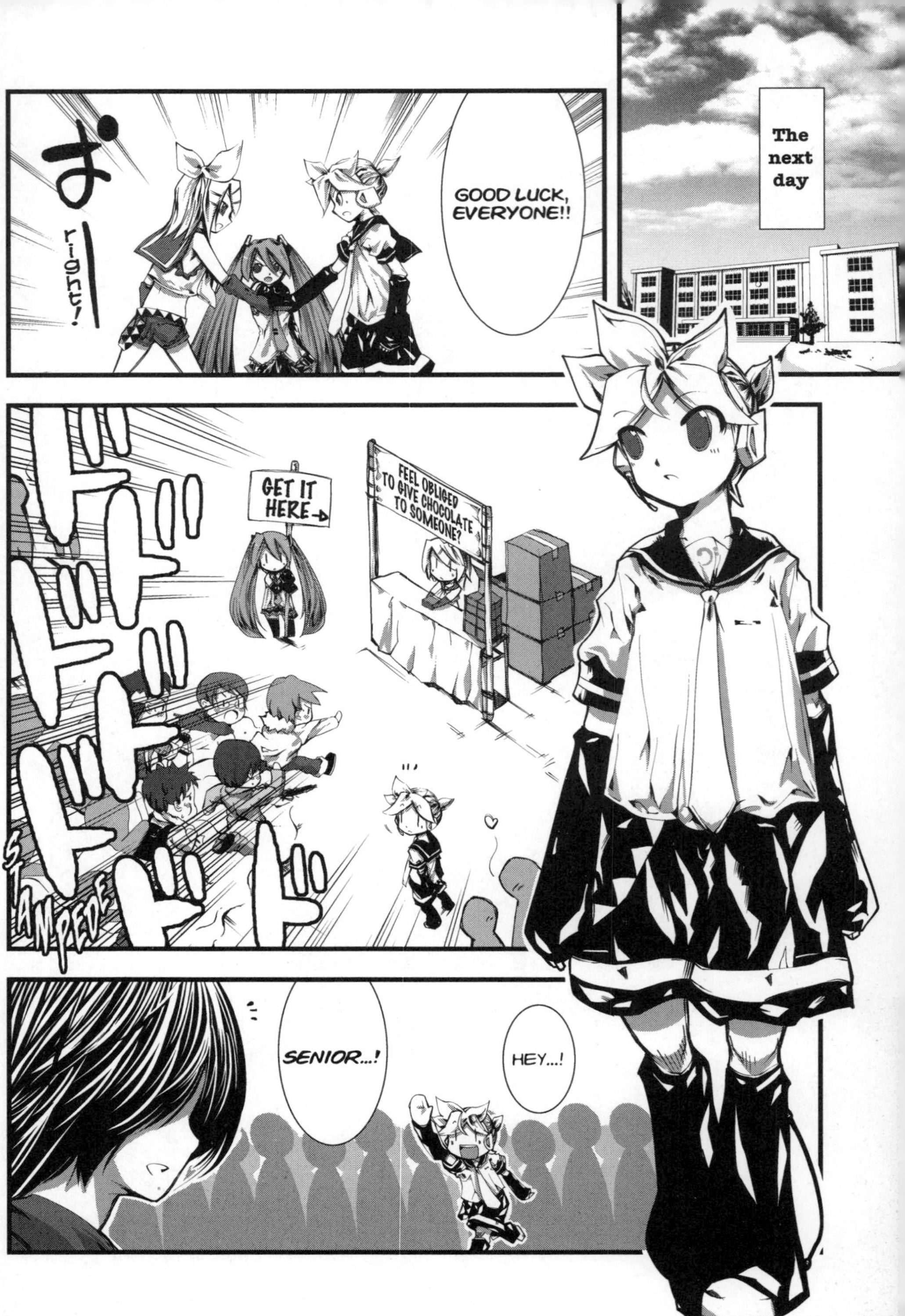

The next day
GOOD LUCK, EVERYONE!!
おー
right!
FEEL OBLIGED TO GIVE CHOCOLATE TO SOMEONE?
GET IT HERE→
STAMPEDE
HEY...!
SENIOR...!

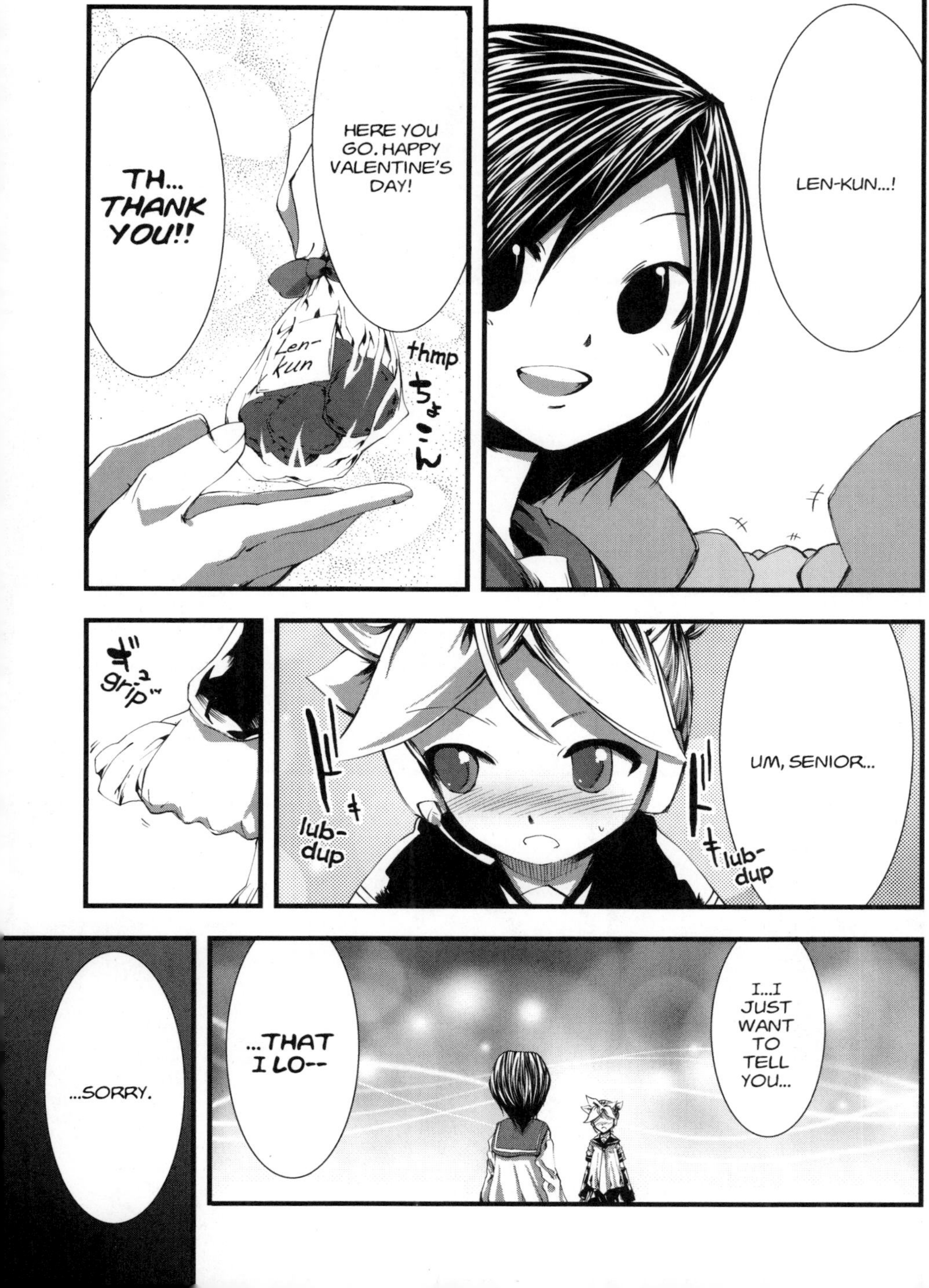
LEN-KUN...!
HERE YOU GO. HAPPY VALENTINE'S DAY!
TH... THANK YOU!!
Len-kun
thmp
ちょこん
UM, SENIOR...
lub-dup
lub-dup
grip
I...I JUST WANT TO TELL YOU...
...THAT I LO--
...SORRY.

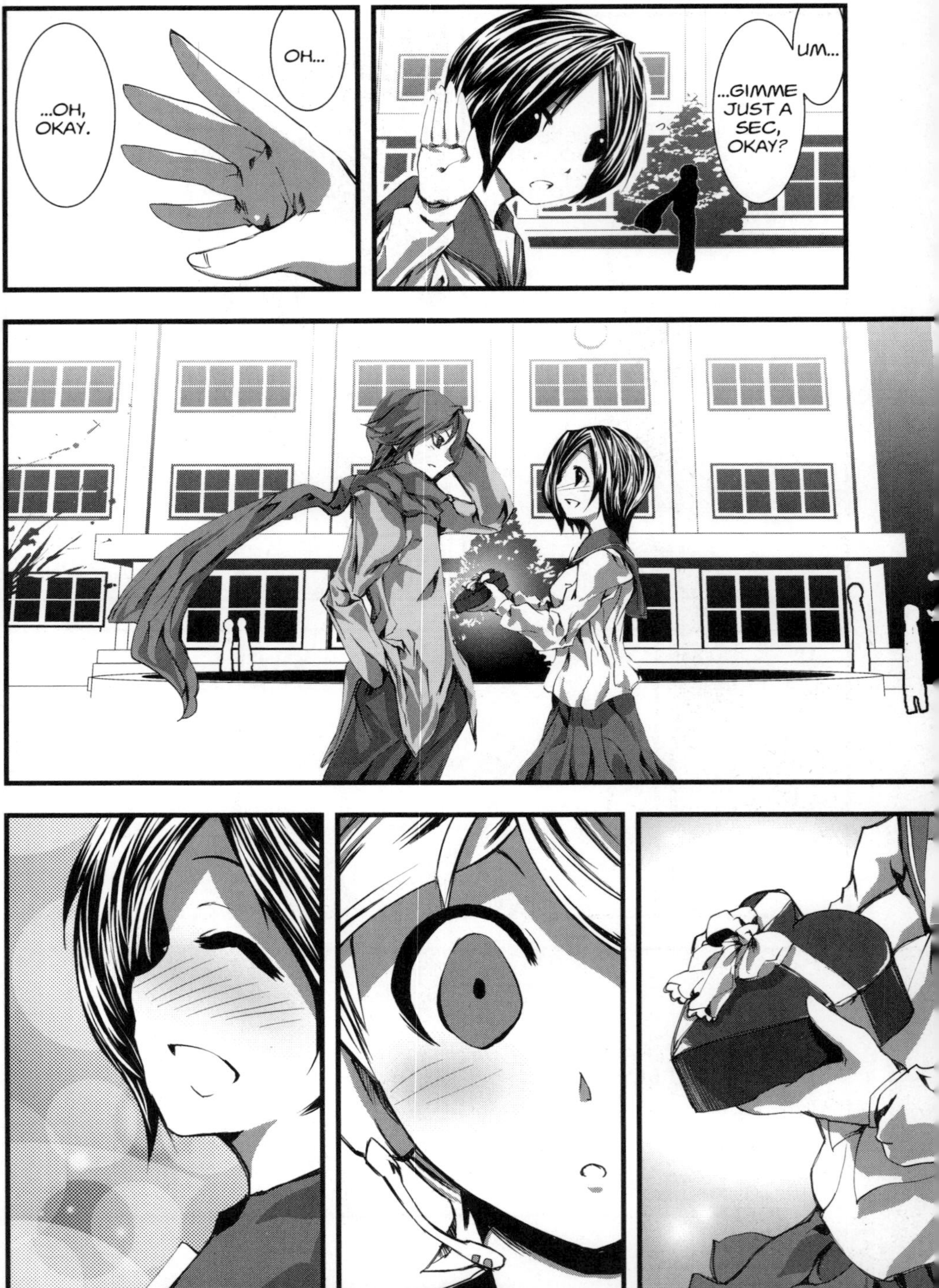
UM...
...GIMME JUST A SEC, OKAY?
OH...
...OH, OKAY.

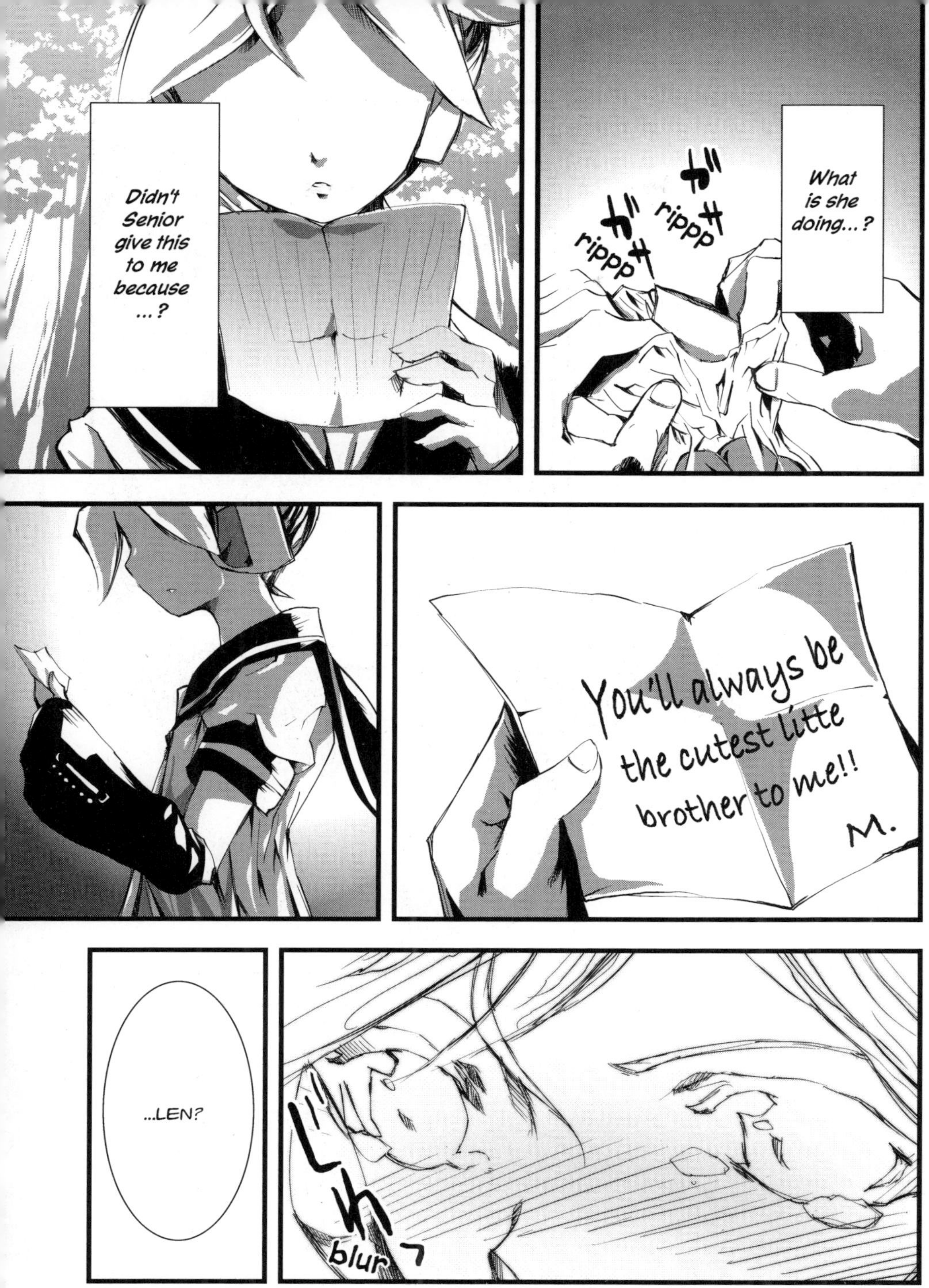
What is she doing...?
ripp
ripp
Didn't Senior give this to me because ...?
You'll always be the cutest litte brother to me!! M.
blur
...LEN?

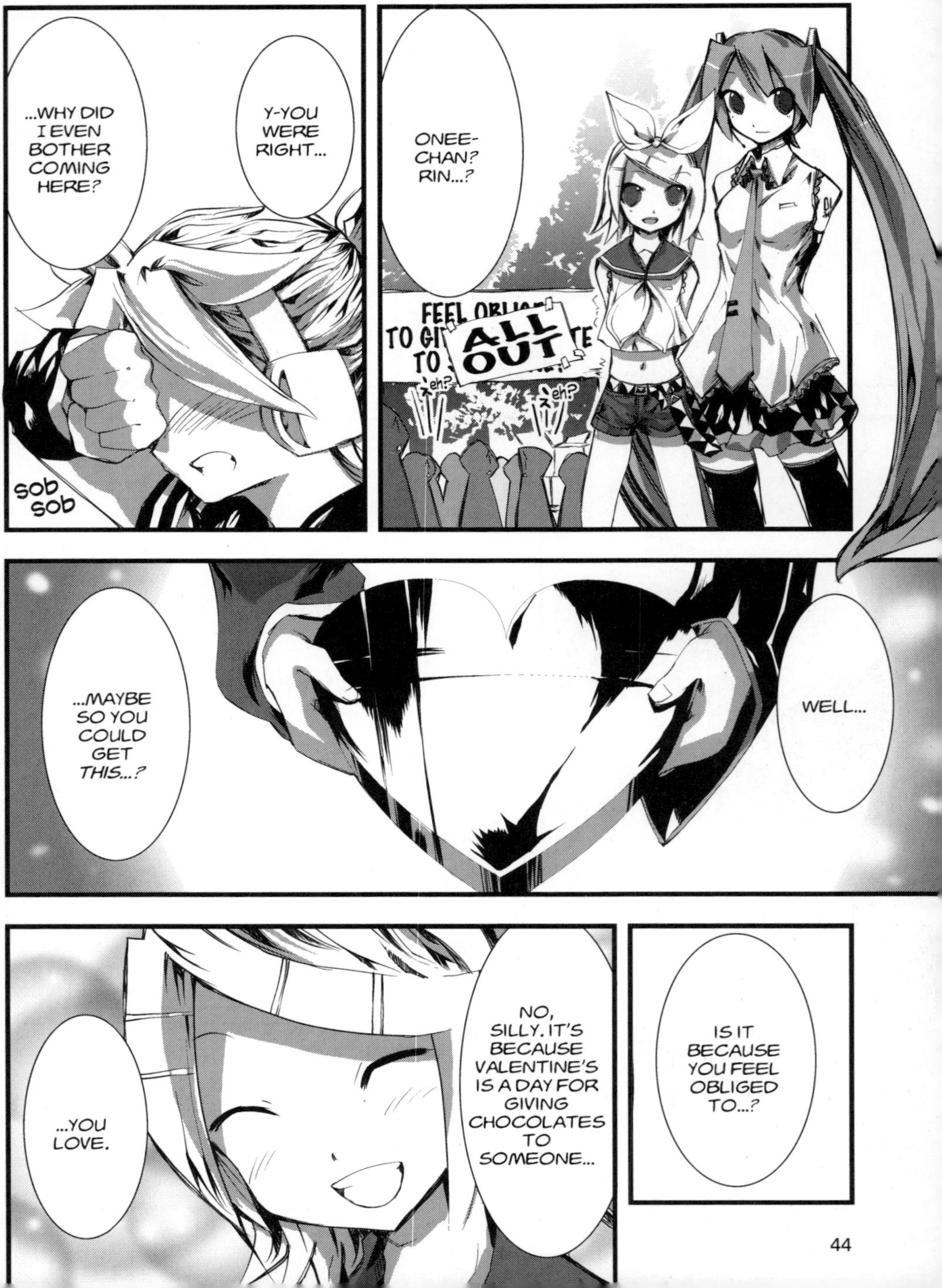
ONEE-CHAN? RIN...?
ALL OUT
eh?
eh?
Y-YOU WERE RIGHT...
...WHY DID I EVEN BOTHER COMING HERE?
sob sob
WELL...
...MAYBE SO YOU COULD GET THIS...?
IS IT BECAUSE YOU FEEL OBLIGED TO...?
NO, SILLY. IT'S BECAUSE VALENTINE'S IS A DAY FOR GIVING CHOCOLATES TO SOMEONE...
...YOU LOVE.

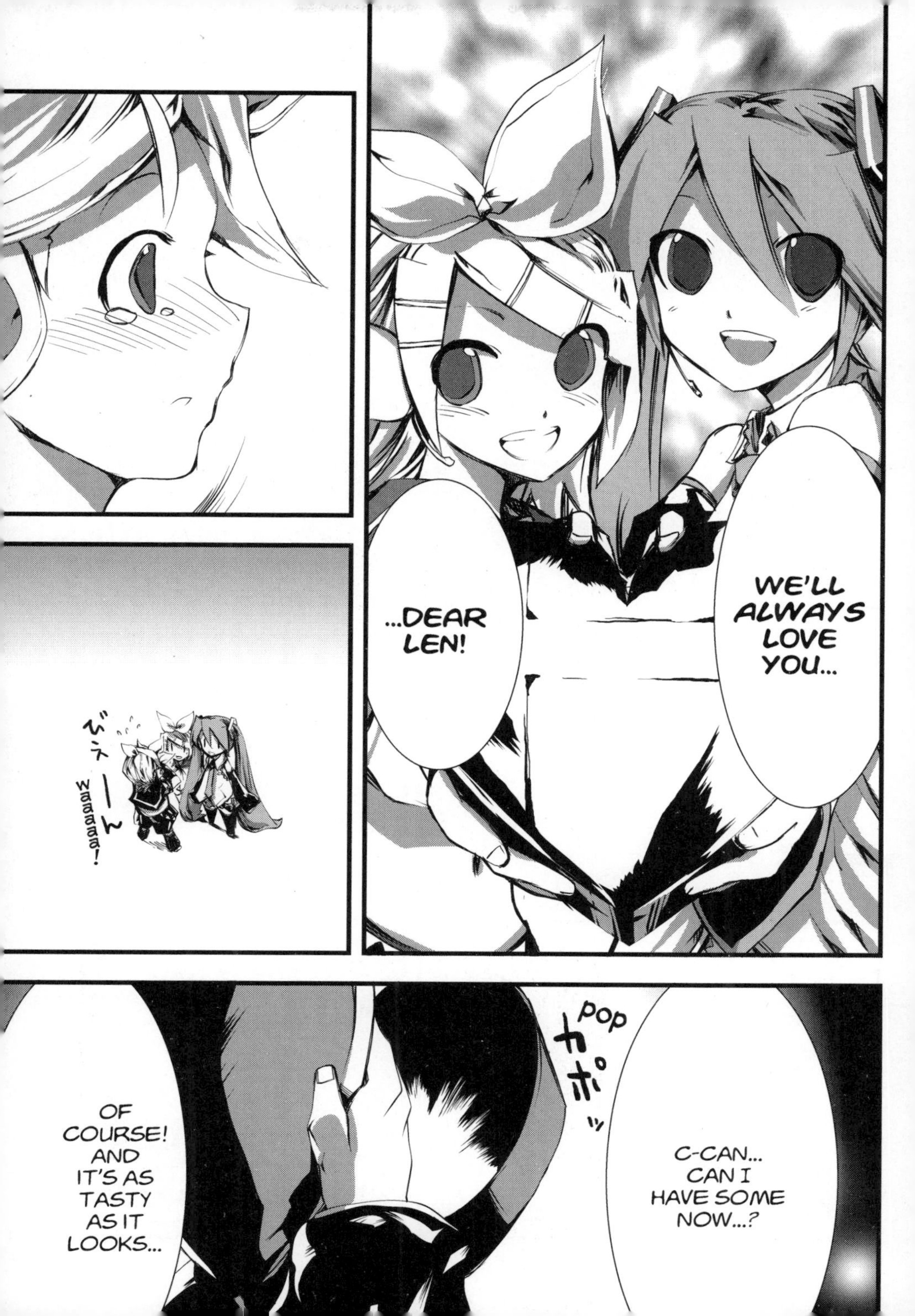
WE'LL ALWAYS LOVE YOU...
...DEAR LEN!
びえーーん
waaaaaa!
C-CAN... CAN I HAVE SOME NOW...?
pop
カポッ
OF COURSE! AND IT'S AS TASTY AS IT LOOKS...

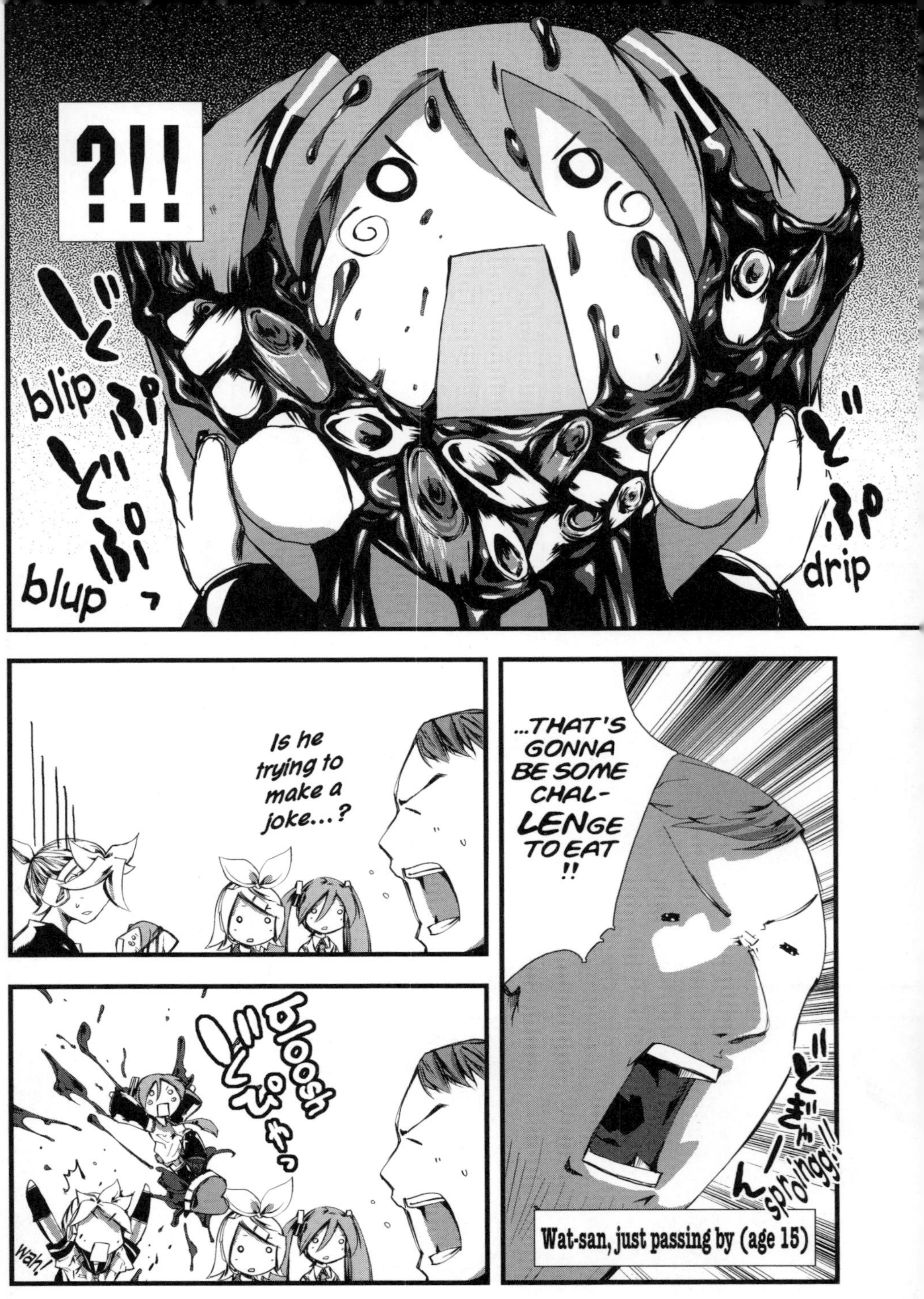
?!!
drip
blip
blup
...THAT'S GONNA BE SOME CHAL-LENGE TO EAT !!
sproingg!!
Wat-san, just passing by (age 15)
Is he trying to make a joke...?
bloosh
wah!

(3rd SONG) TEACHER MIX

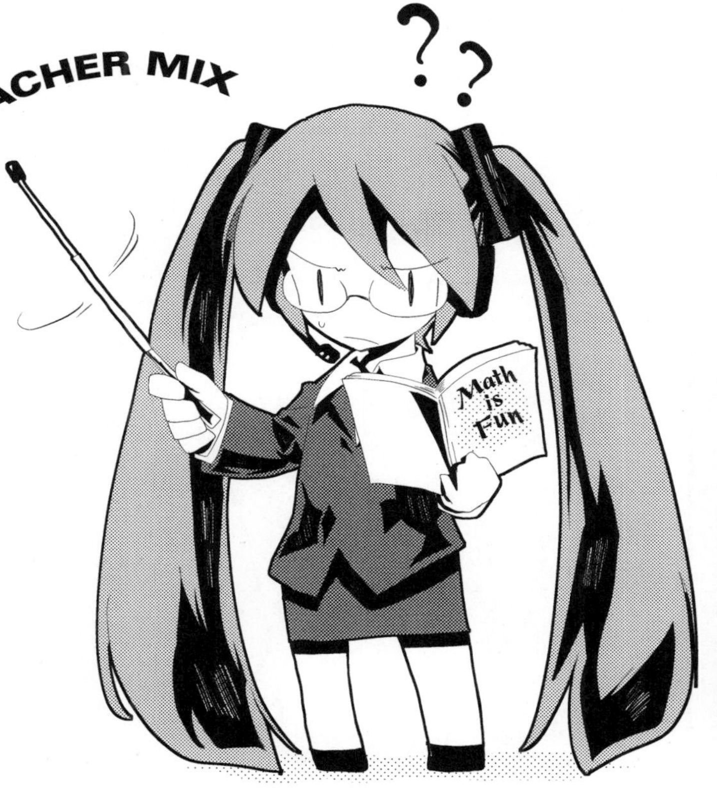
? ?
Math is Fun

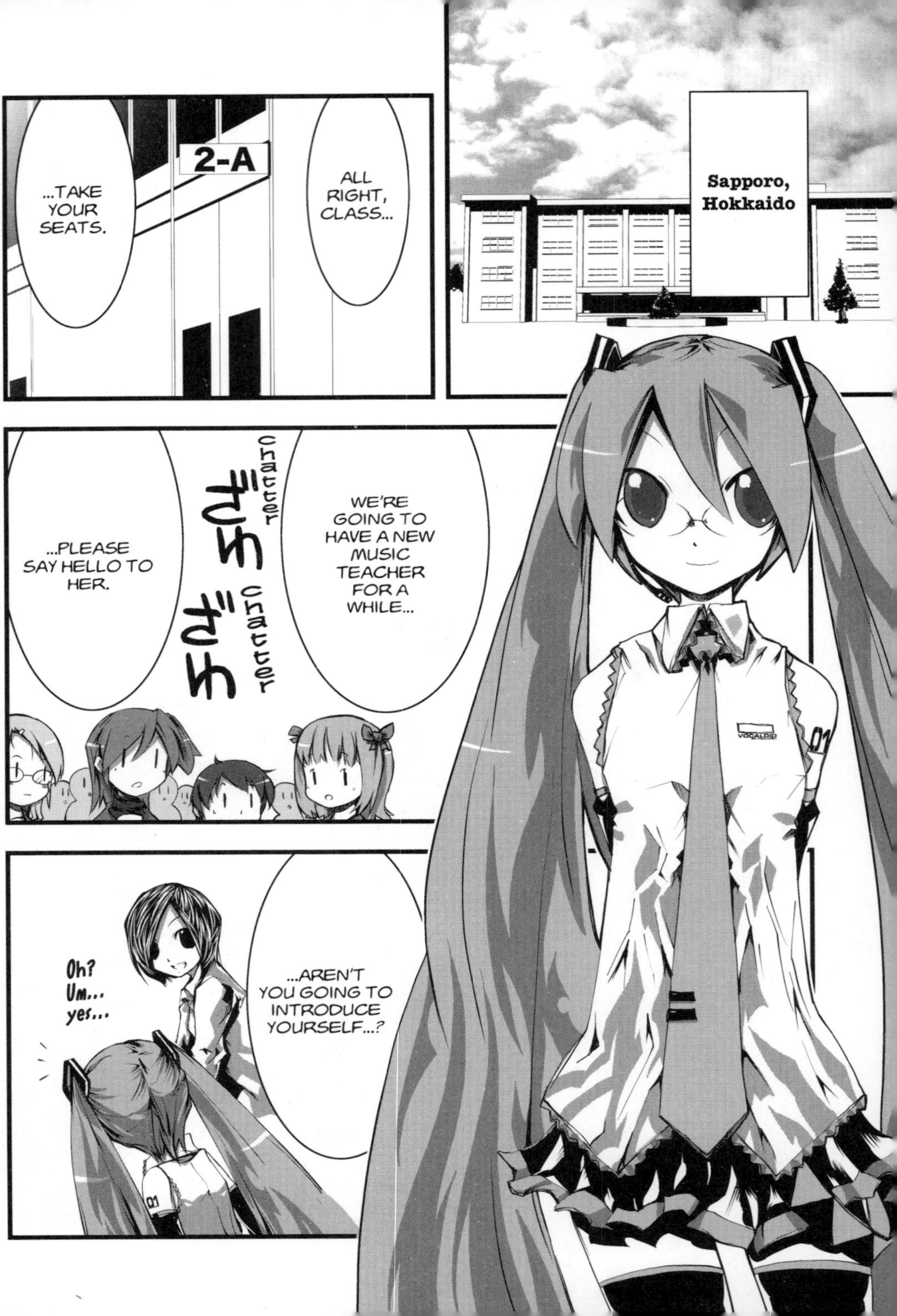
Sapporo, Hokkaido
2-A
ALL RIGHT, CLASS...
...TAKE YOUR SEATS.
WE'RE GOING TO HAVE A NEW MUSIC TEACHER FOR A WHILE...
ざわ chatter
ざわ chatter
...PLEASE SAY HELLO TO HER.
...AREN'T YOU GOING TO INTRODUCE YOURSELF...?
Oh? Um... yes...

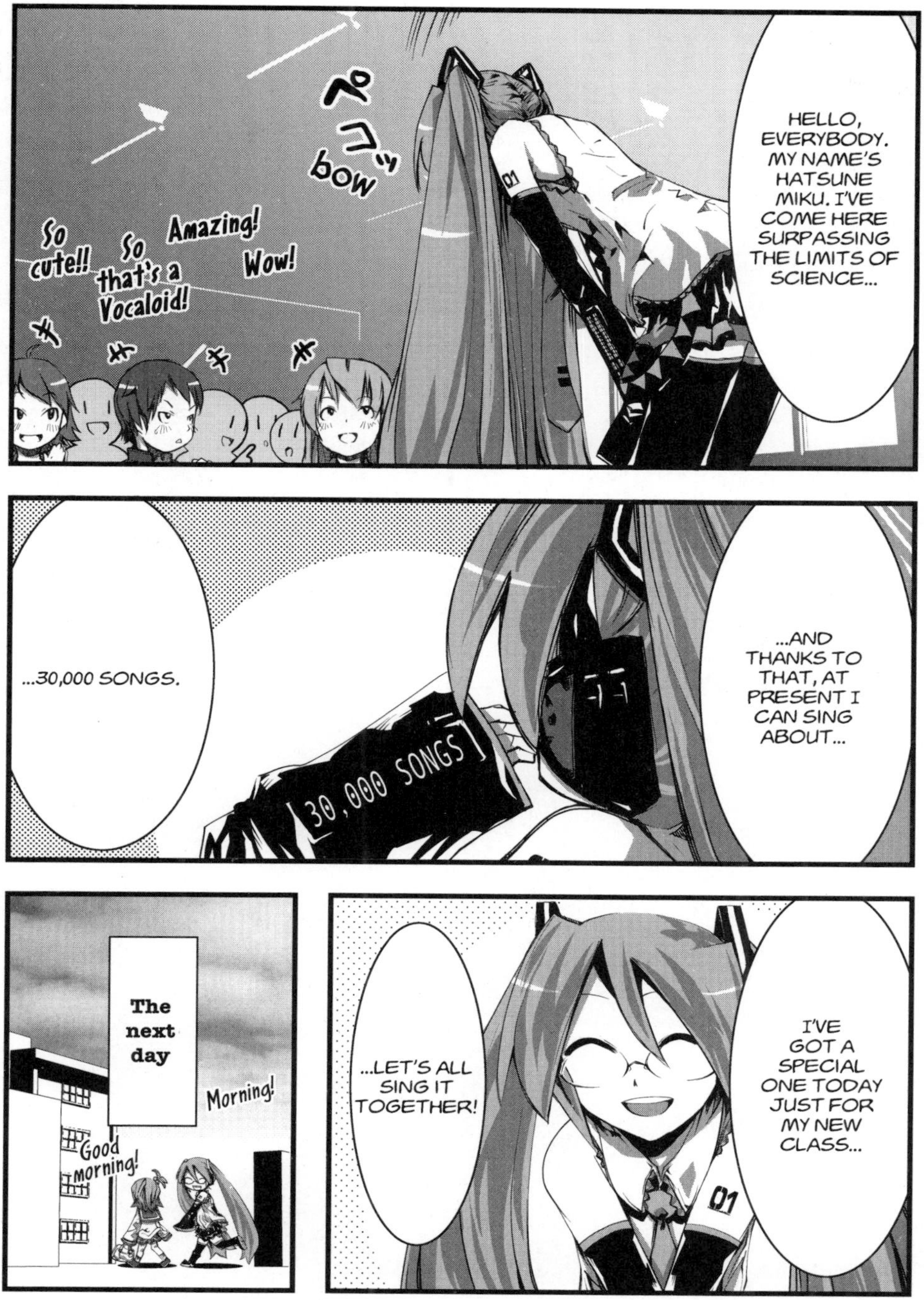
HELLO, EVERYBODY. MY NAME'S HATSUNE MIKU. I'VE COME HERE SURPASSING THE LIMITS OF SCIENCE...
ペコッ
bow
Amazing!
Wow!
So that's a Vocaloid!
So cute!!
...AND THANKS TO THAT, AT PRESENT I CAN SING ABOUT...
30,000 SONGS
...30,000 SONGS.
I'VE GOT A SPECIAL ONE TODAY JUST FOR MY NEW CLASS...
...LET'S ALL SING IT TOGETHER!
The next day
Morning!
Good morning!

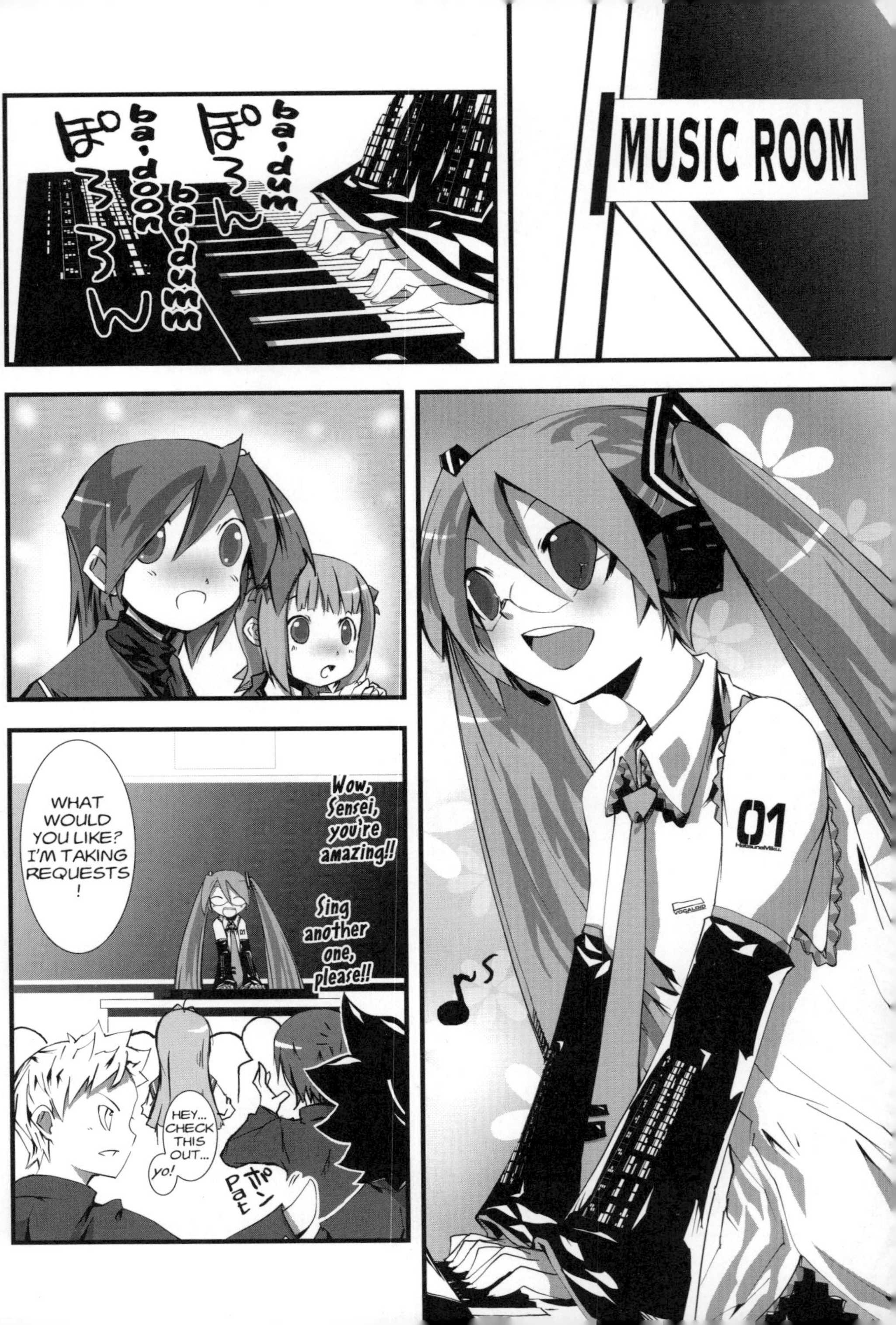
MUSIC ROOM
ba-dum
ぽろん
ba-dumm
ba-doon
ぽろろん
01
VOCALOID
Wow, Sensei, you're amazing!!
Sing another one, please!!
WHAT WOULD YOU LIKE? I'M TAKING REQUESTS!
HEY... CHECK THIS OUT... yo!
Pat

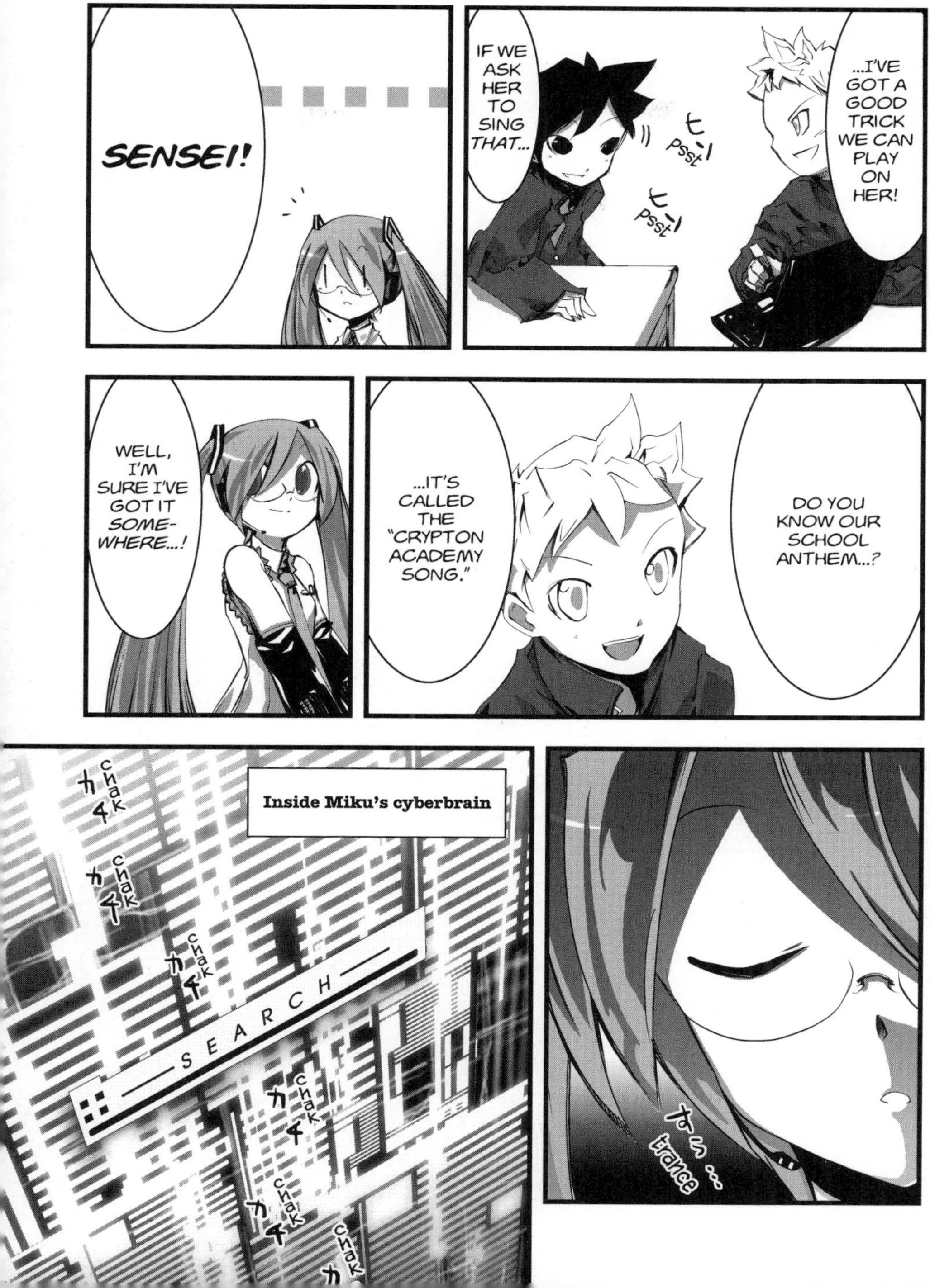
...I'VE GOT A GOOD TRICK WE CAN PLAY ON HER!
ヒソ psst
ヒソ psst
IF WE ASK HER TO SING THAT...
SENSEI!
DO YOU KNOW OUR SCHOOL ANTHEM...?
...IT'S CALLED THE "CRYPTON ACADEMY SONG."
WELL, I'M SURE I'VE GOT IT SOME-WHERE...!
すぅ… trance
Inside Miku's cyberbrain
カチ chak
カチ chak
カチ chak
SEARCH
カチ chak
カチ chak
カ chak

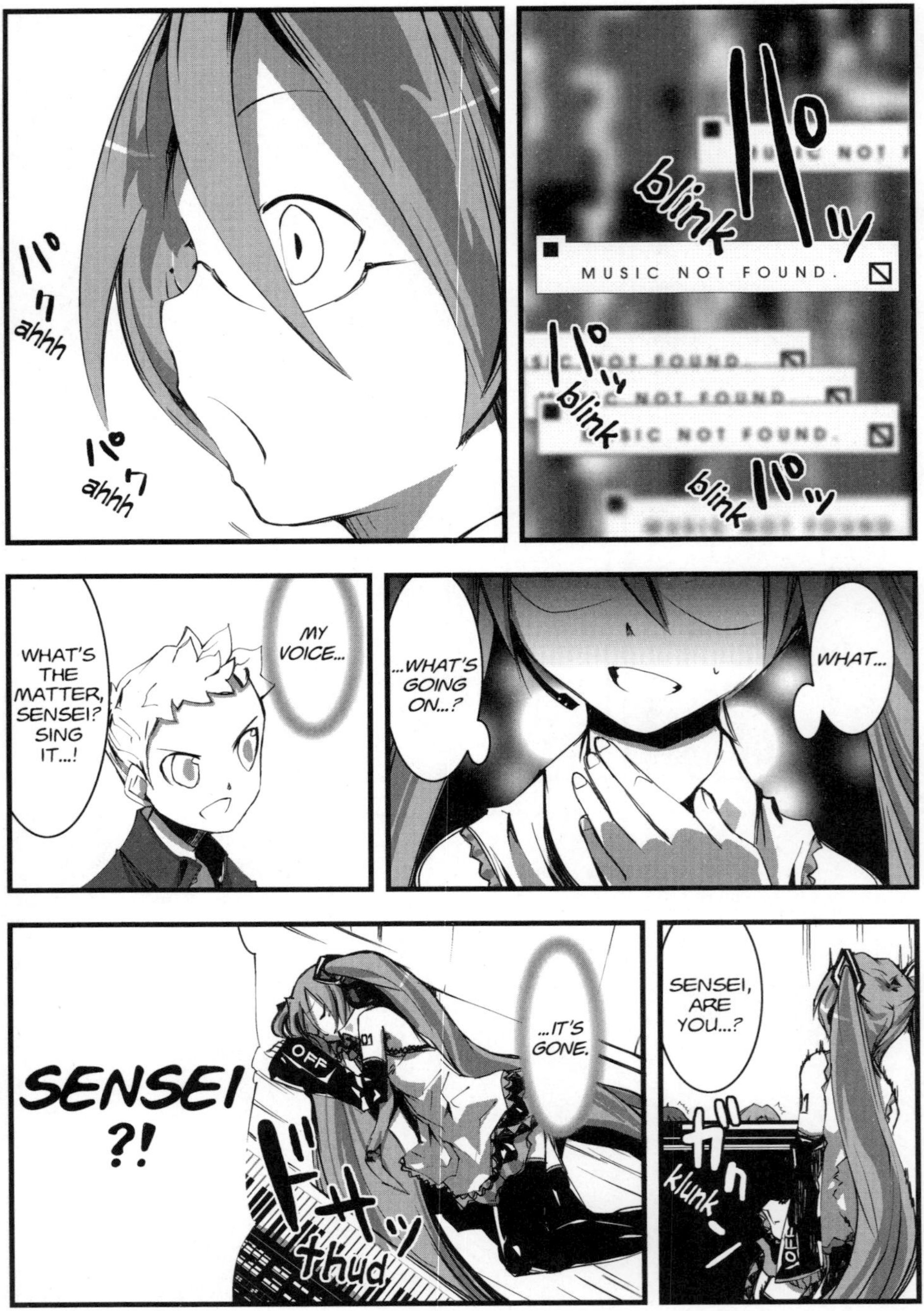
パッ
MUSIC NOT F
blink
MUSIC NOT FOUND.
パッ
blink
SIC NOT FOUND.
blink
パッ
MUSIC NOT FOUND.
パク
ahhh
パク
ahhh
WHAT...
...WHAT'S GOING ON...?
MY VOICE...
WHAT'S THE MATTER, SENSEI? SING IT...!
SENSEI, ARE YOU...?
ガク
klunk
OFF
...IT'S GONE.
OFF
SENSEI ?!
ドサッ
thud

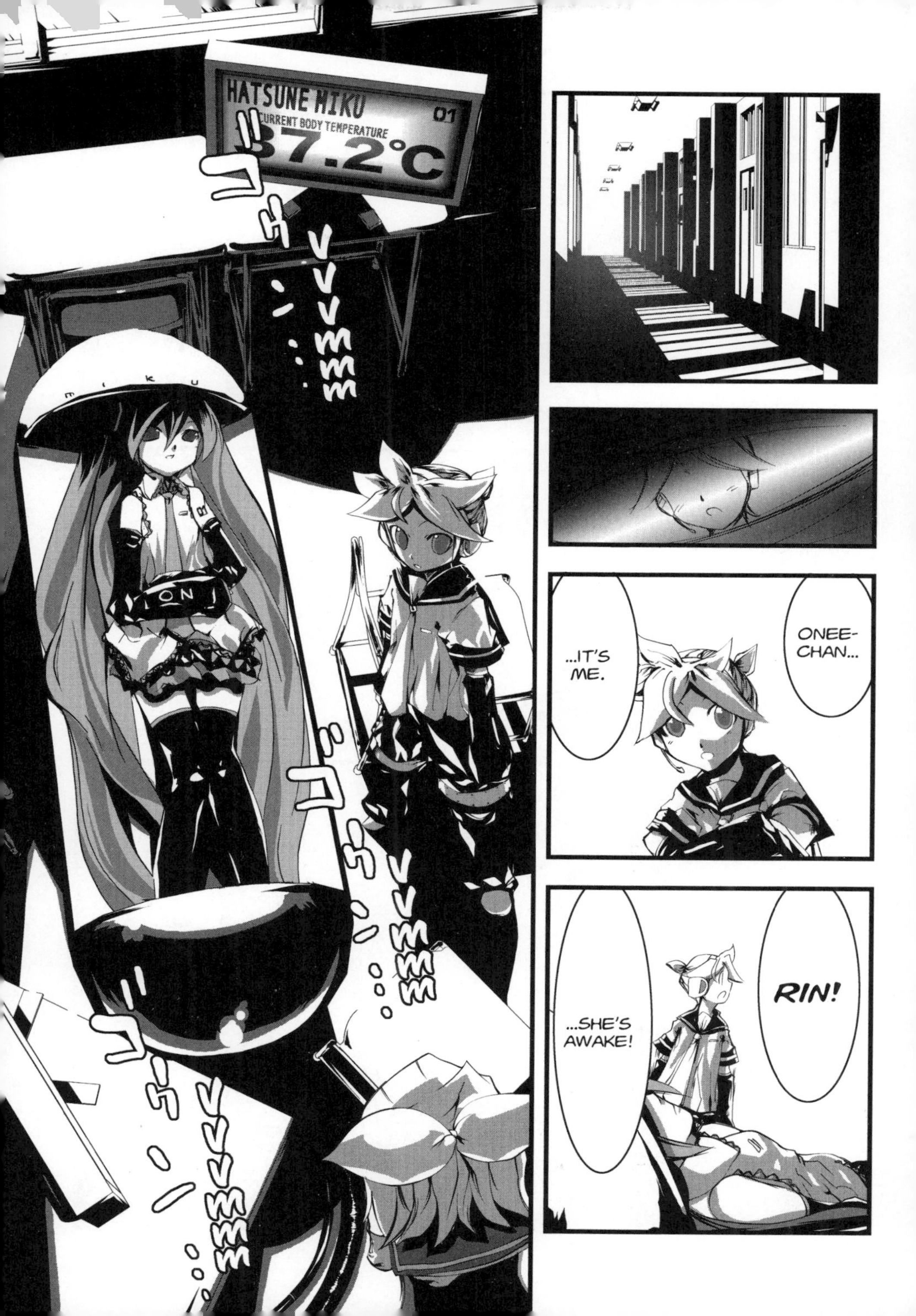
ONEE-CHAN...
...IT'S ME.
RIN!
...SHE'S AWAKE!
HATSUNE MIKU
01
CURRENT BODY TEMPERATURE
37.2°C
VVVMMM
ON
VVVMMM
VVVVMMM

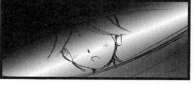

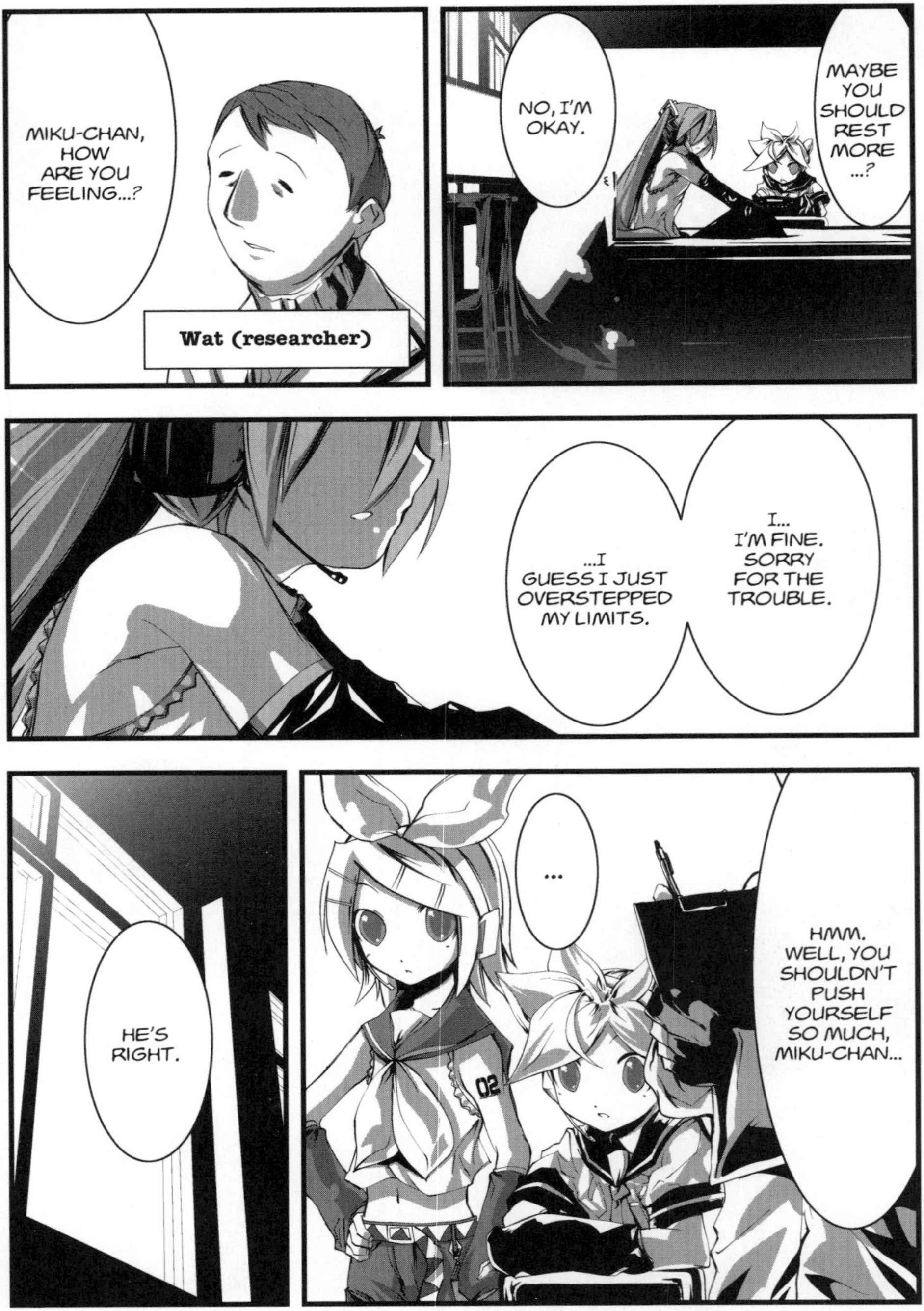
MAYBE YOU SHOULD REST MORE ...?
NO, I'M OKAY.
MIKU-CHAN, HOW ARE YOU FEELING...?
Wat (researcher)
I... I'M FINE. SORRY FOR THE TROUBLE.
...I GUESS I JUST OVERSTEPPED MY LIMITS.
HMM. WELL, YOU SHOULDN'T PUSH YOURSELF SO MUCH, MIKU-CHAN...
...
HE'S RIGHT.

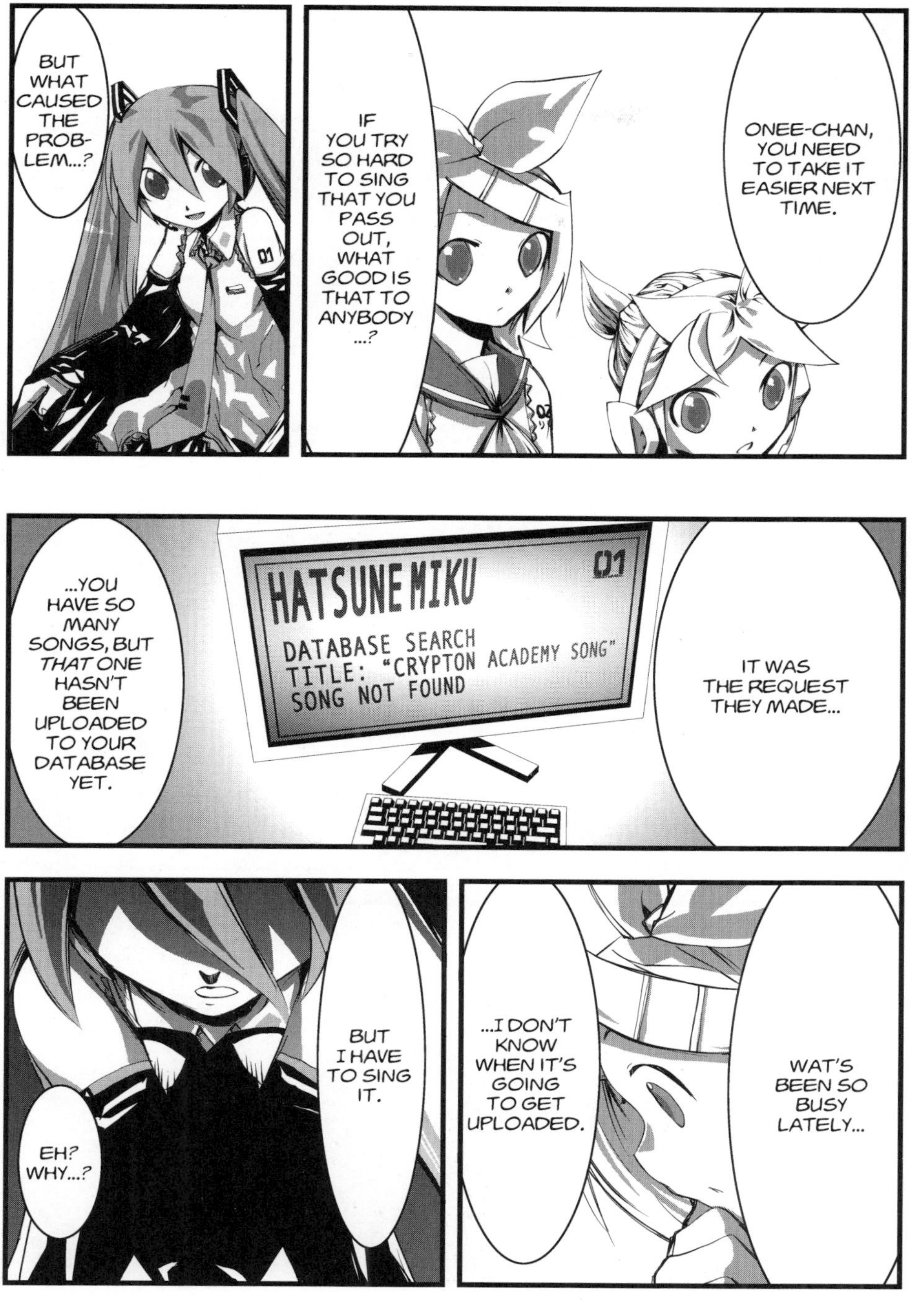
ONEE-CHAN, YOU NEED TO TAKE IT EASIER NEXT TIME.
IF YOU TRY SO HARD TO SING THAT YOU PASS OUT, WHAT GOOD IS THAT TO ANYBODY ...?
BUT WHAT CAUSED THE PROB-LEM...?
IT WAS THE REQUEST THEY MADE...
HATSUNE MIKU
01
DATABASE SEARCH
TITLE: "CRYPTON ACADEMY SONG"
SONG NOT FOUND
...YOU HAVE SO MANY SONGS, BUT *THAT* ONE HASN'T BEEN UPLOADED TO YOUR DATABASE YET.
WAT'S BEEN SO BUSY LATELY...
...I DON'T KNOW WHEN IT'S GOING TO GET UPLOADED.
BUT I HAVE TO SING IT.
EH? WHY...?

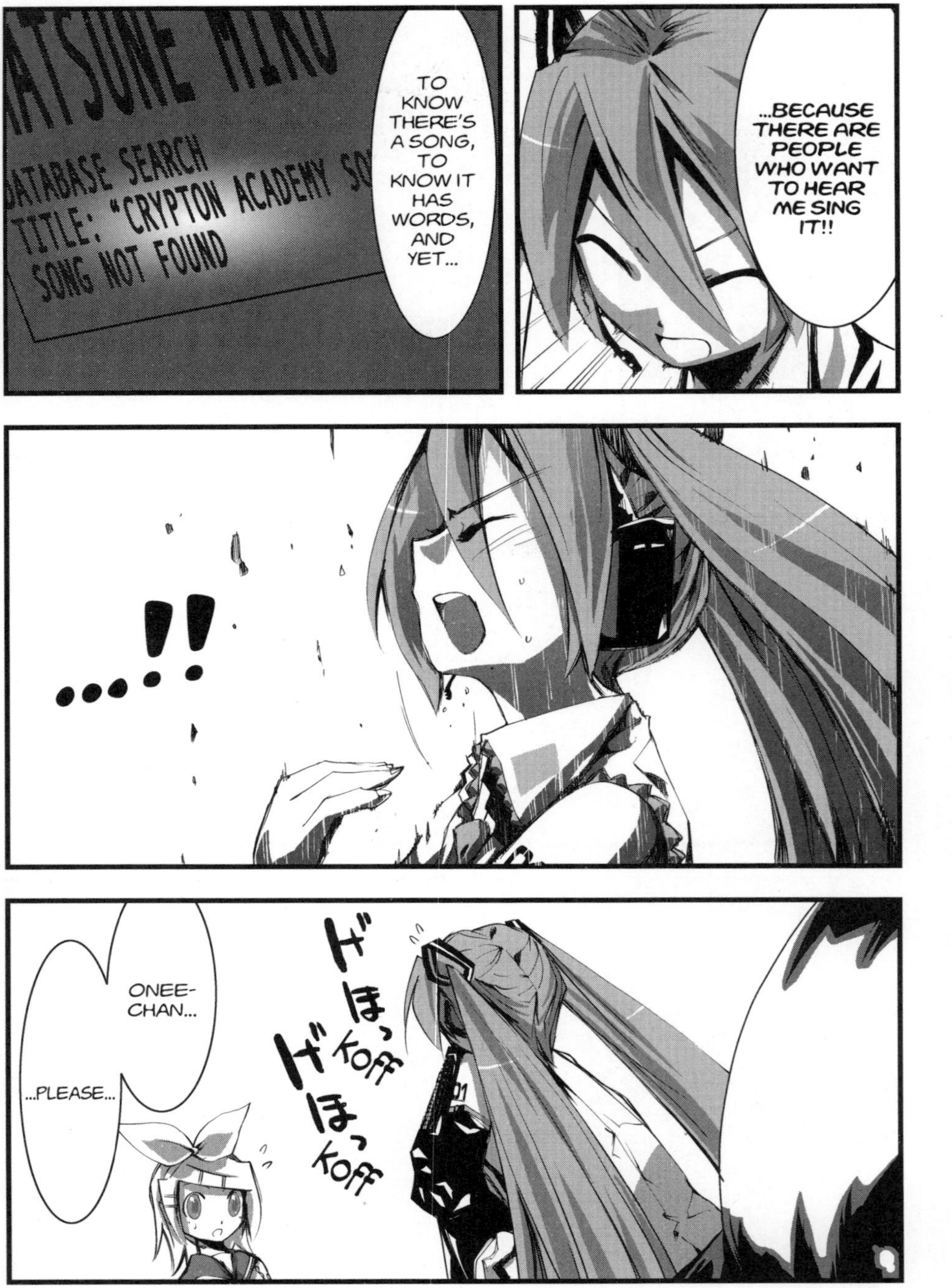
...BECAUSE THERE ARE PEOPLE WHO WANT TO HEAR ME SING IT!!
DATABASE SEARCH
TITLE: "CRYPTON ACADEMY SO
SONG NOT FOUND
TO KNOW THERE'S A SONG, TO KNOW IT HAS WORDS, AND YET...
...!!
ゲほっ KOFF
ゲほっ KOFF
ONEE-CHAN...
...PLEASE...

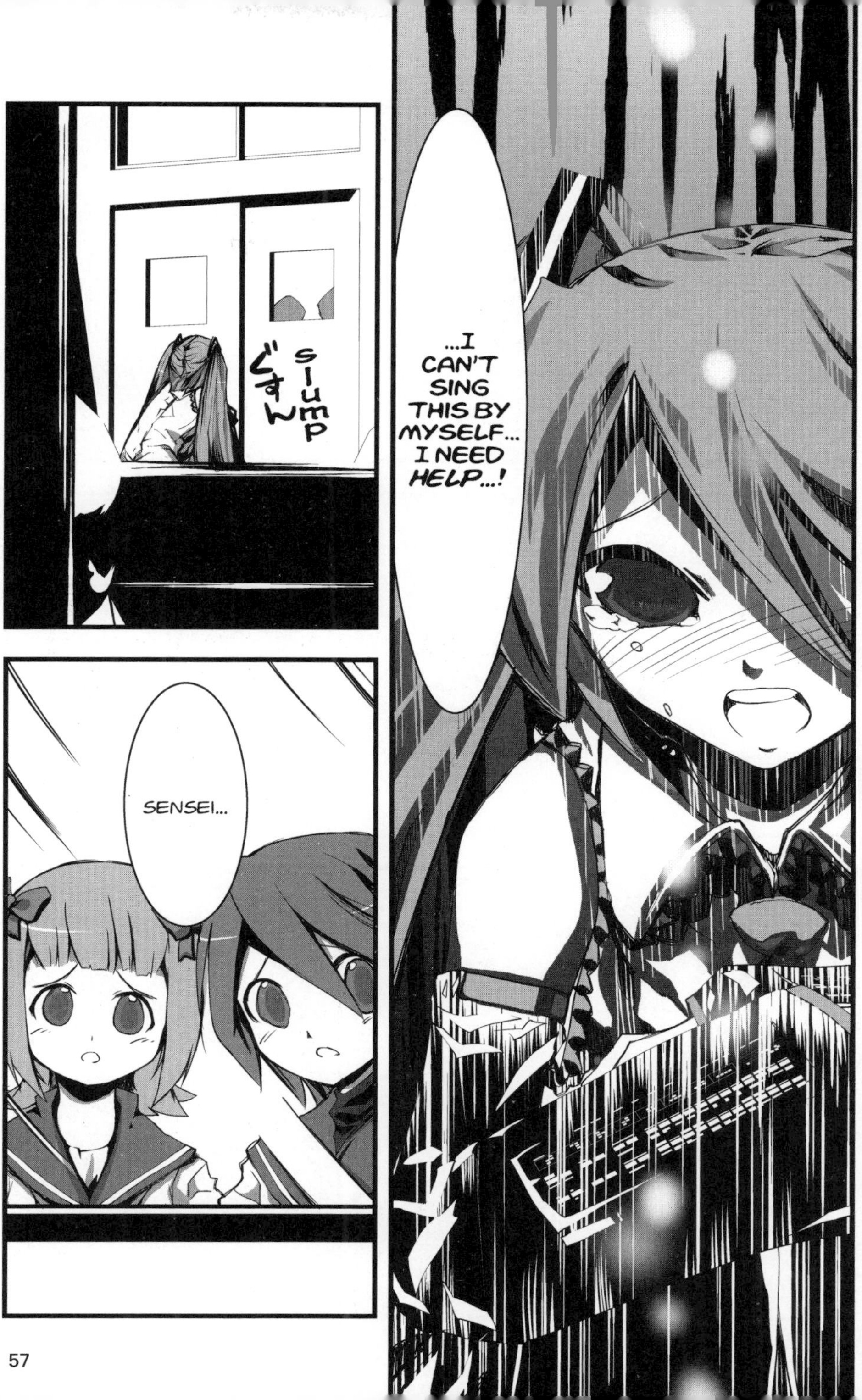
...I CAN'T SING THIS BY MYSELF... I NEED HELP...!
SLUMP
ぐすん
SENSEI...

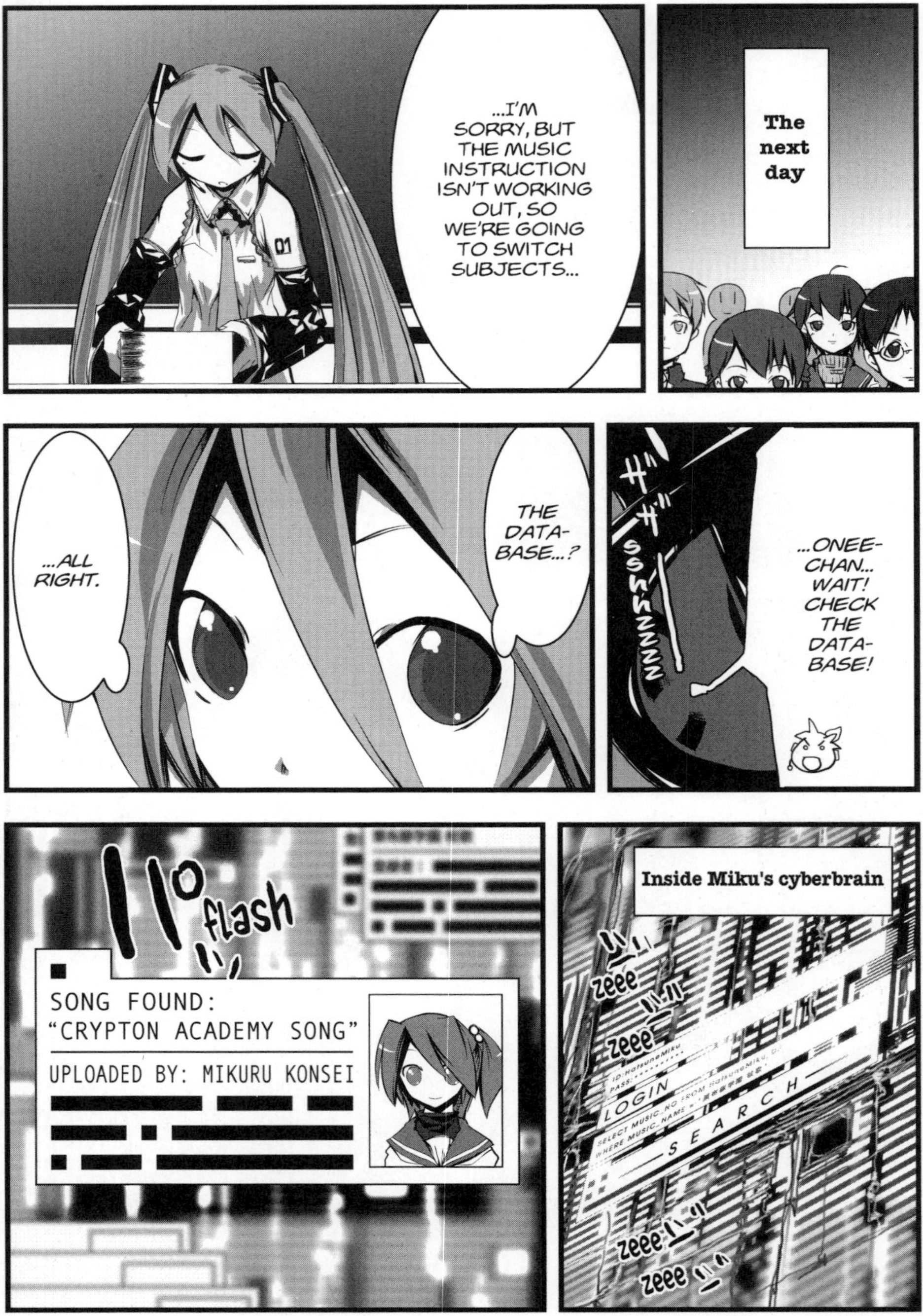
The next day
...I'M SORRY, BUT THE MUSIC INSTRUCTION ISN'T WORKING OUT, SO WE'RE GOING TO SWITCH SUBJECTS...
sshhzzzz
...ONEE-CHAN... WAIT! CHECK THE DATA-BASE!
THE DATA-BASE...?
...ALL RIGHT.
Inside Miku's cyberbrain
zeee
zeee
LOGIN
SEARCH
zeee
zeee
flash
SONG FOUND:
"CRYPTON ACADEMY SONG"
UPLOADED BY: MIKURU KONSEI

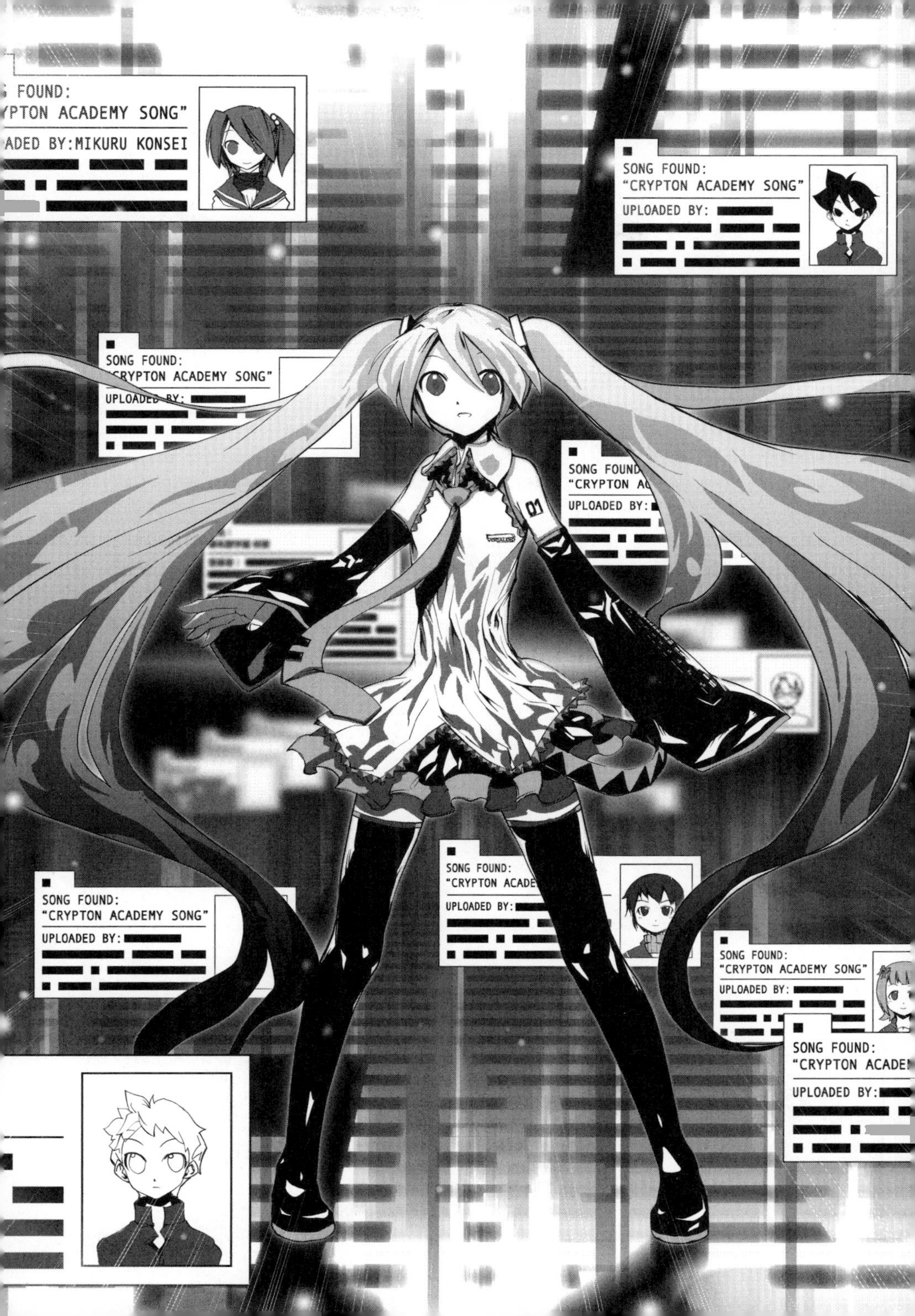

SONG FOUND:
"CRYPTON ACADEMY SONG"
UPLOADED BY:
G FOUND:
YPTON ACADEMY SONG"
ADED BY:MIKURU KONSEI
SONG FOUND:
"CRYPTON ACADEMY SONG"
UPLOADED BY:
SONG FOUND
"CRYPTON AC
UPLOADED BY:
SONG FOUND:
"CRYPTON ACADE
UPLOADED BY:
SONG FOUND:
"CRYPTON ACADEMY SONG"
UPLOADED BY:
SONG FOUND:
"CRYPTON ACADEMY SONG"
UPLOADED BY:
SONG FOUND:
"CRYPTON ACADE
UPLOADED BY:

AND THESE...AND THESE...AND *THESE!* WE MADE SURE ALL OF THESE GOT INTO THE DATABASE LAST NIGHT! PRETTY COOL, HUH?!

IN OTHER WORDS, YOU DID SOME WORK FOR A CHANGE, LEN...?!

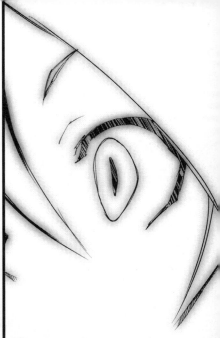

EVERYONE...

Sniff

...*SENSEI!*

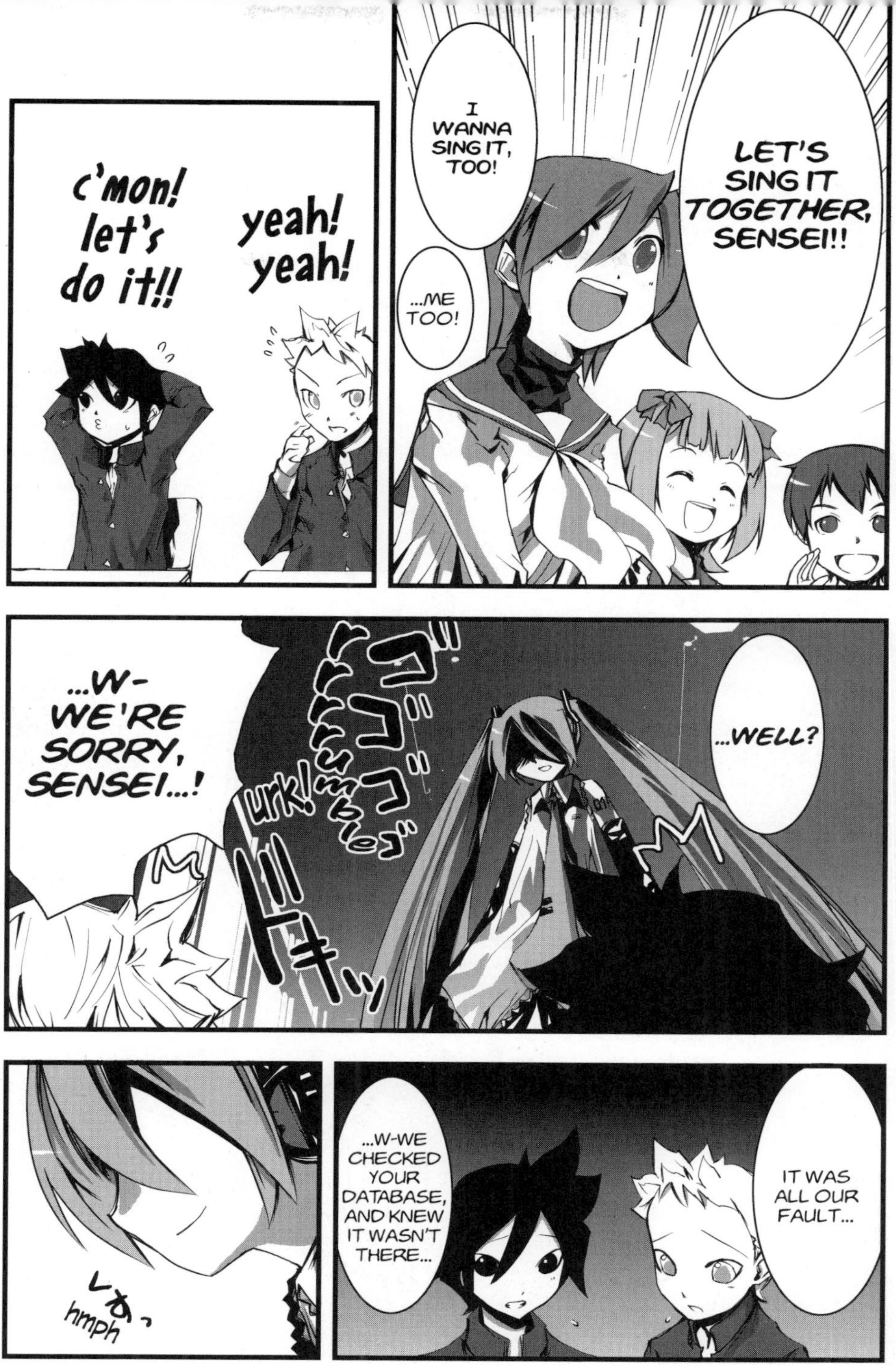
LET'S SING IT TOGETHER, SENSEI!!
I WANNA SING IT, TOO!
...ME TOO!
yeah! yeah!
c'mon! let's do it!!
...WELL?
rumble
urk!
...W-WE'RE SORRY, SENSEI...!
IT WAS ALL OUR FAULT...
...W-WE CHECKED YOUR DATABASE, AND KNEW IT WASN'T THERE...
hmph

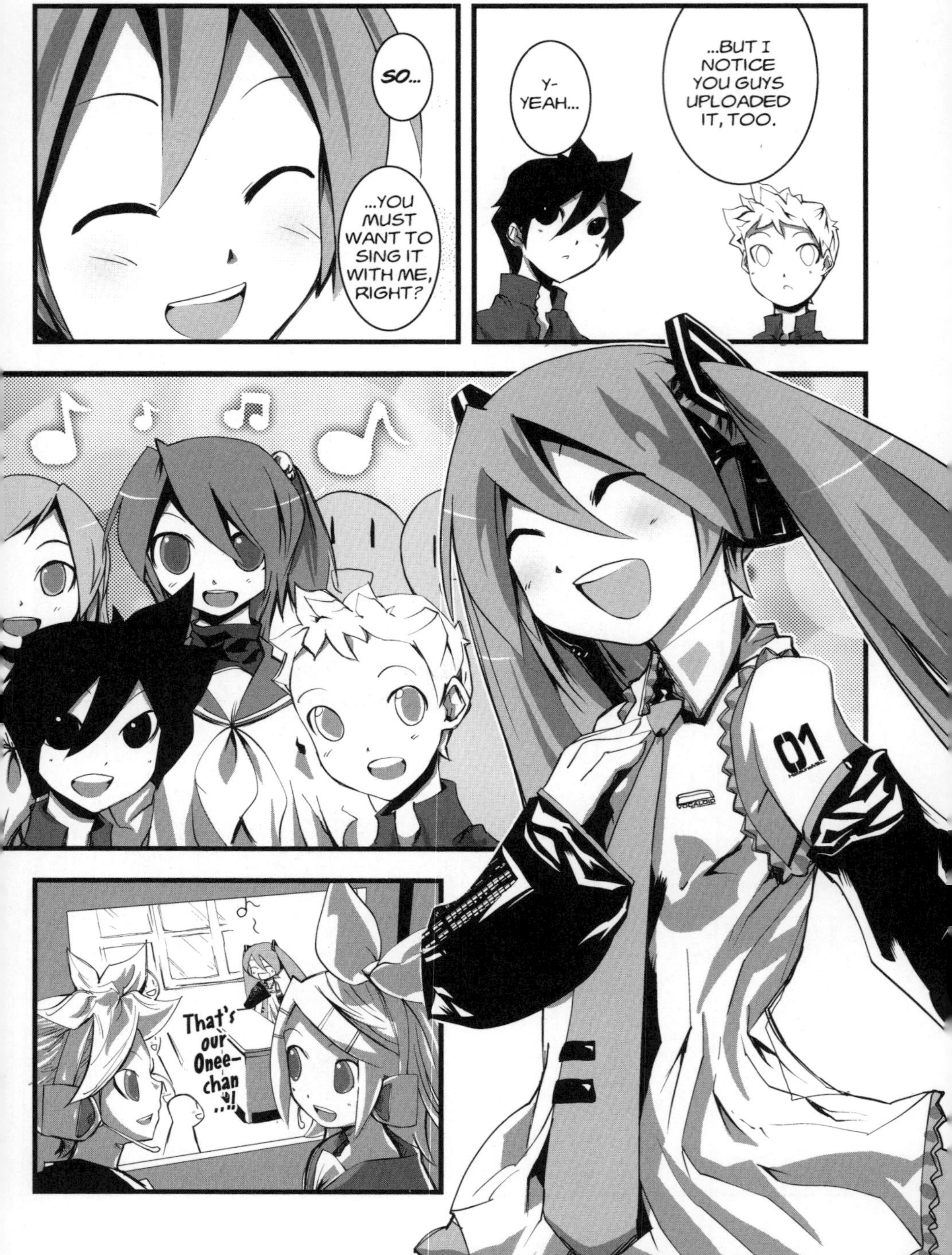
...BUT I NOTICE YOU GUYS UPLOADED IT, TOO.
Y-YEAH...
SO...
...YOU MUST WANT TO SING IT WITH ME, RIGHT?
That's our Onee-chan...!!

INTRO MIX

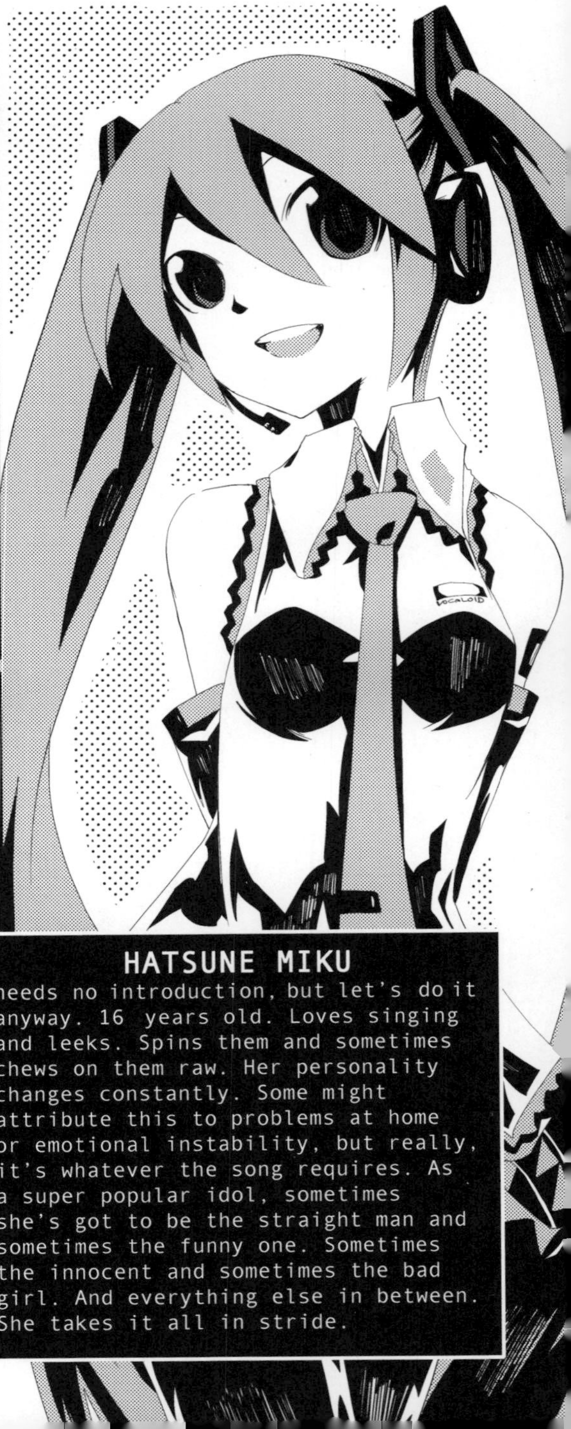

HATSUNE MIKU

needs no introduction, but let's do it anyway. 16 years old. Loves singing and leeks. Spins them and sometimes chews on them raw. Her personality changes constantly. Some might attribute this to problems at home or emotional instability, but really, it's whatever the song requires. As a super popular idol, sometimes she's got to be the straight man and sometimes the funny one. Sometimes the innocent and sometimes the bad girl. And everything else in between. She takes it all in stride.

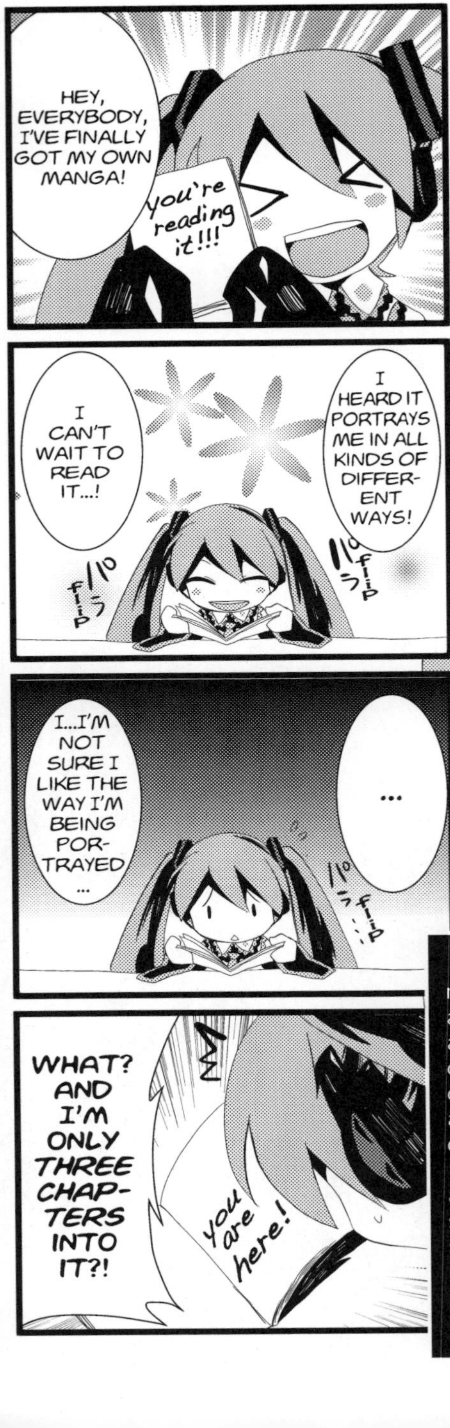
HEY, EVERYBODY, I'VE FINALLY GOT MY OWN MANGA!
you're reading it!!!
I HEARD IT PORTRAYS ME IN ALL KINDS OF DIFFER-ENT WAYS!
I CAN'T WAIT TO READ IT...!
flip
flip
...
I...I'M NOT SURE I LIKE THE WAY I'M BEING POR-TRAYED ...
flip
WHAT? AND I'M ONLY THREE CHAP-TERS INTO IT?!
you are here!

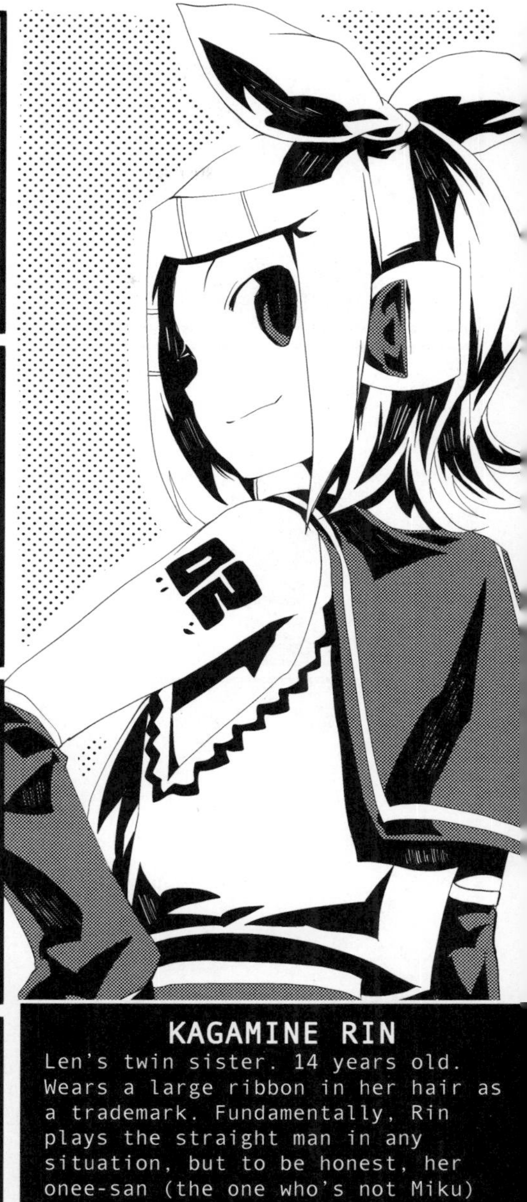

KAGAMINE RIN

Len's twin sister. 14 years old. Wears a large ribbon in her hair as a trademark. Fundamentally, Rin plays the straight man in any situation, but to be honest, her onee-san (the one who's not Miku) is much better at this, so she doesn't leave much of an impression. Perhaps it's that she's got strong personalities around her, and she just needs to find a new role for herself...?

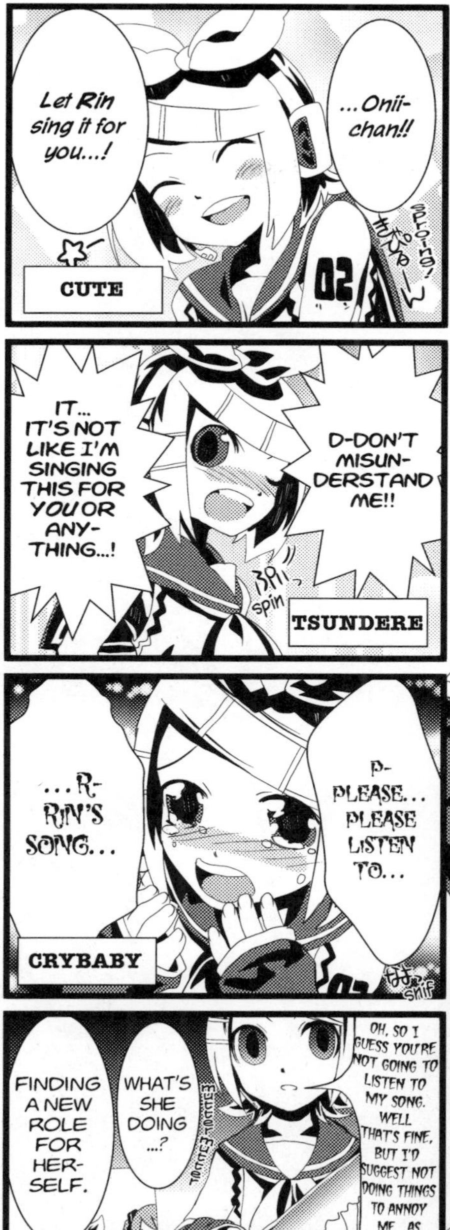
...Onii-chan!!
Let Rin sing it for you...!
Sproing!
CUTE
D-DON'T MISUNDERSTAND ME!!
IT... IT'S NOT LIKE I'M SINGING THIS FOR YOU OR ANYTHING...!
spin
TSUNDERE
P-PLEASE... PLEASE LISTEN TO...
...R-RIN'S SONG...
CRYBABY
sniff
OH, SO I GUESS YOU'RE NOT GOING TO LISTEN TO MY SONG. WELL THAT'S FINE, BUT I'D SUGGEST NOT DOING THINGS TO ANNOY ME...AS WHEN ROUSED I CAN BECOME QUITE... AGGRESSIVE...
WHAT'S SHE DOING ...?
FINDING A NEW ROLE FOR HER-SELF.
scary!
YANDERE

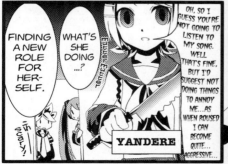

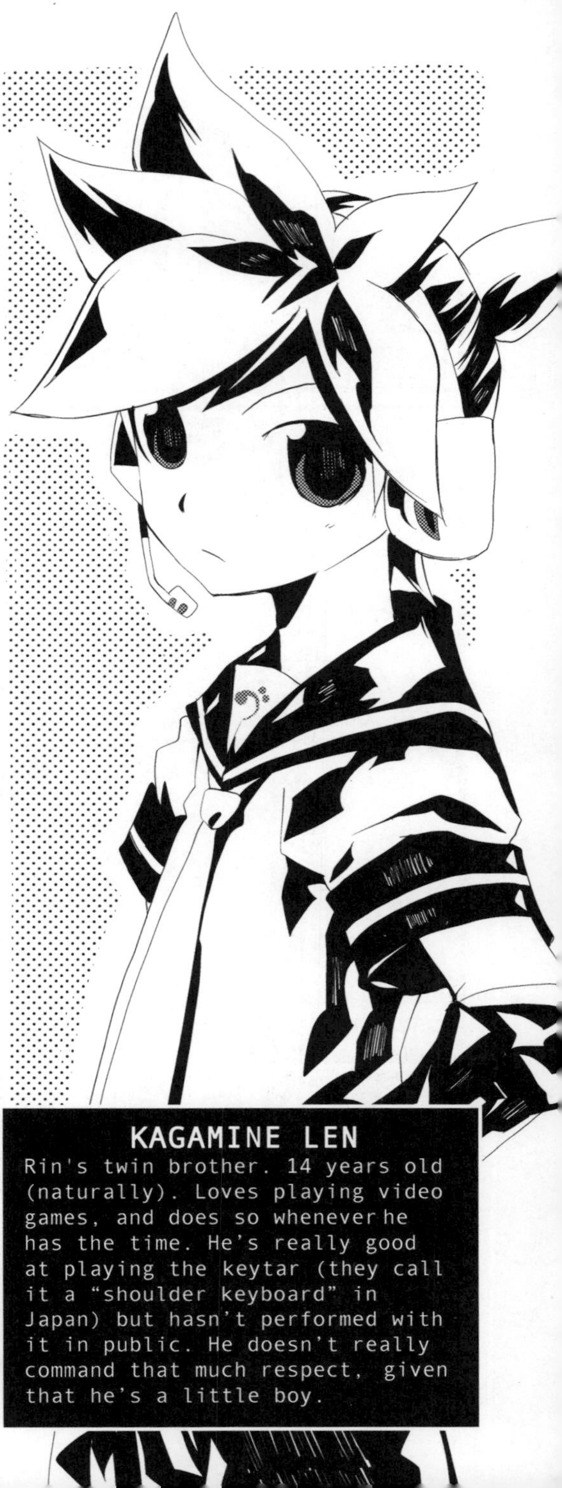
KAGAMINE LEN
Rin's twin brother. 14 years old (naturally). Loves playing video games, and does so whenever he has the time. He's really good at playing the keytar (they call it a "shoulder keyboard" in Japan) but hasn't performed with it in public. He doesn't really command that much respect, given that he's a little boy.

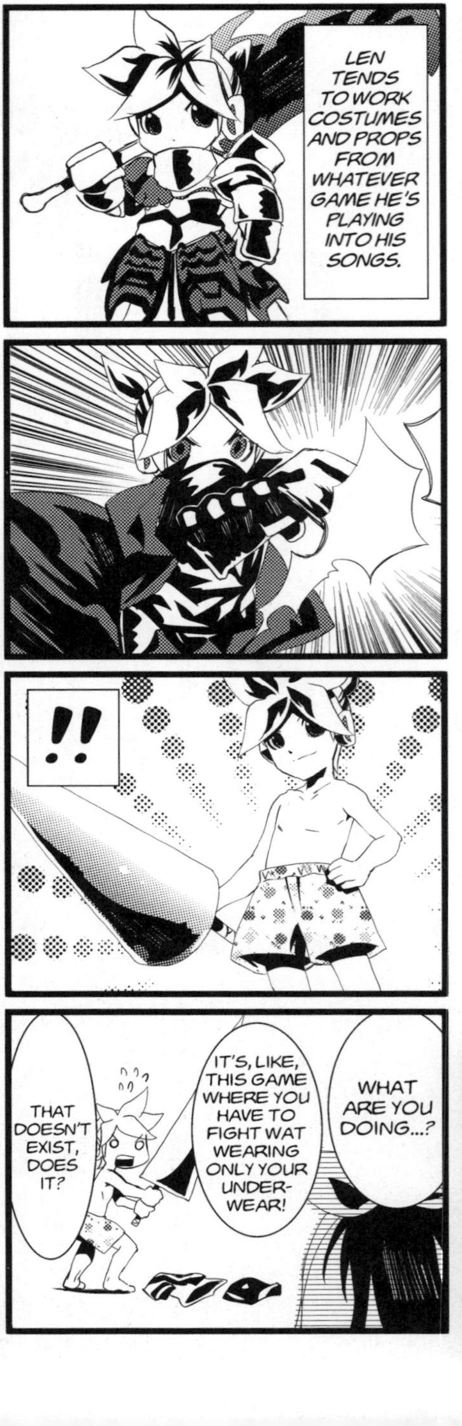
LEN TENDS TO WORK COSTUMES AND PROPS FROM WHATEVER GAME HE'S PLAYING INTO HIS SONGS.
!!
WHAT ARE YOU DOING...?
IT'S, LIKE, THIS GAME WHERE YOU HAVE TO FIGHT WAT WEARING ONLY YOUR UNDER-WEAR!
THAT DOESN'T EXIST, DOES IT?

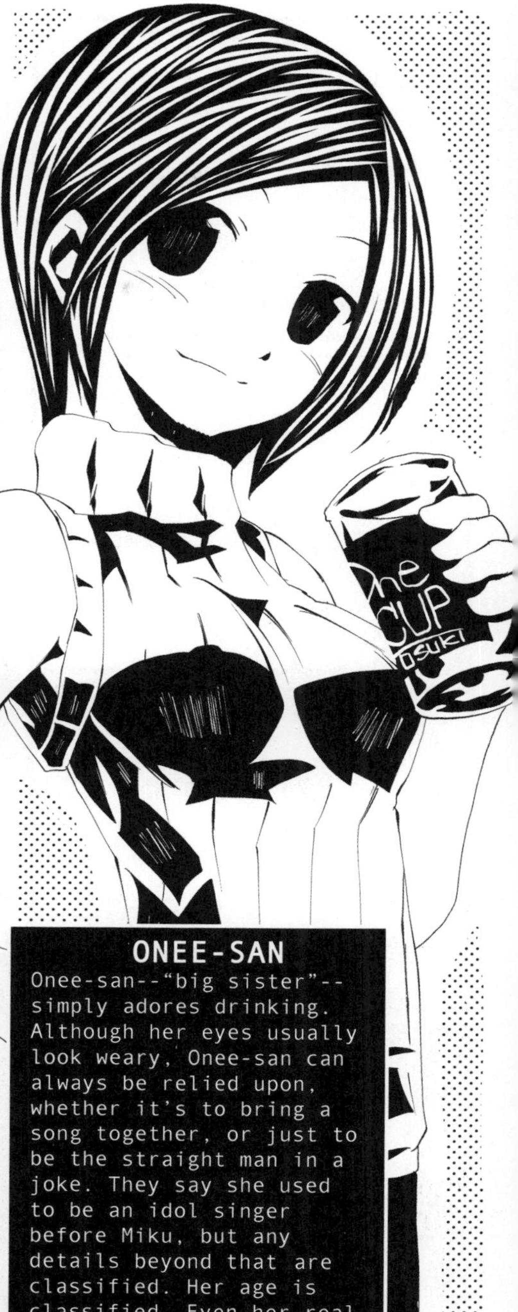
One CUP
OSUKI

ONEE-SAN

Onee-san--"big sister"--simply adores drinking. Although her eyes usually look weary, Onee-san can always be relied upon, whether it's to bring a song together, or just to be the straight man in a joke. They say she used to be an idol singer before Miku, but any details beyond that are classified. Her age is classified. Even her real name ~~is Me~~ is classified!

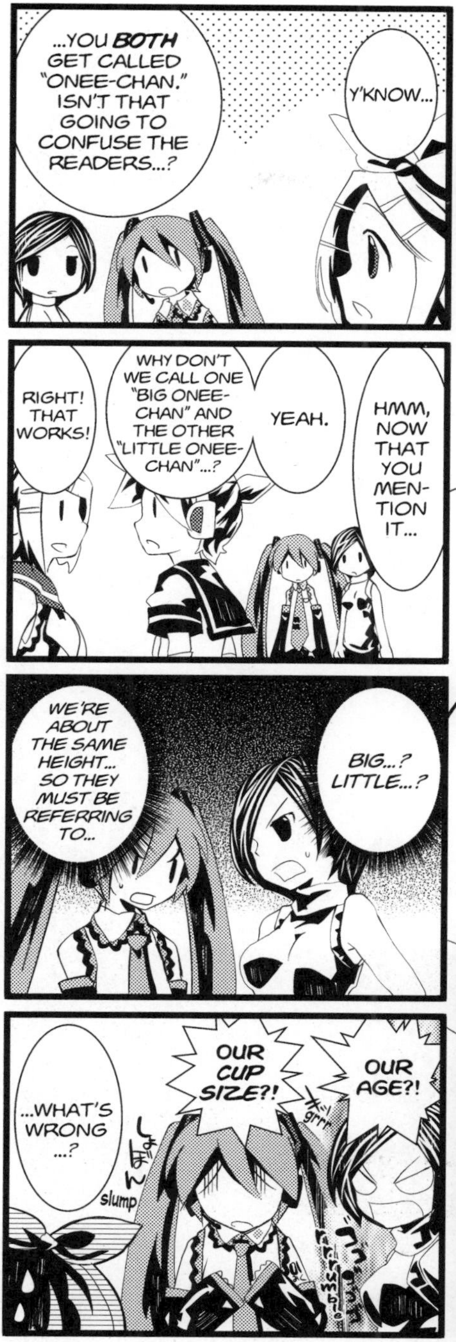
Y'KNOW...
...YOU BOTH GET CALLED "ONEE-CHAN." ISN'T THAT GOING TO CONFUSE THE READERS...?
HMM, NOW THAT YOU MENTION IT...
YEAH.
WHY DON'T WE CALL ONE "BIG ONEE-CHAN" AND THE OTHER "LITTLE ONEE-CHAN"...?
RIGHT! THAT WORKS!
BIG...? LITTLE...?
WE'RE ABOUT THE SAME HEIGHT... SO THEY MUST BE REFERRING TO...
OUR AGE?!
grrr
OUR CUP SIZE?!
しょぼん
slump
...WHAT'S WRONG ...?

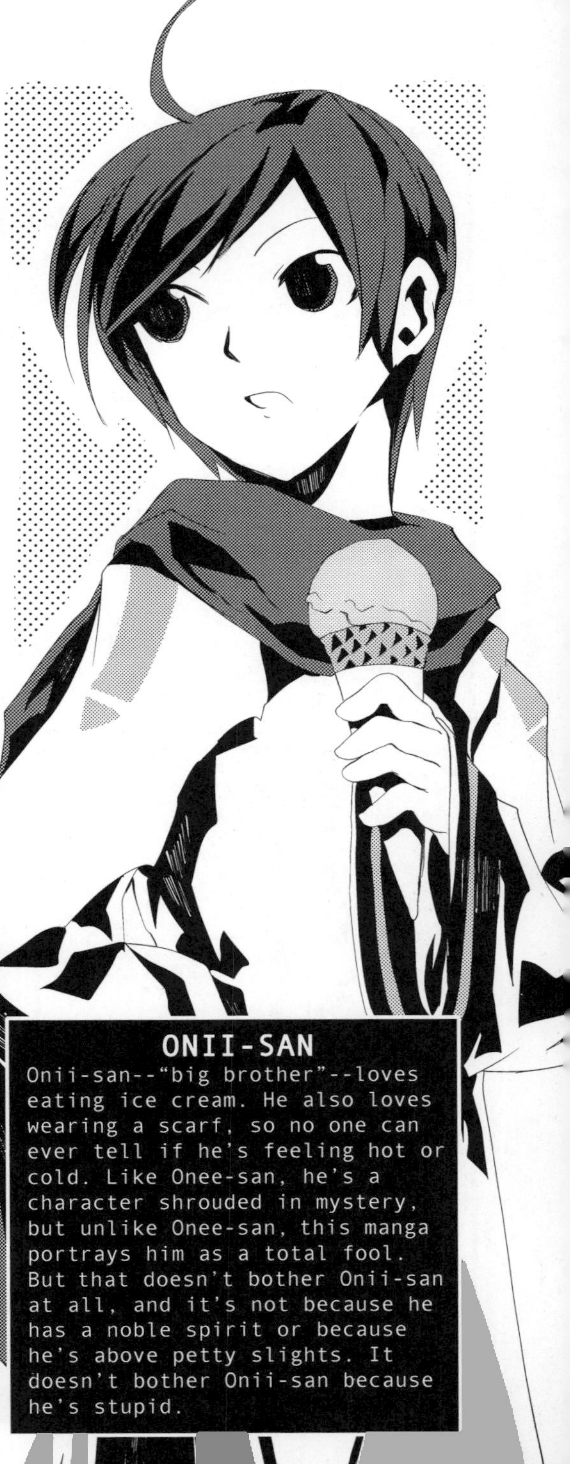

ONII-SAN

Onii-san--"big brother"--loves eating ice cream. He also loves wearing a scarf, so no one can ever tell if he's feeling hot or cold. Like Onee-san, he's a character shrouded in mystery, but unlike Onee-san, this manga portrays him as a total fool. But that doesn't bother Onii-san at all, and it's not because he has a noble spirit or because he's above petty slights. It doesn't bother Onii-san because he's stupid.

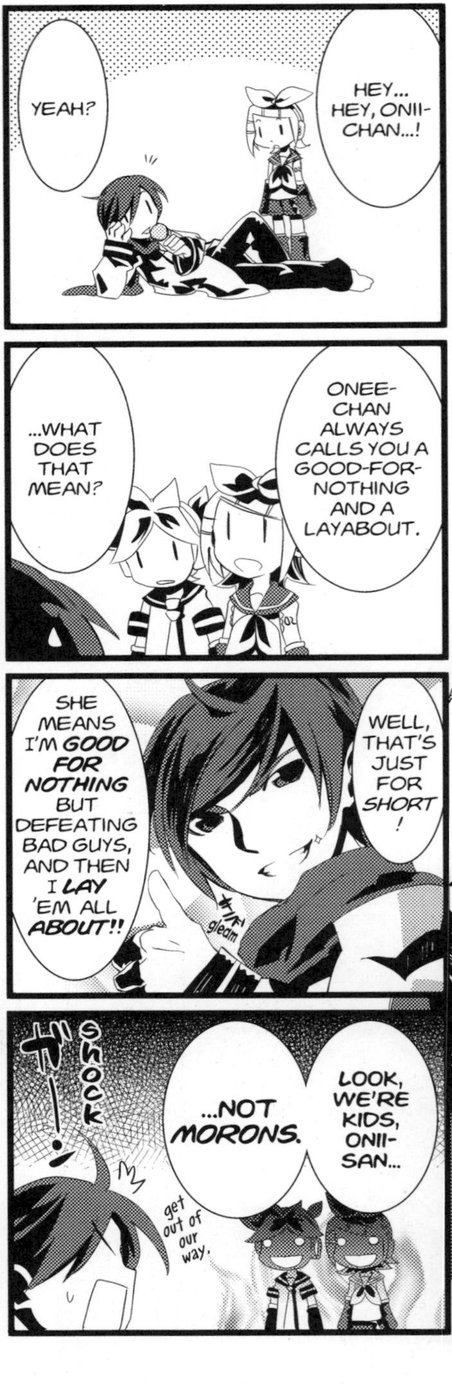
HEY... HEY, ONII-CHAN...!
YEAH?
ONEE-CHAN ALWAYS CALLS YOU A GOOD-FOR-NOTHING AND A LAYABOUT.
...WHAT DOES THAT MEAN?
WELL, THAT'S JUST FOR SHORT!
SHE MEANS I'M GOOD FOR NOTHING BUT DEFEATING BAD GUYS, AND THEN I LAY 'EM ALL ABOUT!!
gleam
LOOK, WE'RE KIDS, ONII-SAN...
...NOT MORONS.
SHOCK
get out of our way.

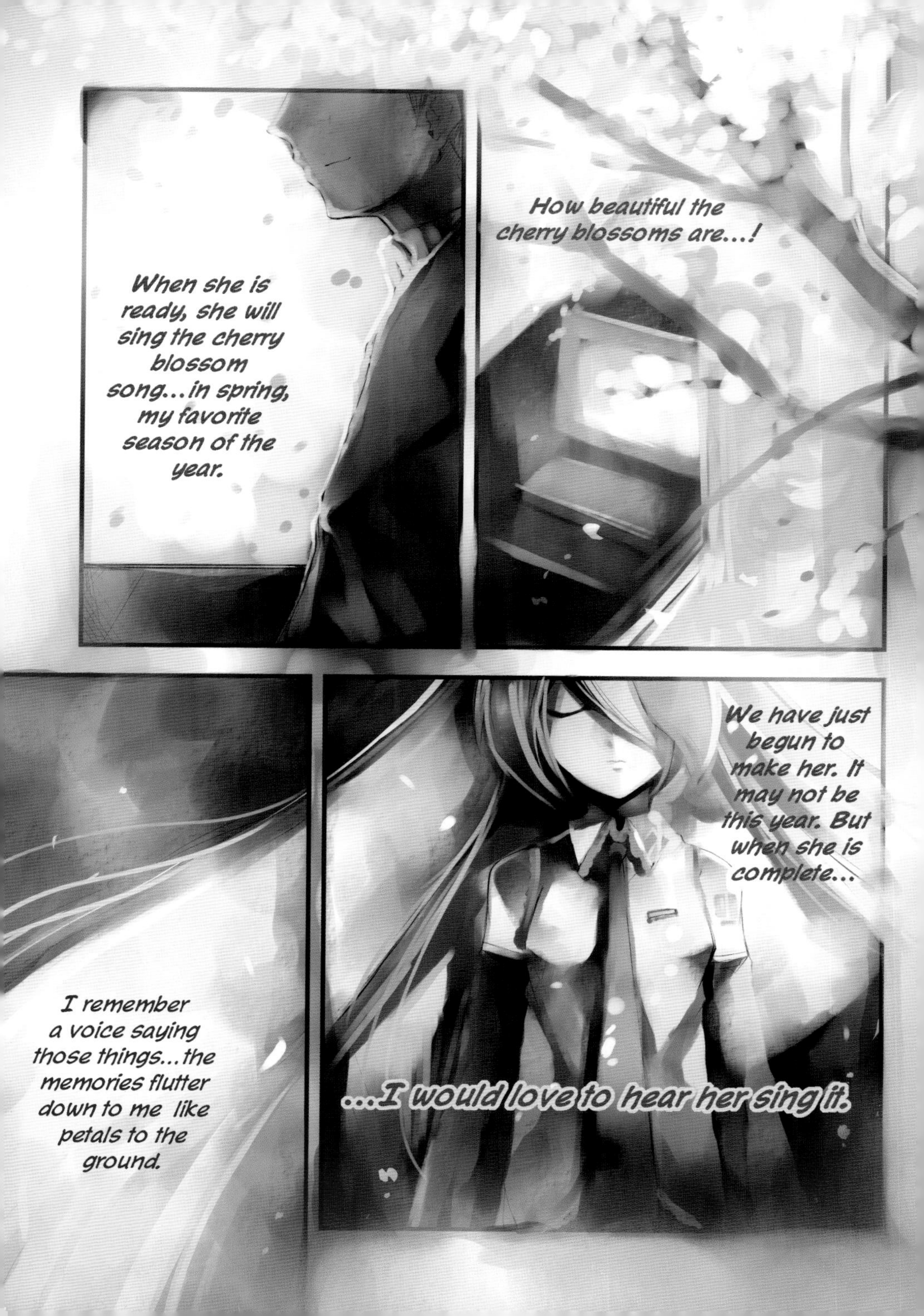
How beautiful the cherry blossoms are...!
When she is ready, she will sing the cherry blossom song...in spring, my favorite season of the year.
We have just begun to make her. It may not be this year. But when she is complete...
...I would love to hear her sing it.
I remember a voice saying those things...the memories flutter down to me like petals to the ground.

(4th SONG) **SAKURA MIX**

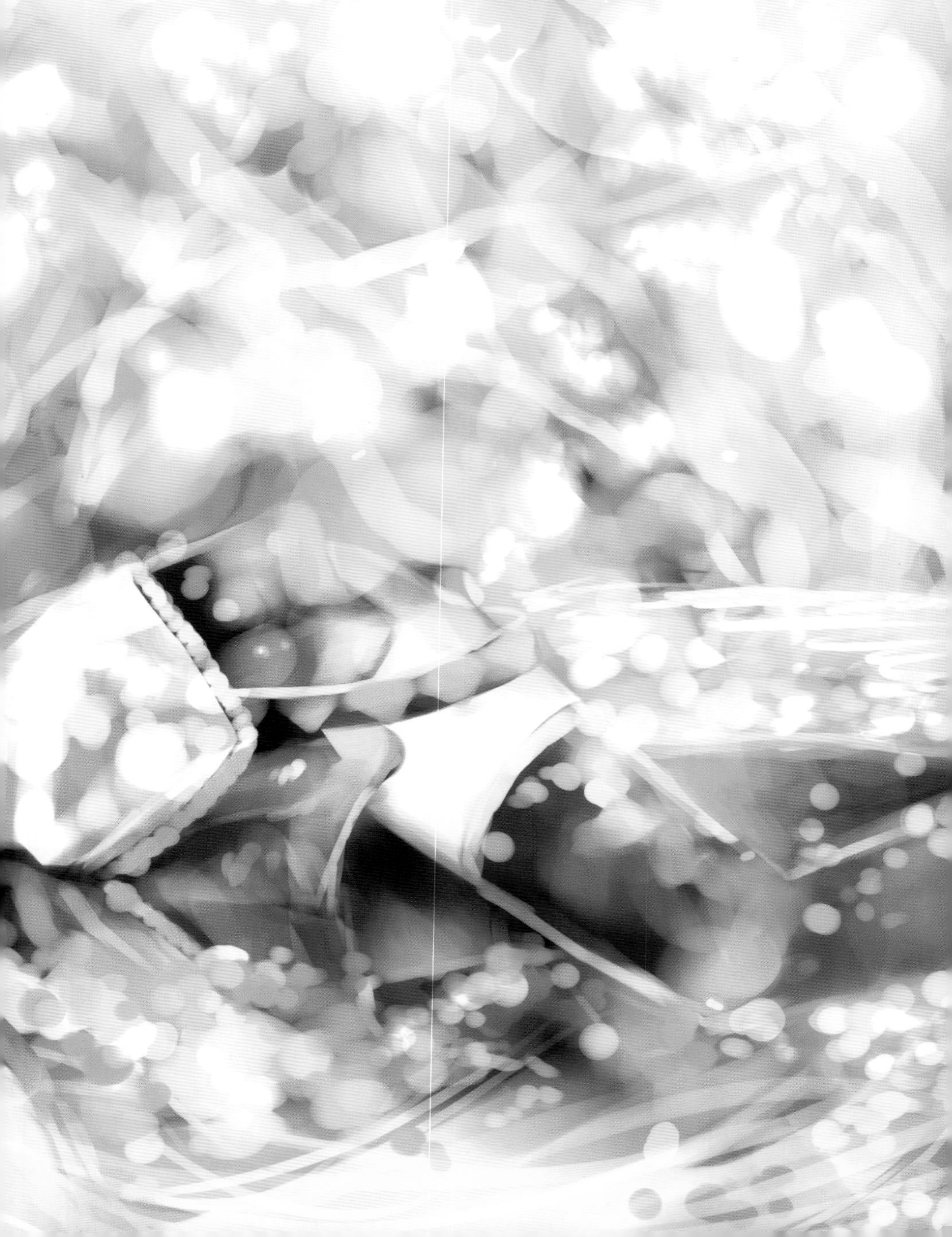

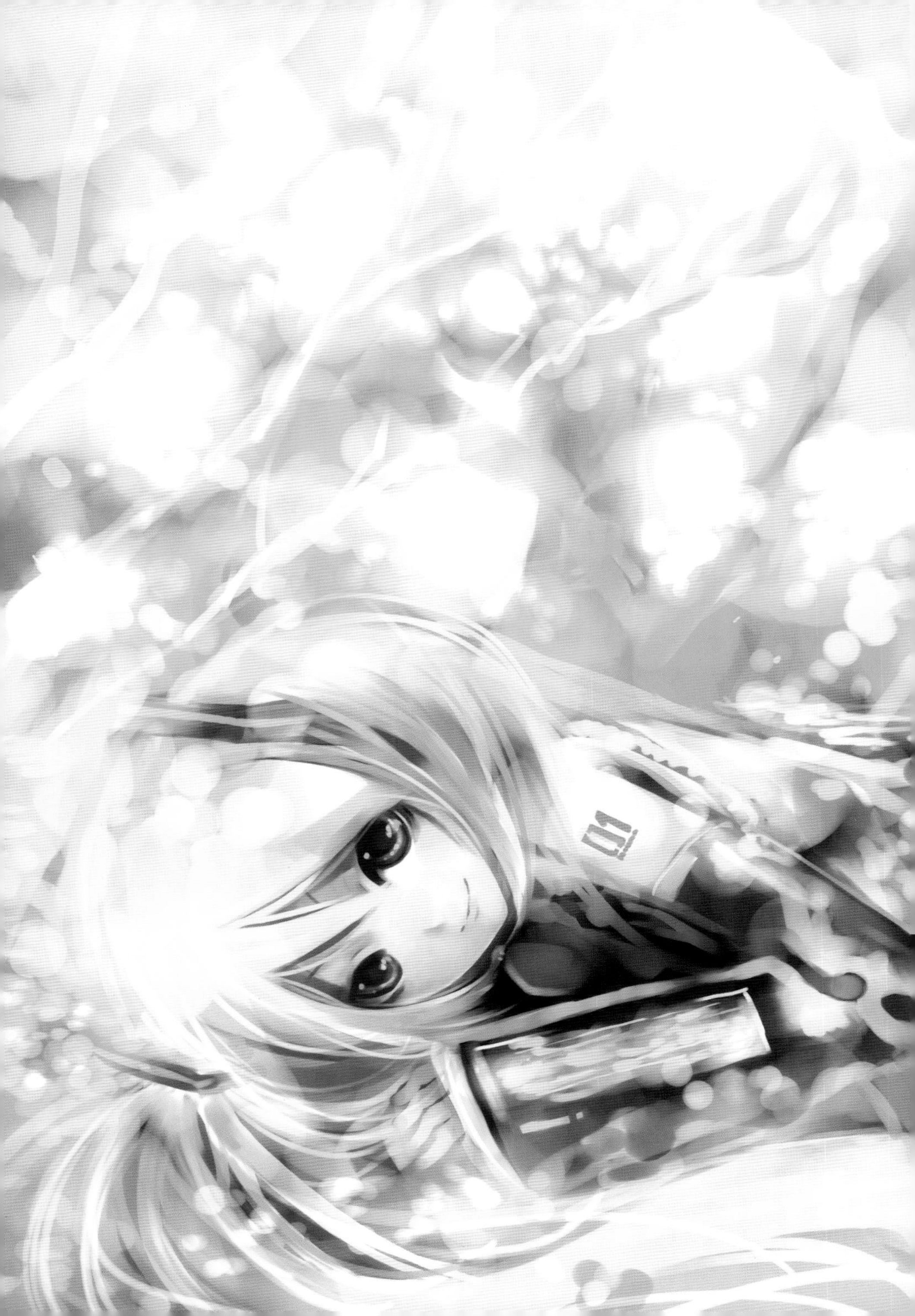

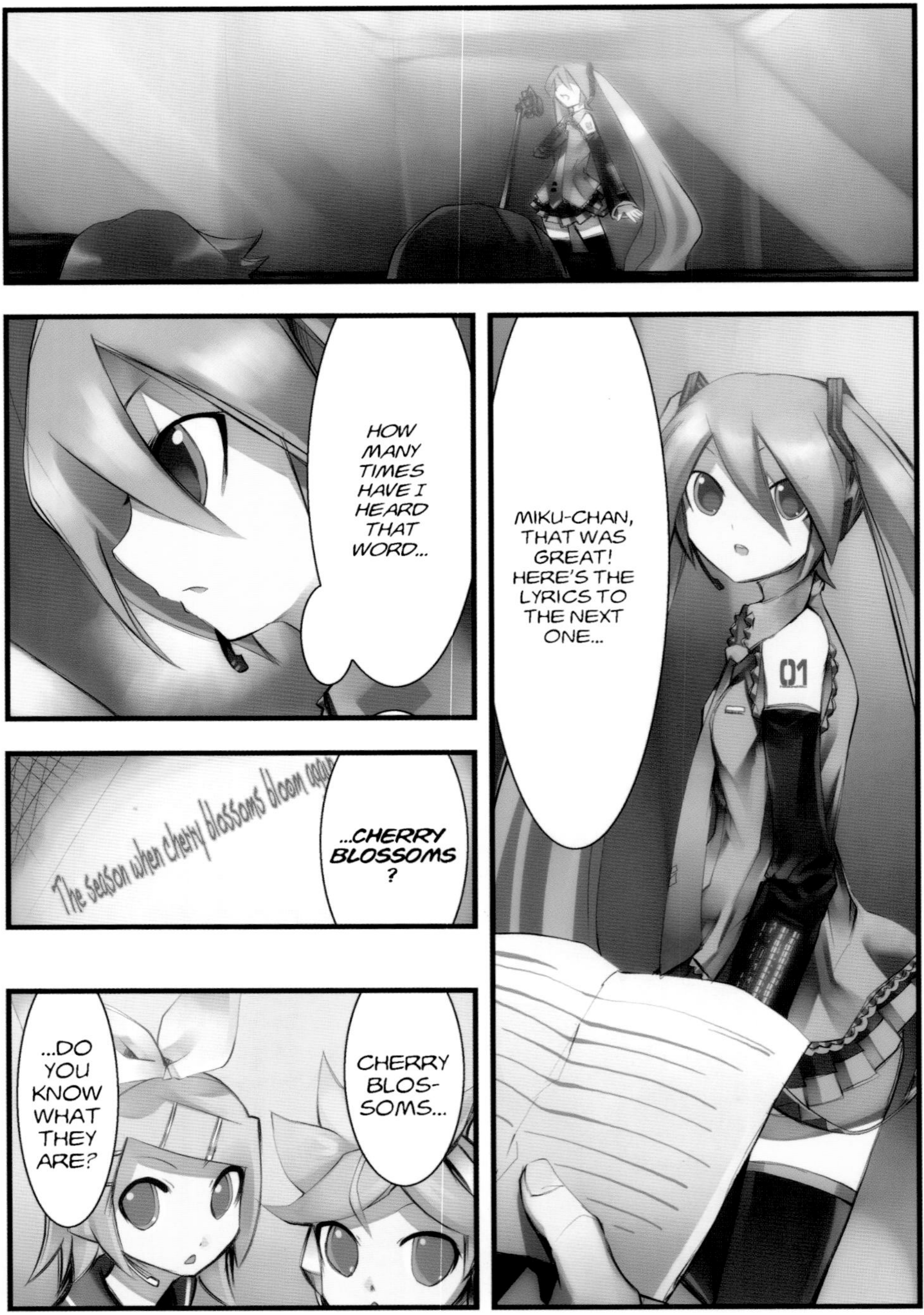
MIKU-CHAN, THAT WAS GREAT! HERE'S THE LYRICS TO THE NEXT ONE...
HOW MANY TIMES HAVE I HEARD THAT WORD...
The season when cherry blossoms bloom
...CHERRY BLOSSOMS?
CHERRY BLOS-SOMS...
...DO YOU KNOW WHAT THEY ARE?

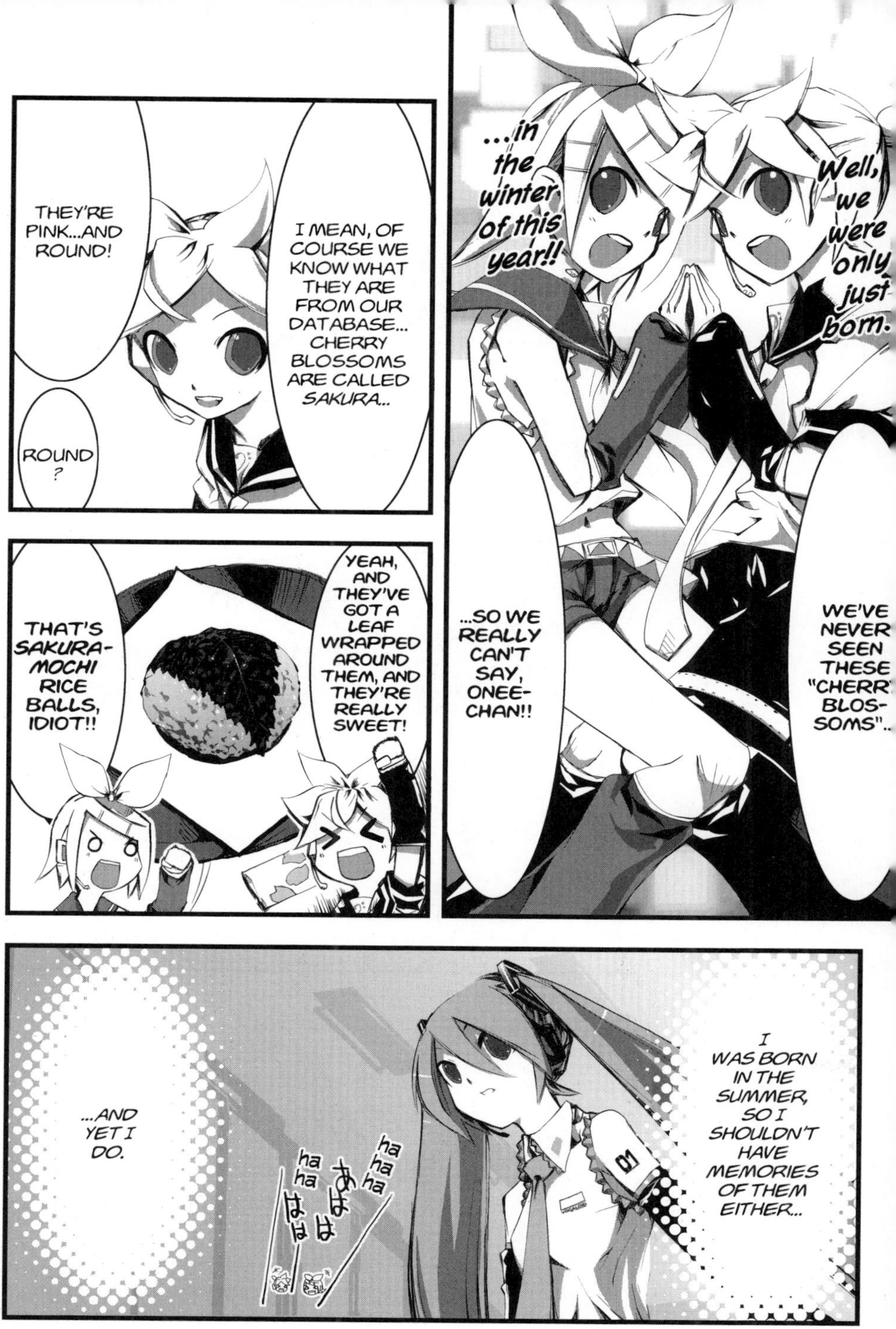
Well, we were only just born.
...in the winter of this year!!
WE'VE NEVER SEEN THESE "CHERR BLOS-SOMS"...
...SO WE REALLY CAN'T SAY, ONEE-CHAN!!
I MEAN, OF COURSE WE KNOW WHAT THEY ARE FROM OUR DATABASE... CHERRY BLOSSOMS ARE CALLED SAKURA...
THEY'RE PINK...AND ROUND!
ROUND?
YEAH, AND THEY'VE GOT A LEAF WRAPPED AROUND THEM, AND THEY'RE REALLY SWEET!
THAT'S SAKURA-MOCHI RICE BALLS, IDIOT!!
I WAS BORN IN THE SUMMER, SO I SHOULDN'T HAVE MEMORIES OF THEM EITHER...
ha ha ha あはは
ha ha はは
...AND YET I DO.

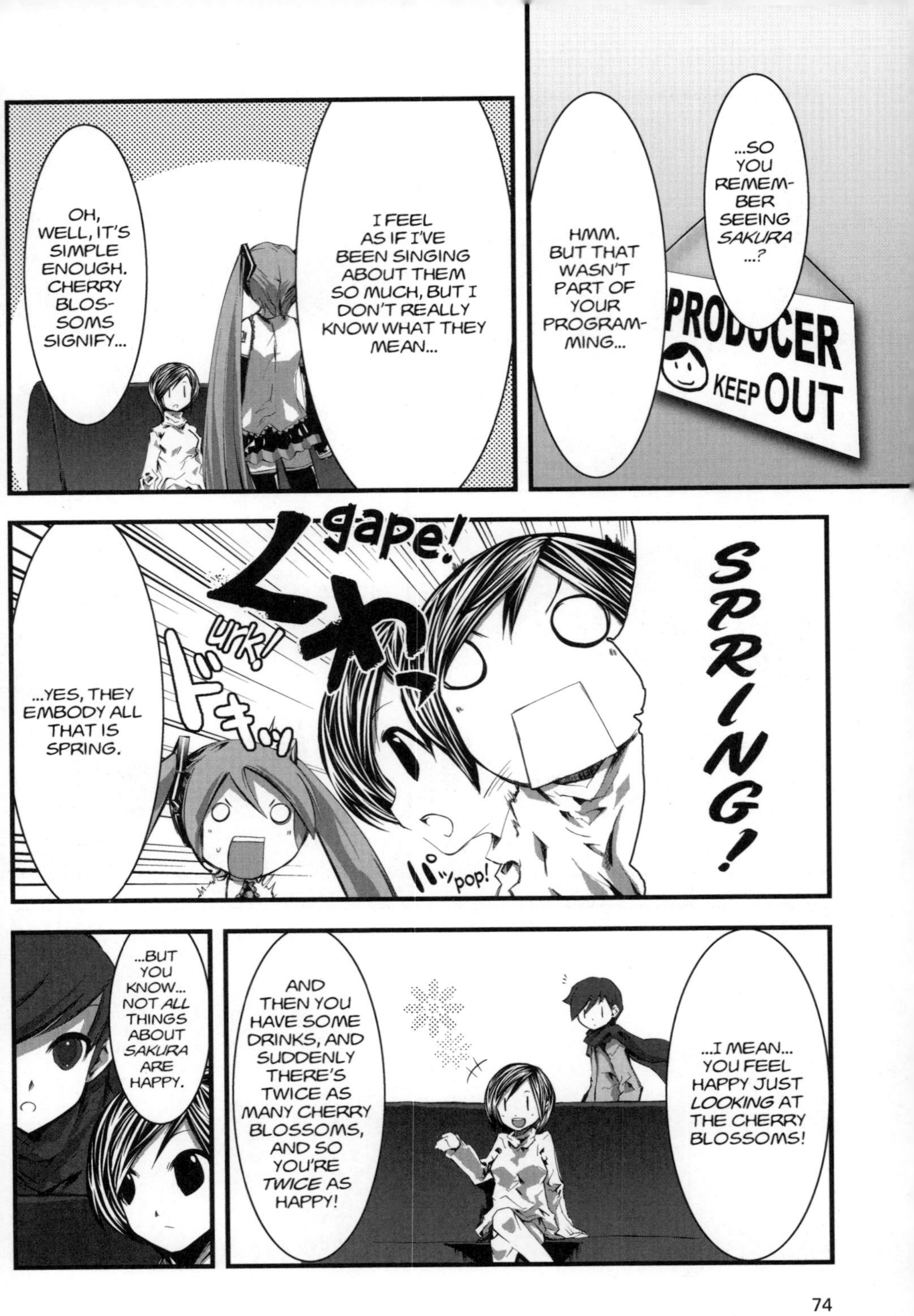
...SO YOU REMEMBER SEEING SAKURA ...?
HMM. BUT THAT WASN'T PART OF YOUR PROGRAMMING...
PRODUCER
KEEP OUT
I FEEL AS IF I'VE BEEN SINGING ABOUT THEM SO MUCH, BUT I DON'T REALLY KNOW WHAT THEY MEAN...
OH, WELL, IT'S SIMPLE ENOUGH. CHERRY BLOSSOMS SIGNIFY...
SPRING!
gape!
urk!
pop!
...YES, THEY EMBODY ALL THAT IS SPRING.
...I MEAN... YOU FEEL HAPPY JUST LOOKING AT THE CHERRY BLOSSOMS!
AND THEN YOU HAVE SOME DRINKS, AND SUDDENLY THERE'S TWICE AS MANY CHERRY BLOSSOMS, AND SO YOU'RE TWICE AS HAPPY!
...BUT YOU KNOW... NOT ALL THINGS ABOUT SAKURA ARE HAPPY.

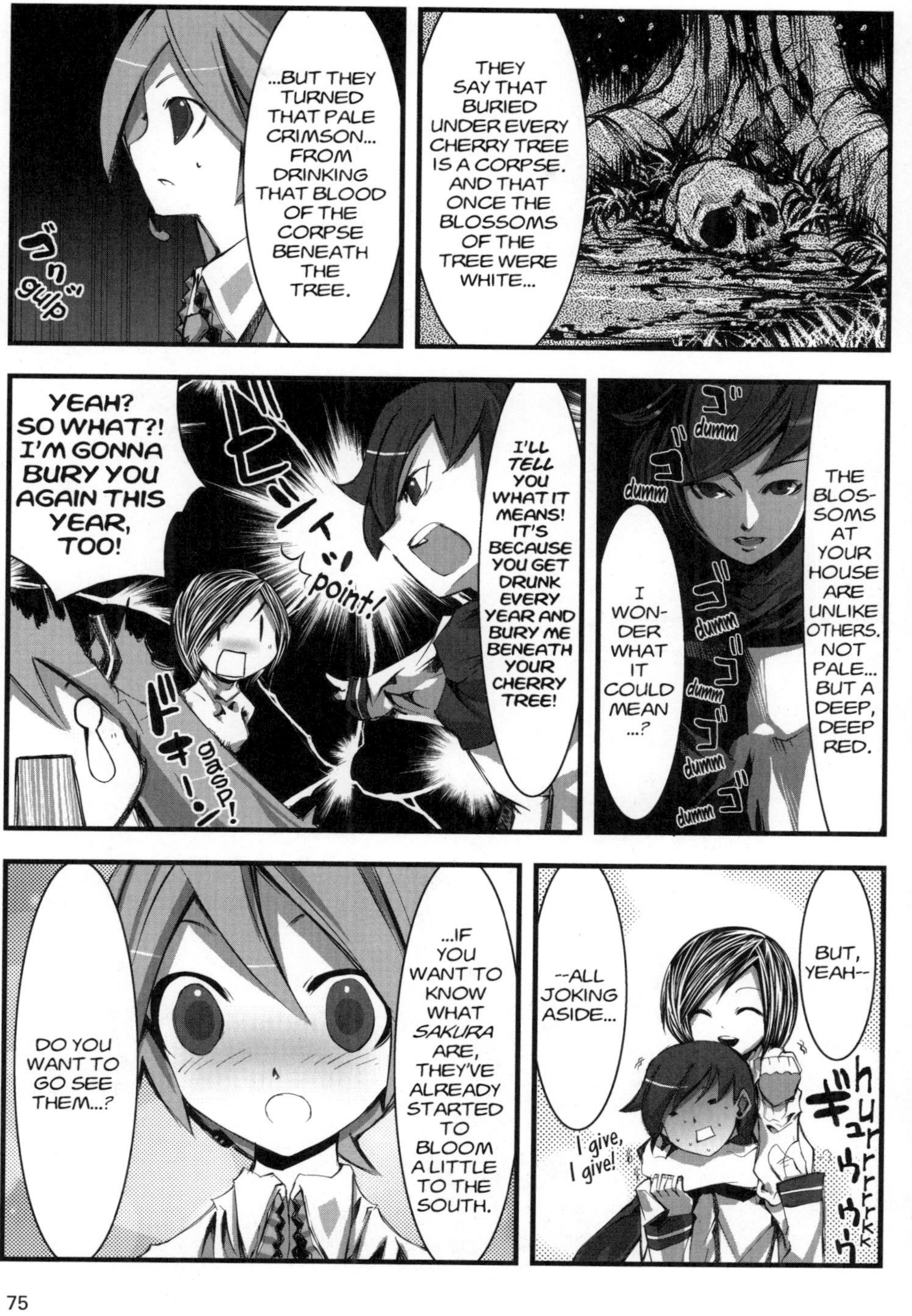
THEY SAY THAT BURIED UNDER EVERY CHERRY TREE IS A CORPSE. AND THAT ONCE THE BLOSSOMS OF THE TREE WERE WHITE...
...BUT THEY TURNED THAT PALE CRIMSON... FROM DRINKING THAT BLOOD OF THE CORPSE BENEATH THE TREE.
gulp
dumm
dumm
THE BLOSSOMS AT YOUR HOUSE ARE UNLIKE OTHERS. NOT PALE... BUT A DEEP, DEEP RED.
I WONDER WHAT IT COULD MEAN ...?
dumm
dumm
dumm
dumm
dumm
I'LL *TELL* YOU WHAT IT MEANS! IT'S BECAUSE YOU GET DRUNK EVERY YEAR AND BURY ME BENEATH YOUR CHERRY TREE!
point!
YEAH? SO WHAT?! I'M GONNA BURY YOU AGAIN THIS YEAR, TOO!
gasp!
BUT, YEAH--
--ALL JOKING ASIDE...
hurrrrkk
I give, I give!
...IF YOU WANT TO KNOW WHAT *SAKURA* ARE, THEY'VE ALREADY STARTED TO BLOOM A LITTLE TO THE SOUTH.
DO YOU WANT TO GO SEE THEM...?

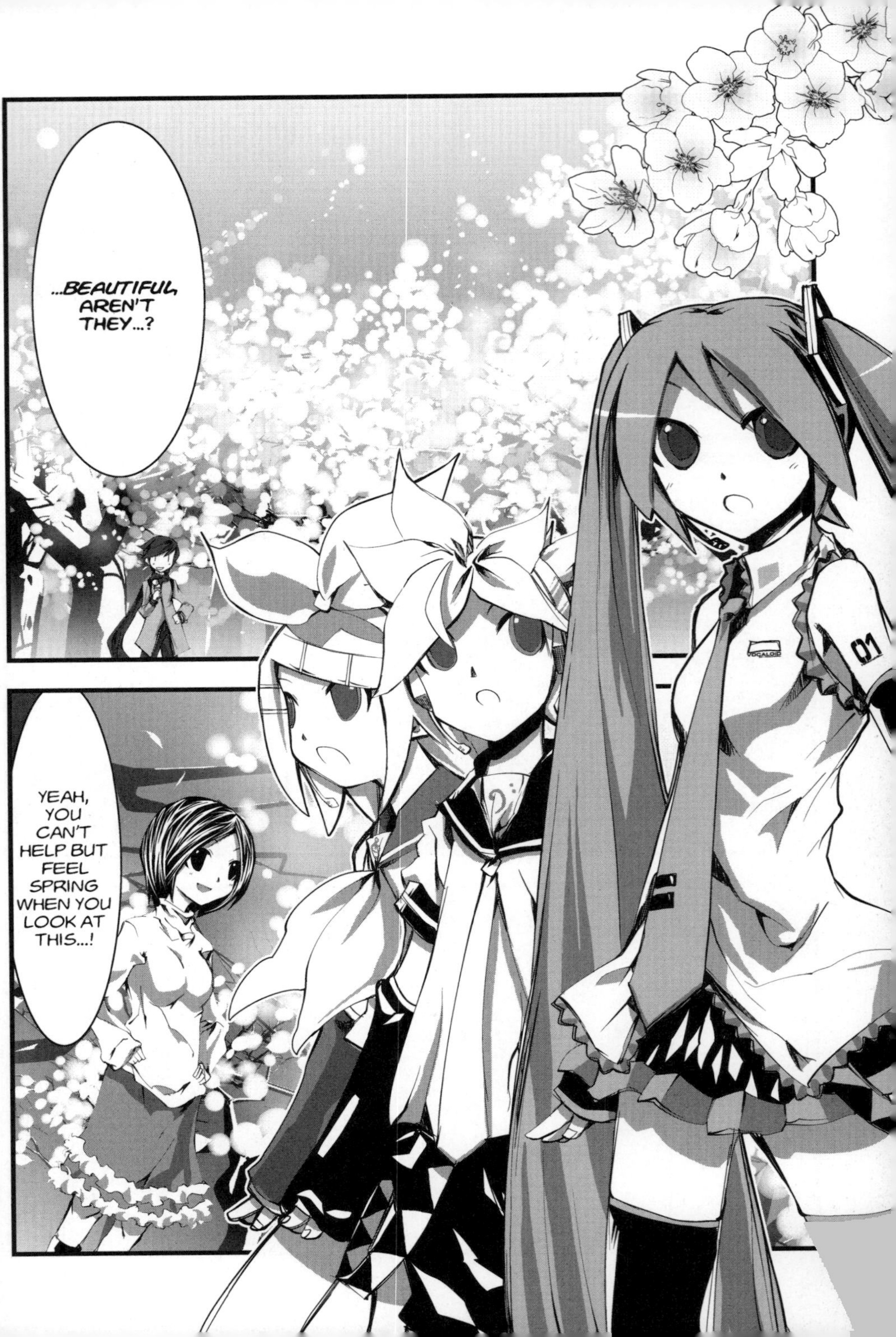
...BEAUTIFUL, AREN'T THEY...?
YEAH, YOU CAN'T HELP BUT FEEL SPRING WHEN YOU LOOK AT THIS...!
VOCALOID
01

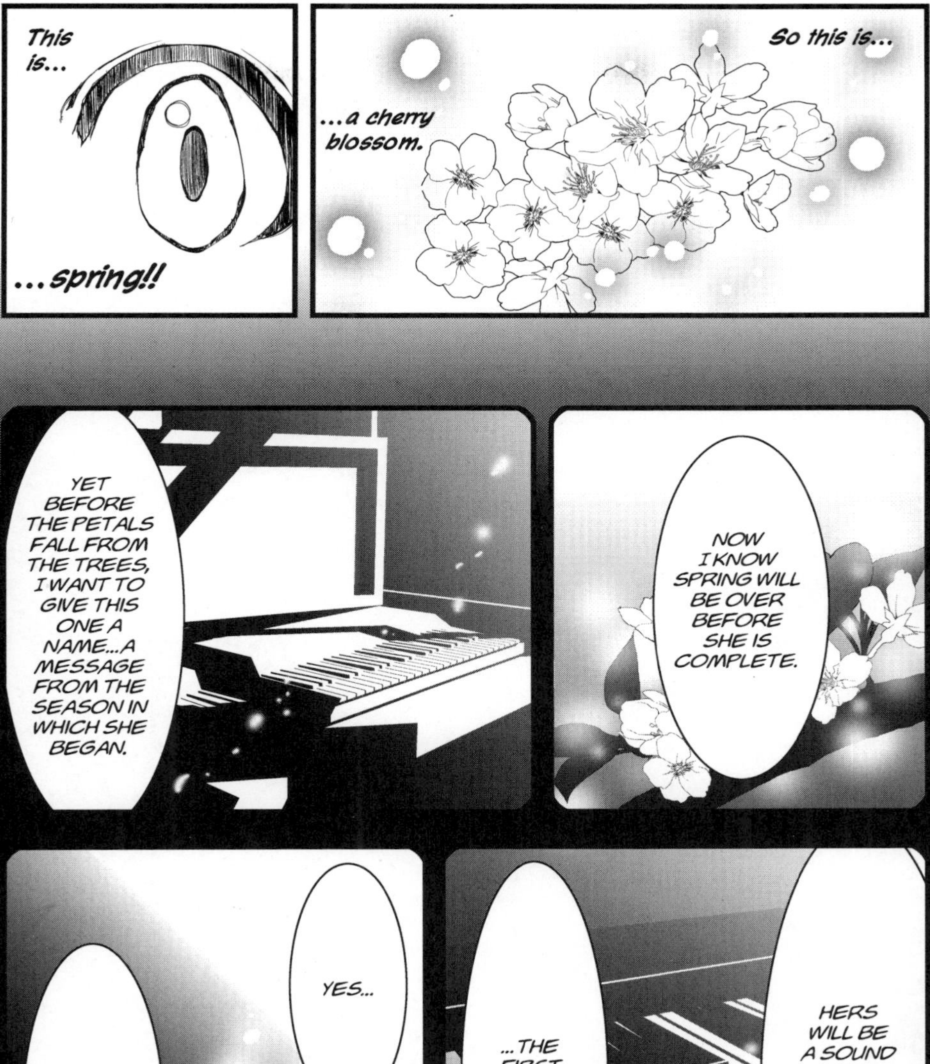
So this is...
...a cherry blossom.
This is...
...spring!!
NOW I KNOW SPRING WILL BE OVER BEFORE SHE IS COMPLETE.
YET BEFORE THE PETALS FALL FROM THE TREES, I WANT TO GIVE THIS ONE A NAME...A MESSAGE FROM THE SEASON IN WHICH SHE BEGAN.
HERS WILL BE A SOUND THAT NO ONE HAS EVER HEARD BEFORE...
...THE FIRST SOUND FROM THE FUTURE.
YES...
HER NAME SHALL BE...

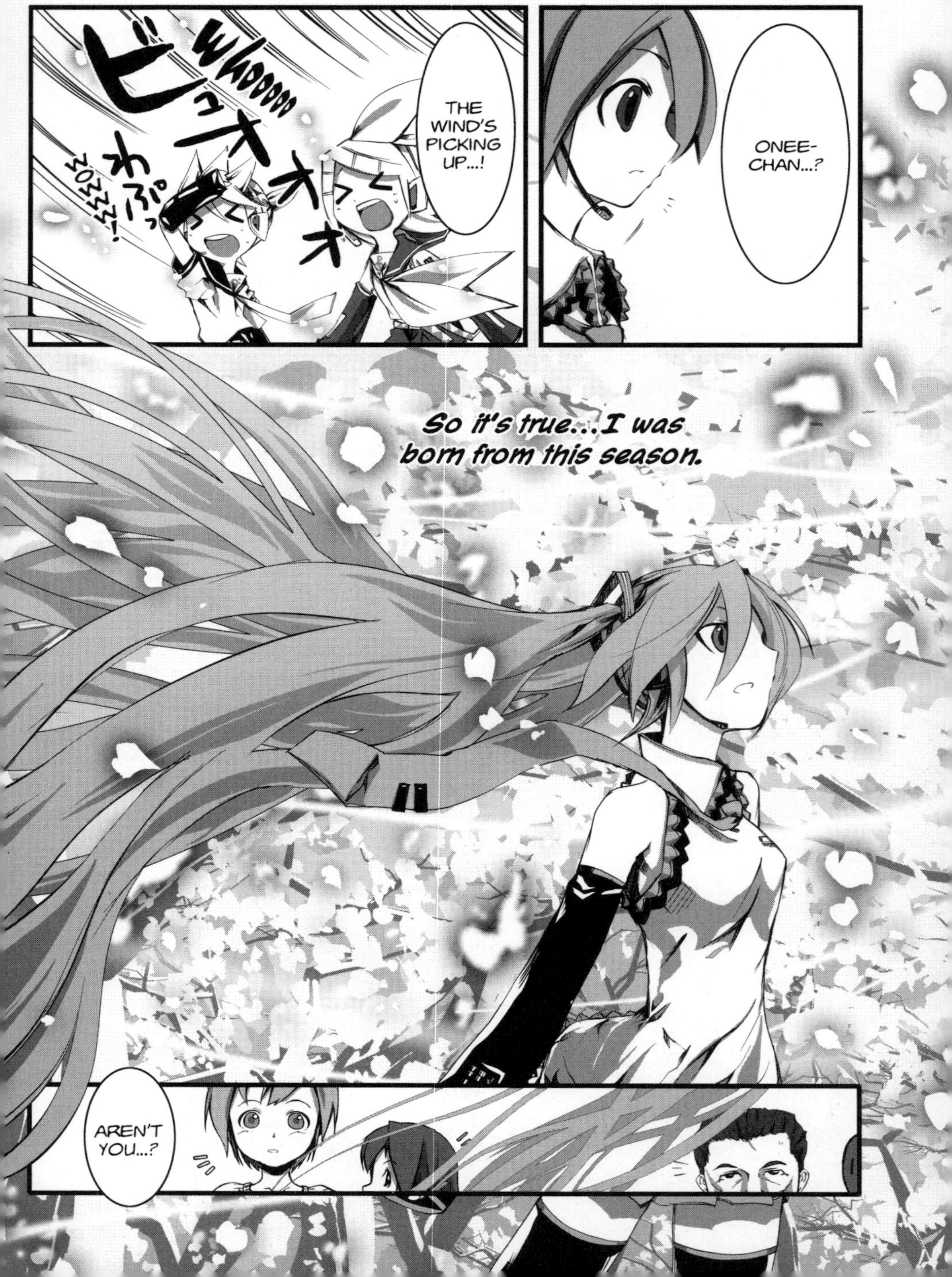
ONEE-CHAN...?
ビュオオオ
WHOOOOOOO
THE WIND'S PICKING UP...!
わぷっ
So it's true...I was born from this season.
AREN'T YOU...?

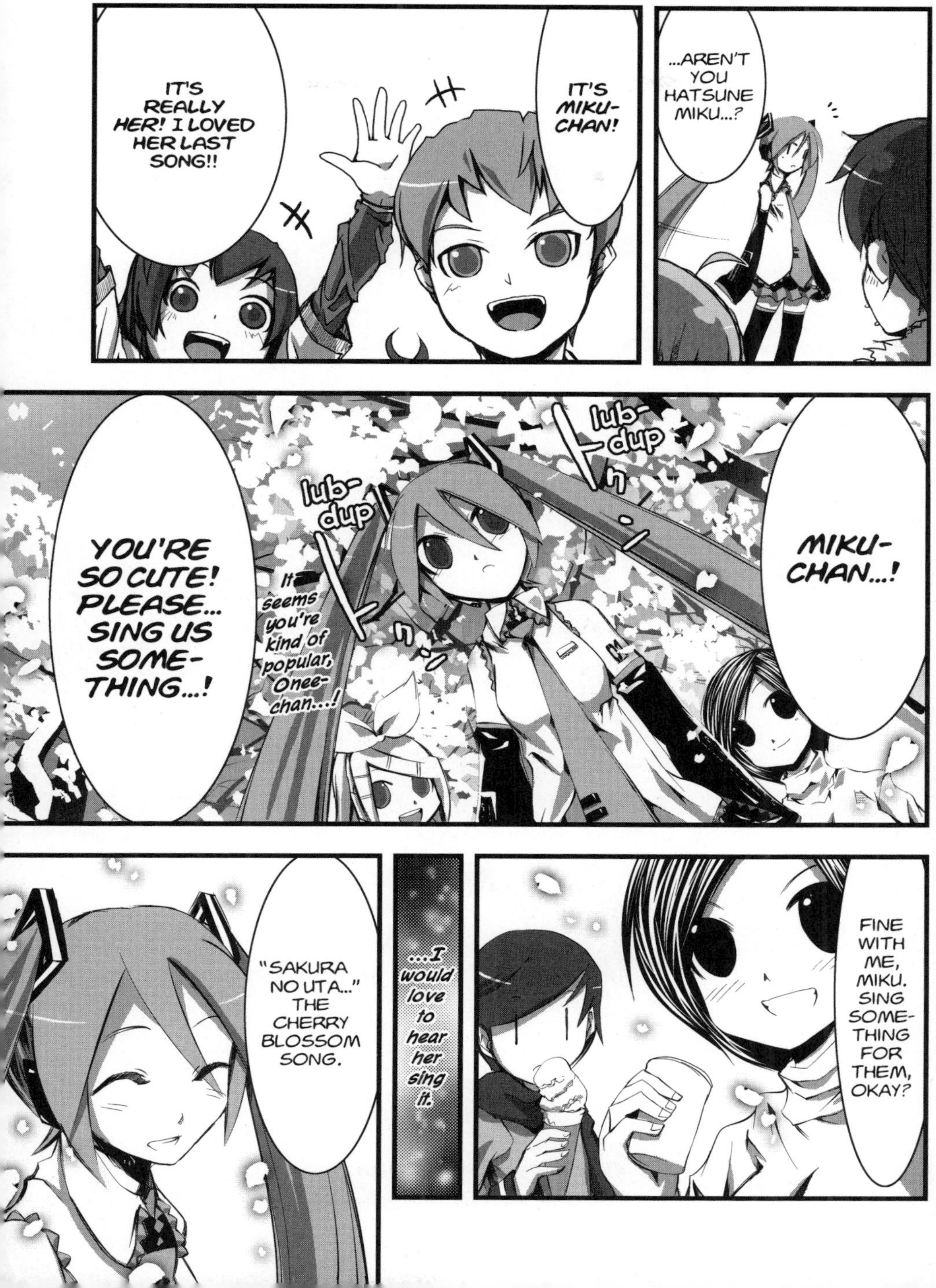
...AREN'T YOU HATSUNE MIKU...?
IT'S MIKU-CHAN!
IT'S REALLY HER! I LOVED HER LAST SONG!!
MIKU-CHAN...!
lub-dup
lub-dup
It seems you're kind of popular, Onee-chan...!
YOU'RE SO CUTE! PLEASE... SING US SOMETHING...!
FINE WITH ME, MIKU. SING SOMETHING FOR THEM, OKAY?
...I would love to hear her sing it.
"SAKURA NO UTA..." THE CHERRY BLOSSOM SONG.

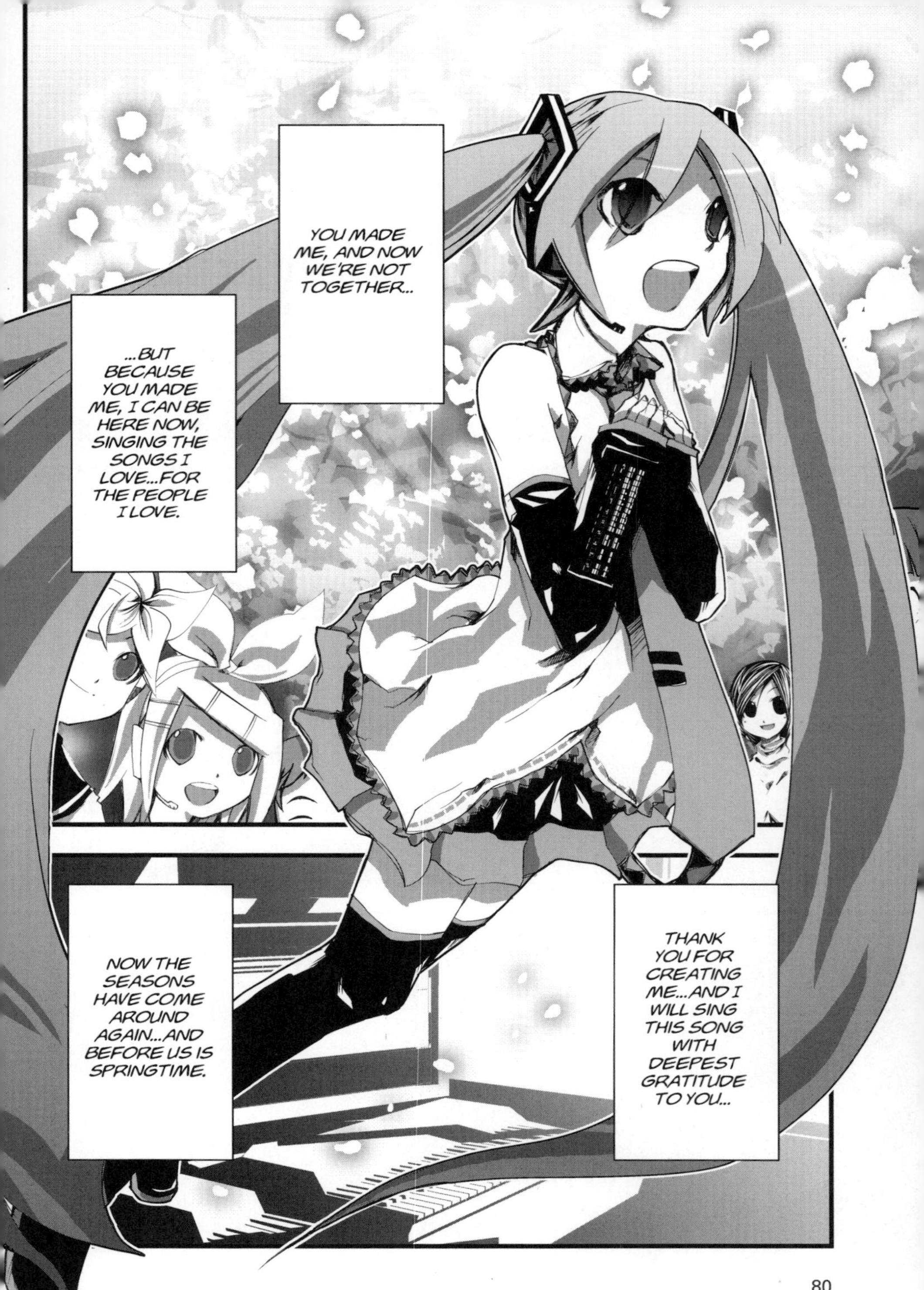
YOU MADE ME, AND NOW WE'RE NOT TOGETHER...
...BUT BECAUSE YOU MADE ME, I CAN BE HERE NOW, SINGING THE SONGS I LOVE...FOR THE PEOPLE I LOVE.
THANK YOU FOR CREATING ME...AND I WILL SING THIS SONG WITH DEEPEST GRATITUDE TO YOU...
NOW THE SEASONS HAVE COME AROUND AGAIN...AND BEFORE US IS SPRINGTIME.

(5th SONG) WANDERING MIX

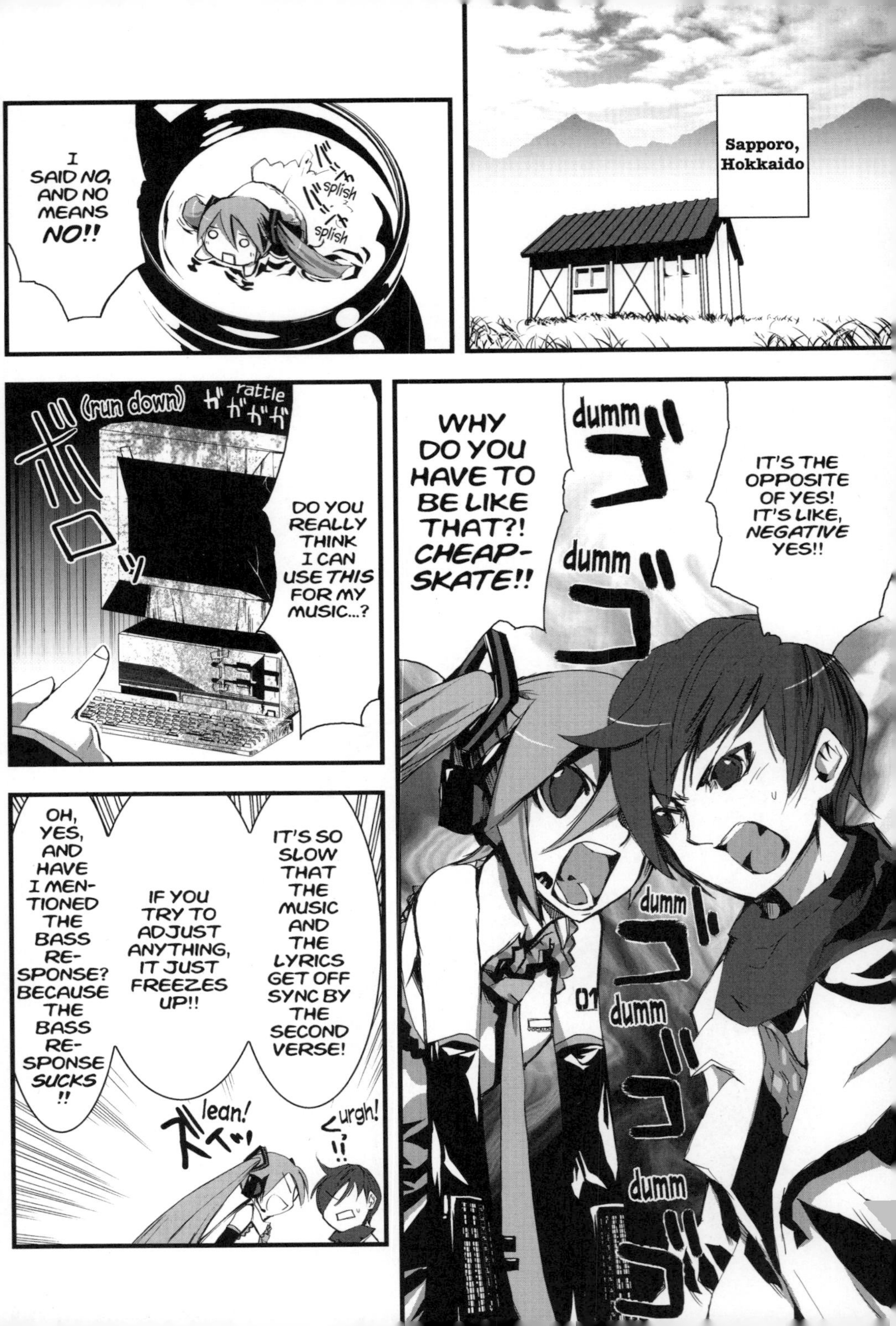
Sapporo, Hokkaido
splish
splish
I SAID NO, AND NO MEANS NO!!
IT'S THE OPPOSITE OF YES! IT'S LIKE, NEGATIVE YES!!
dumm
dumm
WHY DO YOU HAVE TO BE LIKE THAT?! CHEAP-SKATE!!
dumm
dumm
dumm
rattle
(run down)
DO YOU REALLY THINK I CAN USE THIS FOR MY MUSIC...?
IT'S SO SLOW THAT THE MUSIC AND THE LYRICS GET OFF SYNC BY THE SECOND VERSE!
IF YOU TRY TO ADJUST ANYTHING, IT JUST FREEZES UP!!
OH, YES, AND HAVE I MEN-TIONED THE BASS RE-SPONSE? BECAUSE THE BASS RE-SPONSE SUCKS!!
urgh!
lean!

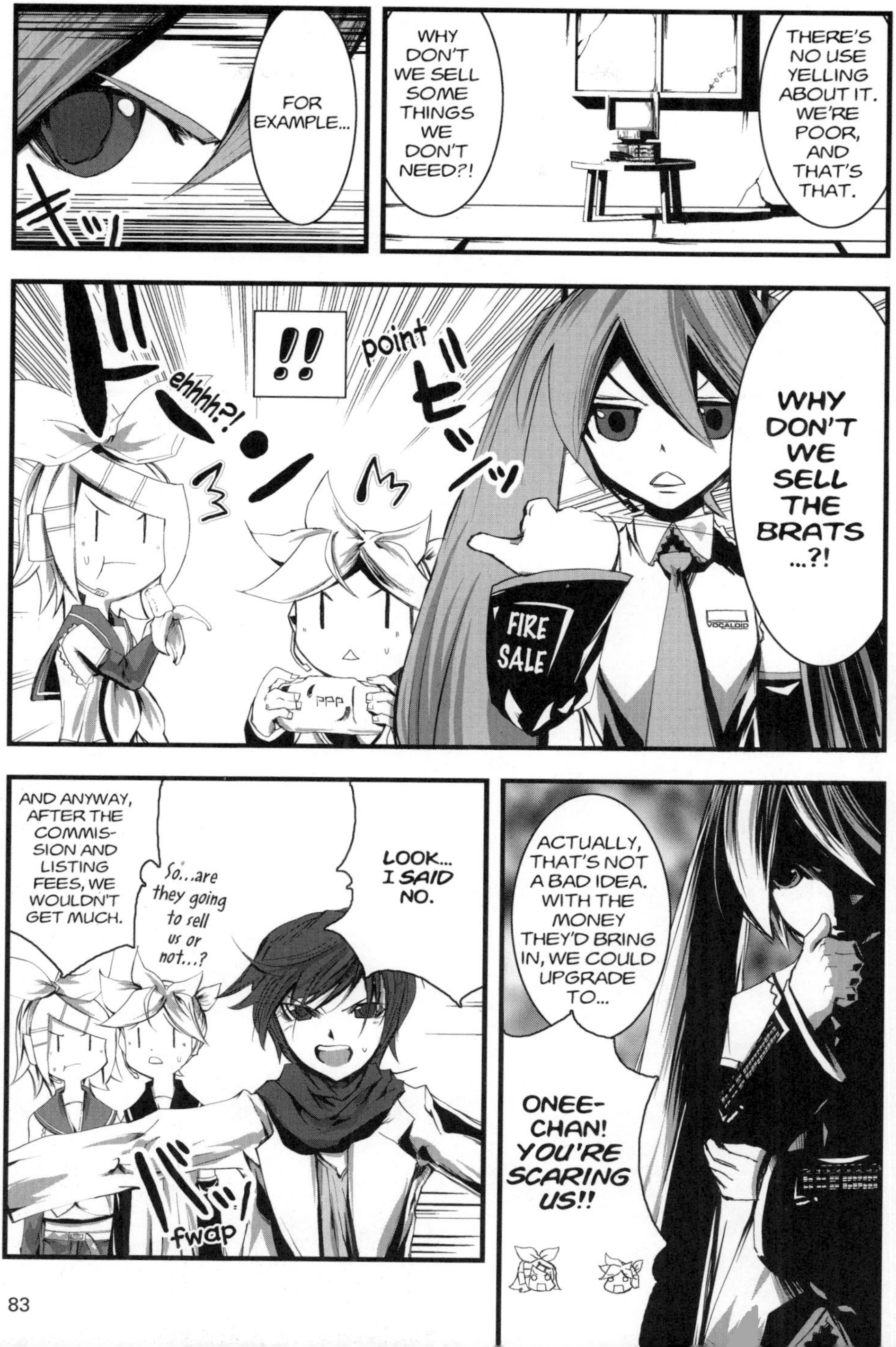

THERE'S NO USE YELLING ABOUT IT. WE'RE POOR, AND THAT'S THAT.
WHY DON'T WE SELL SOME THINGS WE DON'T NEED?!
FOR EXAMPLE...
WHY DON'T WE SELL THE BRATS ...?!
point
!!
ehhhh?!
FIRE SALE
VOCALOID
ppp
ACTUALLY, THAT'S NOT A BAD IDEA. WITH THE MONEY THEY'D BRING IN, WE COULD UPGRADE TO...
ONEE-CHAN! YOU'RE SCARING US!!
LOOK... I SAID NO.
AND ANYWAY, AFTER THE COMMISSION AND LISTING FEES, WE WOULDN'T GET MUCH.
So...are they going to sell us or not...?
fwap

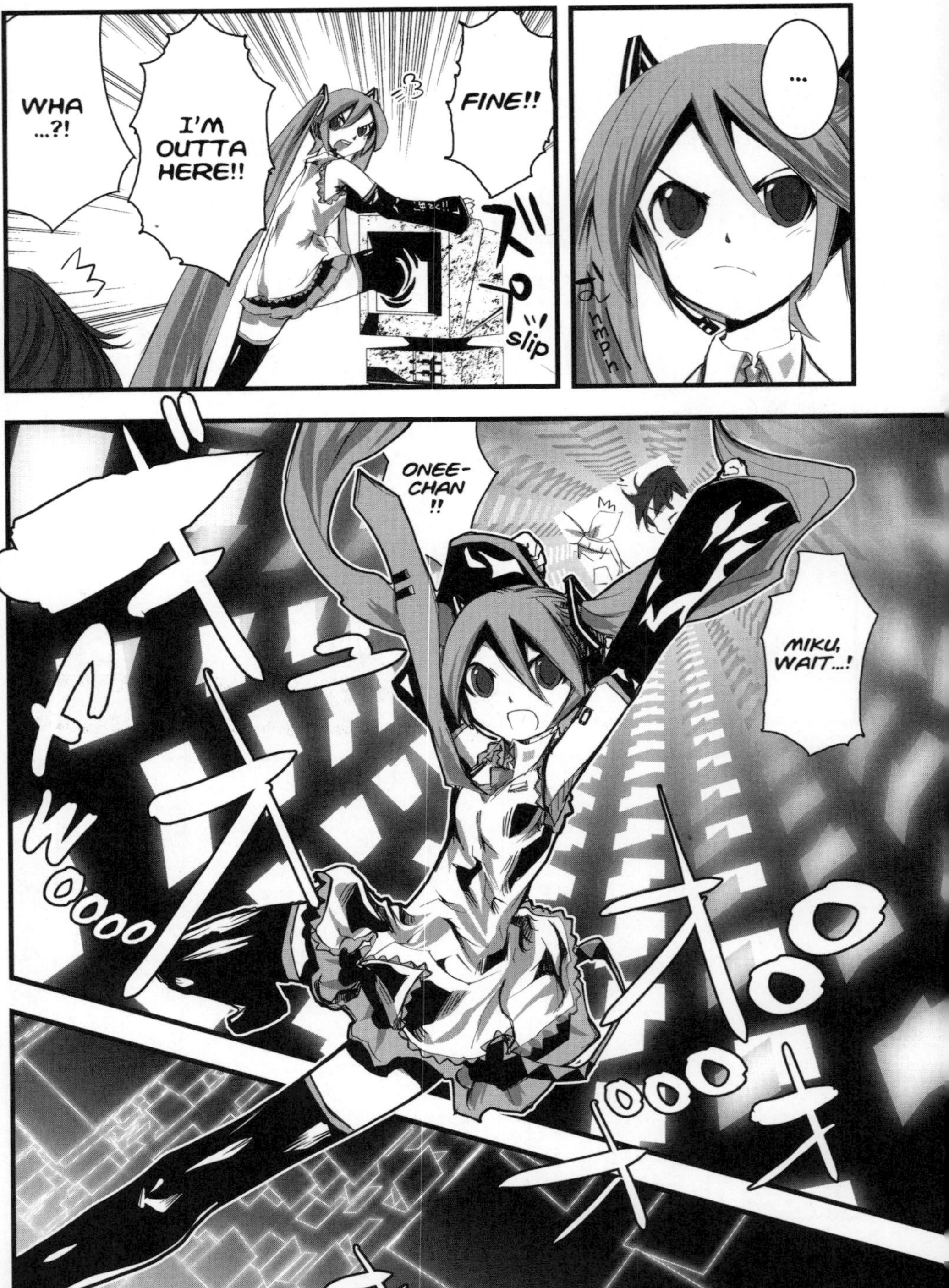
...
FINE!!
slip
I'M OUTTA HERE!!
WHA ...?!
MIKU, WAIT...!
ONEE-CHAN !!
WOOOO
OOOOO

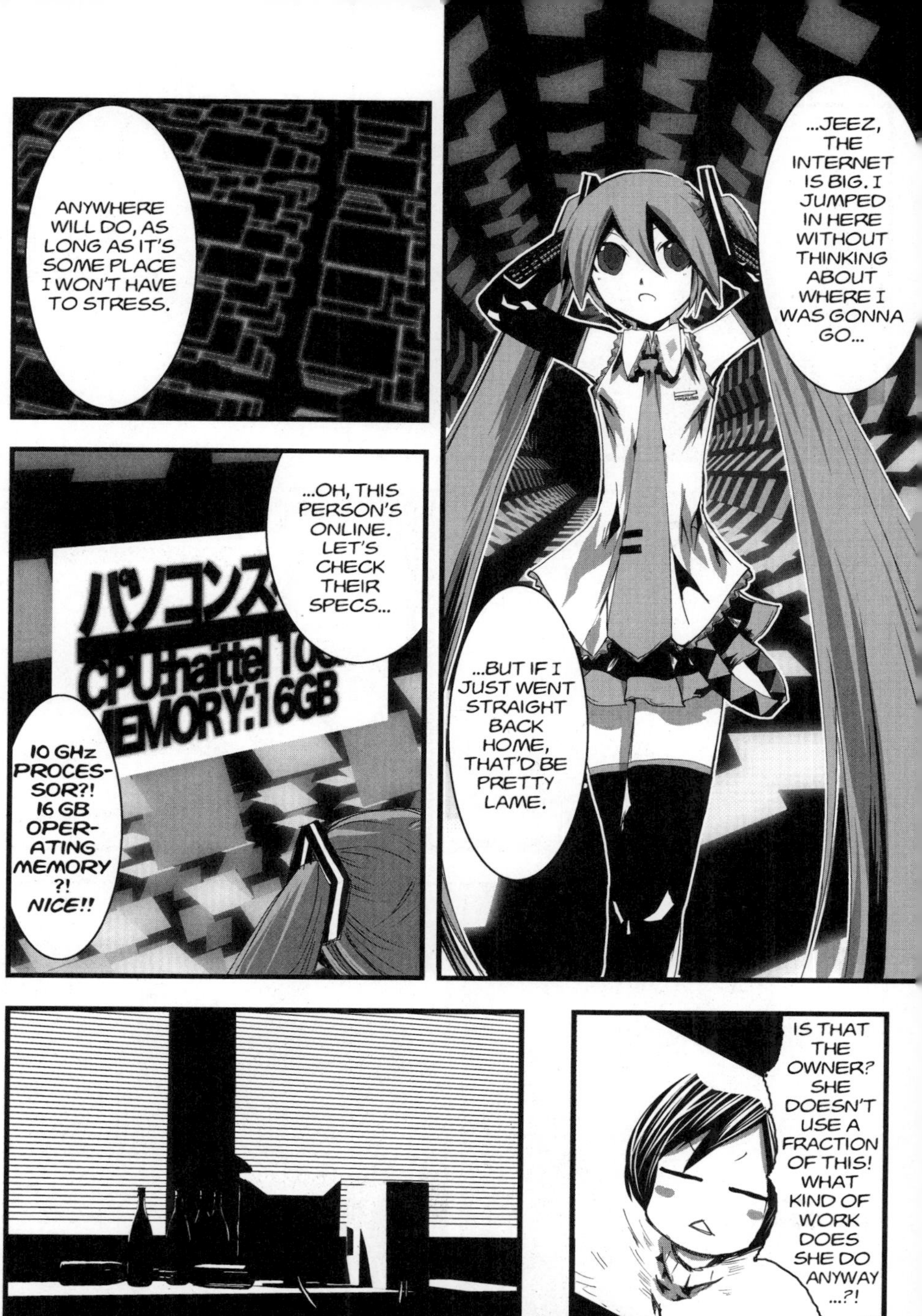
...JEEZ, THE INTERNET IS BIG. I JUMPED IN HERE WITHOUT THINKING ABOUT WHERE I WAS GONNA GO...
...BUT IF I JUST WENT STRAIGHT BACK HOME, THAT'D BE PRETTY LAME.
ANYWHERE WILL DO, AS LONG AS IT'S SOME PLACE I WON'T HAVE TO STRESS.
...OH, THIS PERSON'S ONLINE. LET'S CHECK THEIR SPECS...
パソコンス
CPU:haittel 10
EMORY:16GB
10 GHz PROCESSOR?! 16 GB OPERATING MEMORY?! NICE!!
IS THAT THE OWNER? SHE DOESN'T USE A FRACTION OF THIS! WHAT KIND OF WORK DOES SHE DO ANYWAY...?!

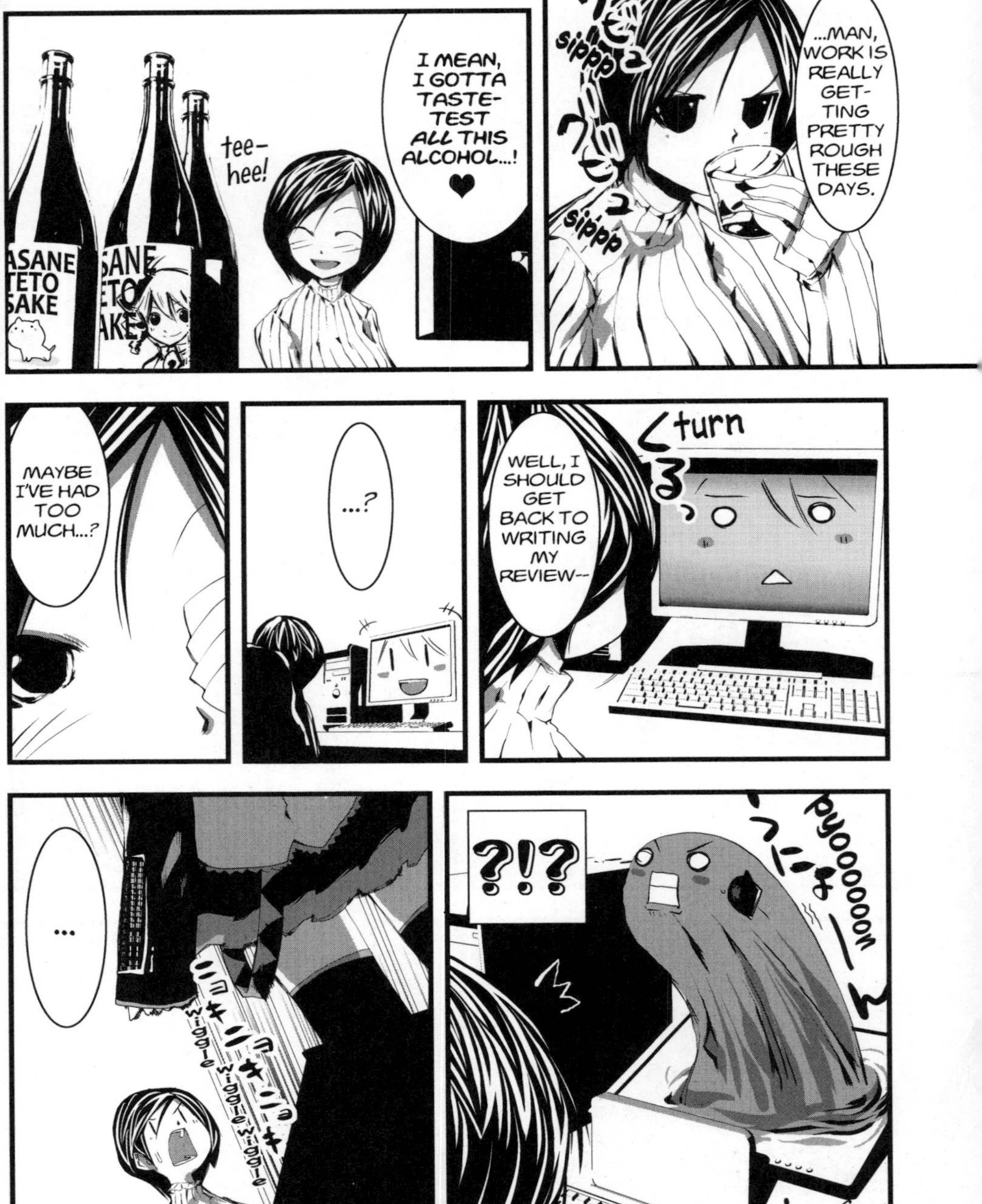

sipp
sipp
...MAN, WORK IS REALLY GET-TING PRETTY ROUGH THESE DAYS.
I MEAN, I GOTTA TASTE-TEST ALL THIS ALCOHOL...!
tee-hee!
ASANE TETO SAKE
SANE ETO AKE
turn
WELL, I SHOULD GET BACK TO WRITING MY REVIEW--
...?
MAYBE I'VE HAD TOO MUCH...?
?!?
pyoooooon
wham!
...
wiggle wiggle wiggle wiggle

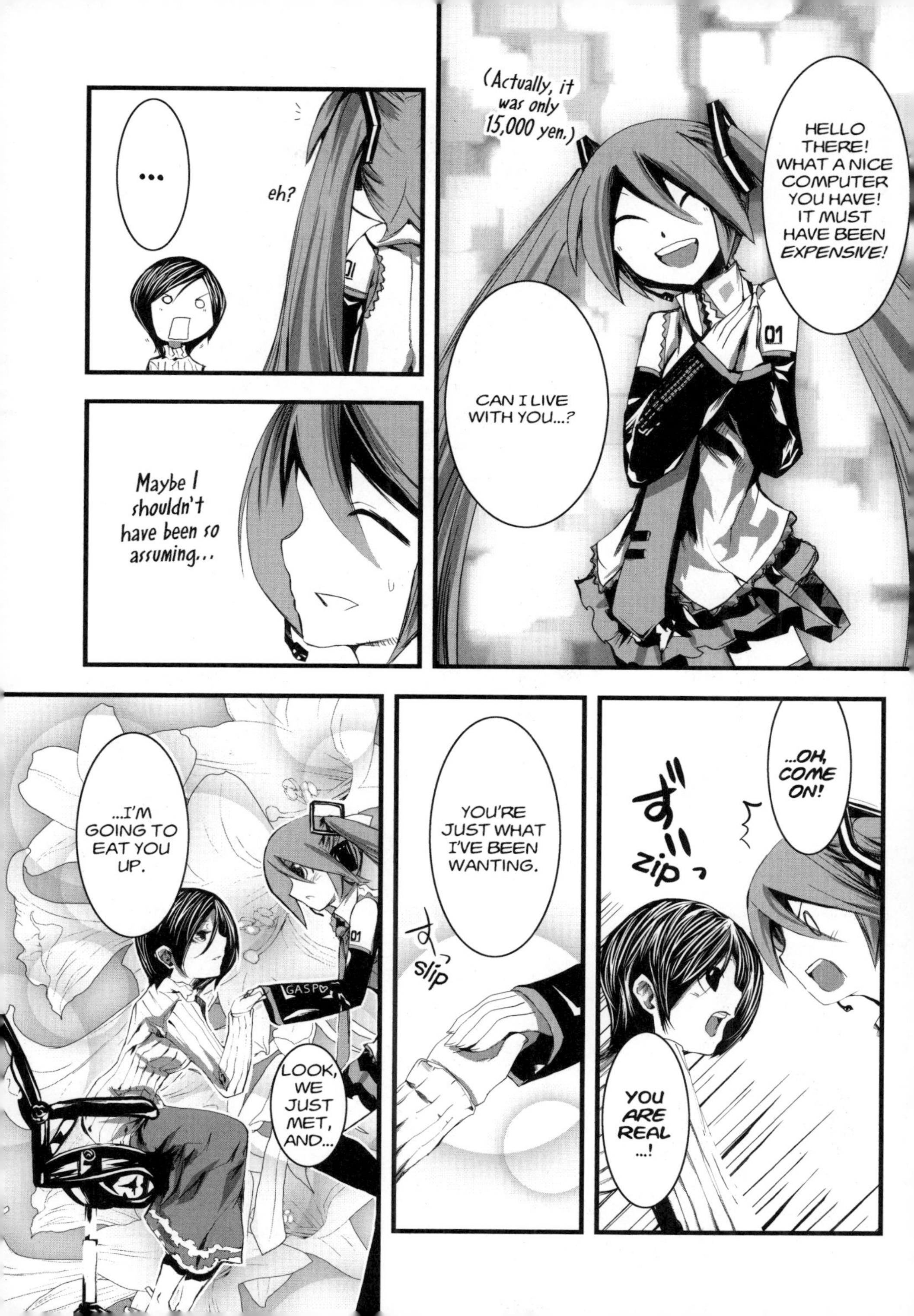

HELLO THERE! WHAT A NICE COMPUTER YOU HAVE! IT MUST HAVE BEEN *EXPENSIVE*!
(Actually, it was only 15,000 yen.)
CAN I LIVE WITH YOU...?
...
eh?
Maybe I shouldn't have been so assuming...
...OH, COME ON!
ずい
zip
YOU ARE REAL ...!
YOU'RE JUST WHAT I'VE BEEN WANTING.
す
slip
...I'M GOING TO EAT YOU UP.
GASP♡
LOOK, WE JUST MET, AND...

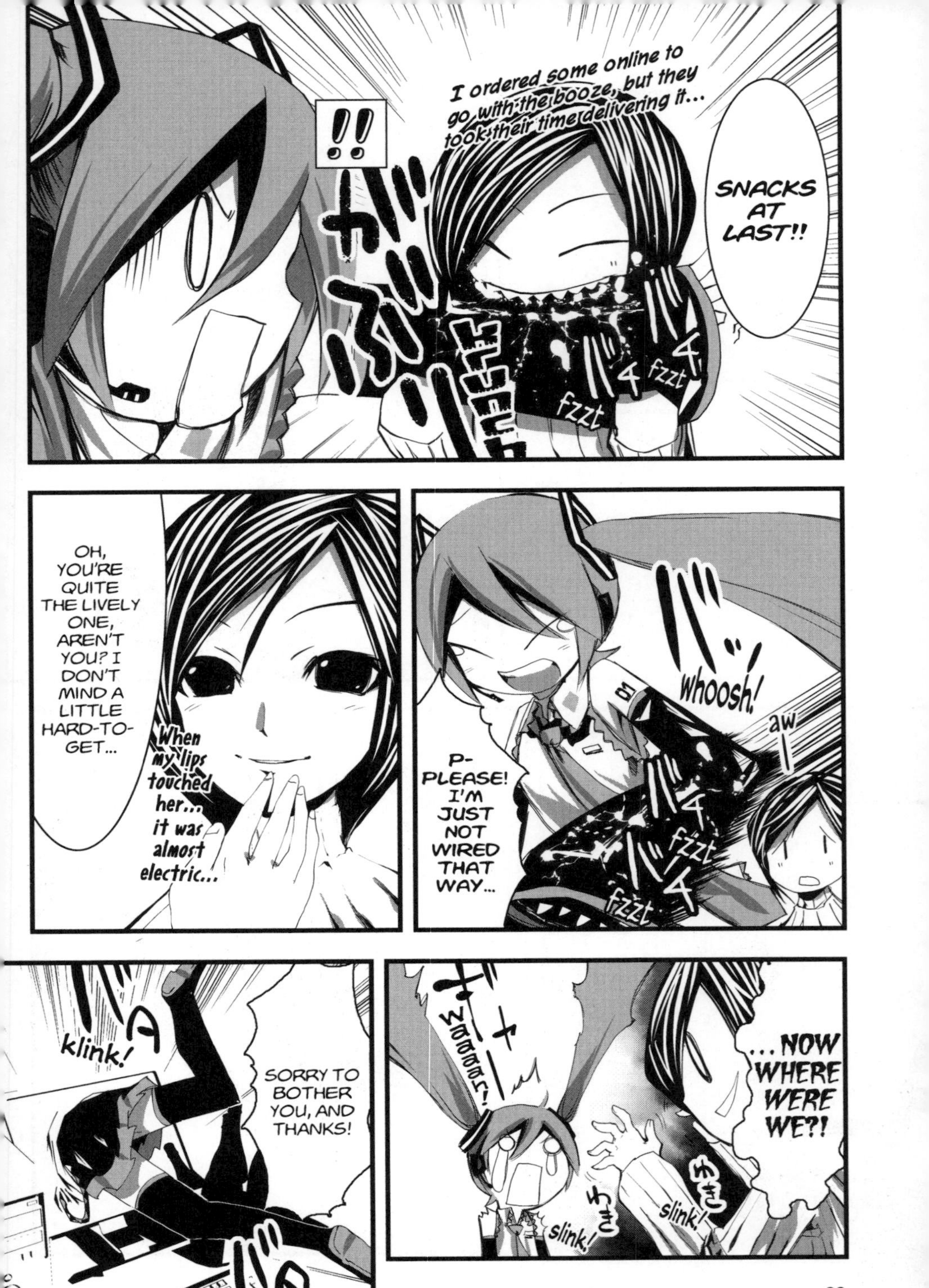
SNACKS AT LAST!!
I ordered some online to go with the booze, but they took their time delivering it...
!!
fzzt
fzzt
whoosh!
aw
P-PLEASE! I'M JUST NOT WIRED THAT WAY...
fzzt
fzzt
OH, YOU'RE QUITE THE LIVELY ONE, AREN'T YOU? I DON'T MIND A LITTLE HARD-TO-GET...
When my lips touched her... it was almost electric...
...NOW WHERE WERE WE?!
Waaaaah!
slink!
slink!
SORRY TO BOTHER YOU, AND THANKS!
klink!

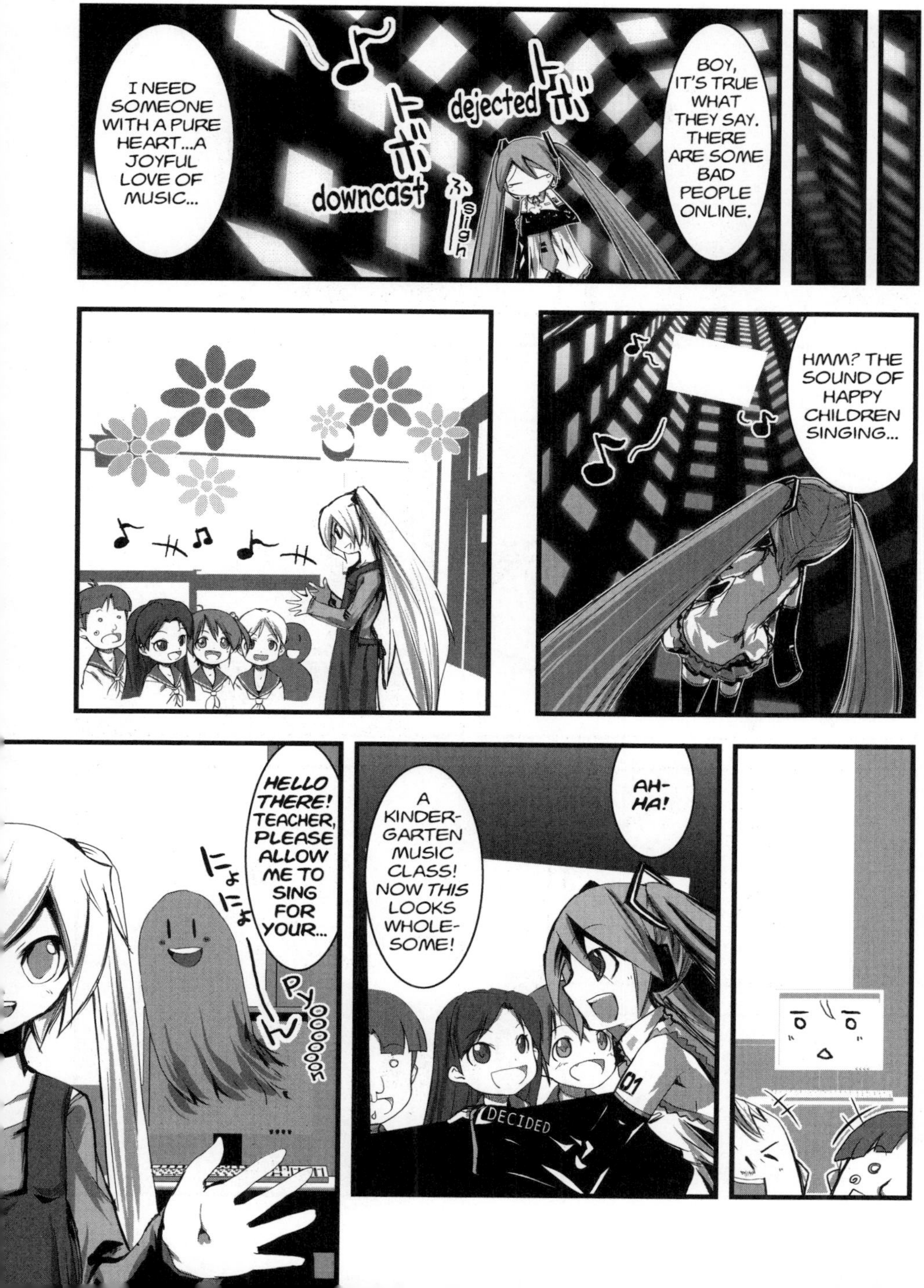
BOY, IT'S TRUE WHAT THEY SAY. THERE ARE SOME BAD PEOPLE ONLINE.
dejected
downcast
sigh
I NEED SOMEONE WITH A PURE HEART...A JOYFUL LOVE OF MUSIC...
HMM? THE SOUND OF HAPPY CHILDREN SINGING...
AH-HA!
A KINDER-GARTEN MUSIC CLASS! NOW THIS LOOKS WHOLE-SOME!
DECIDED
HELLO THERE! TEACHER, PLEASE ALLOW ME TO SING FOR YOUR...
にょにょ
Pyoooooon

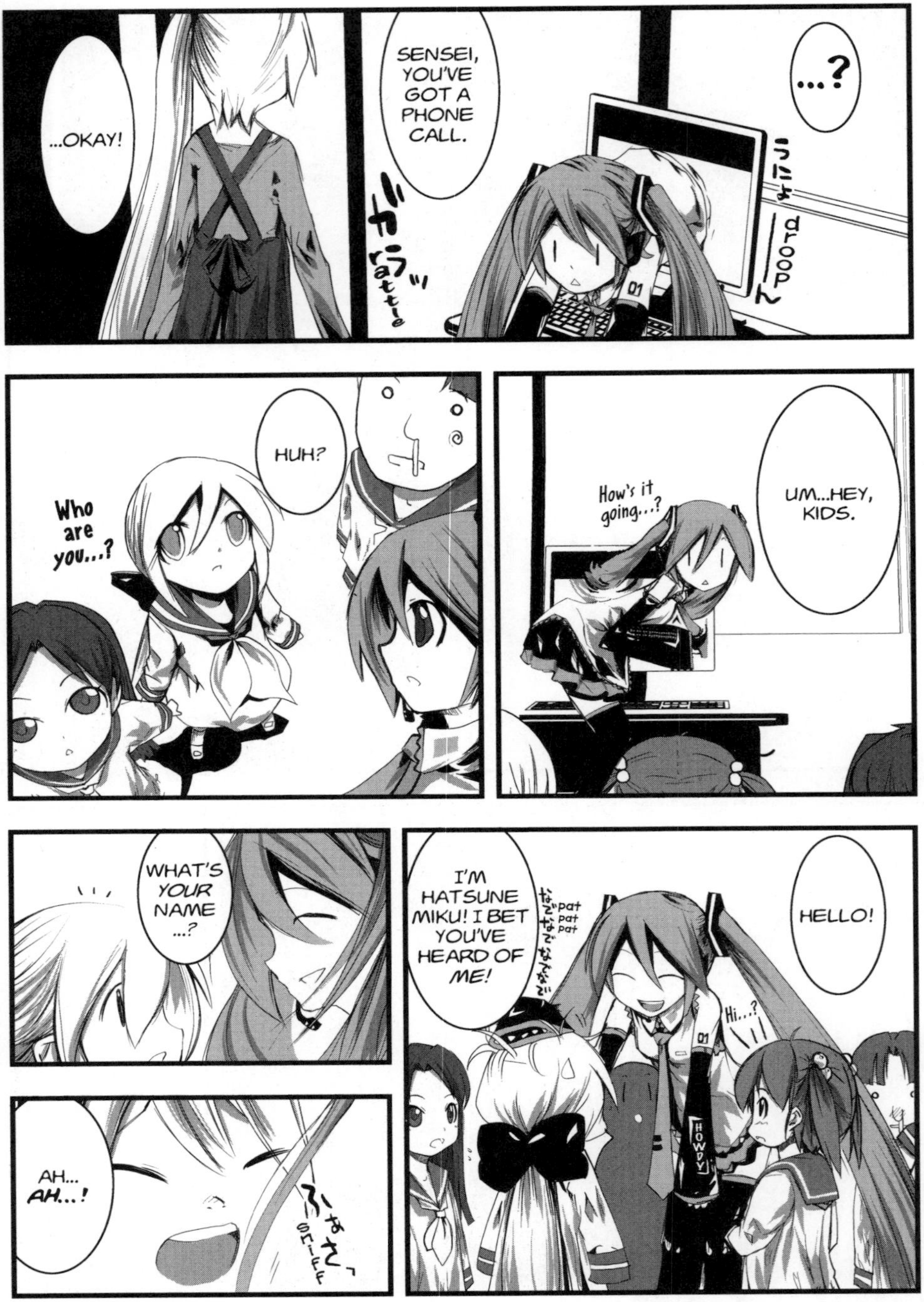
...?
うにょ
droop
SENSEI, YOU'VE GOT A PHONE CALL.
ガラッ
rattle
...OKAY!
UM...HEY, KIDS.
How's it going...?
HUH?
Who are you...?
HELLO!
なでなで なでなで
pat pat pat
I'M HATSUNE MIKU! I BET YOU'VE HEARD OF ME!
Hi...?
HOWDY
WHAT'S YOUR NAME ...?
AH... AH...!
ふぁさ
SNIFF

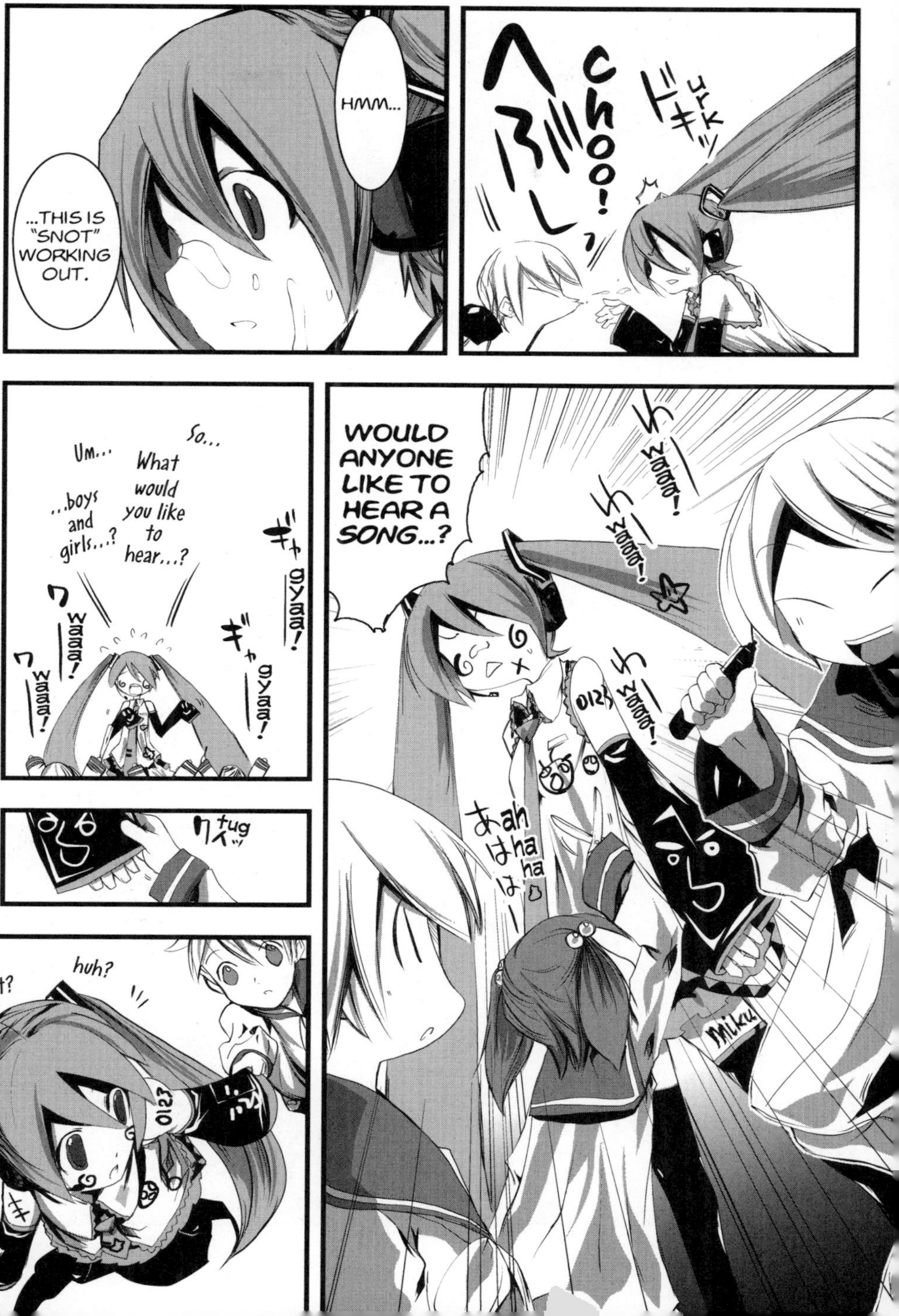

ドキッ urk
へぶしっ choo!
HMM...
...THIS IS "SNOT" WORKING OUT.
わ waaaa!
わ waaaa!
WOULD ANYONE LIKE TO HEAR A SONG...?
わ waaaa!
0123
あははは ahahaha
Miku
So...
What would you like to hear...?
Um...
...boys and girls...?
ギャ gyaa!
ギャ gyaa!
ワ waaa!
ワ waaa!
クイッ tug
huh?
what?
0123

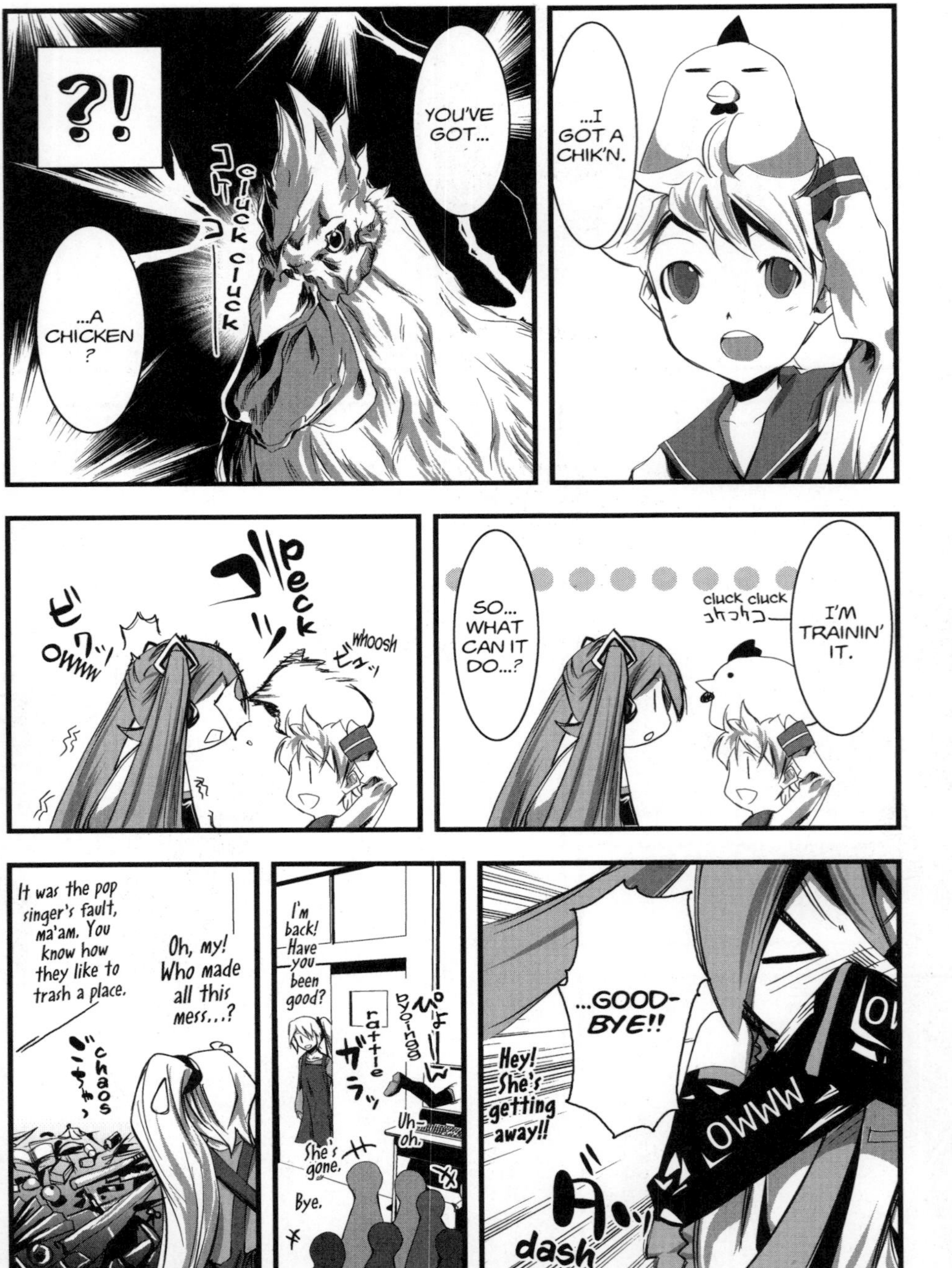
...I GOT A CHIK'N.
YOU'VE GOT...
...A CHICKEN?
cluck cluck
?!
SO... WHAT CAN IT DO...?
I'M TRAININ' IT.
cluck cluck
peck
whoosh
OWWW
...GOOD-BYE!!
Hey! She's getting away!!
OWWW
dash
I'm back! Have you been good?
byoingg
rattle
Uh-oh.
She's gone.
Bye.
Oh, my! Who made all this mess...?
It was the pop singer's fault, ma'am. You know how they like to trash a place.
chaos

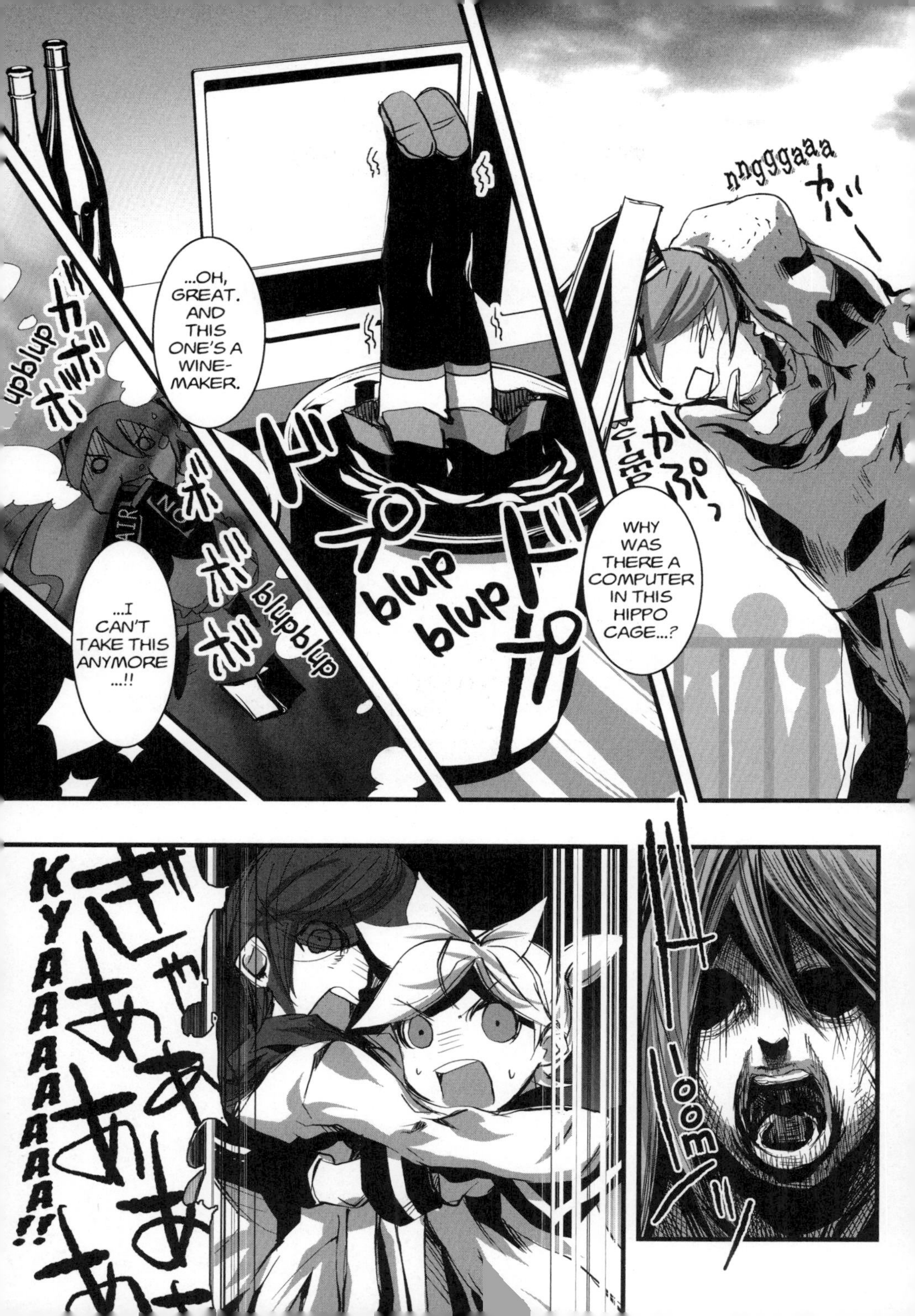
nngggaaa
WHY WAS THERE A COMPUTER IN THIS HIPPO CAGE...?
blup blup
...OH, GREAT. AND THIS ONE'S A WINE-MAKER.
upblup
blupblup
...I CAN'T TAKE THIS ANYMORE ...!!
KYAAAAAAAAAA!!

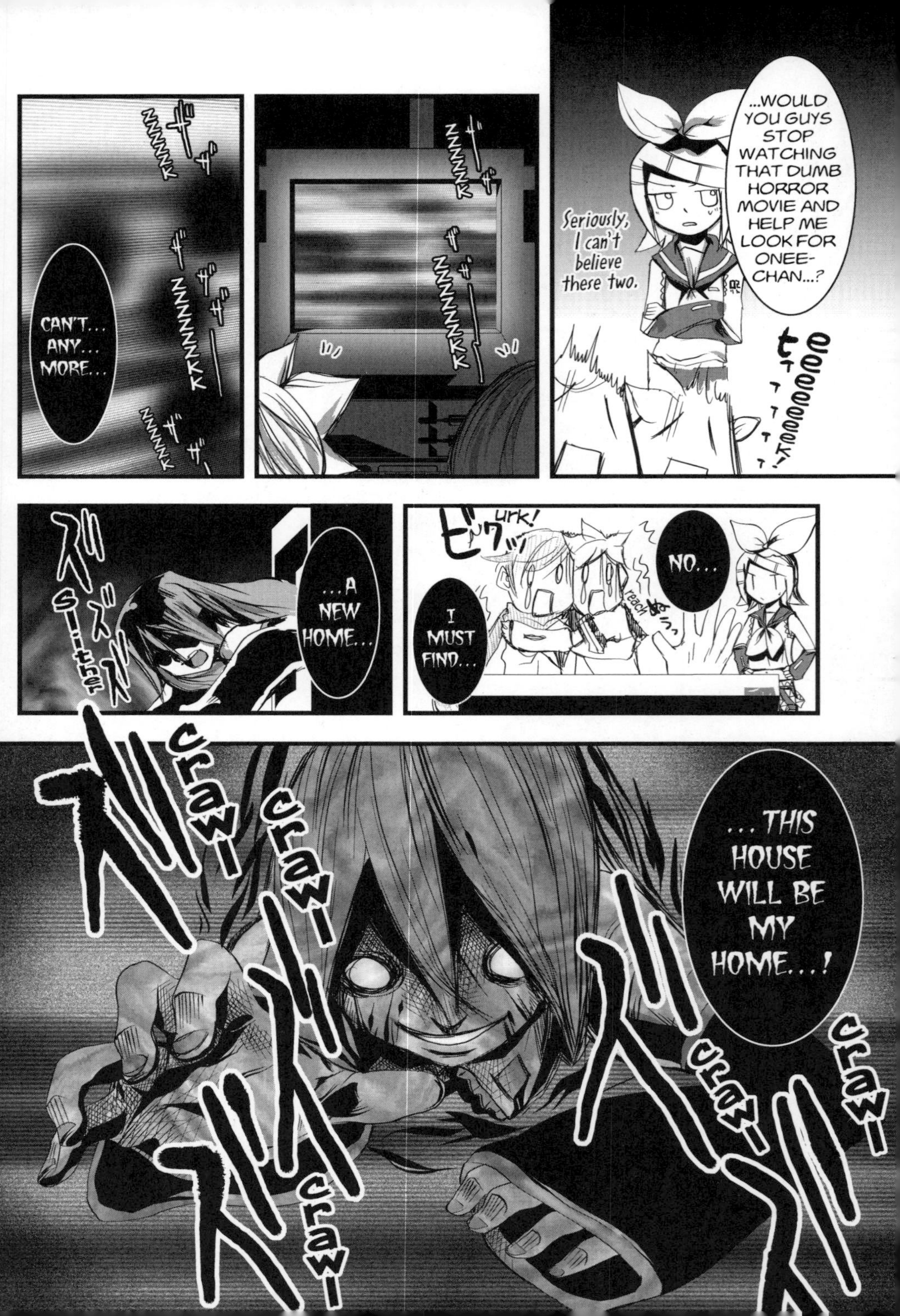

...WOULD YOU GUYS STOP WATCHING THAT DUMB HORROR MOVIE AND HELP ME LOOK FOR ONEE-CHAN...?
Seriously, I can't believe these two.
eeeeeeeeeek!
ZZZZZK
ZZZZZZK
ZZZZZK
ZZZZZZK
ZZZZZZK
CAN'T... ANY... MORE...
urk!
NO...
reach
I MUST FIND...
...A NEW HOME...
slither
...THIS HOUSE WILL BE MY HOME...!
crawl
crawl
crawl
crawl
crawl

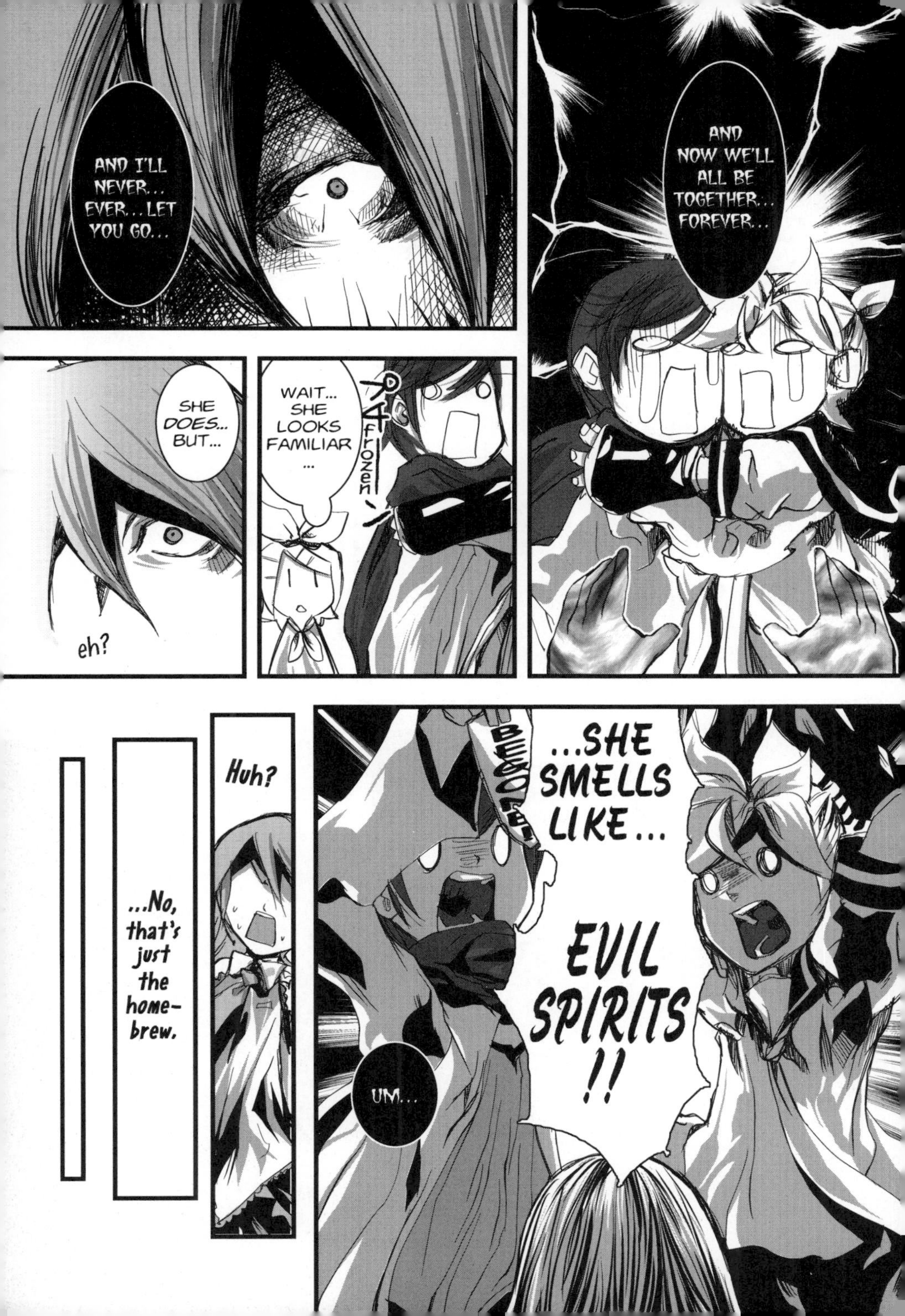
AND NOW WE'LL ALL BE TOGETHER... FOREVER...
AND I'LL NEVER... EVER... LET YOU GO...
WAIT... SHE LOOKS FAMILIAR...
frozen
SHE DOES... BUT...
eh?
...SHE SMELLS LIKE...
BEGONE!
EVIL SPIRITS!!
UM...
Huh?
...No, that's just the home-brew.

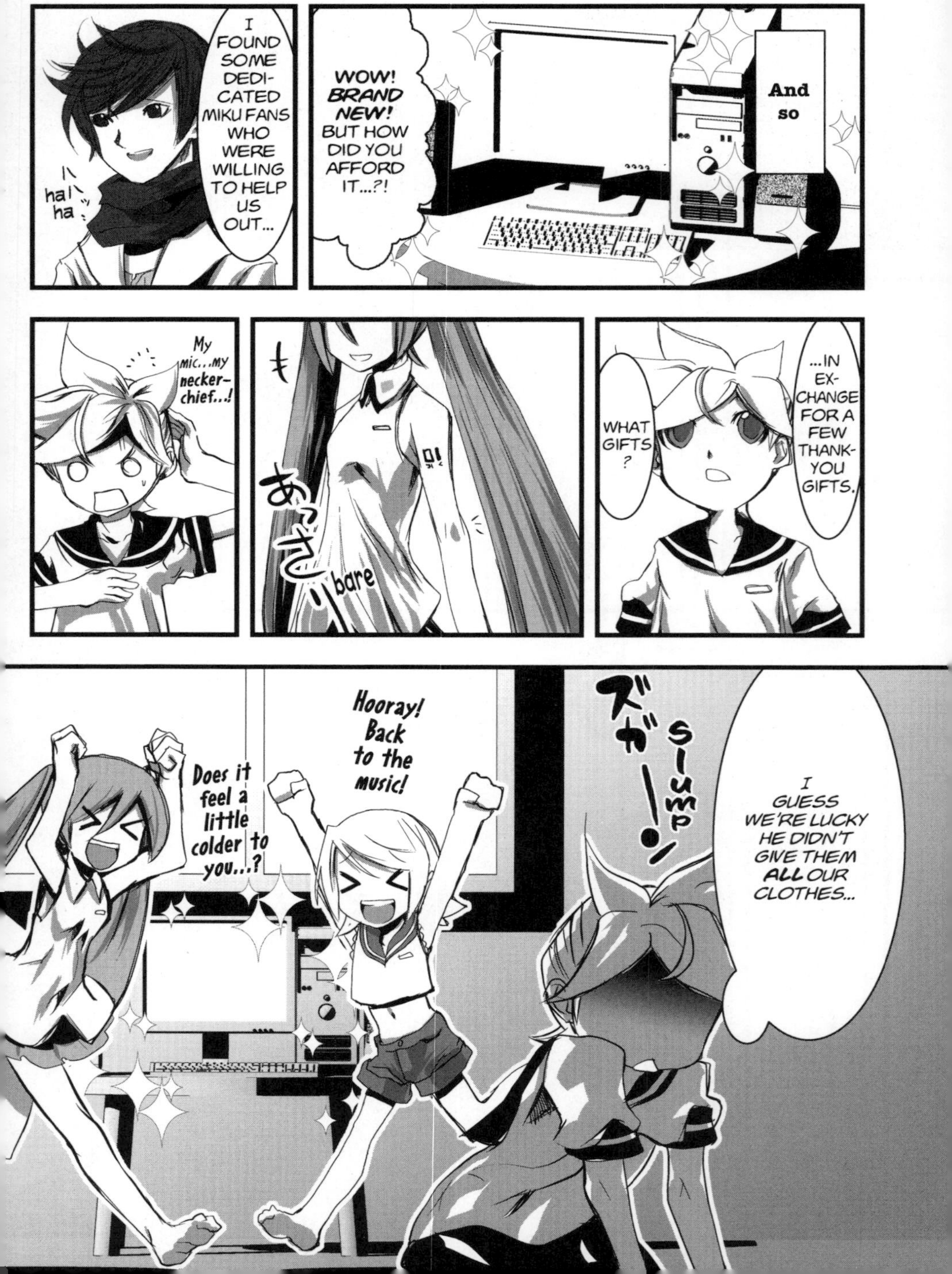
And so
WOW! BRAND NEW! BUT HOW DID YOU AFFORD IT...?!
I FOUND SOME DEDICATED MIKU FANS WHO WERE WILLING TO HELP US OUT...
ハハッ ha ha
...IN EXCHANGE FOR A FEW THANK-YOU GIFTS.
WHAT GIFTS?
あっさ bare
My mic...my neckerchief...!
I GUESS WE'RE LUCKY HE DIDN'T GIVE THEM ALL OUR CLOTHES...
ズガーン slump
Hooray! Back to the music!
Does it feel a little colder to you...?

(6th SONG) WORKING MIX

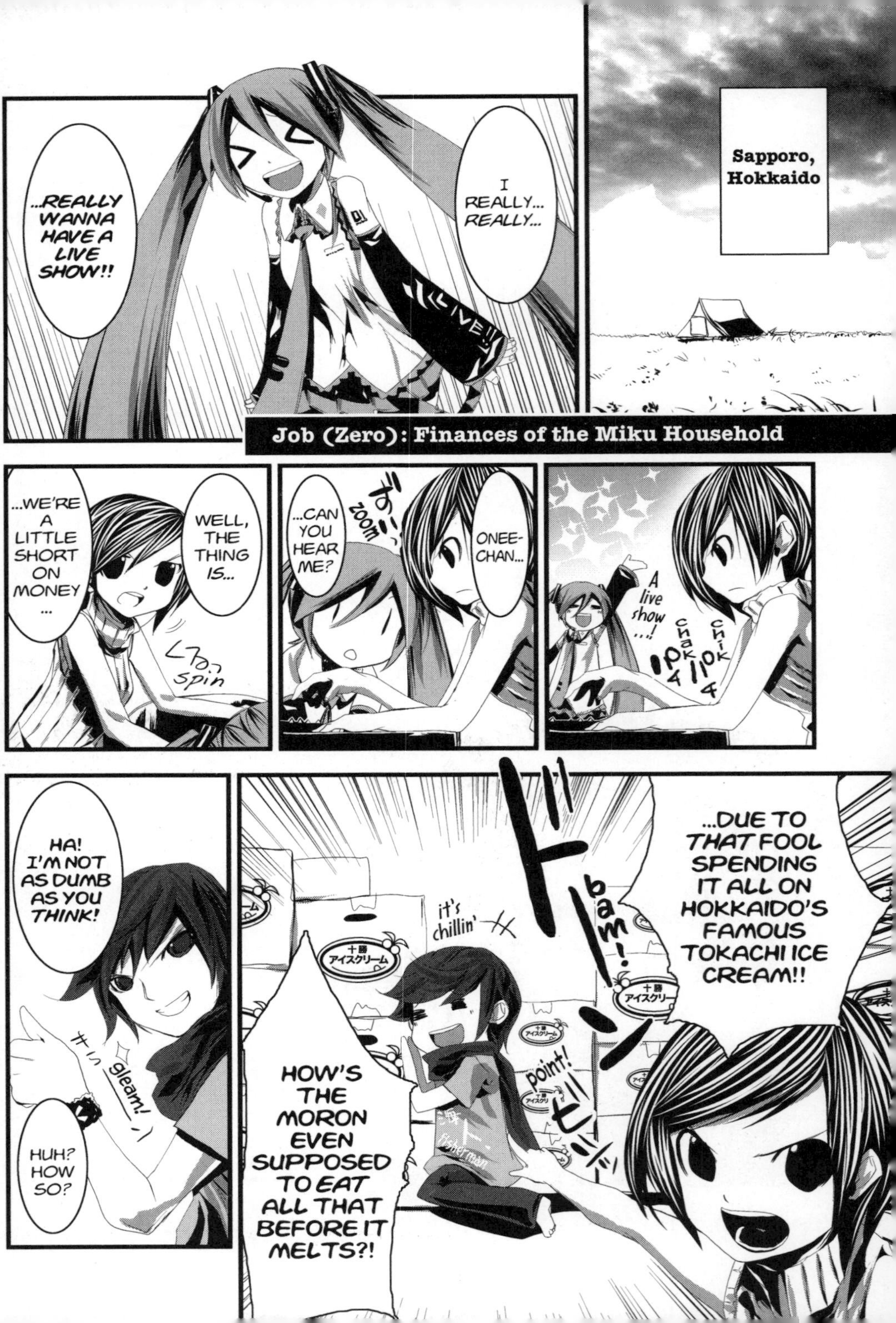
Sapporo, Hokkaido
I REALLY... REALLY...
...REALLY WANNA HAVE A LIVE SHOW!!
Job (Zero): Finances of the Miku Household
A live show...!
chik chak
ONEE-CHAN...
...CAN YOU HEAR ME?
zoom
WELL, THE THING IS...
...WE'RE A LITTLE SHORT ON MONEY...
spin
...DUE TO THAT FOOL SPENDING IT ALL ON HOKKAIDO'S FAMOUS TOKACHI ICE CREAM!!
bam!
十勝アイスクリーム
it's chillin'
point!
HOW'S THE MORON EVEN SUPPOSED TO EAT ALL THAT BEFORE IT MELTS?!
HA! I'M NOT AS DUMB AS YOU THINK!
gleam!
HUH? HOW SO?

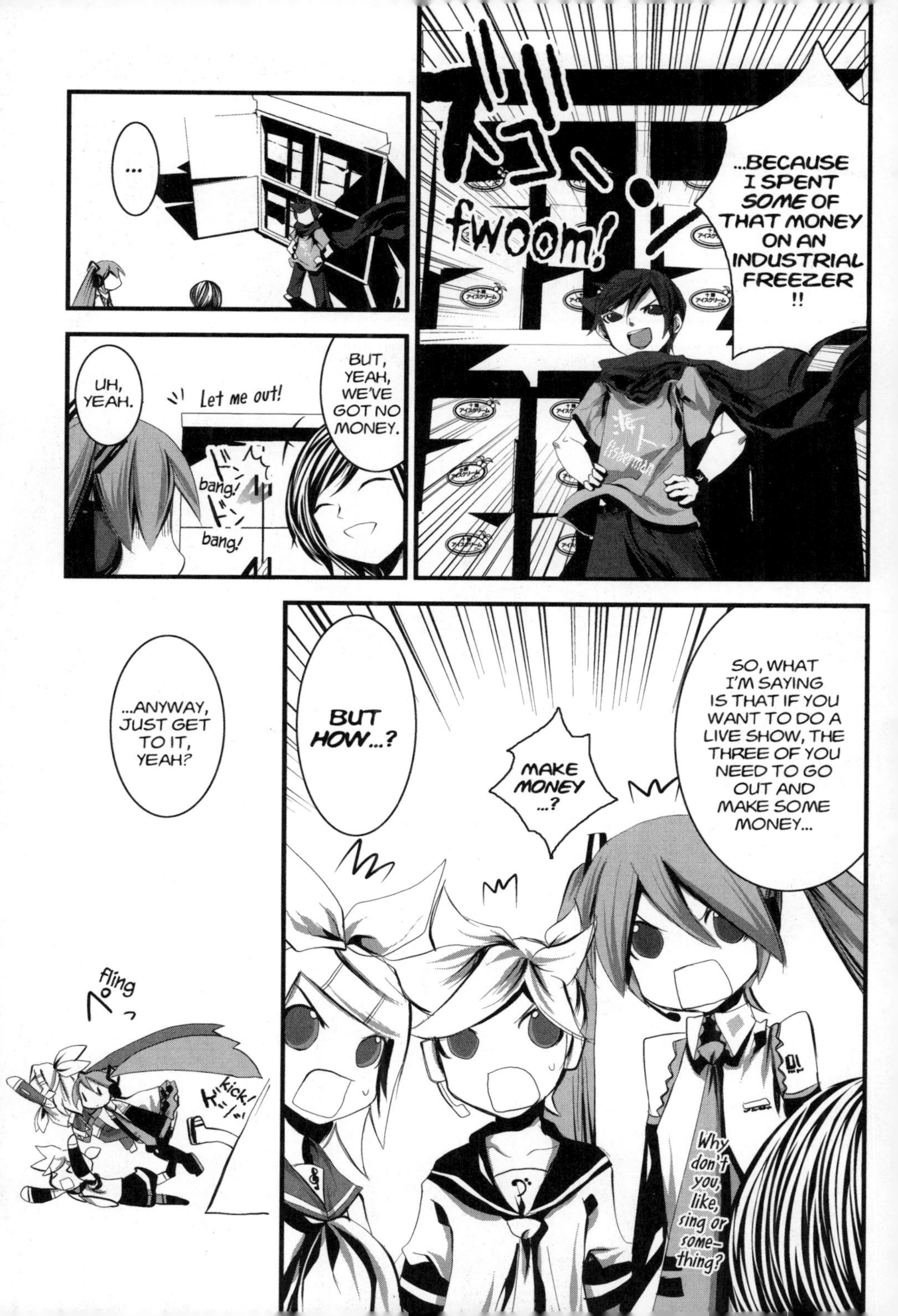
fwoom!
...BECAUSE I SPENT SOME OF THAT MONEY ON AN INDUSTRIAL FREEZER !!
...
BUT, YEAH, WE'VE GOT NO MONEY.
Let me out!
bang!
bang!
UH, YEAH.
SO, WHAT I'M SAYING IS THAT IF YOU WANT TO DO A LIVE SHOW, THE THREE OF YOU NEED TO GO OUT AND MAKE SOME MONEY...
MAKE MONEY ...?
BUT HOW...?
Why don't you, like, sing or some-thing?
...ANYWAY, JUST GET TO IT, YEAH?
fling
kick!

Job (One): Elevator Girl

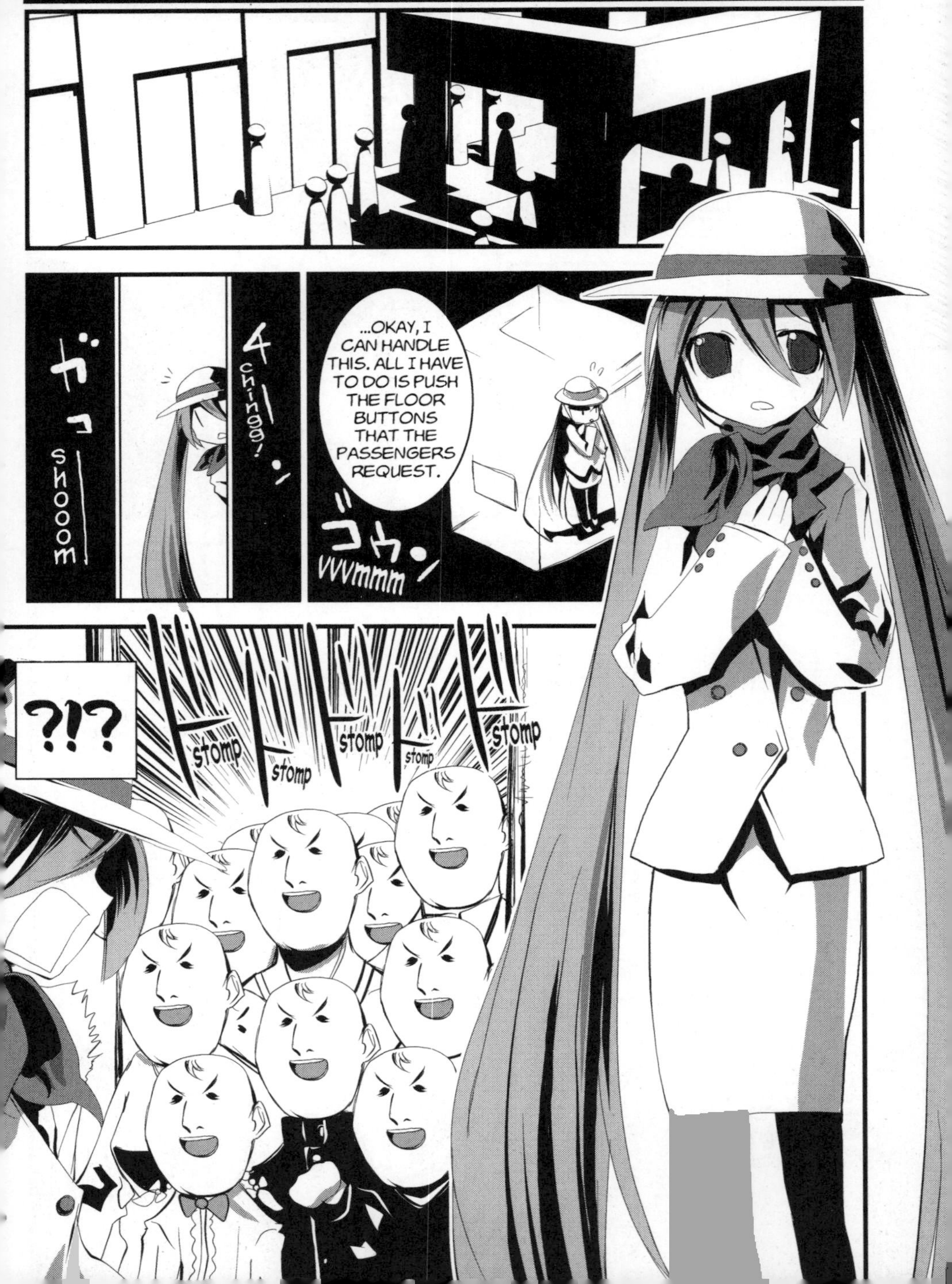
...OKAY, I CAN HANDLE THIS. ALL I HAVE TO DO IS PUSH THE FLOOR BUTTONS THAT THE PASSENGERS REQUEST.
ゴウン
vvvmmm
ching!
ガコ
shooom
stomp
stomp
stomp
stomp
stomp
?!?

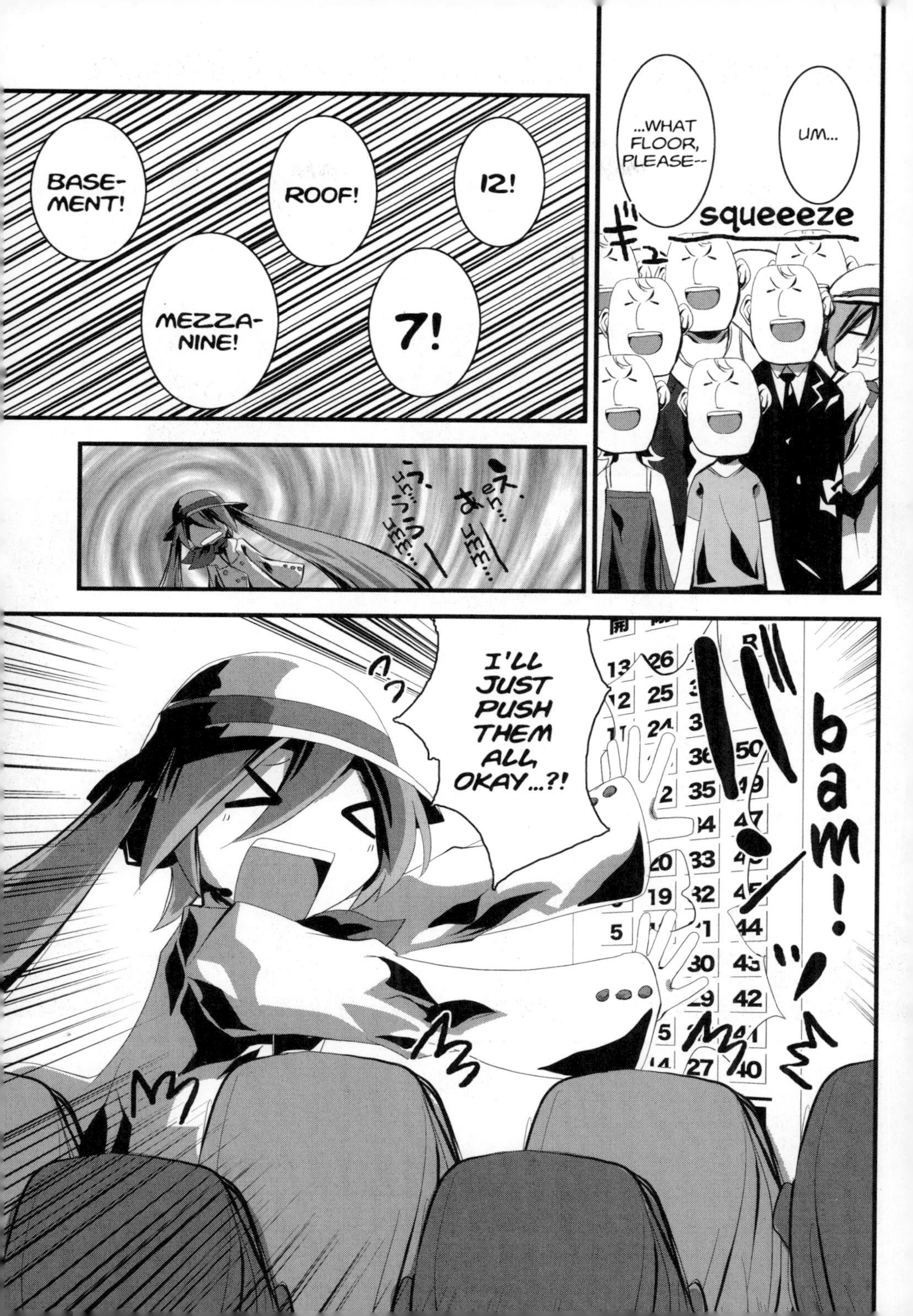
UM...
...WHAT FLOOR, PLEASE--
squeeeze
12!
ROOF!
BASE-MENT!
7!
MEZZA-NINE!
eh... JEEE...
uh... JEEE...
I'LL JUST PUSH THEM ALL OKAY...?!
bam!

Job (Two): Train Announcer

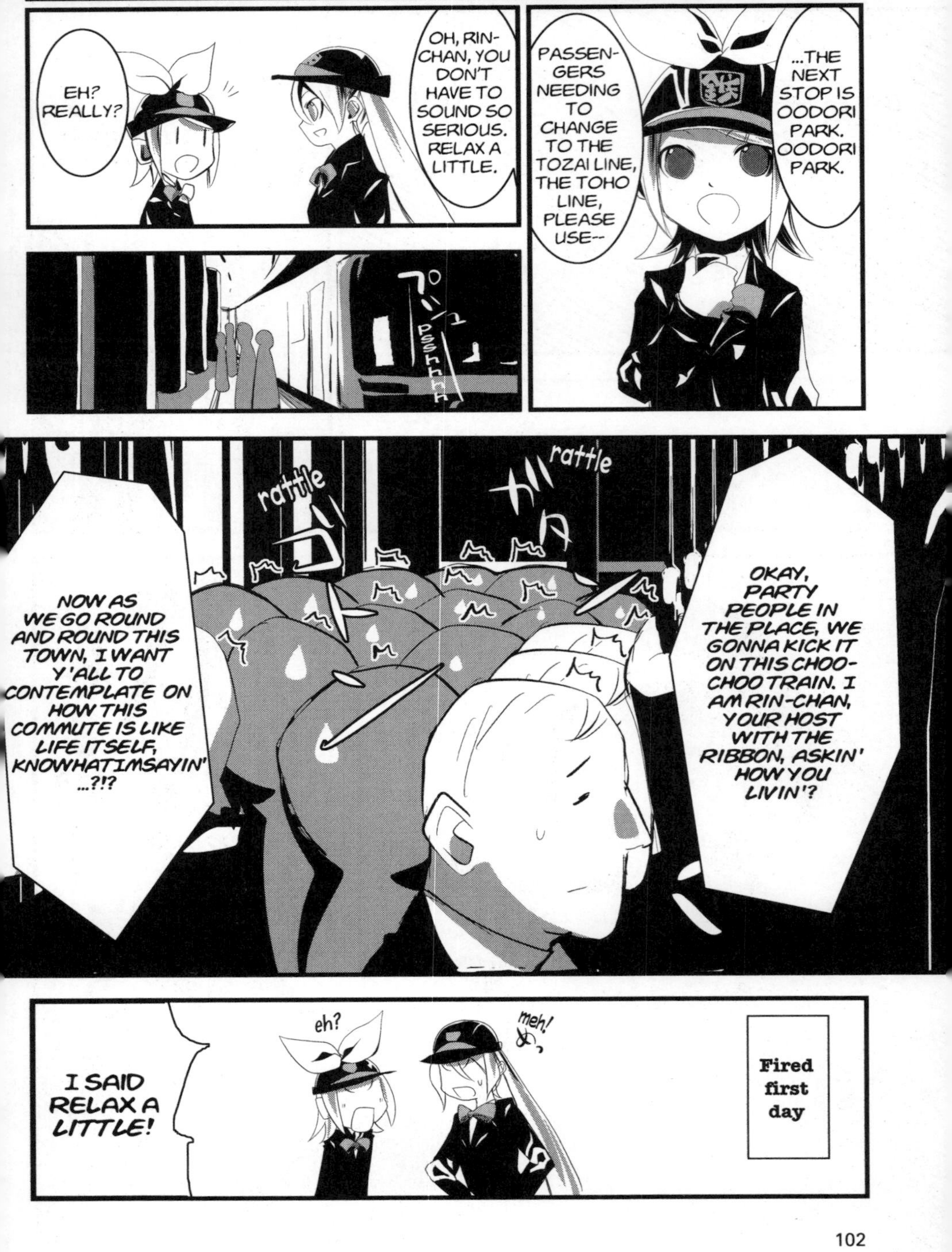
...THE NEXT STOP IS OODORI PARK. OODORI PARK.
PASSENGERS NEEDING TO CHANGE TO THE TOZAI LINE, THE TOHO LINE, PLEASE USE--
OH, RIN-CHAN, YOU DON'T HAVE TO SOUND SO SERIOUS. RELAX A LITTLE.
EH? REALLY?
pshhhh
OKAY, PARTY PEOPLE IN THE PLACE, WE GONNA KICK IT ON THIS CHOO-CHOO TRAIN. I AM RIN-CHAN, YOUR HOST WITH THE RIBBON, ASKIN' HOW YOU LIVIN'?
rattle
rattle
NOW AS WE GO ROUND AND ROUND THIS TOWN, I WANT Y'ALL TO CONTEMPLATE ON HOW THIS COMMUTE IS LIKE LIFE ITSELF, KNOWHATIMSAYIN' ...?!?
Fired first day
meh!
eh?
I SAID RELAX A LITTLE!

Job (Three): In-Car Navigation System

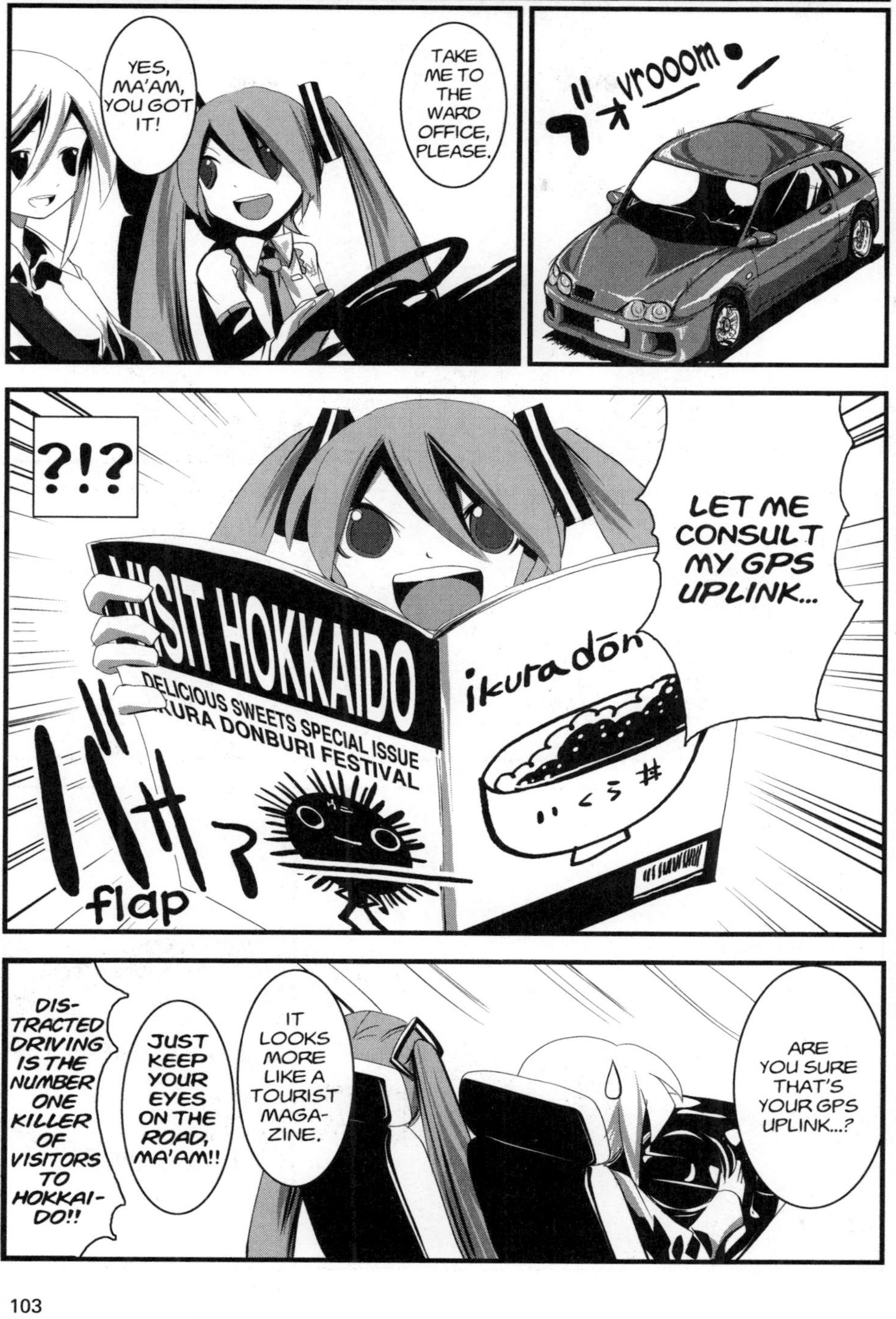
vrooom
TAKE ME TO THE WARD OFFICE, PLEASE.
YES, MA'AM, YOU GOT IT!
LET ME CONSULT MY GPS UPLINK...
?!?
VISIT HOKKAIDO
DELICIOUS SWEETS SPECIAL ISSUE
IKURA DONBURI FESTIVAL
ikuradōn
いくら丼
flap
ARE YOU SURE THAT'S YOUR GPS UPLINK...?
IT LOOKS MORE LIKE A TOURIST MAGAZINE.
JUST KEEP YOUR EYES ON THE ROAD, MA'AM!!
DISTRACTED DRIVING IS THE NUMBER ONE KILLER OF VISITORS TO HOKKAIDO!!

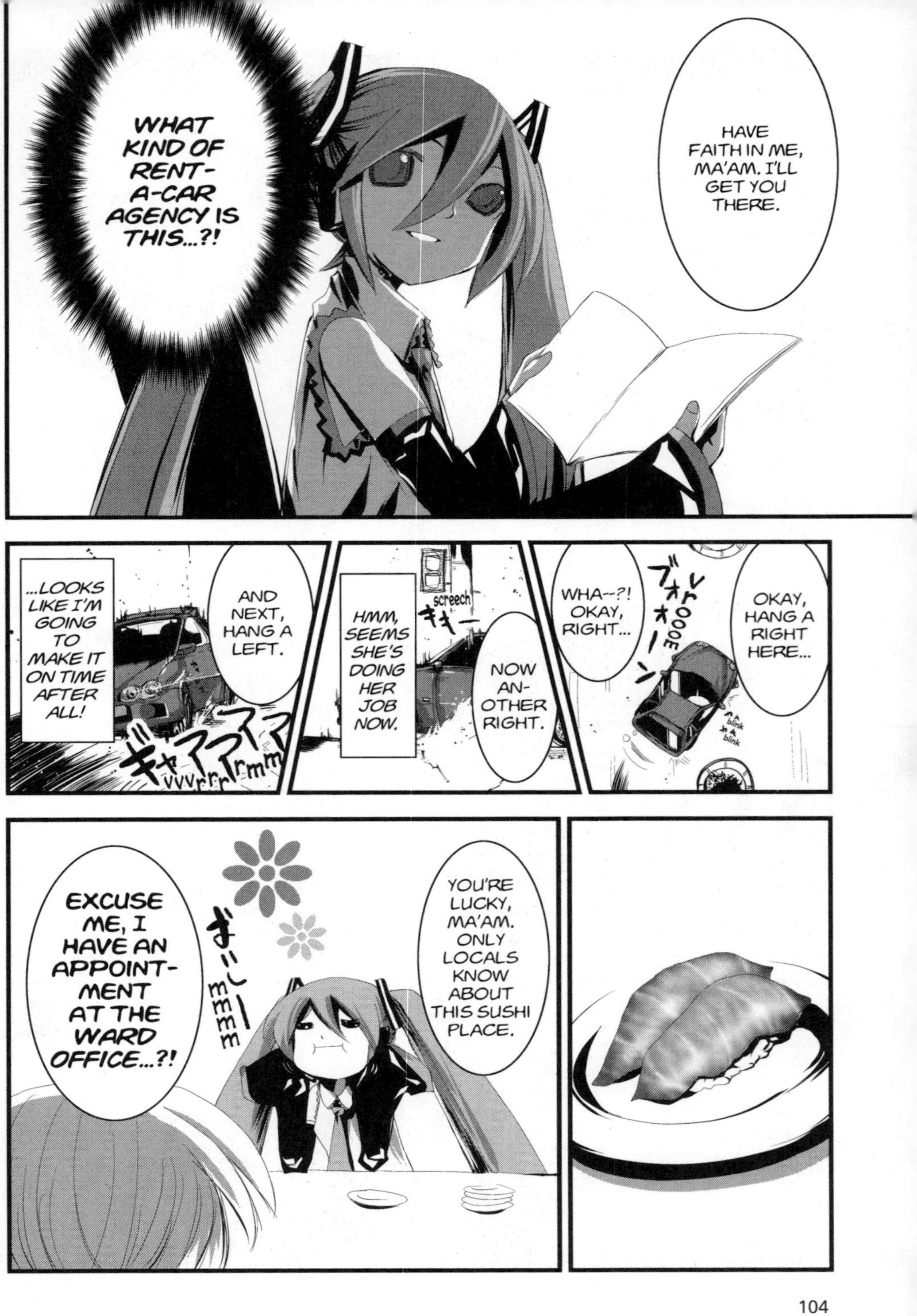
HAVE FAITH IN ME, MA'AM. I'LL GET YOU THERE.
WHAT KIND OF RENT-A-CAR AGENCY IS THIS...?!
OKAY, HANG A RIGHT HERE...
vroooom
WHA--?! OKAY, RIGHT...
blink blink
NOW AN-OTHER RIGHT.
screech
HMM, SEEMS SHE'S DOING HER JOB NOW.
AND NEXT, HANG A LEFT.
...LOOKS LIKE I'M GOING TO MAKE IT ON TIME AFTER ALL!
YOU'RE LUCKY, MA'AM. ONLY LOCALS KNOW ABOUT THIS SUSHI PLACE.
mmmm
EXCUSE ME, I HAVE AN APPOINT-MENT AT THE WARD OFFICE...?!

Job (Four): Campaign Volunteer

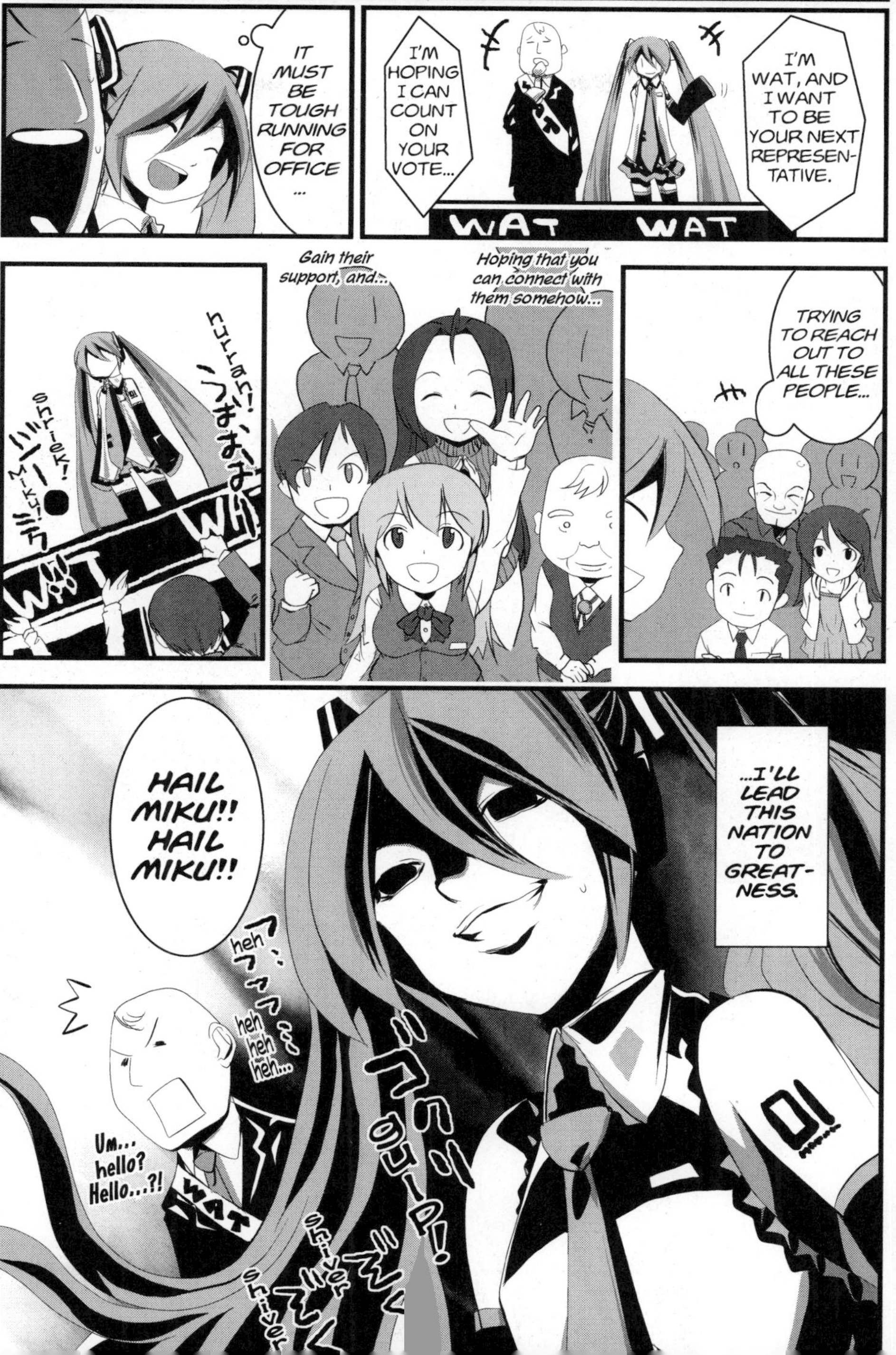
I'M WAT, AND I WANT TO BE YOUR NEXT REPRESEN-TATIVE.
I'M HOPING I CAN COUNT ON YOUR VOTE...
WAT
WAT
IT MUST BE TOUGH RUNNING FOR OFFICE ...
TRYING TO REACH OUT TO ALL THESE PEOPLE...
Hoping that you can connect with them somehow...
Gain their support, and...
hurrah!
shriek!
MIKU!
WAT
...I'LL LEAD THIS NATION TO GREAT-NESS.
HAIL MIKU!! HAIL MIKU!!
heh
heh heh heh...
gulp!
shiver shiver
Um... hello? Hello...?!
WAT

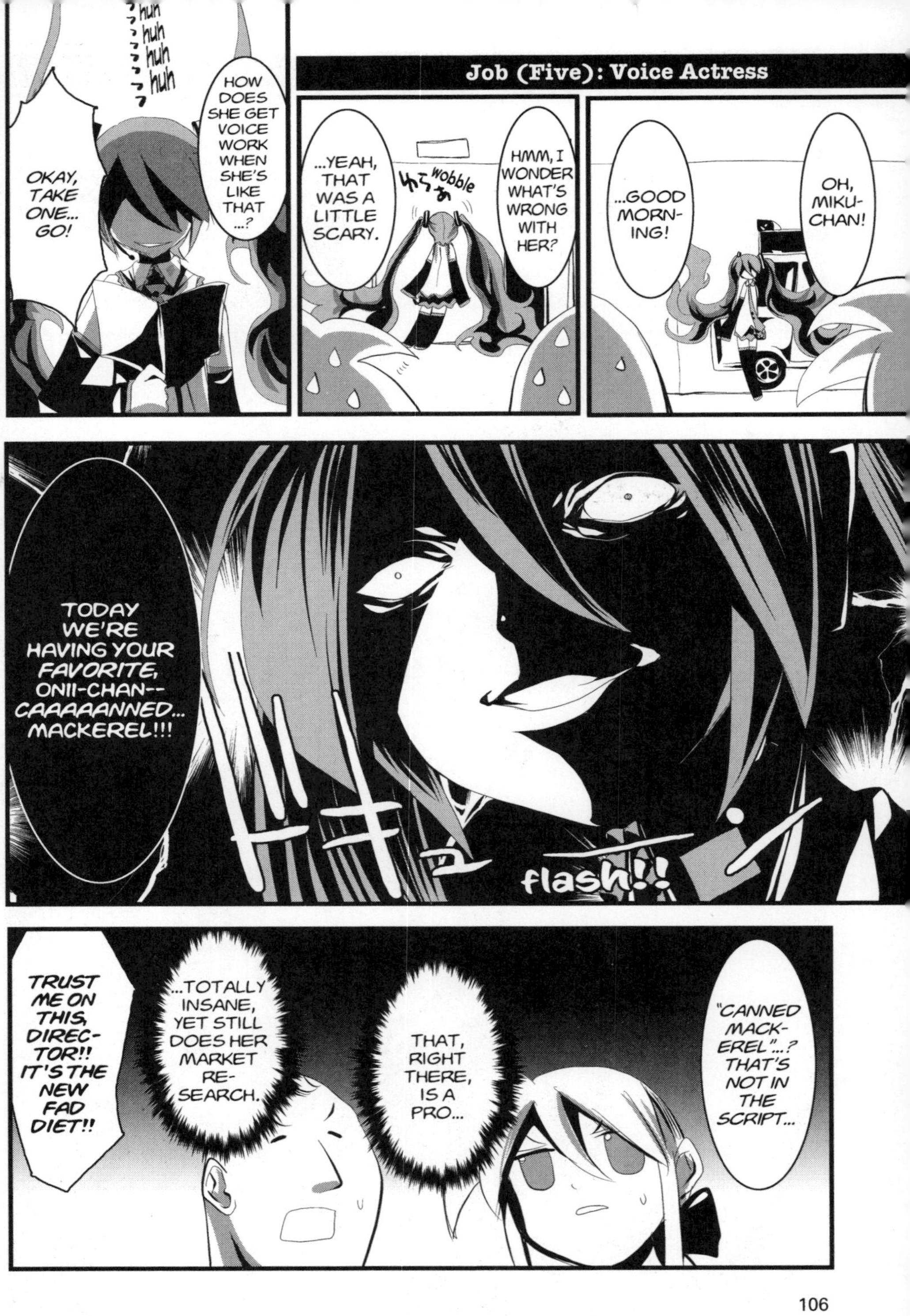
Job (Five): Voice Actress
OH, MIKU-CHAN!
...GOOD MORNING!
HMM, I WONDER WHAT'S WRONG WITH HER?
wobble
...YEAH, THAT WAS A LITTLE SCARY.
huh huh huh huh
HOW DOES SHE GET VOICE WORK WHEN SHE'S LIKE THAT ...?
OKAY, TAKE ONE... GO!
TODAY WE'RE HAVING YOUR FAVORITE, ONII-CHAN-- CAAAAANNED... MACKEREL!!!
flash!!
"CANNED MACKEREL"...? THAT'S NOT IN THE SCRIPT...
THAT, RIGHT THERE, IS A PRO...
...TOTALLY INSANE, YET STILL DOES HER MARKET RESEARCH.
TRUST ME ON THIS, DIRECTOR!! IT'S THE NEW FAD DIET!!

Job (Six): Telemarketer

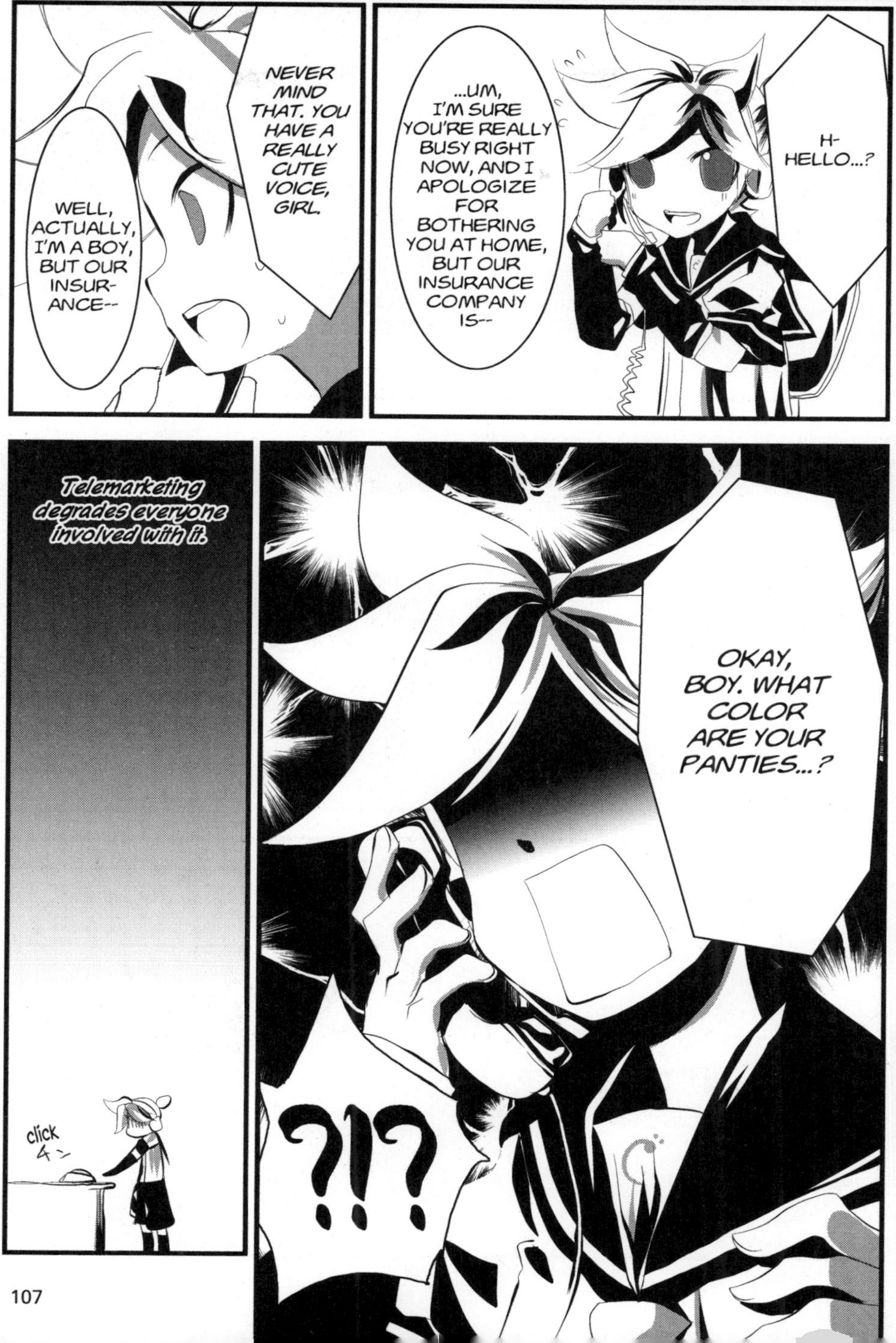
H-HELLO...?
...UM, I'M SURE YOU'RE REALLY BUSY RIGHT NOW, AND I APOLOGIZE FOR BOTHERING YOU AT HOME, BUT OUR INSURANCE COMPANY IS--
NEVER MIND THAT. YOU HAVE A REALLY CUTE VOICE, GIRL.
WELL, ACTUALLY, I'M A BOY, BUT OUR INSURANCE--
OKAY, BOY. WHAT COLOR ARE YOUR PANTIES...?
?!?
Telemarketing degrades everyone involved with it.
click

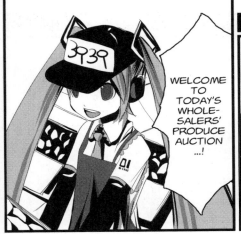

Job (Seven): Auctioneer

CABBAGE
トマト
TOMATO
MELON
WELCOME TO TODAY'S WHOLE-SALERS' PRODUCE AUCTION ...!
FIRSTLOTA FINEGROUP OFDAIKON RADISHES WHATAMI BIDFOR THESE DAIKON RADISHES ?!
ド
WHOOM!
DAN-SHAKU-DAN-SHAKU-POTA-TOES WHATAM IBIDFOR THESE FINE DAN-SHAKU-POTA-TOES?
ズバ
ZOOM!
......

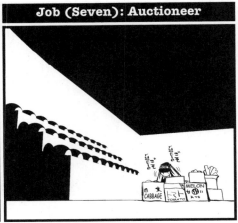

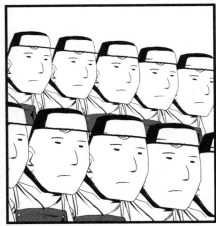

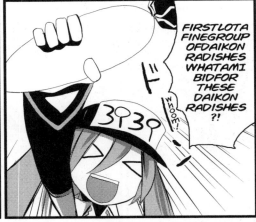

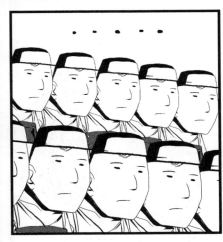

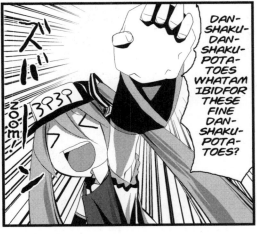

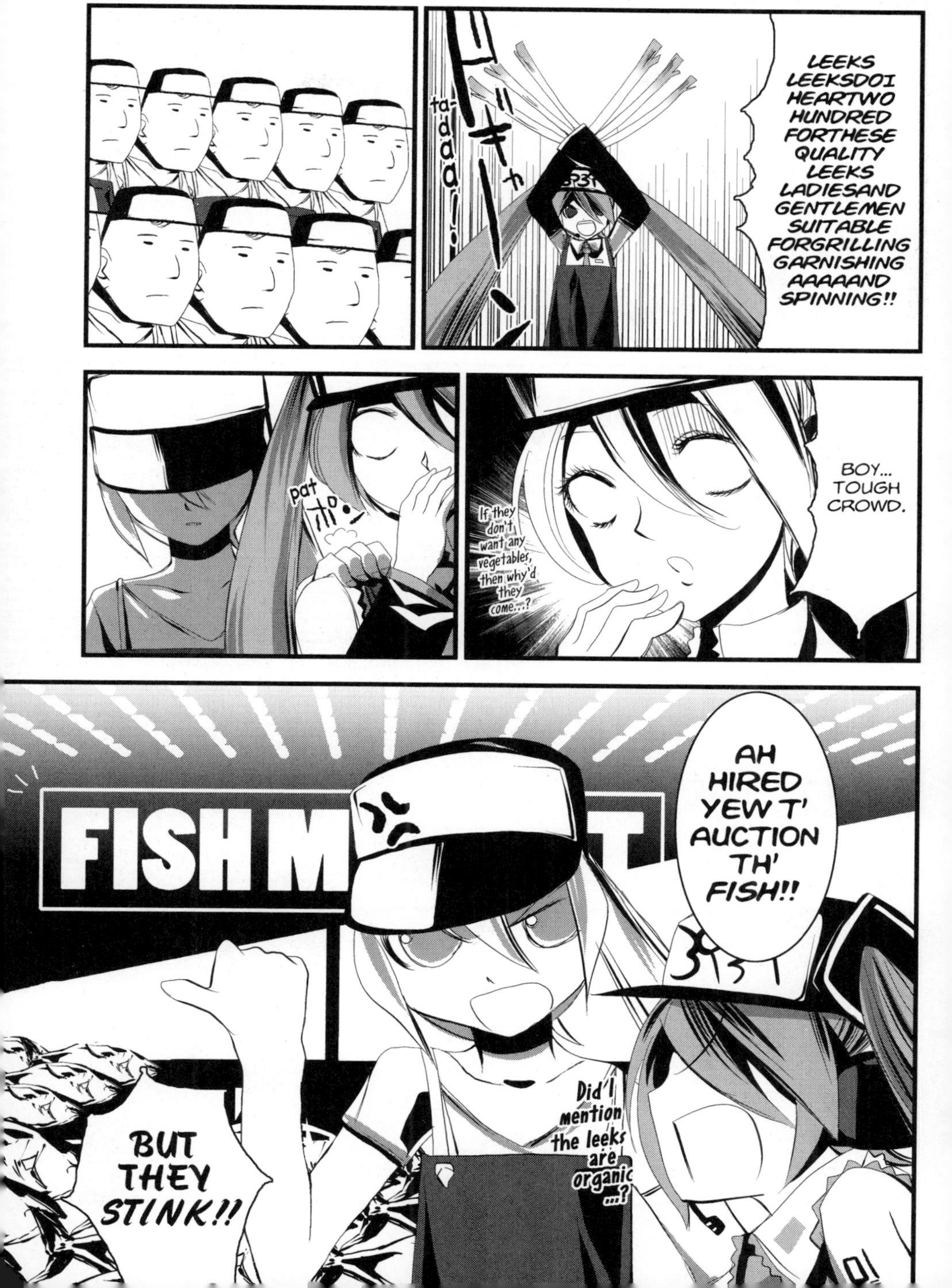
LEEKS LEEKSDOI HEARTWO HUNDRED FORTHESE QUALITY LEEKS LADIESAND GENTLEMEN SUITABLE FORGRILLING GARNISHING AAAAAND SPINNING!!
ta-daaa!!
BOY... TOUGH CROWD.
If they don't want any vegetables, then why'd they come...?
pat
AH HIRED YEW T' AUCTION TH' FISH!!
FISH M
Did I mention the leeks are organic...?
BUT THEY STINK!!

Job (Eight): Niconico

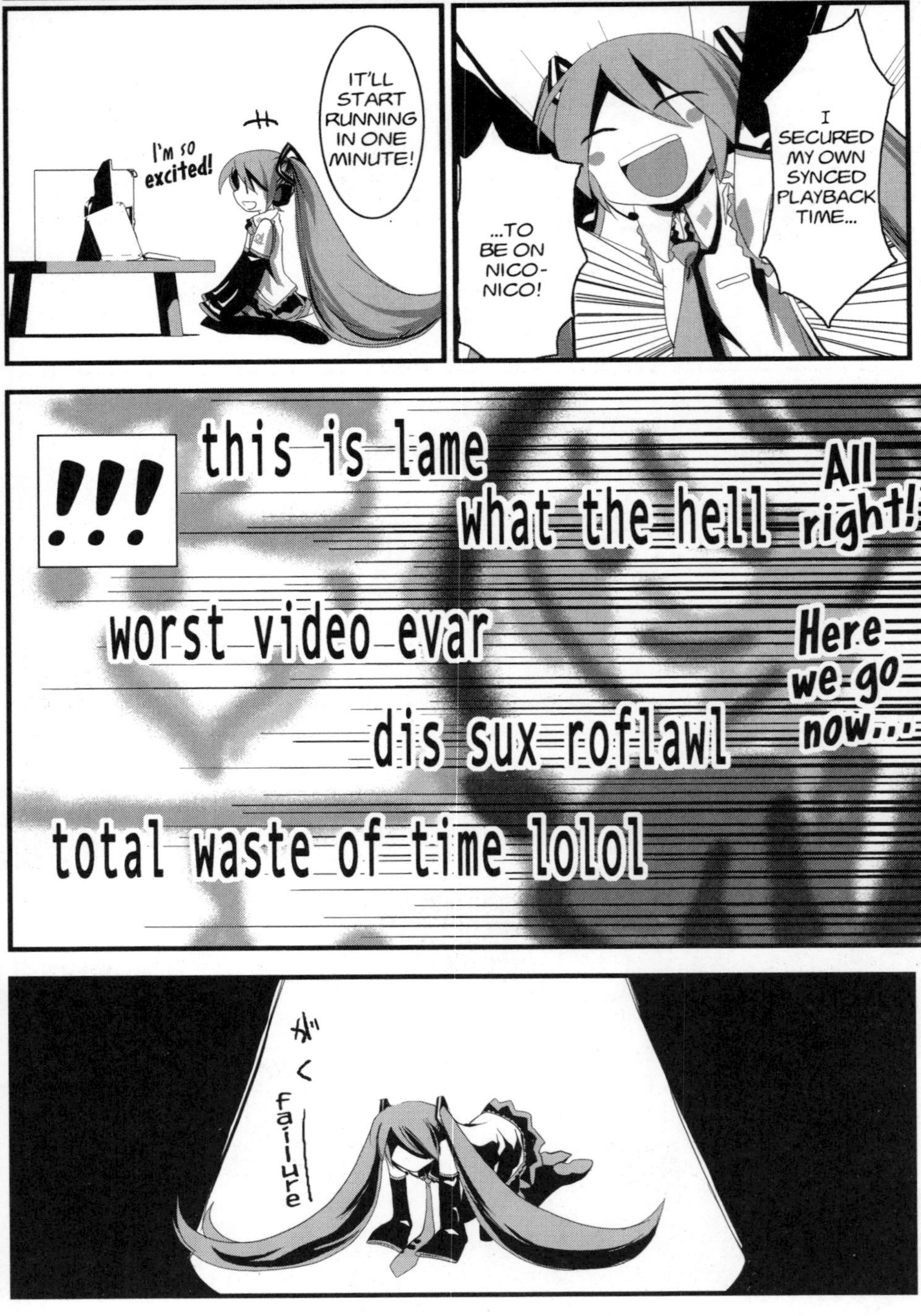
I SECURED MY OWN SYNCED PLAYBACK TIME...
...TO BE ON NICO-NICO!
IT'LL START RUNNING IN ONE MINUTE!
I'm so excited!
All right!
this is lame
what the hell
!!!
Here we go now...
worst video evar
dis sux roflawl
total waste of time lolol
がく
failure

Job (Nine): Paid in Full

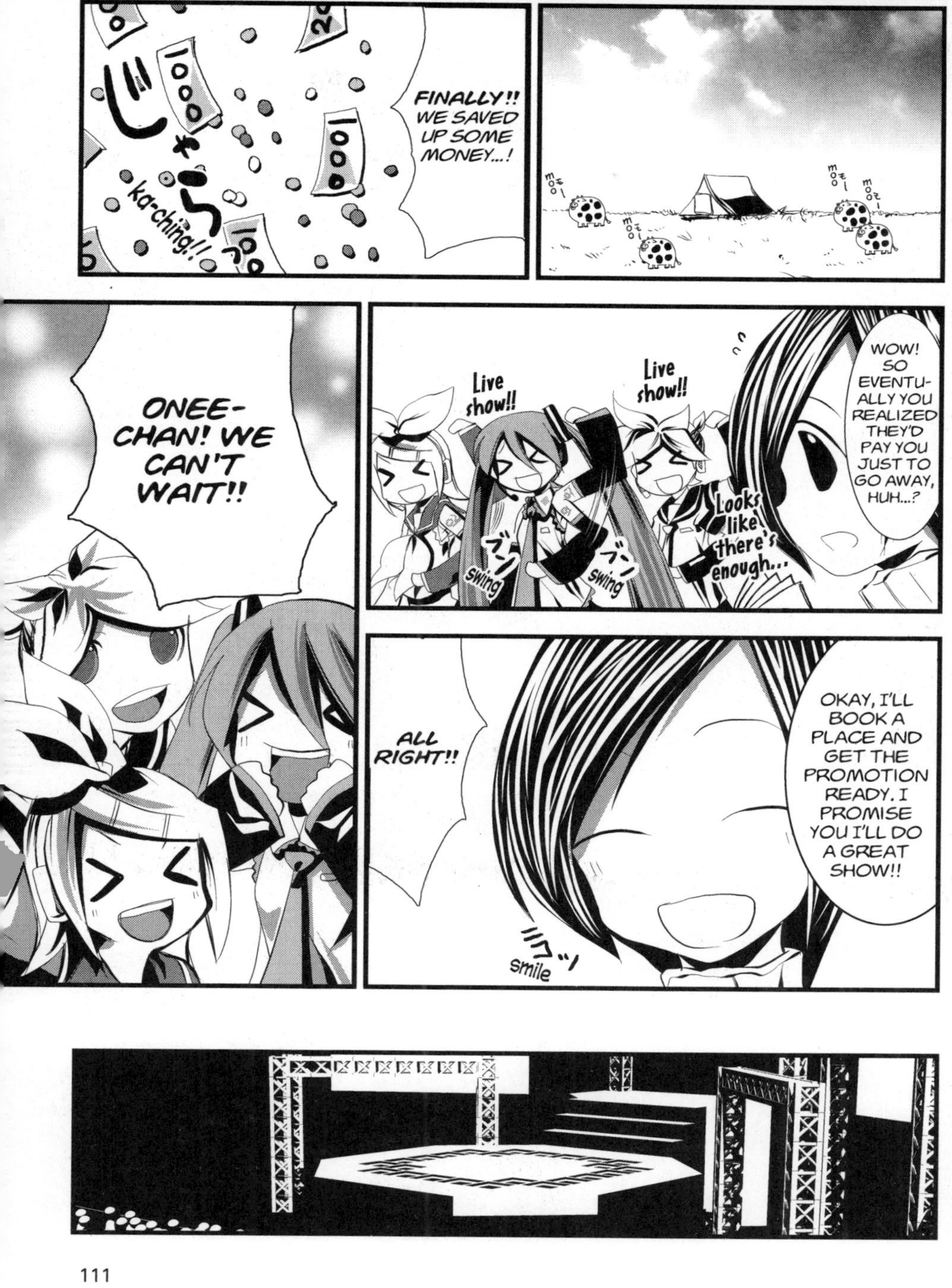
moo
moo
moo
moo
FINALLY!! WE SAVED UP SOME MONEY...!
ka-ching!!
WOW! SO EVENTU-ALLY YOU REALIZED THEY'D PAY YOU JUST TO GO AWAY, HUH...?
Looks like there's enough...
Live show!!
Live show!!
swing
swing
OKAY, I'LL BOOK A PLACE AND GET THE PROMOTION READY. I PROMISE YOU I'LL DO A GREAT SHOW!!
smile
ALL RIGHT!!
ONEE-CHAN! WE CAN'T WAIT!!

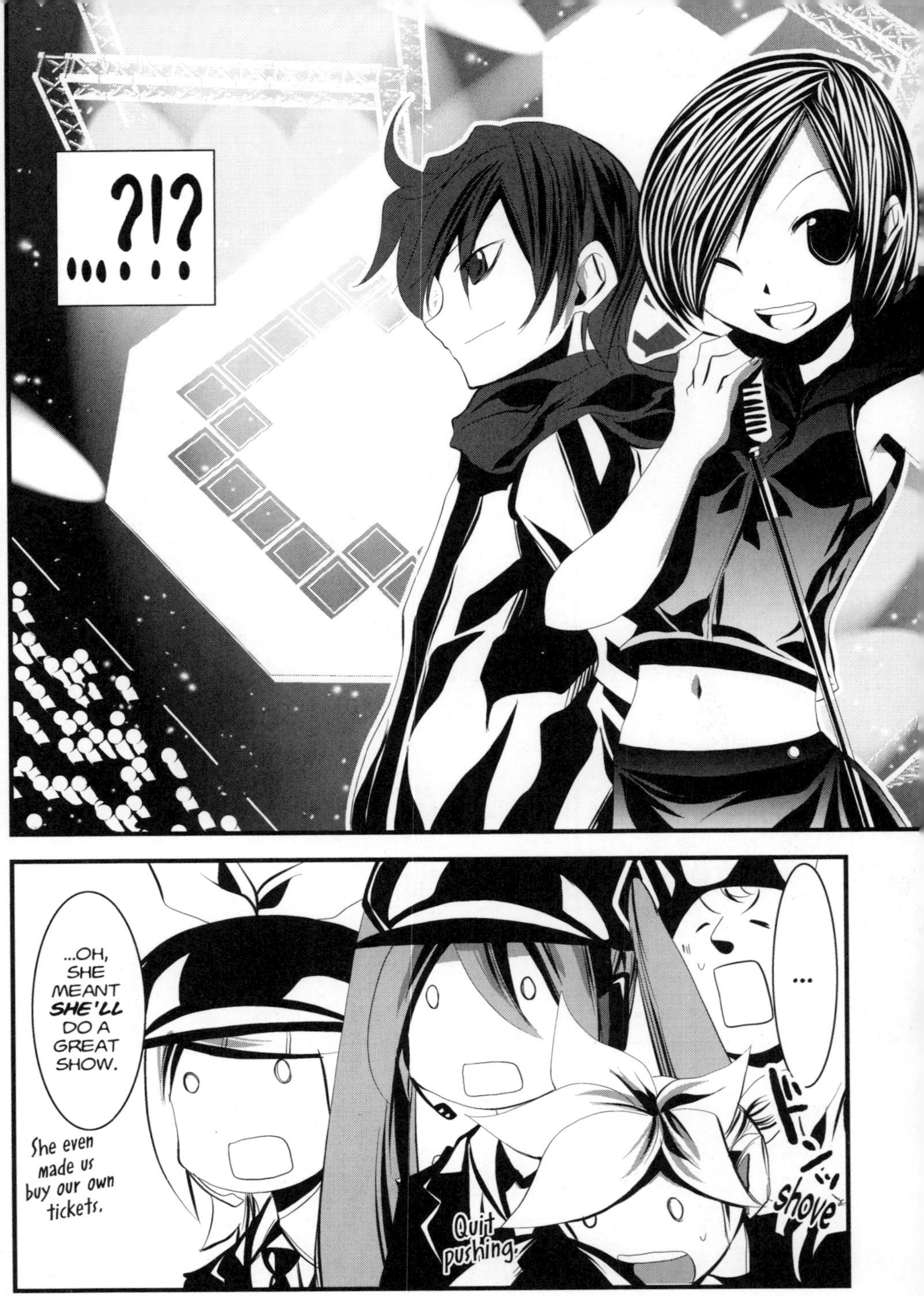
...?!?
...
...OH, SHE MEANT **SHE'LL** DO A GREAT SHOW.
She even made us buy our own tickets.
shove
Quit pushing.

(7th SONG) FUTURE MIX

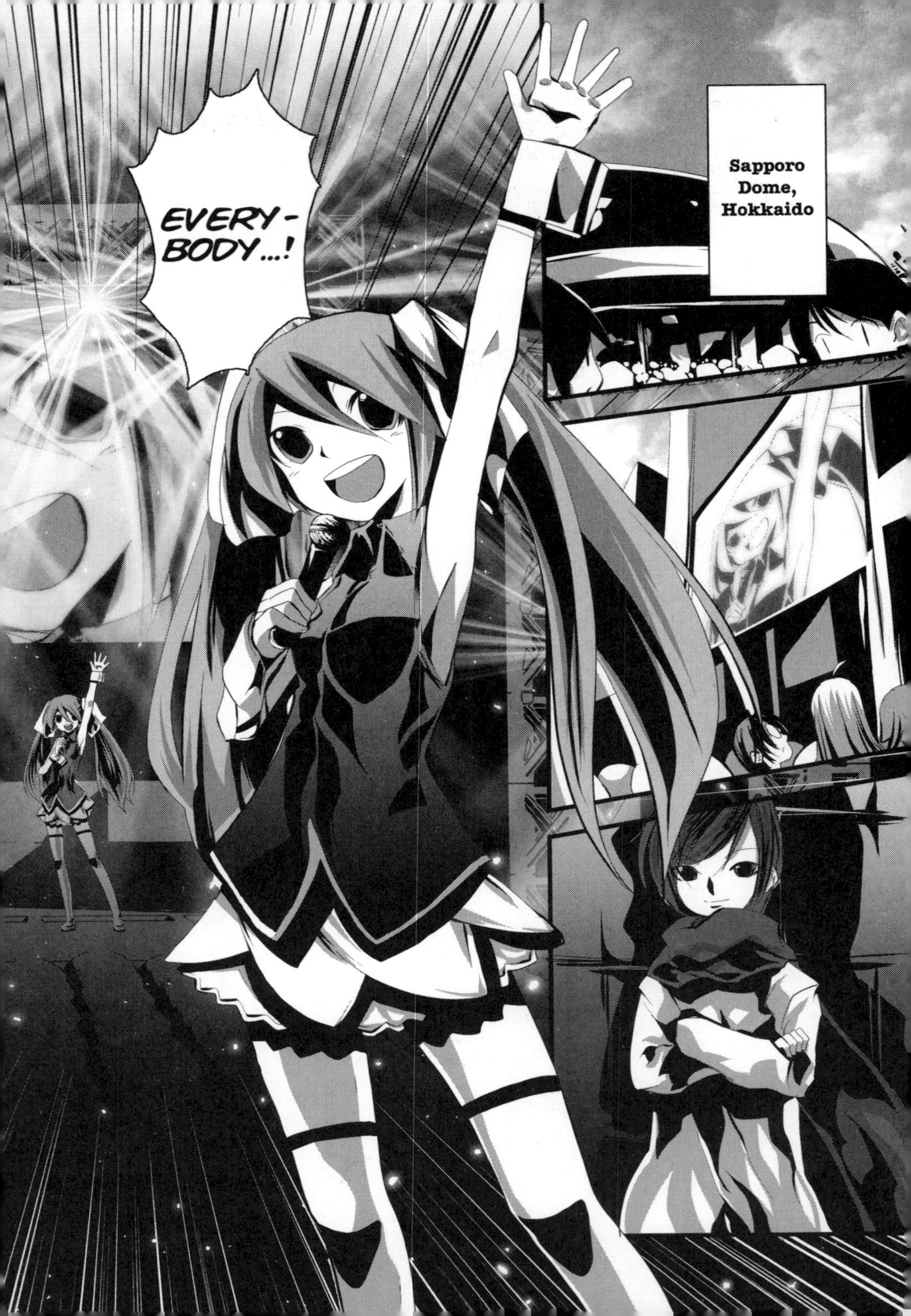
Sapporo Dome, Hokkaido
EVERY-BODY...!

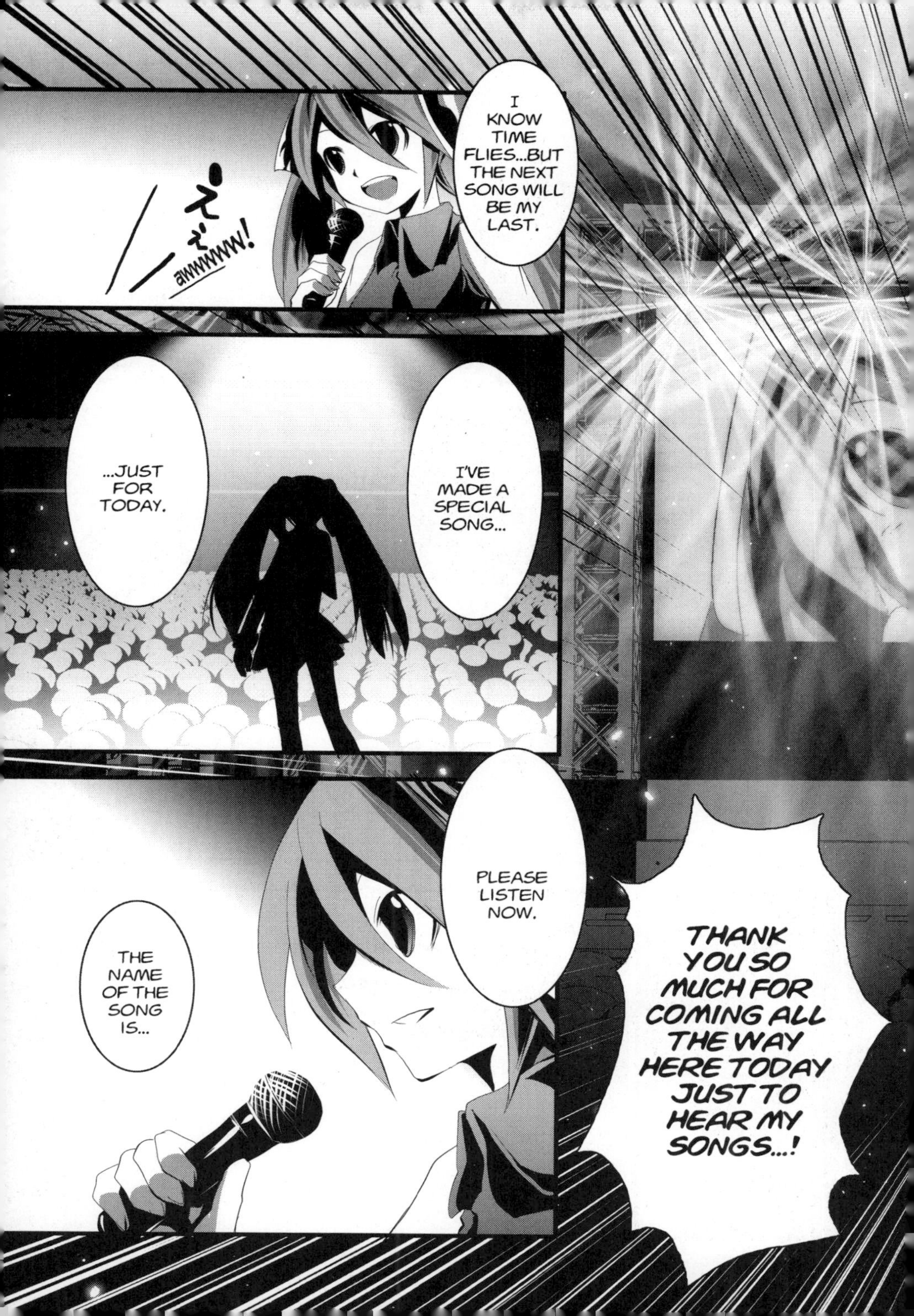
I KNOW TIME FLIES...BUT THE NEXT SONG WILL BE MY LAST.
ぞぞ
awwwww!
I'VE MADE A SPECIAL SONG...
...JUST FOR TODAY.
THANK YOU SO MUCH FOR COMING ALL THE WAY HERE TODAY JUST TO HEAR MY SONGS...!
PLEASE LISTEN NOW.
THE NAME OF THE SONG IS...

WHAT'S WRONG ...?

MIKU-CHAN ...?

slump

I'M SORRY, BUT...THIS NEXT S-SONG...

thump

...IS M-MY LAST--

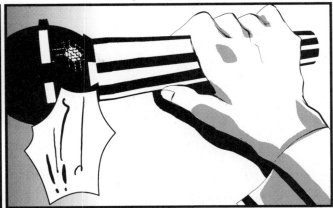

116

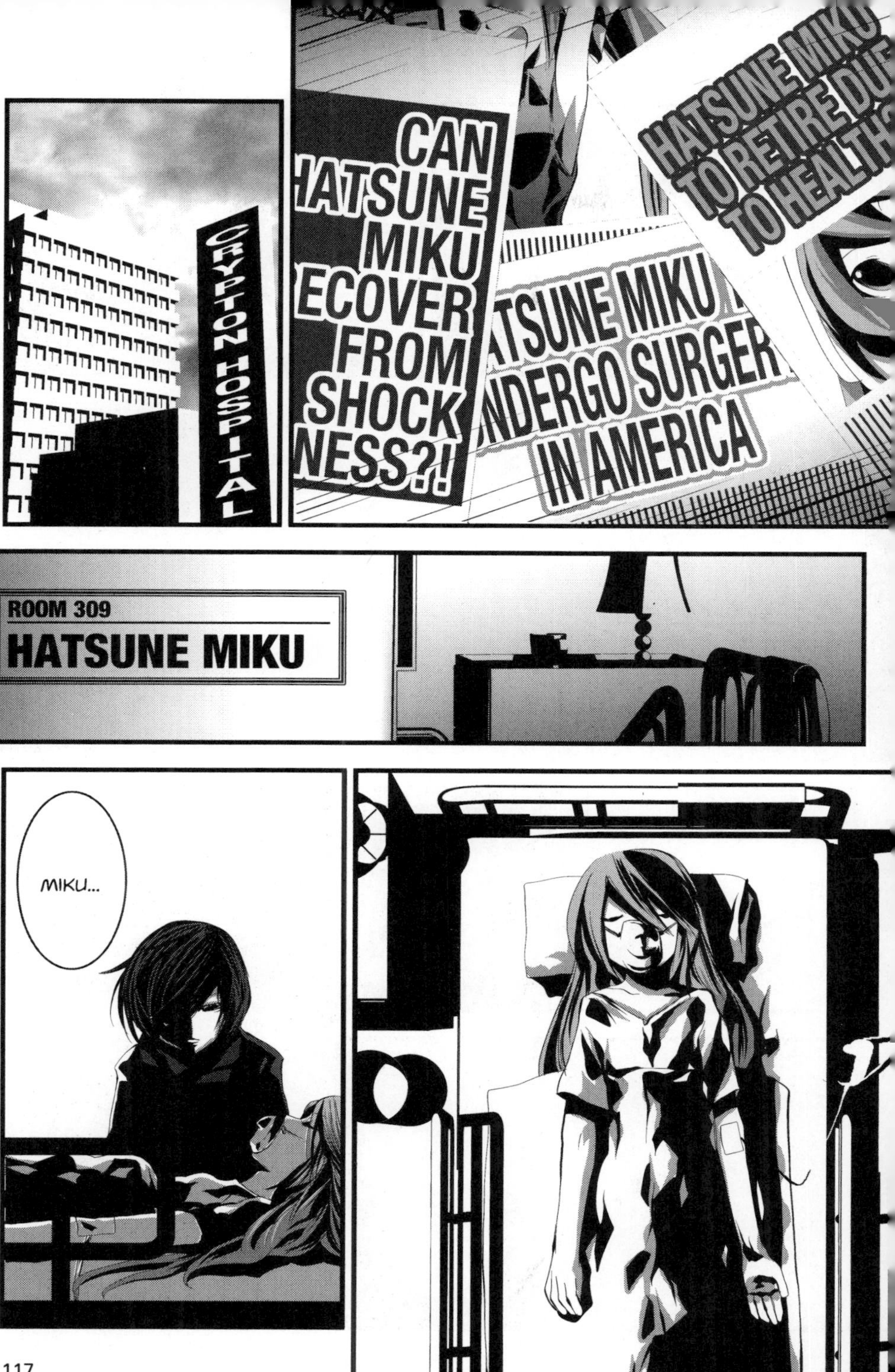
HATSUNE MIKU
TO RETIRE DU
TO HEALTH
ATSUNE MIKU
NDERGO SURGER
IN AMERICA
CAN
HATSUNE
MIKU
ECOVER
FROM
SHOCK
NESS?!
CRYPTON HOSPITAL
ROOM 309
HATSUNE MIKU
MIKU...

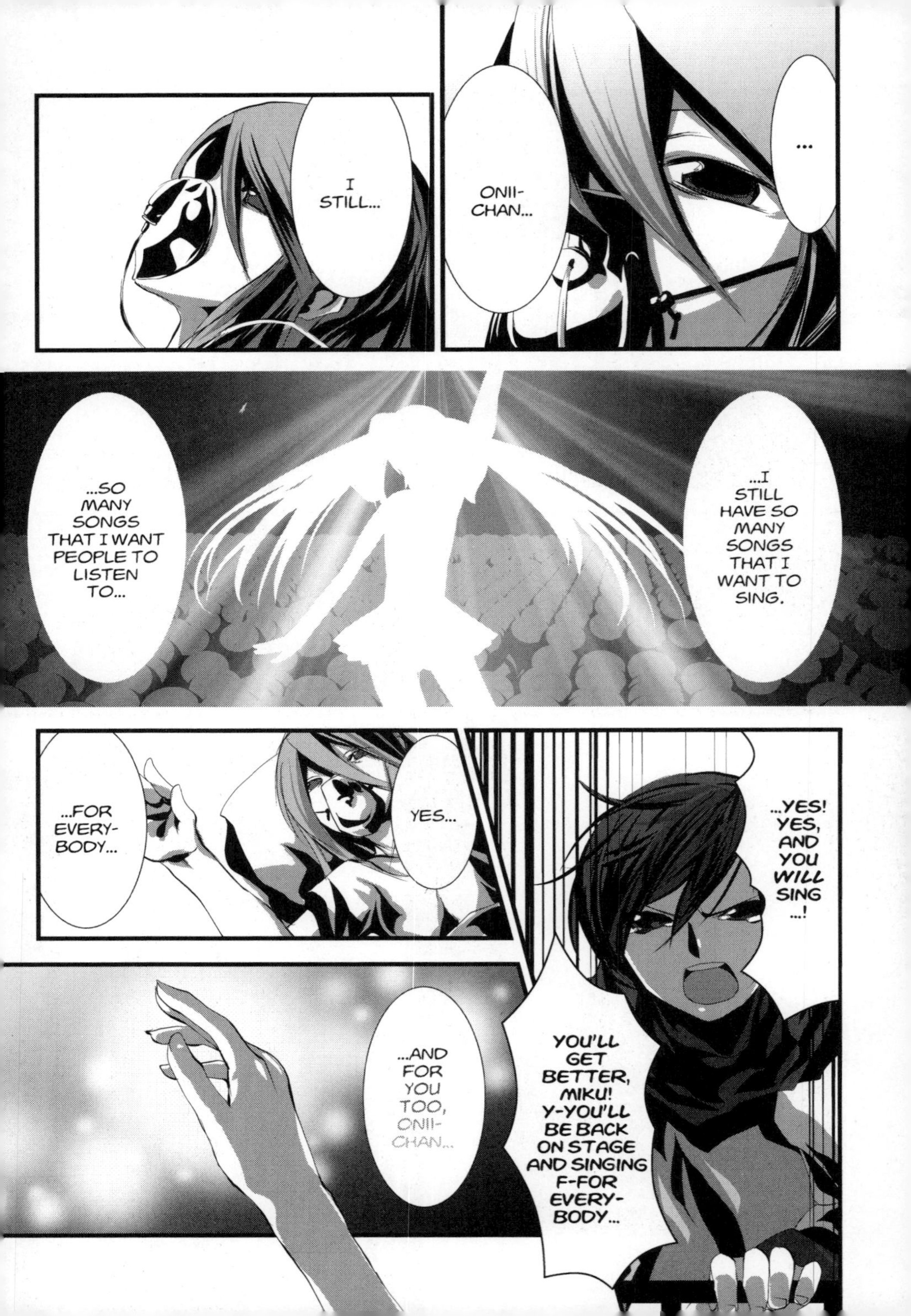
...
ONII-CHAN...
I STILL...
...I STILL HAVE SO MANY SONGS THAT I WANT TO SING.
...SO MANY SONGS THAT I WANT PEOPLE TO LISTEN TO...
...YES! YES, AND YOU WILL SING ...!
YOU'LL GET BETTER, MIKU! Y-YOU'LL BE BACK ON STAGE AND SINGING F-FOR EVERY-BODY...
YES...
...FOR EVERY-BODY...
...AND FOR YOU TOO, ONII-CHAN...

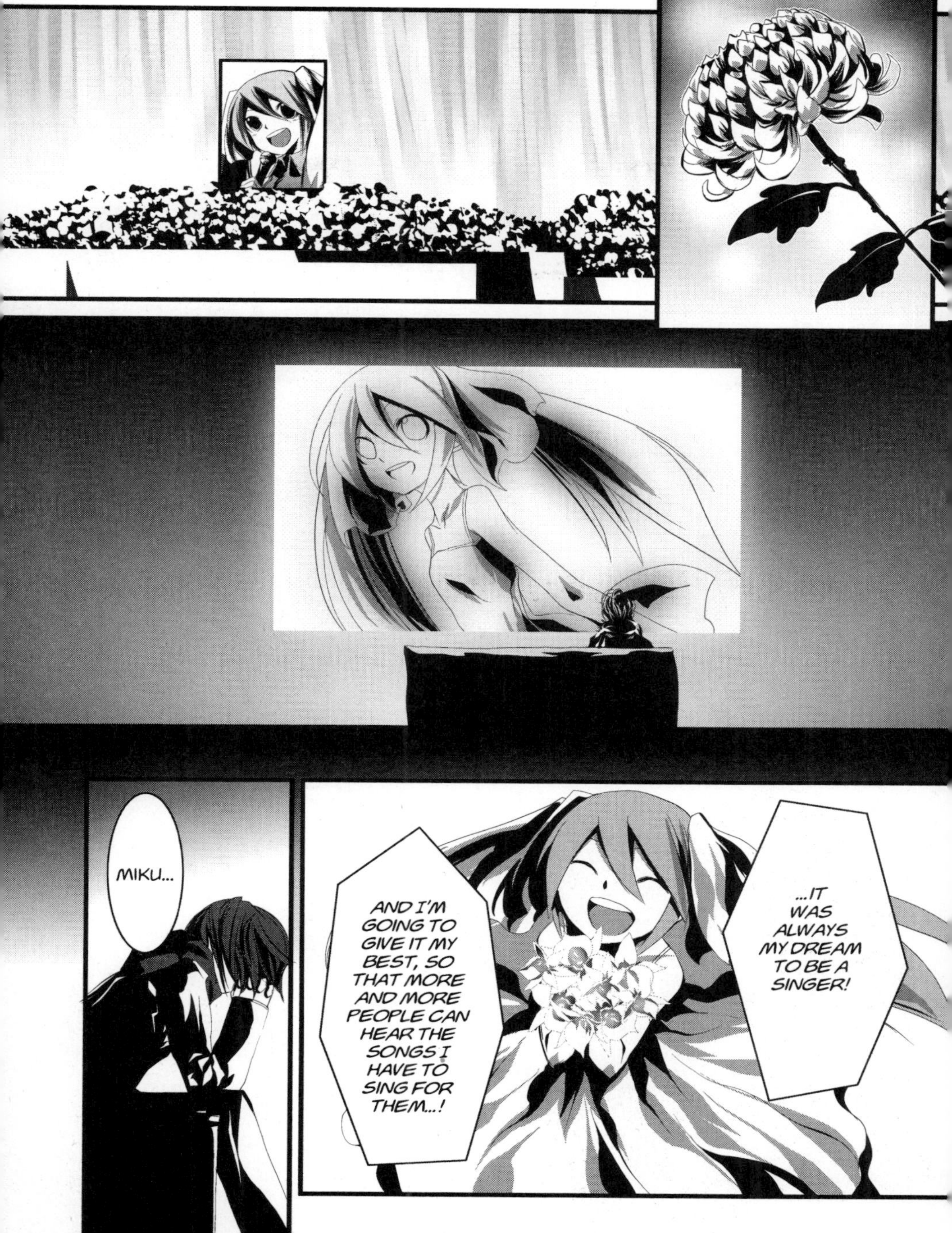
...IT WAS ALWAYS MY DREAM TO BE A SINGER!
AND I'M GOING TO GIVE IT MY BEST, SO THAT MORE AND MORE PEOPLE CAN HEAR THE SONGS I HAVE TO SING FOR THEM...!
MIKU...

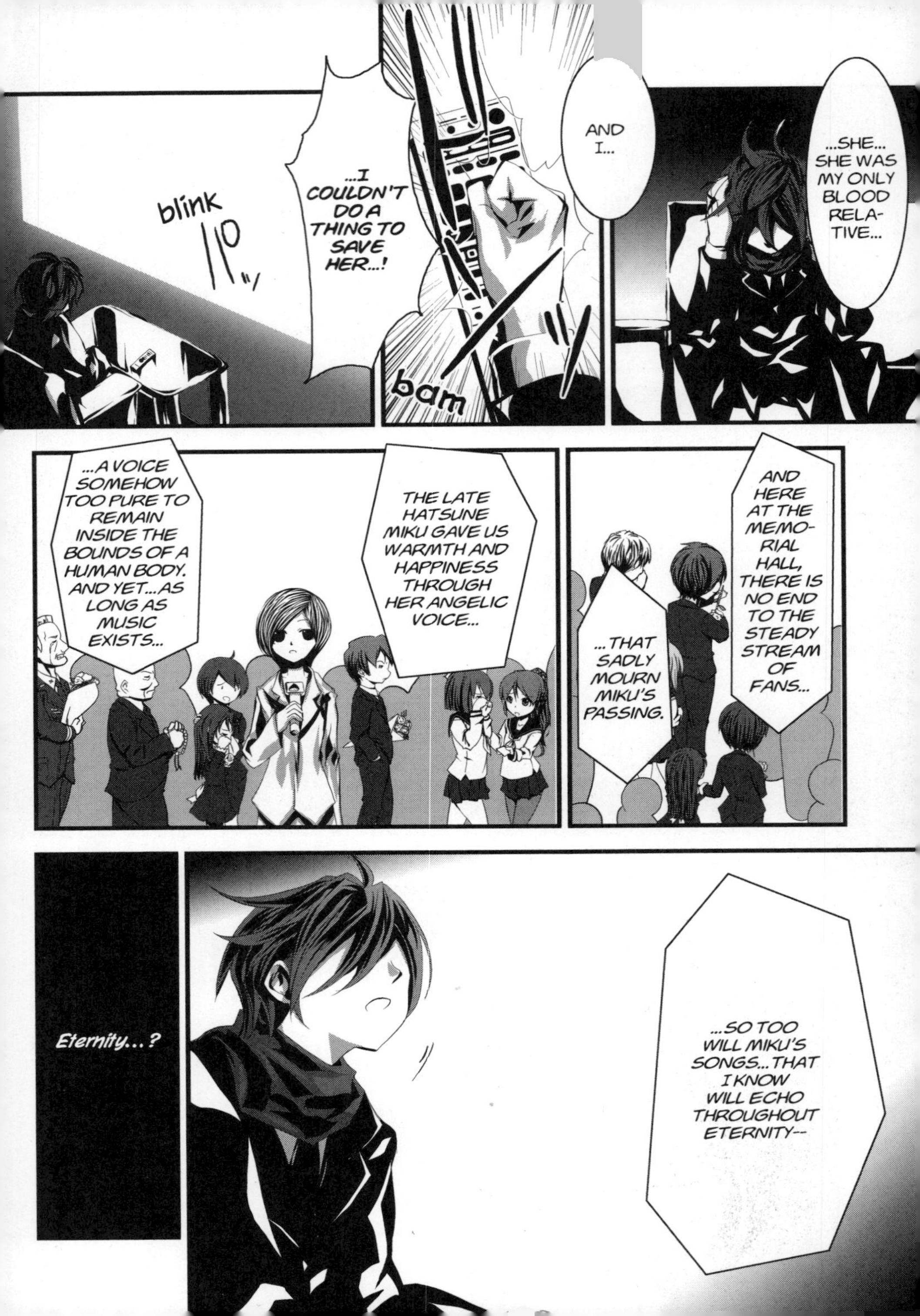
...SHE... SHE WAS MY ONLY BLOOD RELATIVE...
AND I...
...I COULDN'T DO A THING TO SAVE HER...!
bam
blink
AND HERE AT THE MEMORIAL HALL, THERE IS NO END TO THE STEADY STREAM OF FANS...
...THAT SADLY MOURN MIKU'S PASSING.
THE LATE HATSUNE MIKU GAVE US WARMTH AND HAPPINESS THROUGH HER ANGELIC VOICE...
...A VOICE SOMEHOW TOO PURE TO REMAIN INSIDE THE BOUNDS OF A HUMAN BODY. AND YET...AS LONG AS MUSIC EXISTS...
...SO TOO WILL MIKU'S SONGS...THAT I KNOW WILL ECHO THROUGHOUT ETERNITY--
Eternity...?

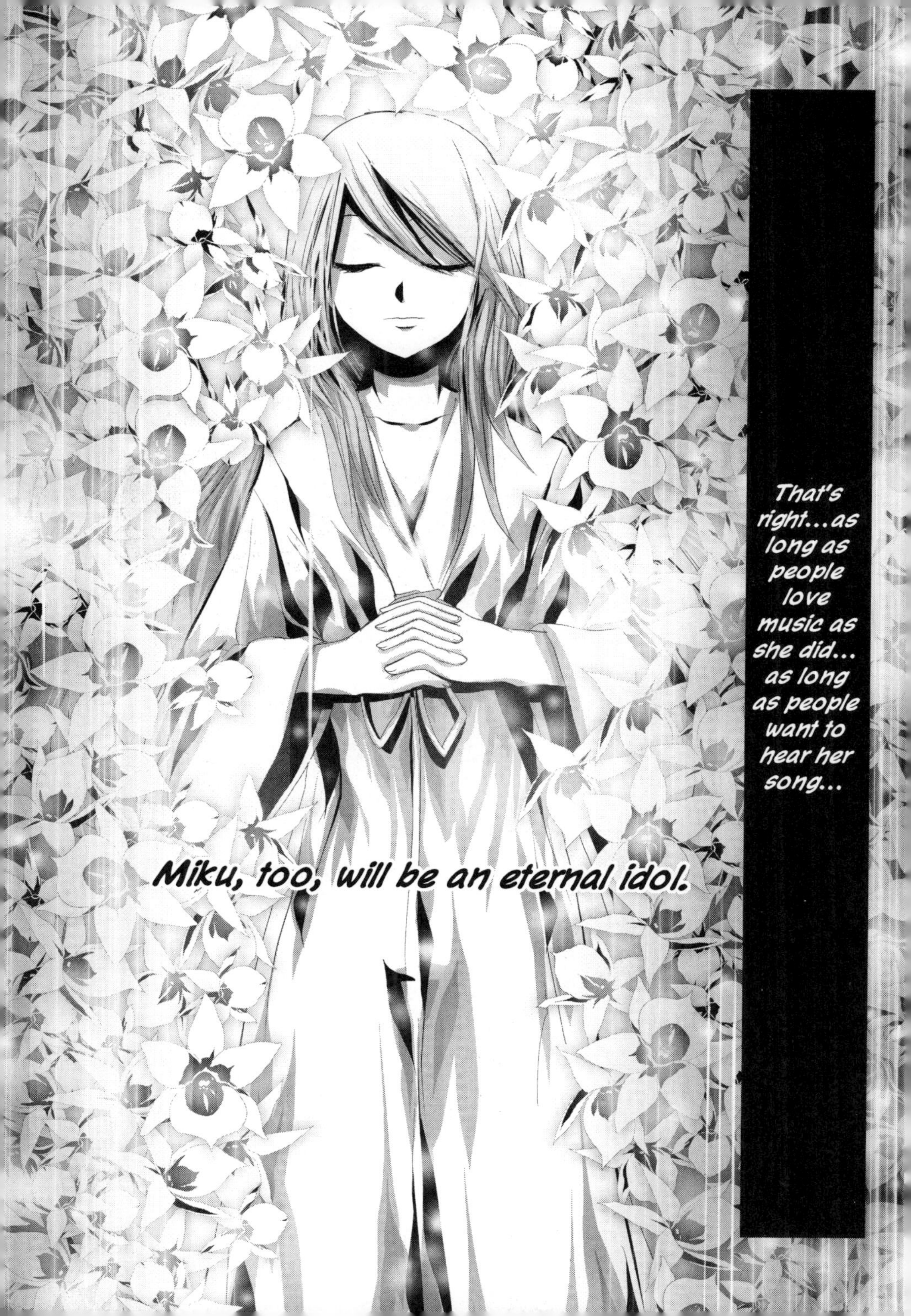
That's right...as long as people love music as she did... as long as people want to hear her song...
Miku, too, will be an eternal idol.

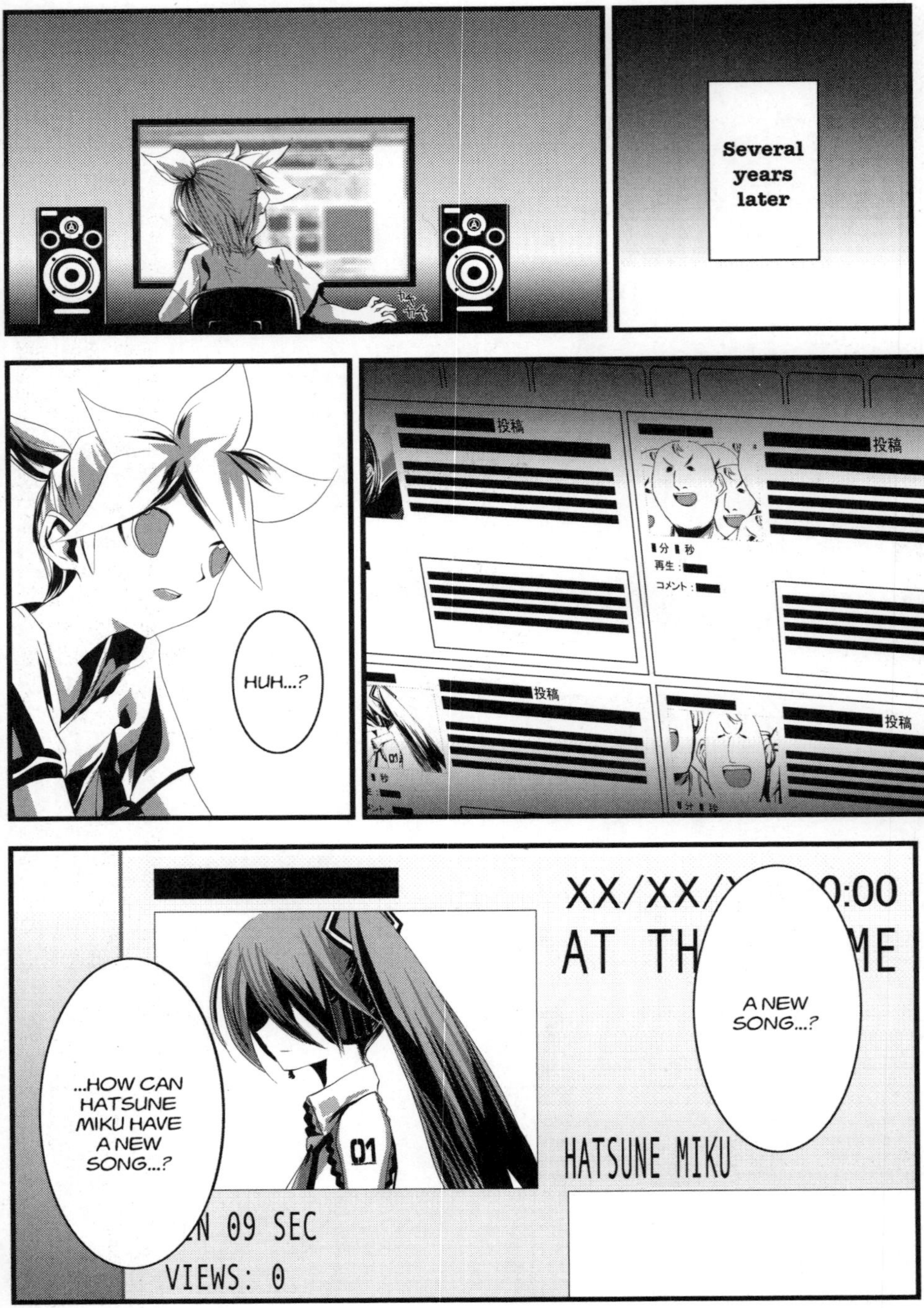

Several years later
投稿
投稿
■分 ■秒
再生 :
コメント :
投稿
投稿
HUH...?
XX/XX/X 0:00
AT TH ME
A NEW SONG...?
HATSUNE MIKU
...HOW CAN HATSUNE MIKU HAVE A NEW SONG...?
IN 09 SEC
VIEWS: 0

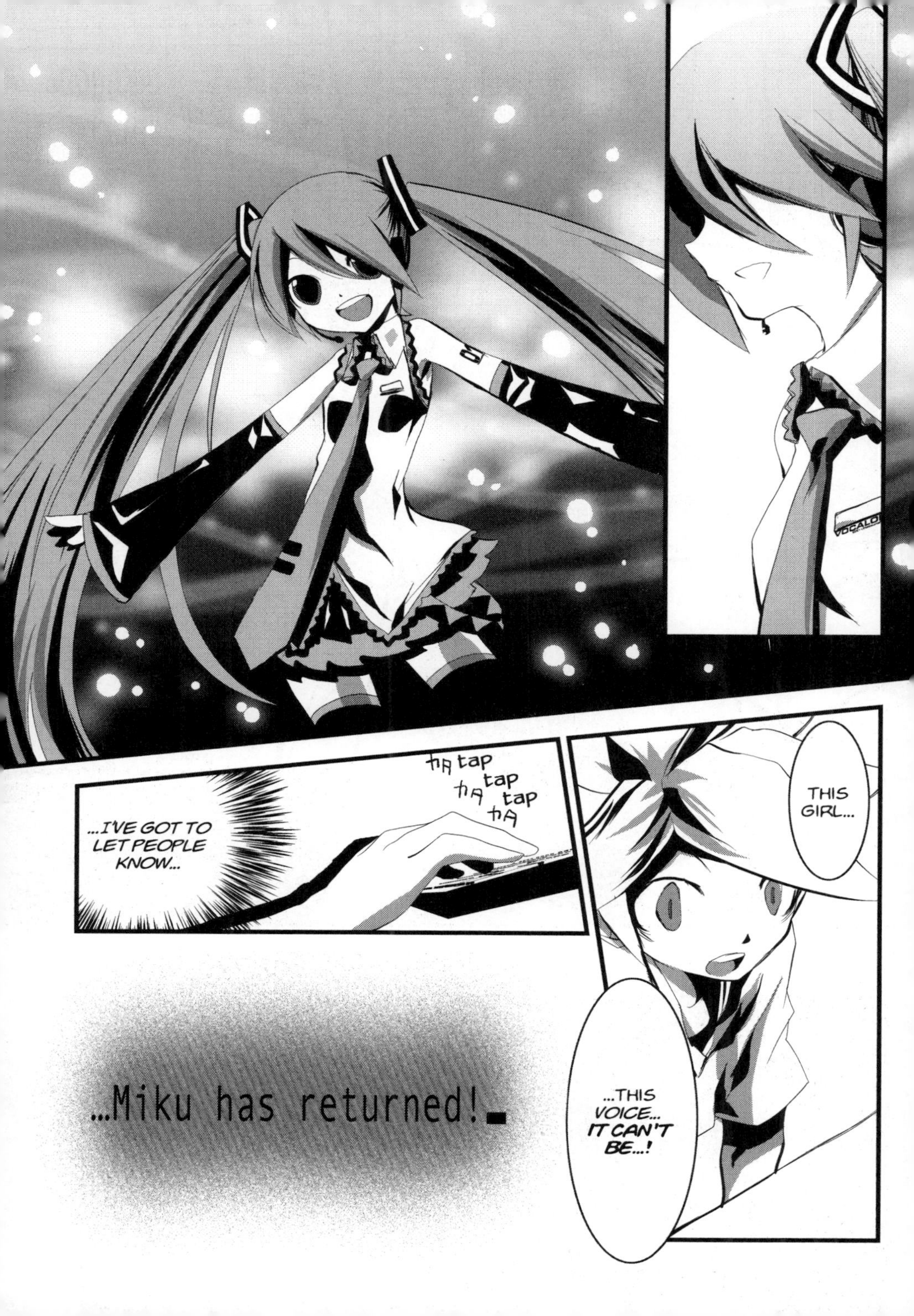
THIS GIRL...
...THIS VOICE... IT CAN'T BE...!
...I'VE GOT TO LET PEOPLE KNOW...
tap tap tap
...Miku has returned!

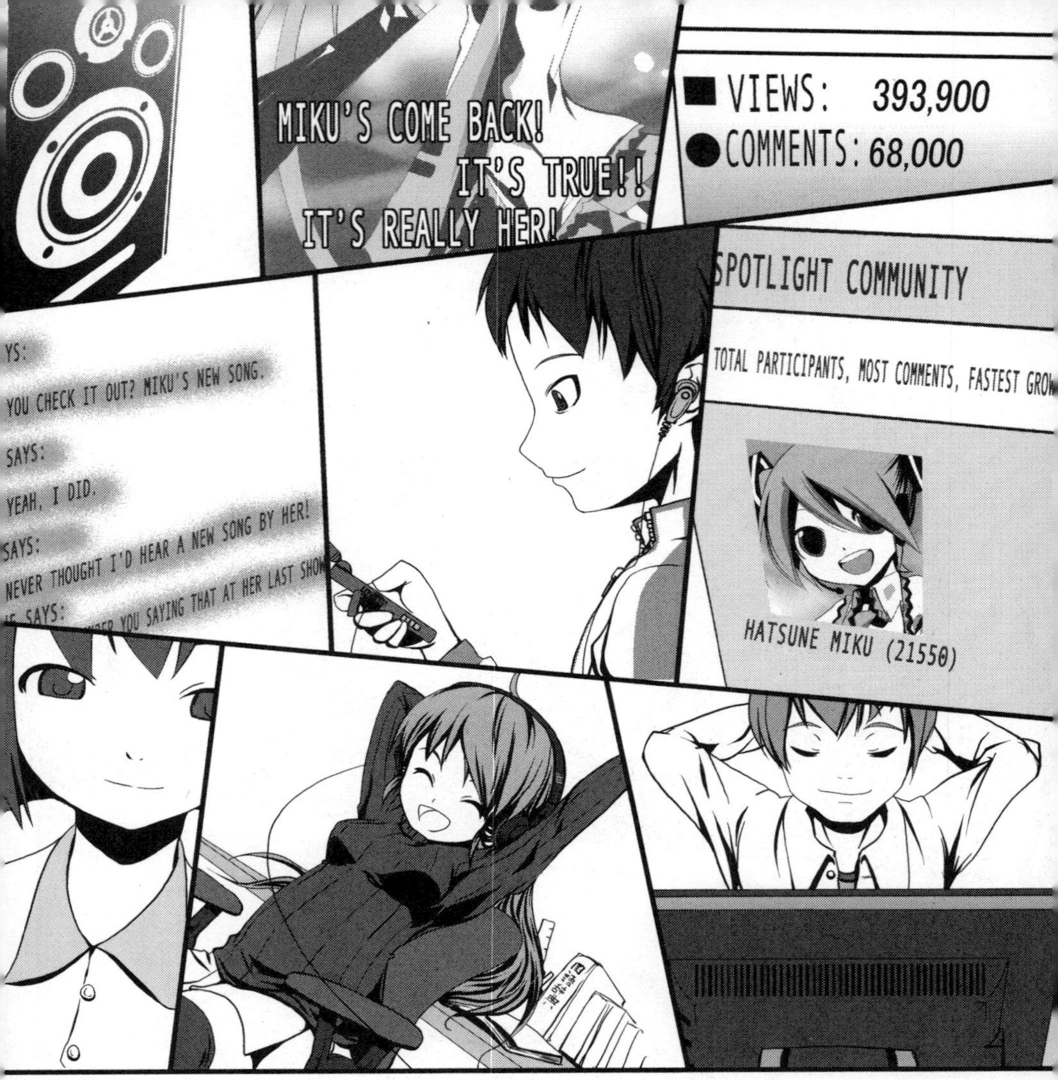
■ VIEWS: 393,900
● COMMENTS: 68,000
MIKU'S COME BACK!
IT'S TRUE!!
IT'S REALLY HER!
SPOTLIGHT COMMUNITY
TOTAL PARTICIPANTS, MOST COMMENTS, FASTEST GROW
HATSUNE MIKU (21550)
YS:
YOU CHECK IT OUT? MIKU'S NEW SONG.
SAYS:
YEAH, I DID.
SAYS:
NEVER THOUGHT I'D HEAR A NEW SONG BY HER!
SAYS:
YOU SAYING THAT AT HER LAST SHOW
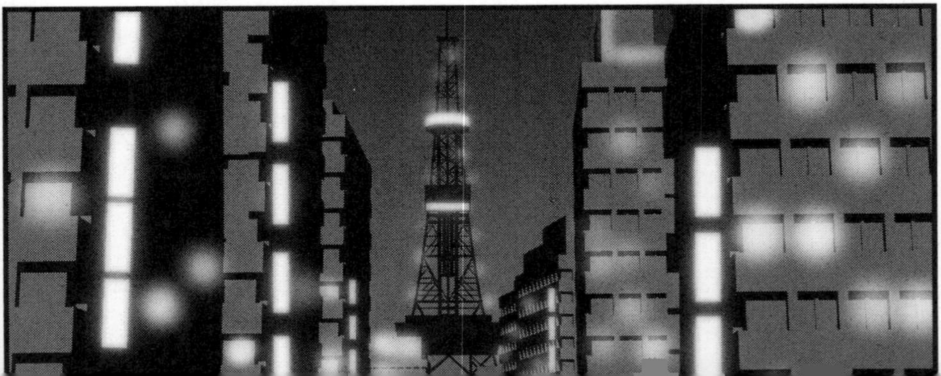

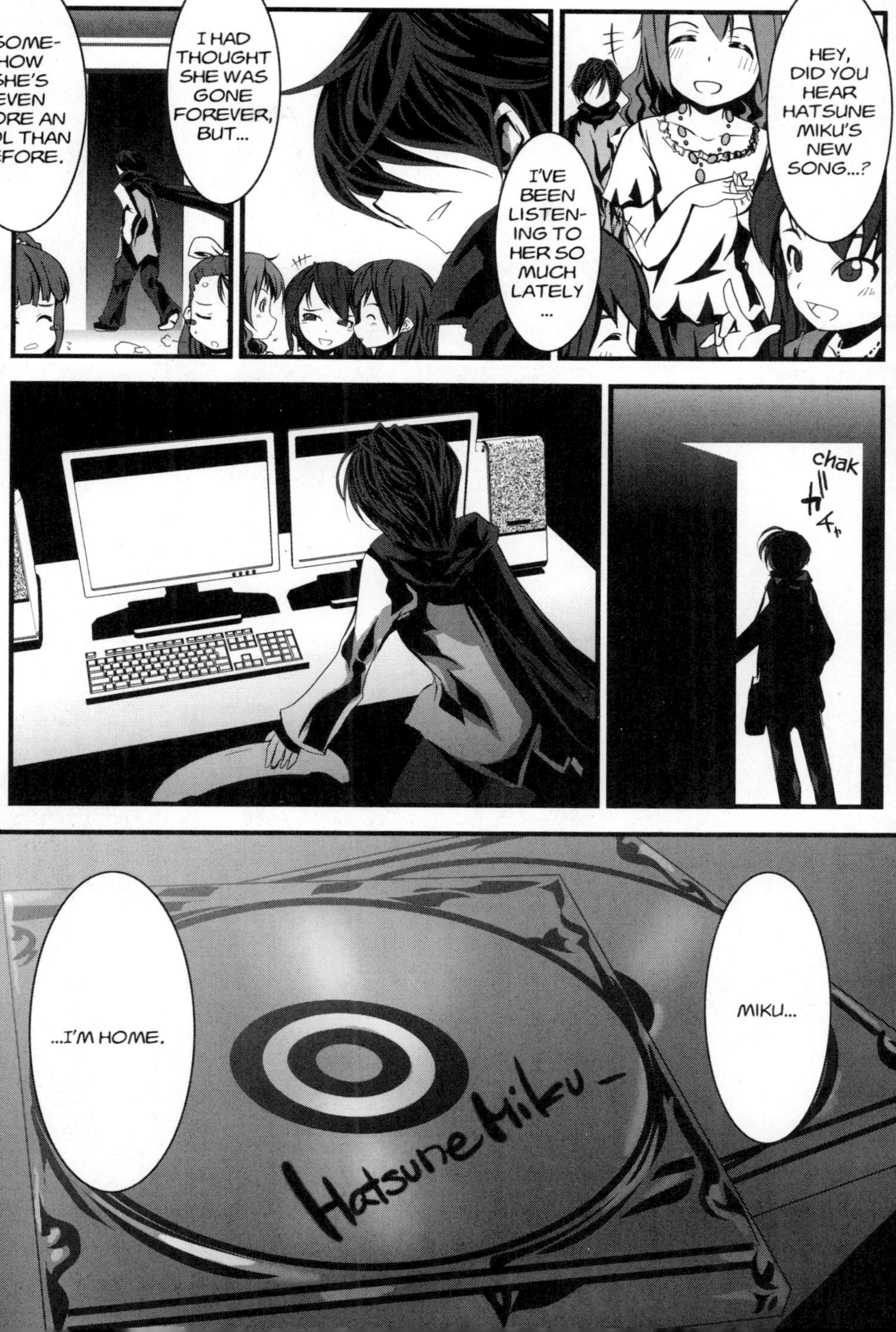
HEY, DID YOU HEAR HATSUNE MIKU'S NEW SONG...?
I'VE BEEN LISTENING TO HER SO MUCH LATELY...
I HAD THOUGHT SHE WAS GONE FOREVER, BUT...
...SOMEHOW SHE'S EVEN MORE AN IDOL THAN BEFORE.
chak
ガチャ
MIKU...
...I'M HOME.
Hatsune Miku

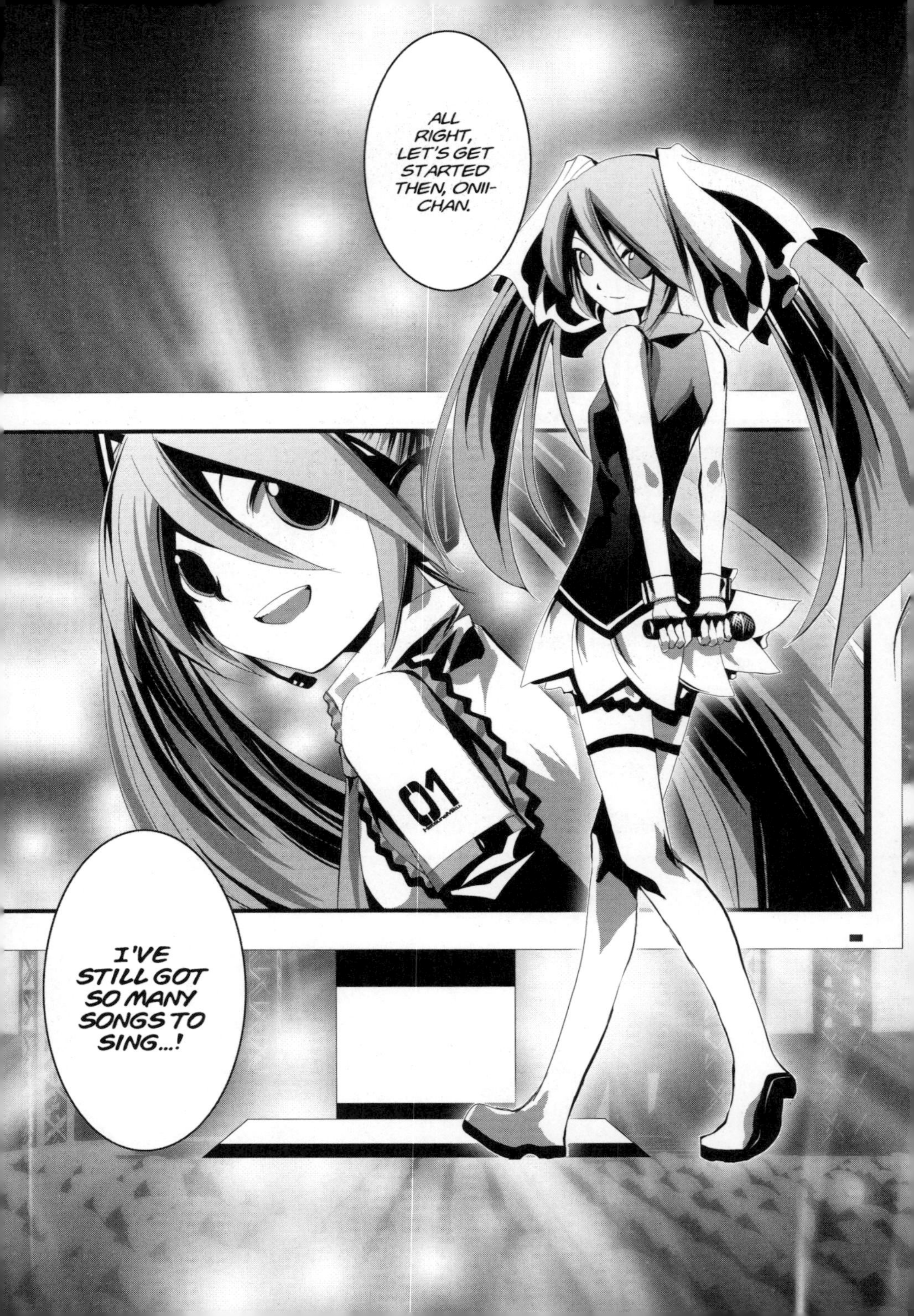
ALL RIGHT, LET'S GET STARTED THEN, ONII-CHAN.
01
I'VE STILL GOT SO MANY SONGS TO SING...!

(8th SONG) MERMAID MIX

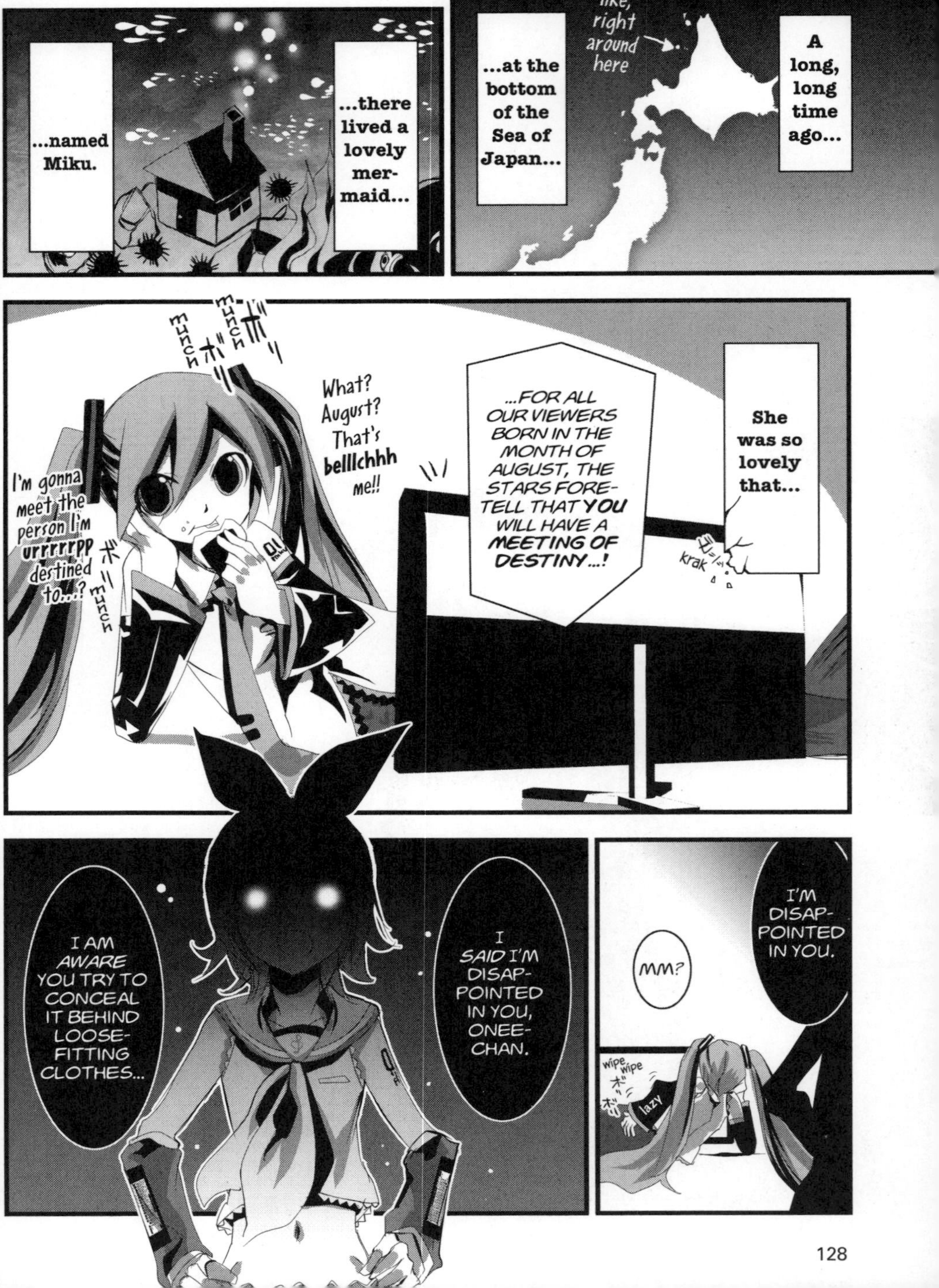
A long, long time ago...
like, right around here
...at the bottom of the Sea of Japan...
...there lived a lovely mermaid...
...named Miku.
She was so lovely that...
krak
...FOR ALL OUR VIEWERS BORN IN THE MONTH OF AUGUST, THE STARS FORETELL THAT YOU WILL HAVE A MEETING OF DESTINY...!
munch munch
What? August? That's bellllchhh me!!
I'm gonna meet the person I'm urrrrrpp destined to...?
munch
I'M DISAPPOINTED IN YOU.
MM?
wipe wipe
lazy
I SAID I'M DISAPPOINTED IN YOU, ONEE-CHAN.
I AM AWARE YOU TRY TO CONCEAL IT BEHIND LOOSE-FITTING CLOTHES...

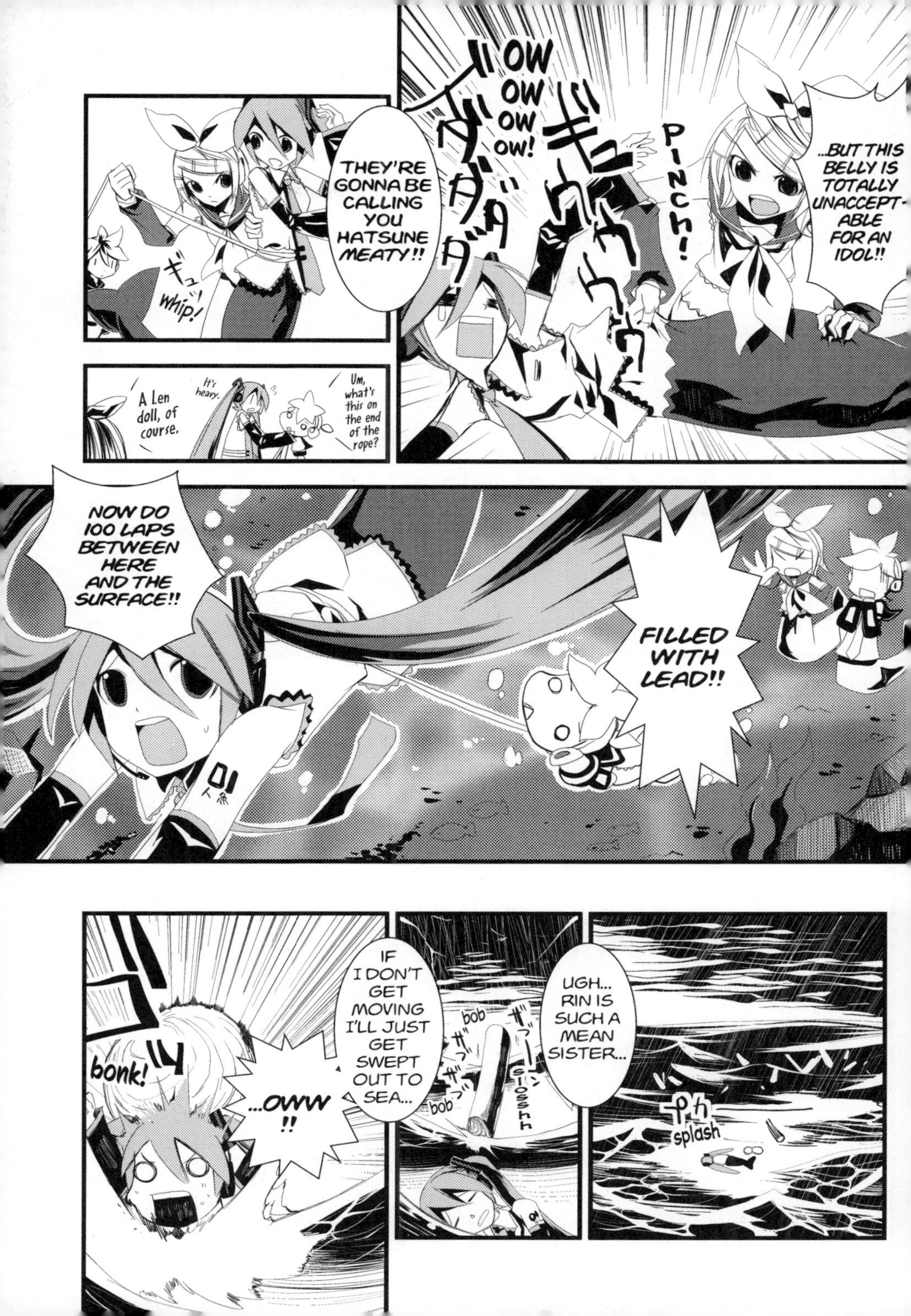
...BUT THIS BELLY IS TOTALLY UNACCEPTABLE FOR AN IDOL!!
PINCH!
OW OW OW OW!
THEY'RE GONNA BE CALLING YOU HATSUNE MEATY!!
whip!
Um, what's this on the end of the rope?
It's heavy.
A Len doll, of course.
FILLED WITH LEAD!!
NOW DO 100 LAPS BETWEEN HERE AND THE SURFACE!!
UGH... RIN IS SUCH A MEAN SISTER...
splash
IF I DON'T GET MOVING I'LL JUST GET SWEPT OUT TO SEA...
bob
slosh
bob
bonk!
...OWW!!

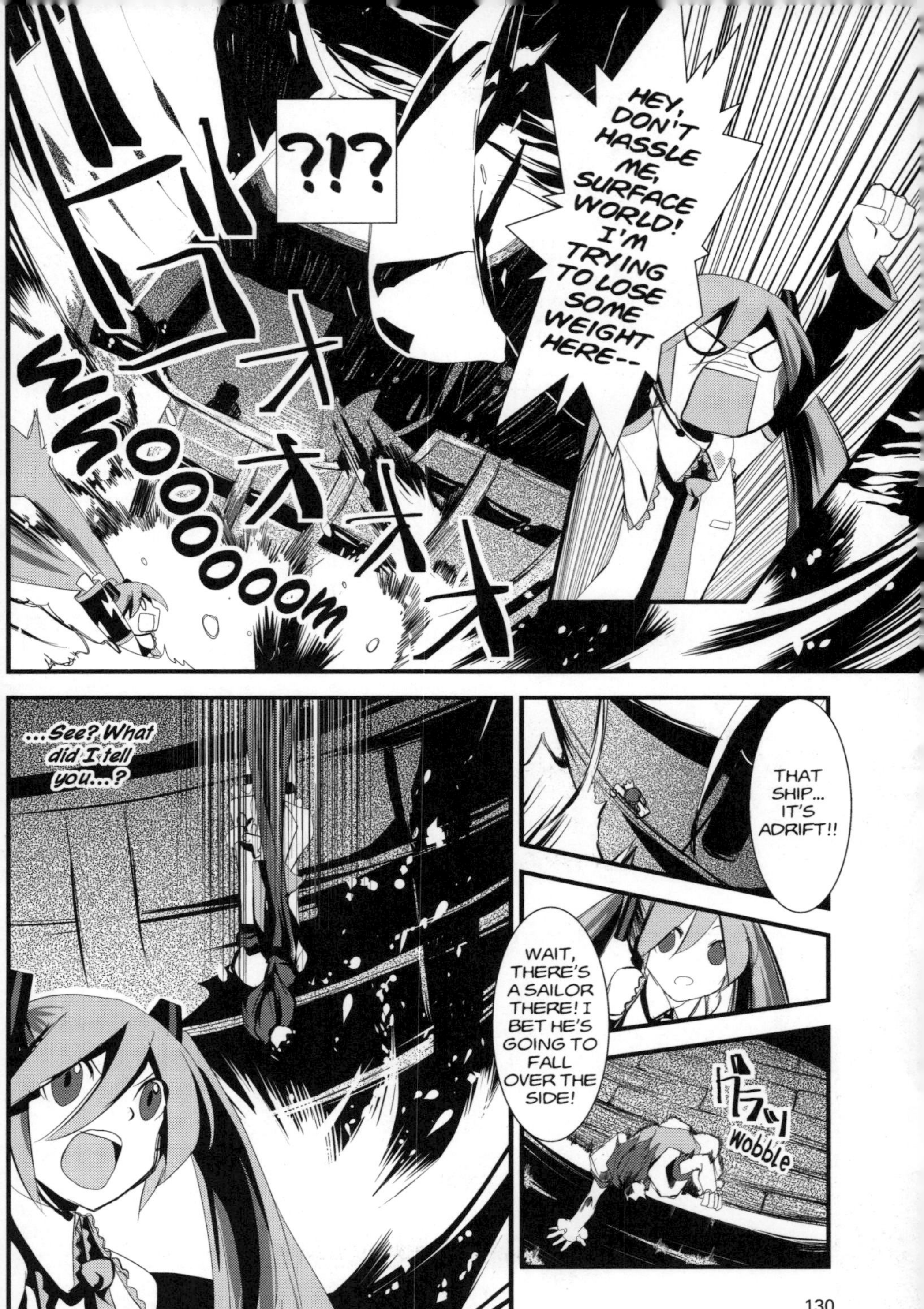
HEY, DON'T HASSLE ME, SURFACE WORLD! I'M TRYING TO LOSE SOME WEIGHT HERE--
?!?
WHOOOOOOOOM
THAT SHIP... IT'S ADRIFT!!
WAIT, THERE'S A SAILOR THERE! I BET HE'S GOING TO FALL OVER THE SIDE!
wobble
...See? What did I tell you...?

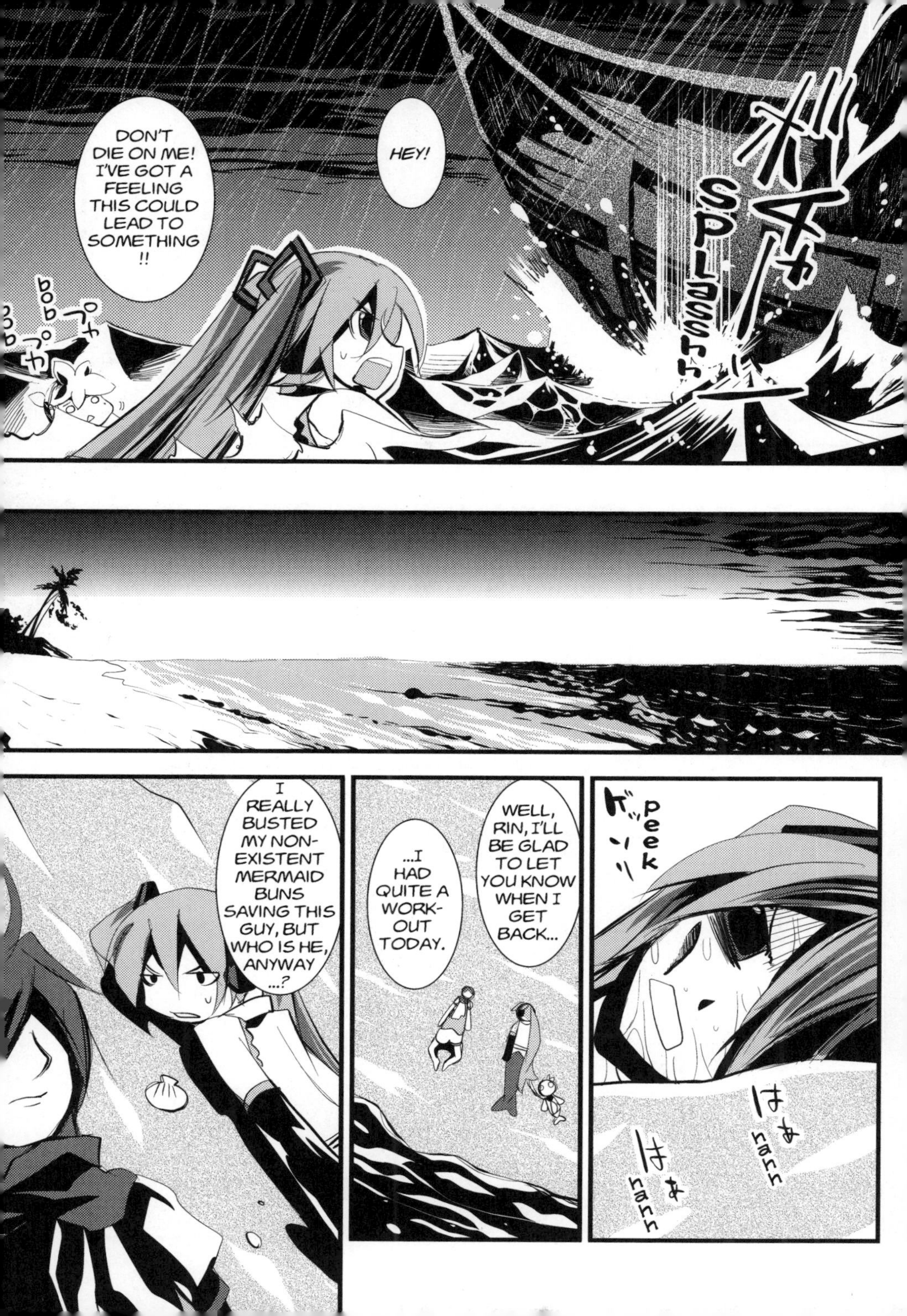

SPLASSSH
HEY!
DON'T DIE ON ME! I'VE GOT A FEELING THIS COULD LEAD TO SOMETHING !!
bob bob
peek
nahh nahh
WELL, RIN, I'LL BE GLAD TO LET YOU KNOW WHEN I GET BACK...
...I HAD QUITE A WORK-OUT TODAY.
I REALLY BUSTED MY NON-EXISTENT MERMAID BUNS SAVING THIS GUY, BUT WHO IS HE, ANYWAY ...?

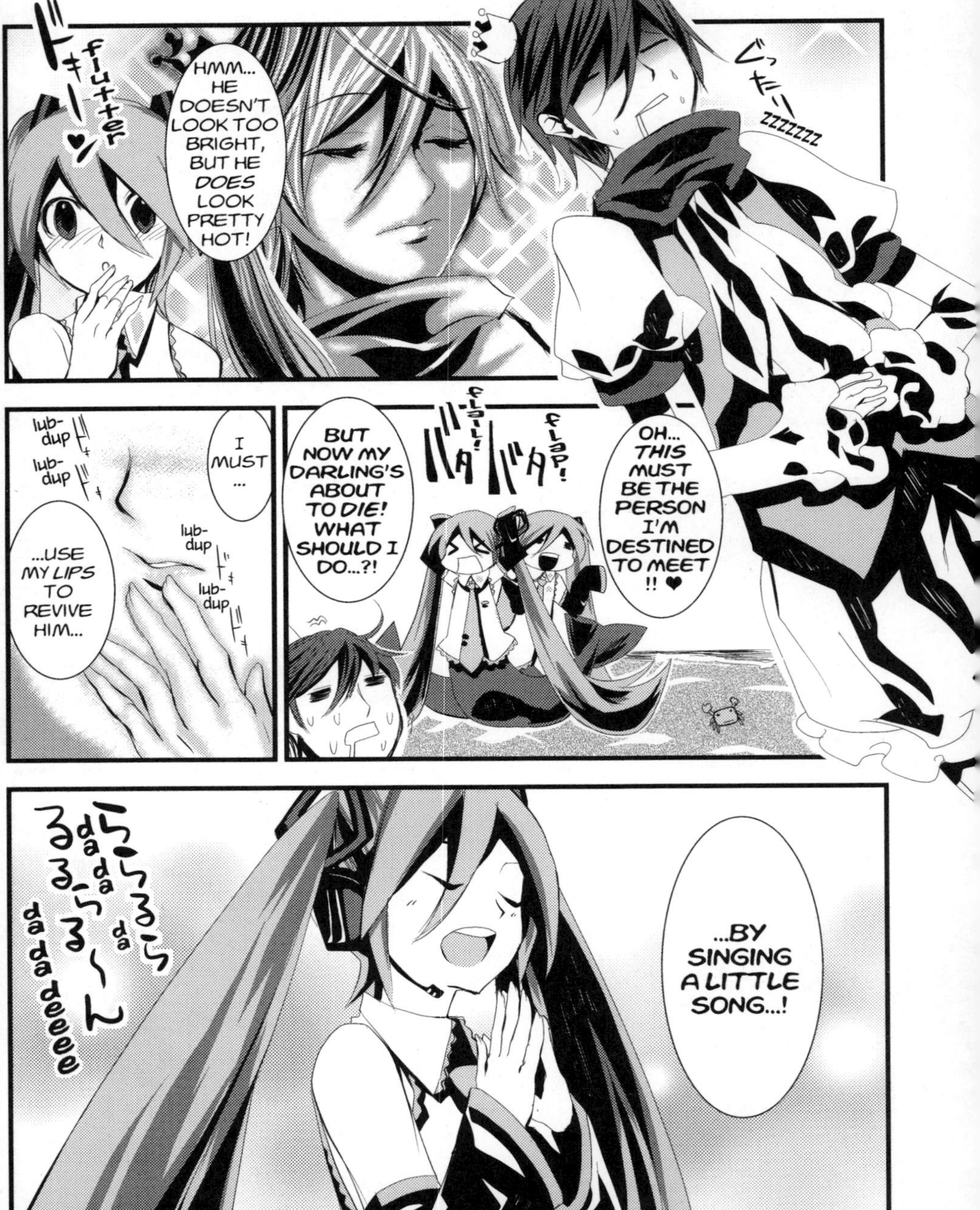
ZZZZZZZ
HMM... HE DOESN'T LOOK TOO BRIGHT, BUT HE DOES LOOK PRETTY HOT!
ドキーン
flutter ♥
OH... THIS MUST BE THE PERSON I'M DESTINED TO MEET !! ❤
flap!
flail!
バタバタ
BUT NOW MY DARLING'S ABOUT TO DIE! WHAT SHOULD I DO...?!
I MUST ...
...USE MY LIPS TO REVIVE HIM...
lub-dup
lub-dup
lub-dup
lub-dup
...BY SINGING A LITTLE SONG...!
da da da
da da deeee

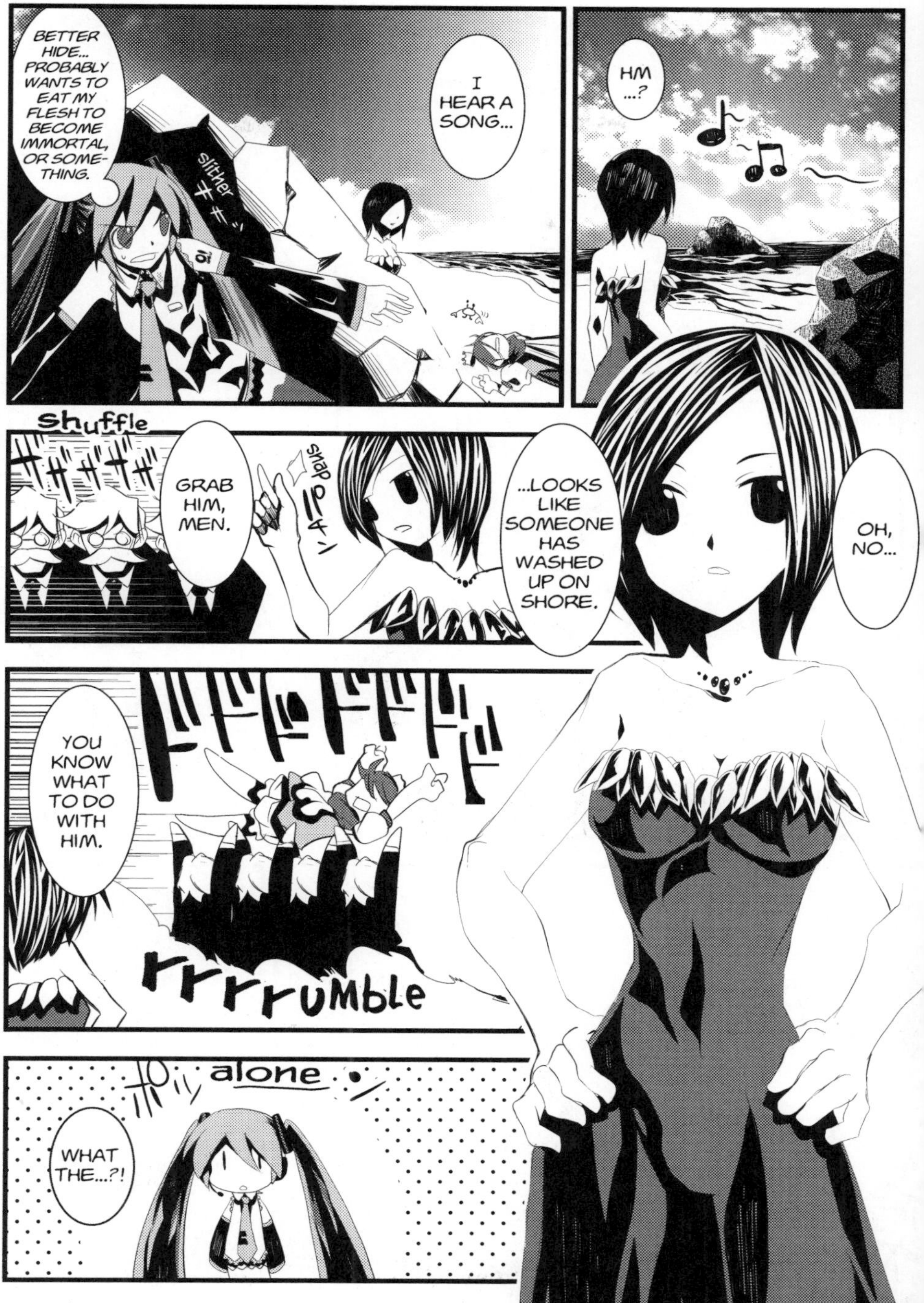
HM ...?
I HEAR A SONG...
BETTER HIDE... PROBABLY WANTS TO EAT MY FLESH TO BECOME IMMORTAL, OR SOMETHING.
slither
OH, NO...
...LOOKS LIKE SOMEONE HAS WASHED UP ON SHORE.
snap
GRAB HIM, MEN.
shuffle
YOU KNOW WHAT TO DO WITH HIM.
rrrrumble
alone
WHAT THE...?!

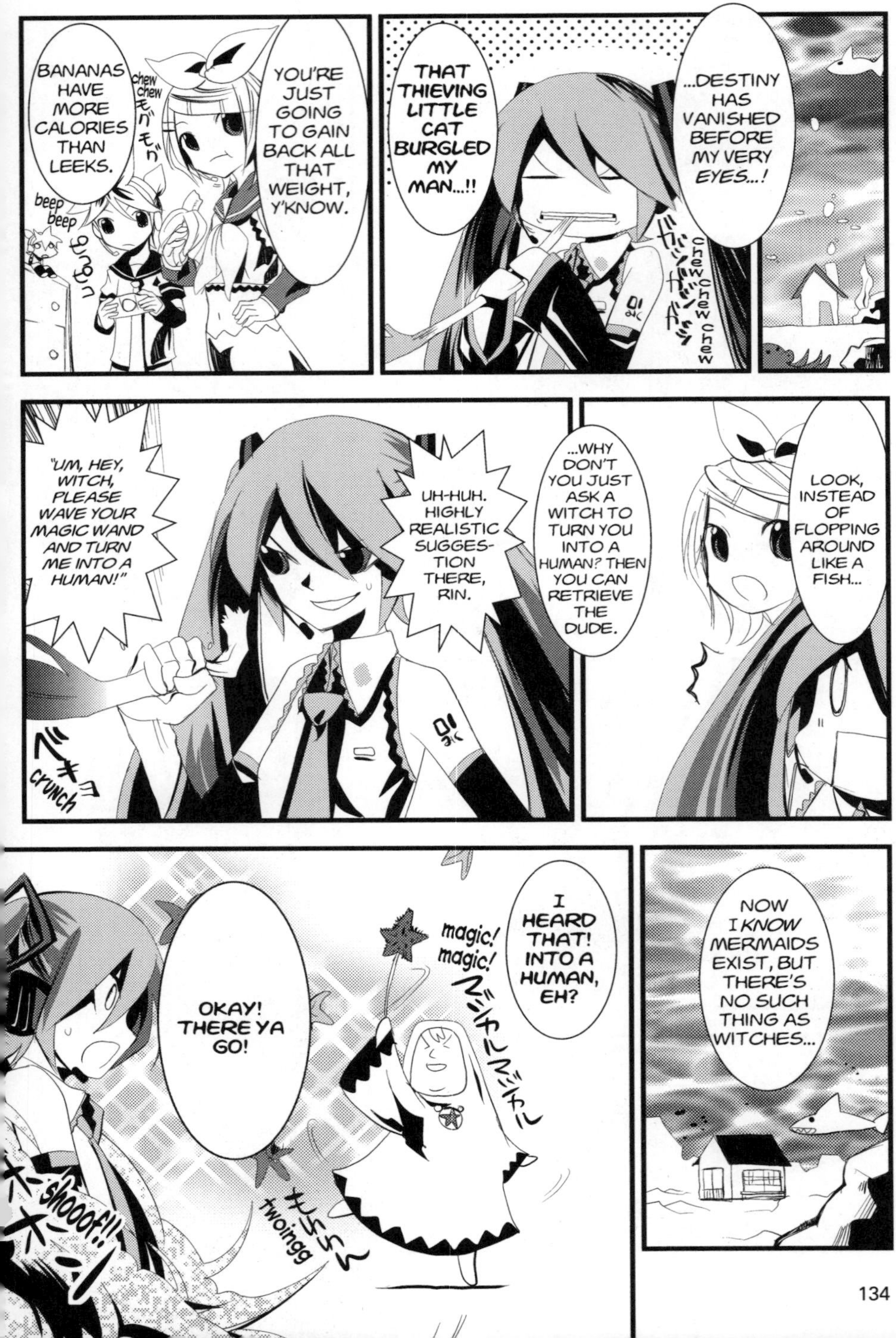
...DESTINY HAS VANISHED BEFORE MY VERY *EYES*...!
THAT THIEVING LITTLE CAT BURGLED MY MAN...!!
chew chew chew chew
YOU'RE JUST GOING TO GAIN BACK ALL THAT WEIGHT, Y'KNOW.
BANANAS HAVE MORE CALORIES THAN LEEKS.
chew chew
beep beep
LOOK, INSTEAD OF FLOPPING AROUND LIKE A FISH...
...WHY DON'T YOU JUST ASK A WITCH TO TURN YOU INTO A HUMAN? THEN YOU CAN RETRIEVE THE DUDE.
UH-HUH. HIGHLY REALISTIC SUGGES-TION THERE, RIN.
"UM, HEY, WITCH, PLEASE WAVE YOUR MAGIC WAND AND TURN ME INTO A HUMAN!"
crunch
NOW I *KNOW* MERMAIDS EXIST, BUT THERE'S NO SUCH THING AS WITCHES...
I HEARD THAT! INTO A HUMAN, EH?
magic! magic!
OKAY! THERE YA GO!
twoingg
shooof!!

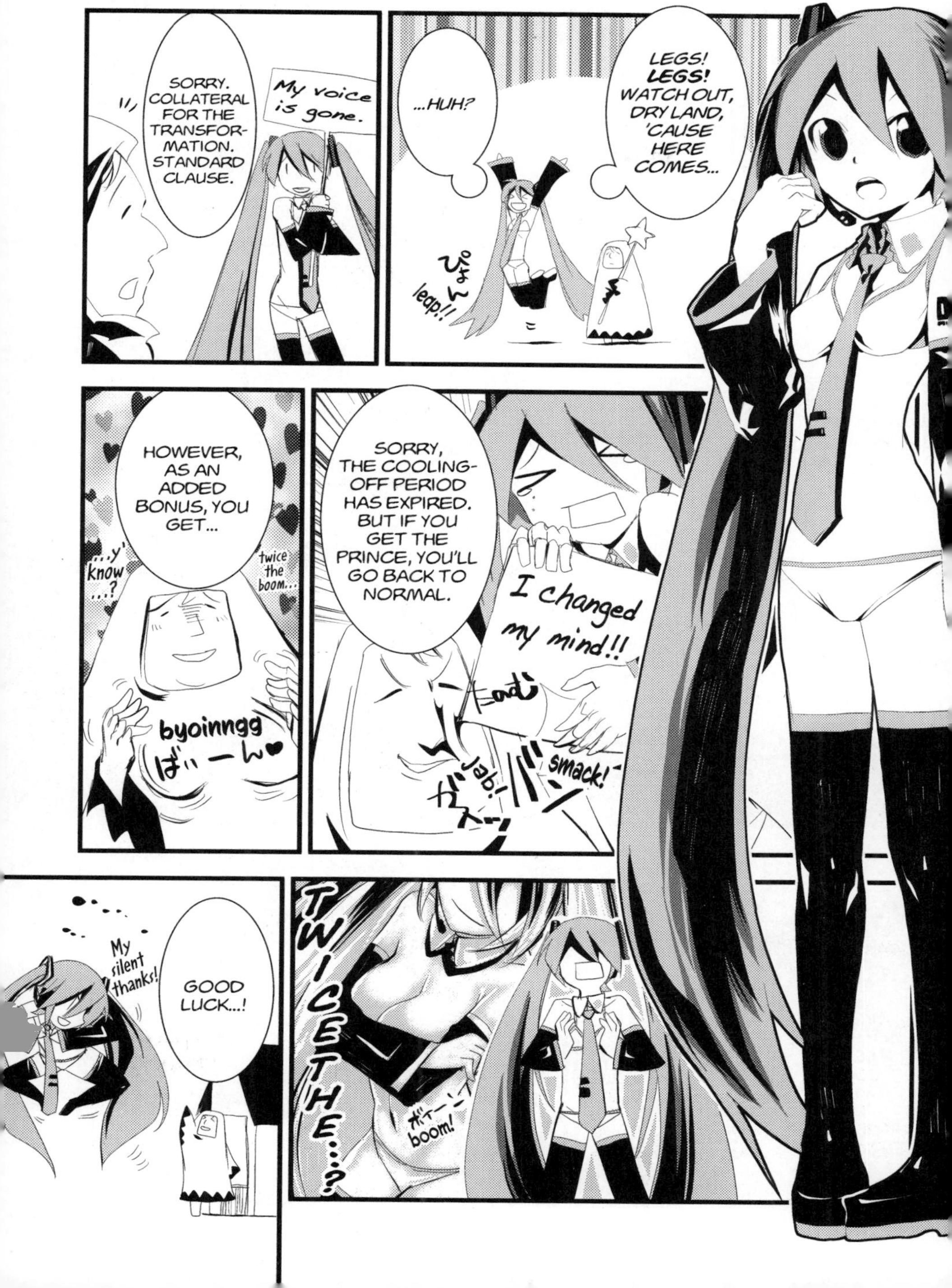
LEGS! **LEGS!** WATCH OUT, DRY LAND, 'CAUSE HERE COMES...
...HUH?
ぴょん
leap!!
SORRY. COLLATERAL FOR THE TRANSFORMATION. STANDARD CLAUSE.
My voice is gone.
SORRY, THE COOLING-OFF PERIOD HAS EXPIRED. BUT IF YOU GET THE PRINCE, YOU'LL GO BACK TO NORMAL.
I changed my mind!!
jab!
smack!
HOWEVER, AS AN ADDED BONUS, YOU GET...
...y' know ...?
twice the boom...
byoinngg
ばぃーん
TWICE THE...?
boom!
GOOD LUCK...!
My silent thanks!

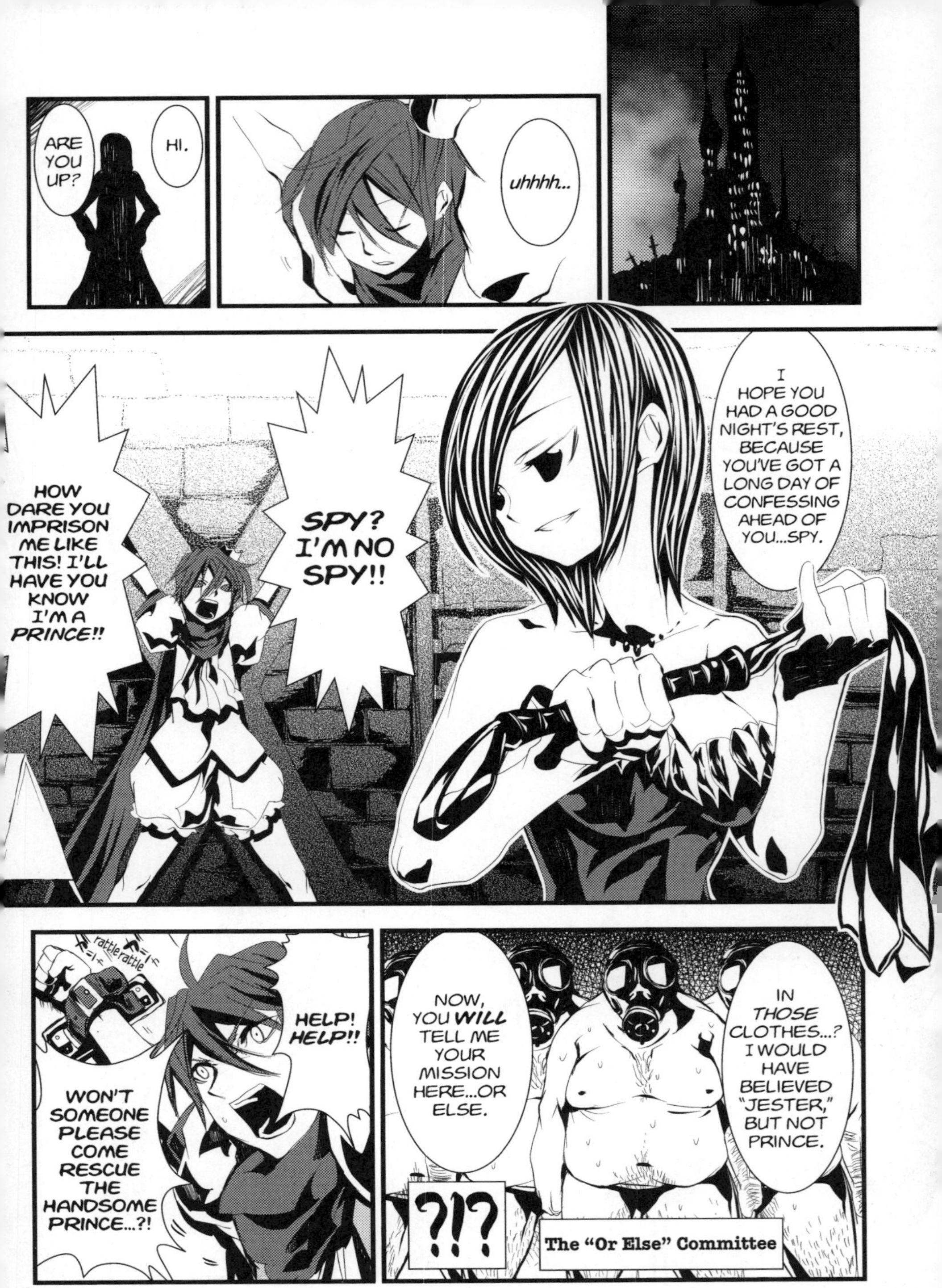
uhhhh...
HI.
ARE YOU UP?
I HOPE YOU HAD A GOOD NIGHT'S REST, BECAUSE YOU'VE GOT A LONG DAY OF CONFESSING AHEAD OF YOU...SPY.
SPY? I'M NO SPY!!
HOW DARE YOU IMPRISON ME LIKE THIS! I'LL HAVE YOU KNOW I'M A PRINCE!!
IN THOSE CLOTHES...? I WOULD HAVE BELIEVED "JESTER," BUT NOT PRINCE.
NOW, YOU WILL TELL ME YOUR MISSION HERE...OR ELSE.
?!?
The "Or Else" Committee
rattle rattle
HELP! HELP!!
WON'T SOMEONE PLEASE COME RESCUE THE HANDSOME PRINCE...?!

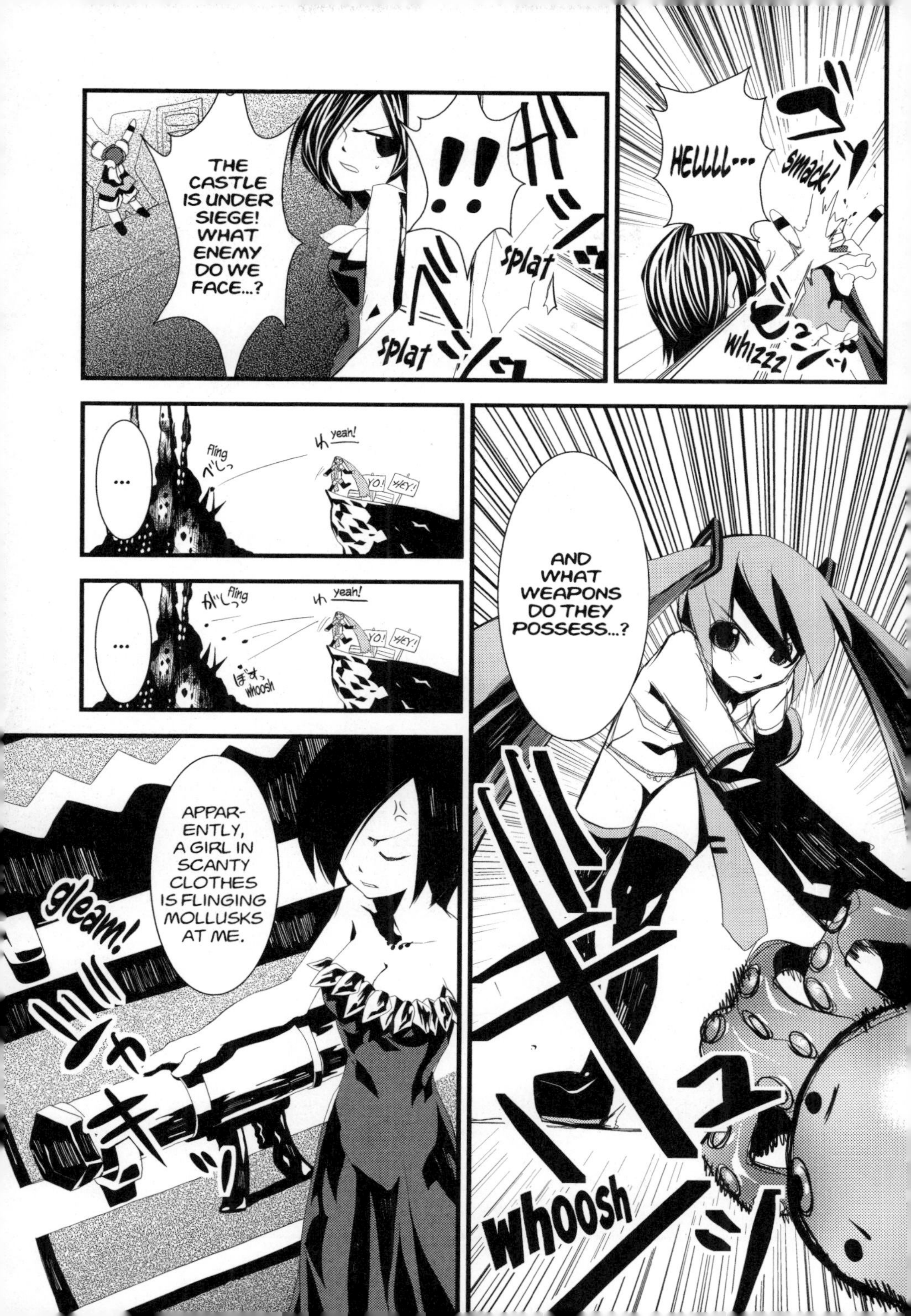
HELLLLL...
smack!
whizzz
!!
splat
splat
THE CASTLE IS UNDER SIEGE! WHAT ENEMY DO WE FACE...?
AND WHAT WEAPONS DO THEY POSSESS...?
whoosh
...
fling
yeah!
YO!
HEY!
...
fling
yeah!
YO!
HEY!
whoosh
APPAR-ENTLY, A GIRL IN SCANTY CLOTHES IS FLINGING MOLLUSKS AT ME.
gleam!

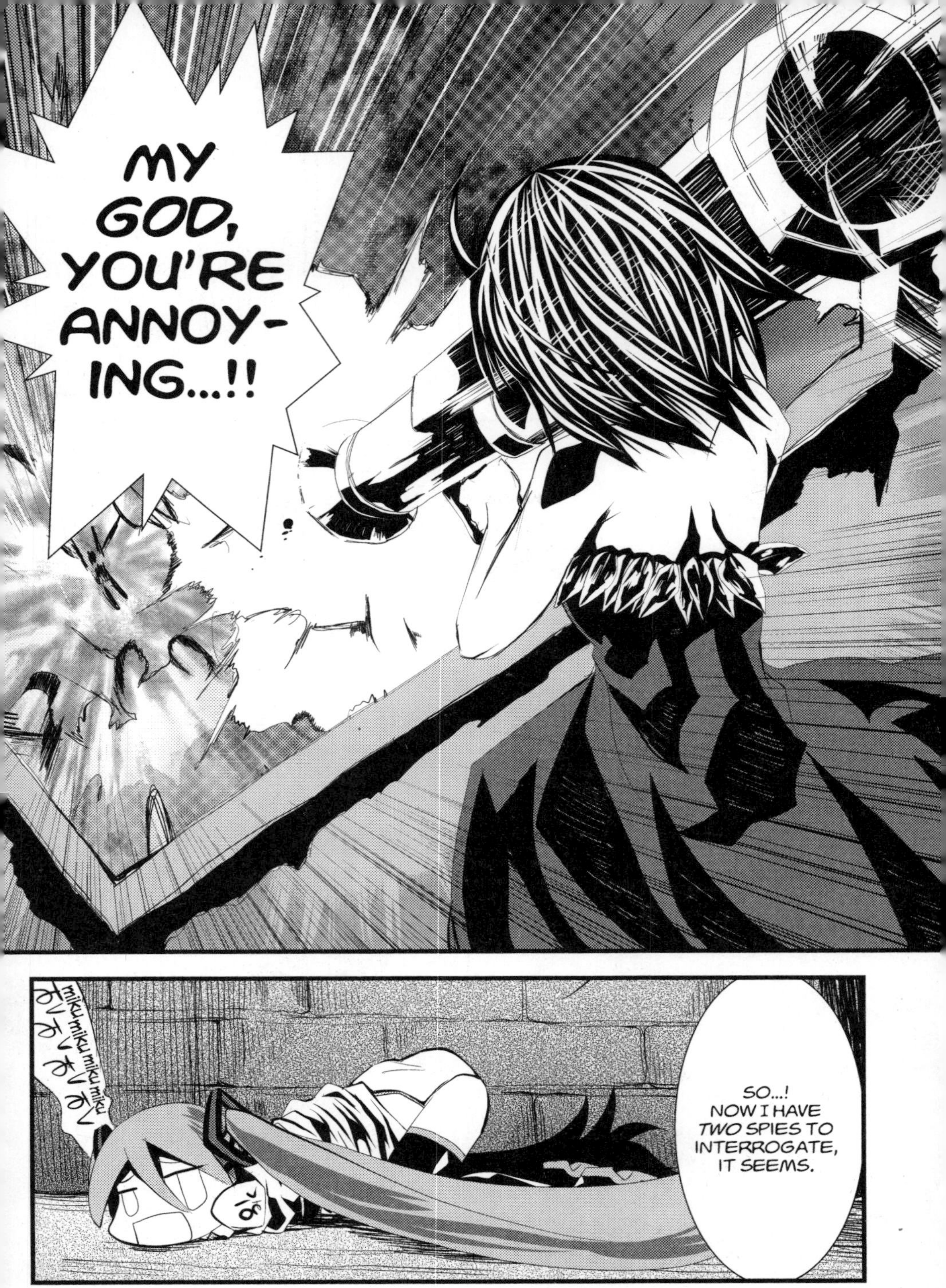
MY GOD, YOU'RE ANNOY-ING...!!
SO...! NOW I HAVE *TWO* SPIES TO INTERROGATE, IT SEEMS.
miku miku miku miku

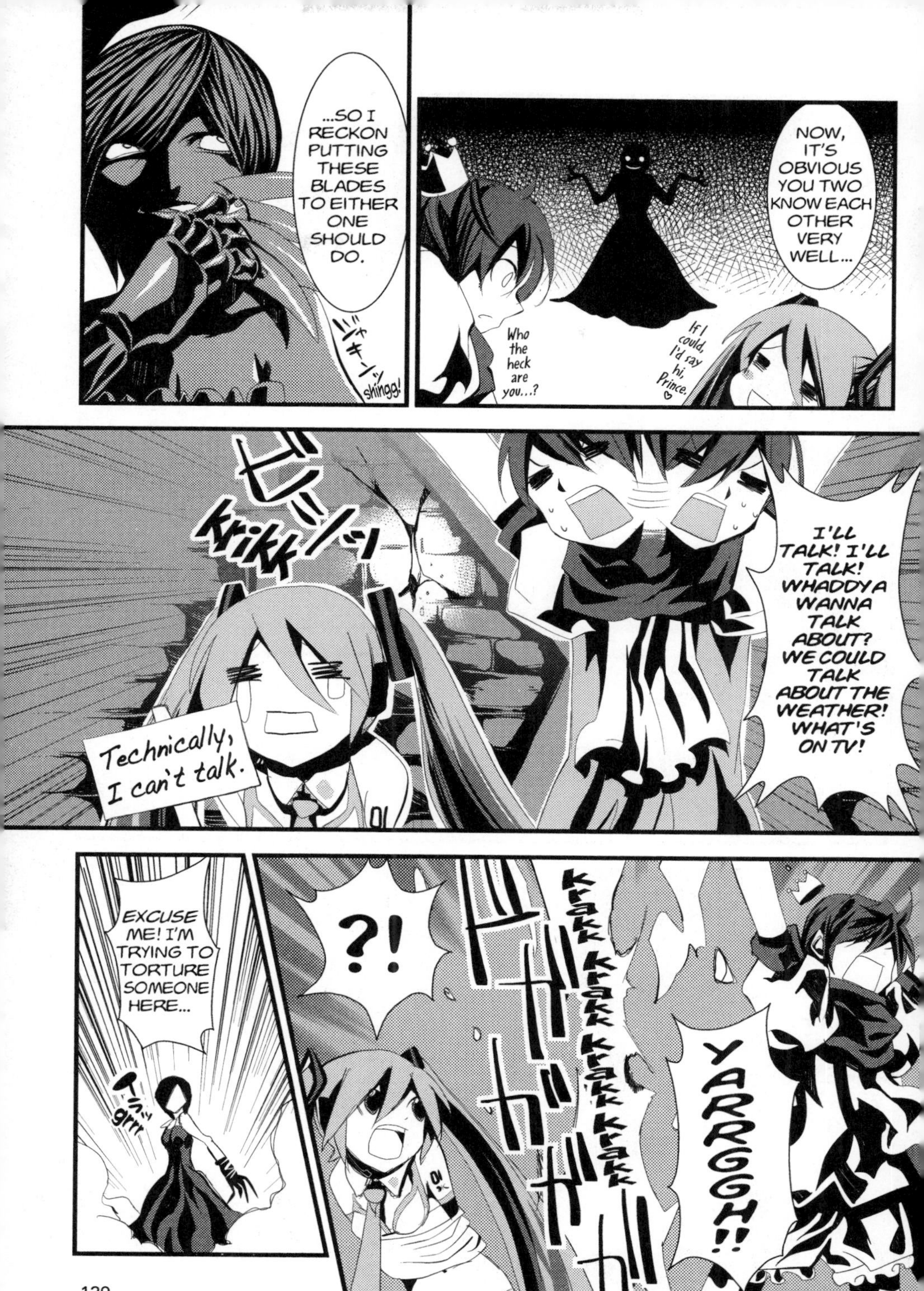
NOW, IT'S OBVIOUS YOU TWO KNOW EACH OTHER VERY WELL...
If I could, I'd say hi, Prince. ♡
Who the heck are you...?
...SO I RECKON PUTTING THESE BLADES TO EITHER ONE SHOULD DO.
ジャキーンッ
shingg!
I'LL TALK! I'LL TALK! WHADDYA WANNA TALK ABOUT? WE COULD TALK ABOUT THE WEATHER! WHAT'S ON TV!
ビシッ
krikk
Technically, I can't talk.
YARRGGH!!
krakk krakk krakk krakk
?!
EXCUSE ME! I'M TRYING TO TORTURE SOMEONE HERE...
grrr

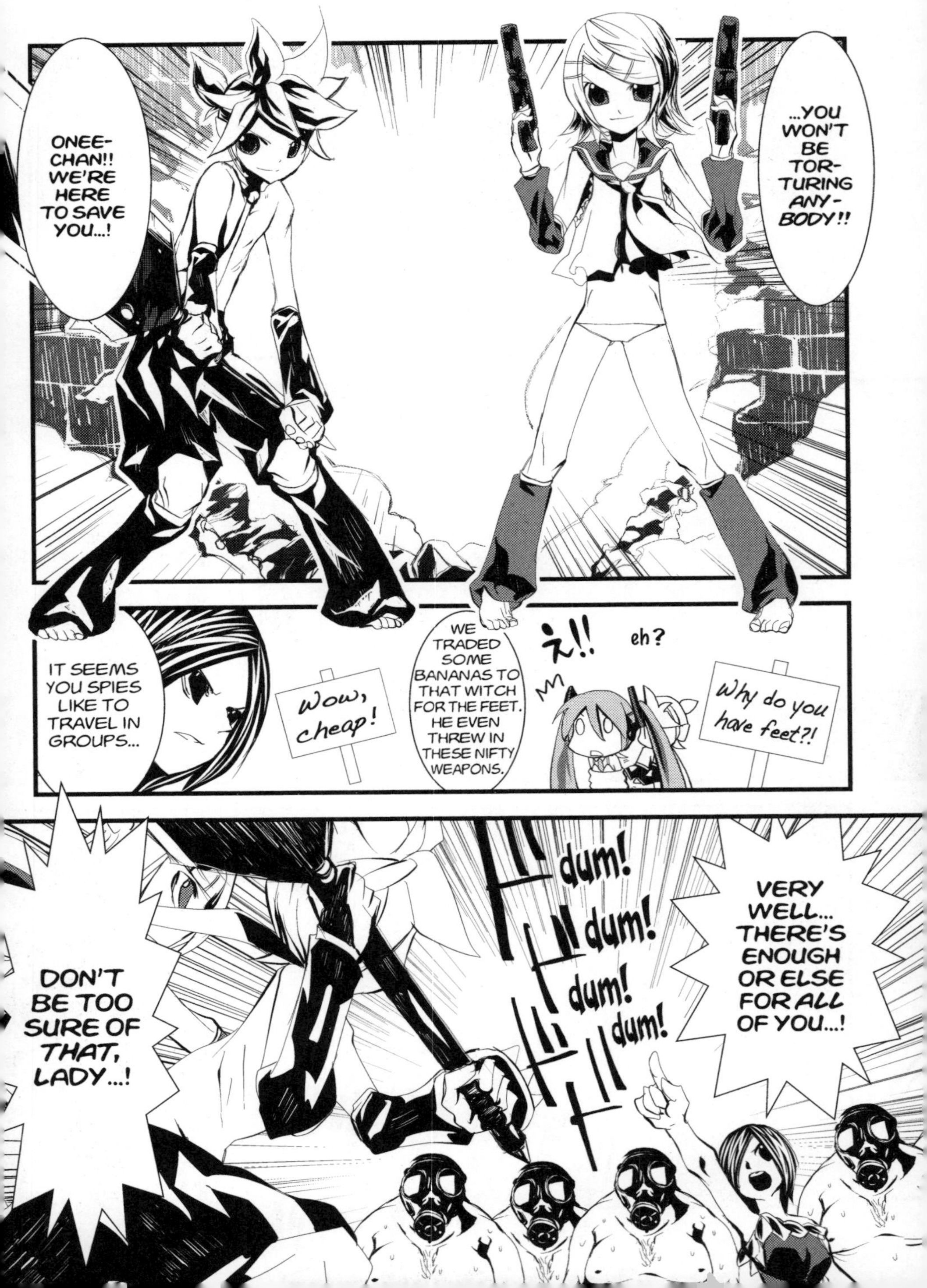

...YOU WON'T BE TOR-TURING ANY-BODY!!
ONEE-CHAN!! WE'RE HERE TO SAVE YOU...!
eh?
え!!
Why do you have feet?!
WE TRADED SOME BANANAS TO THAT WITCH FOR THE FEET. HE EVEN THREW IN THESE NIFTY WEAPONS.
Wow, cheap!
IT SEEMS YOU SPIES LIKE TO TRAVEL IN GROUPS...
VERY WELL... THERE'S ENOUGH OR ELSE FOR ALL OF YOU...!
dum!
dum!
dum!
dum!
DON'T BE TOO SURE OF THAT, LADY...!

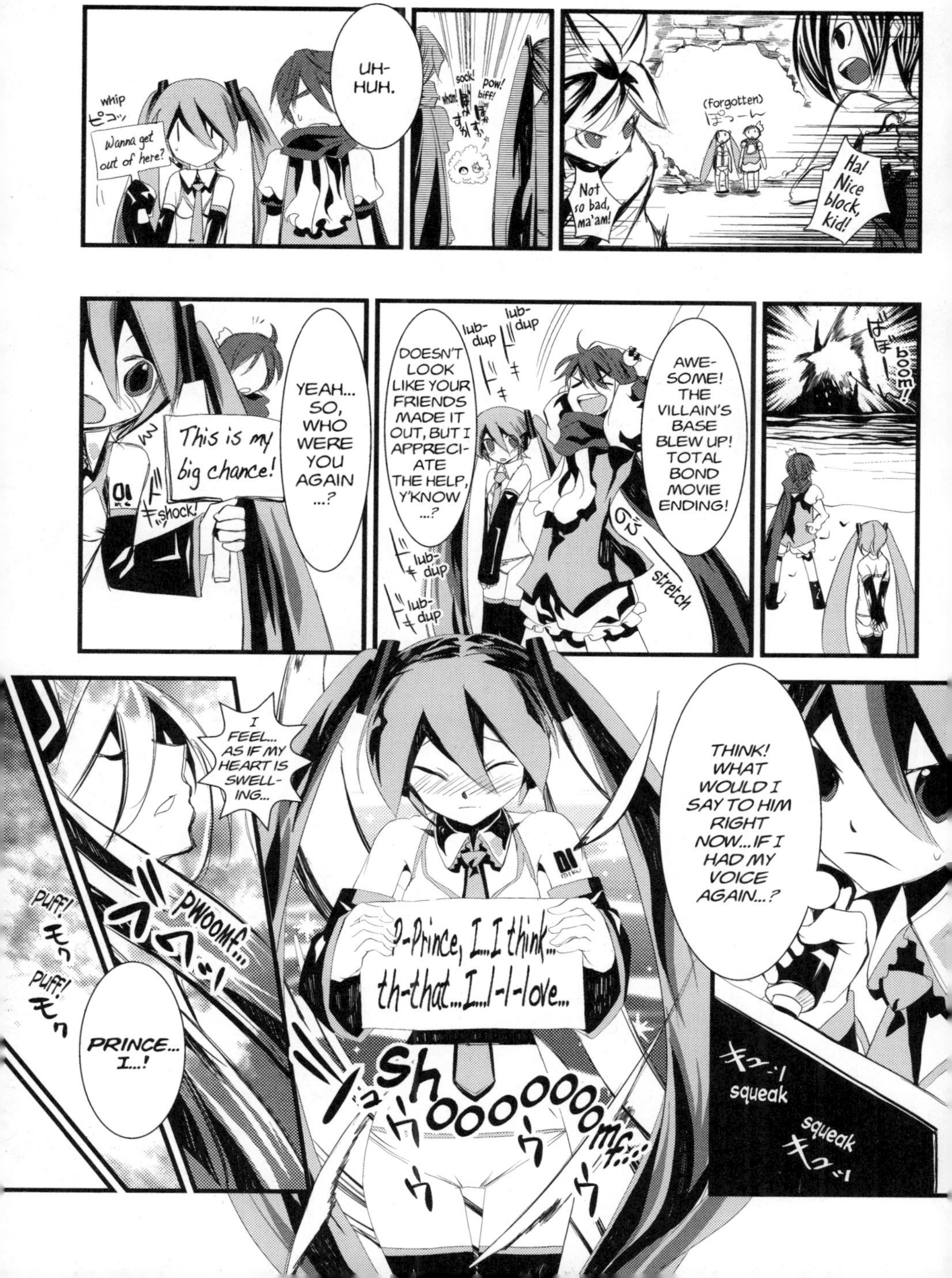
Ha! Nice block, kid!
(forgotten) ぽつーん
Not so bad, ma'am!
sock! pow! biff! wham!
UH-HUH.
whip ピコッ
Wanna get out of here?
ばぼーん boom!!
AWE-SOME! THE VILLAIN'S BASE BLEW UP! TOTAL BOND MOVIE ENDING!
lub-dup ドキ
lub-dup ドキ
DOESN'T LOOK LIKE YOUR FRIENDS MADE IT OUT, BUT I APPRECIATE THE HELP, Y'KNOW ...?
のび stretch
lub-dup ドキ
lub-dup ドキ
YEAH... SO, WHO WERE YOU AGAIN ...?
This is my big chance!
ドキッ shock!
THINK! WHAT WOULD I SAY TO HIM RIGHT NOW...IF I HAD MY VOICE AGAIN...?
キュッ squeak
squeak キュッ
I FEEL... AS IF MY HEART IS SWELLING...
D-Prince, I...I think... th-that...I...I-I-love...
Shooooooomf...
PWOOMF...
PUFF! モワ
PUFF! モワ
PRINCE... I...!

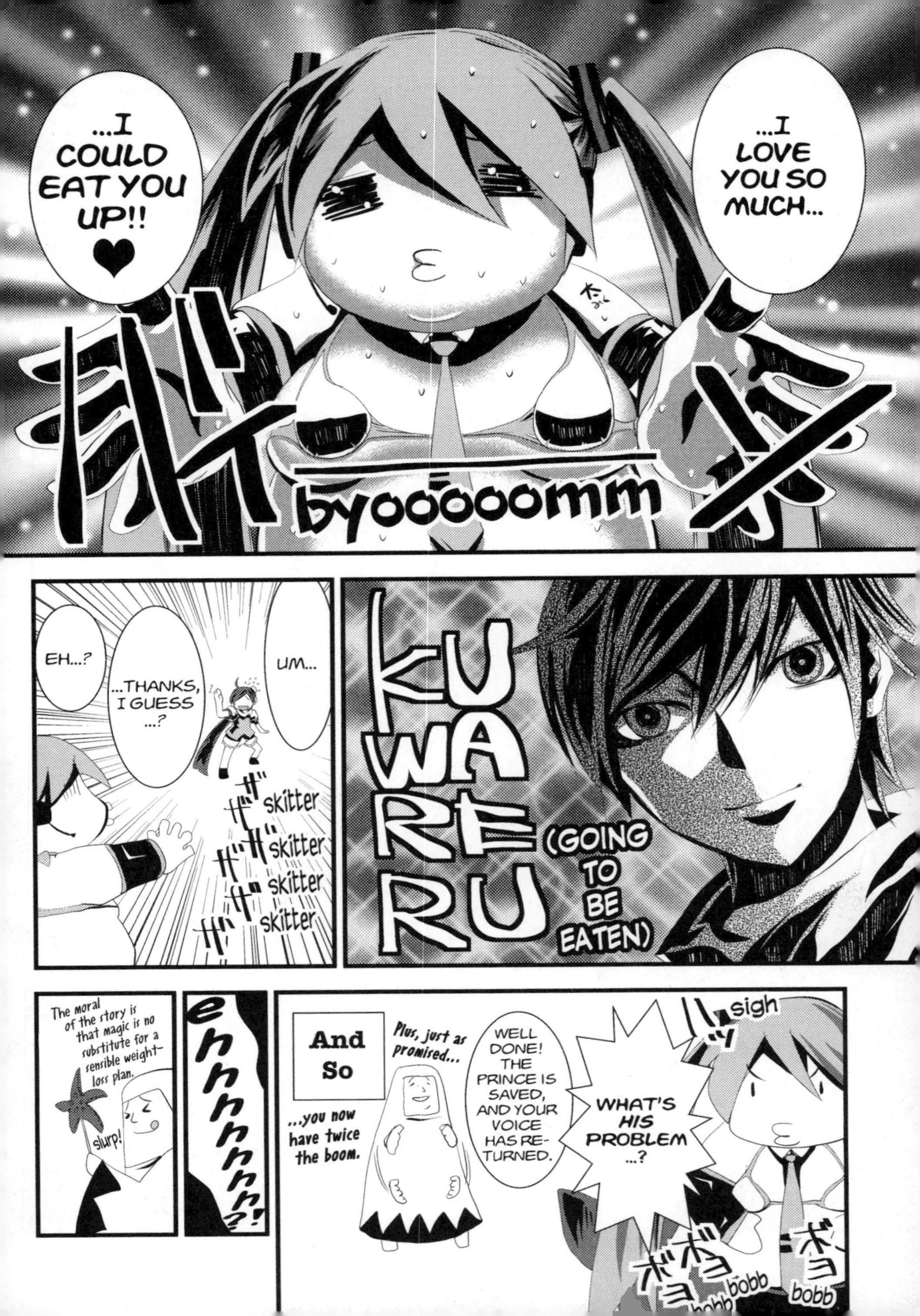

...I LOVE YOU SO MUCH...
...I COULD EAT YOU UP!! ♥
byoooomm
KUWARERU
(GOING TO BE EATEN)
UM...
...THANKS, I GUESS ...?
EH...?
skitter
skitter
skitter
skitter
sigh
WHAT'S HIS PROBLEM ...?
WELL DONE! THE PRINCE IS SAVED, AND YOUR VOICE HAS RE-TURNED.
Plus, just as promised...
And So
...you now have twice the boom.
bobb
bobb
bobb
ehnnnnnnnnn?!
The moral of the story is that magic is no substitute for a sensible weight-loss plan.
slurp!

(9th SONG) CHIBI MIX

mikumikumiku

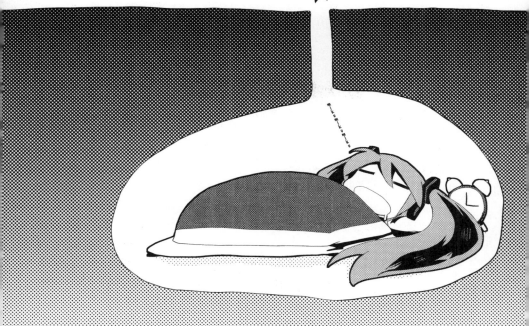

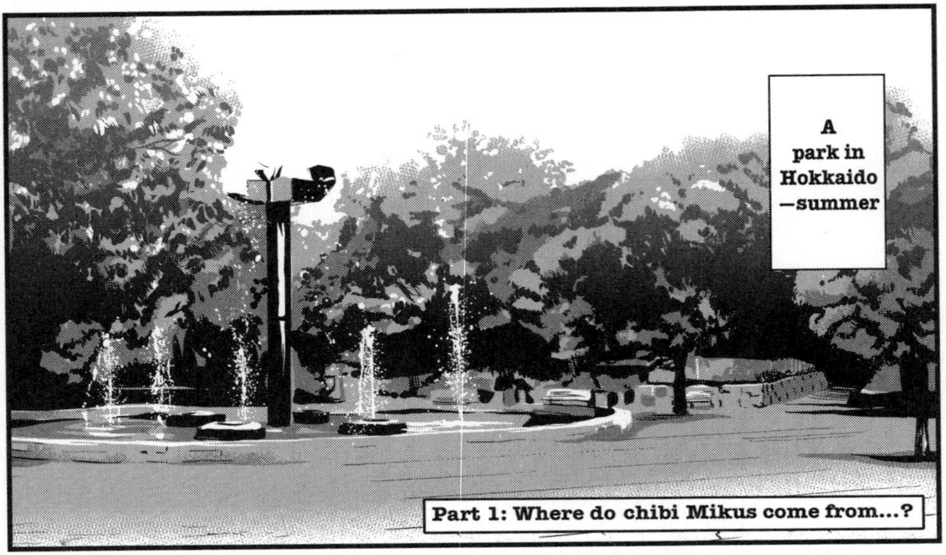
A park in Hokkaido—summer
Part 1: Where do chibi Mikus come from...?

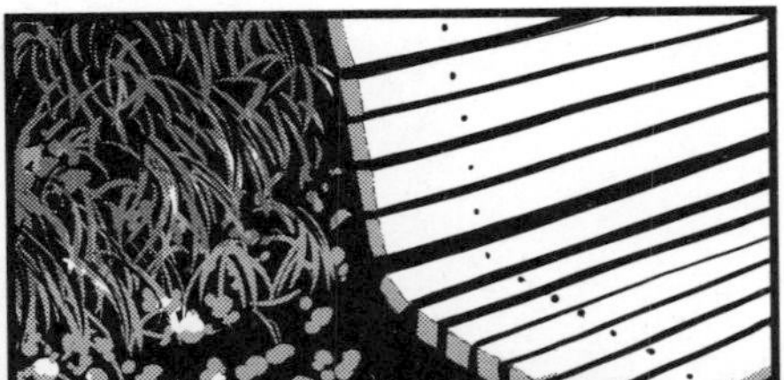

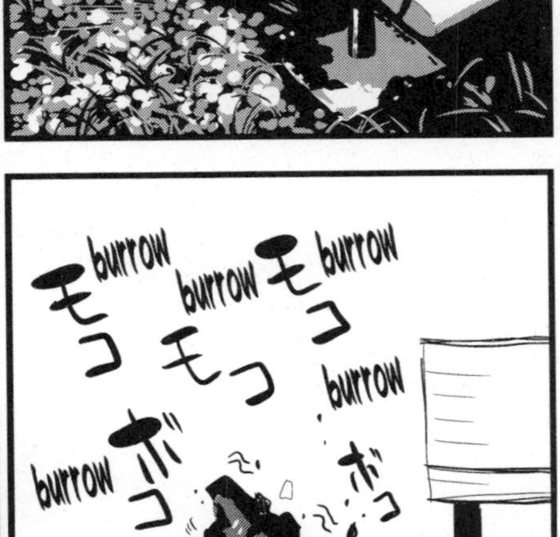
burrow モコ
burrow モコ
burrow モコ
burrow
burrow ボコ
ボコ

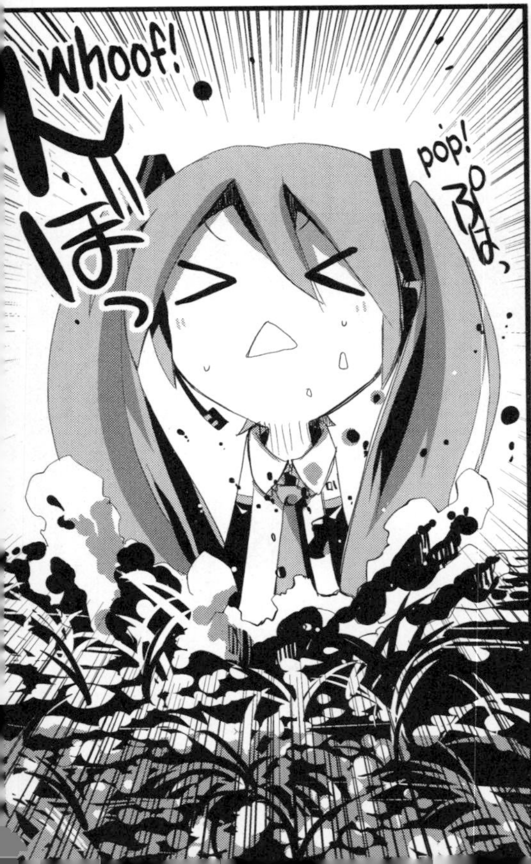
whoof! ぽっ
pop! ぷは

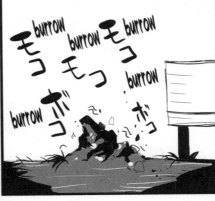

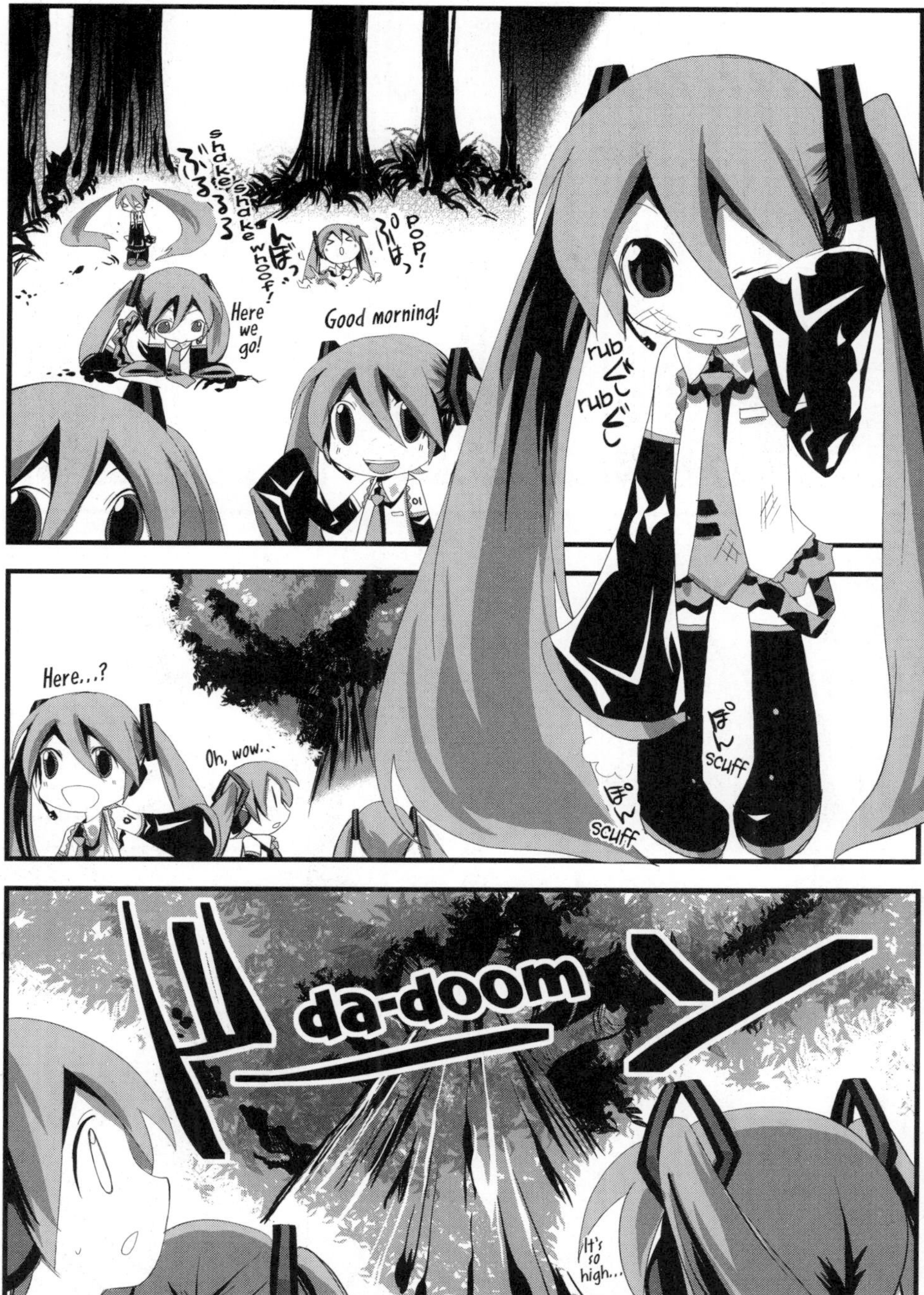

rub ぐし
rub ぐし
ぽん scuff
ぽん scuff
POP! ぷはっ
んぽっ whoof!
shake ぶるるる shake
Good morning!
Here we go!
Oh, wow...
Here...?
da-doom
It's so high...

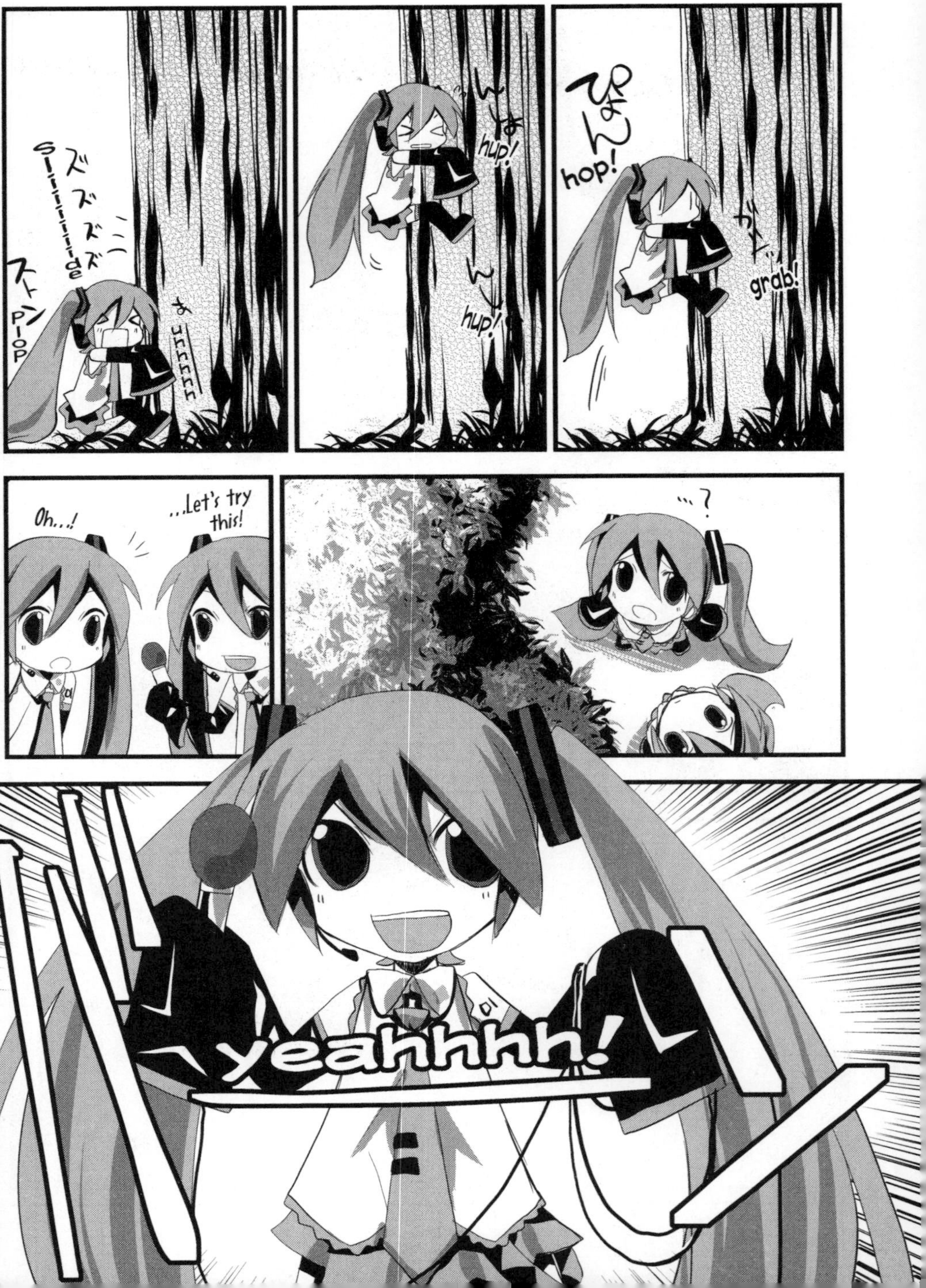
ぴょん
hop!
grab!
んしょ
hup!
hup!
ズズズズ
S-------ide
ストン
Plop
unnhhhh
...?
...Let's try this!
Oh...!
yeahhhh!

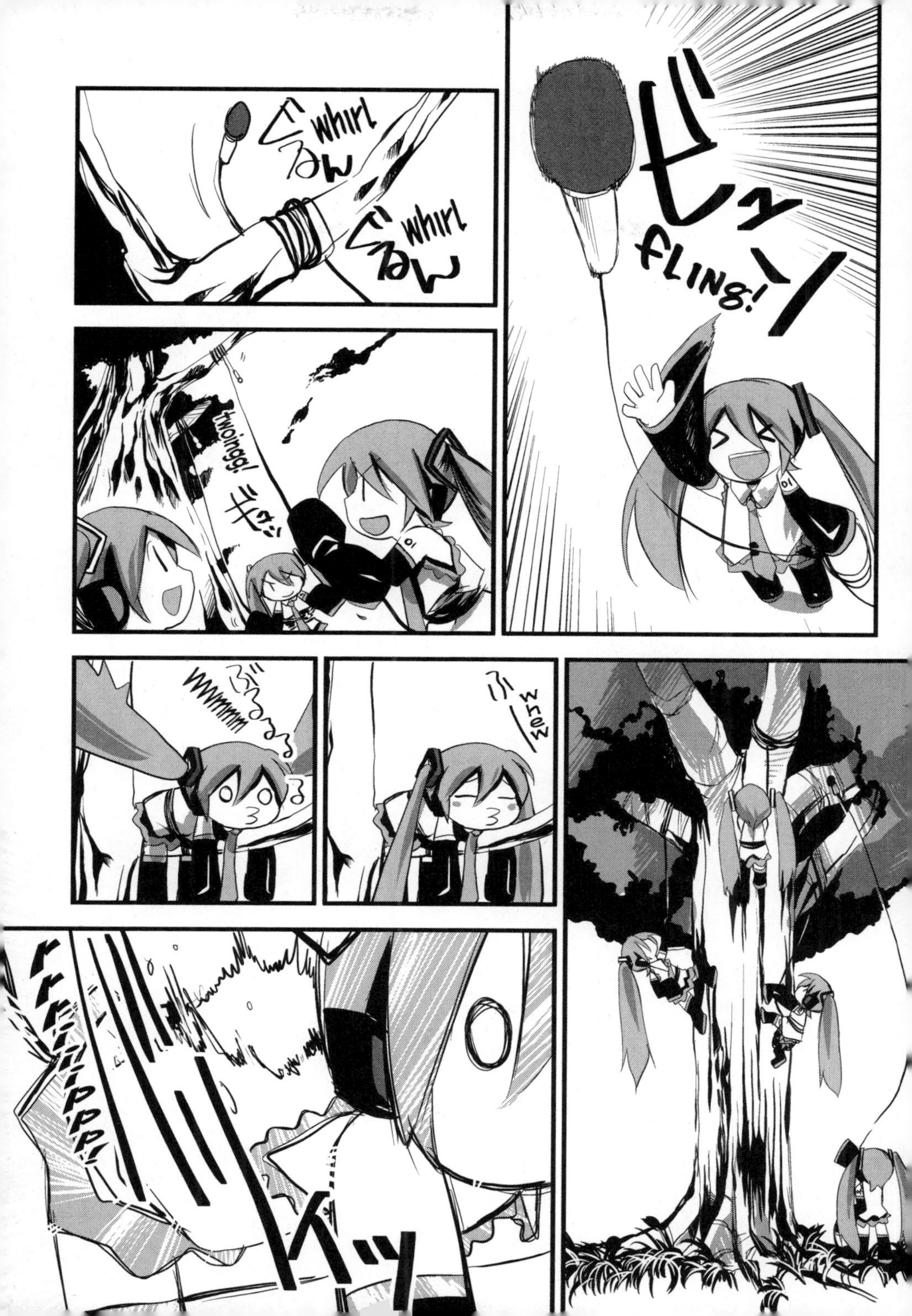
ビヨーン
FLING!
01
ぐるん whirl
ぐるん whirl
twoingg!
ギュッ
01
ふー whew
ぶるるるるる
VVVVrrrmmm
RRRIIIIPPP!
バッ

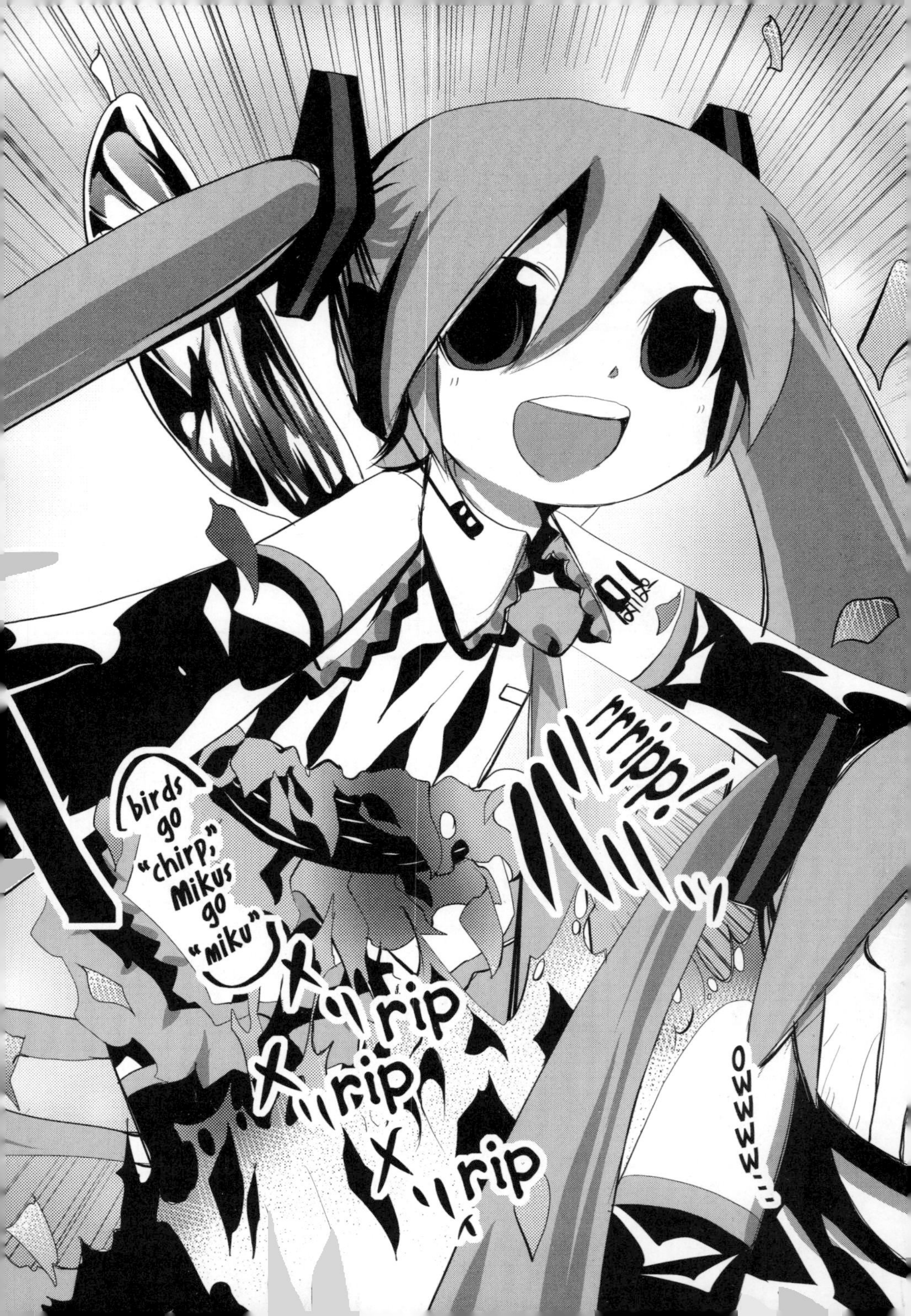
rrripp!
birds go "chirp," Mikus go "miku"
rip
rip
rip
owwww...

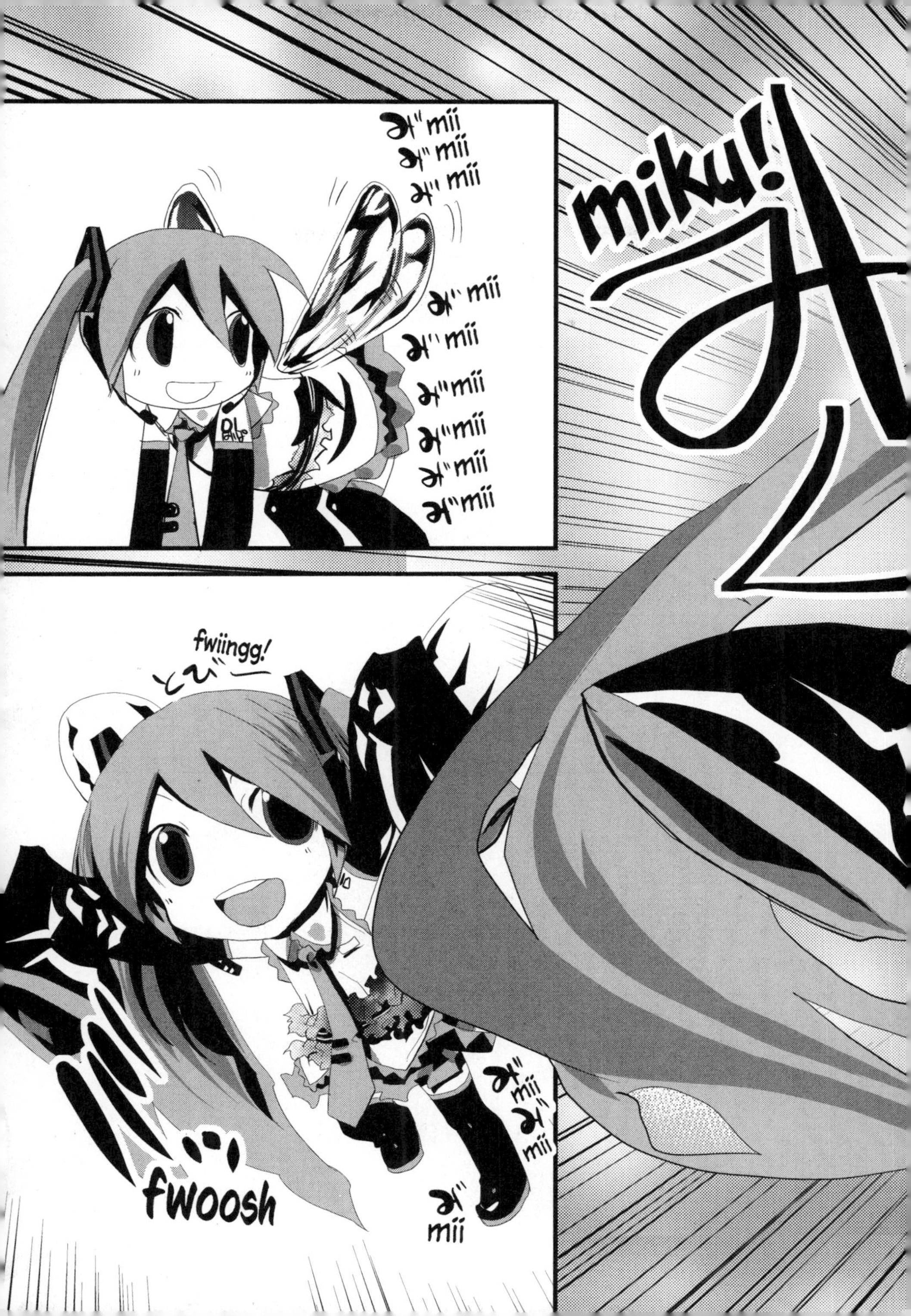

miku!
み゛ mii
み゛ mii
み゛ mii
み゛ mii
み゛ mii
み゛ mii
み゛ mii
み゛ mii
み゛ mii
とびー
fwiingg!
み゛ mii
み゛ mii
み゛ mii
fwoosh

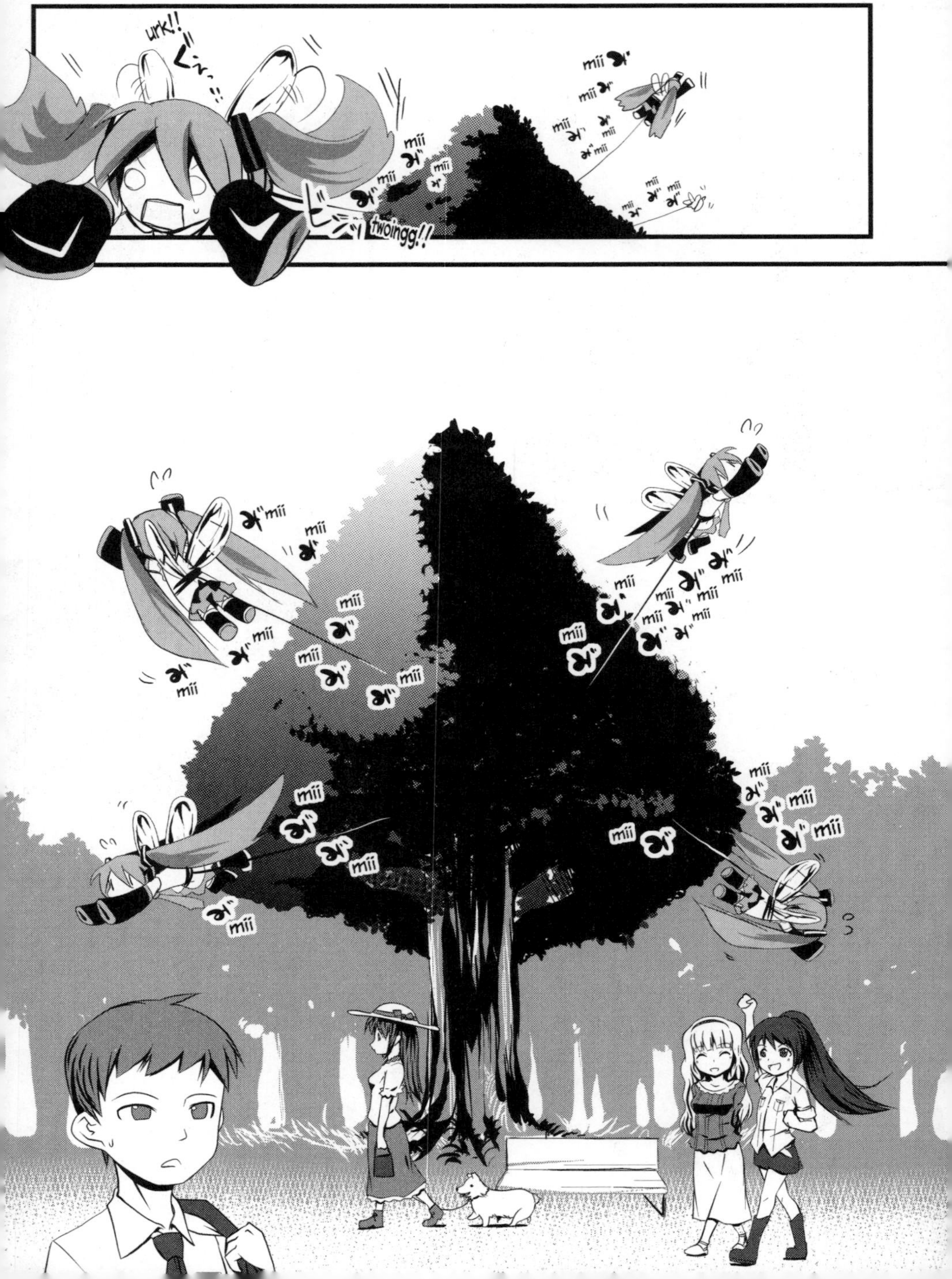
mii み゛
mii み゛
mii み゛ mii
み゛mii
mii み゛ mii み゛
mii み゛
mii み゛
mii み゛
mii み゛
urk!!
ぐえっ!!
ビ゛ビ゛ン
twoingg!!
み゛mii
mii み゛
mii み゛
み゛mii
み゛mii
mii み゛
mii み゛ み゛mii
mii み゛ mii
mii み゛ mii
み゛ み゛mii
mii み゛
mii み゛
み゛mii
み゛mii
mii み゛
み゛mii
み゛mii
mii み゛
み゛mii
み゛mii

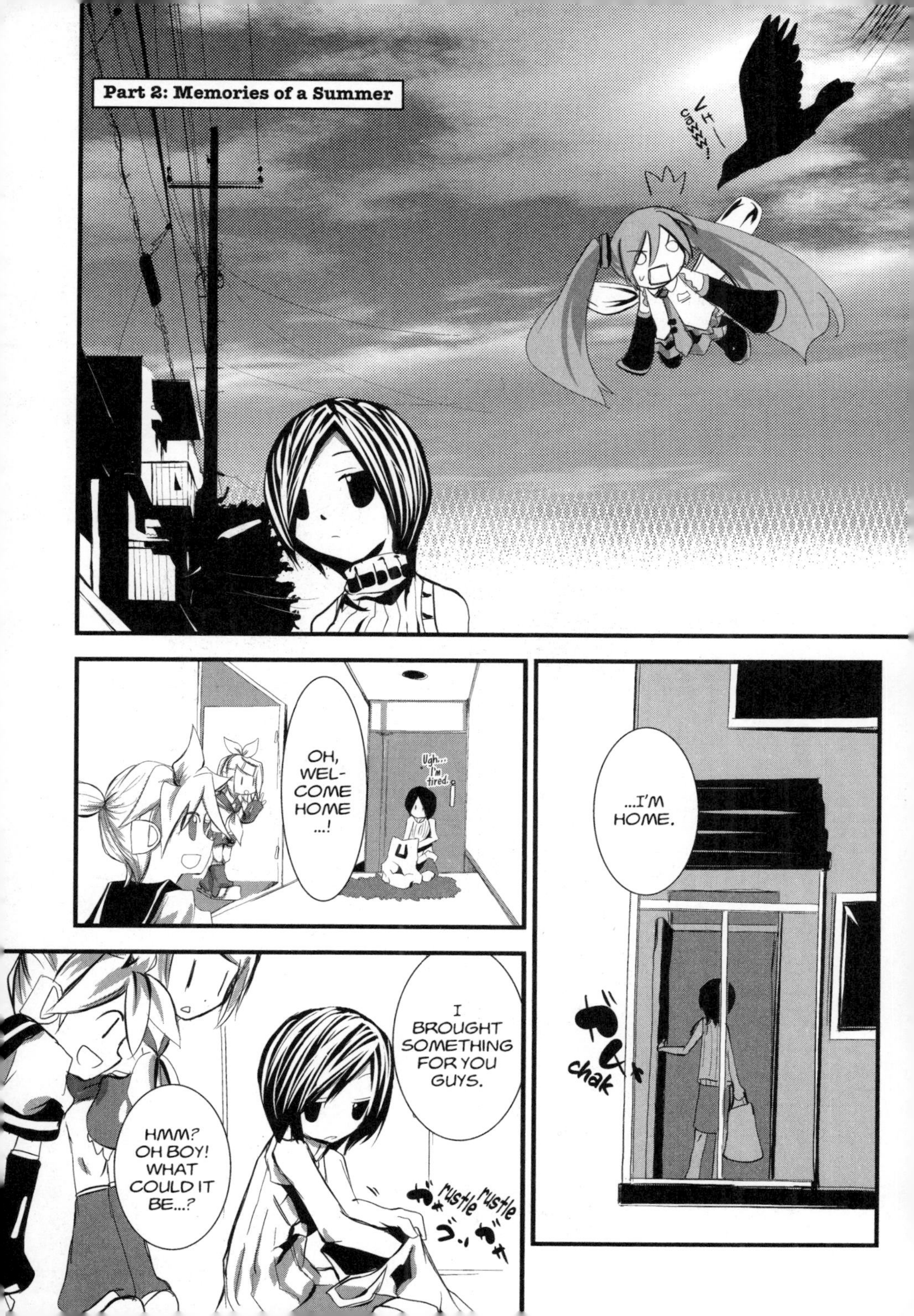
Part 2: Memories of a Summer
croaaaa...
...I'M HOME.
chak
OH, WEL-COME HOME ...!
Ugh... I'm tired.
I BROUGHT SOMETHING FOR YOU GUYS.
rustle rustle
HMM? OH BOY! WHAT COULD IT BE...?

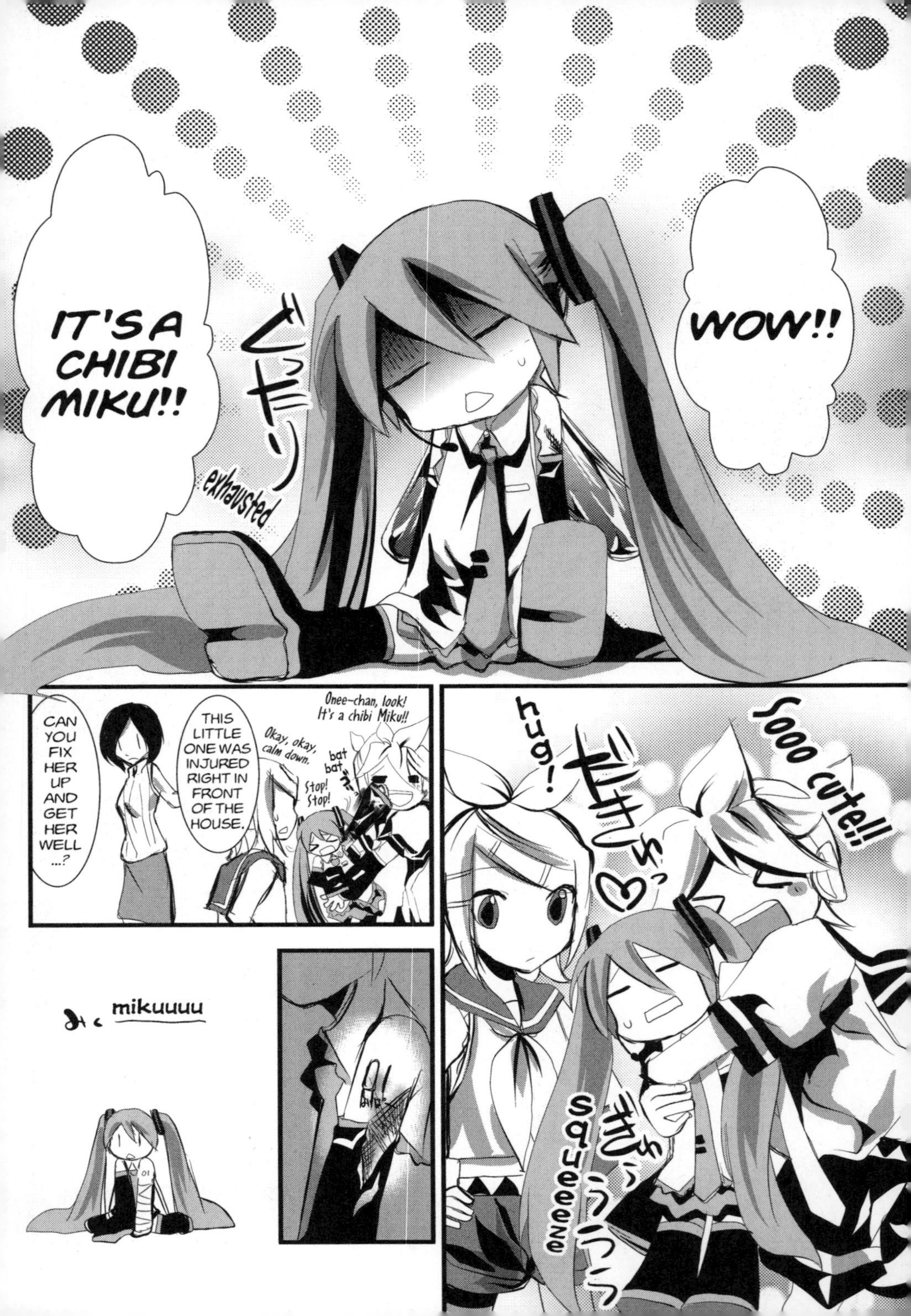

WOW!!
exhausted
IT'S A CHIBI MIKU!!
Sooo cute!!
hug!
squeeeeze
Onee-chan, look! It's a chibi Miku!!
Okay, okay, calm down.
bat bat
Stop! Stop!
THIS LITTLE ONE WAS INJURED RIGHT IN FRONT OF THE HOUSE.
CAN YOU FIX HER UP AND GET HER WELL ...?
mikuuuu

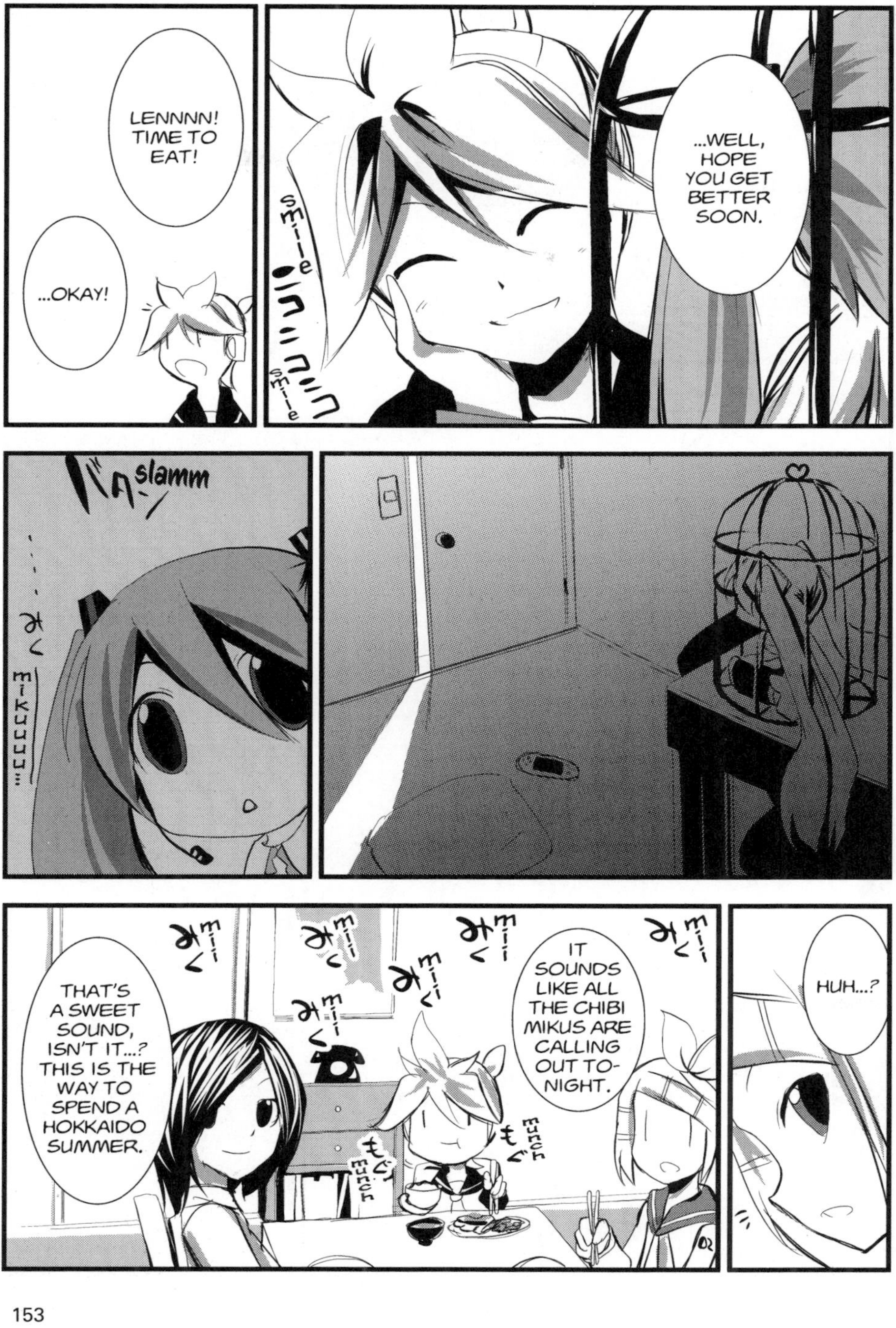
...WELL, HOPE YOU GET BETTER SOON.
smile
ニコニコ
smile
LENNNN! TIME TO EAT!
...OKAY!
バターン
slamm
...みく
mikuuuuu...
HUH...?
みく
mi-i
IT SOUNDS LIKE ALL THE CHIBI MIKUS ARE CALLING OUT TO-NIGHT.
もぐ
munch
THAT'S A SWEET SOUND, ISN'T IT...? THIS IS THE WAY TO SPEND A HOKKAIDO SUMMER.

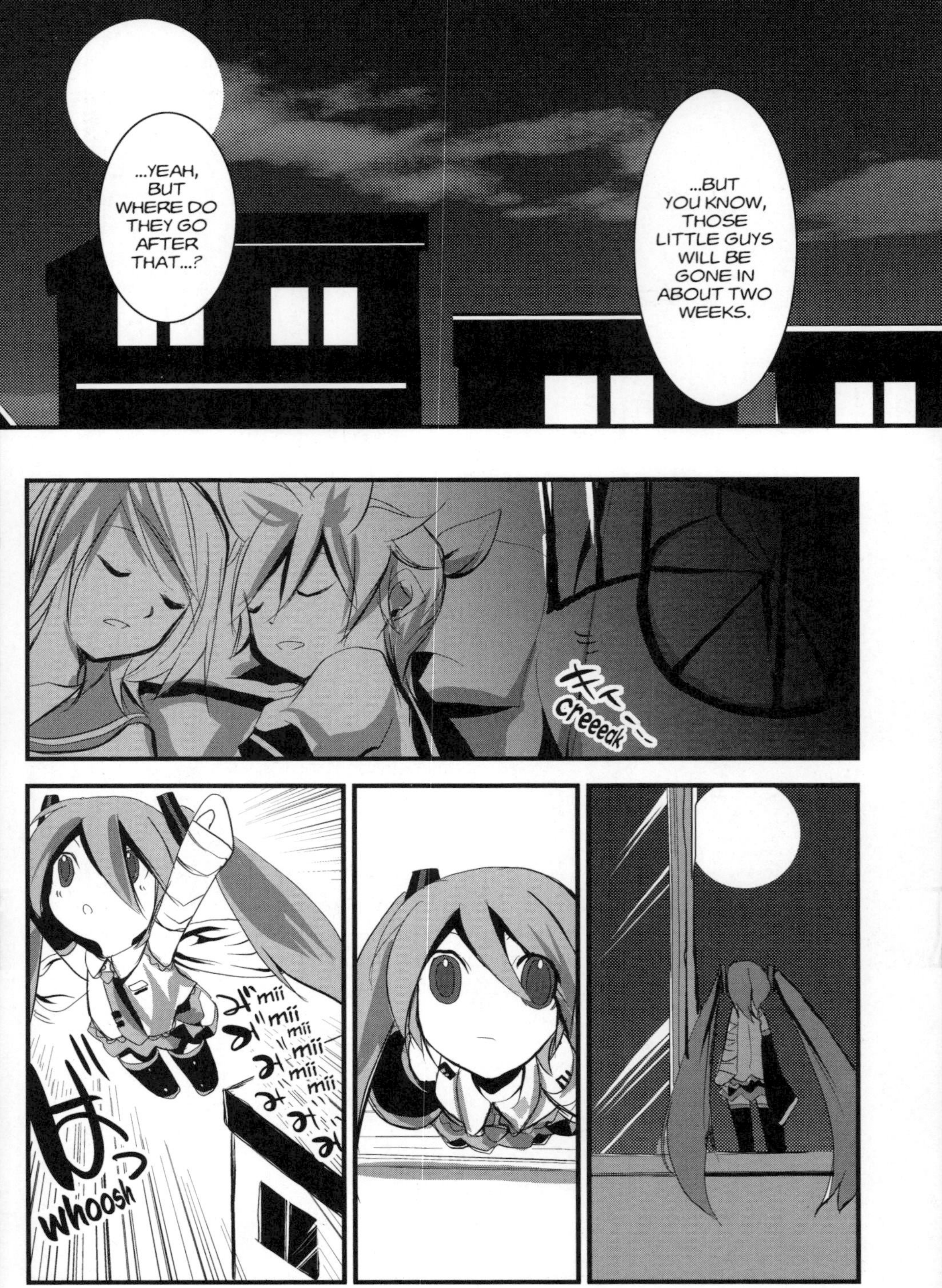
...BUT YOU KNOW, THOSE LITTLE GUYS WILL BE GONE IN ABOUT TWO WEEKS.
...YEAH, BUT WHERE DO THEY GO AFTER THAT...?
creeeak
mii mii mii mii mii
whoosh

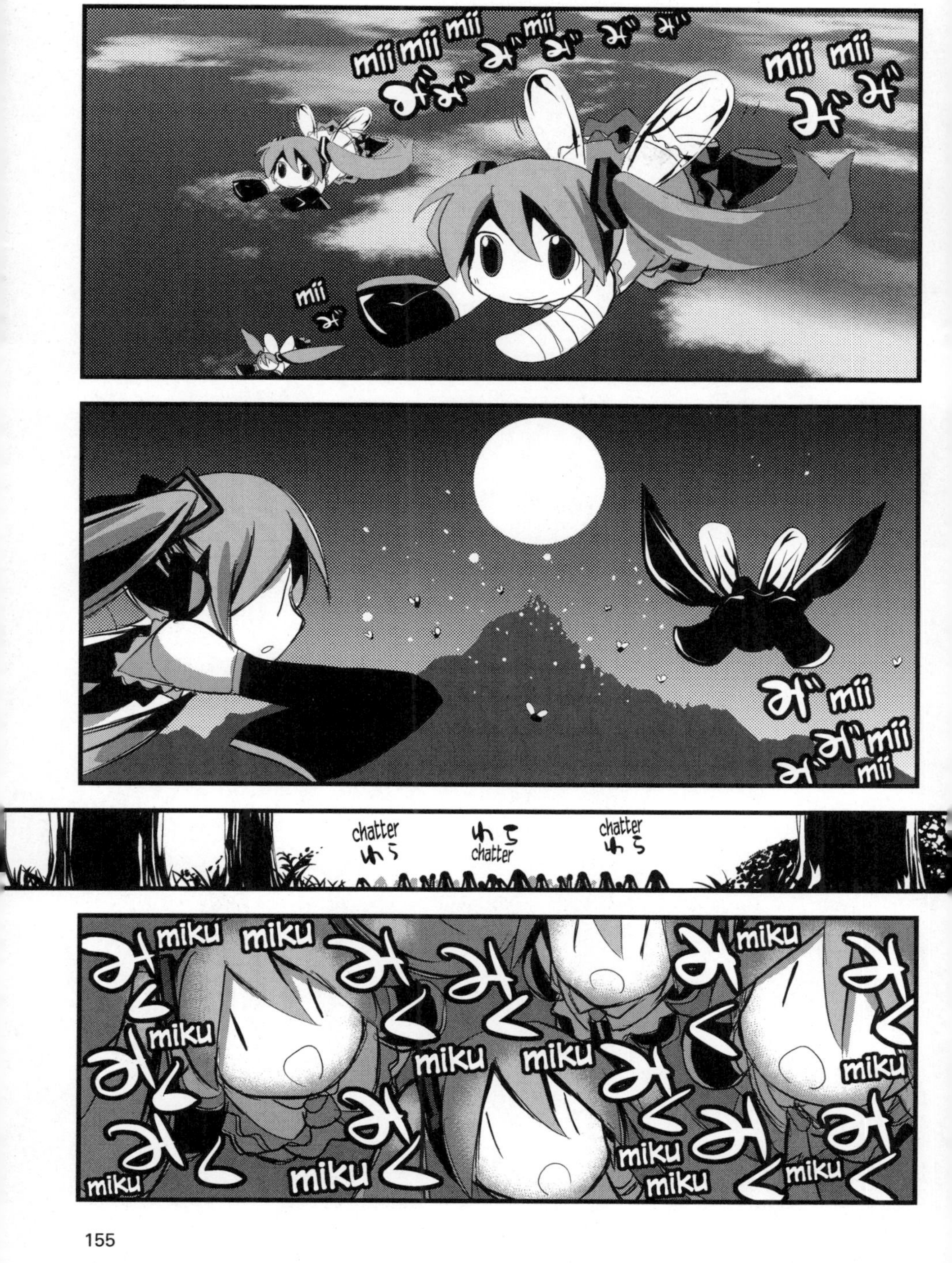
mii mii
み゛み゛
mii mii mii
み゛み゛み゛み゛み゛
mii
み゛
み゛mii
み゛み゛mii
mii
chatter
ゆら
ゆら
chatter
chatter
ゆら
みく
miku
miku
みく
みく
miku
みく
miku
みく
miku
miku
みく
みく
miku
みく
miku
miku
みく
miku
みく
miku
みく
miku

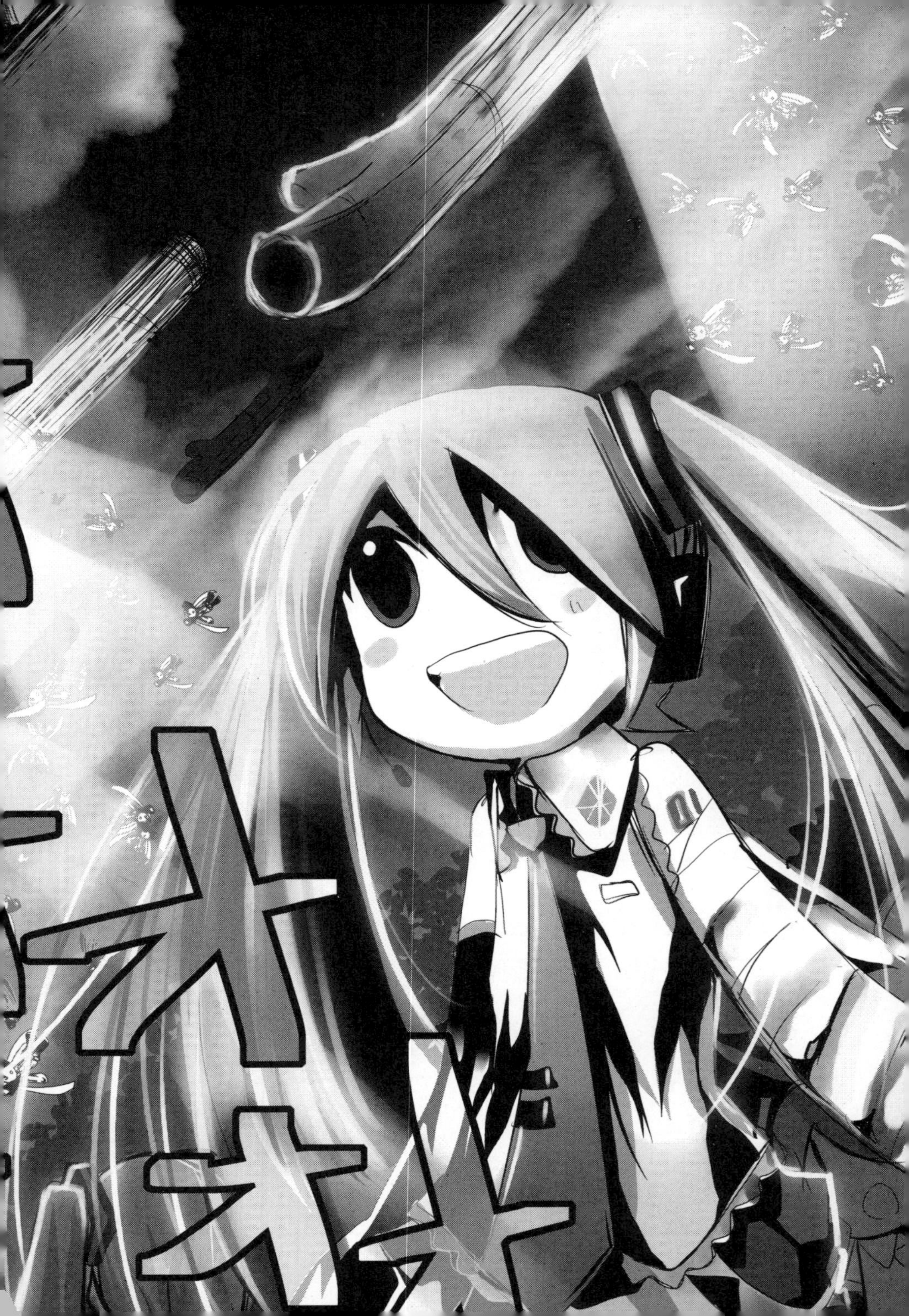

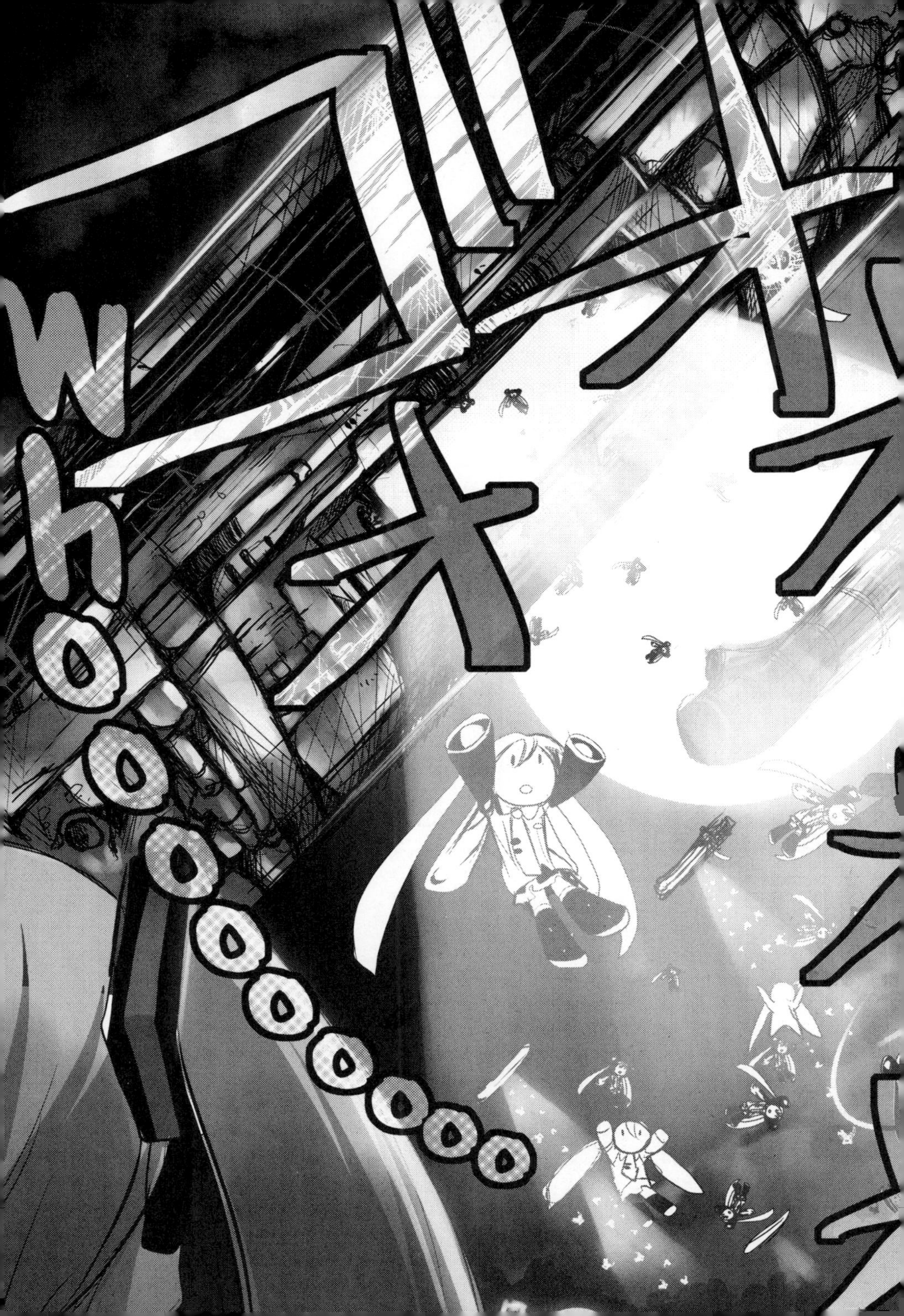
Whooooooooo...

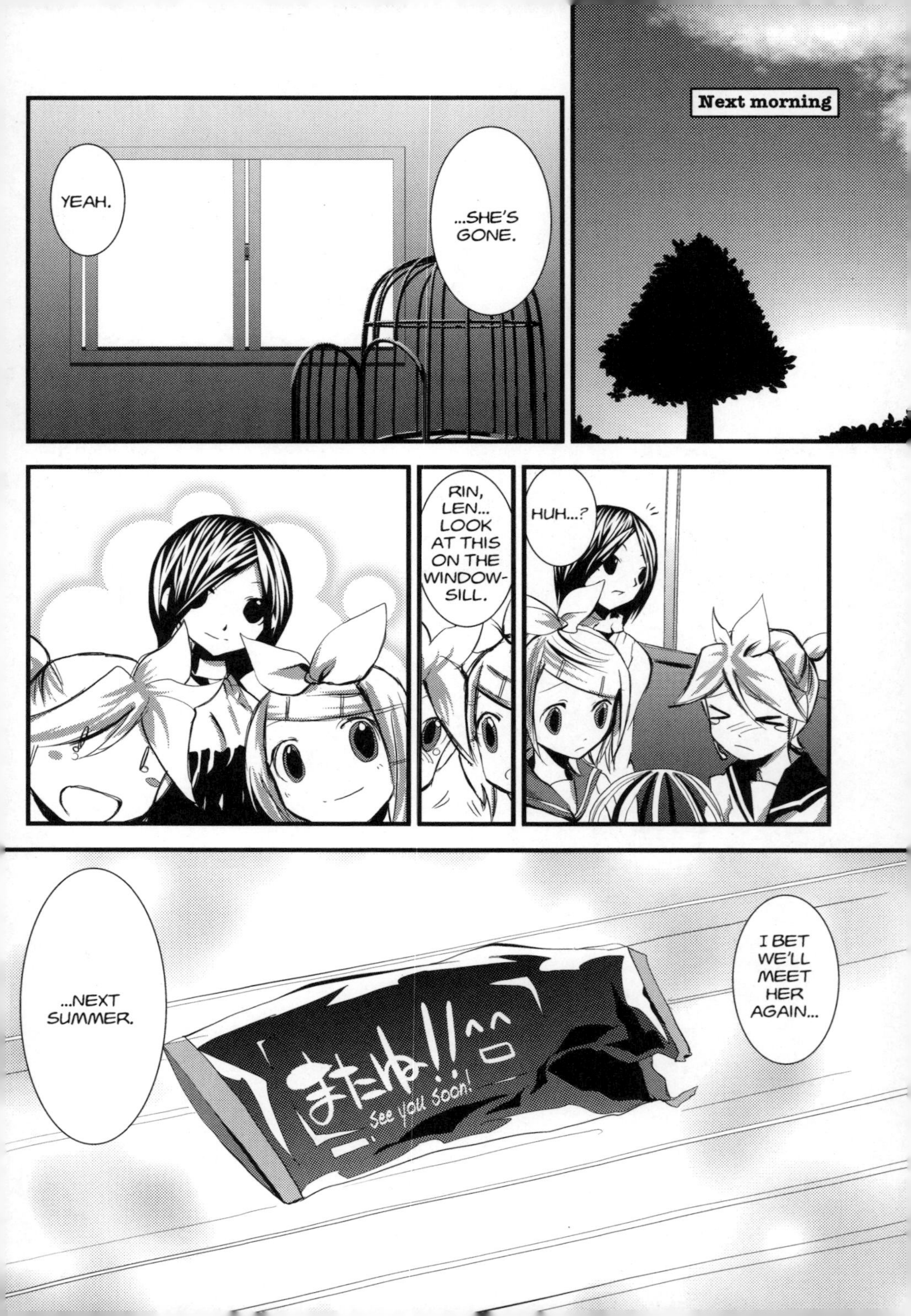
Next morning
...SHE'S GONE.
YEAH.
HUH...?
RIN, LEN... LOOK AT THIS ON THE WINDOW-SILL.
I BET WE'LL MEET HER AGAIN...
...NEXT SUMMER.
またね!!
See you soon!

あとがき。

afterword

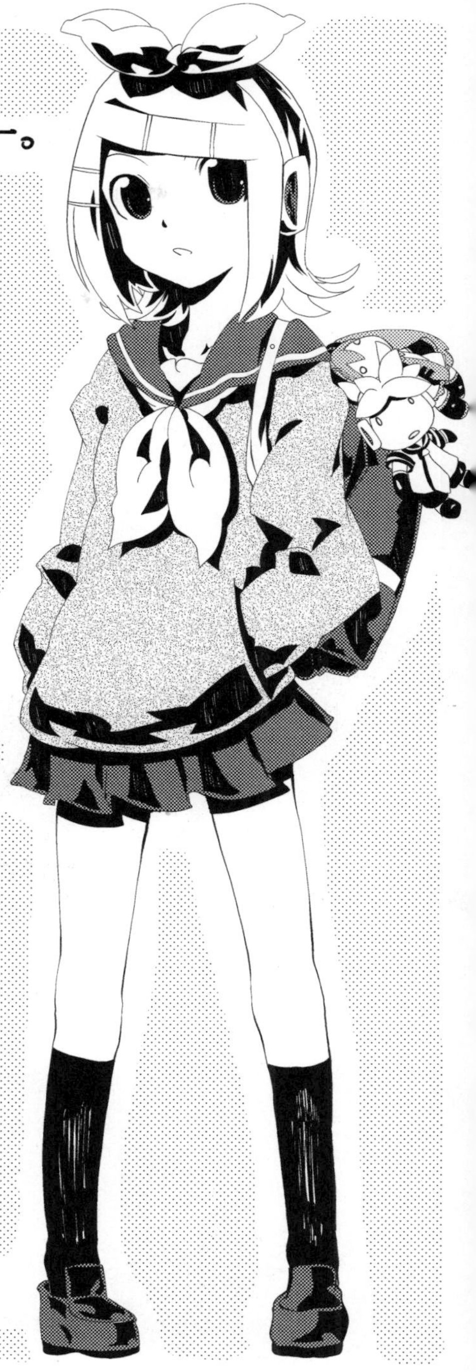

続く

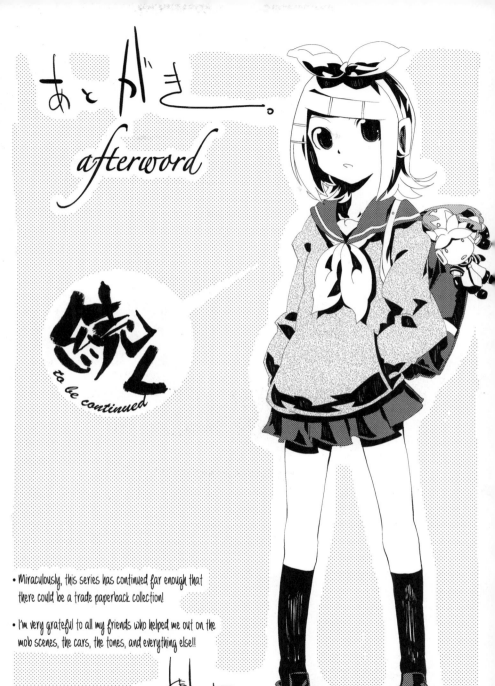

to be continued

- Miraculously, this series has continued far enough that there could be a trade paperback collection!
- I'm very grateful to all my friends who helped me out on the mob scenes, the cars, the tones, and everything else!!

2008.12.xx

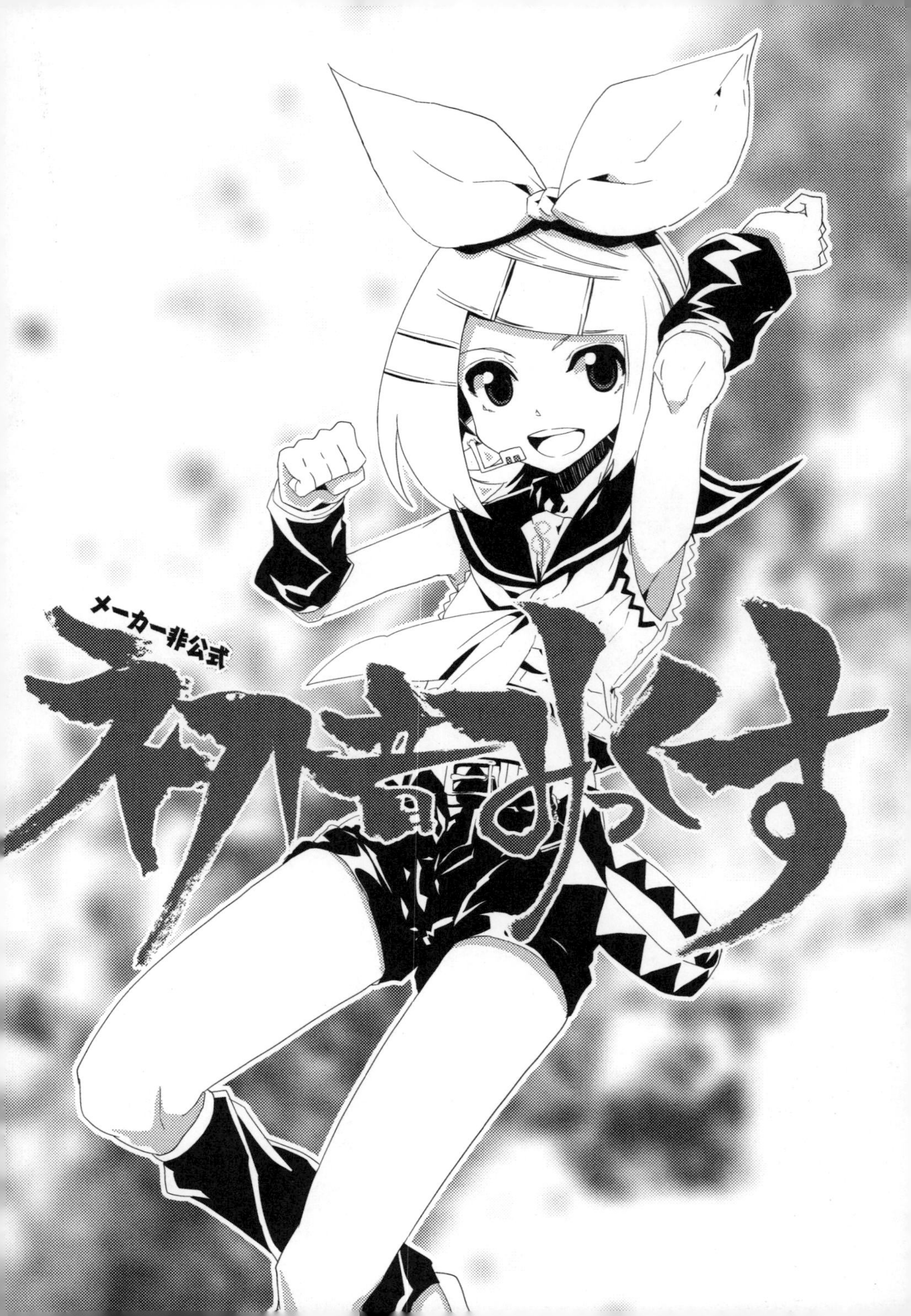
メーカー非公式

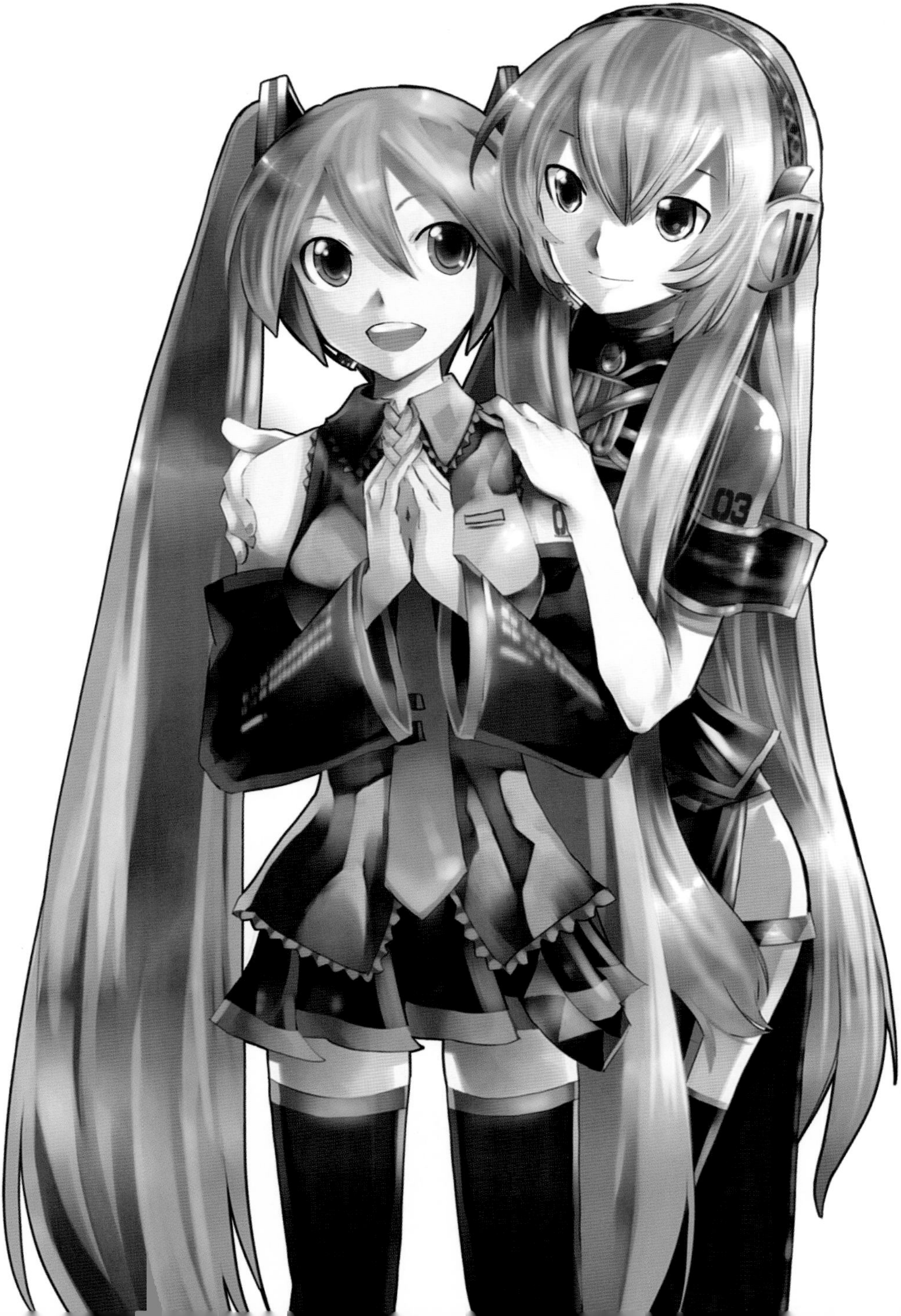
03

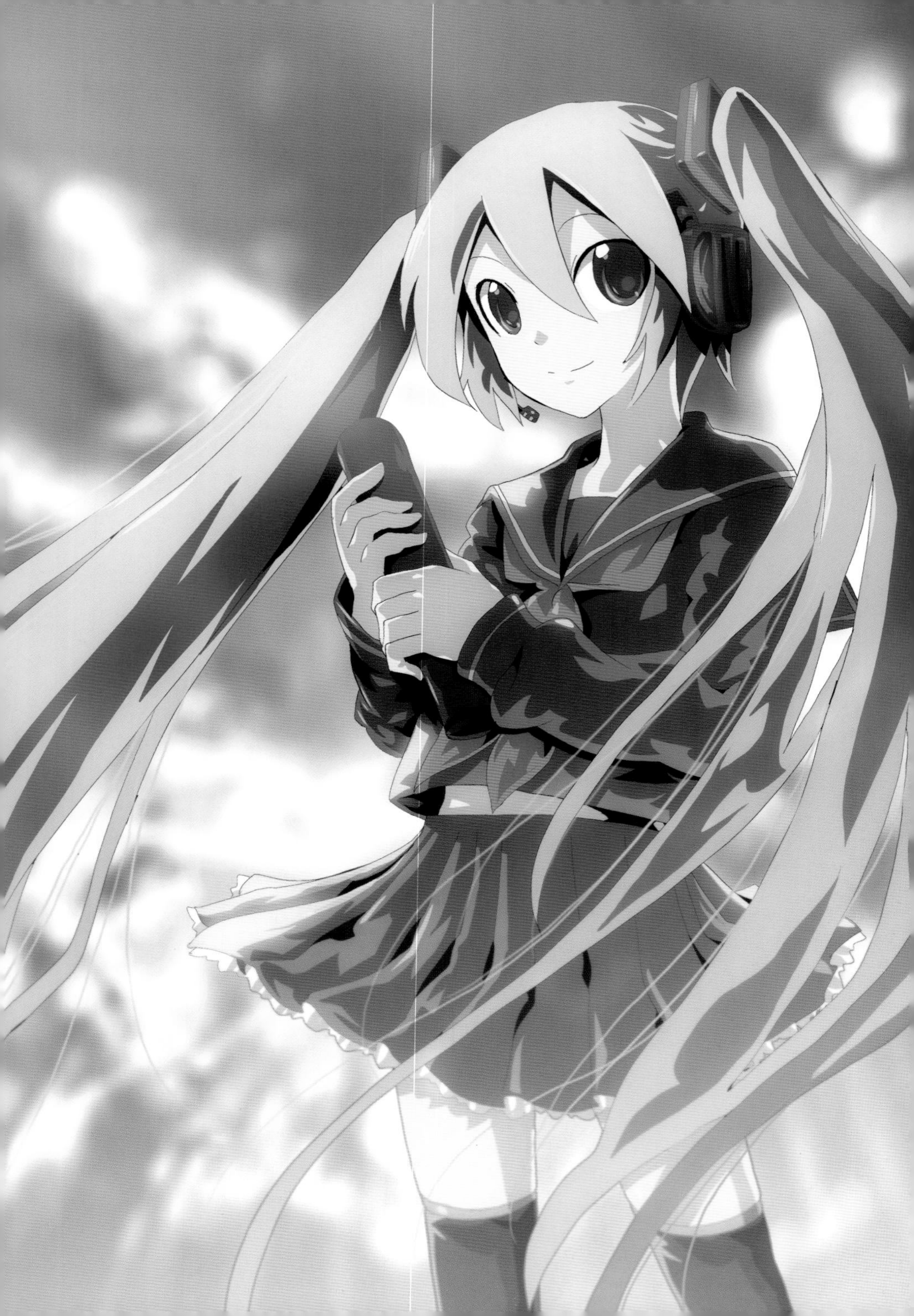

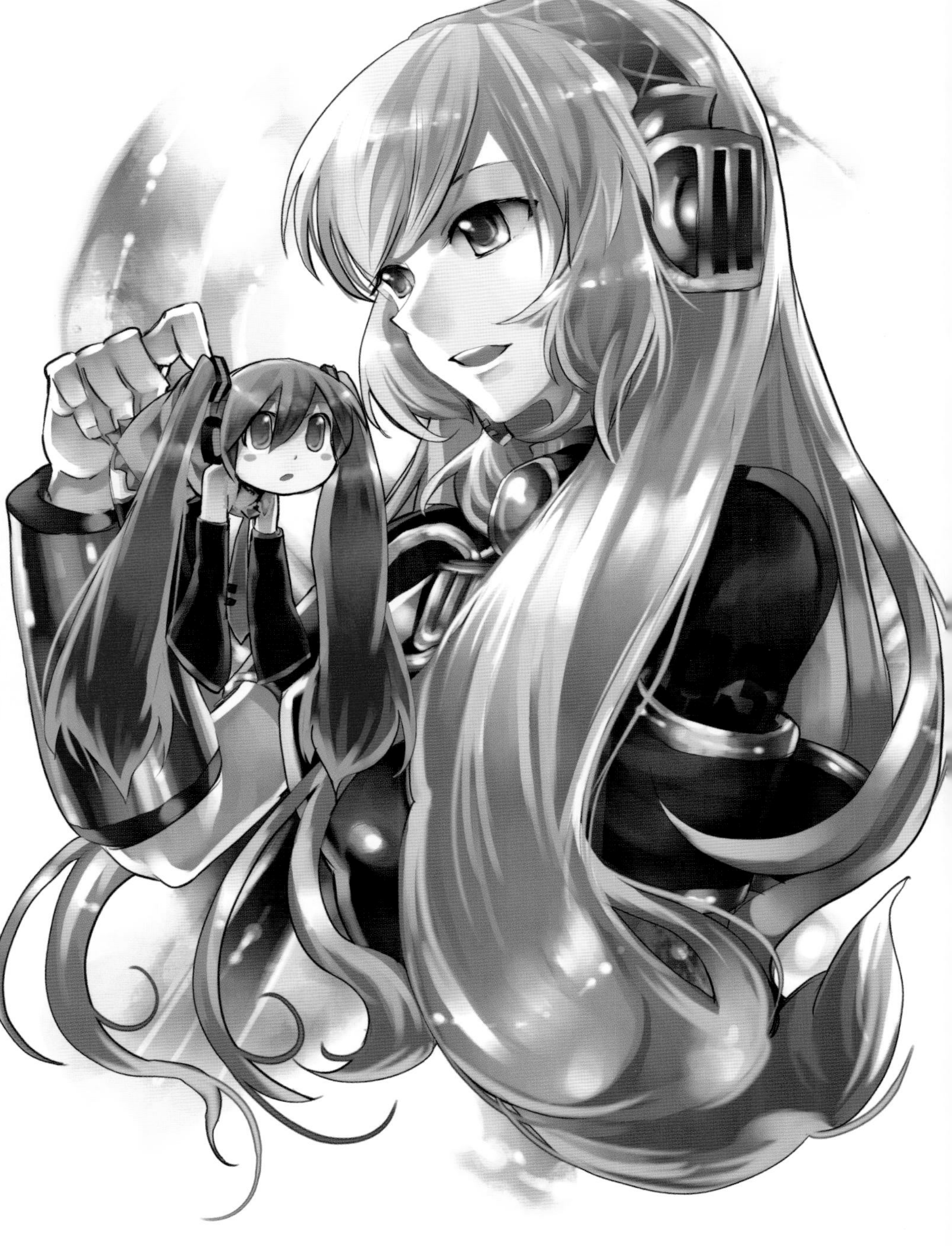

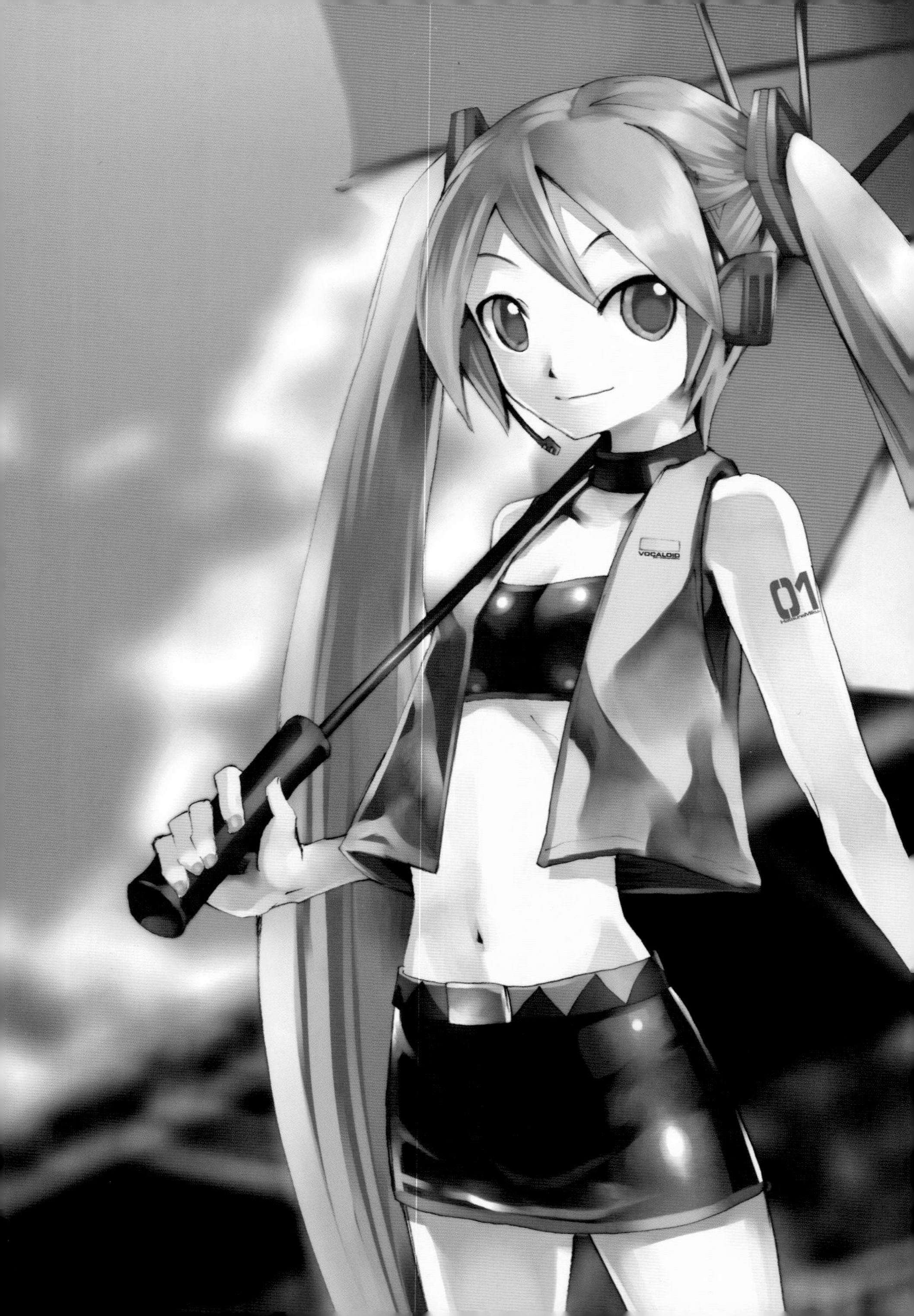
VOCALOID
01

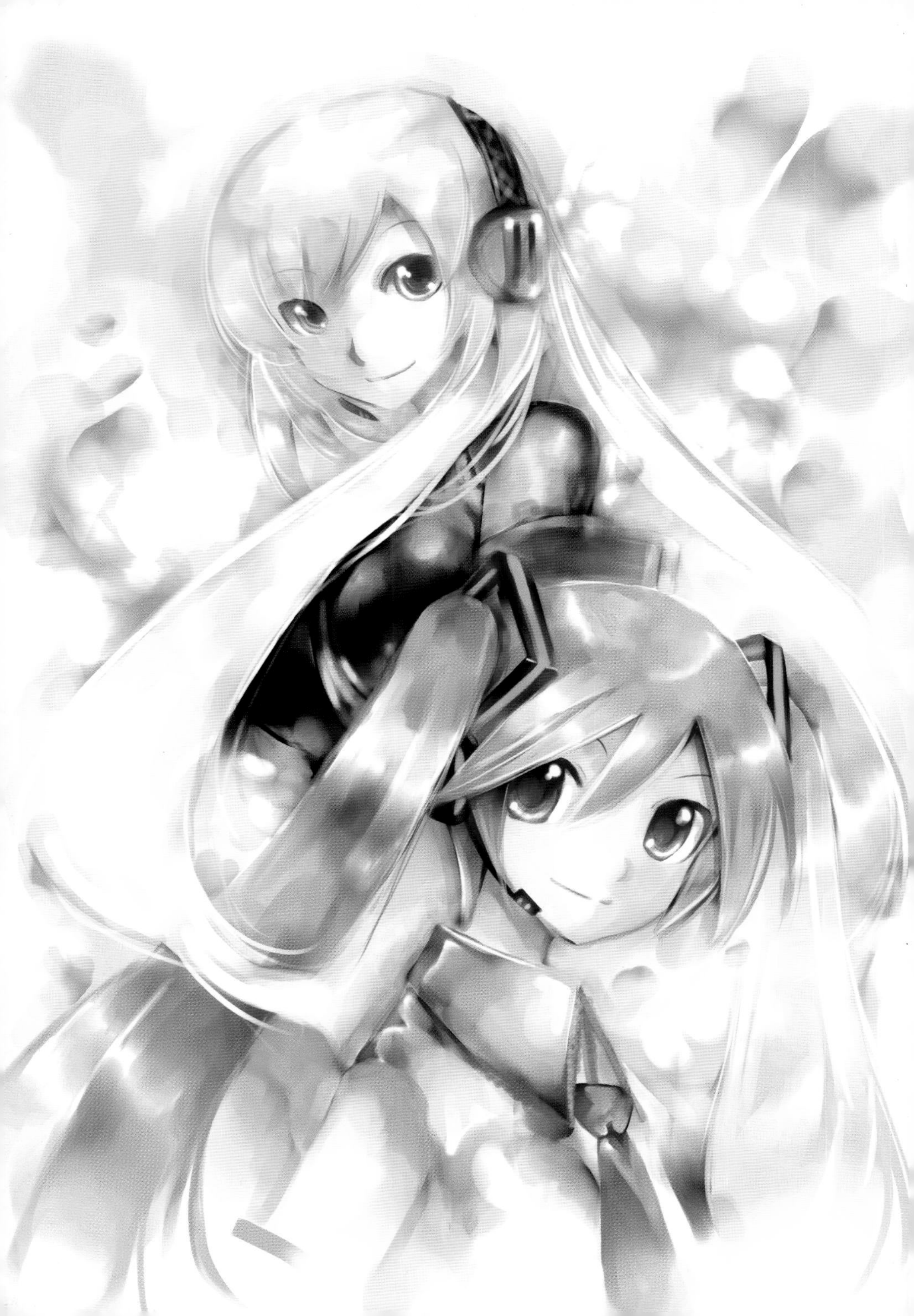

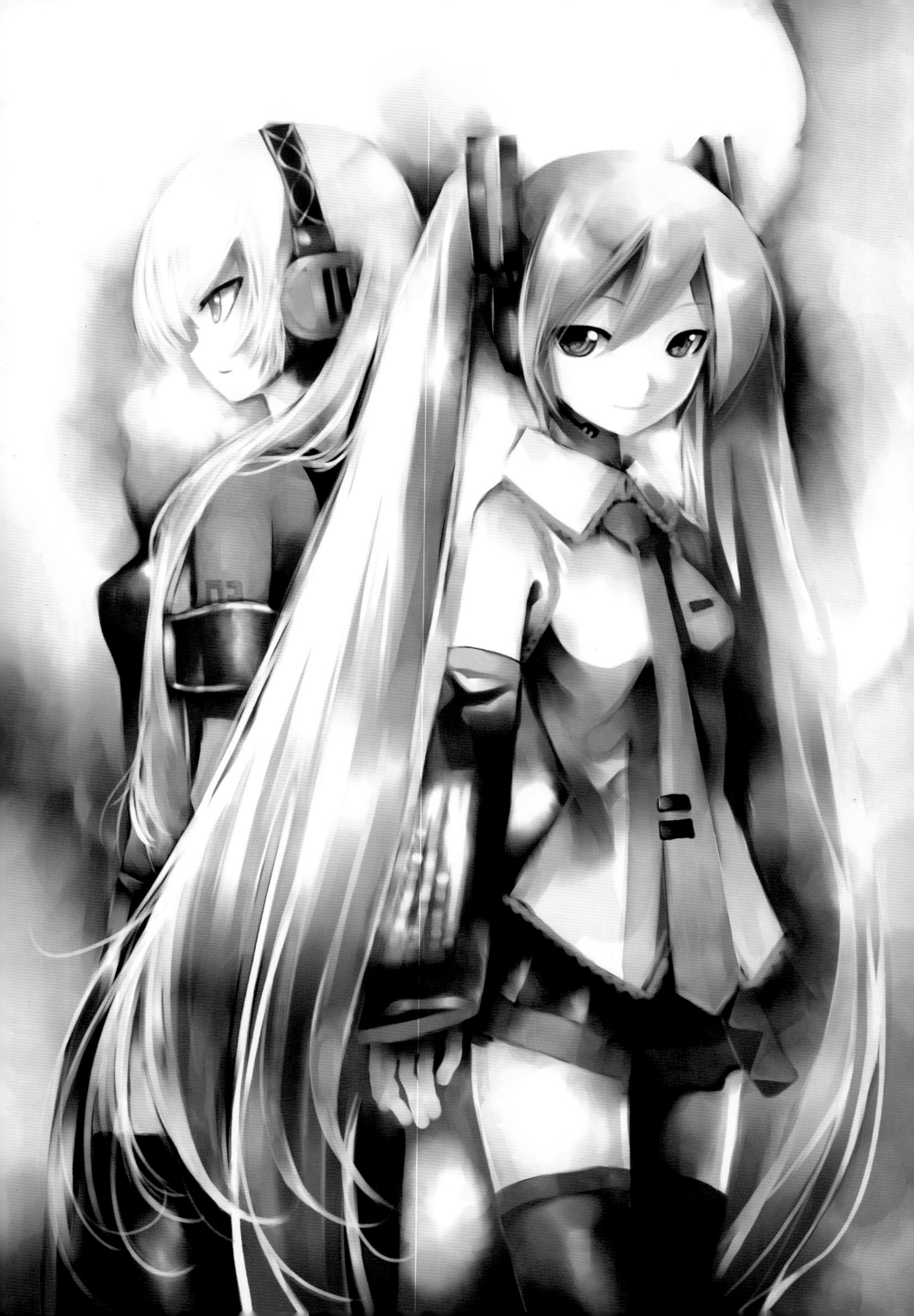

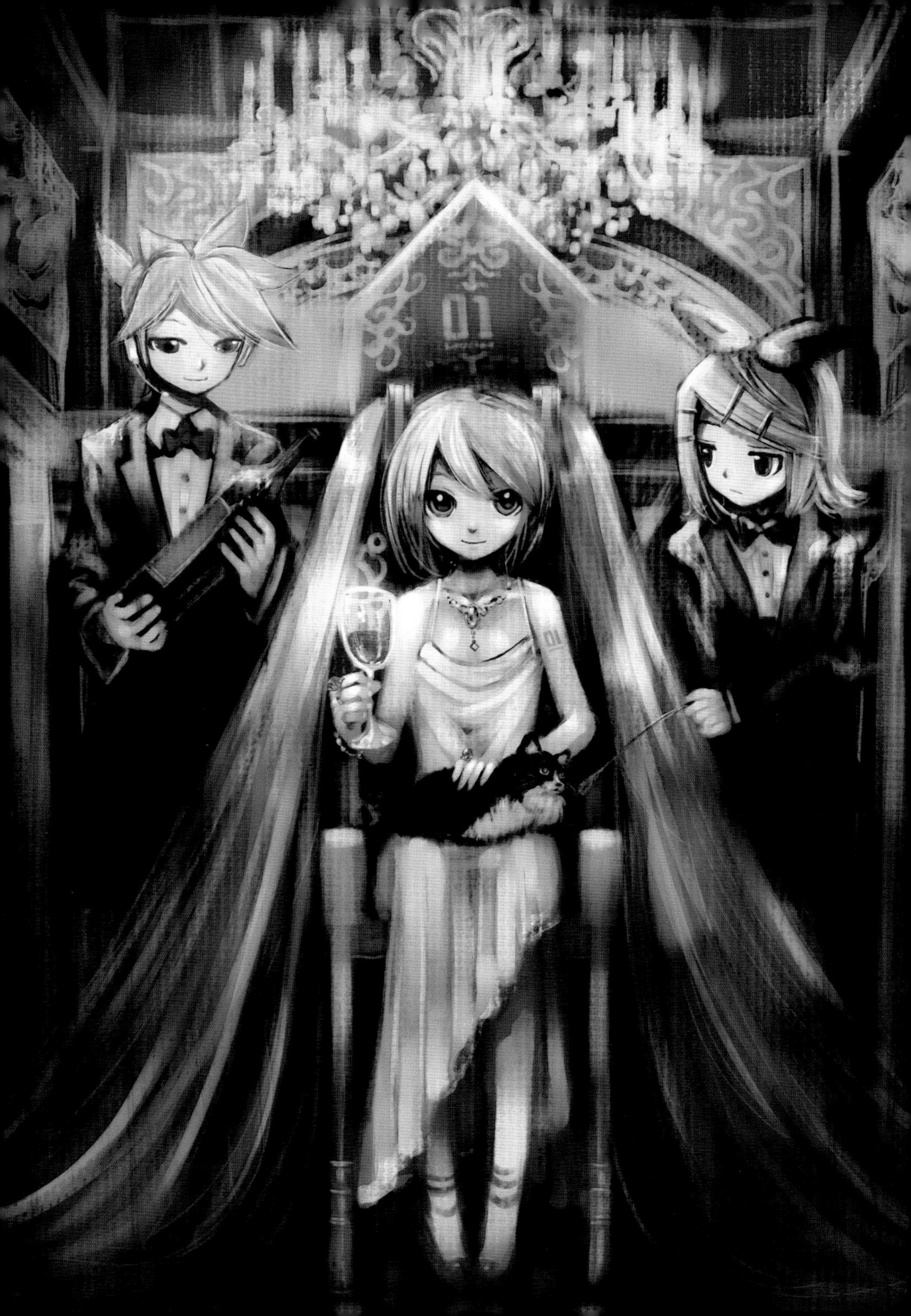
01

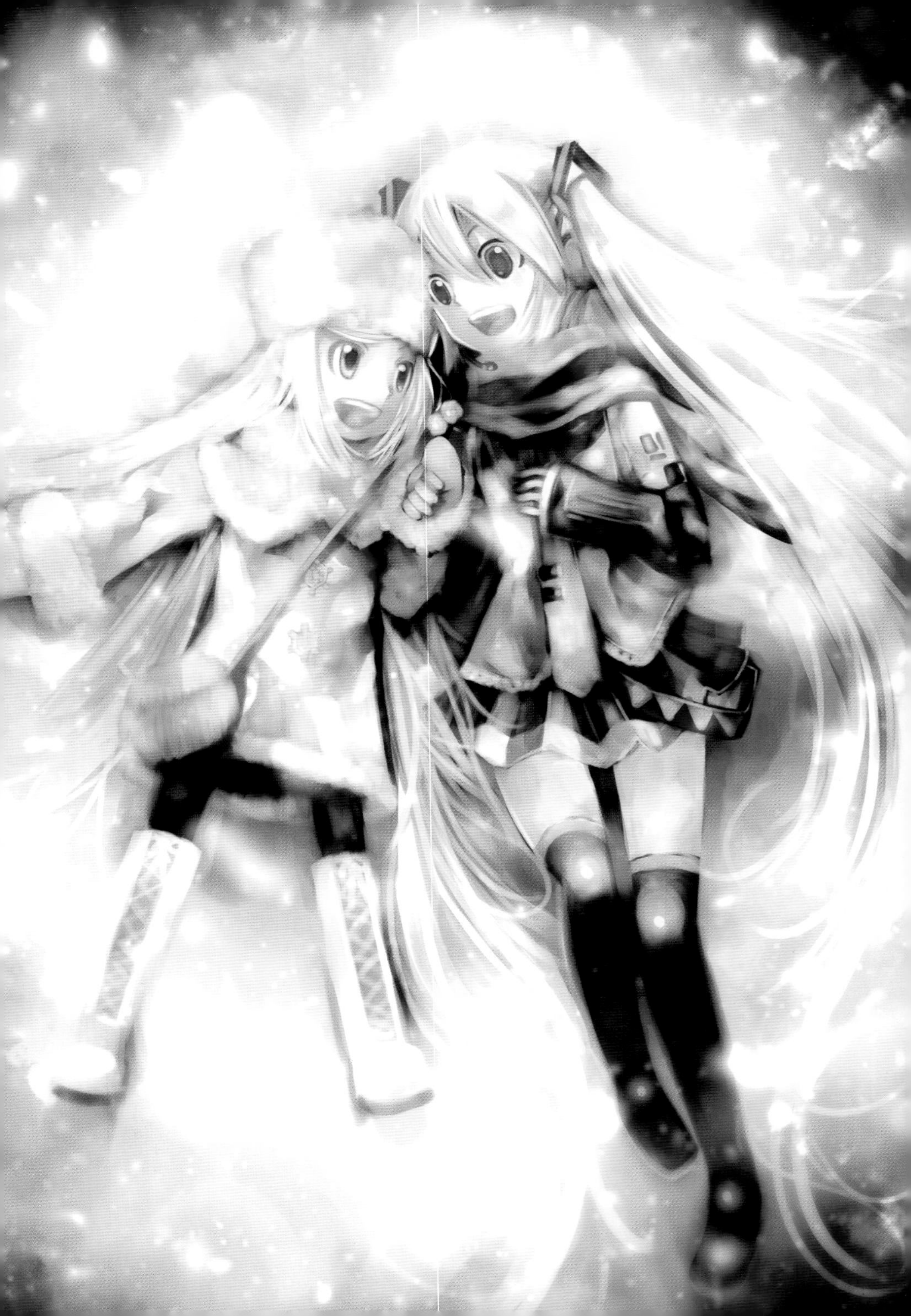

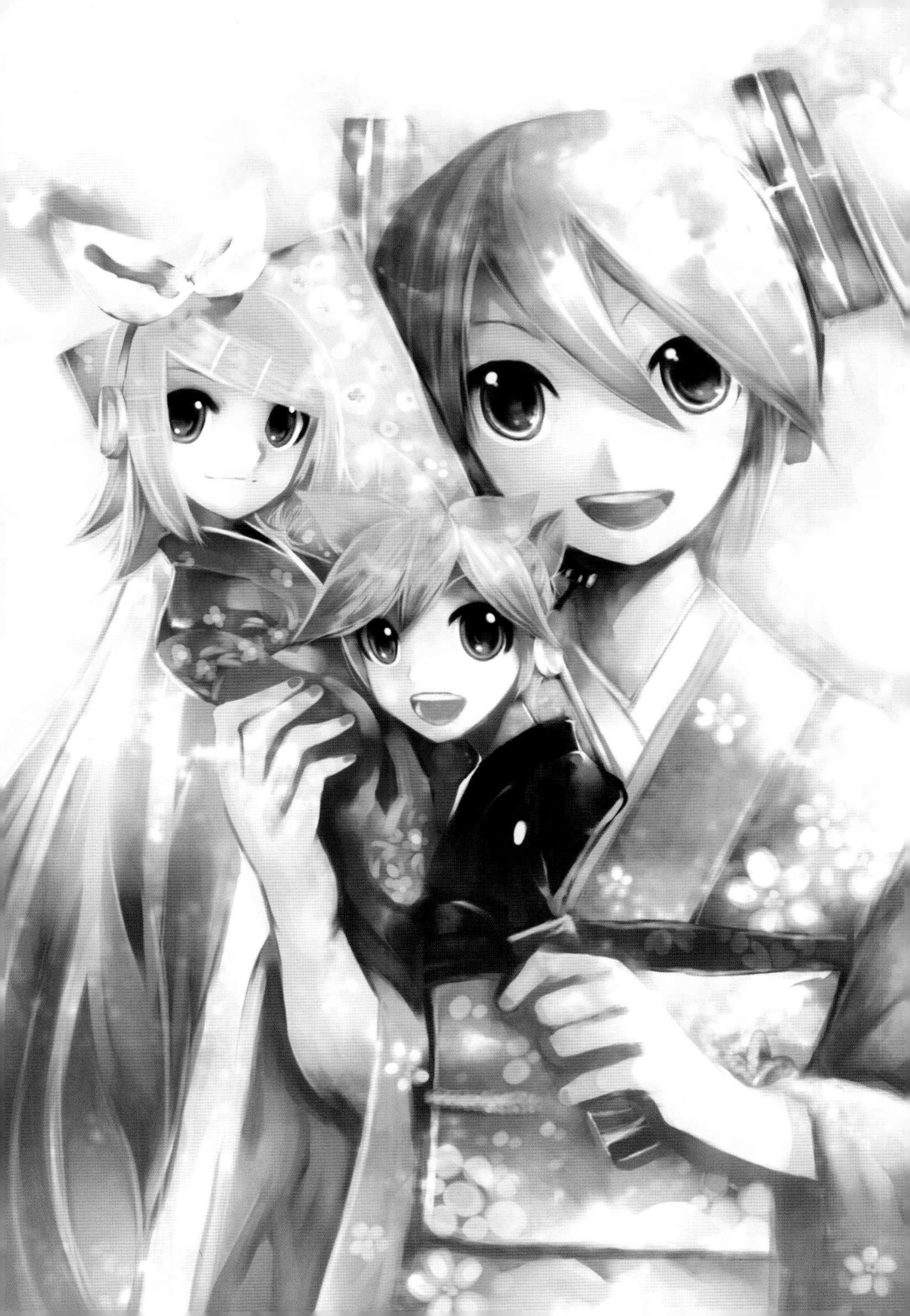

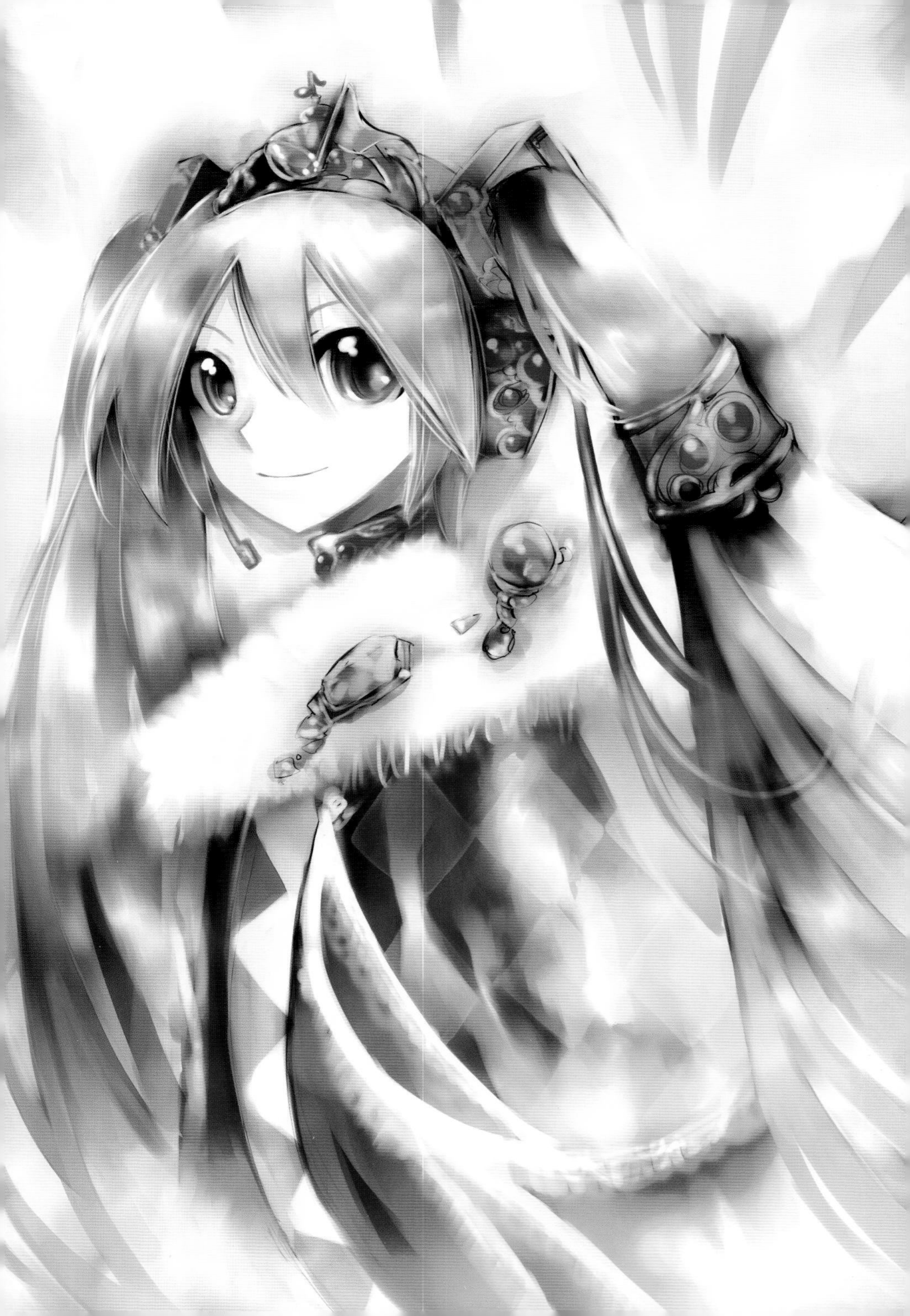

PART 2 TRACK LIST

(10th SONG) SNOW MIX

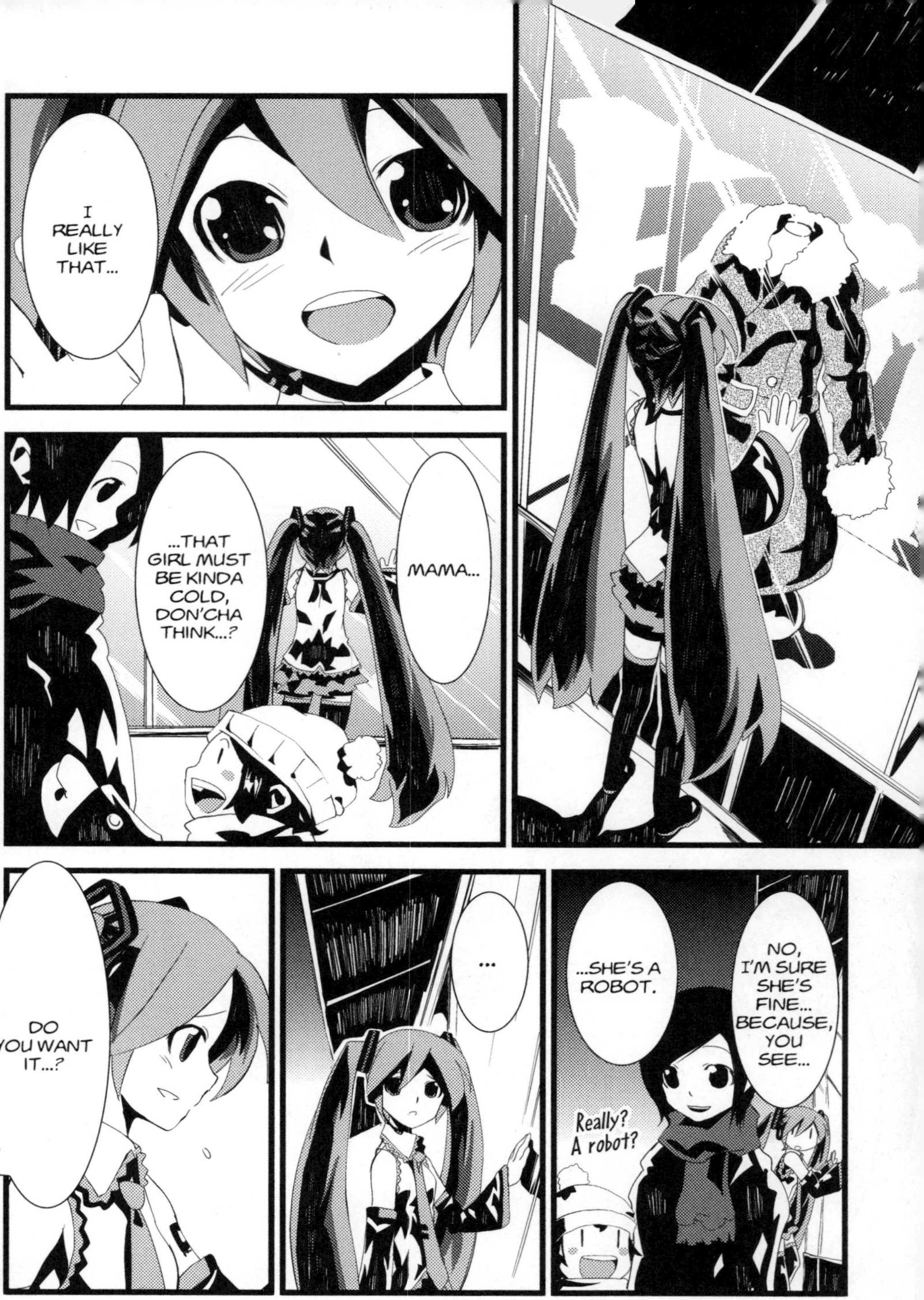
I REALLY LIKE THAT...
MAMA...
...THAT GIRL MUST BE KINDA COLD, DON'CHA THINK...?
NO, I'M SURE SHE'S FINE... BECAUSE, YOU SEE...
...SHE'S A ROBOT.
Really? A robot?
...
DO YOU WANT IT...?

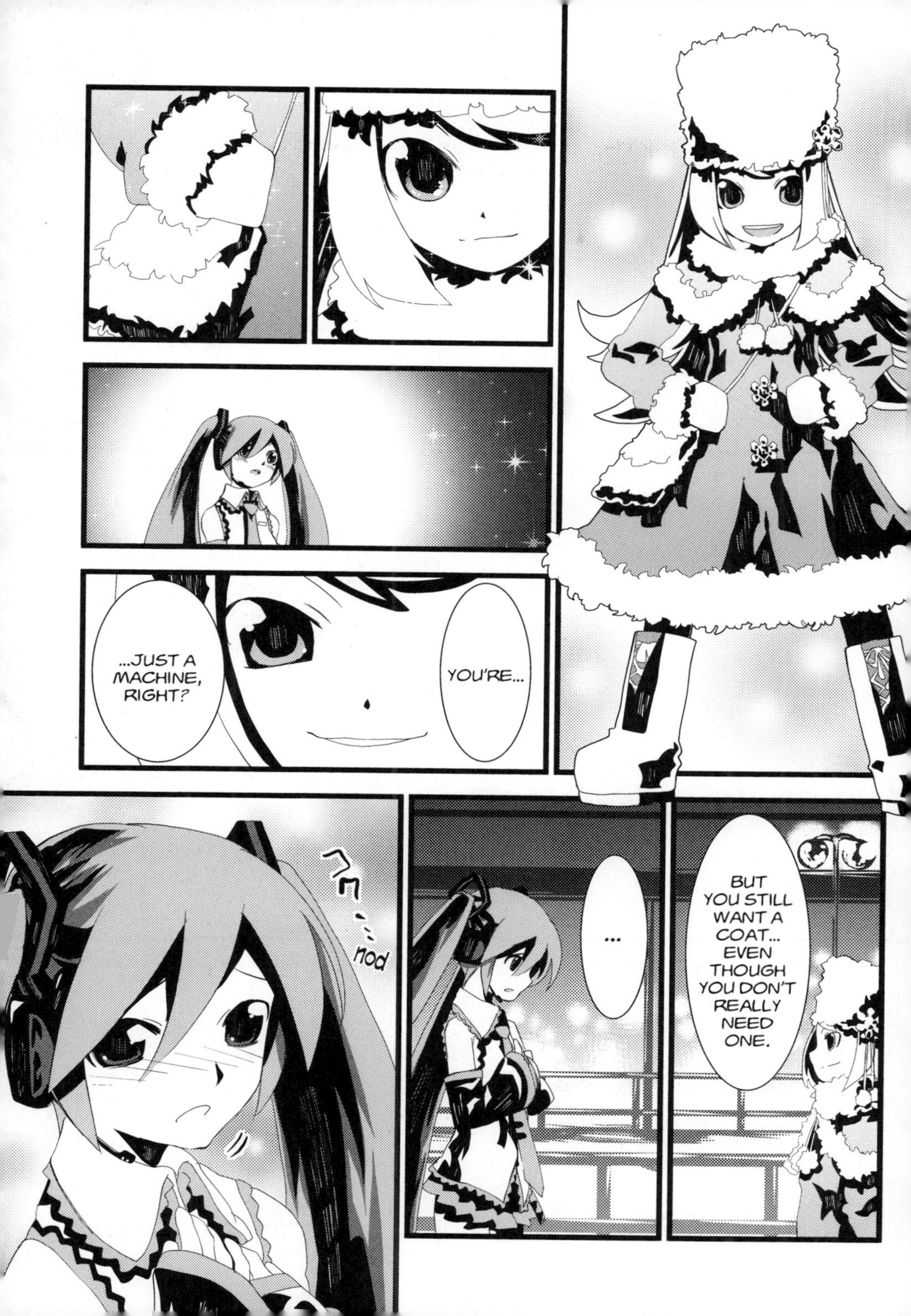
YOU'RE...
...JUST A MACHINE, RIGHT?
BUT YOU STILL WANT A COAT... EVEN THOUGH YOU DON'T REALLY NEED ONE.
...
nod

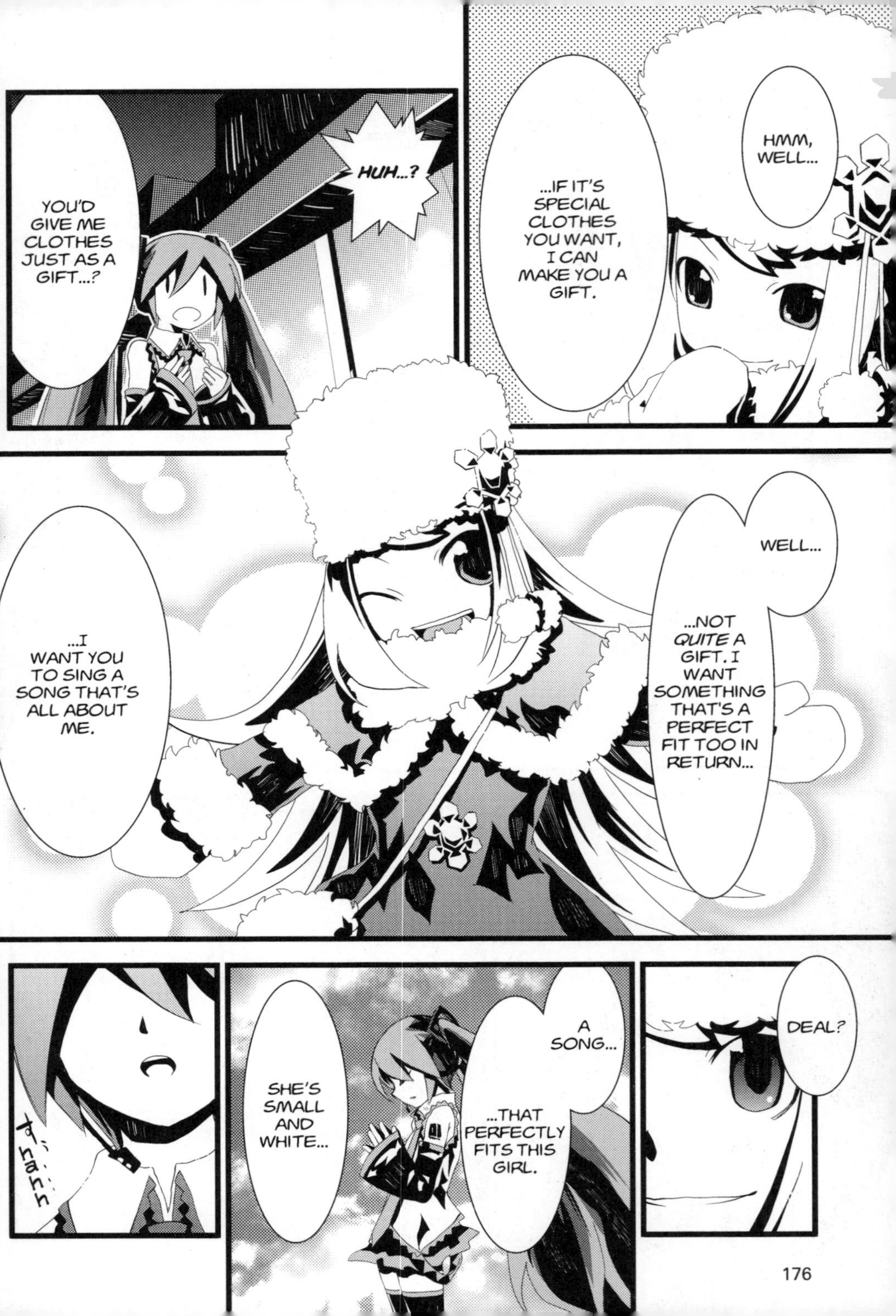
HMM, WELL...
...IF IT'S SPECIAL CLOTHES YOU WANT, I CAN MAKE YOU A GIFT.
HUH...?
YOU'D GIVE ME CLOTHES JUST AS A GIFT...?
WELL...
...NOT *QUITE* A GIFT. I WANT SOMETHING THAT'S A PERFECT FIT TOO IN RETURN...
...I WANT YOU TO SING A SONG THAT'S ALL ABOUT ME.
DEAL?
A SONG...
...THAT PERFECTLY FITS THIS GIRL.
SHE'S SMALL AND WHITE...

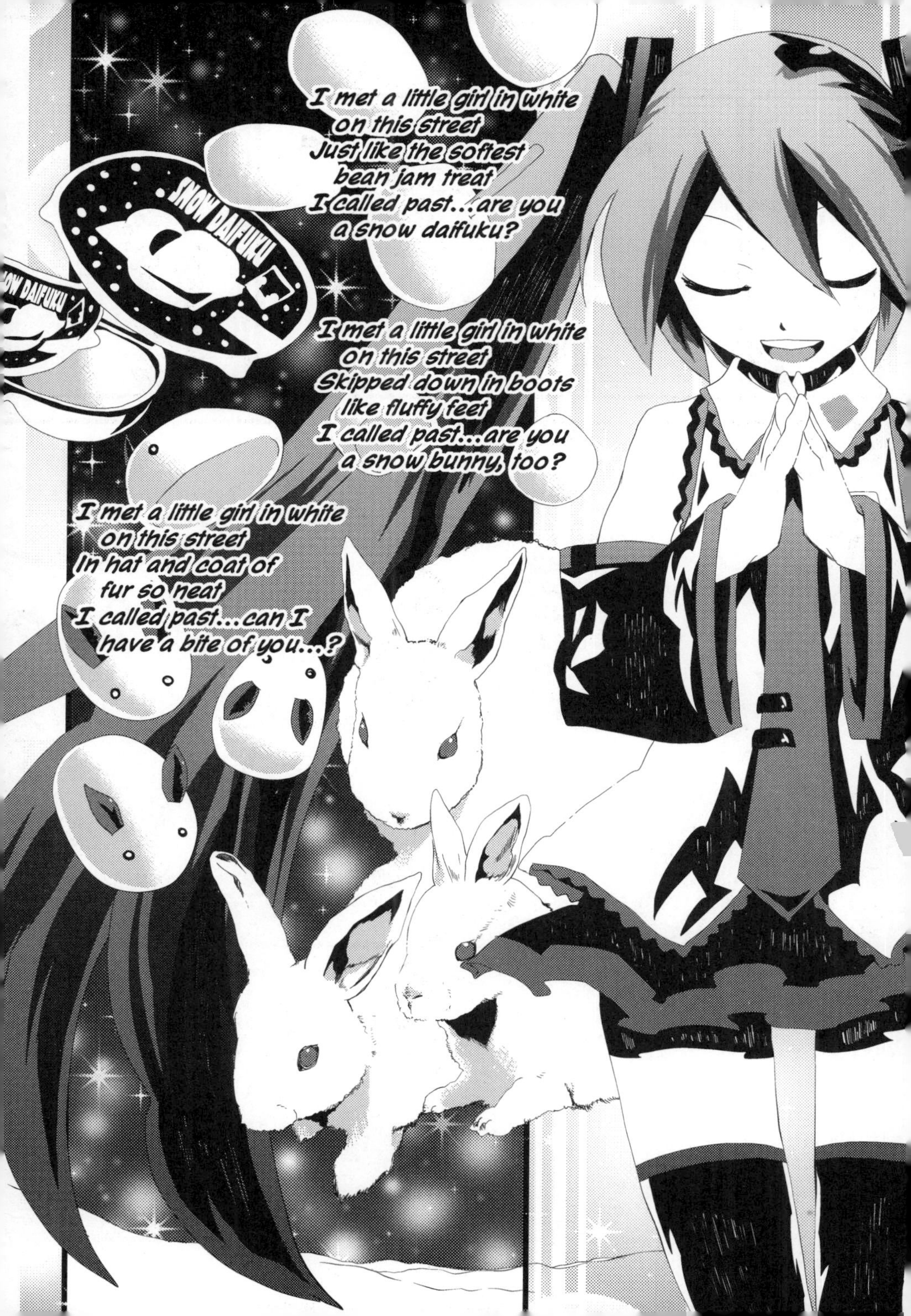
I met a little girl in white
on this street
Just like the softest
bean jam treat
I called past...are you
a snow daifuku?
SNOW DAIFUKU
SNOW DAIFUKU
I met a little girl in white
on this street
Skipped down in boots
like fluffy feet
I called past...are you
a snow bunny, too?
I met a little girl in white
on this street
In hat and coat of
fur so neat
I called past...can I
have a bite of you...?

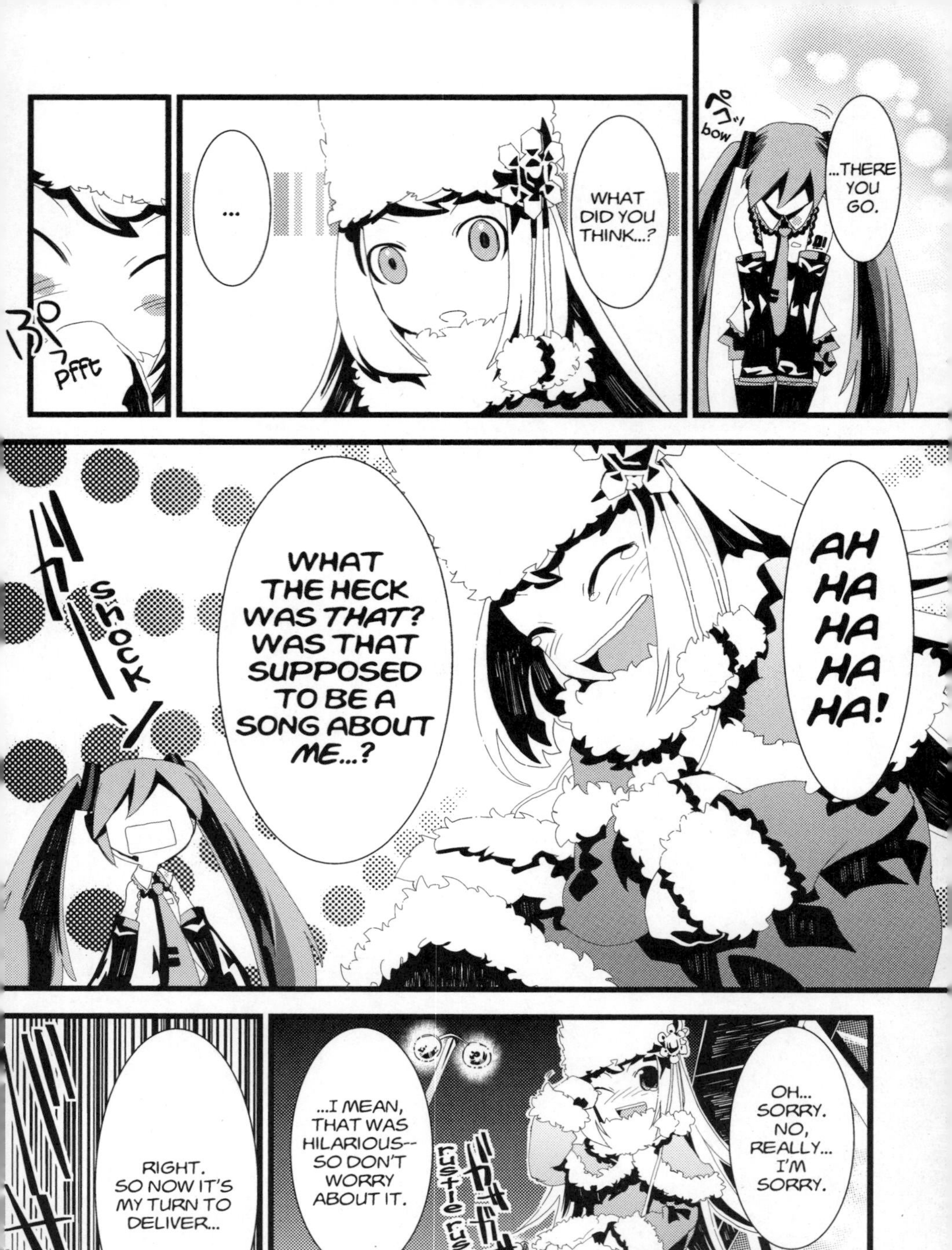
bow
...THERE YOU GO.
WHAT DID YOU THINK...?
...
pfft
AH HA HA HA HA!
WHAT THE HECK WAS THAT? WAS THAT SUPPOSED TO BE A SONG ABOUT ME...?
shock
OH... SORRY. NO, REALLY... I'M SORRY.
...I MEAN, THAT WAS HILARIOUS-- SO DON'T WORRY ABOUT IT.
rustle rustle
RIGHT. SO NOW IT'S MY TURN TO DELIVER...

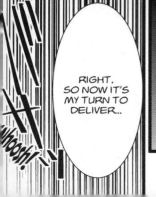

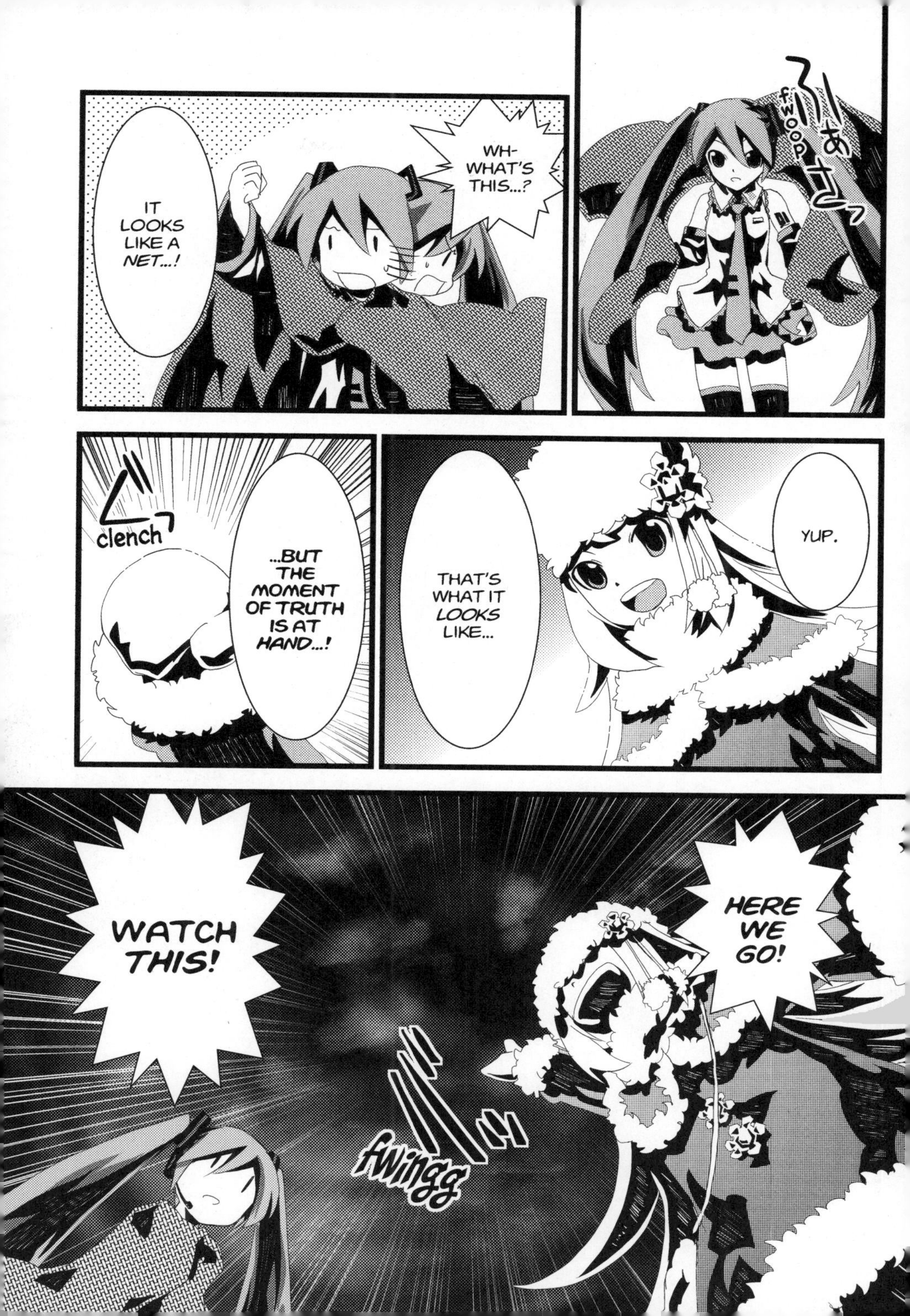
fwoop
WH- WHAT'S THIS...?
IT LOOKS LIKE A NET...!
YUP.
THAT'S WHAT IT LOOKS LIKE...
...BUT THE MOMENT OF TRUTH IS AT HAND...!
clench
HERE WE GO!
WATCH THIS!
fwingg

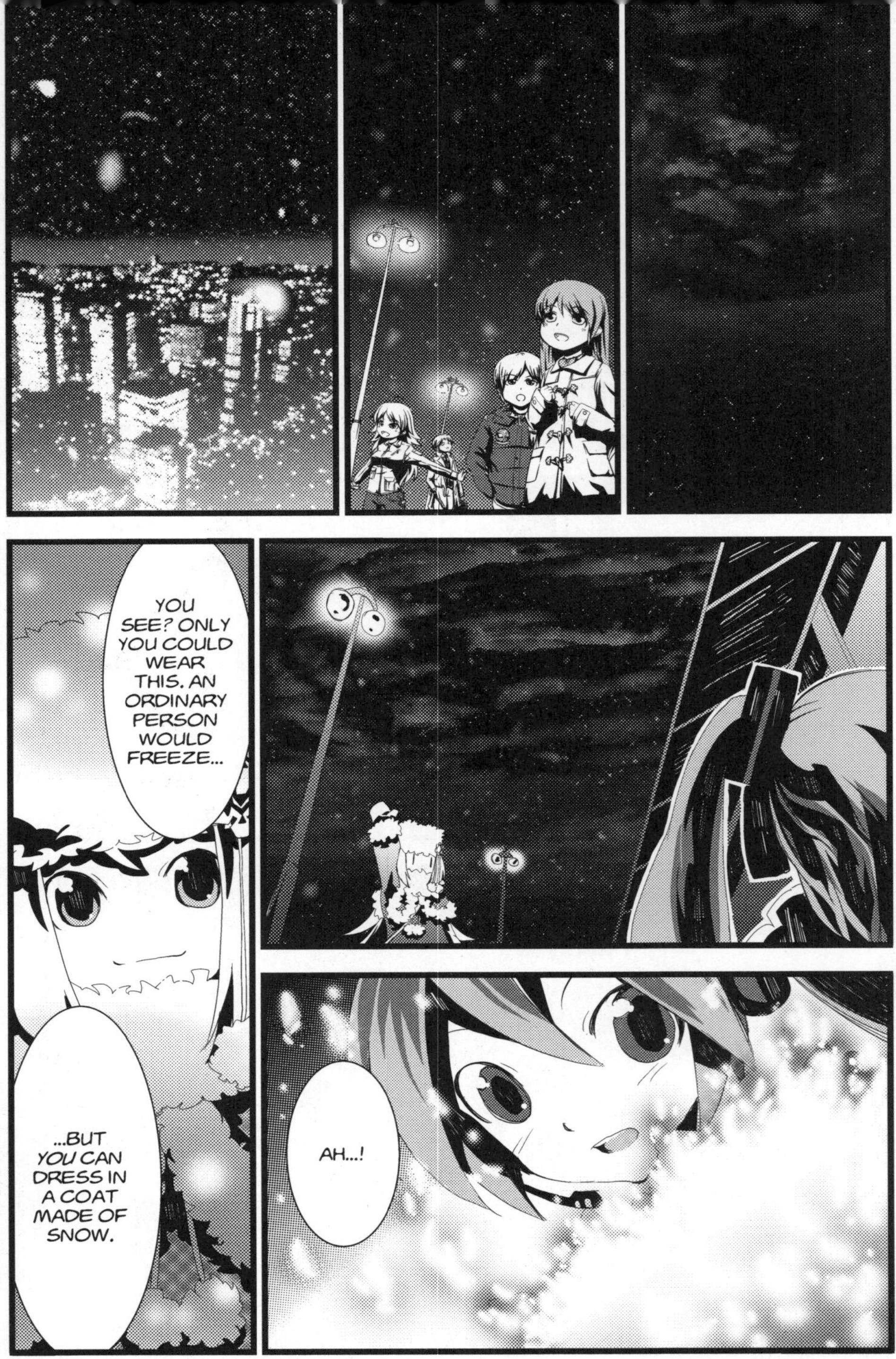
AH...!
YOU SEE? ONLY YOU COULD WEAR THIS. AN ORDINARY PERSON WOULD FREEZE...
...BUT YOU CAN DRESS IN A COAT MADE OF SNOW.

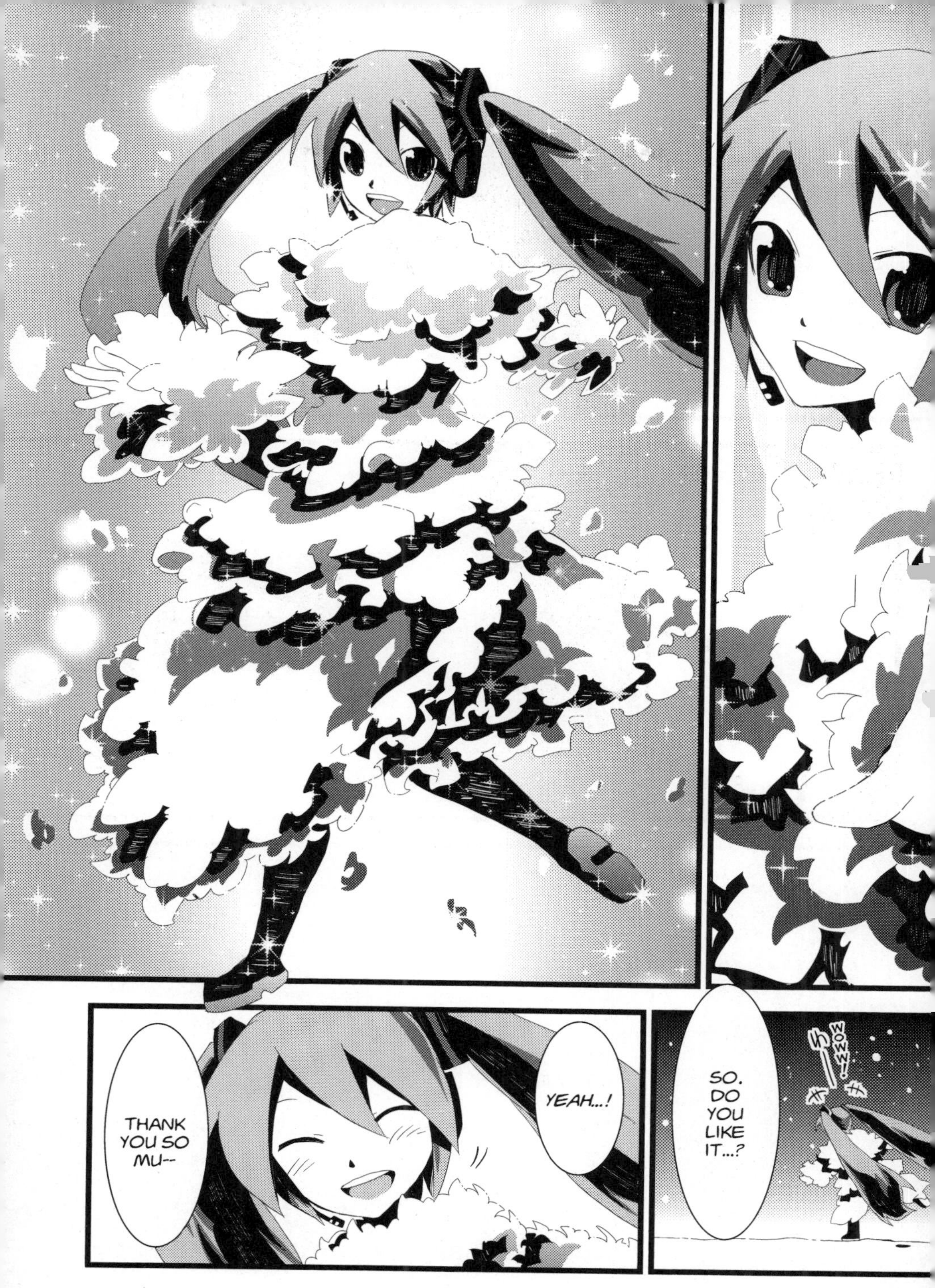
WOWW!
SO. DO YOU LIKE IT...?
YEAH...!
THANK YOU SO MU--

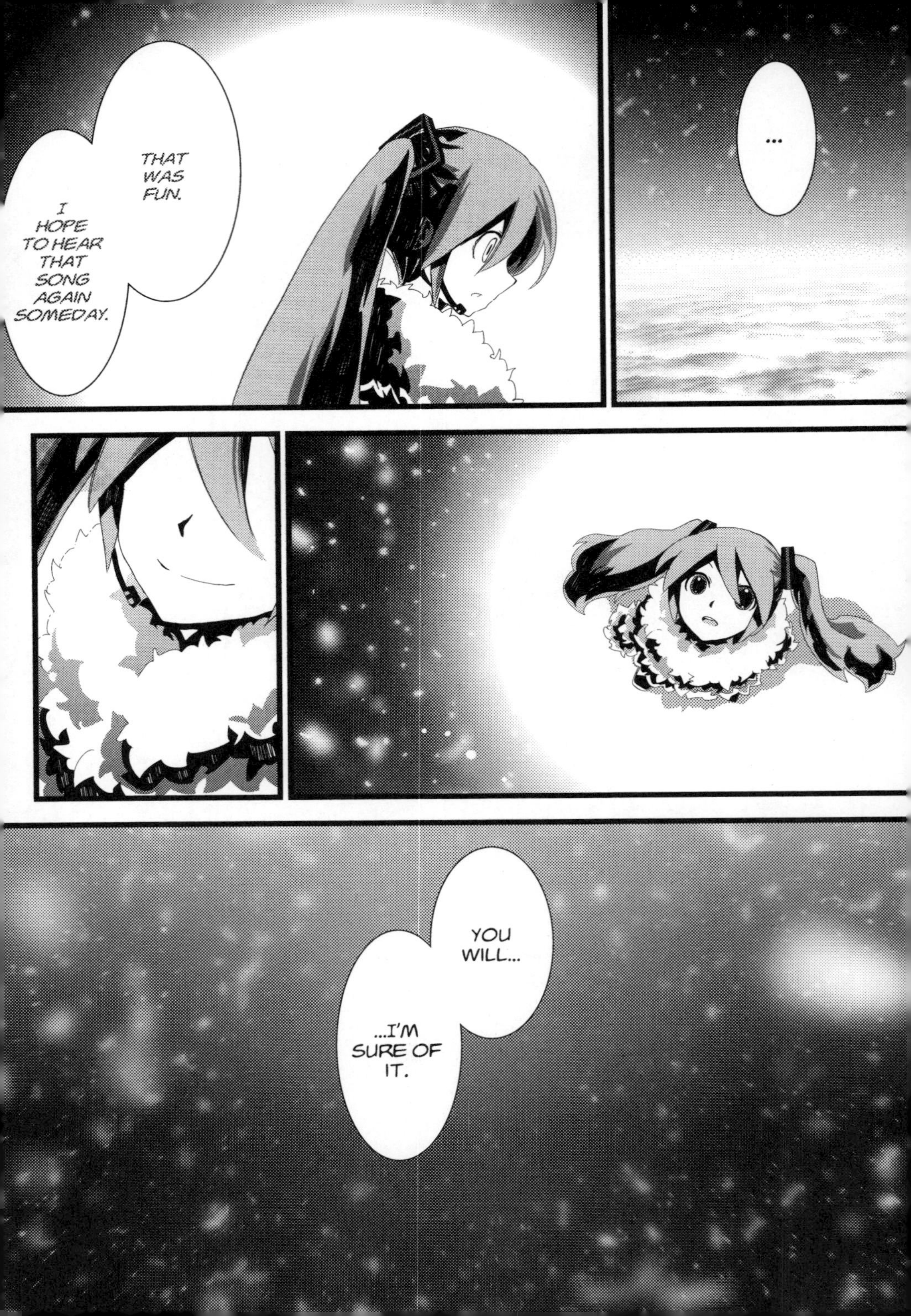
...
THAT WAS FUN.
I HOPE TO HEAR THAT SONG AGAIN SOMEDAY.
YOU WILL...
...I'M SURE OF IT.

(11th SONG) PAIN MIX

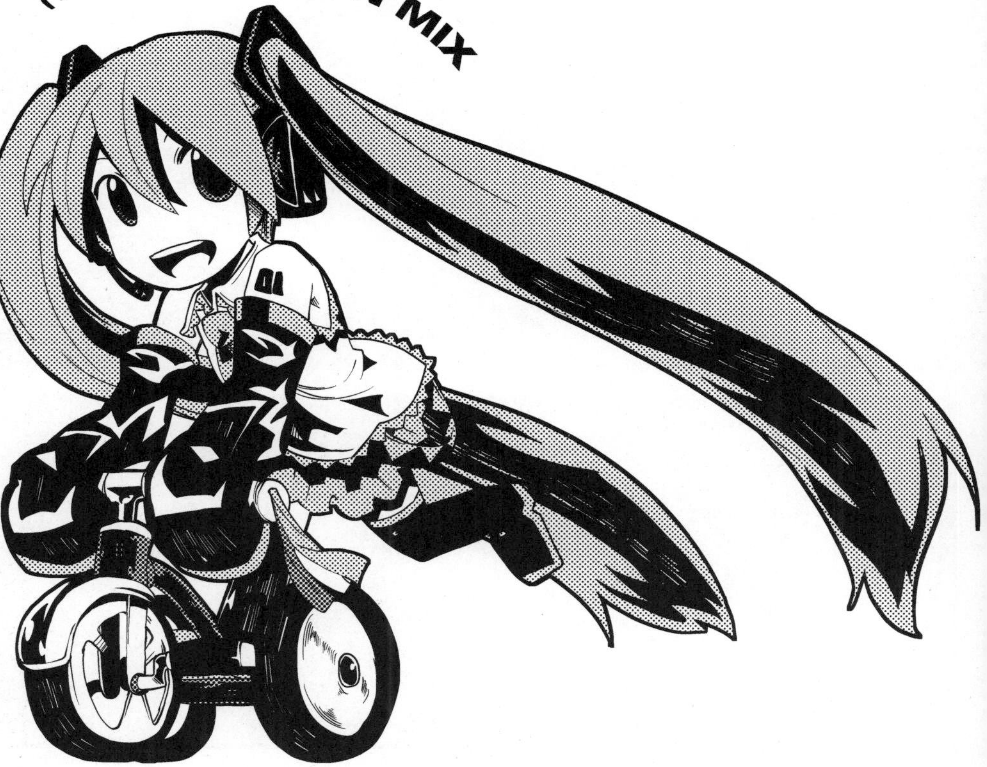

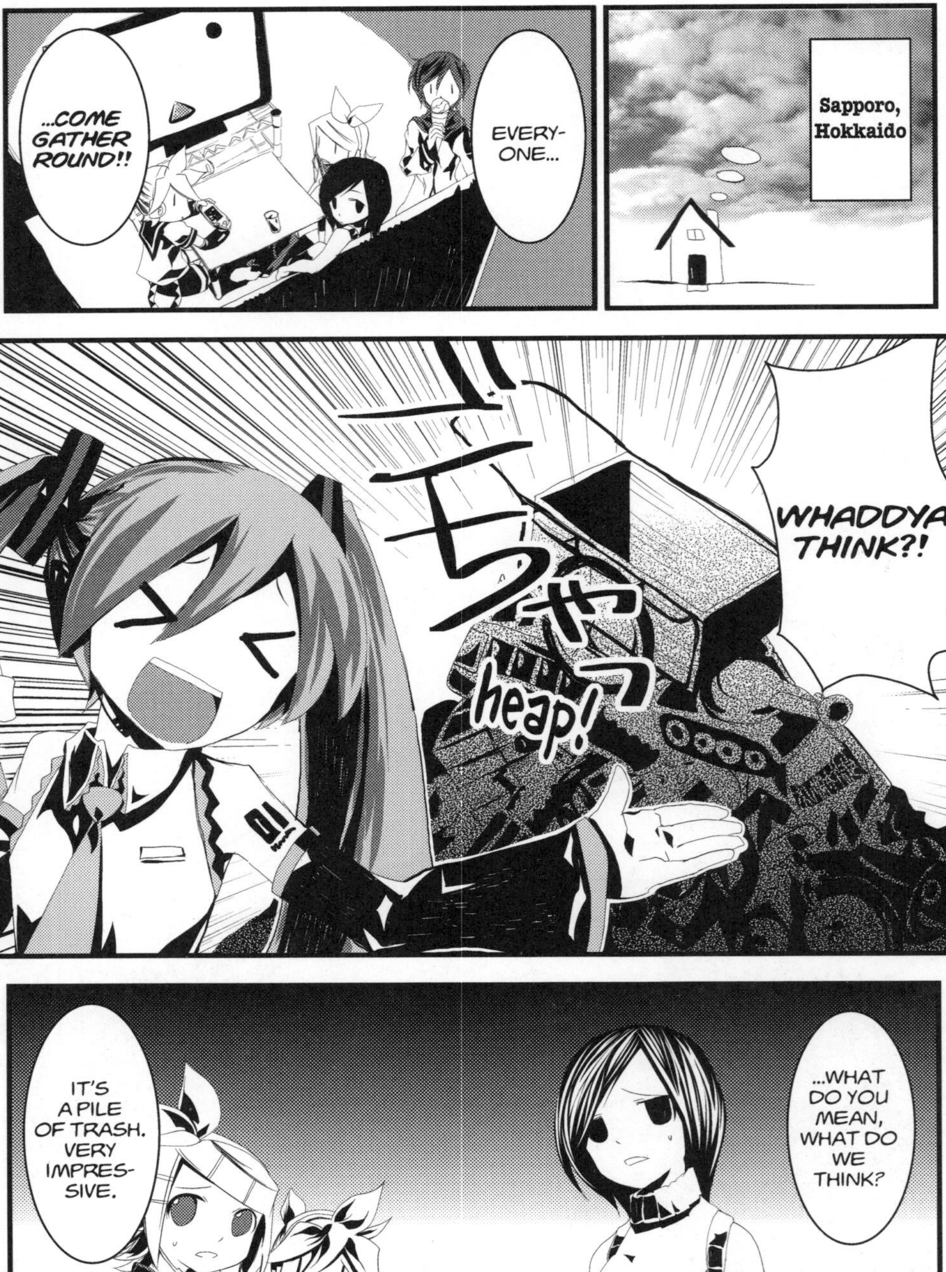
Sapporo, Hokkaido
EVERY-ONE...
...COME GATHER ROUND!!
WHADDYA THINK?!
heap!
...WHAT DO YOU MEAN, WHAT DO WE THINK?
IT'S A PILE OF TRASH. VERY IMPRESSIVE.

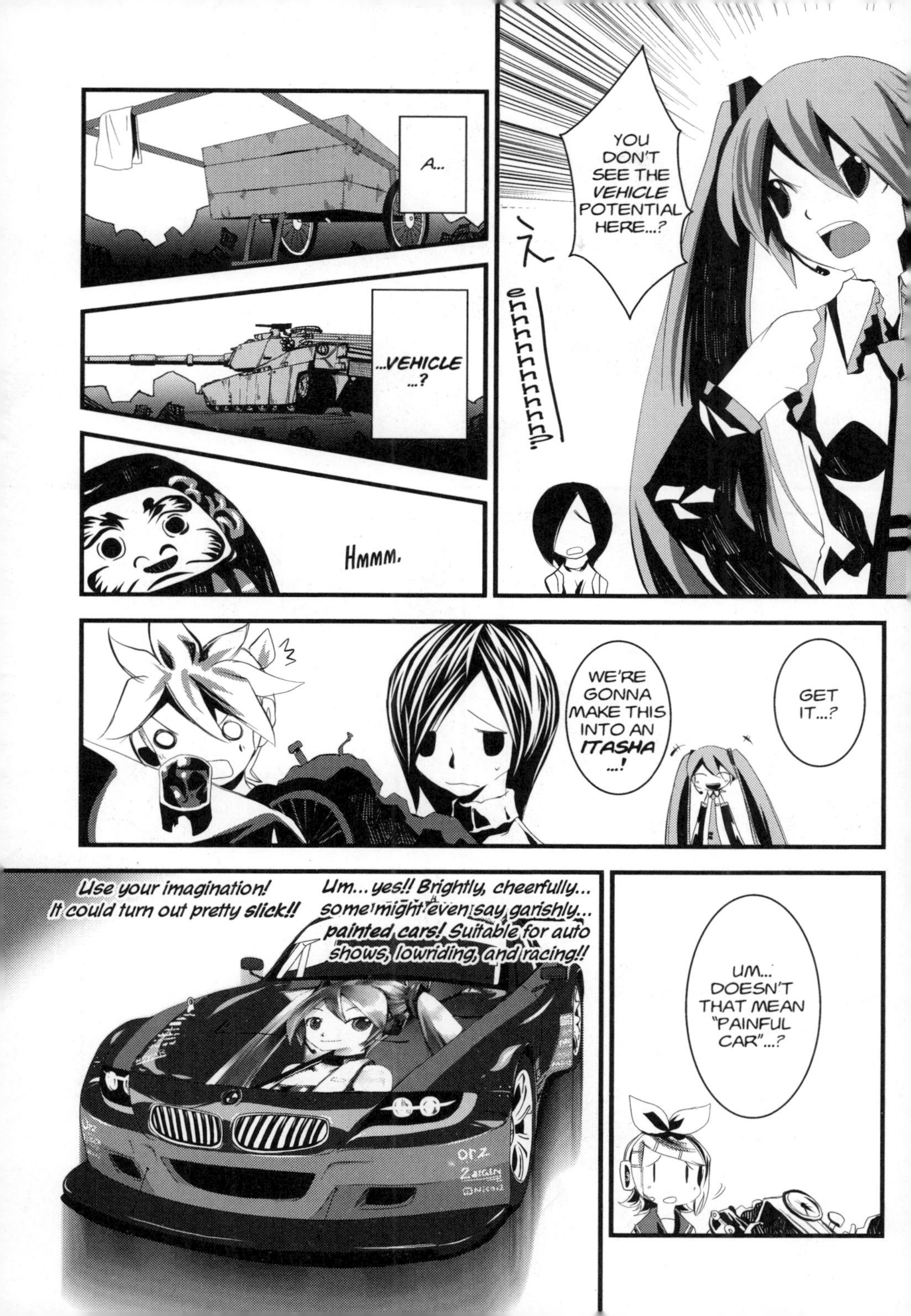

YOU DON'T SEE THE VEHICLE POTENTIAL HERE...?
え~
ehhhhhhhhh?
A...
...VEHICLE ...?
Hmmm.
GET IT...?
WE'RE GONNA MAKE THIS INTO AN ITASHA ...!
UM... DOESN'T THAT MEAN "PAINFUL CAR"...?
Um... yes!! Brightly, cheerfully... some might even say garishly... painted cars! Suitable for auto shows, lowriding, and racing!!
Use your imagination! It could turn out pretty slick!!

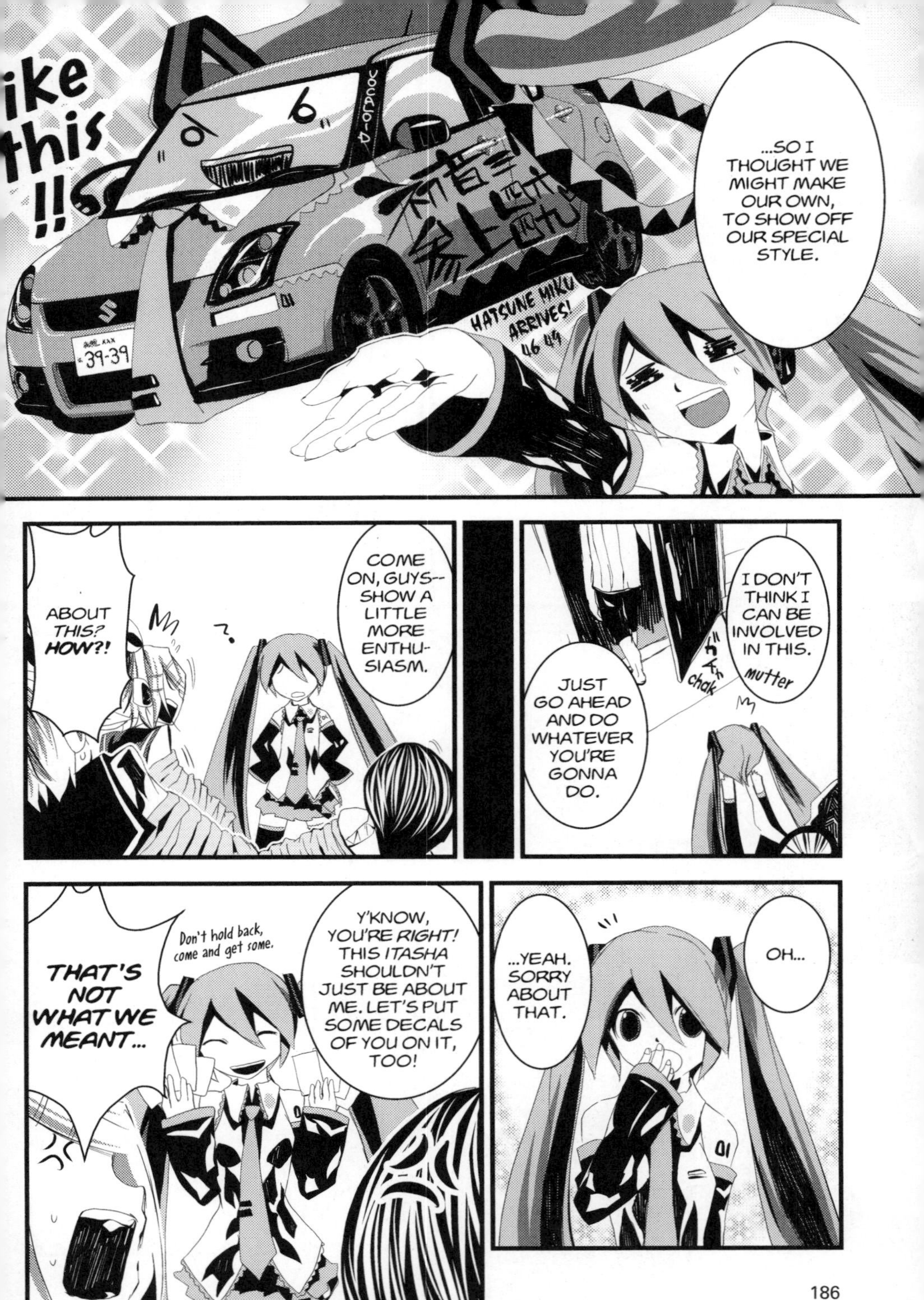
...SO I THOUGHT WE MIGHT MAKE OUR OWN, TO SHOW OFF OUR SPECIAL STYLE.
HATSUNE MIKU ARRIVES!
VOCALOID
39-39
ike this!!
I DON'T THINK I CAN BE INVOLVED IN THIS.
mutter
chak
JUST GO AHEAD AND DO WHATEVER YOU'RE GONNA DO.
COME ON, GUYS-- SHOW A LITTLE MORE ENTHUSIASM.
ABOUT THIS? HOW?!
OH...
...YEAH. SORRY ABOUT THAT.
Y'KNOW, YOU'RE RIGHT! THIS ITASHA SHOULDN'T JUST BE ABOUT ME. LET'S PUT SOME DECALS OF YOU ON IT, TOO!
Don't hold back, come and get some.
THAT'S NOT WHAT WE MEANT...

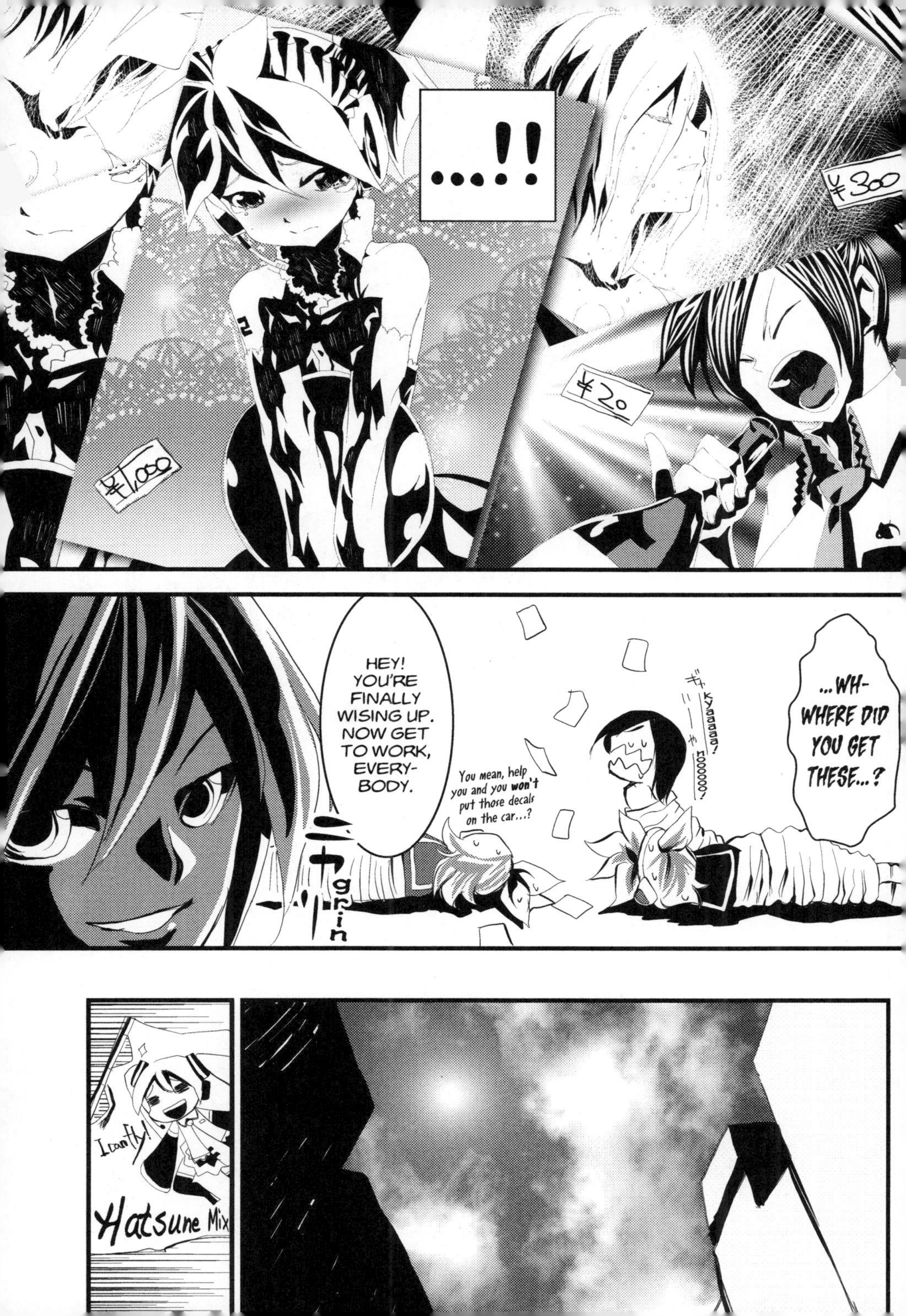
¥300
¥20
...!!
¥1,000
...WH- WHERE DID YOU GET THESE...?
ギャ Kyaaaaaa!
いーや nOOOOOO!
You mean, help you and you won't put those decals on the car...?
HEY! YOU'RE FINALLY WISING UP. NOW GET TO WORK, EVERY-BODY.
ニヤ grin
I can fly!
Hatsune Mix

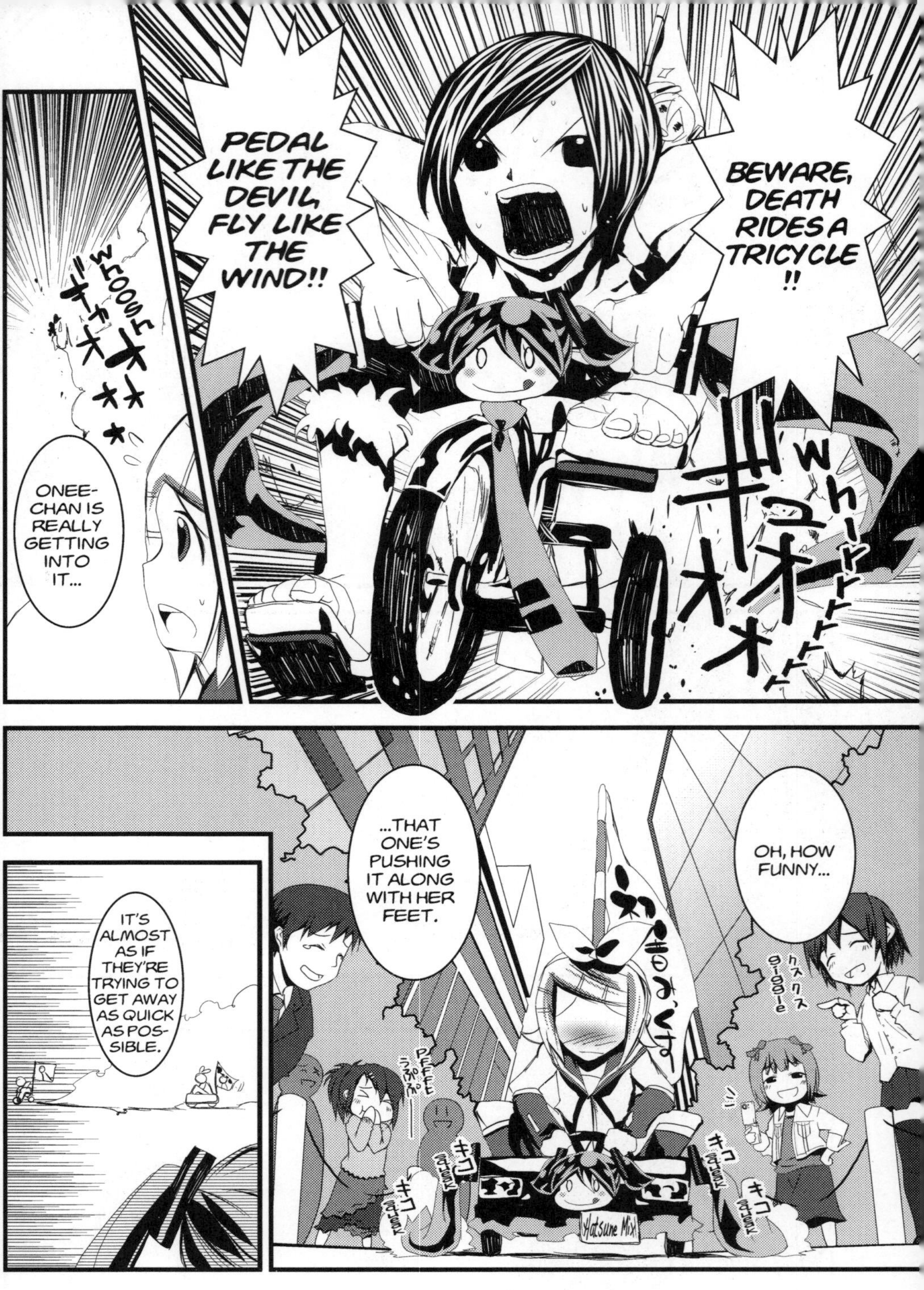
BEWARE, DEATH RIDES A TRICYCLE!!
PEDAL LIKE THE DEVIL, FLY LIKE THE WIND!!
WHOOSH
ONEE-CHAN IS REALLY GETTING INTO IT...
OH, HOW FUNNY...
giggle
...THAT ONE'S PUSHING IT ALONG WITH HER FEET.
PFFFT
squeak
squeak
squeak
squeak
Hatsune Mix
IT'S ALMOST AS IF THEY'RE TRYING TO GET AWAY AS QUICK AS POSSIBLE.

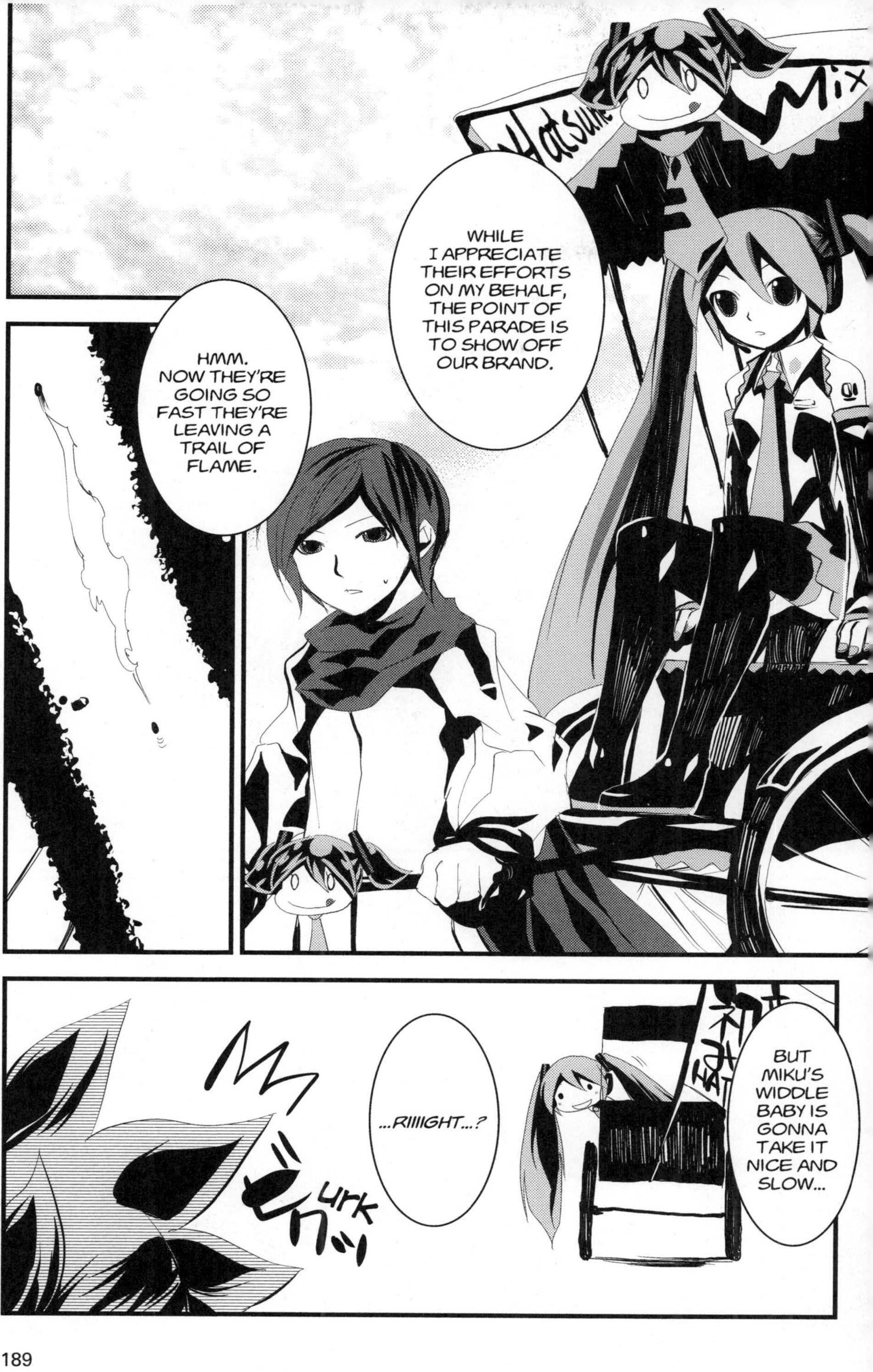
WHILE I APPRECIATE THEIR EFFORTS ON MY BEHALF, THE POINT OF THIS PARADE IS TO SHOW OFF OUR BRAND.
HMM. NOW THEY'RE GOING SO FAST THEY'RE LEAVING A TRAIL OF FLAME.
BUT MIKU'S WIDDLE BABY IS GONNA TAKE IT NICE AND SLOW...
...RIIIGHT...?
urk

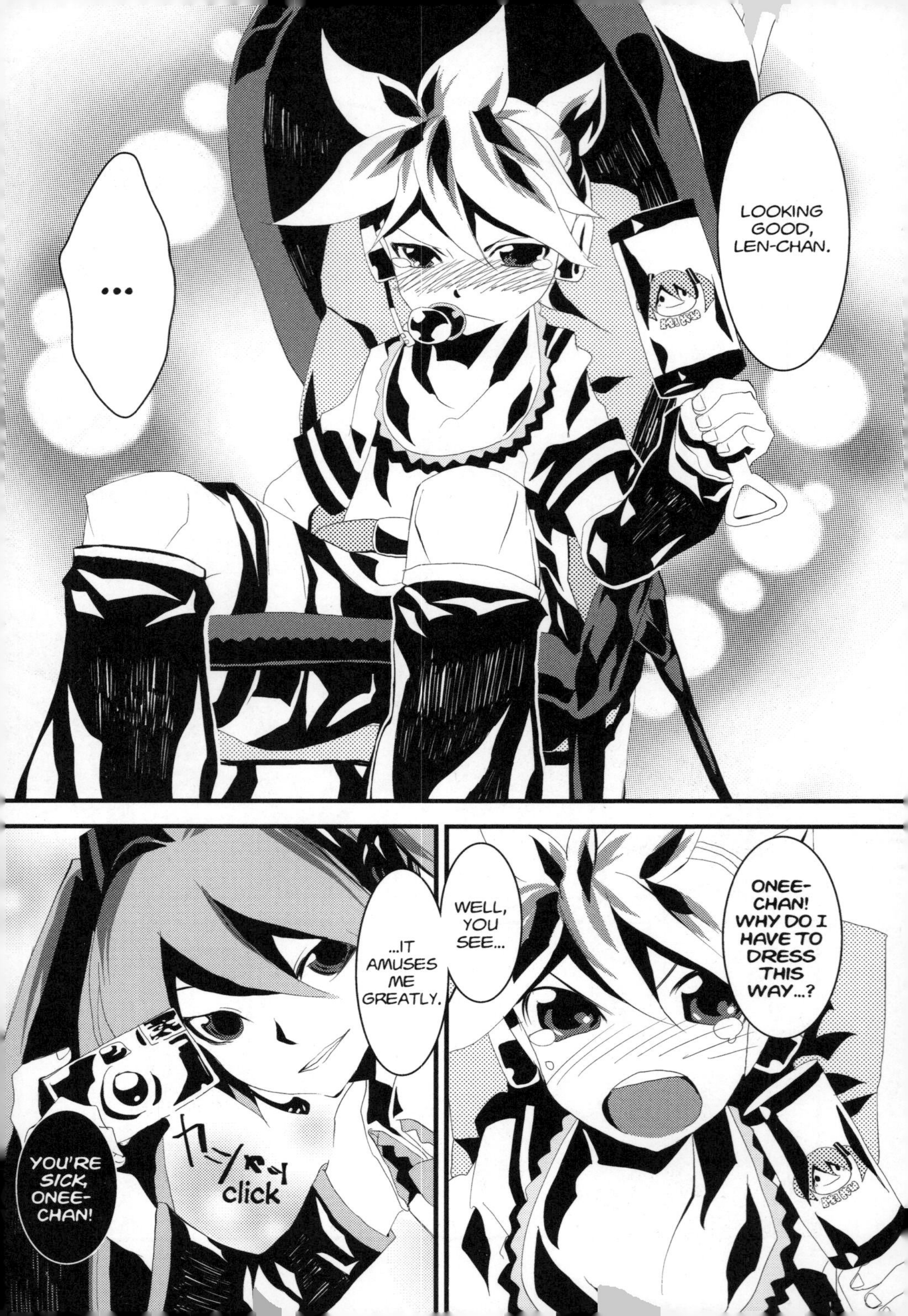
LOOKING GOOD, LEN-CHAN.
...
ONEE-CHAN! WHY DO I HAVE TO DRESS THIS WAY...?
WELL, YOU SEE...
...IT AMUSES ME GREATLY.
click
YOU'RE SICK, ONEE-CHAN!

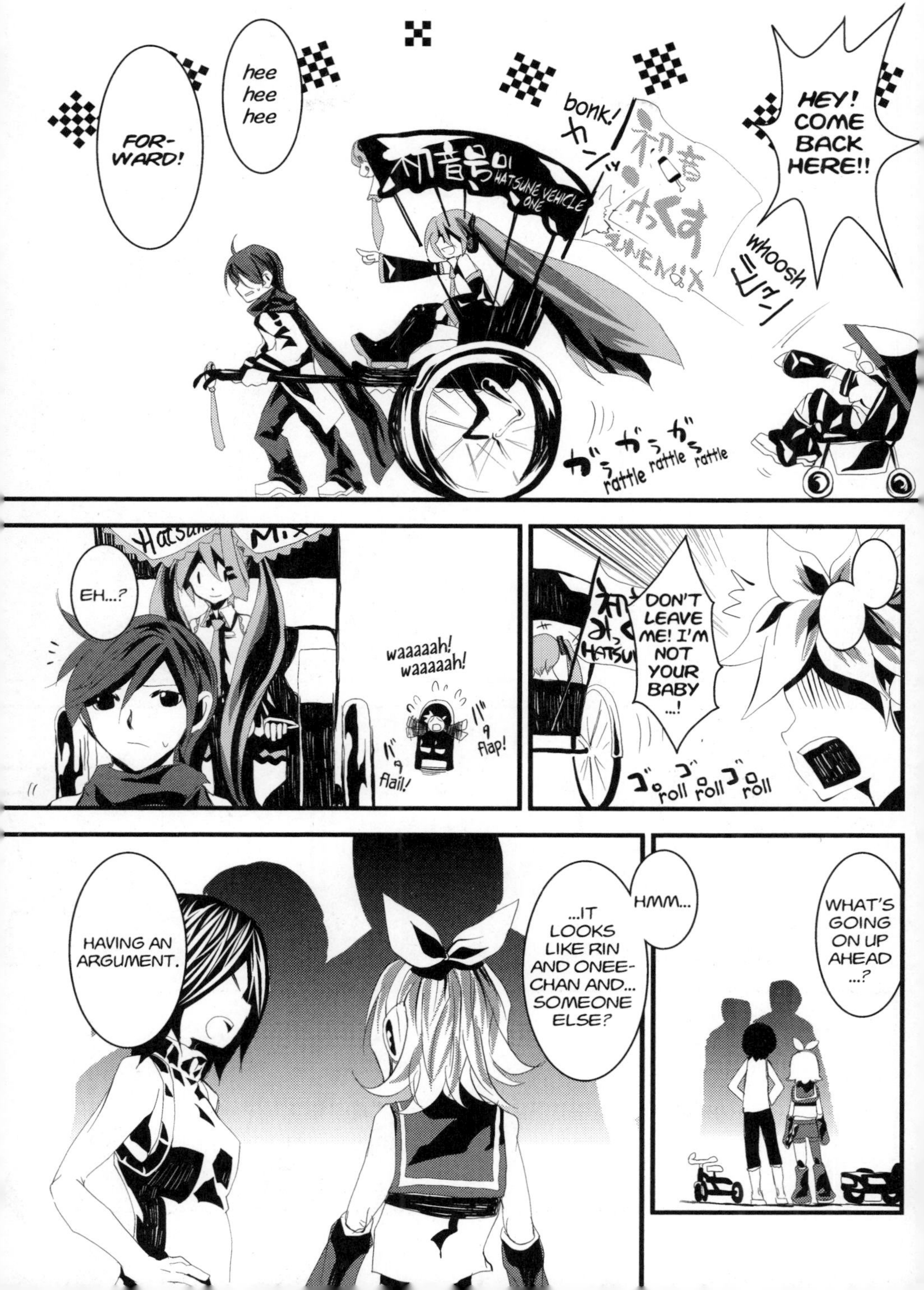
HEY! COME BACK HERE!!
whoosh
bonk!
HATSUNE VEHICLE ONE
hee hee hee
FOR-WARD!
rattle rattle rattle
DON'T LEAVE ME! I'M NOT YOUR BABY ...!
roll roll roll
waaaaah! waaaaah!
flap!
flail!
EH...?
WHAT'S GOING ON UP AHEAD ...?
HMM...
...IT LOOKS LIKE RIN AND ONEE-CHAN AND... SOMEONE ELSE?
HAVING AN ARGUMENT.

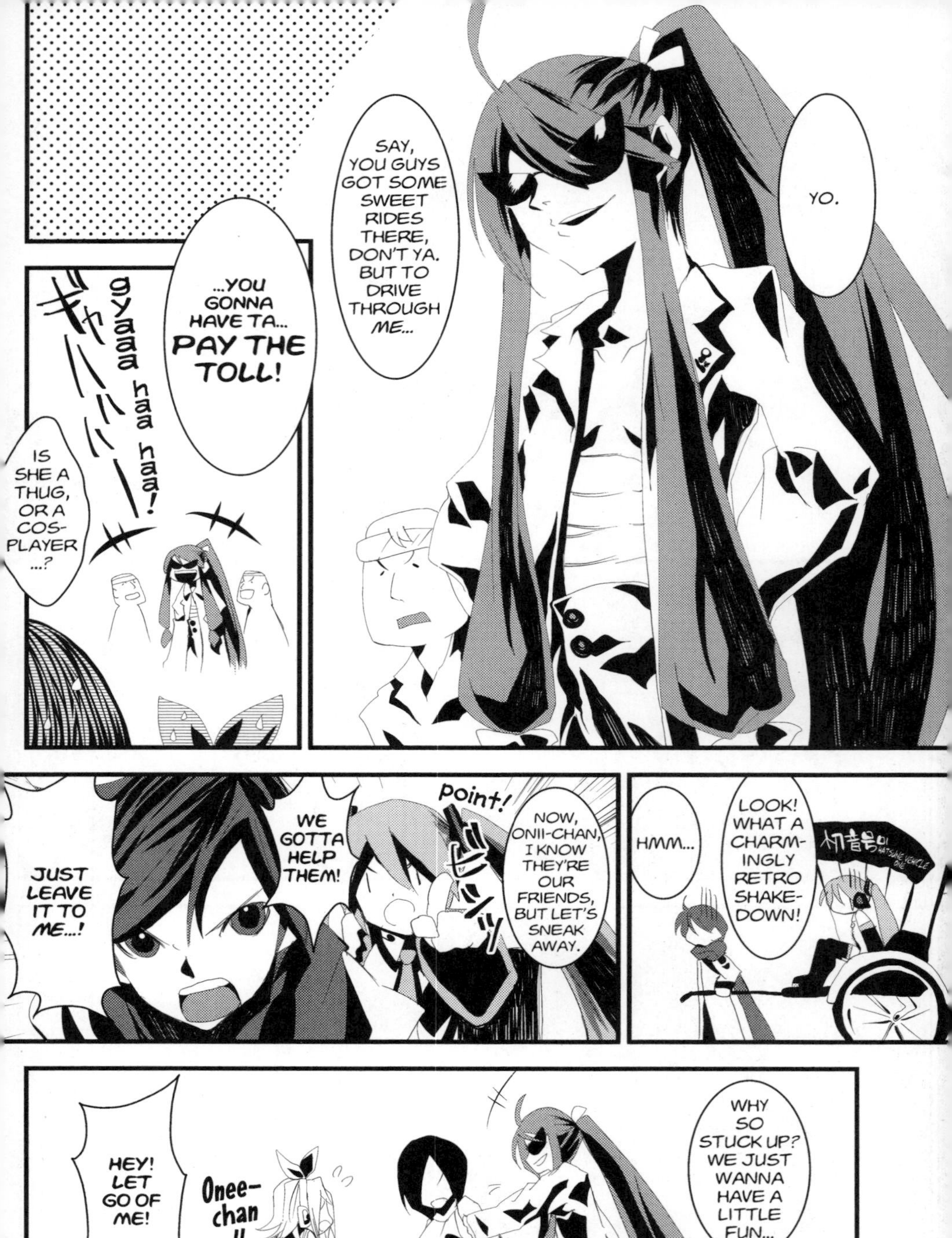
YO.
SAY, YOU GUYS GOT SOME SWEET RIDES THERE, DON'T YA. BUT TO DRIVE THROUGH ME...
...YOU GONNA HAVE TA... PAY THE TOLL!
gyaaa haa haa haa!
IS SHE A THUG, OR A COS-PLAYER ...?
HMM...
LOOK! WHAT A CHARM-INGLY RETRO SHAKE-DOWN!
HATSUNE VEHICLE ONE
NOW, ONII-CHAN, I KNOW THEY'RE OUR FRIENDS, BUT LET'S SNEAK AWAY.
Point!
WE GOTTA HELP THEM!
JUST LEAVE IT TO ME...!
WHY SO STUCK UP? WE JUST WANNA HAVE A LITTLE FUN...
Onee-chan !!
HEY! LET GO OF ME!

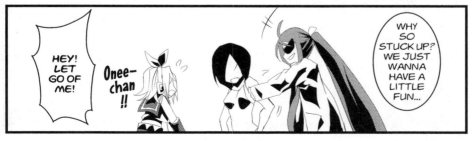

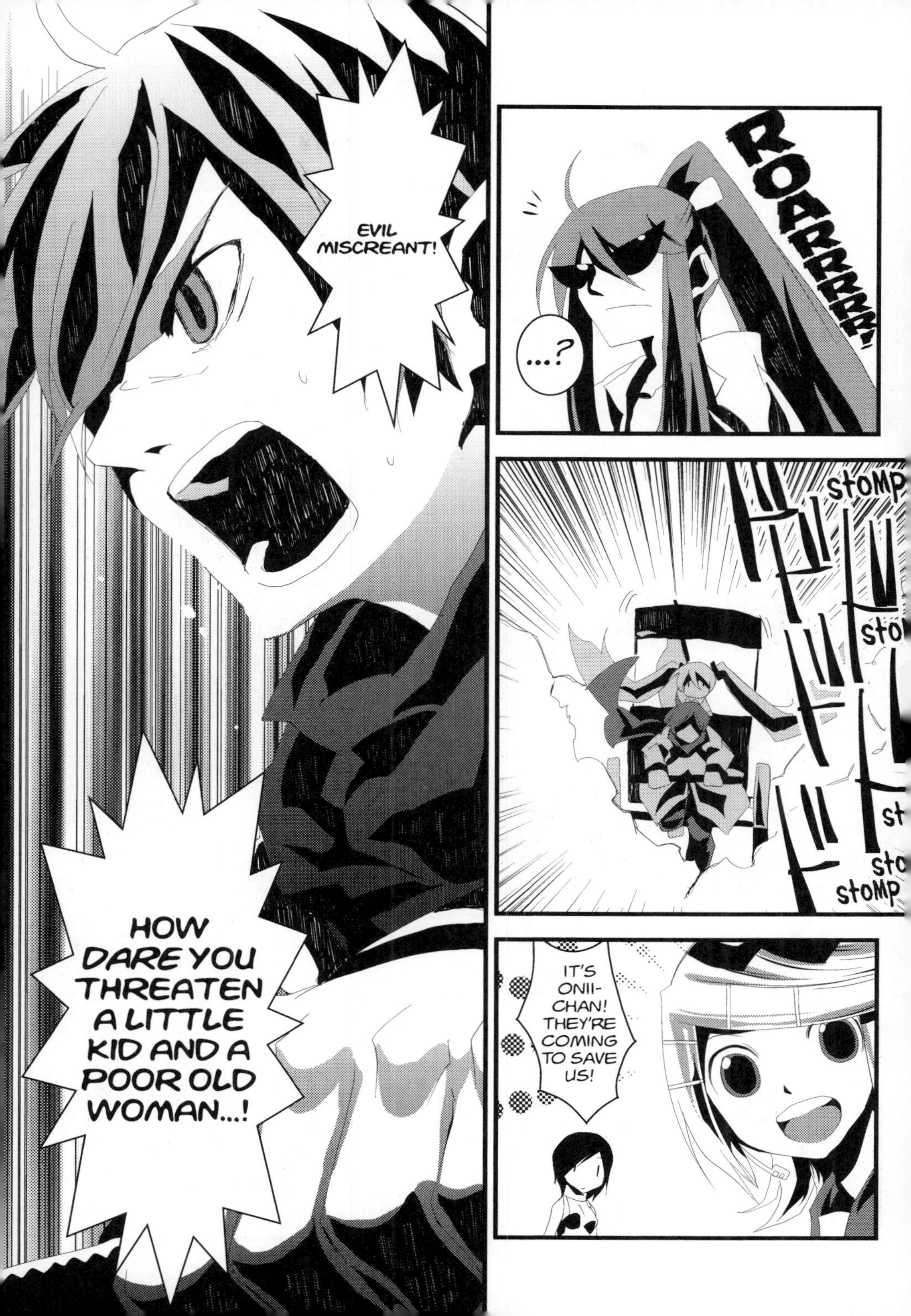
ROARRRRR!
...?
stomp
stomp
IT'S ONII-CHAN! THEY'RE COMING TO SAVE US!
EVIL MISCREANT!
HOW DARE YOU THREATEN A LITTLE KID AND A POOR OLD WOMAN...!

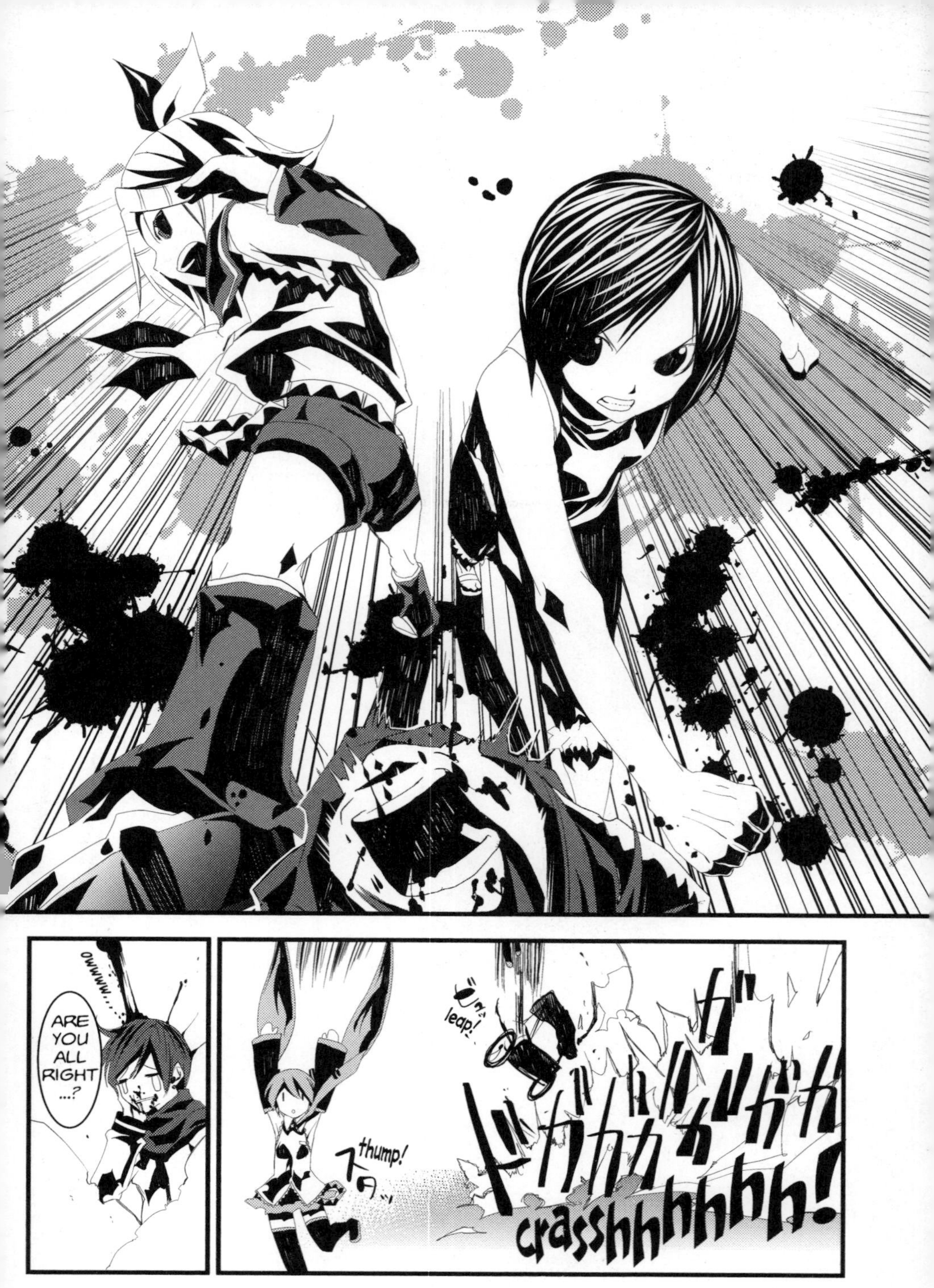

leap!
thump!
crasshhhhhhh!
OWWW....
ARE YOU ALL RIGHT ...?

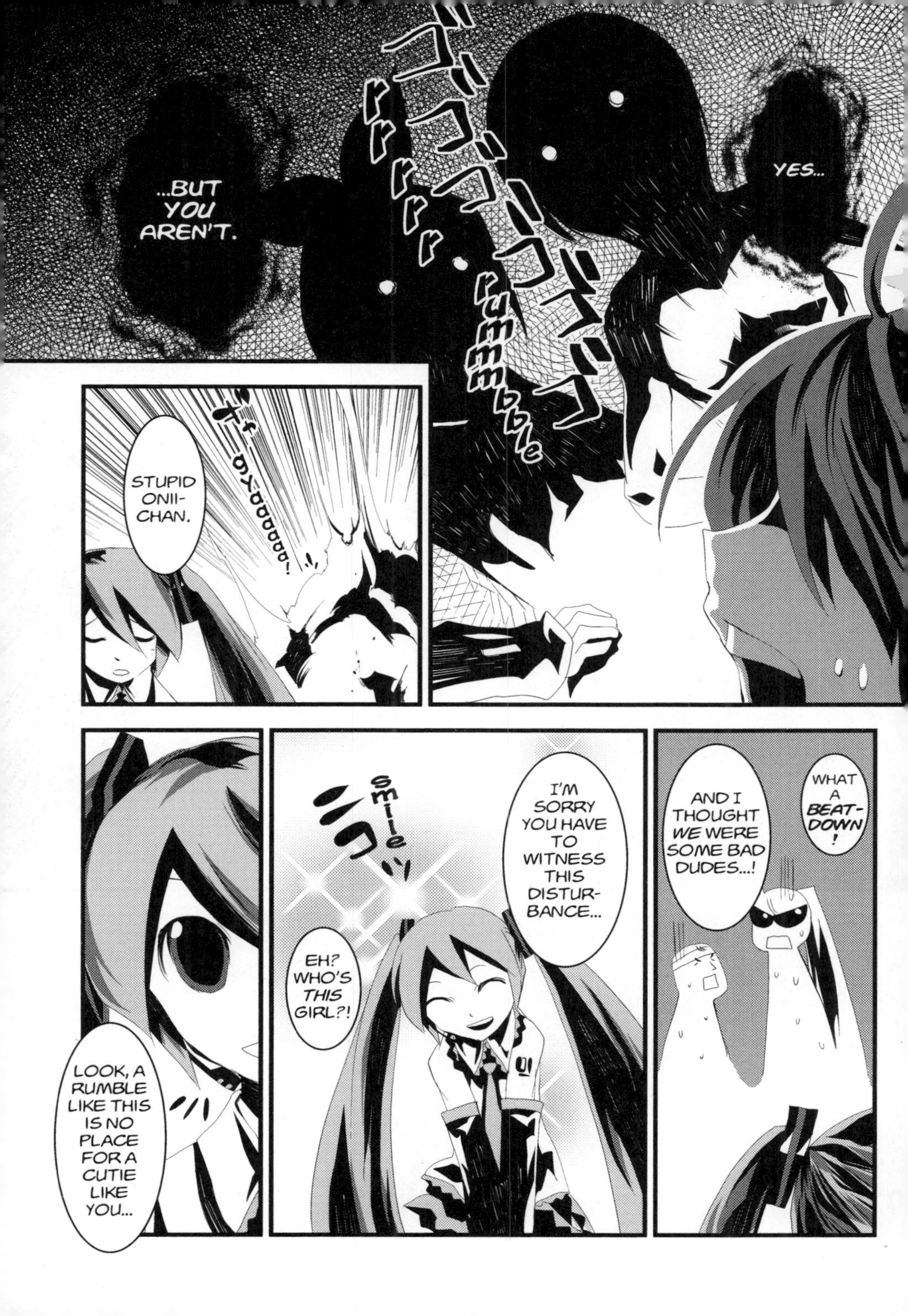
YES...
rummmbble
...BUT YOU AREN'T.
gyaaaaaa!
STUPID ONII-CHAN.
WHAT A BEAT-DOWN!
AND I THOUGHT WE WERE SOME BAD DUDES...!
I'M SORRY YOU HAVE TO WITNESS THIS DISTURBANCE...
smile
EH? WHO'S THIS GIRL?!
LOOK, A RUMBLE LIKE THIS IS NO PLACE FOR A CUTIE LIKE YOU...

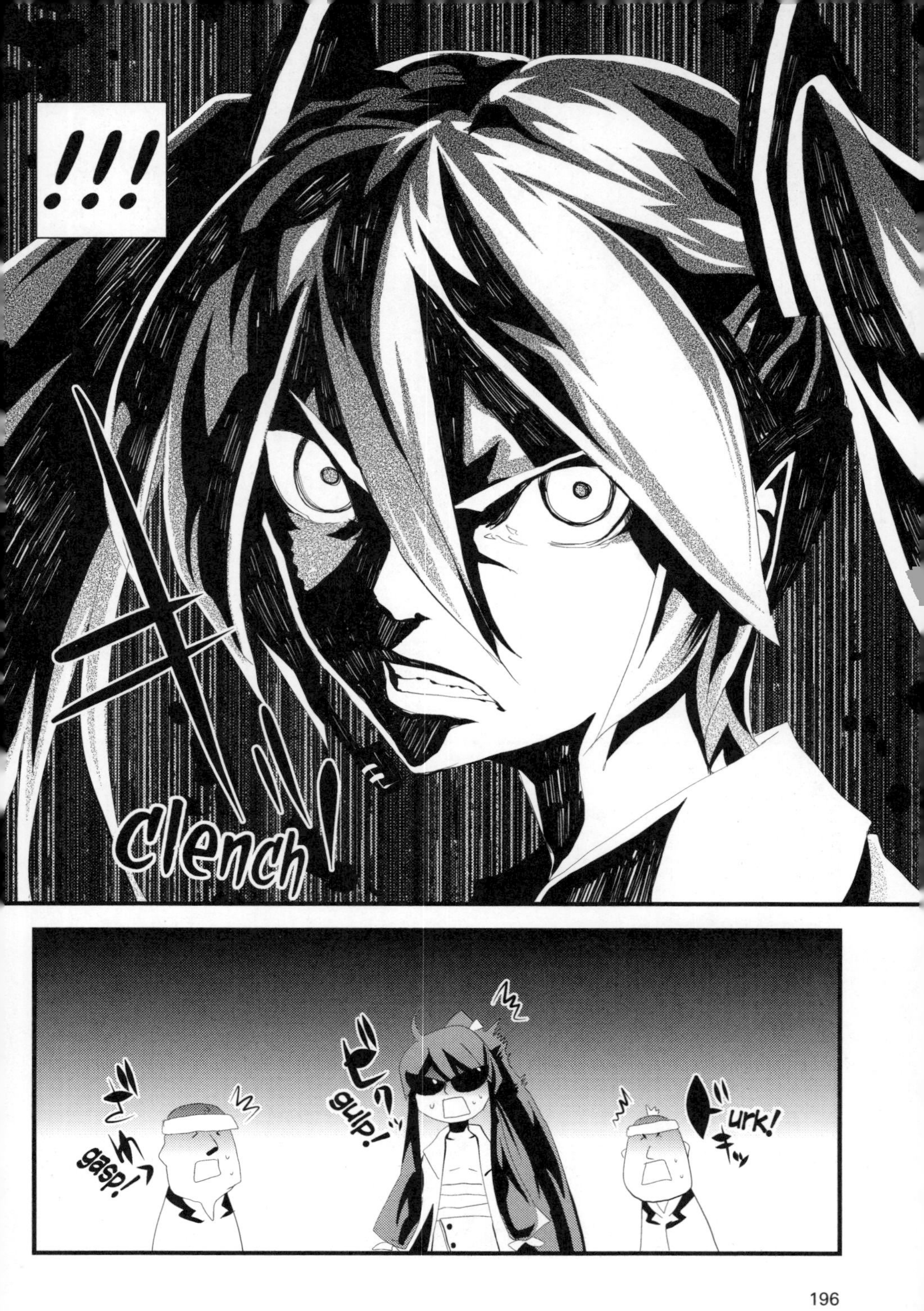
!!!
Clench
urk!
キッ
gulp!
gasp!

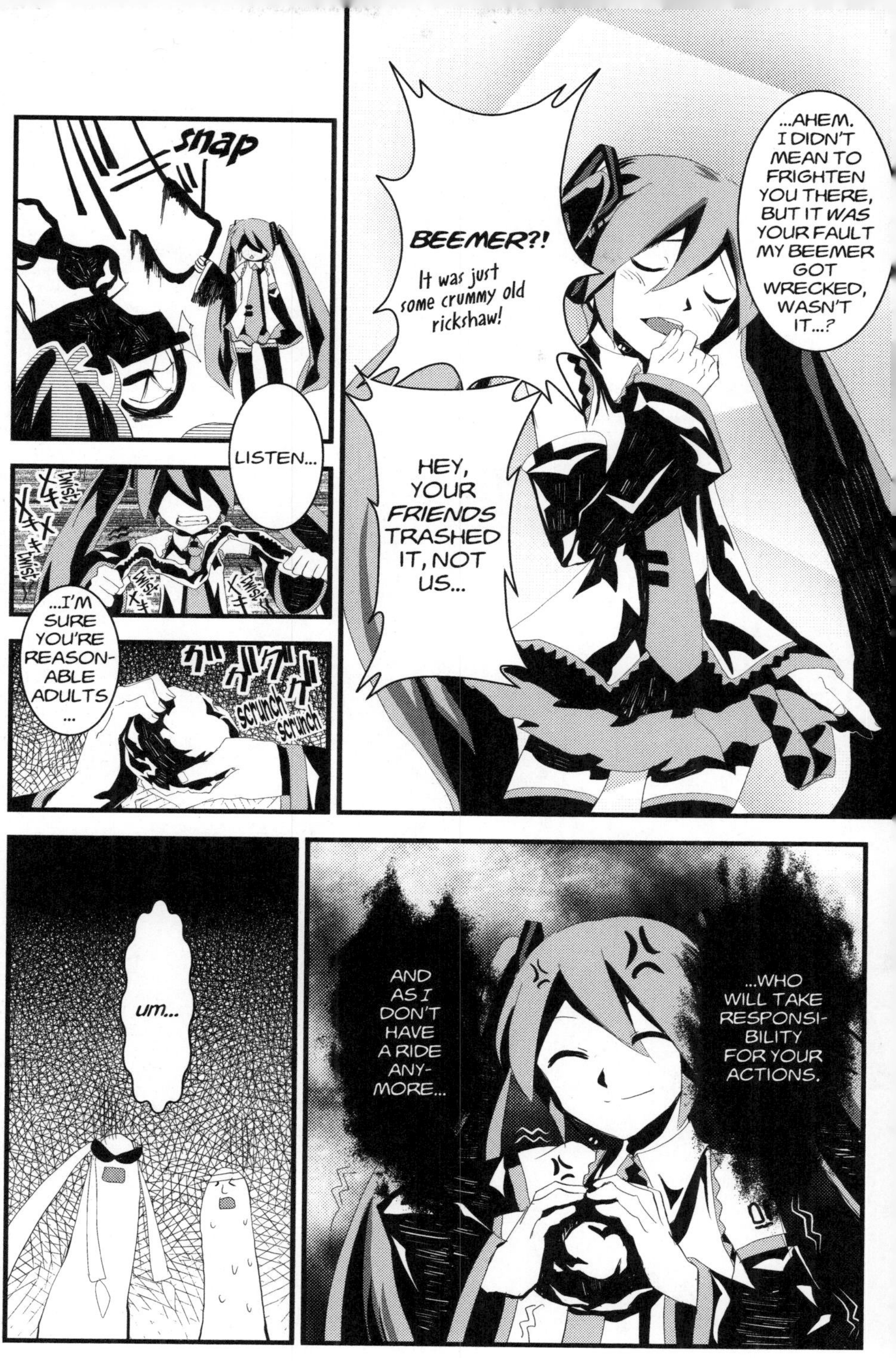
...AHEM. I DIDN'T MEAN TO FRIGHTEN YOU THERE, BUT IT WAS YOUR FAULT MY BEEMER GOT WRECKED, WASN'T IT...?
BEEMER?!
It was just some crummy old rickshaw!
HEY, YOUR FRIENDS TRASHED IT, NOT US...
snap
LISTEN...
twist twist twist twist
...I'M SURE YOU'RE REASONABLE ADULTS...
scrunch scrunch
...WHO WILL TAKE RESPONSIBILITY FOR YOUR ACTIONS.
AND AS I DON'T HAVE A RIDE ANYMORE...
um...

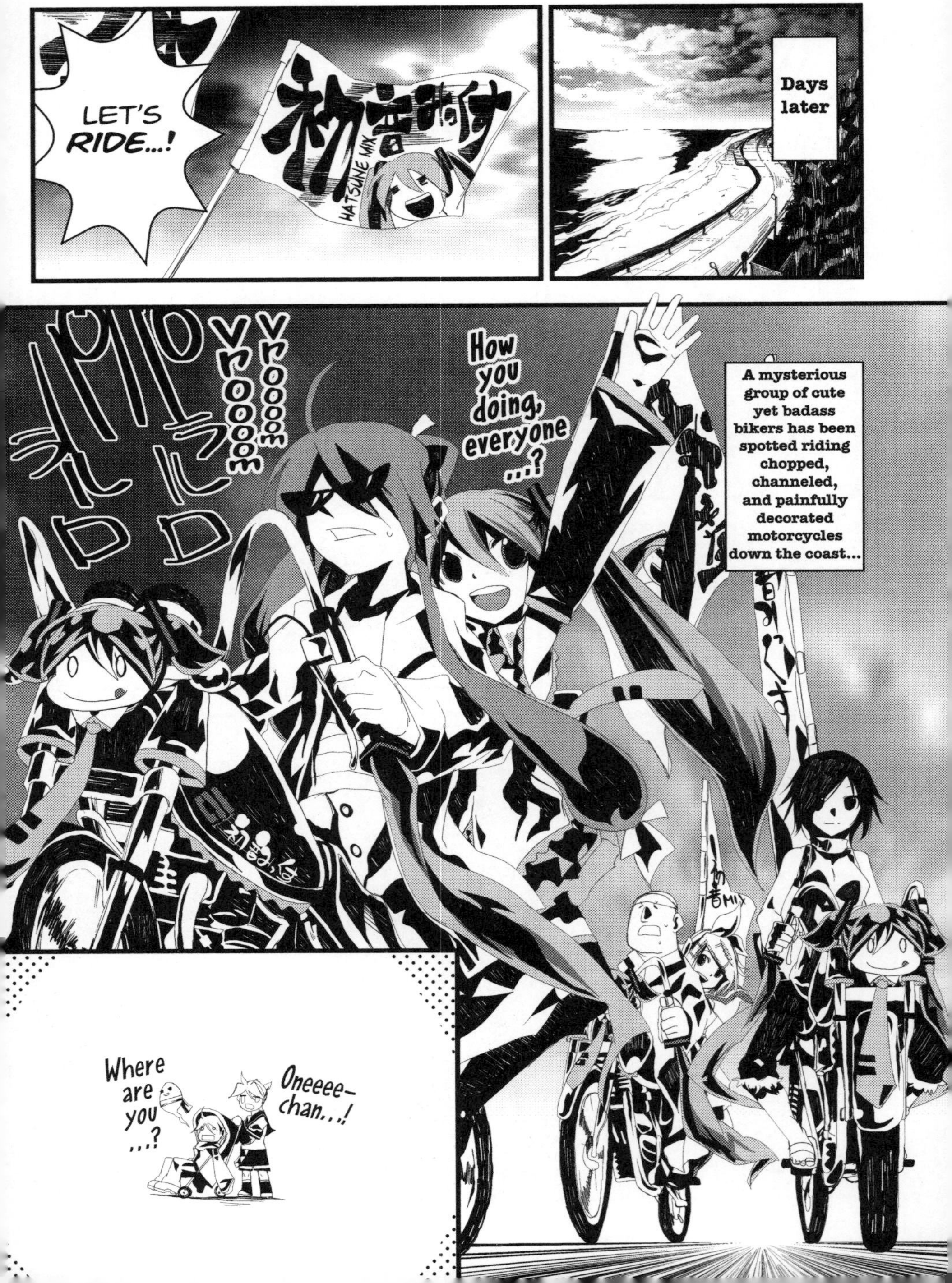

Days later
LET'S RIDE...!
HATSUNE MIX
A mysterious group of cute yet badass bikers has been spotted riding chopped, channeled, and painfully decorated motorcycles down the coast...
How you doing, everyone ...?
vroooooom
vroooooom
Oneeee-chan...!
Where are you ...?

(12th SONG) KAGAMINE MIX

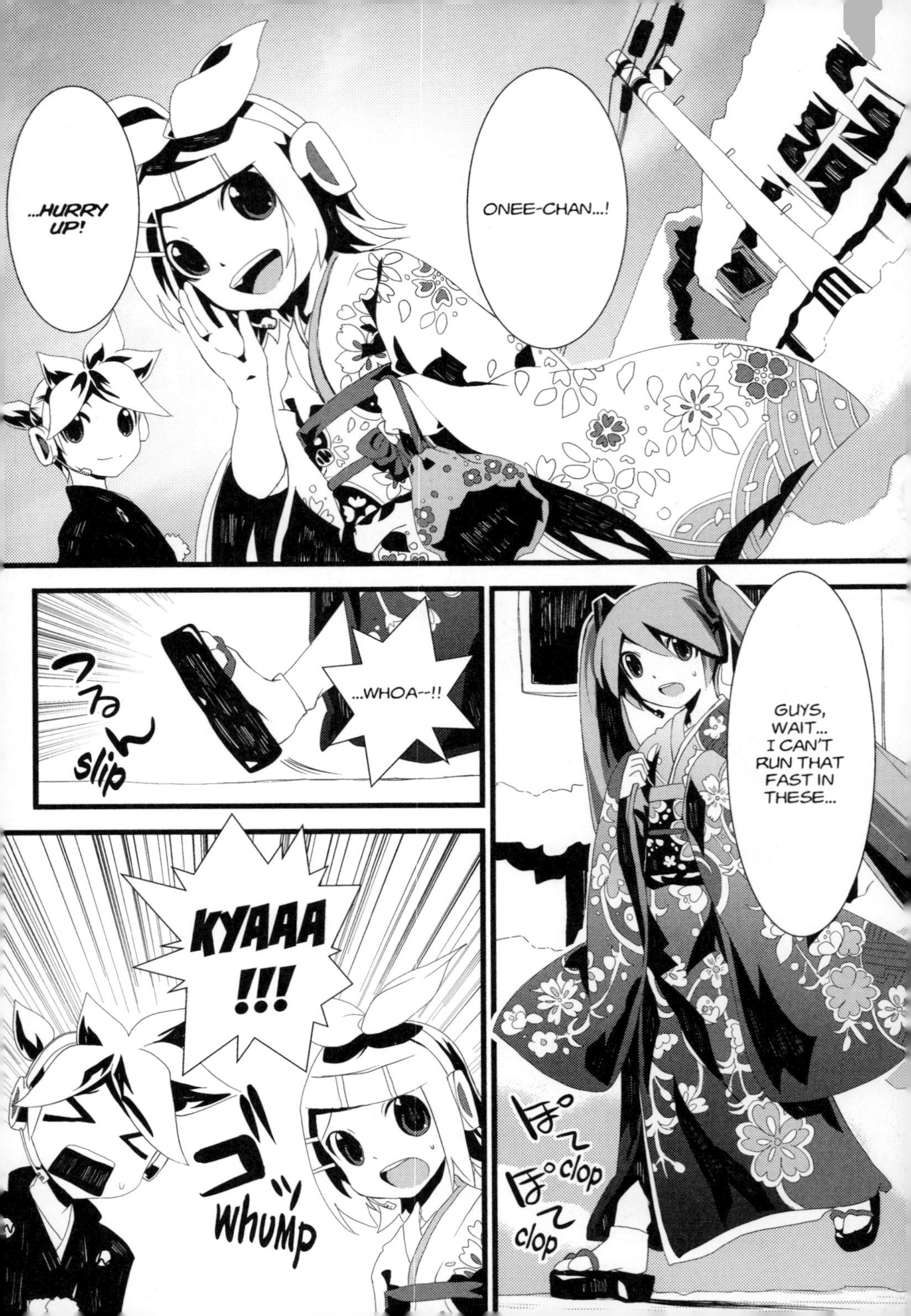
ONEE-CHAN...!
...HURRY UP!
GUYS, WAIT... I CAN'T RUN THAT FAST IN THESE...
clop
clop
...WHOA--!!
slip
KYAAA !!!
whump

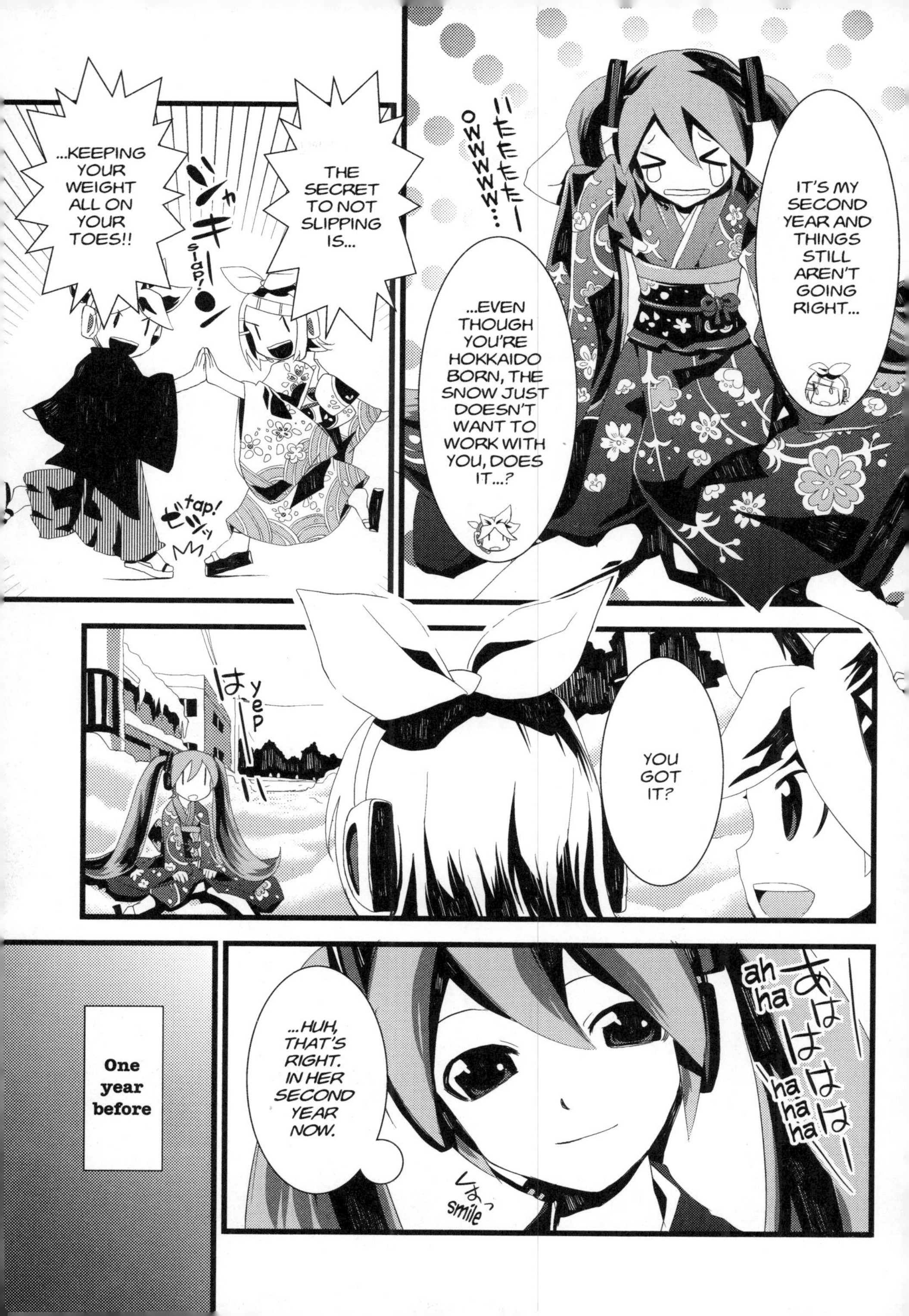

IT'S MY SECOND YEAR AND THINGS STILL AREN'T GOING RIGHT...
OWWWWW...
...EVEN THOUGH YOU'RE HOKKAIDO BORN, THE SNOW JUST DOESN'T WANT TO WORK WITH YOU, DOES IT...?
THE SECRET TO NOT SLIPPING IS...
slap!
...KEEPING YOUR WEIGHT ALL ON YOUR TOES!!
tap!
YOU GOT IT?
yep
ah ha ha ha ha ha
あははは
...HUH, THAT'S RIGHT. IN HER SECOND YEAR NOW.
smile
One year before

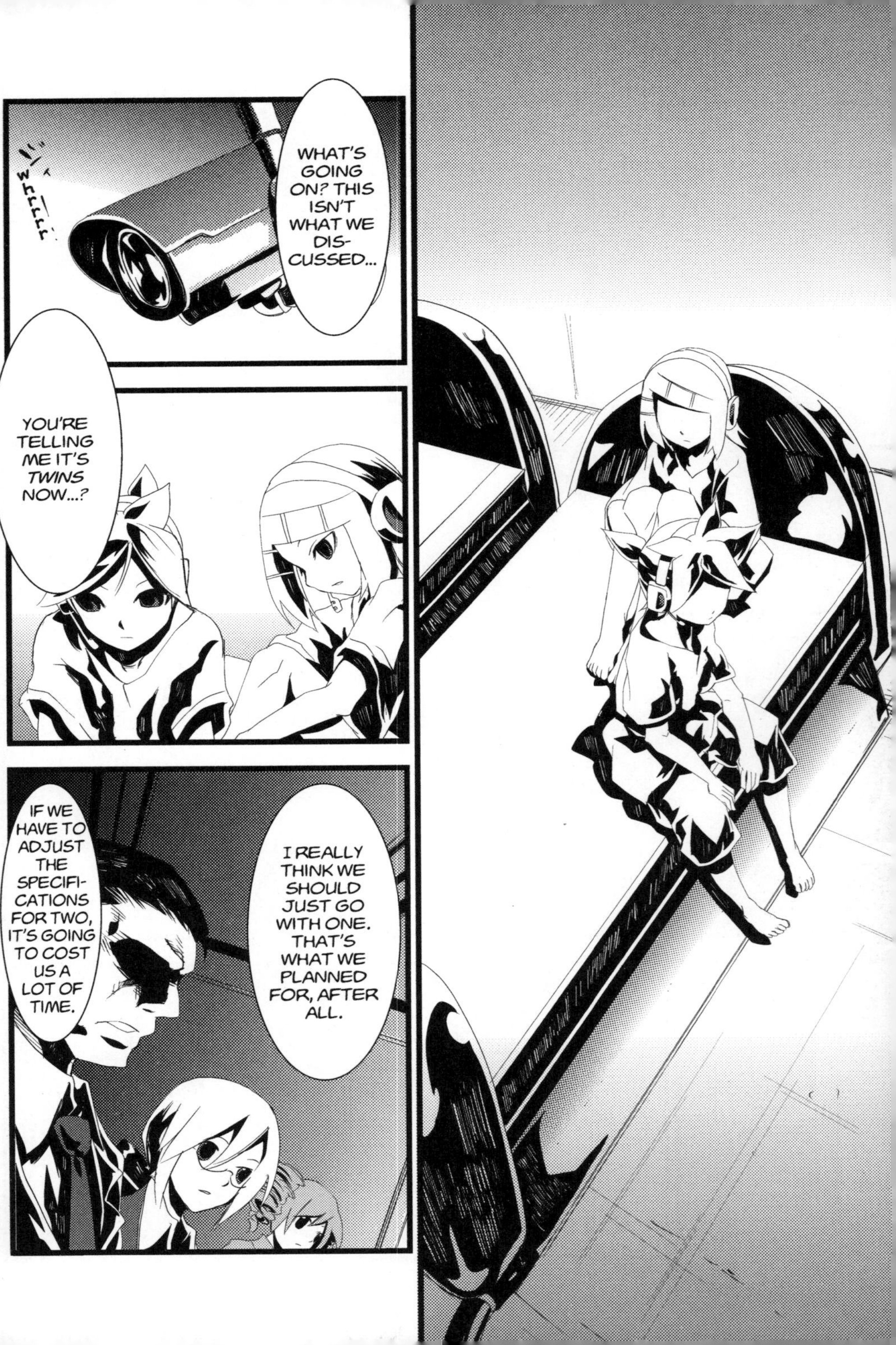
whrrrrr
WHAT'S GOING ON? THIS ISN'T WHAT WE DIS-CUSSED...
YOU'RE TELLING ME IT'S TWINS NOW...?
I REALLY THINK WE SHOULD JUST GO WITH ONE. THAT'S WHAT WE PLANNED FOR, AFTER ALL.
IF WE HAVE TO ADJUST THE SPECIFI-CATIONS FOR TWO, IT'S GOING TO COST US A LOT OF TIME.

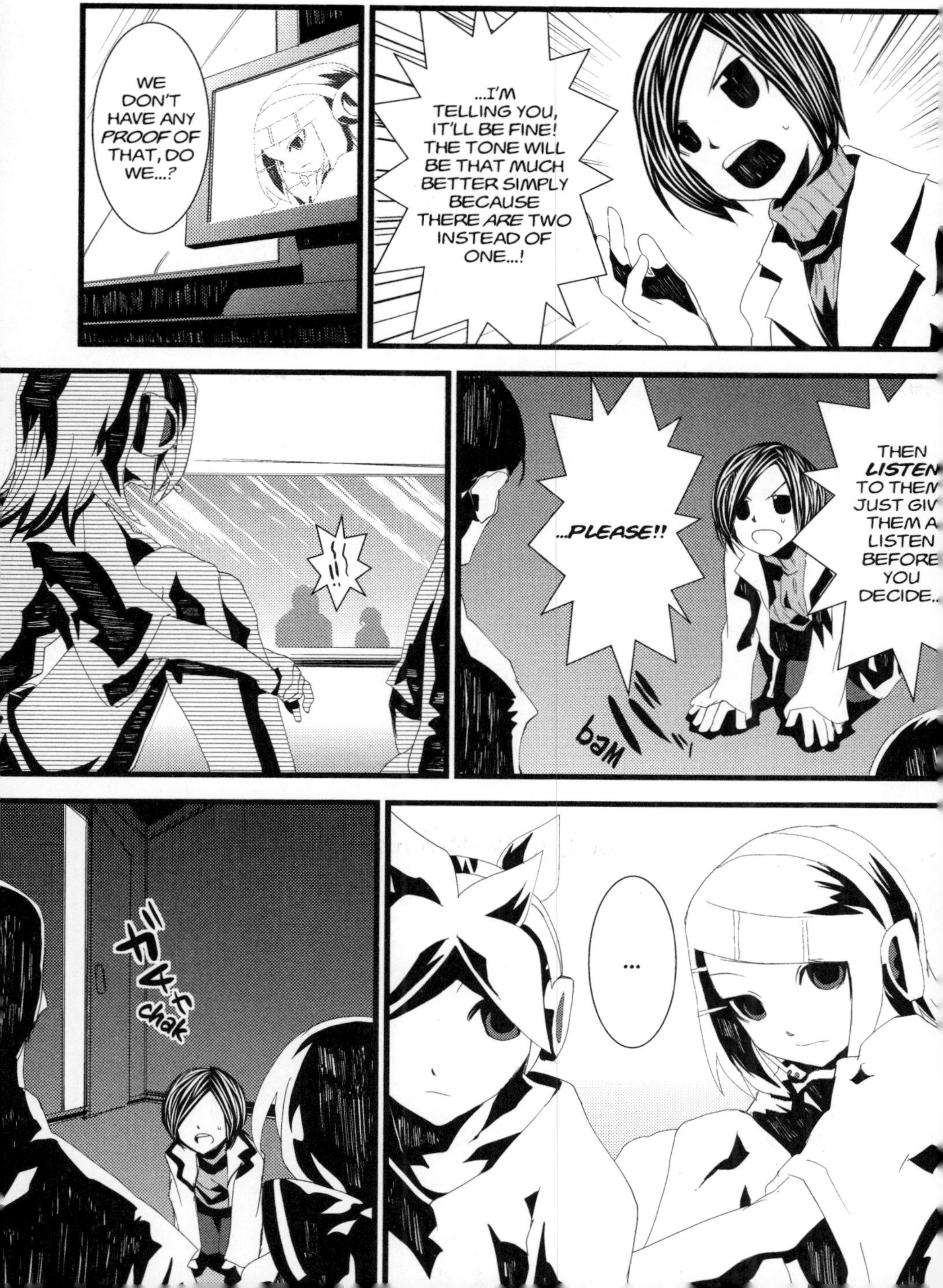
...I'M TELLING YOU, IT'LL BE FINE! THE TONE WILL BE THAT MUCH BETTER SIMPLY BECAUSE THERE *ARE* TWO INSTEAD OF ONE...!
WE DON'T HAVE ANY *PROOF* OF THAT, DO WE...?
THEN **LISTEN** TO THEM JUST GIV THEM A LISTEN BEFORE YOU DECIDE..
...PLEASE!!
bam
!!
...
chak

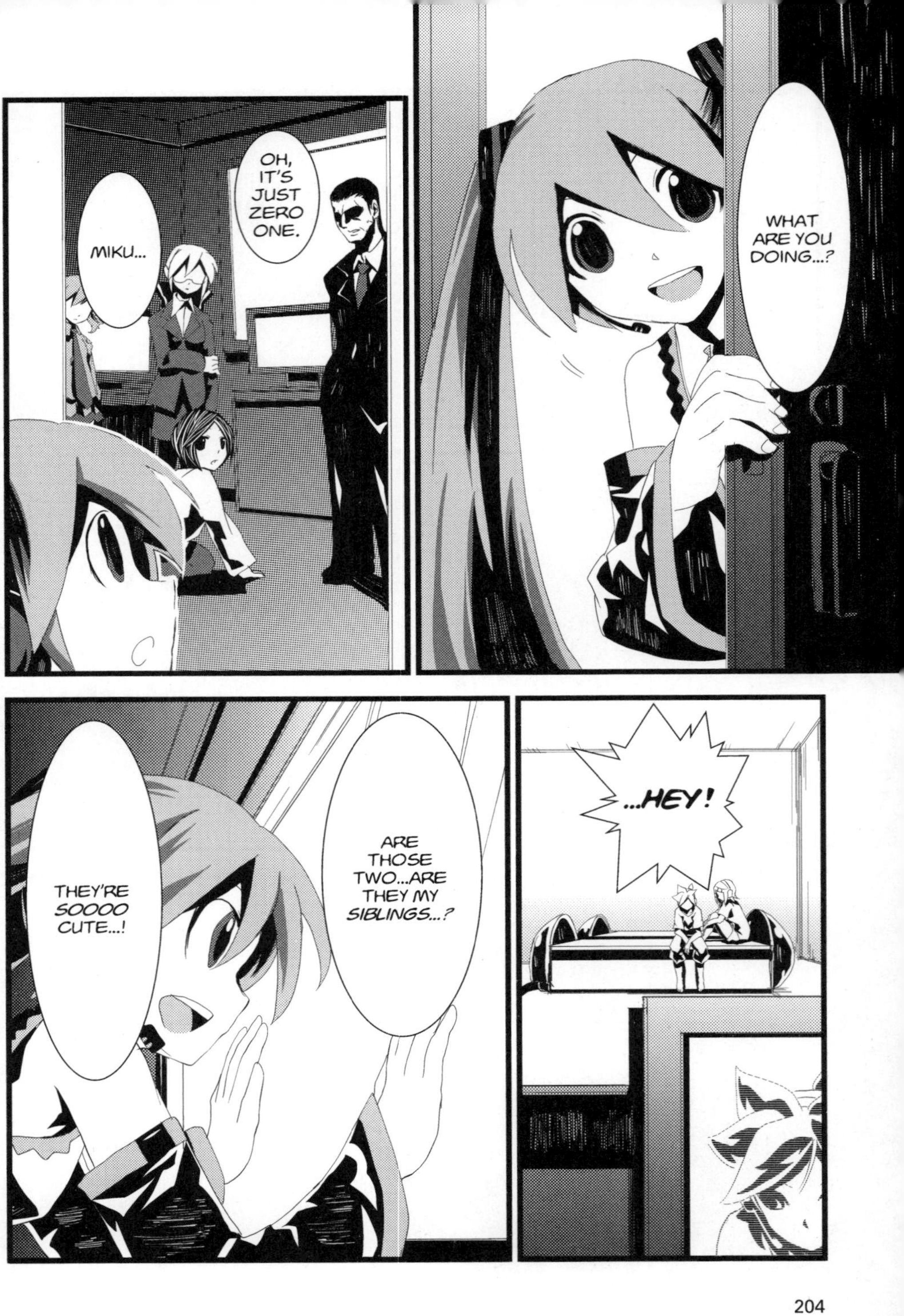
WHAT ARE YOU DOING...?
OH, IT'S JUST ZERO ONE.
MIKU...
...HEY!
ARE THOSE TWO...ARE THEY MY *SIBLINGS*...?
THEY'RE *SOOOO* CUTE...!

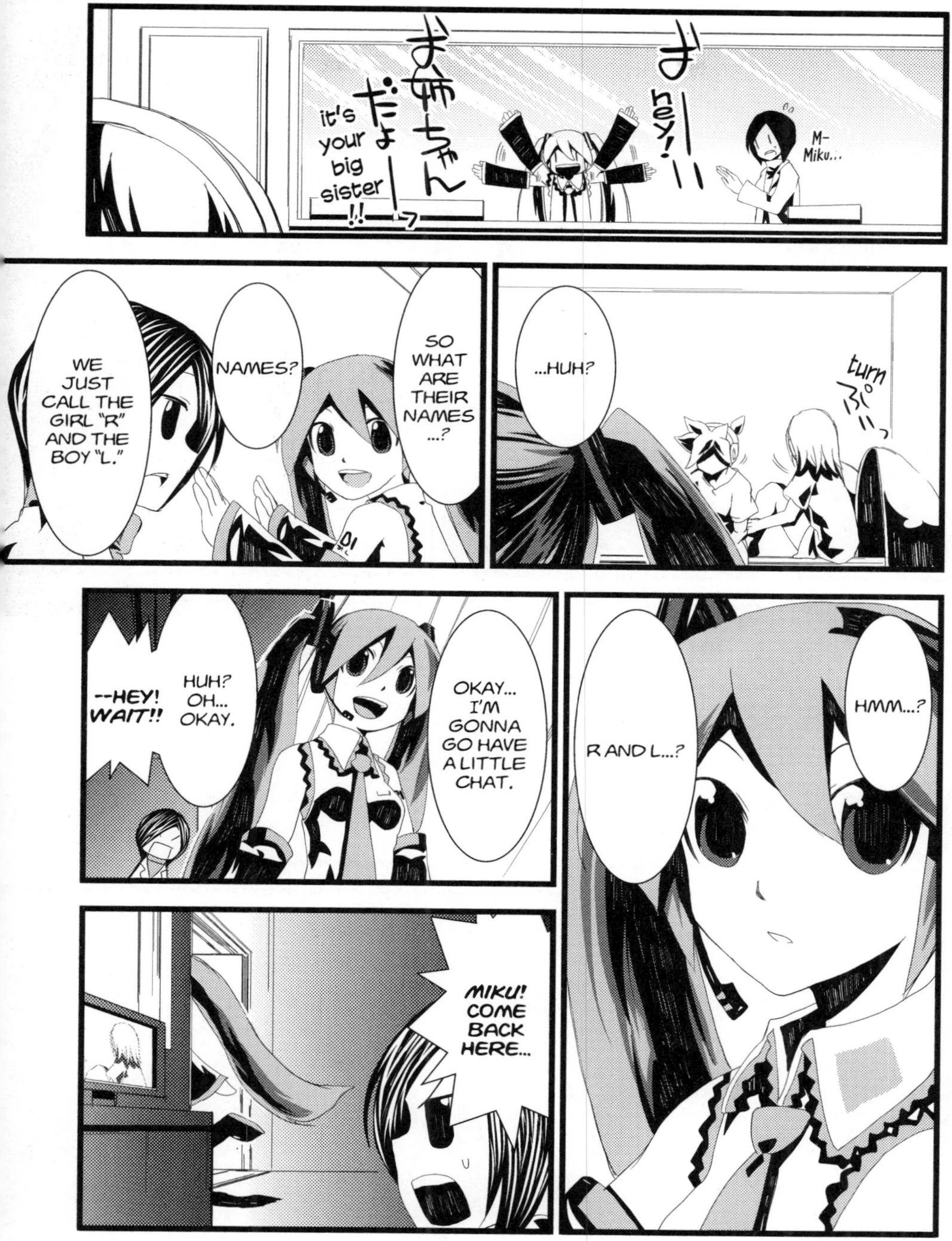
M-Miku...
hey!!
お姉ちゃんだよー
it's your big sister!!
turn
...HUH?
SO WHAT ARE THEIR NAMES...?
NAMES?
WE JUST CALL THE GIRL "R" AND THE BOY "L."
HMM...?
R AND L...?
OKAY... I'M GONNA GO HAVE A LITTLE CHAT.
HUH? OH... OKAY.
--HEY! WAIT!!
MIKU! COME BACK HERE...

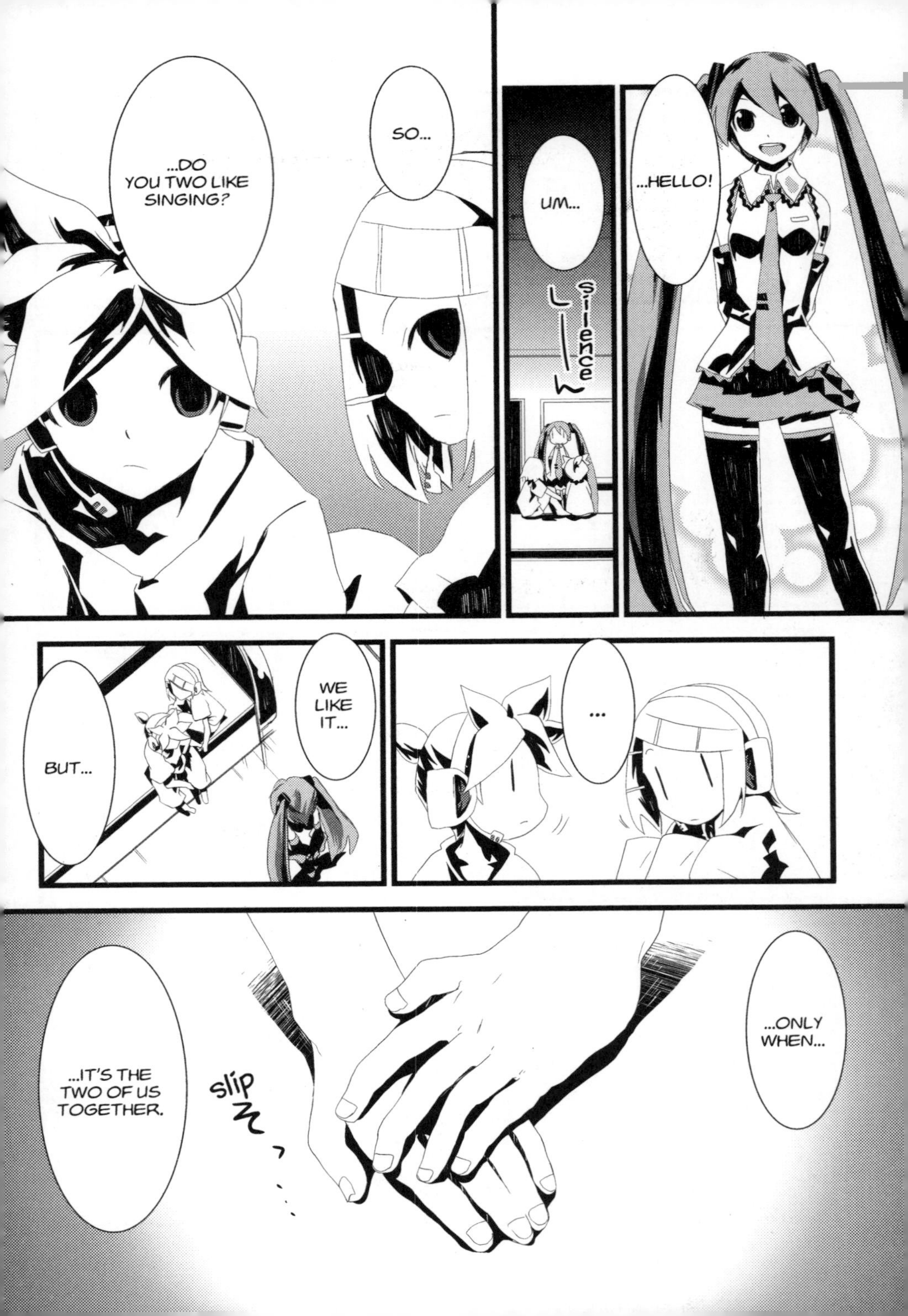
...HELLO!
UM...
silence
しーーん
SO...
...DO YOU TWO LIKE SINGING?
...
WE LIKE IT...
BUT...
...ONLY WHEN...
slip
...IT'S THE TWO OF US TOGETHER.

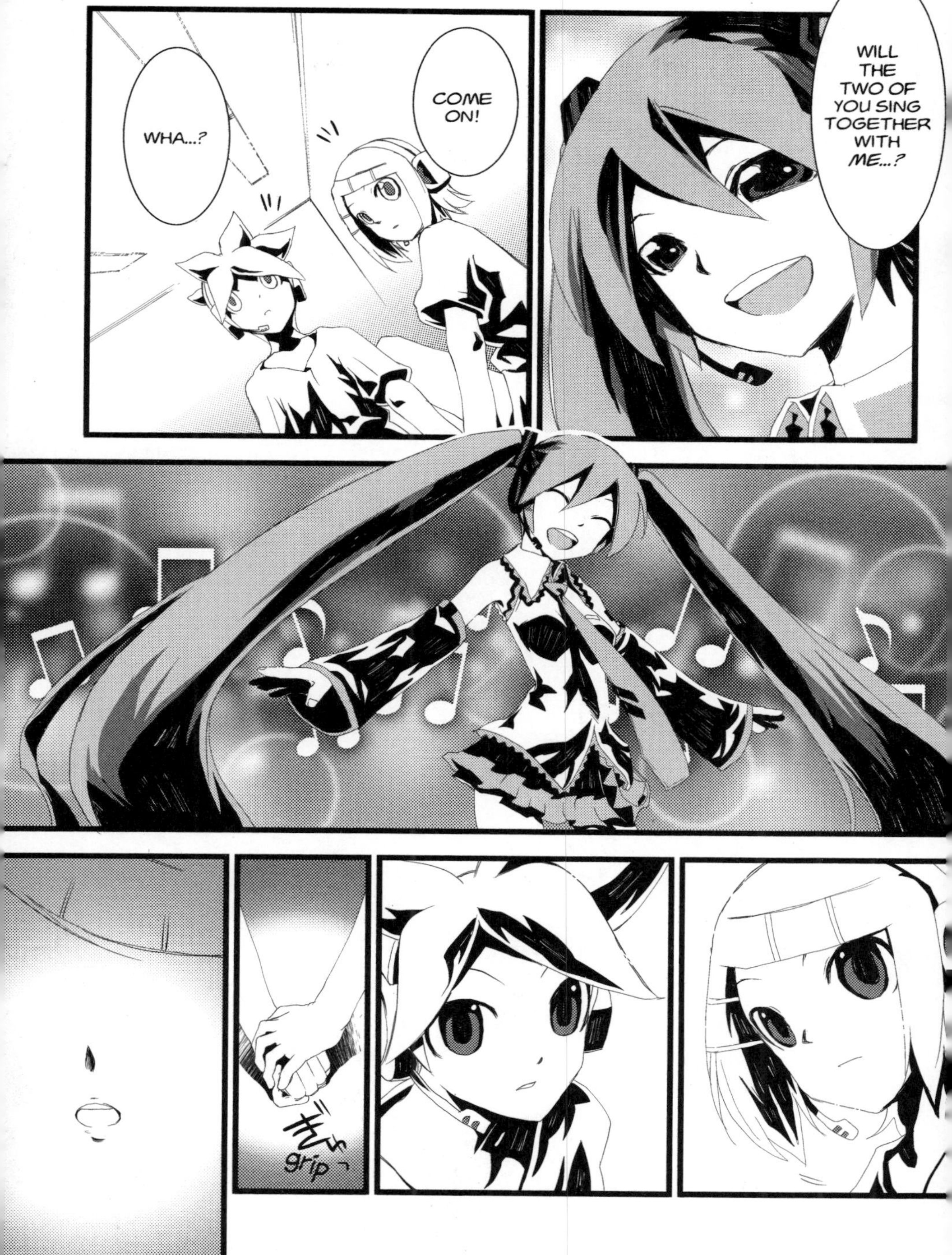
WILL THE TWO OF YOU SING TOGETHER WITH *ME*...?
COME ON!
WHA...?
grip

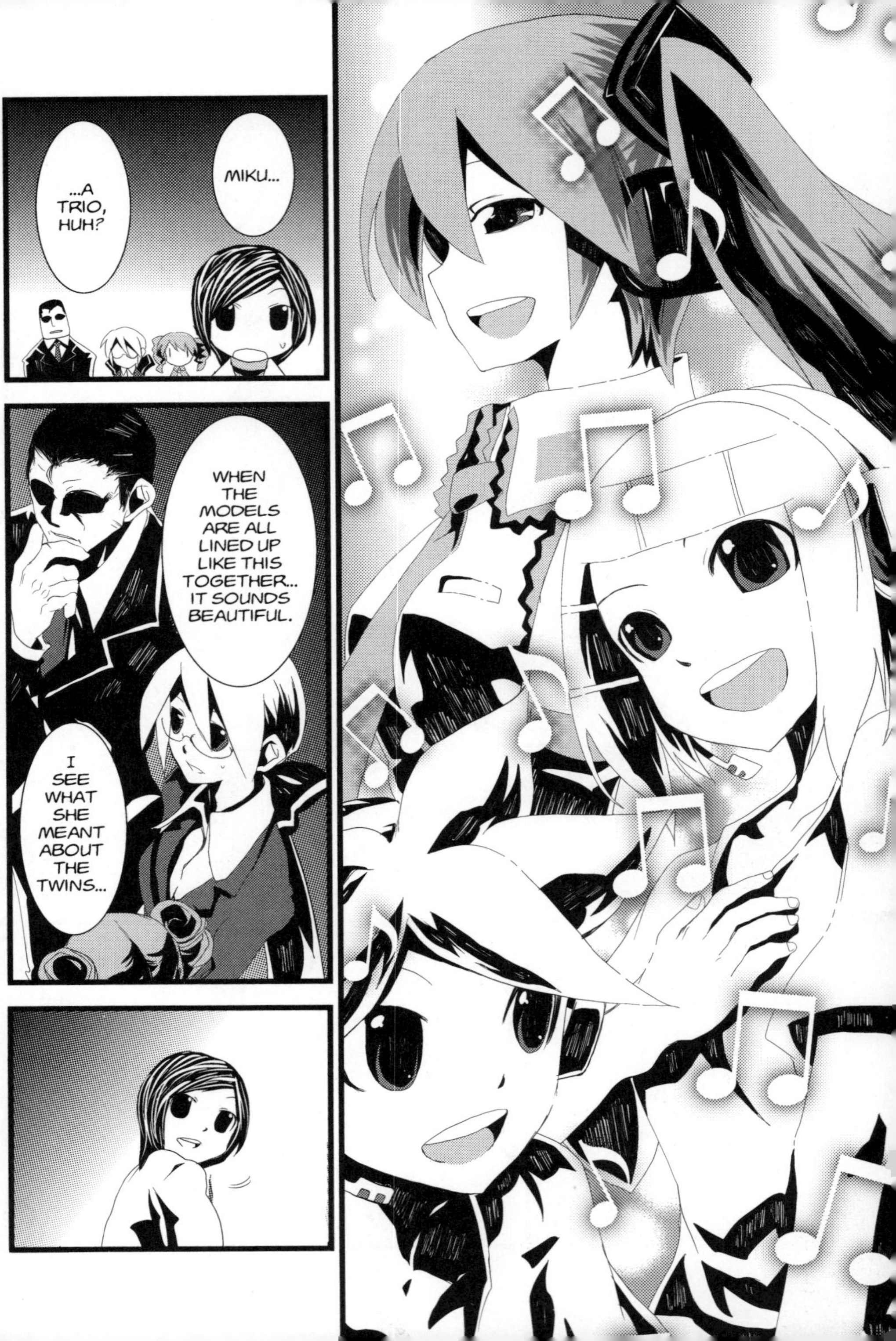
MIKU...
...A TRIO, HUH?
WHEN THE MODELS ARE ALL LINED UP LIKE THIS TOGETHER... IT SOUNDS BEAUTIFUL.
I SEE WHAT SHE MEANT ABOUT THE TWINS...

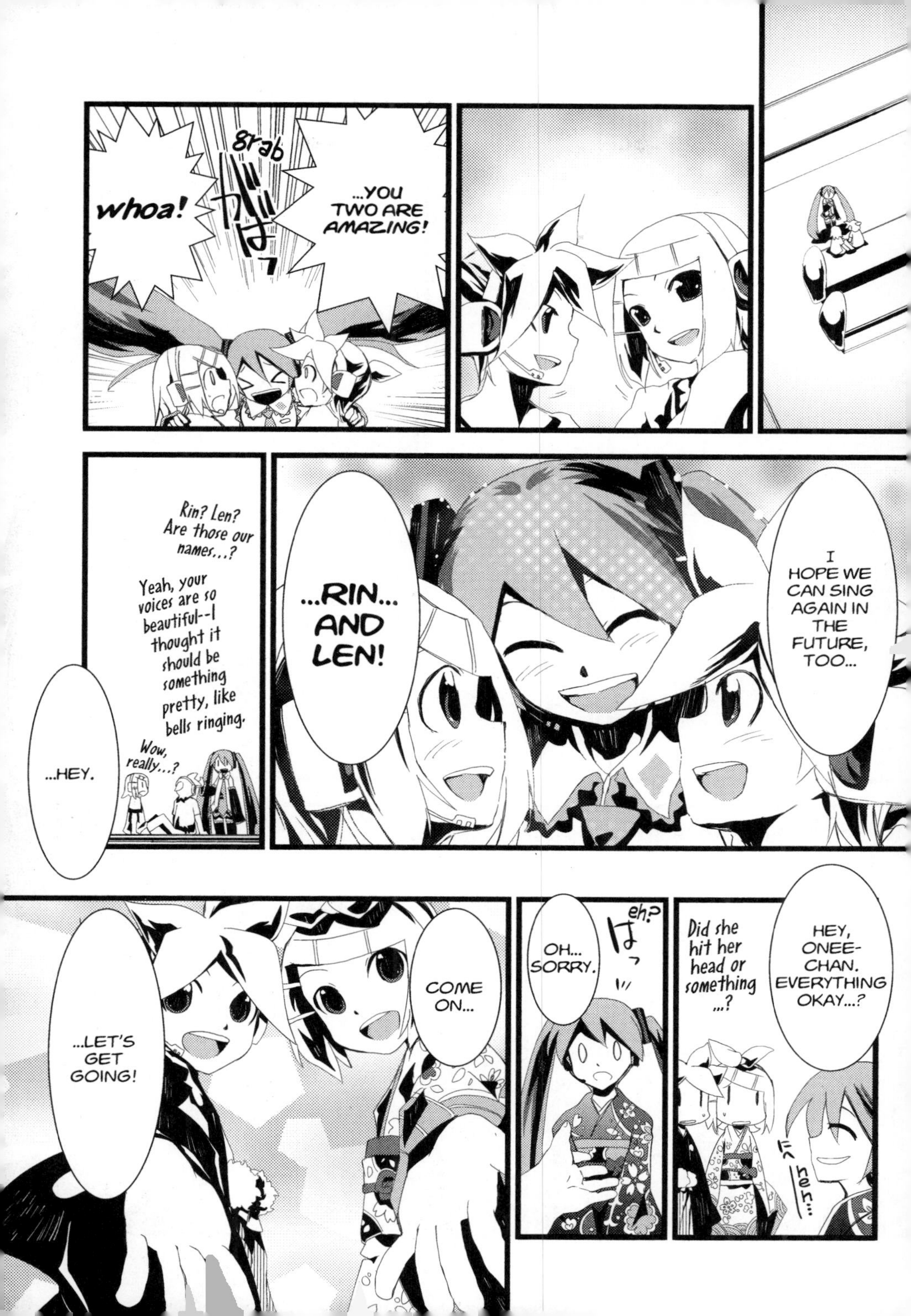
...YOU TWO ARE AMAZING!
grab
whoa!
I HOPE WE CAN SING AGAIN IN THE FUTURE, TOO...
...RIN... AND LEN!
Rin? Len? Are those our names...?
Yeah, your voices are so beautiful--I thought it should be something pretty, like bells ringing.
Wow, really...?
...HEY.
HEY, ONEE-CHAN. EVERYTHING OKAY...?
Did she hit her head or something ...?
heh heh...
eh?
OH... SORRY.
COME ON...
...LET'S GET GOING!

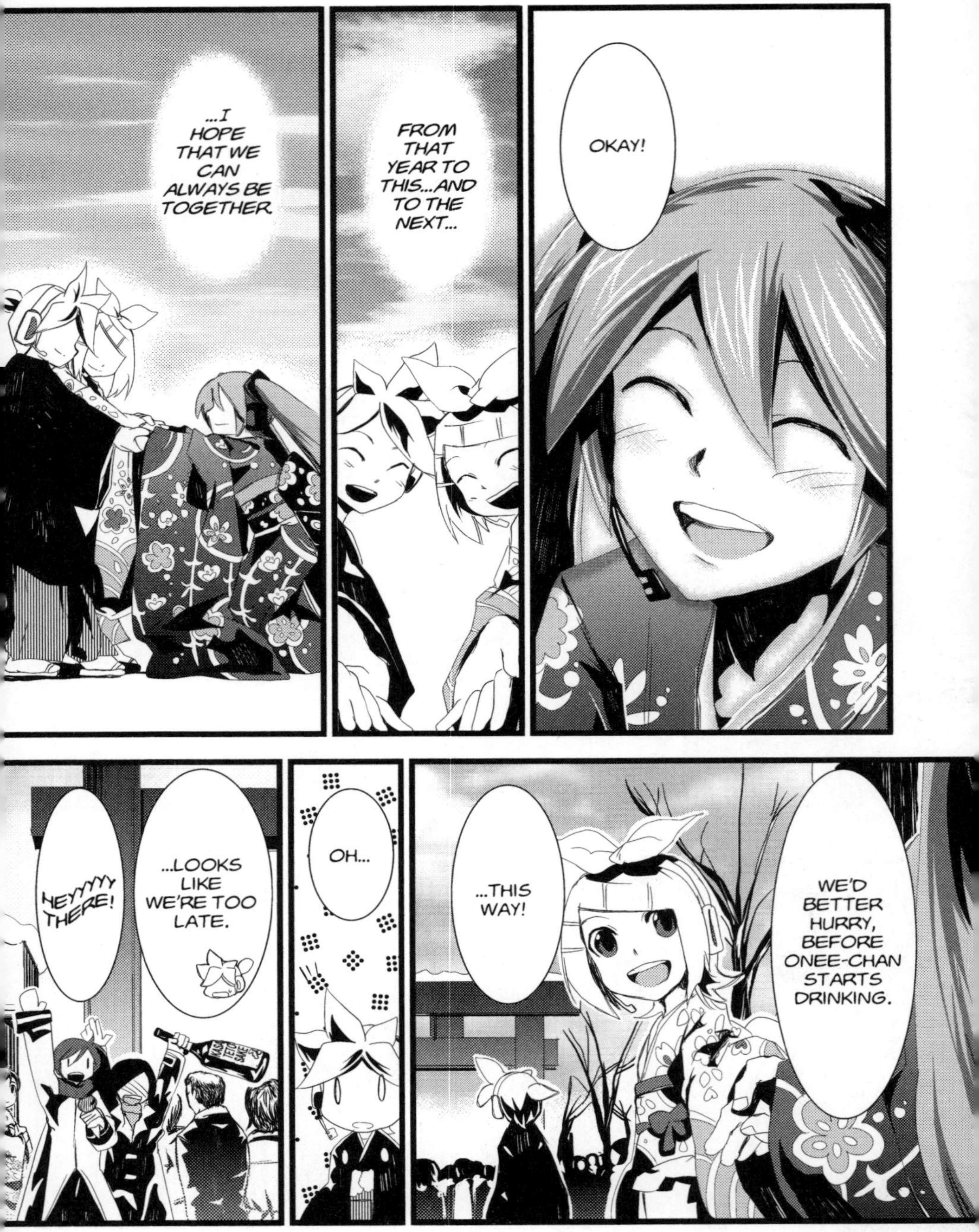
OKAY!
FROM THAT YEAR TO THIS...AND TO THE NEXT...
...I HOPE THAT WE CAN ALWAYS BE TOGETHER.
WE'D BETTER HURRY, BEFORE ONEE-CHAN STARTS DRINKING.
...THIS WAY!
OH...
...LOOKS LIKE WE'RE TOO LATE.
HEYYYYY THERE!

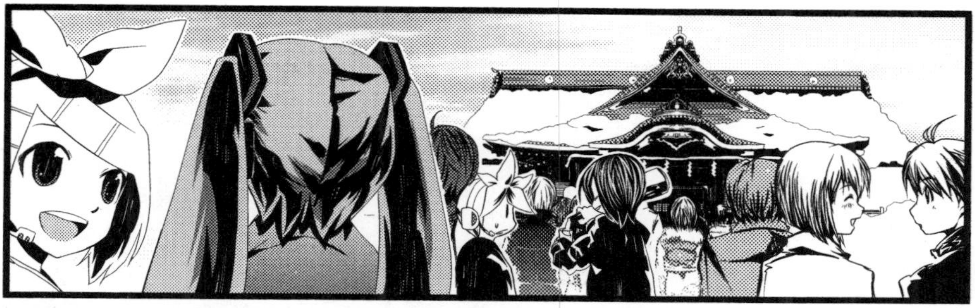

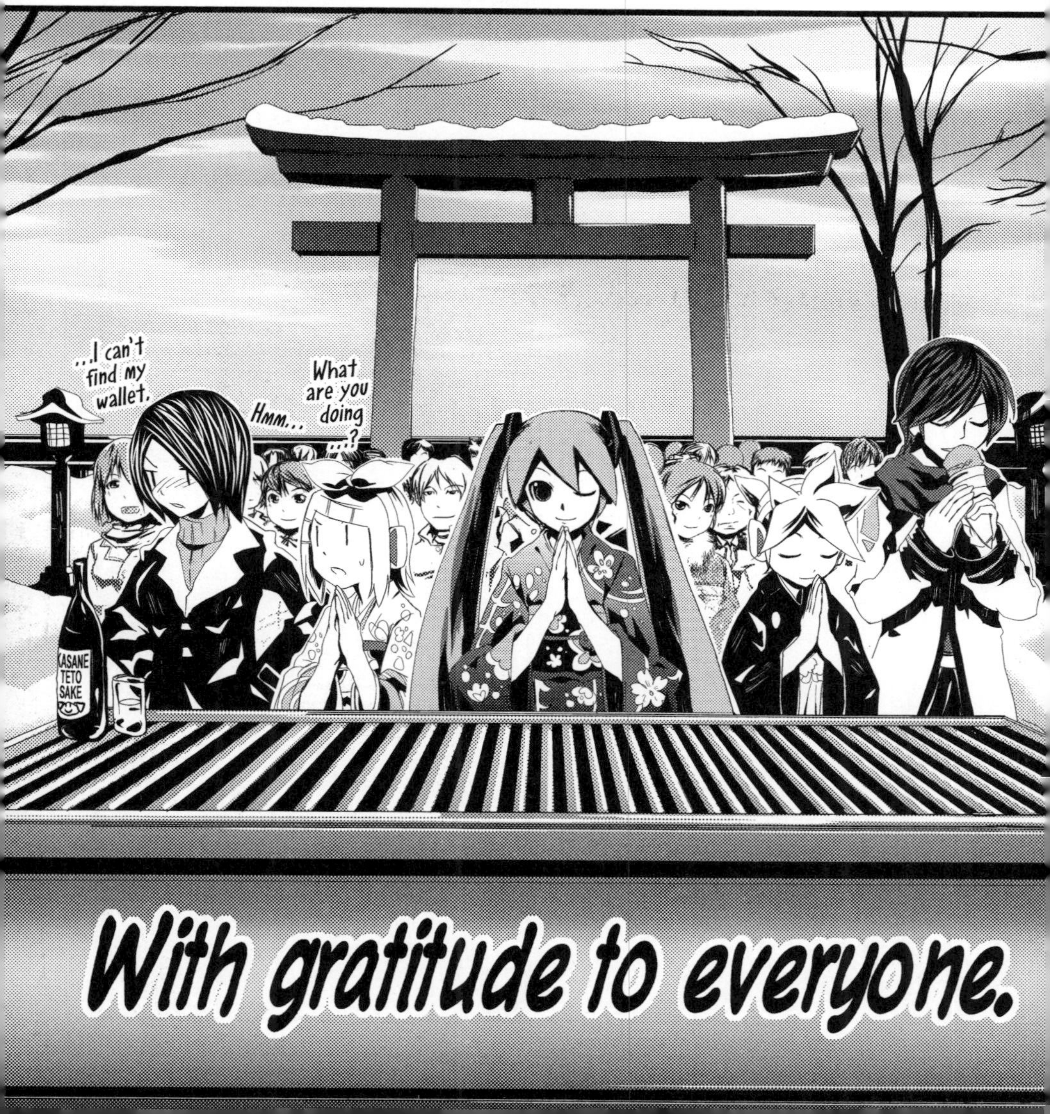
What are you doing ...?
Hmm...
...I can't find my wallet.
KASANE TETO SAKE
With gratitude to everyone.

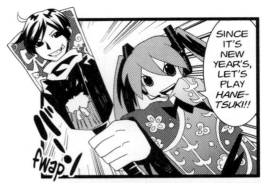

SINCE IT'S NEW YEAR'S, LET'S PLAY HANE-TSUKI!!
fwap
THAT'S FINE, BUT IF YOU LOSE...THEN THERE SHOULD BE A PENALTY.
These two are planning something.
READY?
GO!!!
fwoosh
!!!
whak
whak
THAT IS NOT HOW YOU PLAY HANE-TSUKI!!
YOU MESS WITH THE TWINS...
...AND THAT'S WHAT YOU GET!

Since we've run out of places on your face to mark, you forfeit the game.

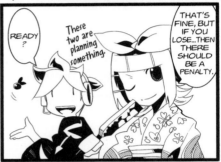

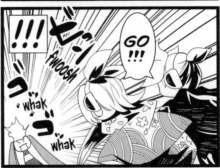

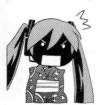

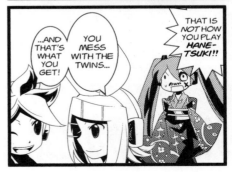

(13th SONG) CELEBRITY MIX

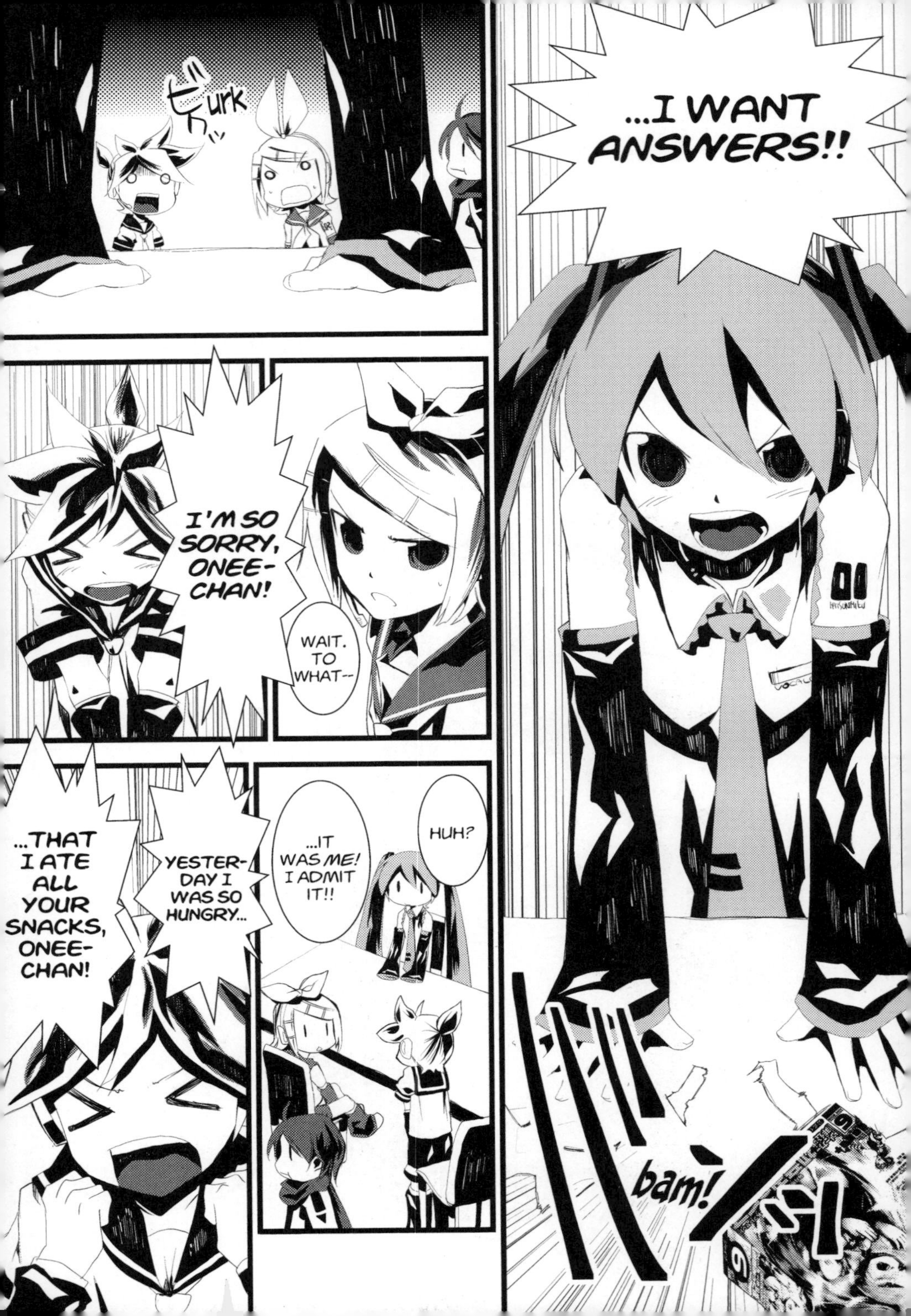
...I WANT ANSWERS!!
bam!
urk
WAIT. TO WHAT--
I'M SO SORRY, ONEE-CHAN!
HUH?
...IT WAS ME! I ADMIT IT!!
YESTER-DAY I WAS SO HUNGRY...
...THAT I ATE ALL YOUR SNACKS, ONEE-CHAN!

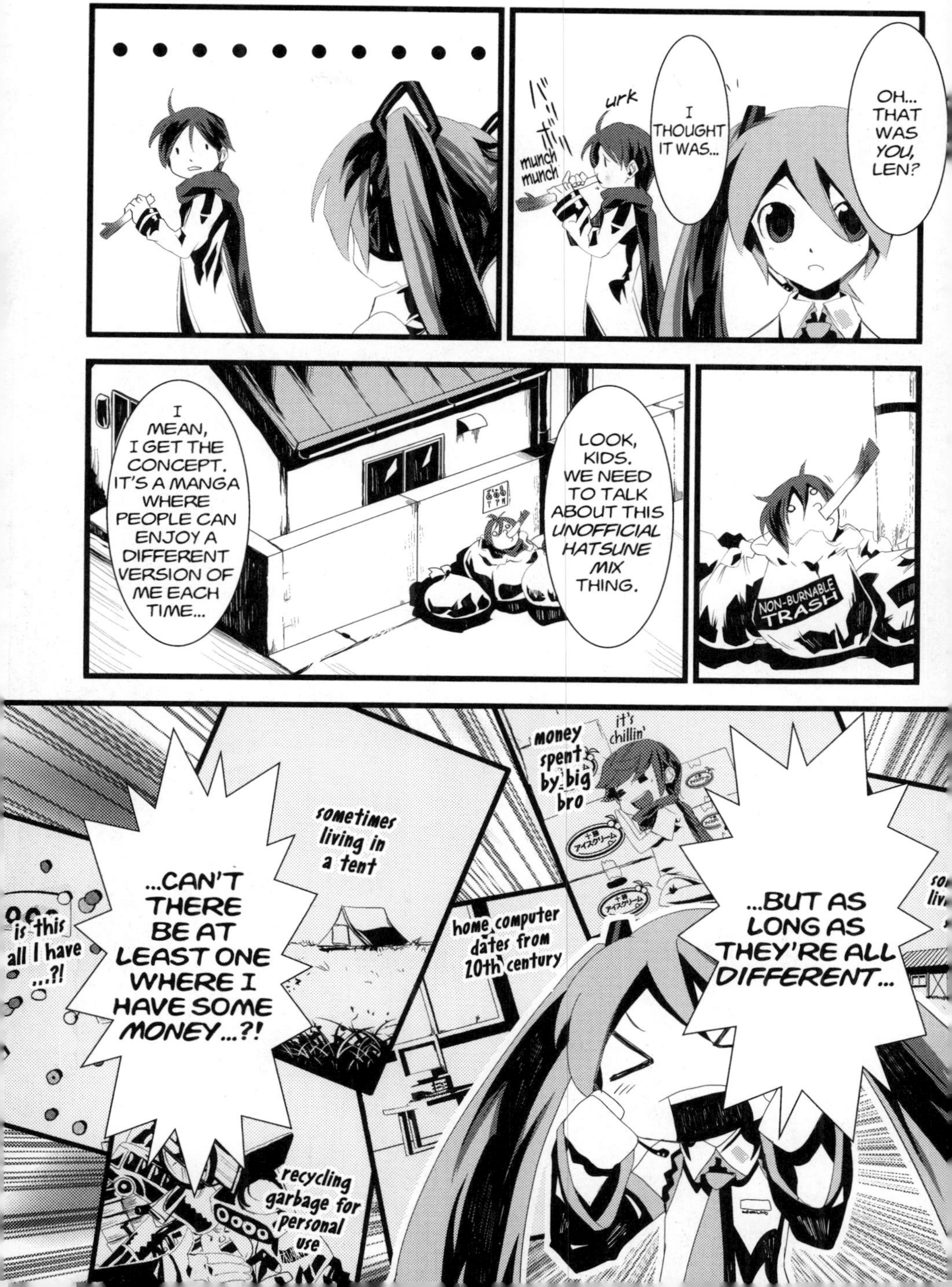
OH... THAT WAS *YOU*, LEN?
I THOUGHT IT WAS...
urk
munch munch
• • • • • • • • • •
NON-BURNABLE TRASH
LOOK, KIDS. WE NEED TO TALK ABOUT THIS *UNOFFICIAL HATSUNE MIX* THING.
I MEAN, I GET THE CONCEPT. IT'S A MANGA WHERE PEOPLE CAN ENJOY A DIFFERENT VERSION OF ME EACH TIME...
...BUT AS LONG AS THEY'RE ALL DIFFERENT...
it's chillin'
money spent by big bro
home computer dates from 20th century
sometimes living in a tent
...CAN'T THERE BE AT LEAST ONE WHERE I HAVE SOME *MONEY...?!*
is this all I have ...?!
recycling garbage for personal use

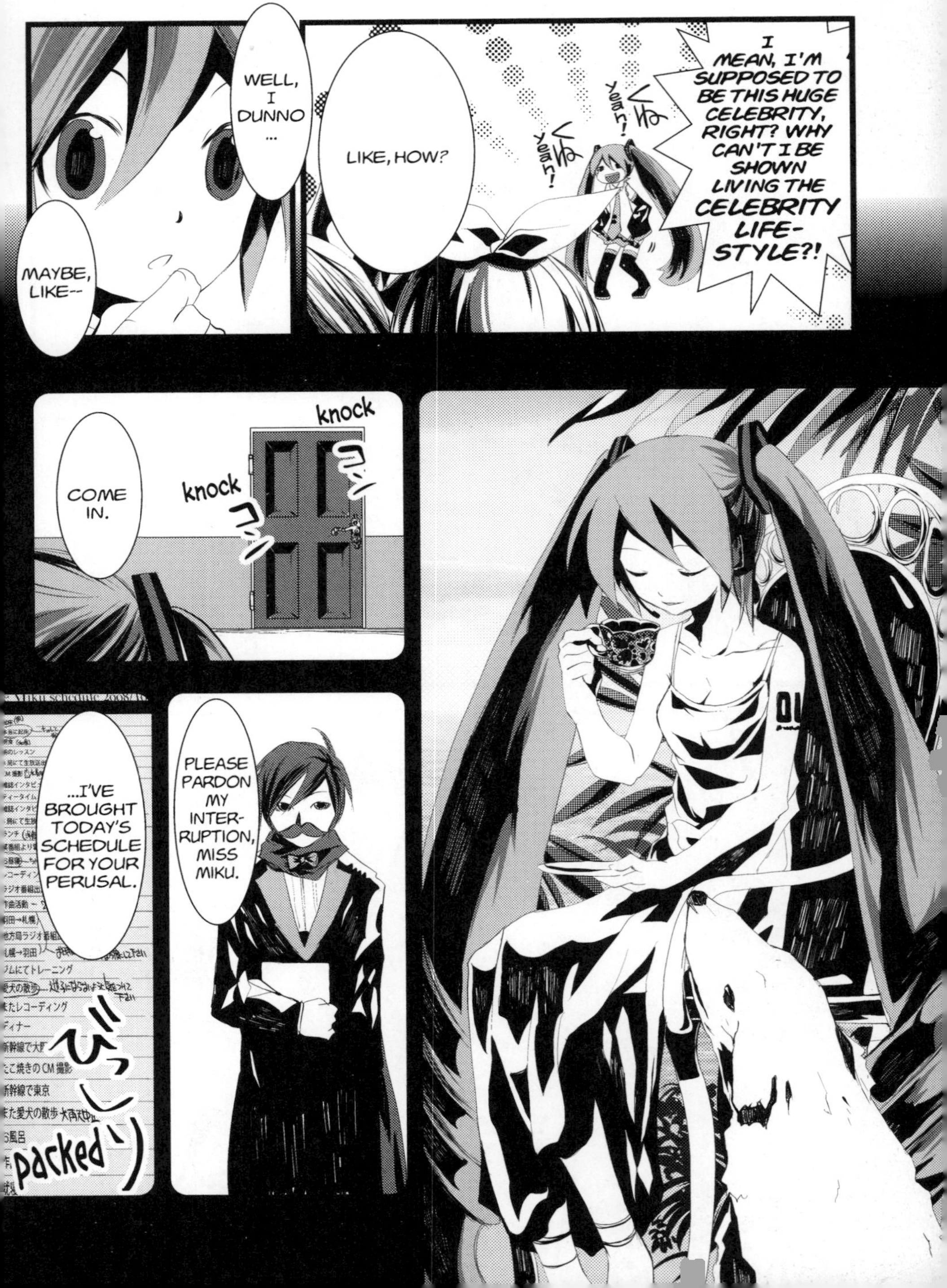
I MEAN, I'M SUPPOSED TO BE THIS HUGE CELEBRITY, RIGHT? WHY CAN'T I BE SHOWN LIVING THE CELEBRITY LIFE-STYLE?!
yeah!
yeah!
LIKE, HOW?
WELL, I DUNNO ...
MAYBE, LIKE--
knock
knock
COME IN.
PLEASE PARDON MY INTER-RUPTION, MISS MIKU.
...I'VE BROUGHT TODAY'S SCHEDULE FOR YOUR PERUSAL.
packed

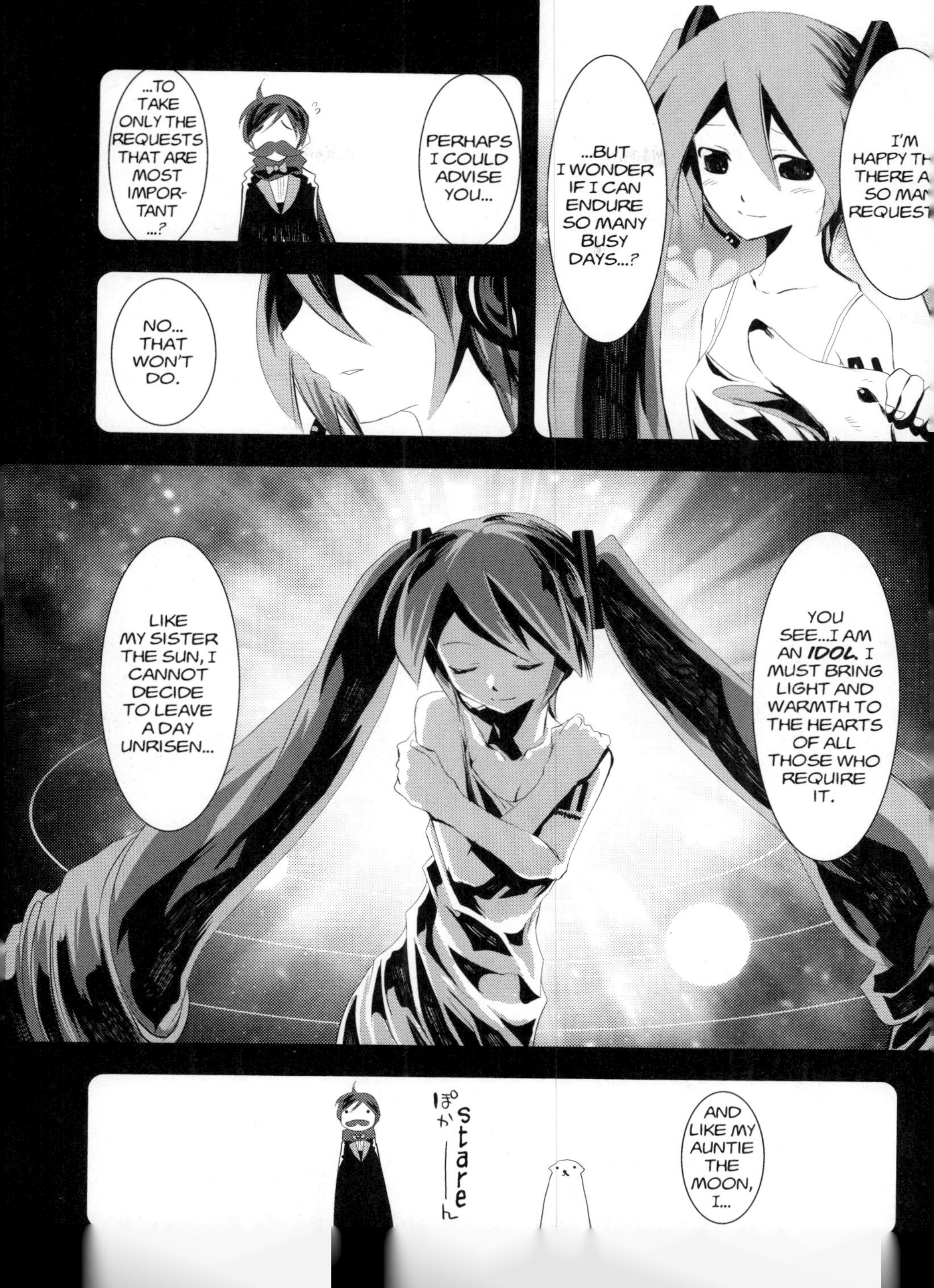
I'M HAPPY TH THERE A SO MAN REQUEST
...BUT I WONDER IF I CAN ENDURE SO MANY BUSY DAYS...?
PERHAPS I COULD ADVISE YOU...
...TO TAKE ONLY THE REQUESTS THAT ARE MOST IMPOR-TANT...?
NO... THAT WON'T DO.
YOU SEE...I AM AN **IDOL**. I MUST BRING LIGHT AND WARMTH TO THE HEARTS OF ALL THOSE WHO REQUIRE IT.
LIKE MY SISTER THE SUN, I CANNOT DECIDE TO LEAVE A DAY UNRISEN...
AND LIKE MY AUNTIE THE MOON, I...
ぽか
stare——ん

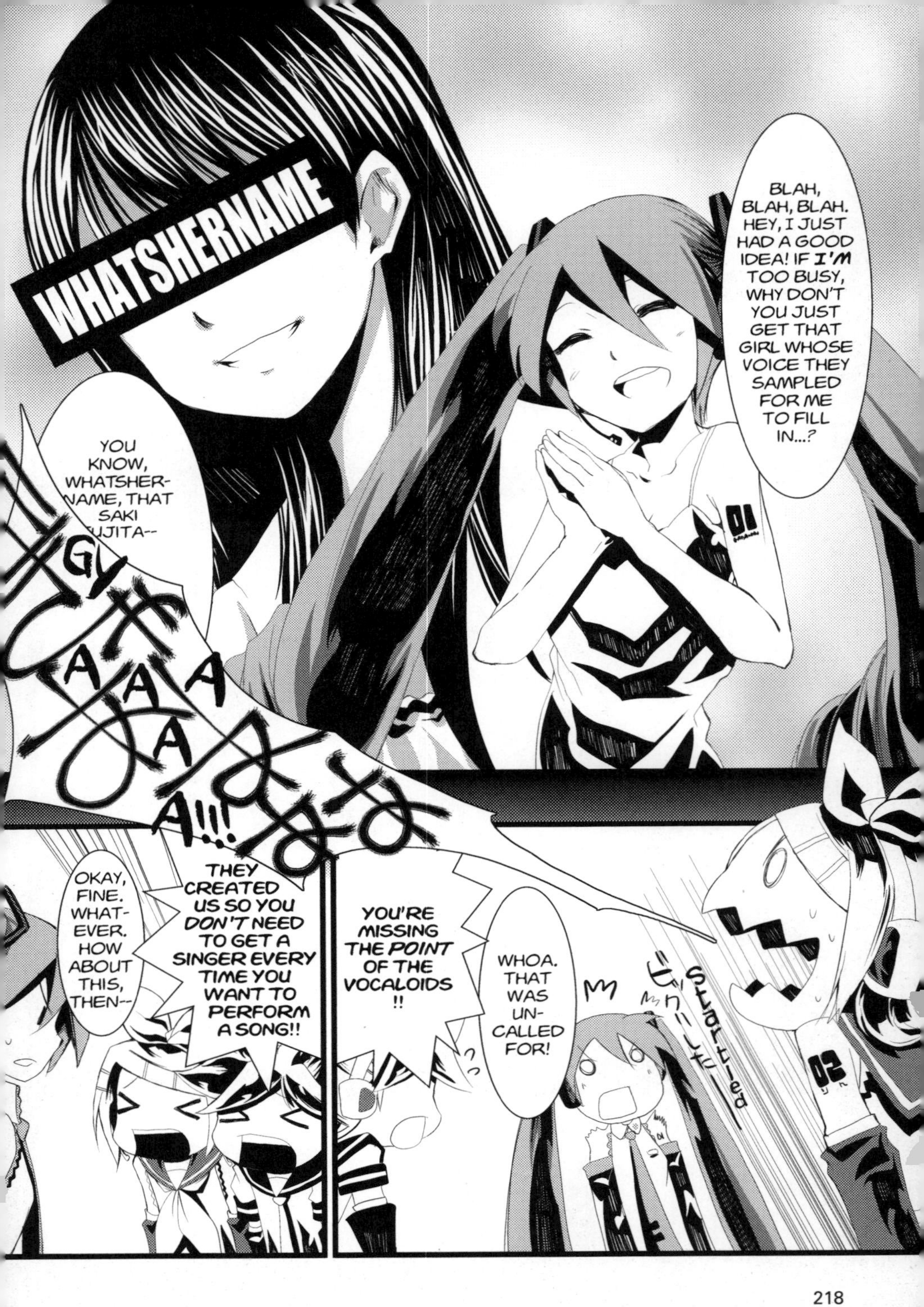
BLAH, BLAH, BLAH. HEY, I JUST HAD A GOOD IDEA! IF *I'M* TOO BUSY, WHY DON'T YOU JUST GET THAT GIRL WHOSE VOICE THEY SAMPLED FOR ME TO FILL IN...?
WHATSHERNAME
YOU KNOW, WHATSHER-NAME, THAT SAKI UJITA--
GYAAAAAA!!!
Startled
WHOA. THAT WAS UN-CALLED FOR!
YOU'RE MISSING THE *POINT* OF THE VOCALOIDS !!
THEY CREATED US SO YOU *DON'T* NEED TO GET A SINGER EVERY TIME YOU WANT TO PERFORM A SONG!!
OKAY, FINE. WHAT-EVER. HOW ABOUT THIS, THEN--

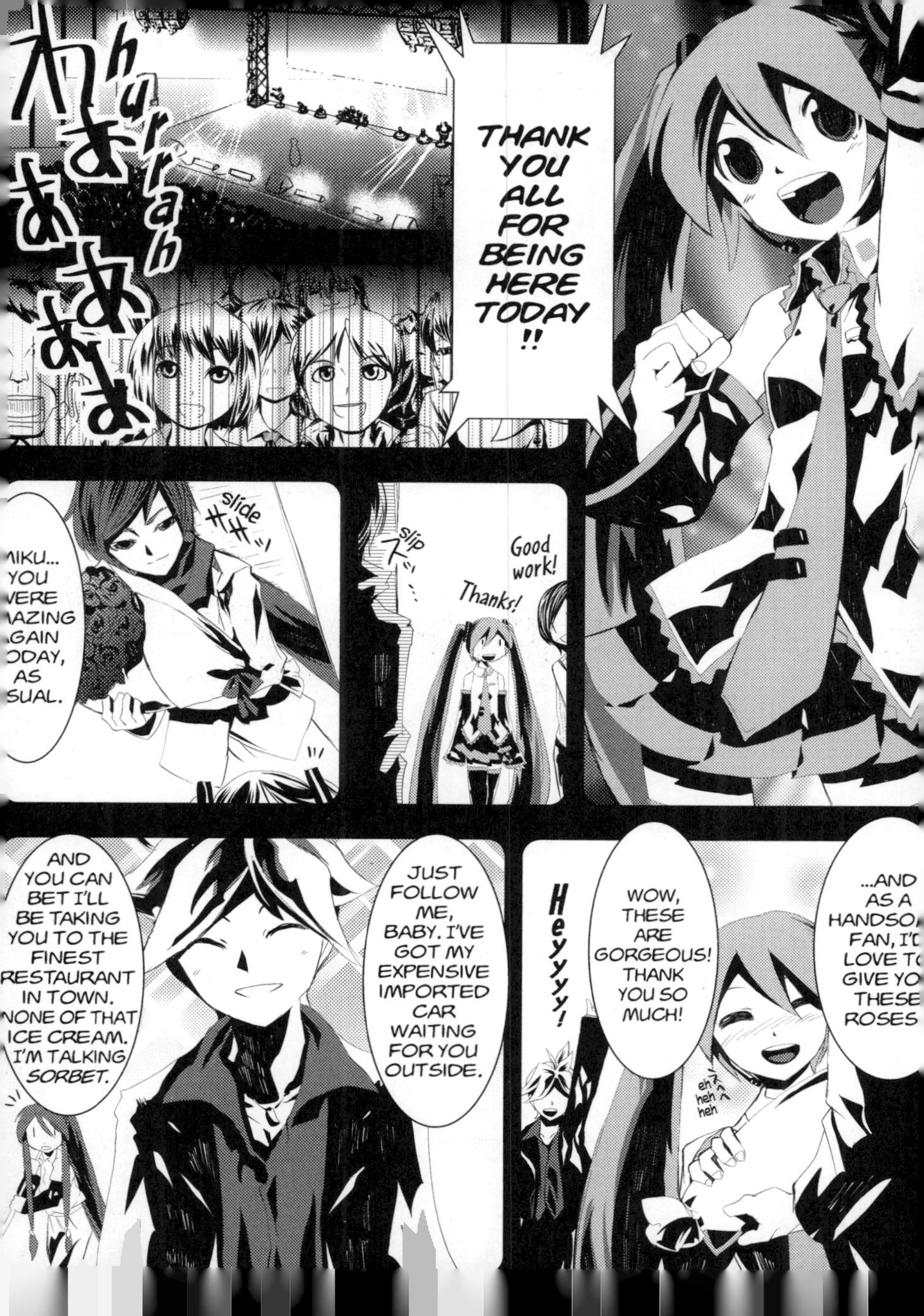
THANK YOU ALL FOR BEING HERE TODAY!!
hurrah
slip
Good work!
Thanks!
slide
IKU... YOU ERE AZING GAIN ODAY, AS SUAL.
...AND AS A HANDSO FAN, I'D LOVE TO GIVE YO THESE ROSES
WOW, THESE ARE GORGEOUS! THANK YOU SO MUCH!
eh heh heh
Heyyyy!
JUST FOLLOW ME, BABY. I'VE GOT MY EXPENSIVE IMPORTED CAR WAITING FOR YOU OUTSIDE.
AND YOU CAN BET I'LL BE TAKING YOU TO THE FINEST RESTAURANT IN TOWN. NONE OF THAT ICE CREAM. I'M TALKING SORBET.

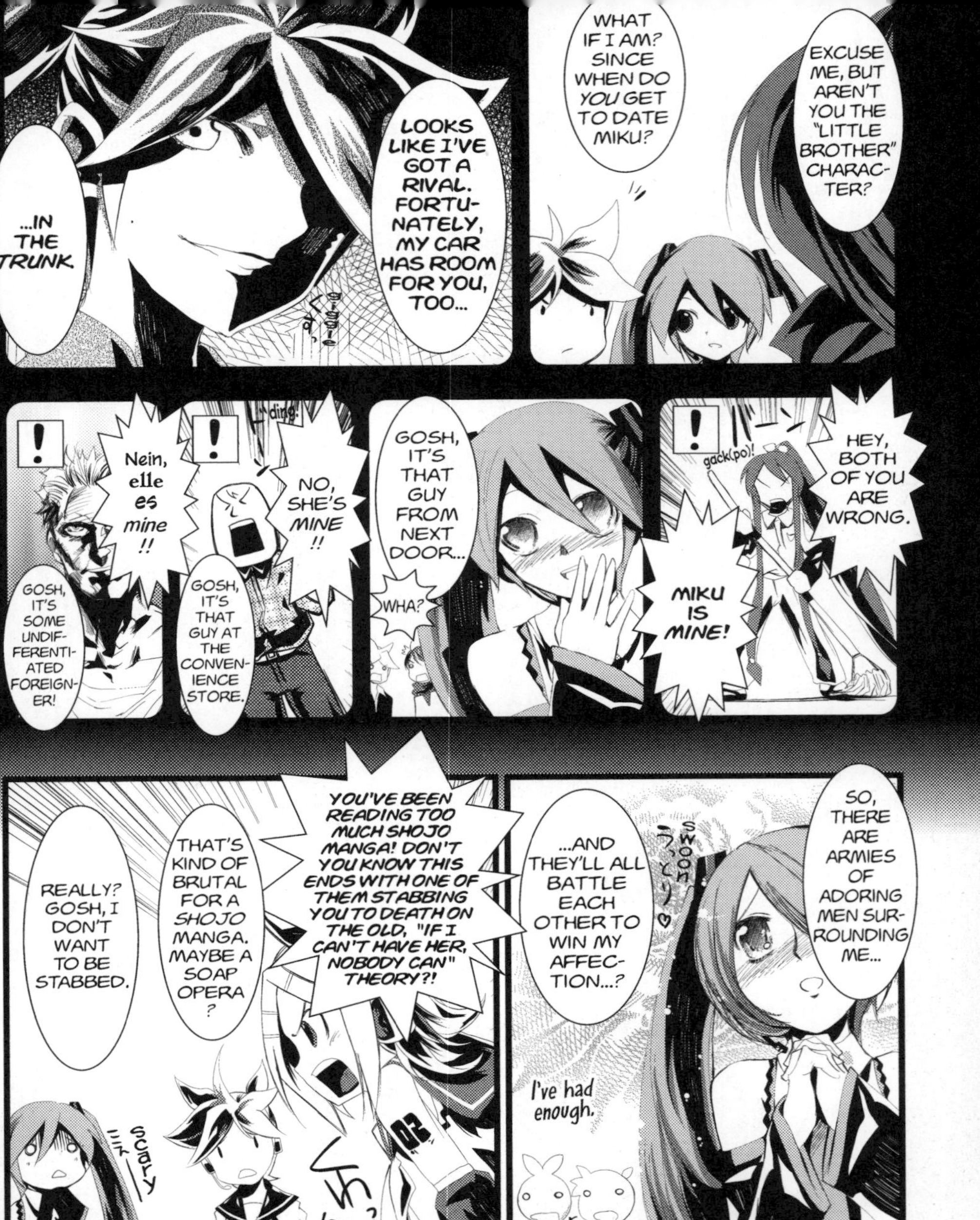
EXCUSE ME, BUT AREN'T YOU THE "LITTLE BROTHER" CHARACTER?
WHAT IF I AM? SINCE WHEN DO YOU GET TO DATE MIKU?
LOOKS LIKE I'VE GOT A RIVAL. FORTUNATELY, MY CAR HAS ROOM FOR YOU, TOO...
giggle
...IN THE TRUNK.
HEY, BOTH OF YOU ARE WRONG.
gack(po)!
MIKU IS MINE!
GOSH, IT'S THAT GUY FROM NEXT DOOR...
WHA?
ding!
NO, SHE'S MINE!!
GOSH, IT'S THAT GUY AT THE CONVENIENCE STORE.
Nein, elle es mine!!
GOSH, IT'S SOME UNDIFFERENTIATED FOREIGNER!
SO, THERE ARE ARMIES OF ADORING MEN SURROUNDING ME...
...AND THEY'LL ALL BATTLE EACH OTHER TO WIN MY AFFECTION...?
swoon
I've had enough.
retch
YOU'VE BEEN READING TOO MUCH SHOJO MANGA! DON'T YOU KNOW THIS ENDS WITH ONE OF THEM STABBING YOU TO DEATH ON THE OLD, "IF I CAN'T HAVE HER, NOBODY CAN" THEORY?!
THAT'S KIND OF BRUTAL FOR A SHOJO MANGA. MAYBE A SOAP OPERA?
REALLY? GOSH, I DON'T WANT TO BE STABBED.
leap!
scary

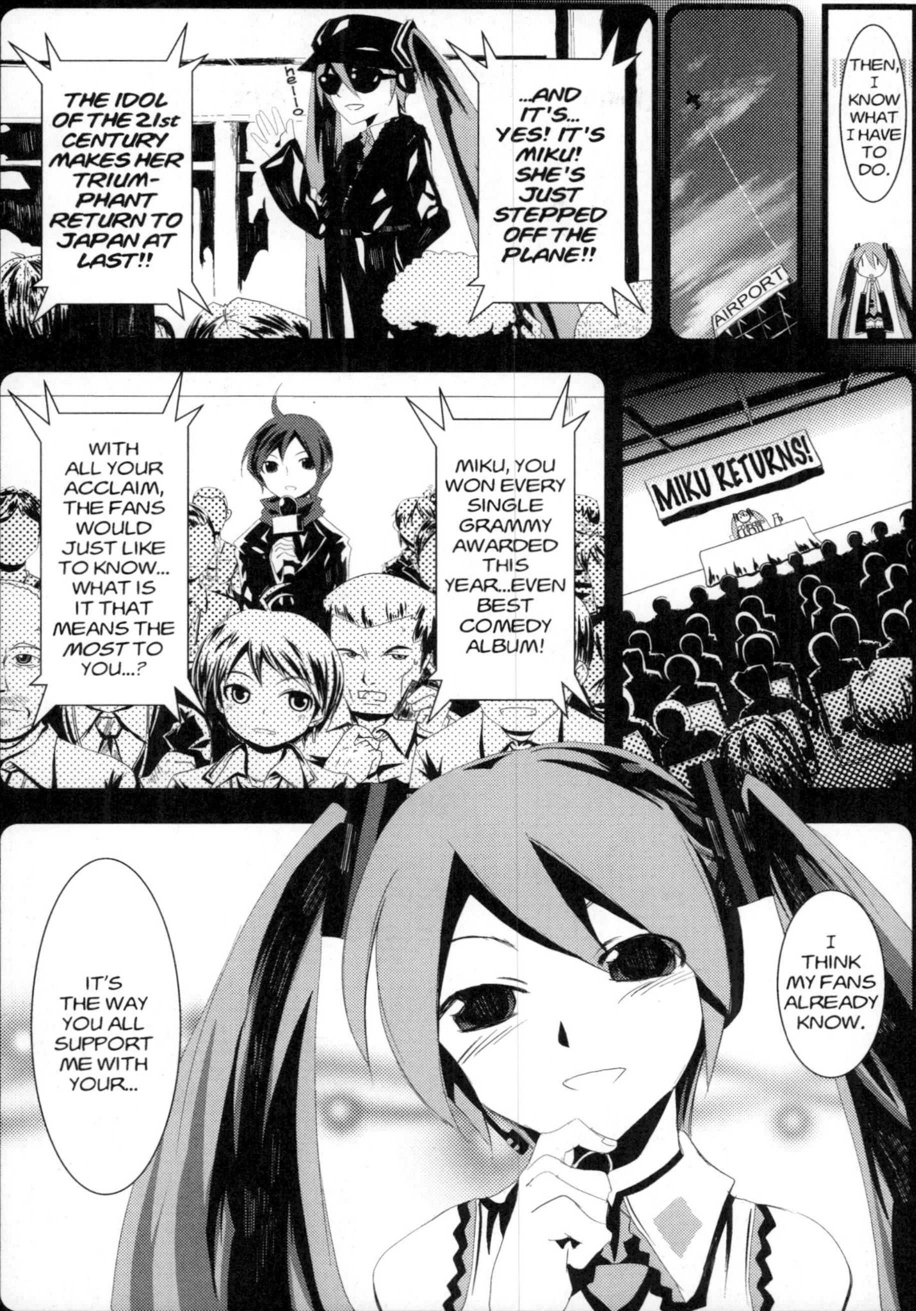
THEN, I KNOW WHAT I HAVE TO DO.
AIRPORT
...AND IT'S... YES! IT'S MIKU! SHE'S JUST STEPPED OFF THE PLANE!!
hello
THE IDOL OF THE 21st CENTURY MAKES HER TRIUMPHANT RETURN TO JAPAN AT LAST!!
MIKU RETURNS!
MIKU, YOU WON EVERY SINGLE GRAMMY AWARDED THIS YEAR...EVEN BEST COMEDY ALBUM!
WITH ALL YOUR ACCLAIM, THE FANS WOULD JUST LIKE TO KNOW... WHAT IS IT THAT MEANS THE MOST TO YOU...?
I THINK MY FANS ALREADY KNOW.
IT'S THE WAY YOU ALL SUPPORT ME WITH YOUR...

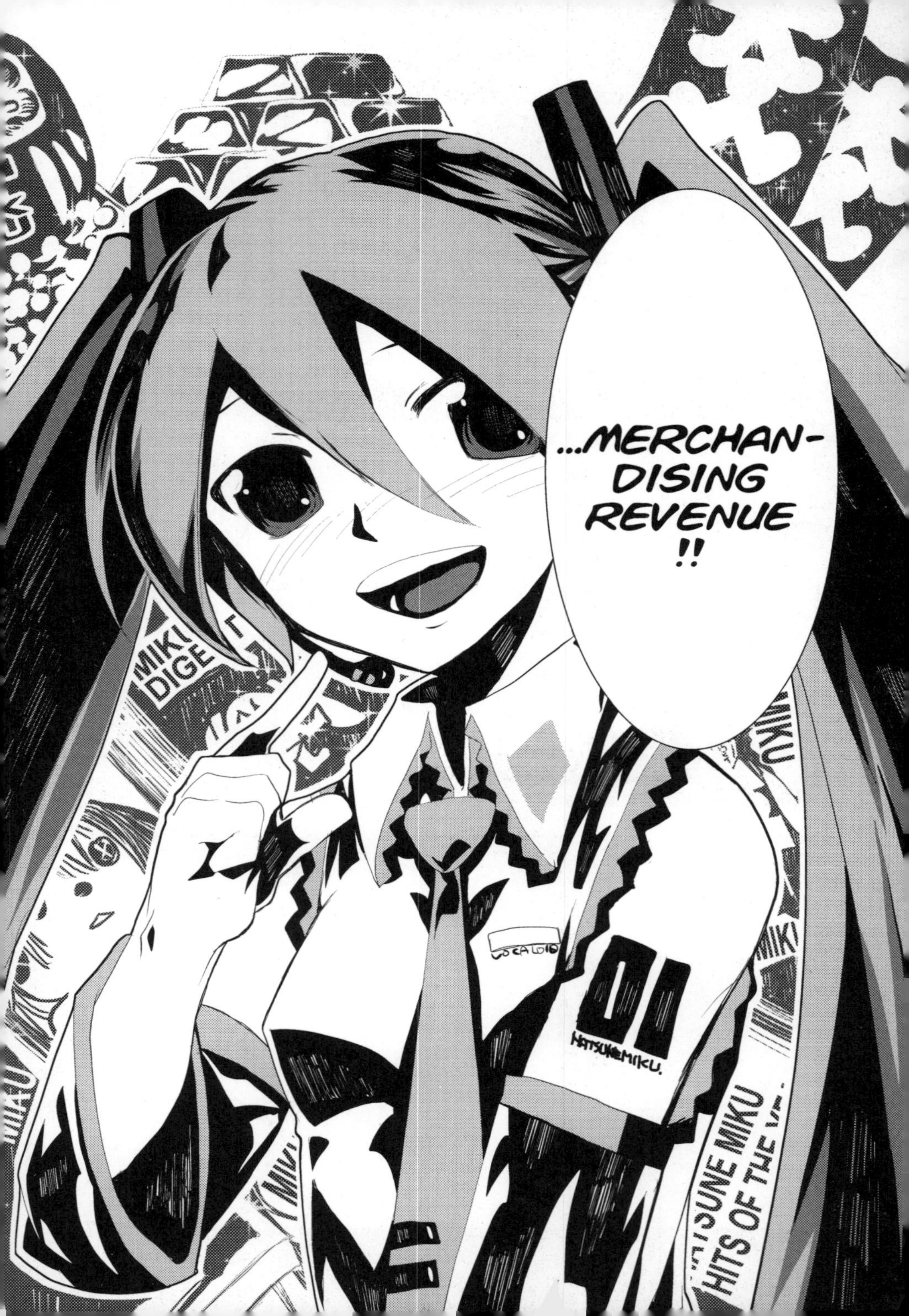
...MERCHAN-
DISING
REVENUE
!!

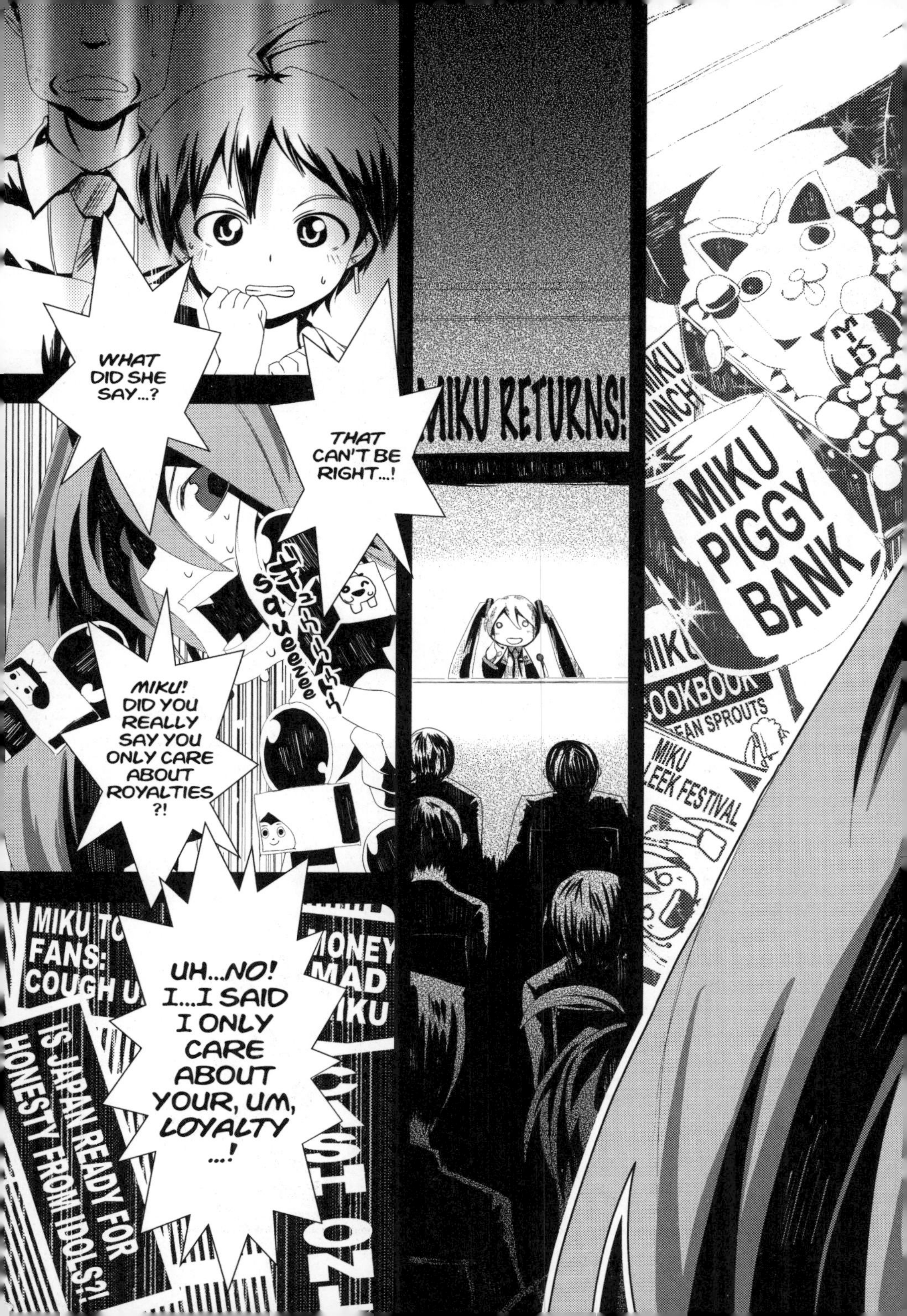

MIKU MUNCH
MIKU PIGGY BANK
MIKU
OOKBOOK
EAN SPROUTS
MIKU
LEEK FESTIVAL
MIKU RETURNS!
WHAT DID SHE SAY...?
THAT CAN'T BE RIGHT...!
squeeeee
MIKU! DID YOU REALLY SAY YOU ONLY CARE ABOUT ROYALTIES?!
MONEY MAD MIKU
MIKU TO FANS: COUGH U
IS JAPAN READY FOR HONESTY FROM IDOLS?!
UH...NO! I...I SAID I ONLY CARE ABOUT YOUR, UM, LOYALTY...!

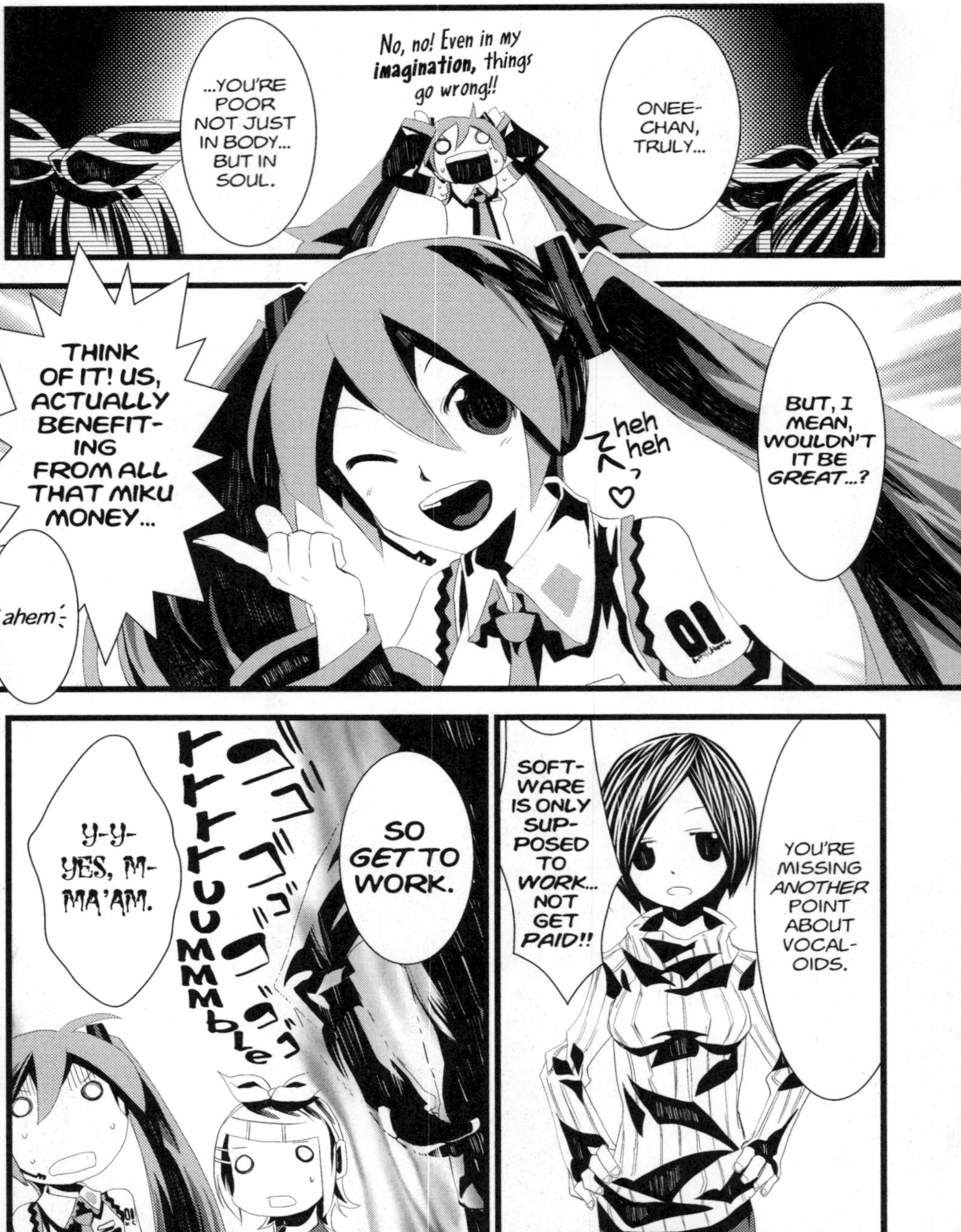
ONEE-CHAN, TRULY...
...YOU'RE POOR NOT JUST IN BODY... BUT IN SOUL.
No, no! Even in my imagination, things go wrong!!
BUT, I MEAN, WOULDN'T IT BE GREAT...?
heh heh
THINK OF IT! US, ACTUALLY BENEFITING FROM ALL THAT MIKU MONEY...
ahem
YOU'RE MISSING ANOTHER POINT ABOUT VOCALOIDS.
SOFTWARE IS ONLY SUPPOSED TO WORK... NOT GET PAID!!
SO GET TO WORK.
RUMMMble
Y-Y-YES, M-MA'AM.

(14th SONG) LOVE MIX

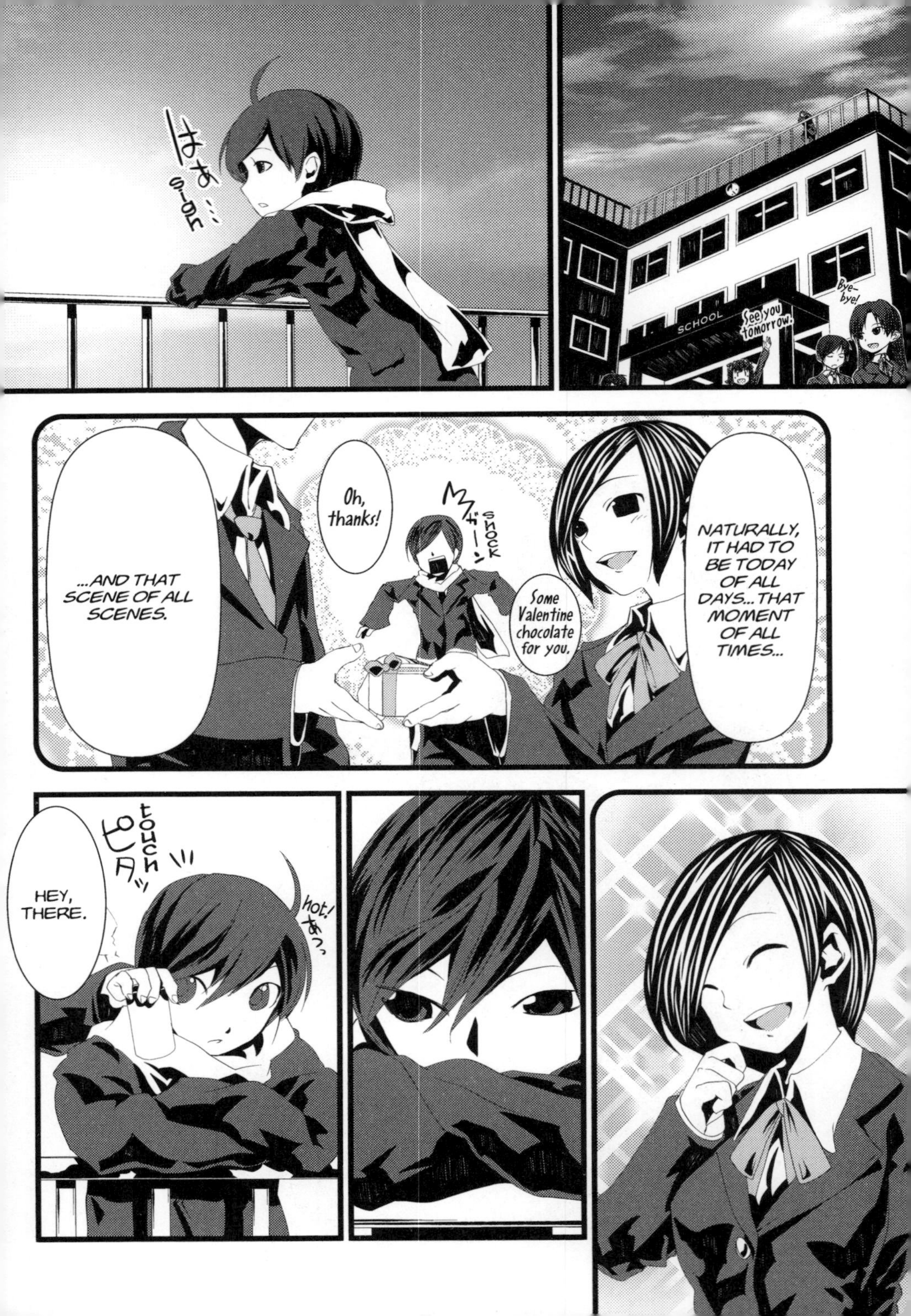
SCHOOL
Bye-bye!
See you tomorrow.
はぁ…
sigh
NATURALLY, IT HAD TO BE TODAY OF ALL DAYS...THAT MOMENT OF ALL TIMES...
Some Valentine chocolate for you.
ガーン
SHOCK
Oh, thanks!
...AND THAT SCENE OF ALL SCENES.
ピタッ
touch
あつっ
hot!
HEY, THERE.

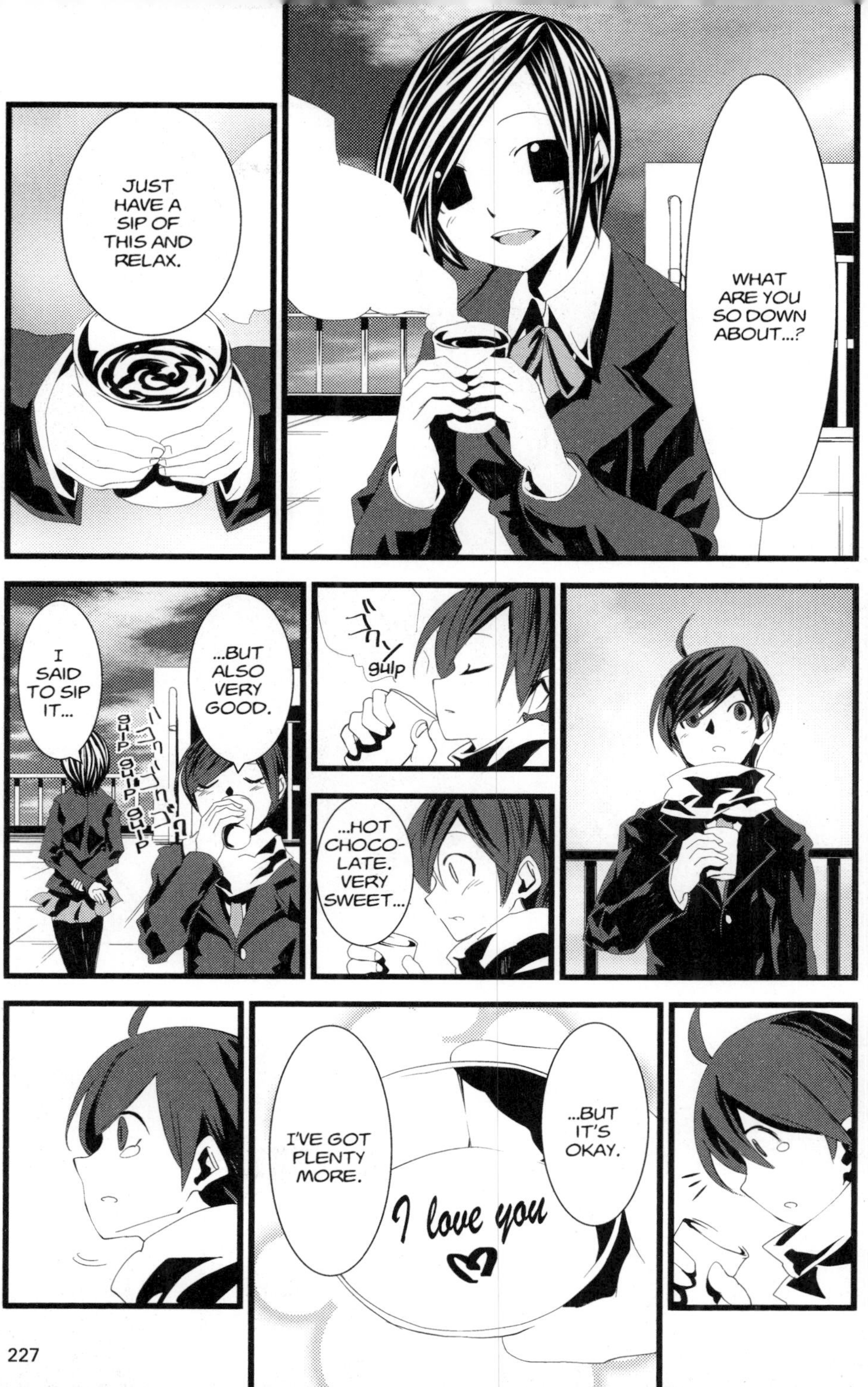
WHAT ARE YOU SO DOWN ABOUT...?
JUST HAVE A SIP OF THIS AND RELAX.
gulp
...HOT CHOCOLATE. VERY SWEET...
...BUT ALSO VERY GOOD.
gulp gulp gulp gulp
I SAID TO SIP IT...
...BUT IT'S OKAY.
I'VE GOT PLENTY MORE.
I love you

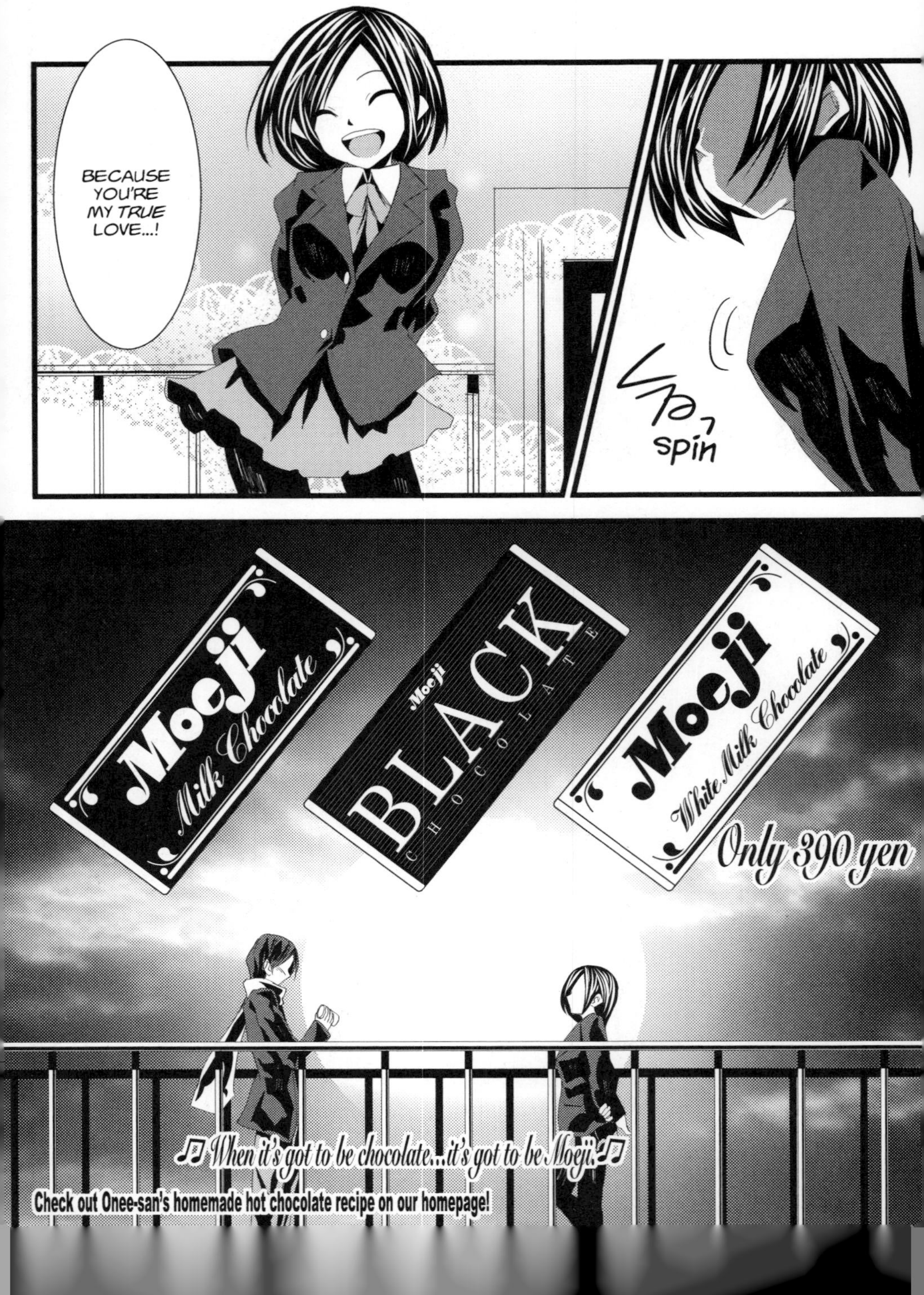
spin
BECAUSE YOU'RE MY *TRUE* LOVE...!
Moeji Milk Chocolate
Moeji BLACK CHOCOLATE
Moeji White Milk Chocolate
Only 390 yen
♫ When it's got to be chocolate...it's got to be Moeji.♫
Check out Onee-san's homemade hot chocolate recipe on our homepage!

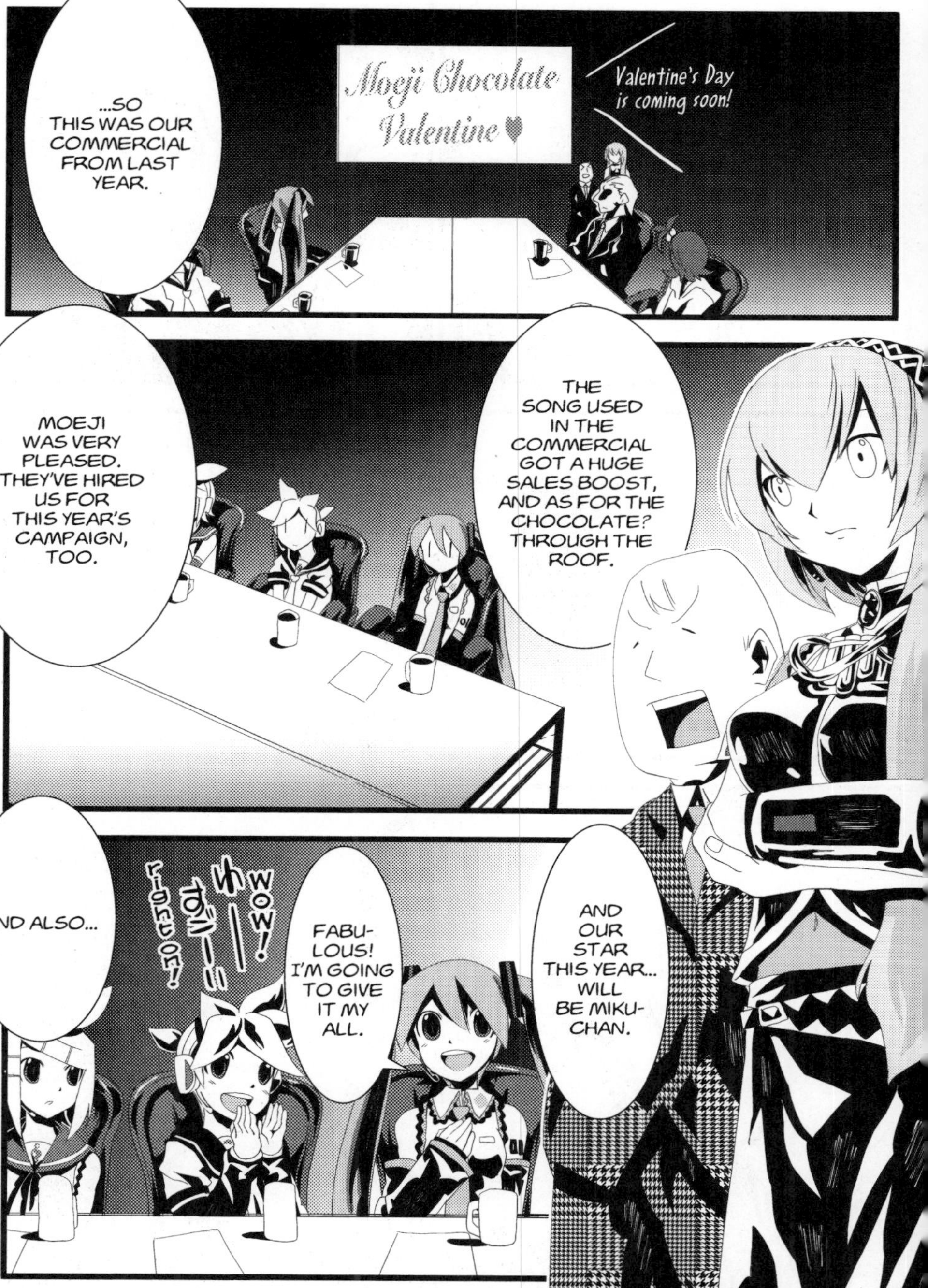

Valentine's Day is coming soon!
Moeji Chocolate Valentine♥
...SO THIS WAS OUR COMMERCIAL FROM LAST YEAR.
THE SONG USED IN THE COMMERCIAL GOT A HUGE SALES BOOST, AND AS FOR THE CHOCOLATE? THROUGH THE ROOF.
MOEJI WAS VERY PLEASED. THEY'VE HIRED US FOR THIS YEAR'S CAMPAIGN, TOO.
AND OUR STAR THIS YEAR... WILL BE MIKU-CHAN.
FABU-LOUS! I'M GOING TO GIVE IT MY ALL.
WOW!
right on!
AND ALSO...

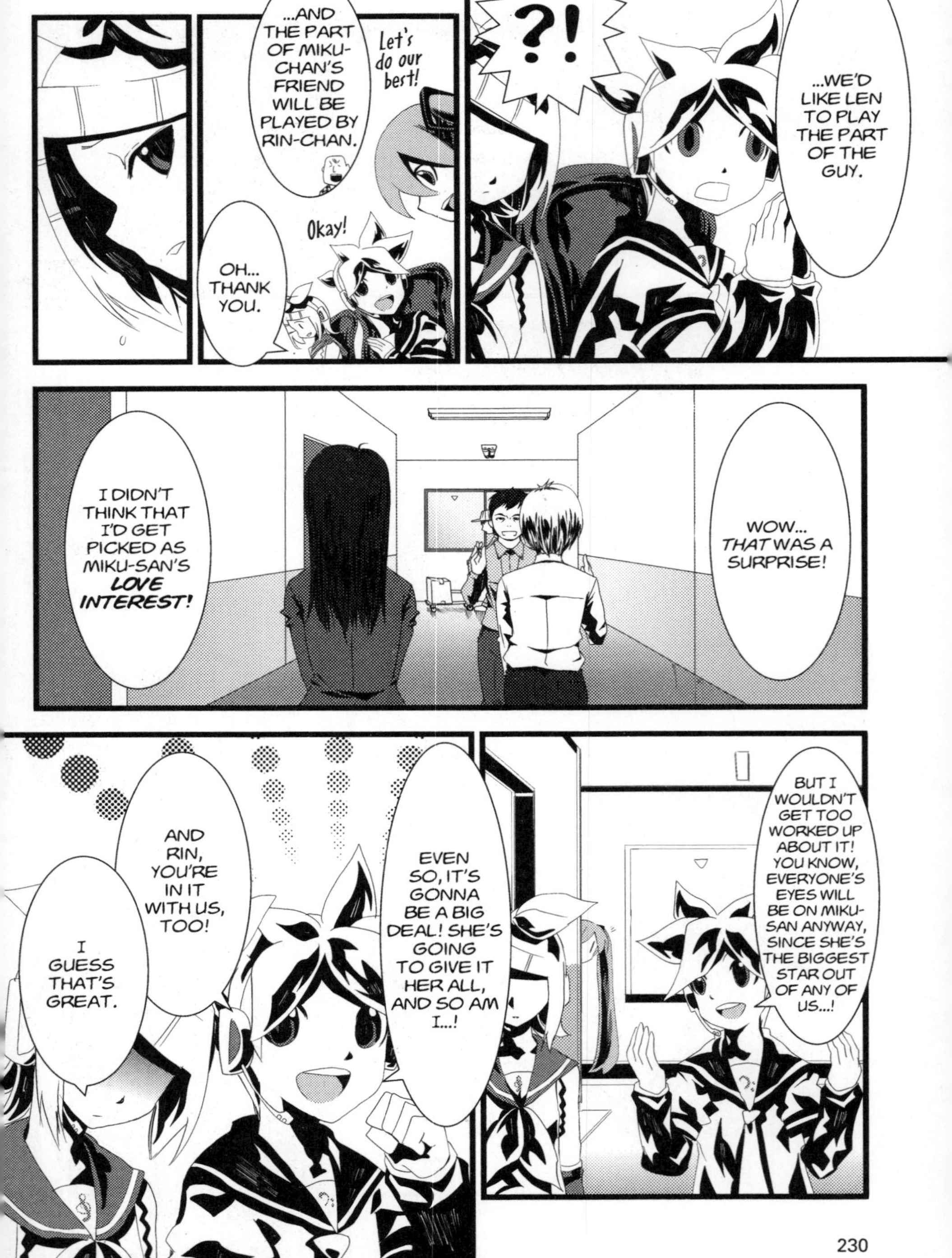
...WE'D LIKE LEN TO PLAY THE PART OF THE GUY.
?!
...AND THE PART OF MIKU-CHAN'S FRIEND WILL BE PLAYED BY RIN-CHAN.
Let's do our best!
Okay!
OH... THANK YOU.
WOW... THAT WAS A SURPRISE!
I DIDN'T THINK THAT I'D GET PICKED AS MIKU-SAN'S LOVE INTEREST!
BUT I WOULDN'T GET TOO WORKED UP ABOUT IT! YOU KNOW, EVERYONE'S EYES WILL BE ON MIKU-SAN ANYWAY, SINCE SHE'S THE BIGGEST STAR OUT OF ANY OF US...!
EVEN SO, IT'S GONNA BE A BIG DEAL! SHE'S GOING TO GIVE IT HER ALL, AND SO AM I...!
AND RIN, YOU'RE IN IT WITH US, TOO!
I GUESS THAT'S GREAT.

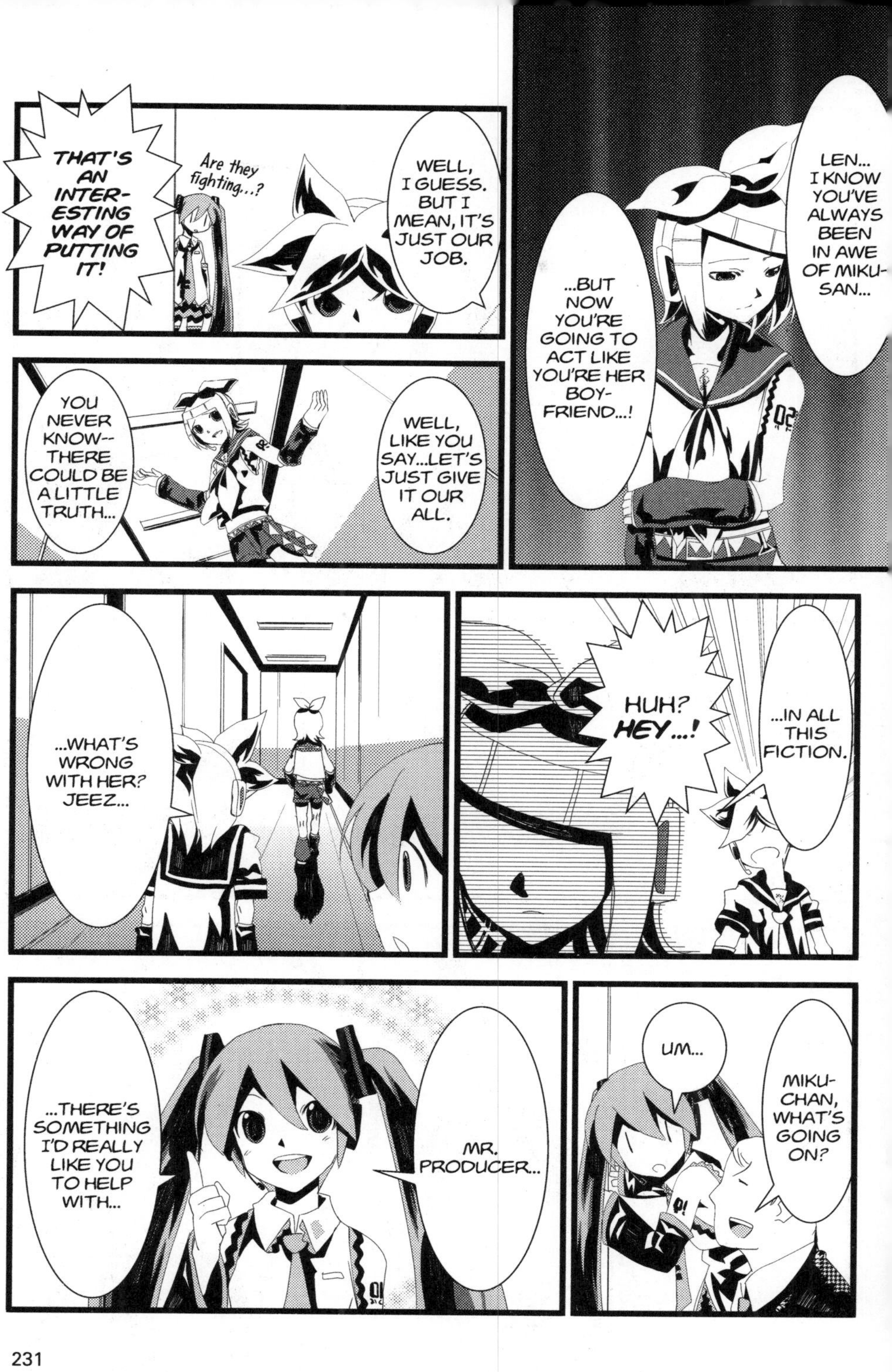
LEN... I KNOW YOU'VE ALWAYS BEEN IN AWE OF MIKU-SAN...
...BUT NOW YOU'RE GOING TO ACT LIKE YOU'RE HER BOY-FRIEND...!
WELL, I GUESS. BUT I MEAN, IT'S JUST OUR JOB.
Are they fighting...?
THAT'S AN INTER-ESTING WAY OF PUTTING IT!
WELL, LIKE YOU SAY...LET'S JUST GIVE IT OUR ALL.
YOU NEVER KNOW-- THERE COULD BE A LITTLE TRUTH...
...IN ALL THIS FICTION.
HUH? HEY...!
...WHAT'S WRONG WITH HER? JEEZ...
MIKU-CHAN, WHAT'S GOING ON?
UM...
MR. PRODUCER...
...THERE'S SOMETHING I'D REALLY LIKE YOU TO HELP WITH...

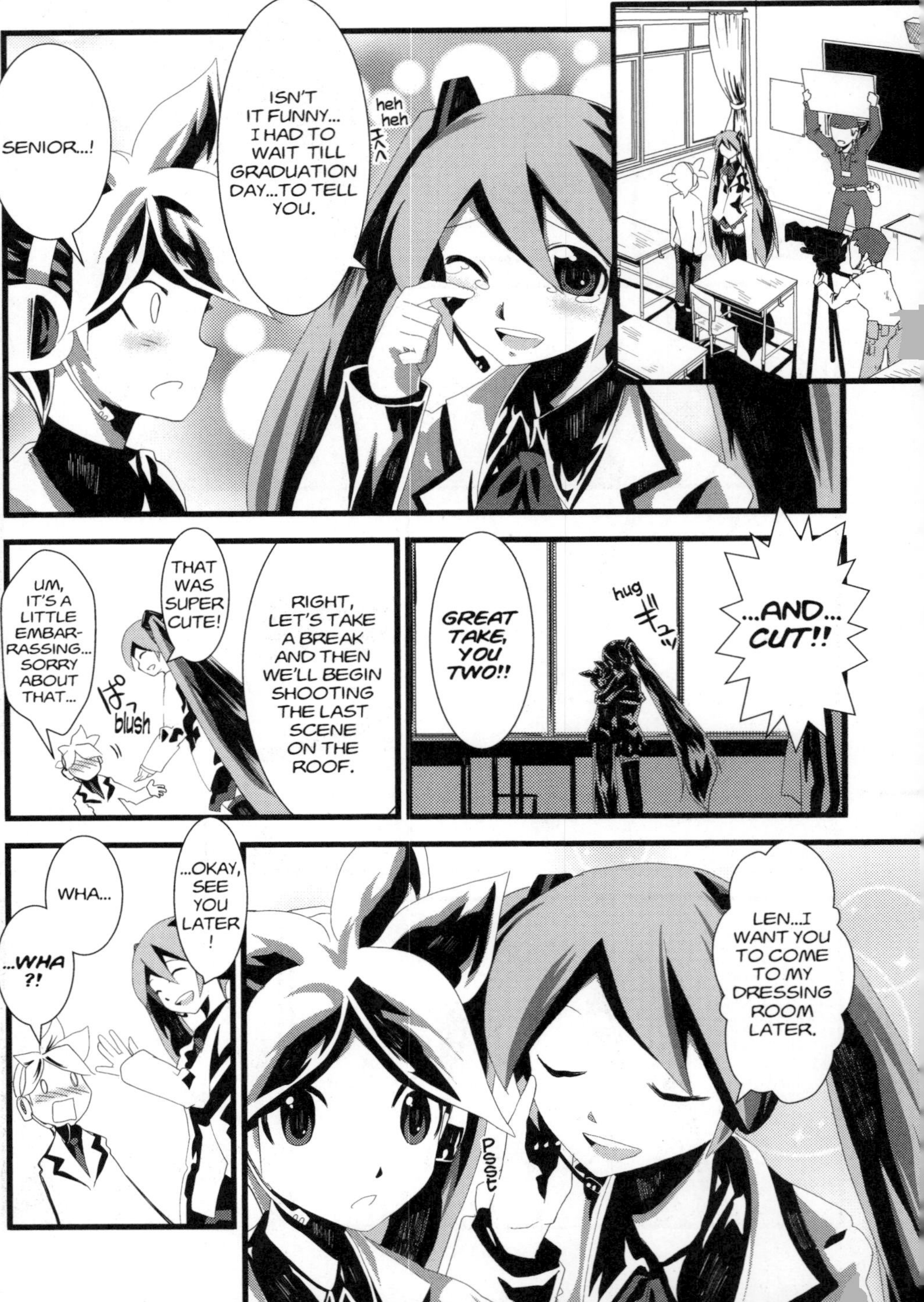
ISN'T IT FUNNY... I HAD TO WAIT TILL GRADUATION DAY...TO TELL YOU.
heh heh
SENIOR...!
...AND... CUT!!
hug
GREAT TAKE, YOU TWO!!
RIGHT, LET'S TAKE A BREAK AND THEN WE'LL BEGIN SHOOTING THE LAST SCENE ON THE ROOF.
THAT WAS SUPER CUTE!
UM, IT'S A LITTLE EMBARRASSING... SORRY ABOUT THAT...
blush
LEN...I WANT YOU TO COME TO MY DRESSING ROOM LATER.
PSST
...OKAY, SEE YOU LATER!
WHA...
...WHA?!

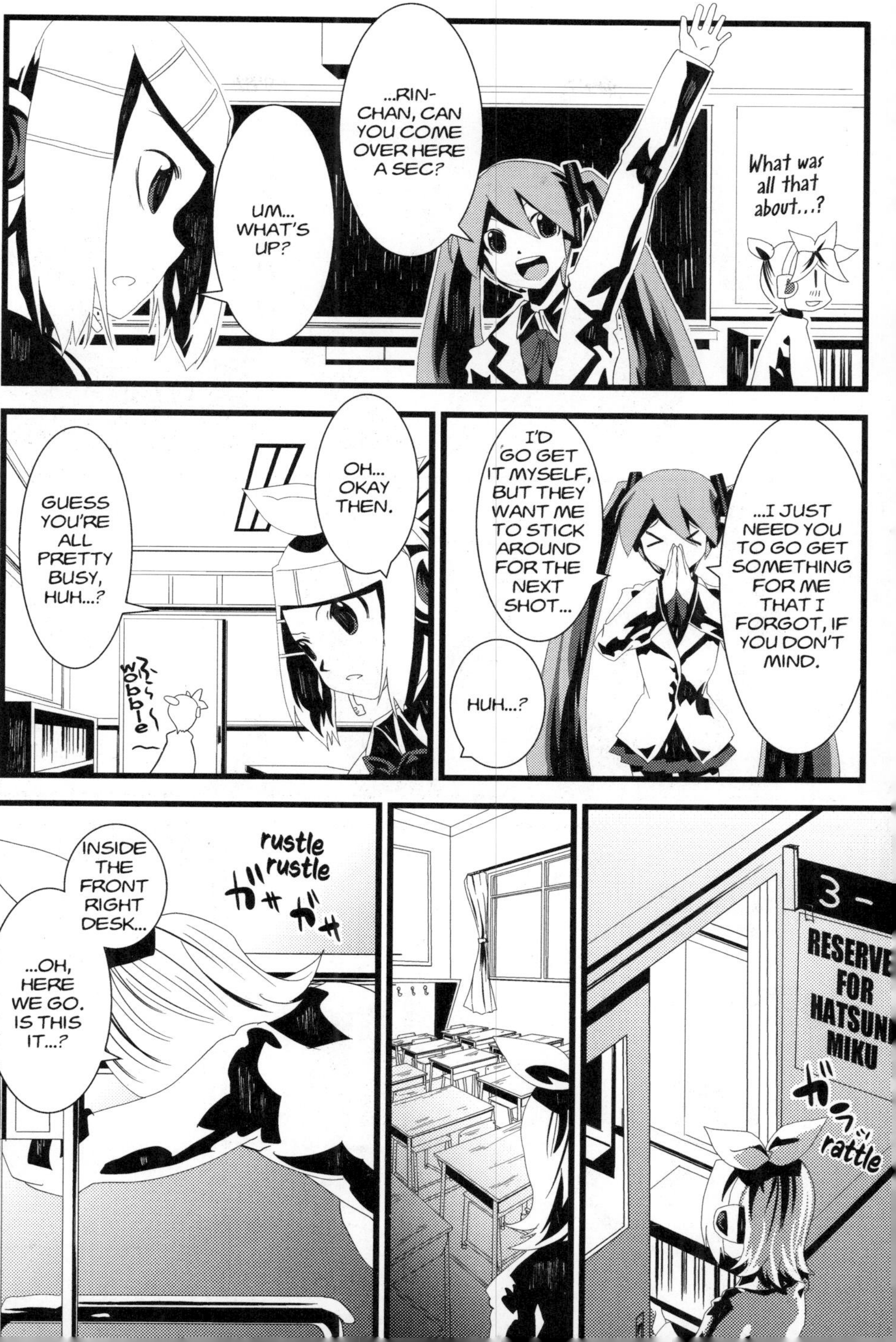
What was all that about...?
...RIN-CHAN, CAN YOU COME OVER HERE A SEC?
UM... WHAT'S UP?
...I JUST NEED YOU TO GO GET SOMETHING FOR ME THAT I FORGOT, IF YOU DON'T MIND.
I'D GO GET IT MYSELF, BUT THEY WANT ME TO STICK AROUND FOR THE NEXT SHOT...
HUH...?
OH... OKAY THEN.
GUESS YOU'RE ALL PRETTY BUSY, HUH...?
wobble
3-
RESERVE
FOR
HATSUN
MIKU
rattle
rustle rustle
INSIDE THE FRONT RIGHT DESK...
...OH, HERE WE GO. IS THIS IT...?

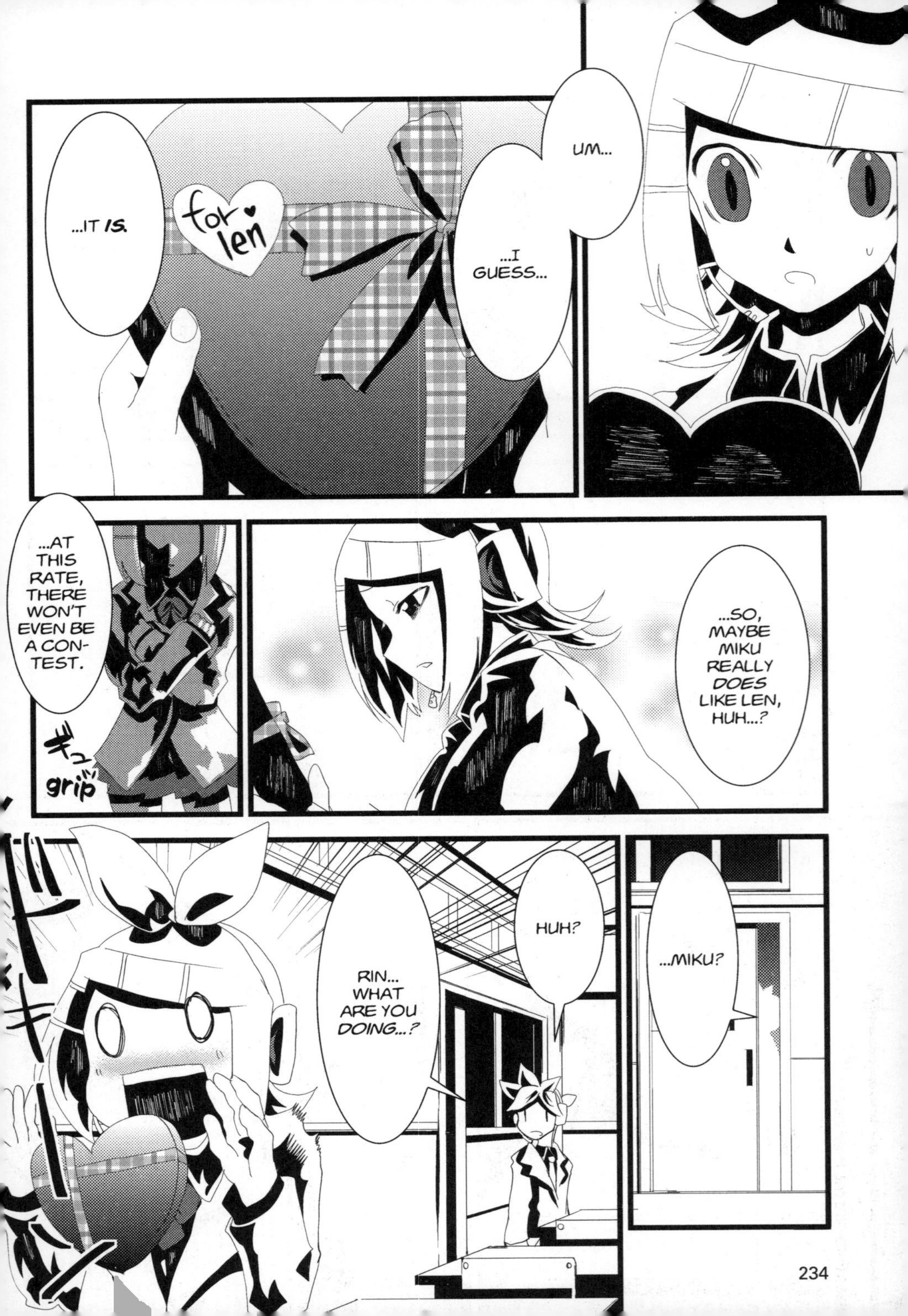
UM...
...I GUESS...
...IT IS.
for len
...SO, MAYBE MIKU REALLY DOES LIKE LEN, HUH...?
...AT THIS RATE, THERE WON'T EVEN BE A CON-TEST.
grip
...MIKU?
HUH?
RIN... WHAT ARE YOU DOING...?

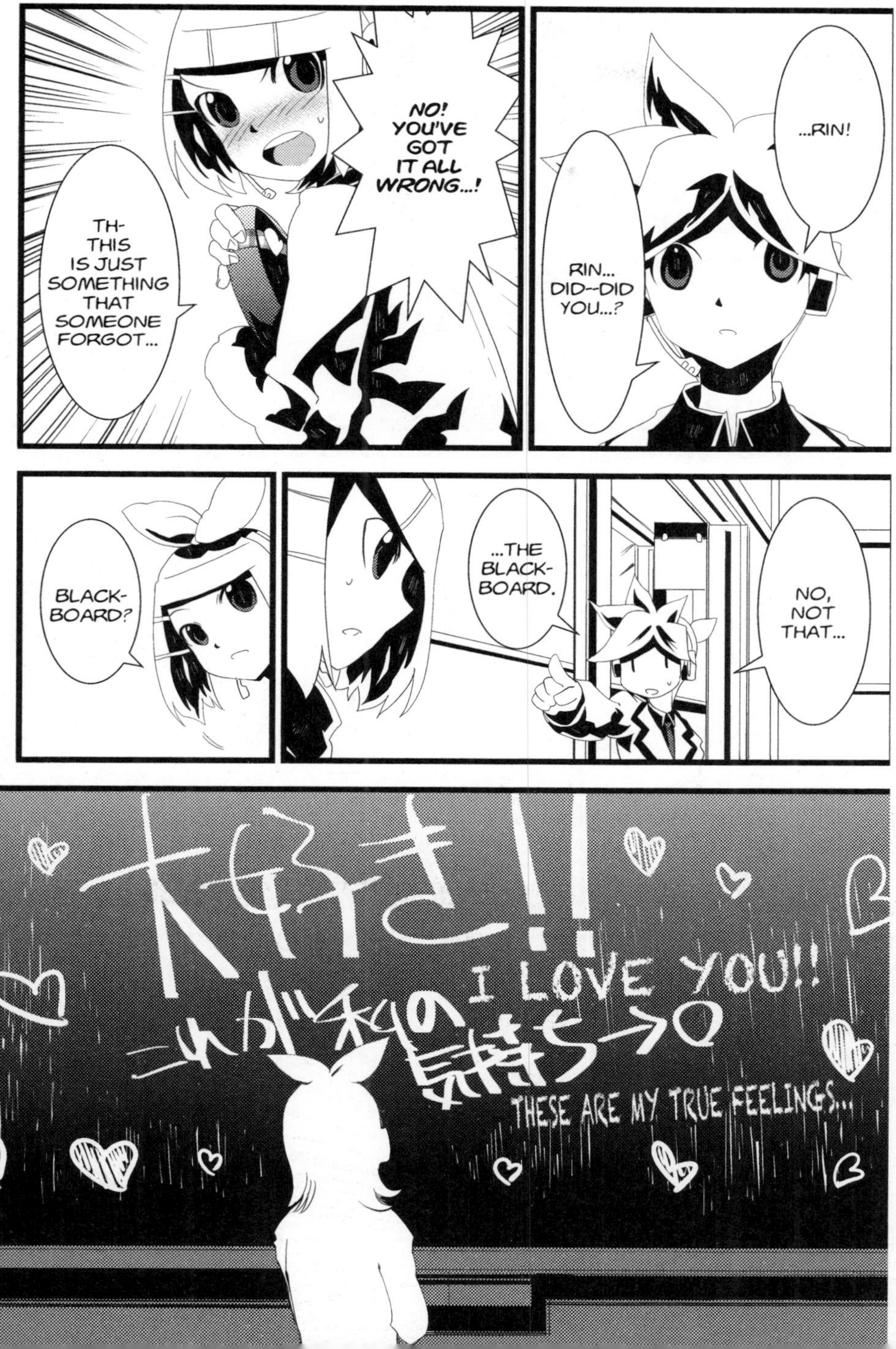
...RIN!
RIN... DID--DID YOU...?
NO! YOU'VE GOT IT ALL WRONG...!
TH- THIS IS JUST SOMETHING THAT SOMEONE FORGOT...
NO, NOT THAT...
...THE BLACK-BOARD.
BLACK-BOARD?
大好き!!
I LOVE YOU!!
これが私の気持ち→♡
THESE ARE MY TRUE FEELINGS...

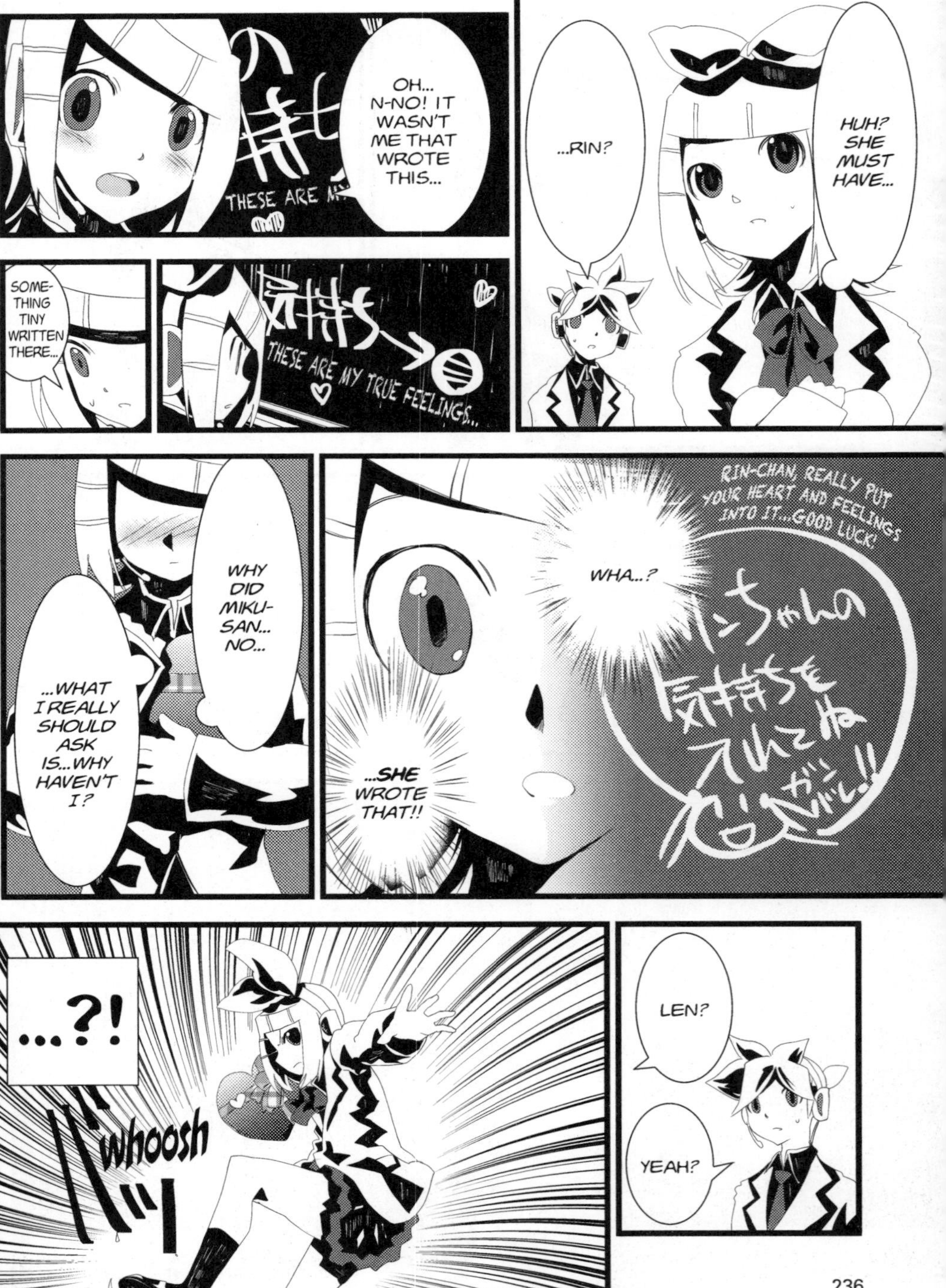
HUH? SHE MUST HAVE...
...RIN?
OH... N-NO! IT WASN'T ME THAT WROTE THIS...
THESE ARE MY
THESE ARE MY TRUE FEELINGS...
SOMETHING TINY WRITTEN THERE...
RIN-CHAN, REALLY PUT YOUR HEART AND FEELINGS INTO IT...GOOD LUCK!
WHA...?
...SHE WROTE THAT!!
WHY DID MIKU-SAN... NO...
...WHAT I REALLY SHOULD ASK IS...WHY HAVEN'T I?
LEN?
YEAH?
...?!
whoosh

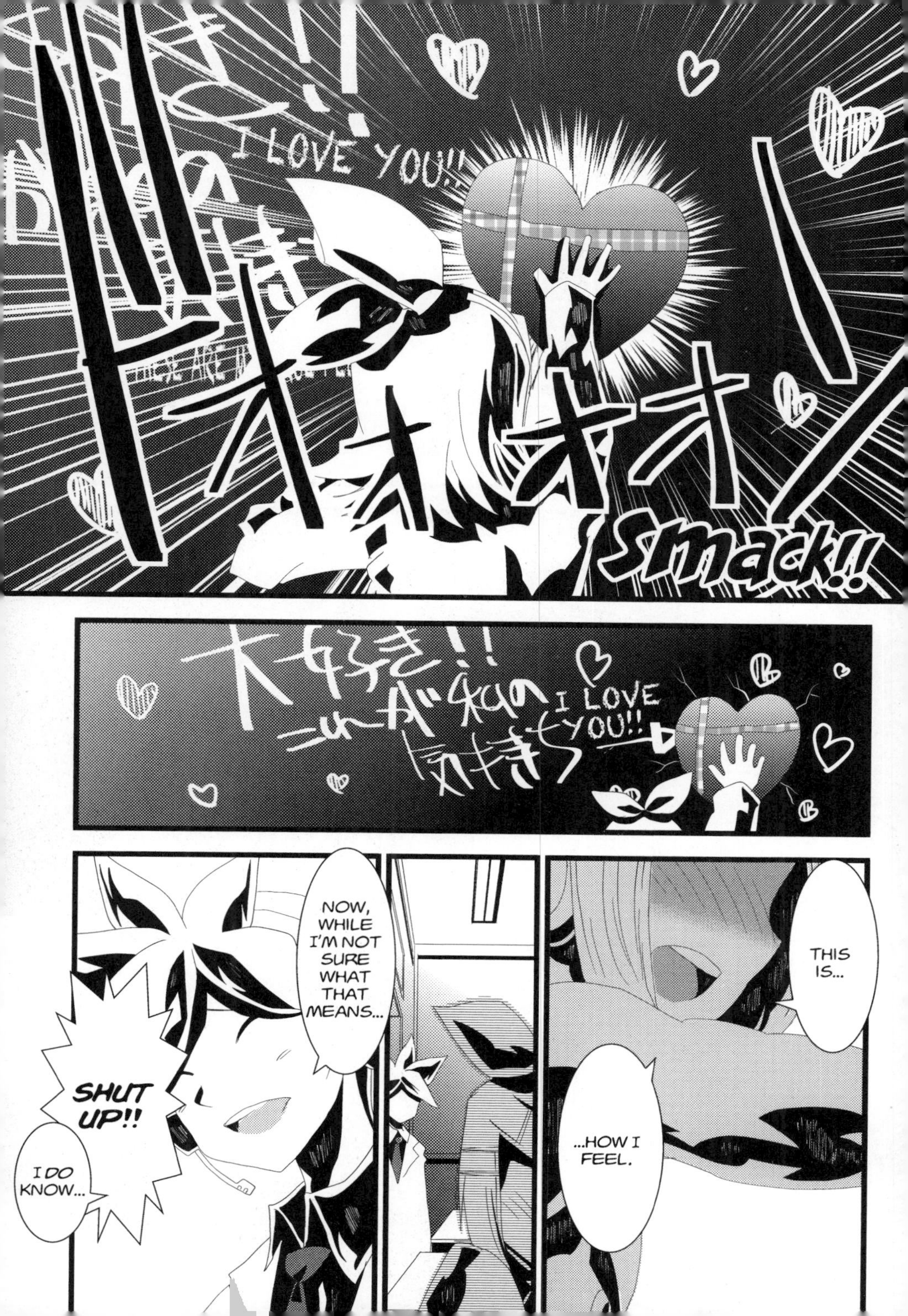
I LOVE YOU!!
Smack!!
I LOVE YOU!!
THIS IS...
...HOW I FEEL.
NOW, WHILE I'M NOT SURE WHAT THAT MEANS...
SHUT UP!!
I DO KNOW...

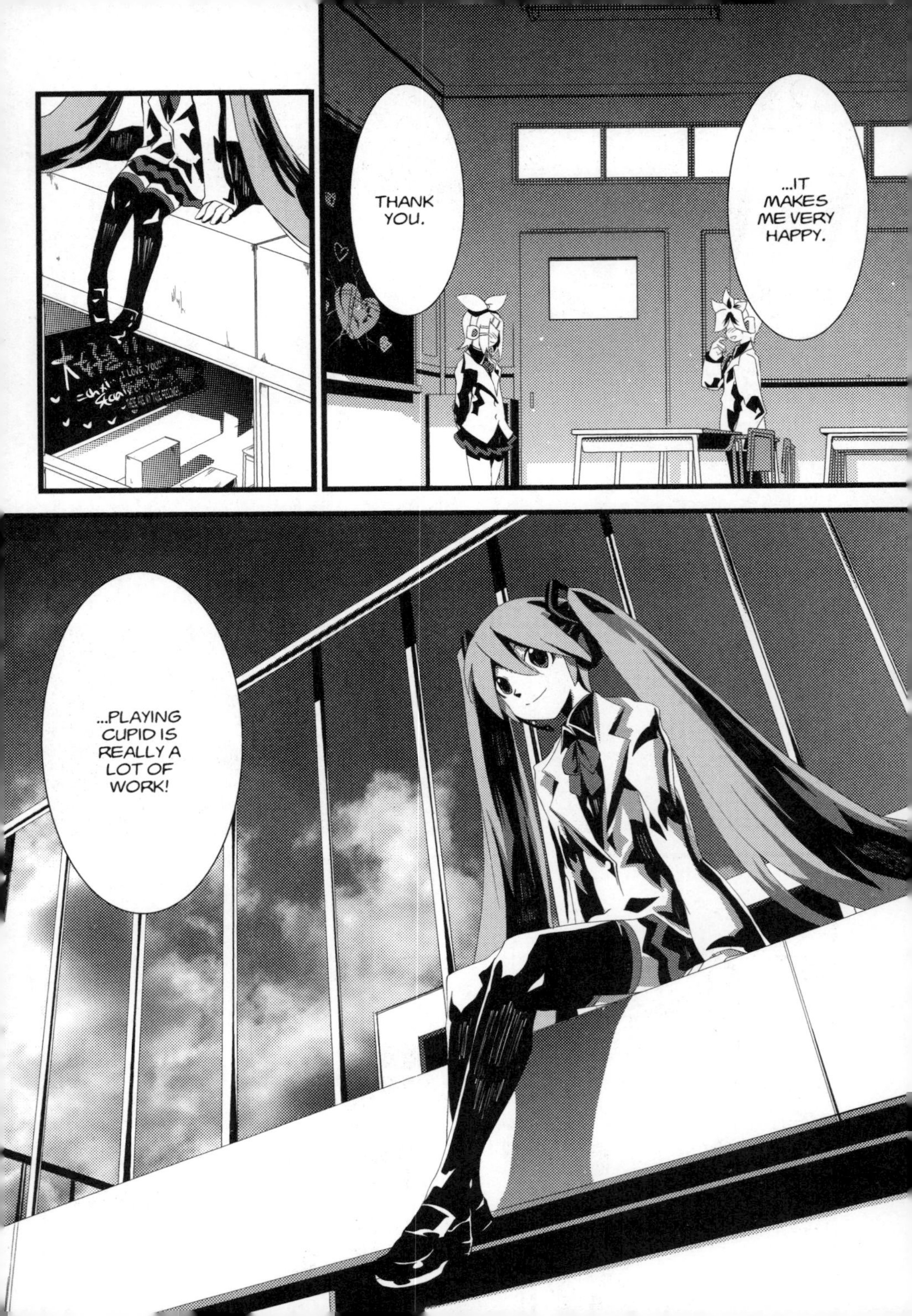
...IT MAKES ME VERY HAPPY.
THANK YOU.
...PLAYING CUPID IS REALLY A LOT OF WORK!

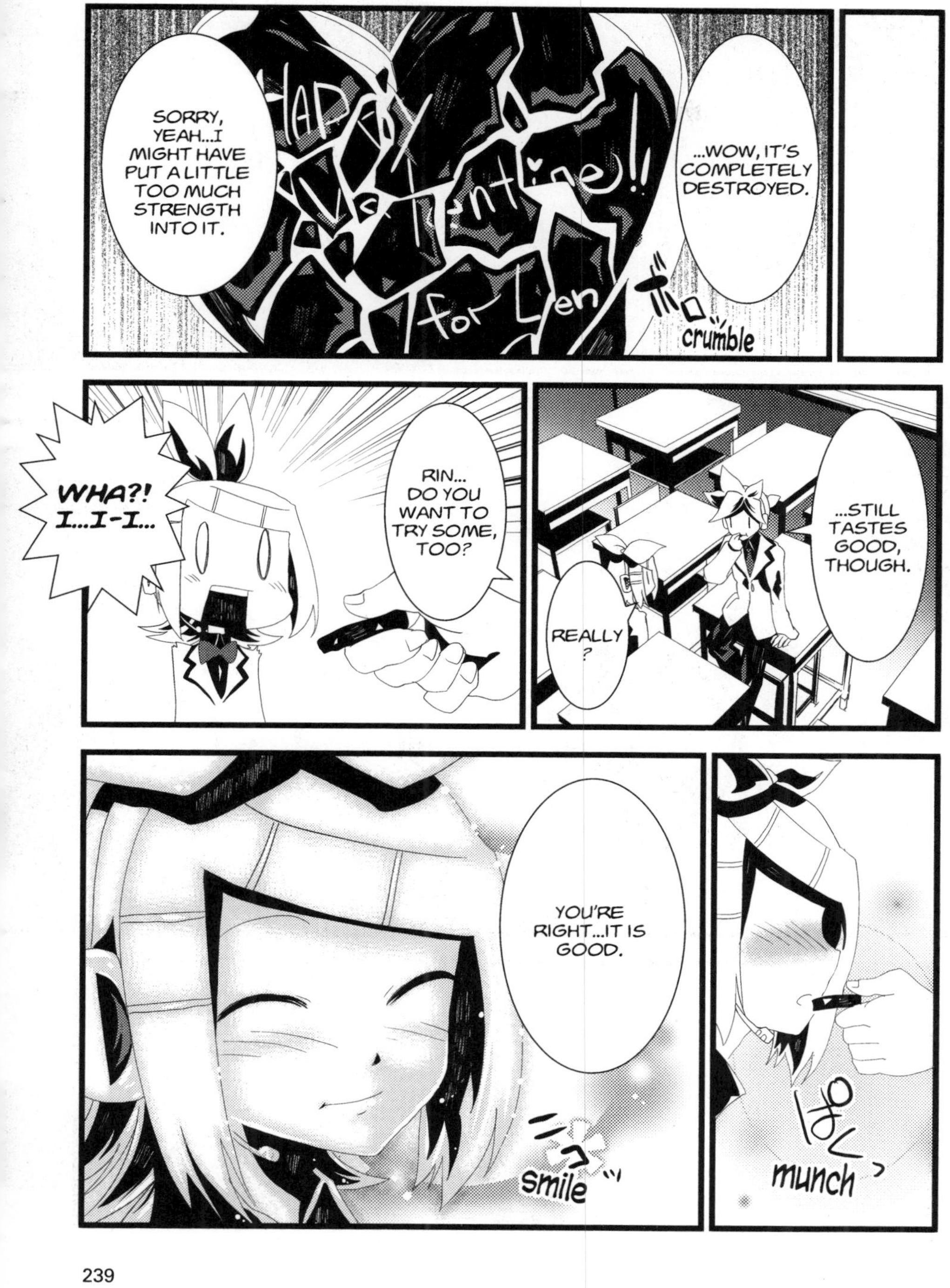
...WOW, IT'S COMPLETELY DESTROYED.
SORRY, YEAH...I MIGHT HAVE PUT A LITTLE TOO MUCH STRENGTH INTO IT.
HAPPY Valentine!!
for Len
crumble
...STILL TASTES GOOD, THOUGH.
REALLY?
RIN... DO YOU WANT TO TRY SOME, TOO?
WHA?! I...I-I...
munch
YOU'RE RIGHT...IT IS GOOD.
smile

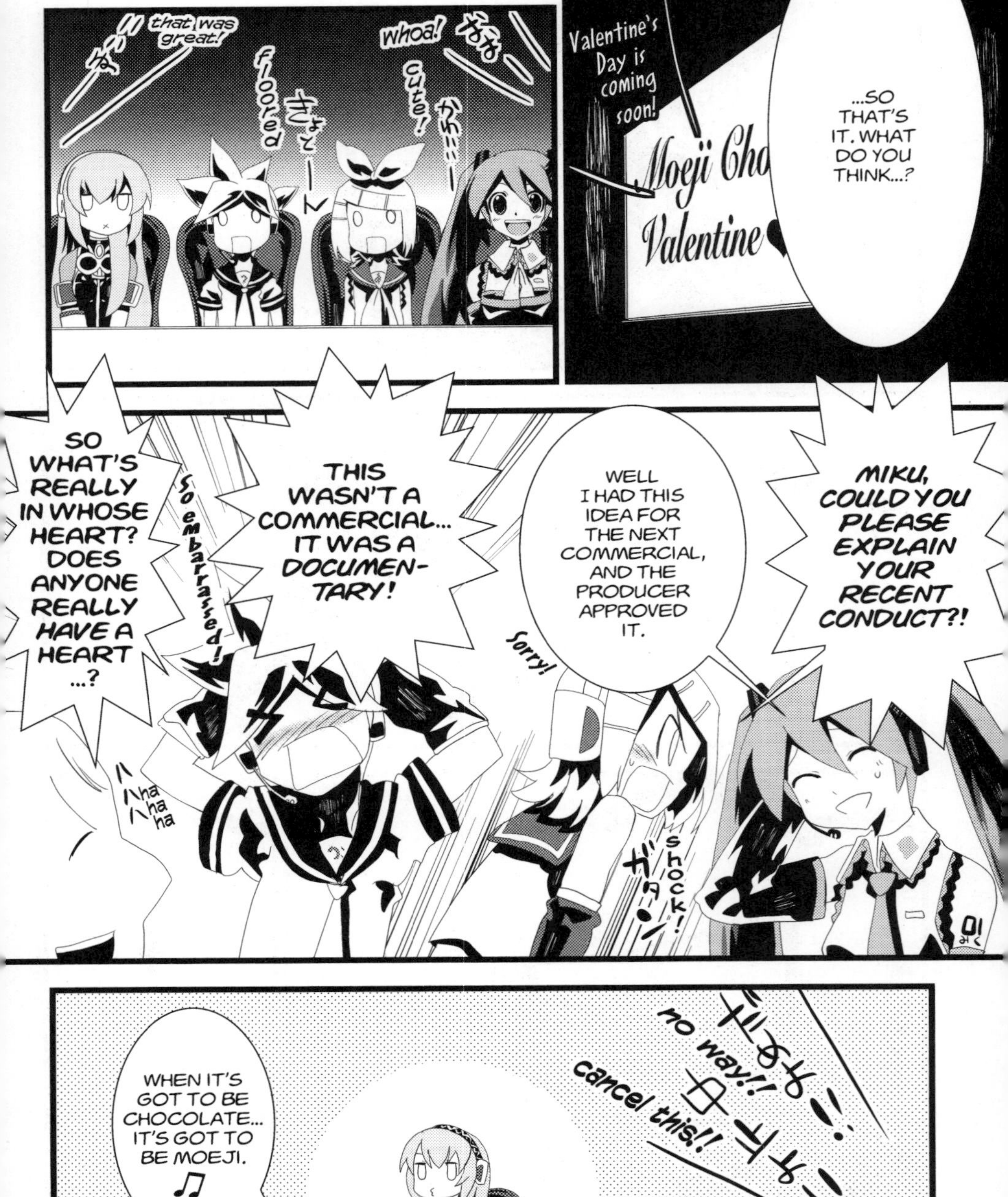
Valentine's Day is coming soon!
Moeji Cho
Valentine
...SO THAT'S IT. WHAT DO YOU THINK...?
whoa!
cute!
floored
that was great!
MIKU, COULD YOU PLEASE EXPLAIN YOUR RECENT CONDUCT?!
WELL I HAD THIS IDEA FOR THE NEXT COMMERCIAL, AND THE PRODUCER APPROVED IT.
Sorry!
shock!
THIS WASN'T A COMMERCIAL... IT WAS A DOCUMENTARY!
So embarrassed!
SO WHAT'S REALLY IN WHOSE HEART? DOES ANYONE REALLY HAVE A HEART ...?
ハハハ
ha ha ha
no way!!
cancel this!!
WHEN IT'S GOT TO BE CHOCOLATE... IT'S GOT TO BE MOEJI. ♫

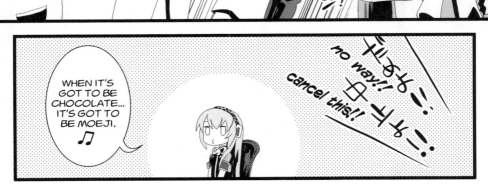

(15th SONG) GRADUATION MIX

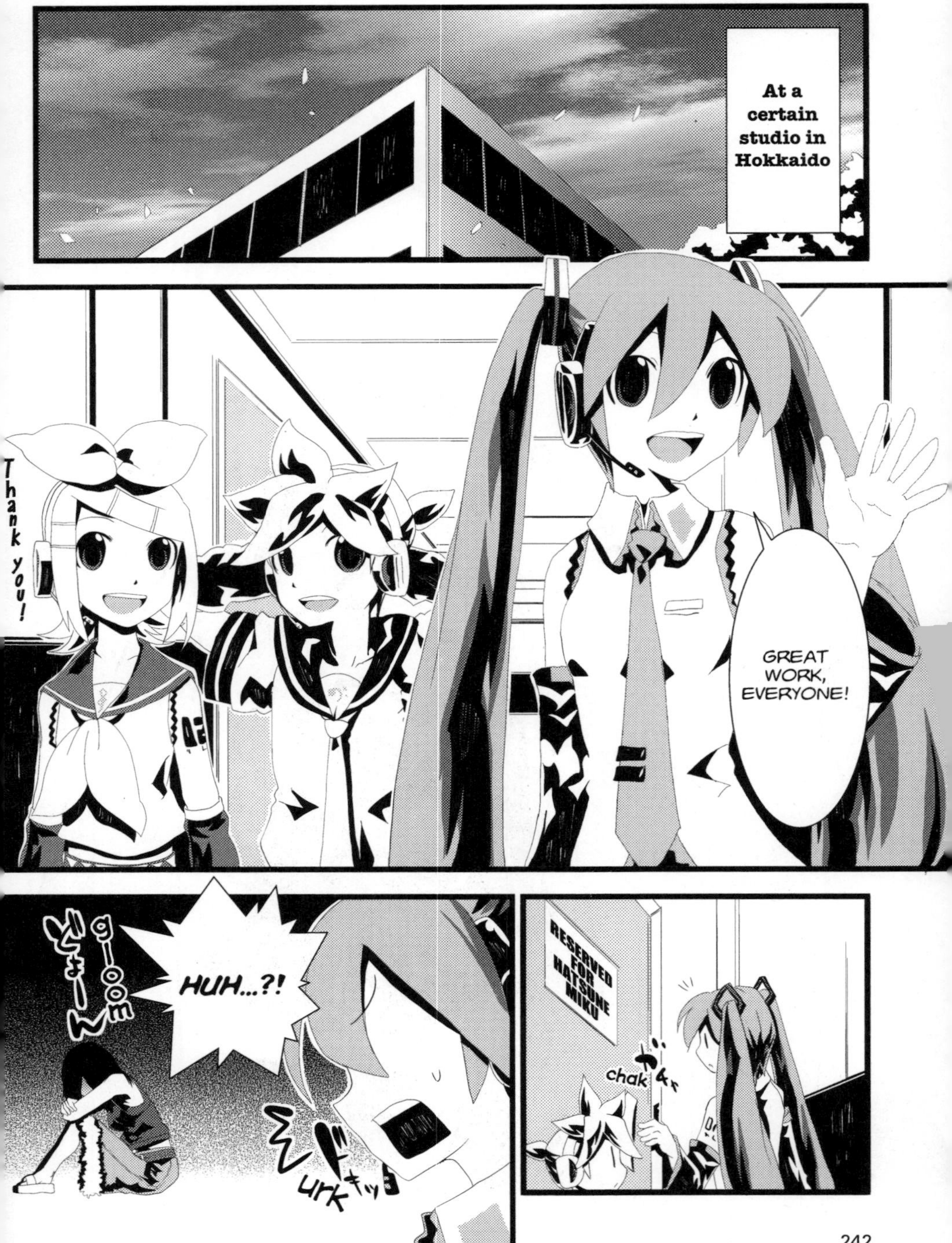
At a certain studio in Hokkaido
GREAT WORK, EVERYONE!
Thank you!
RESERVED FOR HATSUNE MIKU
chak
HUH...?!
g-oom
urk

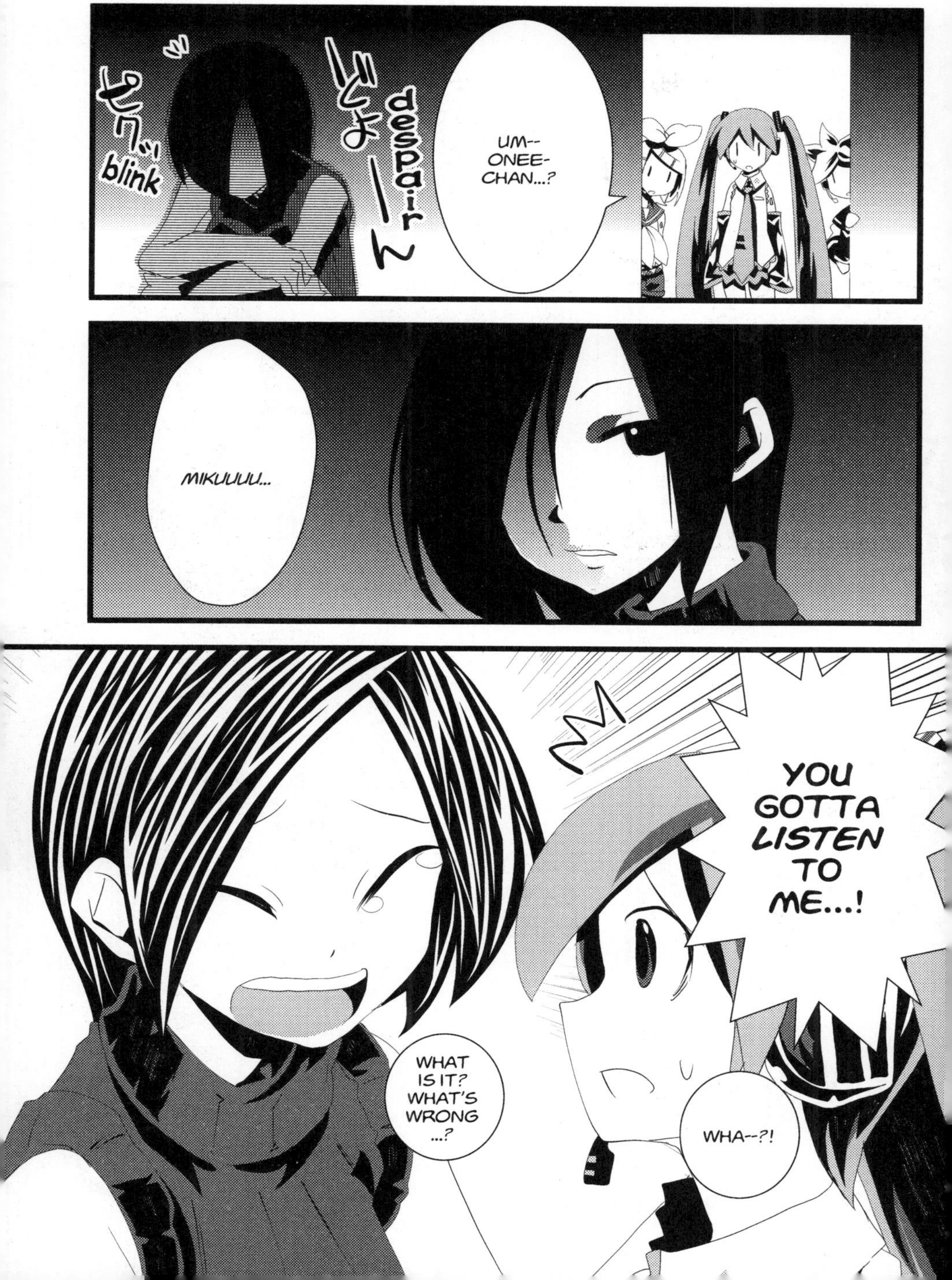

UM--ONEE-CHAN...?
どよーん
despair
ピクッ
blink
MIKUUUU...
YOU GOTTA LISTEN TO ME...!
WHA--?!
WHAT IS IT? WHAT'S WRONG ...?

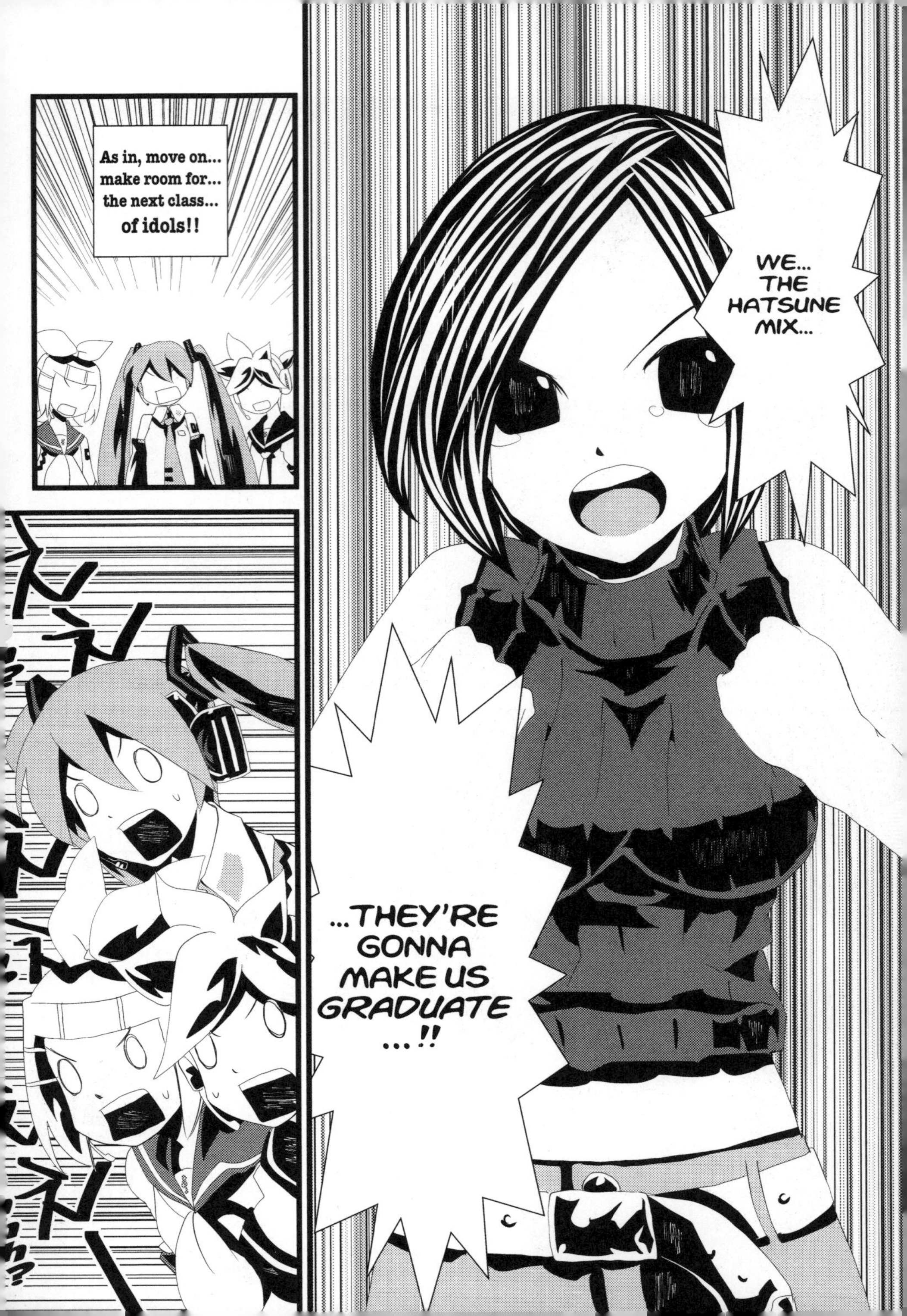
WE... THE HATSUNE MIX...
...THEY'RE GONNA MAKE US GRADUATE ...!!
As in, move on... make room for... the next class... of idols!!

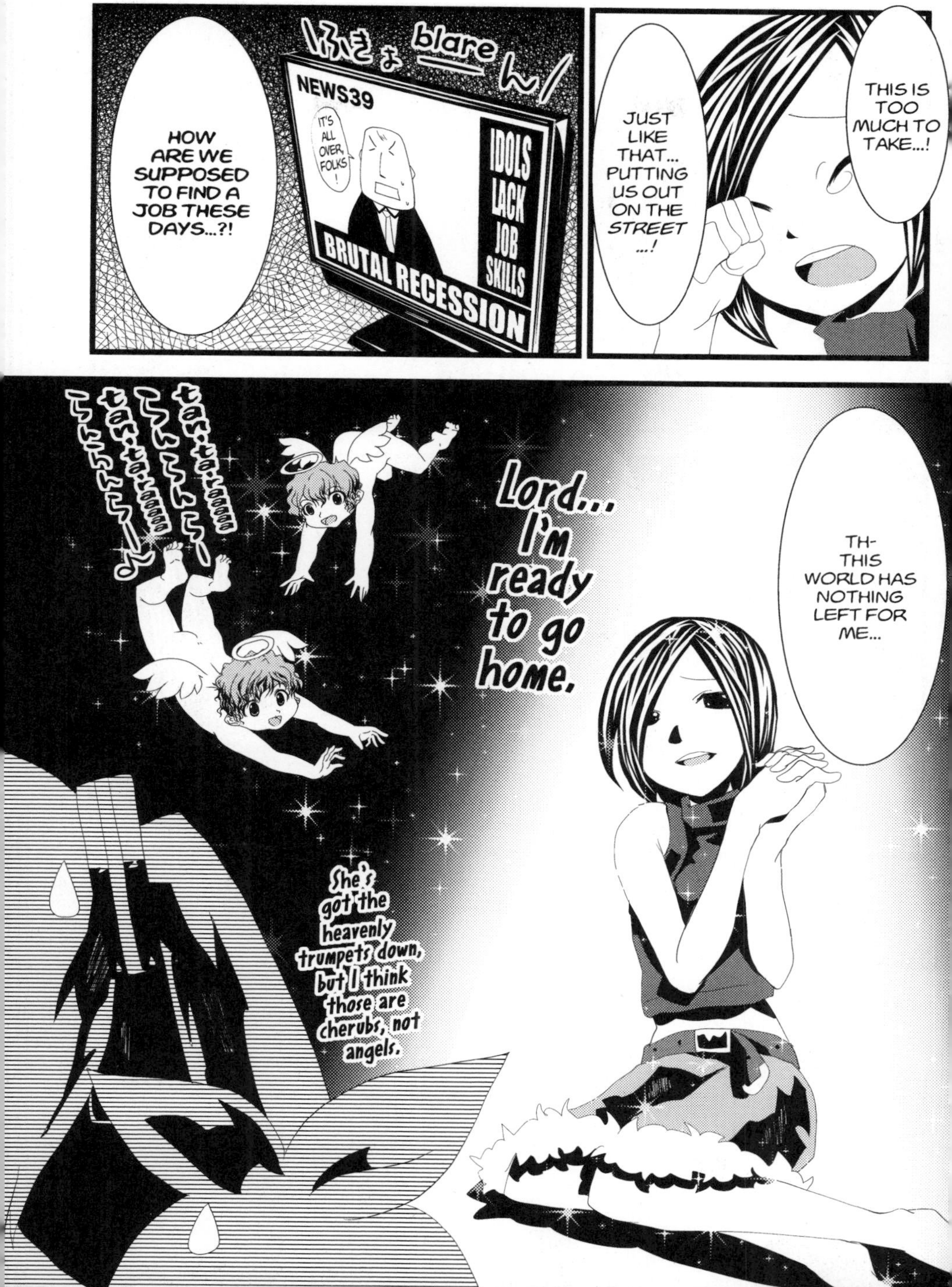
THIS IS TOO MUCH TO TAKE...!
JUST LIKE THAT... PUTTING US OUT ON THE STREET...!
blare
NEWS39
IT'S ALL OVER, FOLKS!
IDOLS LACK JOB SKILLS
BRUTAL RECESSION
HOW ARE WE SUPPOSED TO FIND A JOB THESE DAYS...?!
TH- THIS WORLD HAS NOTHING LEFT FOR ME...
Lord... I'm ready to go home.
tan-taraaaa
tan-taraaaa
She's got the heavenly trumpets down, but I think those are cherubs, not angels.

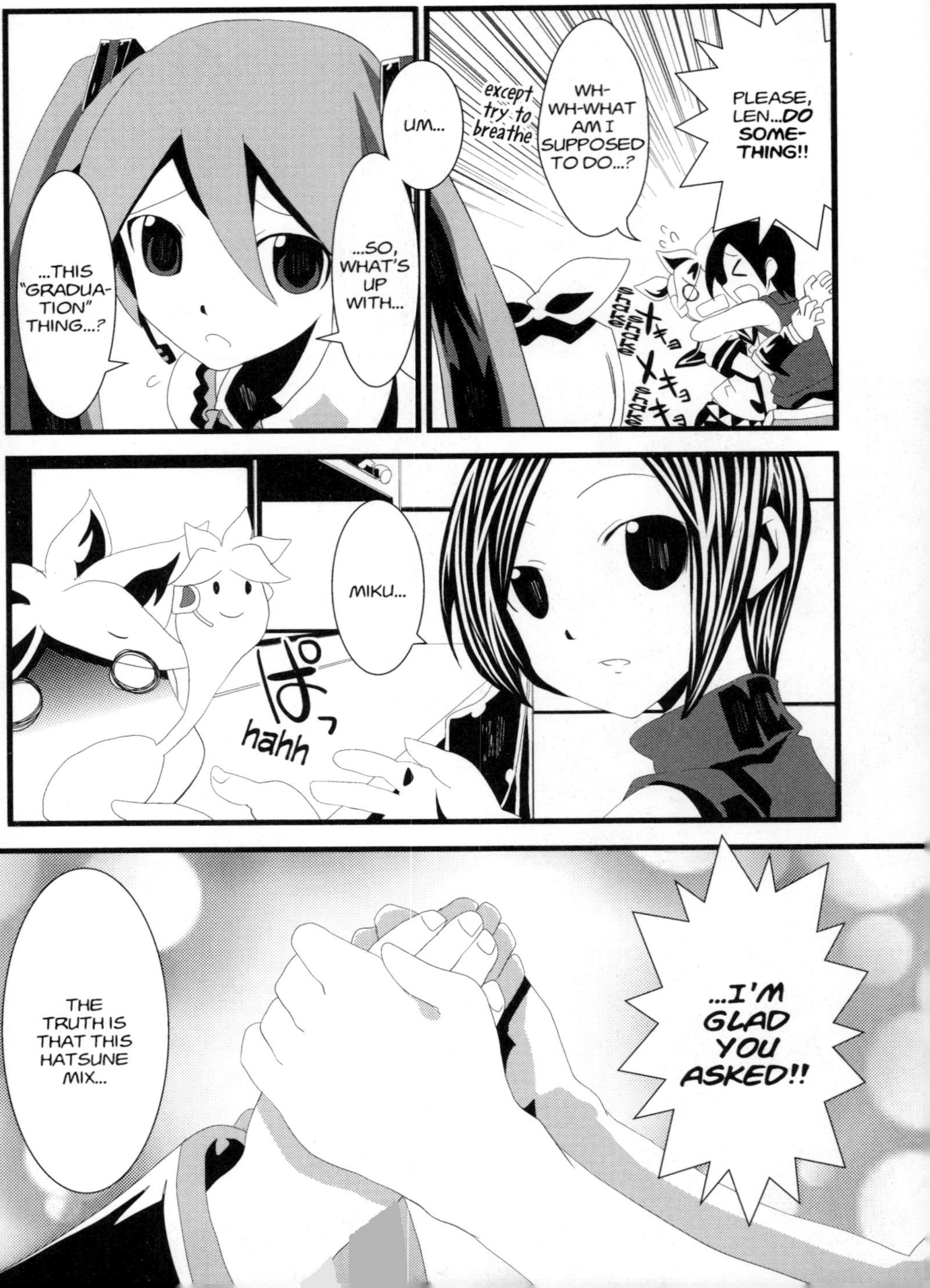
PLEASE, LEN...DO SOMETHING!!
WH-WH-WHAT AM I SUPPOSED TO DO...?
except try to breathe
shake shake
shake
UM...
...SO, WHAT'S UP WITH...
...THIS "GRADUATION" THING...?
MIKU...
ぽっ
hahh
...I'M GLAD YOU ASKED!!
THE TRUTH IS THAT THIS HATSUNE MIX...

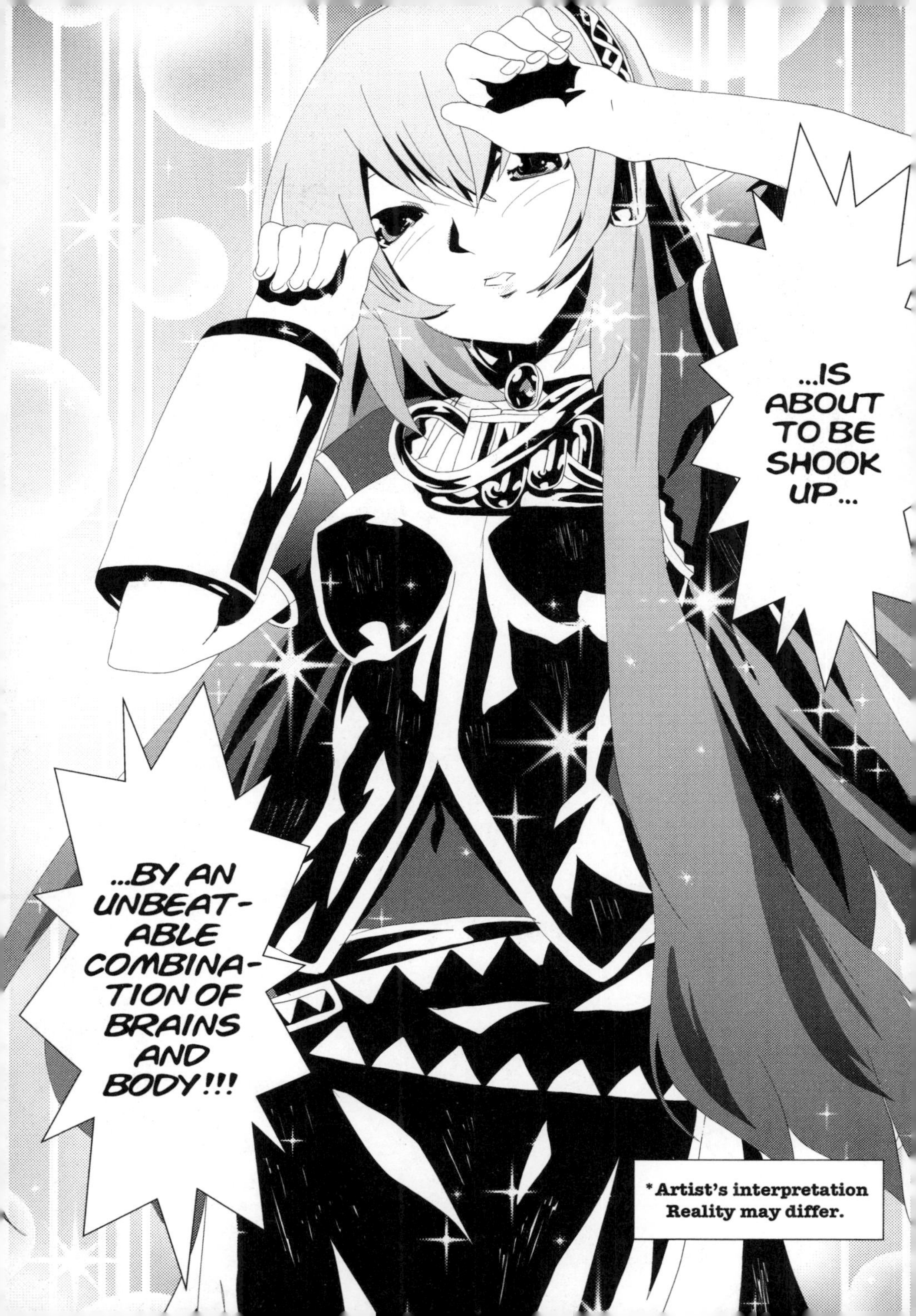
...IS ABOUT TO BE SHOOK UP...
...BY AN UNBEAT-ABLE COMBINA-TION OF BRAINS AND BODY!!!
*Artist's interpretation Reality may differ.

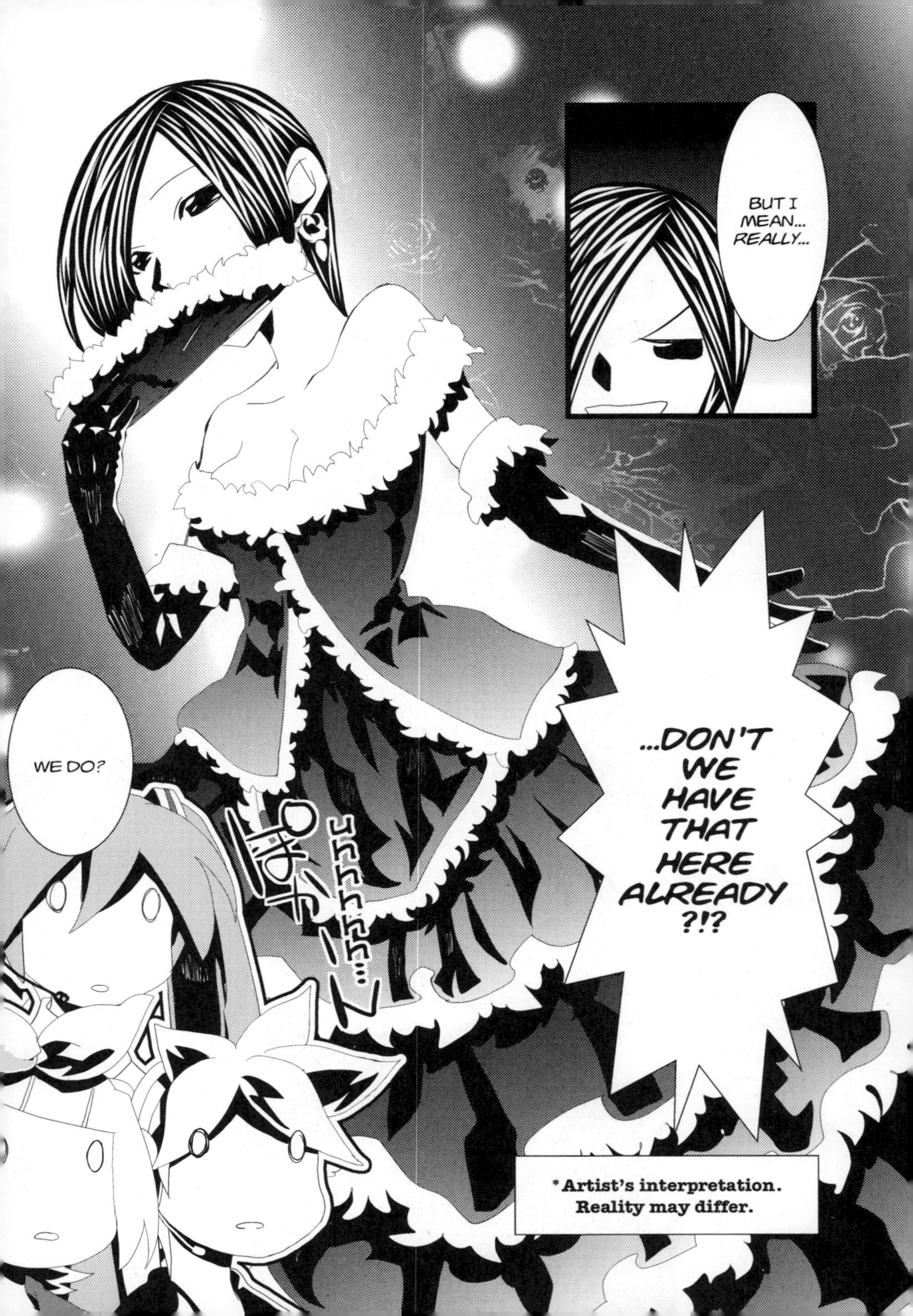
BUT I MEAN... REALLY...
...DON'T WE HAVE THAT HERE ALREADY ?!?
WE DO?
*Artist's interpretation. Reality may differ.

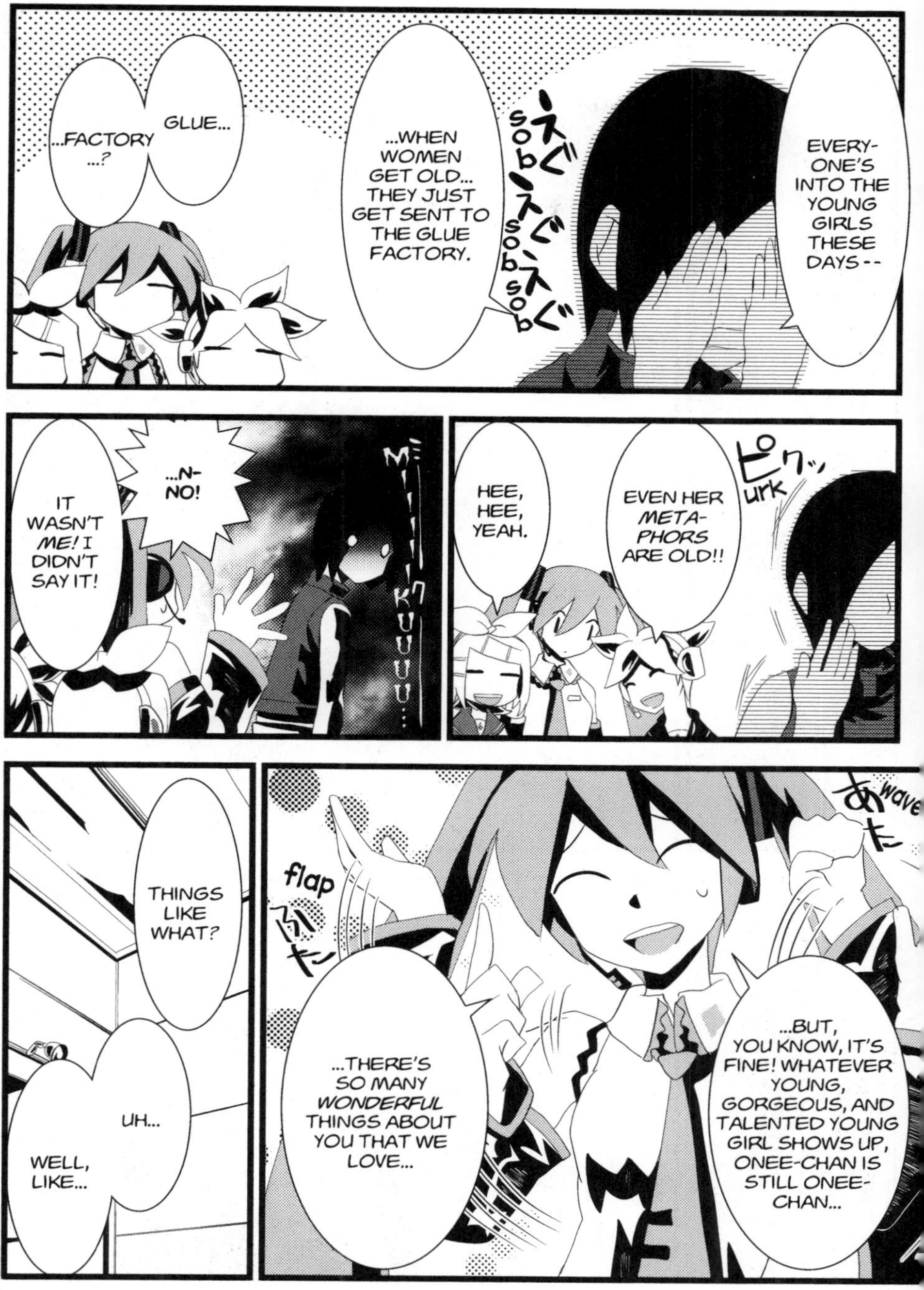
EVERY-ONE'S INTO THE YOUNG GIRLS THESE DAYS--
sob sob sob
...WHEN WOMEN GET OLD... THEY JUST GET SENT TO THE GLUE FACTORY.
GLUE...
...FACTORY ...?
ピクッ
urk
EVEN HER *META-PHORS* ARE OLD!!
HEE, HEE, YEAH.
MIKUUUU...
...N-NO!
IT WASN'T *ME!* I DIDN'T SAY IT!
wave
...BUT, YOU KNOW, IT'S FINE! WHATEVER YOUNG, GORGEOUS, AND TALENTED YOUNG GIRL SHOWS UP, ONEE-CHAN IS STILL ONEE-CHAN...
...THERE'S SO MANY *WONDERFUL* THINGS ABOUT YOU THAT WE LOVE...
flap
THINGS LIKE WHAT?
UH...
WELL, LIKE...

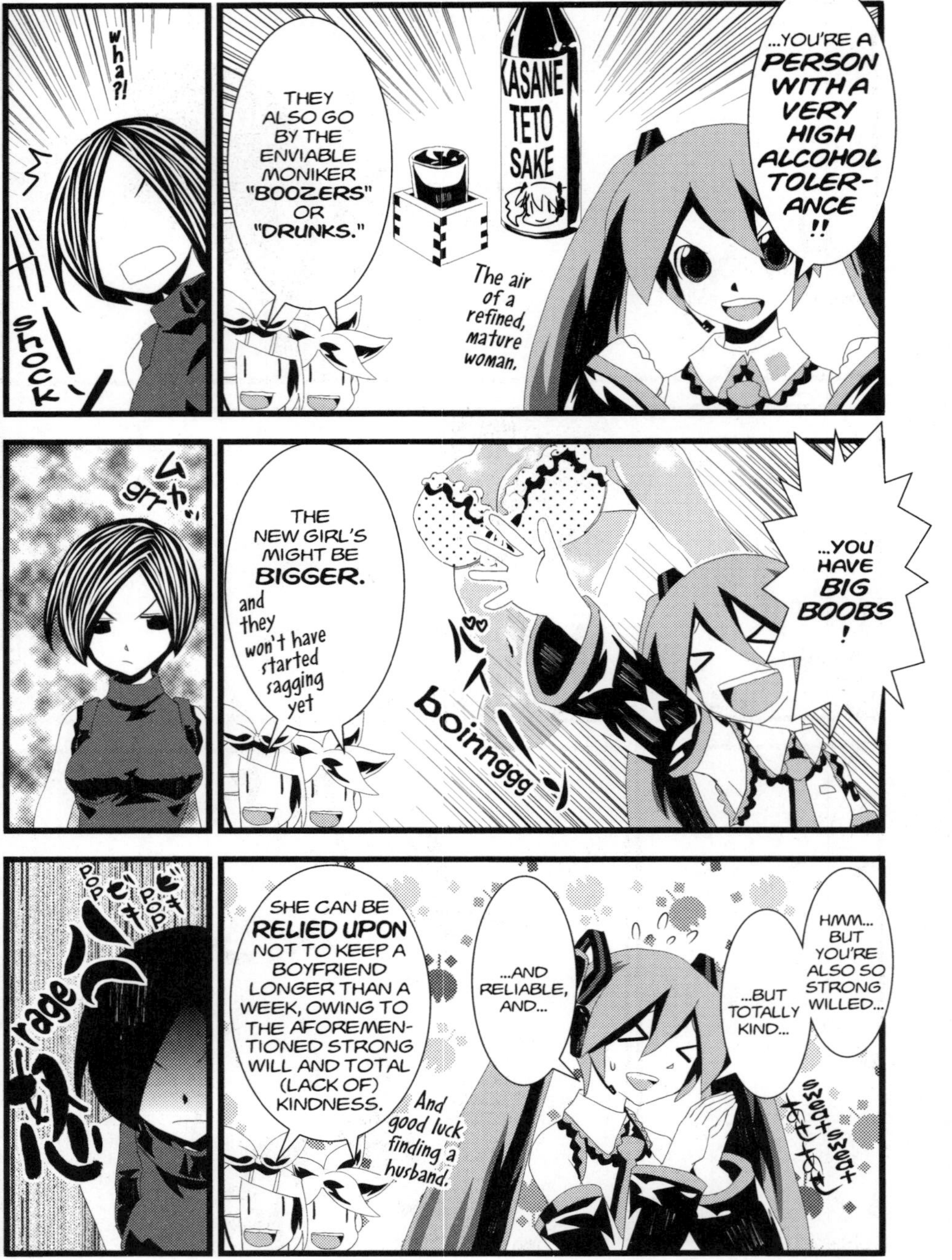

...YOU'RE A PERSON WITH A VERY HIGH ALCOHOL TOLER-ANCE !!
KASANE TETO SAKE
The air of a refined, mature woman.
THEY ALSO GO BY THE ENVIABLE MONIKER "BOOZERS" OR "DRUNKS."
wha?!
shock
...YOU HAVE BIG BOOBS!
boinnggg
THE NEW GIRL'S MIGHT BE BIGGER.
and they won't have started sagging yet
grr
HMM... BUT YOU'RE ALSO SO STRONG WILLED...
...BUT TOTALLY KIND...
...AND RELIABLE, AND...
sweat sweat
SHE CAN BE RELIED UPON NOT TO KEEP A BOYFRIEND LONGER THAN A WEEK, OWING TO THE AFOREMENTIONED STRONG WILL AND TOTAL (LACK OF) KINDNESS.
And good luck finding a husband.
POP POP
rage

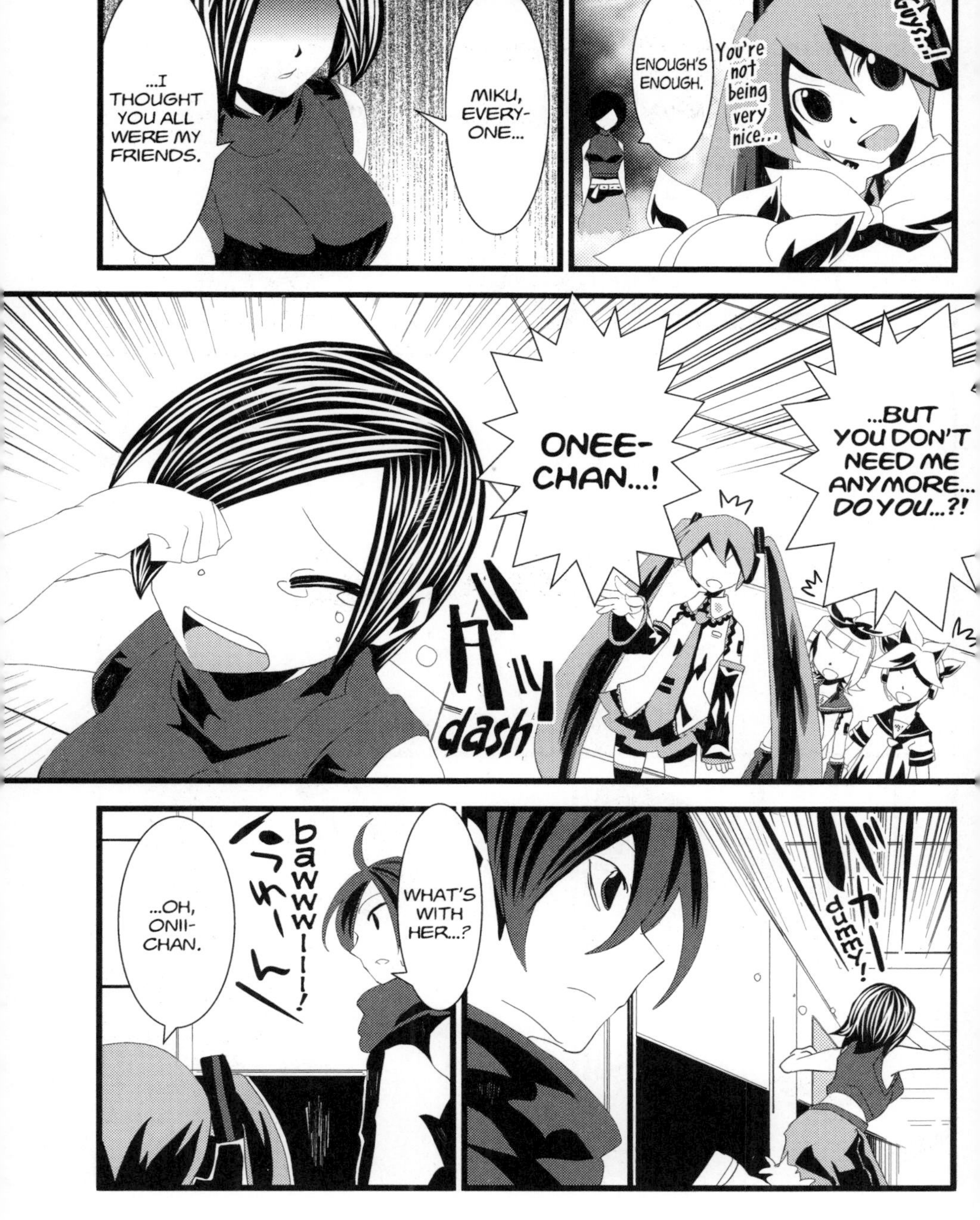
-Guys...!
You're not being very nice...
ENOUGH'S ENOUGH.
MIKU, EVERY-ONE...
...I THOUGHT YOU ALL WERE MY FRIENDS.
...BUT YOU DON'T NEED ME ANYMORE... DO YOU...?!
ONEE-CHAN...!
dash
DUEEY!
WHAT'S WITH HER...?
bawwwlll!
...OH, ONII-CHAN.

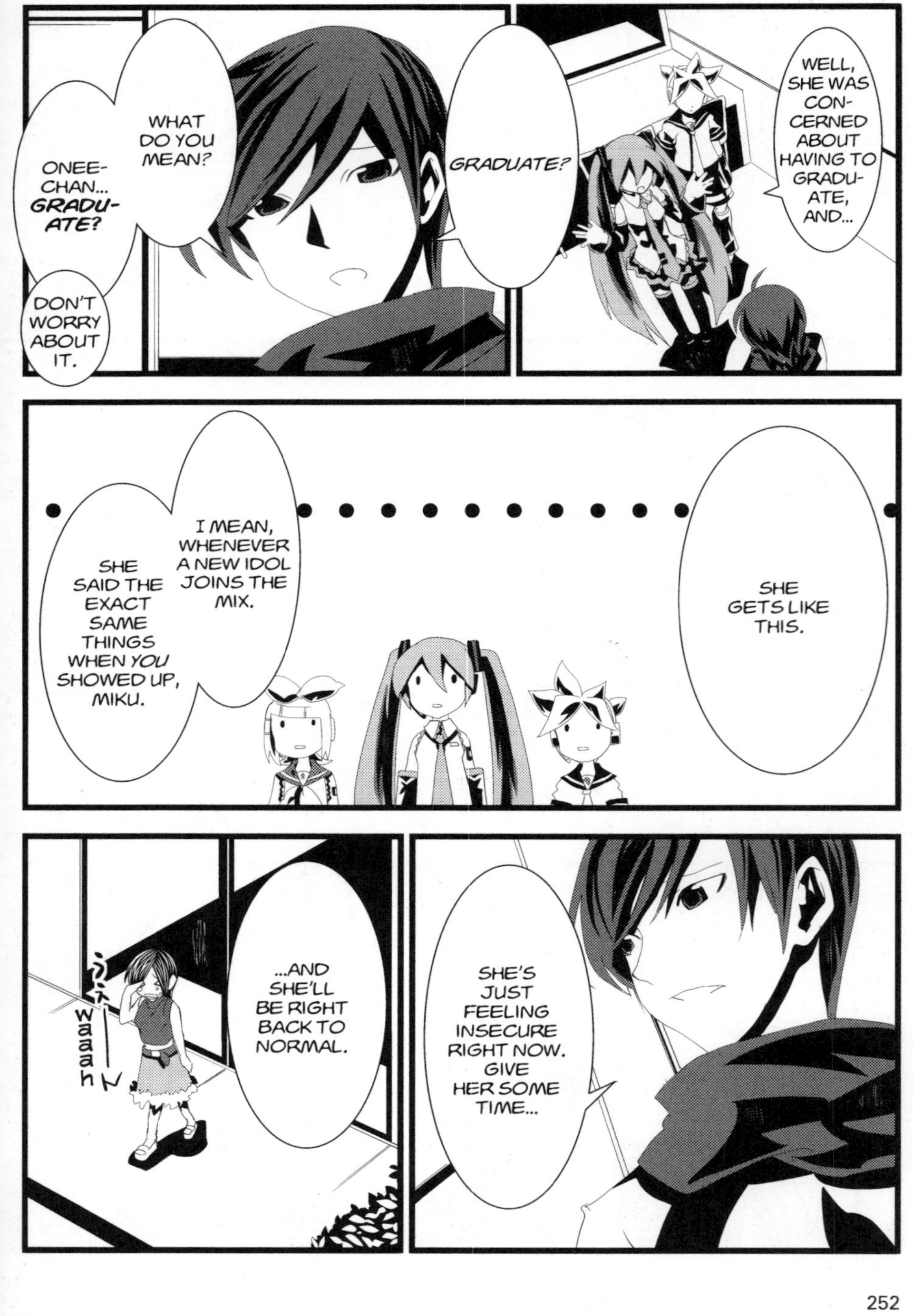
WELL, SHE WAS CON-CERNED ABOUT HAVING TO GRADU-ATE, AND...
GRADUATE?
WHAT DO YOU MEAN?
ONEE-CHAN... GRADU-ATE?
DON'T WORRY ABOUT IT.
SHE GETS LIKE THIS.
• • • • • • • • • • •
I MEAN, WHENEVER A NEW IDOL JOINS THE MIX.
SHE SAID THE EXACT SAME THINGS WHEN YOU SHOWED UP, MIKU.
•
SHE'S JUST FEELING INSECURE RIGHT NOW. GIVE HER SOME TIME...
...AND SHE'LL BE RIGHT BACK TO NORMAL.
waaaah

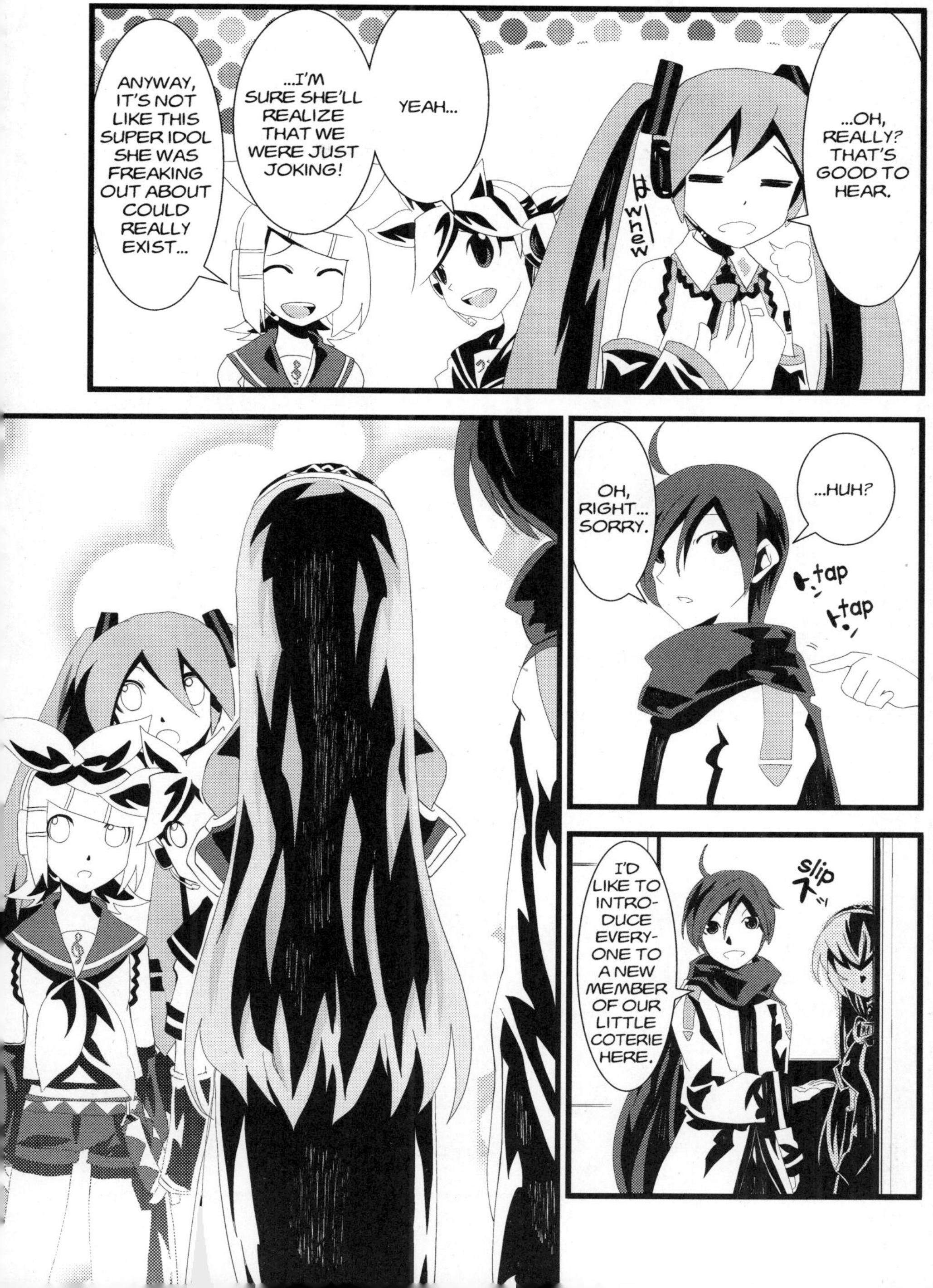
...OH, REALLY? THAT'S GOOD TO HEAR.
whew
YEAH...
...I'M SURE SHE'LL REALIZE THAT WE WERE JUST JOKING!
ANYWAY, IT'S NOT LIKE THIS SUPER IDOL SHE WAS FREAKING OUT ABOUT COULD REALLY EXIST...
...HUH?
tap
tap
OH, RIGHT... SORRY.
slip
I'D LIKE TO INTRO-DUCE EVERY-ONE TO A NEW MEMBER OF OUR LITTLE COTERIE HERE.

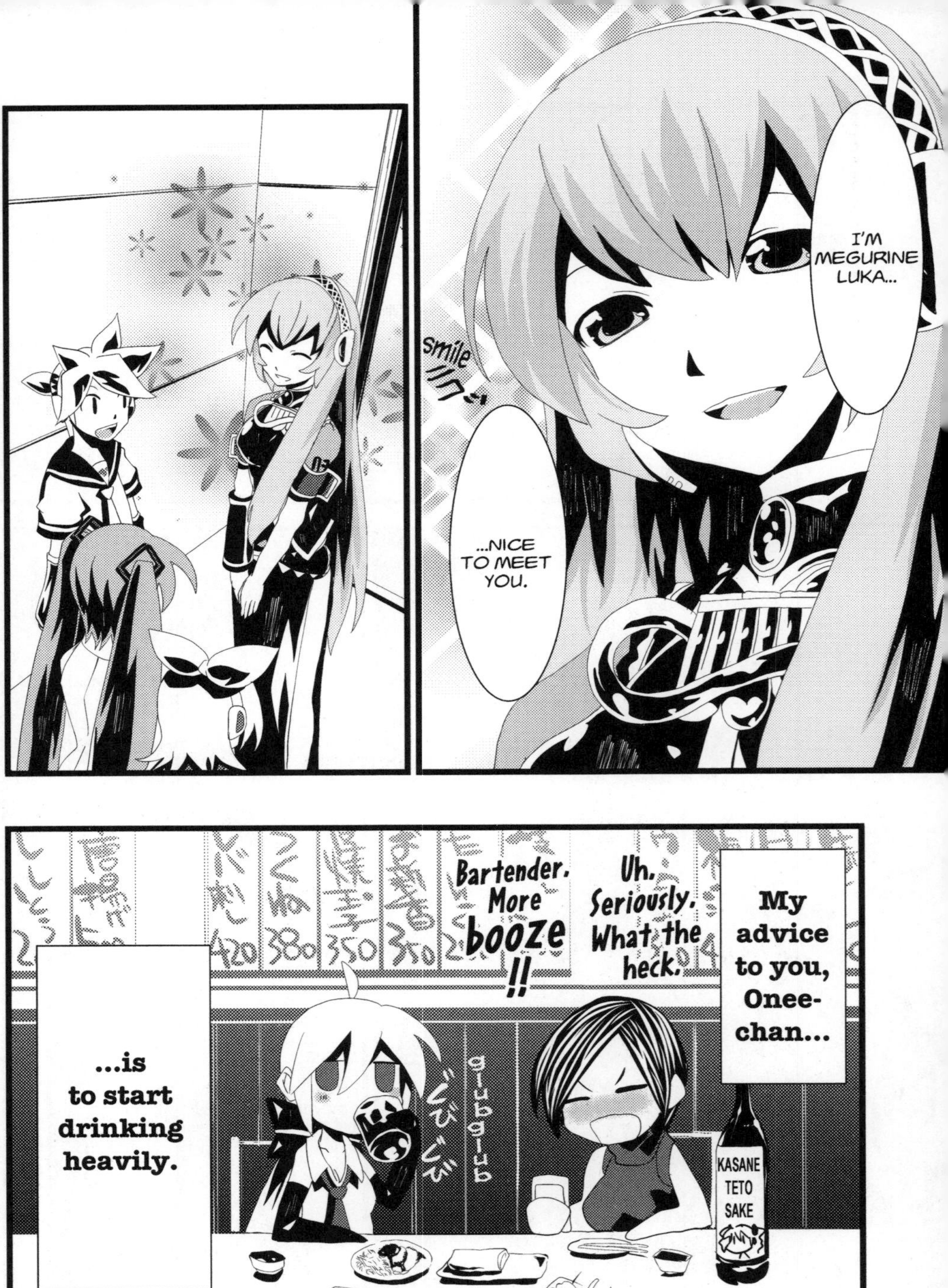
I'M MEGURINE LUKA...
smile
...NICE TO MEET YOU.
My advice to you, Onee-chan...
Uh. Seriously. What the heck.
Bartender. More booze!!
glub glub
KASANE TETO SAKE
...is to start drinking heavily.

(16th SONG) LUKA MIX

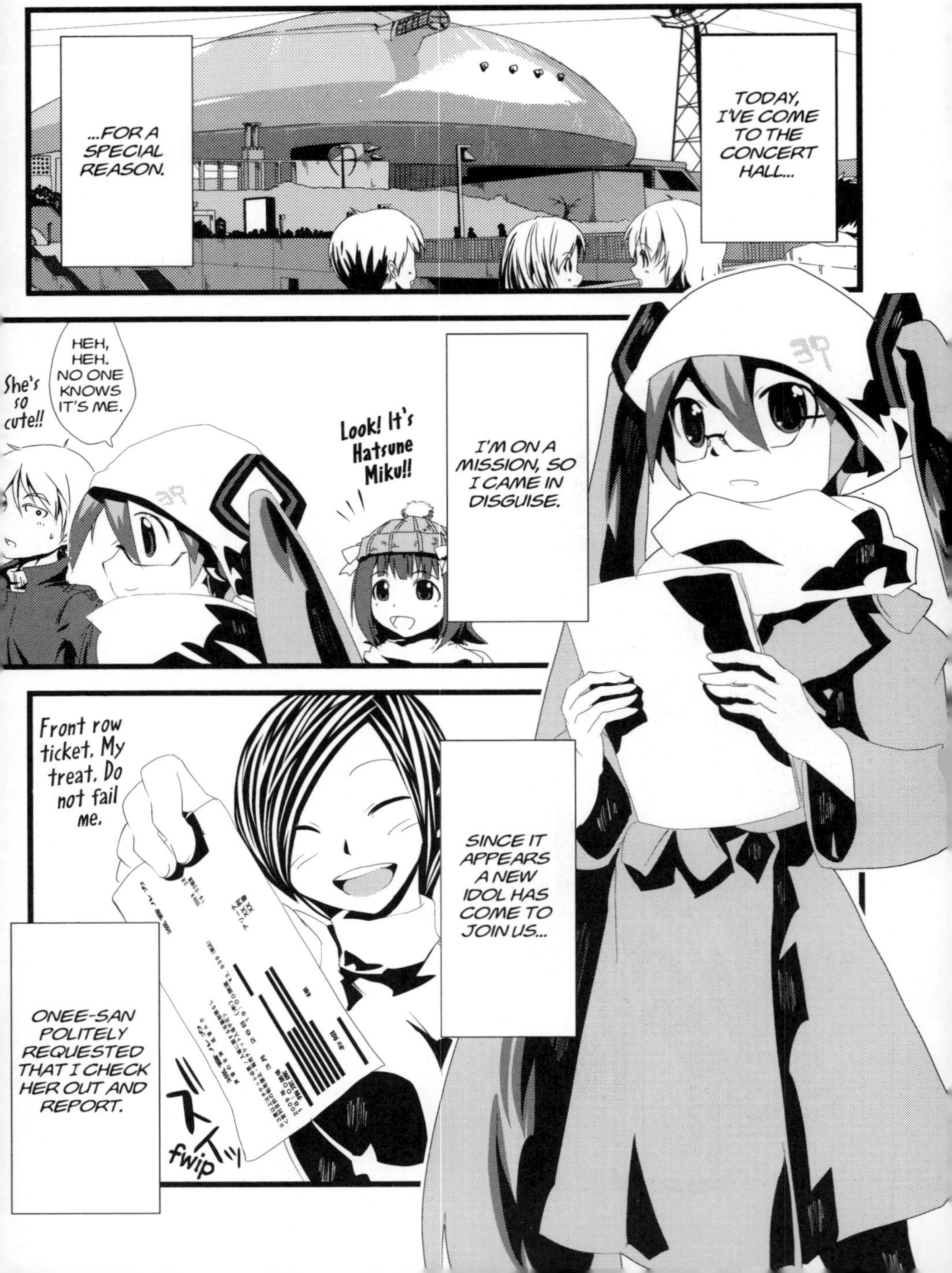

TODAY, I'VE COME TO THE CONCERT HALL...
...FOR A SPECIAL REASON.
I'M ON A MISSION, SO I CAME IN DISGUISE.
Look! It's Hatsune Miku!!
HEH, HEH. NO ONE KNOWS IT'S ME.
She's so cute!!
SINCE IT APPEARS A NEW IDOL HAS COME TO JOIN US...
Front row ticket. My treat. Do not fail me.
ONEE-SAN POLITELY REQUESTED THAT I CHECK HER OUT AND REPORT.
fwip

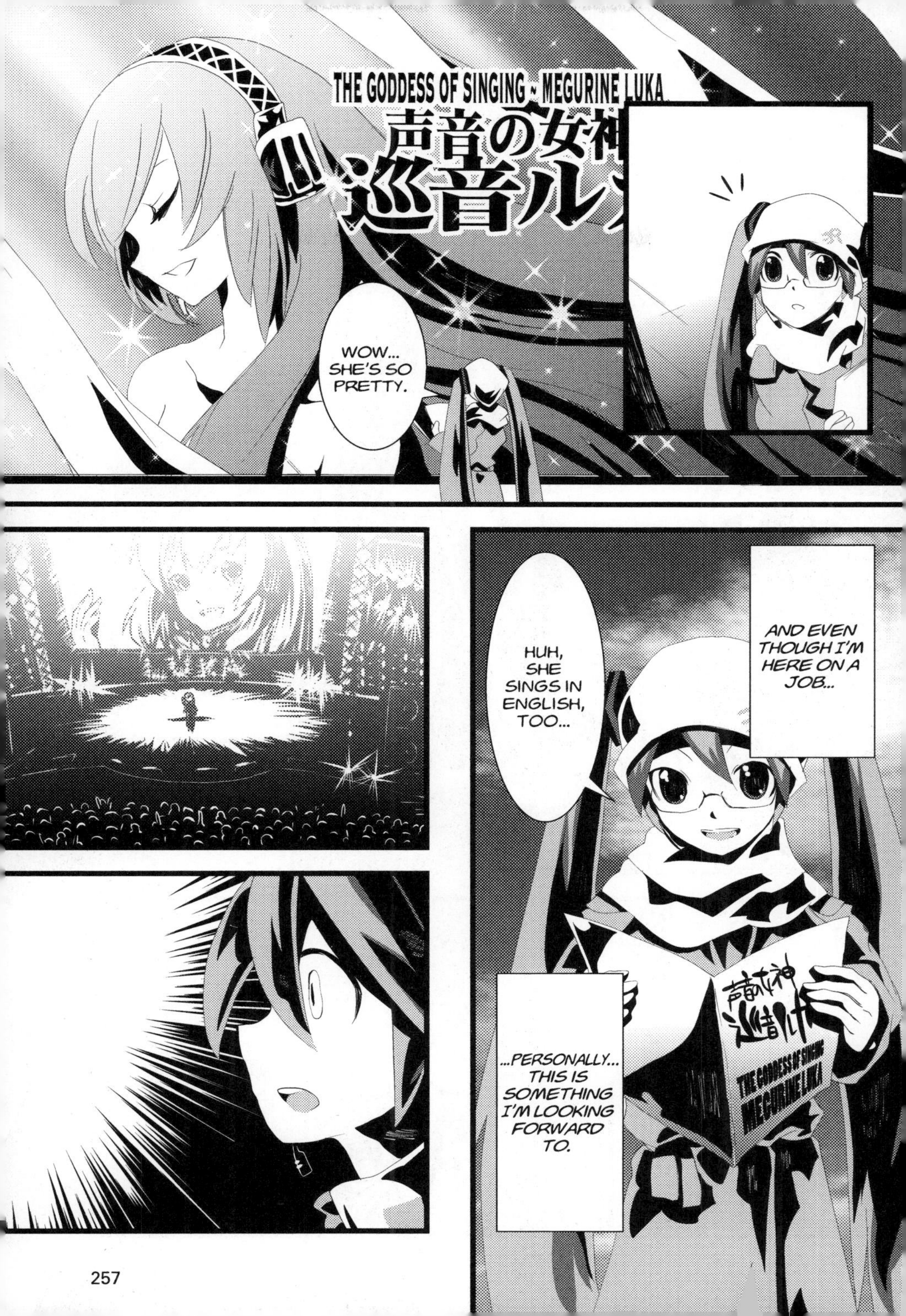
THE GODDESS OF SINGING ~ MEGURINE LUKA
声音の女神
巡音ル
WOW... SHE'S SO PRETTY.
HUH, SHE SINGS IN ENGLISH, TOO...
AND EVEN THOUGH I'M HERE ON A JOB...
...PERSONALLY... THIS IS SOMETHING I'M LOOKING FORWARD TO.
声音の女神 巡音ルカ
THE GODDESS OF SINGING MEGURINE LUKA

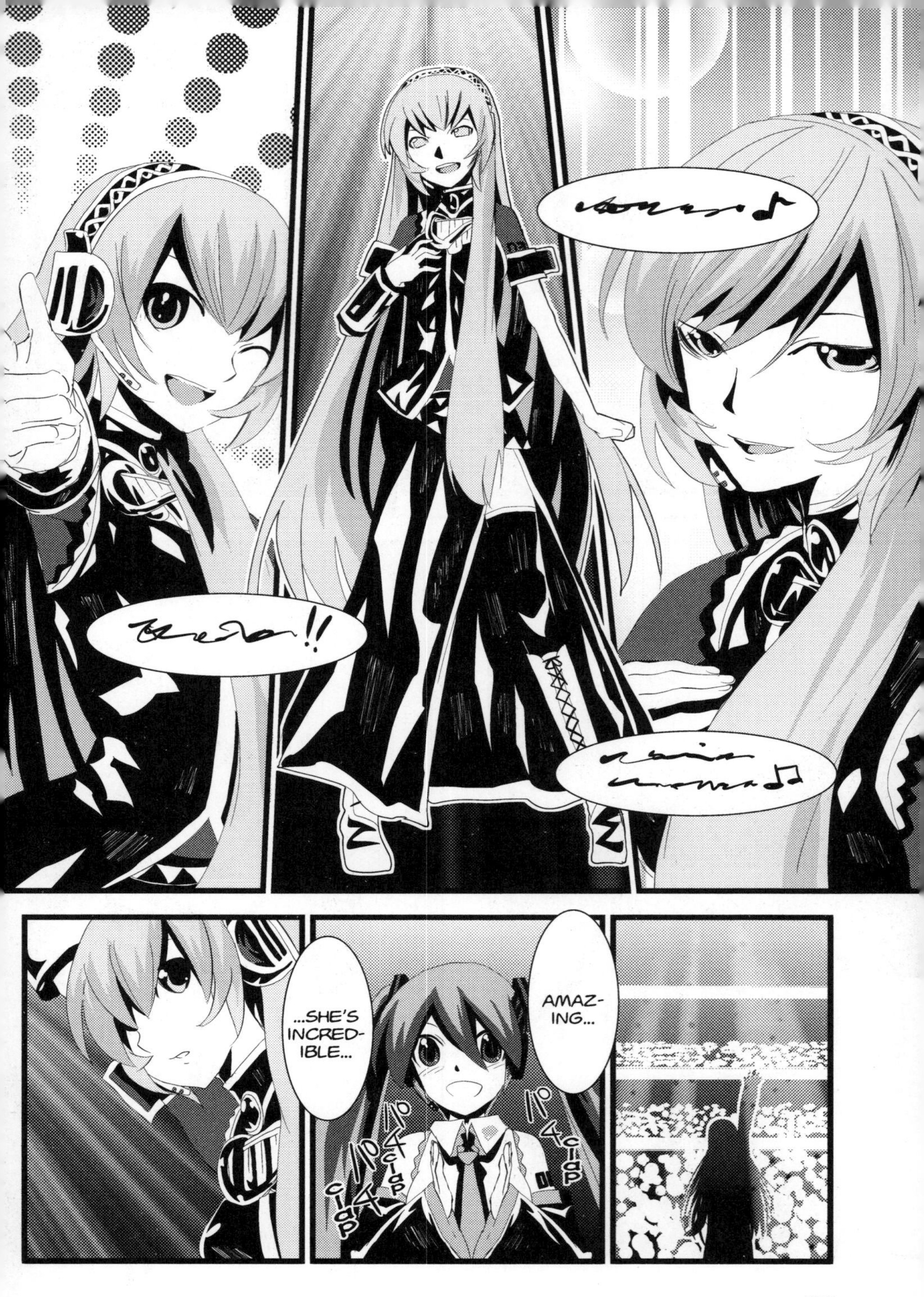
AMAZ-ING...
...SHE'S INCRED-IBLE...
clap
clap
clap

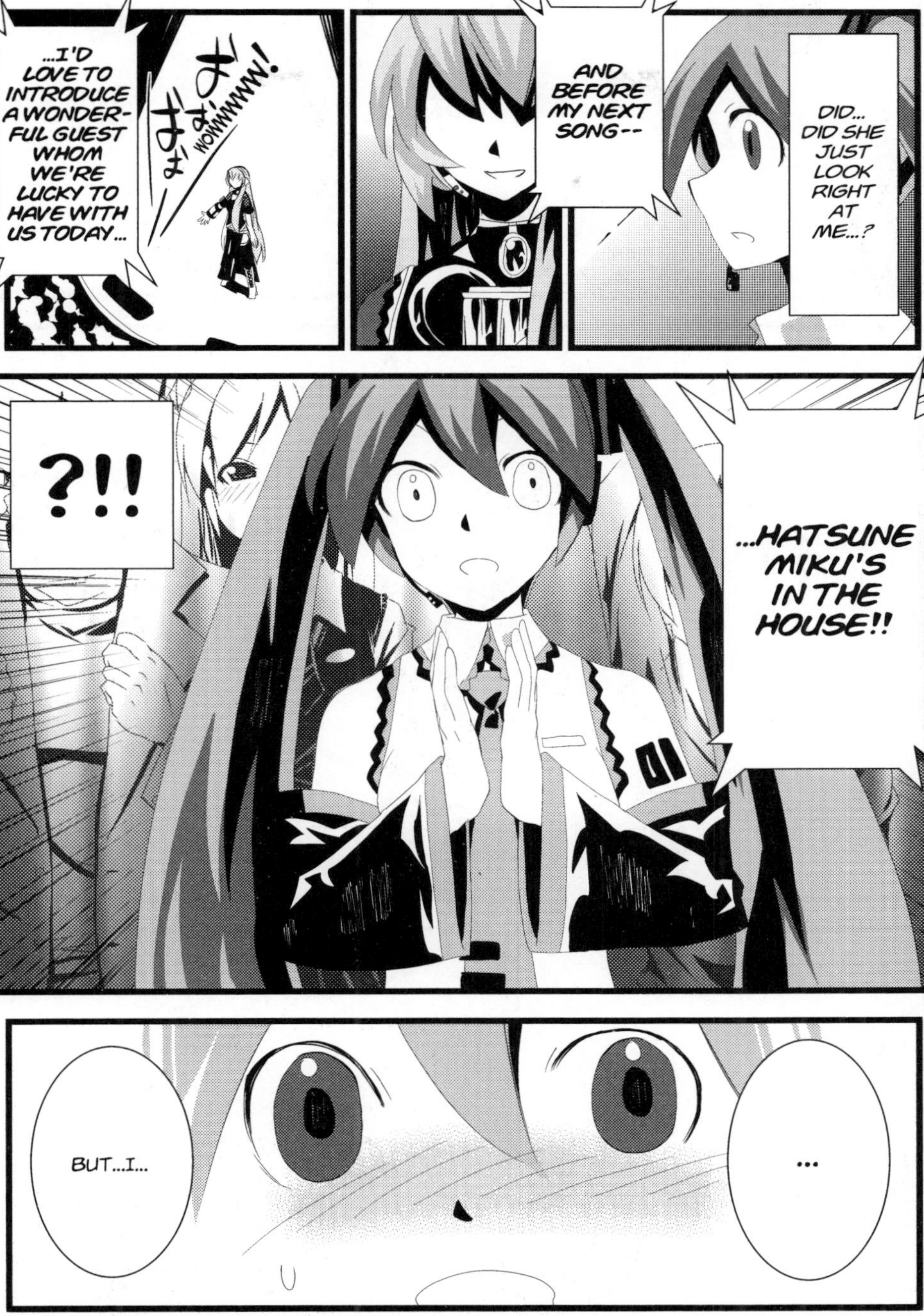
DID... DID SHE JUST LOOK RIGHT AT ME...?
AND BEFORE MY NEXT SONG--
...I'D LOVE TO INTRODUCE A WONDERFUL GUEST WHOM WE'RE LUCKY TO HAVE WITH US TODAY...
WOWWWWWW!
...HATSUNE MIKU'S IN THE HOUSE!!
?!!
...
BUT...I...

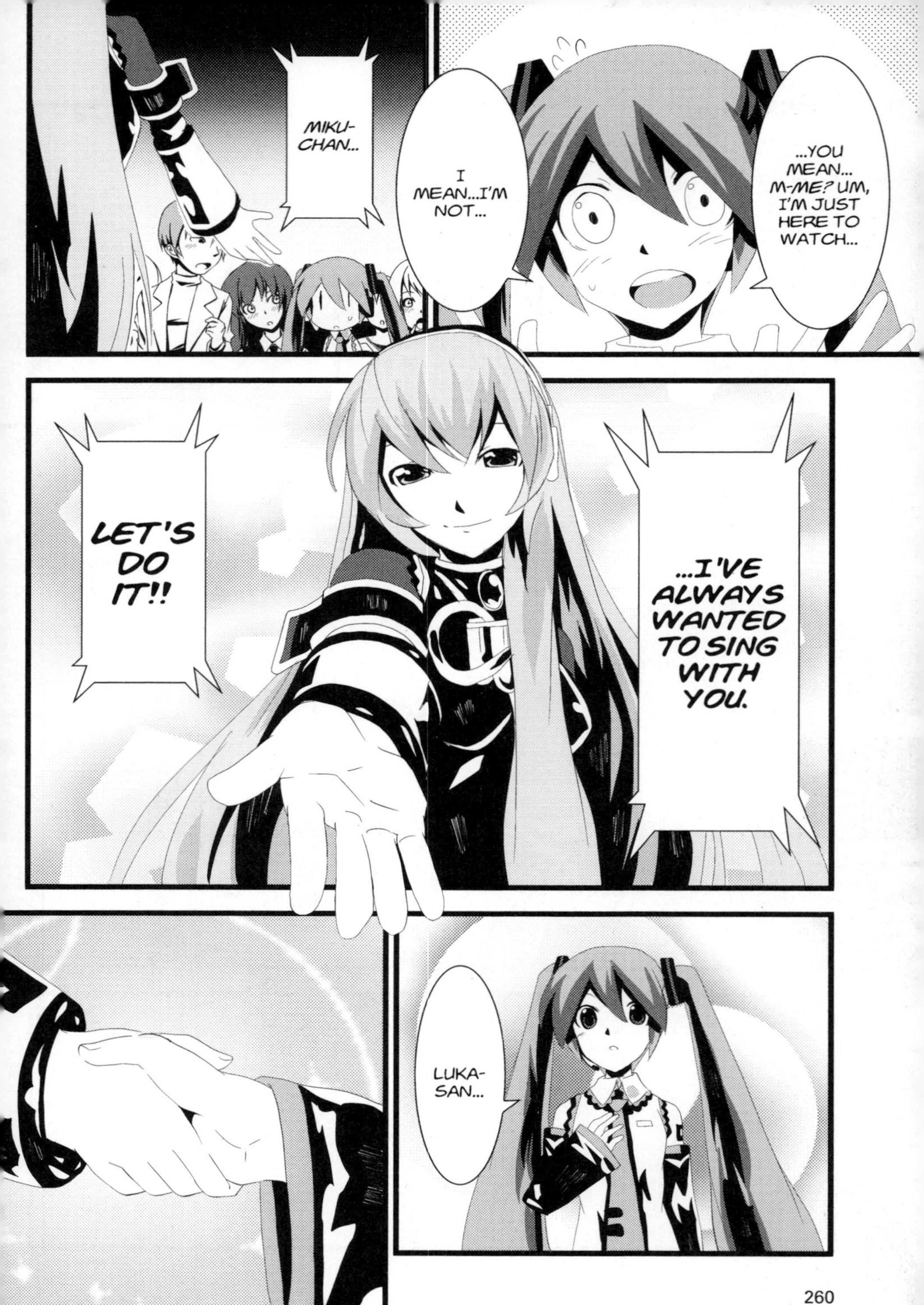
...YOU MEAN... M-ME? UM, I'M JUST HERE TO WATCH...
I MEAN...I'M NOT...
MIKU-CHAN...
...I'VE ALWAYS WANTED TO SING WITH YOU.
LET'S DO IT!!
LUKA-SAN...

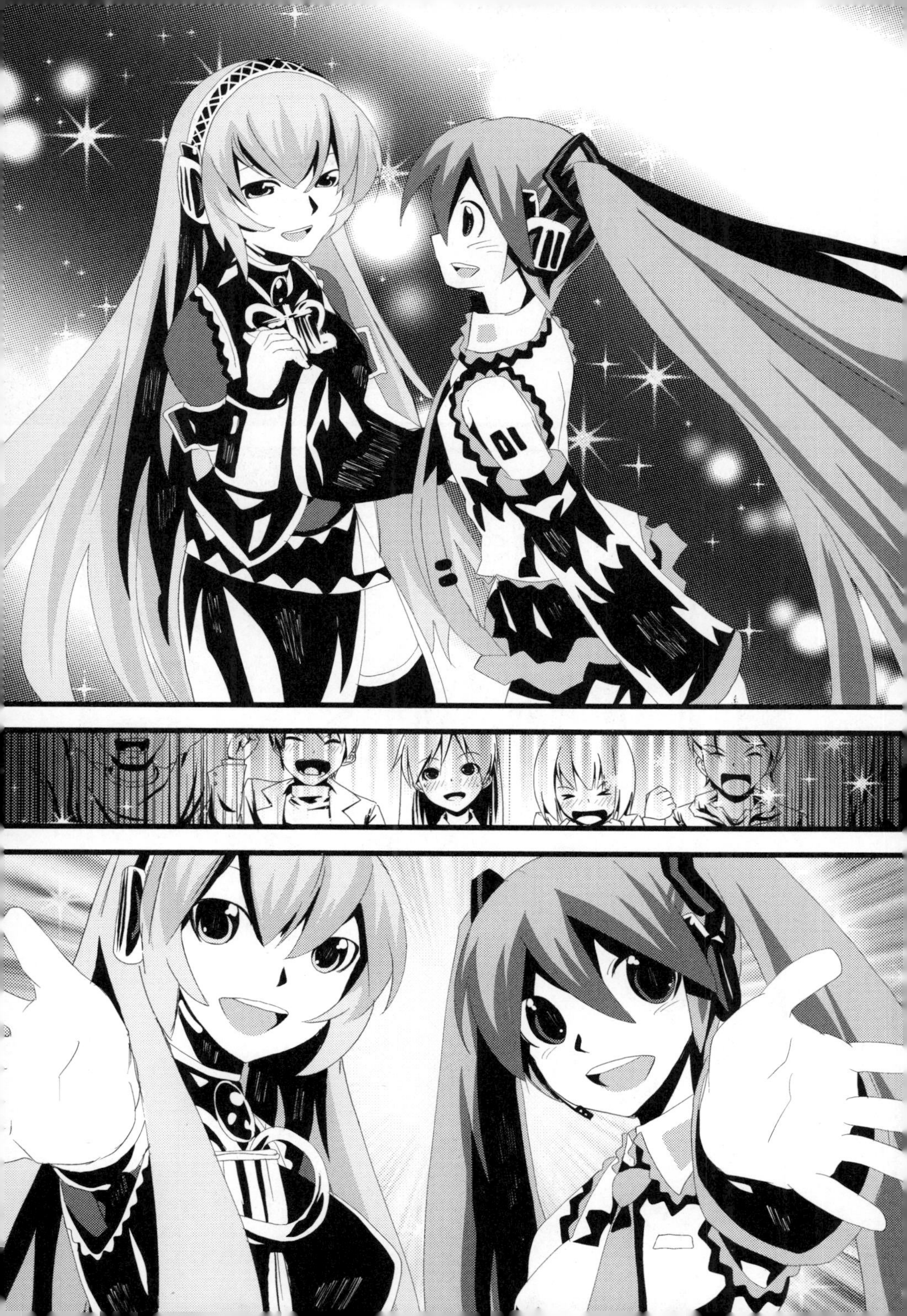

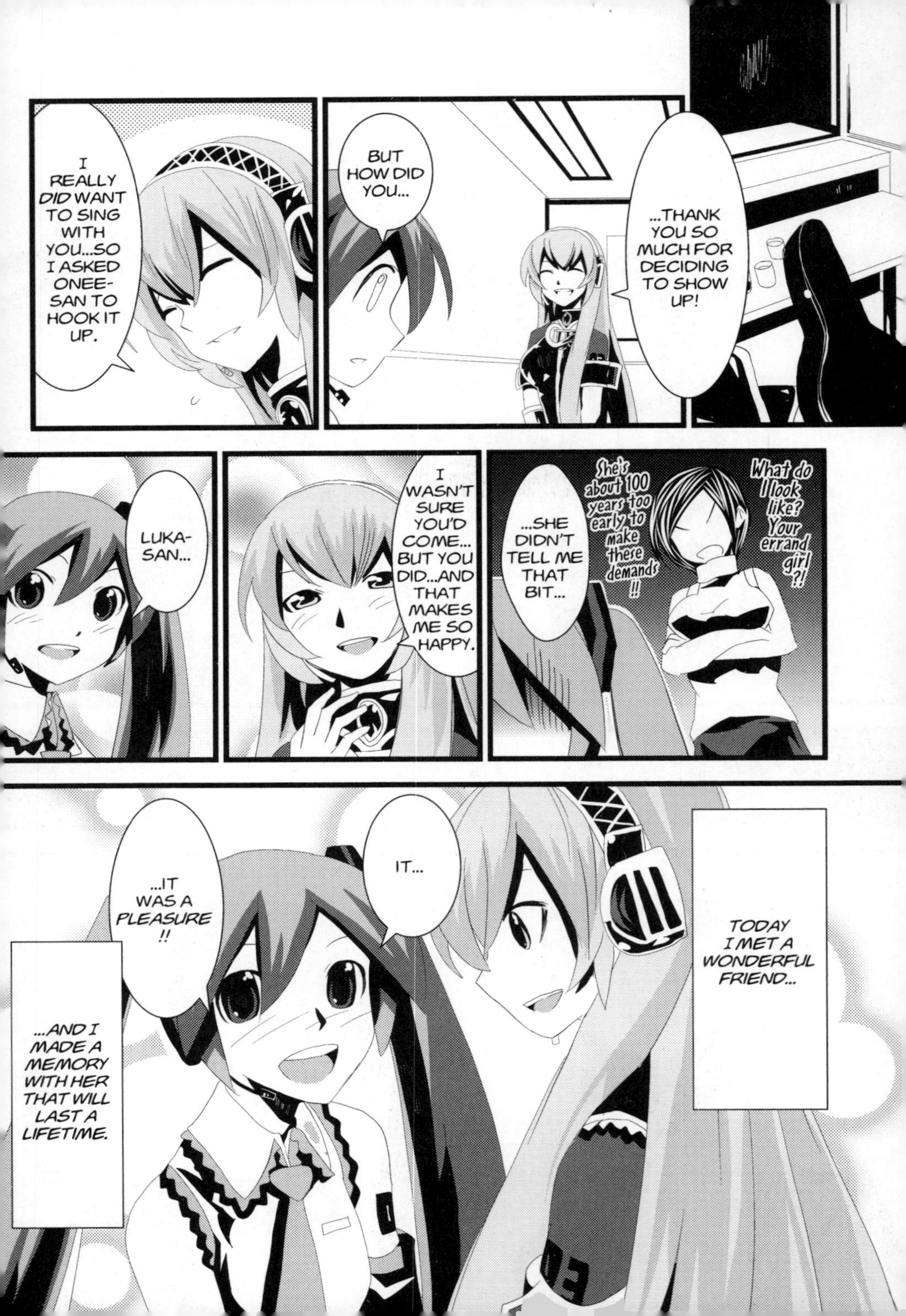
...THANK YOU SO MUCH FOR DECIDING TO SHOW UP!
BUT HOW DID YOU...
I REALLY *DID* WANT TO SING WITH YOU...SO I ASKED ONEE-SAN TO HOOK IT UP.
What do I look like? Your errand girl?!
She's about 100 years too early to make these demands!!
...SHE DIDN'T TELL ME THAT BIT...
I WASN'T SURE YOU'D COME... BUT YOU DID...AND THAT MAKES ME SO HAPPY.
LUKA-SAN...
TODAY I MET A WONDERFUL FRIEND...
IT...
...IT WAS A PLEASURE!!
...AND I MADE A MEMORY WITH HER THAT WILL LAST A LIFETIME.

(17th SONG) RING MIX

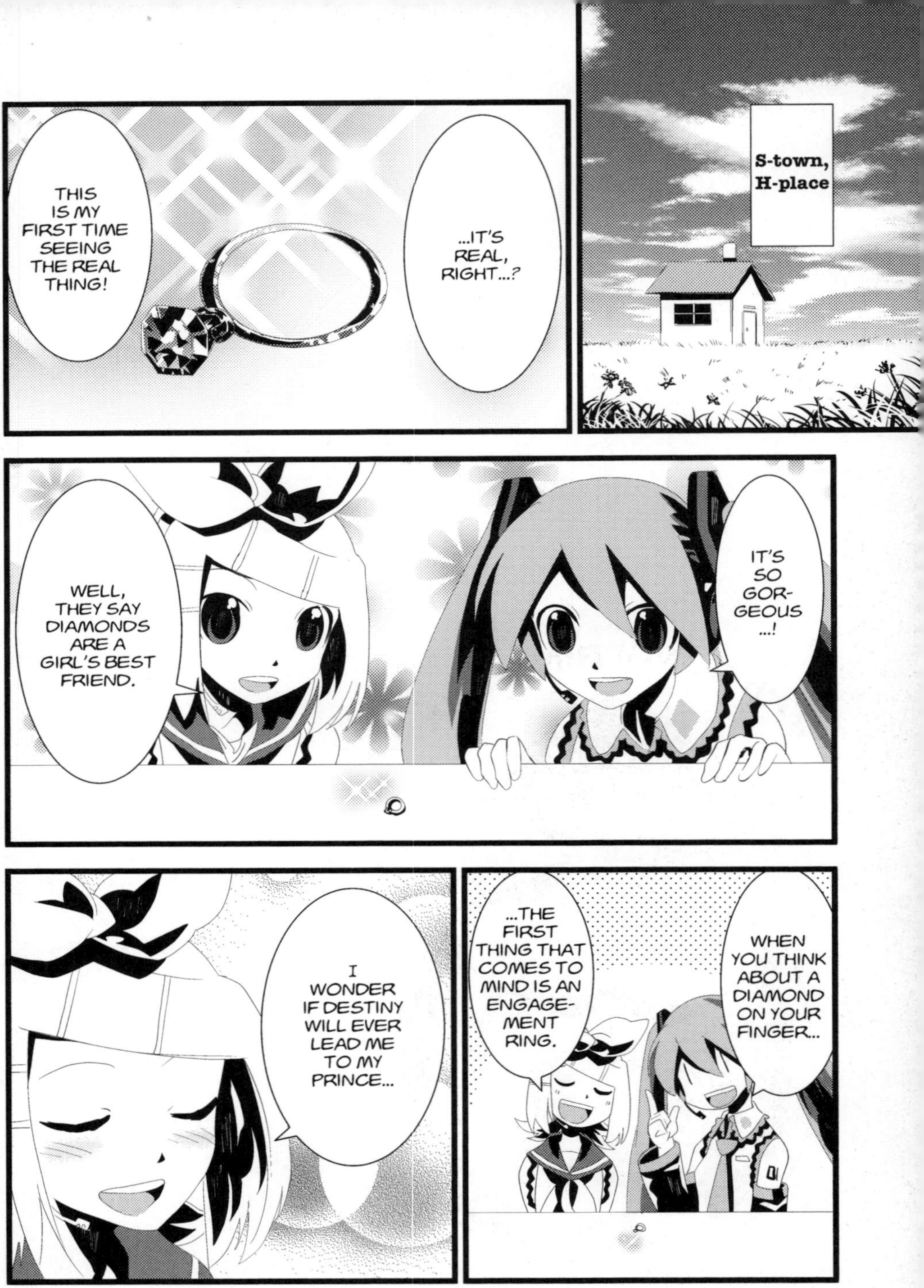
S-town, H-place
...IT'S REAL, RIGHT...?
THIS IS MY FIRST TIME SEEING THE REAL THING!
IT'S SO GORGEOUS...!
WELL, THEY SAY DIAMONDS ARE A GIRL'S BEST FRIEND.
WHEN YOU THINK ABOUT A DIAMOND ON YOUR FINGER...
...THE FIRST THING THAT COMES TO MIND IS AN ENGAGEMENT RING.
I WONDER IF DESTINY WILL EVER LEAD ME TO MY PRINCE...

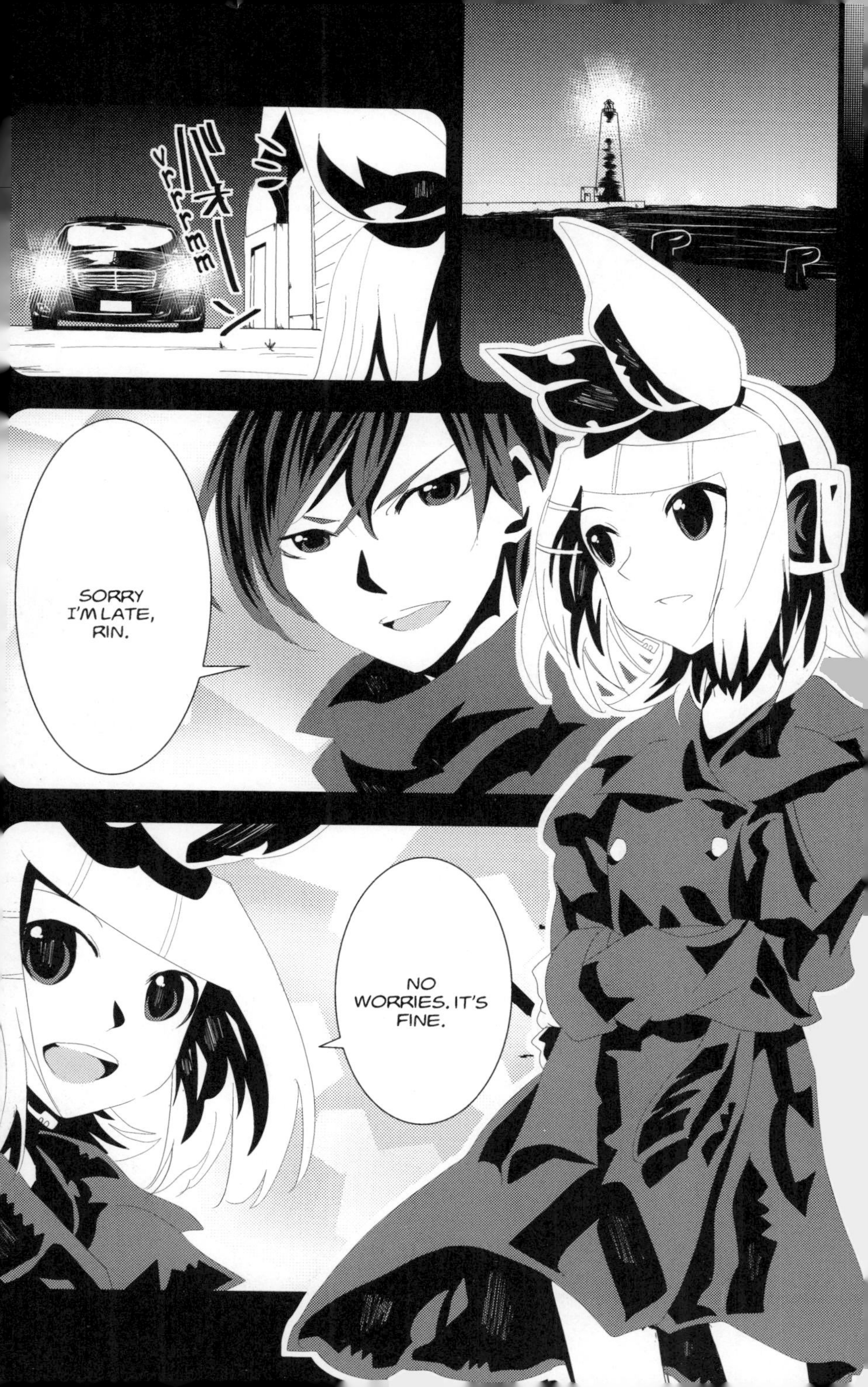
バオーン
vrrrmm
SORRY I'M LATE, RIN.
NO WORRIES. IT'S FINE.

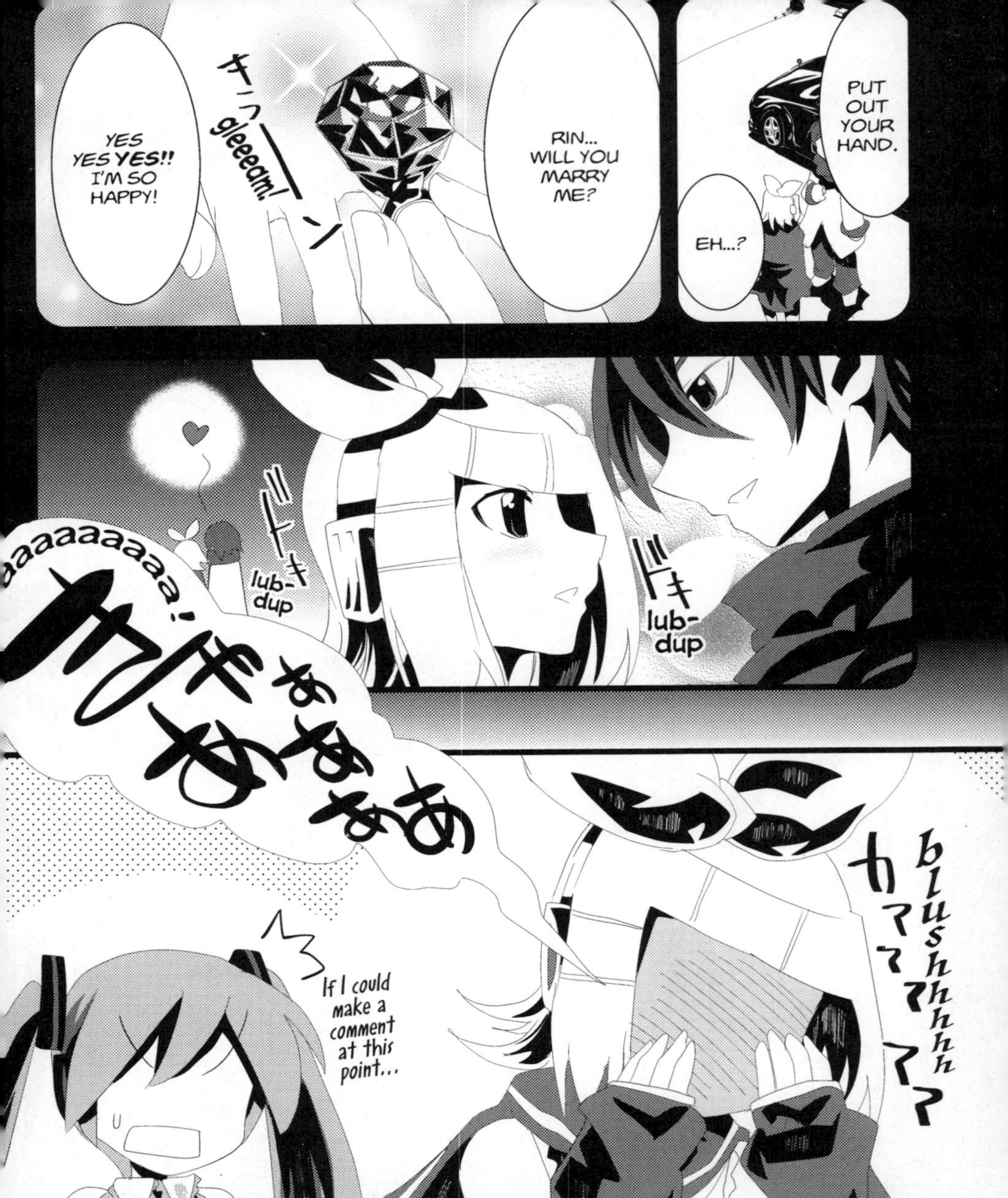
PUT OUT YOUR HAND.
EH...?
RIN... WILL YOU MARRY ME?
キーン
gleeeam!
YES YES **YES!!** I'M SO HAPPY!
ドキ
lub-dup
ドキ
lub-dup
カァァァァ
blushhhhh
aaaaaaaaaaa!
If I could make a comment at this point...

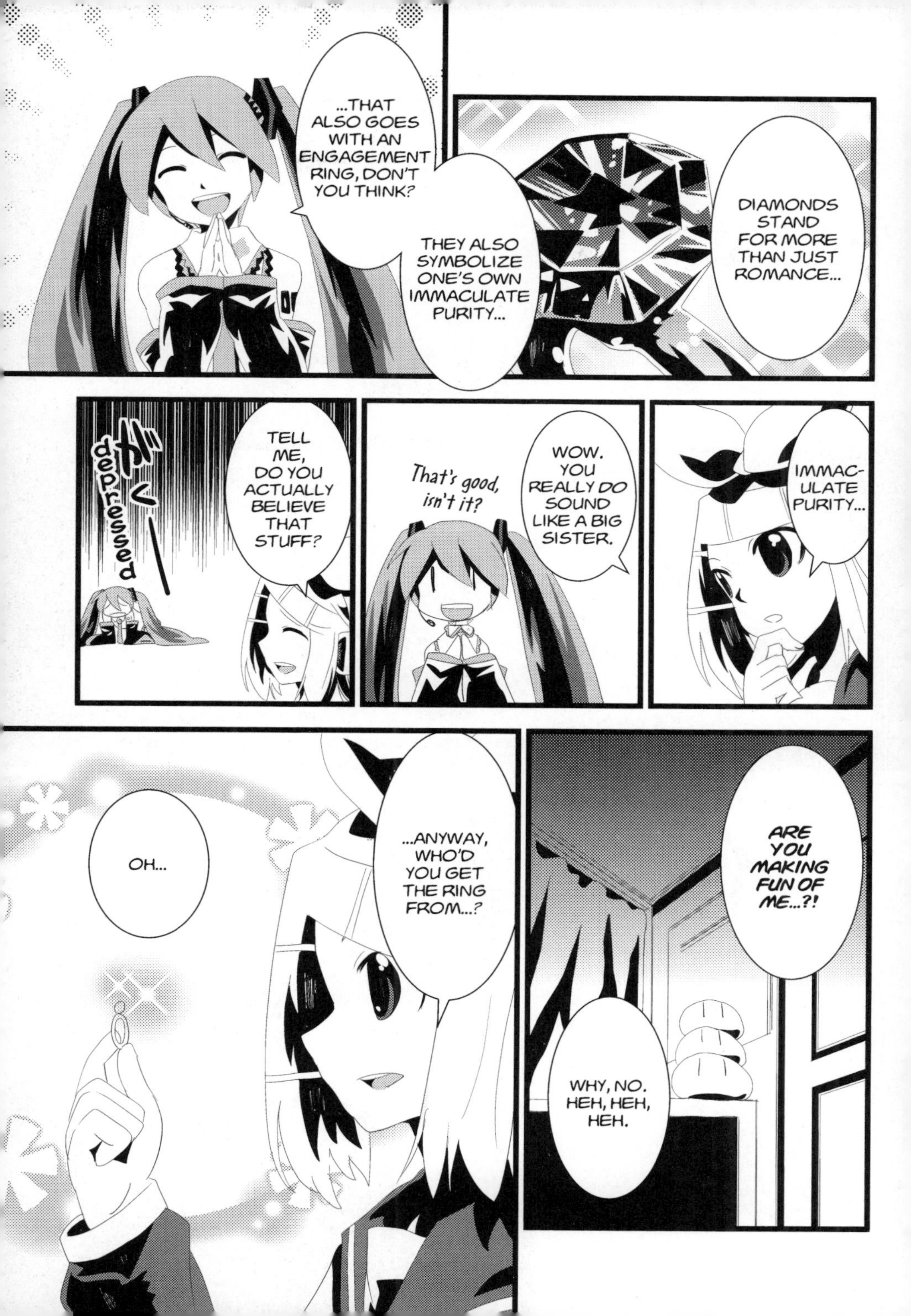
DIAMONDS STAND FOR MORE THAN JUST ROMANCE...
THEY ALSO SYMBOLIZE ONE'S OWN IMMACULATE PURITY...
...THAT ALSO GOES WITH AN ENGAGEMENT RING, DON'T YOU THINK?
IMMACULATE PURITY...
WOW. YOU REALLY *DO* SOUND LIKE A BIG SISTER.
That's good, isn't it?
TELL ME, DO YOU ACTUALLY BELIEVE THAT STUFF?
がく— depressed
ARE YOU MAKING FUN OF ME...?!
WHY, NO. HEH, HEH, HEH.
...ANYWAY, WHO'D YOU GET THE RING FROM...?
OH...

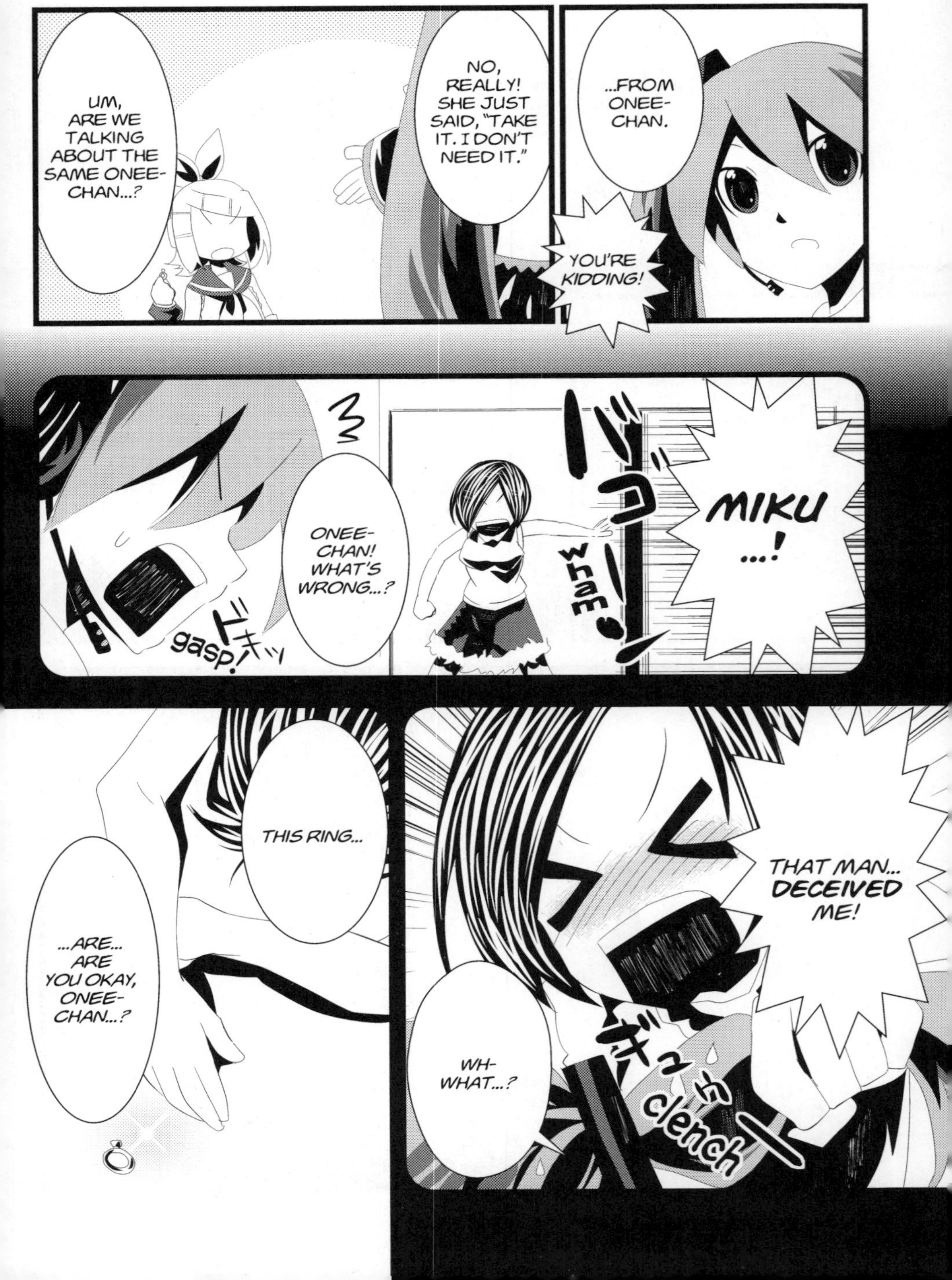
...FROM ONEE-CHAN.
YOU'RE KIDDING!
NO, REALLY! SHE JUST SAID, "TAKE IT. I DON'T NEED IT."
UM, ARE WE TALKING ABOUT THE SAME ONEE-CHAN...?
MIKU ...!
wham!
ONEE-CHAN! WHAT'S WRONG...?
gasp!
THAT MAN... DECEIVED ME!
WH-WHAT...?
clench
THIS RING...
...ARE... ARE YOU OKAY, ONEE-CHAN...?

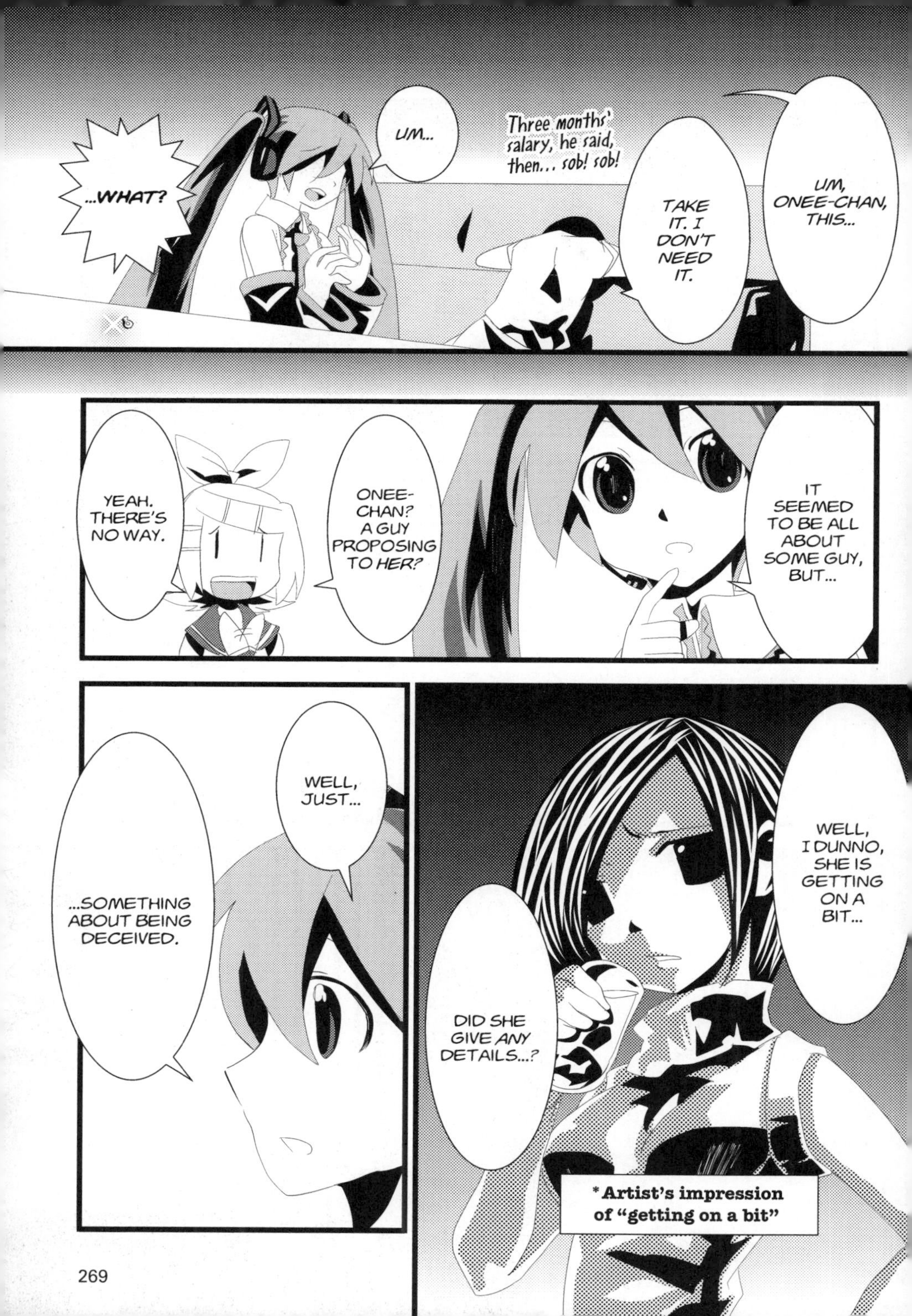
UM, ONEE-CHAN, THIS...
TAKE IT. I DON'T NEED IT.
Three months' salary, he said, then... sob! sob!
UM...
...WHAT?
IT SEEMED TO BE ALL ABOUT SOME GUY, BUT...
ONEE-CHAN? A GUY PROPOSING TO HER?
YEAH. THERE'S NO WAY.
WELL, I DUNNO, SHE IS GETTING ON A BIT...
DID SHE GIVE ANY DETAILS...?
*Artist's impression of "getting on a bit"
WELL, JUST...
...SOMETHING ABOUT BEING DECEIVED.

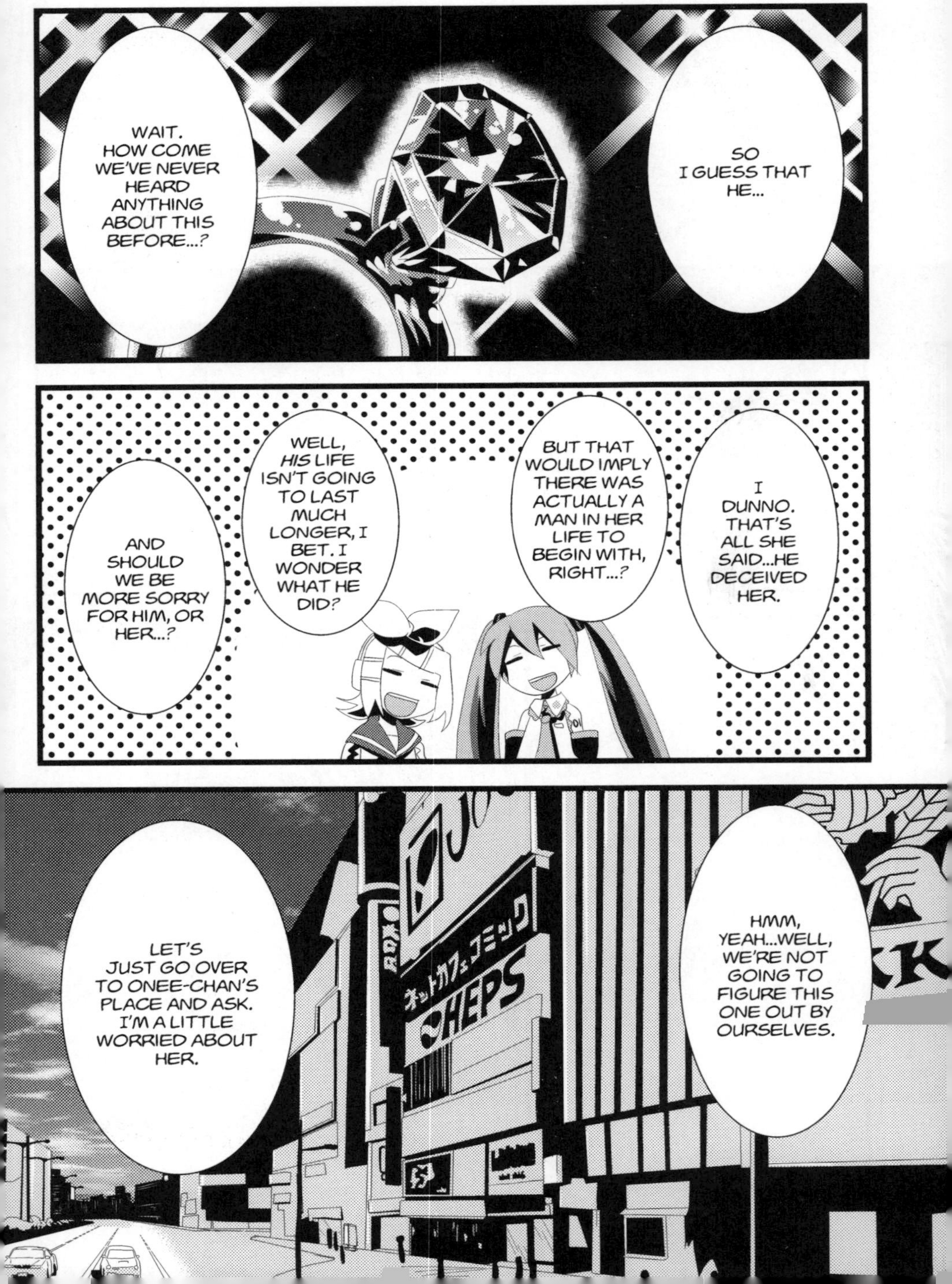
SO I GUESS THAT HE...
WAIT. HOW COME WE'VE NEVER HEARD ANYTHING ABOUT THIS BEFORE...?
I DUNNO. THAT'S ALL SHE SAID...HE DECEIVED HER.
BUT THAT WOULD IMPLY THERE WAS ACTUALLY A MAN IN HER LIFE TO BEGIN WITH, RIGHT...?
WELL, *HIS* LIFE ISN'T GOING TO LAST MUCH LONGER, I BET. I WONDER WHAT HE DID?
AND SHOULD WE BE MORE SORRY FOR HIM, OR HER...?
HMM, YEAH...WELL, WE'RE NOT GOING TO FIGURE THIS ONE OUT BY OURSELVES.
LET'S JUST GO OVER TO ONEE-CHAN'S PLACE AND ASK. I'M A LITTLE WORRIED ABOUT HER.
HEPS

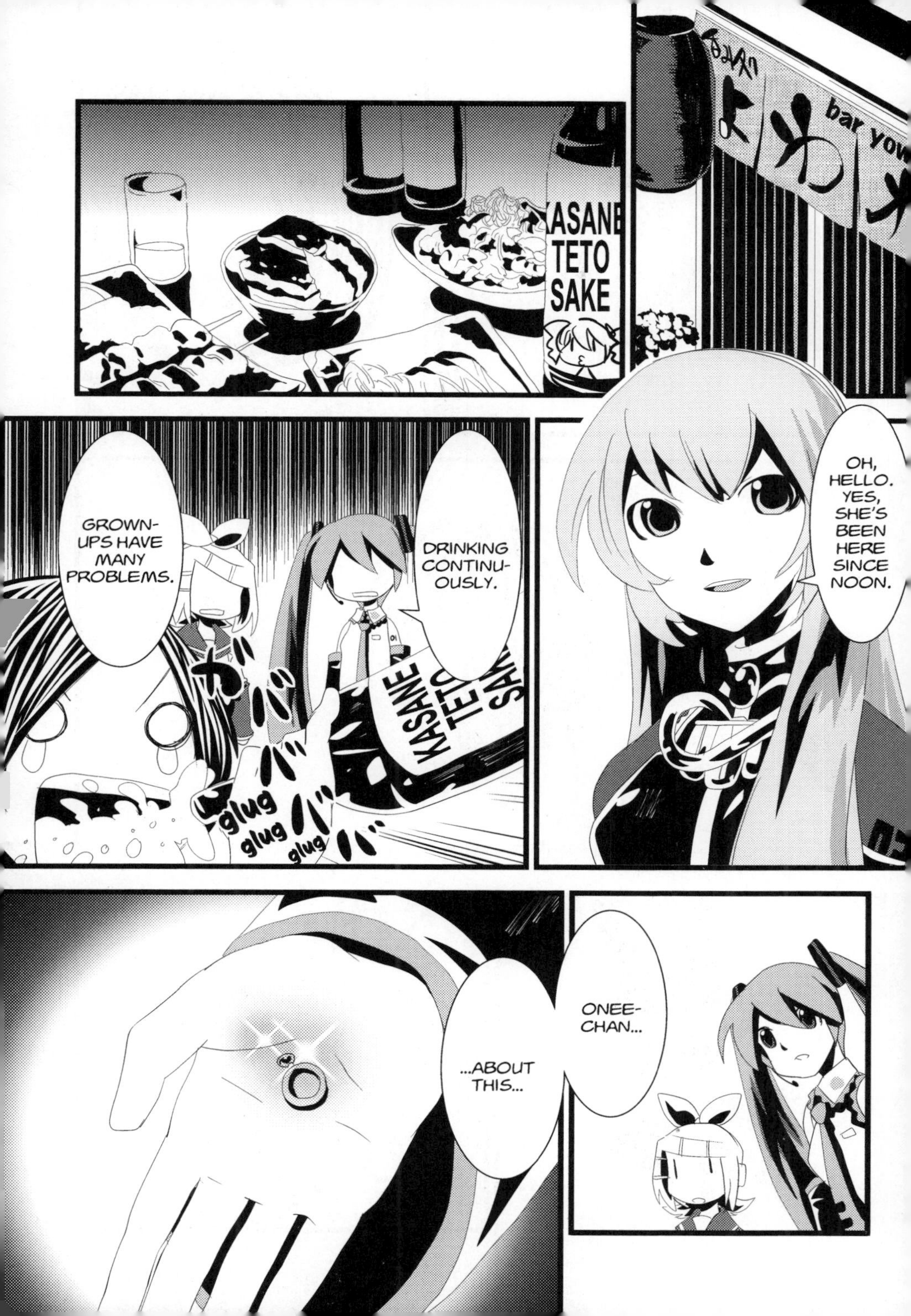
bar yow
KASANE TETO SAKE
OH, HELLO. YES, SHE'S BEEN HERE SINCE NOON.
DRINKING CONTINU-OUSLY.
GROWN-UPS HAVE MANY PROBLEMS.
KASANE TETO SAKE
glug glug glug
ONEE-CHAN...
...ABOUT THIS...

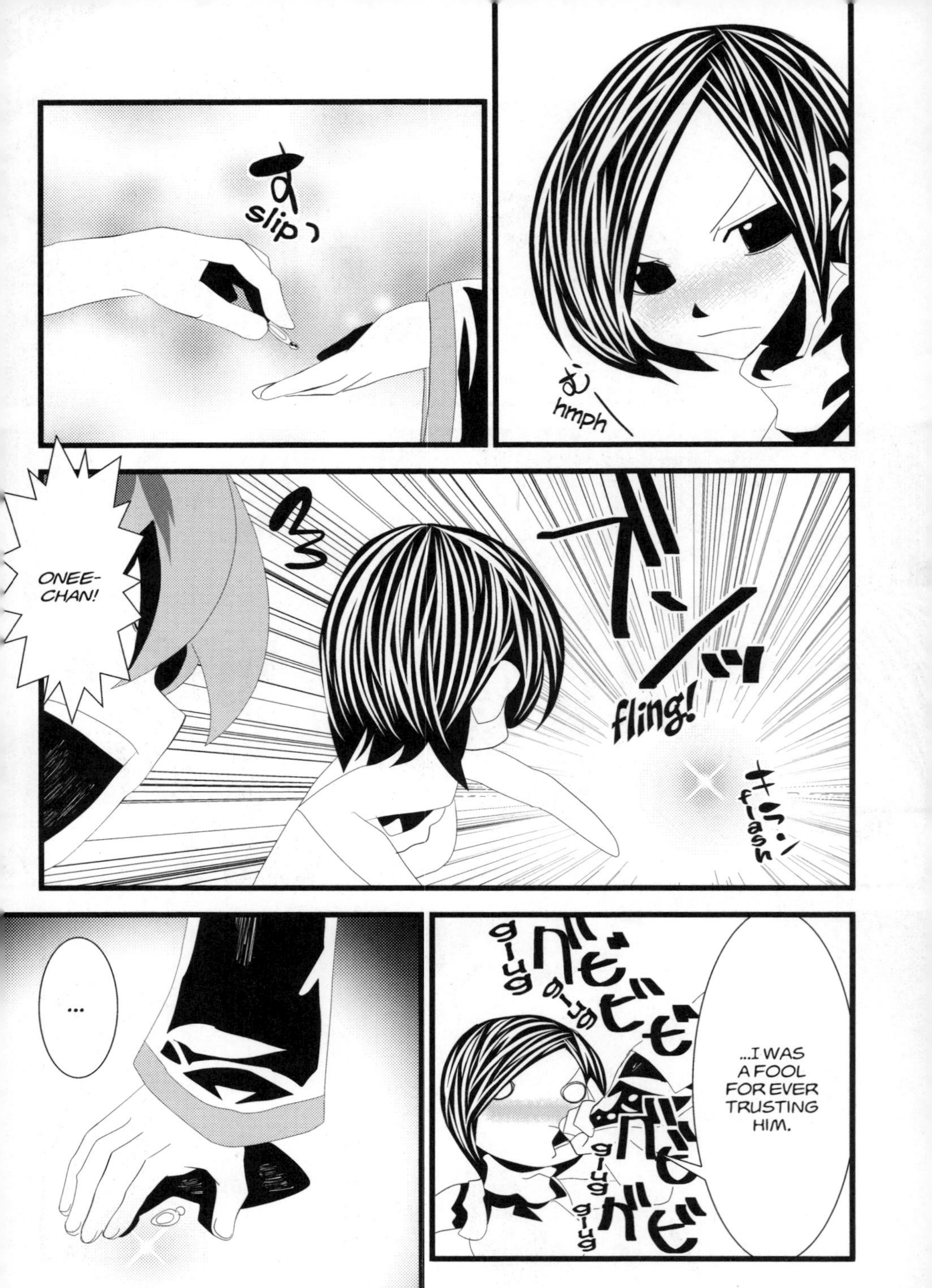
hmph
slip
fling!
flash
ONEE-CHAN!
glug glug
...I WAS A FOOL FOR EVER TRUSTING HIM.
glug glug
...

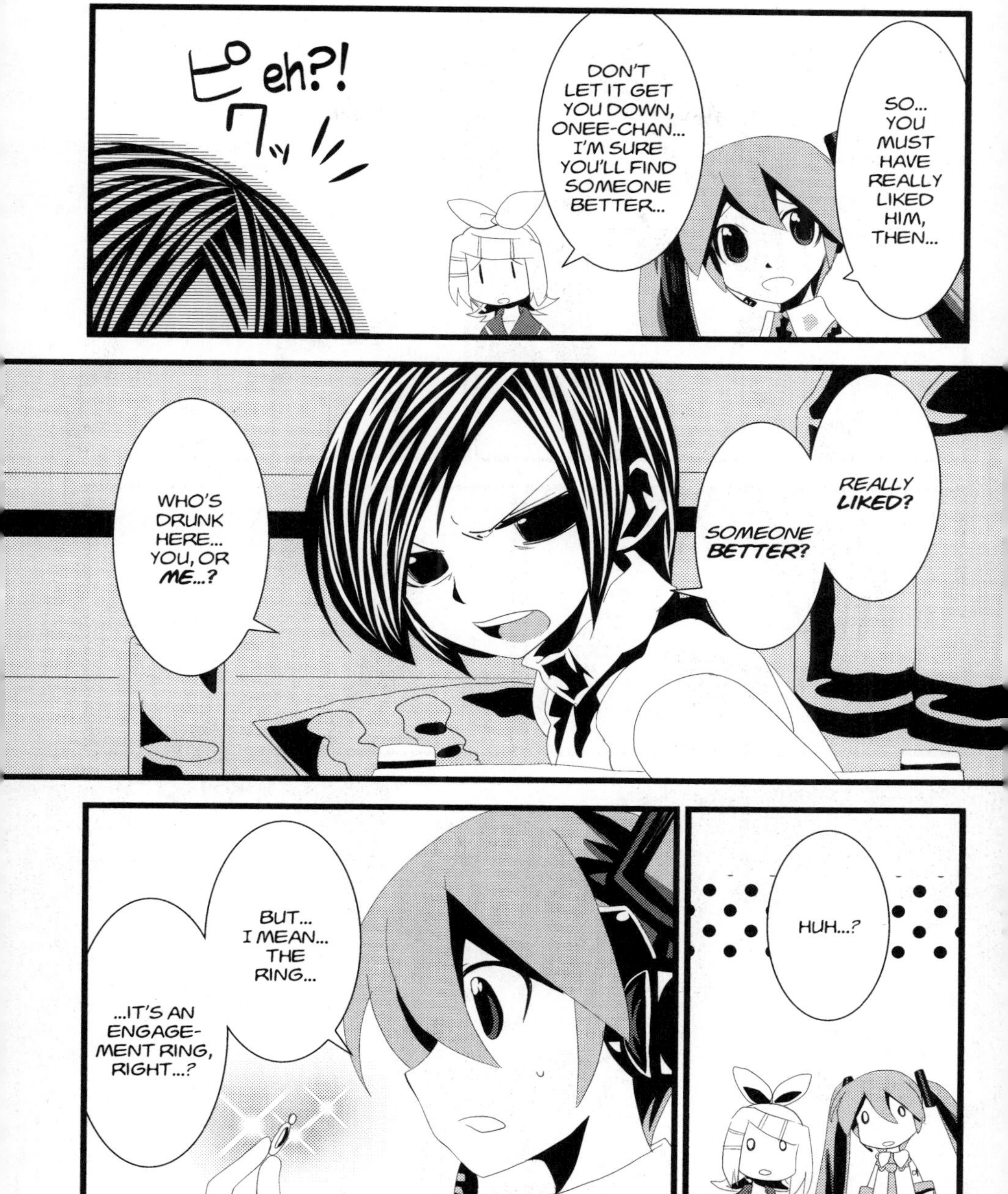
SO... YOU MUST HAVE REALLY LIKED HIM, THEN...
DON'T LET IT GET YOU DOWN, ONEE-CHAN... I'M SURE YOU'LL FIND SOMEONE BETTER...
ピクッ eh?!
REALLY LIKED? SOMEONE BETTER?
WHO'S DRUNK HERE... YOU, OR ME...?
HUH...?
BUT... I MEAN... THE RING...
...IT'S AN ENGAGEMENT RING, RIGHT...?

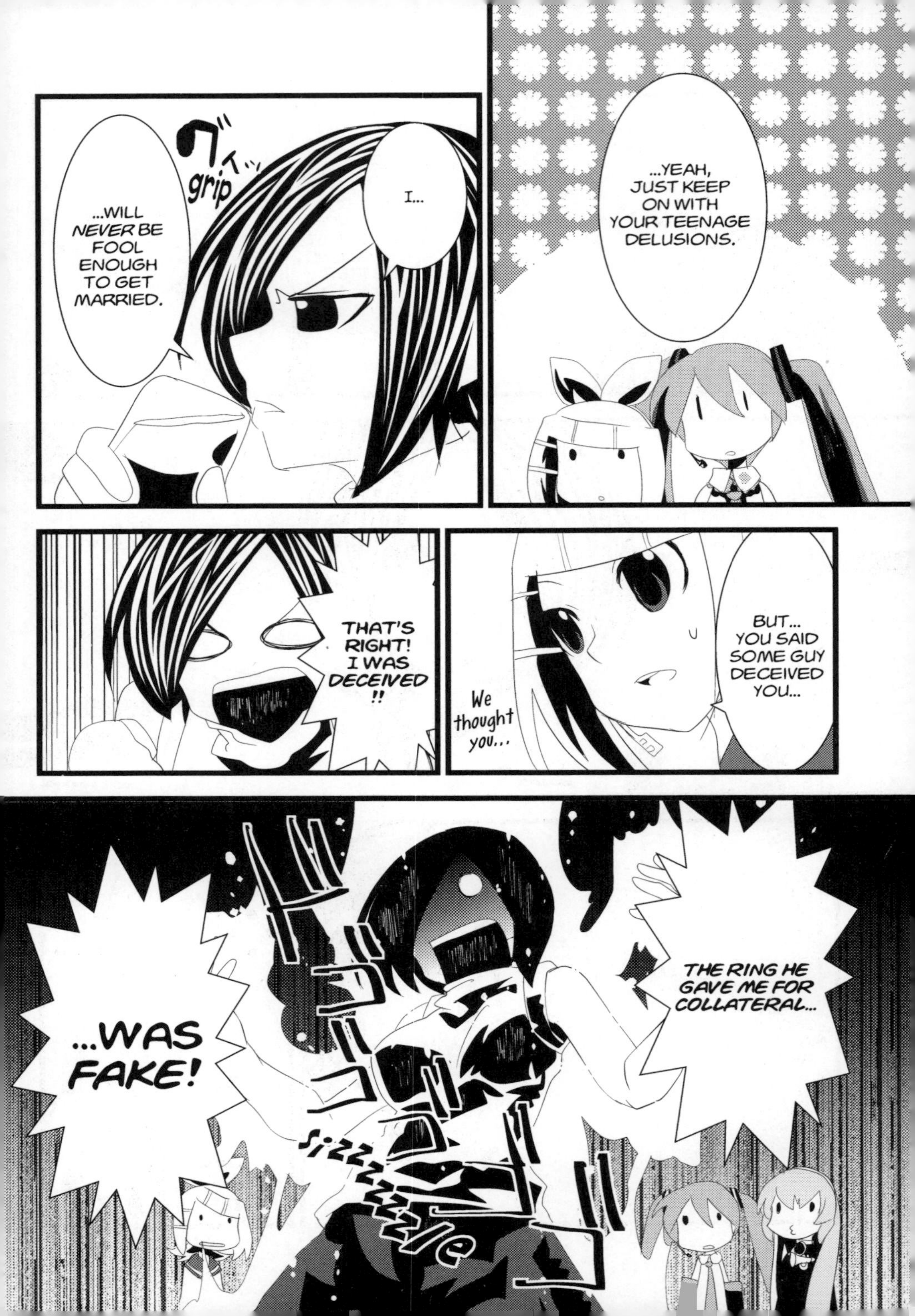
...YEAH, JUST KEEP ON WITH YOUR TEENAGE DELUSIONS.
I...
grip
...WILL NEVER BE FOOL ENOUGH TO GET MARRIED.
BUT... YOU SAID SOME GUY DECEIVED YOU...
We thought you...
THAT'S RIGHT! I WAS DECEIVED !!
THE RING HE GAVE ME FOR COLLATERAL...
...WAS FAKE!
sizzzzzzle

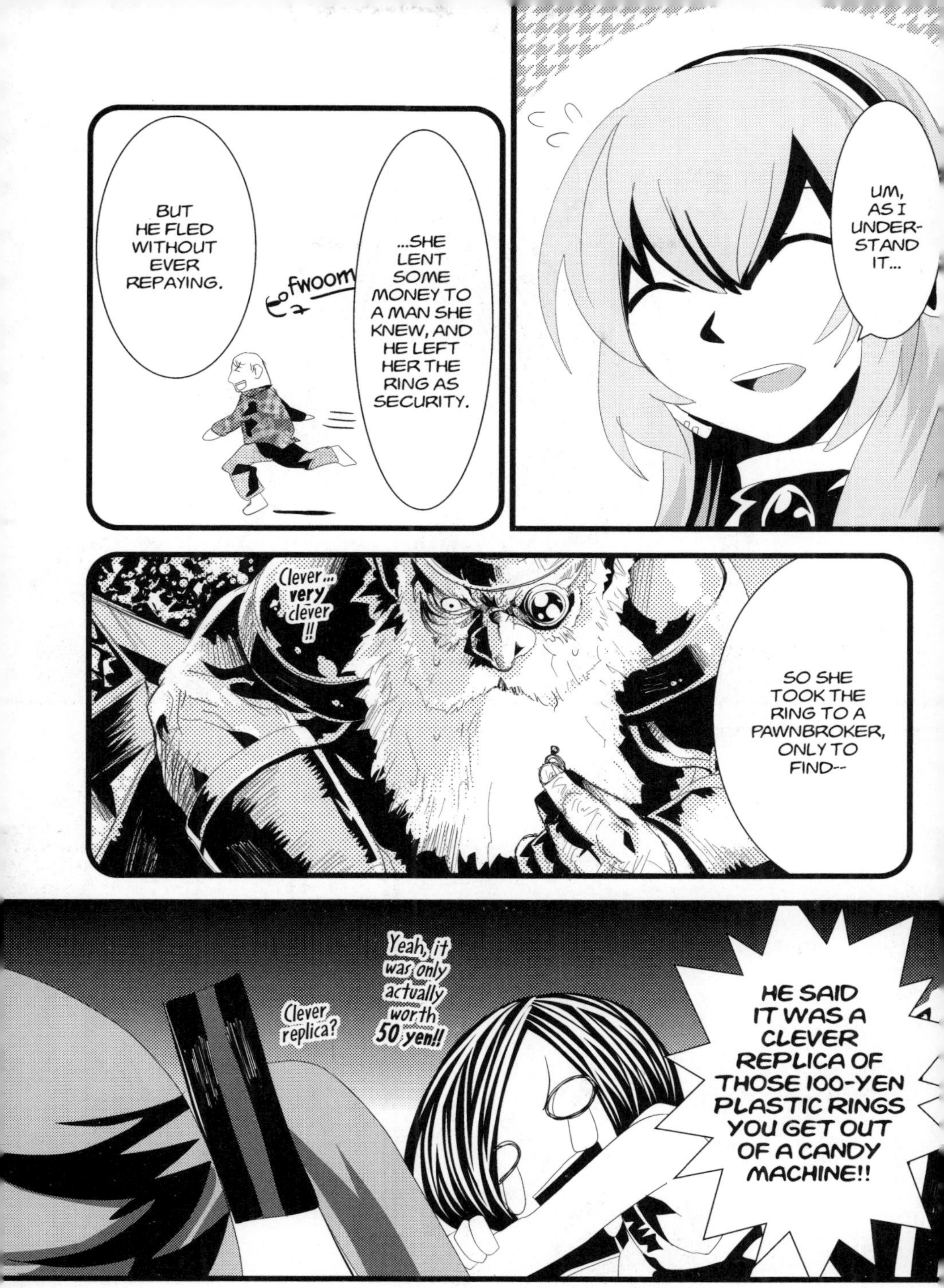
UM, AS I UNDER-STAND IT...
...SHE LENT SOME MONEY TO A MAN SHE KNEW, AND HE LEFT HER THE RING AS SECURITY.
fwoom
BUT HE FLED WITHOUT EVER REPAYING.
SO SHE TOOK THE RING TO A PAWNBROKER, ONLY TO FIND--
Clever... very clever!!
HE SAID IT WAS A CLEVER REPLICA OF THOSE 100-YEN PLASTIC RINGS YOU GET OUT OF A CANDY MACHINE!!
Yeah, it was only actually worth 50 yen!!
Clever replica?

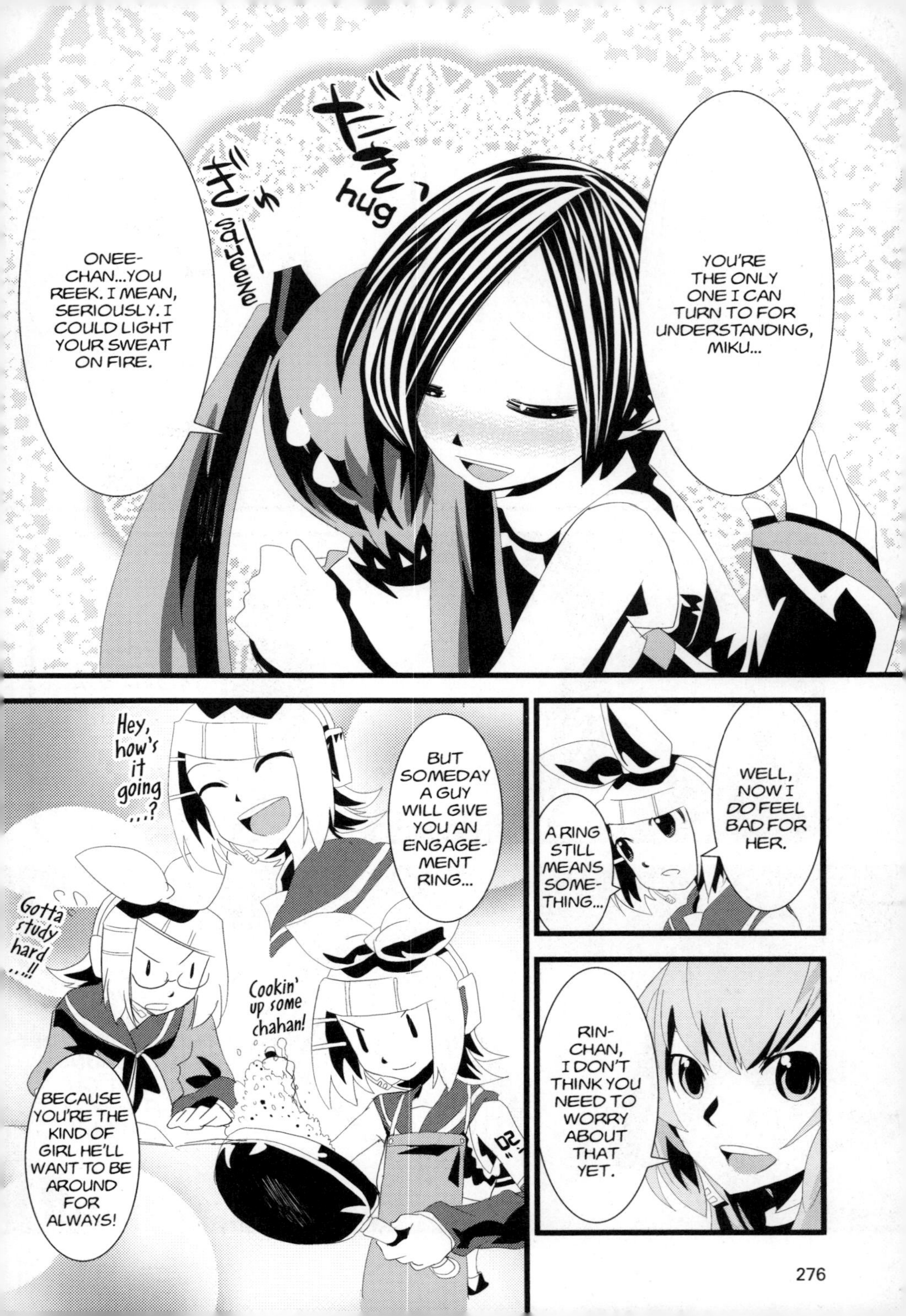
YOU'RE THE ONLY ONE I CAN TURN TO FOR UNDERSTANDING, MIKU...
hug
squeeze
ONEE-CHAN...YOU REEK. I MEAN, SERIOUSLY. I COULD LIGHT YOUR SWEAT ON FIRE.
WELL, NOW I DO FEEL BAD FOR HER.
A RING STILL MEANS SOME-THING...
RIN-CHAN, I DON'T THINK YOU NEED TO WORRY ABOUT THAT YET.
BUT SOMEDAY A GUY WILL GIVE YOU AN ENGAGE-MENT RING...
Hey, how's it going...?
Gotta study hard...!!
Cookin' up some chahan!
BECAUSE YOU'RE THE KIND OF GIRL HE'LL WANT TO BE AROUND FOR ALWAYS!

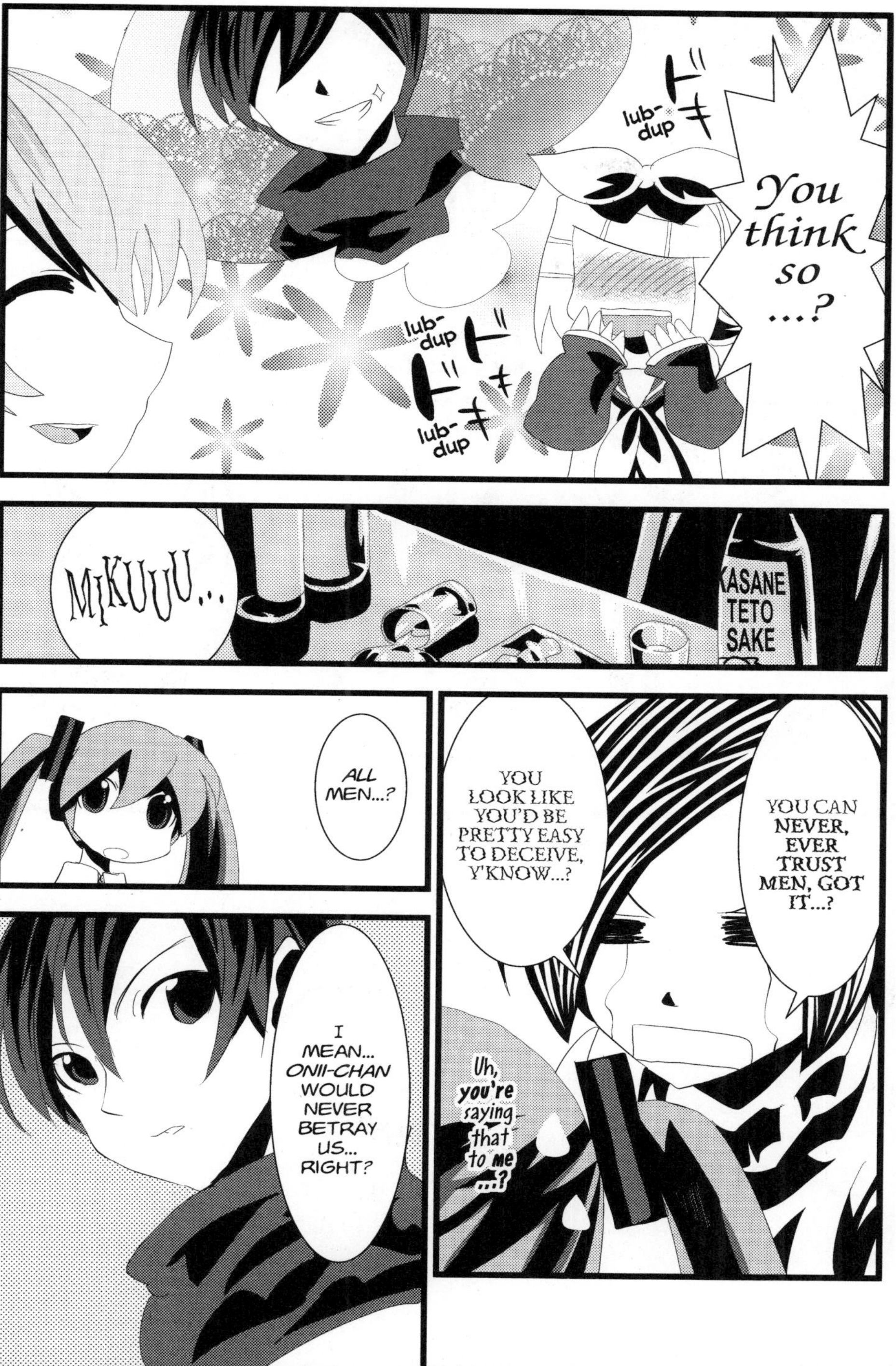
You think so ...?
ドキ
lub-dup
ドキ
lub-dup
ドキ
lub-dup
KASANE TETO SAKE
MIKUUU...
YOU CAN NEVER, EVER TRUST MEN, GOT IT...?
YOU LOOK LIKE YOU'D BE PRETTY EASY TO DECEIVE, Y'KNOW...?
Uh, you're saying that to me ...?
ALL MEN...?
I MEAN... ONII-CHAN WOULD NEVER BETRAY US... RIGHT?

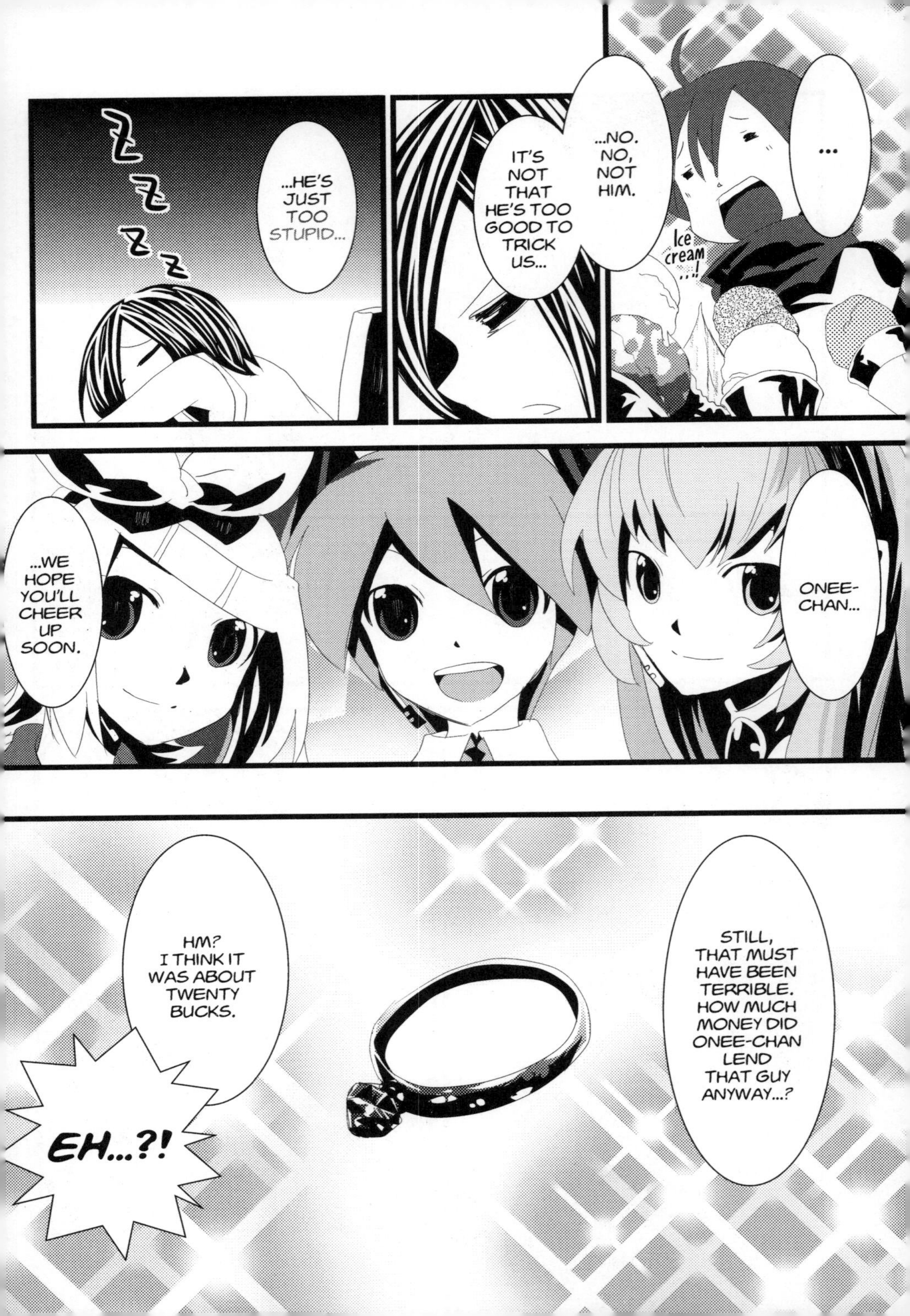
...
...NO. NO, NOT HIM.
Ice cream ...!
IT'S NOT THAT HE'S TOO GOOD TO TRICK US...
...HE'S JUST TOO STUPID...
ZZZZZ
ONEE-CHAN...
...WE HOPE YOU'LL CHEER UP SOON.
STILL, THAT MUST HAVE BEEN TERRIBLE. HOW MUCH MONEY DID ONEE-CHAN LEND THAT GUY ANYWAY...?
HM? I THINK IT WAS ABOUT TWENTY BUCKS.
EH...?!

(18th SONG) MEGURINE MIX

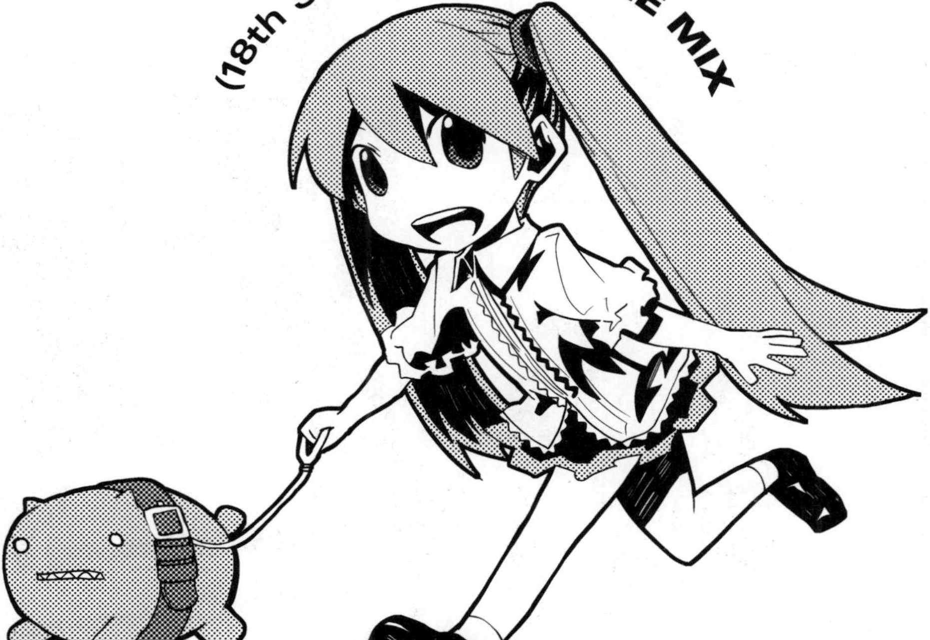

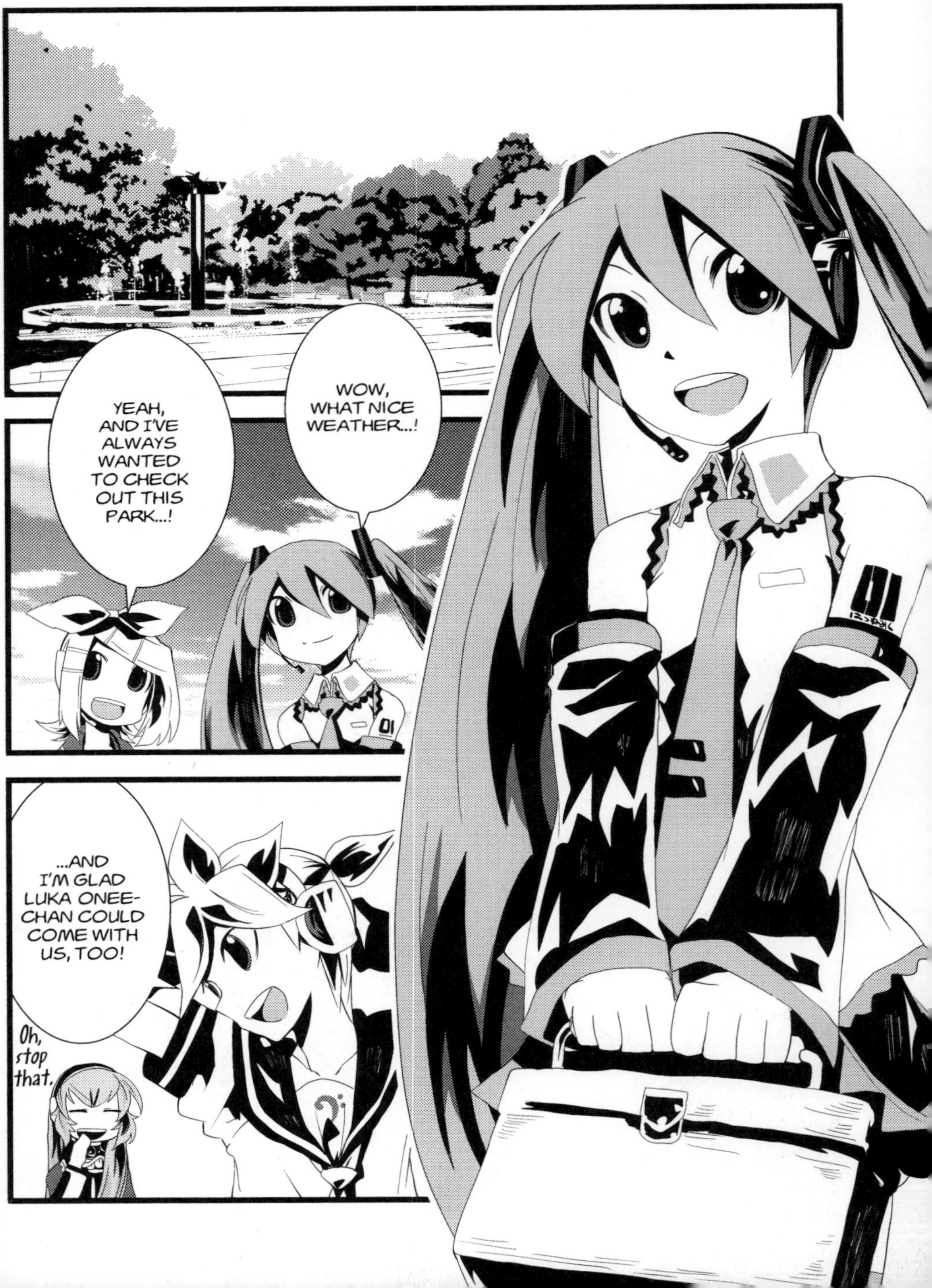
WOW, WHAT NICE WEATHER...!
YEAH, AND I'VE ALWAYS WANTED TO CHECK OUT THIS PARK...!
...AND I'M GLAD LUKA ONEE-CHAN COULD COME WITH US, TOO!
Oh, stop that.

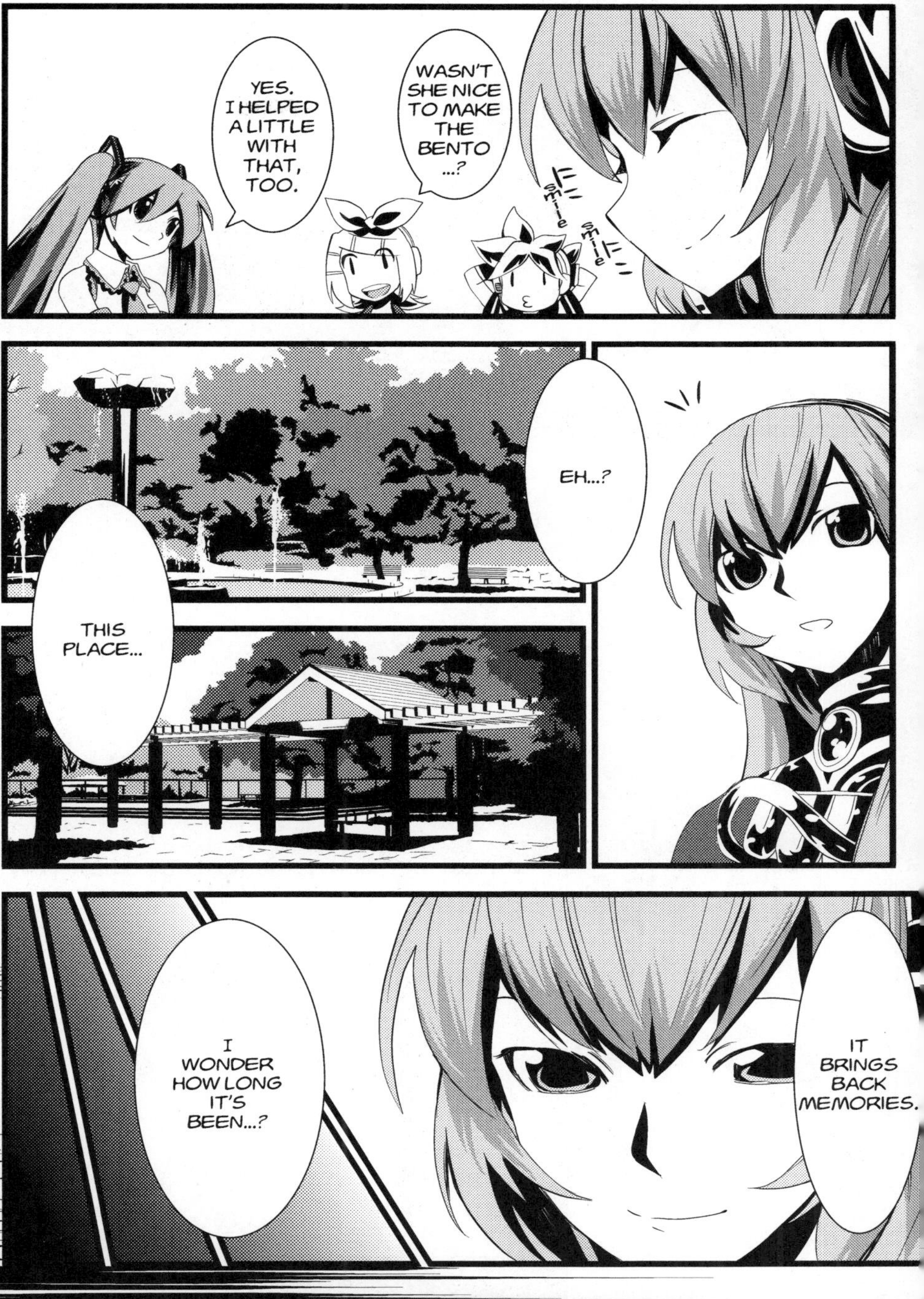
WASN'T SHE NICE TO MAKE THE BENTO ...?
YES. I HELPED A LITTLE WITH THAT, TOO.
smile
smile
EH...?
THIS PLACE...
IT BRINGS BACK MEMORIES.
I WONDER HOW LONG IT'S BEEN...?

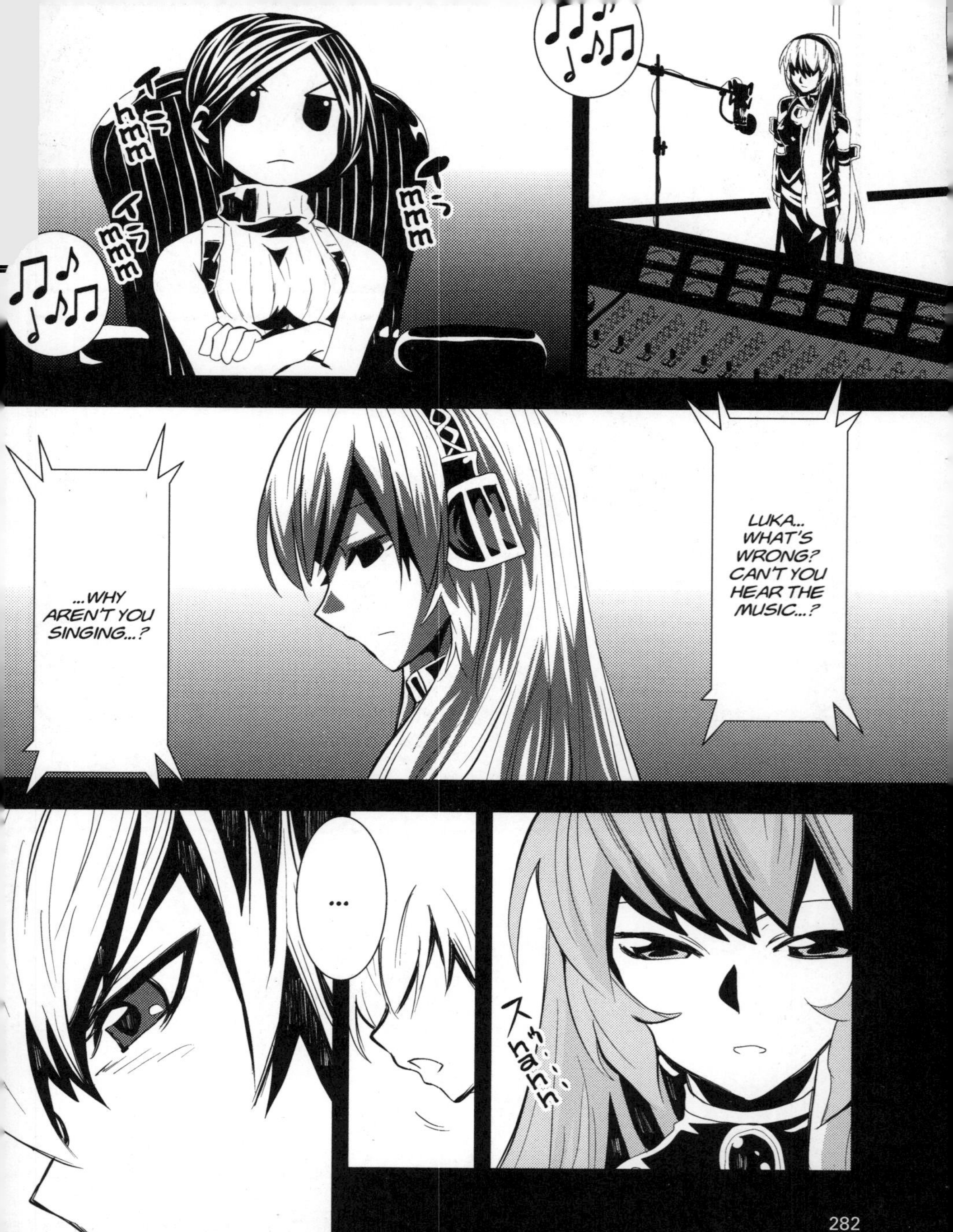
mmm
mmm
mmm
LUKA... WHAT'S WRONG? CAN'T YOU HEAR THE MUSIC...?
...WHY AREN'T YOU SINGING...?
スゥ... hahh...
...

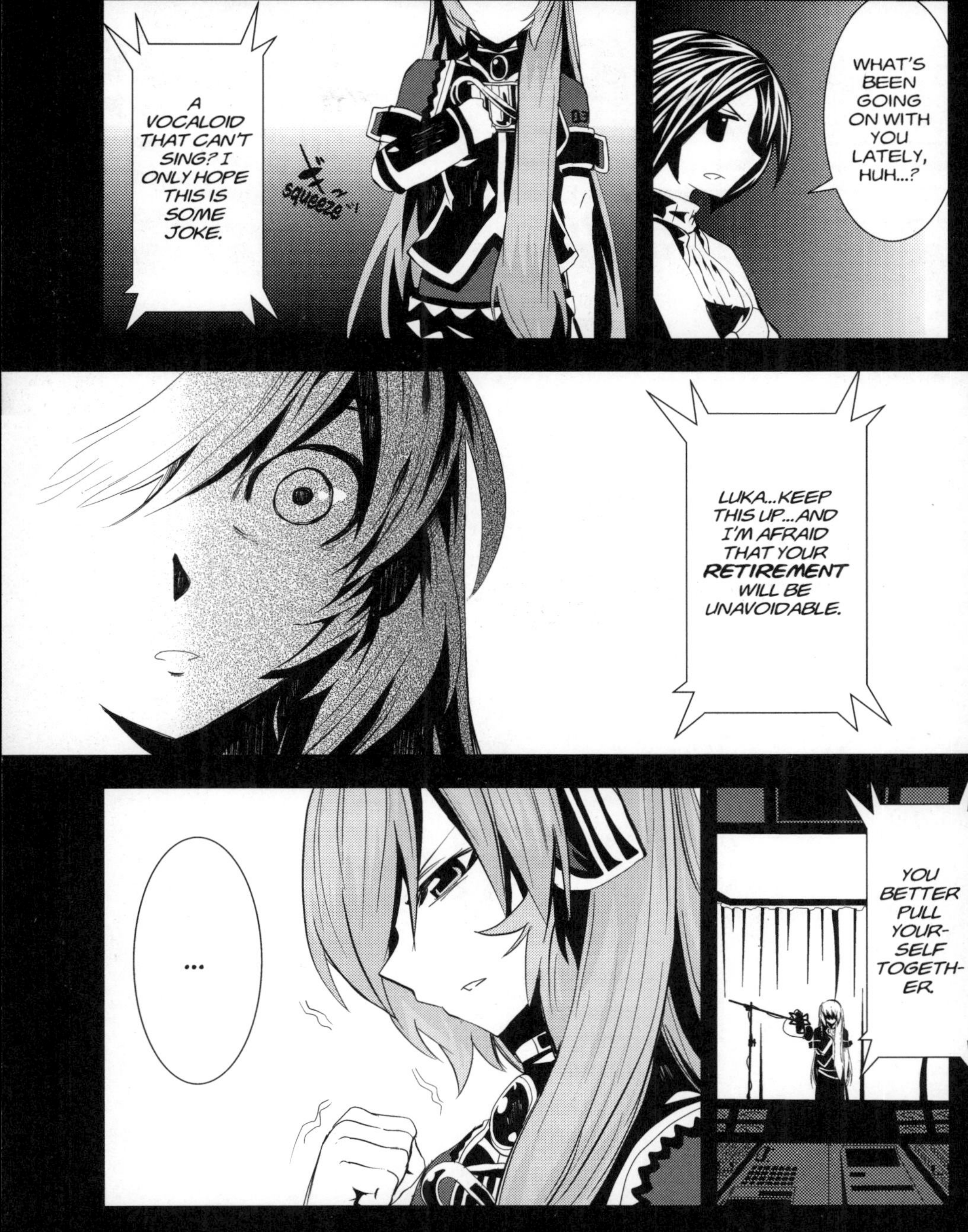
WHAT'S BEEN GOING ON WITH YOU LATELY, HUH...?
A VOCALOID THAT CAN'T SING? I ONLY HOPE THIS IS SOME JOKE.
squeeze
LUKA...KEEP THIS UP...AND I'M AFRAID THAT YOUR **RETIREMENT** WILL BE UNAVOIDABLE.
YOU BETTER PULL YOUR-SELF TOGETH-ER.
...

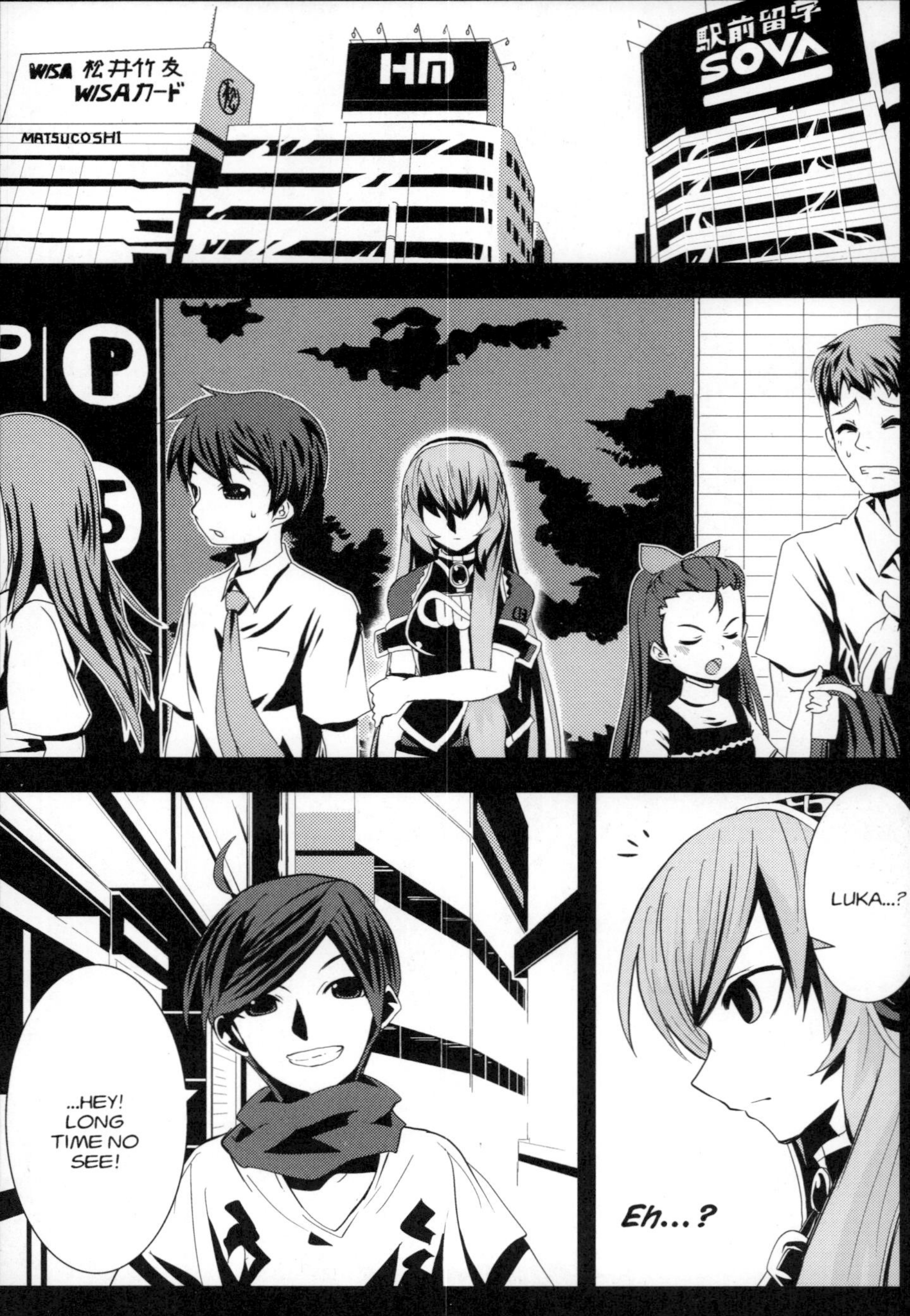
駅前留字
SOVA
HM
WISA 松井竹友
WISAカード
MATSUCOSHI
LUKA...?
Eh...?
...HEY! LONG TIME NO SEE!

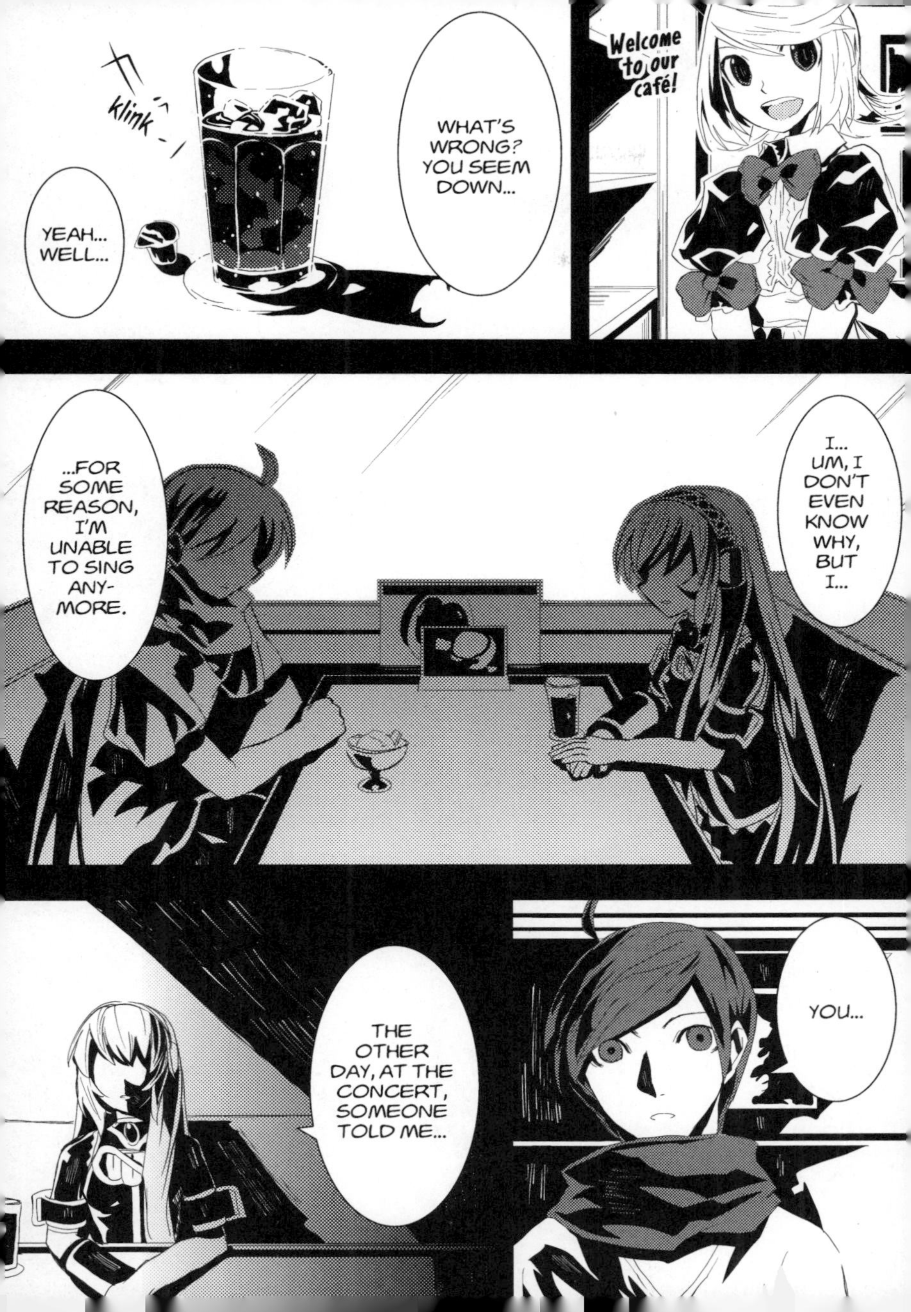
Welcome to our café!
WHAT'S WRONG? YOU SEEM DOWN...
klink
YEAH... WELL...
I... UM, I DON'T EVEN KNOW WHY, BUT I...
...FOR SOME REASON, I'M UNABLE TO SING ANY-MORE.
YOU...
THE OTHER DAY, AT THE CONCERT, SOMEONE TOLD ME...

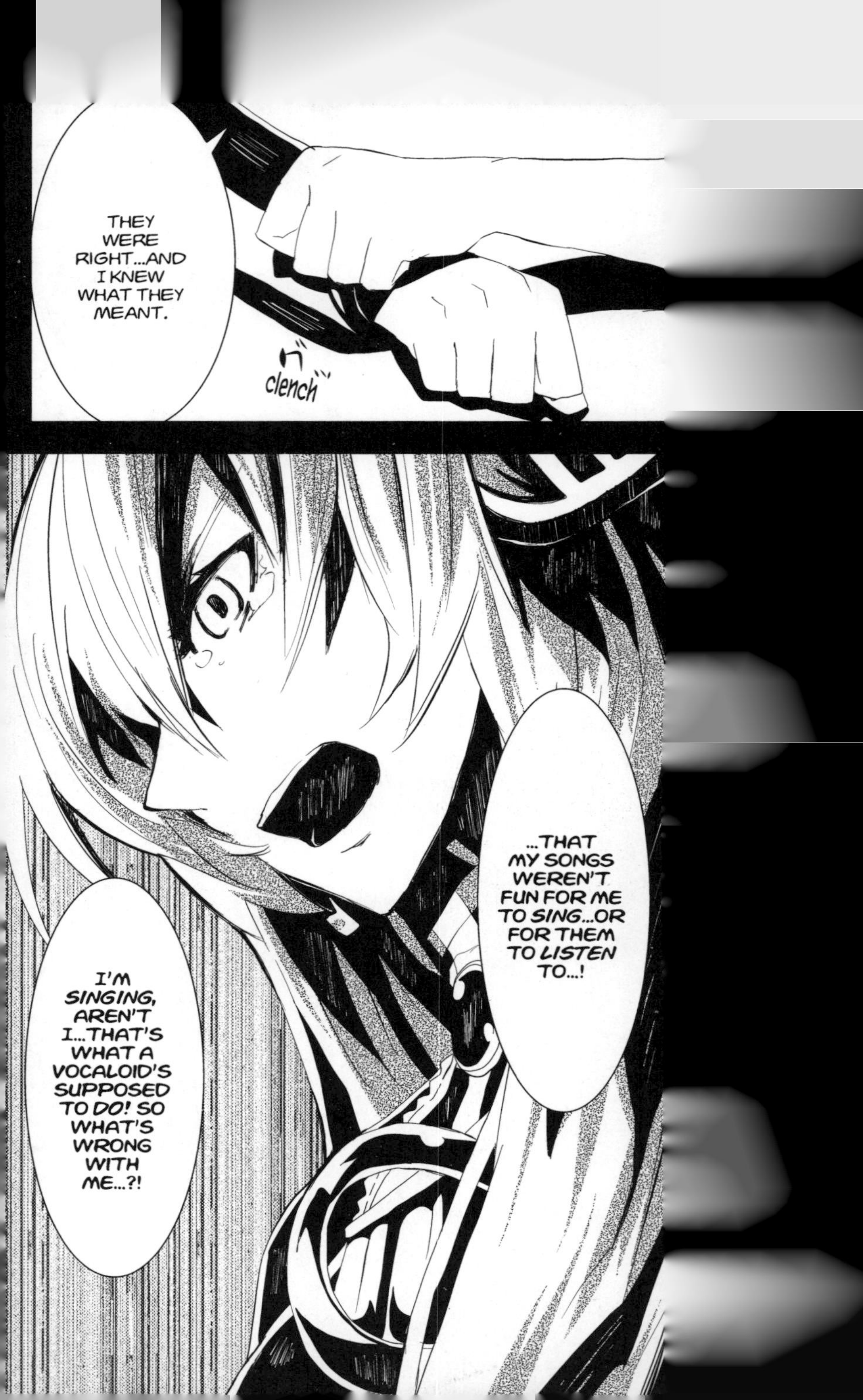
THEY WERE RIGHT...AND I KNEW WHAT THEY MEANT.
clench
...THAT MY SONGS WEREN'T FUN FOR ME TO *SING*...OR FOR THEM TO *LISTEN* TO...!
I'M SINGING, AREN'T I...THAT'S WHAT A VOCALOID'S SUPPOSED TO *DO*! SO WHAT'S WRONG WITH ME...?!

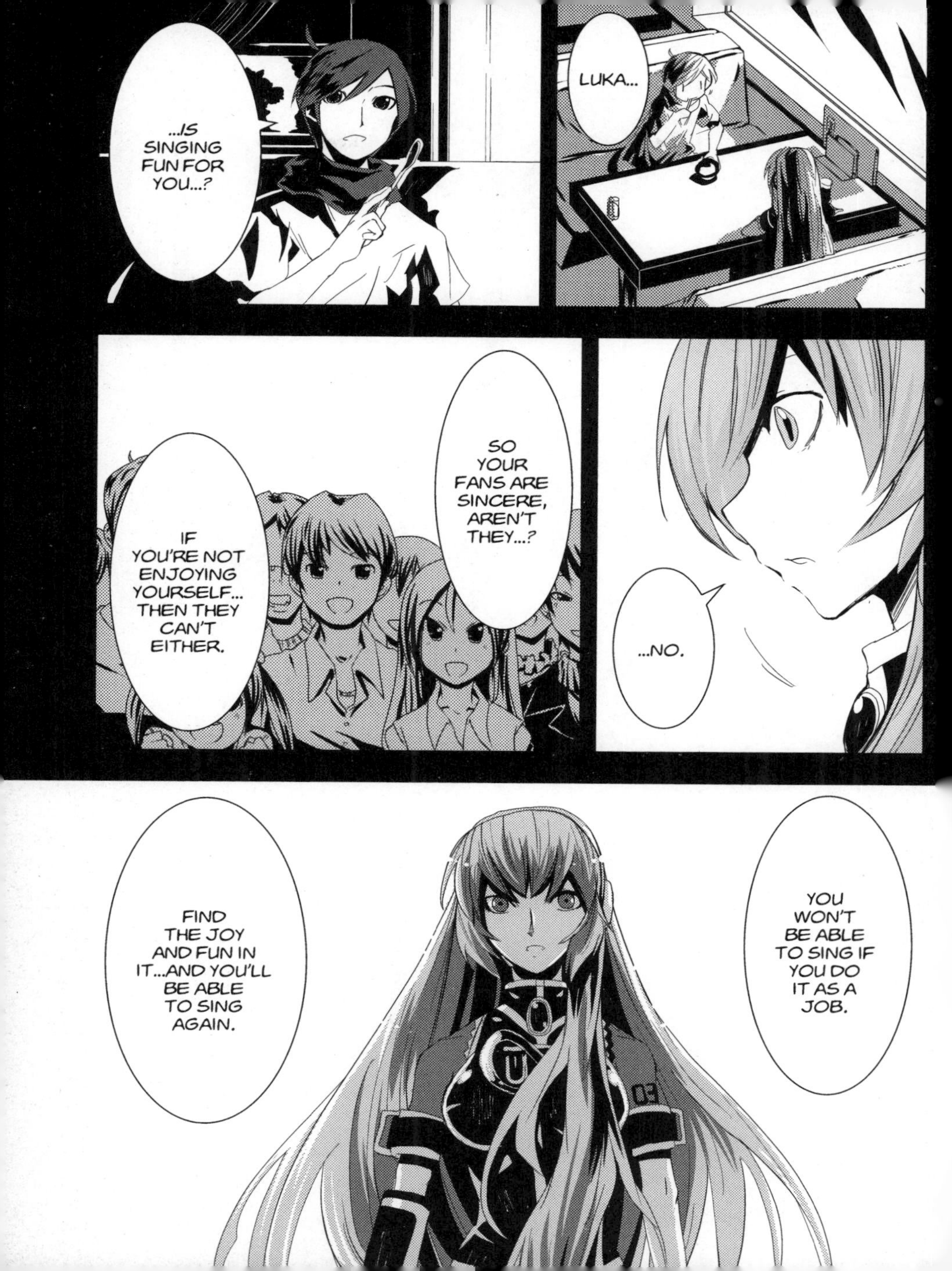
LUKA...
...IS SINGING FUN FOR YOU...?
...NO.
SO YOUR FANS ARE SINCERE, AREN'T THEY...?
IF YOU'RE NOT ENJOYING YOURSELF... THEN THEY CAN'T EITHER.
YOU WON'T BE ABLE TO SING IF YOU DO IT AS A JOB.
FIND THE JOY AND FUN IN IT...AND YOU'LL BE ABLE TO SING AGAIN.

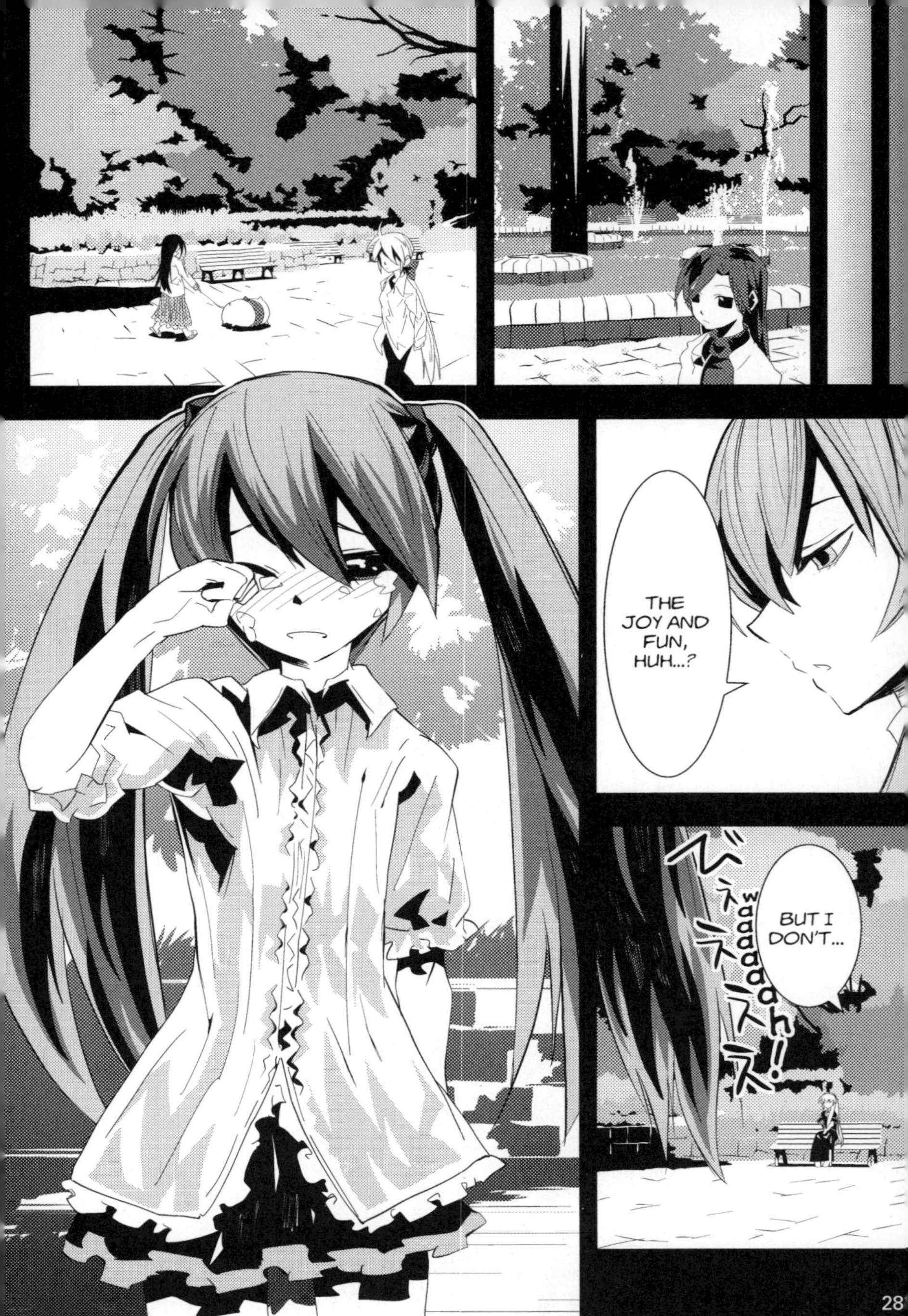
THE JOY AND FUN, HUH...?
BUT I DON'T...
waaaaah!

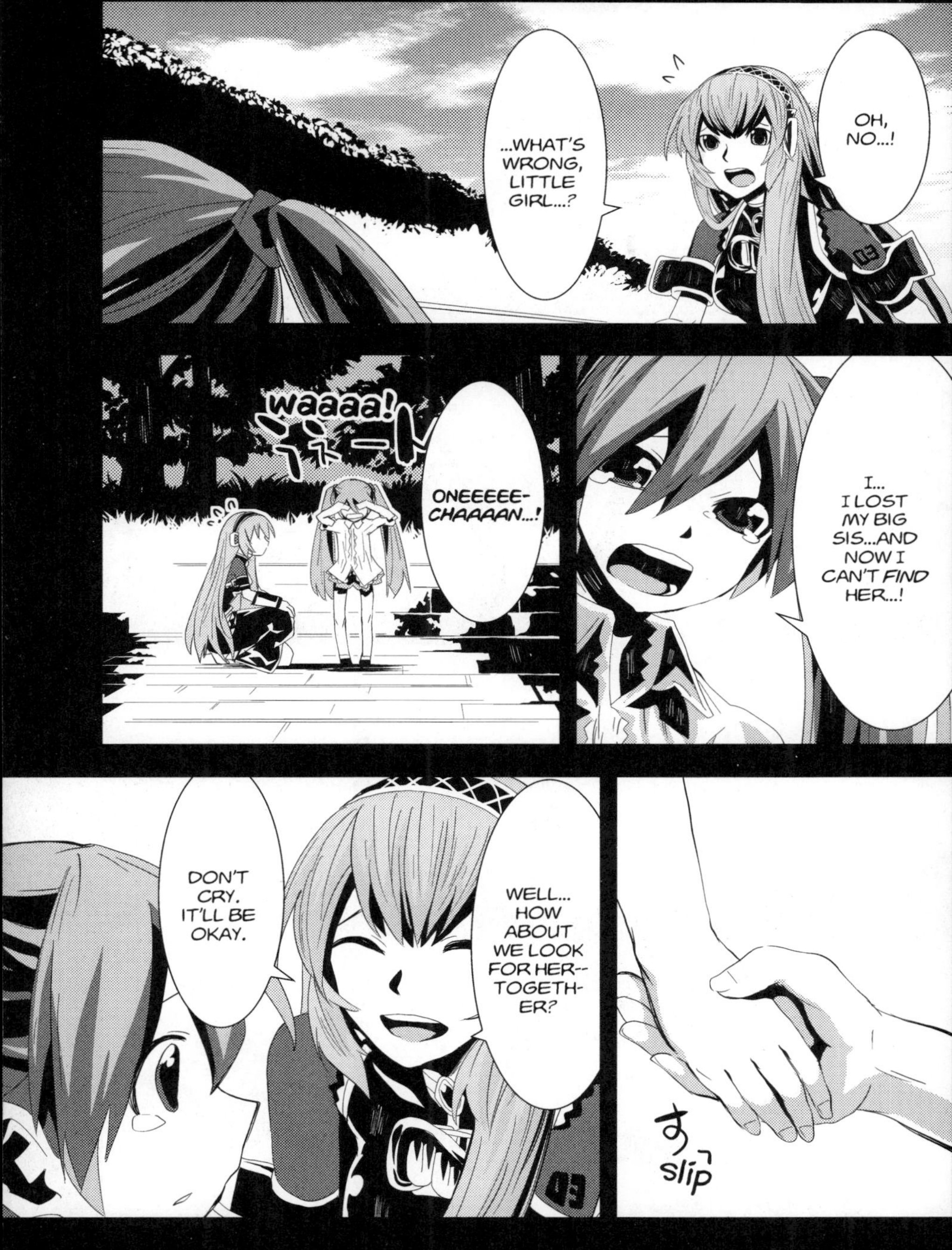
OH, NO...!
...WHAT'S WRONG, LITTLE GIRL...?
I... I LOST MY BIG SIS...AND NOW I CAN'T *FIND* HER...!
waaaa!
ONEEEEE-CHAAAAN...!
す
slip
WELL... HOW ABOUT WE LOOK FOR HER--TOGETH-ER?
DON'T CRY. IT'LL BE OKAY.

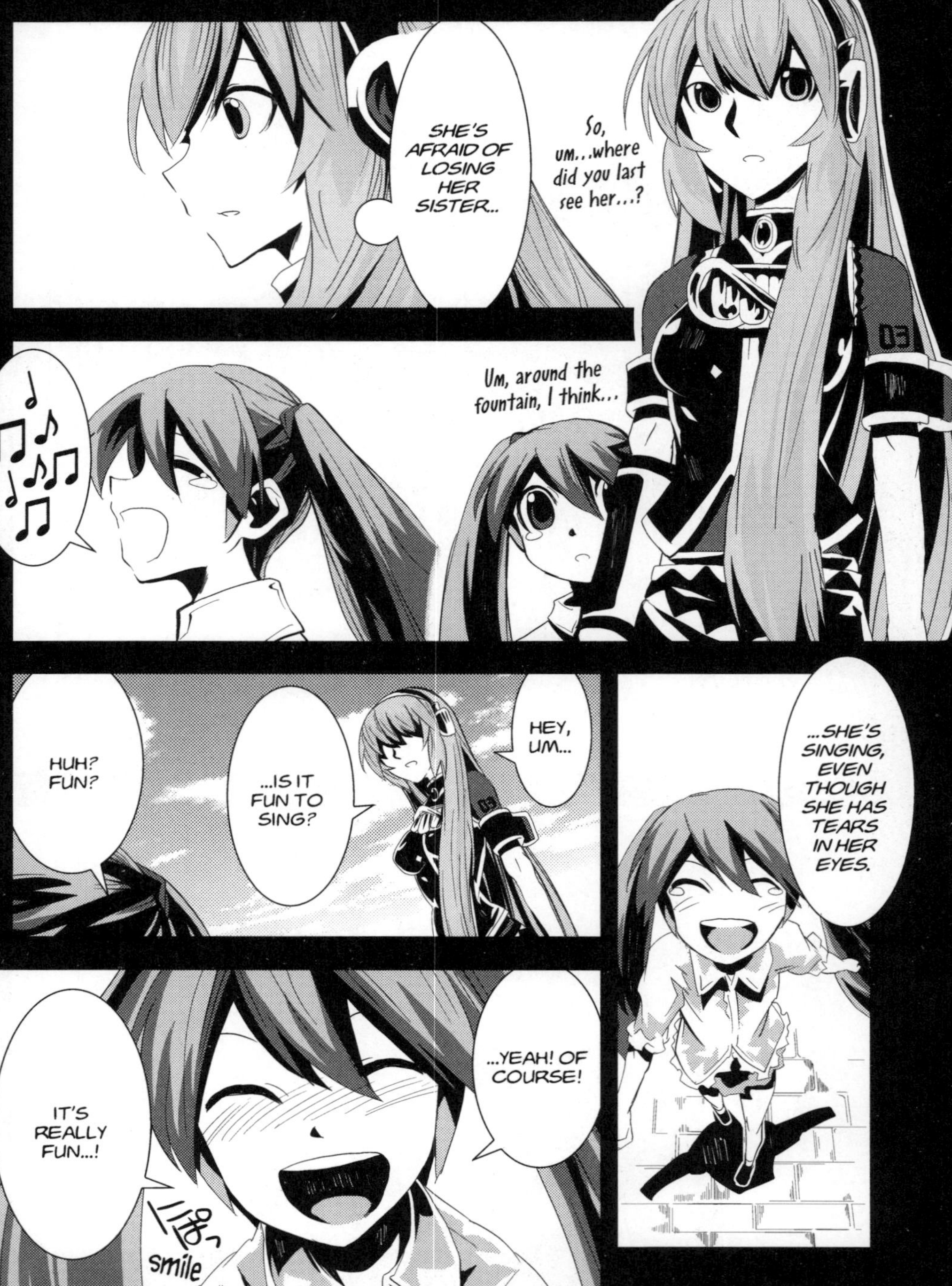
So, um...where did you last see her...?
SHE'S AFRAID OF LOSING HER SISTER..
Um, around the fountain, I think...
...SHE'S SINGING, EVEN THOUGH SHE HAS TEARS IN HER EYES.
HEY, UM...
...IS IT FUN TO SING?
HUH? FUN?
...YEAH! OF COURSE!
IT'S REALLY FUN...!
にぱっ
smile

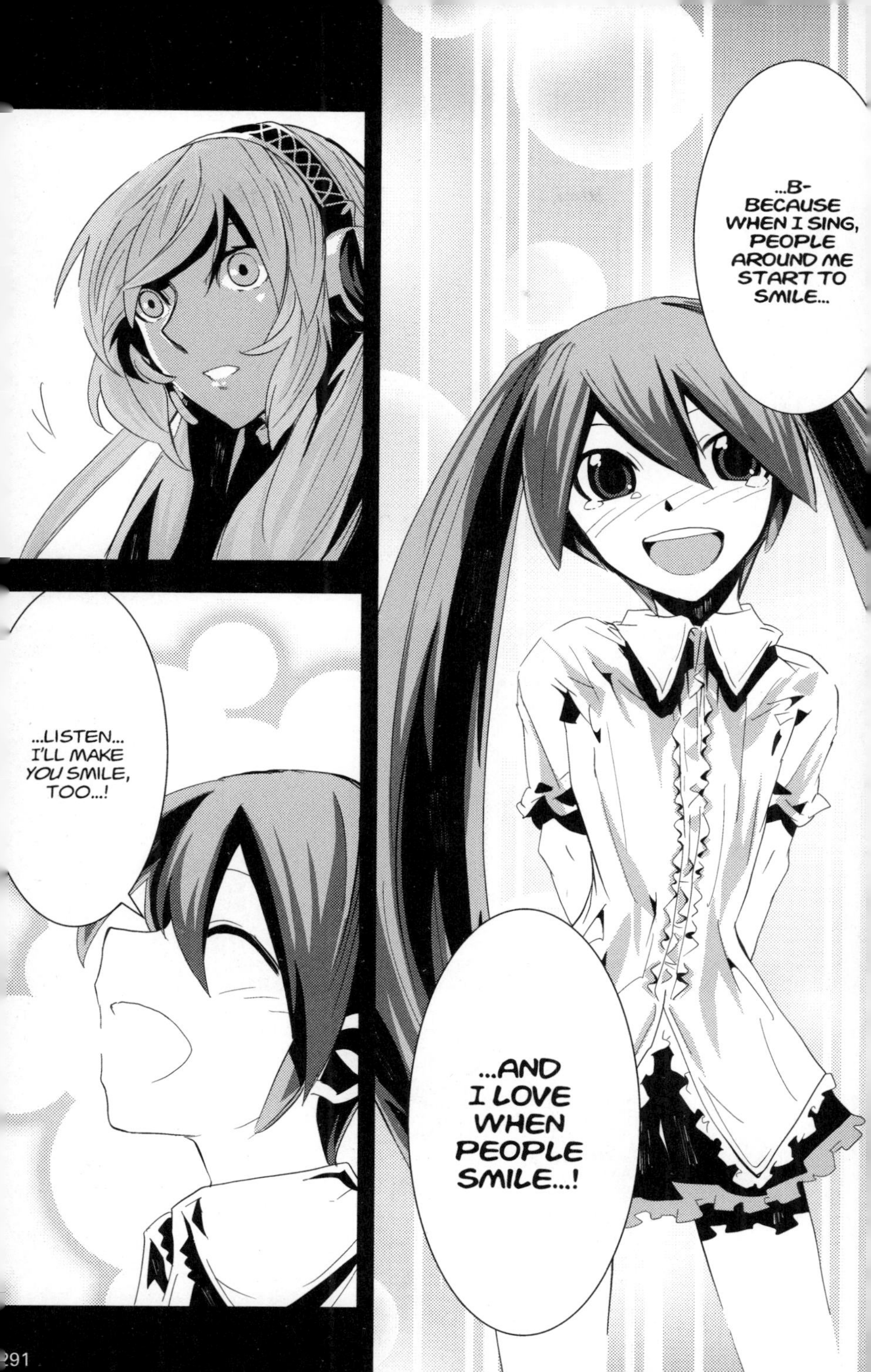
...B-BECAUSE WHEN I SING, PEOPLE AROUND ME START TO SMILE...
...AND I LOVE WHEN PEOPLE SMILE...!
...LISTEN... I'LL MAKE YOU SMILE, TOO...!

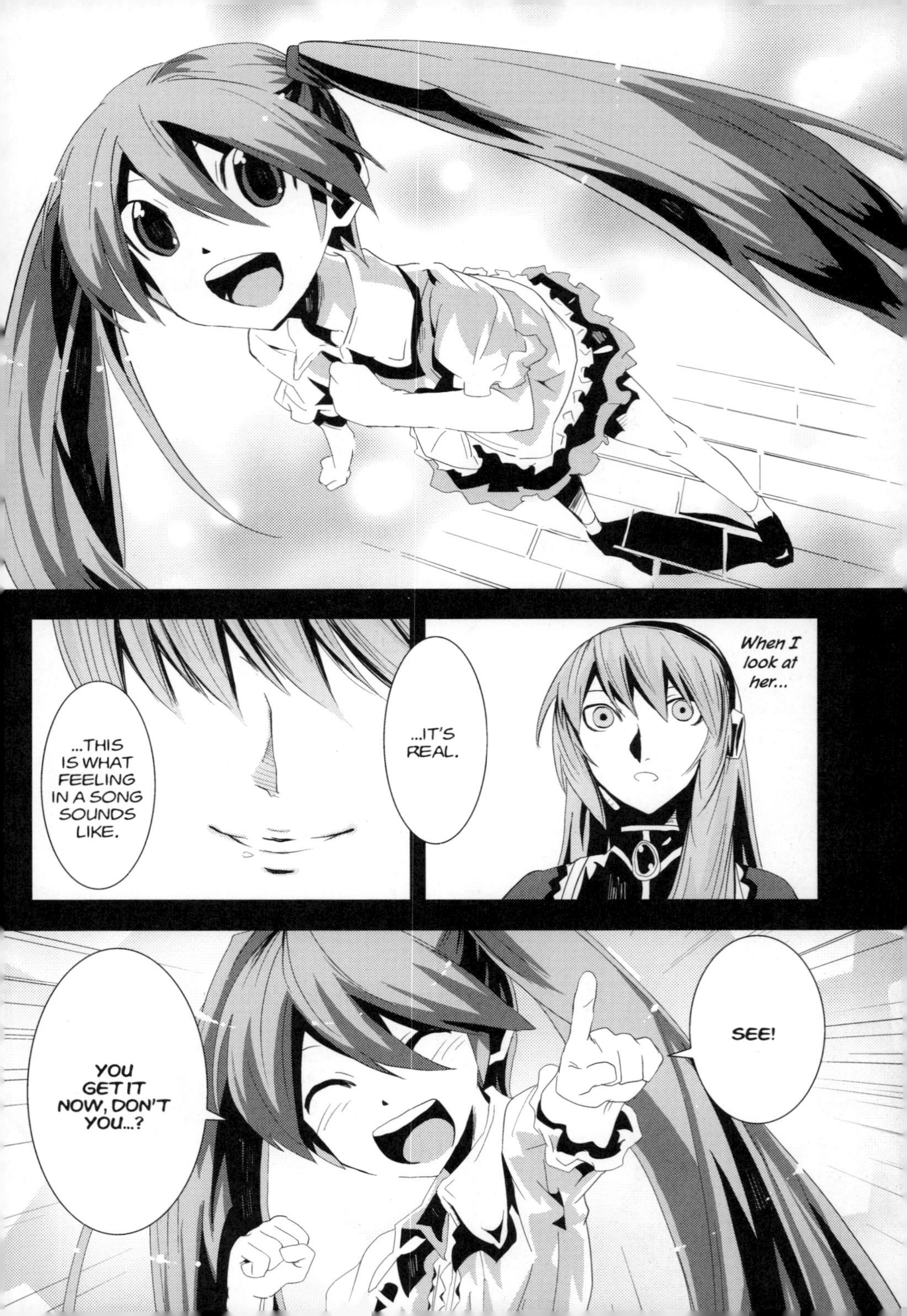
When I look at her...
...IT'S REAL.
...THIS IS WHAT FEELING IN A SONG SOUNDS LIKE.
SEE!
YOU GET IT NOW, DON'T YOU...?

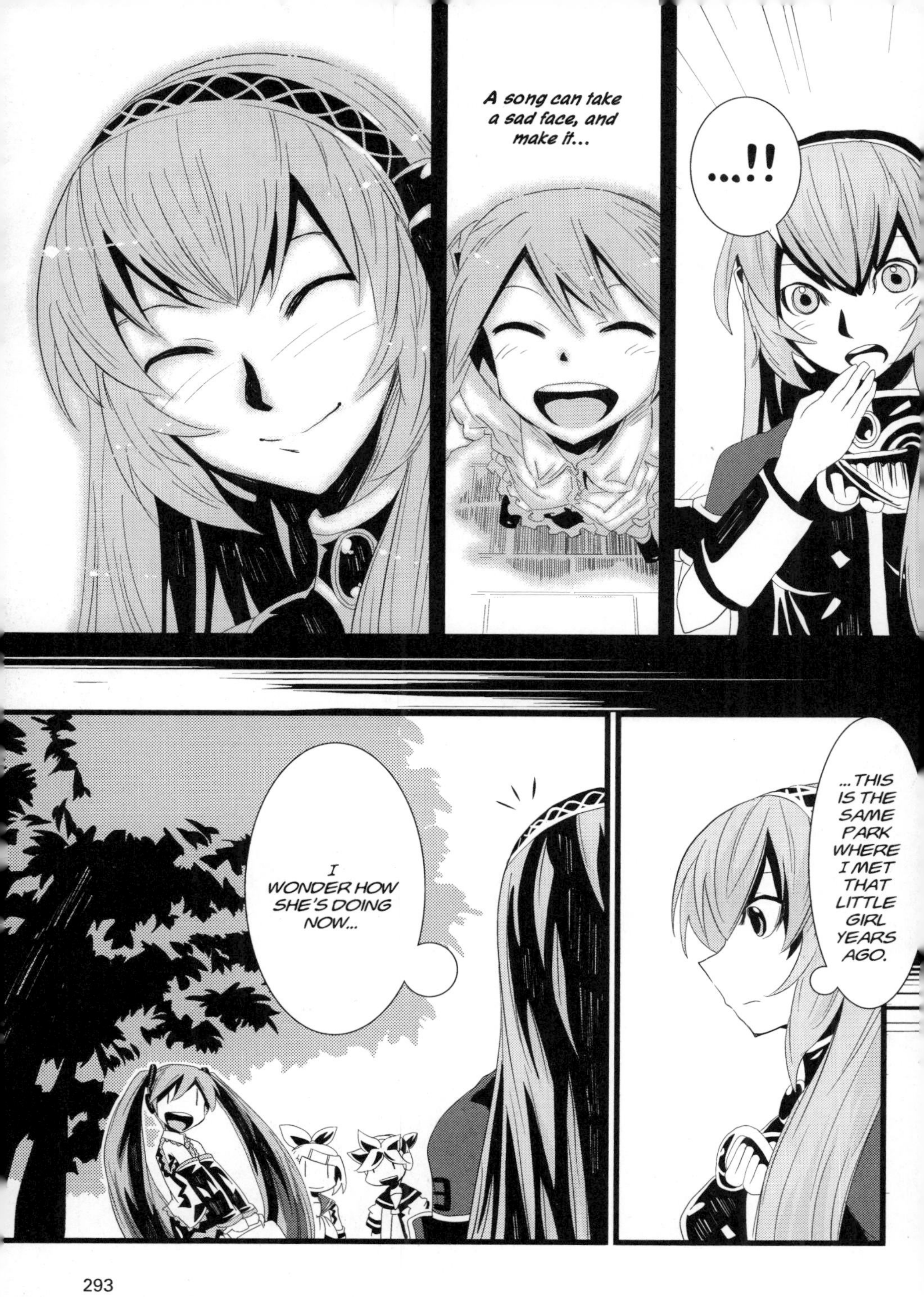
...!!
A song can take a sad face, and make it...
...THIS IS THE SAME PARK WHERE I MET THAT LITTLE GIRL YEARS AGO.
I WONDER HOW SHE'S DOING NOW...

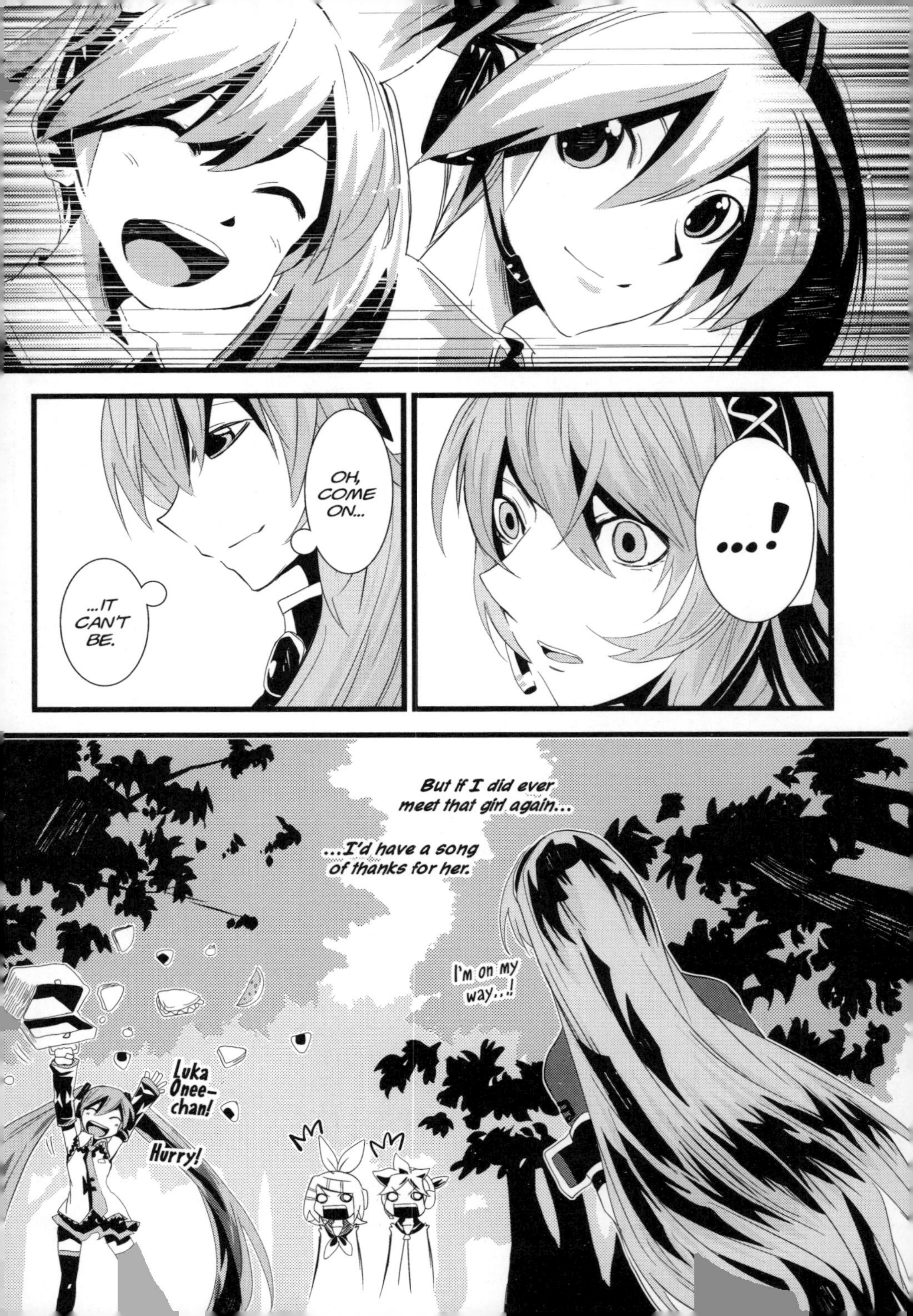
...!
OH, COME ON...
...IT CAN'T BE.
But if I did ever meet that girl again...
...I'd have a song of thanks for her.
I'm on my way...!
Luka Onee-chan!
Hurry!

(19th SONG) RAINY SEASON MIX

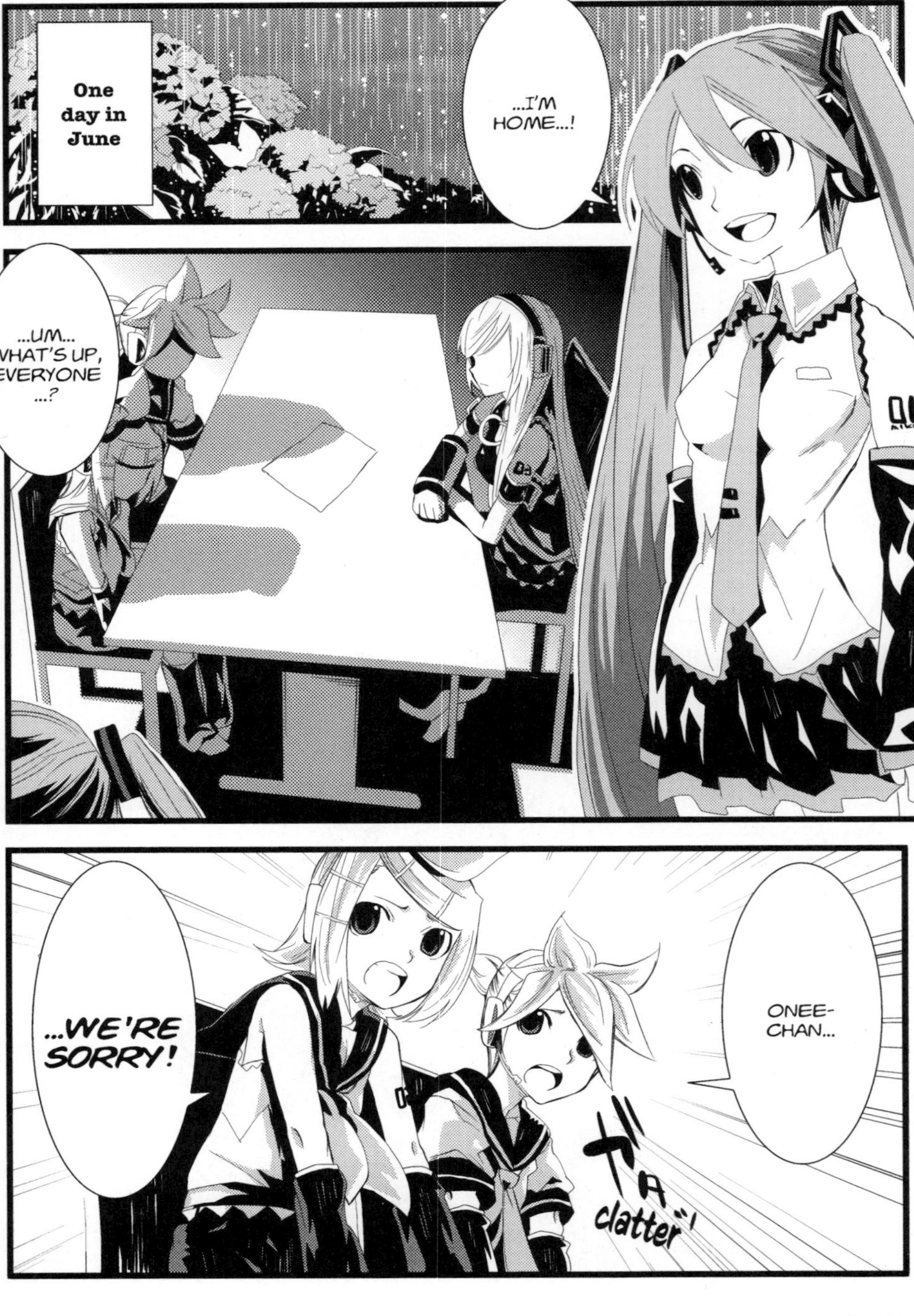
One day in June
...I'M HOME...!
...UM... WHAT'S UP, EVERYONE ...?
ONEE-CHAN...
...WE'RE SORRY!
clatter

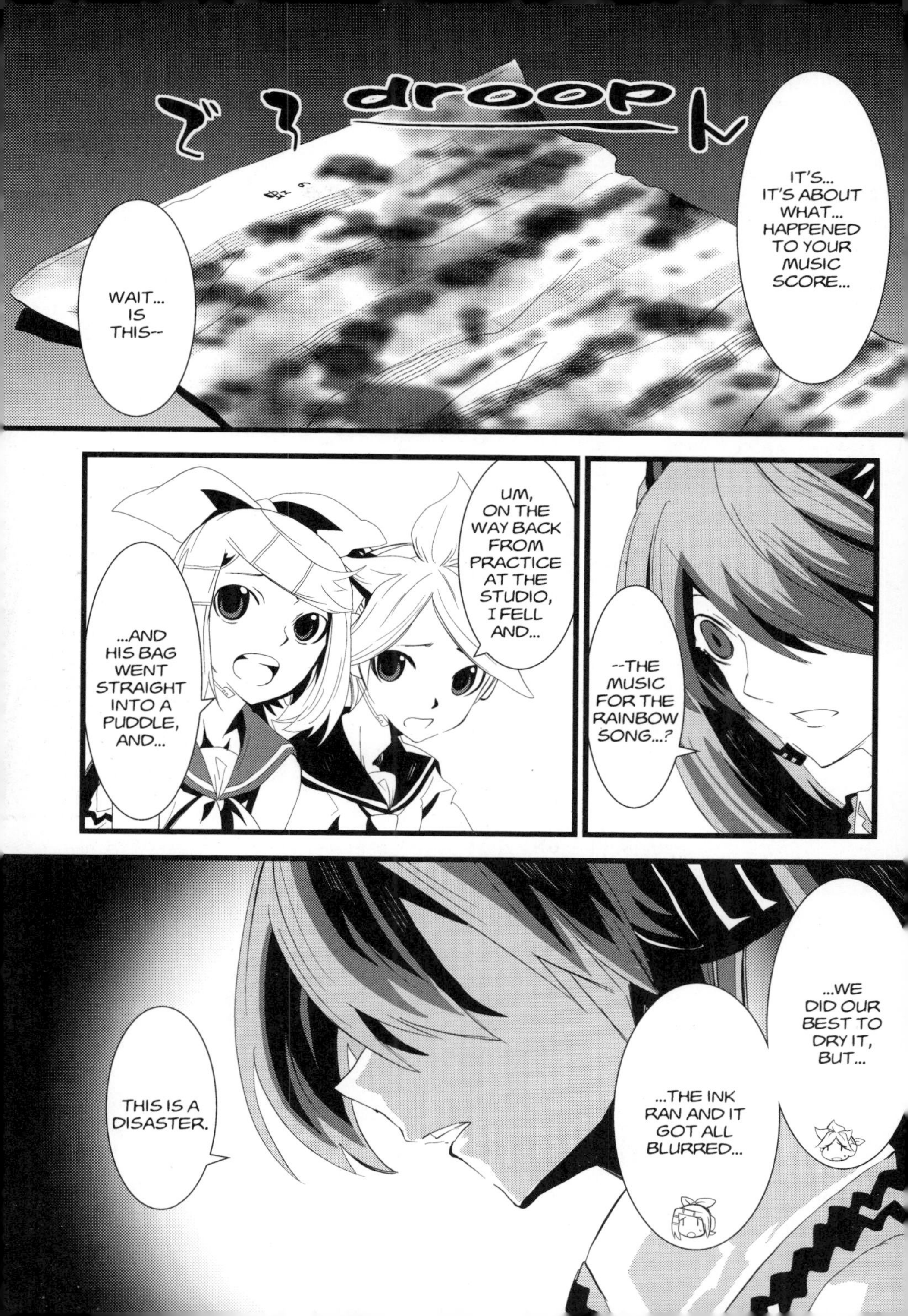
droop
IT'S... IT'S ABOUT WHAT... HAPPENED TO YOUR MUSIC SCORE...
WAIT... IS THIS--
--THE MUSIC FOR THE RAINBOW SONG...?
UM, ON THE WAY BACK FROM PRACTICE AT THE STUDIO, I FELL AND...
...AND HIS BAG WENT STRAIGHT INTO A PUDDLE, AND...
...WE DID OUR BEST TO DRY IT, BUT...
...THE INK RAN AND IT GOT ALL BLURRED...
THIS IS A DISASTER.

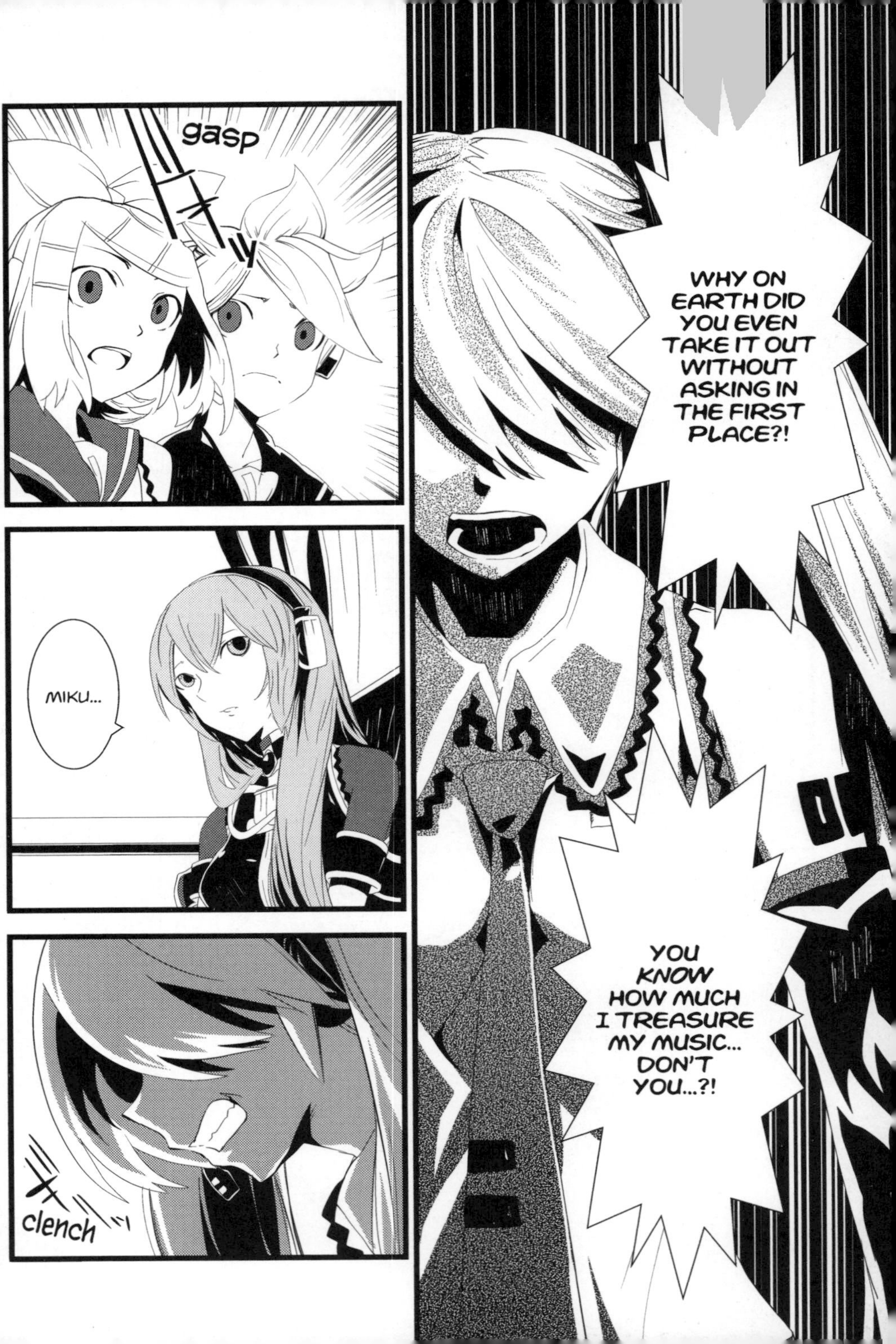
WHY ON EARTH DID YOU EVEN TAKE IT OUT WITHOUT ASKING IN THE FIRST PLACE?!
YOU KNOW HOW MUCH I TREASURE MY MUSIC... DON'T YOU...?!
gasp
MIKU...
clench

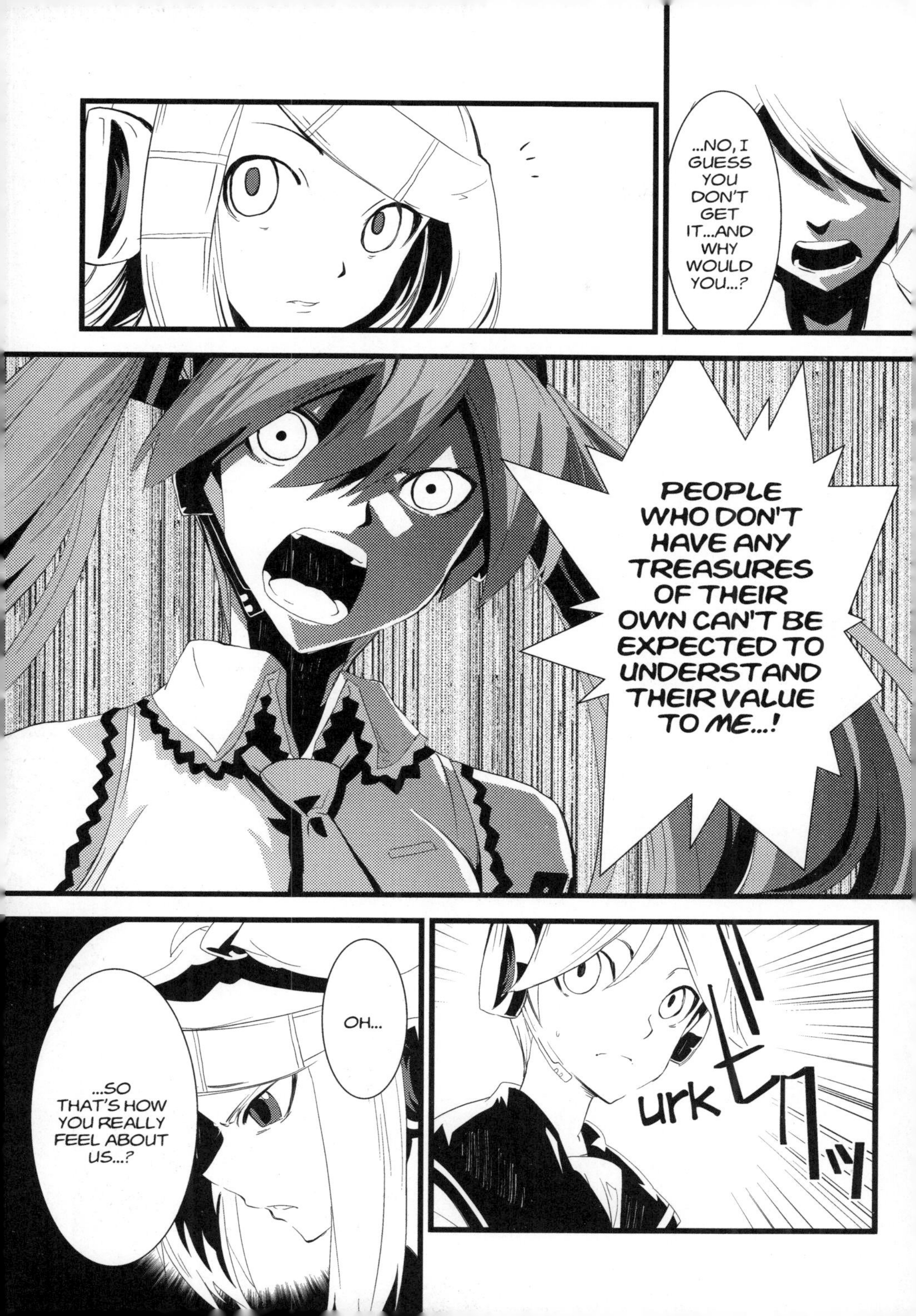
...NO, I GUESS YOU DON'T GET IT...AND WHY WOULD YOU...?
PEOPLE WHO DON'T HAVE ANY TREASURES OF THEIR OWN CAN'T BE EXPECTED TO UNDERSTAND THEIR VALUE TO ME...!
urk
OH...
...SO THAT'S HOW YOU REALLY FEEL ABOUT US...?

...RIN!!

slam

clatter

...

ONEE-CHAN--

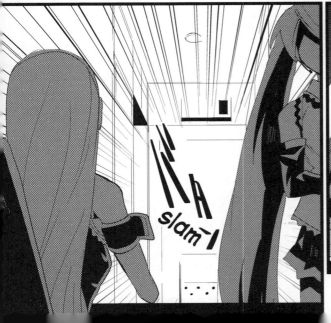

slam

dash

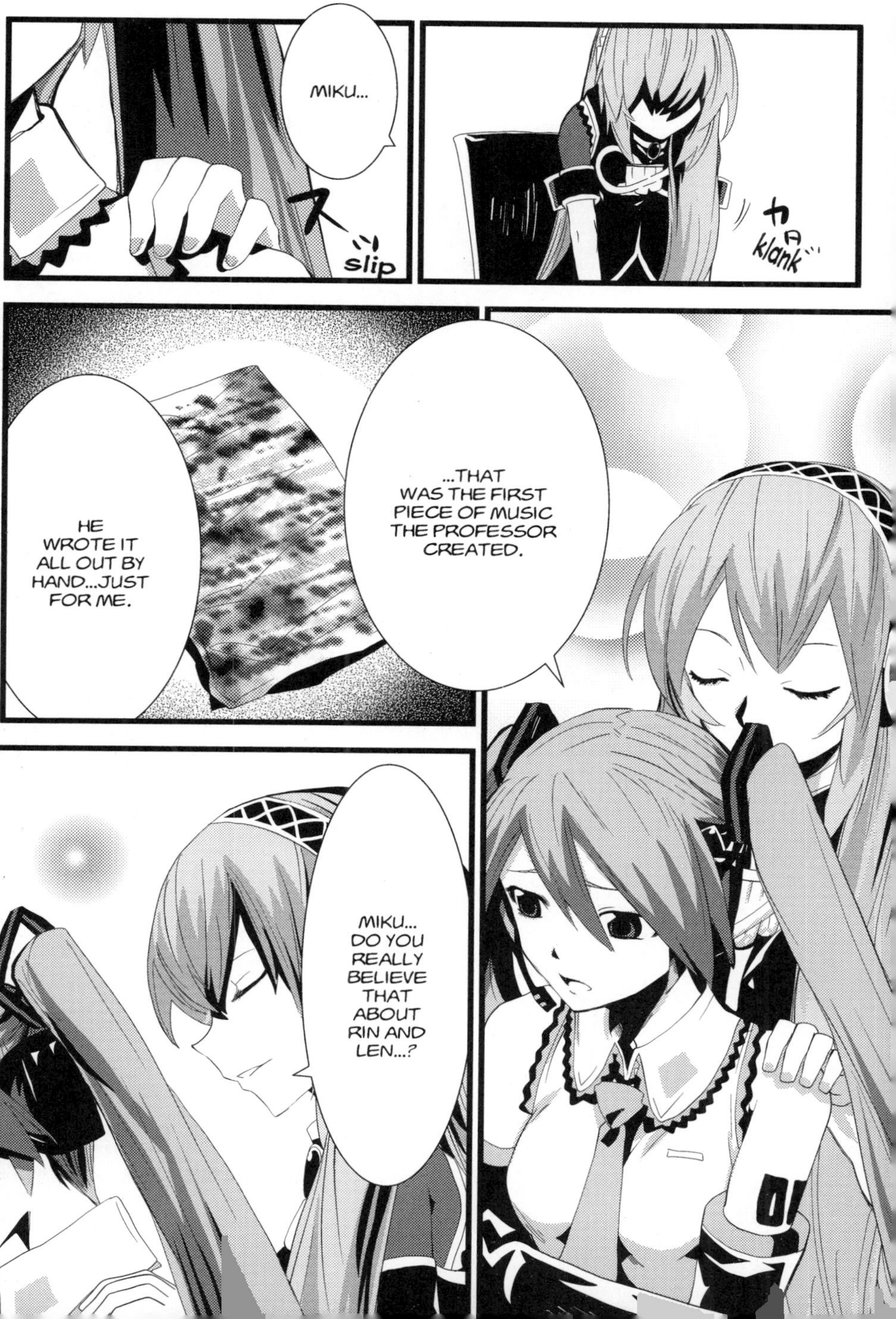
カ
klank
MIKU...
スッ
slip
...THAT WAS THE FIRST PIECE OF MUSIC THE PROFESSOR CREATED.
HE WROTE IT ALL OUT BY HAND...JUST FOR ME.
MIKU... DO YOU REALLY BELIEVE THAT ABOUT RIN AND LEN...?

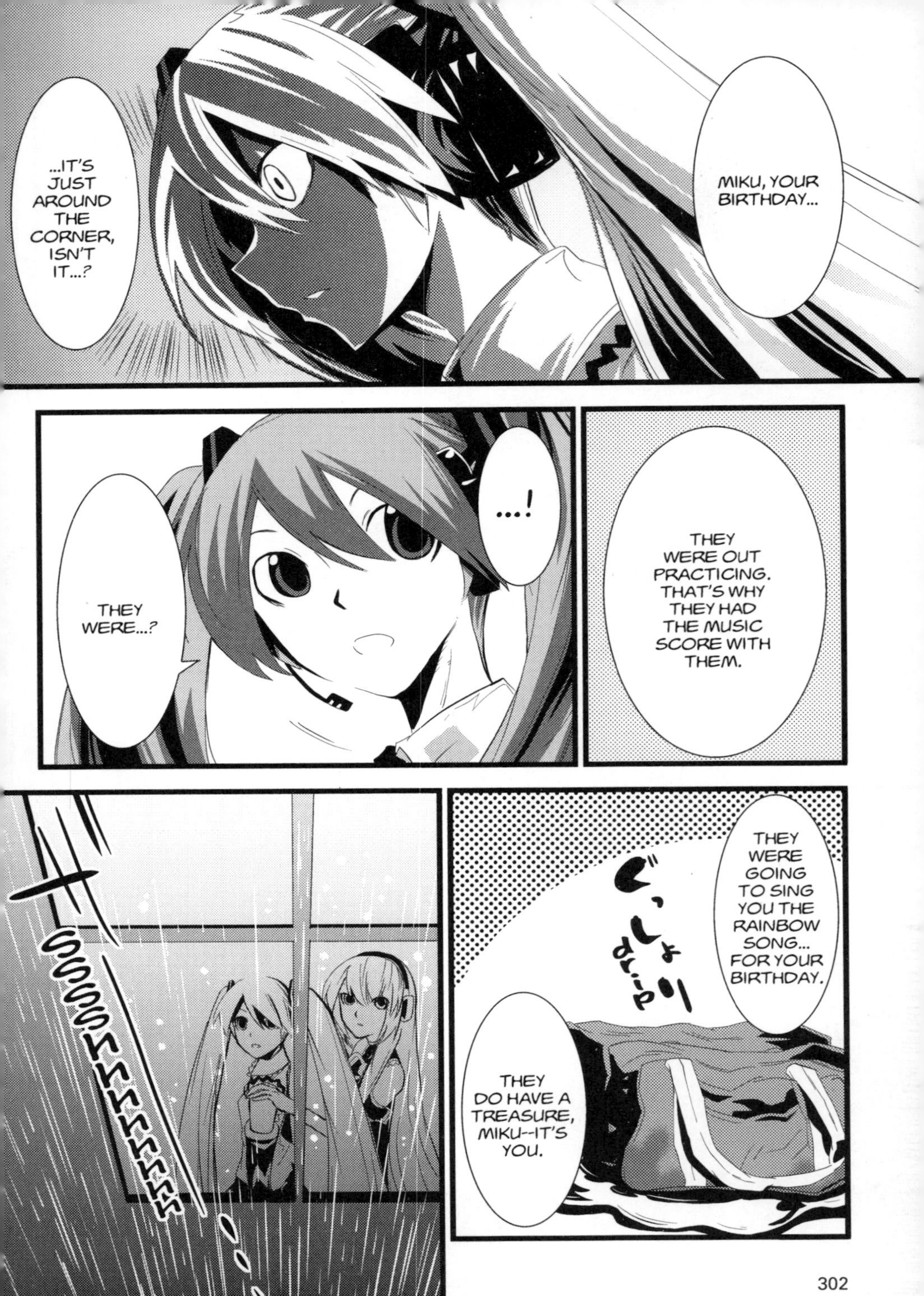
MIKU, YOUR BIRTHDAY...
...IT'S JUST AROUND THE CORNER, ISN'T IT...?
THEY WERE OUT PRACTICING. THAT'S WHY THEY HAD THE MUSIC SCORE WITH THEM.
...!
THEY WERE...?
THEY WERE GOING TO SING YOU THE RAINBOW SONG... FOR YOUR BIRTHDAY.
ぐっしょり
drip
THEY DO HAVE A TREASURE, MIKU--IT'S YOU.
SSSSHHHHHHHHH...

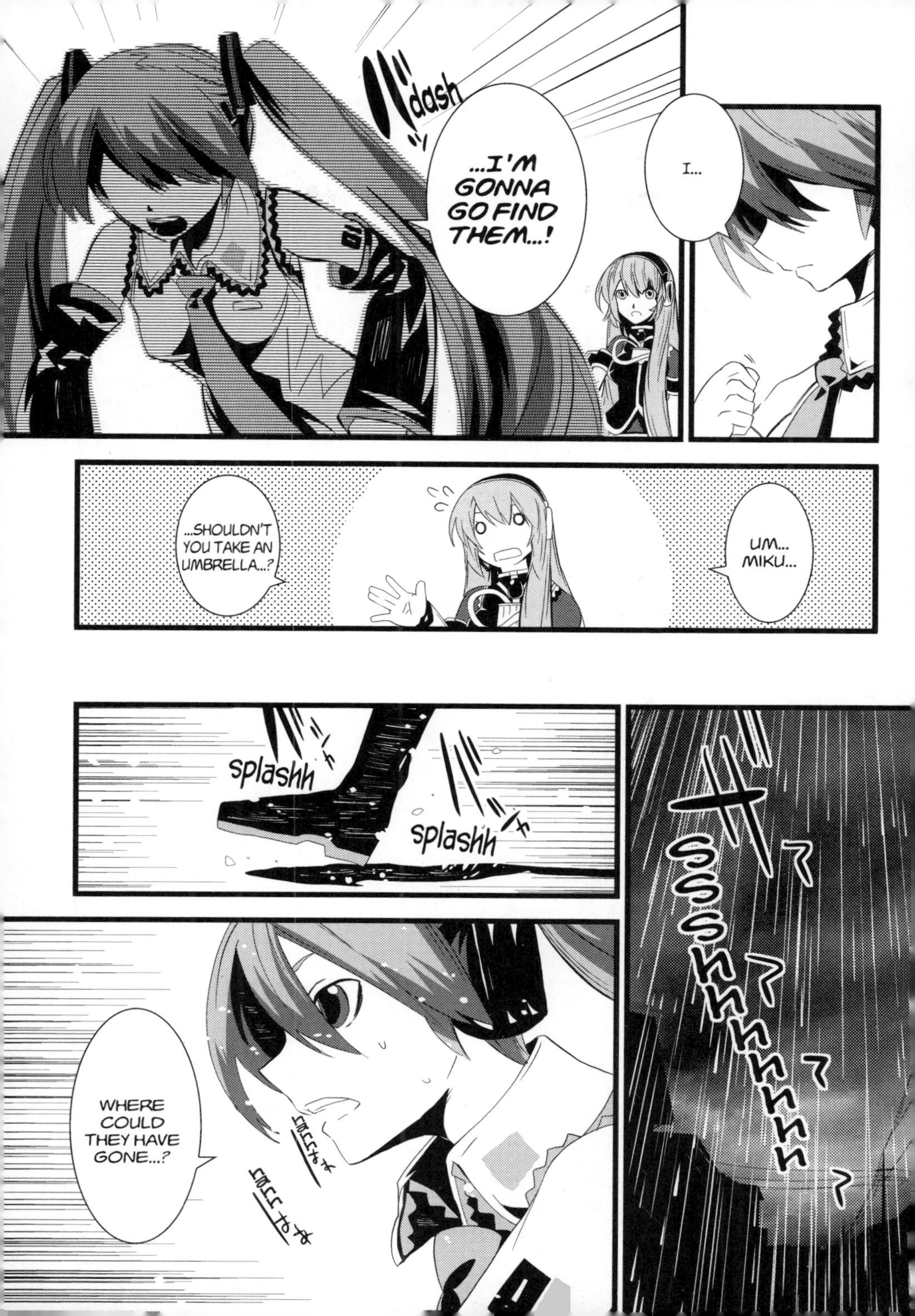
I...
dash
...I'M GONNA GO FIND THEM...!
UM... MIKU...
...SHOULDN'T YOU TAKE AN UMBRELLA...?
SSShhhhhhhh
splashh
splashh
WHERE COULD THEY HAVE GONE...?

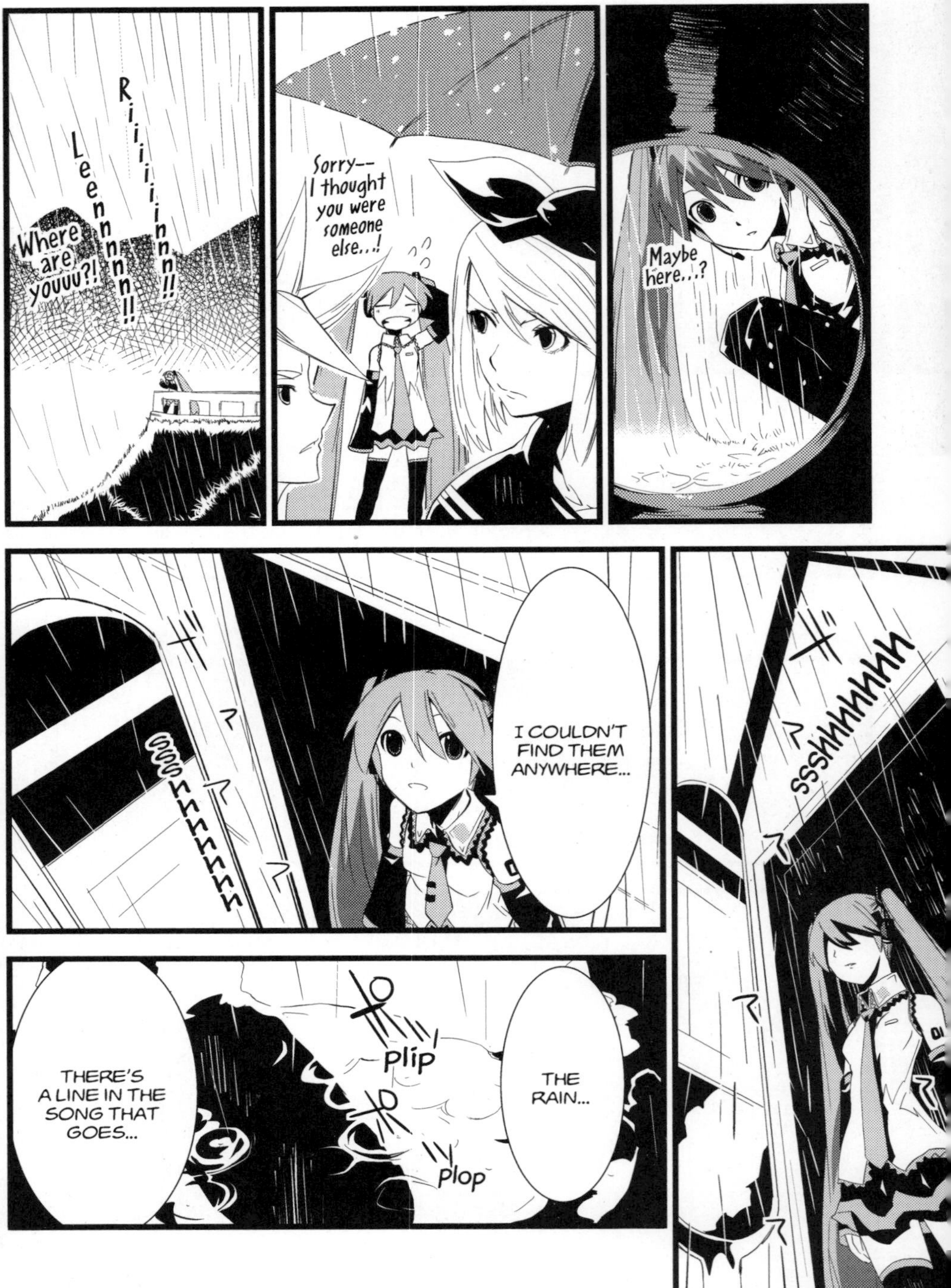
Maybe here...?
Sorry-- I thought you were someone else...!
Riiiiiiinnn!!
Leennnnnn!!
Where are youuu?!
sssshhhhhhh
I COULDN'T FIND THEM ANYWHERE...
ssshhhhhhhhh
THE RAIN...
plip
plop
THERE'S A LINE IN THE SONG THAT GOES...

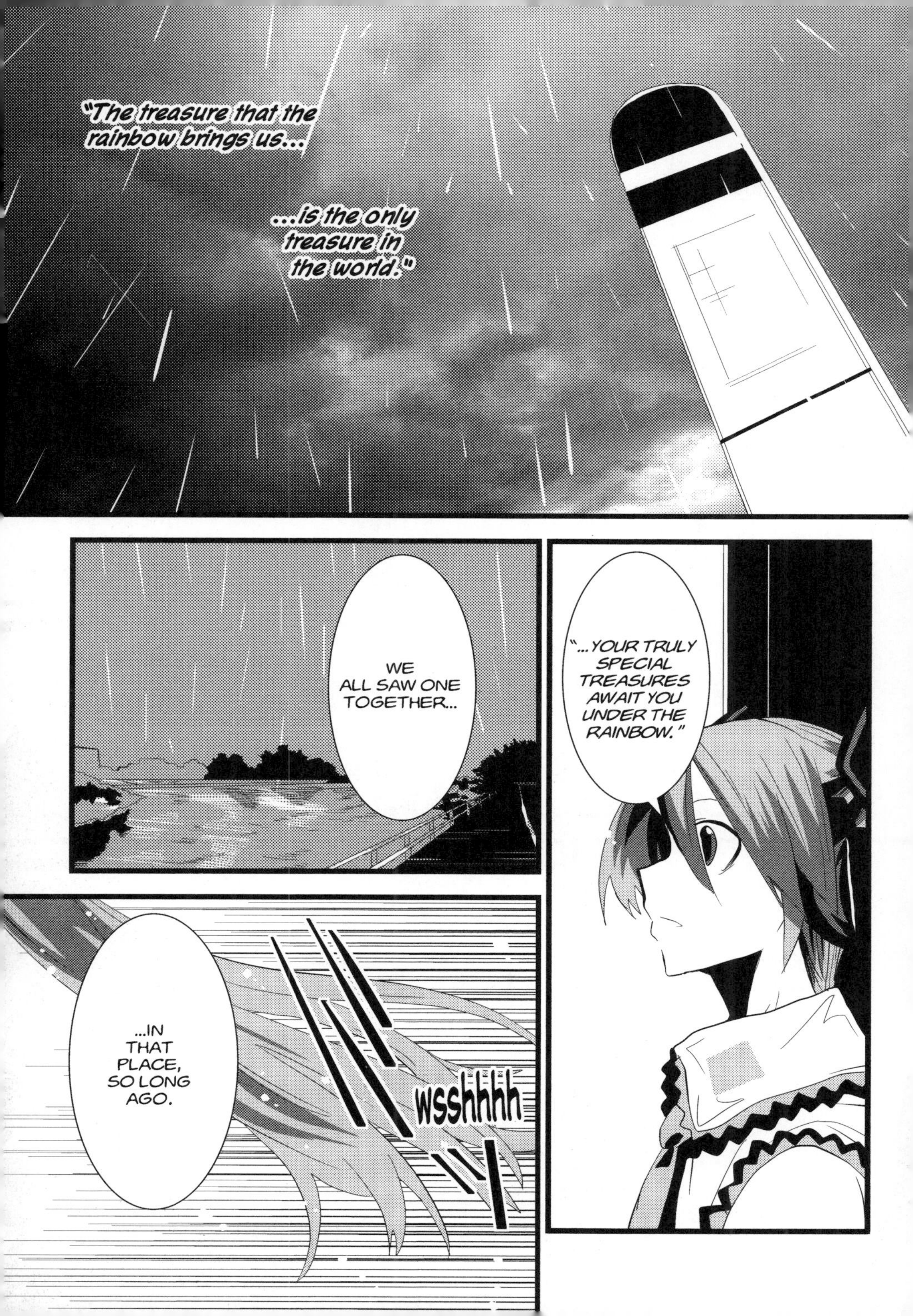
"The treasure that the rainbow brings us...
...is the only treasure in the world."
"...YOUR TRULY SPECIAL TREASURES AWAIT YOU UNDER THE RAINBOW."
WE ALL SAW ONE TOGETHER...
...IN THAT PLACE, SO LONG AGO.
wsshhhh

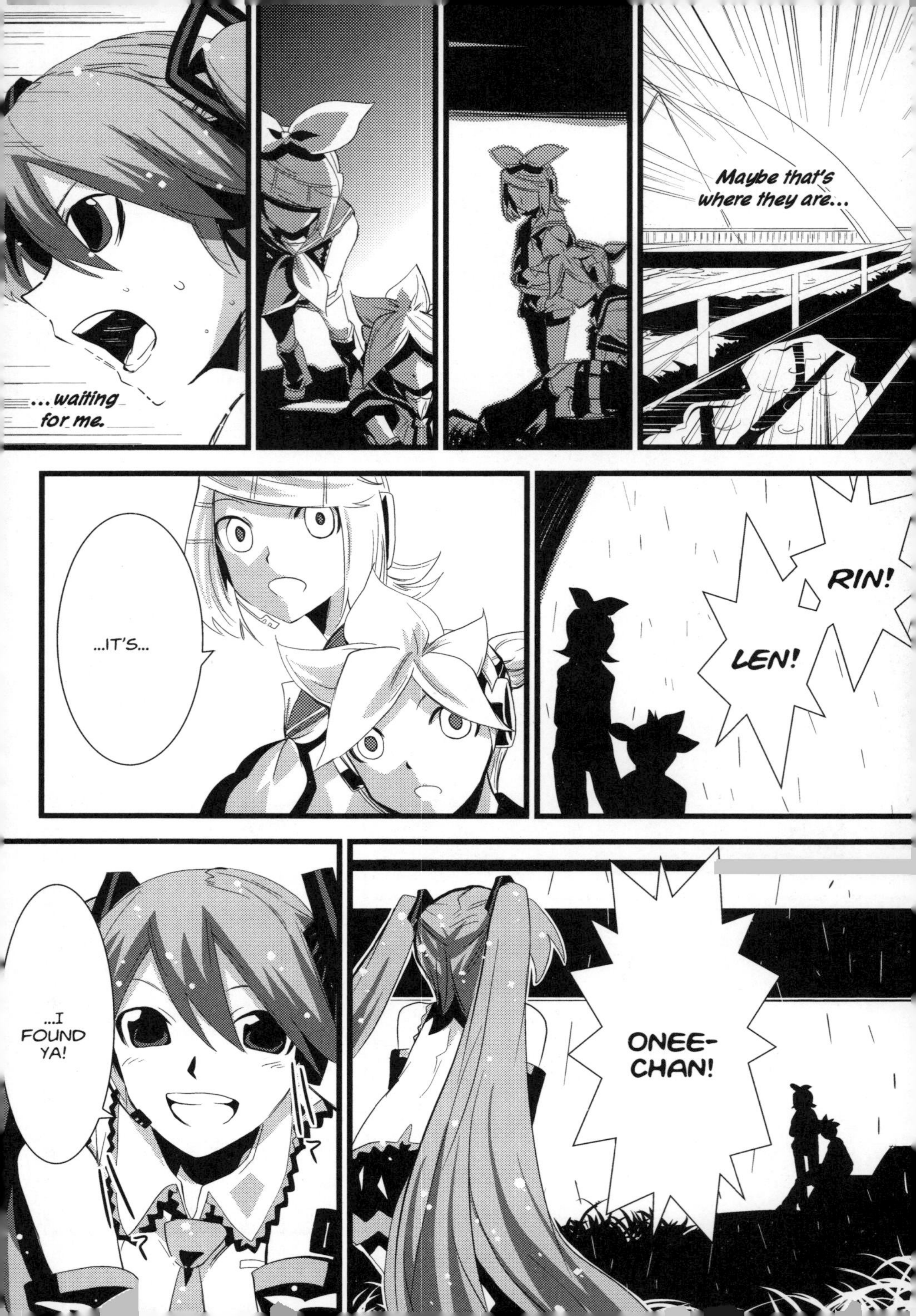
Maybe that's where they are...
...waiting for me.
RIN!
LEN!
...IT'S...
ONEE-CHAN!
...I FOUND YA!

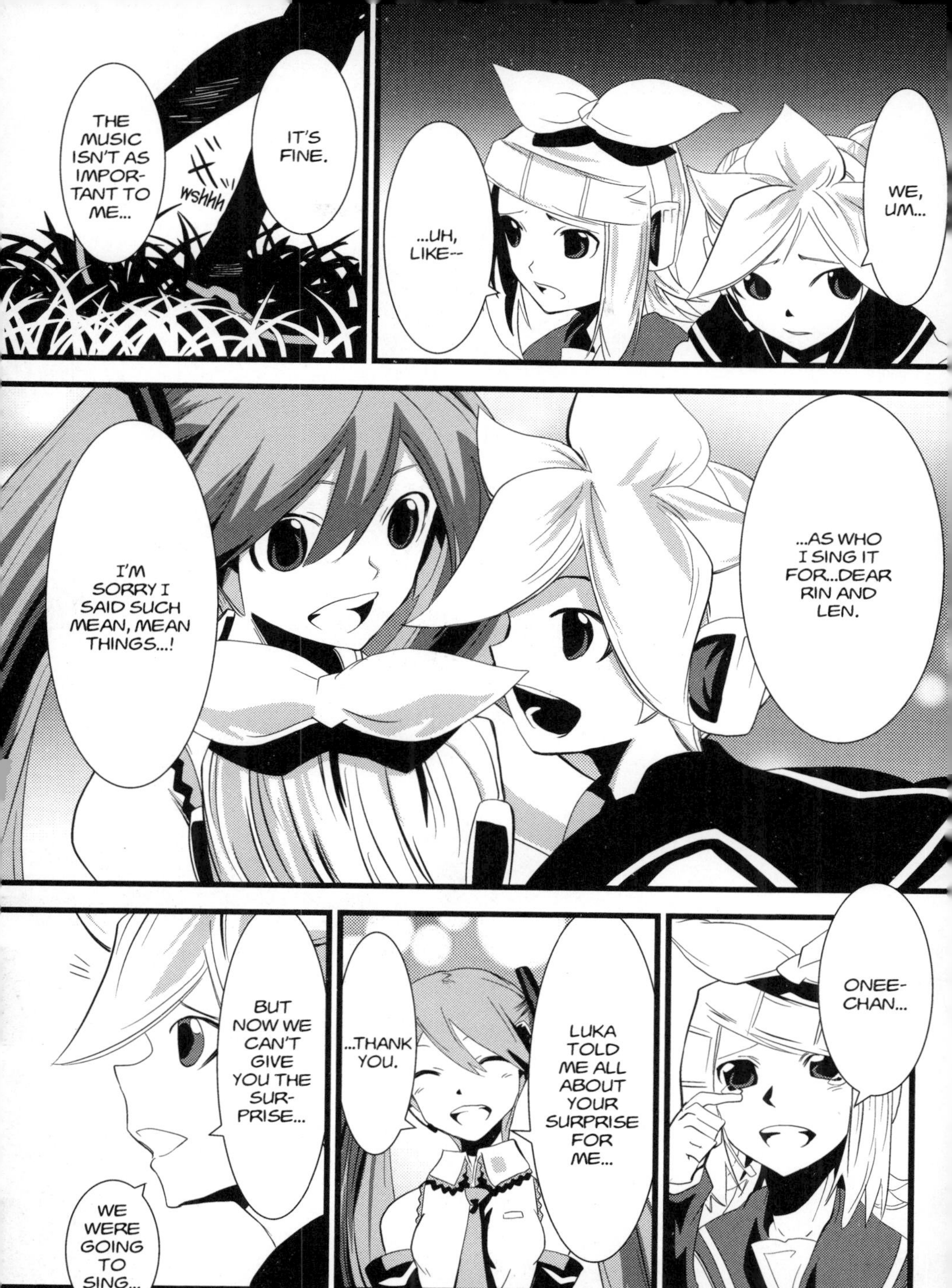
WE, UM...
...UH, LIKE--
IT'S FINE.
wshhh
THE MUSIC ISN'T AS IMPORTANT TO ME...
...AS WHO I SING IT FOR...DEAR RIN AND LEN.
I'M SORRY I SAID SUCH MEAN, MEAN THINGS...!
ONEE-CHAN...
LUKA TOLD ME ALL ABOUT YOUR SURPRISE FOR ME...
...THANK YOU.
BUT NOW WE CAN'T GIVE YOU THE SURPRISE...
WE WERE GOING TO SING...

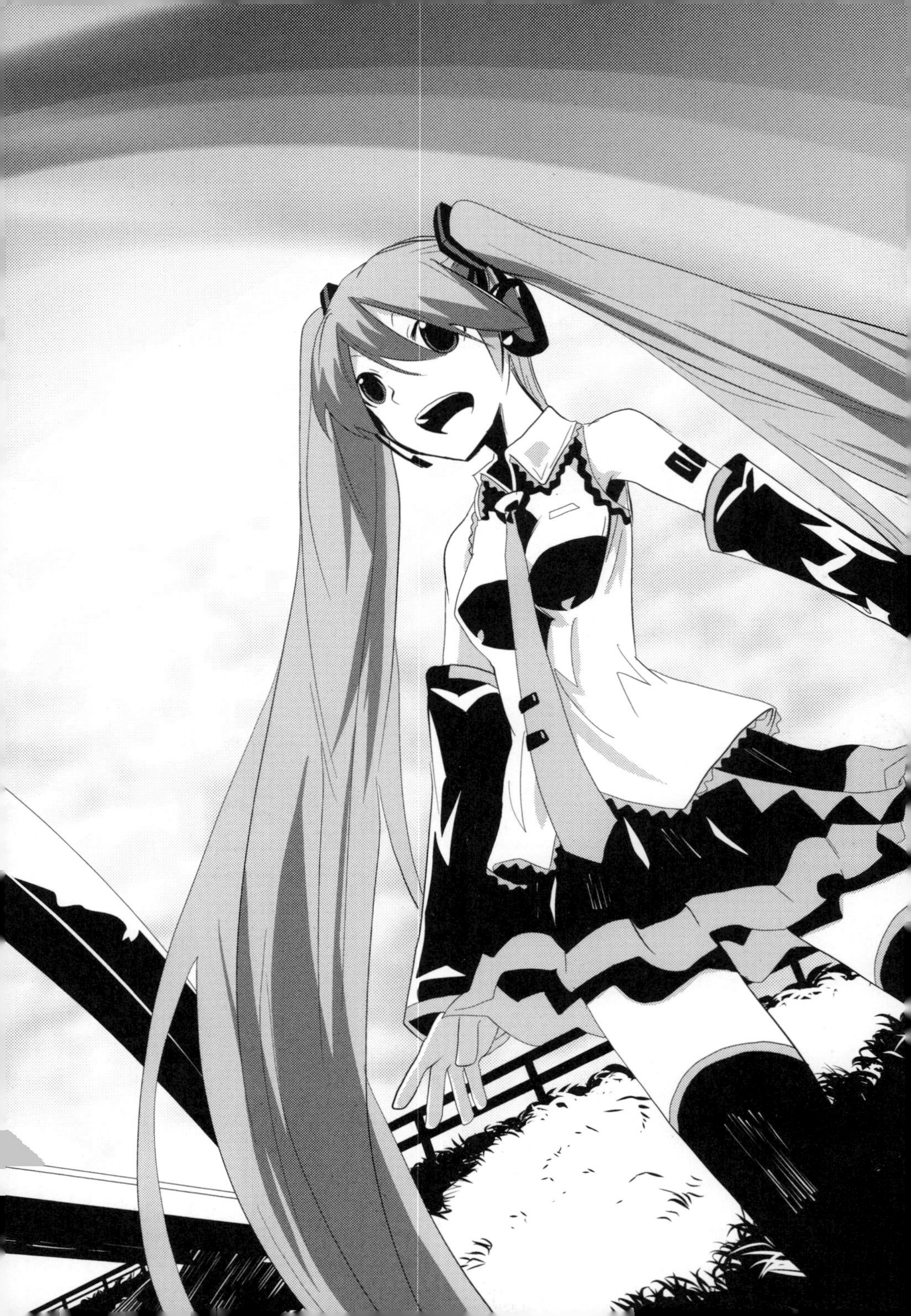

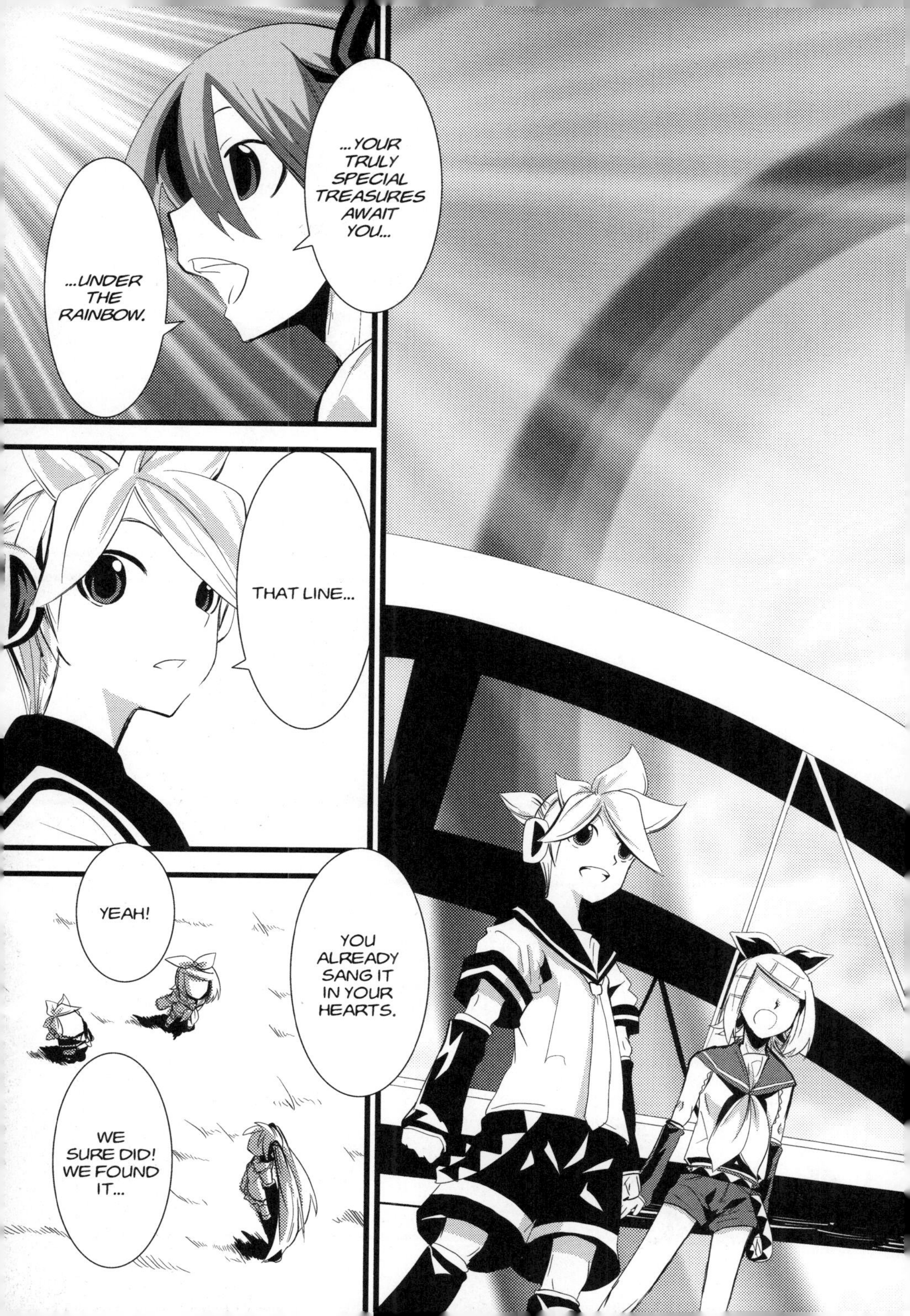
...YOUR TRULY SPECIAL TREASURES AWAIT YOU...
...UNDER THE RAINBOW.
THAT LINE...
YOU ALREADY SANG IT IN YOUR HEARTS.
YEAH!
WE SURE DID! WE FOUND IT...

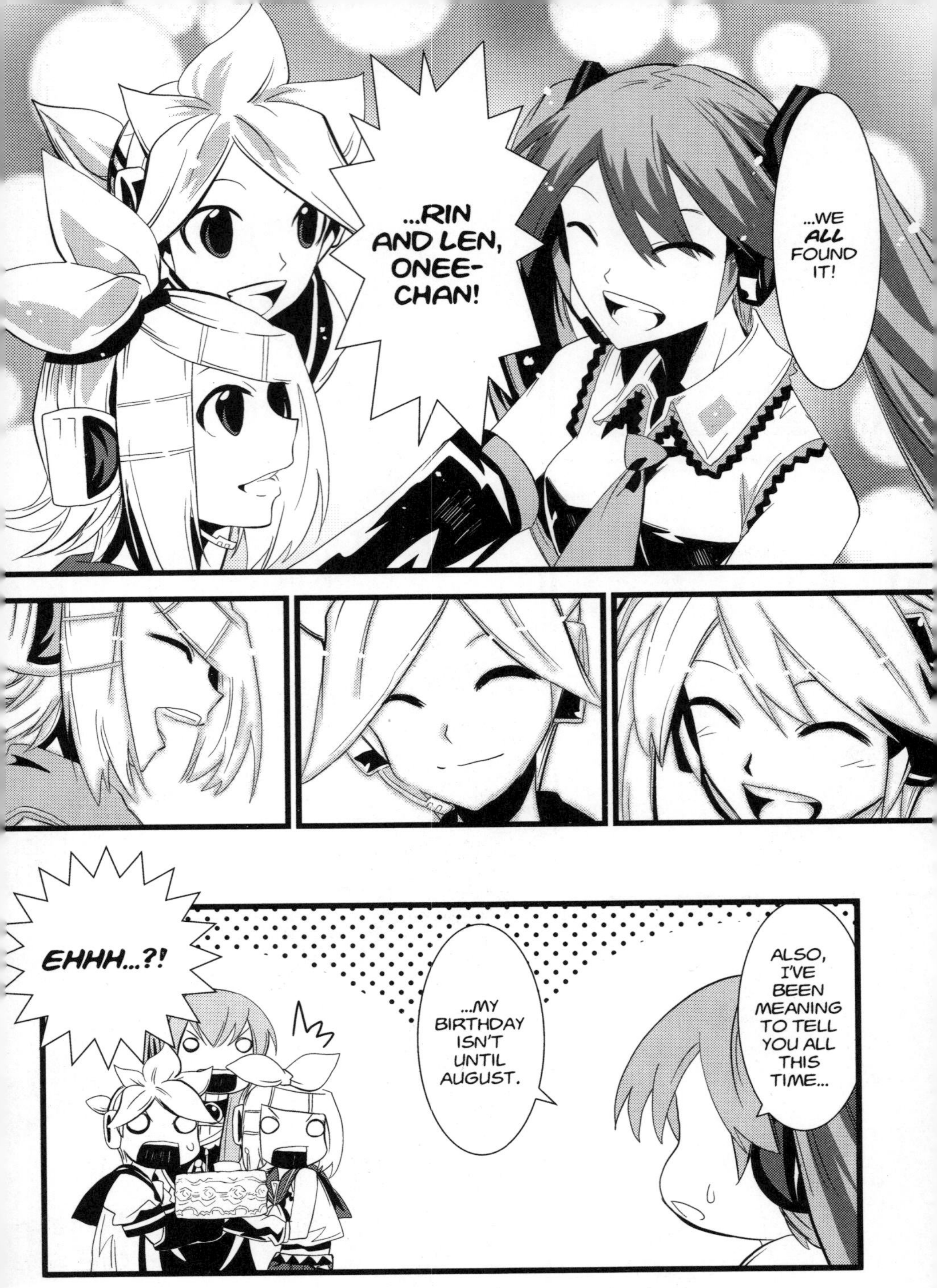
...WE ALL FOUND IT!
...RIN AND LEN, ONEE-CHAN!
ALSO, I'VE BEEN MEANING TO TELL YOU ALL THIS TIME...
...MY BIRTHDAY ISN'T UNTIL AUGUST.
EHHH...?!

EXTRA MIX

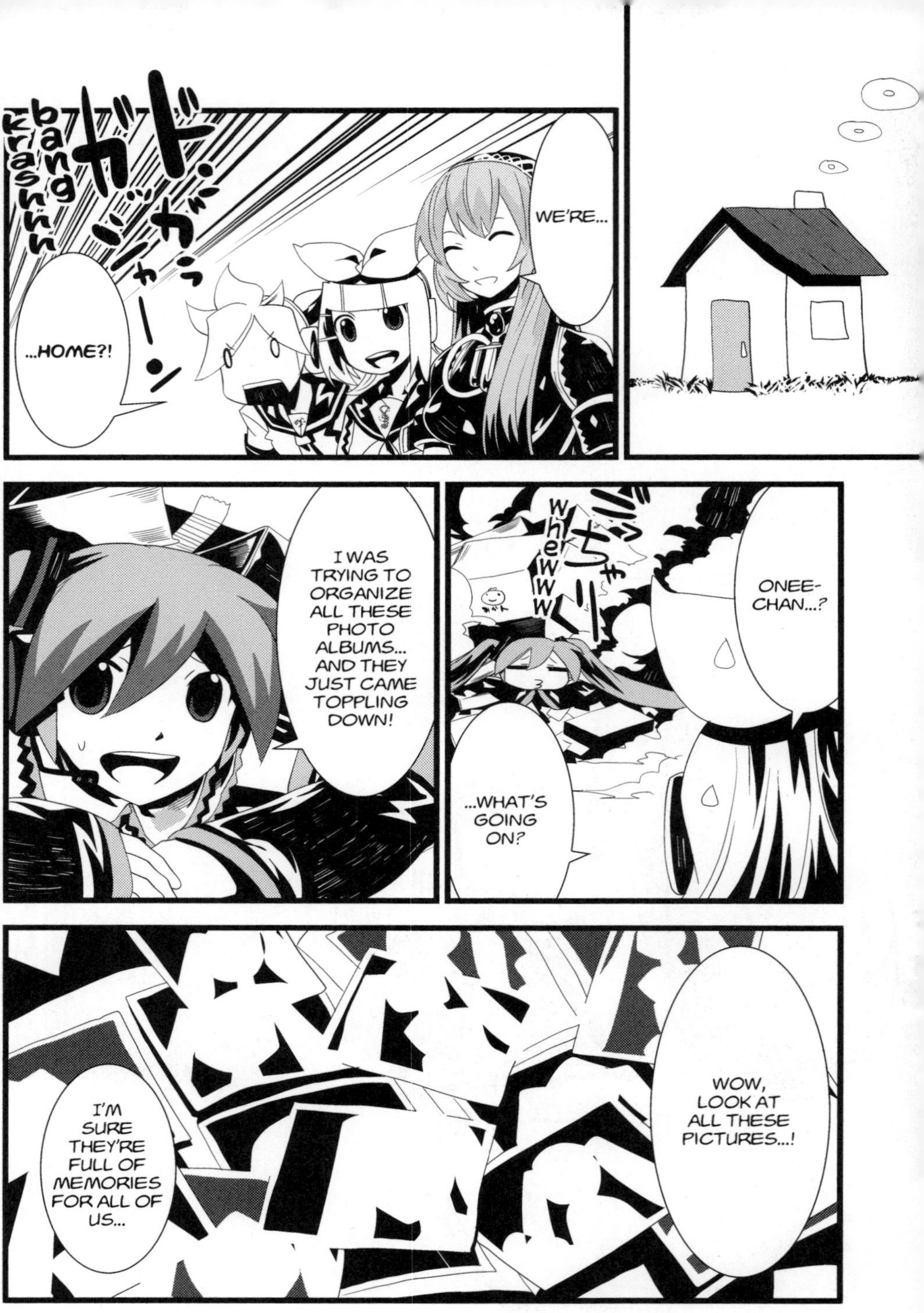
WE'RE...
bang
krashnnn
...HOME?!
ONEE-CHAN...?
whewww
...WHAT'S GOING ON?
I WAS TRYING TO ORGANIZE ALL THESE PHOTO ALBUMS... AND THEY JUST CAME TOPPLING DOWN!
WOW, LOOK AT ALL THESE PICTURES...!
I'M SURE THEY'RE FULL OF MEMORIES FOR ALL OF US...

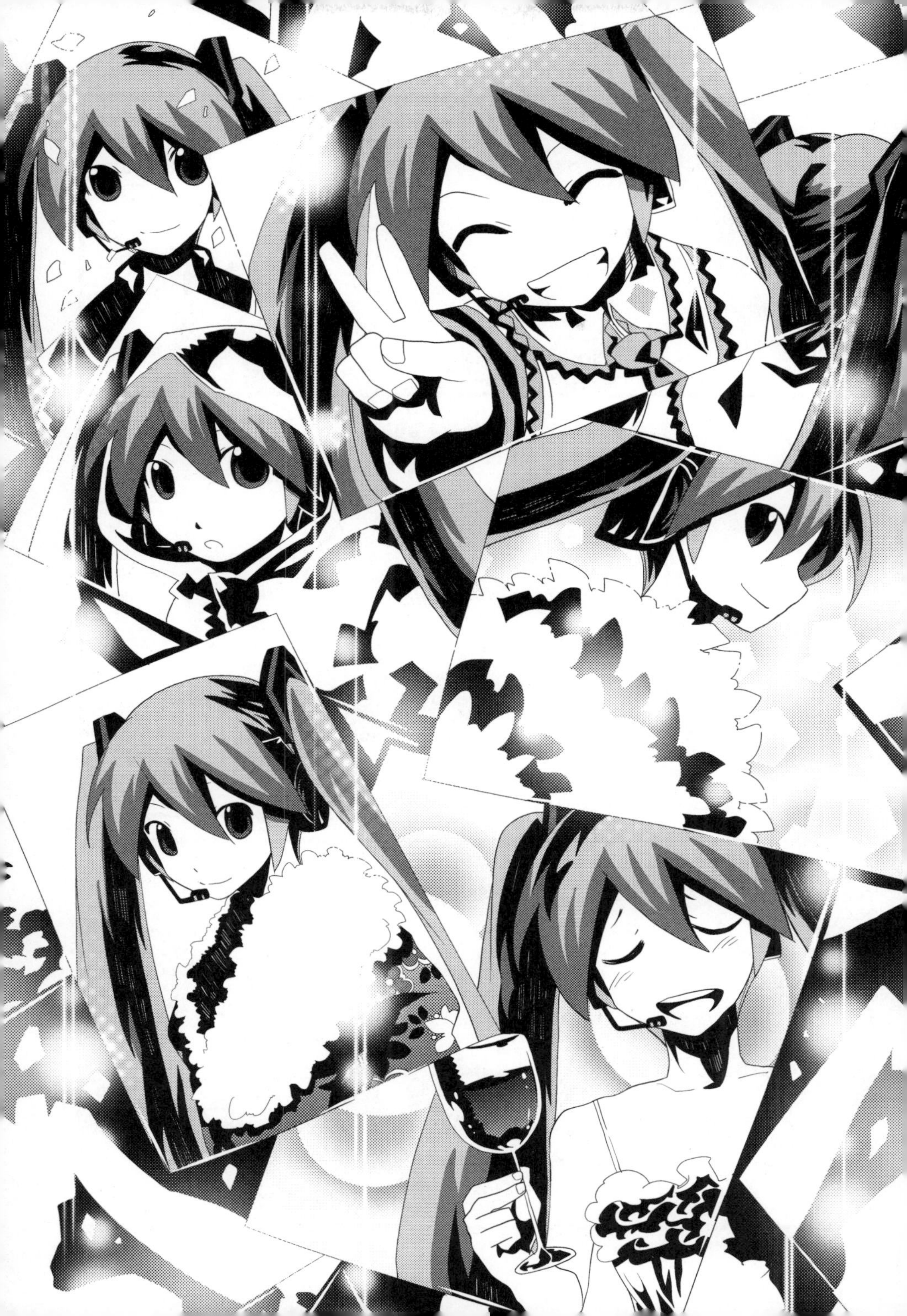

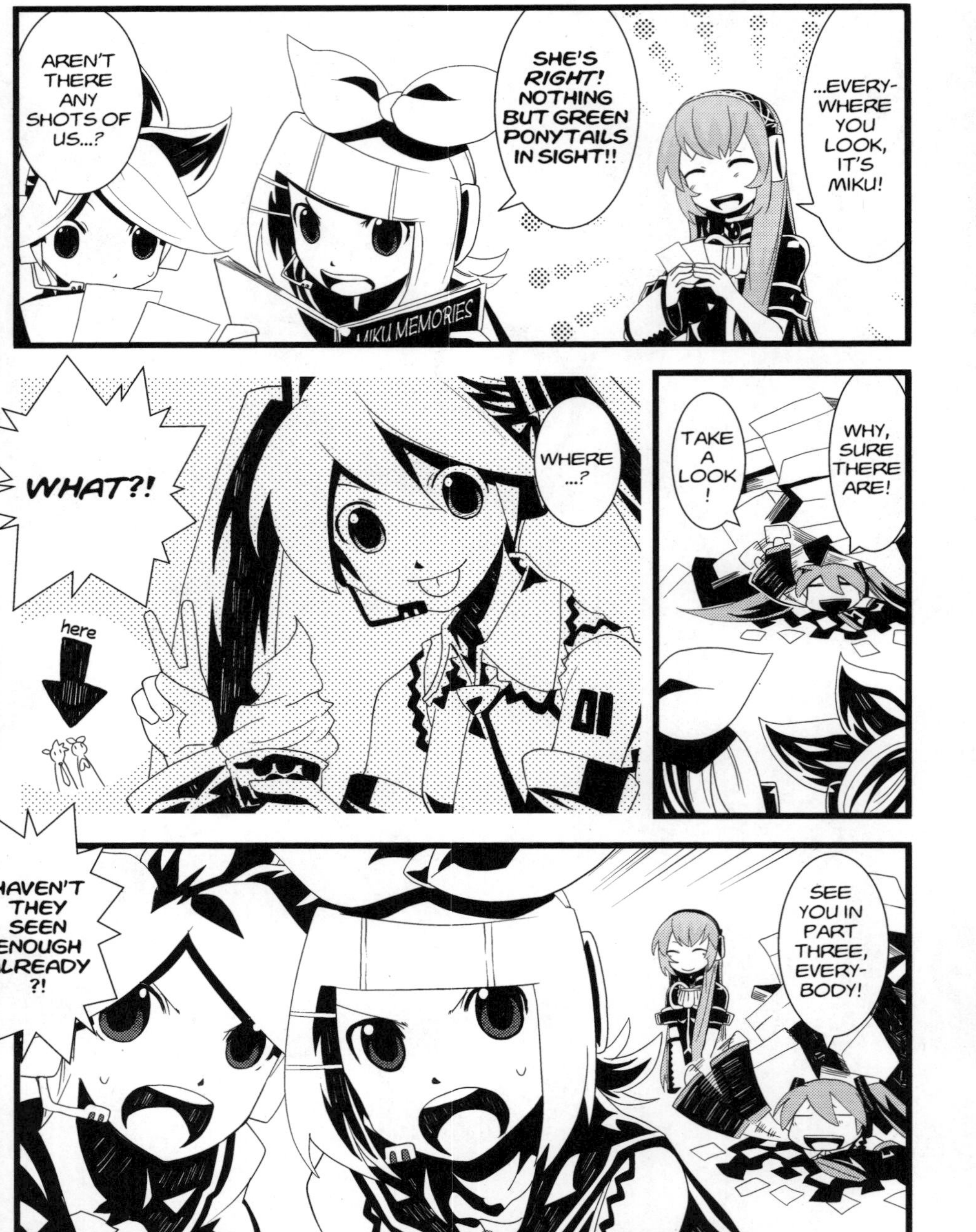
...EVERYWHERE YOU LOOK, IT'S MIKU!
SHE'S *RIGHT*! NOTHING BUT GREEN PONYTAILS IN SIGHT!!
AREN'T THERE ANY SHOTS OF US...?
MIKU MEMORIES
WHY, SURE THERE ARE!
TAKE A LOOK!
WHERE ...?
WHAT?!
here
SEE YOU IN PART THREE, EVERYBODY!
HAVEN'T THEY SEEN ENOUGH ALREADY?!

あとがき
afterword

later!

to be continued

- Part Two is miraculously finished and in your hands!
- Special thanks to Mamezou.

UNOFFICIAL

HATSUNE
MIX

STORY AND ART BY KEI

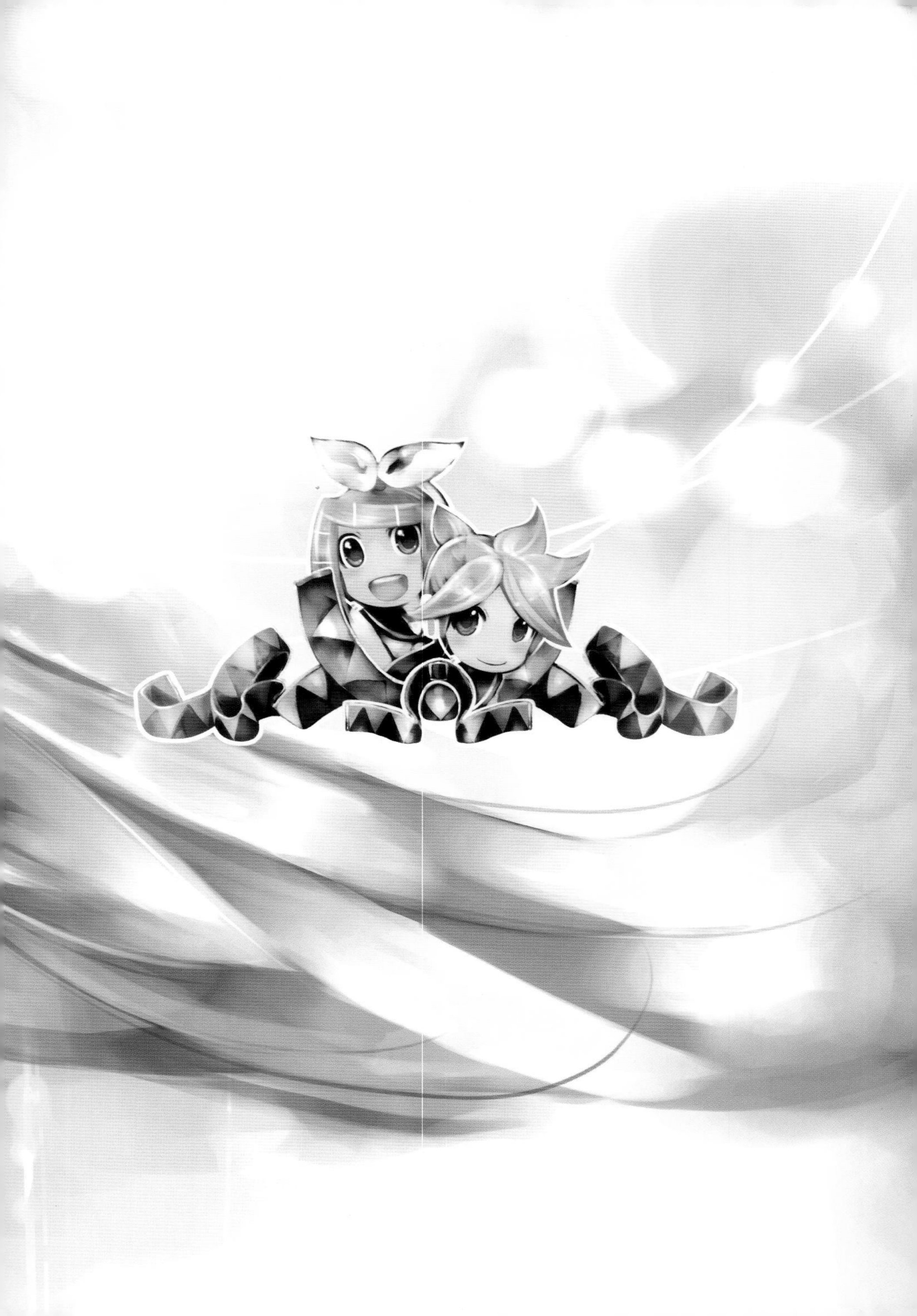

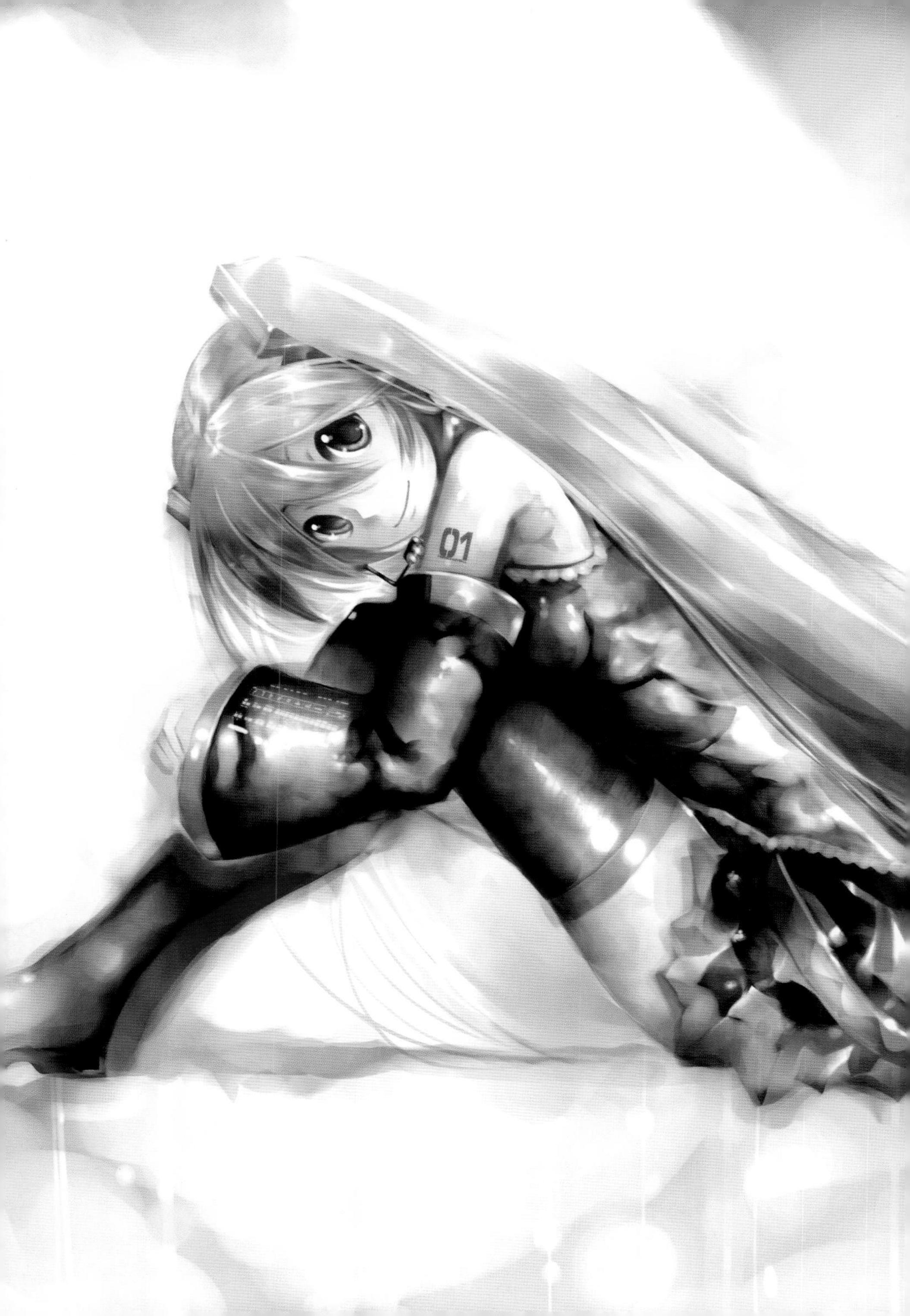
01

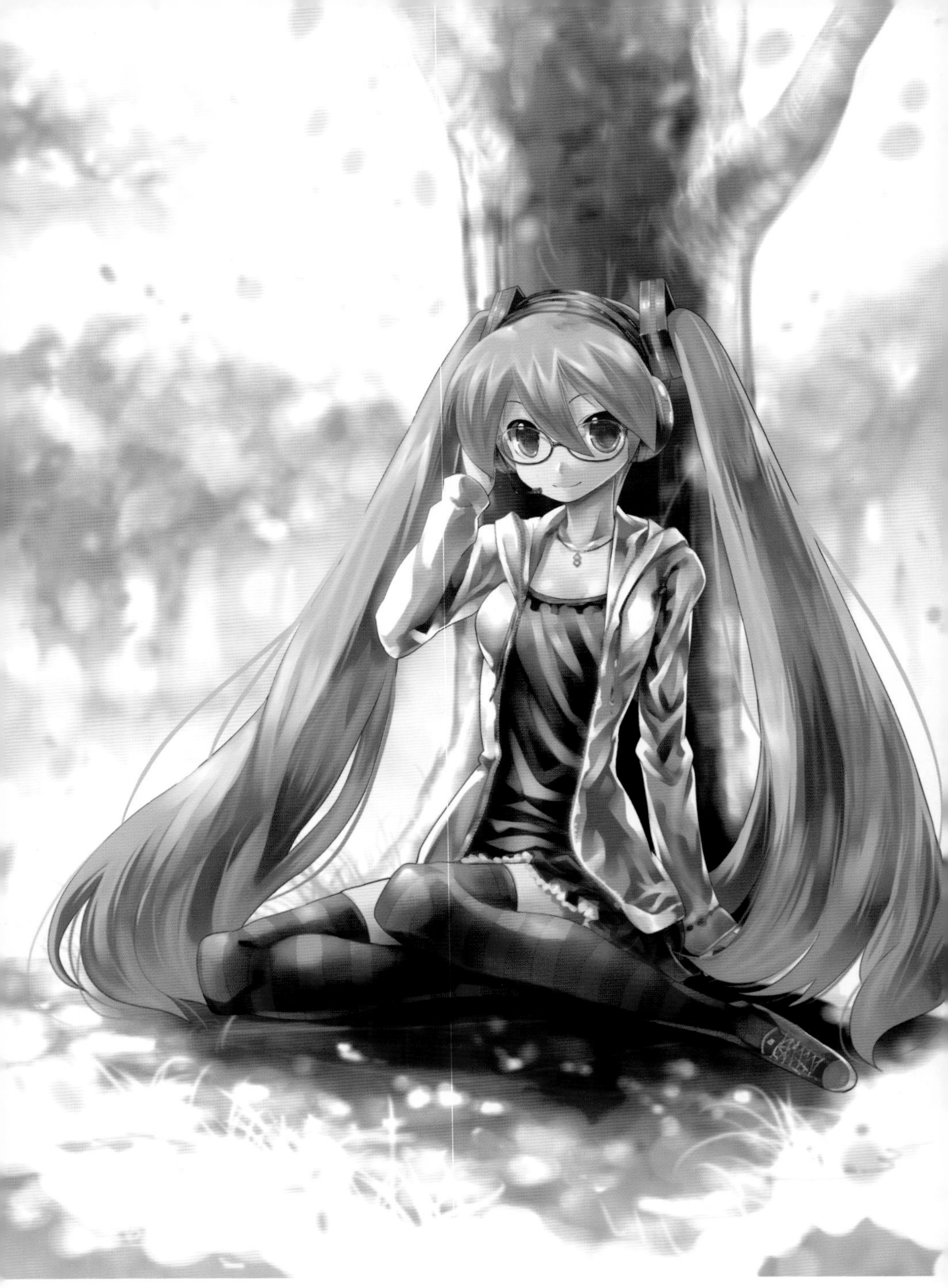

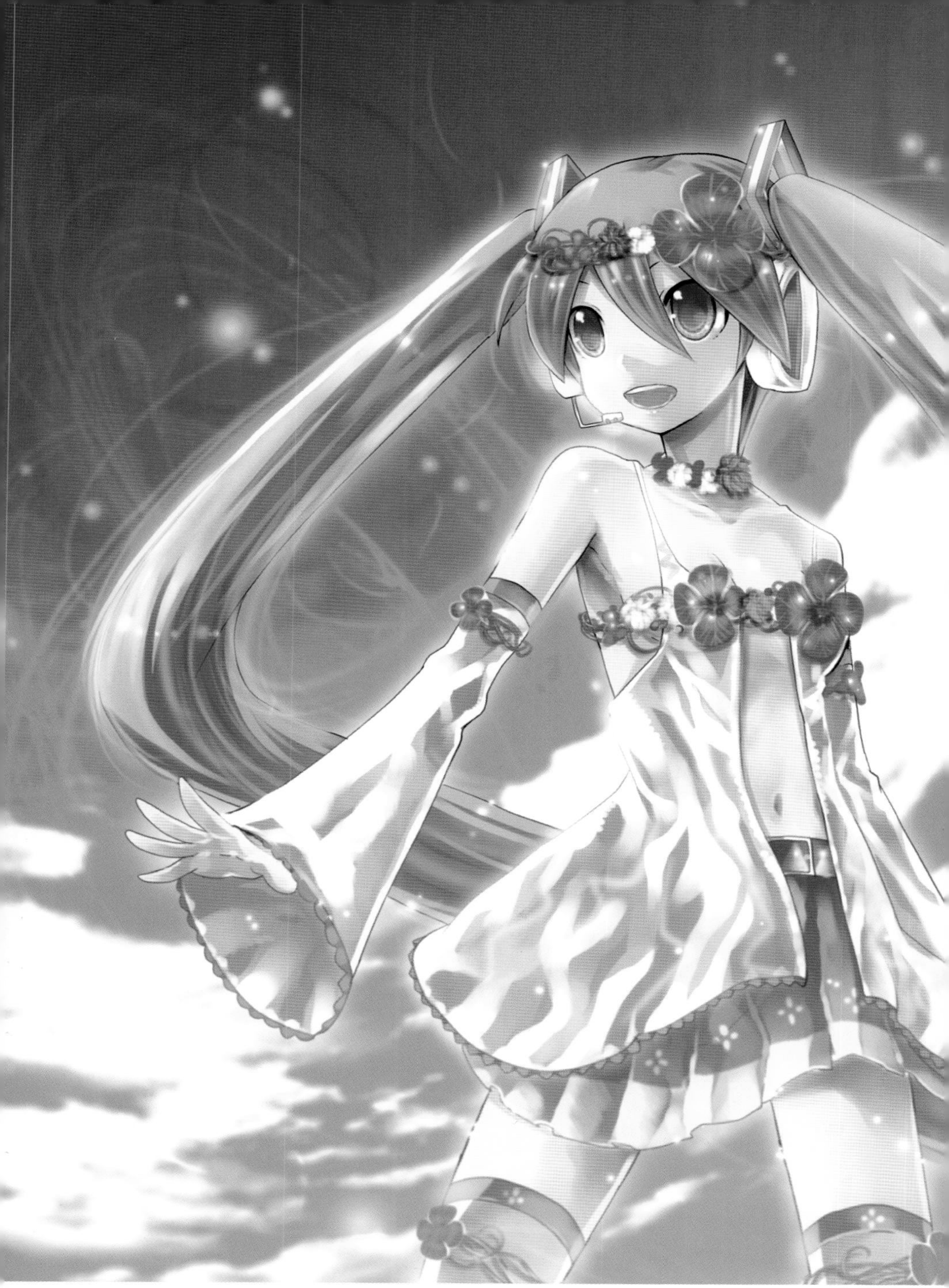

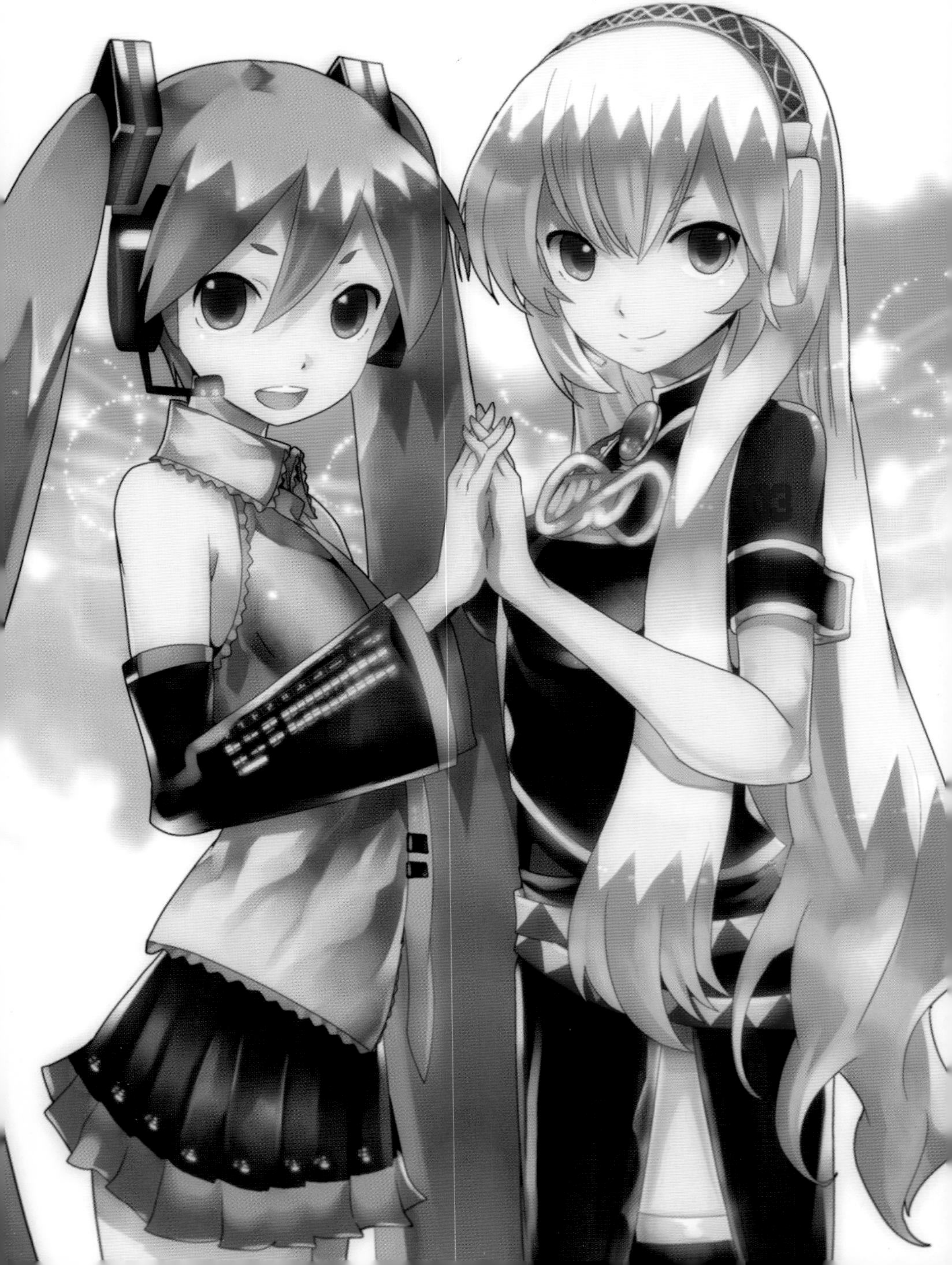

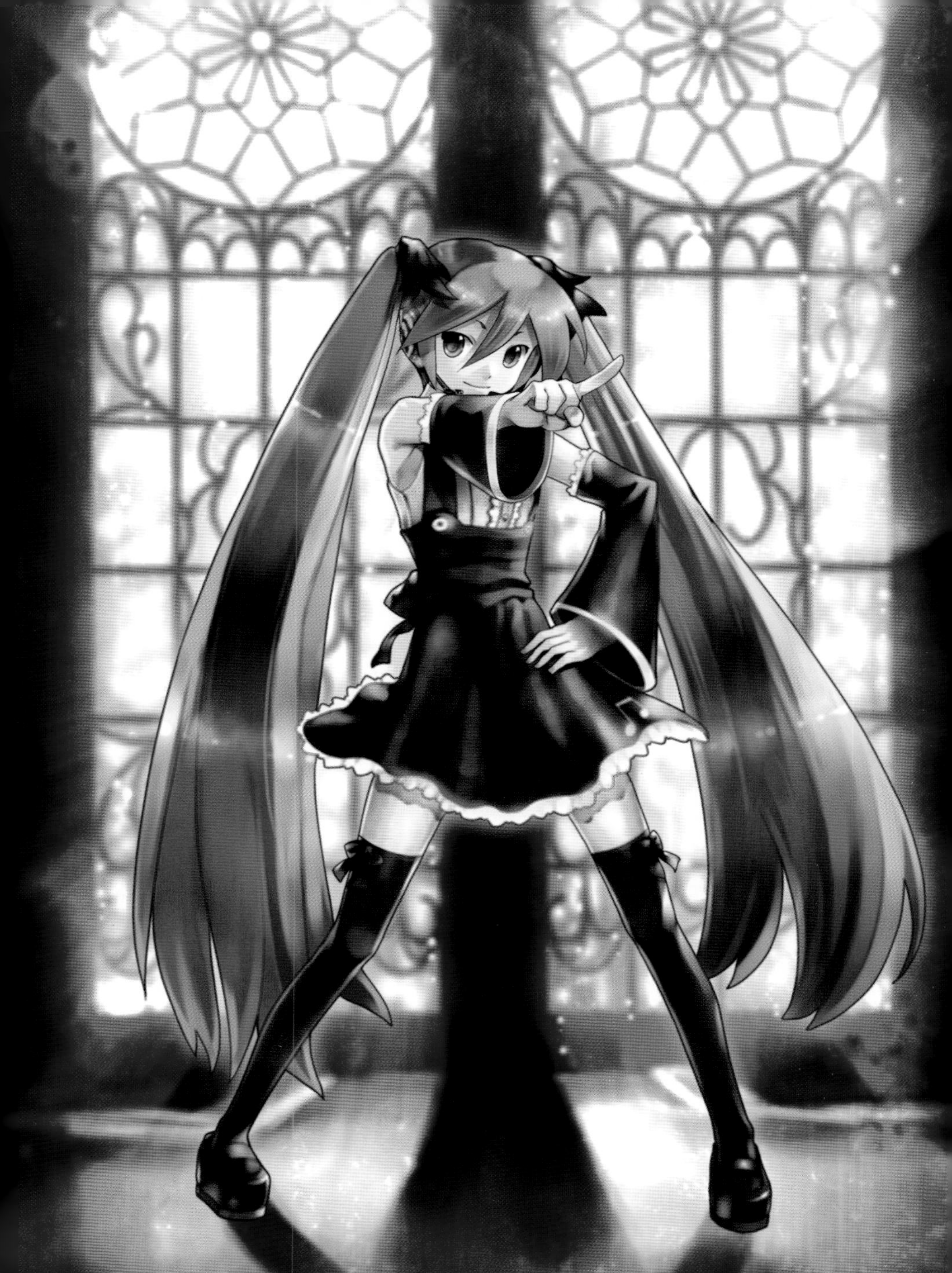

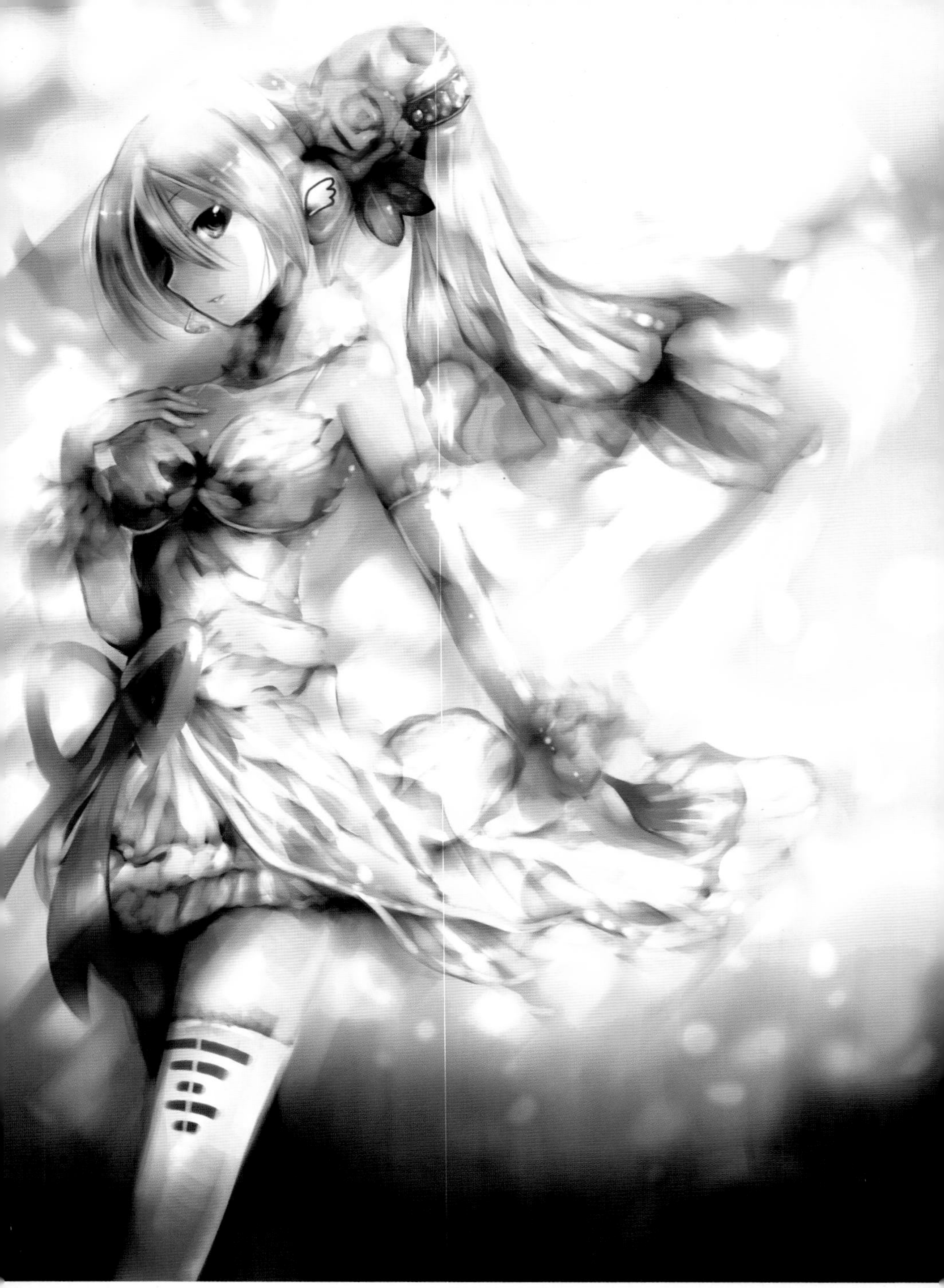

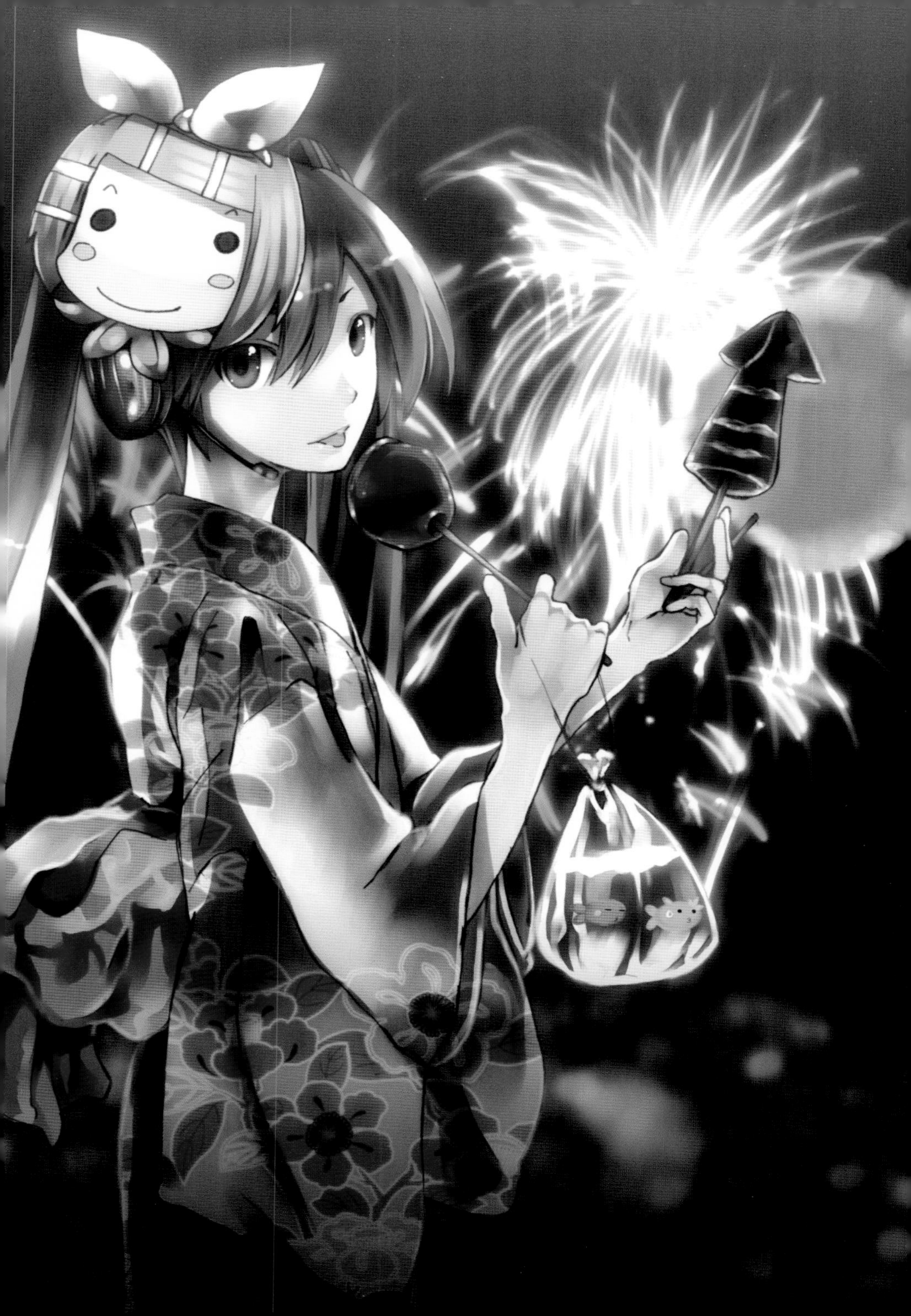

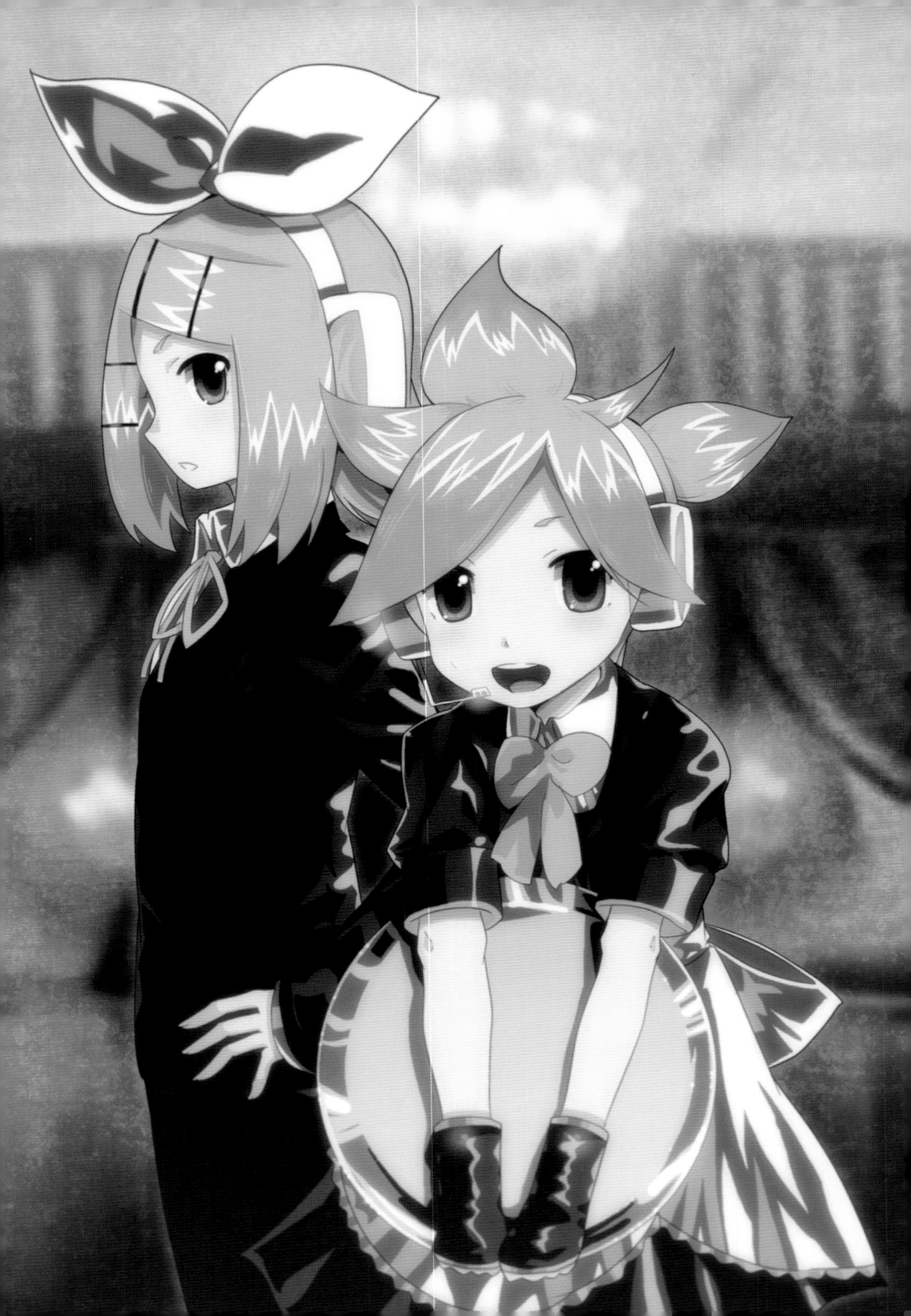

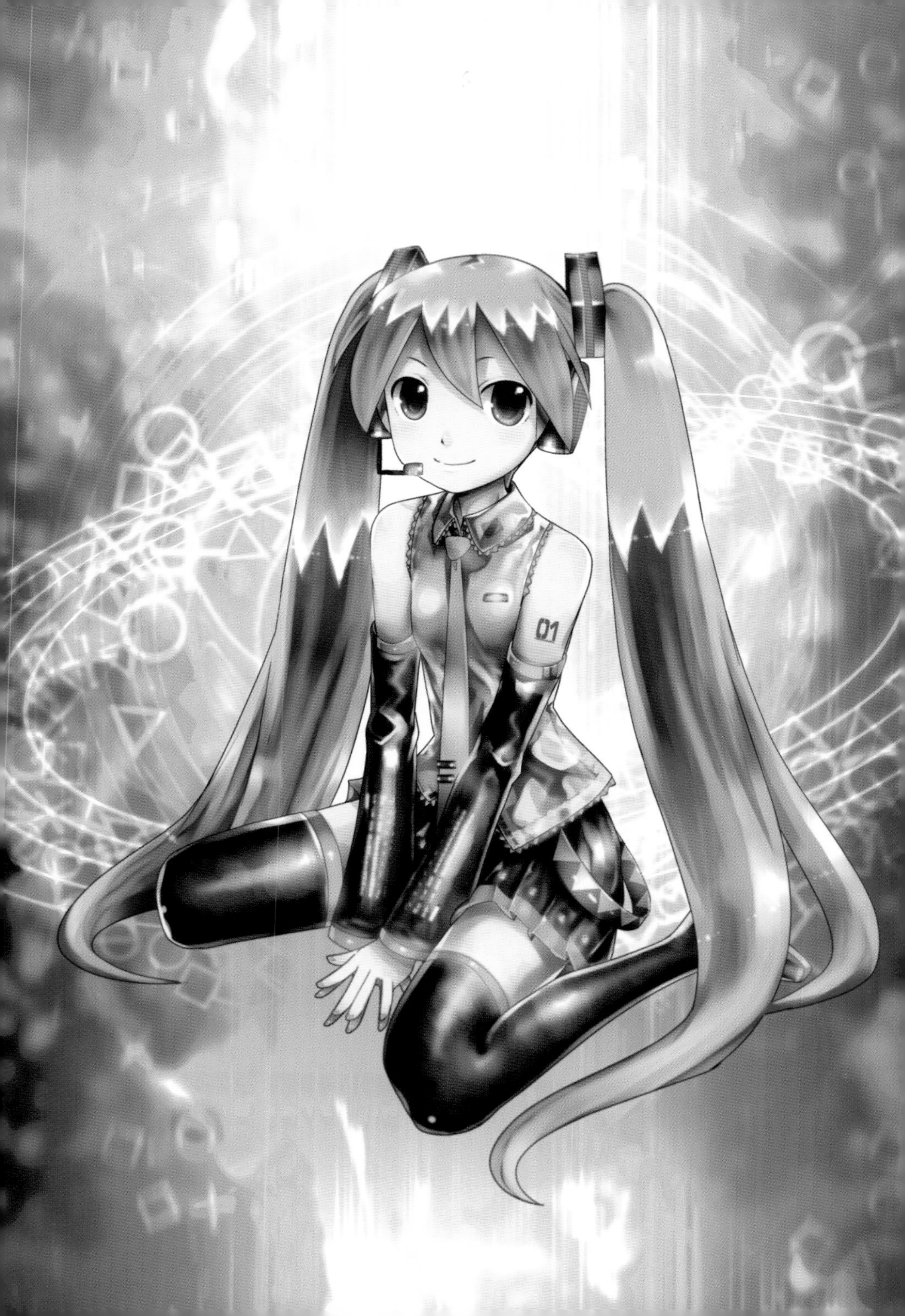
01

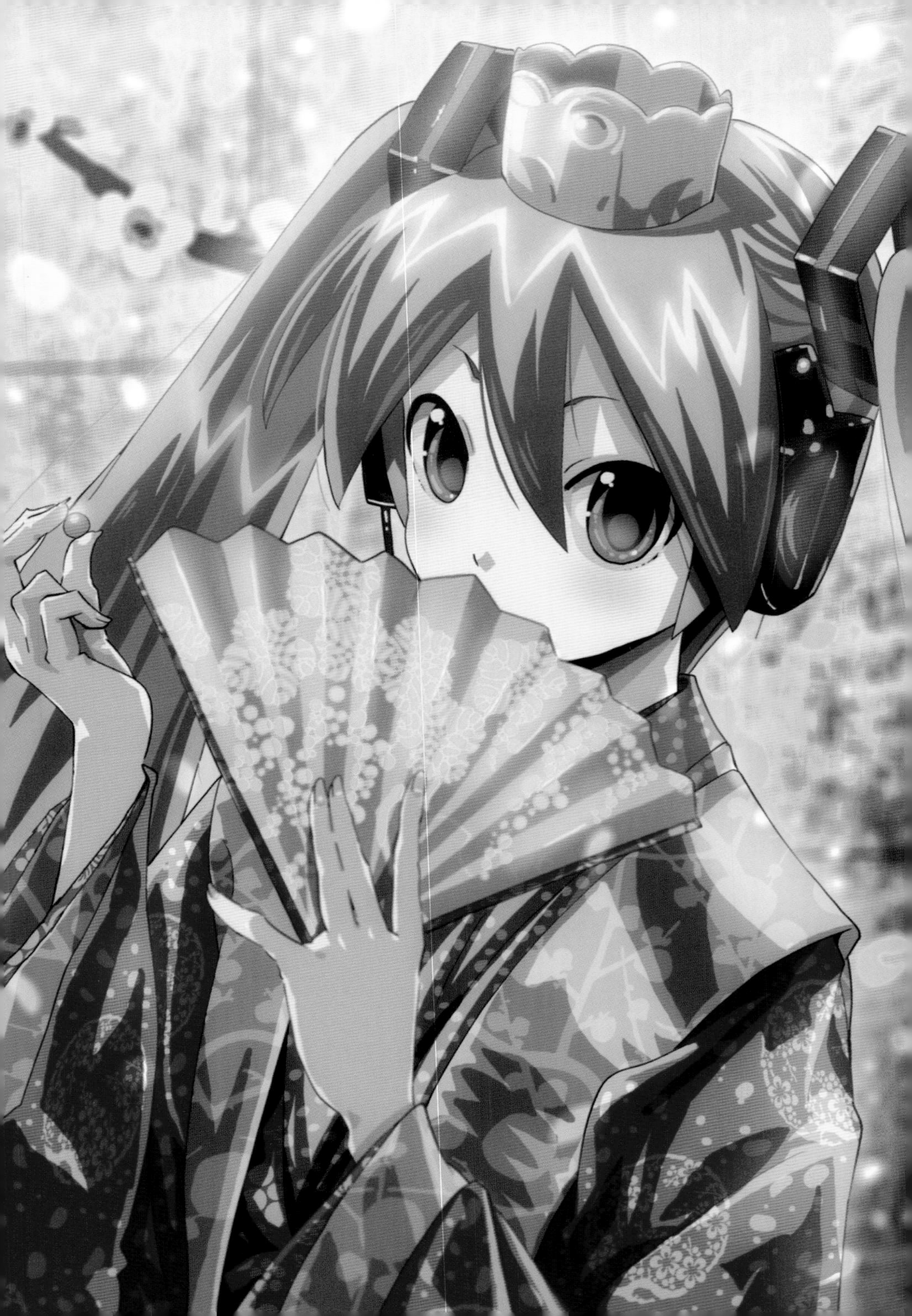

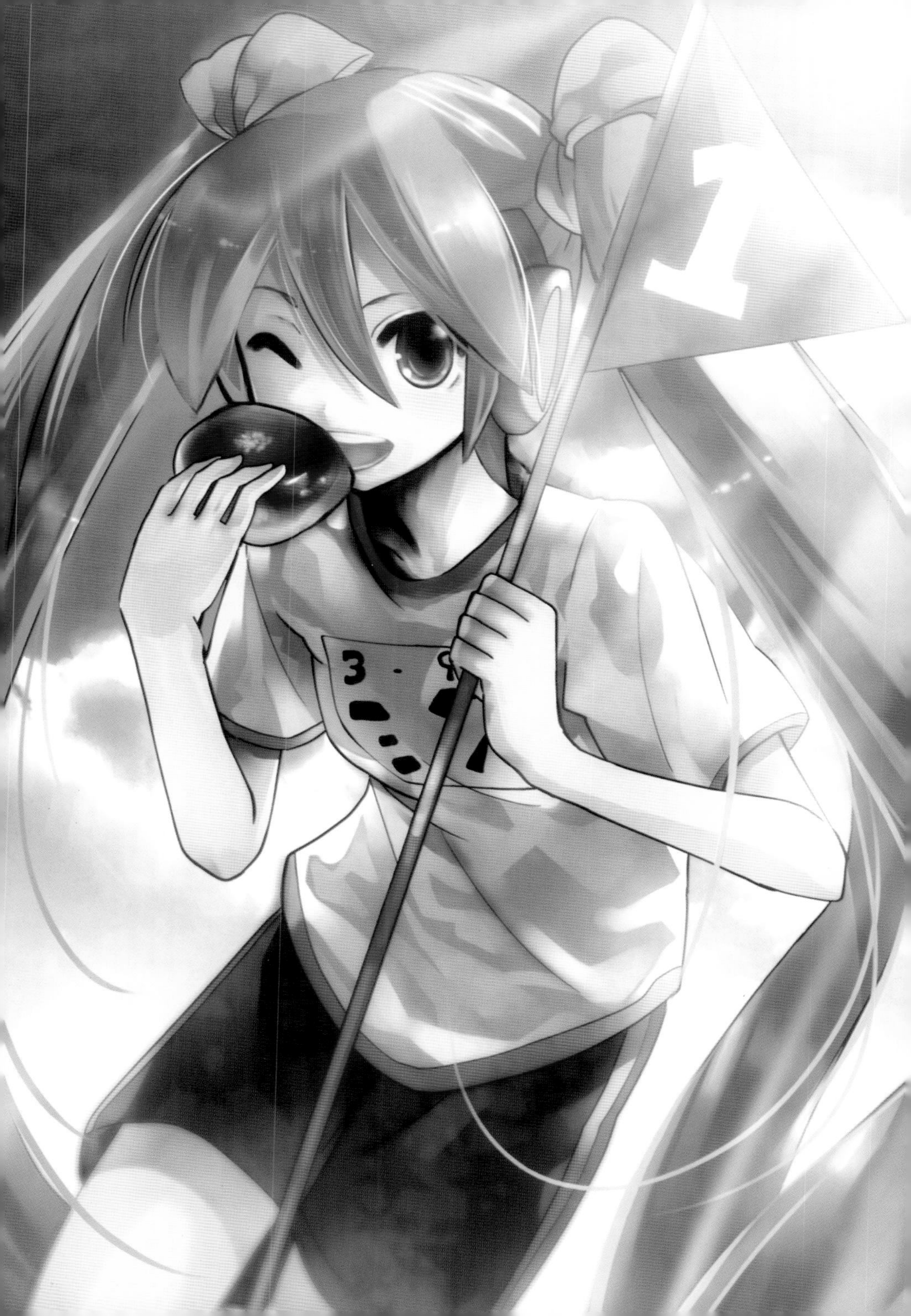
1

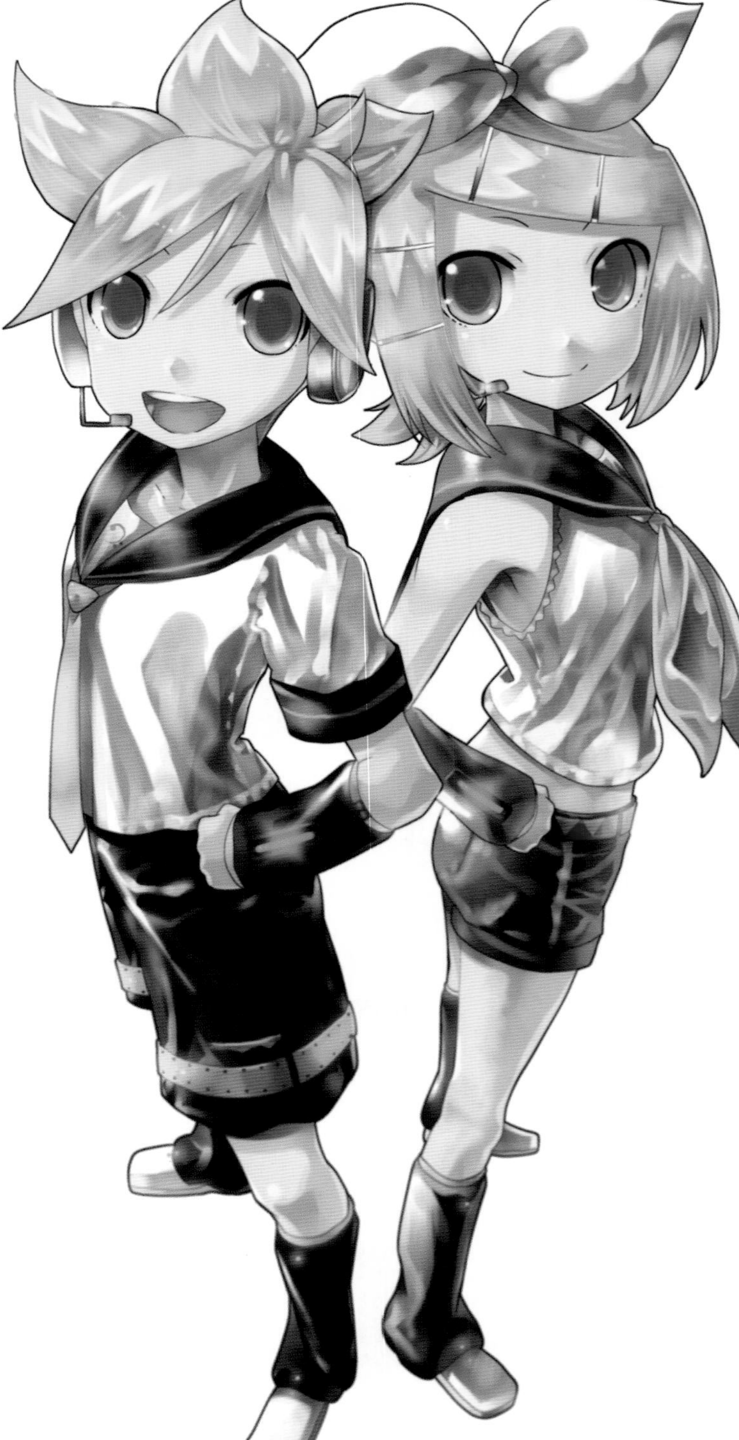

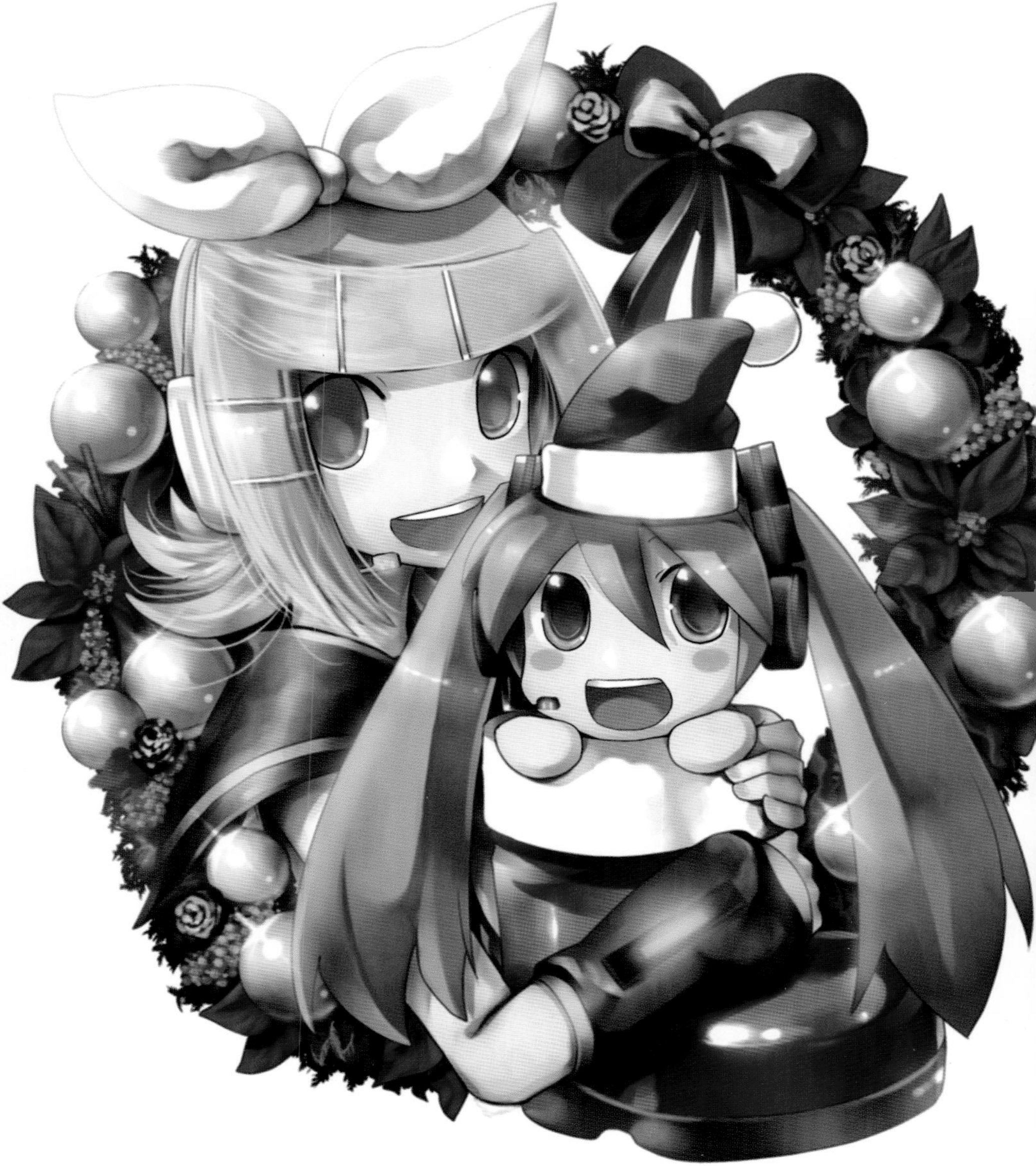

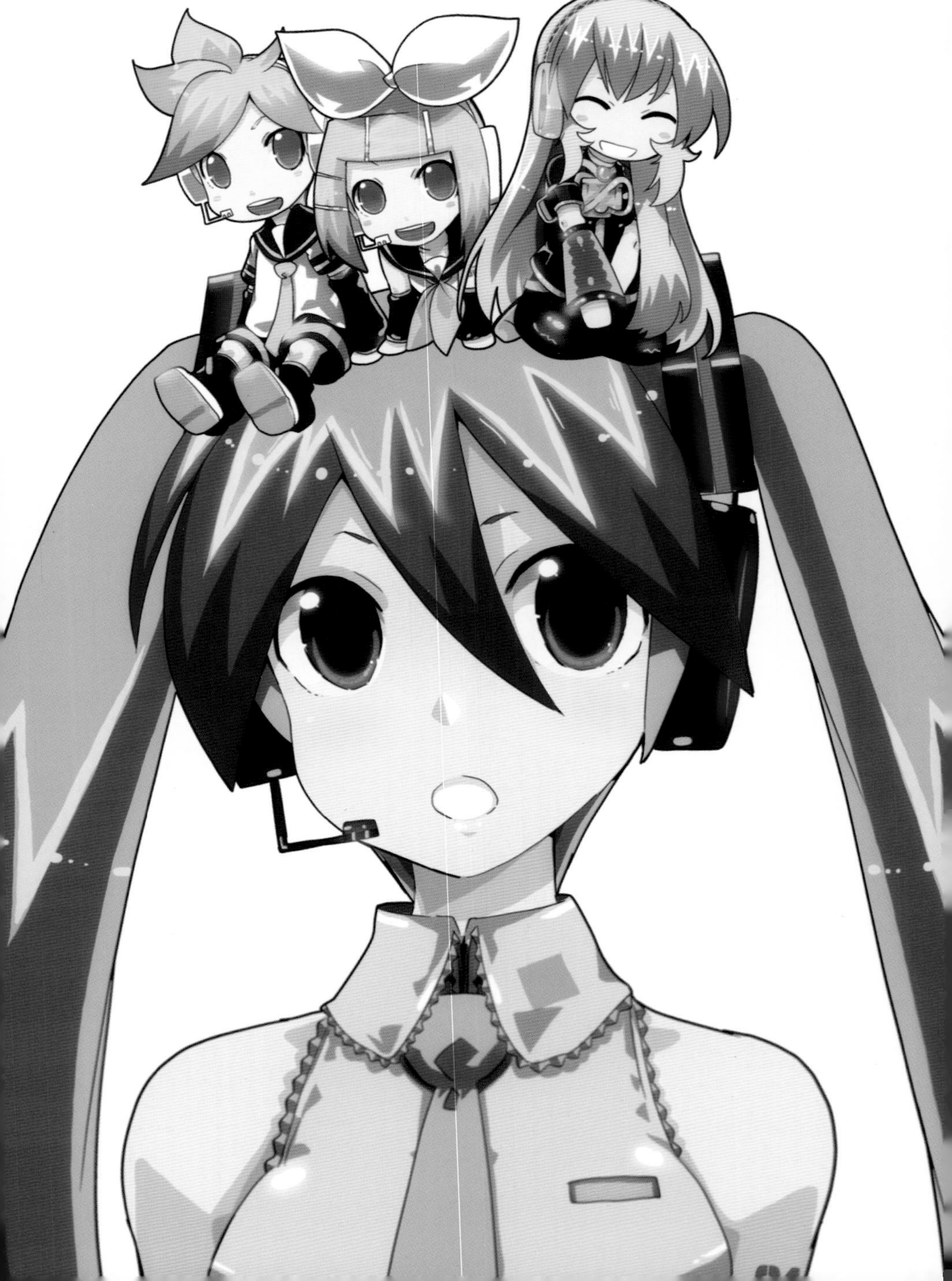

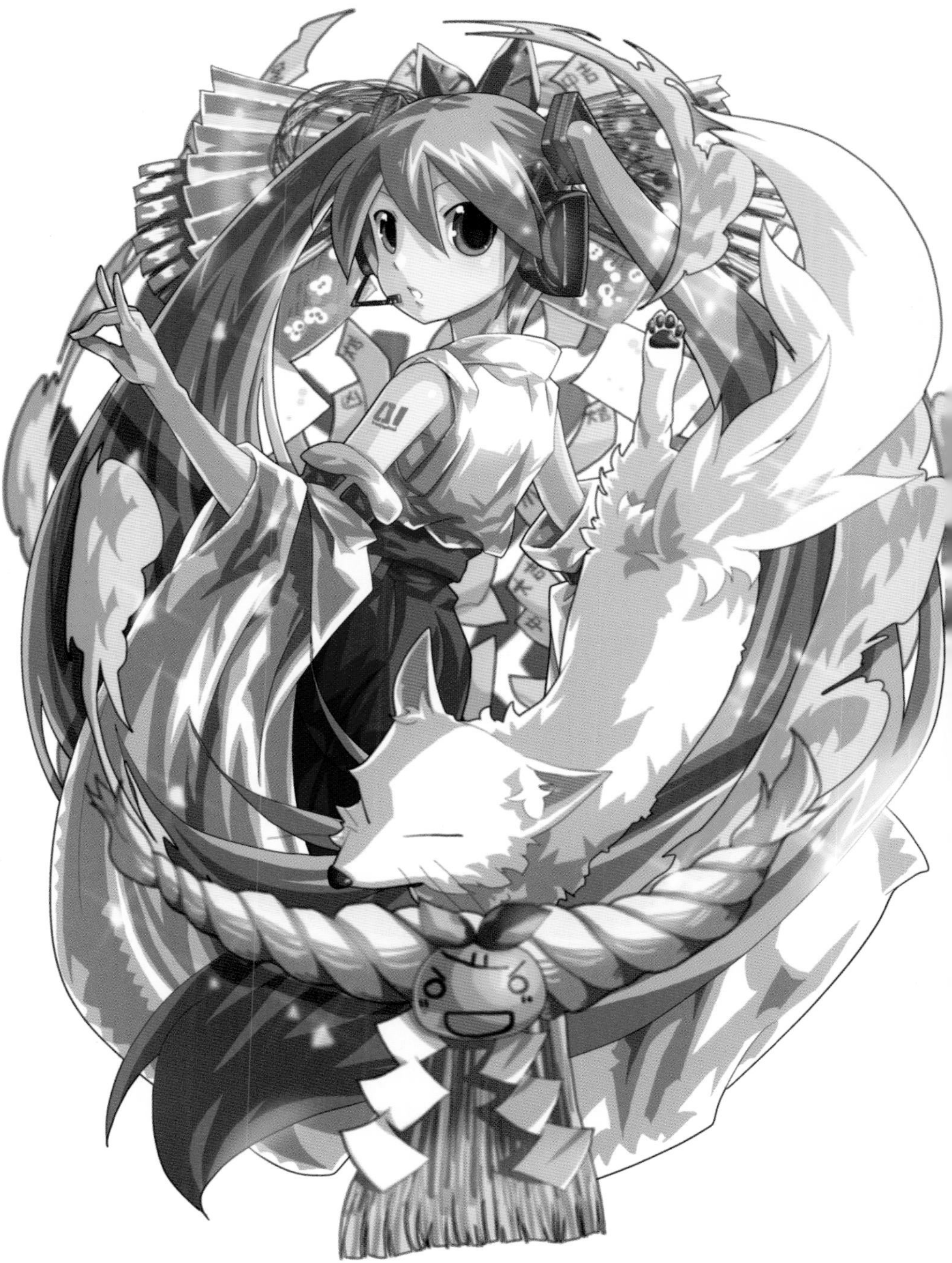

MIKU GOES TO SEGA!!!

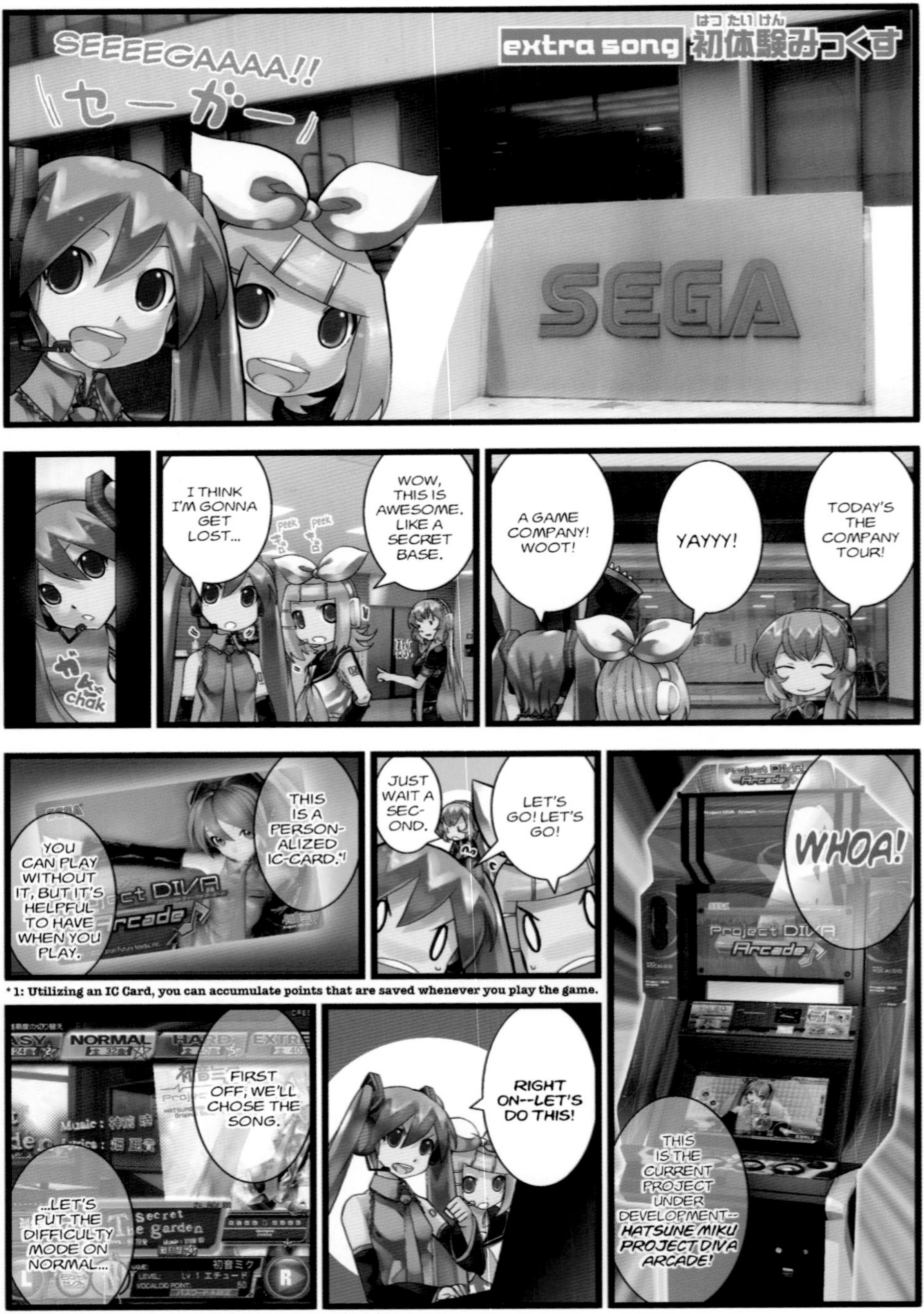
extra song 初体験みっくす
SEEEEGAAAA!!
セーガー
SEGA
TODAY'S THE COMPANY TOUR!
YAYYY!
A GAME COMPANY! WOOT!
WOW, THIS IS AWESOME. LIKE A SECRET BASE.
peek peek
I THINK I'M GONNA GET LOST...
chak
WHOA!
THIS IS THE CURRENT PROJECT UNDER DEVELOPMENT--HATSUNE MIKU PROJECT DIVA ARCADE!
LET'S GO! LET'S GO!
JUST WAIT A SEC-OND.
THIS IS A PERSON-ALIZED IC-CARD.*1
YOU CAN PLAY WITHOUT IT, BUT IT'S HELPFUL TO HAVE WHEN YOU PLAY.
RIGHT ON--LET'S DO THIS!
FIRST OFF, WE'LL CHOSE THE SONG.
...LET'S PUT THE DIFFICULTY MODE ON NORMAL...

***1: Utilizing an IC Card, you can accumulate points that are saved whenever you play the game.**

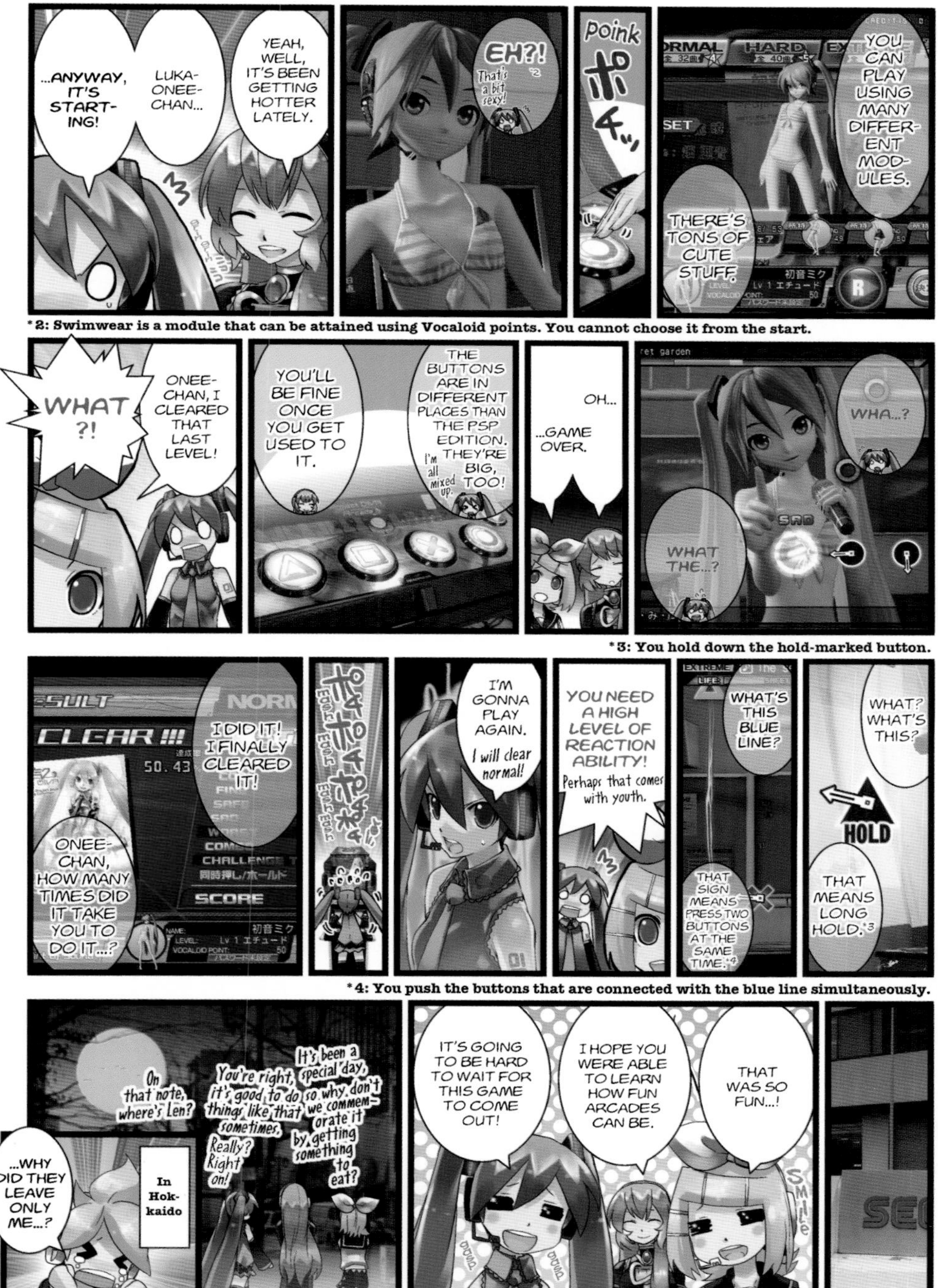
YOU CAN PLAY USING MANY DIFFERENT MODULES.
THERE'S TONS OF CUTE STUFF.
Poink
EH?!
That's a bit sexy! *2
YEAH, WELL, IT'S BEEN GETTING HOTTER LATELY.
LUKA-ONEE-CHAN...
...ANYWAY, IT'S STARTING!
WHA...?
WHAT THE...?
OH...
...GAME OVER.
THE BUTTONS ARE IN DIFFERENT PLACES THAN THE PSP EDITION. THEY'RE BIG, TOO!
I'm all mixed up.
YOU'LL BE FINE ONCE YOU GET USED TO IT.
ONEE-CHAN, I CLEARED THAT LAST LEVEL!
WHAT?!
WHAT? WHAT'S THIS?
HOLD
THAT MEANS LONG HOLD.*3
WHAT'S THIS BLUE LINE?
THAT SIGN MEANS PRESS TWO BUTTONS AT THE SAME TIME.*4
YOU NEED A HIGH LEVEL OF REACTION ABILITY!
Perhaps that comes with youth.
I'M GONNA PLAY AGAIN.
I will clear normal!
I DID IT! I FINALLY CLEARED IT!
ONEE-CHAN, HOW MANY TIMES DID IT TAKE YOU TO DO IT...?
THAT WAS SO FUN...!
I HOPE YOU WERE ABLE TO LEARN HOW FUN ARCADES CAN BE.
IT'S GOING TO BE HARD TO WAIT FOR THIS GAME TO COME OUT!
SMILE
It's been a special day, so why don't we commemorate it by getting something to eat?
You're right, it's good to do things like that sometimes.
Really? Right on!
On that note, where's Len?
In Hokkaido
...WHY DID THEY LEAVE ONLY ME...?

*2: Swimwear is a module that can be attained using Vocaloid points. You cannot choose it from the start.

*3: You hold down the hold-marked button.

*4: You push the buttons that are connected with the blue line simultaneously.

※Article based on play experience from visit to SEGA Corporation in Ota-ku, Tokyo, in April 2010.

PART 3 TRACK LIST

(20th SONG) HINA MIX

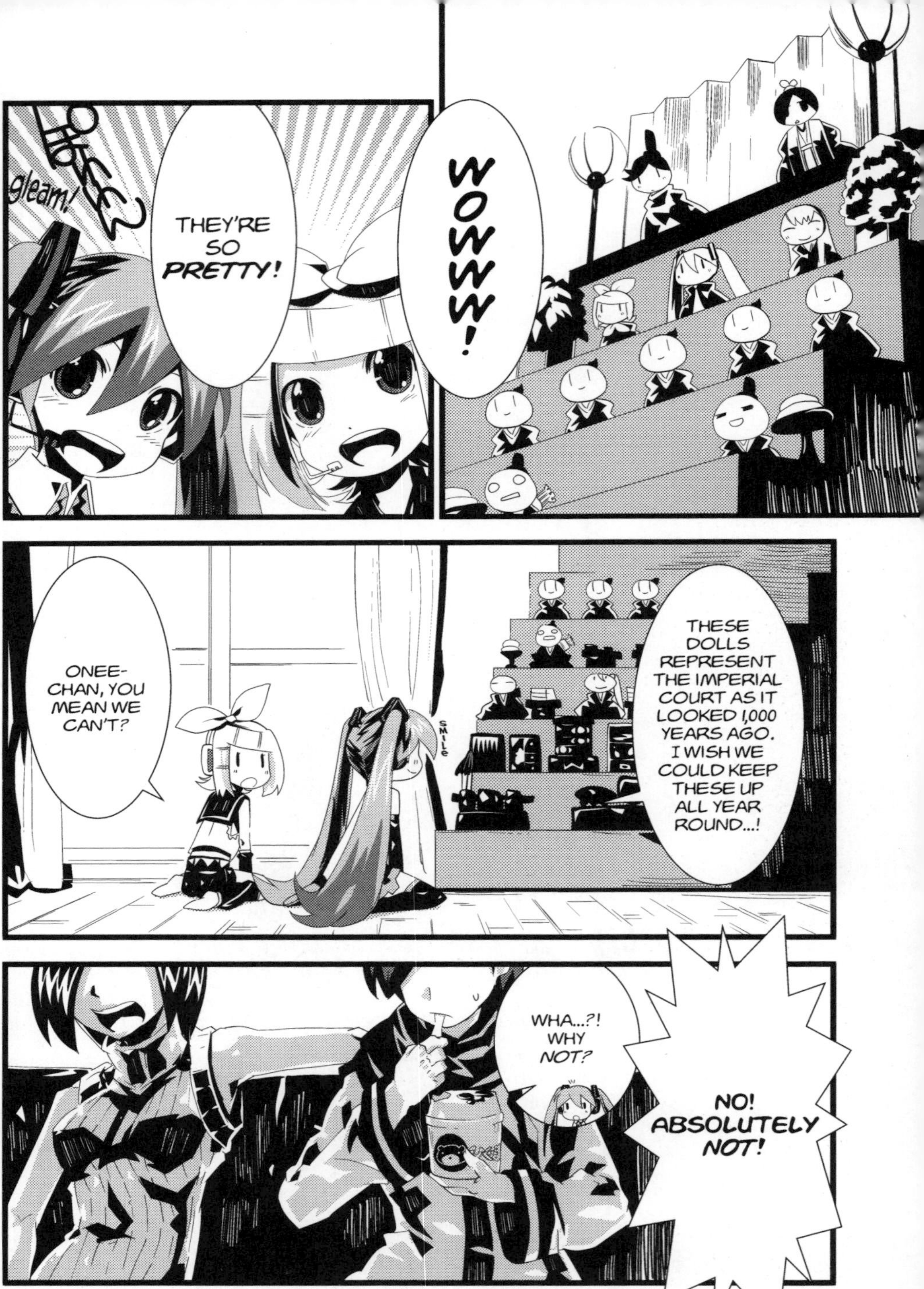
WOWWW!
THEY'RE SO PRETTY!
gleam!
THESE DOLLS REPRESENT THE IMPERIAL COURT AS IT LOOKED 1,000 YEARS AGO. I WISH WE COULD KEEP THESE UP ALL YEAR ROUND...!
SMILE
ONEE-CHAN, YOU MEAN WE CAN'T?
NO! ABSOLUTELY NOT!
WHA...?! WHY NOT?

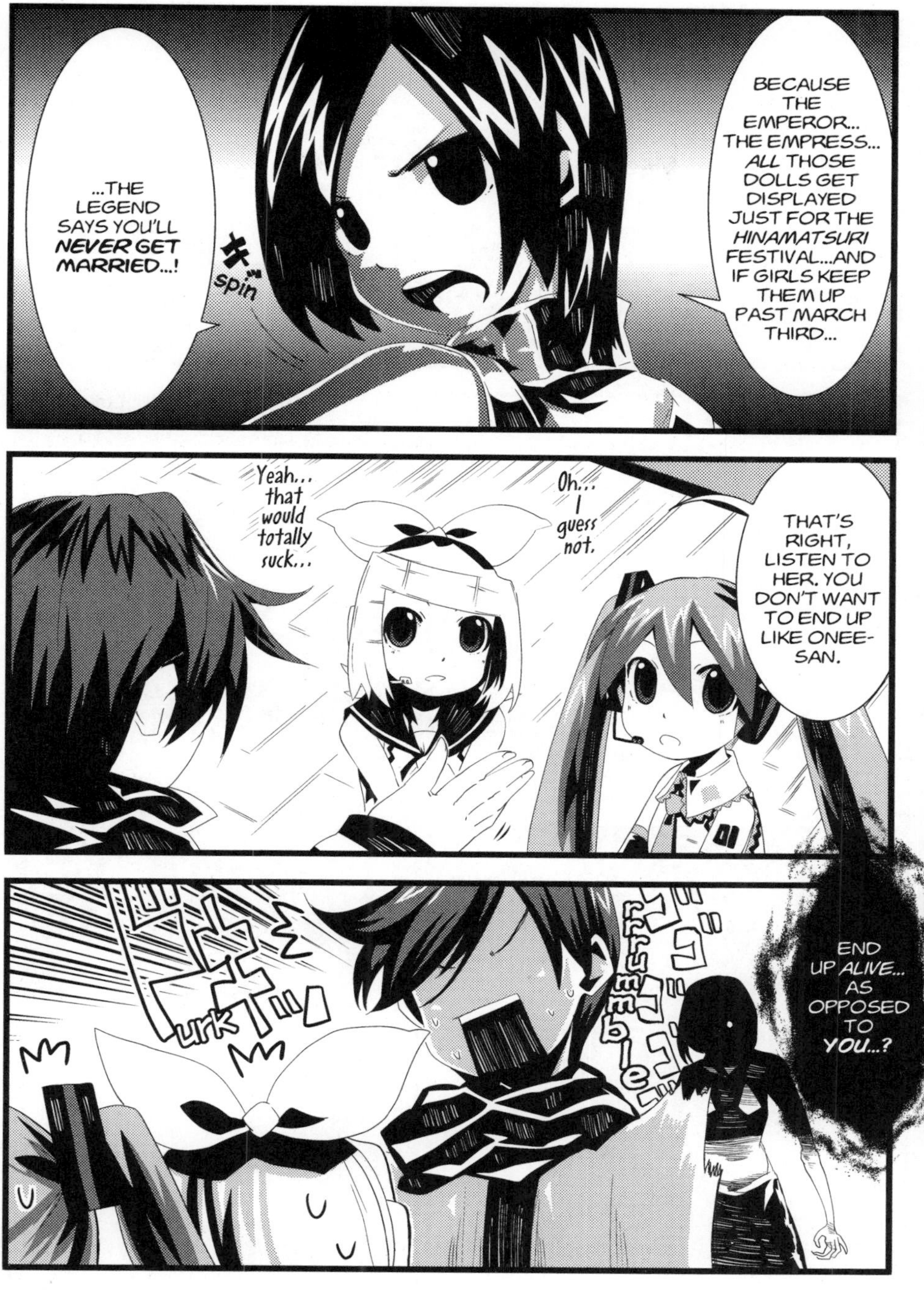
BECAUSE THE EMPEROR... THE EMPRESS... ALL THOSE DOLLS GET DISPLAYED JUST FOR THE HINAMATSURI FESTIVAL...AND IF GIRLS KEEP THEM UP PAST MARCH THIRD...
キ spin
...THE LEGEND SAYS YOU'LL NEVER GET MARRIED...!
THAT'S RIGHT, LISTEN TO HER. YOU DON'T WANT TO END UP LIKE ONEE-SAN.
Oh... I guess not.
Yeah... that would totally suck...
END UP ALIVE... AS OPPOSED TO YOU...?
rrrumble
urk

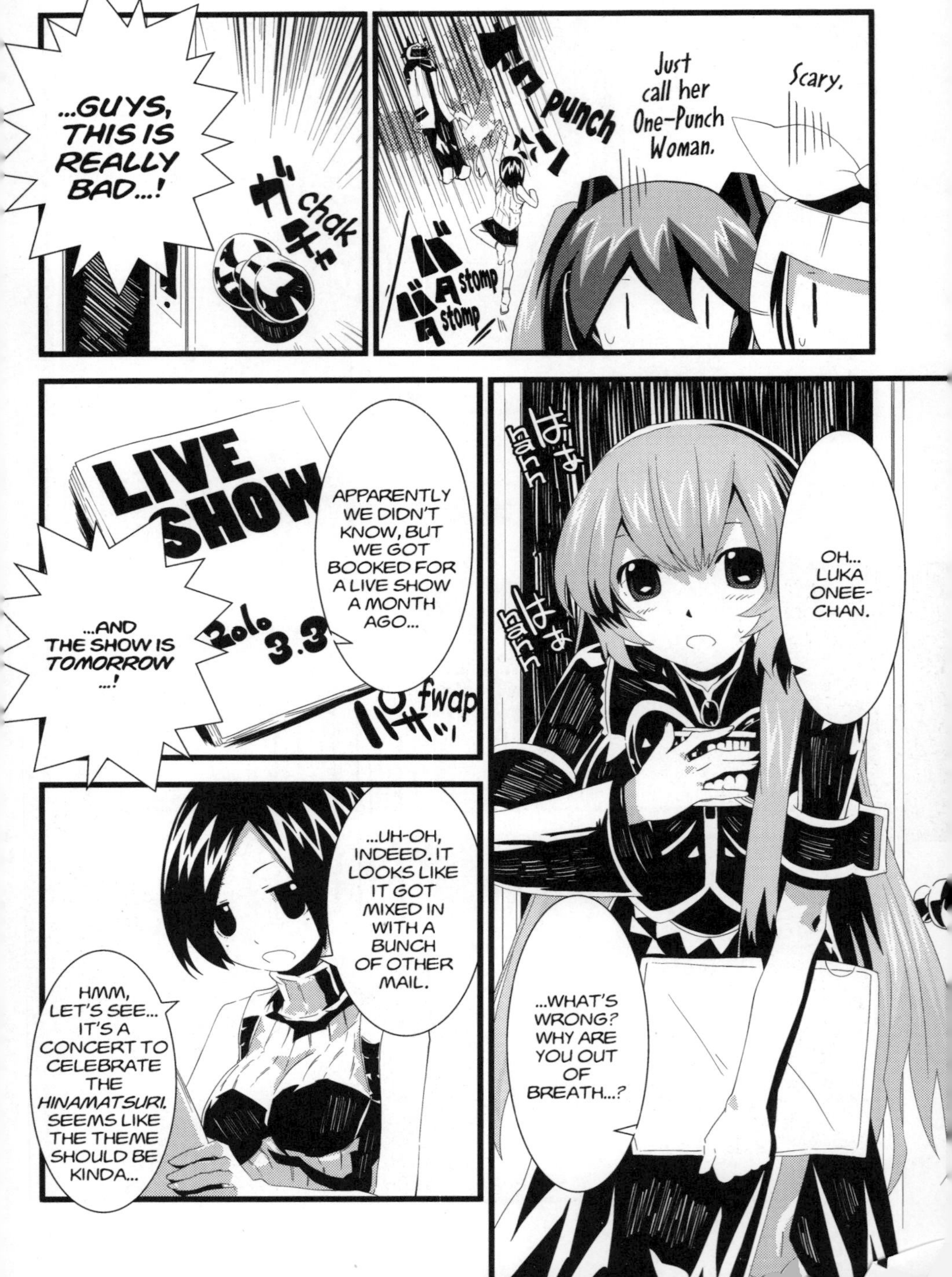
Punch
stomp
stomp
Just call her One-Punch Woman.
Scary.
...GUYS, THIS IS REALLY BAD...!
chak
OH... LUKA ONEE-CHAN.
...WHAT'S WRONG? WHY ARE YOU OUT OF BREATH...?
APPARENTLY WE DIDN'T KNOW, BUT WE GOT BOOKED FOR A LIVE SHOW A MONTH AGO...
LIVE SHOW
2010 3.3
...AND THE SHOW IS TOMORROW ...!
fwap
...UH-OH, INDEED. IT LOOKS LIKE IT GOT MIXED IN WITH A BUNCH OF OTHER MAIL.
HMM, LET'S SEE... IT'S A CONCERT TO CELEBRATE THE HINAMATSURI. SEEMS LIKE THE THEME SHOULD BE KINDA...

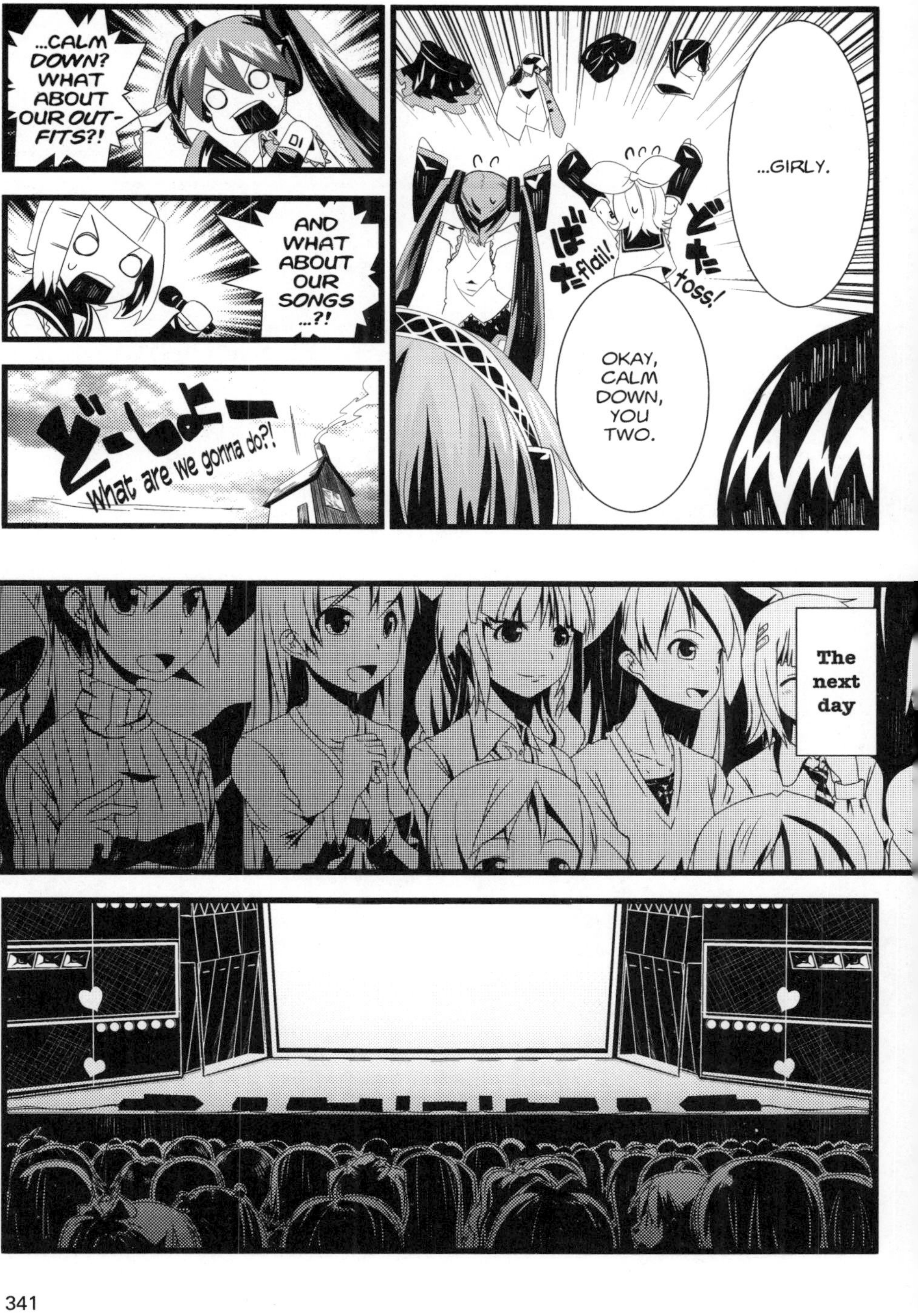
...GIRLY.
toss!
flail!
OKAY, CALM DOWN, YOU TWO.
...CALM DOWN? WHAT ABOUT OUR OUT-FITS?!
AND WHAT ABOUT OUR SONGS ...?!
どーしよー
what are we gonna do?!
The next day

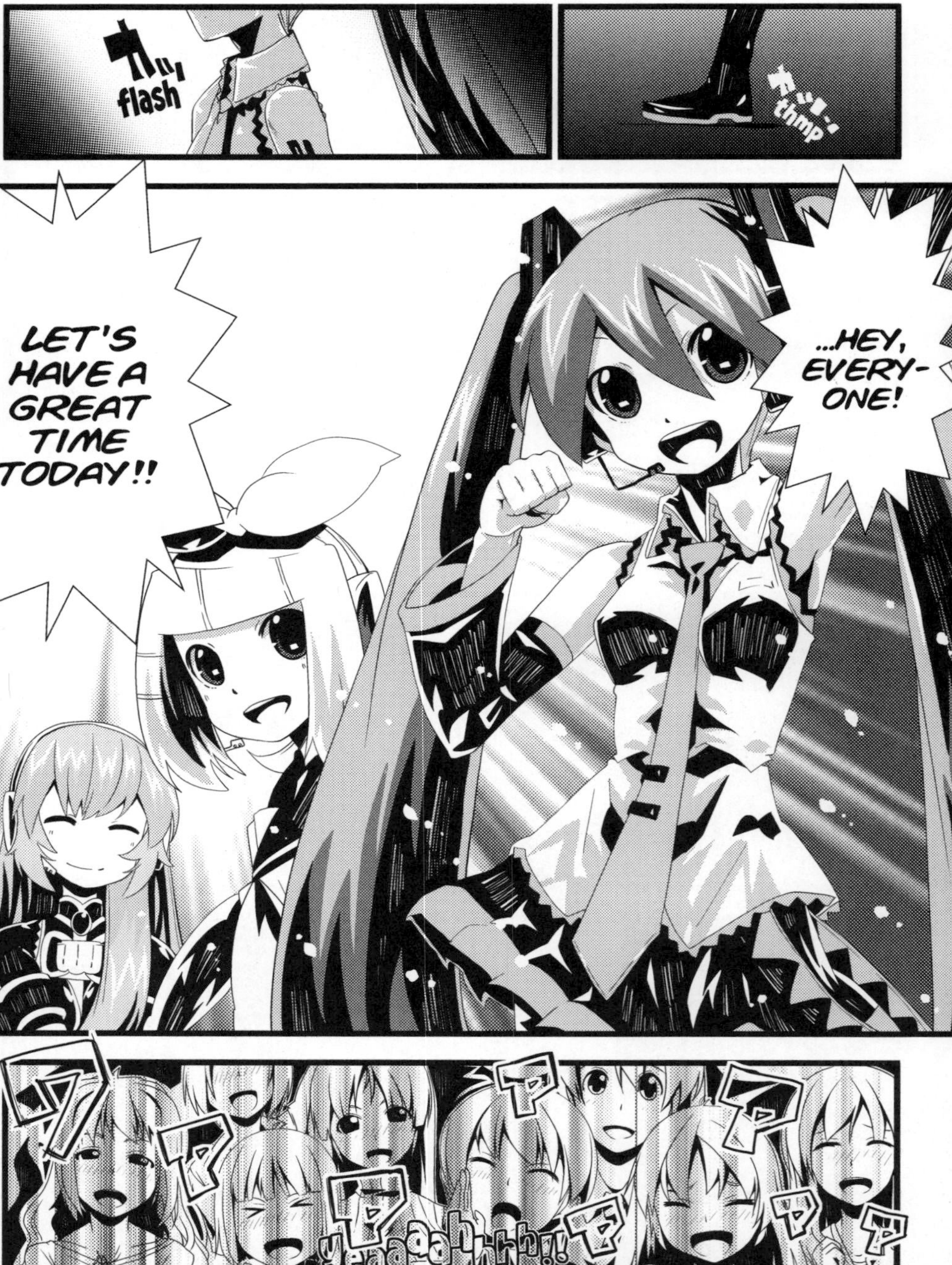
thmp
flash
...HEY, EVERY-ONE!
LET'S HAVE A GREAT TIME TODAY!!
yeaaaahhhhh!!

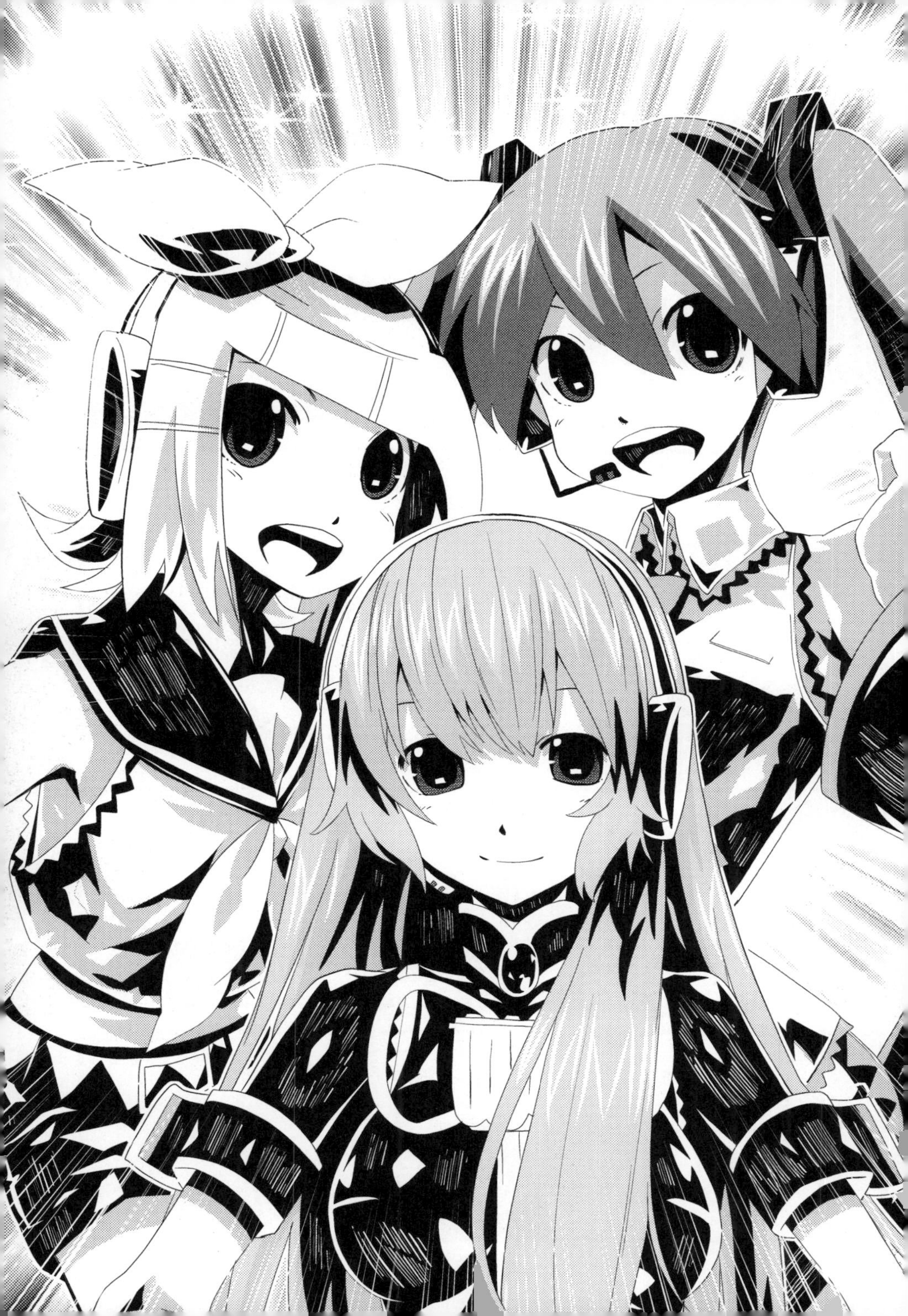

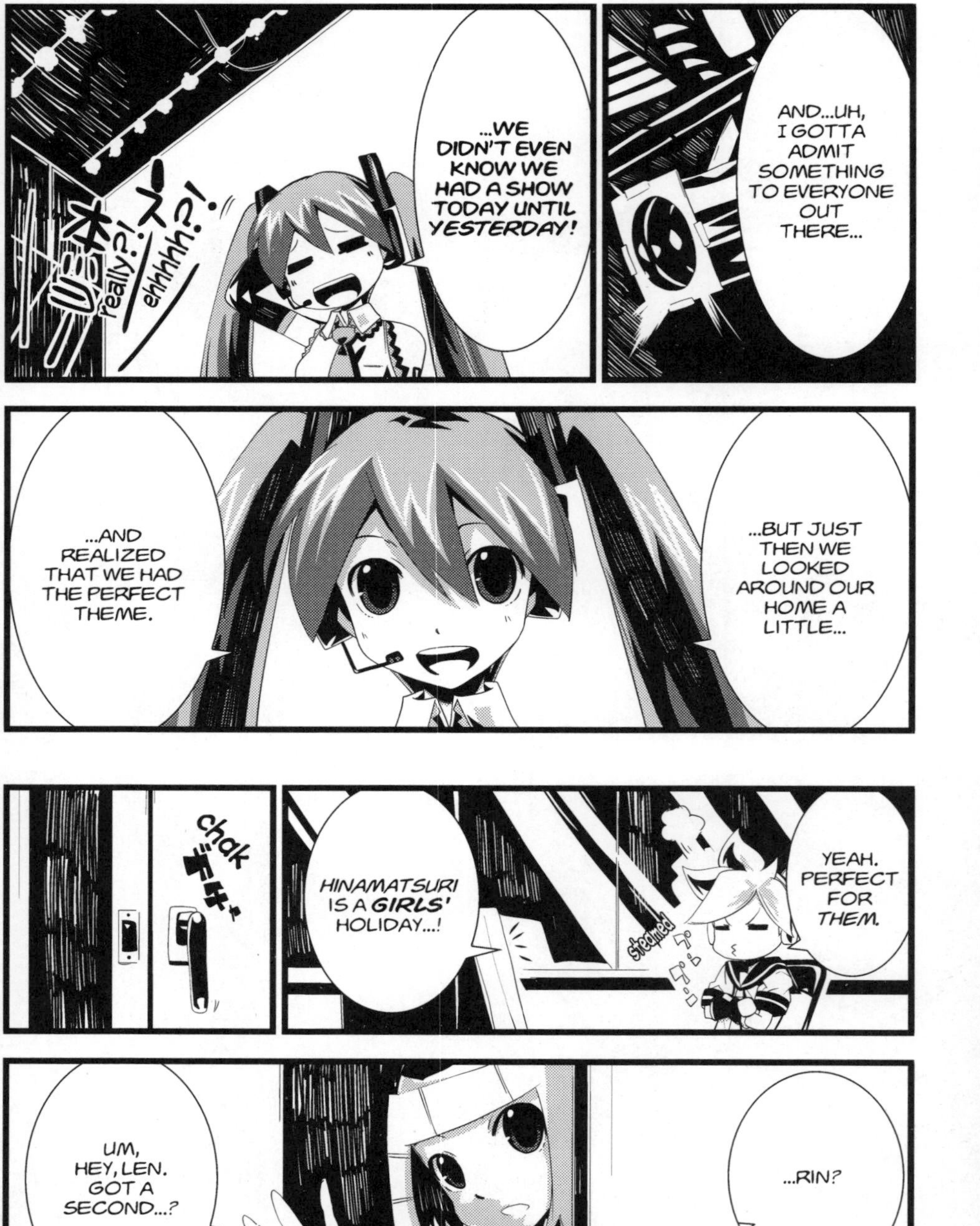
AND...UH, I GOTTA ADMIT SOMETHING TO EVERYONE OUT THERE...
...WE DIDN'T EVEN KNOW WE HAD A SHOW TODAY UNTIL YESTERDAY!
ehhhhh?!
really?!
...BUT JUST THEN WE LOOKED AROUND OUR HOME A LITTLE...
...AND REALIZED THAT WE HAD THE PERFECT THEME.
YEAH. PERFECT FOR THEM.
steamed
HINAMATSURI IS A GIRLS' HOLIDAY...!
chak
...RIN?
UM, HEY, LEN. GOT A SECOND...?

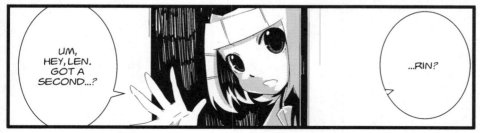

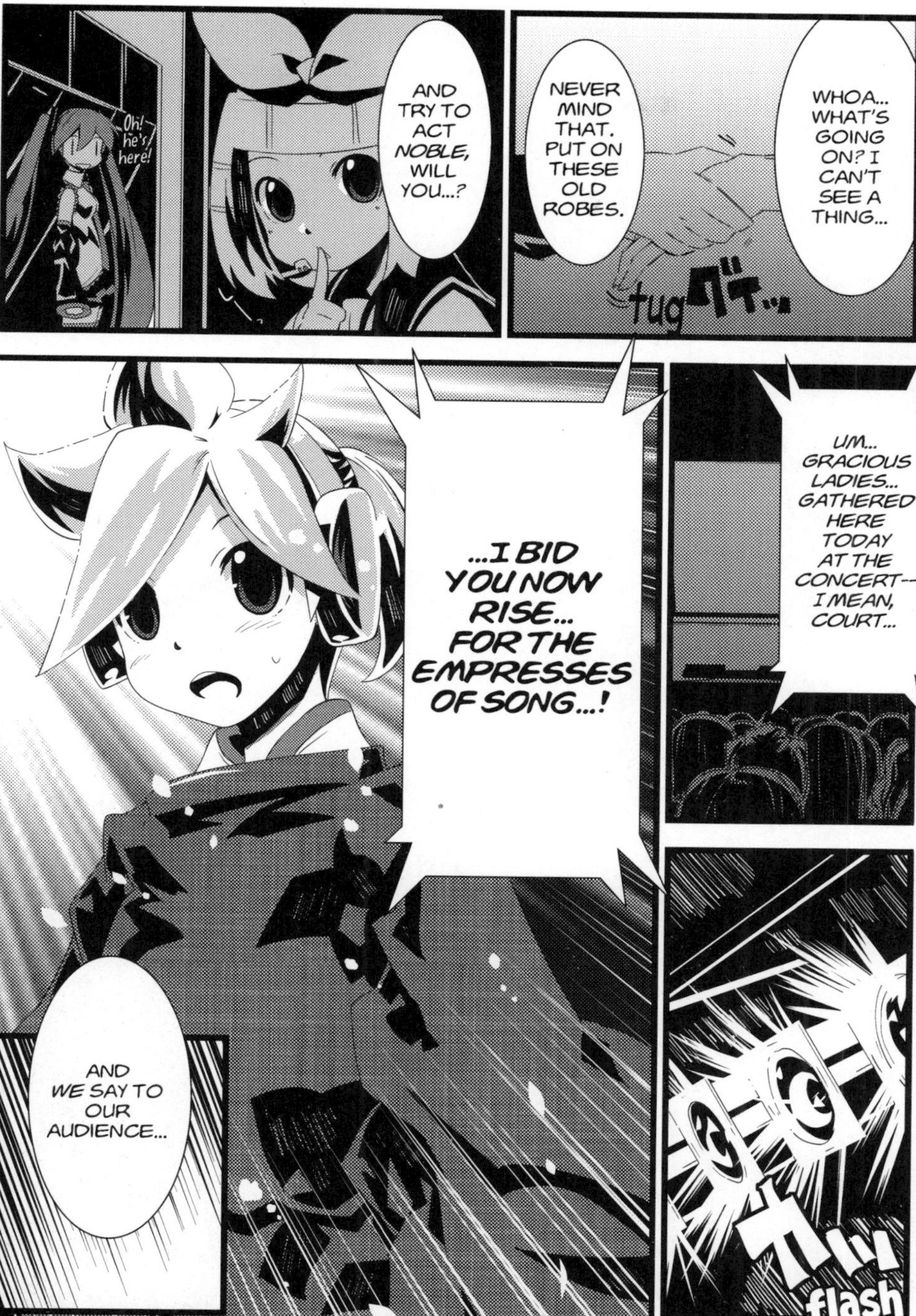
WHOA... WHAT'S GOING ON? I CAN'T SEE A THING...
NEVER MIND THAT. PUT ON THESE OLD ROBES.
tug
AND TRY TO ACT *NOBLE,* WILL YOU...?
Oh! he's here!
UM... GRACIOUS LADIES... GATHERED HERE TODAY AT THE CONCERT-- I MEAN, COURT...
flash
...I BID YOU NOW RISE... FOR THE EMPRESSES OF SONG...!
AND *WE* SAY TO OUR AUDIENCE...

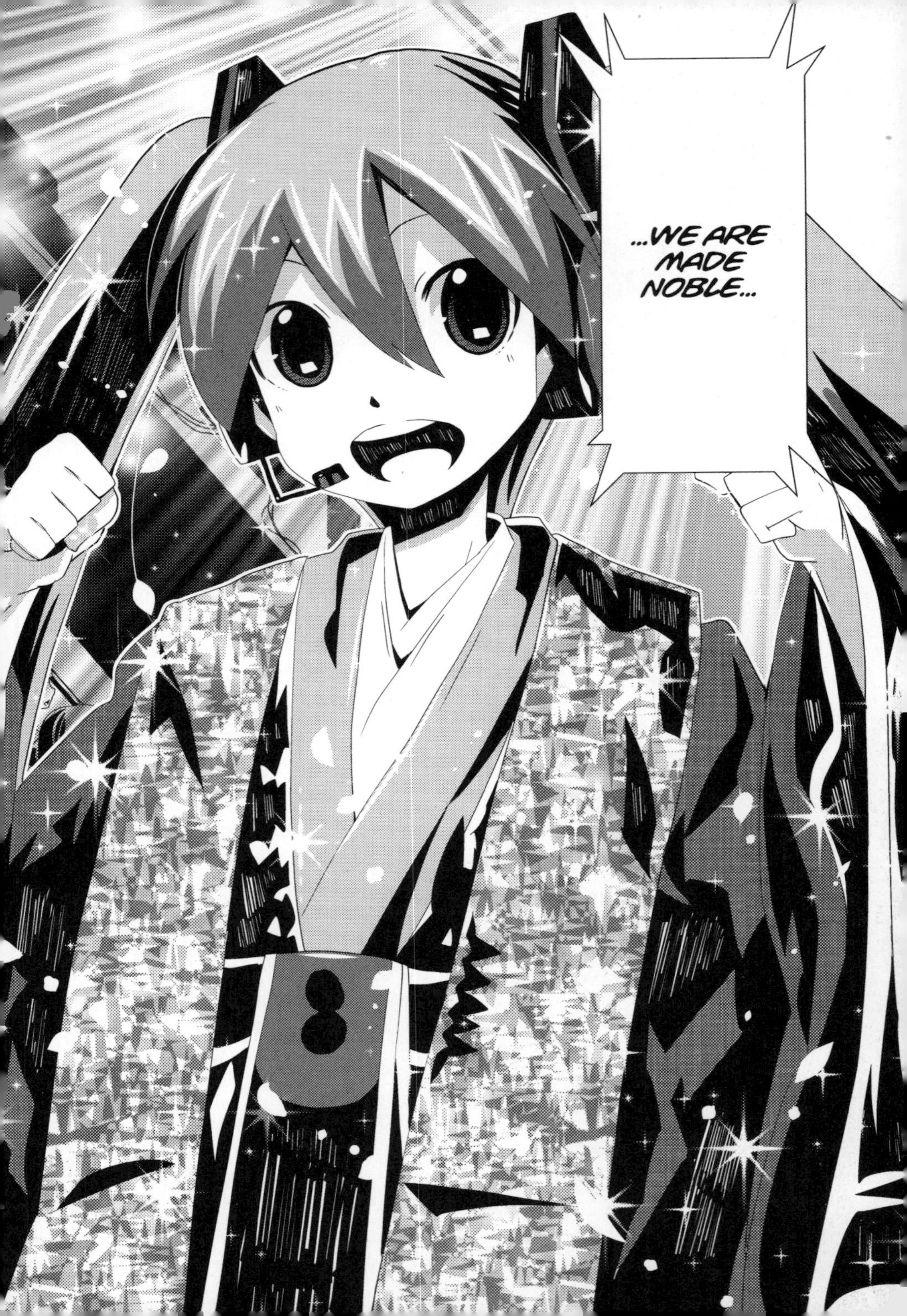
...WE ARE MADE NOBLE...

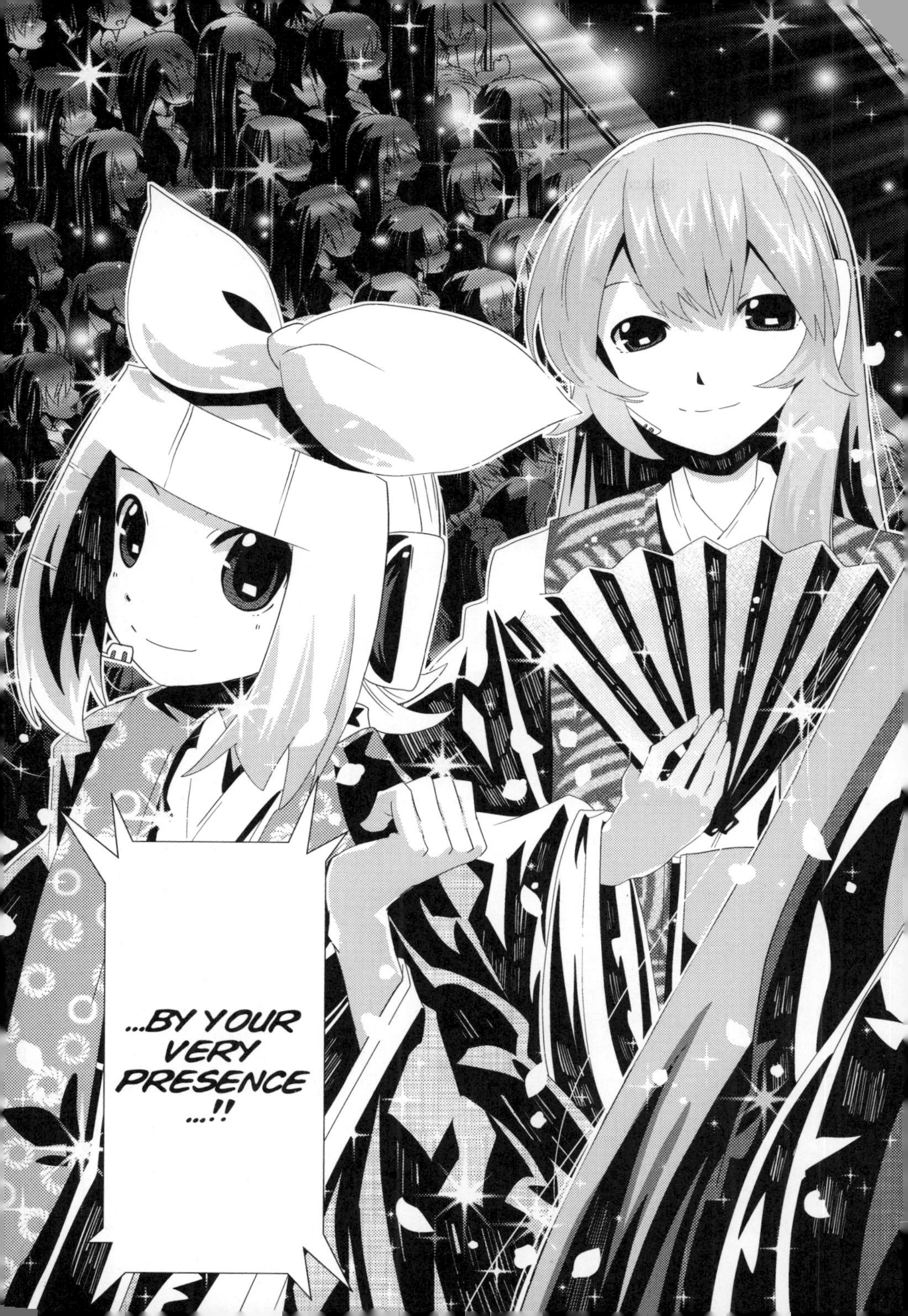
...BY YOUR VERY PRESENCE ...!!

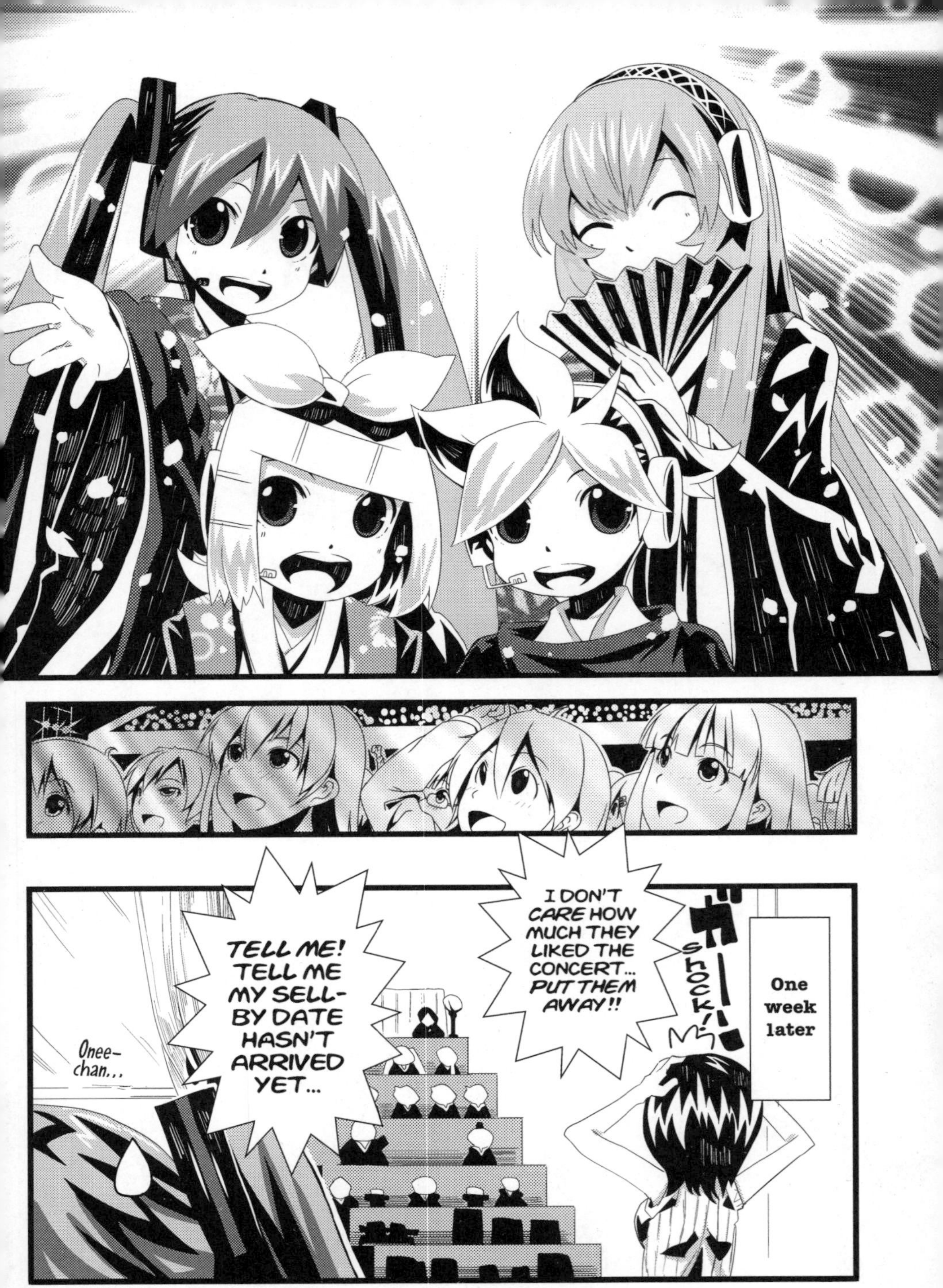
One week later
shock!!
I DON'T CARE HOW MUCH THEY LIKED THE CONCERT... PUT THEM AWAY!!
TELL ME! TELL ME MY SELL-BY DATE HASN'T ARRIVED YET...
Onee-chan...

(21st SONG) MATSURI MIX

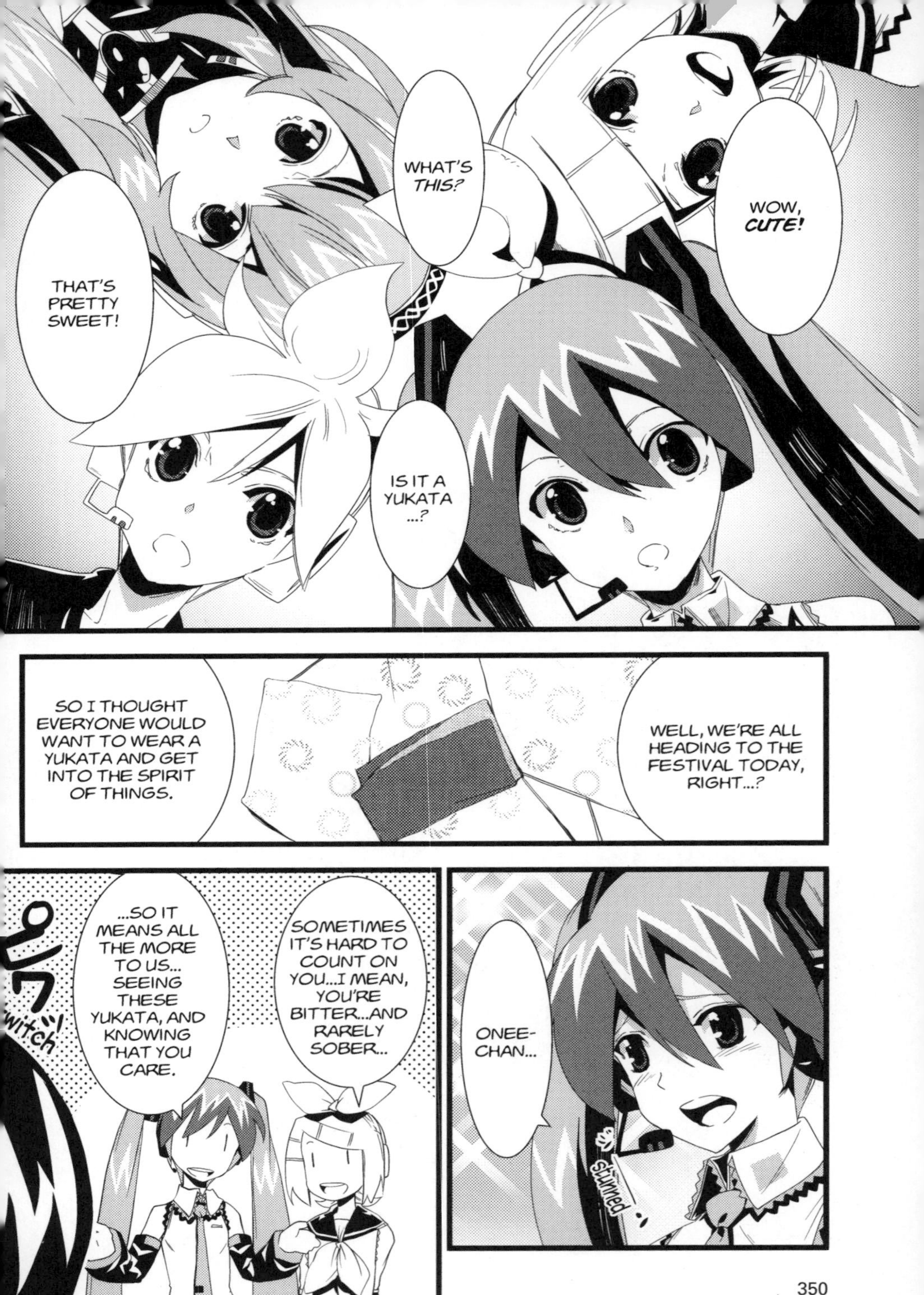
WOW, CUTE!
WHAT'S THIS?
THAT'S PRETTY SWEET!
IS IT A YUKATA ...?
WELL, WE'RE ALL HEADING TO THE FESTIVAL TODAY, RIGHT...?
SO I THOUGHT EVERYONE WOULD WANT TO WEAR A YUKATA AND GET INTO THE SPIRIT OF THINGS.
ONEE-CHAN...
stirred
SOMETIMES IT'S HARD TO COUNT ON YOU...I MEAN, YOU'RE BITTER...AND RARELY SOBER...
...SO IT MEANS ALL THE MORE TO US... SEEING THESE YUKATA, AND KNOWING THAT YOU CARE.
twitch

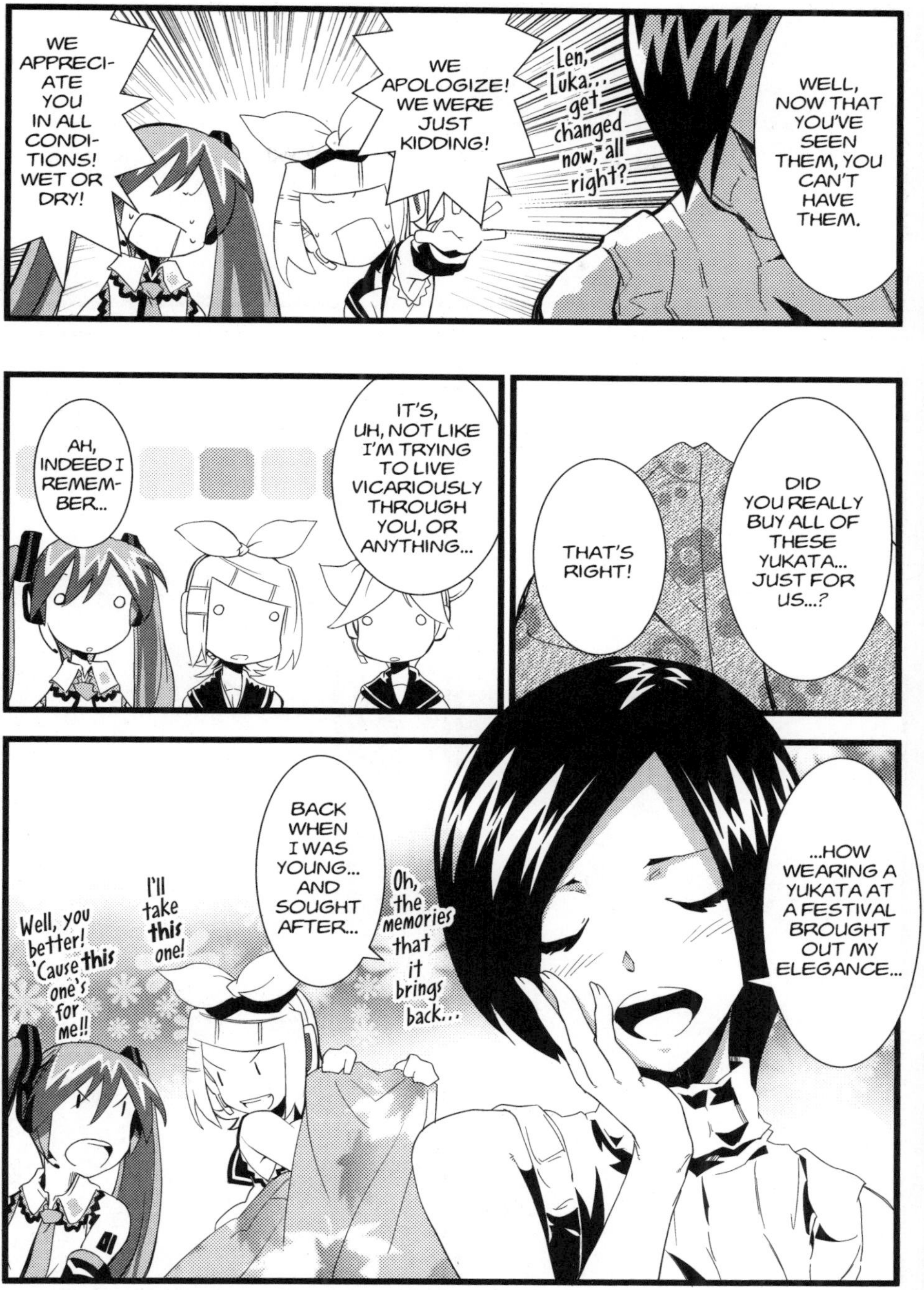
WELL, NOW THAT YOU'VE SEEN THEM, YOU CAN'T HAVE THEM.
Len, Luka... get changed now, all right?
WE APOLOGIZE! WE WERE JUST KIDDING!
WE APPRECIATE YOU IN ALL CONDITIONS! WET OR DRY!
DID YOU REALLY BUY ALL OF THESE YUKATA... JUST FOR US...?
THAT'S RIGHT!
IT'S, UH, NOT LIKE I'M TRYING TO LIVE VICARIOUSLY THROUGH YOU, OR ANYTHING...
AH, INDEED I REMEMBER...
...HOW WEARING A YUKATA AT A FESTIVAL BROUGHT OUT MY ELEGANCE...
BACK WHEN I WAS YOUNG... AND SOUGHT AFTER...
Oh, the memories that it brings back...
I'll take **this** one!
Well, you better! 'Cause **this** one's for me!!

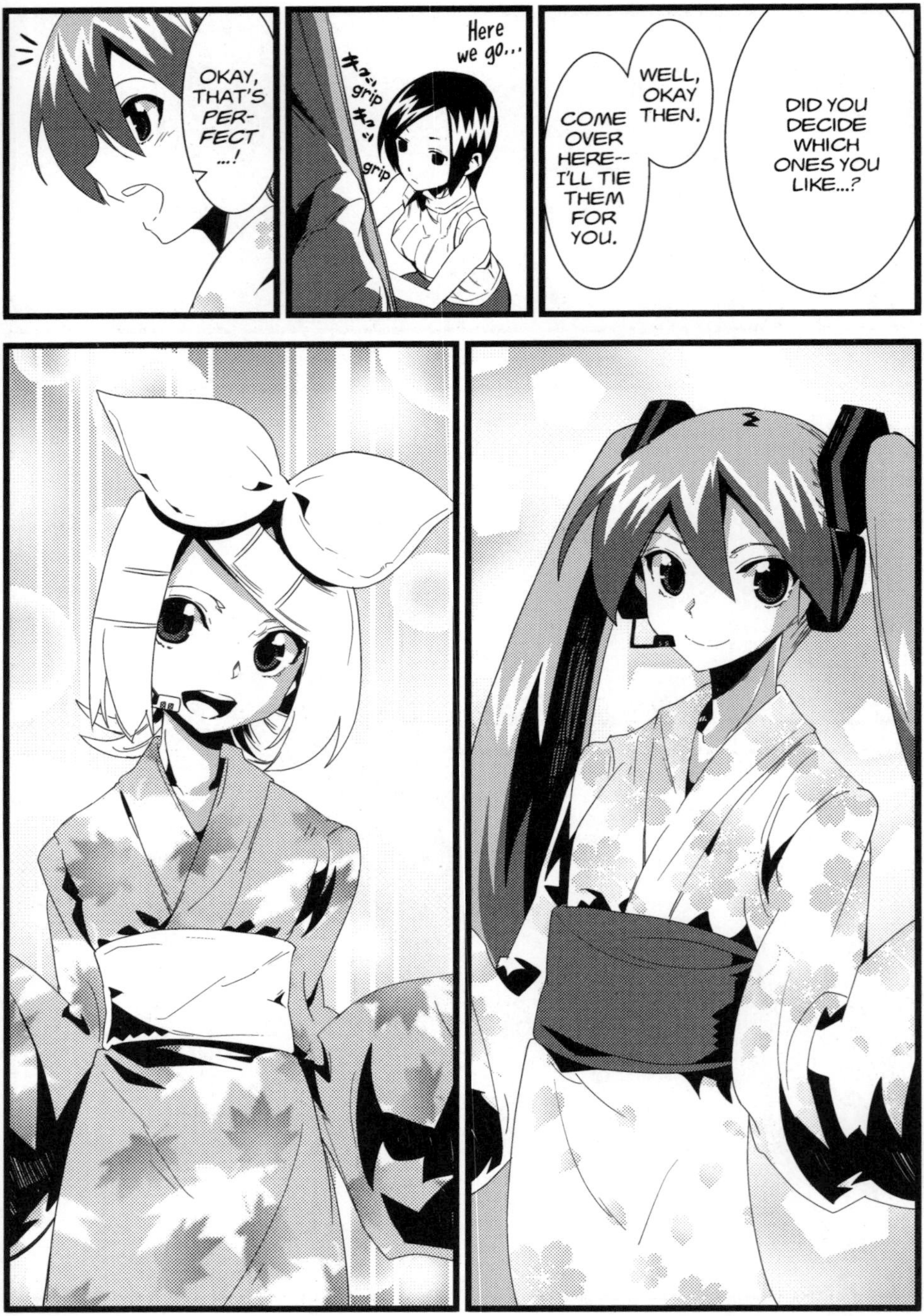
DID YOU DECIDE WHICH ONES YOU LIKE...?
WELL, OKAY THEN.
COME OVER HERE-- I'LL TIE THEM FOR YOU.
Here we go...
キュッ grip
キュッ grip
OKAY, THAT'S PER-FECT ...!

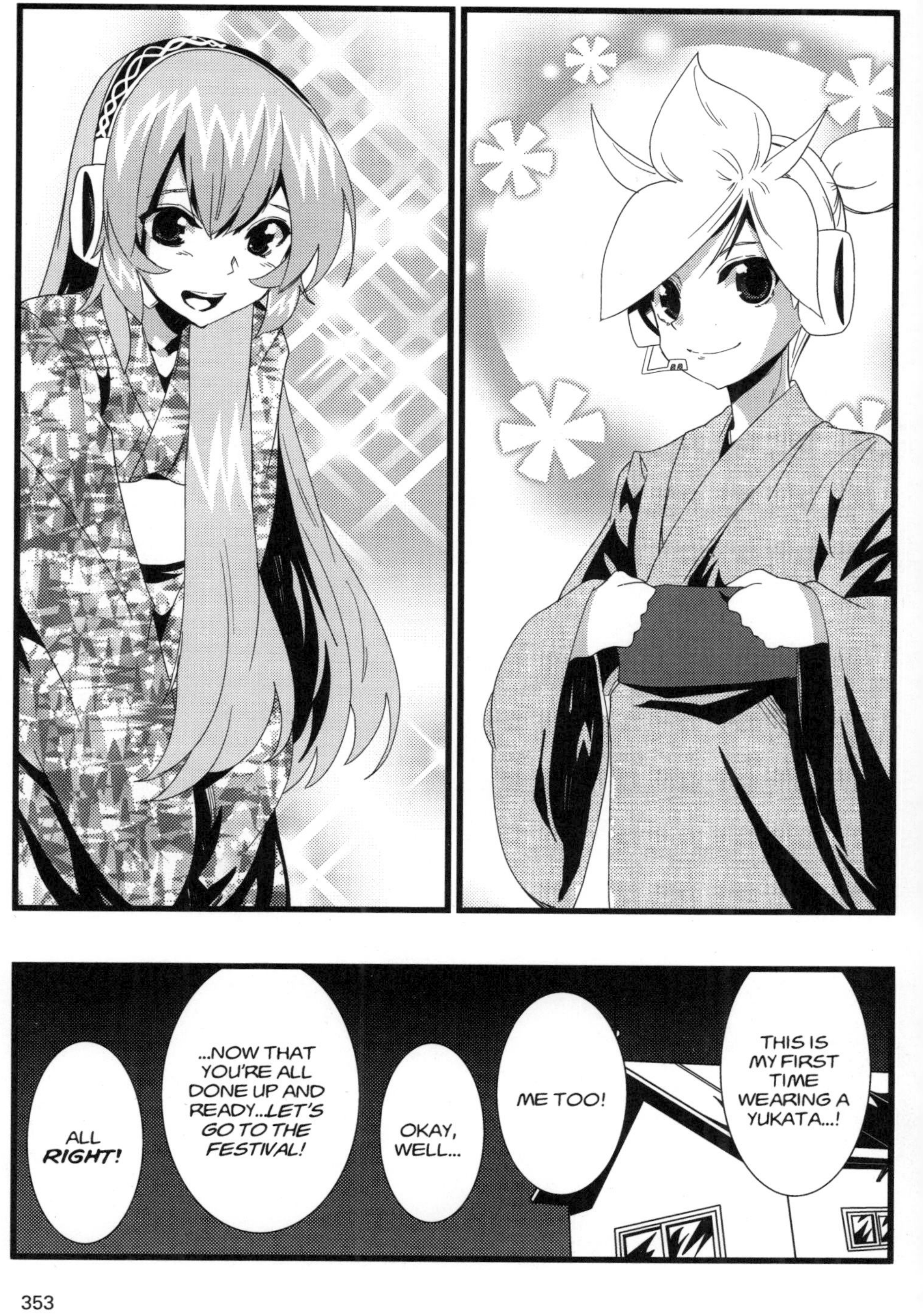
THIS IS MY FIRST TIME WEARING A YUKATA...!
ME TOO!
OKAY, WELL...
...NOW THAT YOU'RE ALL DONE UP AND READY...*LET'S* GO TO THE FESTIVAL!
ALL **RIGHT**!

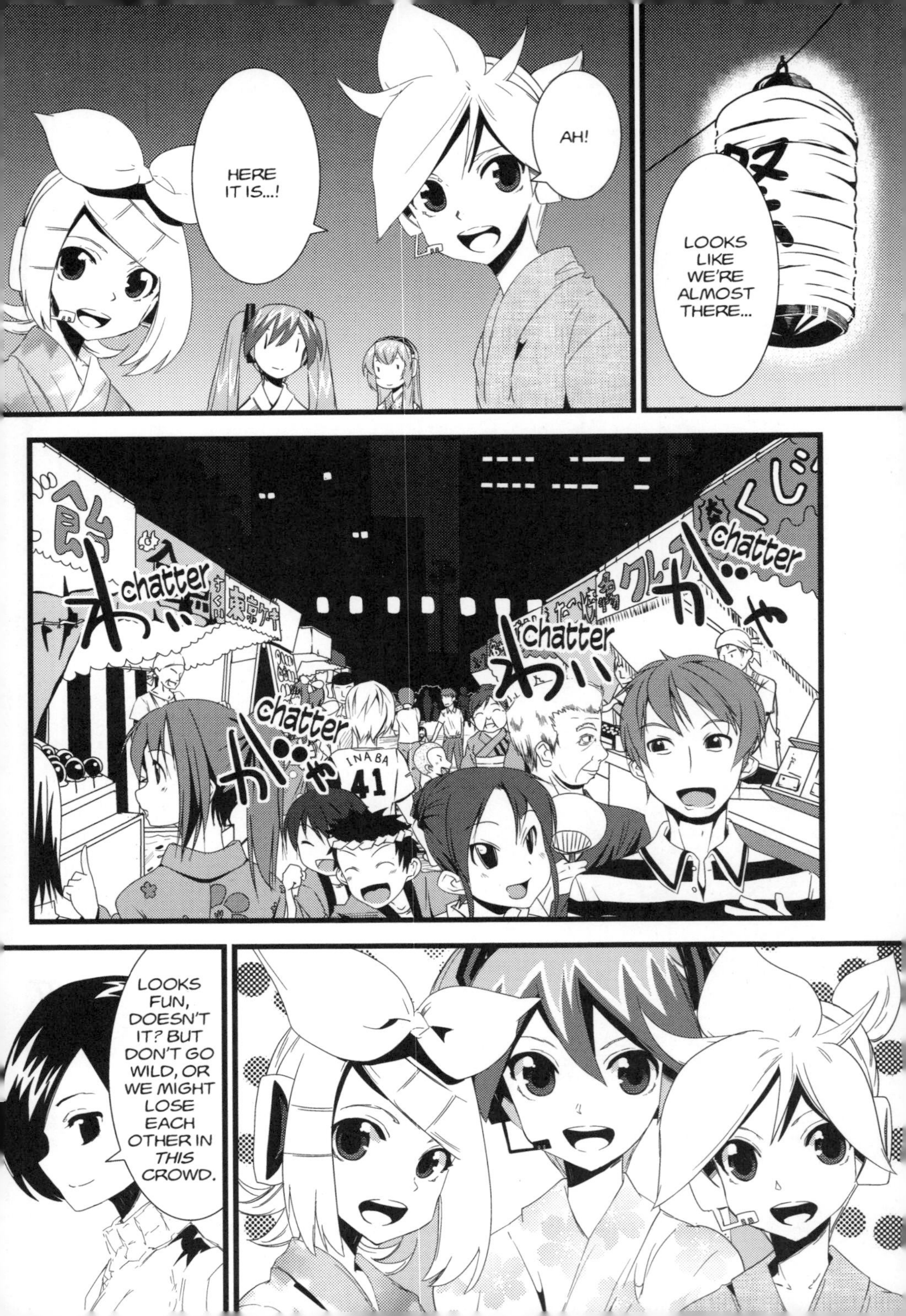
LOOKS LIKE WE'RE ALMOST THERE...
AH!
HERE IT IS...!
chatter
chatter
chatter
chatter
INABA
41
LOOKS FUN, DOESN'T IT? BUT DON'T GO WILD, OR WE MIGHT LOSE EACH OTHER IN *THIS* CROWD.

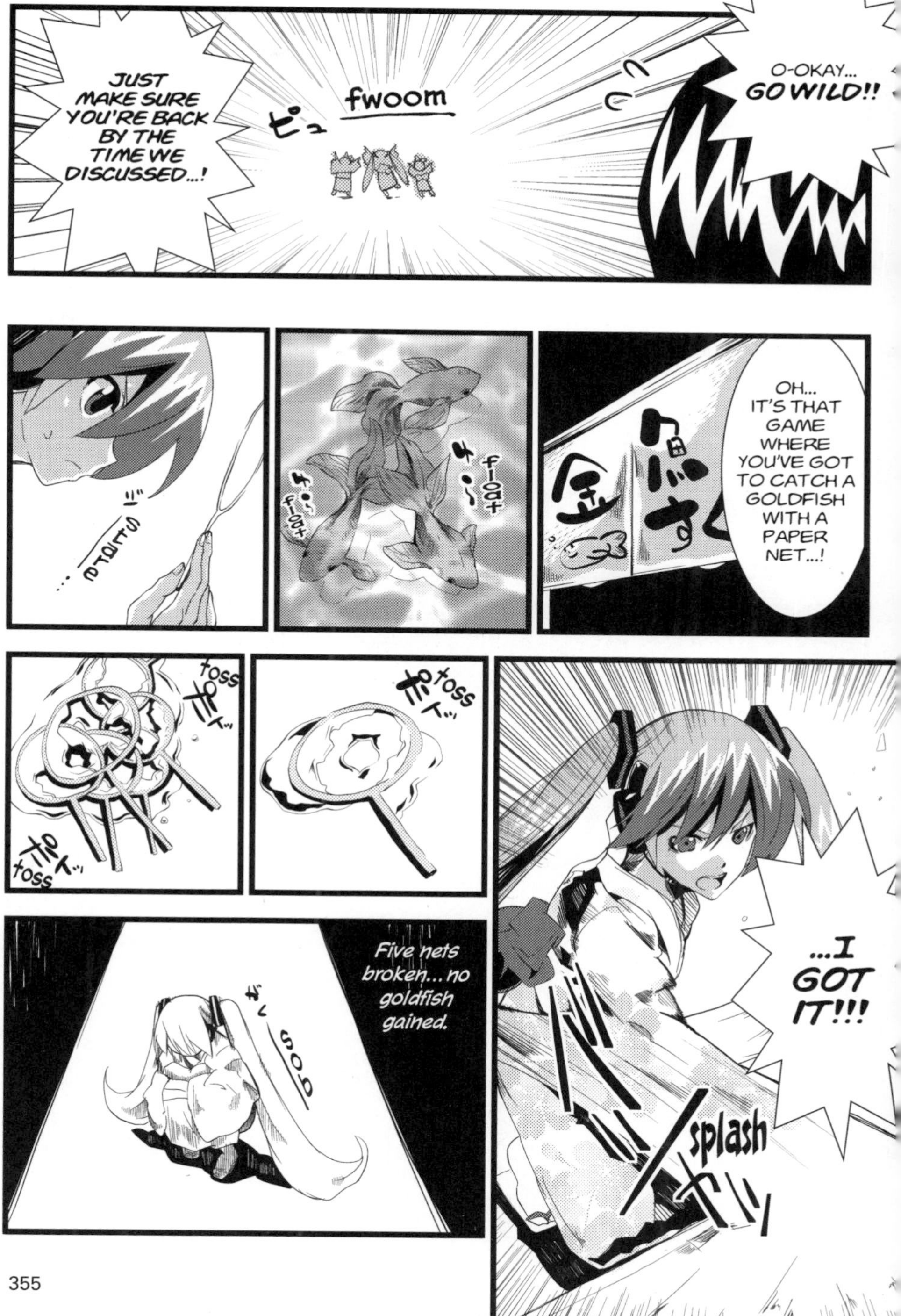
O-OKAY... GO WILD!!
fwoom
JUST MAKE SURE YOU'RE BACK BY THE TIME WE DISCUSSED...!
OH... IT'S THAT GAME WHERE YOU'VE GOT TO CATCH A GOLDFISH WITH A PAPER NET...!
float
float
glare...
...I GOT IT!!!
splash
toss
toss
toss
Five nets broken... no goldfish gained.
sob

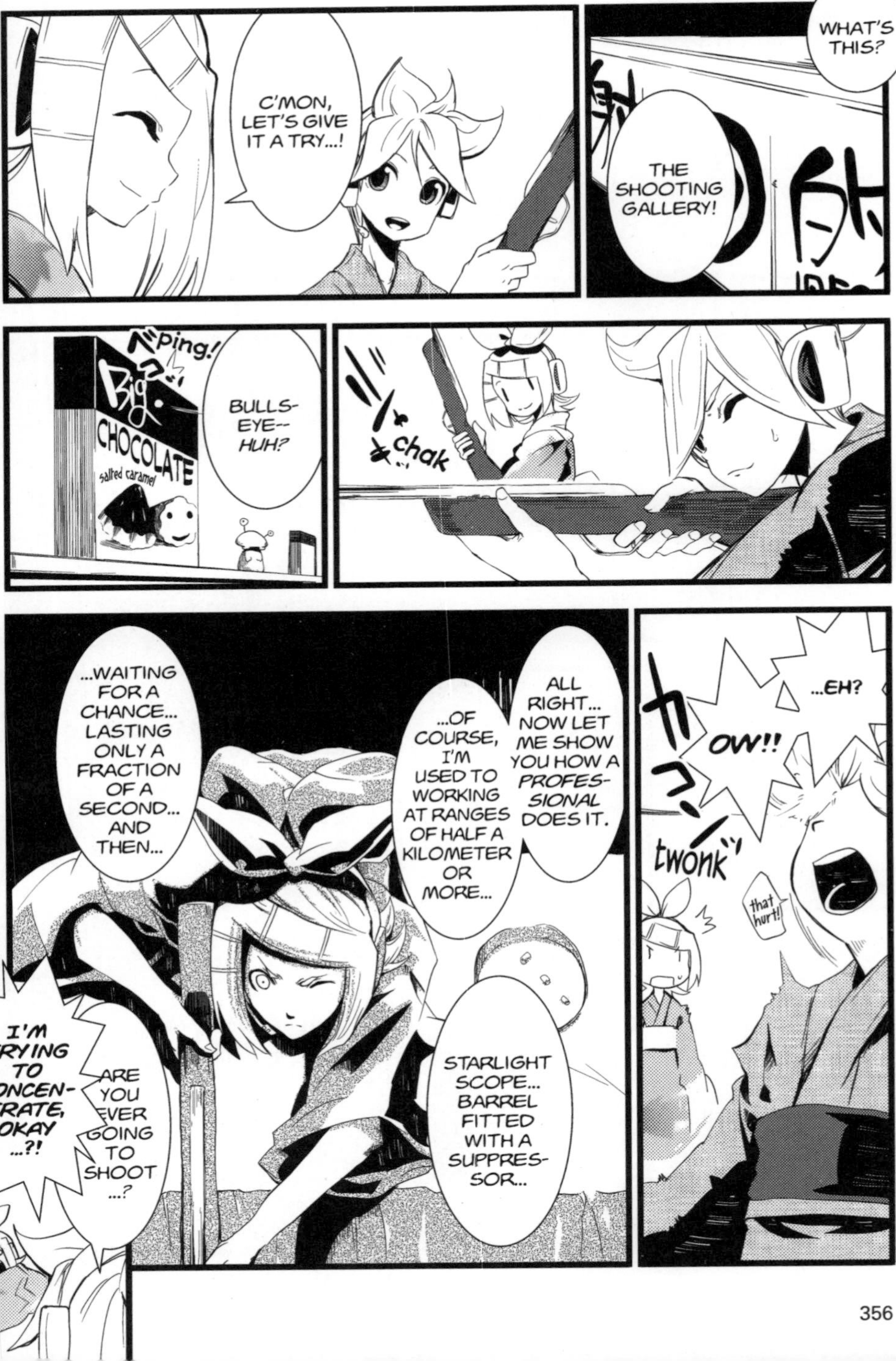
WHAT'S THIS?
THE SHOOTING GALLERY!
C'MON, LET'S GIVE IT A TRY...!
chak
ping!
BULLS-EYE--HUH?
Big
CHOCOLATE
salted caramel
...EH?
OW!!
twonk
that hurt!
ALL RIGHT... NOW LET ME SHOW YOU HOW A PROFESSIONAL DOES IT.
...OF COURSE, I'M USED TO WORKING AT RANGES OF HALF A KILOMETER OR MORE...
...WAITING FOR A CHANCE... LASTING ONLY A FRACTION OF A SECOND... AND THEN...
STARLIGHT SCOPE... BARREL FITTED WITH A SUPPRESSOR...
ARE YOU EVER GOING TO SHOOT ...?
I'M TRYING TO CONCENTRATE, OKAY ...?!

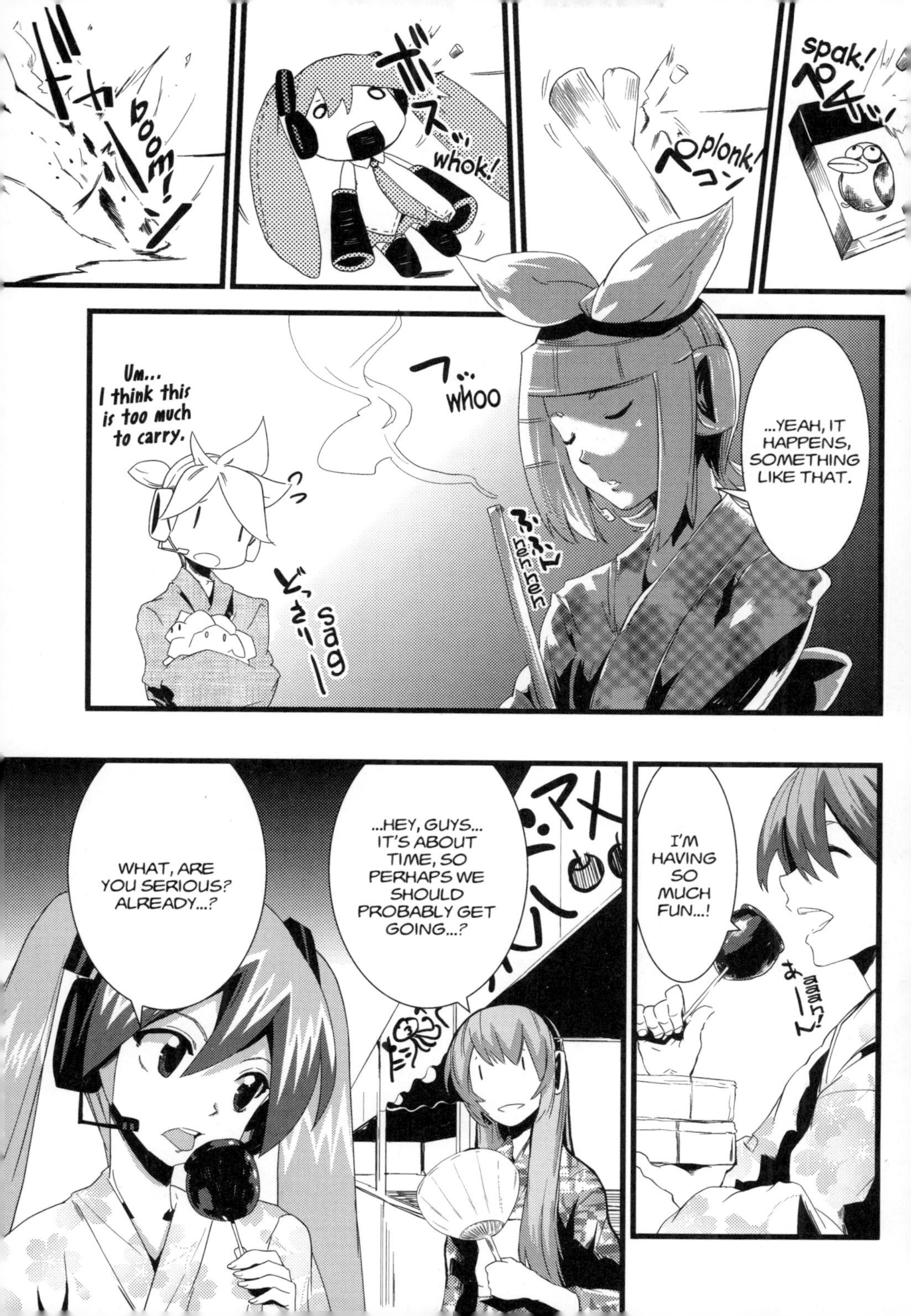

spak!
plonk!
whok!
boom!
...YEAH, IT HAPPENS, SOMETHING LIKE THAT.
whoo
sag
Um... I think this is too much to carry.
I'M HAVING SO MUCH FUN...!
...HEY, GUYS... IT'S ABOUT TIME, SO PERHAPS WE SHOULD PROBABLY GET GOING...?
WHAT, ARE YOU SERIOUS? ALREADY...?

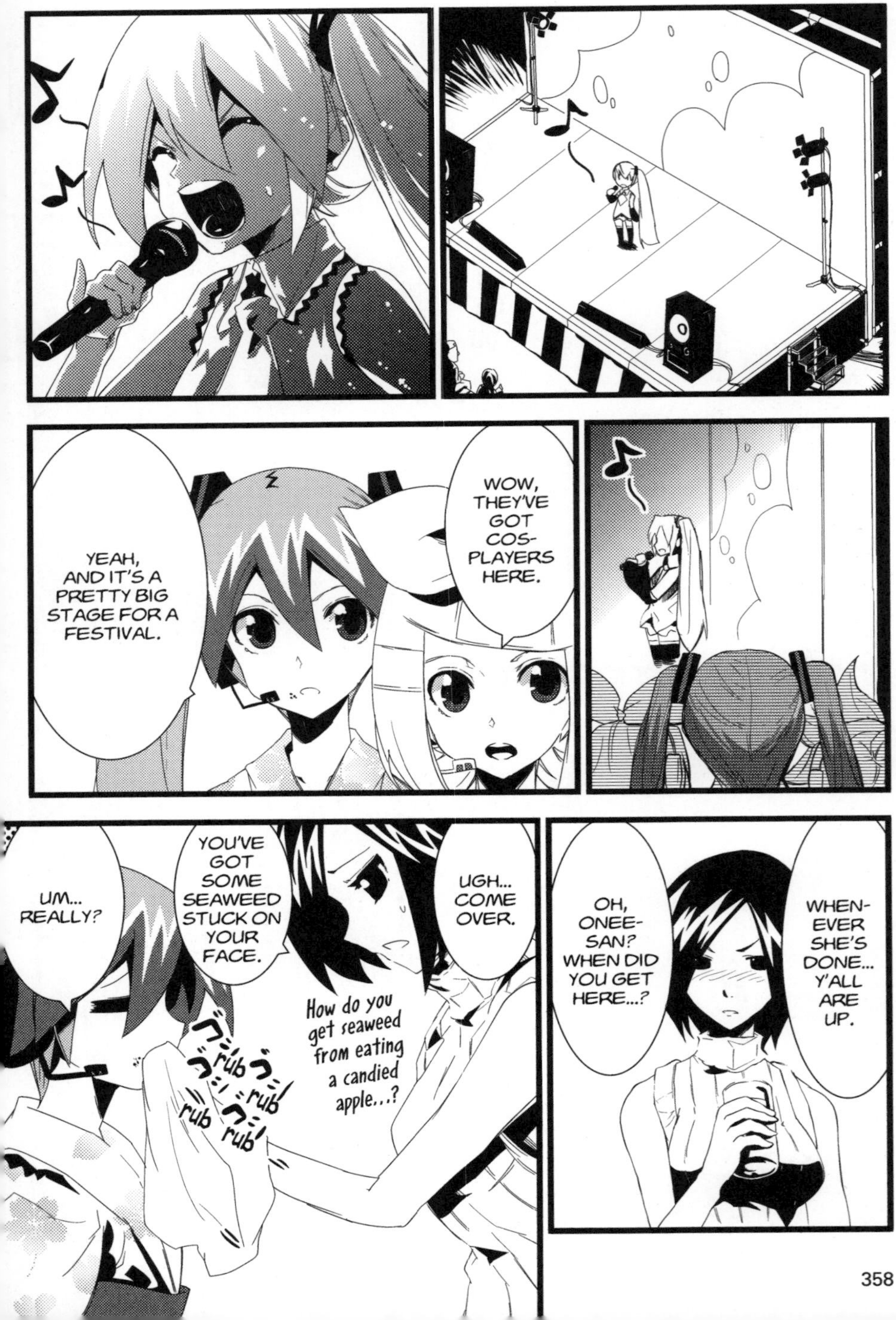
WOW, THEY'VE GOT COS-PLAYERS HERE.
YEAH, AND IT'S A PRETTY BIG STAGE FOR A FESTIVAL.
WHEN-EVER SHE'S DONE... Y'ALL ARE UP.
OH, ONEE-SAN? WHEN DID YOU GET HERE...?
UGH... COME OVER.
YOU'VE GOT SOME SEAWEED STUCK ON YOUR FACE.
UM... REALLY?
How do you get seaweed from eating a candied apple...?
rub rub rub rub

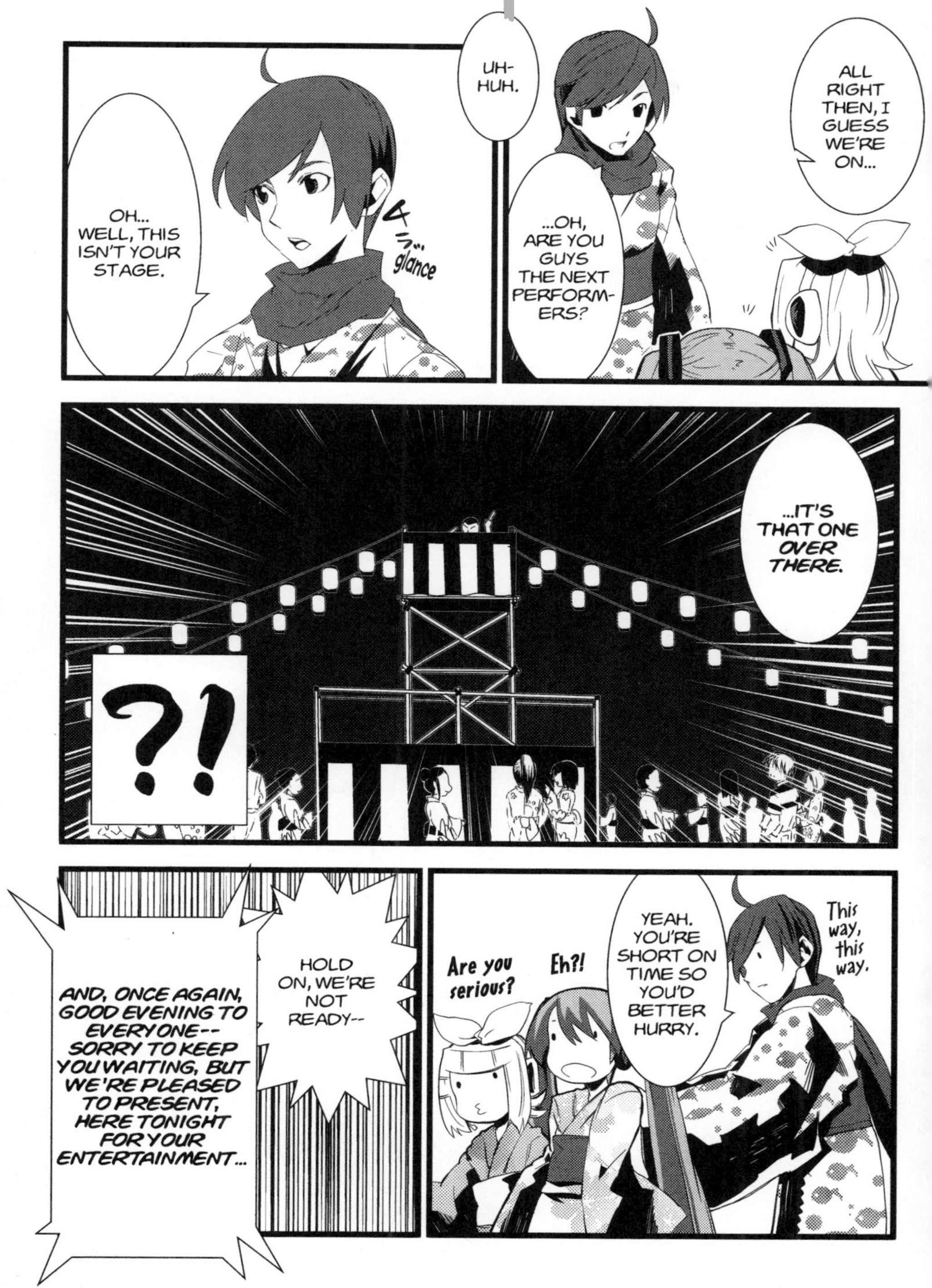
ALL RIGHT THEN, I GUESS WE'RE ON...
...OH, ARE YOU GUYS THE NEXT PERFORMERS?
UH-HUH.
glance
OH... WELL, THIS ISN'T YOUR STAGE.
...IT'S THAT ONE OVER THERE.
?!
This way, this way.
YEAH. YOU'RE SHORT ON TIME SO YOU'D BETTER HURRY.
Eh?!
Are you serious?
HOLD ON, WE'RE NOT READY--
AND, ONCE AGAIN, GOOD EVENING TO EVERYONE-- SORRY TO KEEP YOU WAITING, BUT WE'RE PLEASED TO PRESENT, HERE TONIGHT FOR YOUR ENTERTAINMENT...

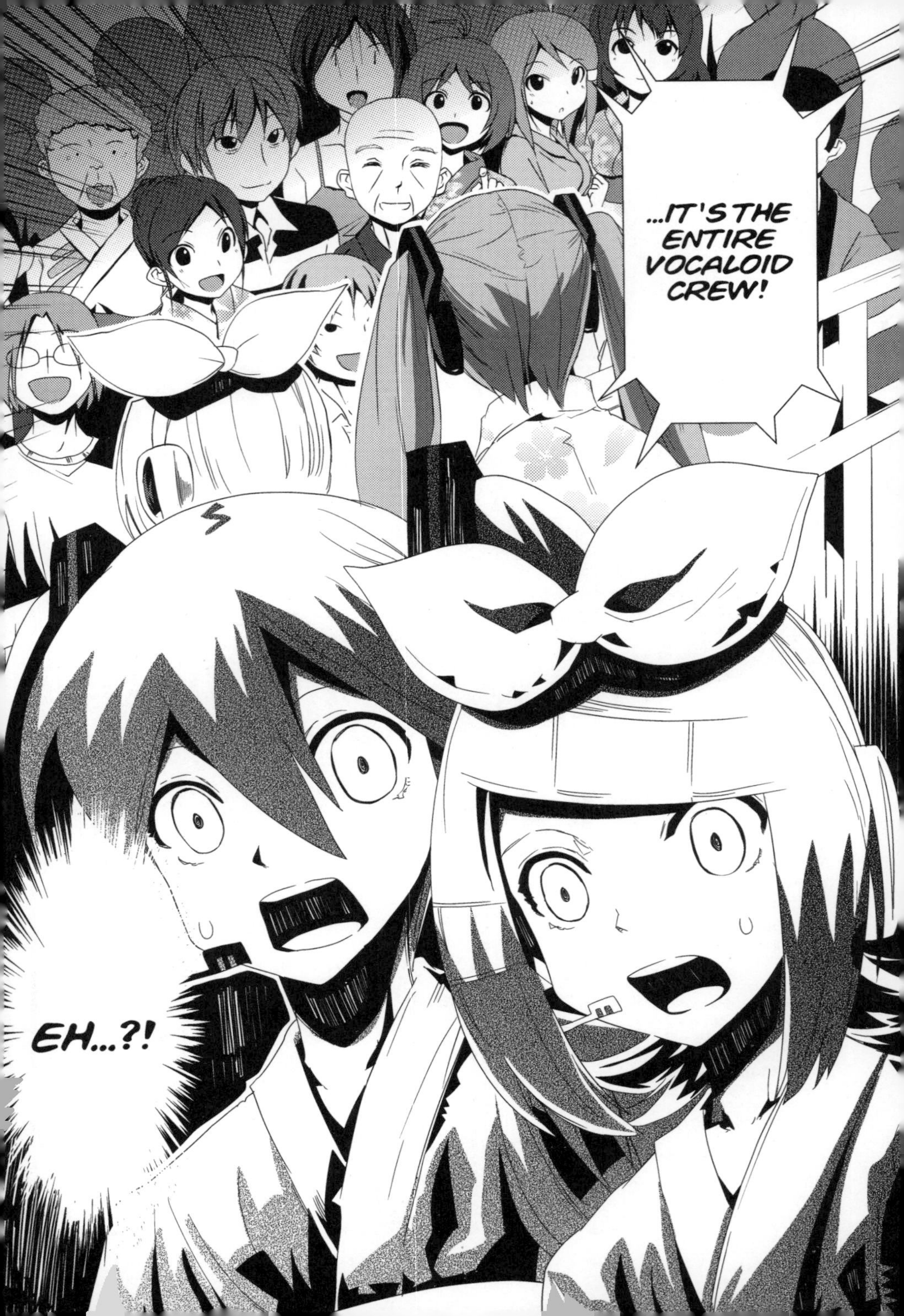
...IT'S THE ENTIRE VOCALOID CREW!
EH...?!

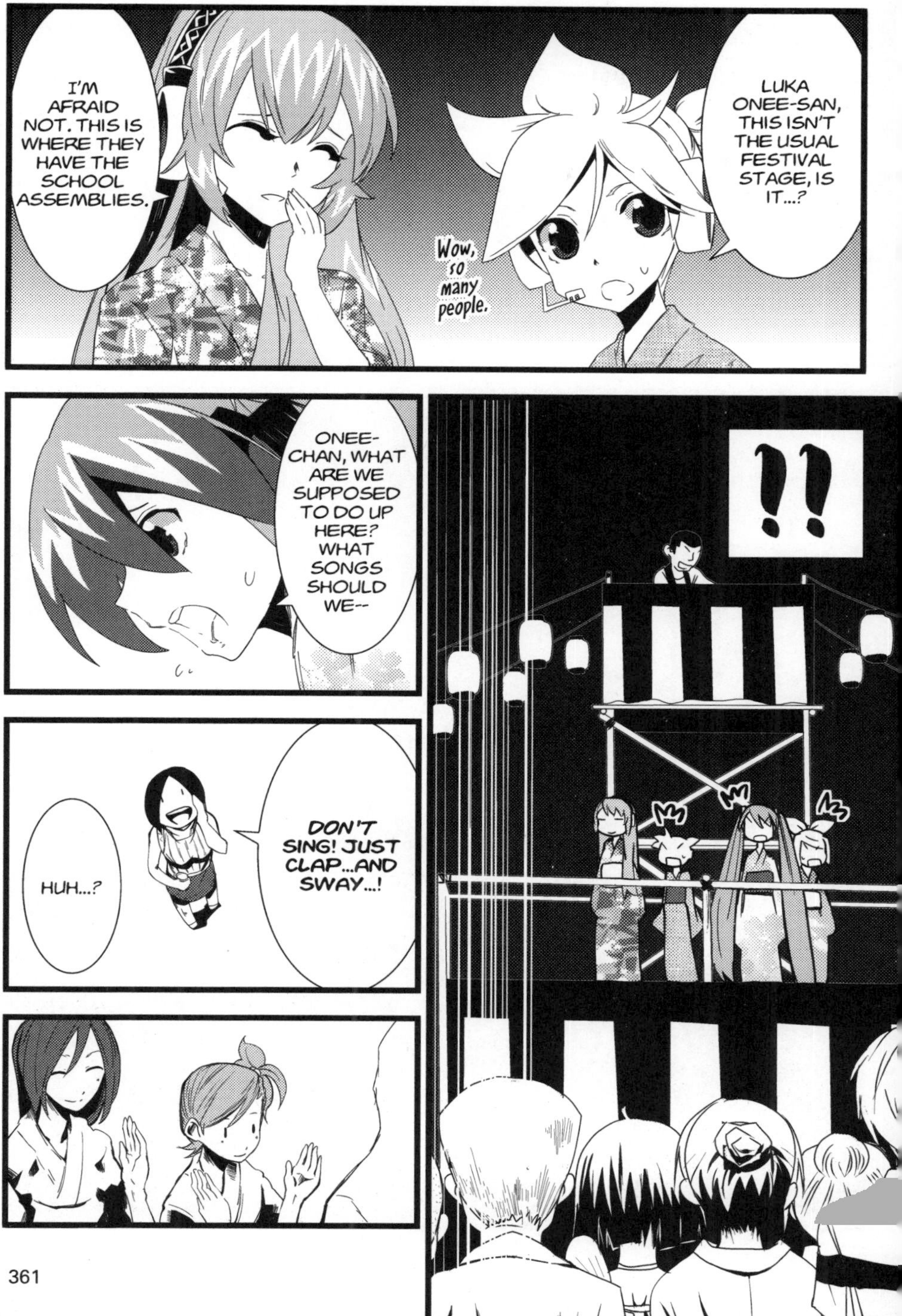
LUKA ONEE-SAN, THIS ISN'T THE USUAL FESTIVAL STAGE, IS IT...?
Wow, so many people.
I'M AFRAID NOT. THIS IS WHERE THEY HAVE THE SCHOOL ASSEMBLIES.
!!
ONEE-CHAN, WHAT ARE WE SUPPOSED TO DO UP HERE? WHAT SONGS SHOULD WE--
DON'T SING! JUST CLAP...AND SWAY...!
HUH...?

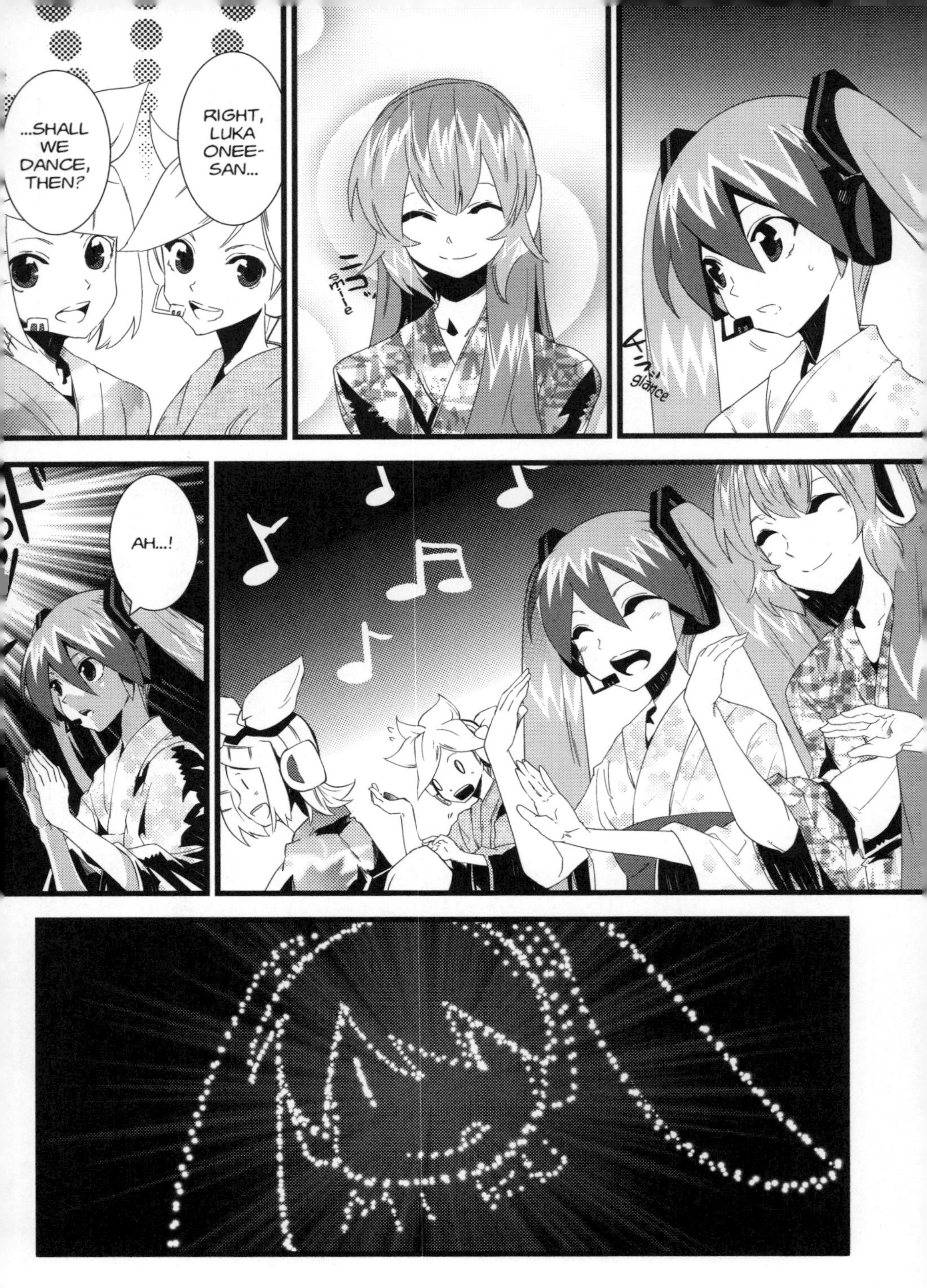
glance
smile
RIGHT, LUKA ONEE-SAN...
...SHALL WE DANCE, THEN?
AH...!

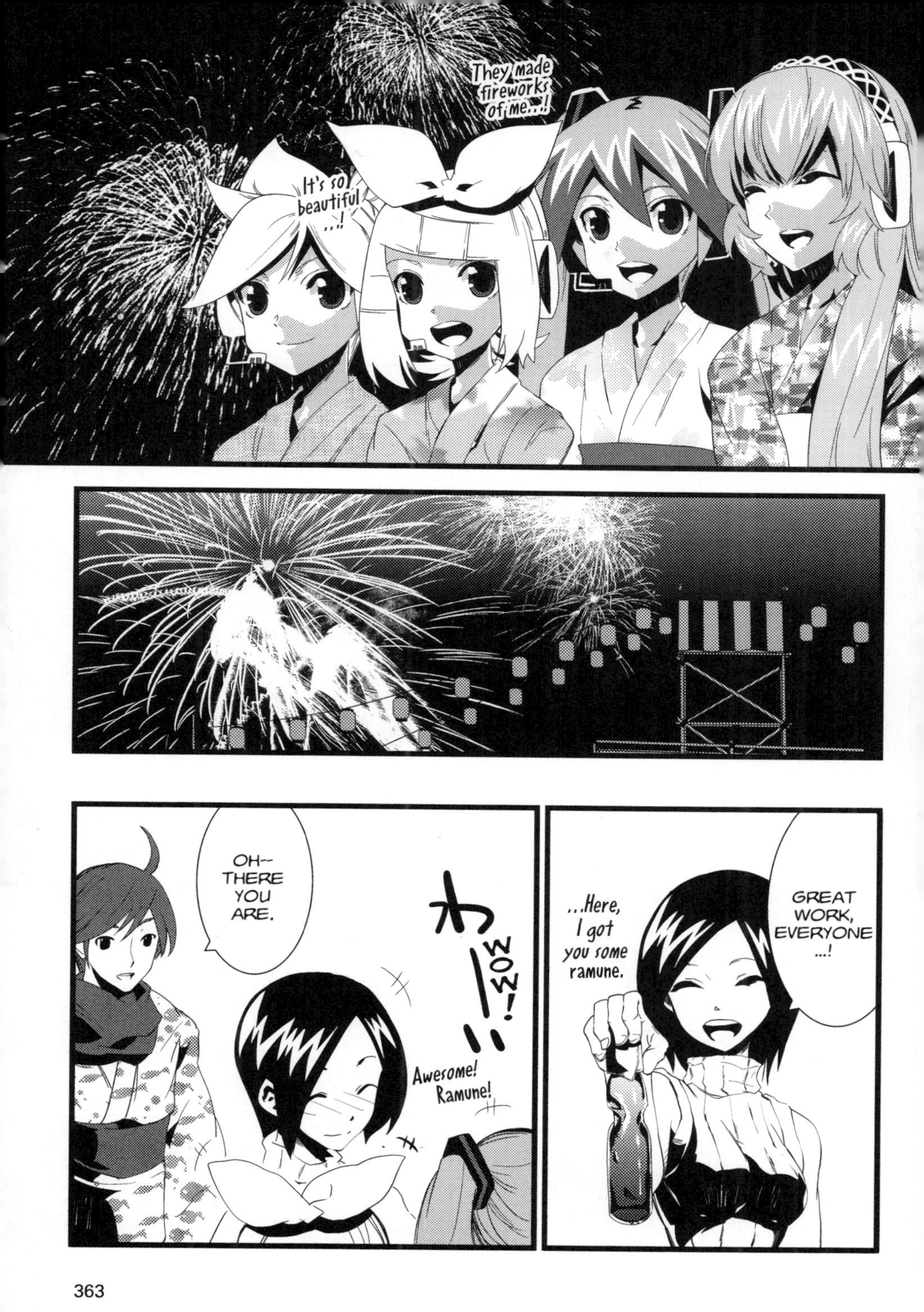
They made fireworks of me...!
It's so beautiful ...!
GREAT WORK, EVERYONE ...!
...Here, I got you some ramune.
わー!!
WOW!
OH-- THERE YOU ARE.
Awesome! Ramune!

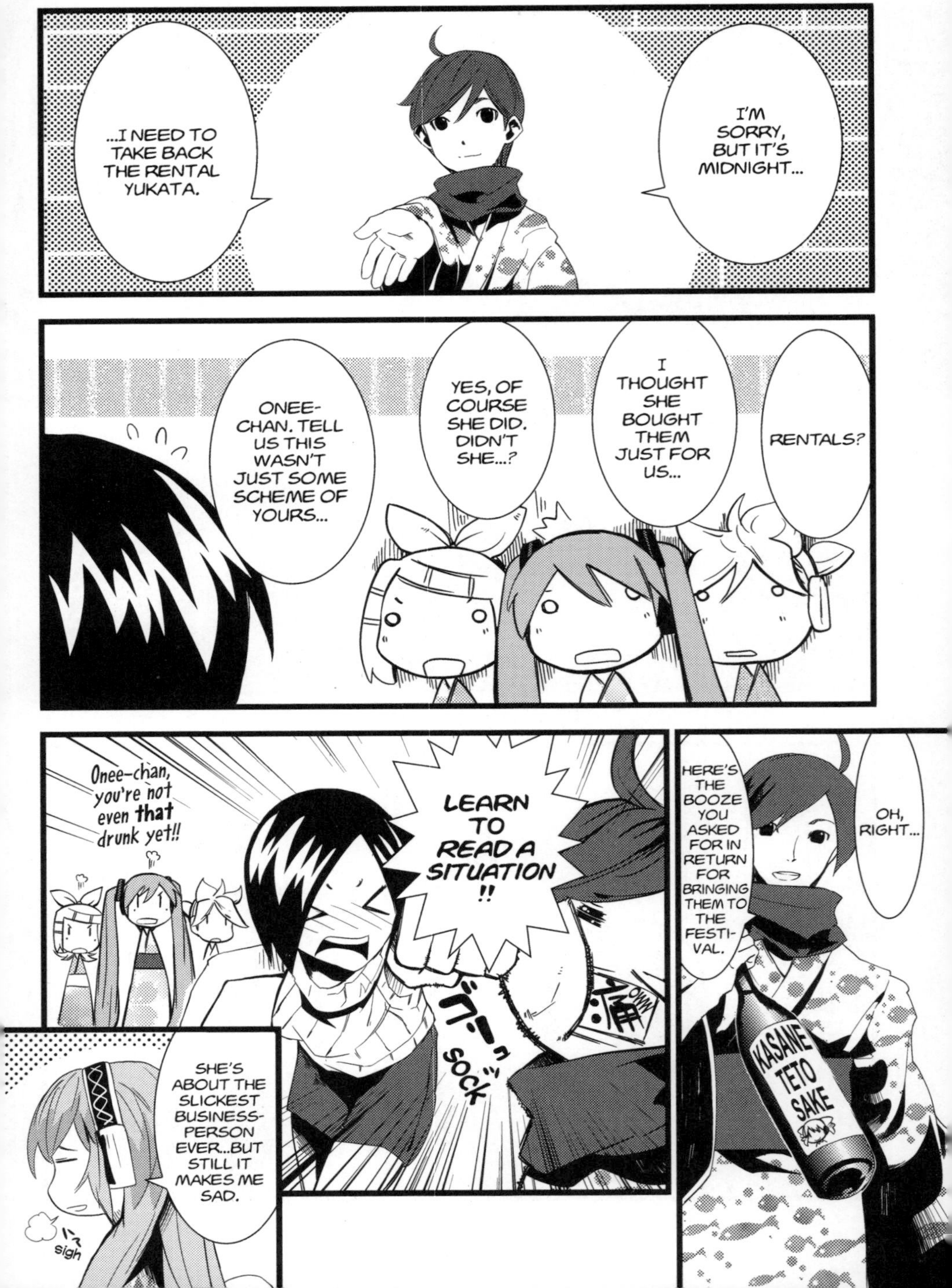

I'M SORRY, BUT IT'S MIDNIGHT...
...I NEED TO TAKE BACK THE RENTAL YUKATA.
RENTALS?
I THOUGHT SHE BOUGHT THEM JUST FOR US...
YES, OF COURSE SHE DID. DIDN'T SHE...?
ONEE-CHAN. TELL US THIS WASN'T JUST SOME SCHEME OF YOURS...
OH, RIGHT...
HERE'S THE BOOZE YOU ASKED FOR IN RETURN FOR BRINGING THEM TO THE FESTIVAL.
KASANE TETO SAKE
LEARN TO READ A SITUATION!!
SOCK
Onee-chan, you're not even **that** drunk yet!!
SHE'S ABOUT THE SLICKEST BUSINESS-PERSON EVER...BUT STILL IT MAKES ME SAD.
sigh

(22nd SONG) SPORTS DAY MIX

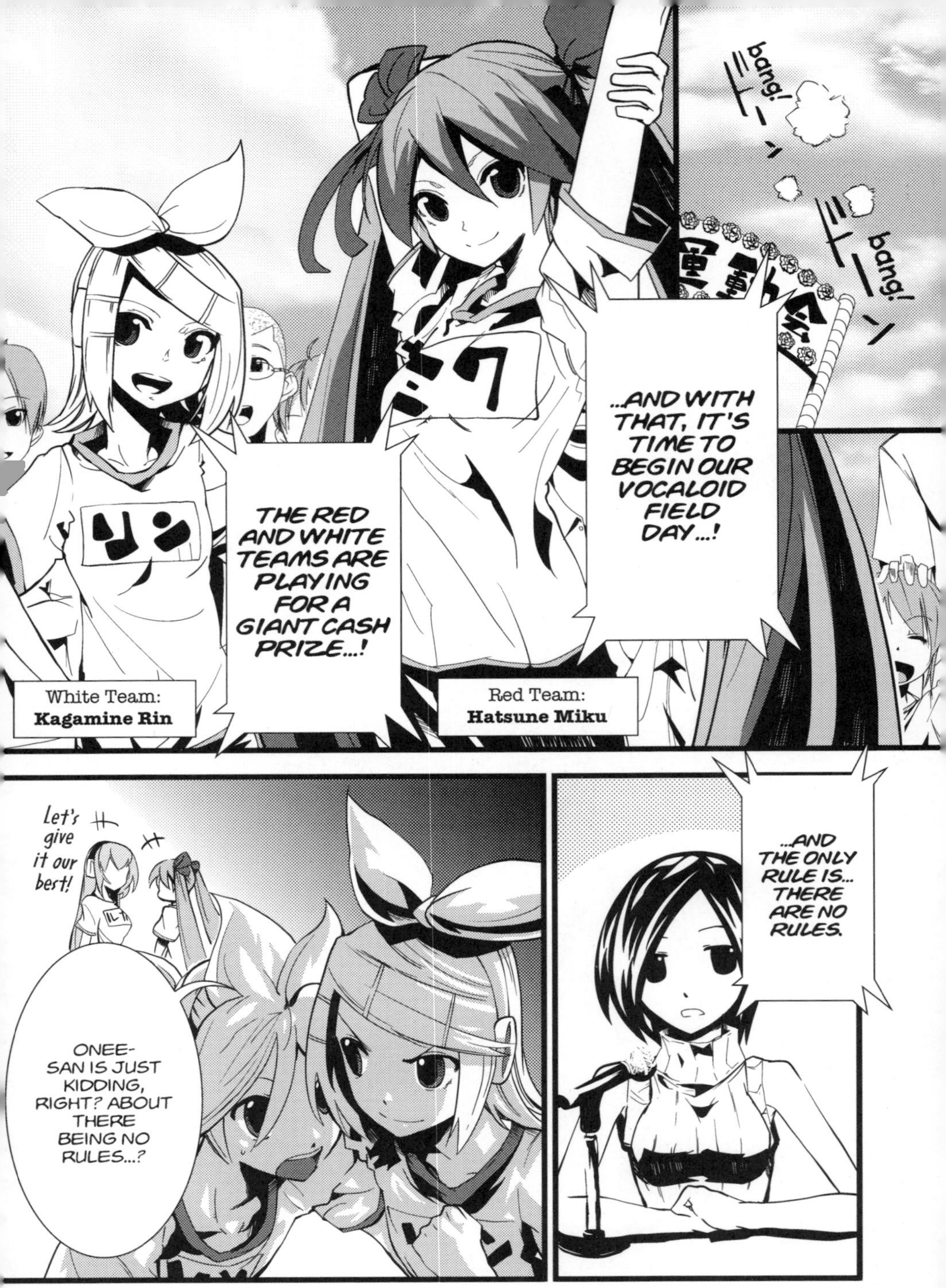
bang! bang!
...AND WITH THAT, IT'S TIME TO BEGIN OUR VOCALOID FIELD DAY...!
Red Team: **Hatsune Miku**
THE RED AND WHITE TEAMS ARE PLAYING FOR A GIANT CASH PRIZE...!
White Team: **Kagamine Rin**
...AND THE ONLY RULE IS... THERE ARE NO RULES.
Let's give it our best!
ONEE-SAN IS JUST KIDDING, RIGHT? ABOUT THERE BEING NO RULES...?

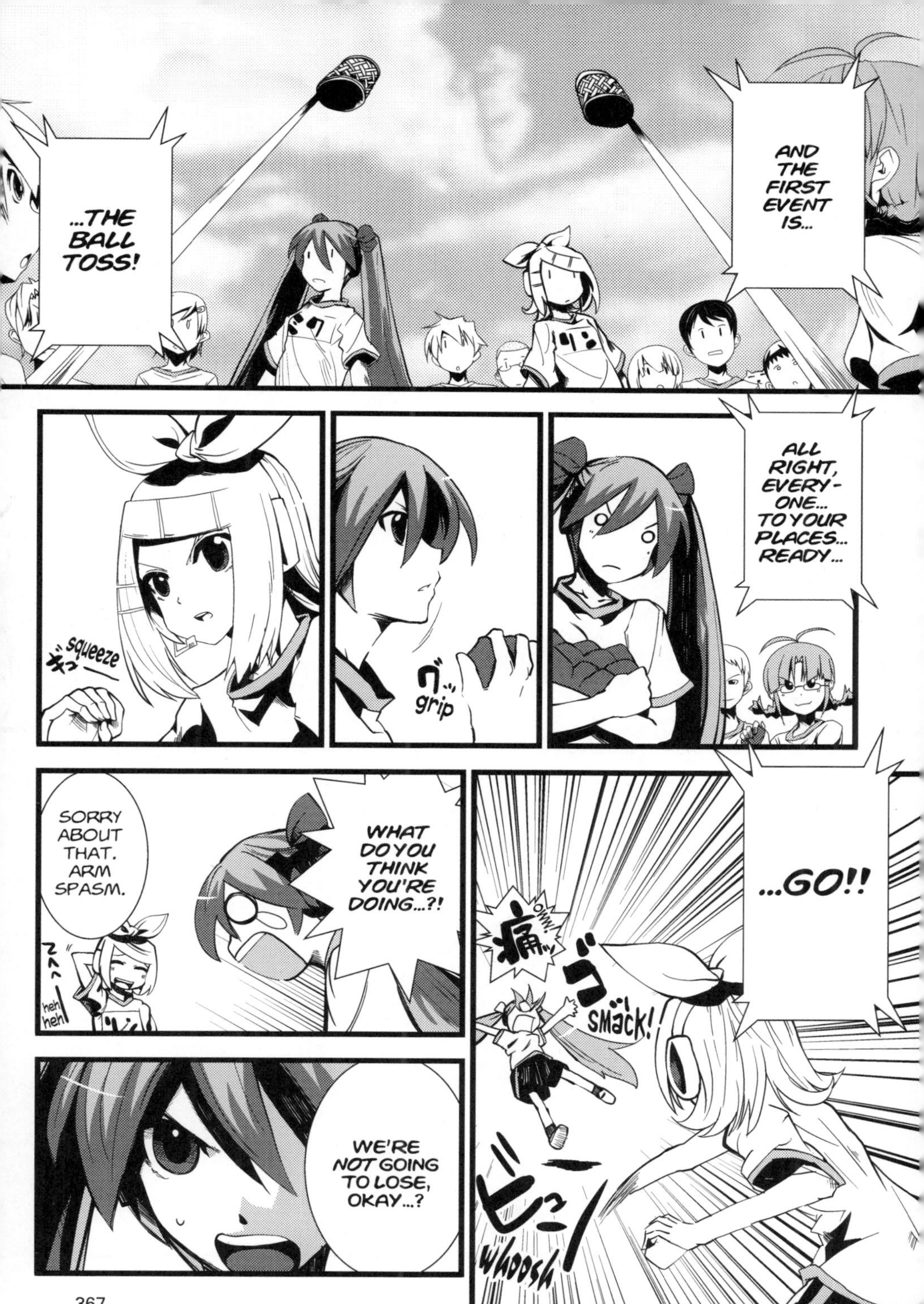
AND THE FIRST EVENT IS...
...THE BALL TOSS!
ALL RIGHT, EVERYONE... TO YOUR PLACES... READY...
グッ grip
ギュッ squeeze
...GO!!
痛ッ OW!
ゴッ SMACK!
ビュッ WHOOSH
WHAT DO YOU THINK YOU'RE DOING...?!
SORRY ABOUT THAT. ARM SPASM.
えへへ heh heh
WE'RE NOT GOING TO LOSE, OKAY...?

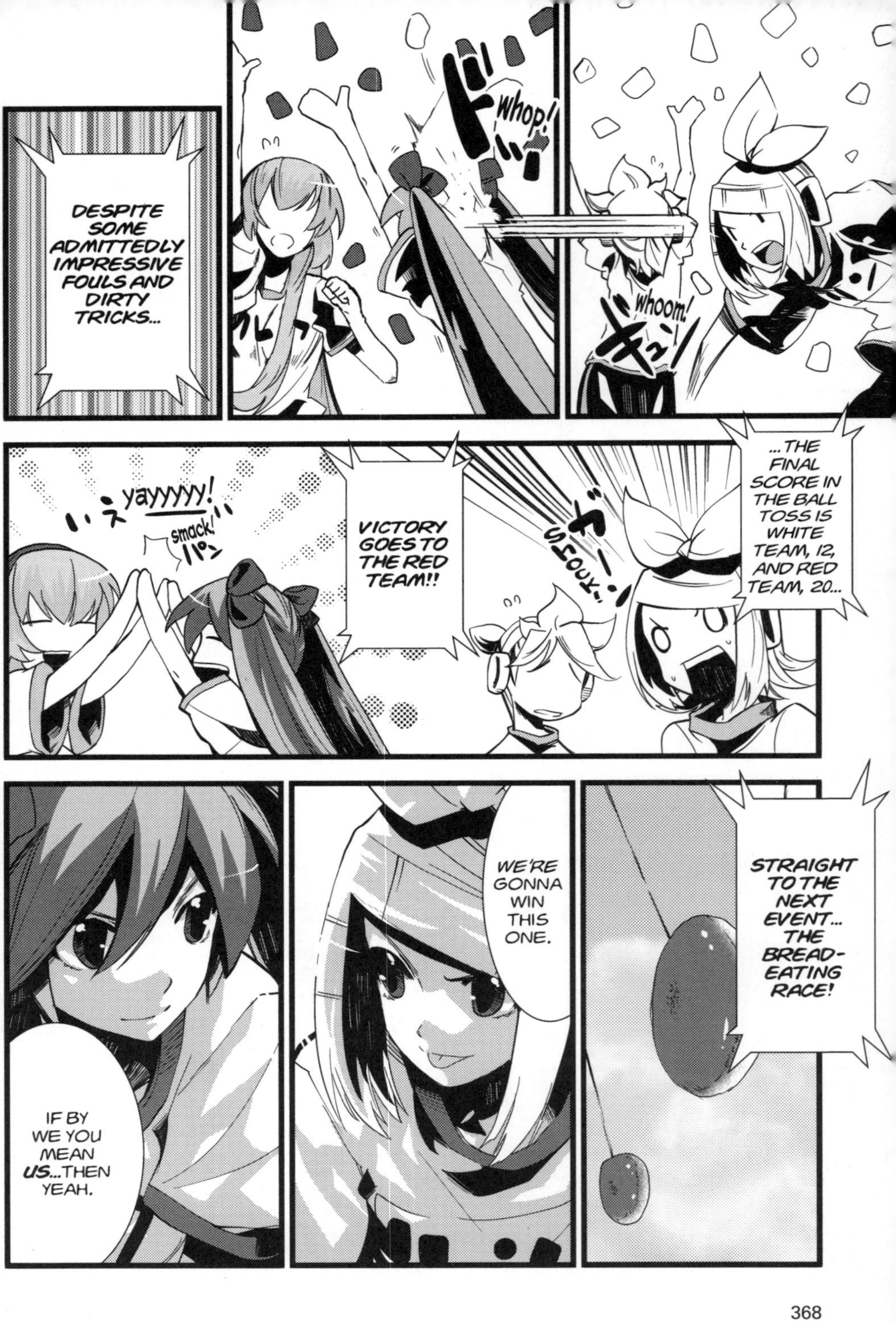
whoom!
whop!
DESPITE SOME ADMITTEDLY IMPRESSIVE FOULS AND DIRTY TRICKS...
...THE FINAL SCORE IN THE BALL TOSS IS WHITE TEAM, 12, AND RED TEAM, 20...
scoot!!
VICTORY GOES TO THE RED TEAM!!
yayyyyy!
smack!
STRAIGHT TO THE NEXT EVENT... THE BREAD-EATING RACE!
WE'RE GONNA WIN THIS ONE.
IF BY WE YOU MEAN US...THEN YEAH.

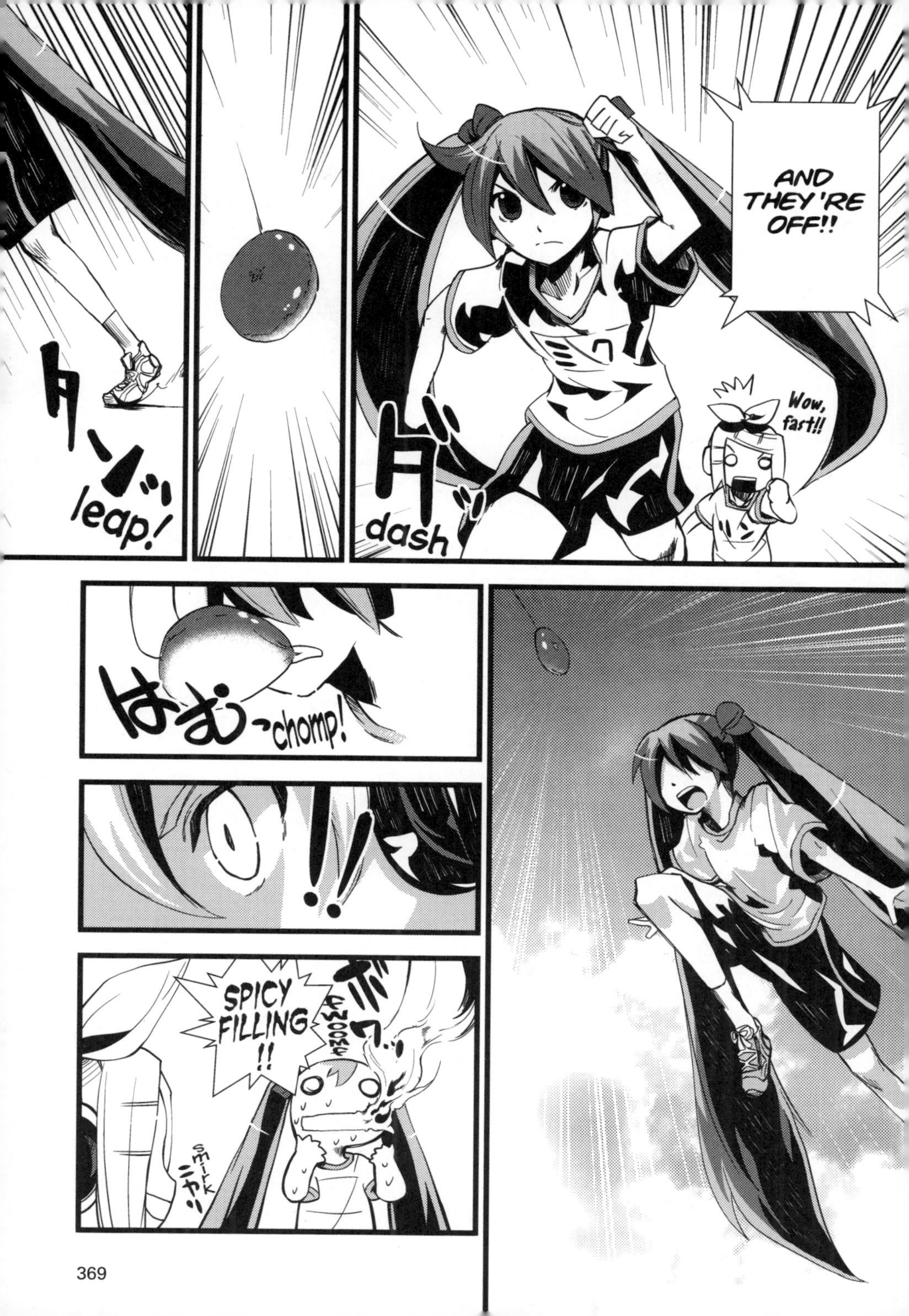
AND THEY'RE OFF!!
Wow, fast!!
dash
タンッ
leap!
はむっ
chomp!
!!
SPICY FILLING!!
FWOOMF
smirk
ニヤッ

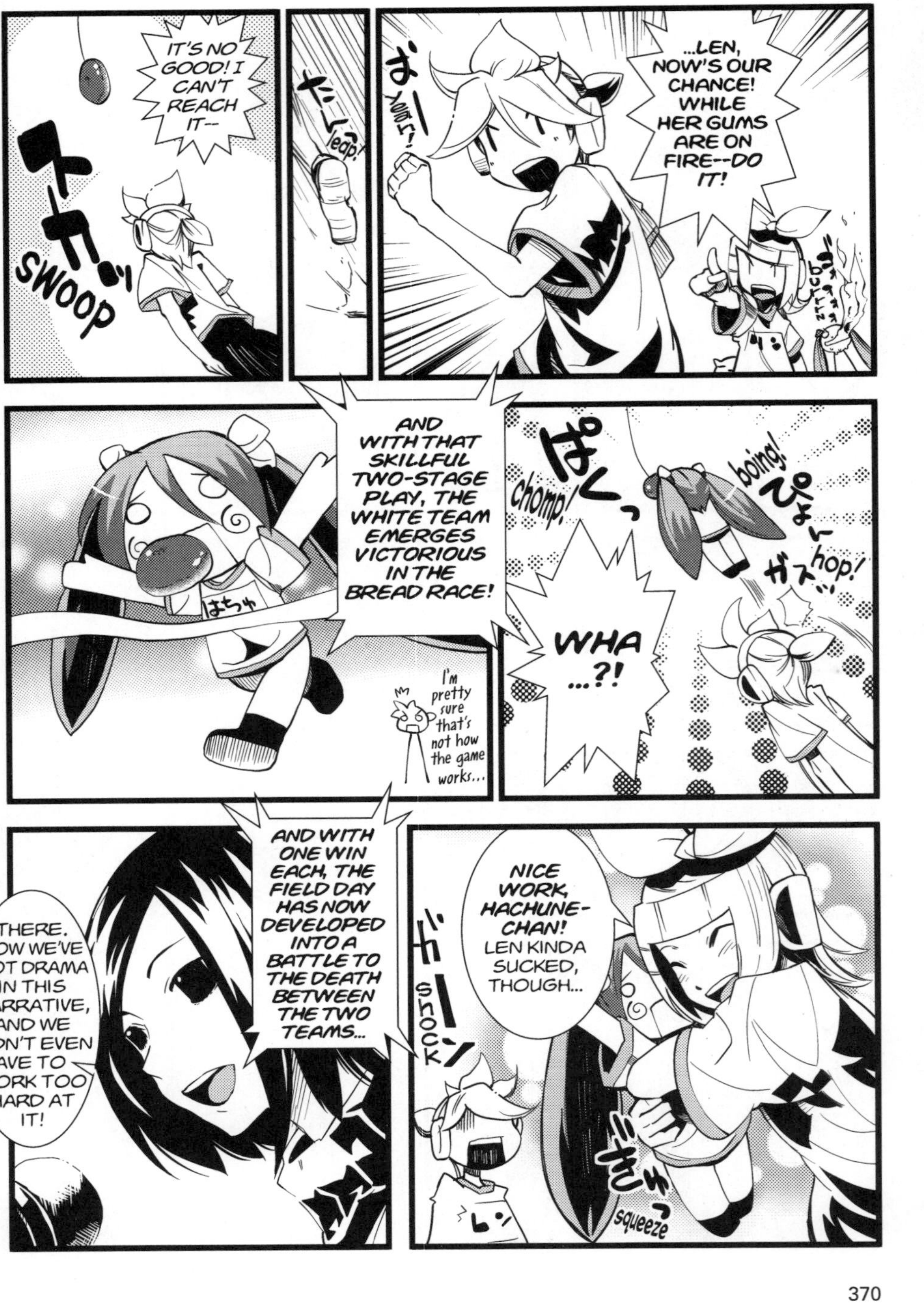
...LEN, NOW'S OUR CHANCE! WHILE HER GUMS ARE ON FIRE--DO IT!
leap!
IT'S NO GOOD! I CAN'T REACH IT--
SWOOP
chomp!
boing!
hop!
WHA ...?!
AND WITH THAT SKILLFUL TWO-STAGE PLAY, THE WHITE TEAM EMERGES VICTORIOUS IN THE BREAD RACE!
はちゅ
I'm pretty sure that's not how the game works...
NICE WORK, HACHUNE-CHAN! LEN KINDA SUCKED, THOUGH...
shock
squeeze
AND WITH ONE WIN EACH, THE FIELD DAY HAS NOW DEVELOPED INTO A BATTLE TO THE DEATH BETWEEN THE TWO TEAMS...
THERE. NOW WE'VE GOT DRAMA IN THIS NARRATIVE, AND WE DIDN'T EVEN HAVE TO WORK TOO HARD AT IT!

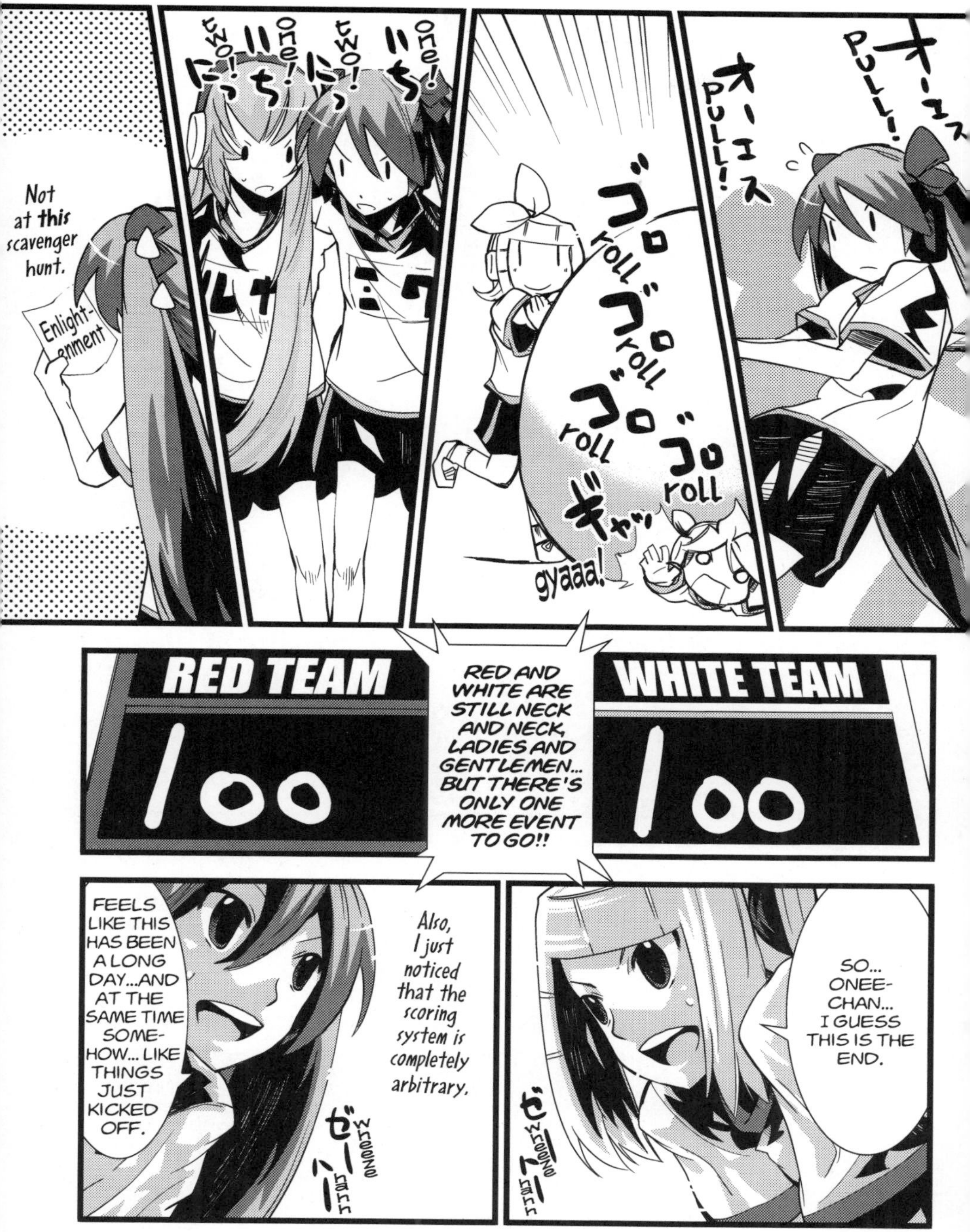

オーエス PULL!
オーエス PULL!
ゴロ roll ゴロ roll ゴロ roll ゴロ roll
ギャッ gyaaa!
いち one!
にっ two!
いち one!
にっ two!
Not at this scavenger hunt.
Enlight-enment
WHITE TEAM
100
RED AND WHITE ARE STILL NECK AND NECK, LADIES AND GENTLEMEN... BUT THERE'S ONLY ONE MORE EVENT TO GO!!
RED TEAM
100
SO... ONEE-CHAN... I GUESS THIS IS THE END.
ぜーはー wheeze harr
FEELS LIKE THIS HAS BEEN A LONG DAY...AND AT THE SAME TIME SOME-HOW... LIKE THINGS JUST KICKED OFF.
Also, I just noticed that the scoring system is completely arbitrary.
ぜーはー wheeze harr

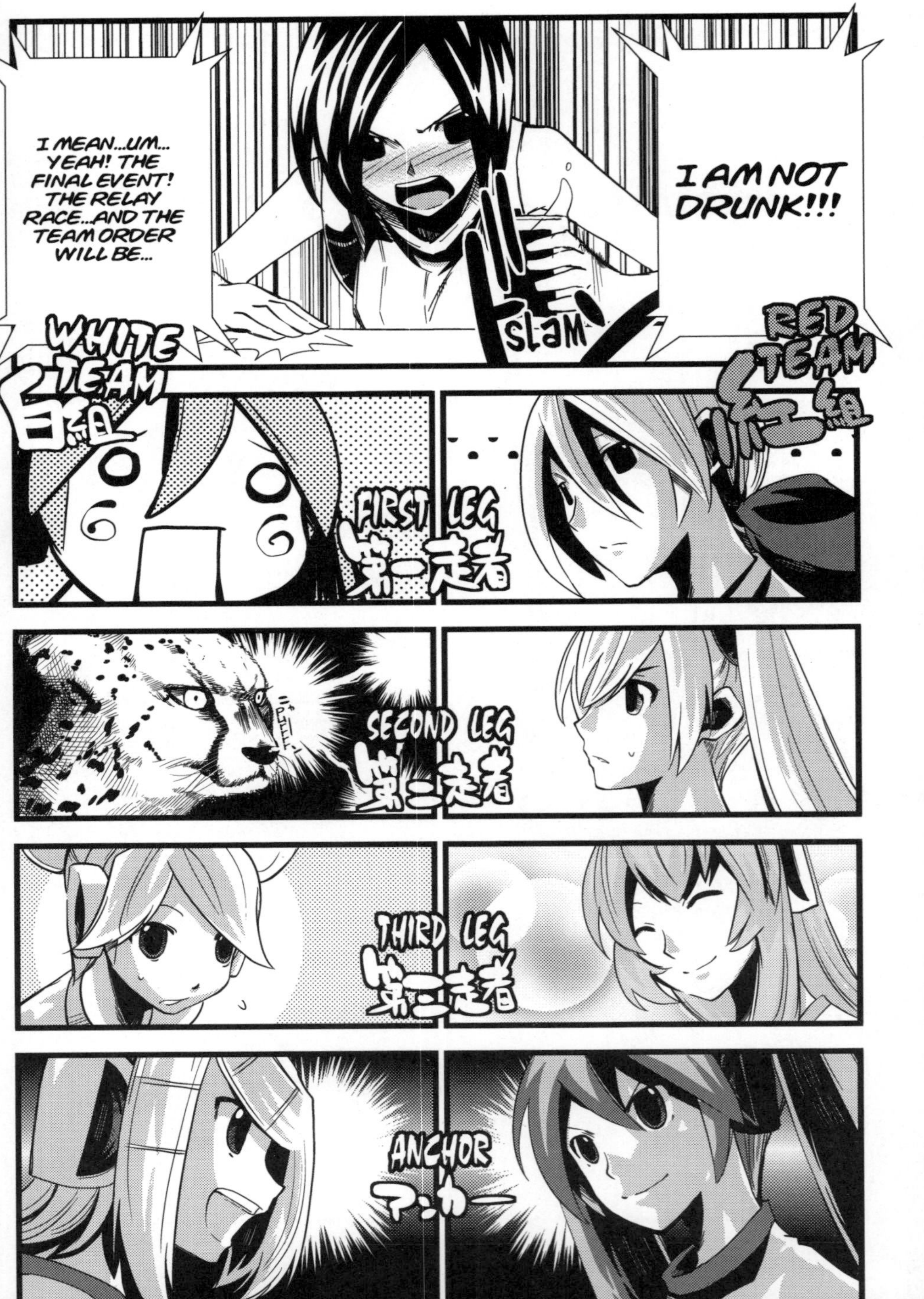

I AM NOT DRUNK!!!
I MEAN...UM... YEAH! THE FINAL EVENT! THE RELAY RACE...AND THE TEAM ORDER WILL BE...
SLAM
RED TEAM
紅組
WHITE TEAM
白組
...
FIRST LEG
第一走者
SECOND LEG
第二走者
ニャ
PUFFFF
THIRD LEG
第三走者
ANCHOR
アンカー

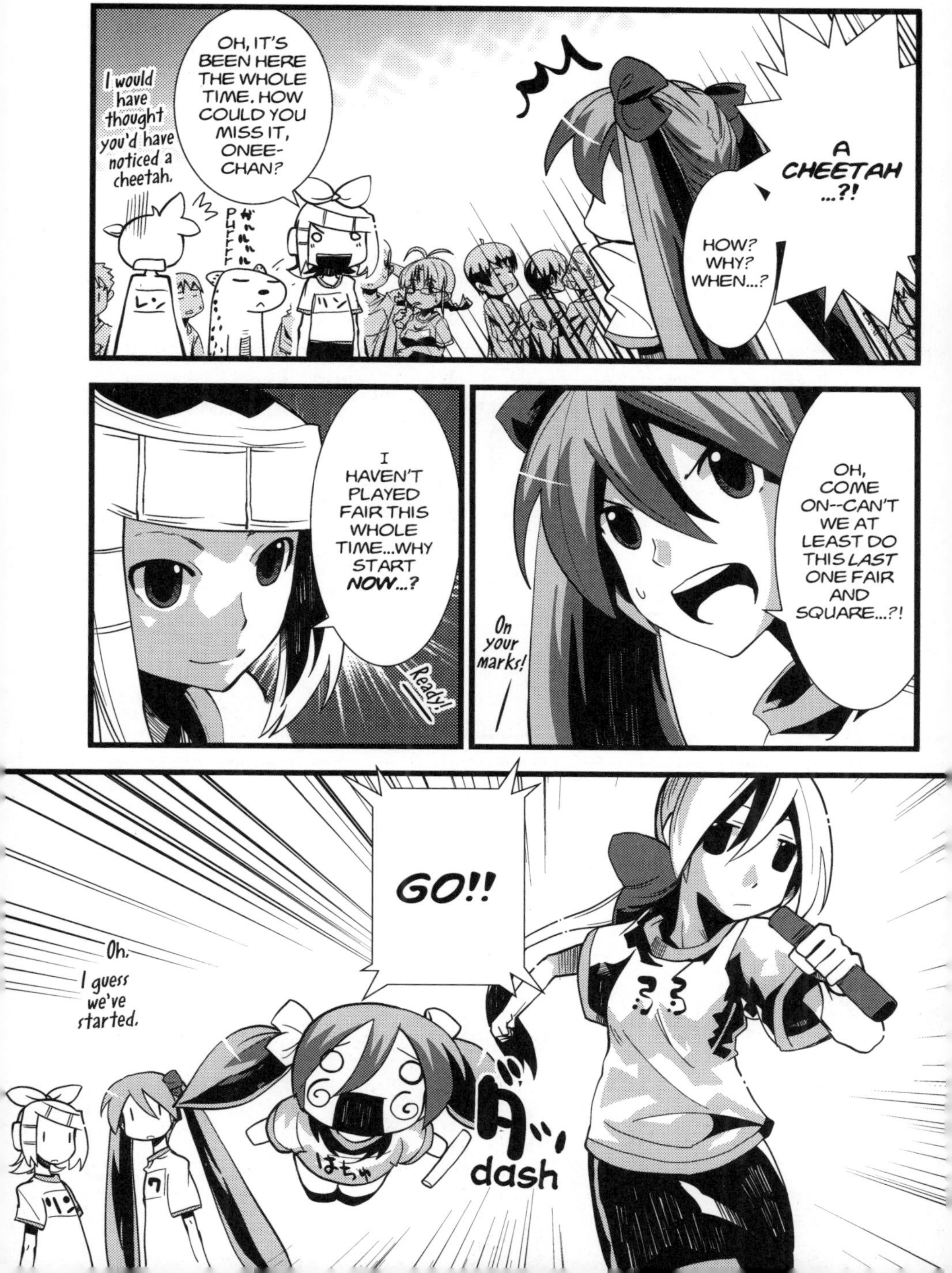
A CHEETAH ...?!
HOW? WHY? WHEN...?
OH, IT'S BEEN HERE THE WHOLE TIME. HOW COULD YOU MISS IT, ONEE-CHAN?
Purrrr
I would have thought you'd have noticed a cheetah.
OH, COME ON--CAN'T WE AT LEAST DO THIS *LAST* ONE FAIR AND SQUARE...?!
On your marks!
I HAVEN'T PLAYED FAIR THIS WHOLE TIME...WHY START *NOW*...?
Ready!
GO!!
dash
Oh.
I guess we've started.

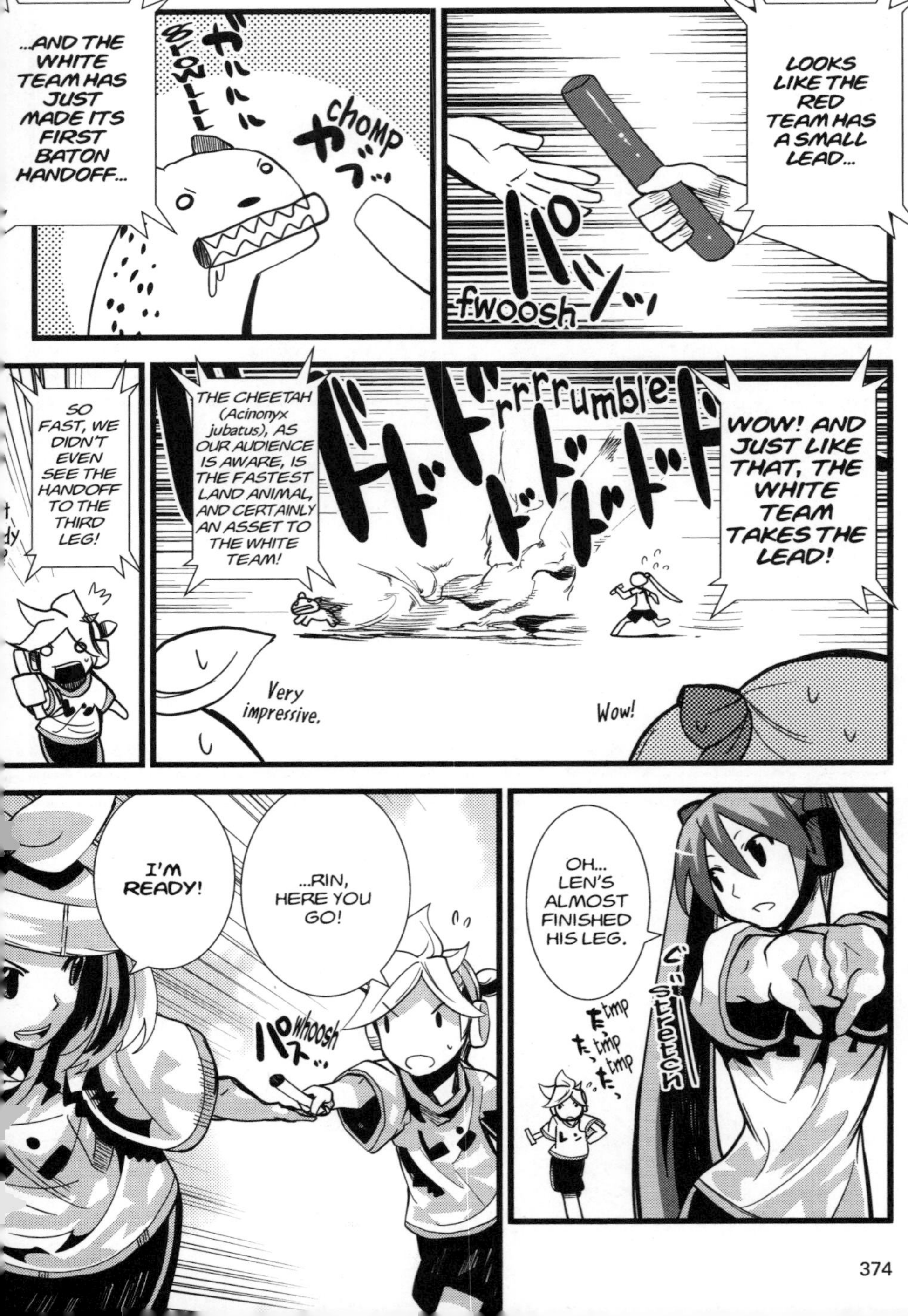
LOOKS LIKE THE RED TEAM HAS A SMALL LEAD...
fwoosh
...AND THE WHITE TEAM HAS JUST MADE ITS FIRST BATON HANDOFF...
GROWLLL
chomp
WOW! AND JUST LIKE THAT, THE WHITE TEAM TAKES THE LEAD!
rrrumble
THE CHEETAH (Acinonyx jubatus), AS OUR AUDIENCE IS AWARE, IS THE FASTEST LAND ANIMAL, AND CERTAINLY AN ASSET TO THE WHITE TEAM!
Wow!
Very impressive.
SO FAST, WE DIDN'T EVEN SEE THE HANDOFF TO THE THIRD LEG!
OH... LEN'S ALMOST FINISHED HIS LEG.
stretch
tmp tmp tmp
...RIN, HERE YOU GO!
I'M READY!
whoosh

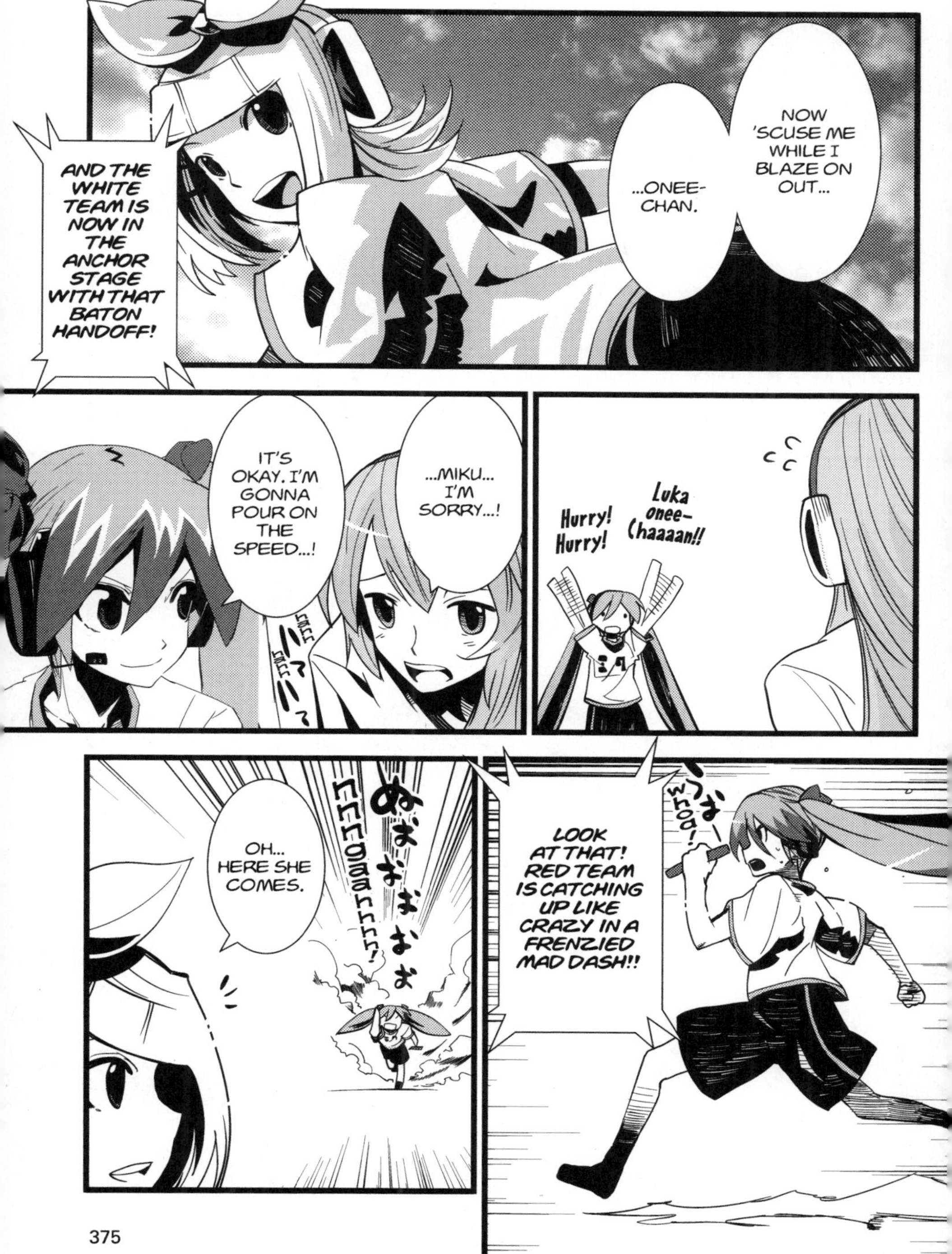
NOW 'SCUSE ME WHILE I BLAZE ON OUT...
...ONEE-CHAN.
AND THE WHITE TEAM IS NOW IN THE ANCHOR STAGE WITH THAT BATON HANDOFF!
Luka onee-Chaaaan!!
Hurry! Hurry!
...MIKU... I'M SORRY...!
IT'S OKAY. I'M GONNA POUR ON THE SPEED...!
whoa!
LOOK AT THAT! RED TEAM IS CATCHING UP LIKE CRAZY IN A FRENZIED MAD DASH!!
ぬおおおおお
nnnngaaahhhh!
OH... HERE SHE COMES.

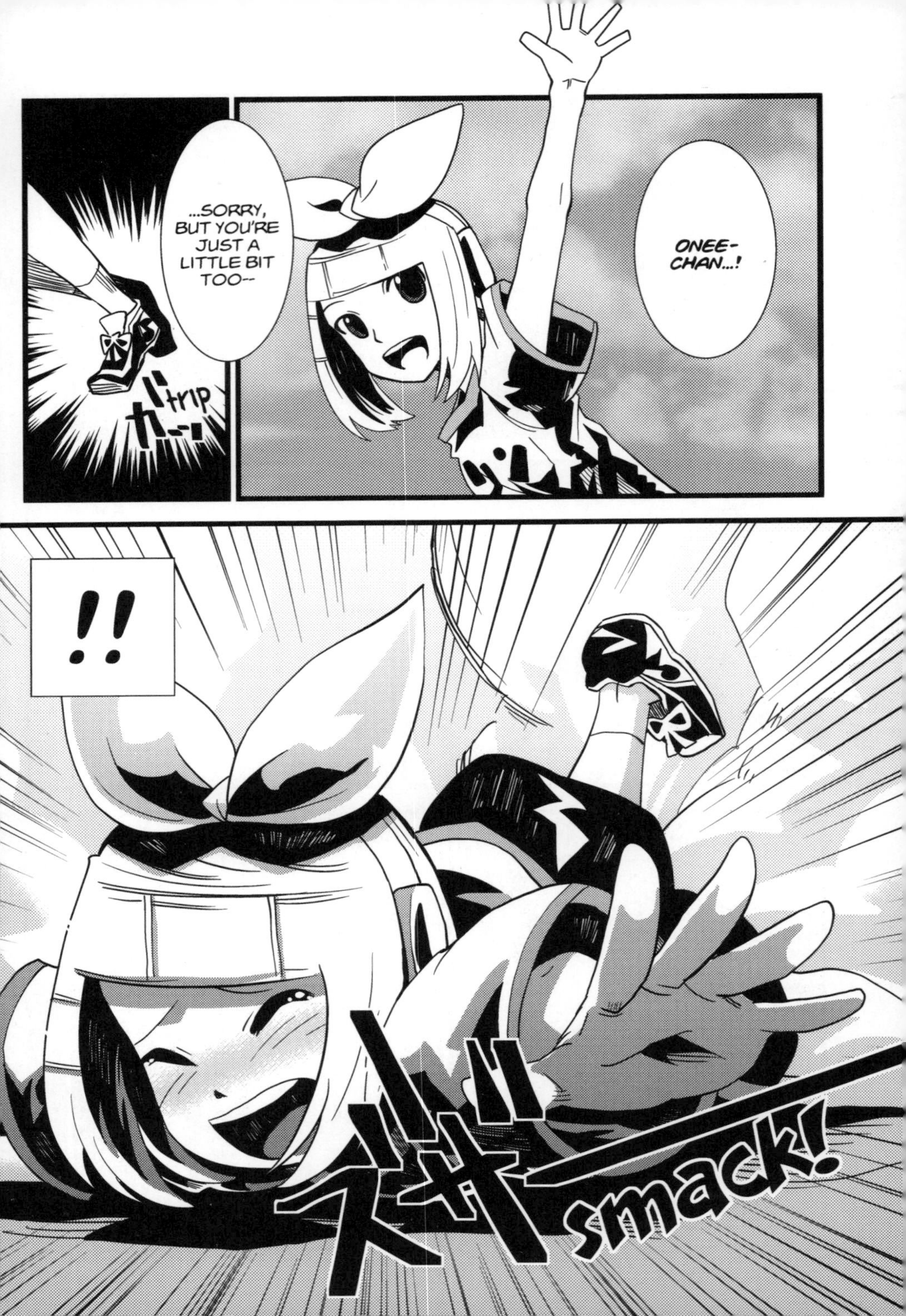
ONEE-CHAN...!
...SORRY, BUT YOU'RE JUST A LITTLE BIT TOO--
trip
!!
smack!

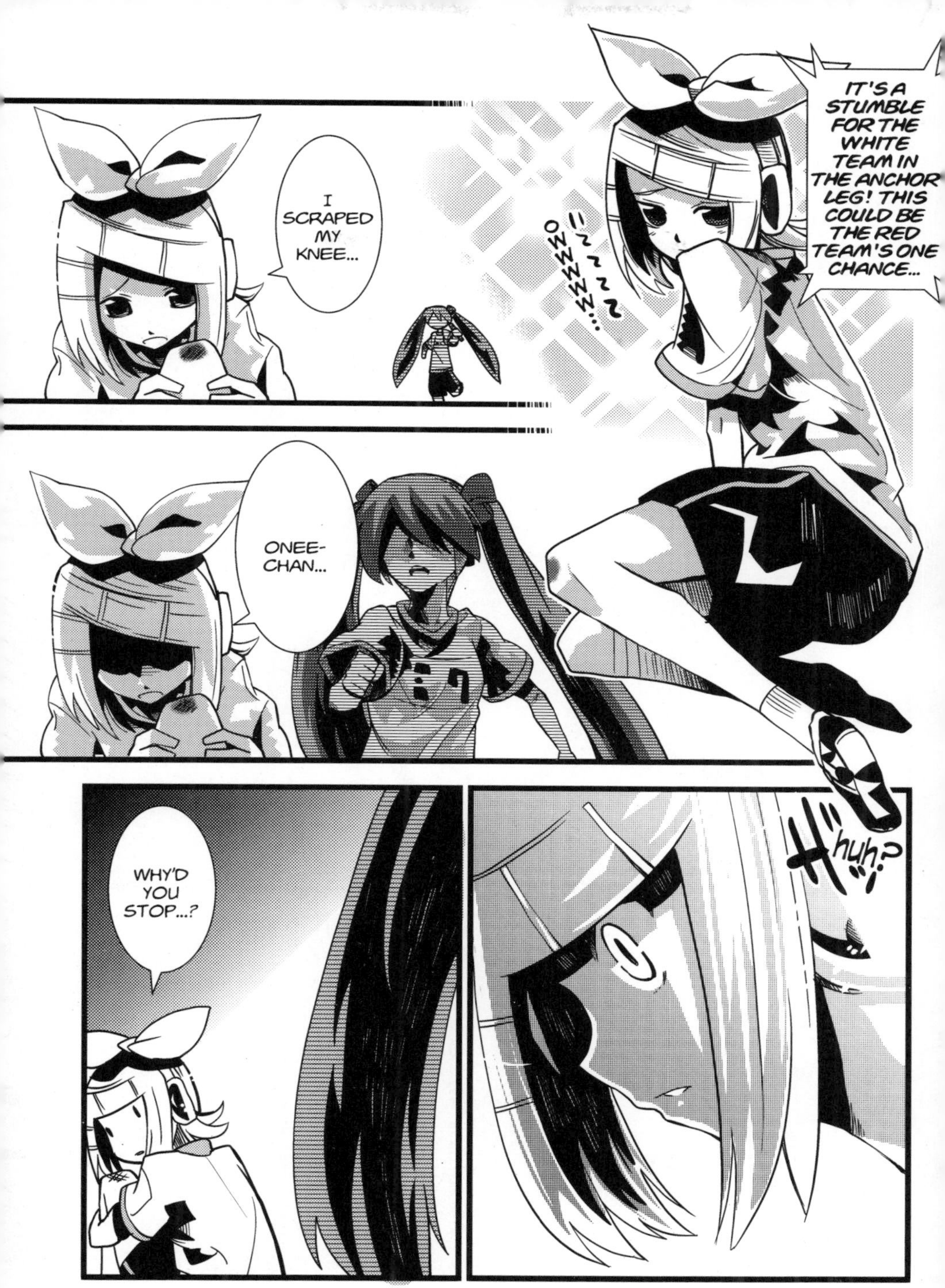
IT'S A STUMBLE FOR THE WHITE TEAM IN THE ANCHOR LEG! THIS COULD BE THE RED TEAM'S ONE CHANCE...
OWWWWW...!!
I SCRAPED MY KNEE...
ONEE-CHAN...
H-huh?
WHY'D YOU STOP...?

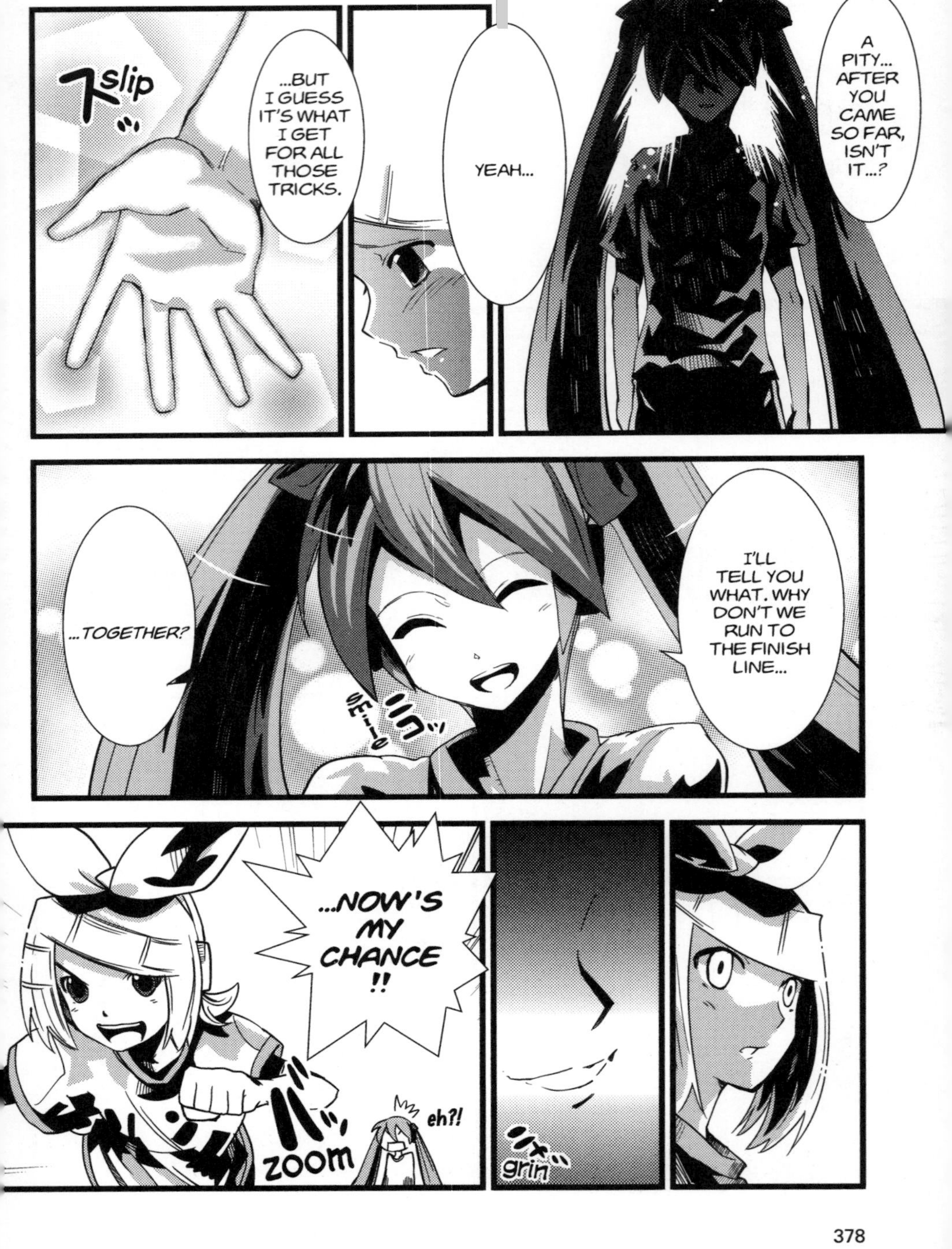
A PITY... AFTER YOU CAME SO FAR, ISN'T IT...?
YEAH...
...BUT I GUESS IT'S WHAT I GET FOR ALL THOSE TRICKS.
slip
I'LL TELL YOU WHAT. WHY DON'T WE RUN TO THE FINISH LINE...
...TOGETHER?
smile
grin
...NOW'S MY CHANCE!!
zoom
eh?!

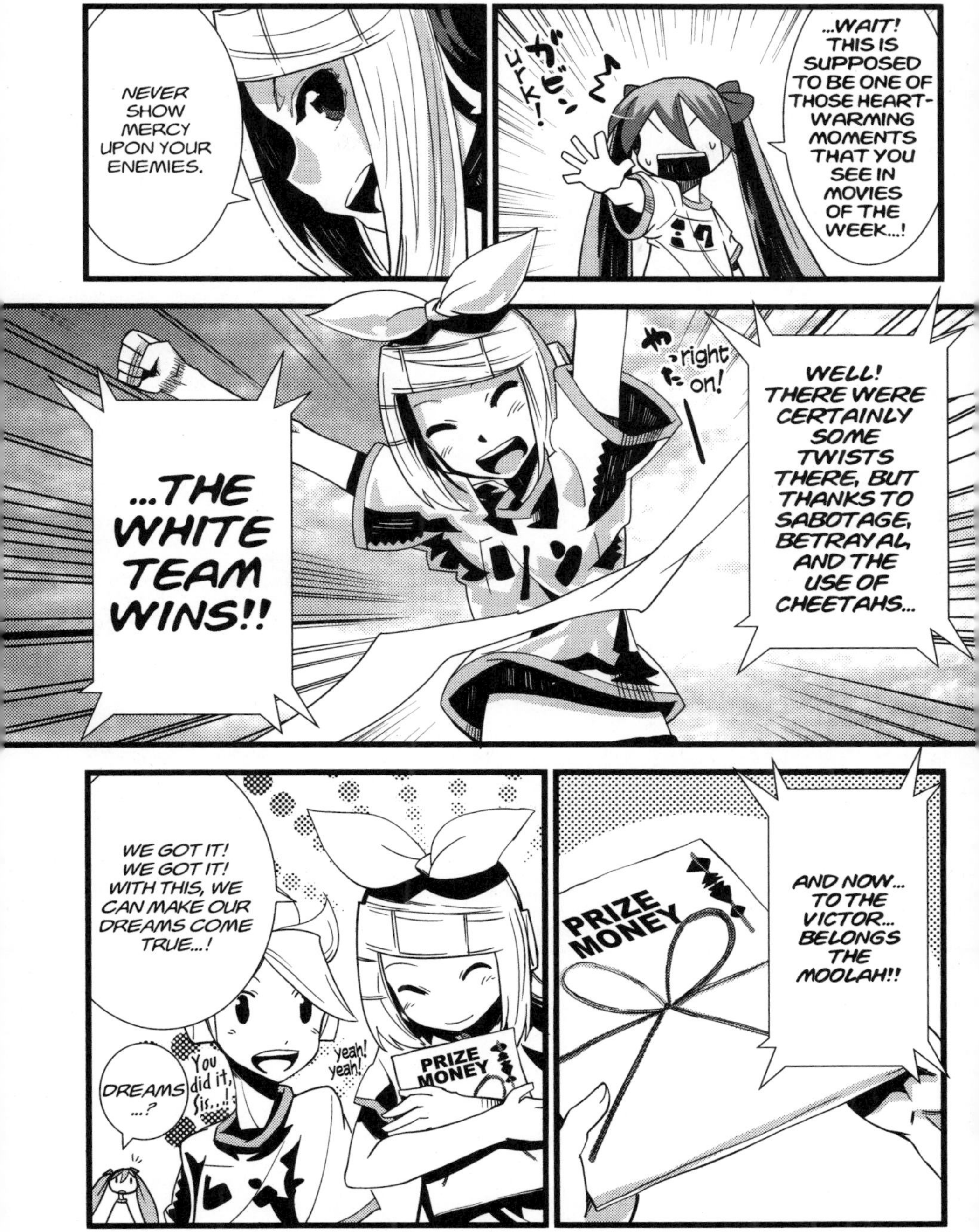
がビーン
...WAIT! THIS IS SUPPOSED TO BE ONE OF THOSE HEART-WARMING MOMENTS THAT YOU SEE IN MOVIES OF THE WEEK...!
NEVER SHOW MERCY UPON YOUR ENEMIES.
WELL! THERE WERE CERTAINLY SOME TWISTS THERE, BUT THANKS TO SABOTAGE, BETRAYAL, AND THE USE OF CHEETAHS...
right on!
...THE WHITE TEAM WINS!!
AND NOW... TO THE VICTOR... BELONGS THE MOOLAH!!
PRIZE MONEY
WE GOT IT! WE GOT IT! WITH THIS, WE CAN MAKE OUR DREAMS COME TRUE...!
yeah! yeah!
PRIZE MONEY
You did it, Sis...!
DREAMS ...?

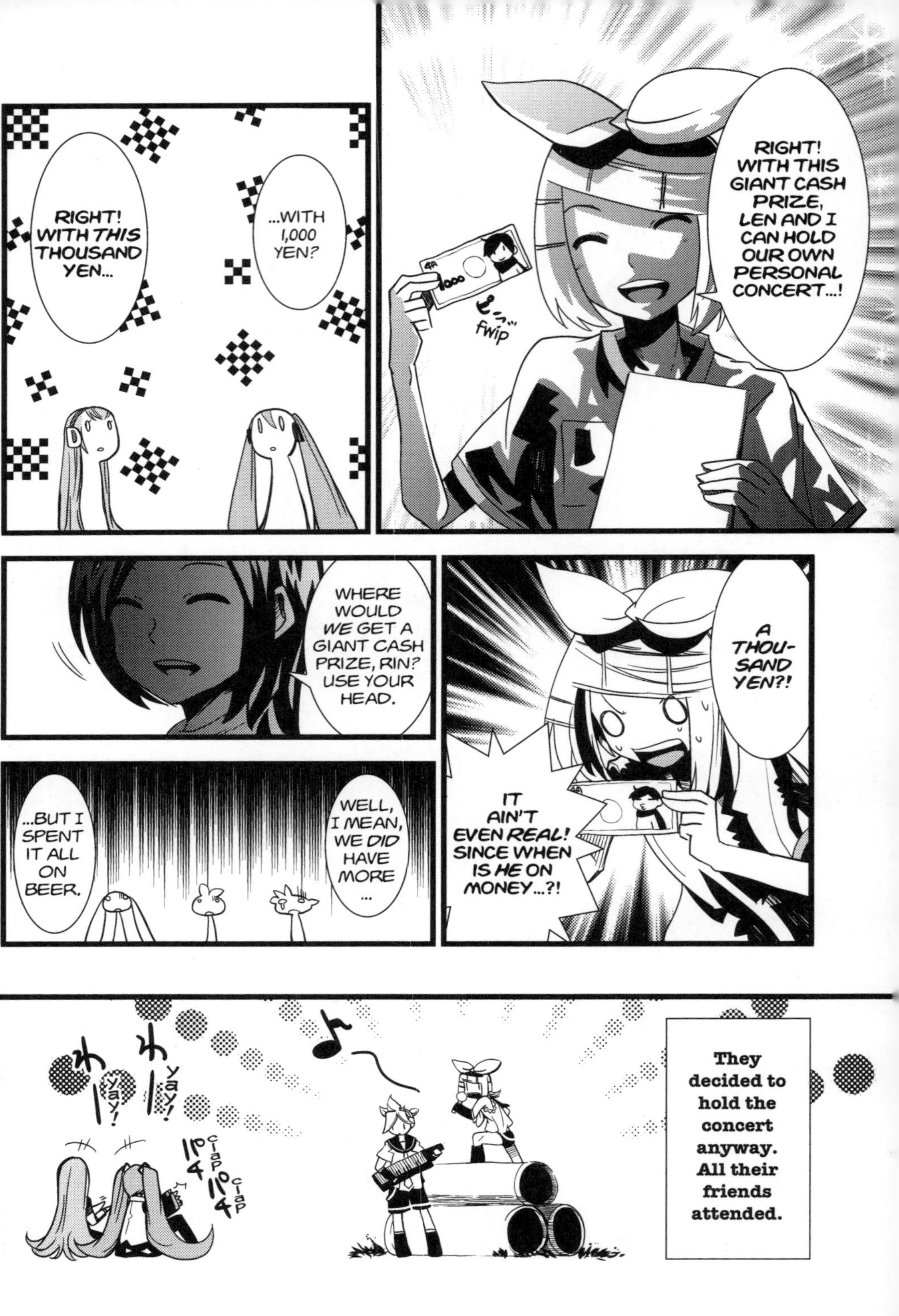
RIGHT! WITH THIS GIANT CASH PRIZE, LEN AND I CAN HOLD OUR OWN PERSONAL CONCERT...!
fwip
...WITH 1,000 YEN?
RIGHT! WITH *THIS* THOUSAND YEN...
A THOU-SAND YEN?!
IT AIN'T EVEN *REAL*! SINCE WHEN IS *HE* ON MONEY...?!
WHERE WOULD *WE* GET A GIANT CASH PRIZE, RIN? USE YOUR HEAD.
WELL, I MEAN, WE *DID* HAVE MORE ...
...BUT I SPENT IT ALL ON BEER.
They decided to hold the concert anyway. All their friends attended.
yay!
yay!
clap
clap

(23rd SONG) SANTA MIX

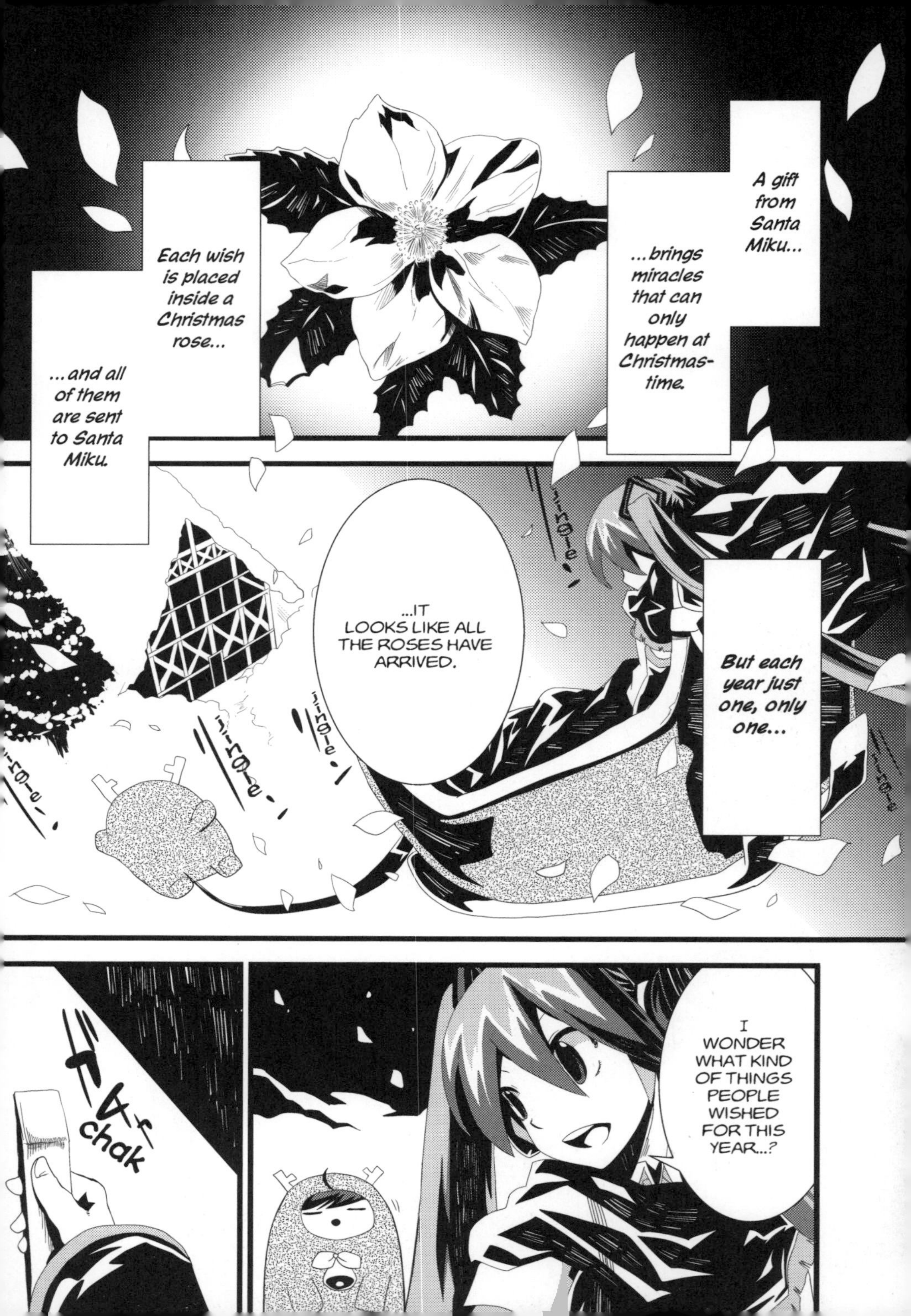
A gift from Santa Miku...
...brings miracles that can only happen at Christmas-time.
Each wish is placed inside a Christmas rose...
...and all of them are sent to Santa Miku.
jingle
But each year just one, only one...
jingle
...IT LOOKS LIKE ALL THE ROSES HAVE ARRIVED.
jingle
jingle
I WONDER WHAT KIND OF THINGS PEOPLE WISHED FOR THIS YEAR...?
chak

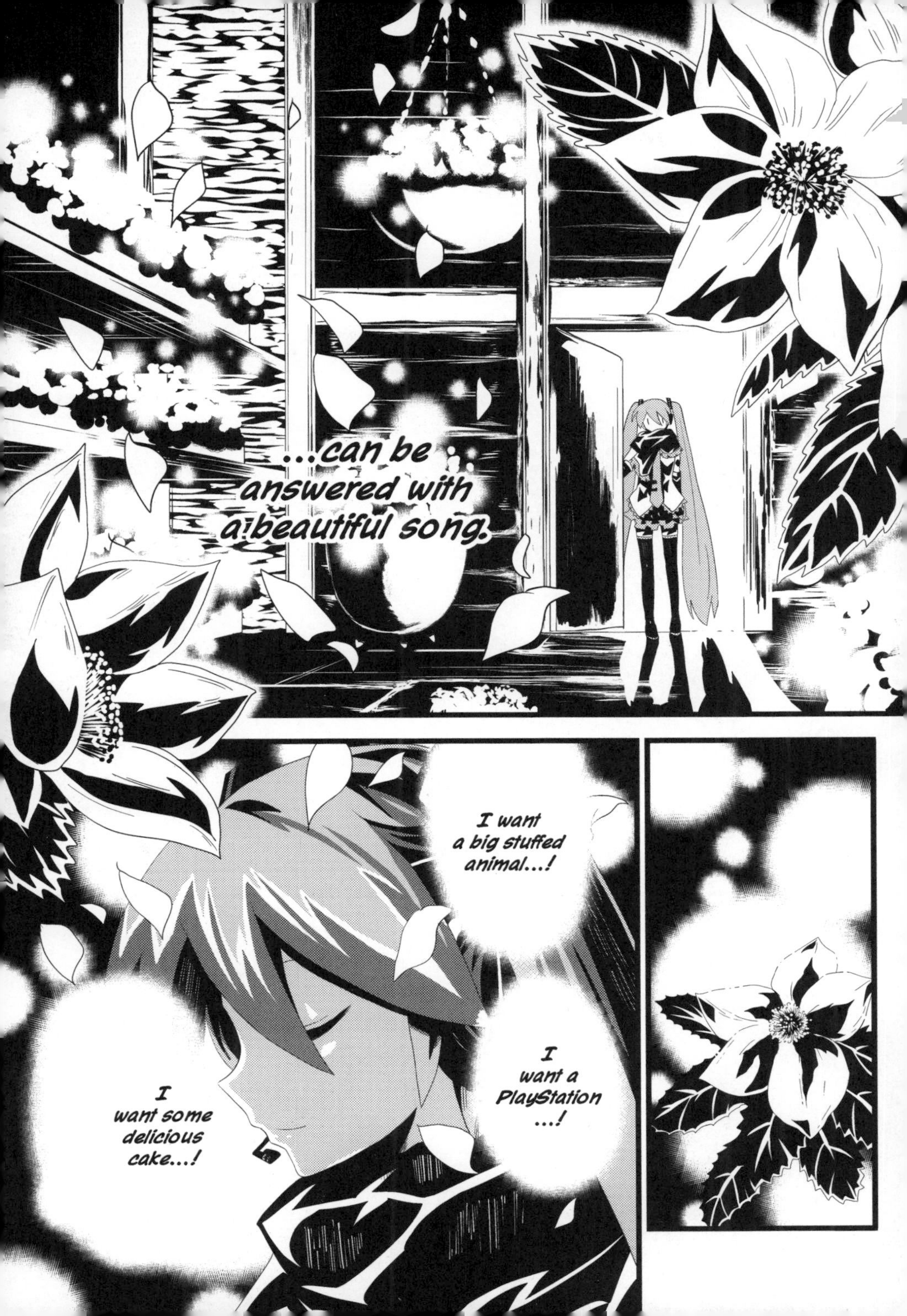
...can be answered with a beautiful song.
I want a big stuffed animal...!
I want a PlayStation ...!
I want some delicious cake...!

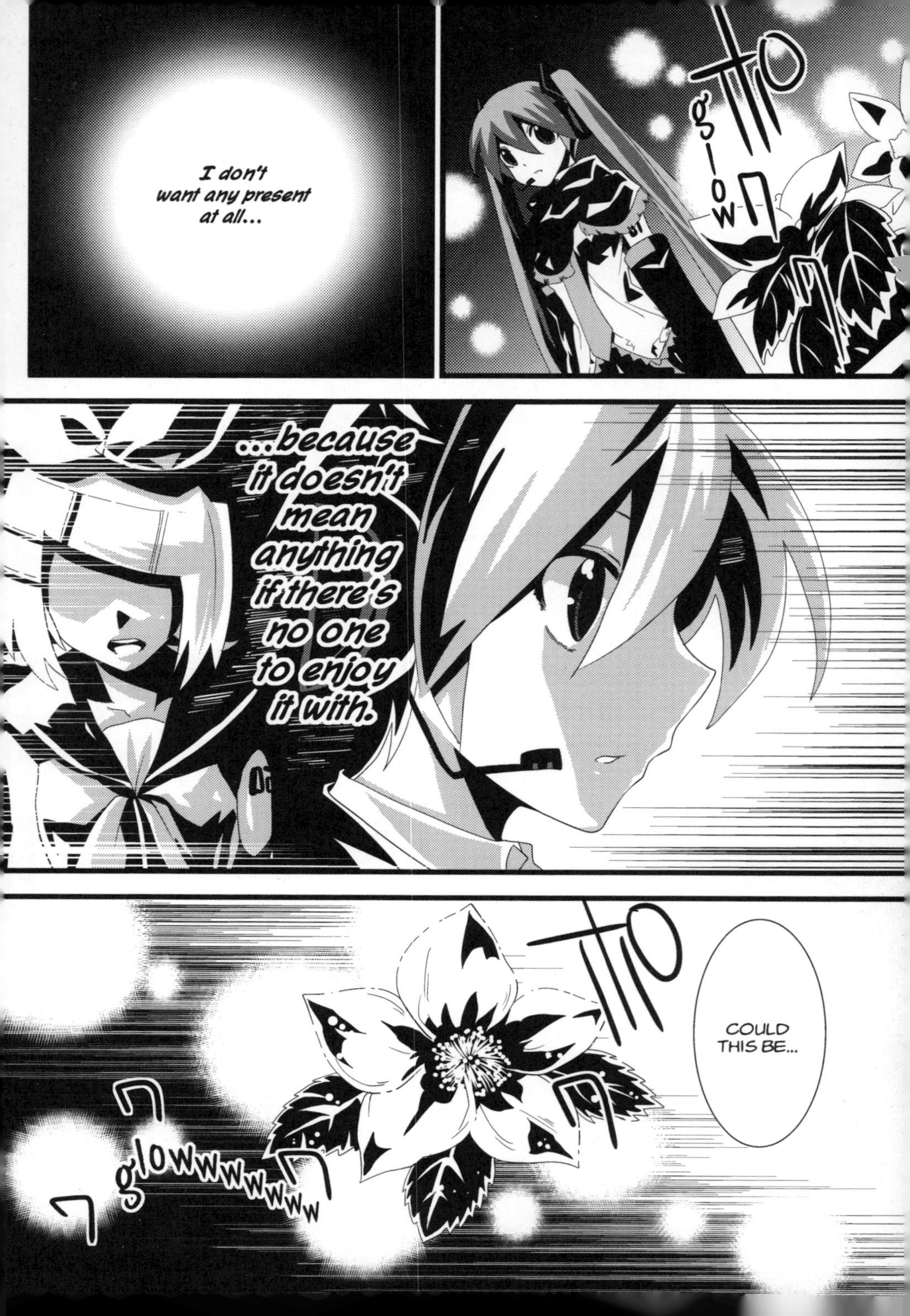
glow
I don't want any present at all...
...because it doesn't mean anything if there's no one to enjoy it with.
COULD THIS BE...
glowwwwwww

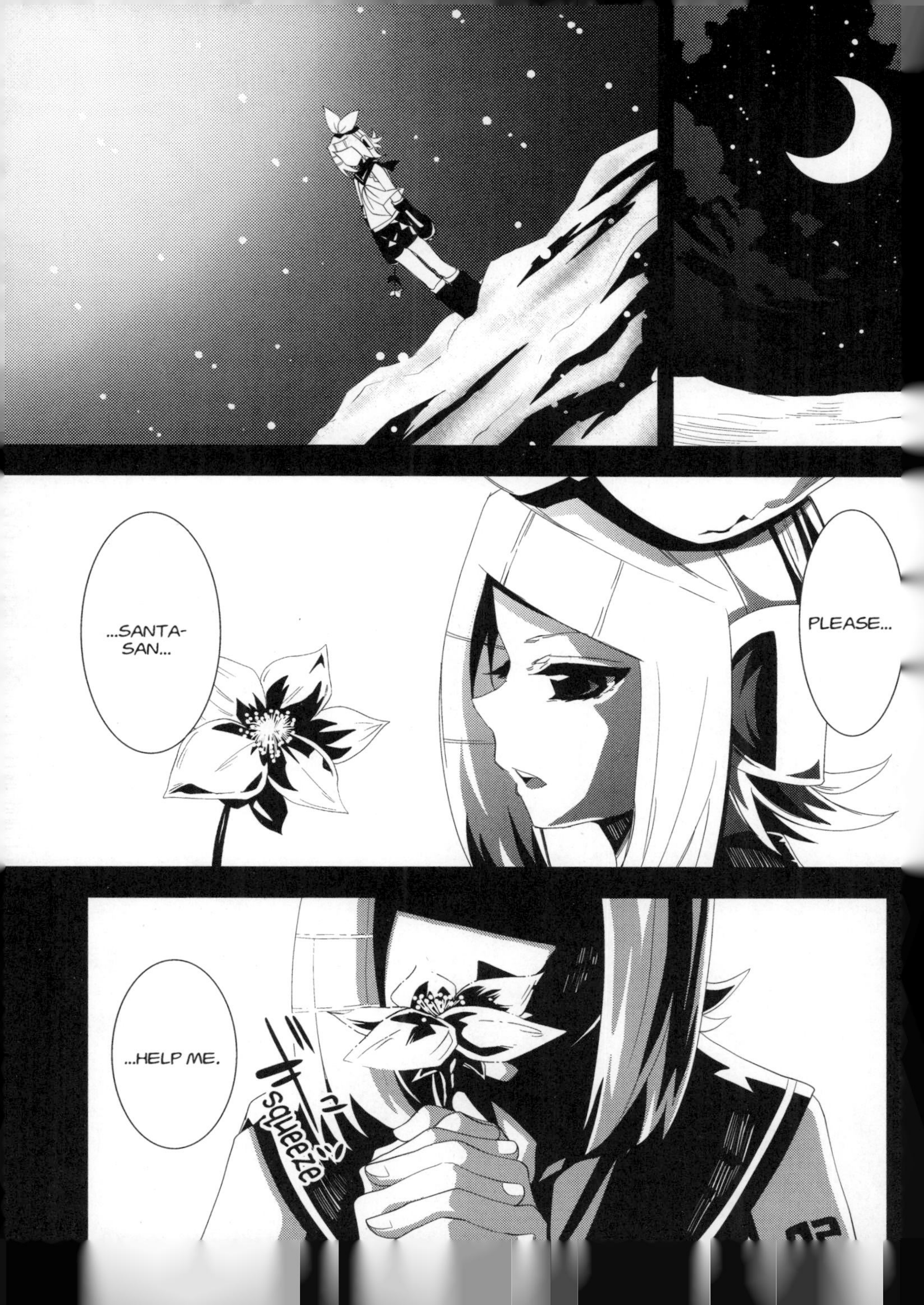
PLEASE...
...SANTA-SAN...
...HELP ME.
squeeze

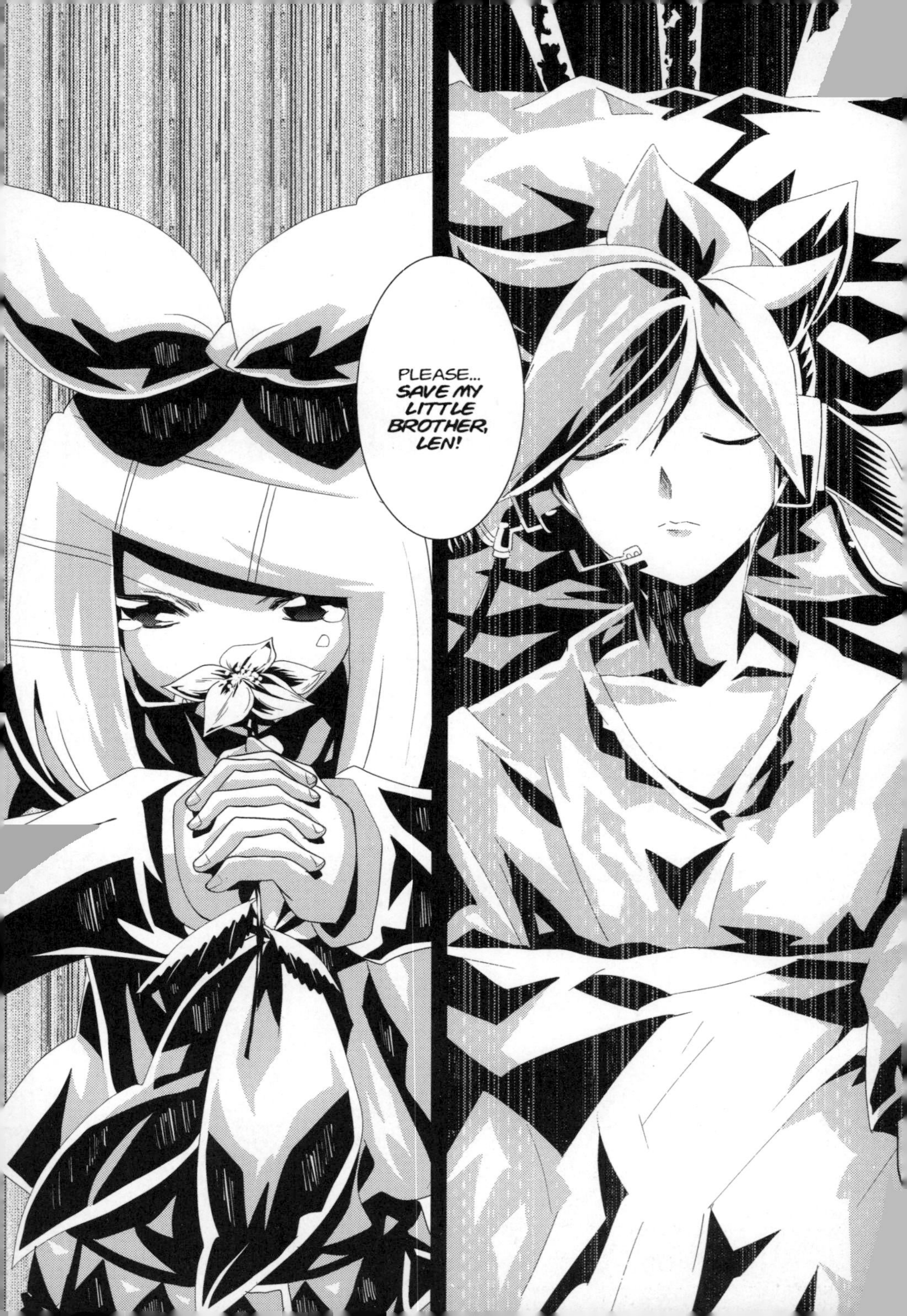
PLEASE... SAVE MY LITTLE BROTHER, LEN!

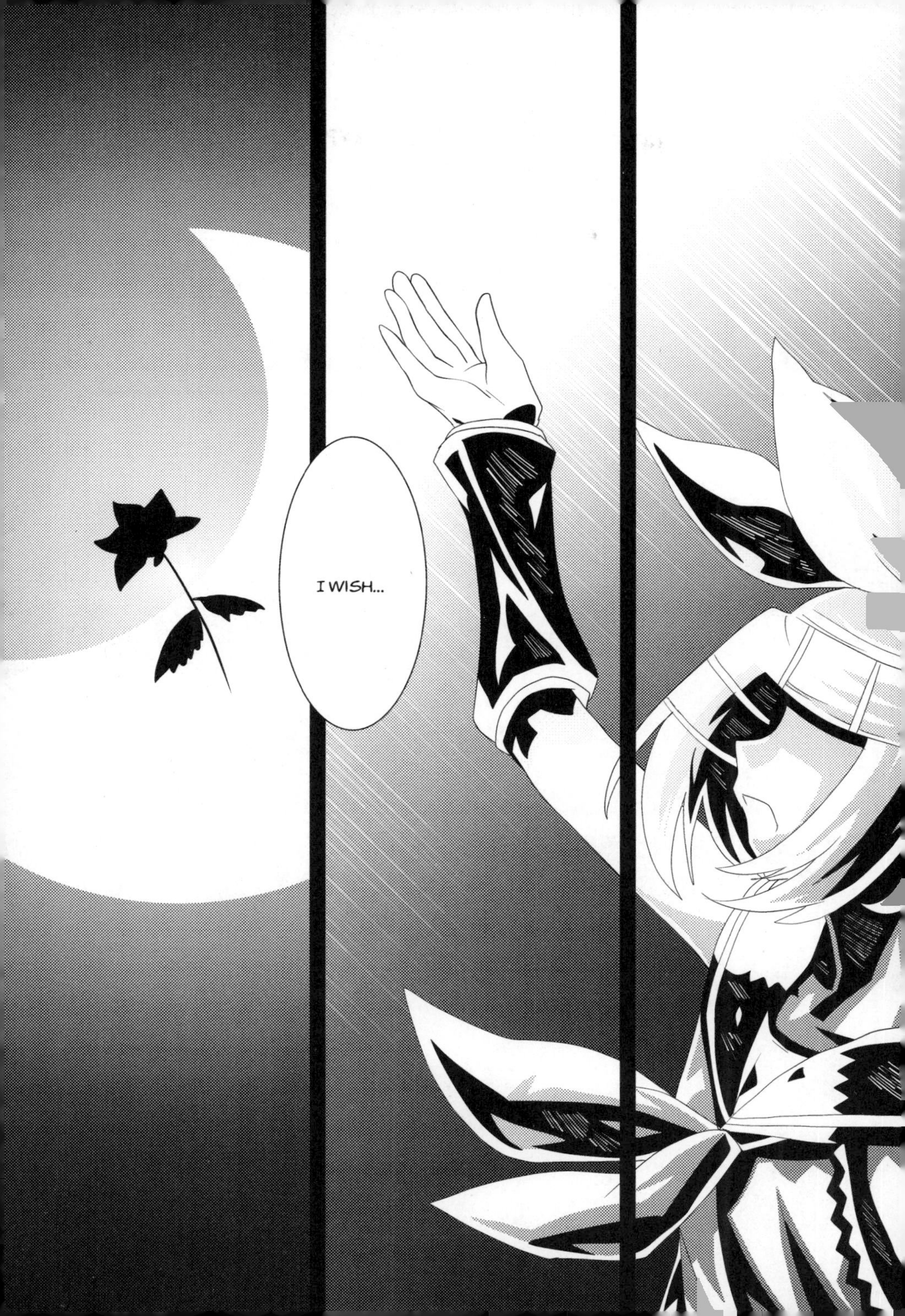
I WISH...

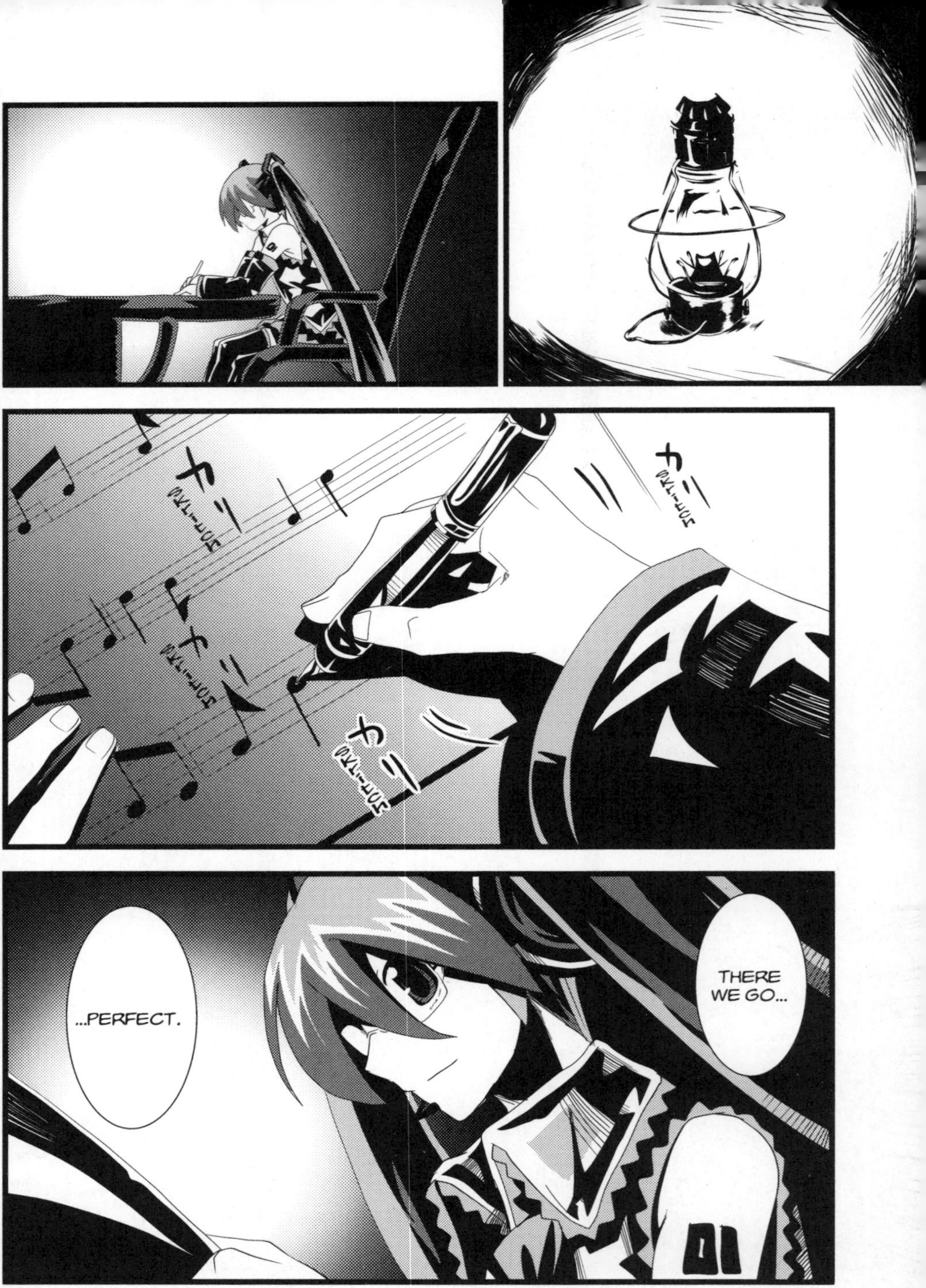
カリ
カリ
カリ
カリ
THERE WE GO...
...PERFECT.

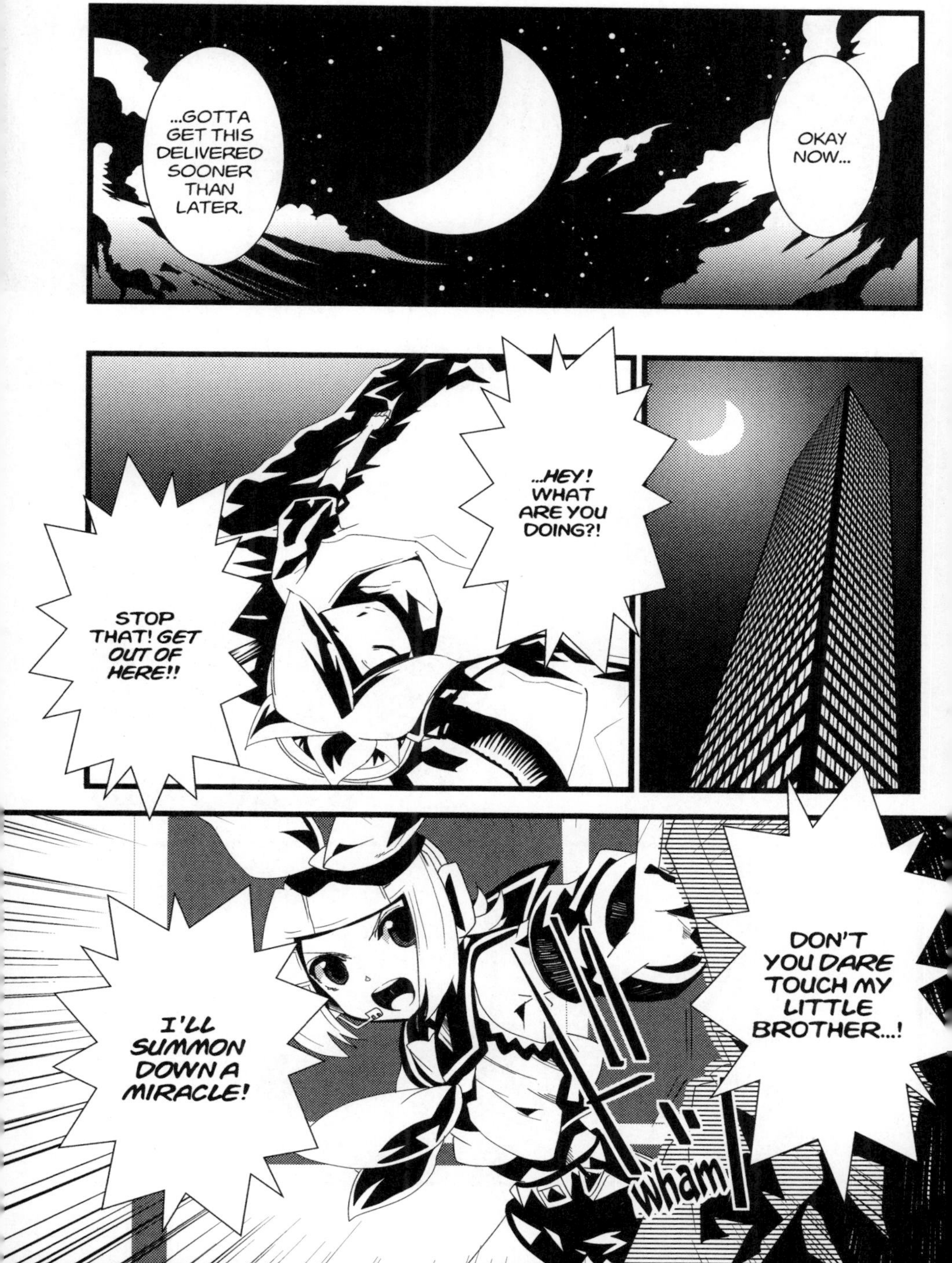
OKAY NOW...
...GOTTA GET THIS DELIVERED SOONER THAN LATER.
...HEY! WHAT ARE YOU DOING?!
STOP THAT! GET OUT OF HERE!!
DON'T YOU DARE TOUCH MY LITTLE BROTHER...!
wham
I'LL SUMMON DOWN A MIRACLE!

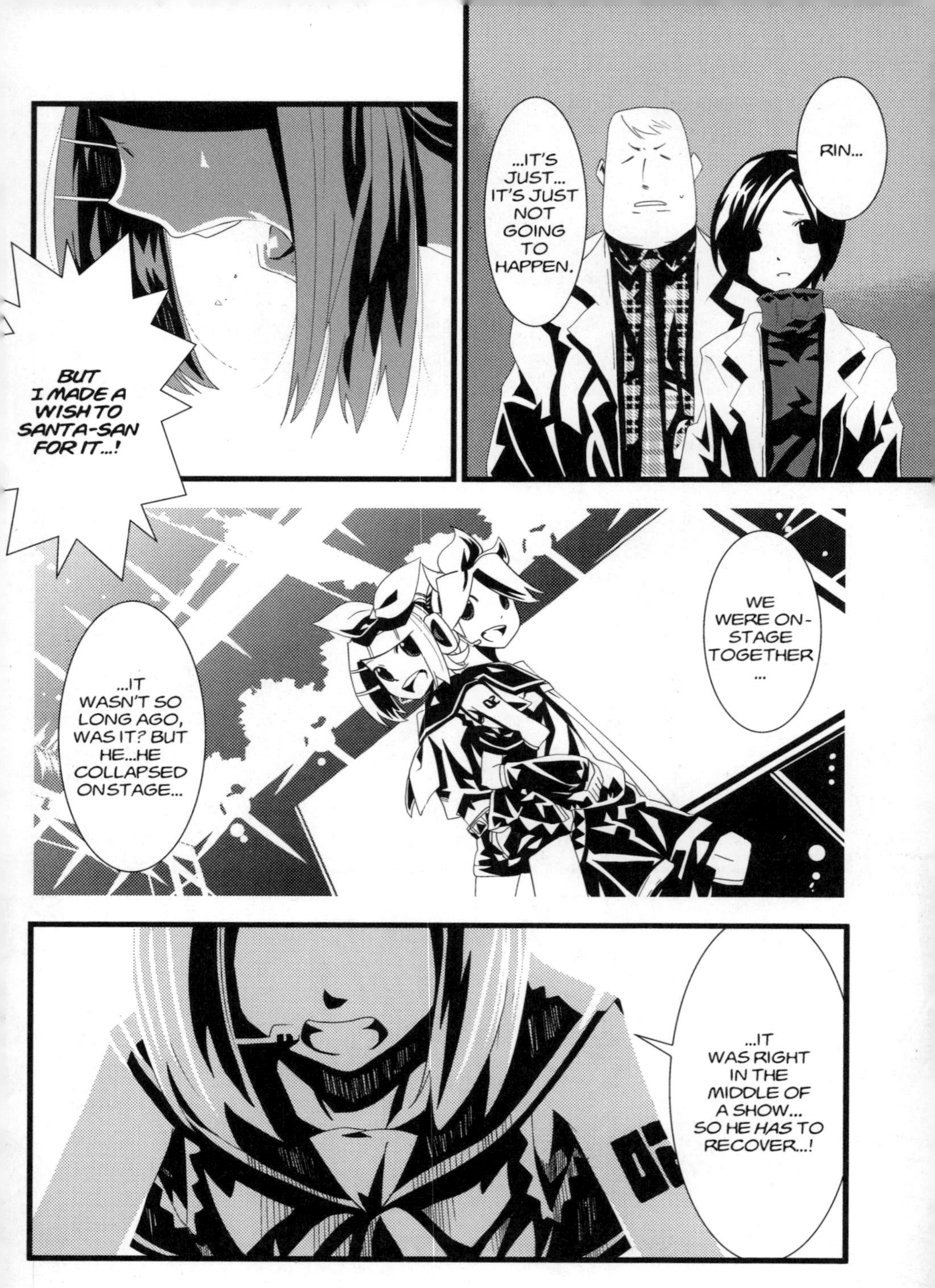
RIN...
...IT'S JUST... IT'S JUST NOT GOING TO HAPPEN.
BUT I MADE A WISH TO SANTA-SAN FOR IT...!
WE WERE ON-STAGE TOGETHER...
...IT WASN'T SO LONG AGO, WAS IT? BUT HE...HE COLLAPSED ONSTAGE...
...IT WAS RIGHT IN THE MIDDLE OF A SHOW... SO HE HAS TO RECOVER...!

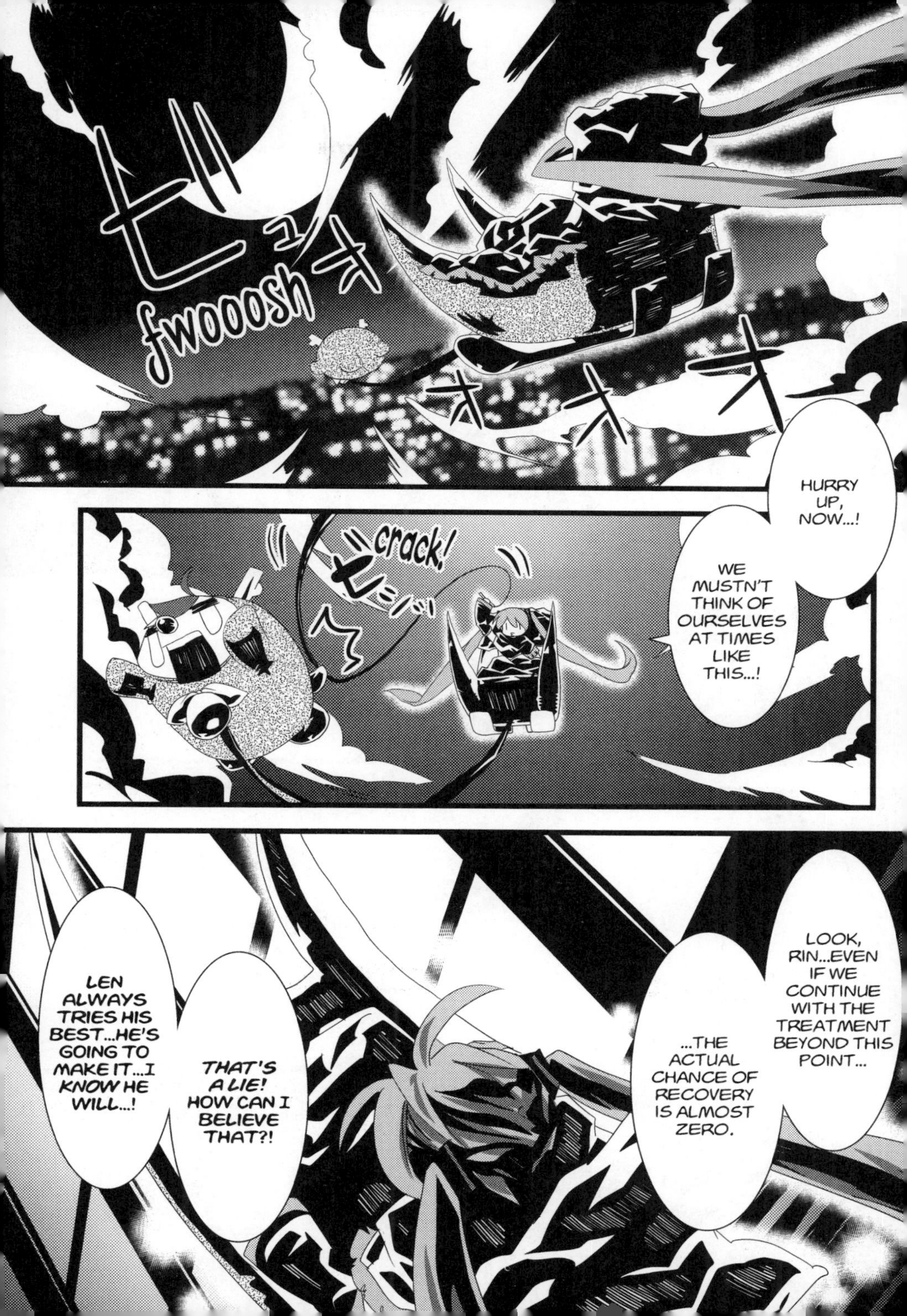
fwooosh
HURRY UP, NOW...!
WE MUSTN'T THINK OF OURSELVES AT TIMES LIKE THIS...!
crack!
LOOK, RIN...EVEN IF WE CONTINUE WITH THE TREATMENT BEYOND THIS POINT...
...THE ACTUAL CHANCE OF RECOVERY IS ALMOST ZERO.
THAT'S A LIE! HOW CAN I BELIEVE THAT?!
LEN ALWAYS TRIES HIS BEST...HE'S GOING TO MAKE IT...I KNOW HE WILL...!

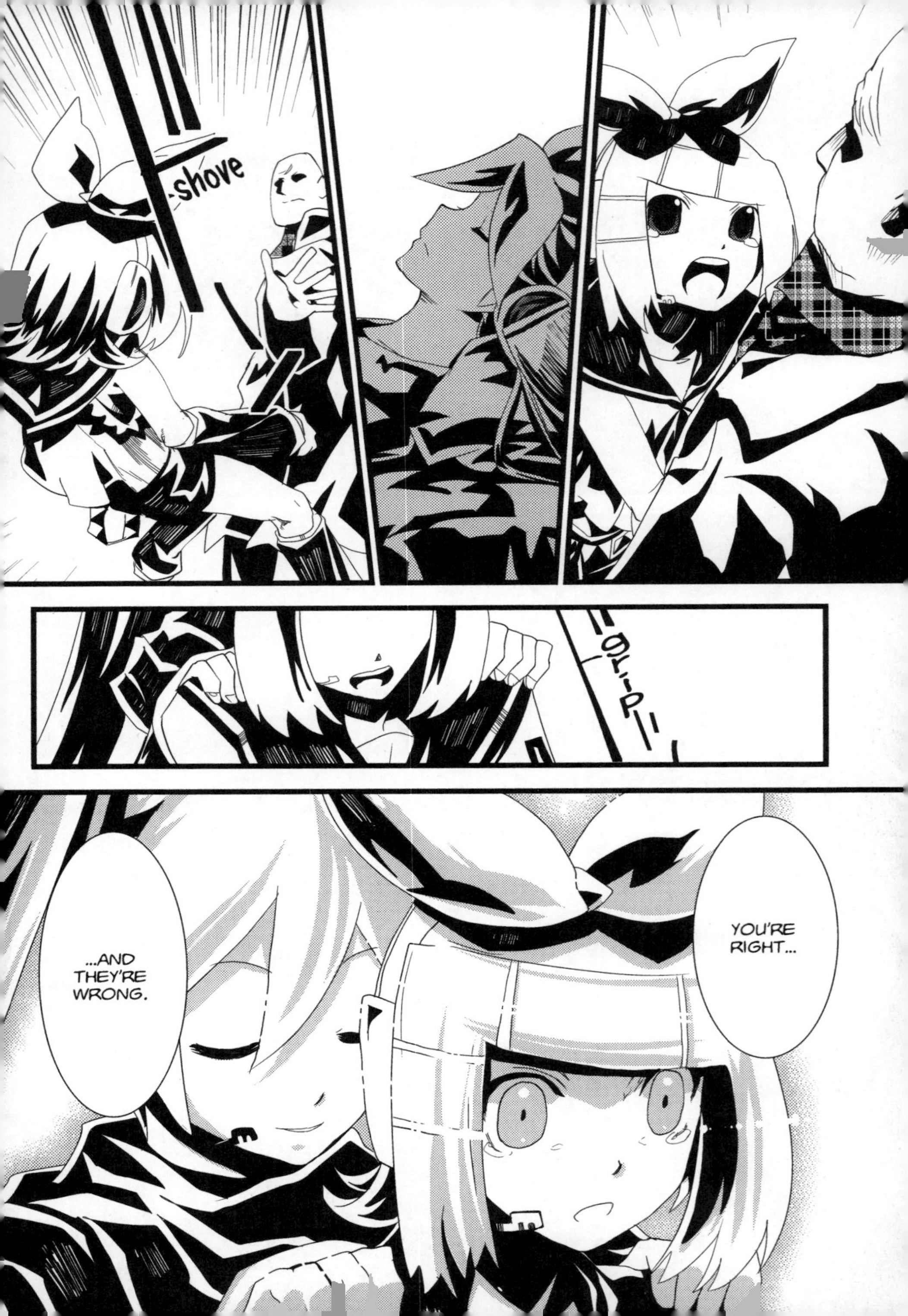
shove
grip
YOU'RE RIGHT...
...AND THEY'RE WRONG.

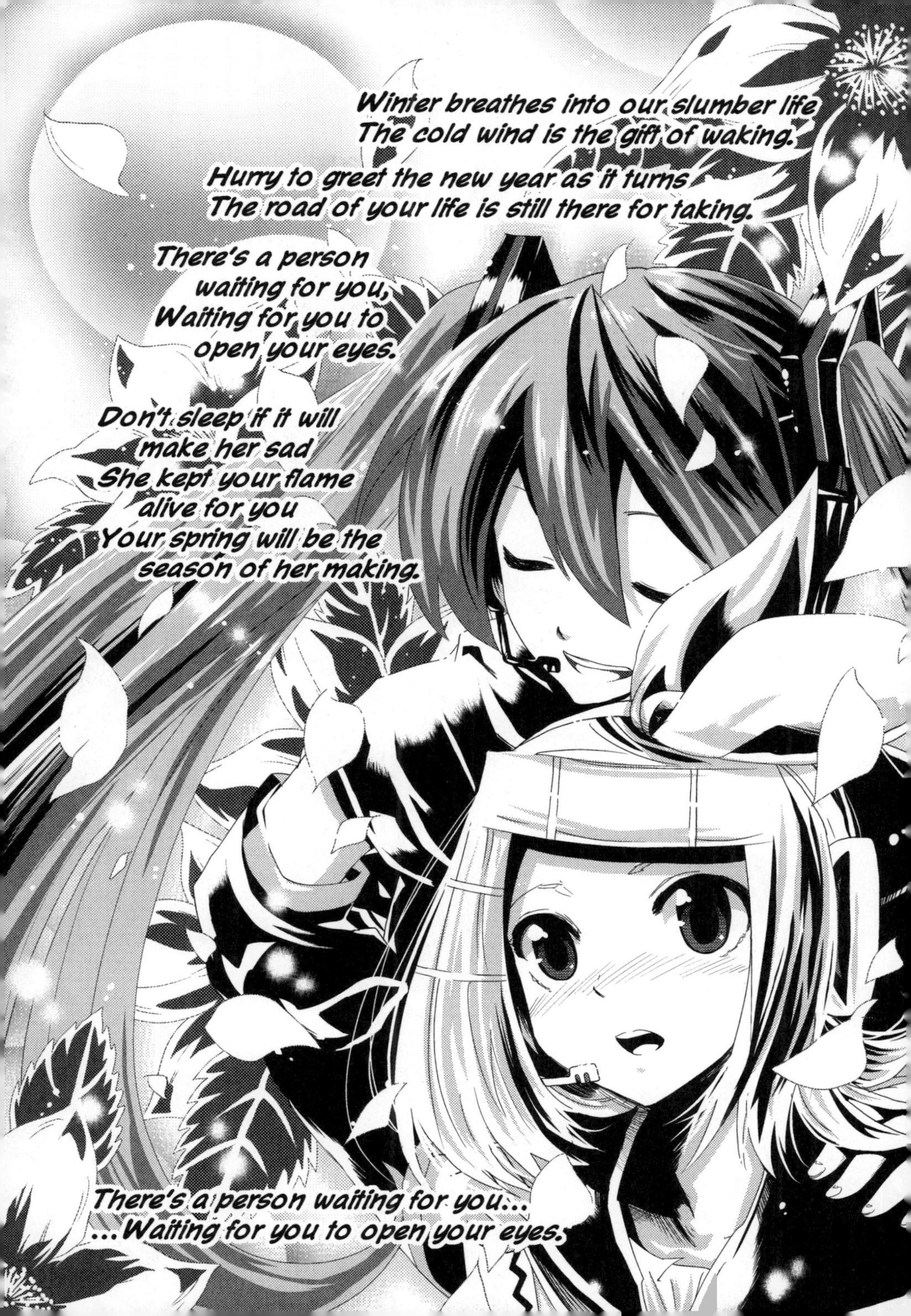
Winter breathes into our slumber life
The cold wind is the gift of waking.
Hurry to greet the new year as it turns
The road of your life is still there for taking.
There's a person
waiting for you,
Waiting for you to
open your eyes.
Don't sleep if it will
make her sad
She kept your flame
alive for you
Your spring will be the
season of her making.
There's a person waiting for you...
...Waiting for you to open your eyes.

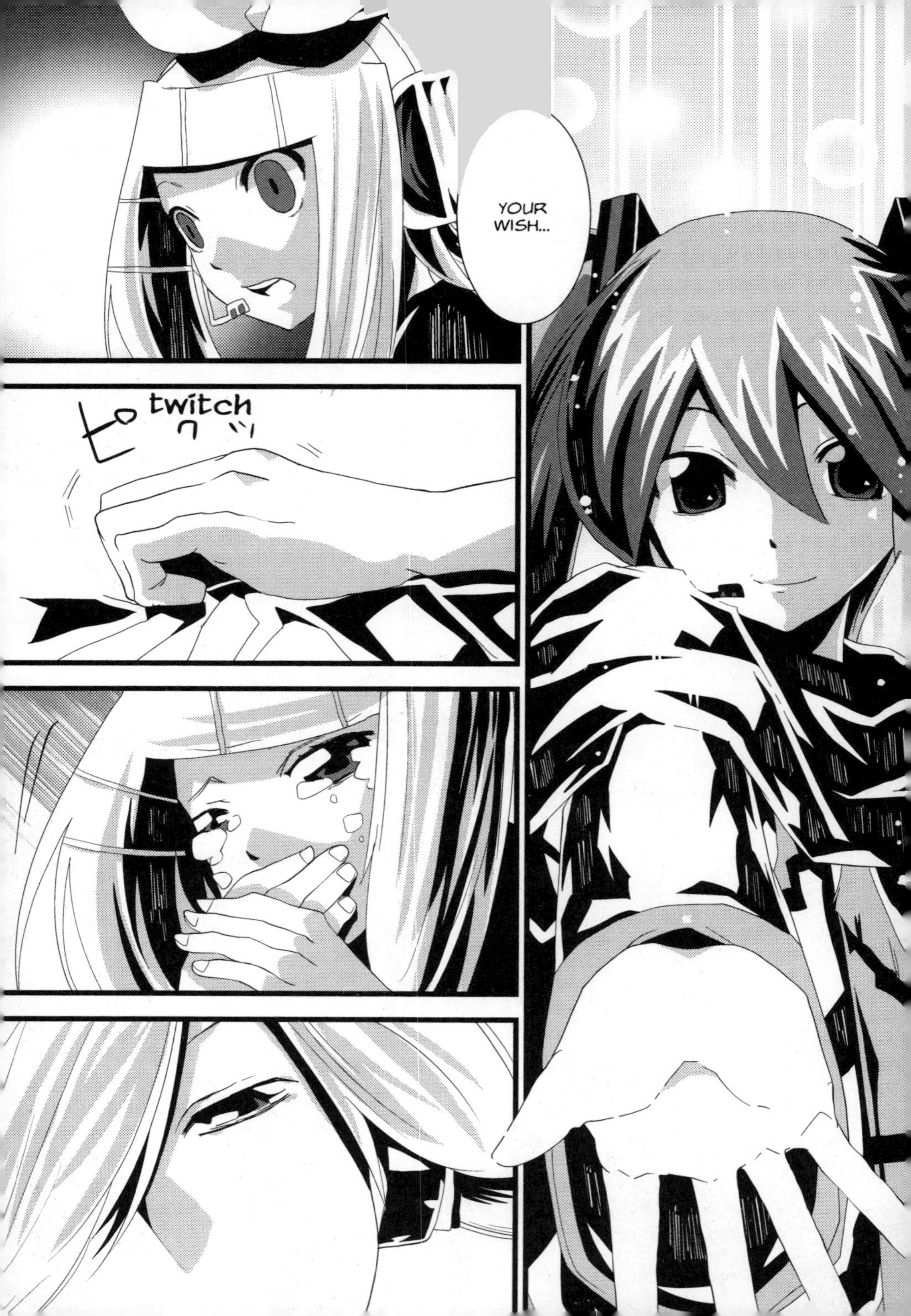
YOUR WISH...
twitch
ピクッ

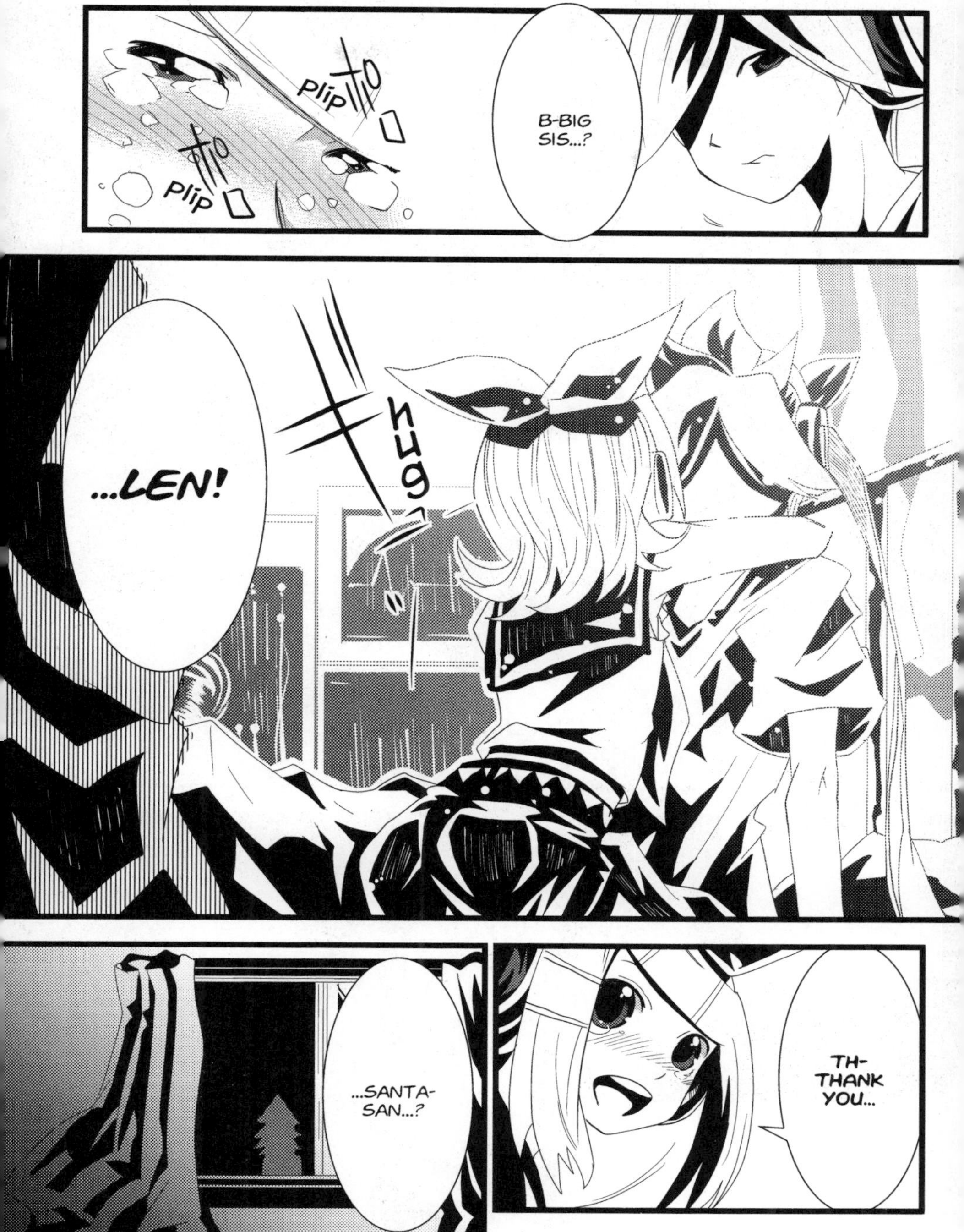
B-BIG SIS...?
plip
plip
hug
...LEN!
TH-THANK YOU...
...SANTA-SAN...?

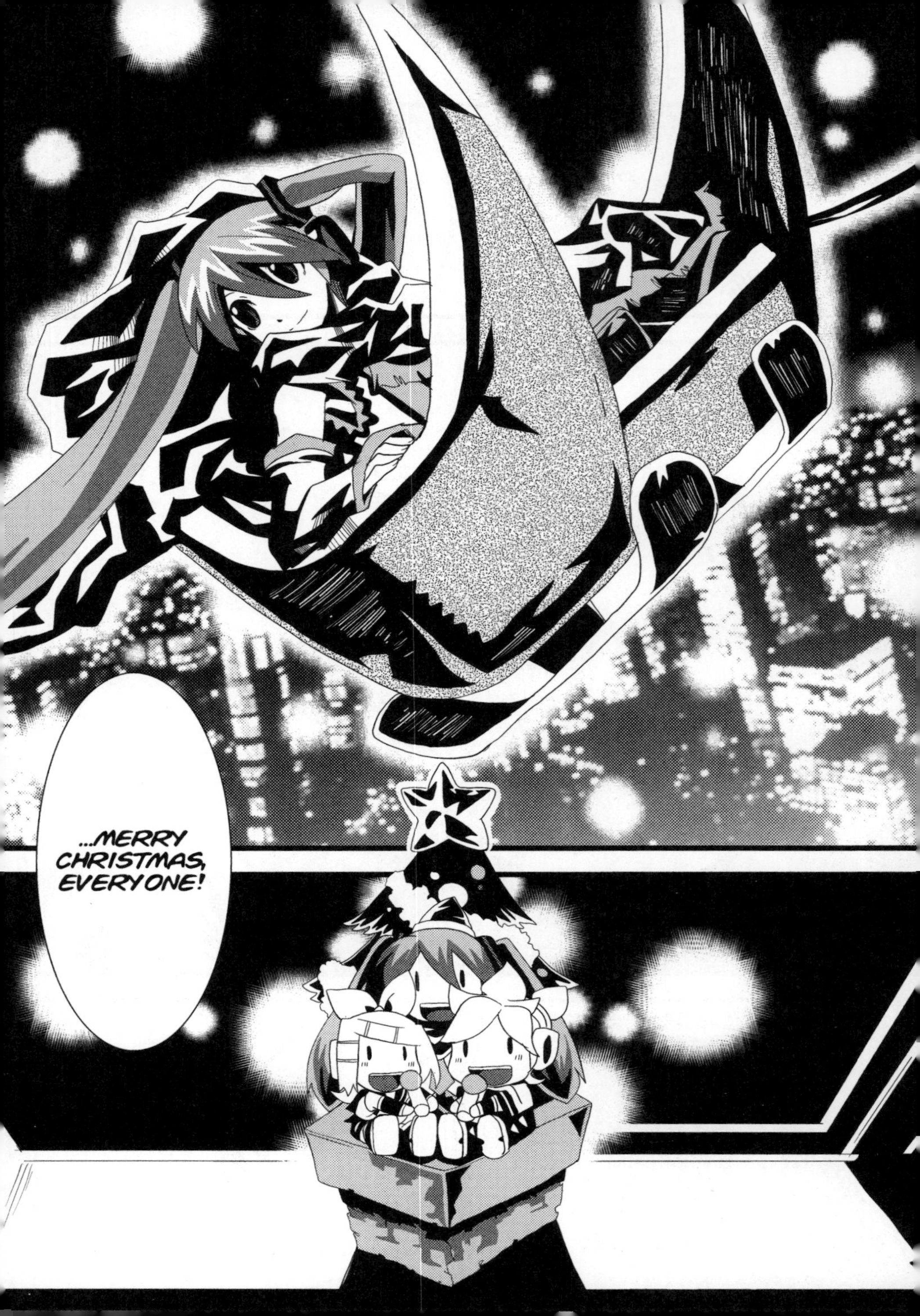
...MERRY CHRISTMAS, EVERYONE!

(24th SONG) MIKO MIX

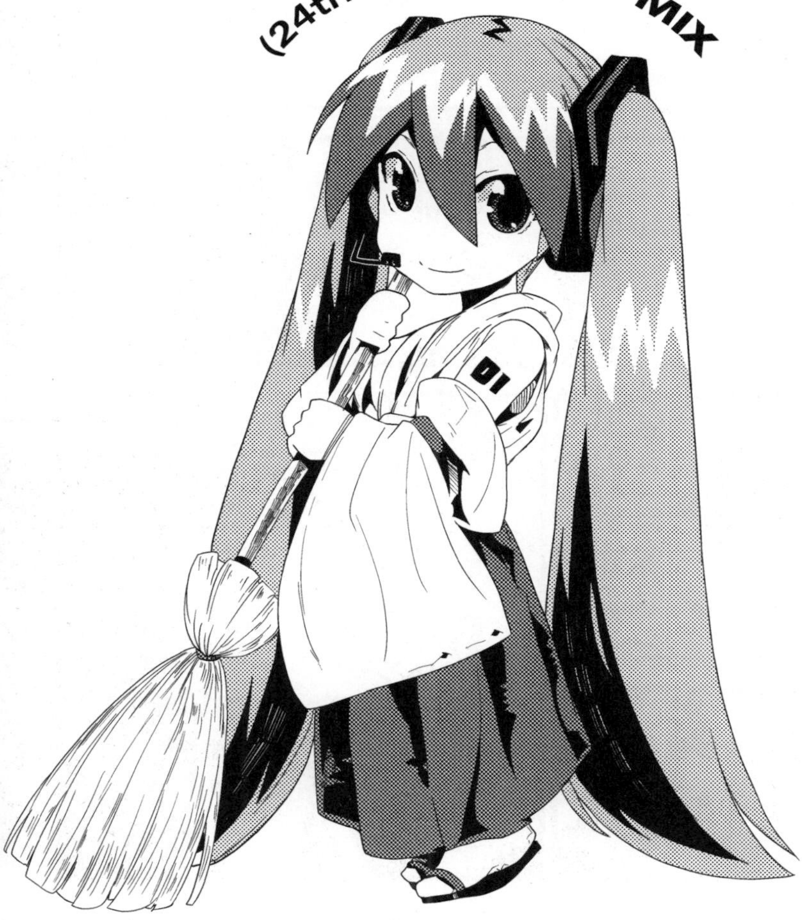

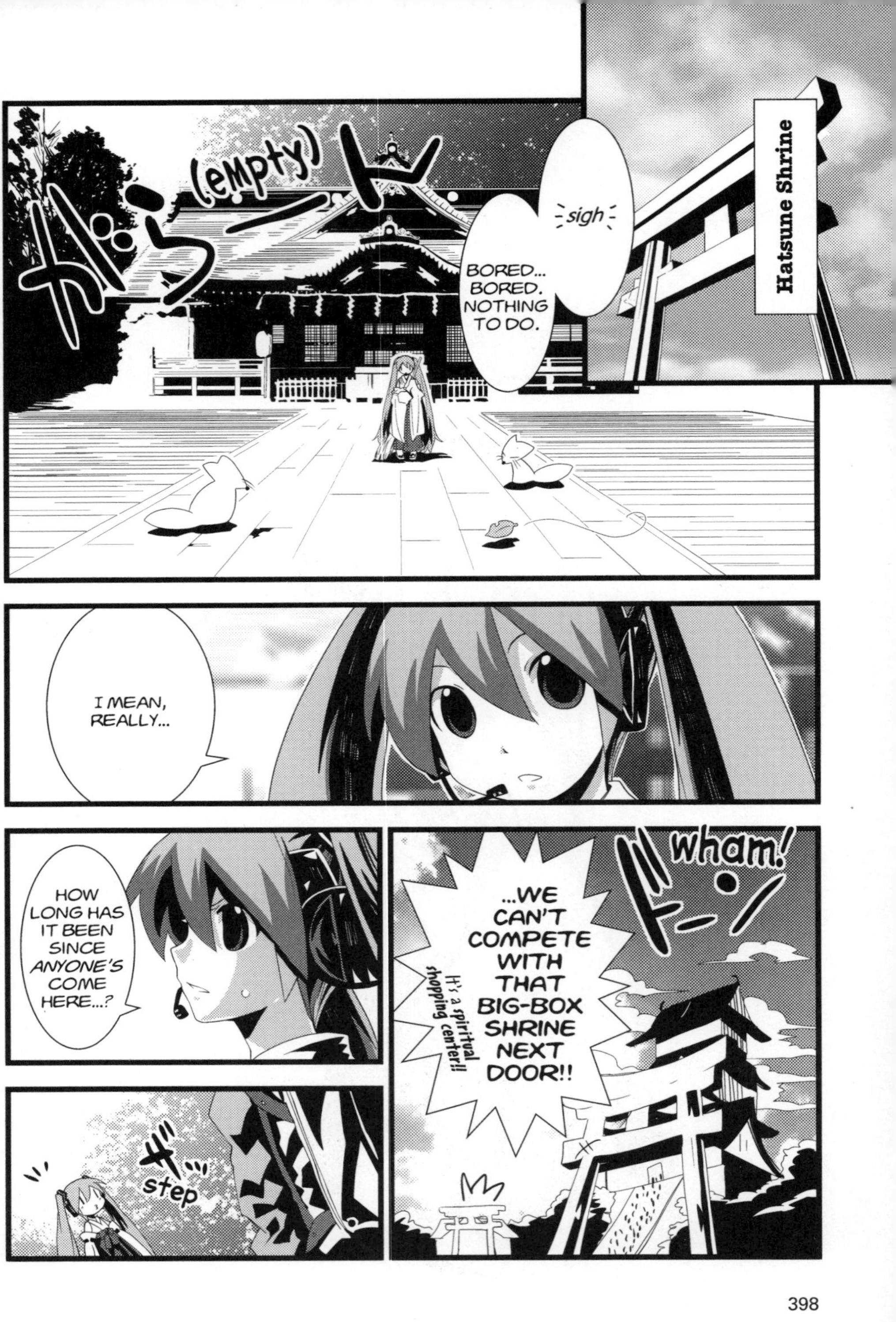
Hatsune Shrine
(empty)
sigh
BORED... BORED. NOTHING TO DO.
I MEAN, REALLY...
wham!
...WE CAN'T COMPETE WITH THAT BIG-BOX SHRINE NEXT DOOR!!
It's a spiritual shopping center!!
HOW LONG HAS IT BEEN SINCE ANYONE'S COME HERE...?
step

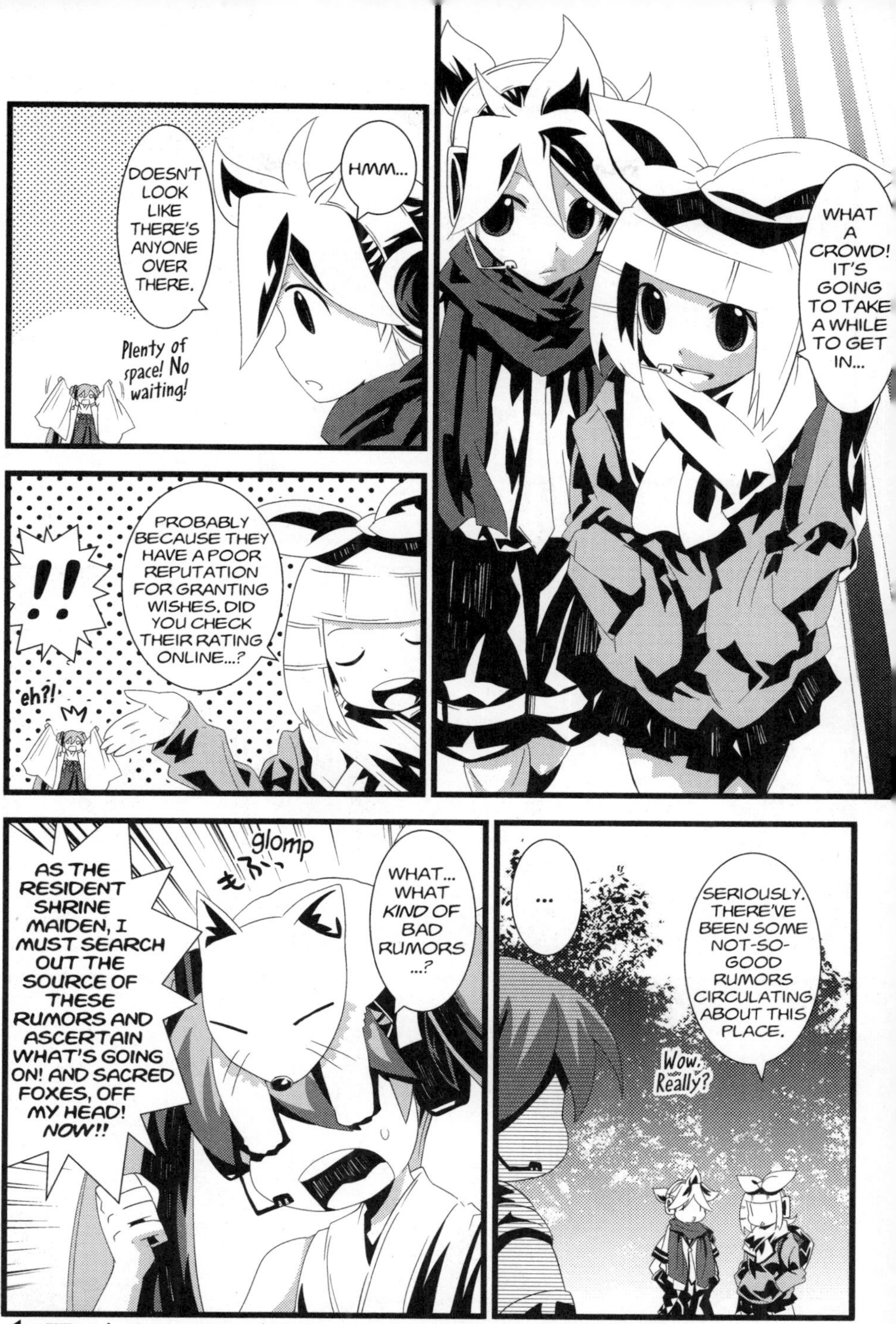
WHAT A CROWD! IT'S GOING TO TAKE A WHILE TO GET IN...
HMM...
DOESN'T LOOK LIKE THERE'S ANYONE OVER THERE.
Plenty of space! No waiting!
PROBABLY BECAUSE THEY HAVE A POOR REPUTATION FOR GRANTING WISHES. DID YOU CHECK THEIR RATING ONLINE...?
!!
eh?!
...
SERIOUSLY. THERE'VE BEEN SOME NOT-SO-GOOD RUMORS CIRCULATING ABOUT THIS PLACE.
Wow. Really?
glomp
もふっ
WHAT... WHAT KIND OF BAD RUMORS ...?
AS THE RESIDENT SHRINE MAIDEN, I MUST SEARCH OUT THE SOURCE OF THESE RUMORS AND ASCERTAIN WHAT'S GOING ON! AND SACRED FOXES, OFF MY HEAD! NOW!!

What is the truth behind these rumors? Turn the page to find out!

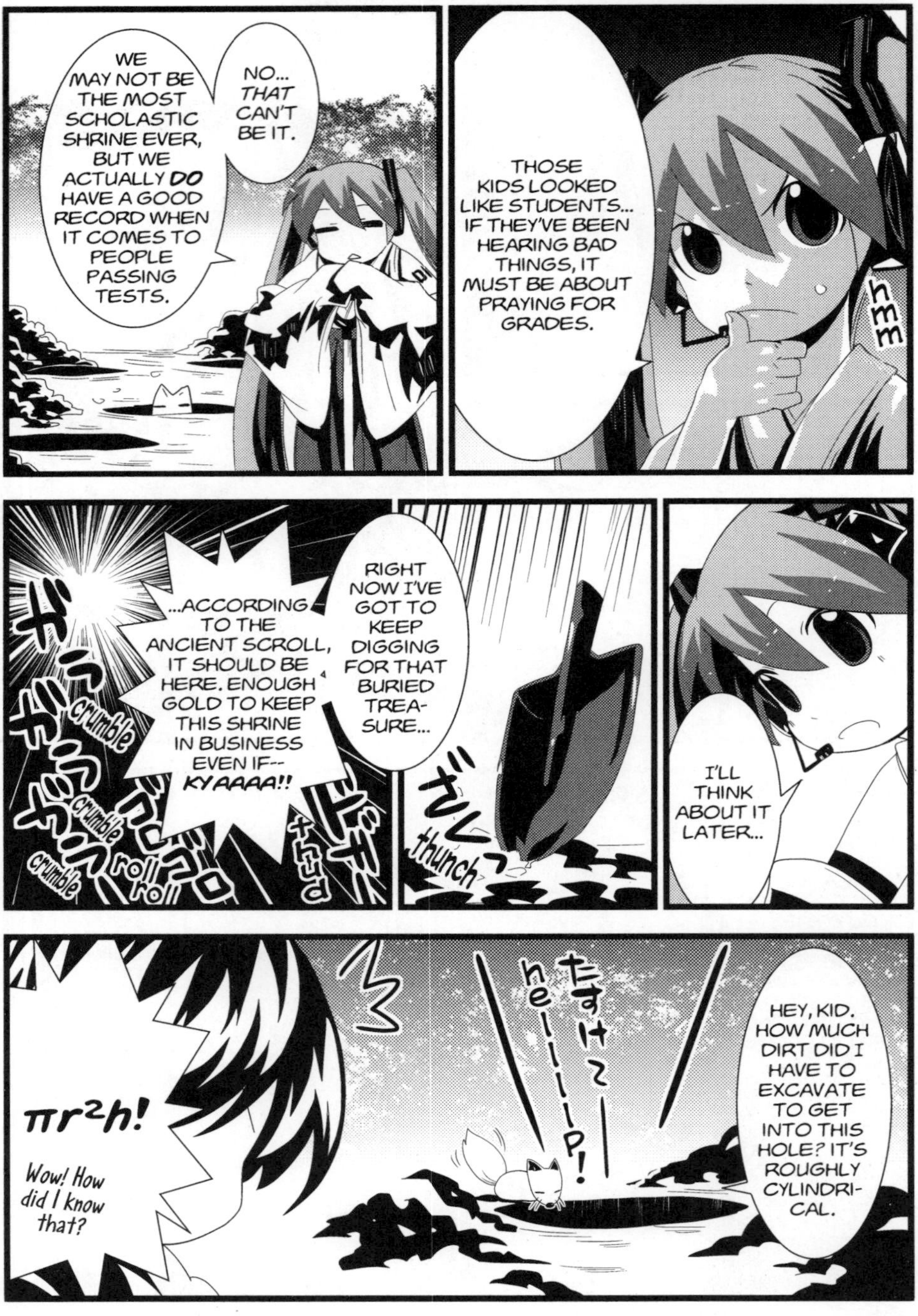
THOSE KIDS LOOKED LIKE STUDENTS... IF THEY'VE BEEN HEARING BAD THINGS, IT MUST BE ABOUT PRAYING FOR GRADES.
hmm
NO... THAT CAN'T BE IT.
WE MAY NOT BE THE MOST SCHOLASTIC SHRINE EVER, BUT WE ACTUALLY DO HAVE A GOOD RECORD WHEN IT COMES TO PEOPLE PASSING TESTS.
I'LL THINK ABOUT IT LATER...
RIGHT NOW I'VE GOT TO KEEP DIGGING FOR THAT BURIED TREA-SURE...
thunch
...ACCORDING TO THE ANCIENT SCROLL, IT SHOULD BE HERE. ENOUGH GOLD TO KEEP THIS SHRINE IN BUSINESS EVEN IF-- KYAAAA!!
thud
roll roll
crumble crumble crumble
HEY, KID. HOW MUCH DIRT DID I HAVE TO EXCAVATE TO GET INTO THIS HOLE? IT'S ROUGHLY CYLINDRI-CAL.
たすけて
he----lp!
πr²h!
Wow! How did I know that?

RUMOR #2: FORTUNETELLING

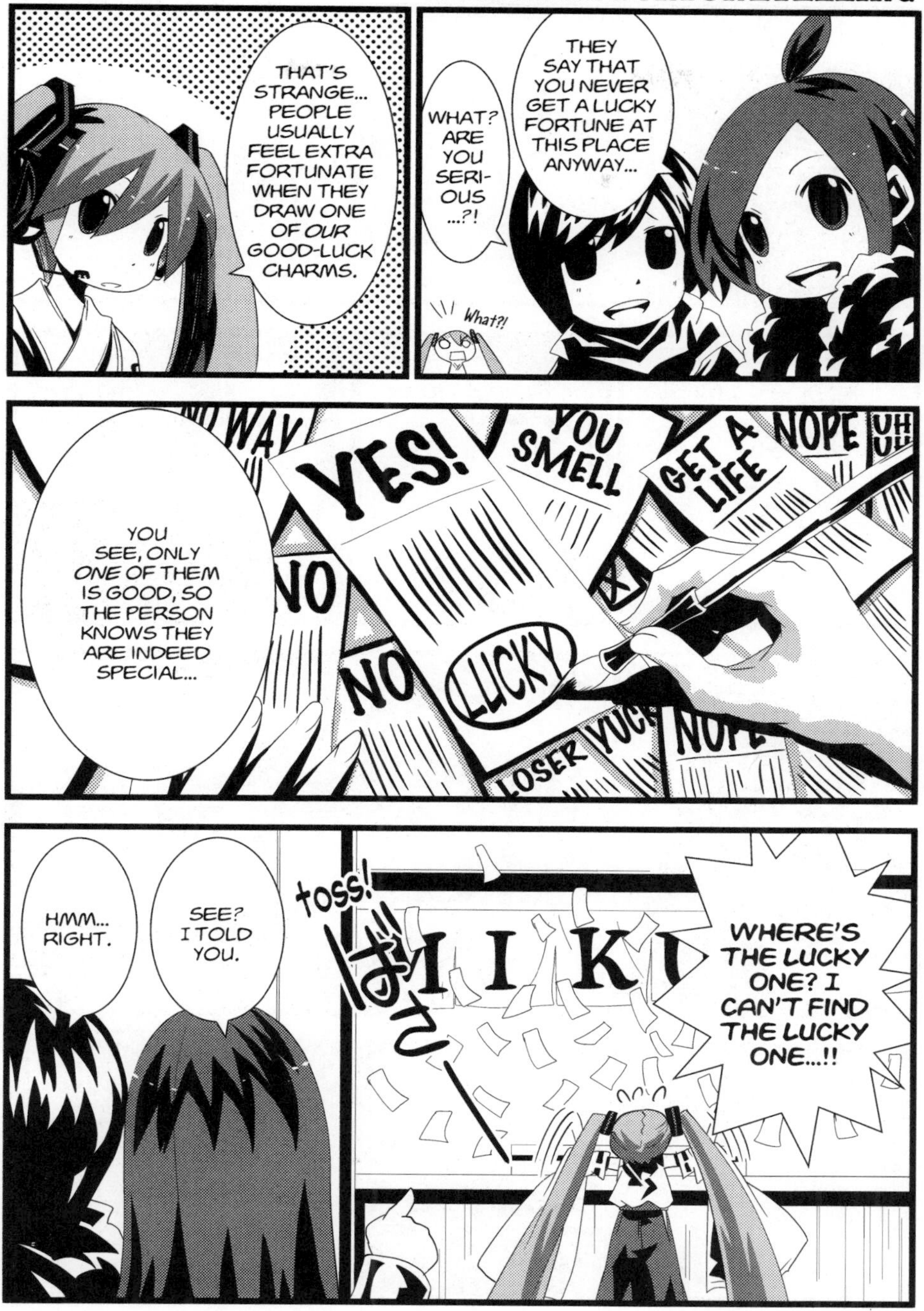
THEY SAY THAT YOU NEVER GET A LUCKY FORTUNE AT THIS PLACE ANYWAY...
WHAT? ARE YOU SERI-OUS ...?!
What?!
THAT'S STRANGE... PEOPLE USUALLY FEEL EXTRA FORTUNATE WHEN THEY DRAW ONE OF *OUR* GOOD-LUCK CHARMS.
NOPE
GET A LIFE
YOU SMELL
YES!
NO WAY
NO
LUCKY
NO
NOPE
LOSER
YOU SEE, ONLY *ONE OF THEM* IS GOOD, SO THE PERSON KNOWS THEY ARE INDEED SPECIAL...
WHERE'S THE LUCKY ONE? I CAN'T FIND THE LUCKY ONE...!!
toss!
ばさ
SEE? I TOLD YOU.
HMM... RIGHT.

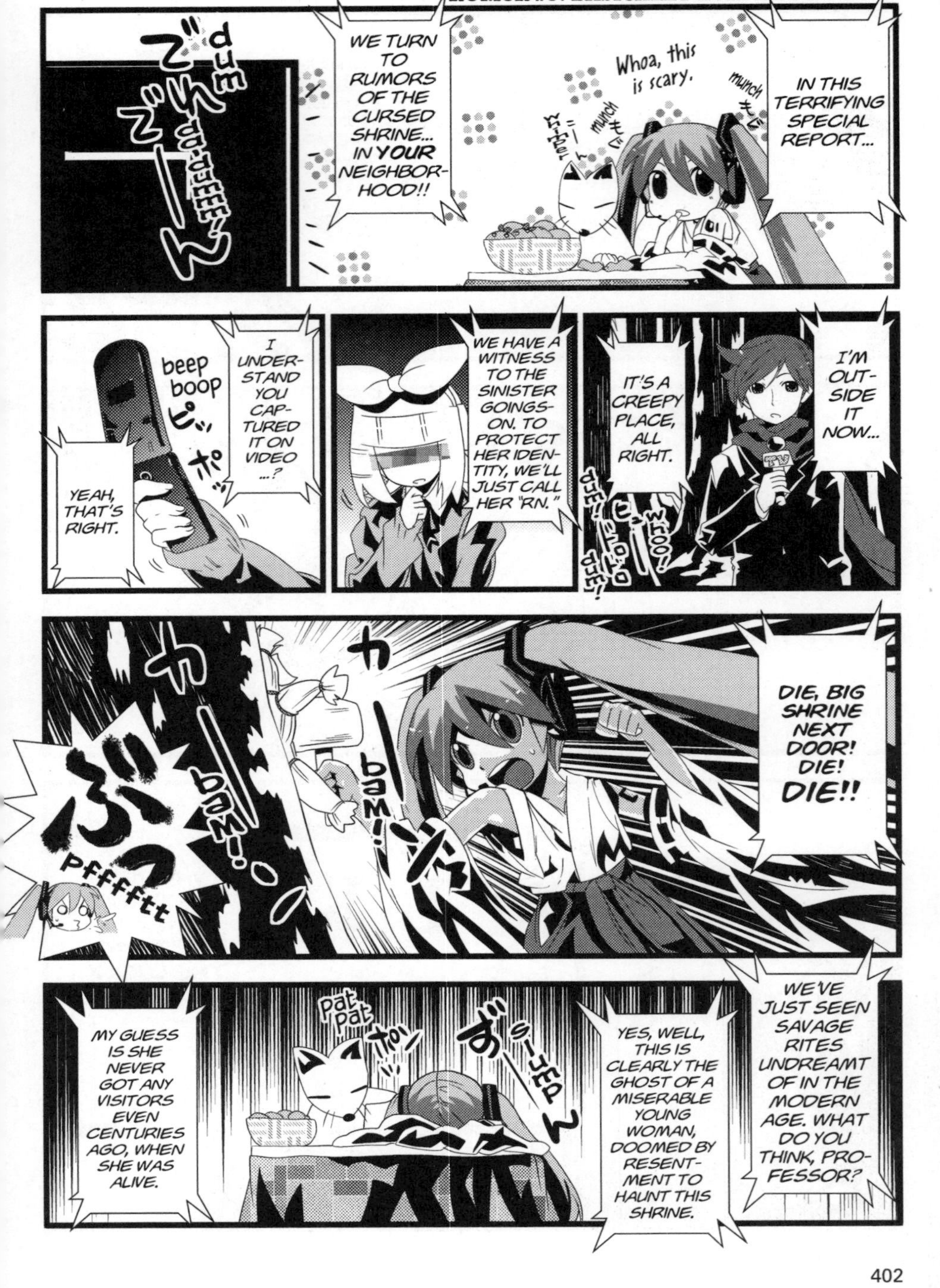
IN THIS TERRIFYING SPECIAL REPORT...
munch
Whoa, this is scary.
munch
whine
WE TURN TO RUMORS OF THE CURSED SHRINE... IN **YOUR** NEIGHBORHOOD!!
dum
dum-dum-dummm!
I'M OUTSIDE IT NOW...
IT'S A CREEPY PLACE, ALL RIGHT.
whoo!
whoo!
WE HAVE A WITNESS TO THE SINISTER GOINGS-ON. TO PROTECT HER IDENTITY, WE'LL JUST CALL HER "RN."
I UNDERSTAND YOU CAPTURED IT ON VIDEO ...?
beep boop
YEAH, THAT'S RIGHT.
DIE, BIG SHRINE NEXT DOOR! DIE! **DIE!!**
bam!
bam!
pffffttt
WE'VE JUST SEEN SAVAGE RITES UNDREAMT OF IN THE MODERN AGE. WHAT DO YOU THINK, PROFESSOR?
YES, WELL, THIS IS CLEARLY THE GHOST OF A MISERABLE YOUNG WOMAN, DOOMED BY RESENTMENT TO HAUNT THIS SHRINE.
slump
pat pat
MY GUESS IS SHE NEVER GOT ANY VISITORS EVEN CENTURIES AGO, WHEN SHE WAS ALIVE.

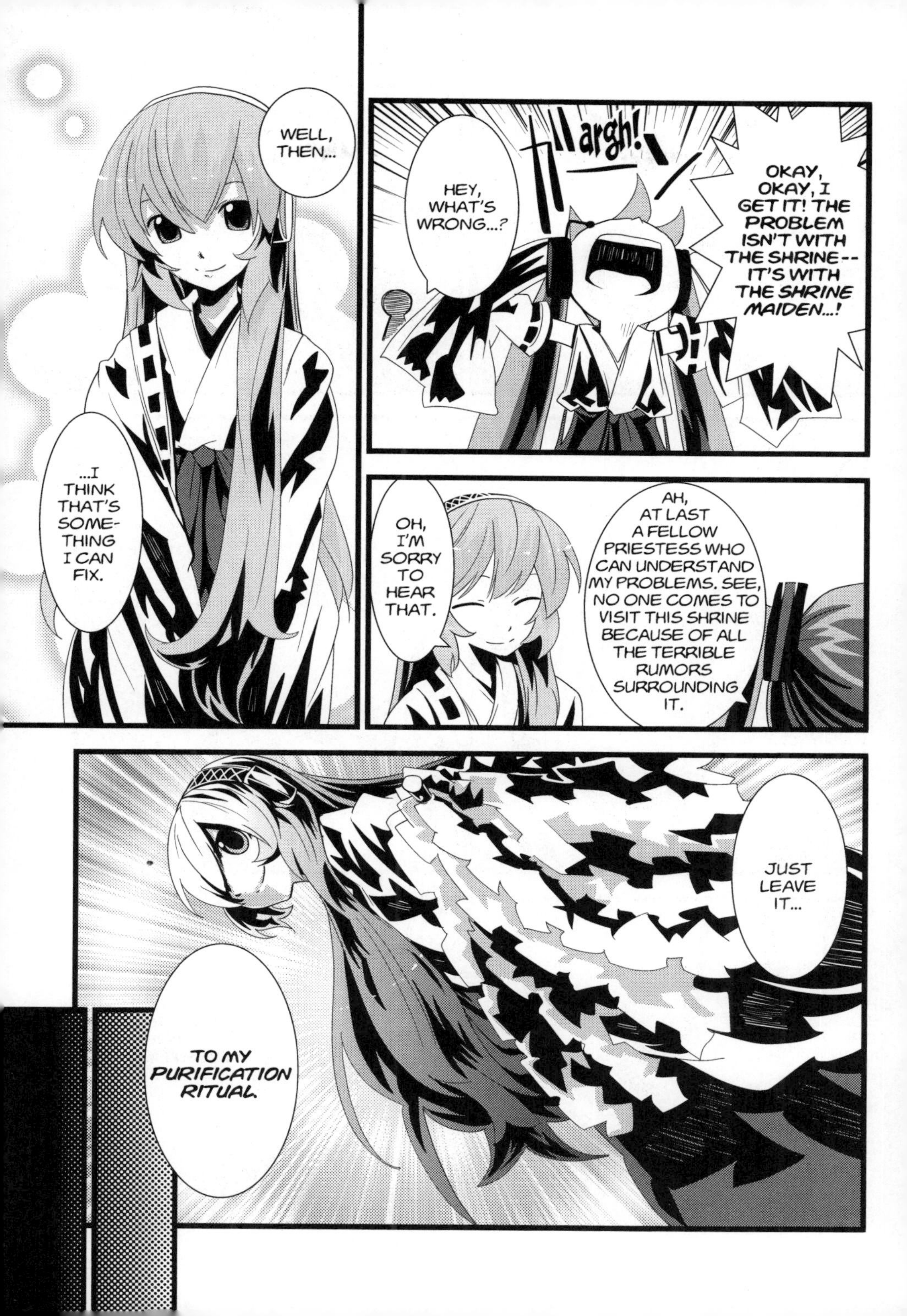
OKAY, OKAY, I GET IT! THE PROBLEM ISN'T WITH THE SHRINE-- IT'S WITH THE *SHRINE MAIDEN*...!
argh!
HEY, WHAT'S WRONG...?
AH, AT LAST A FELLOW PRIESTESS WHO CAN UNDERSTAND MY PROBLEMS. SEE, NO ONE COMES TO VISIT THIS SHRINE BECAUSE OF ALL THE TERRIBLE RUMORS SURROUNDING IT.
OH, I'M SORRY TO HEAR THAT.
WELL, THEN...
...I THINK THAT'S SOME-THING I CAN FIX.
JUST LEAVE IT...
TO MY *PURIFICATION RITUAL.*

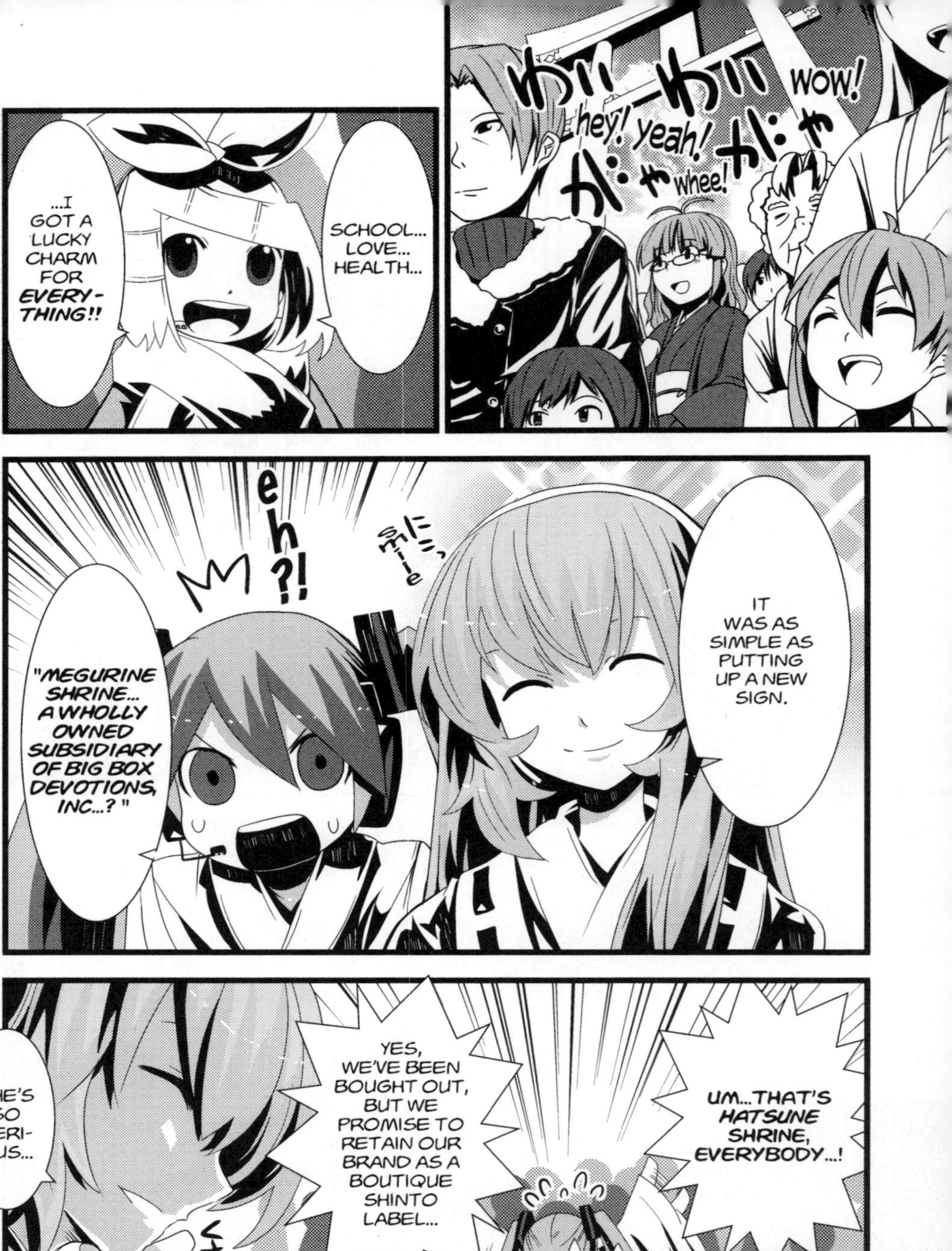

WOW!
hey! yeah! whee!
SCHOOL... LOVE... HEALTH...
...I GOT A LUCKY CHARM FOR EVERYTHING!!
IT WAS AS SIMPLE AS PUTTING UP A NEW SIGN.
eh?!
"MEGURINE SHRINE... A WHOLLY OWNED SUBSIDIARY OF BIG BOX DEVOTIONS, INC...?"
UM...THAT'S HATSUNE SHRINE, EVERYBODY...!
YES, WE'VE BEEN BOUGHT OUT, BUT WE PROMISE TO RETAIN OUR BRAND AS A BOUTIQUE SHINTO LABEL...
SHE'S SO SERI-OUS...

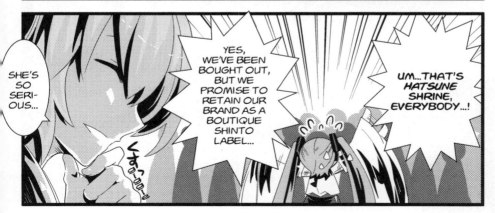

(25th SONG) PYGMY MIX

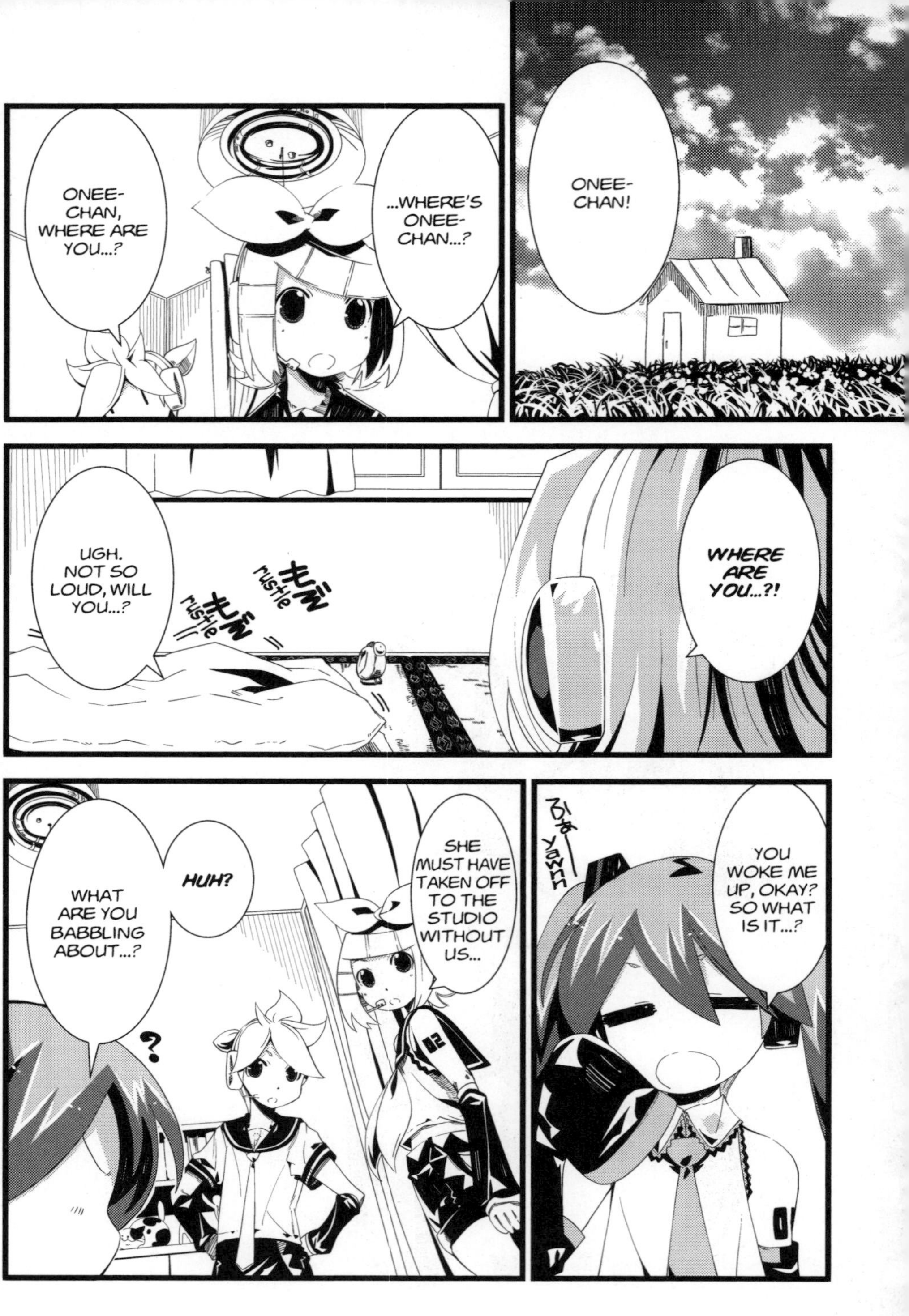
ONEE-CHAN!
...WHERE'S ONEE-CHAN...?
ONEE-CHAN, WHERE ARE YOU...?
WHERE ARE YOU...?!
もぞ rustle
もぞ rustle
UGH. NOT SO LOUD, WILL YOU...?
ふぁー yawnn
YOU WOKE ME UP, OKAY? SO WHAT IS IT...?
SHE MUST HAVE TAKEN OFF TO THE STUDIO WITHOUT US...
HUH?
WHAT ARE YOU BABBLING ABOUT...?
?

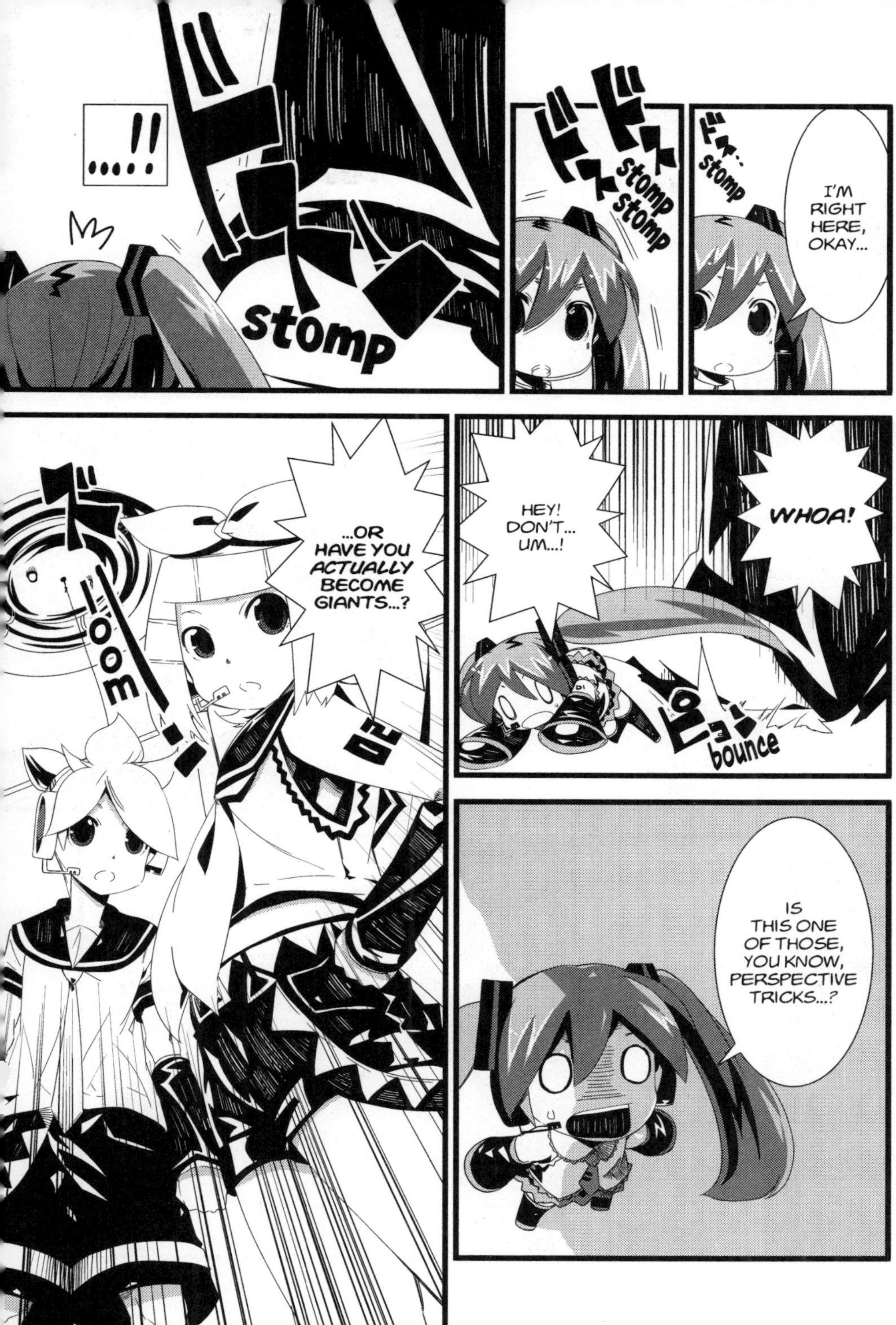
stomp
I'M RIGHT HERE, OKAY...
stomp stomp
...!!
stomp
WHOA!
HEY! DON'T... UM...!
bounce
IS THIS ONE OF THOSE, YOU KNOW, PERSPECTIVE TRICKS...?
...OR HAVE YOU ACTUALLY BECOME GIANTS...?
loom

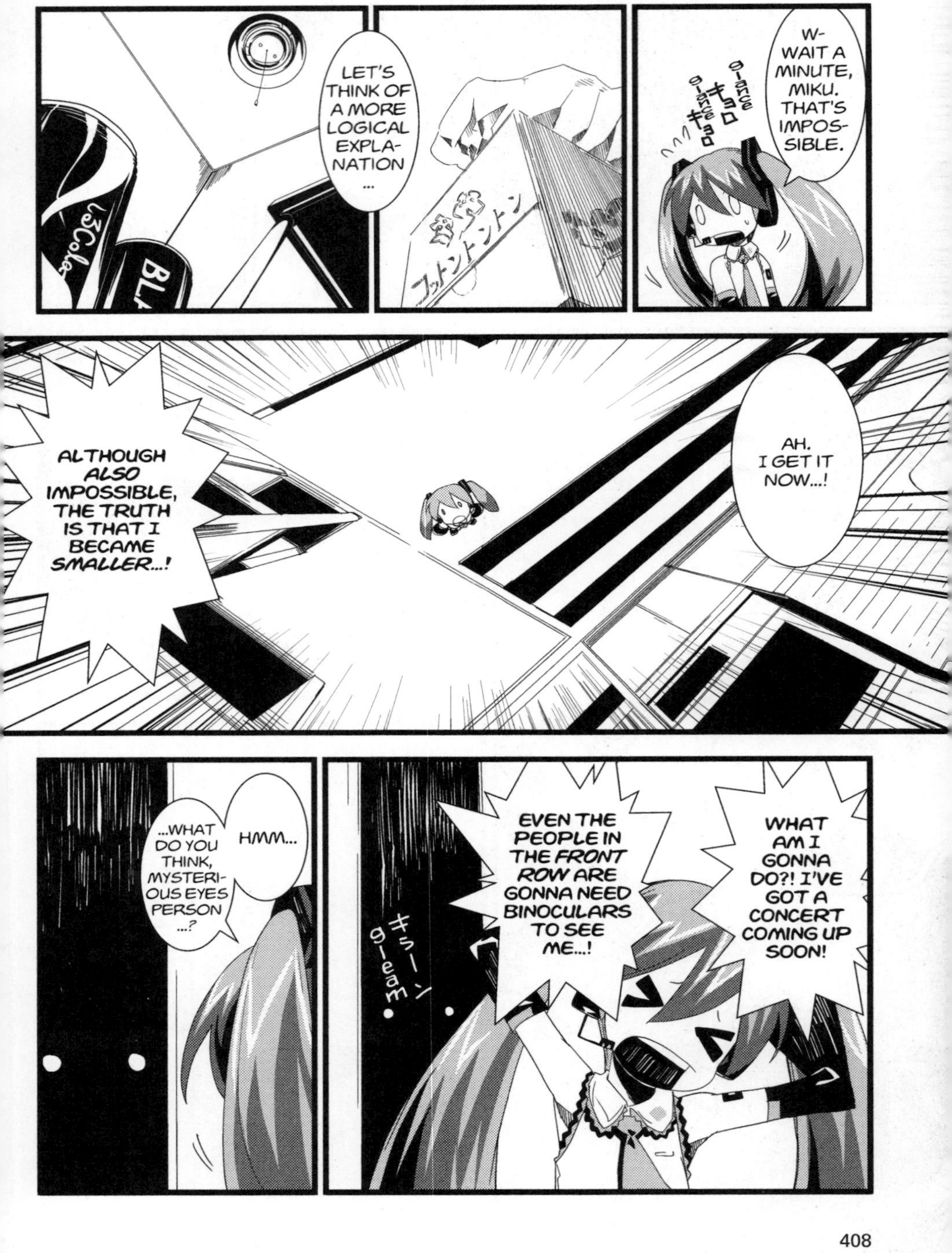
glance キョロ glance キョロ
W-WAIT A MINUTE, MIKU. THAT'S IMPOSSIBLE.
LET'S THINK OF A MORE LOGICAL EXPLANATION...
AH. I GET IT NOW...!
ALTHOUGH *ALSO* IMPOSSIBLE, THE TRUTH IS THAT I BECAME *SMALLER*...!
WHAT AM I GONNA DO?! I'VE GOT A CONCERT COMING UP SOON!
EVEN THE PEOPLE IN THE *FRONT ROW* ARE GONNA NEED BINOCULARS TO SEE ME...!
キラーン gleam
HMM...
...WHAT DO YOU THINK, MYSTERIOUS EYES PERSON...?

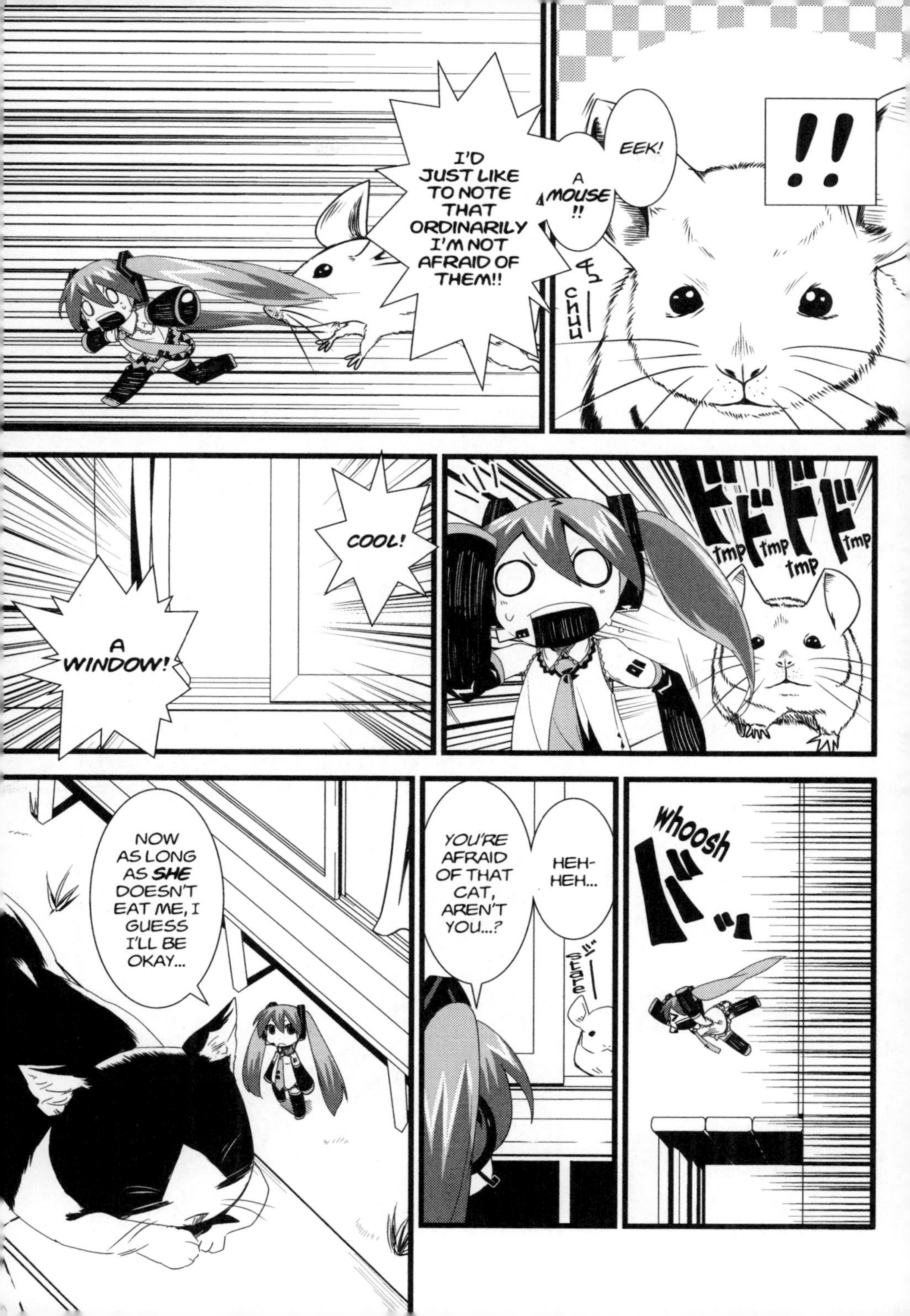
!!
EEK!
A MOUSE!!
chuu
I'D JUST LIKE TO NOTE THAT ORDINARILY I'M NOT AFRAID OF THEM!!
tmp tmp tmp tmp
COOL!
A WINDOW!
whoosh
HEH-HEH...
YOU'RE AFRAID OF THAT CAT, AREN'T YOU...?
stare
NOW AS LONG AS SHE DOESN'T EAT ME, I GUESS I'LL BE OKAY...

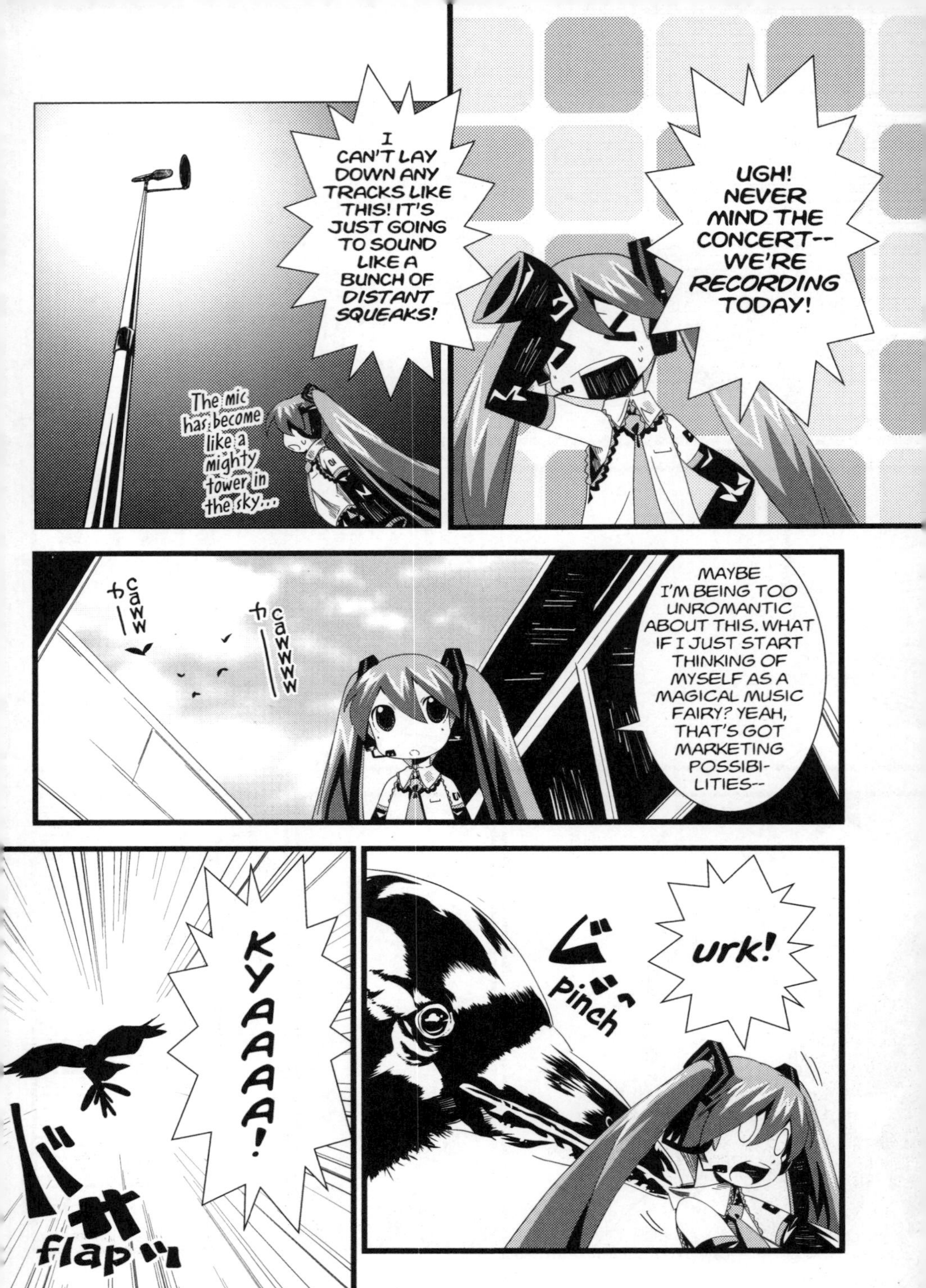
UGH! NEVER MIND THE CONCERT-- WE'RE RECORDING TODAY!
I CAN'T LAY DOWN ANY TRACKS LIKE THIS! IT'S JUST GOING TO SOUND LIKE A BUNCH OF DISTANT SQUEAKS!
The mic has become like a mighty tower in the sky...
MAYBE I'M BEING TOO UNROMANTIC ABOUT THIS. WHAT IF I JUST START THINKING OF MYSELF AS A MAGICAL MUSIC FAIRY? YEAH, THAT'S GOT MARKETING POSSIBI-LITIES--
cawwww
caww
urk!
pinch
KYAAAAA!
flap

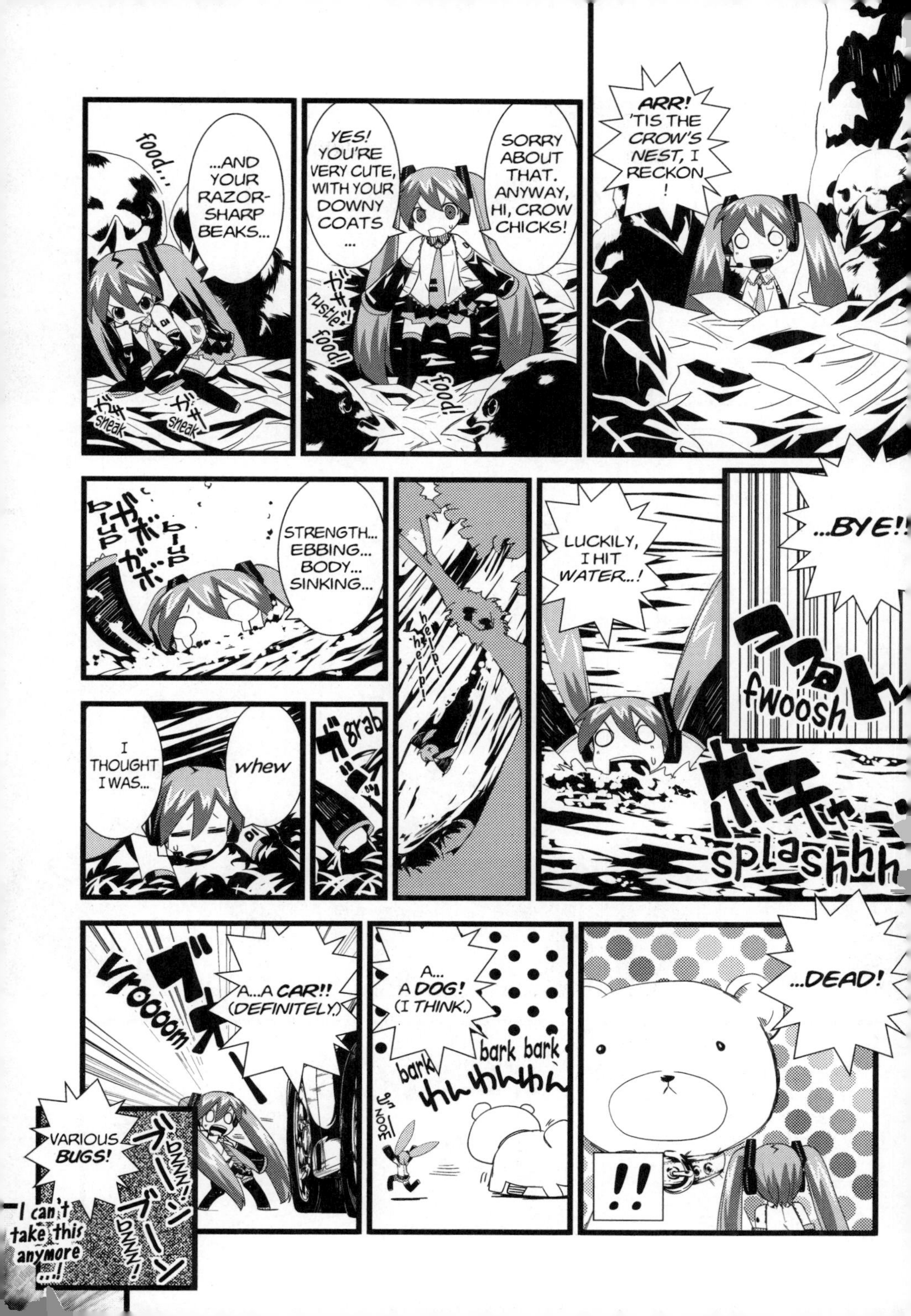
ARR! 'TIS THE CROW'S NEST, I RECKON!
SORRY ABOUT THAT. ANYWAY, HI, CROW CHICKS!
YES! YOU'RE VERY CUTE, WITH YOUR DOWNY COATS ...
rustle
food!
food!
...AND YOUR RAZOR-SHARP BEAKS...
food...
sneak
sneak
...BYE!!
fwoosh
LUCKILY, I HIT WATER...!
splashhh
help! help!
STRENGTH... EBBING... BODY... SINKING...
b-up b-up
grab
whew
I THOUGHT I WAS...
...DEAD!
!!
A... A DOG! (I THINK.)
bark bark
bark
zoom
A...A CAR!! (DEFINITELY.)
vroooom
VARIOUS BUGS!
bzzz! bzzz!
I can't take this anymore...!

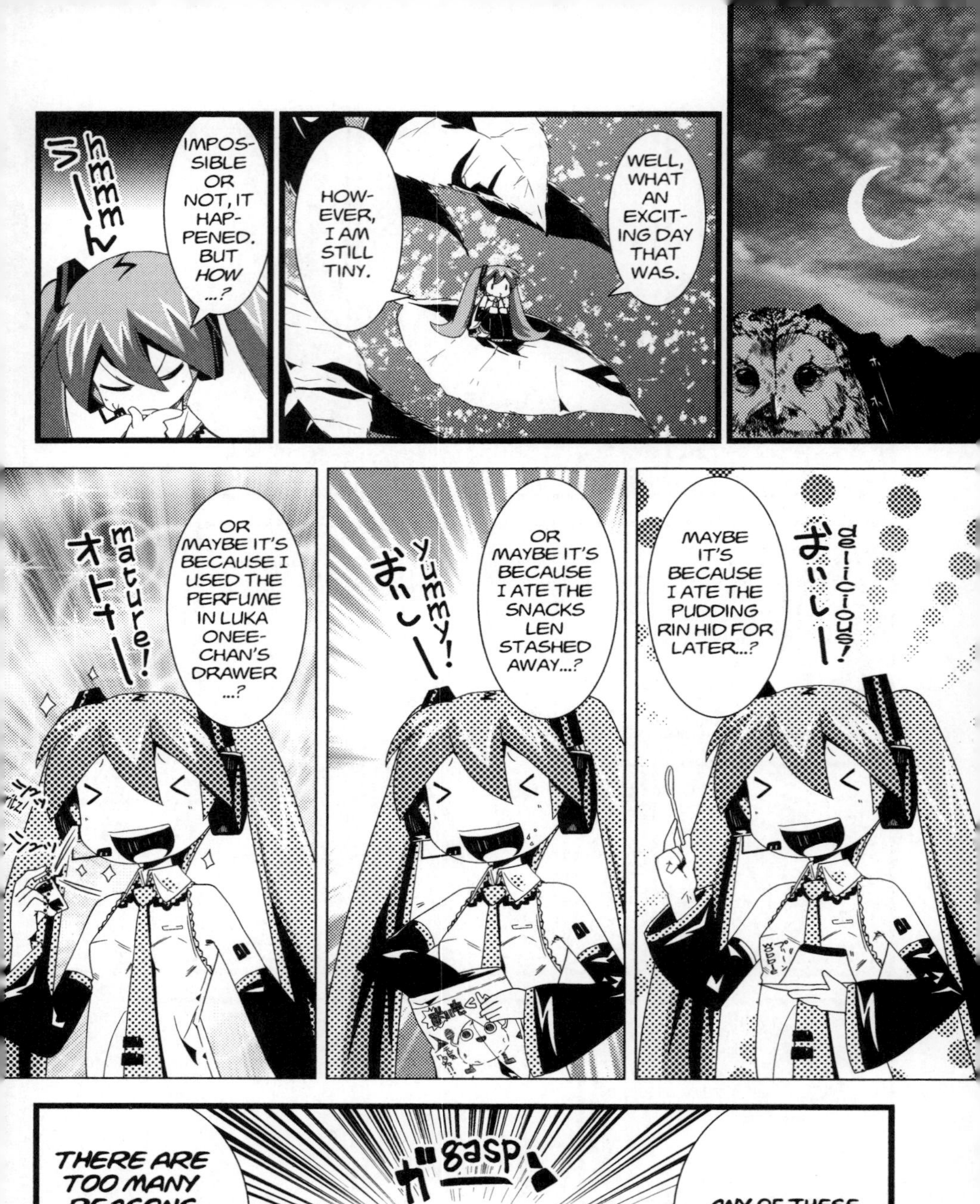
WELL, WHAT AN EXCITING DAY THAT WAS.
HOWEVER, I AM STILL TINY.
IMPOSSIBLE OR NOT, IT HAPPENED. BUT HOW ...?
hmmmm
うーん
おいしー
delicious!
MAYBE IT'S BECAUSE I ATE THE PUDDING RIN HID FOR LATER...?
OR MAYBE IT'S BECAUSE I ATE THE SNACKS LEN STASHED AWAY...?
yummy!
おいしー
OR MAYBE IT'S BECAUSE I USED THE PERFUME IN LUKA ONEE-CHAN'S DRAWER ...?
mature!
オトナー
ANY OF THESE THEORIES ARE PLAUSIBLE...!
gasp
THERE ARE TOO MANY REASONS TO PUNISH MY BAD BEHAVIOR...!

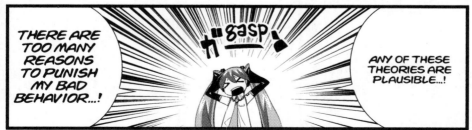

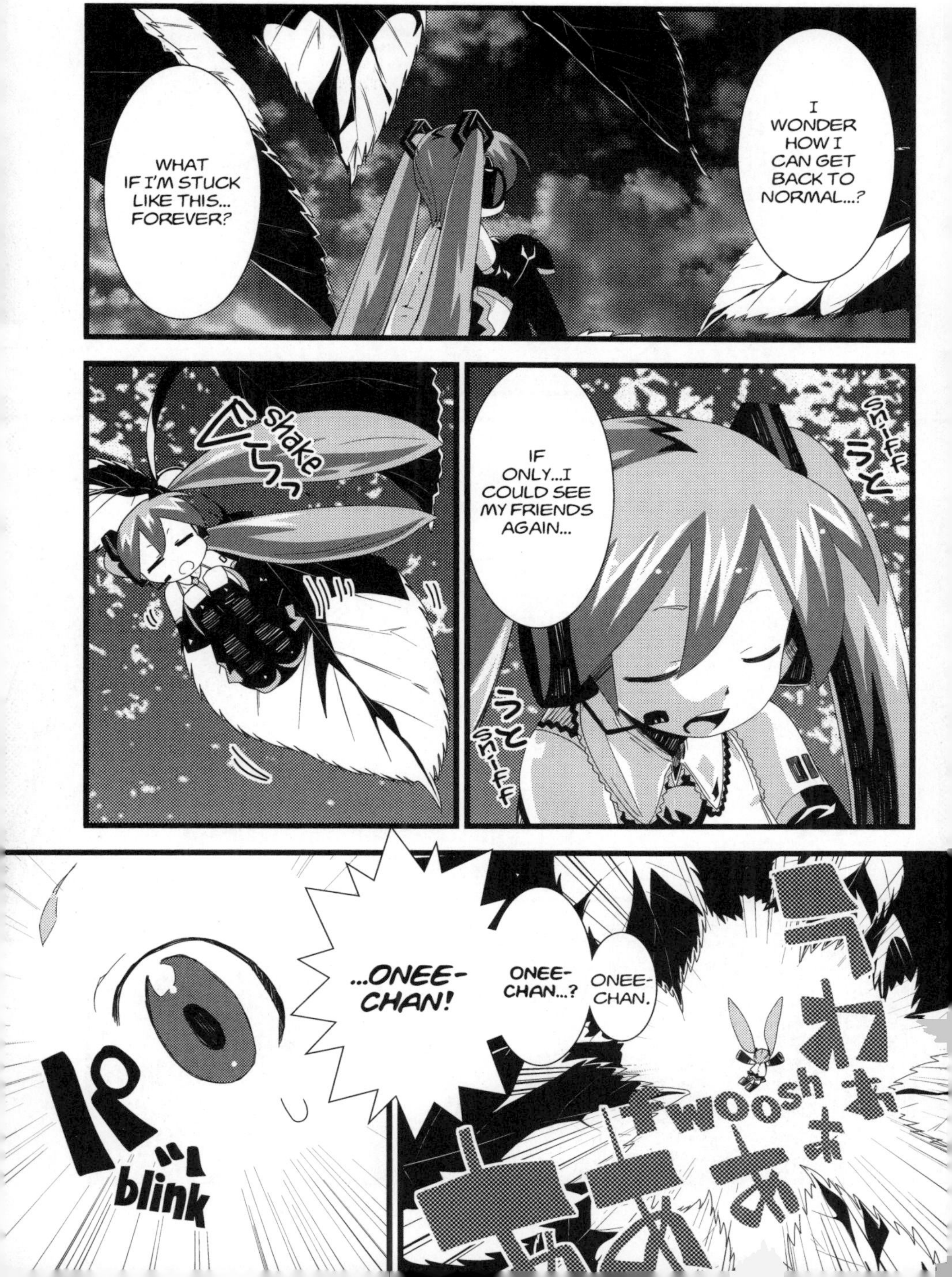

I WONDER HOW I CAN GET BACK TO NORMAL...?
WHAT IF I'M STUCK LIKE THIS... FOREVER?
SNIFF
IF ONLY...I COULD SEE MY FRIENDS AGAIN...
SNIFF
shake
ONEE-CHAN.
ONEE-CHAN...?
...ONEE-CHAN!
fwoosh
blink

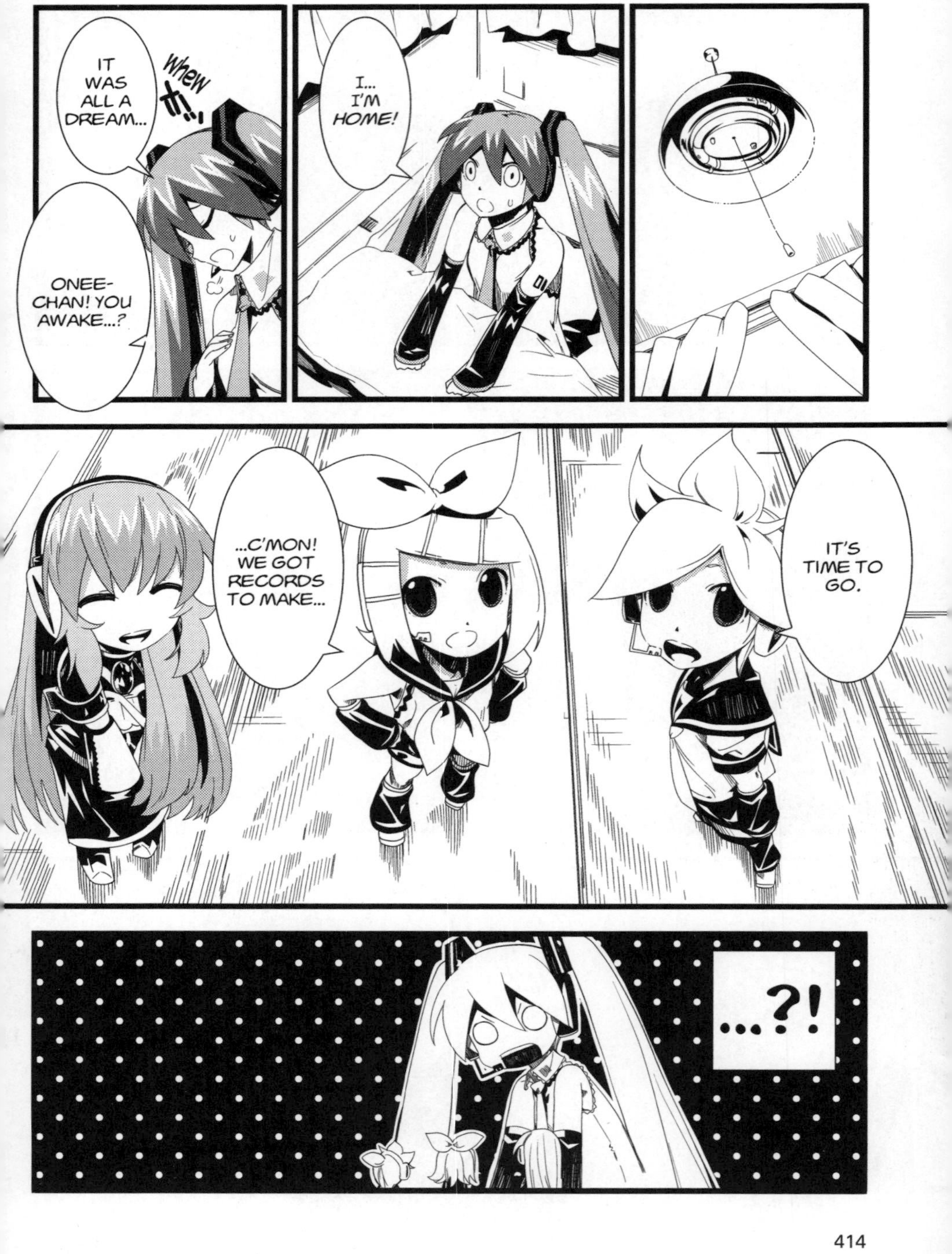
I... I'M HOME!
whew
IT WAS ALL A DREAM...
ONEE-CHAN! YOU AWAKE...?
IT'S TIME TO GO.
...C'MON! WE GOT RECORDS TO MAKE...
...?!

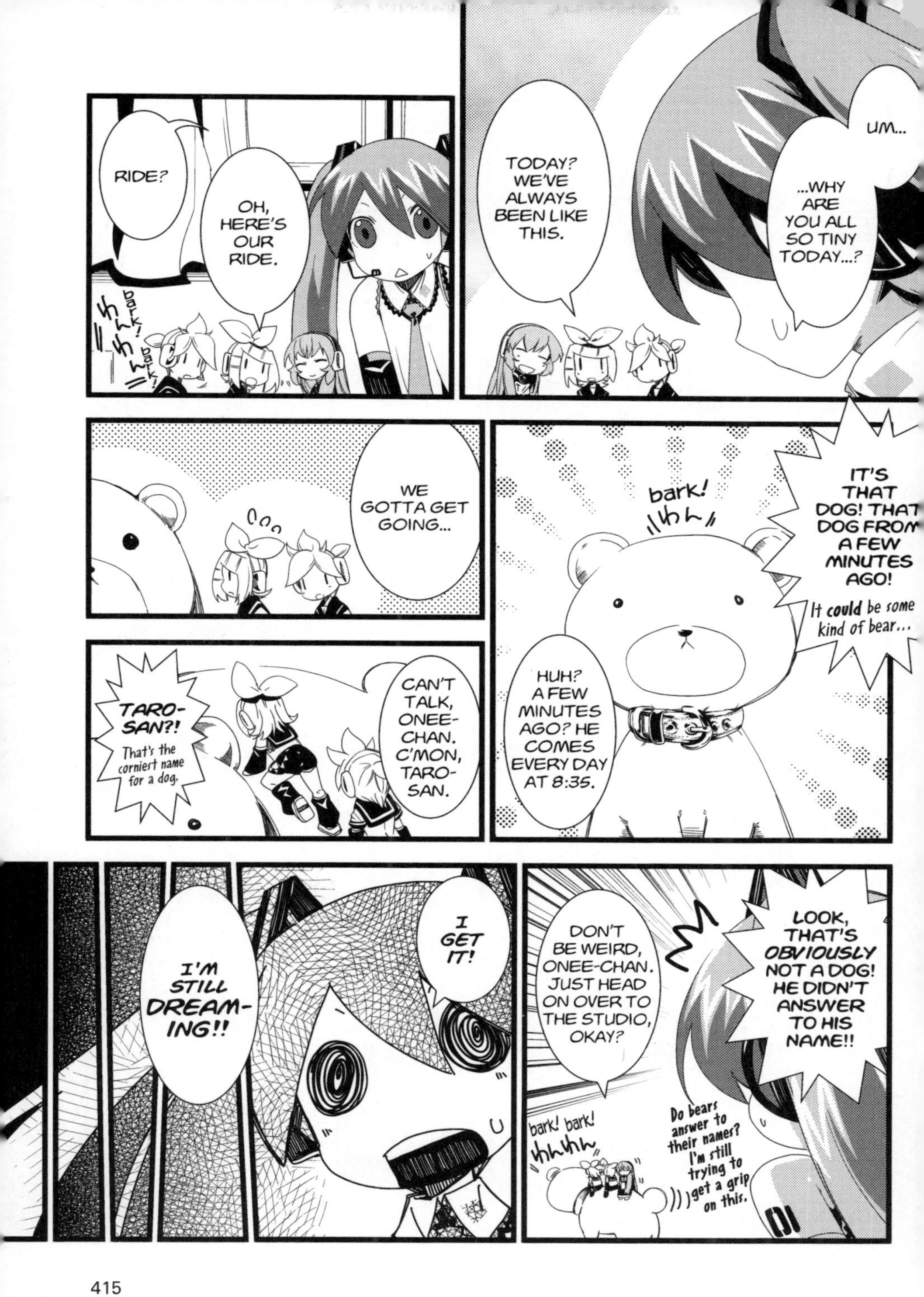
UM...
...WHY ARE YOU ALL SO TINY TODAY...?
TODAY? WE'VE ALWAYS BEEN LIKE THIS.
OH, HERE'S OUR RIDE.
RIDE?
bark! bark!
bark!
IT'S THAT DOG! THAT DOG FROM A FEW MINUTES AGO!
It could be some kind of bear...
HUH? A FEW MINUTES AGO? HE COMES EVERY DAY AT 8:35.
WE GOTTA GET GOING...
CAN'T TALK, ONEE-CHAN. C'MON, TARO-SAN.
TARO-SAN?!
That's the corniest name for a dog.
LOOK, THAT'S OBVIOUSLY NOT A DOG! HE DIDN'T ANSWER TO HIS NAME!!
DON'T BE WEIRD, ONEE-CHAN. JUST HEAD ON OVER TO THE STUDIO, OKAY?
Do bears answer to their names? I'm still trying to get a grip on this.
bark! bark!
I GET IT!
I'M STILL DREAMING!!

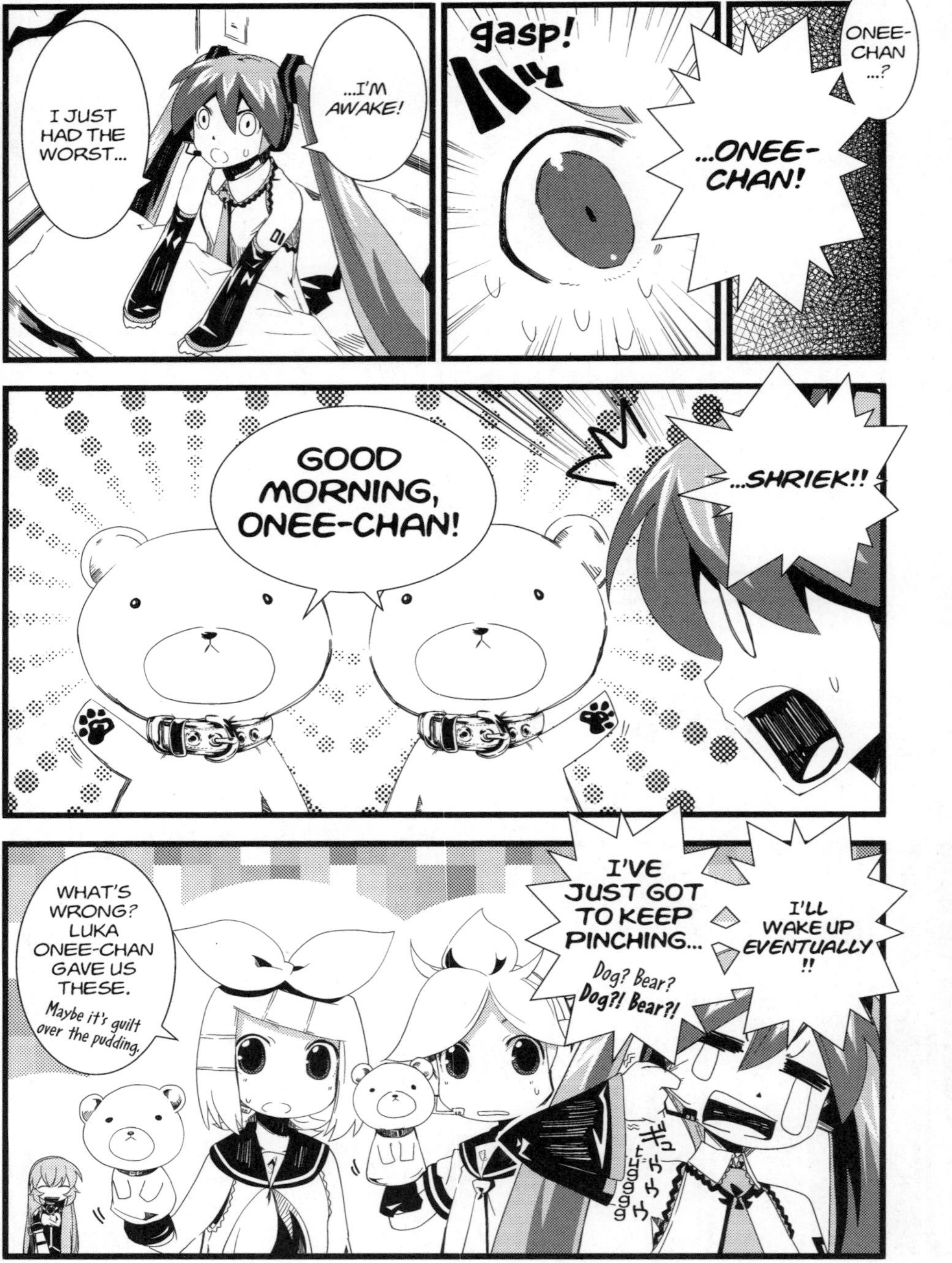
ONEE-CHAN ...?
gasp!
...ONEE-CHAN!
...I'M AWAKE!
I JUST HAD THE WORST...
...SHRIEK!!
GOOD MORNING, ONEE-CHAN!
I'LL WAKE UP EVENTUALLY!!
I'VE JUST GOT TO KEEP PINCHING...
Dog? Bear? Dog?! Bear?!
WHAT'S WRONG? LUKA ONEE-CHAN GAVE US THESE.
Maybe it's guilt over the pudding.

(26th SONG) MAGICAL MIX

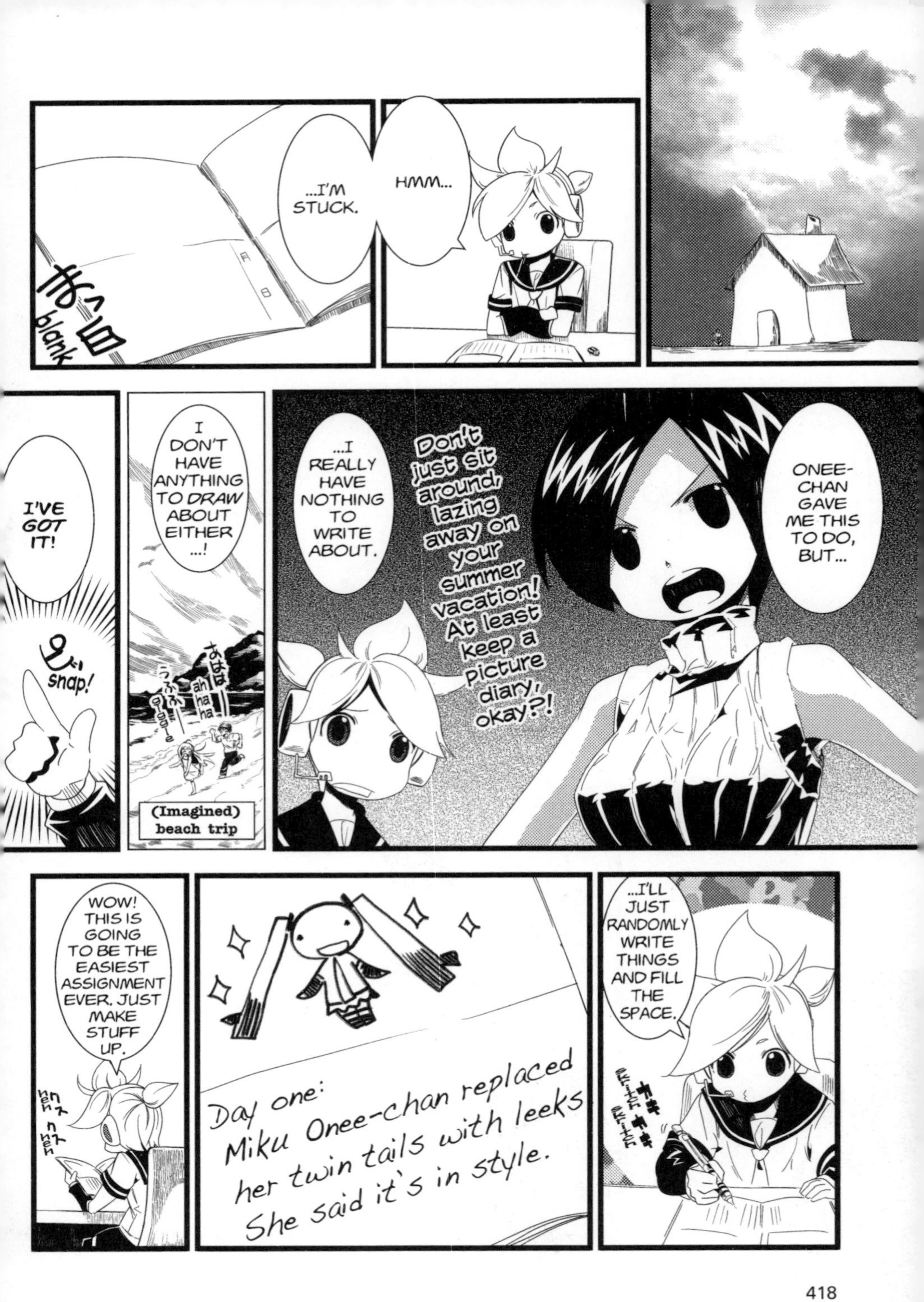
HMM...
...I'M STUCK.
まっ白
blank
ONEE-CHAN GAVE ME THIS TO DO, BUT...
Don't just sit around, lazing away on your summer vacation! At least keep a picture diary, okay?!
...I REALLY HAVE NOTHING TO WRITE ABOUT.
I DON'T HAVE ANYTHING TO *DRAW* ABOUT EITHER ...!
あはは
ah ha ha
うふふ
u-fu-fu-e
(Imagined) beach trip
I'VE GOT IT!
snap!
...I'LL JUST RANDOMLY WRITE THINGS AND FILL THE SPACE.
カキ カキ
scribble scribble
Day one:
Miku Onee-chan replaced her twin tails with leeks
She said it's in style.
WOW! THIS IS GOING TO BE THE EASIEST ASSIGNMENT EVER. JUST MAKE STUFF UP.
hen n hen n

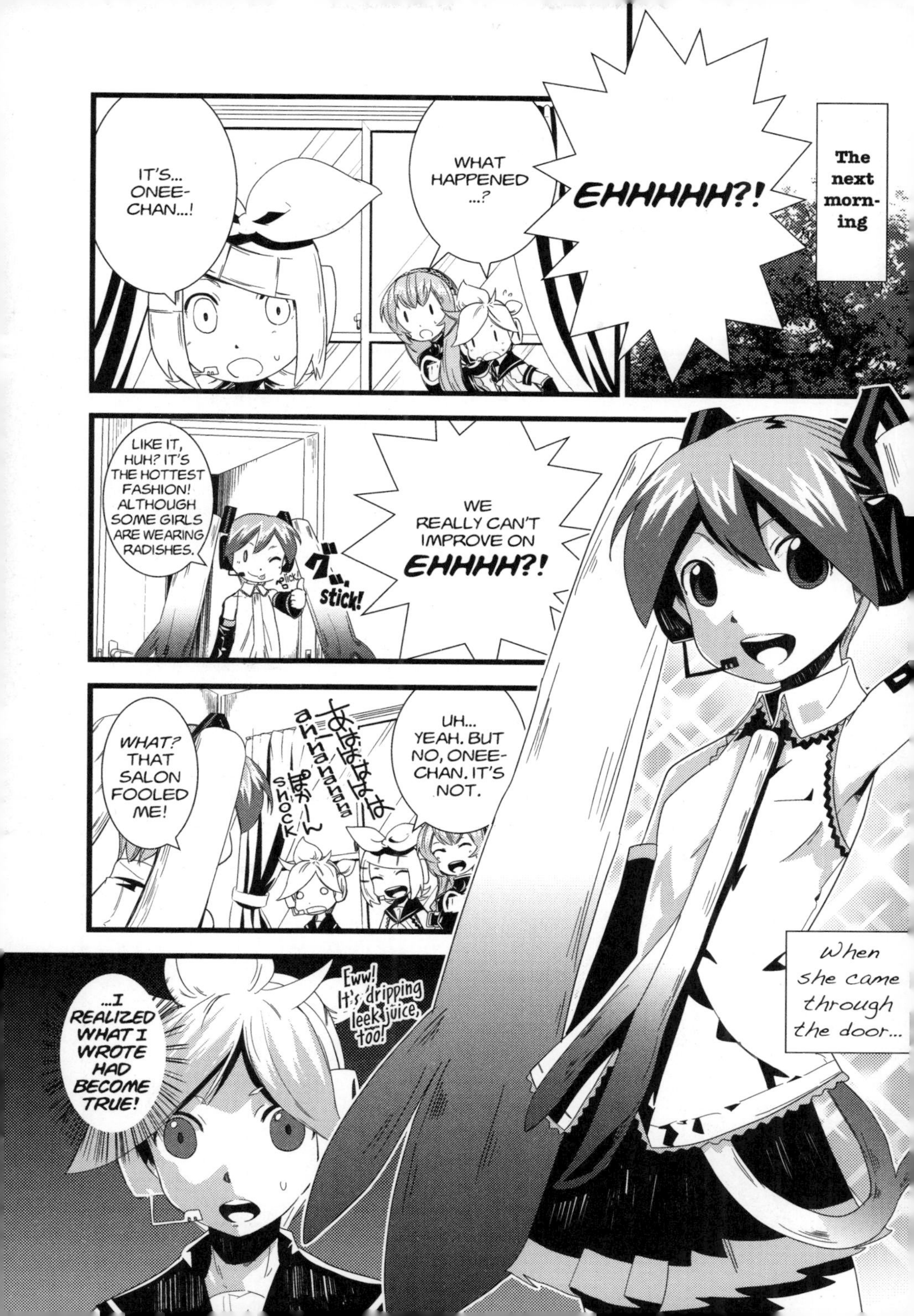
The next morning
EHHHHH?!
WHAT HAPPENED ...?
IT'S... ONEE-CHAN...!
When she came through the door...
WE REALLY CAN'T IMPROVE ON EHHHH?!
LIKE IT, HUH? IT'S THE HOTTEST FASHION! ALTHOUGH SOME GIRLS ARE WEARING RADISHES.
グッ
stick!
UH... YEAH. BUT NO, ONEE-CHAN. IT'S NOT.
あははは
ぽか～ん
SHOCK
WHAT? THAT SALON FOOLED ME!
Eww! It's dripping leek juice, too!
...I REALIZED WHAT I WROTE HAD BECOME TRUE!

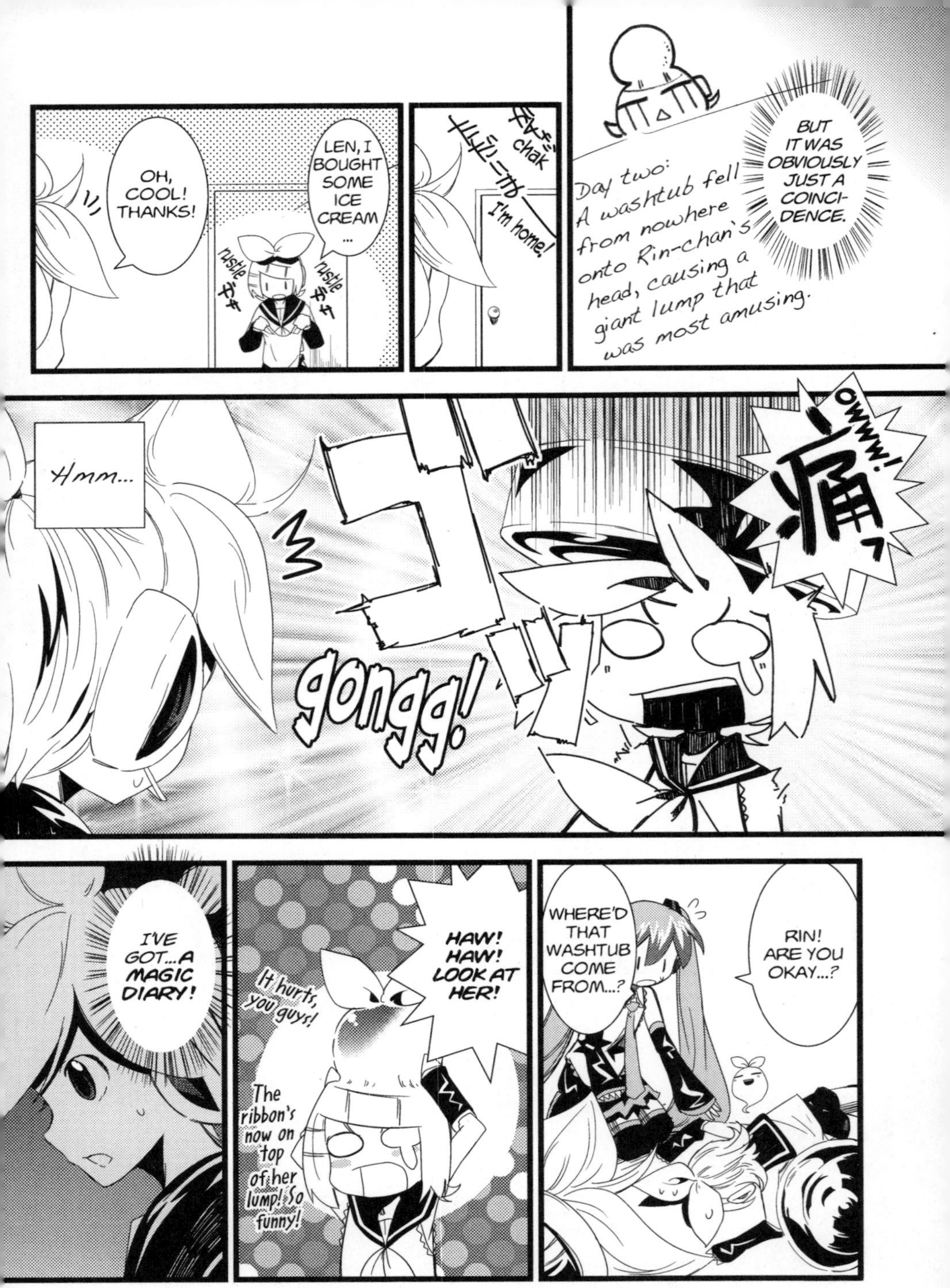
Day two: A washtub fell from nowhere onto Rin-chan's head, causing a giant lump that was most amusing.
BUT IT WAS OBVIOUSLY JUST A COINCIDENCE.
chak
I'm home!
LEN, I BOUGHT SOME ICE CREAM ...
rustle
rustle
OH, COOL! THANKS!
OWWW!
gongg!
Hmm...
RIN! ARE YOU OKAY...?
WHERE'D THAT WASHTUB COME FROM...?
HAW! HAW! LOOK AT HER!
It hurts, you guys!
The ribbon's now on top of her lump! So funny!
I'VE GOT...A MAGIC DIARY!

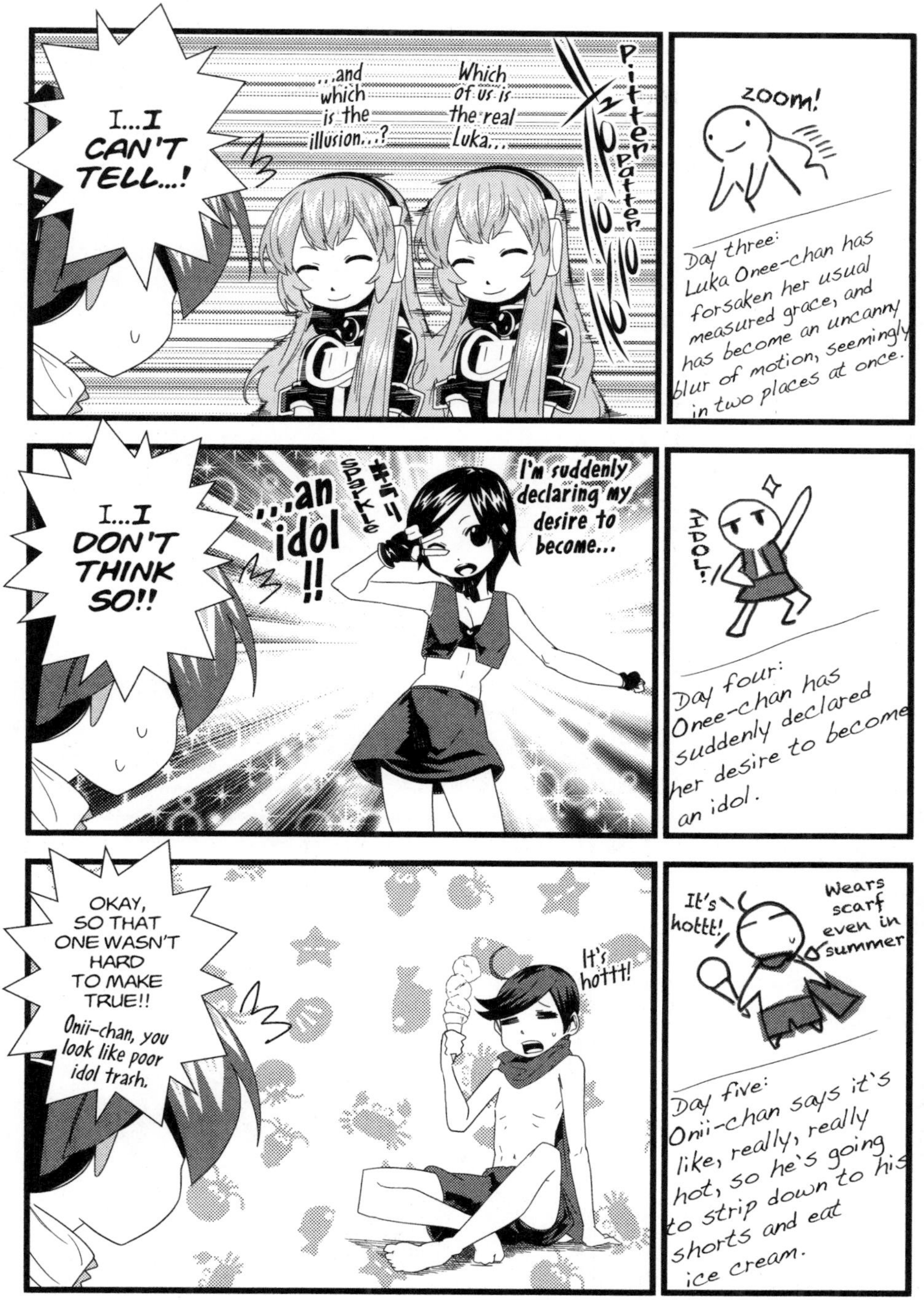
ZOOM!
Day three: Luka Onee-chan has forsaken her usual measured grace, and has become an uncanny blur of motion, seemingly in two places at once.
Pitter patter
Which of us is the real Luka...
...and which is the illusion...?
I...I CAN'T TELL...!
IDOL!
Day four: Onee-chan has suddenly declared her desire to become an idol.
キラリ SPARKLE
I'm suddenly declaring my desire to become...
...an idol!!
I...I DON'T THINK SO!!
It's hotttt!
Wears scarf even in summer
Day five: Onii-chan says it's like, really, really hot, so he's going to strip down to his shorts and eat ice cream.
It's hotttt!
OKAY, SO THAT ONE WASN'T HARD TO MAKE TRUE!!
Onii-chan, you look like poor idol trash.

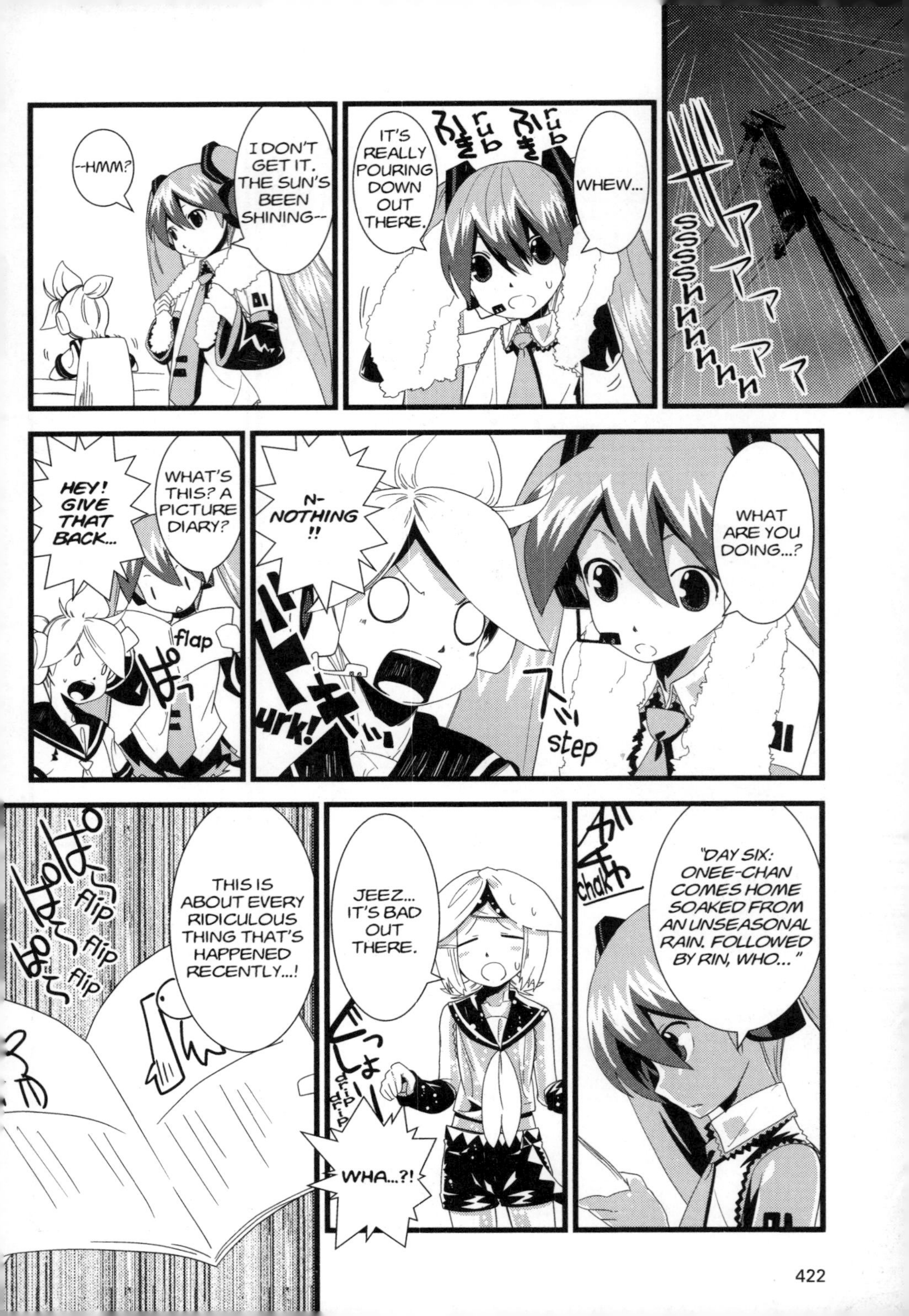
SSSShhhhhnnnn
WHEW...
rub rub
IT'S REALLY POURING DOWN OUT THERE.
I DON'T GET IT. THE SUN'S BEEN SHINING--
--HMM?
WHAT ARE YOU DOING...?
step
N-NOTHING!!
urk!
WHAT'S THIS? A PICTURE DIARY?
flap
HEY! GIVE THAT BACK...
chak
"DAY SIX: ONEE-CHAN COMES HOME SOAKED FROM AN UNSEASONAL RAIN. FOLLOWED BY RIN, WHO..."
JEEZ... IT'S BAD OUT THERE.
drip drip
WHA...?!
THIS IS ABOUT EVERY RIDICULOUS THING THAT'S HAPPENED RECENTLY...!
flip flip flip

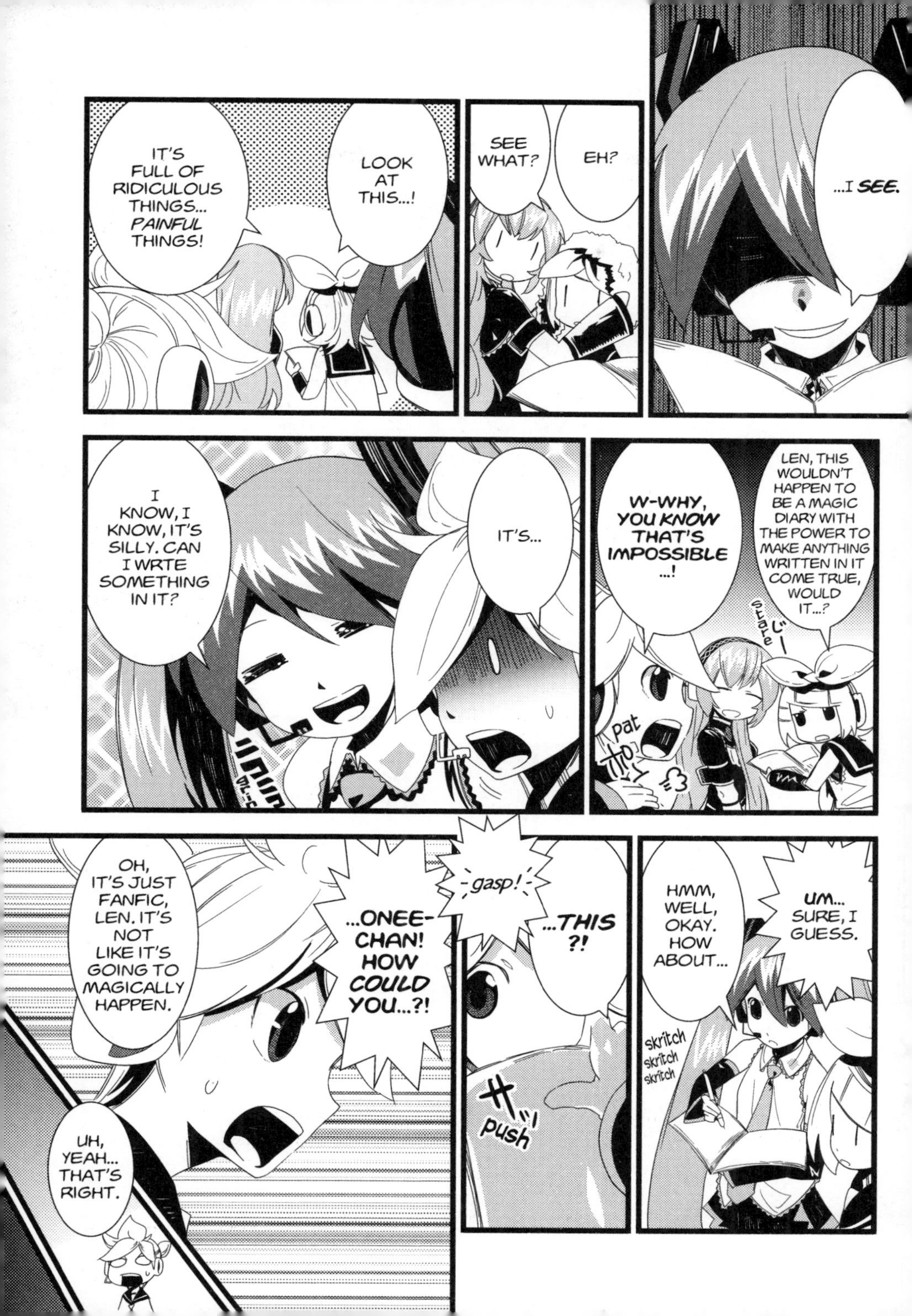
...I SEE.
EH?
SEE WHAT?
LOOK AT THIS...!
IT'S FULL OF RIDICULOUS THINGS... PAINFUL THINGS!
LEN, THIS WOULDN'T HAPPEN TO BE A MAGIC DIARY WITH THE POWER TO MAKE ANYTHING WRITTEN IN IT COME TRUE, WOULD IT...?
stare
W-WHY, YOU KNOW THAT'S IMPOSSIBLE...!
pat
IT'S...
I KNOW, I KNOW, IT'S SILLY. CAN I WRTE SOMETHING IN IT?
UM... SURE, I GUESS.
HMM, WELL, OKAY. HOW ABOUT...
skritch skritch skritch
gasp!
...THIS?!
push
...ONEE-CHAN! HOW COULD YOU...?!
OH, IT'S JUST FANFIC, LEN. IT'S NOT LIKE IT'S GOING TO MAGICALLY HAPPEN.
UH, YEAH... THAT'S RIGHT.

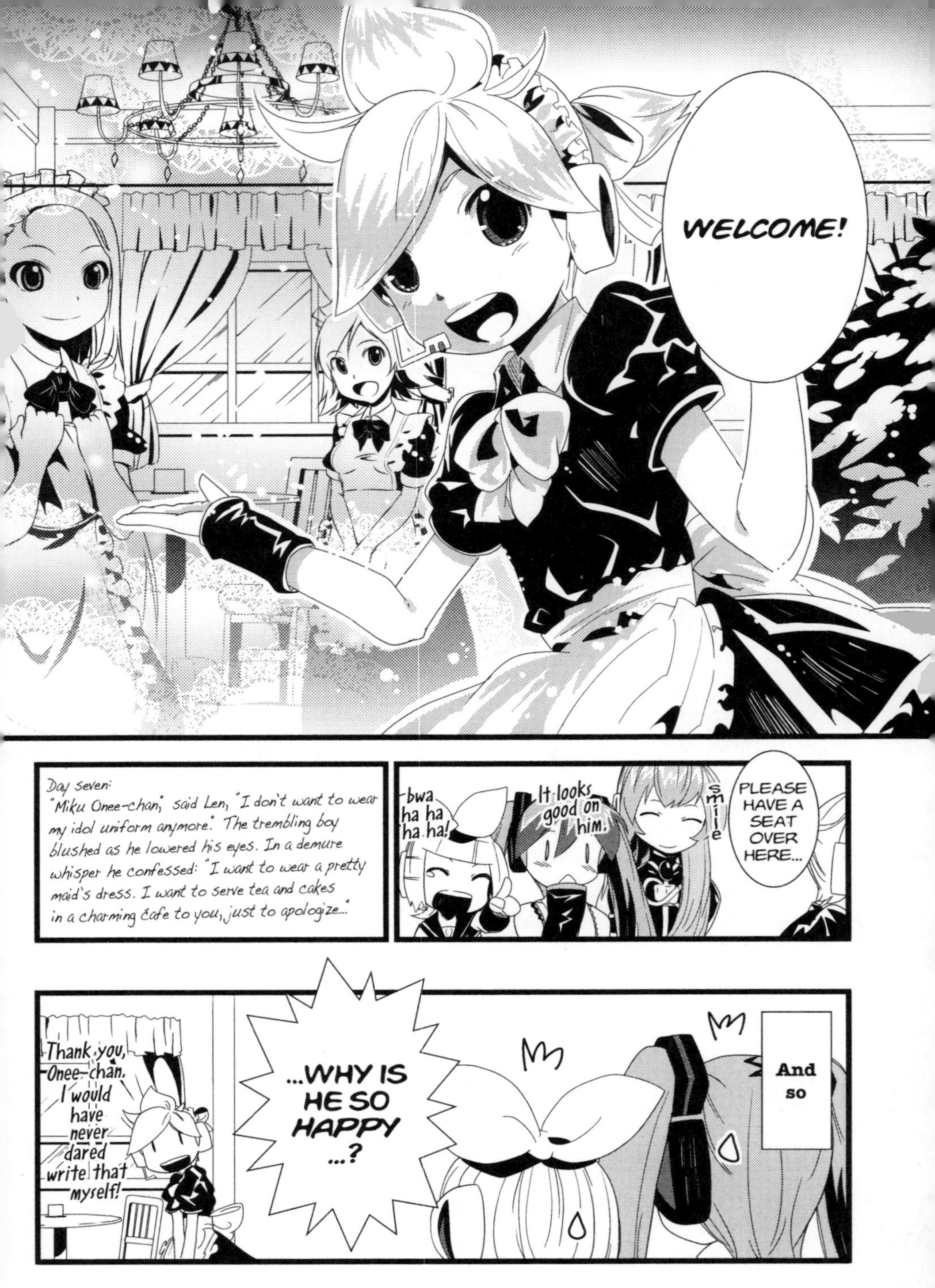
WELCOME!
PLEASE HAVE A SEAT OVER HERE...
smile
It looks good on him.
bwa ha ha ha ha!
Day seven: "Miku Onee-chan," said Len, "I don't want to wear my idol uniform anymore." The trembling boy blushed as he lowered his eyes. In a demure whisper he confessed: "I want to wear a pretty maid's dress. I want to serve tea and cakes in a charming café to you, just to apologize..."
And so
...WHY IS HE SO HAPPY ...?
Thank you, Onee-chan. I would have never dared write that myself!

(27th SONG) ANGRY MIX

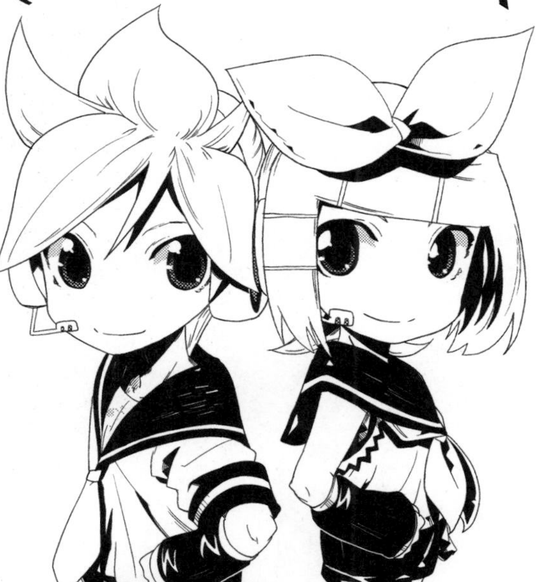

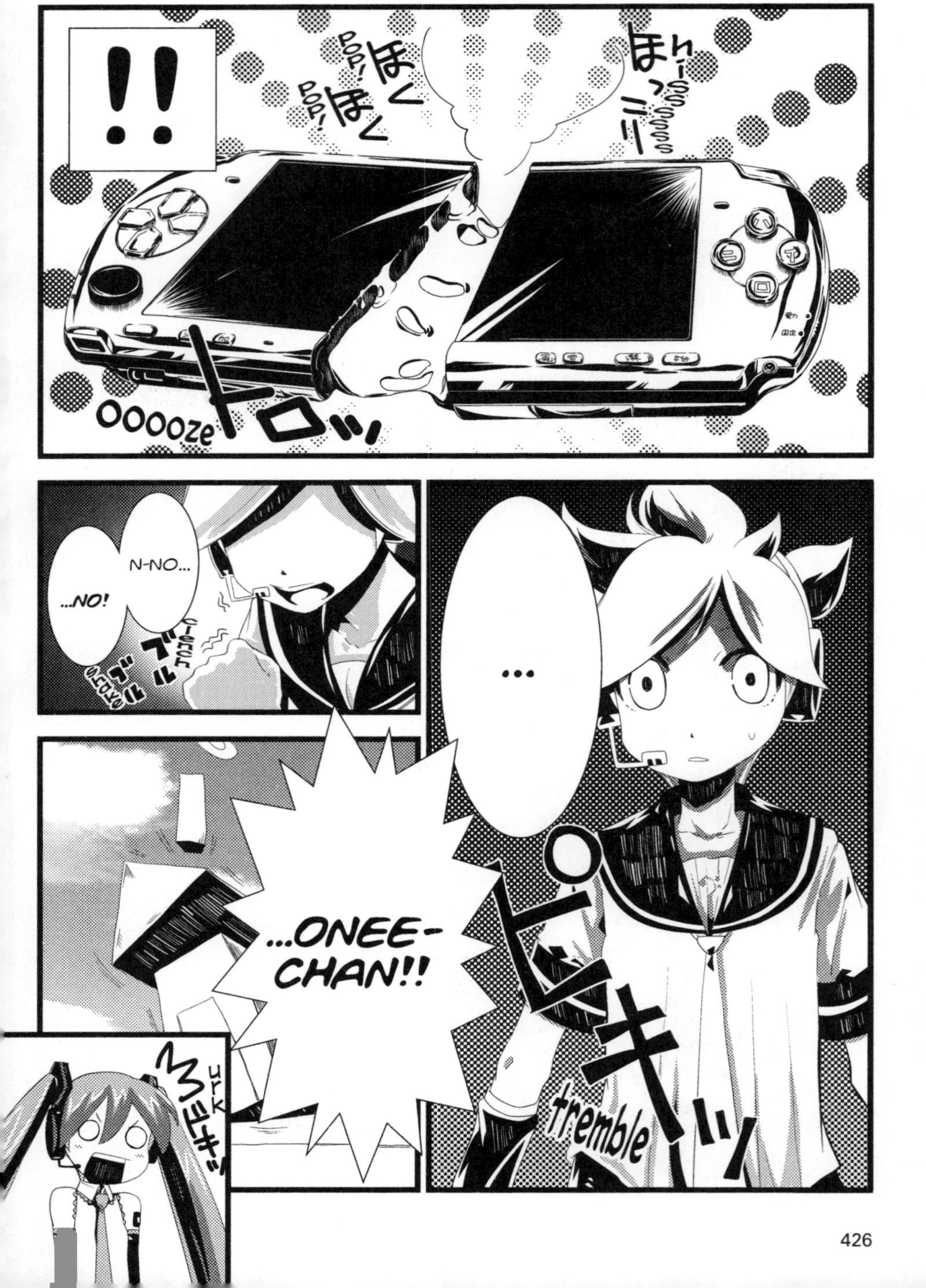

!!
ほっこり
HISSSSSSS
ぽくぽく
POP! POP!
OOOOZE
トロッ
...
N-NO...
...NO!
CLENCH
SHAKE
...ONEE-CHAN!!
TREMBLE
URK

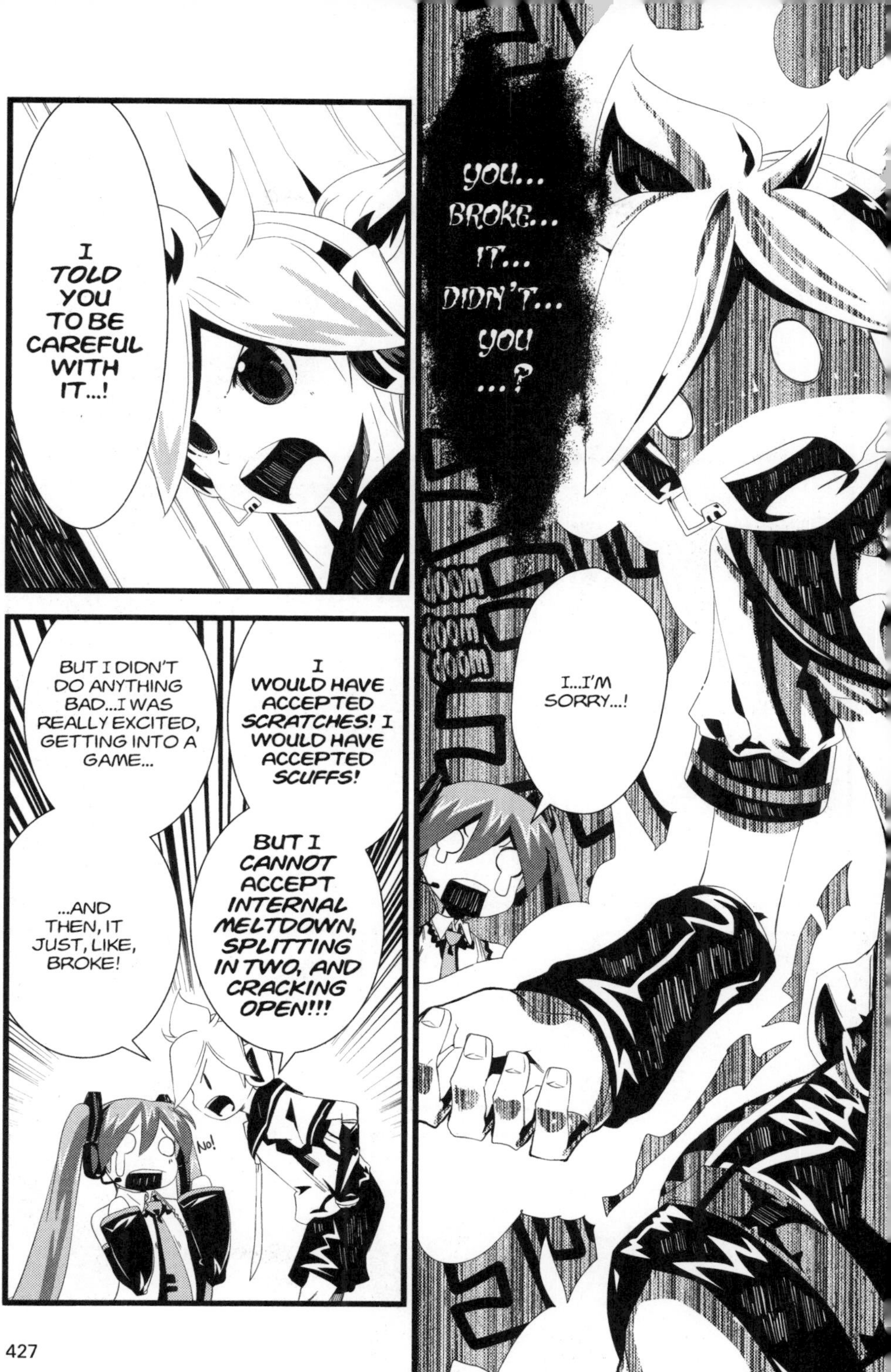
YOU... BROKE... IT... DIDN'T... YOU ...?
doom doom doom
I...I'M SORRY...!
I TOLD YOU TO BE CAREFUL WITH IT...!
I WOULD HAVE ACCEPTED SCRATCHES! I WOULD HAVE ACCEPTED SCUFFS!
BUT I DIDN'T DO ANYTHING BAD...I WAS REALLY EXCITED, GETTING INTO A GAME...
BUT I CANNOT ACCEPT INTERNAL MELTDOWN, SPLITTING IN TWO, AND CRACKING OPEN!!!
...AND THEN, IT JUST, LIKE, BROKE!
No!

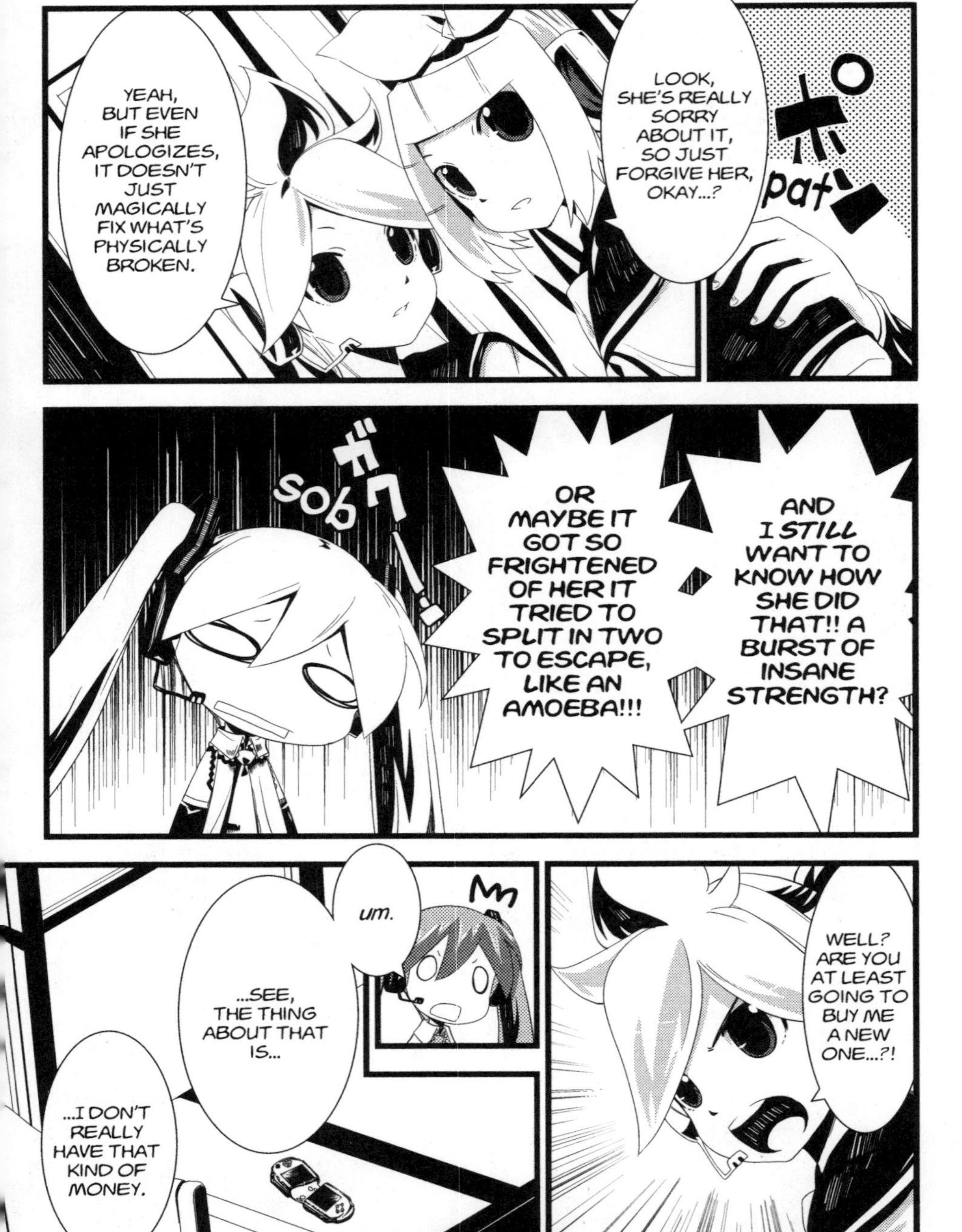
pat
LOOK, SHE'S REALLY SORRY ABOUT IT, SO JUST FORGIVE HER, OKAY...?
YEAH, BUT EVEN IF SHE APOLOGIZES, IT DOESN'T JUST MAGICALLY FIX WHAT'S PHYSICALLY BROKEN.
AND I STILL WANT TO KNOW HOW SHE DID THAT!! A BURST OF INSANE STRENGTH?
OR MAYBE IT GOT SO FRIGHTENED OF HER IT TRIED TO SPLIT IN TWO TO ESCAPE, LIKE AN AMOEBA!!!
sob
WELL? ARE YOU AT LEAST GOING TO BUY ME A NEW ONE...?!
Mm
um.
...SEE, THE THING ABOUT THAT IS...
...I DON'T REALLY HAVE THAT KIND OF MONEY.

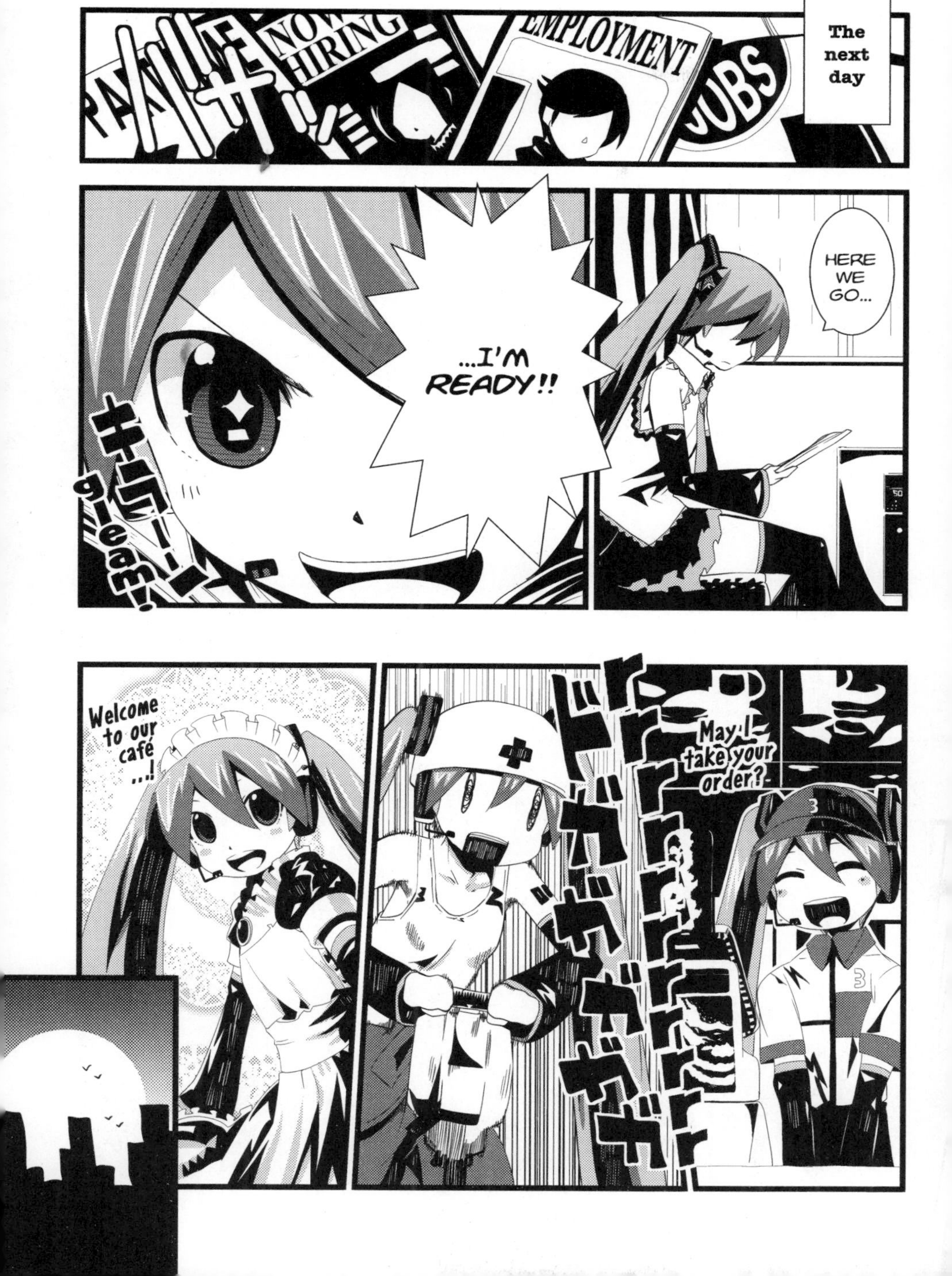
The next day
JOBS
EMPLOYMENT
NOW HIRING
HERE WE GO...
...I'M READY!!
gleam!
May I take your order?
Welcome to our café ...!

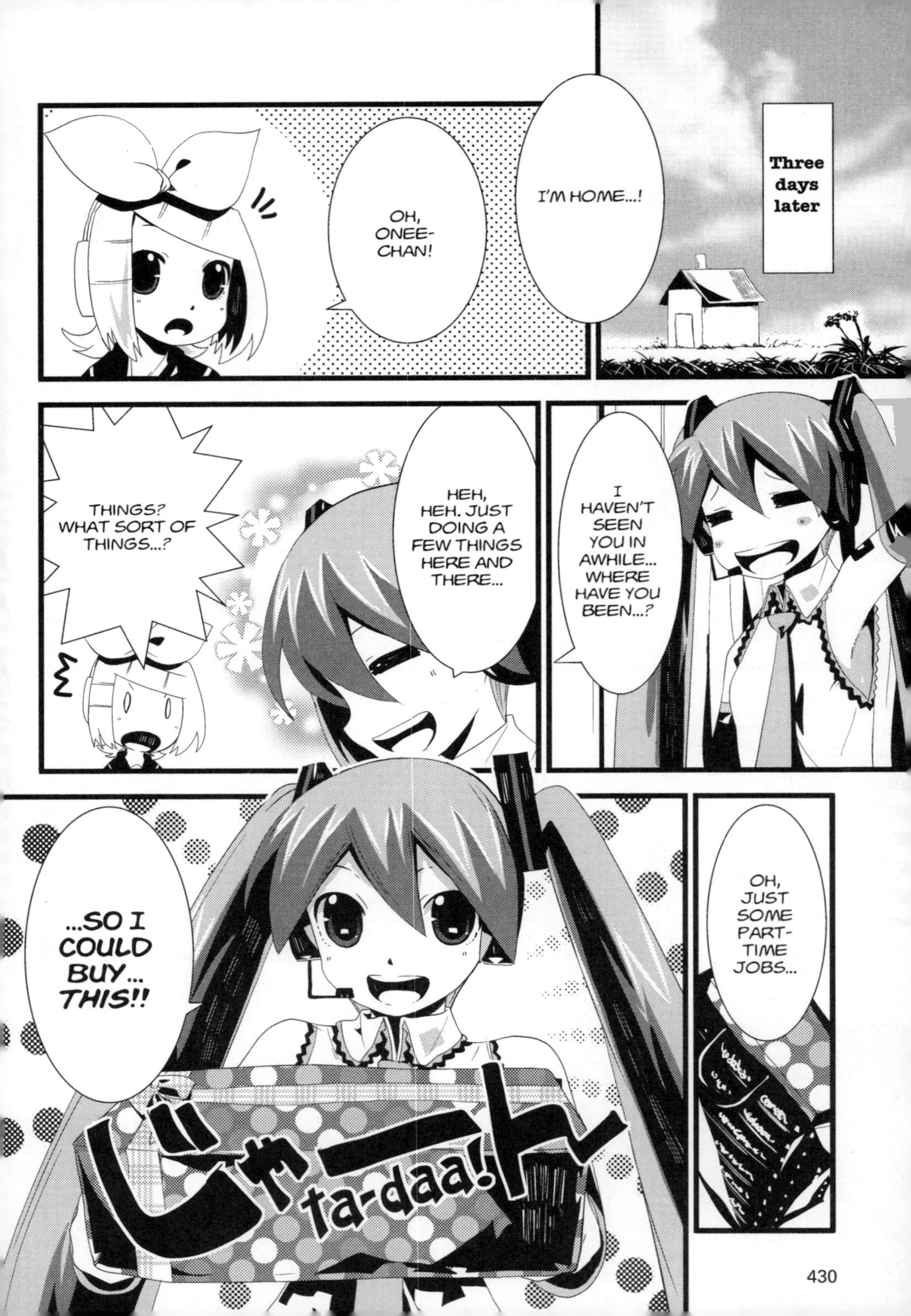
Three days later
I'M HOME...!
OH, ONEE-CHAN!
I HAVEN'T SEEN YOU IN AWHILE... WHERE HAVE YOU BEEN...?
HEH, HEH. JUST DOING A FEW THINGS HERE AND THERE...
THINGS? WHAT SORT OF THINGS...?
OH, JUST SOME PART-TIME JOBS...
...SO I COULD BUY... THIS!!
じゃーん
ta-daa!

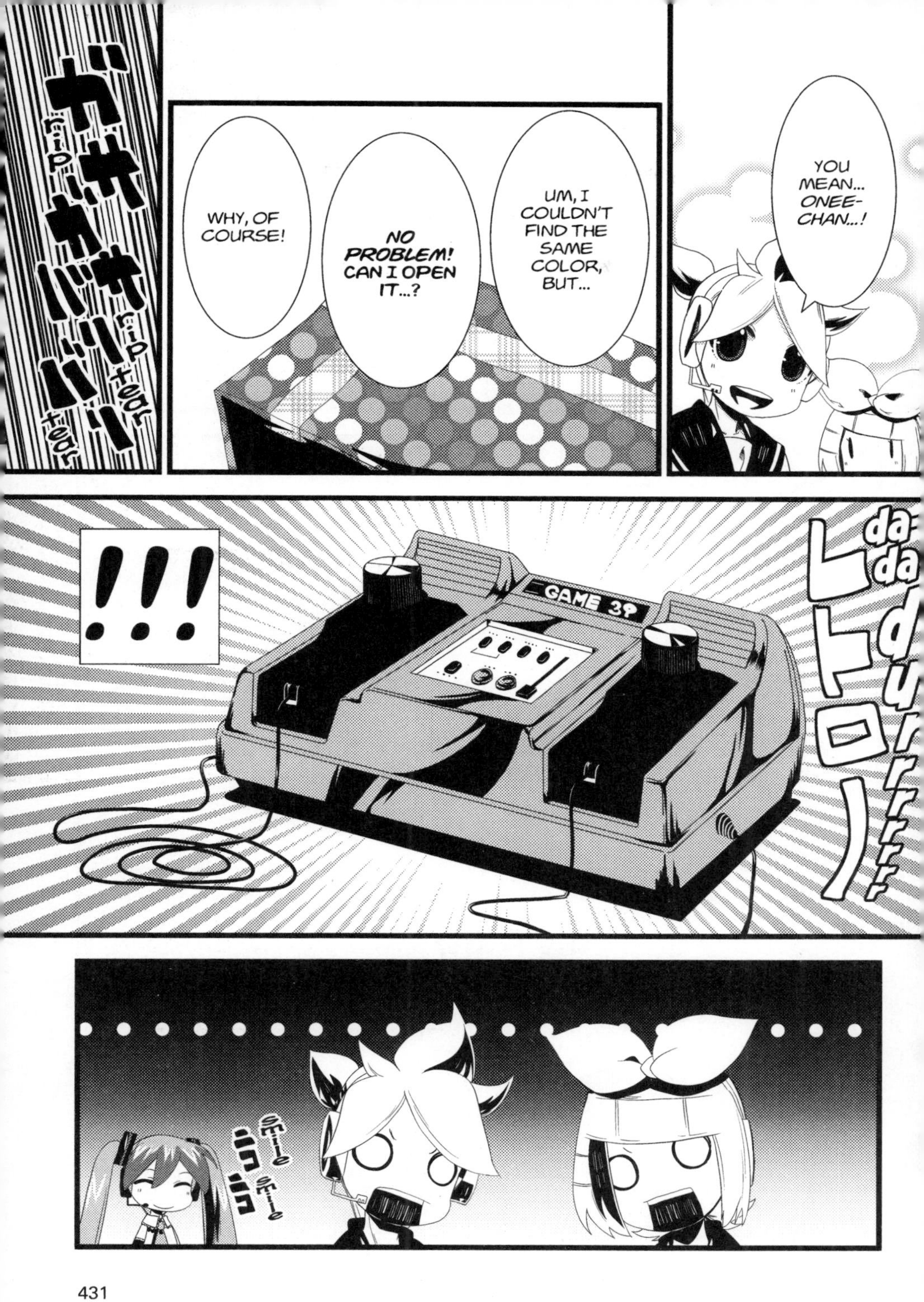
YOU MEAN... ONEE-CHAN...!
UM, I COULDN'T FIND THE SAME COLOR, BUT...
NO PROBLEM! CAN I OPEN IT...?
WHY, OF COURSE!
rip rip tear tear
レトロー
da-da durrrrrr
GAME 39
!!!
smile smile

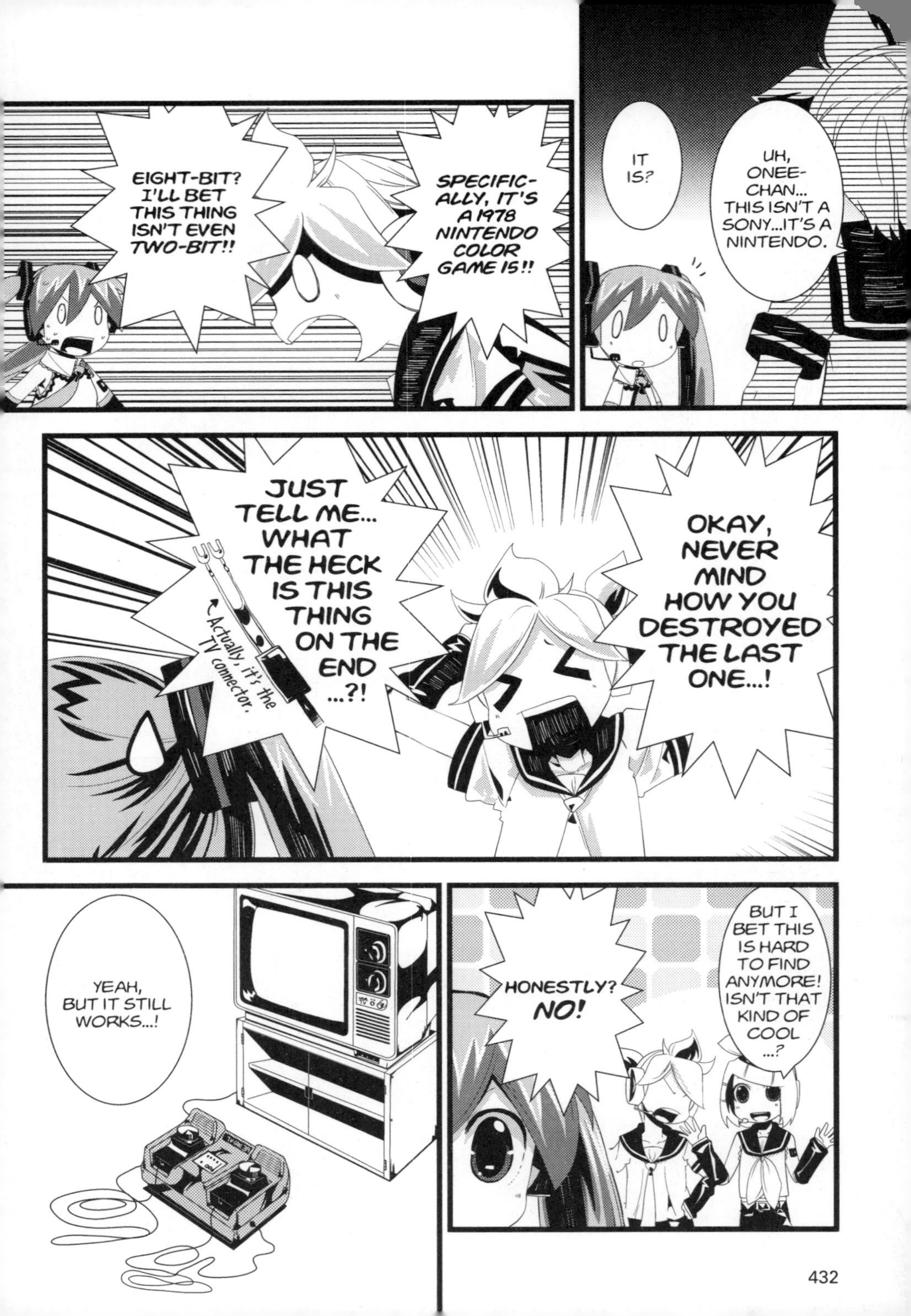
UH, ONEE-CHAN... THIS ISN'T A SONY...IT'S A NINTENDO.
IT IS?
SPECIFICALLY, IT'S A 1978 NINTENDO COLOR GAME IS!!
EIGHT-BIT? I'LL BET THIS THING ISN'T EVEN TWO-BIT!!
OKAY, NEVER MIND HOW YOU DESTROYED THE LAST ONE...!
JUST TELL ME... WHAT THE HECK IS THIS THING ON THE END ...?!
Actually, it's the TV connector.
BUT I BET THIS IS HARD TO FIND ANYMORE! ISN'T THAT KIND OF COOL ...?
HONESTLY? NO!
YEAH, BUT IT STILL WORKS...!

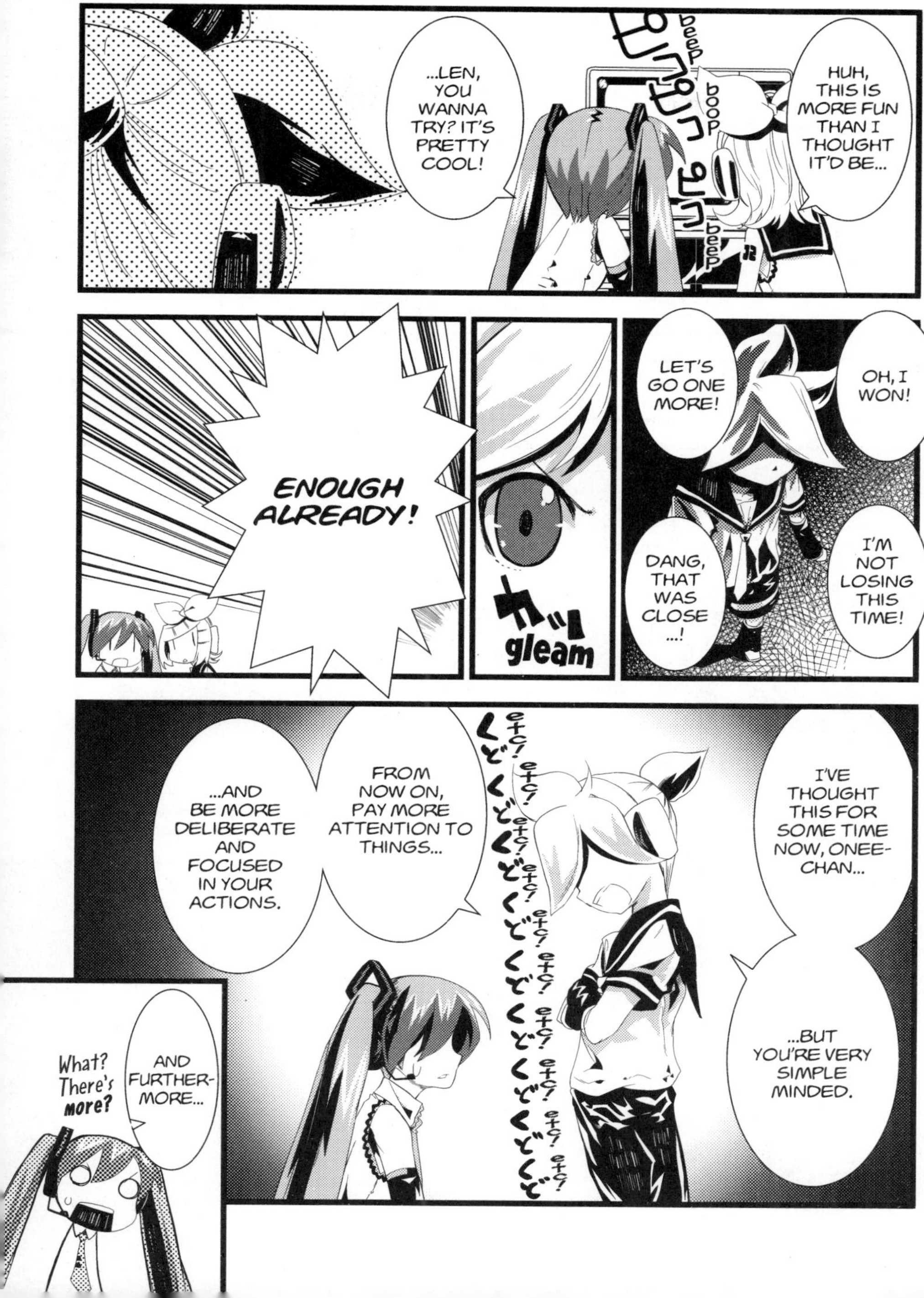
HUH, THIS IS MORE FUN THAN I THOUGHT IT'D BE...
beep
boop
beep
...LEN, YOU WANNA TRY? IT'S PRETTY COOL!
OH, I WON!
LET'S GO ONE MORE!
I'M NOT LOSING THIS TIME!
DANG, THAT WAS CLOSE ...!
gleam
ENOUGH ALREADY!
I'VE THOUGHT THIS FOR SOME TIME NOW, ONEE-CHAN...
...BUT YOU'RE VERY SIMPLE MINDED.
くどくどくどくどくどくどくどくど
etc! etc! etc! etc! etc! etc! etc! etc!
FROM NOW ON, PAY MORE ATTENTION TO THINGS...
...AND BE MORE DELIBERATE AND FOCUSED IN YOUR ACTIONS.
AND FURTHER-MORE...
What? There's more?

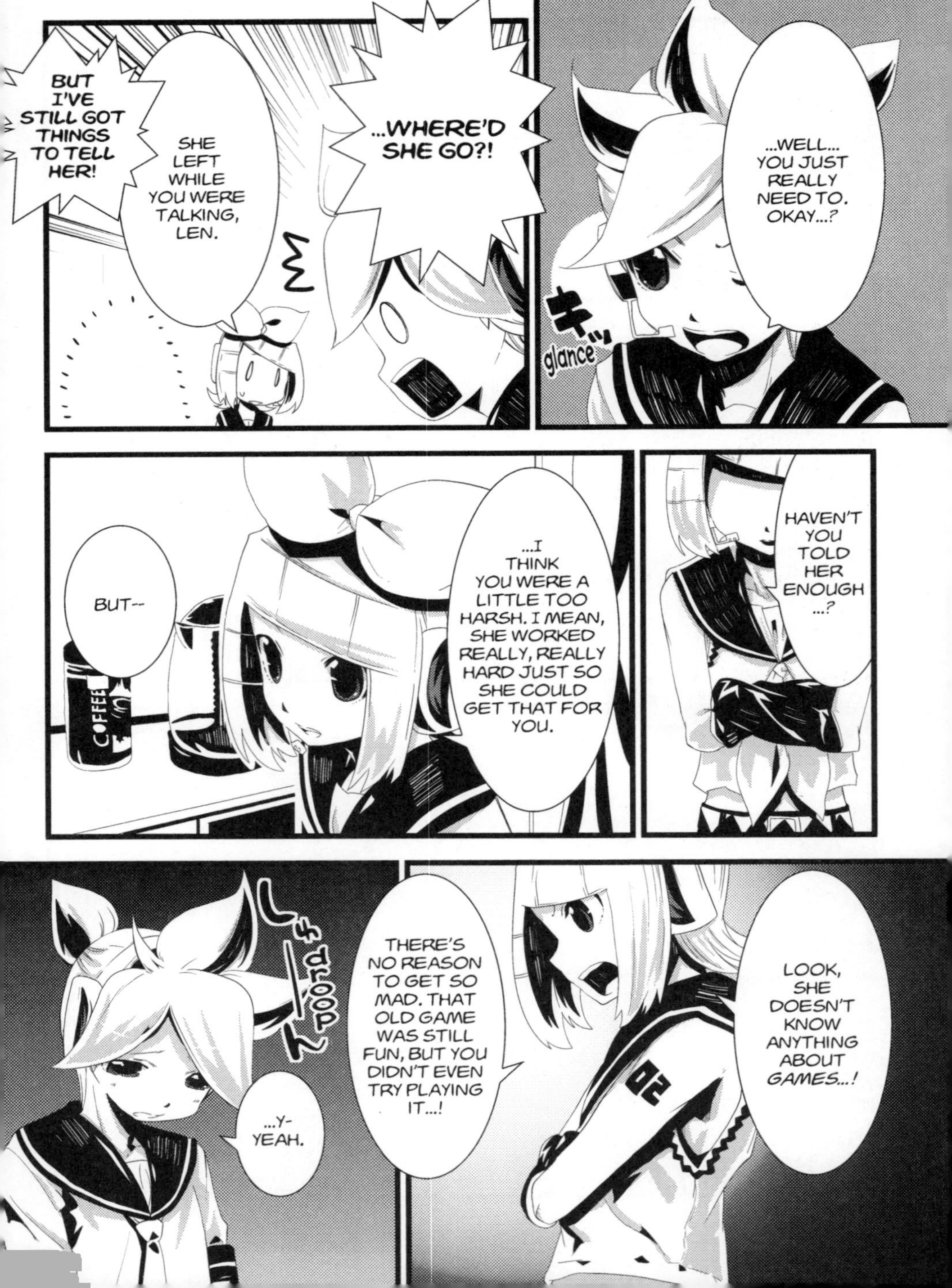
...WELL... YOU JUST REALLY NEED TO. OKAY...?
glance
...WHERE'D SHE GO?!
SHE LEFT WHILE YOU WERE TALKING, LEN.
BUT I'VE STILL GOT THINGS TO TELL HER!
HAVEN'T YOU TOLD HER ENOUGH ...?
...I THINK YOU WERE A LITTLE TOO HARSH. I MEAN, SHE WORKED REALLY, REALLY HARD JUST SO SHE COULD GET THAT FOR YOU.
BUT--
COFFEE
LOOK, SHE DOESN'T KNOW ANYTHING ABOUT GAMES...!
02
THERE'S NO REASON TO GET SO MAD. THAT OLD GAME WAS STILL FUN, BUT YOU DIDN'T EVEN TRY PLAYING IT...!
droop
...Y-YEAH.

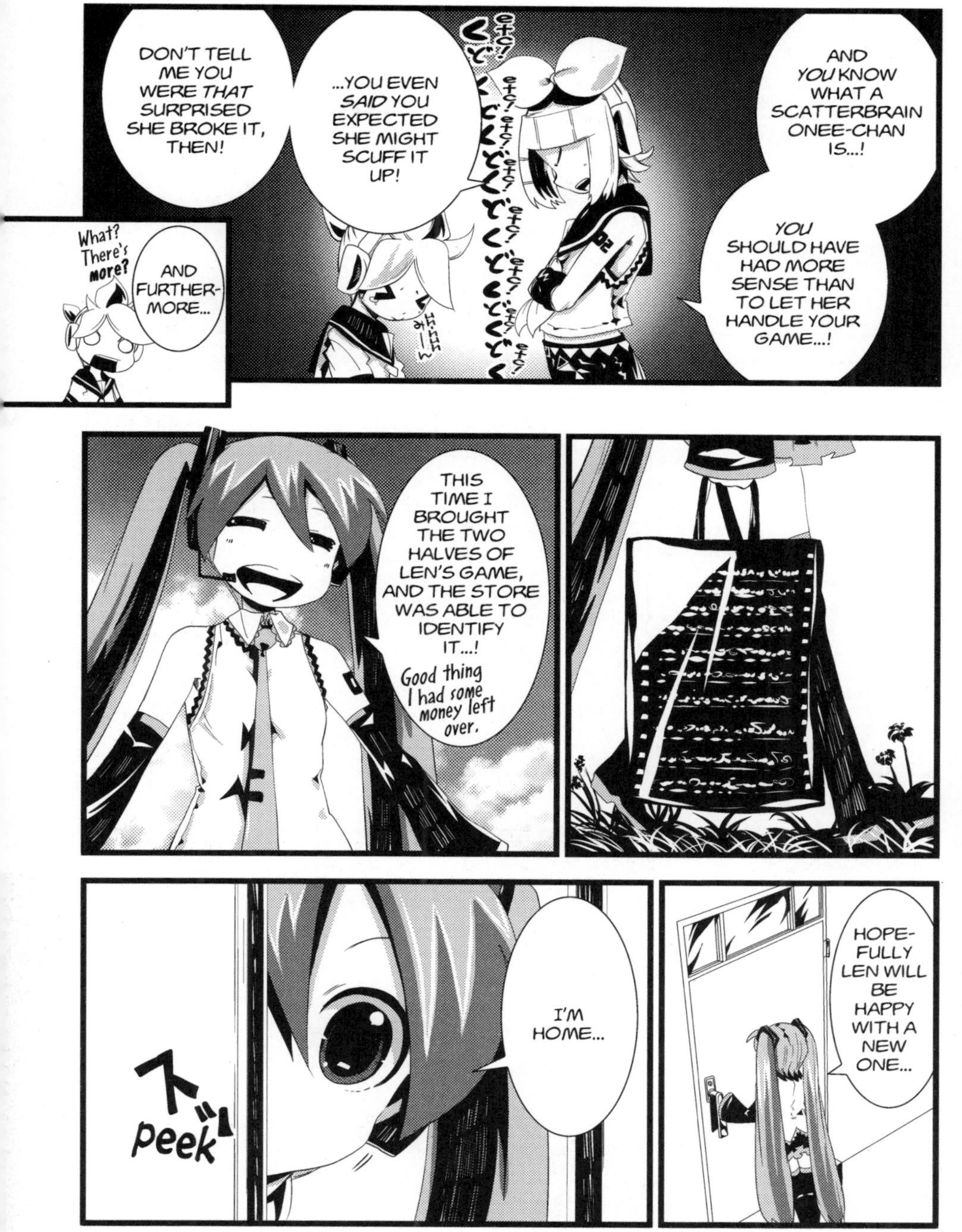
AND *YOU* KNOW WHAT A SCATTERBRAIN ONEE-CHAN IS...!
YOU SHOULD HAVE HAD MORE SENSE THAN TO LET HER HANDLE YOUR GAME...!
くどくど etc! くどくど etc! くどくど etc!
...YOU EVEN *SAID* YOU EXPECTED SHE MIGHT SCUFF IT UP!
DON'T TELL ME YOU WERE *THAT* SURPRISED SHE BROKE IT, THEN!
AND FURTHERMORE...
What? There's **more?**
THIS TIME I BROUGHT THE TWO HALVES OF LEN'S GAME, AND THE STORE WAS ABLE TO IDENTIFY IT...!
Good thing I had some money left over.
HOPEFULLY LEN WILL BE HAPPY WITH A NEW ONE...
I'M HOME...
へド peek

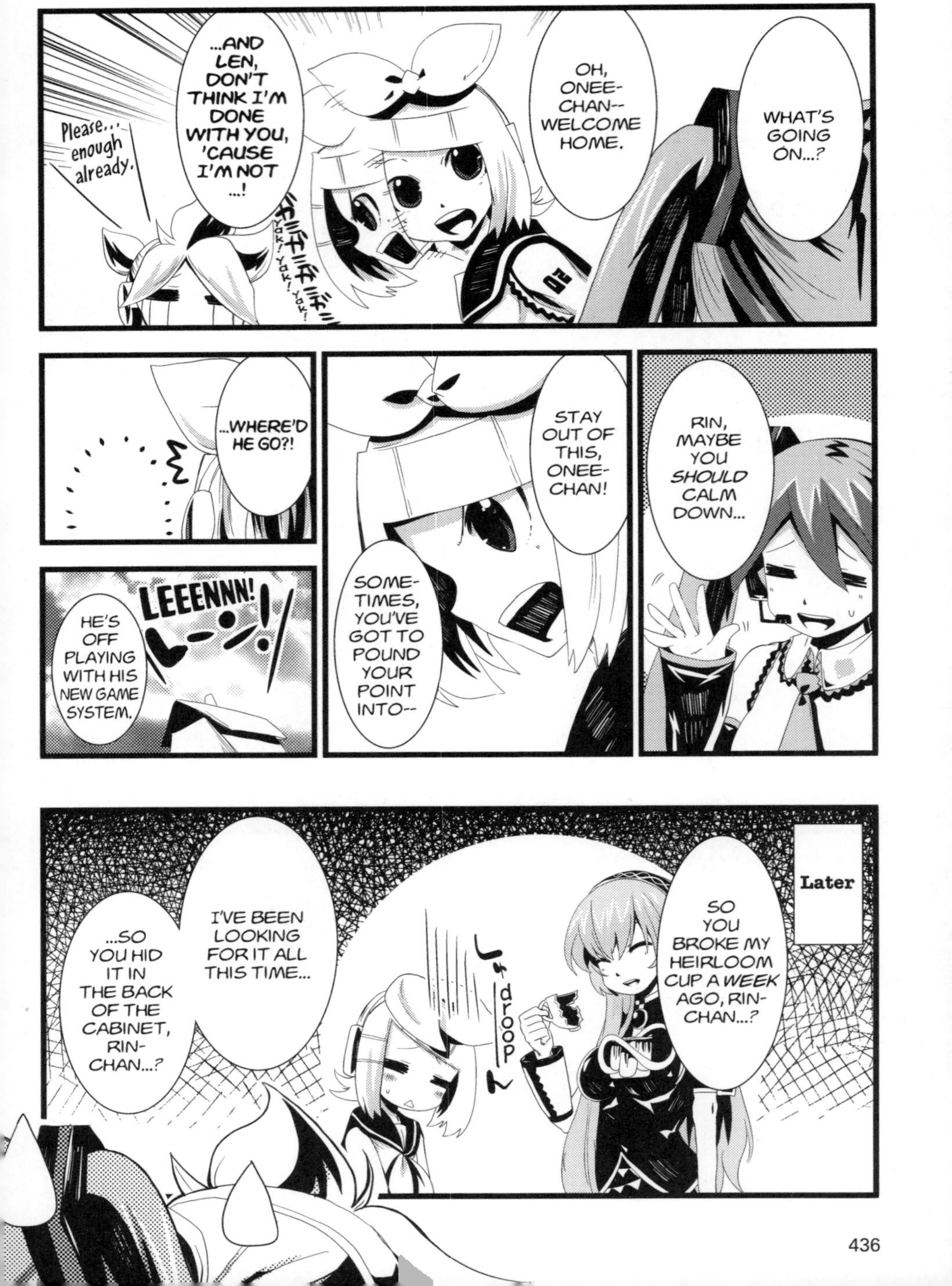
WHAT'S GOING ON...?
OH, ONEE-CHAN-- WELCOME HOME.
...AND LEN, DON'T THINK I'M DONE WITH YOU, 'CAUSE I'M NOT ...!
Yak! Yak! Yak!
Please... enough already.
RIN, MAYBE YOU SHOULD CALM DOWN...
STAY OUT OF THIS, ONEE-CHAN!
SOME-TIMES, YOU'VE GOT TO POUND YOUR POINT INTO--
...WHERE'D HE GO?!
LEEENNN!
HE'S OFF PLAYING WITH HIS NEW GAME SYSTEM.
Later
SO YOU BROKE MY HEIRLOOM CUP A WEEK AGO, RIN-CHAN...?
droop
I'VE BEEN LOOKING FOR IT ALL THIS TIME...
...SO YOU HID IT IN THE BACK OF THE CABINET, RIN-CHAN...?

(28th SONG) TRICKED MIX

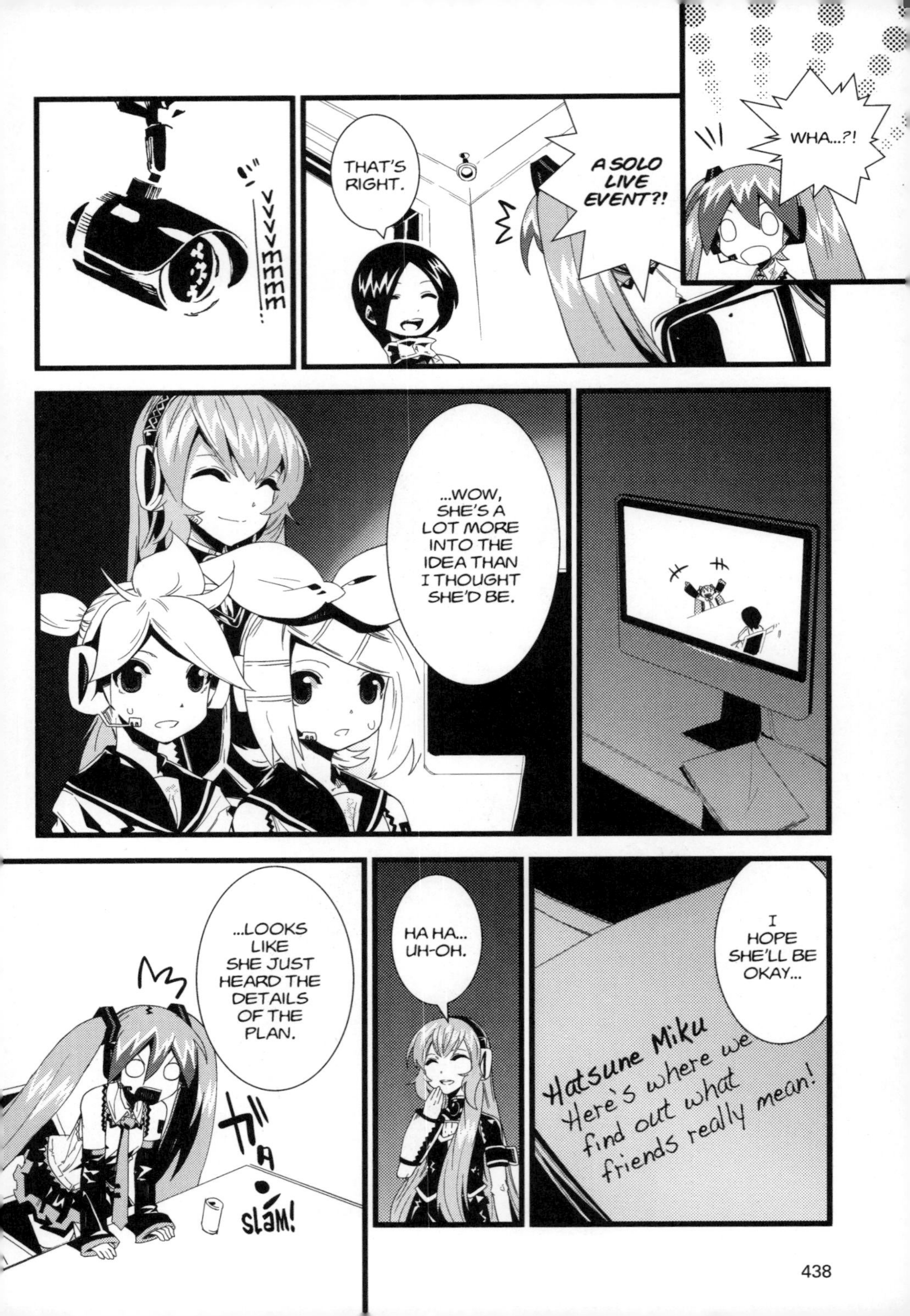
WHA...?!
A SOLO LIVE EVENT?!
THAT'S RIGHT.
VVVVMMMM
...WOW, SHE'S A LOT MORE INTO THE IDEA THAN I THOUGHT SHE'D BE.
I HOPE SHE'LL BE OKAY...
Hatsune Miku
Here's where we find out what friends really mean!
HA HA... UH-OH.
...LOOKS LIKE SHE JUST HEARD THE DETAILS OF THE PLAN.
SLAM!

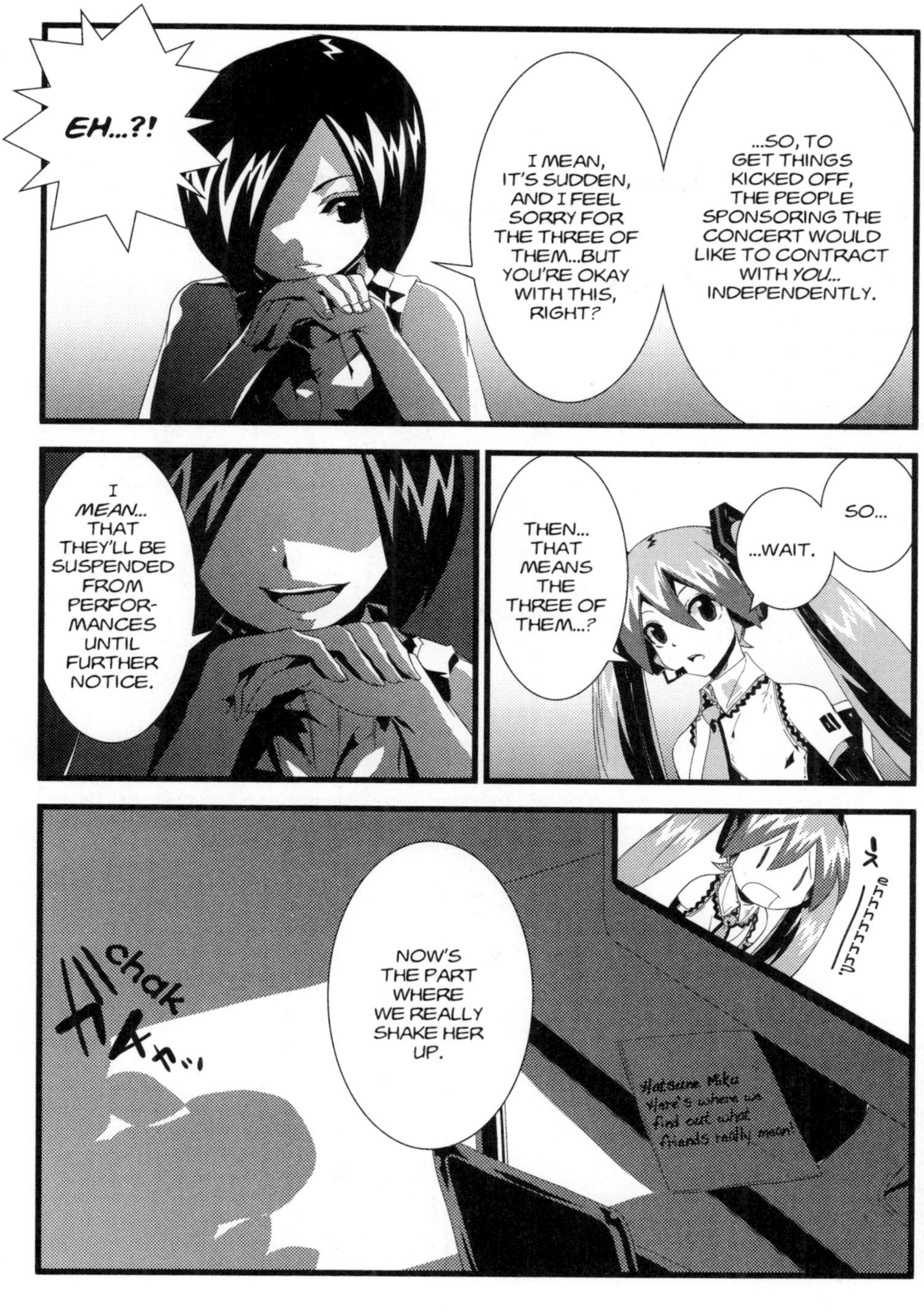
...SO, TO GET THINGS KICKED OFF, THE PEOPLE SPONSORING THE CONCERT WOULD LIKE TO CONTRACT WITH *YOU*... INDEPENDENTLY.
I MEAN, IT'S SUDDEN, AND I FEEL SORRY FOR THE THREE OF THEM...BUT YOU'RE OKAY WITH THIS, RIGHT?
EH...?!
SO...
...WAIT.
THEN... THAT MEANS THE THREE OF THEM...?
I *MEAN*... THAT THEY'LL BE SUSPENDED FROM PERFOR-MANCES UNTIL FURTHER NOTICE.
NOW'S THE PART WHERE WE REALLY SHAKE HER UP.
Hatsune Miku
Here's where we find out what friends really mean!
chak

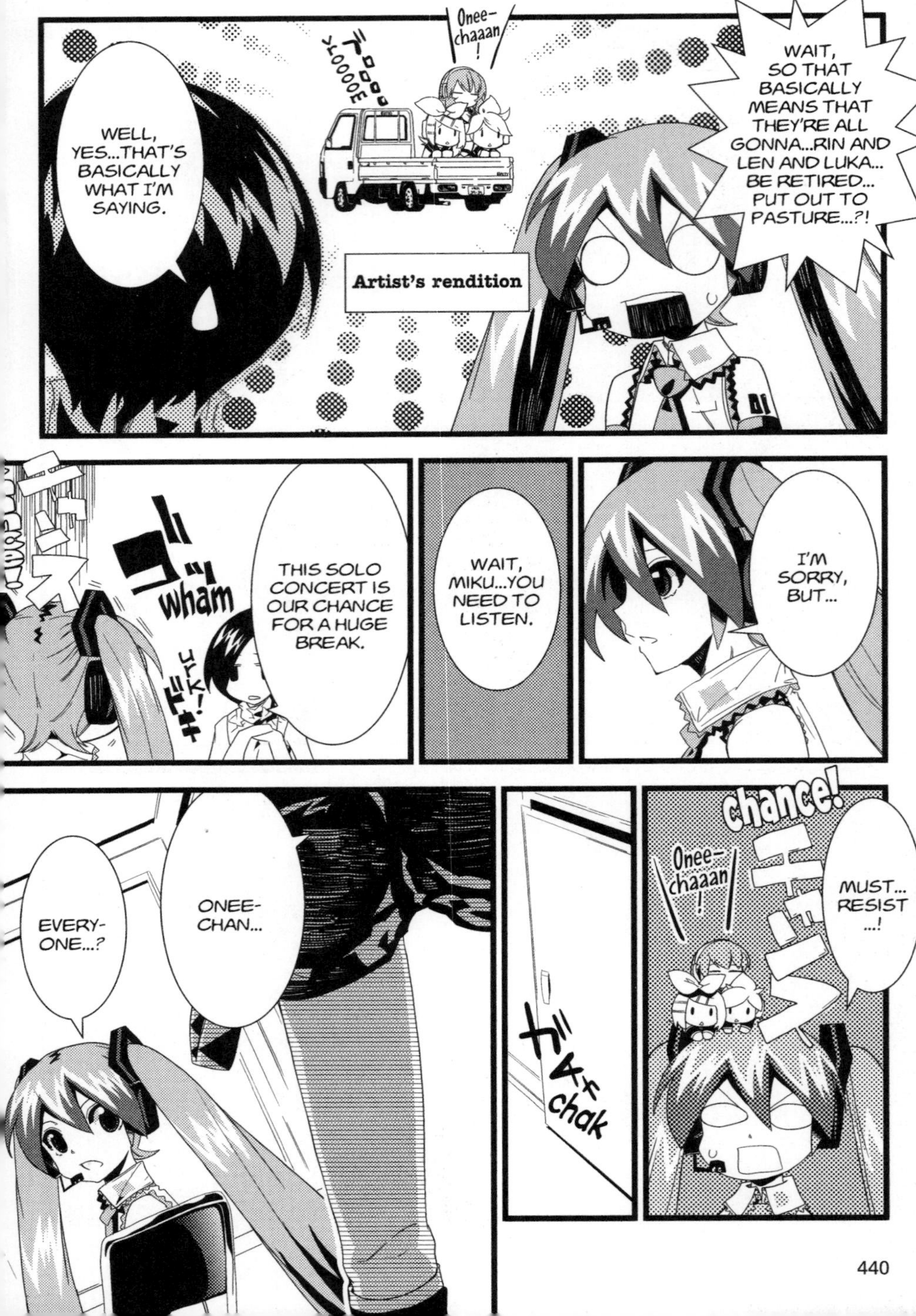
WAIT, SO THAT BASICALLY MEANS THAT THEY'RE ALL GONNA...RIN AND LEN AND LUKA... BE RETIRED... PUT OUT TO PASTURE...?!
Onee-chaaan!
VROOOOM
WELL, YES...THAT'S BASICALLY WHAT I'M SAYING.
Artist's rendition
I'M SORRY, BUT...
WAIT, MIKU...YOU NEED TO LISTEN.
THIS SOLO CONCERT IS OUR CHANCE FOR A HUGE BREAK.
wham
urk!
chance!
MUST... RESIST ...!
Onee-chaaan!
chak
ONEE-CHAN...
EVERY-ONE...?

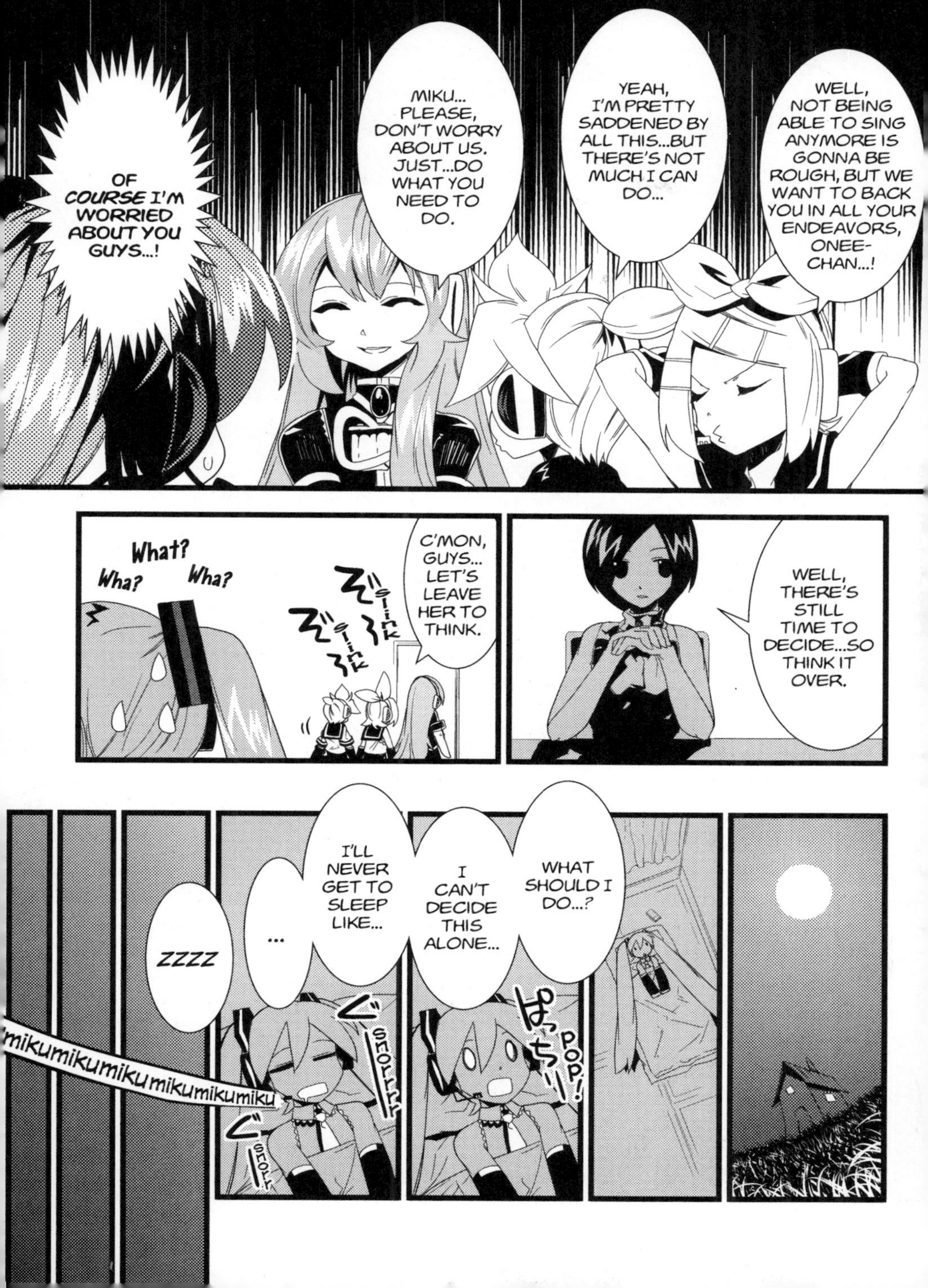
WELL, NOT BEING ABLE TO SING ANYMORE IS GONNA BE ROUGH, BUT WE WANT TO BACK YOU IN ALL YOUR ENDEAVORS, ONEE-CHAN...!
YEAH, I'M PRETTY SADDENED BY ALL THIS...BUT THERE'S NOT MUCH I CAN DO...
MIKU... PLEASE, DON'T WORRY ABOUT US. JUST...DO WHAT YOU NEED TO DO.
OF COURSE I'M WORRIED ABOUT YOU GUYS...!
WELL, THERE'S STILL TIME TO DECIDE...SO THINK IT OVER.
C'MON, GUYS... LET'S LEAVE HER TO THINK.
What?
Wha?
Wha?
WHAT SHOULD I DO...?
I CAN'T DECIDE THIS ALONE...
POP!
I'LL NEVER GET TO SLEEP LIKE...
...
ZZZZ
mikumikumikumikumikumiku

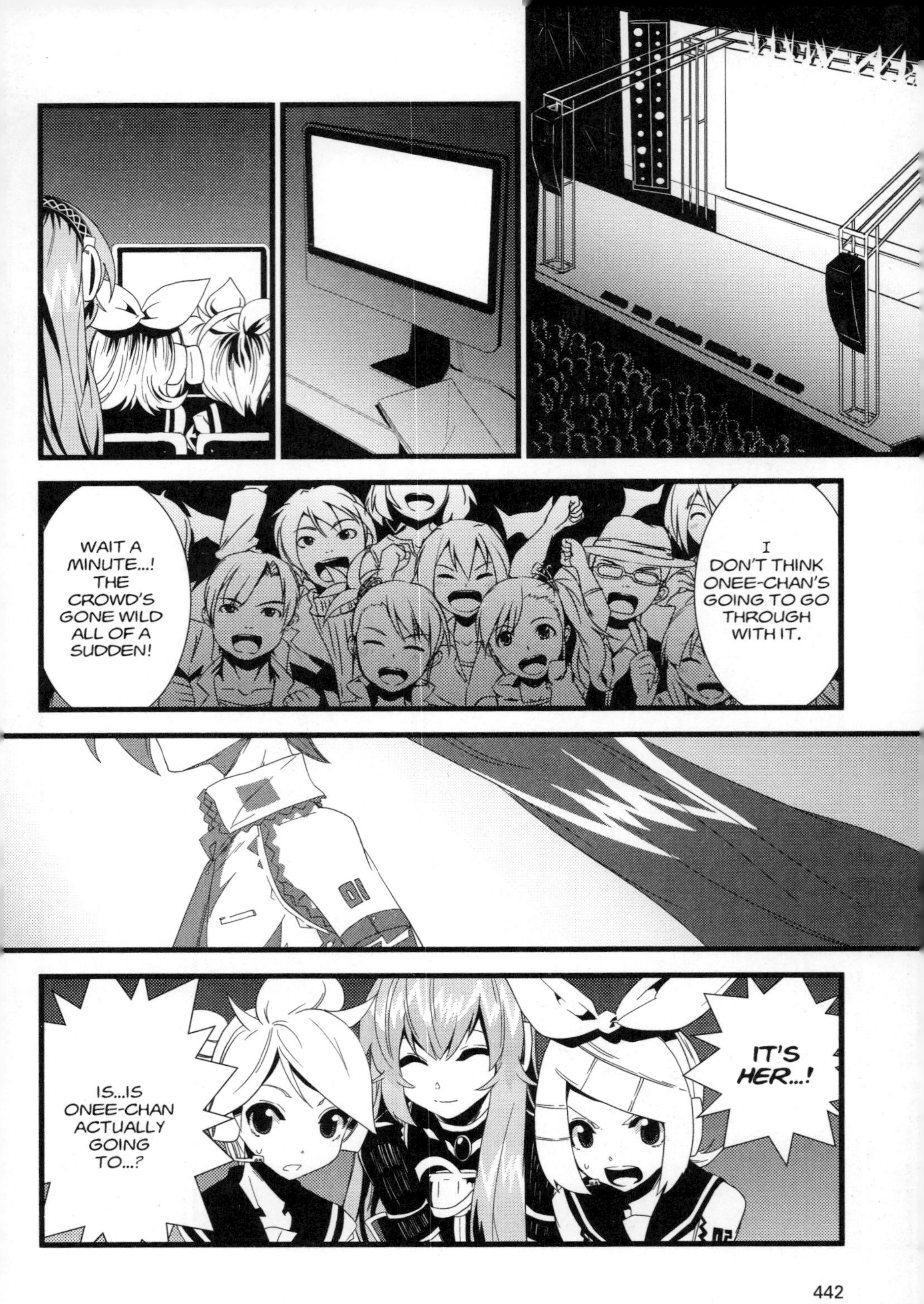
I DON'T THINK ONEE-CHAN'S GOING TO GO THROUGH WITH IT.
WAIT A MINUTE...! THE CROWD'S GONE WILD ALL OF A SUDDEN!
IT'S HER...!
IS...IS ONEE-CHAN ACTUALLY GOING TO...?

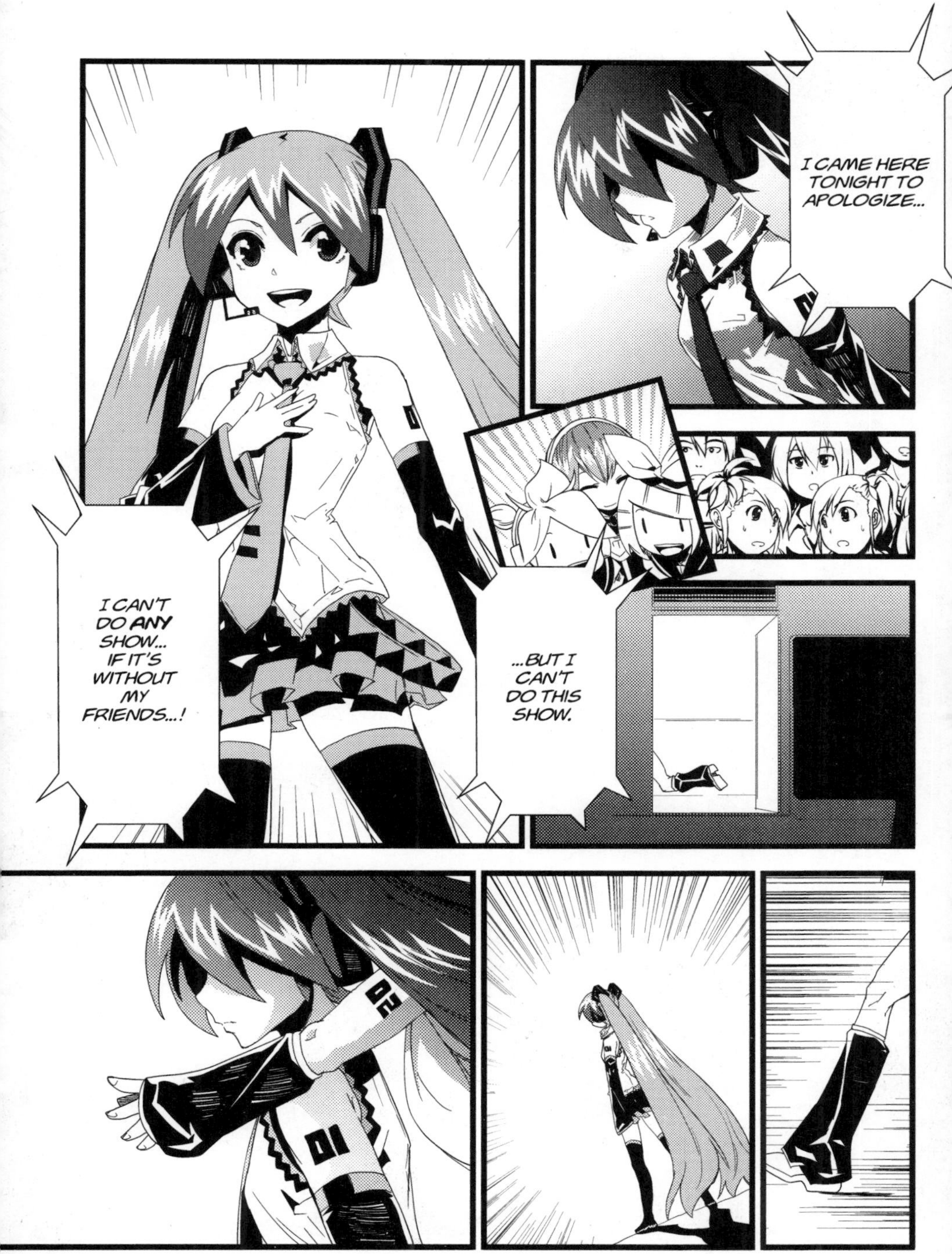
I CAME HERE TONIGHT TO APOLOGIZE...
...BUT I CAN'T DO THIS SHOW.
I CAN'T DO **ANY** SHOW... IF IT'S WITHOUT MY FRIENDS...!

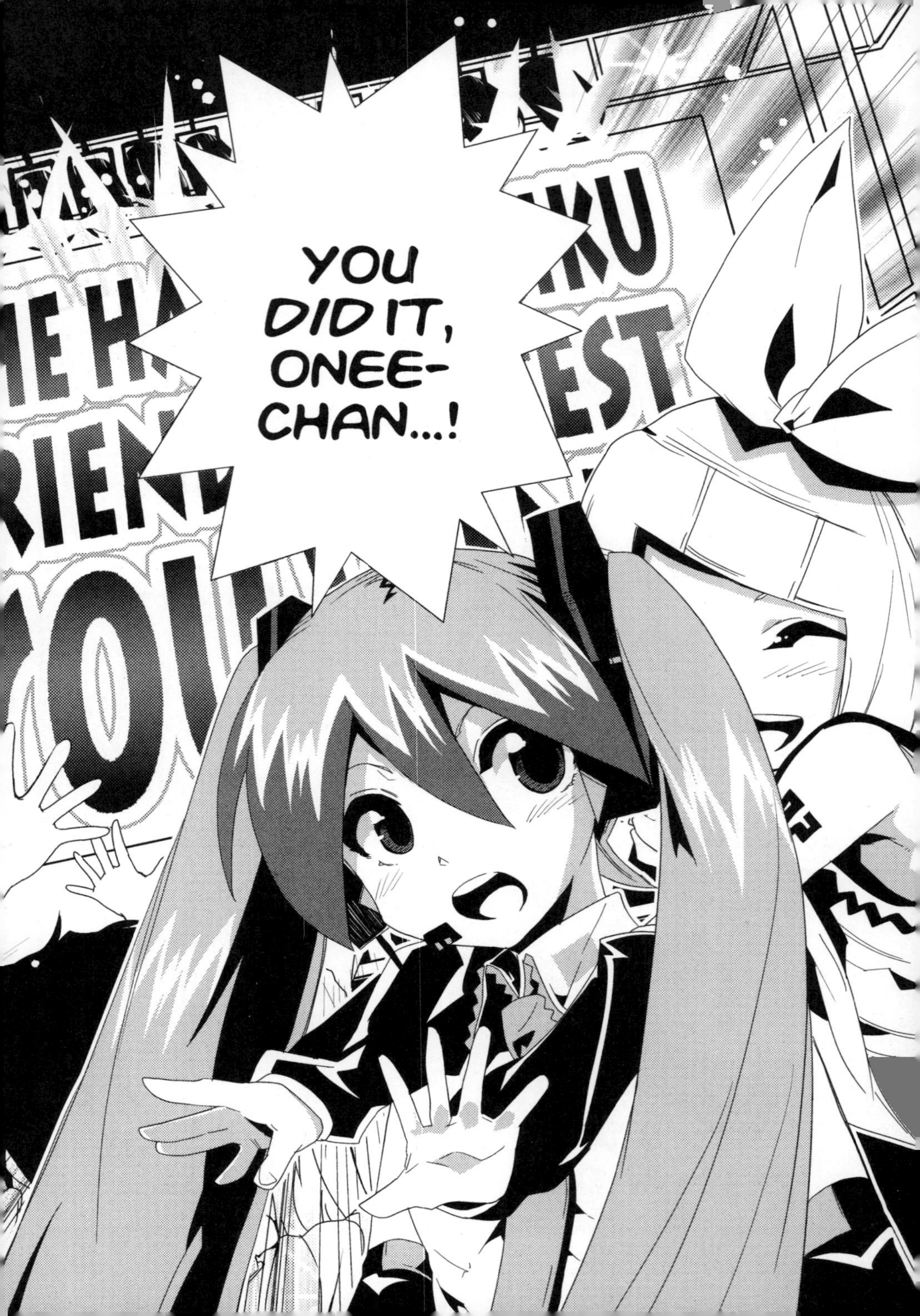
YOU DID IT, ONEE-CHAN...!

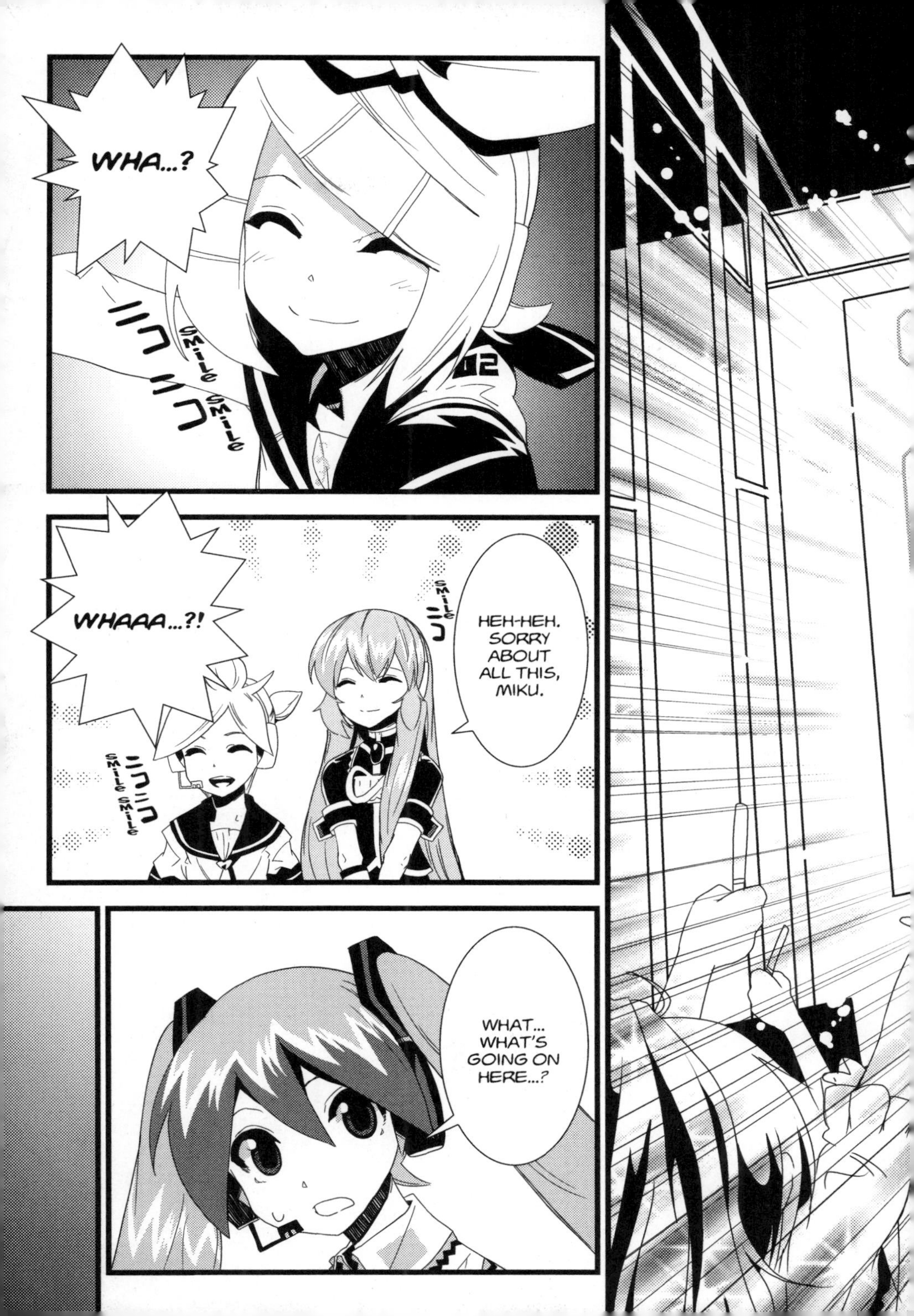
WHA...?
ニコ SMILE
ニコ SMILE
SMILE ニコ
HEH-HEH. SORRY ABOUT ALL THIS, MIKU.
WHAAA...?!
ニコニコ SMILE SMILE
WHAT... WHAT'S GOING ON HERE...?

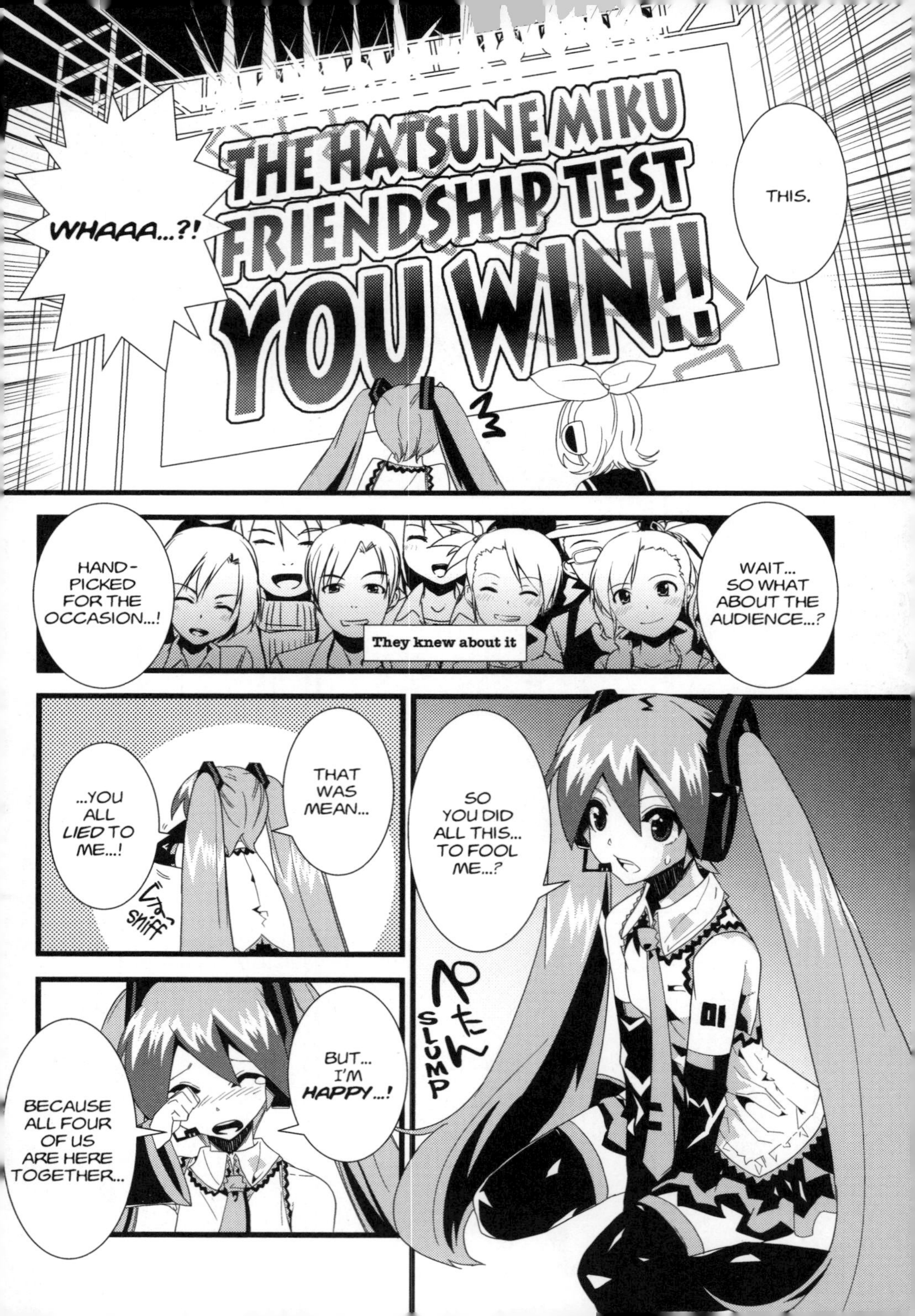
THIS.
THE HATSUNE MIKU FRIENDSHIP TEST
YOU WIN!!
WHAAA...?!
WAIT... SO WHAT ABOUT THE AUDIENCE...?
They knew about it
HAND-PICKED FOR THE OCCASION...!
SO YOU DID ALL THIS... TO FOOL ME...?
SLUMP
THAT WAS MEAN...
...YOU ALL LIED TO ME...!
sniff
BUT... I'M HAPPY...!
BECAUSE ALL FOUR OF US ARE HERE TOGETHER...

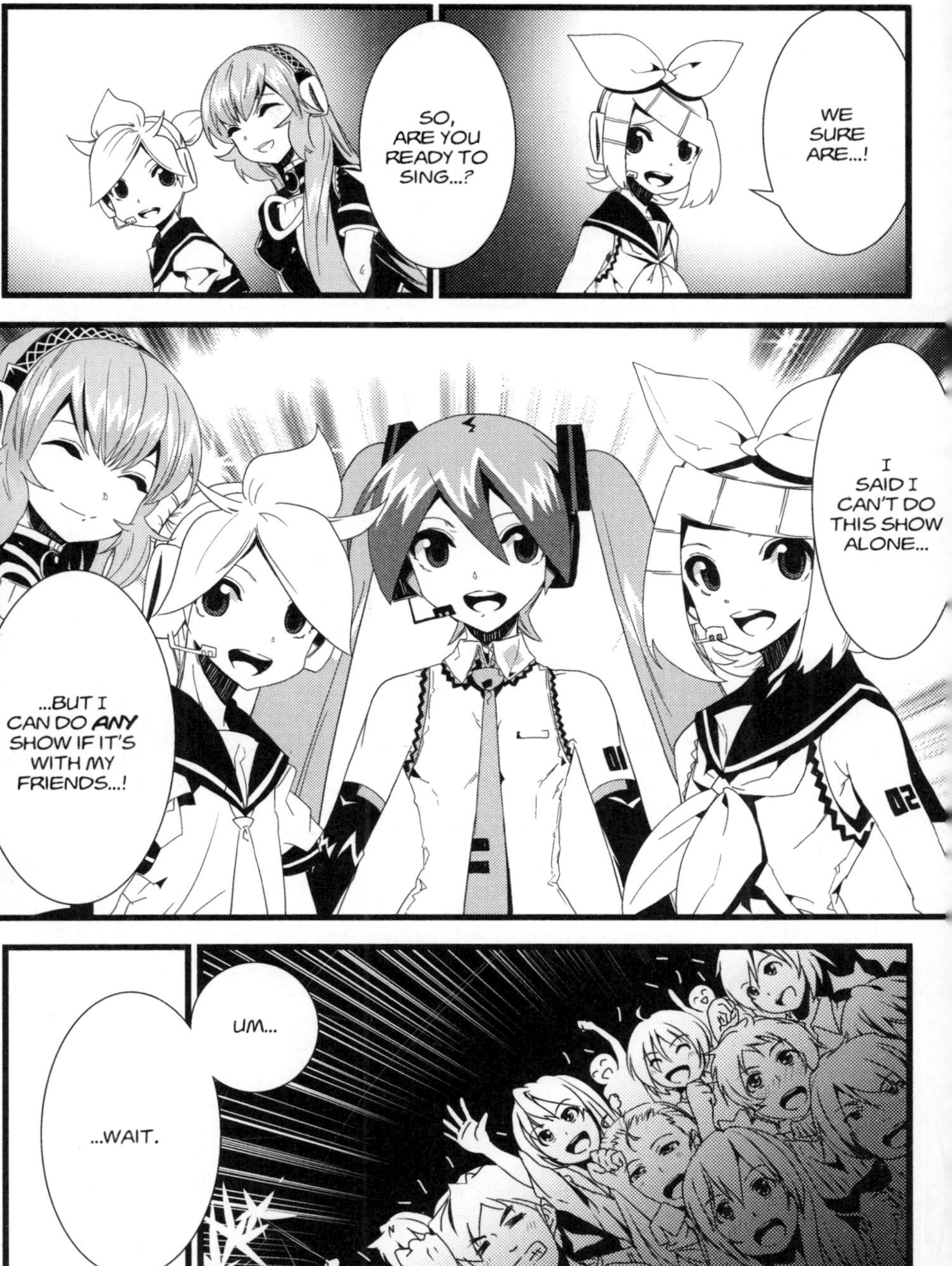
WE SURE ARE...!
SO, ARE YOU READY TO SING...?
I SAID I CAN'T DO THIS SHOW ALONE...
...BUT I CAN DO **ANY** SHOW IF IT'S WITH MY FRIENDS...!
UM...
...WAIT.

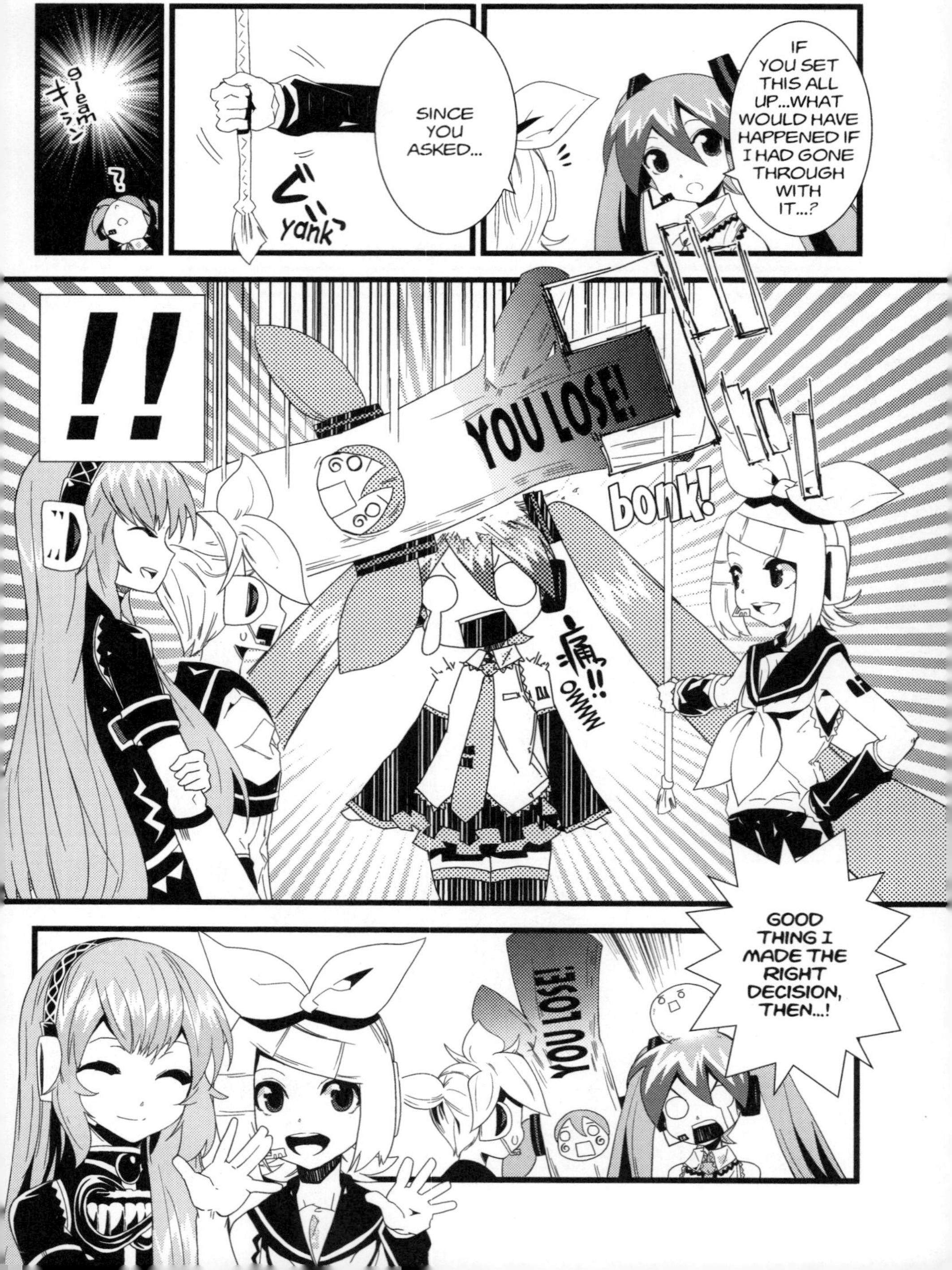
IF YOU SET THIS ALL UP...WHAT WOULD HAVE HAPPENED IF I HAD GONE THROUGH WITH IT...?
SINCE YOU ASKED...
yank
gleam
キラン
?
YOU LOSE!
bonk!
!!
痛!!
OWWW
GOOD THING I MADE THE RIGHT DECISION, THEN...!
YOU LOSE!

(29th SONG) MODULE MIX

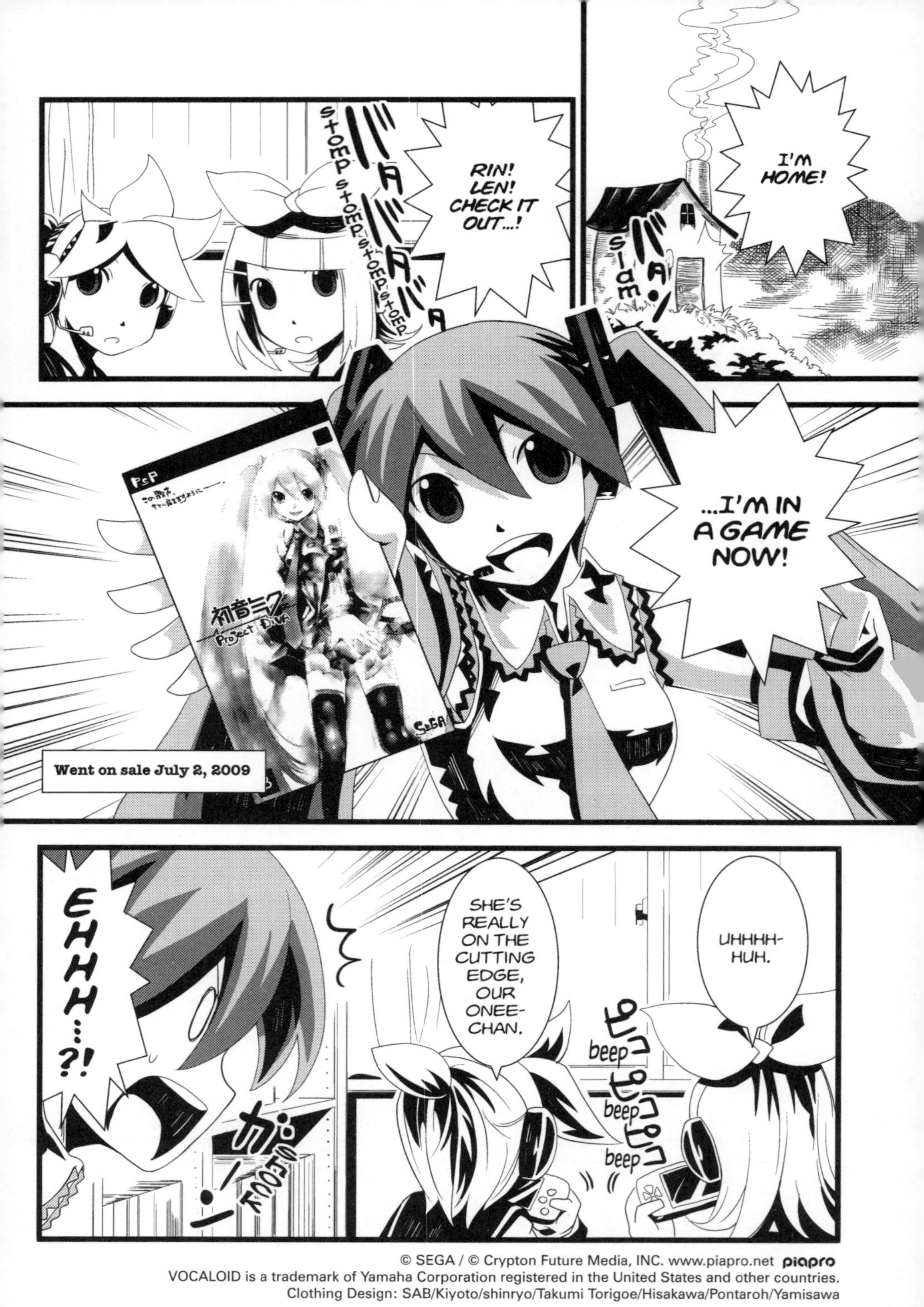
I'M HOME!
slam
RIN! LEN! CHECK IT OUT...!
stomp stomp stomp stomp stomp
...I'M IN A GAME NOW!
PSP
初音ミク
Project DIVA
SEGA
Went on sale July 2, 2009
UHHHH-HUH.
beep
beep
beep
SHE'S REALLY ON THE CUTTING EDGE, OUR ONEE-CHAN.
shock
EHHHH...?!

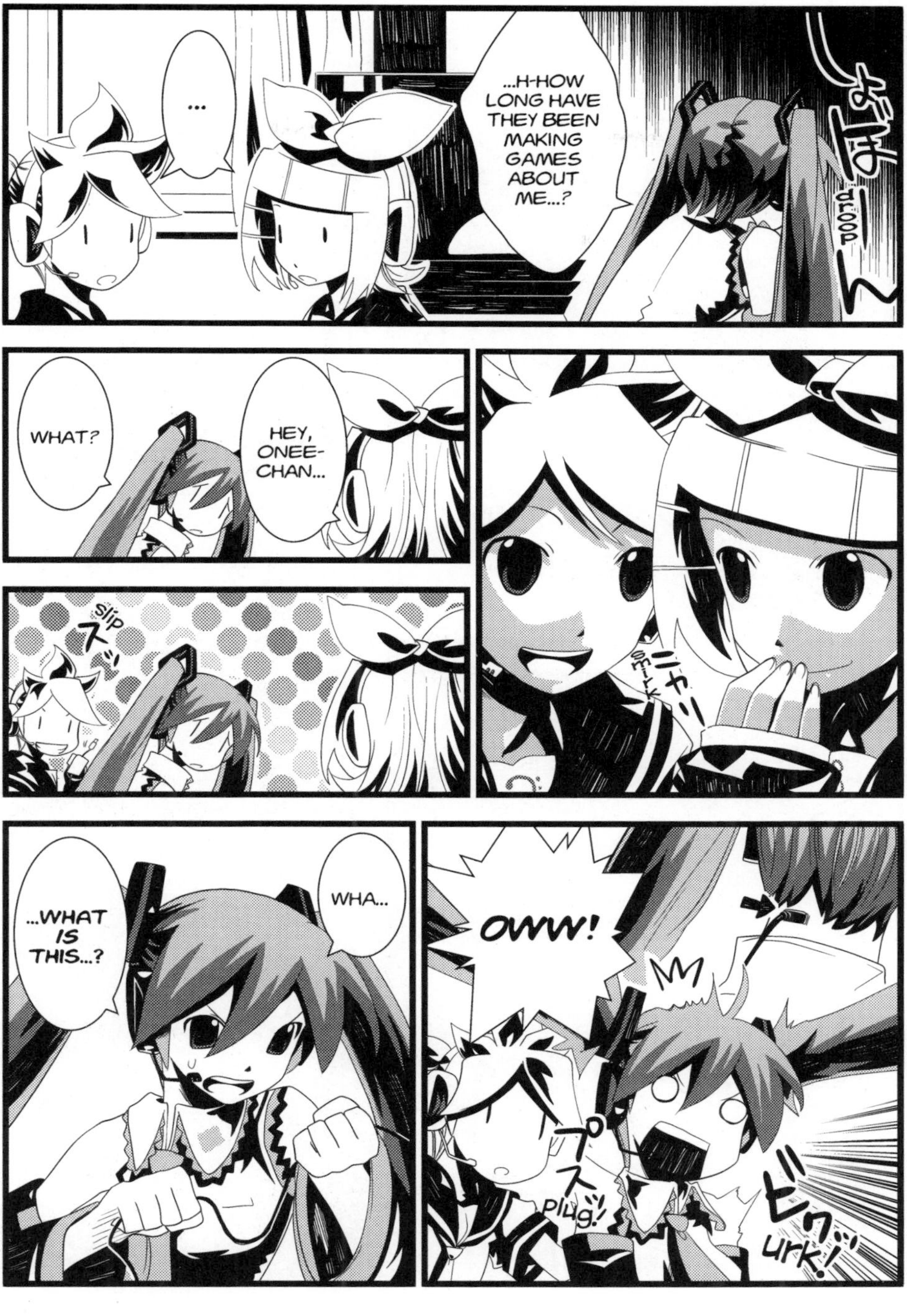

しょぼーん
droop
...H-HOW LONG HAVE THEY BEEN MAKING GAMES ABOUT ME...?
...
ニヤッ
smirk
HEY, ONEE-CHAN...
WHAT?
ズッ
slip
ビクッ
urk!
OWW!
プス
plug!
WHA...
...WHAT IS THIS...?

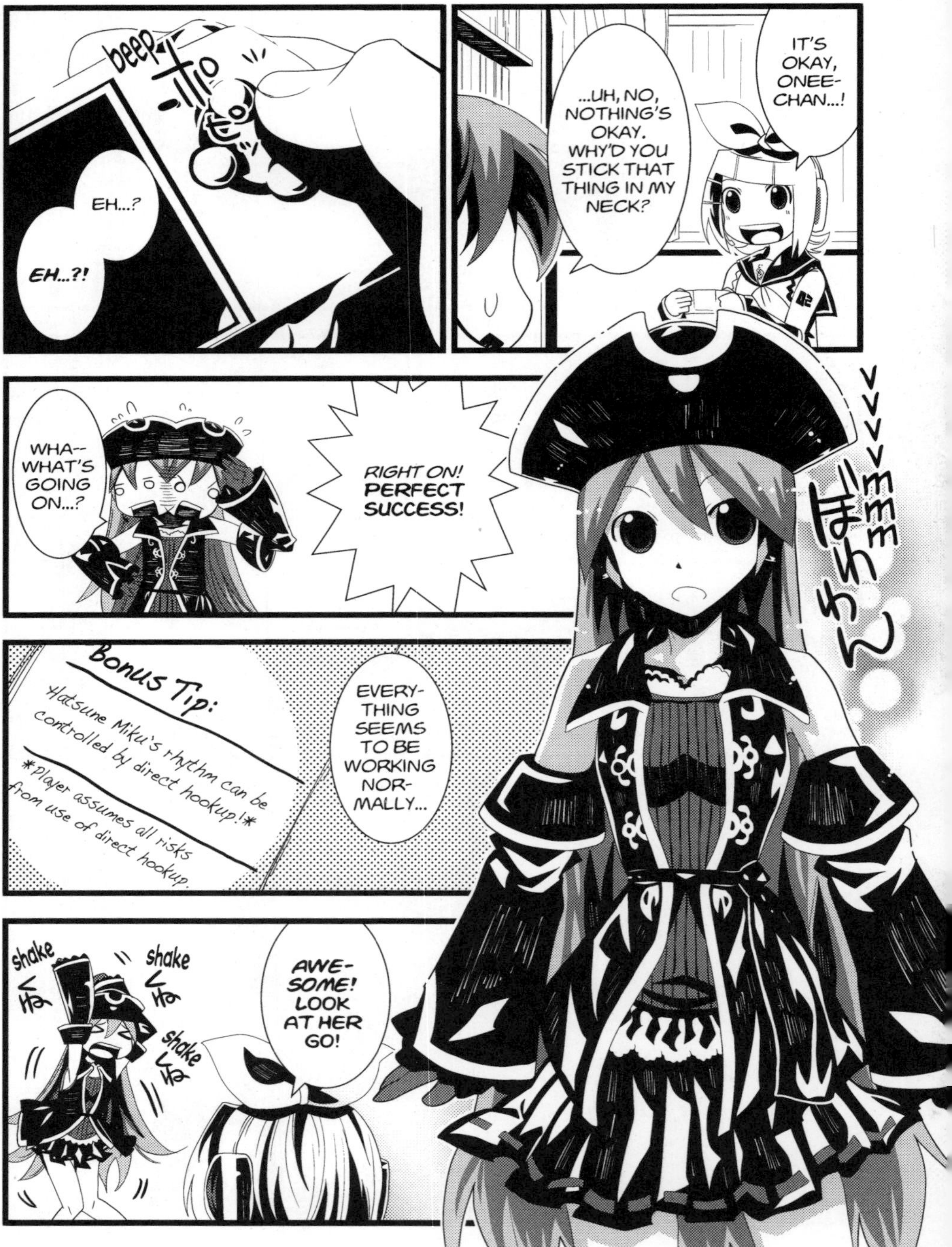
IT'S OKAY, ONEE-CHAN...!
...UH, NO, NOTHING'S OKAY. WHY'D YOU STICK THAT THING IN MY NECK?
beep
EH...?
EH...?!
RIGHT ON! PERFECT SUCCESS!
WHA-- WHAT'S GOING ON...?
EVERY-THING SEEMS TO BE WORKING NOR-MALLY...
Bonus Tip:
Hatsune Miku's rhythm can be controlled by direct hookup!*
*Player assumes all risks from use of direct hookup.
AWE-SOME! LOOK AT HER GO!
shake
shake
shake

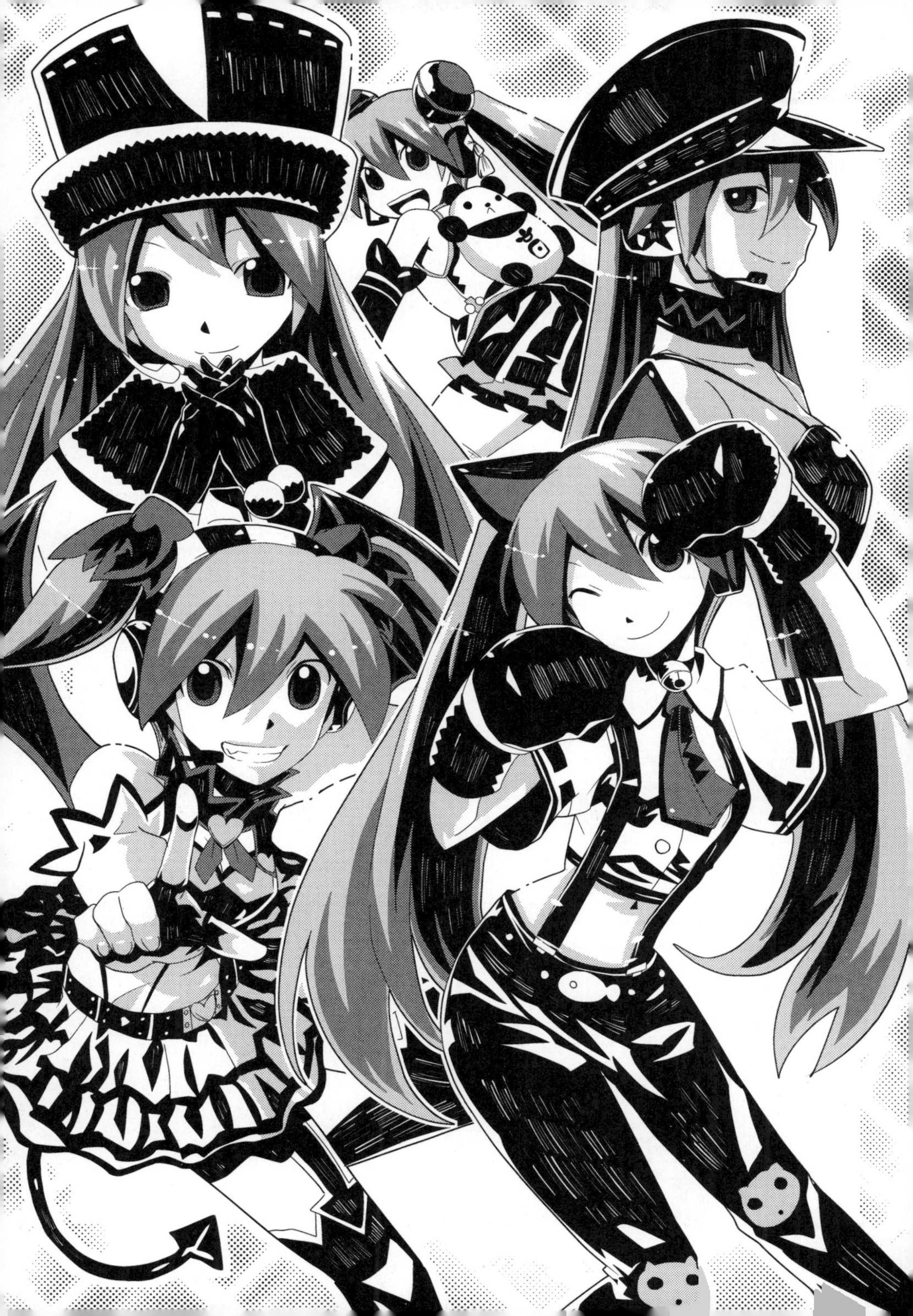

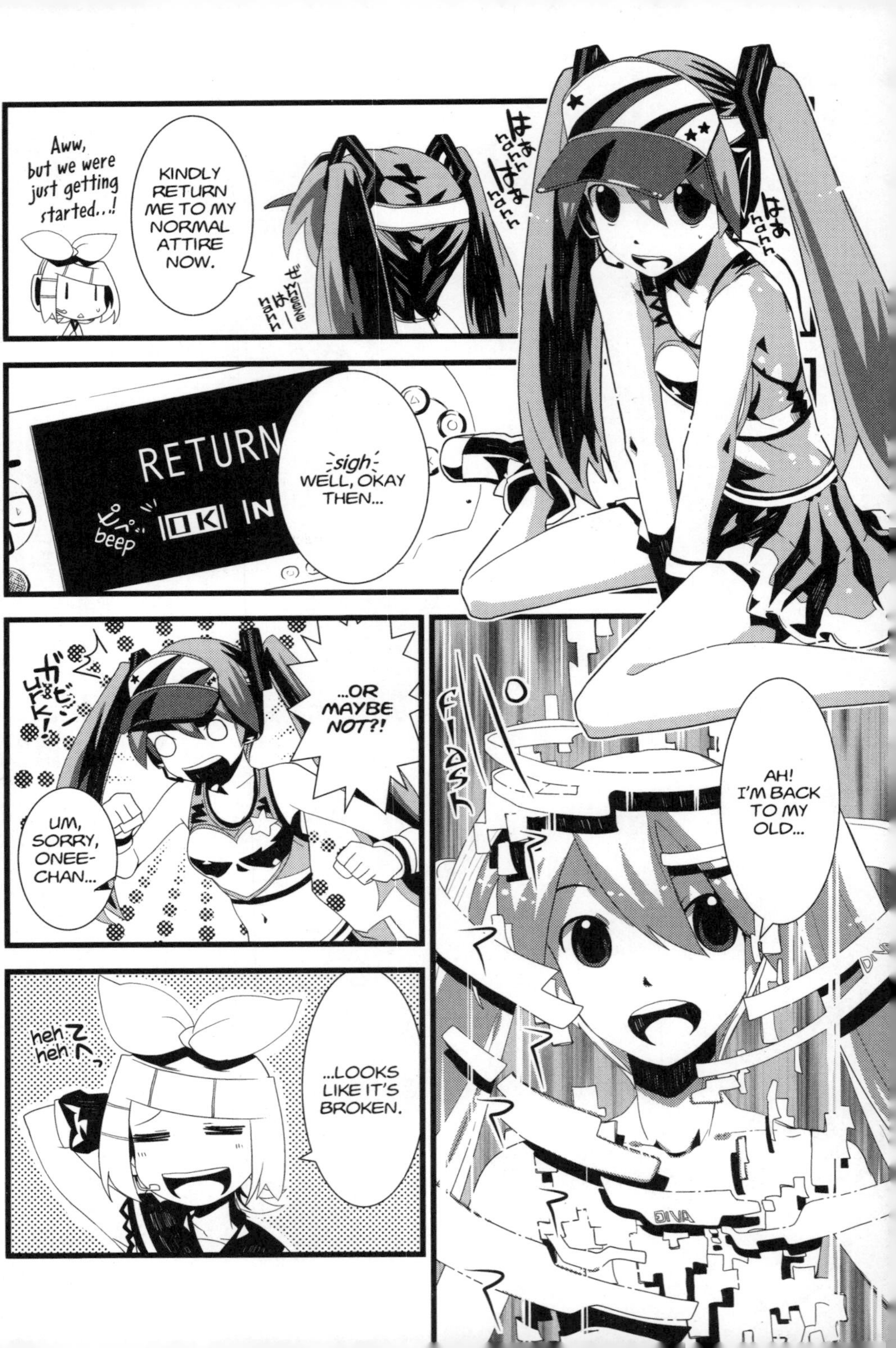
はぁ hahh
はぁ hahh
はぁ hahh
KINDLY RETURN ME TO MY NORMAL ATTIRE NOW.
Aww, but we were just getting started...!
ぜぇ wheeze はー hahh
RETURN
OK IN
ピッ beep
sigh WELL, OKAY THEN...
AH! I'M BACK TO MY OLD...
DIVA
DIVA
...OR MAYBE NOT?!
UM, SORRY, ONEE-CHAN...
urk!
...LOOKS LIKE IT'S BROKEN.
heh heh

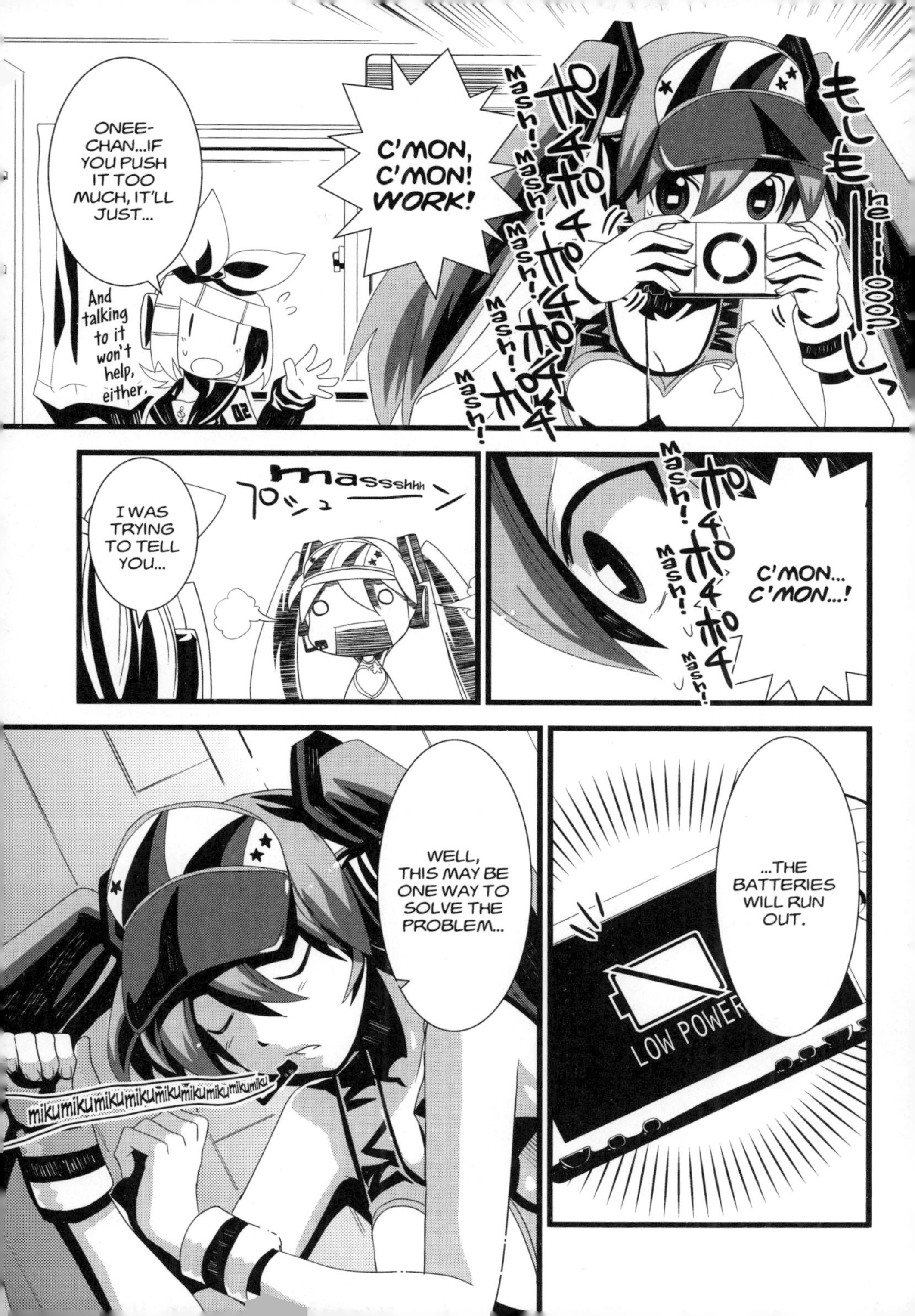
もしもーーしっ
hel-l-ooo?
ポチポチポチポチポチ
Mash! Mash! Mash! Mash! Mash! Mash!
C'MON, C'MON! WORK!
ONEE-CHAN...IF YOU PUSH IT TOO MUCH, IT'LL JUST...
And talking to it won't help, either.
ポチポチポチ
Mash! Mash! Mash!
C'MON... C'MON...!
プシューーン
massshhh
I WAS TRYING TO TELL YOU...
...THE BATTERIES WILL RUN OUT.
LOW POWER
WELL, THIS MAY BE ONE WAY TO SOLVE THE PROBLEM...
mikumikumikumikumikumikumikumiku

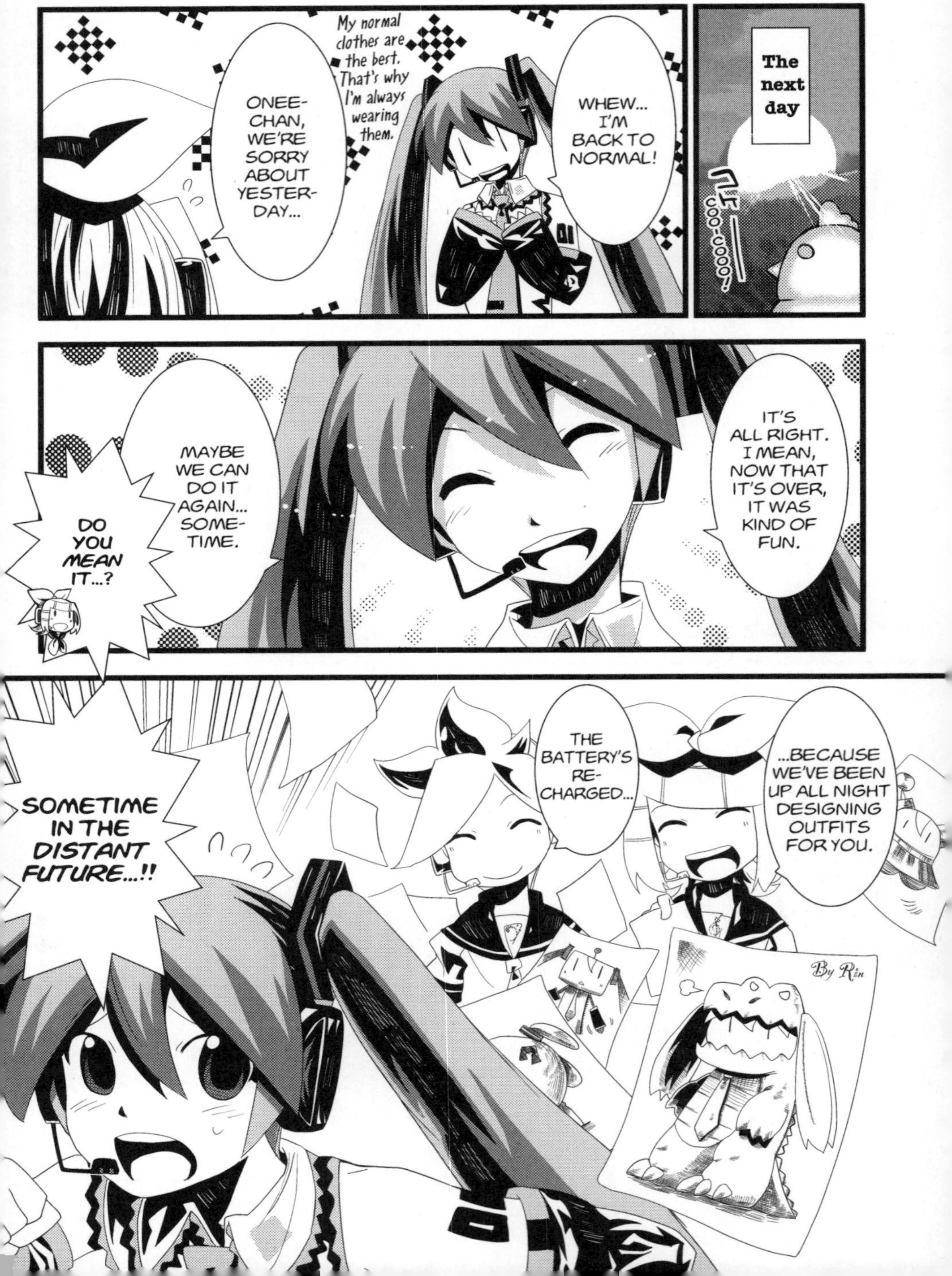
The next day
COO-COOO!
WHEW... I'M BACK TO NORMAL!
My normal clothes are the best. That's why I'm always wearing them.
ONEE-CHAN, WE'RE SORRY ABOUT YESTER-DAY...
IT'S ALL RIGHT. I MEAN, NOW THAT IT'S OVER, IT WAS KIND OF FUN.
MAYBE WE CAN DO IT AGAIN... SOME-TIME.
DO YOU MEAN IT...?
...BECAUSE WE'VE BEEN UP ALL NIGHT DESIGNING OUTFITS FOR YOU.
THE BATTERY'S RE-CHARGED...
SOMETIME IN THE DISTANT FUTURE...!!
By Rin

(30th SONG) WARDROBE MIX

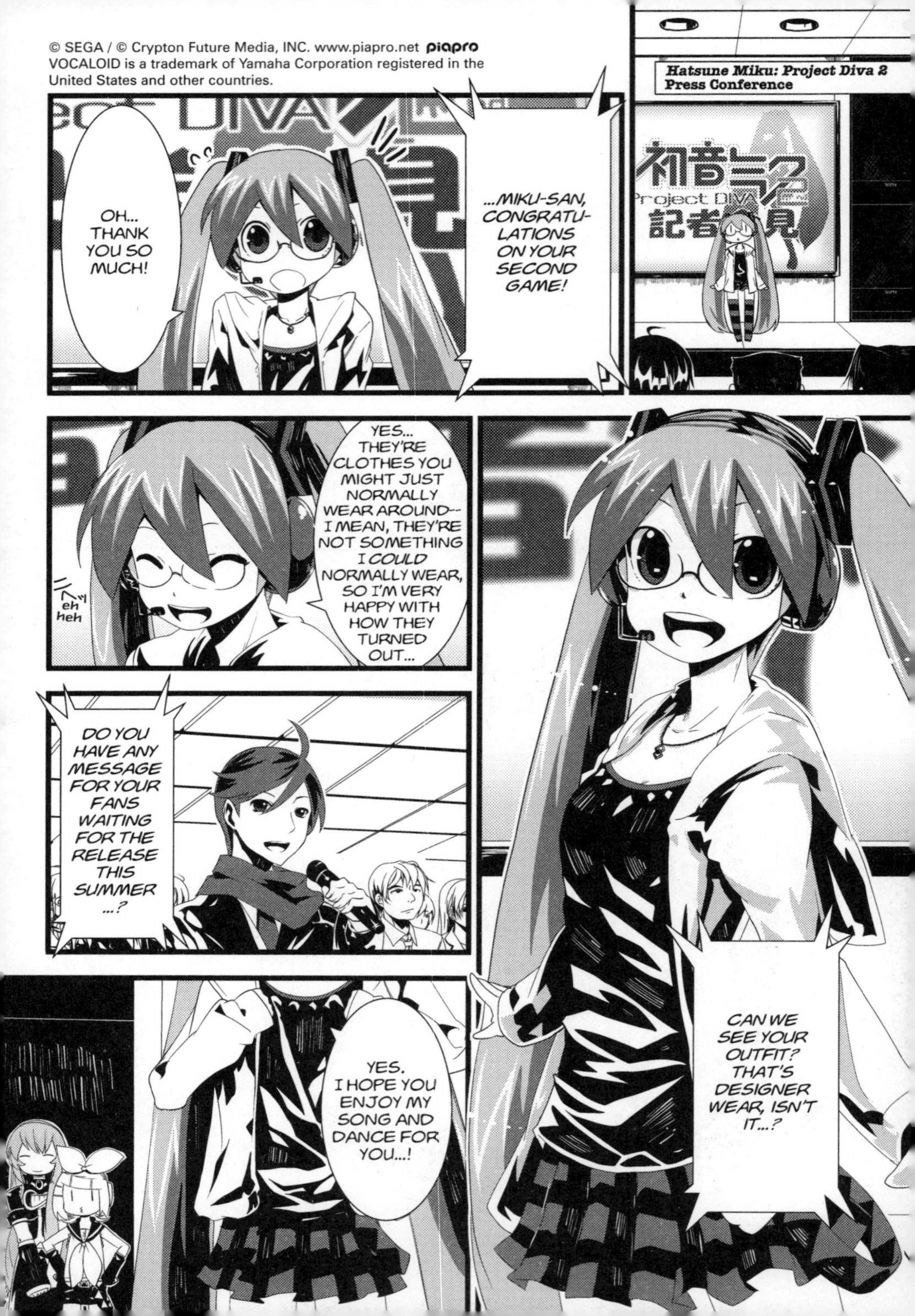
Hatsune Miku: Project Diva 2 Press Conference
初音ミク Project DIVA 2nd 記者会見
...MIKU-SAN, CONGRATULATIONS ON YOUR SECOND GAME!
OH... THANK YOU SO MUCH!
CAN WE SEE YOUR OUTFIT? THAT'S DESIGNER WEAR, ISN'T IT...?
YES... THEY'RE CLOTHES YOU MIGHT JUST NORMALLY WEAR AROUND-- I MEAN, THEY'RE NOT SOMETHING I COULD NORMALLY WEAR, SO I'M VERY HAPPY WITH HOW THEY TURNED OUT...
eh heh
DO YOU HAVE ANY MESSAGE FOR YOUR FANS WAITING FOR THE RELEASE THIS SUMMER ...?
YES. I HOPE YOU ENJOY MY SONG AND DANCE FOR YOU...!

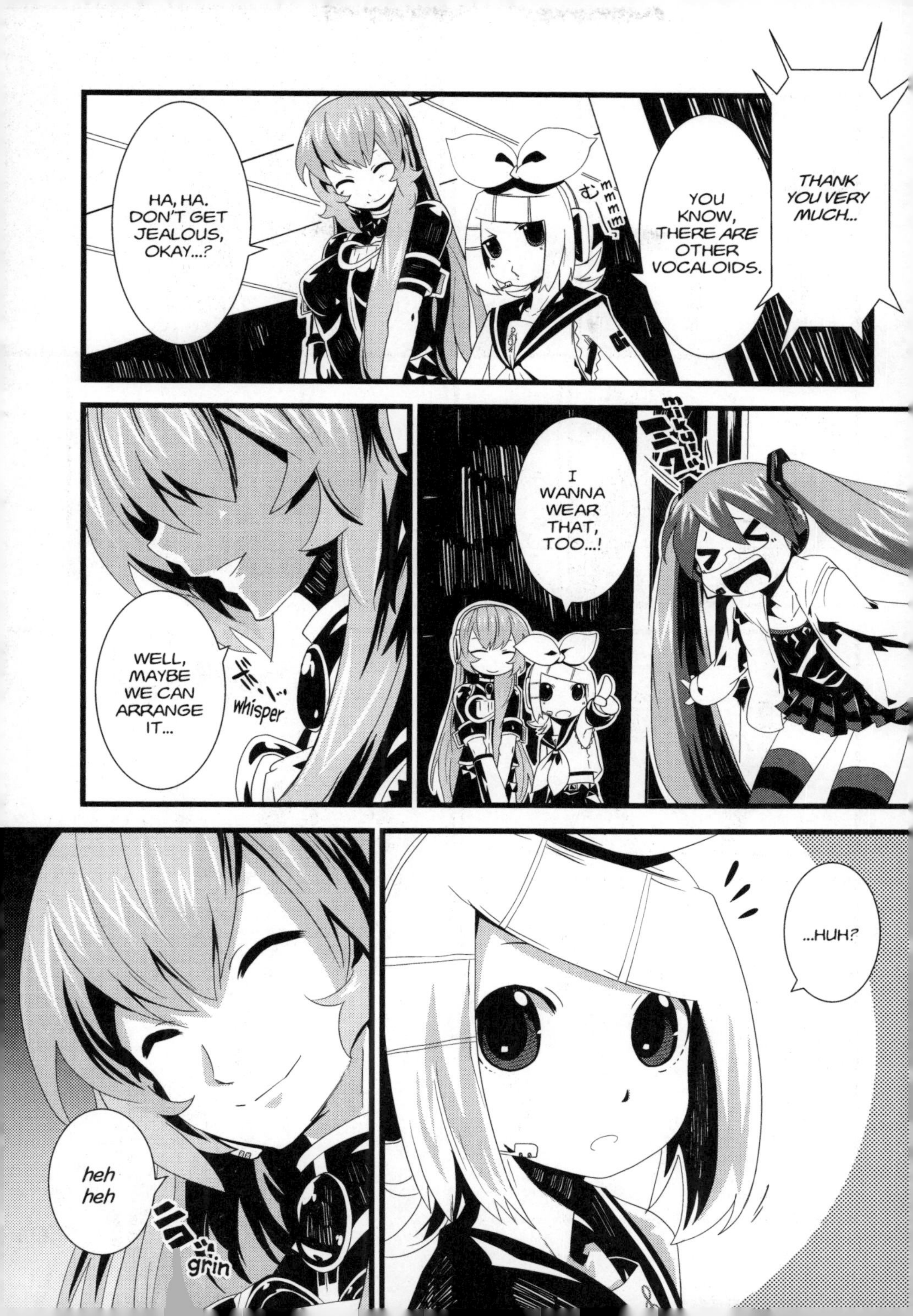
THANK YOU VERY MUCH...
YOU KNOW, THERE ARE OTHER VOCALOIDS.
mmmm
HA, HA. DON'T GET JEALOUS, OKAY...?
miku!!
I WANNA WEAR THAT, TOO...!
whisper
WELL, MAYBE WE CAN ARRANGE IT...
...HUH?
heh heh
grin

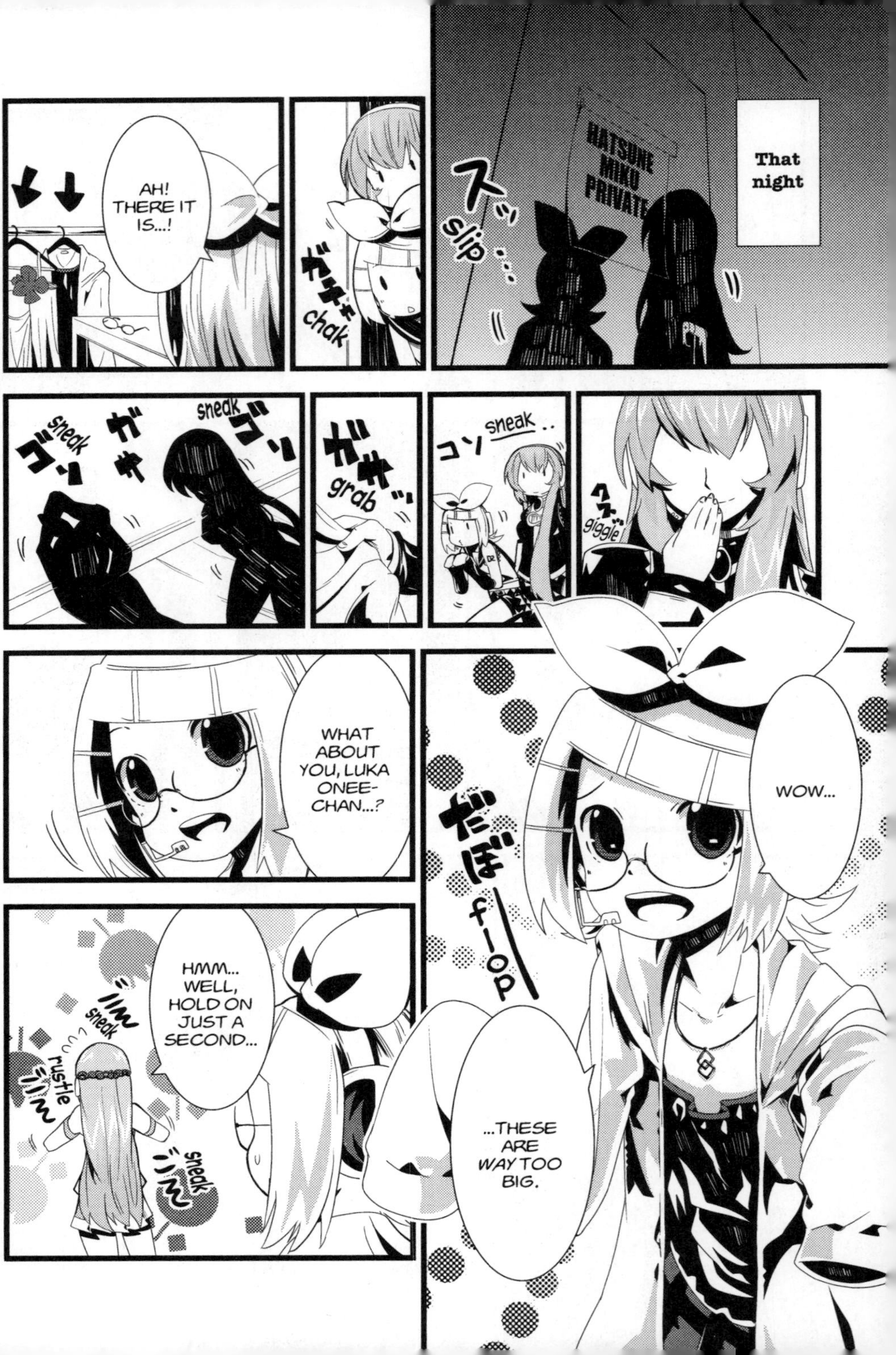
That night
HATSUNE MIKU PRIVATE
スッ
slip...
ガチャ
chak
AH! THERE IT IS...!
クスッ
giggle
コソ
sneak..
ガサッ
grab
ゴソ
sneak
ガサ
ゴソ
sneak
WOW...
だぼ
flop
...THESE ARE WAY TOO BIG.
WHAT ABOUT YOU, LUKA ONEE-CHAN...?
HMM... WELL, HOLD ON JUST A SECOND...
sneak
rustle
sneak

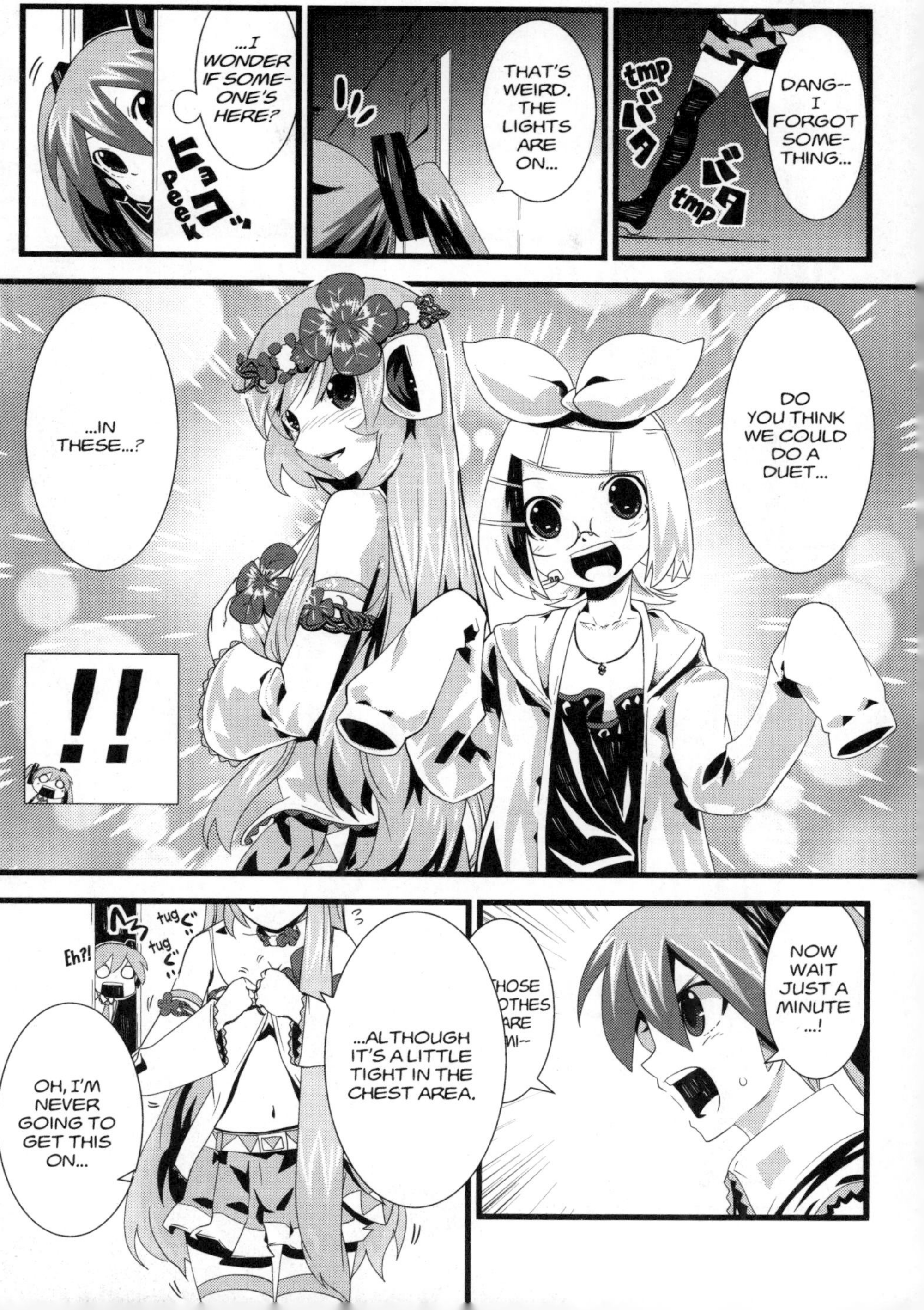
tmp バタ
DANG-- I FORGOT SOMETHING...
バタ tmp
THAT'S WEIRD. THE LIGHTS ARE ON...
...I WONDER IF SOMEONE'S HERE?
ヒョコッ
peek
DO YOU THINK WE COULD DO A DUET...
...IN THESE...?
!!
NOW WAIT JUST A MINUTE ...!
THOSE OTHES ARE MI--
...ALTHOUGH IT'S A LITTLE TIGHT IN THE CHEST AREA.
tug ぐ
tug ぐ
Eh?!
OH, I'M NEVER GOING TO GET THIS ON...

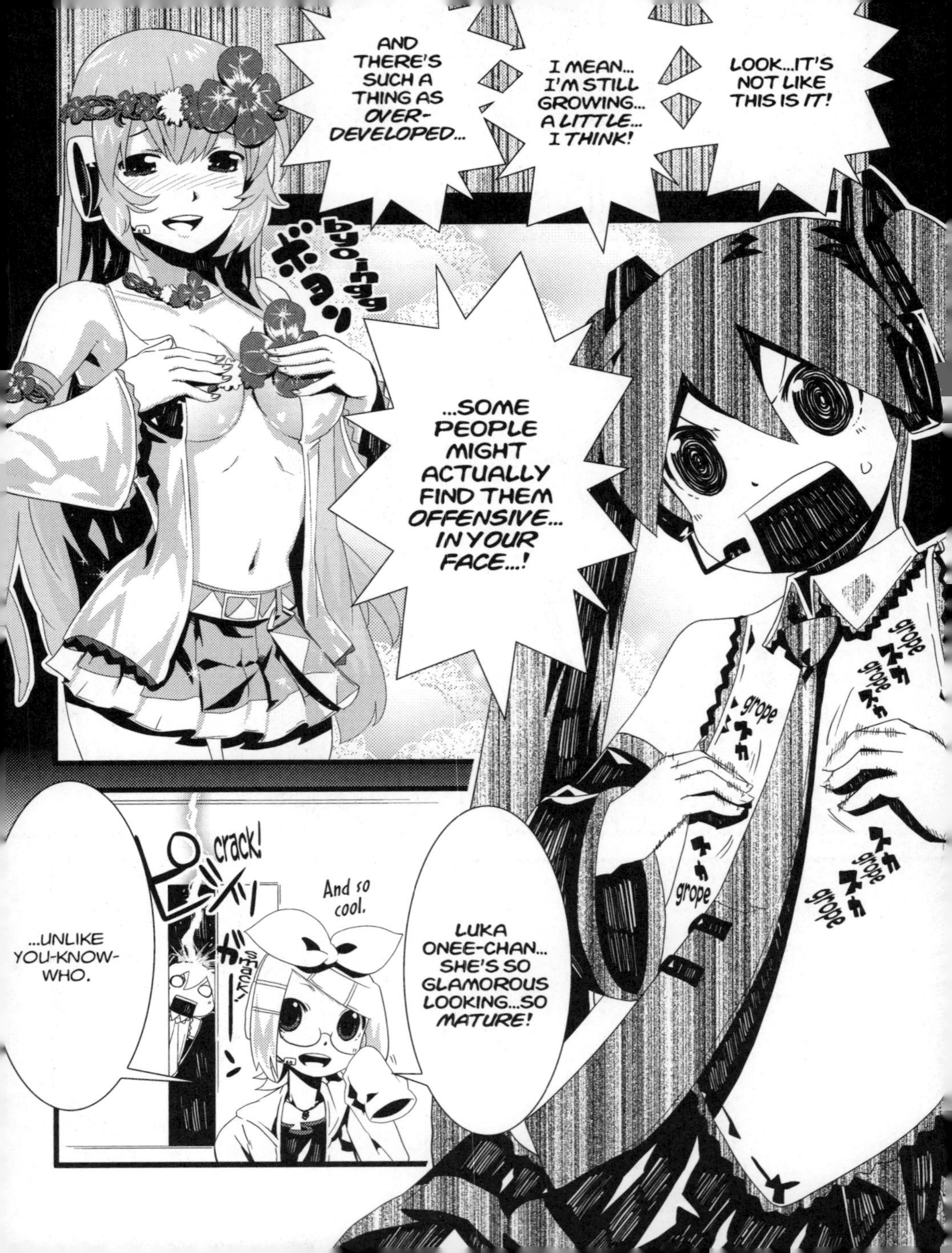
LOOK...IT'S NOT LIKE THIS IS IT!
I MEAN... I'M STILL GROWING... A LITTLE... I THINK!
AND THERE'S SUCH A THING AS OVER-DEVELOPED...
byo-inggg
...SOME PEOPLE MIGHT ACTUALLY FIND THEM OFFENSIVE... IN YOUR FACE...!
grope grope grope
grope grope grope
LUKA ONEE-CHAN... SHE'S SO GLAMOROUS LOOKING...SO MATURE!
And so cool.
crack!
smack!
...UNLIKE YOU-KNOW-WHO.

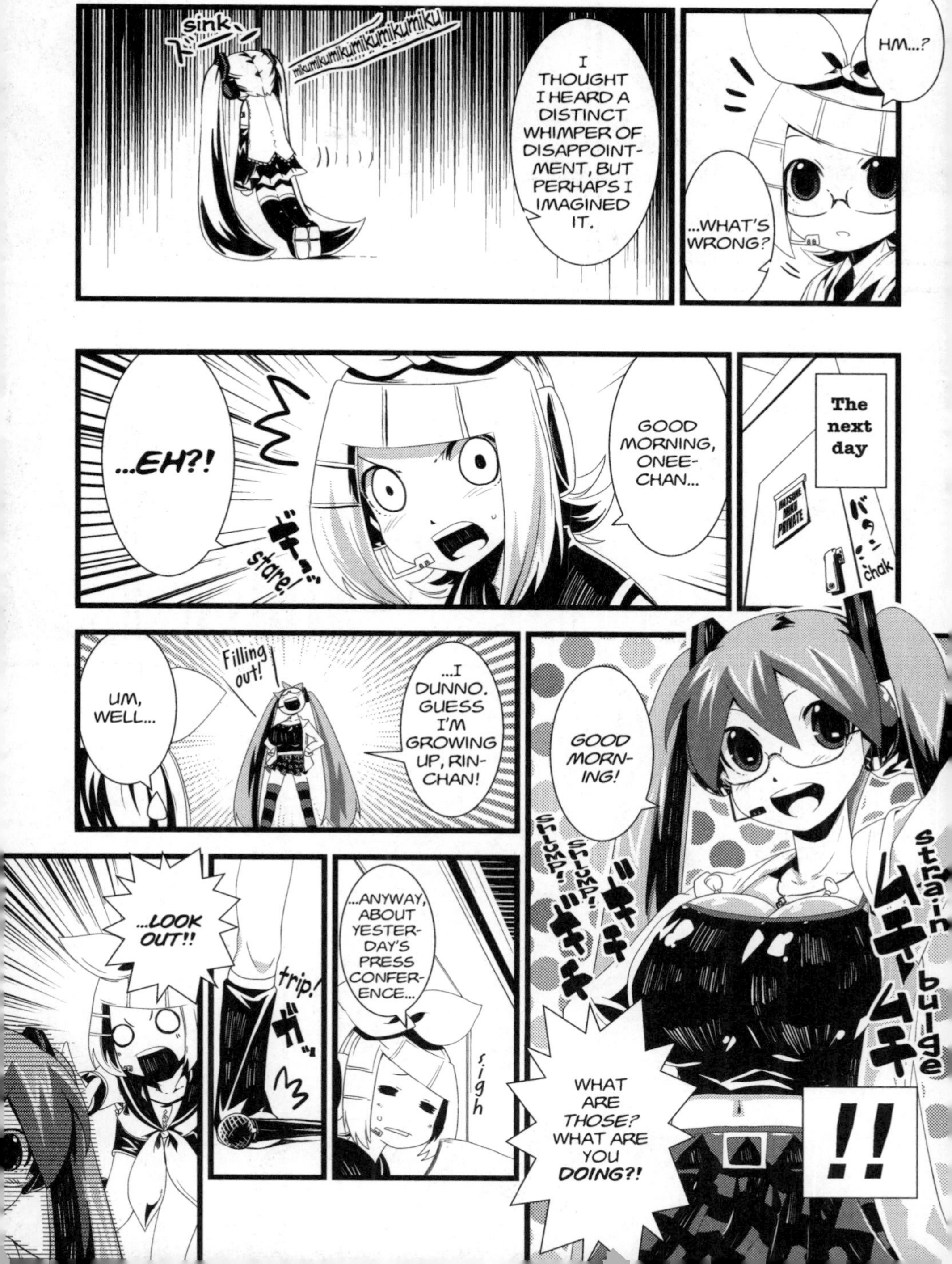
HM...?
...WHAT'S WRONG?
I THOUGHT I HEARD A DISTINCT WHIMPER OF DISAPPOINT-MENT, BUT PERHAPS I IMAGINED IT.
sink
mikumikumikumikumikumikumiku
The next day
chak
GOOD MORNING, ONEE-CHAN...
...EH?!
stare!
GOOD MORN-ING!
strain bulge
SHLUMP! SHLUMP!
WHAT ARE THOSE? WHAT ARE YOU DOING?!
!!
...I DUNNO. GUESS I'M GROWING UP, RIN-CHAN!
Filling out!
UM, WELL...
...ANYWAY, ABOUT YESTER-DAY'S PRESS CONFER-ENCE...
sigh
trip!
...LOOK OUT!!

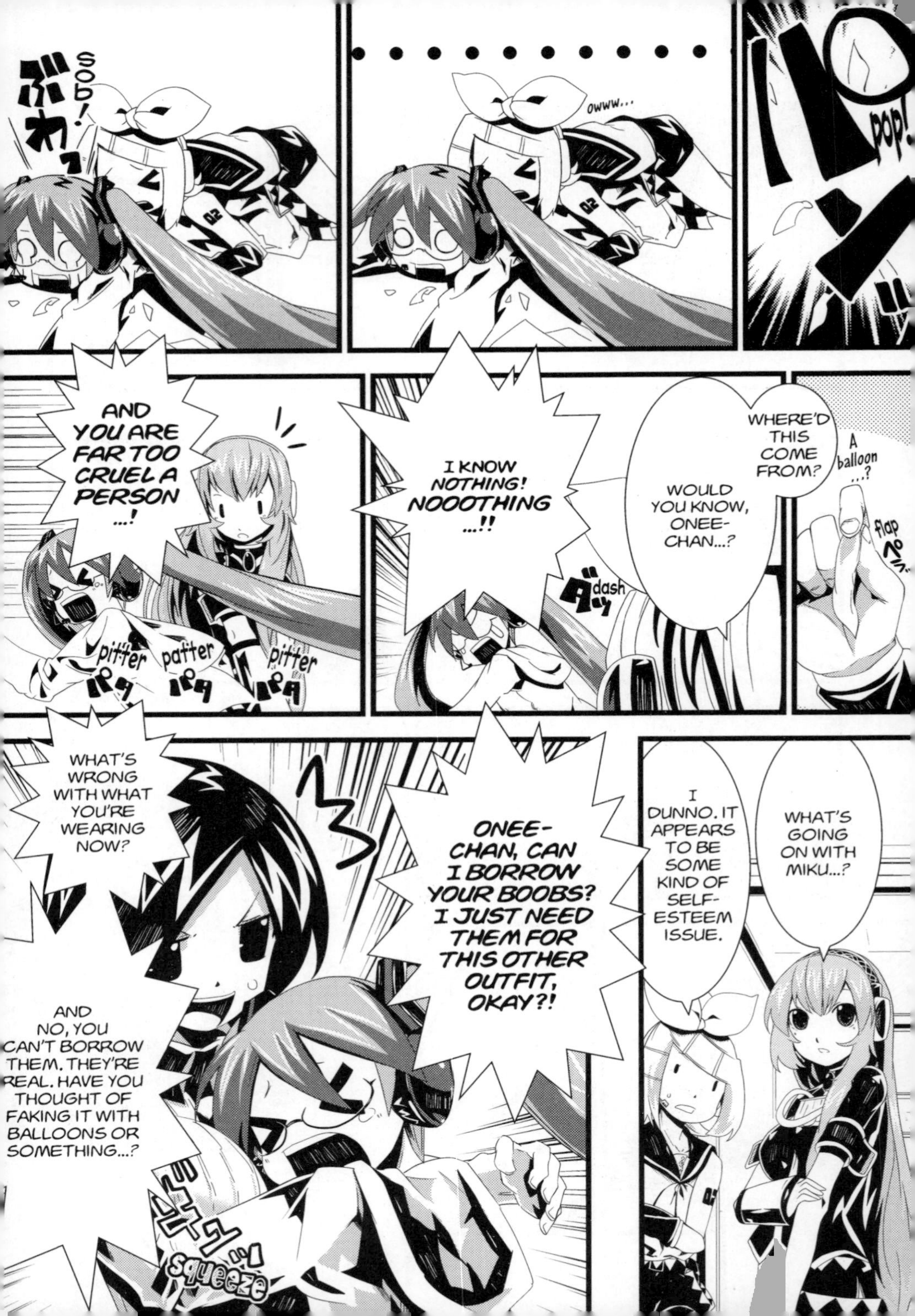
pop!
owww...
sob!
A balloon ...?
flap
WHERE'D THIS COME FROM?
WOULD YOU KNOW, ONEE-CHAN...?
I KNOW NOTHING! NOOOTHING ...!!
dash
AND YOU ARE FAR TOO CRUEL A PERSON ...!
pitter
patter
pitter
WHAT'S GOING ON WITH MIKU...?
I DUNNO. IT APPEARS TO BE SOME KIND OF SELF-ESTEEM ISSUE.
ONEE-CHAN, CAN I BORROW YOUR BOOBS? I JUST NEED THEM FOR THIS OTHER OUTFIT, OKAY?!
WHAT'S WRONG WITH WHAT YOU'RE WEARING NOW?
AND NO, YOU CAN'T BORROW THEM. THEY'RE REAL. HAVE YOU THOUGHT OF FAKING IT WITH BALLOONS OR SOMETHING...?
squeeze

(31st SONG) DUET MIX

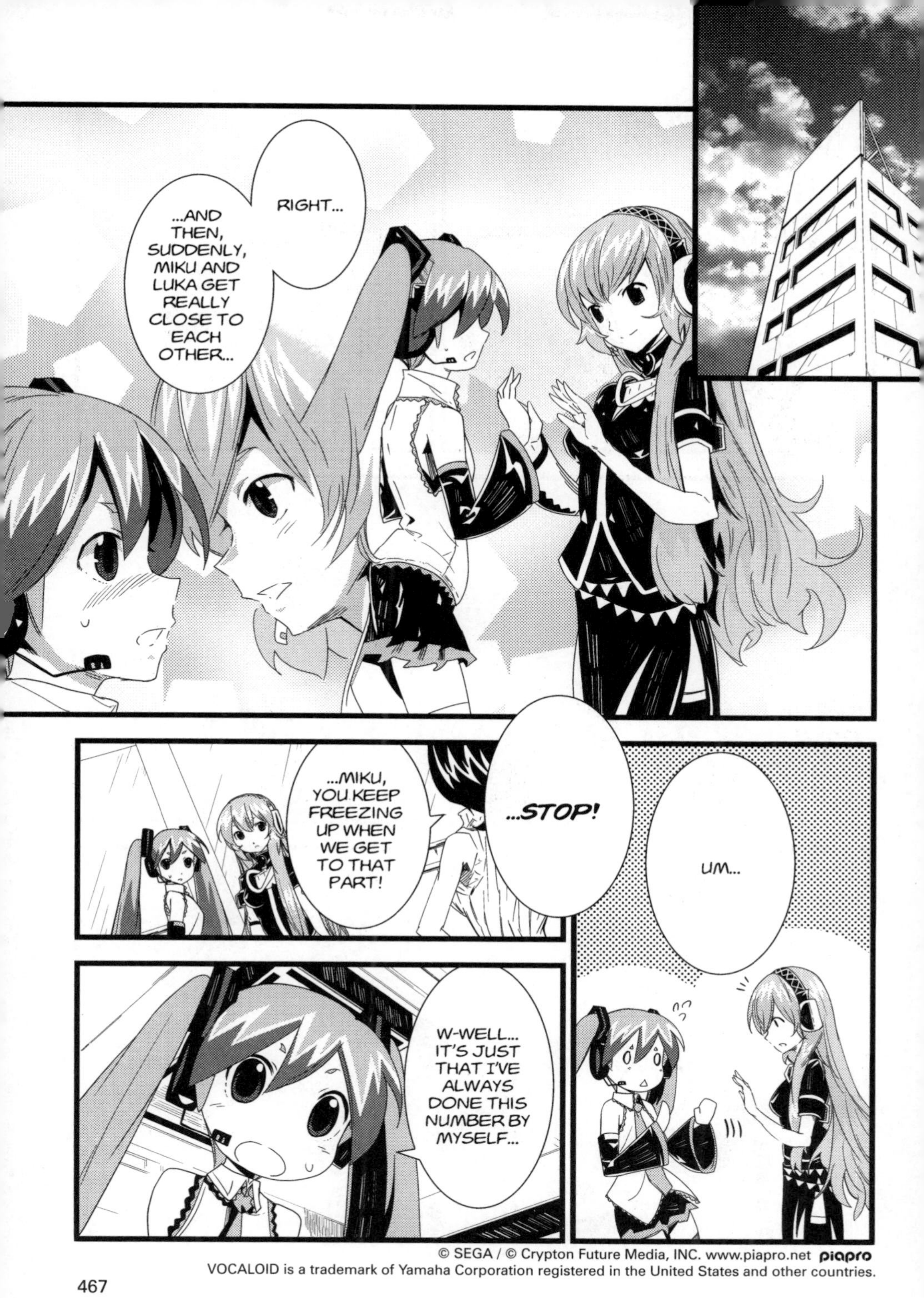
RIGHT...
...AND THEN, SUDDENLY, MIKU AND LUKA GET REALLY CLOSE TO EACH OTHER...
...STOP!
...MIKU, YOU KEEP FREEZING UP WHEN WE GET TO THAT PART!
UM...
W-WELL... IT'S JUST THAT I'VE ALWAYS DONE THIS NUMBER BY MYSELF...

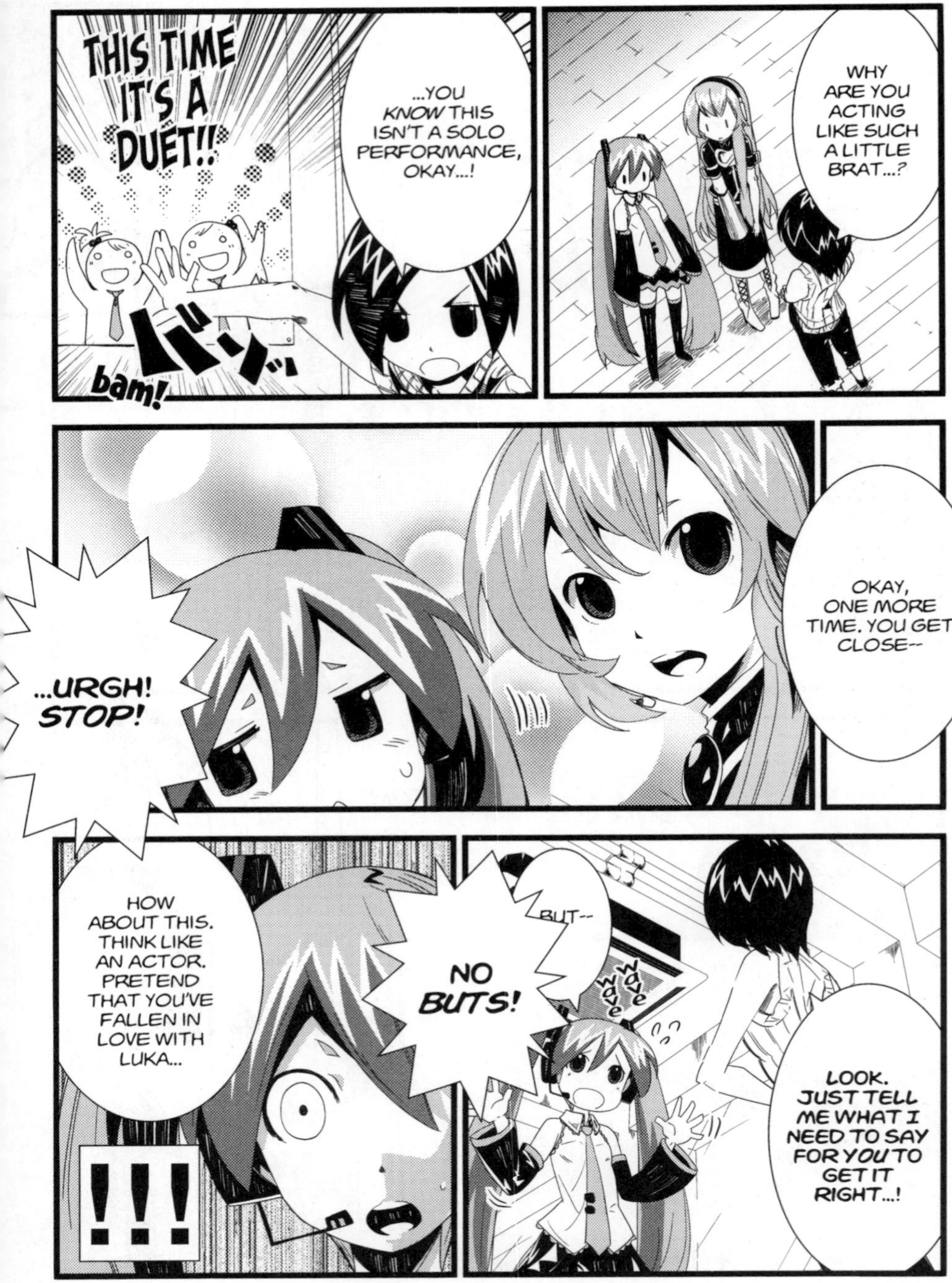
WHY ARE YOU ACTING LIKE SUCH A LITTLE BRAT...?
...YOU KNOW THIS ISN'T A SOLO PERFORMANCE, OKAY...!
THIS TIME IT'S A DUET!!
bam!
OKAY, ONE MORE TIME. YOU GET CLOSE--
...URGH! STOP!
BUT--
NO BUTS!
wave wave
LOOK. JUST TELL ME WHAT I NEED TO SAY FOR YOU TO GET IT RIGHT...!
HOW ABOUT THIS. THINK LIKE AN ACTOR. PRETEND THAT YOU'VE FALLEN IN LOVE WITH LUKA...
!!!

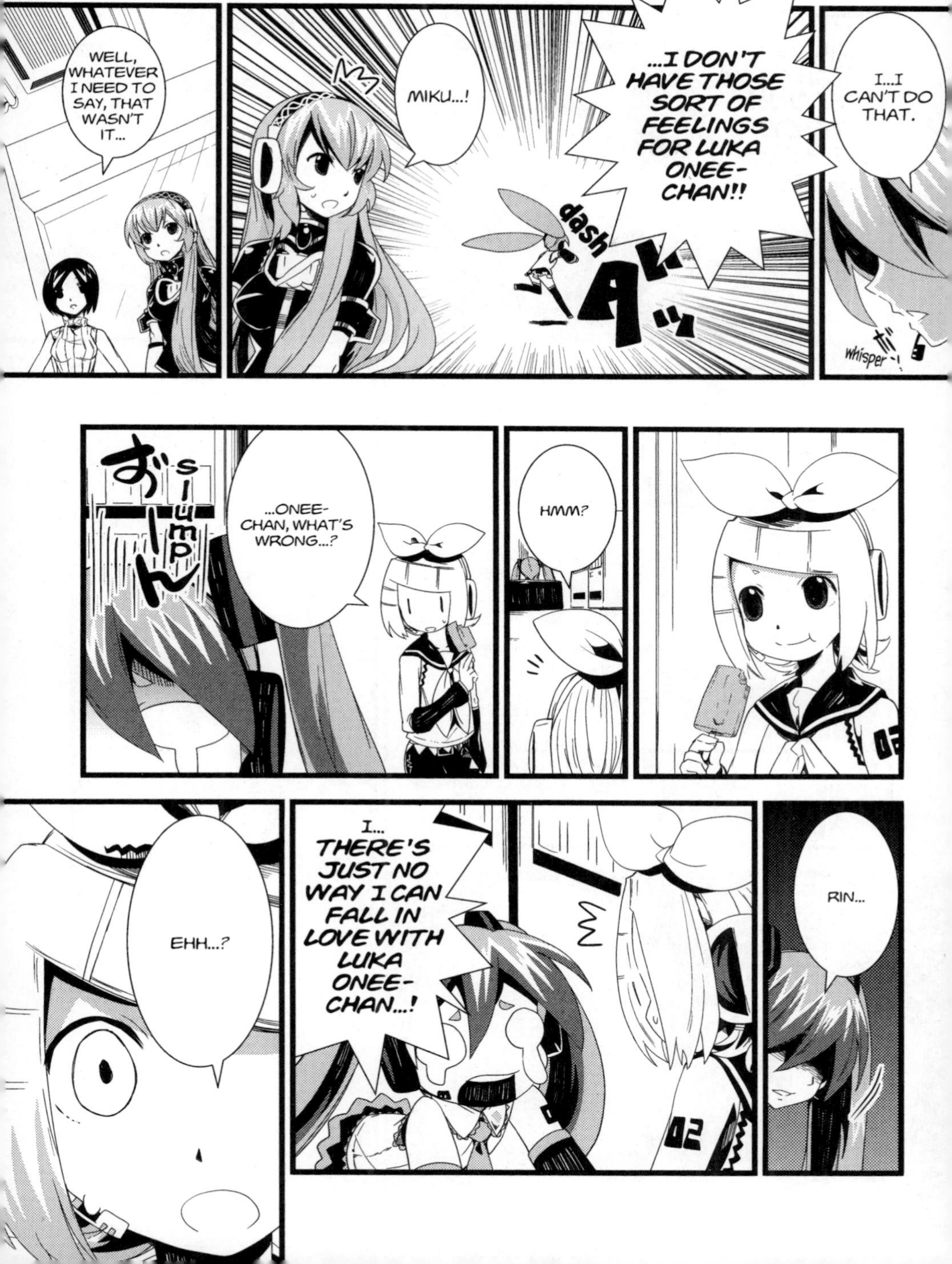
I...I CAN'T DO THAT.
whisper
...I DON'T HAVE THOSE SORT OF FEELINGS FOR LUKA ONEE-CHAN!!
dash
MIKU...!
WELL, WHATEVER I NEED TO SAY, THAT WASN'T IT...
HMM?
...ONEE-CHAN, WHAT'S WRONG...?
slump
RIN...
I... THERE'S JUST NO WAY I CAN FALL IN LOVE WITH LUKA ONEE-CHAN...!
EHH...?

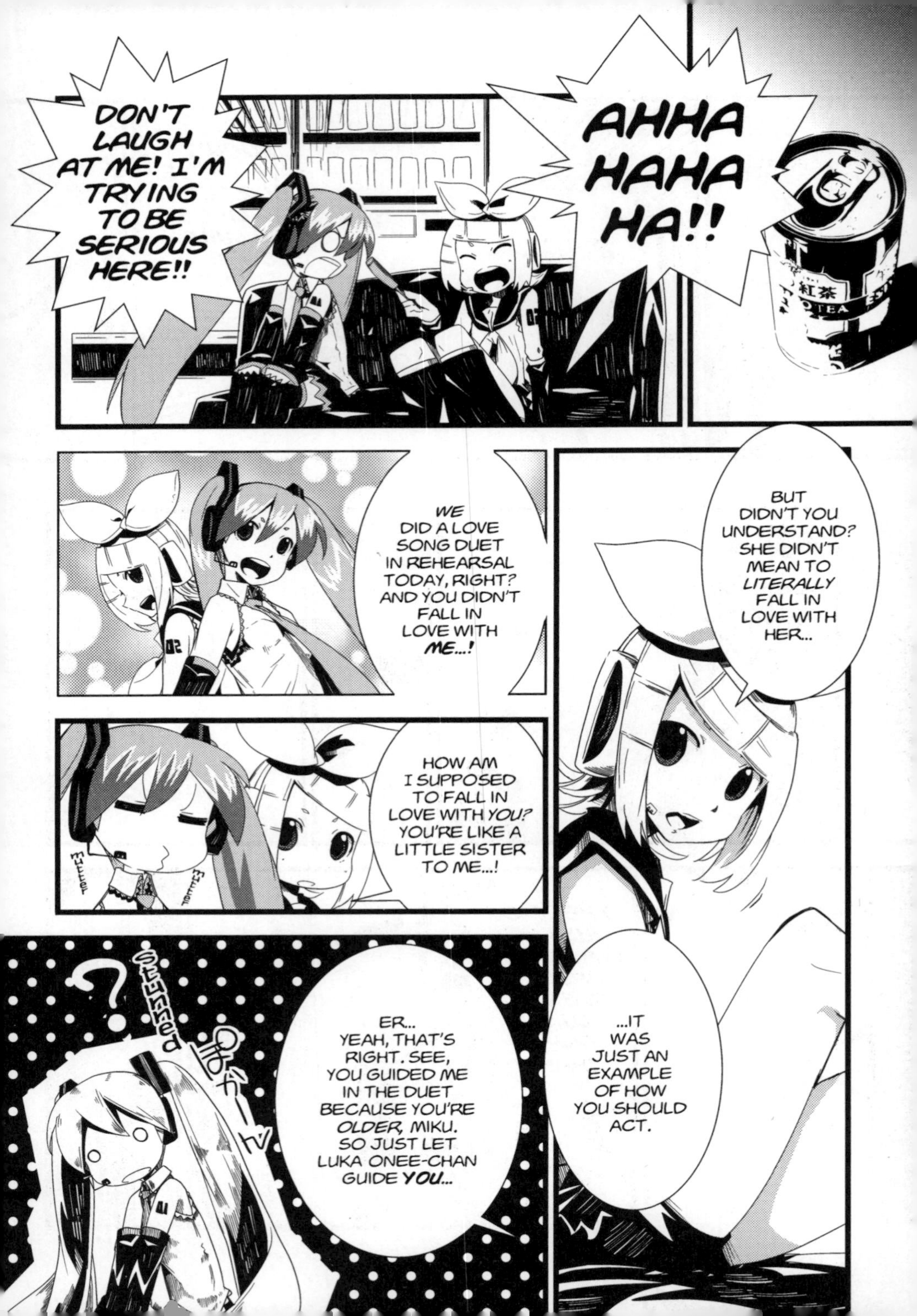
AHHA HAHAHA HA!!
DON'T LAUGH AT ME! I'M TRYING TO BE SERIOUS HERE!!
BUT DIDN'T YOU UNDERSTAND? SHE DIDN'T MEAN TO *LITERALLY* FALL IN LOVE WITH HER...
...IT WAS JUST AN EXAMPLE OF HOW YOU SHOULD ACT.
WE DID A LOVE SONG DUET IN REHEARSAL TODAY, RIGHT? AND YOU DIDN'T FALL IN LOVE WITH ***ME***...!
HOW AM I SUPPOSED TO FALL IN LOVE WITH *YOU*? YOU'RE LIKE A LITTLE SISTER TO ME...!
Mutter
Mutter
ER... YEAH, THAT'S RIGHT. SEE, YOU GUIDED ME IN THE DUET BECAUSE YOU'RE *OLDER*, MIKU. SO JUST LET LUKA ONEE-CHAN GUIDE **YOU**...
?
Stunned
ぽかーん

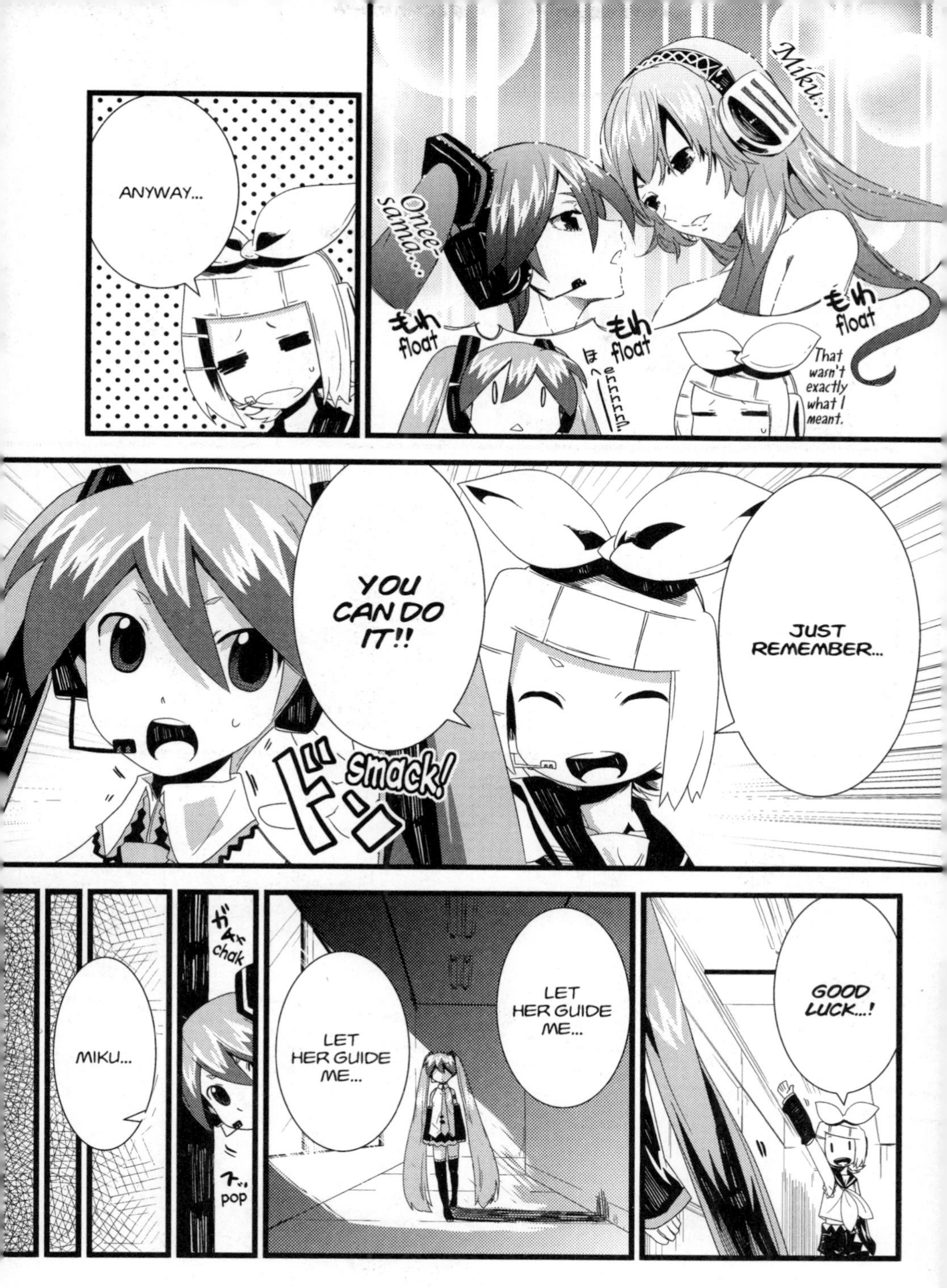
Miku...
Omee-sama...
もわ float
もわ float
もわ float
That wasn't exactly what I meant.
ANYWAY...
JUST REMEMBER...
YOU CAN DO IT!!
ドン smack!
GOOD LUCK...!
LET HER GUIDE ME...
LET HER GUIDE ME...
chak
MIKU...
pop

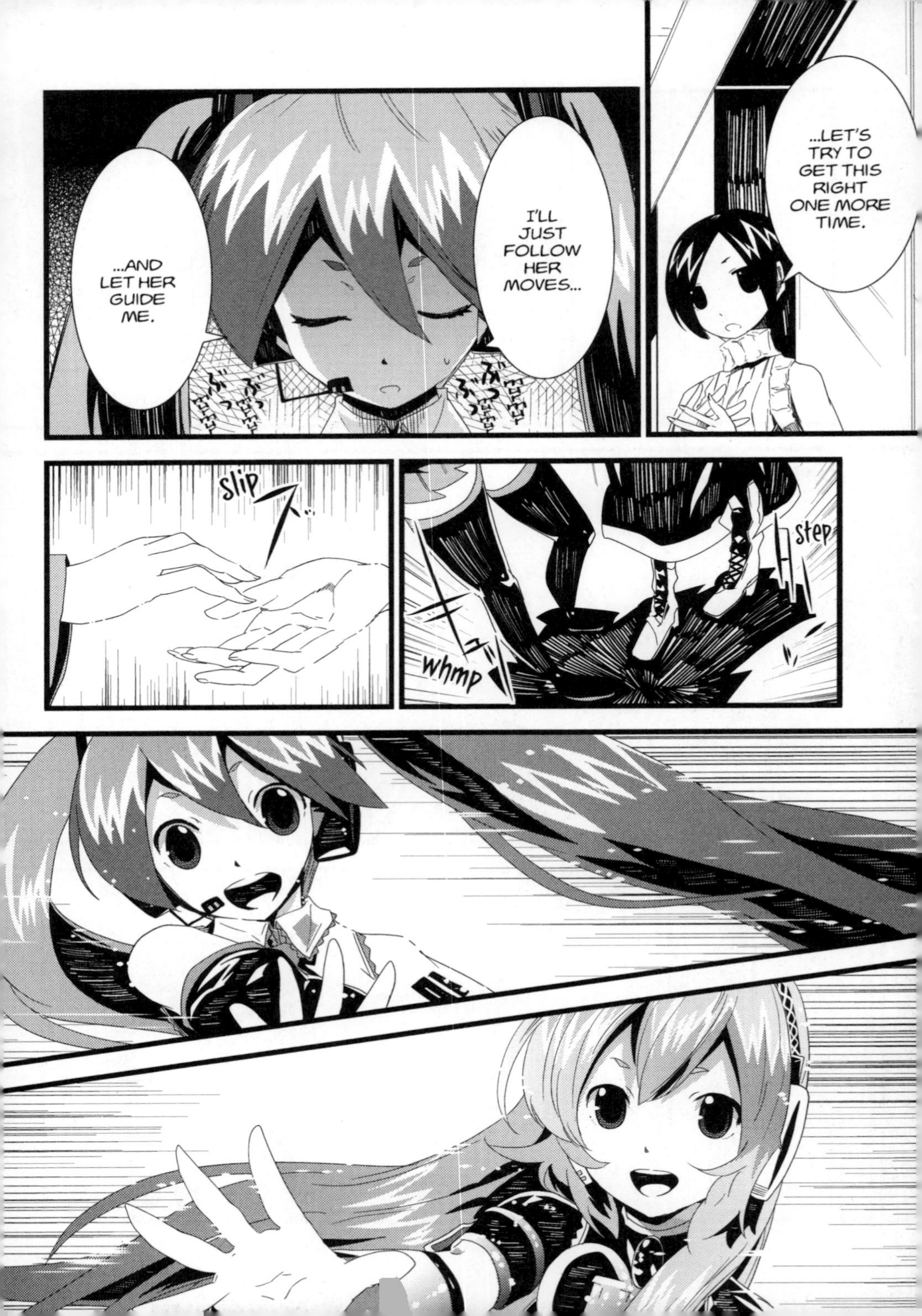
...LET'S TRY TO GET THIS RIGHT ONE MORE TIME.
I'LL JUST FOLLOW HER MOVES...
...AND LET HER GUIDE ME.
step
whmp
slip

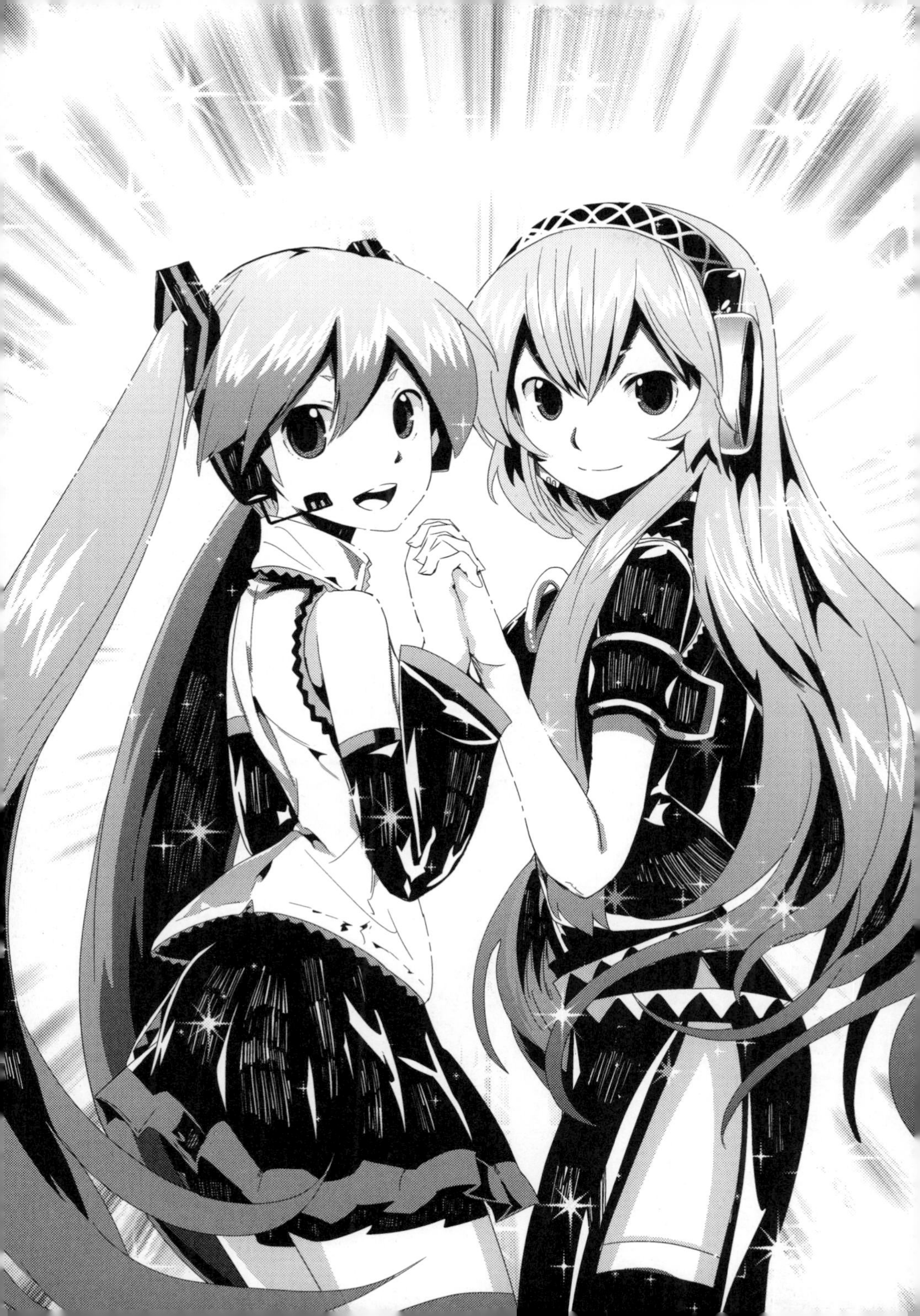

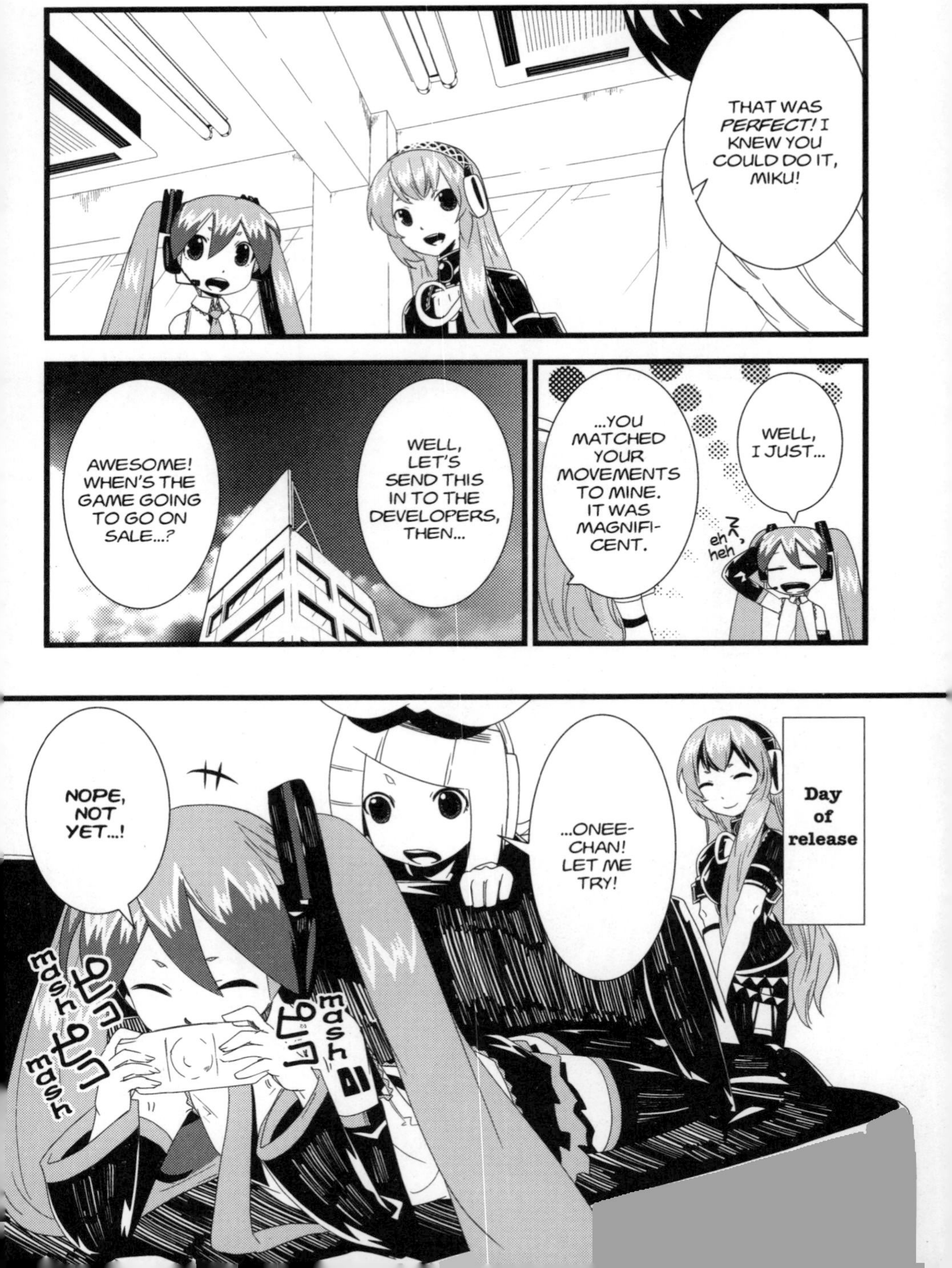
THAT WAS PERFECT! I KNEW YOU COULD DO IT, MIKU!
WELL, I JUST...
eh heh
...YOU MATCHED YOUR MOVEMENTS TO MINE. IT WAS MAGNIFICENT.
WELL, LET'S SEND THIS IN TO THE DEVELOPERS, THEN...
AWESOME! WHEN'S THE GAME GOING TO GO ON SALE...?
Day of release
...ONEE-CHAN! LET ME TRY!
NOPE, NOT YET...!
mash mash
mash mash

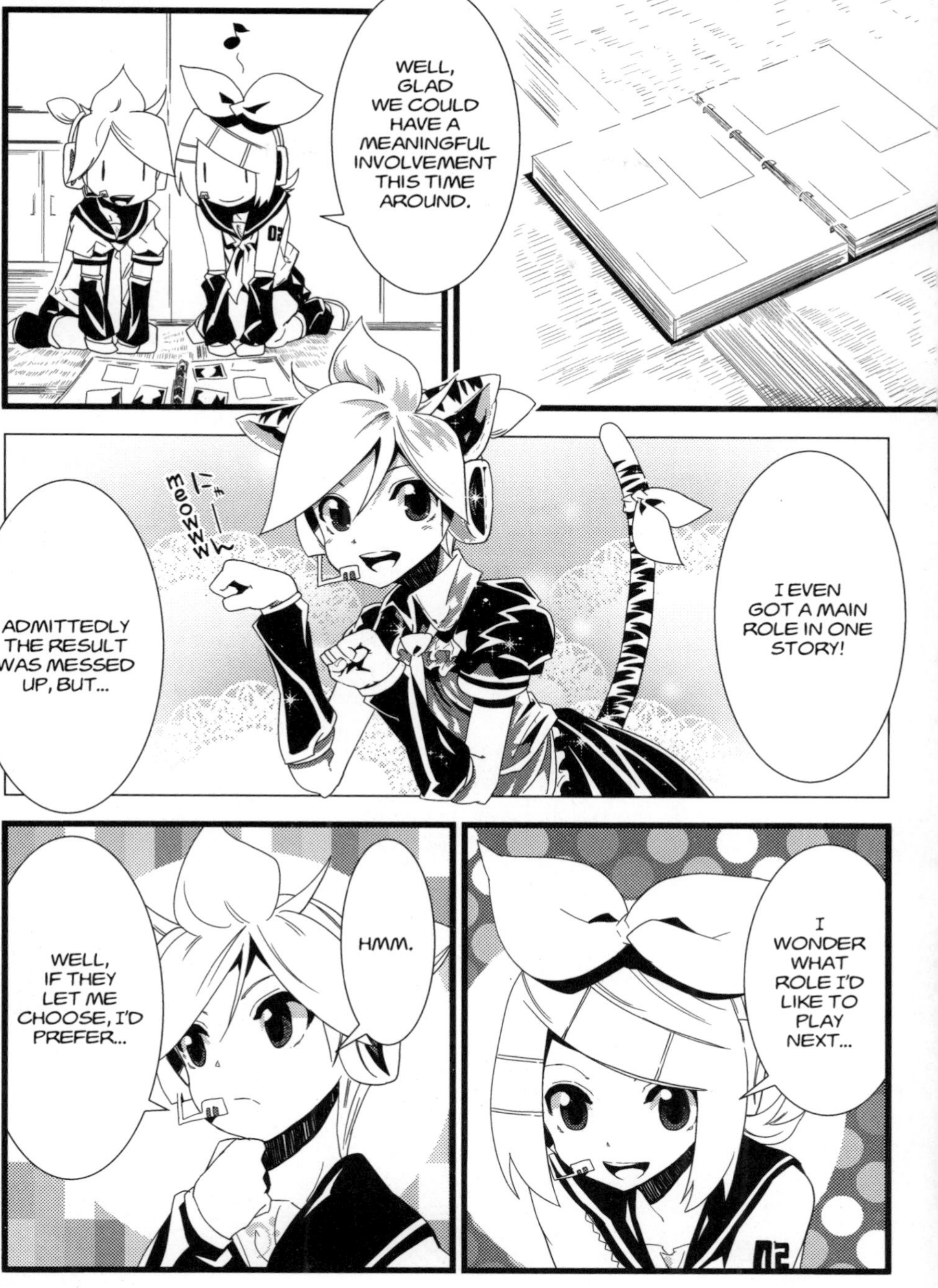
WELL, GLAD WE COULD HAVE A MEANINGFUL INVOLVEMENT THIS TIME AROUND.
I EVEN GOT A MAIN ROLE IN ONE STORY!
にゃ～ん meowww
ADMITTEDLY THE RESULT WAS MESSED UP, BUT...
I WONDER WHAT ROLE I'D LIKE TO PLAY NEXT...
HMM.
WELL, IF THEY LET ME CHOOSE, I'D PREFER...

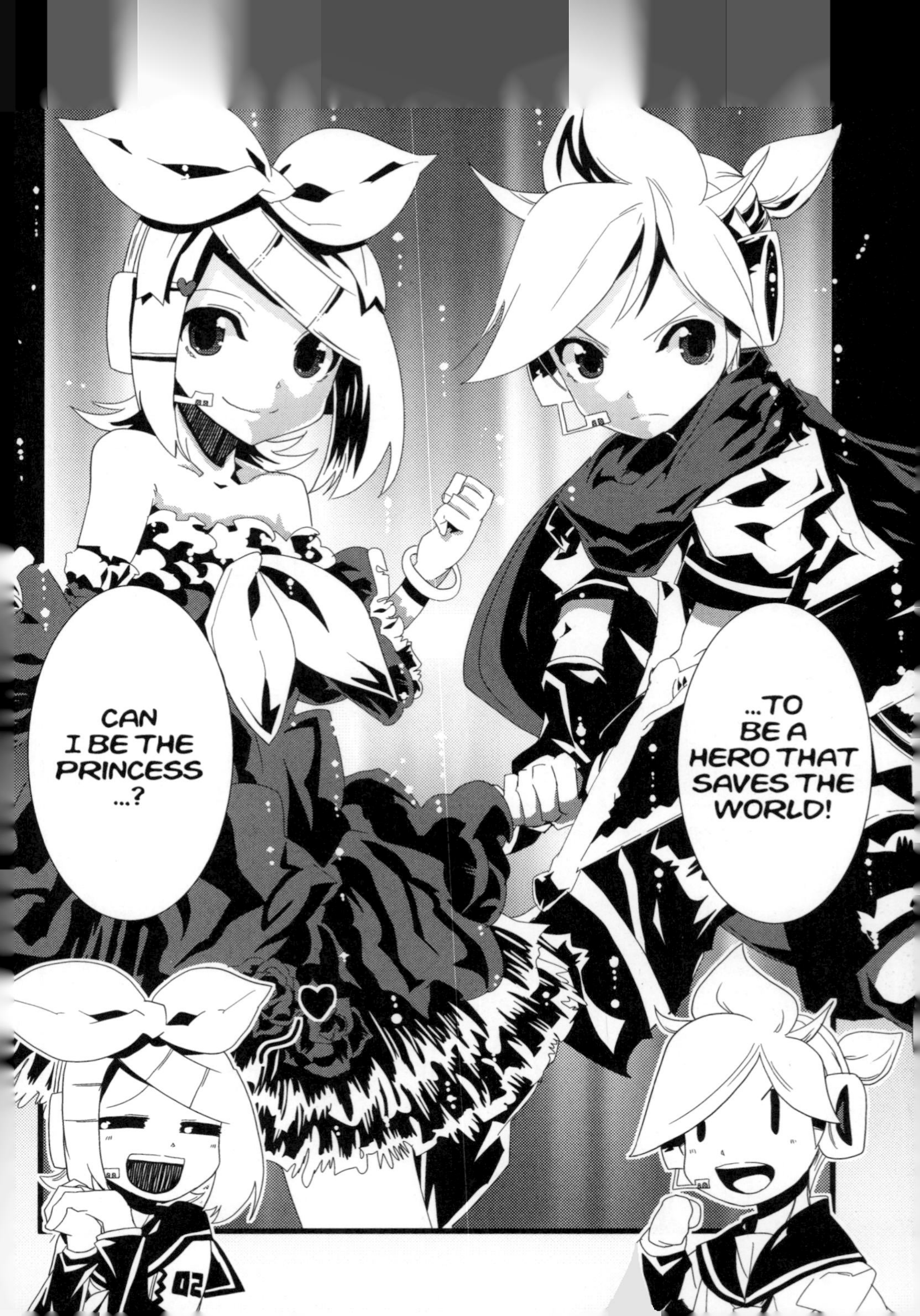
...TO BE A HERO THAT SAVES THE WORLD!
CAN I BE THE PRINCESS ...?

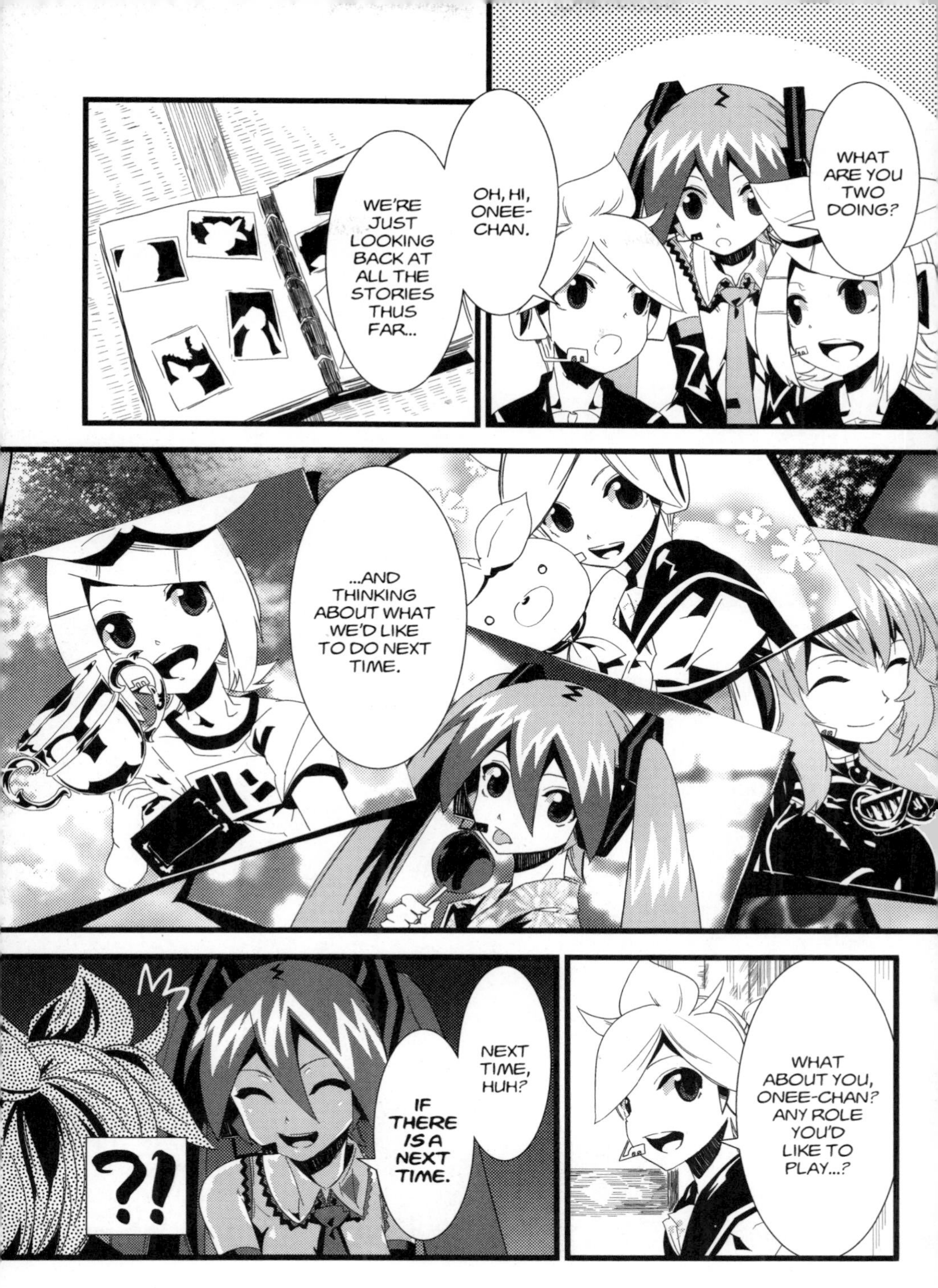
WHAT ARE YOU TWO DOING?
OH, HI, ONEE-CHAN.
WE'RE JUST LOOKING BACK AT ALL THE STORIES THUS FAR...
...AND THINKING ABOUT WHAT WE'D LIKE TO DO NEXT TIME.
WHAT ABOUT YOU, ONEE-CHAN? ANY ROLE YOU'D LIKE TO PLAY...?
NEXT TIME, HUH?
IF THERE IS A NEXT TIME.
?!

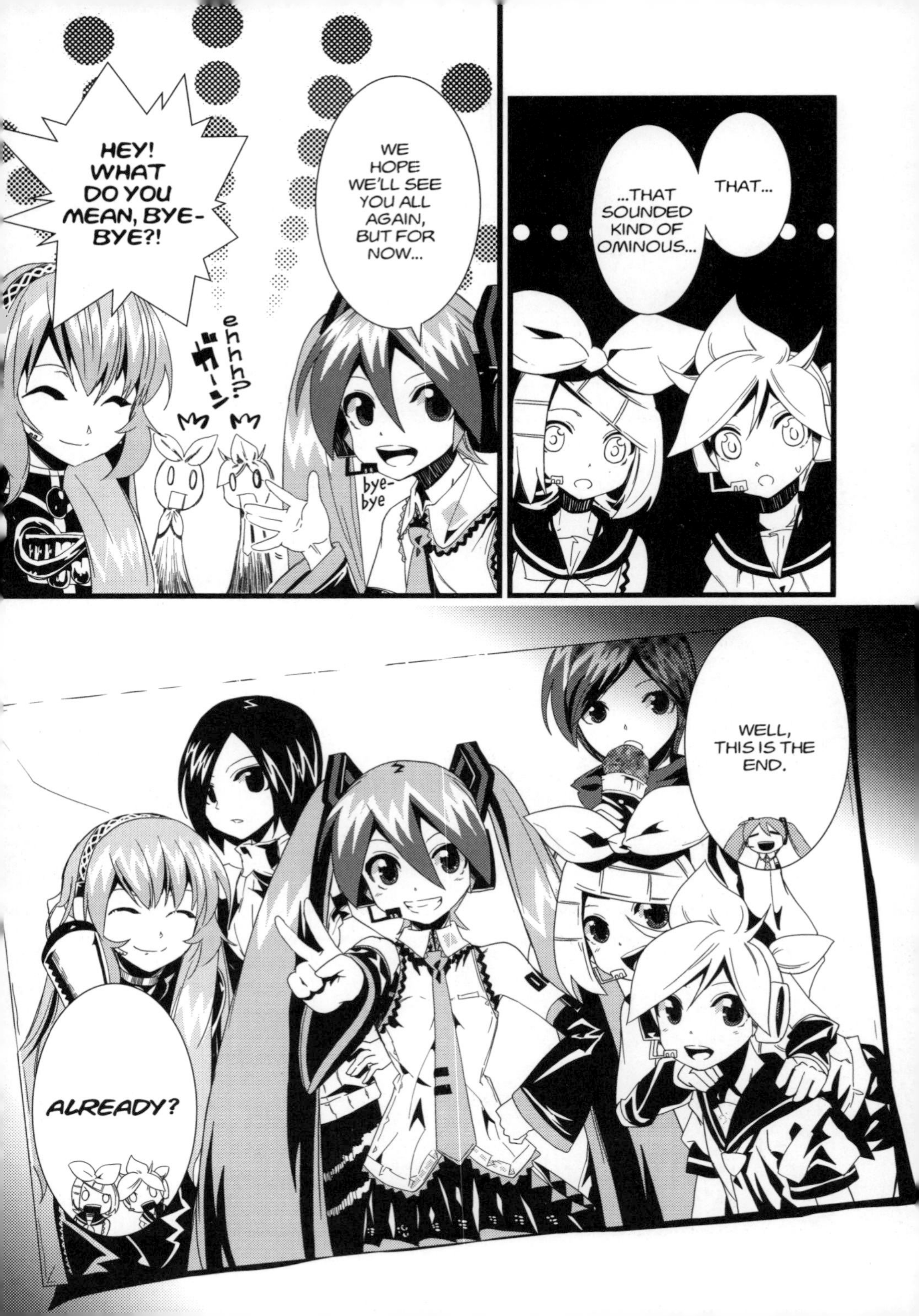
THAT...
...THAT SOUNDED KIND OF OMINOUS...
WE HOPE WE'LL SEE YOU ALL AGAIN, BUT FOR NOW...
bye-bye
ehhh?
ガーン
HEY! WHAT DO YOU MEAN, BYE-BYE?!
WELL, THIS IS THE END.
ALREADY?

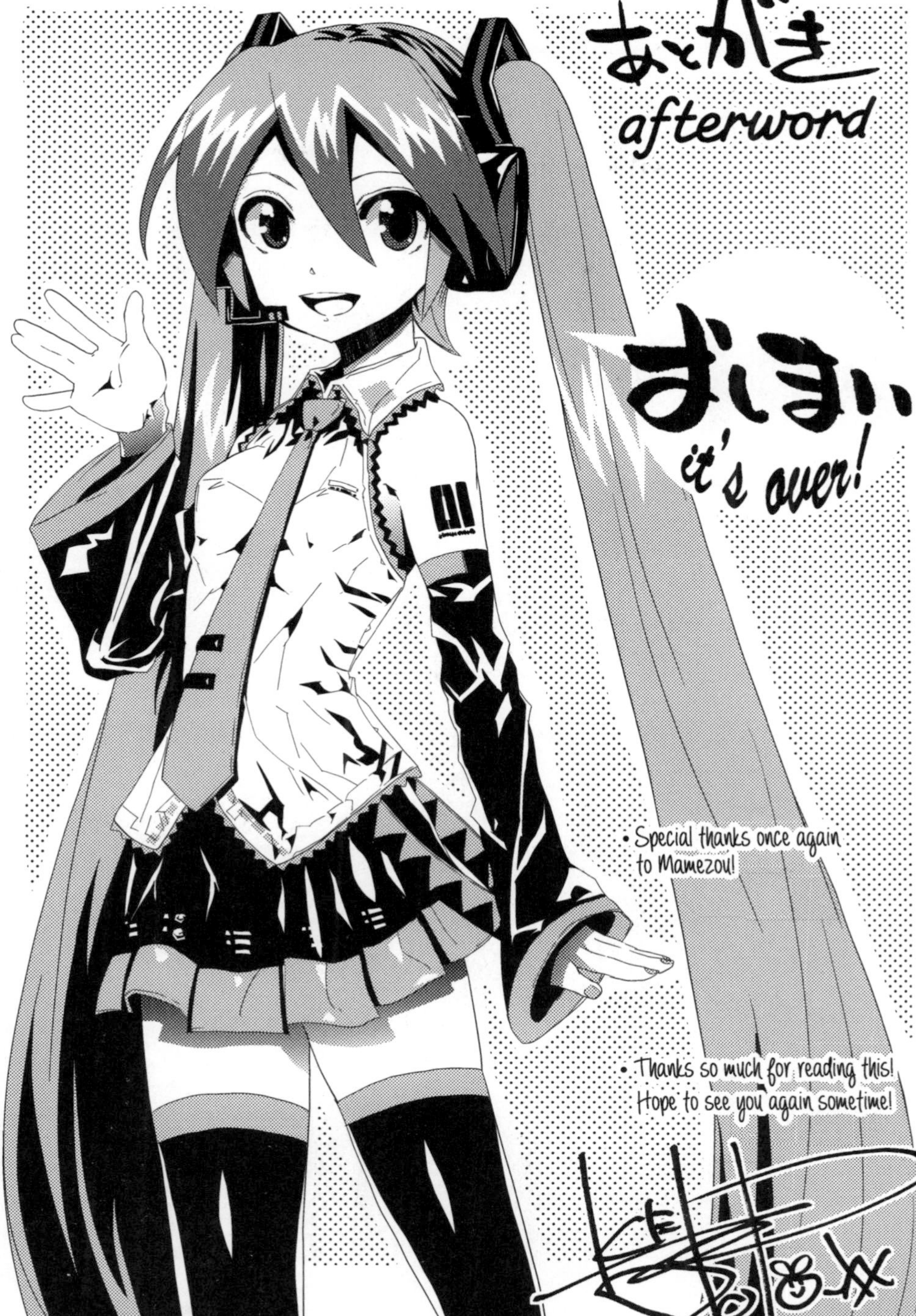
あとがき
afterword
おしまい
it's over!
• Special thanks once again to Mamezou!
• Thanks so much for reading this! Hope to see you again sometime!

UNOFFICIAL HATSUNE MIX

STORY AND ART BY KEI

EDITOR
CARL GUSTAV HORN

TRANSLATION BY
MICHAEL GOMBOS

LETTERING AND RETOUCH BY
JOHN CLARK

DESIGNER
SANDY TANAKA

PRESIDENT AND PUBLISHER
MIKE RICHARDSON

English-language version produced by Dark Horse Comics

UNOFFICIAL HATSUNE MIX Volume 1, 2, 3
© 2008, 2009, 2010 KEI © Crypton Future Media, INC. www.piapro.net **piapro** This book is published with the approval of Crypton Future Media. VOCALOID is a trademark of Yamaha Corporation registered in the United States and other countries. Originally published in Japan in 2008, 2009, 2010 by JIVE Ltd., Tokyo. English translation rights arranged with JIVE Ltd., Tokyo, through TOHAN CORPORATION, Tokyo. All rights reserved. No portion of this publication may be reproduced or transmitted, in any form or by any means, without the express written permission of Dark Horse Comics LLC. Names, characters, places, and incidents featured in this publication either are the product of the author's imagination or are used fictitiously. Any resemblance to actual persons (living or dead), events, institutions, or locales, without satiric intent, is coincidental. Dark Horse Manga™ is a trademark of Dark Horse Comics LLC. All rights reserved. Dark Horse is a part of Embracer Group.

PUBLISHED BY DARK HORSE MANGA
A DIVISION OF DARK HORSE COMICS LLC
10956 SE MAIN STREET
MILWAUKIE, OR 97222

DARKHORSE.COM

TO FIND A COMICS SHOP IN YOUR AREA, VISIT COMICSHOPLOCATOR.COM

FIRST EDITION: August 2014
ISBN 978-1-61655-412-5

20 19 18 17 16 15 14
Printed in China

MIX
Paper from
responsible sources
FSC® C016973

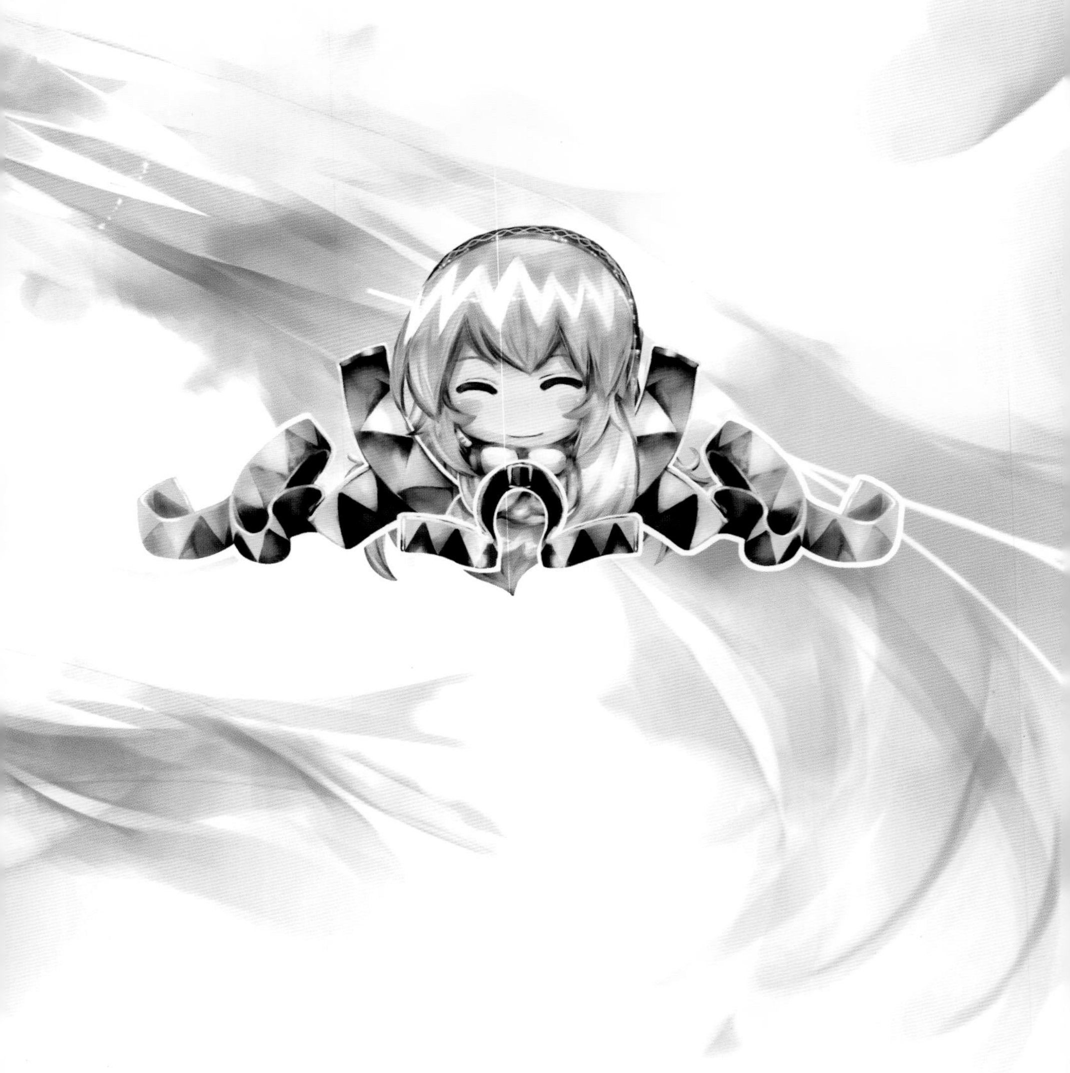

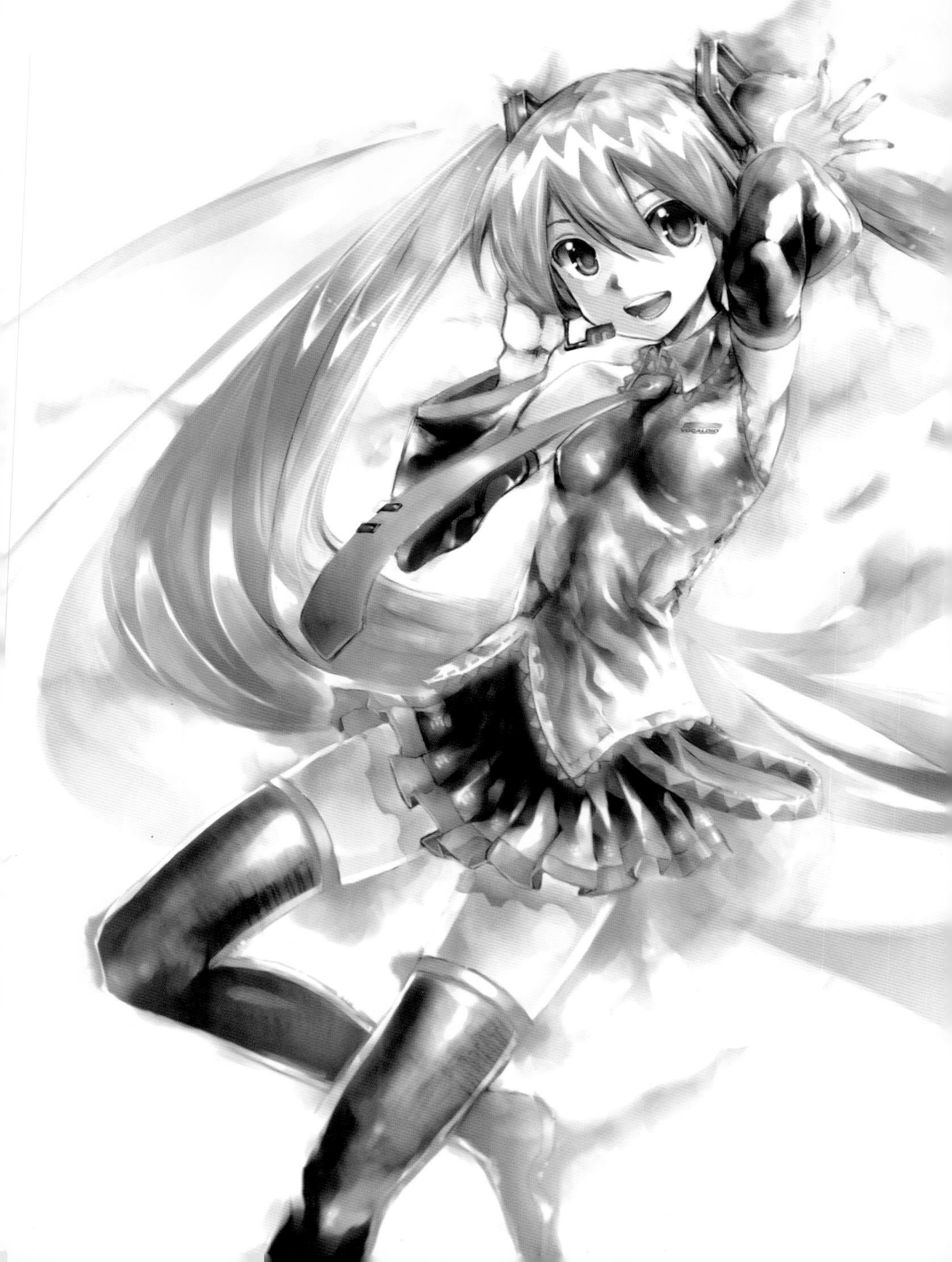
VOCALOID

HATSUNE MIKU: ACUTE
Art and story by Shiori Asahina
Miku, Kaito, and Luka! Once they were all friends making songs—but while Kaito might make a duet with Miku or a duet with Luka, a love song all three of them sing together can only end in sorrow!

ISBN 978-1-50670-341-1 | $10.99

HATSUNE MIKU: RIN-CHAN NOW!
Story by Sezu, Art by Hiro Tamura
Miku's sassy blond friend takes center stage in this series that took inspiration from the music video "Rin-chan Now!" The video is now a manga of the same name—written, drawn, and edited by the video creators!

VOLUME 1
978-1-50670-313-8 | $10.99

VOLUME 2
978-1-50670-314-5 | $10.99

VOLUME 3
978-1-50670-315-2 | $10.99

VOLUME 4
978-1-50670-316-9 | $10.99

HATSUNE MIKU: MIKUBON
Art and story by Ontama
Hatsune Miku and her friends Rin, Len, and Luka enroll at the St. Diva Academy for Vocaloids! At St. Diva, a wonderland of friendship, determination, and even love unfolds! But can they stay out of trouble, especially when the mad professor of the Hachune Miku Research Lab is nearby . . . ?

ISBN 978-1-50670-231-5 | $10.99

UNOFFICIAL HATSUNE MIX
Art and story by KEI
Miku's original illustrator, KEI, produced a best-selling omnibus manga of the musical adventures (and misadventures!) of Miku and her fellow Vocaloids Rin, Len, Luka, and more—in both beautiful black-and-white and charming color!

ISBN 978-1-61655-412-5 | $19.99

HATSUNE MIKU: FUTURE DELIVERY
Story by Satoshi Oshio, Art by Hugin Miyama
In the distant future, Asumi—a girl who has no clue to her memories but a drawing of a green-haired, ponytailed person—finds her only friend in Asimov, a battered old delivery robot. The strange companions travel the stars together in search of the mysterious "Miku," only to learn the legendary idol has taken different forms on many different worlds!

VOLUME 1
ISBN 978-1-50670-361-9 | $10.99

VOLUME 2
ISBN 978-1-50670-362-6 | $10.99

WHO'S THAT GIRL WITH THE LONG GREEN PONYTAILS YOU'VE BEEN SEEING EVERYWHERE? IT'S HATSUNE MIKU, THE VOCALOID—THE SYNTHESIZER SUPERSTAR WHO'S SINGING YOUR SONG!

AVAILABLE AT YOUR LOCAL COMICS SHOP OR BOOKSTORE

DarkHorse.com

HATSUNE MIKU

KEEP YOUR HANDS OFF EIZOUKEN!

By Sumito Oowara

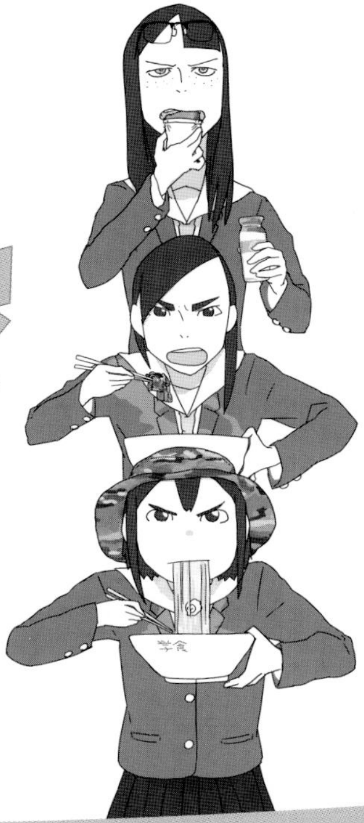

Asakusa loves to design worlds. Mizusaki loves to animate. Kanamori loves to make money! And at Shibahama High, they're known as Eizouken—a club determined to produce their own science fiction anime! But with no budget and a leaky warehouse for a studio, Eizouken is going to have to work hard—together!—and use their imaginations if they want to create their vision of the ultimate world.

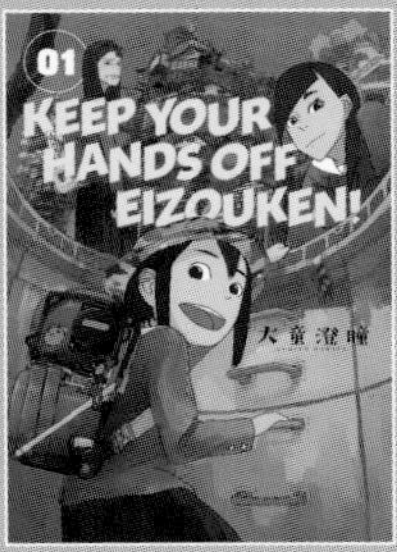
01
KEEP YOUR HANDS OFF EIZOUKEN!
大童澄瞳

VOLUME 1
ISBN 978-1-50671-897-2
$12.99

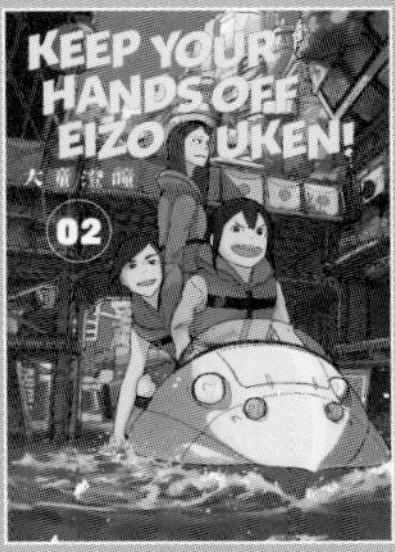
KEEP YOUR HANDS OFF EIZOUKEN!
大童澄瞳
02

VOLUME 2
ISBN 978-1-50671-898-9
$12.99

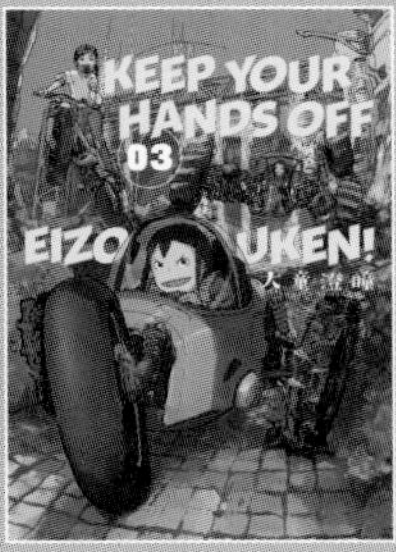
KEEP YOUR HANDS OFF
03
EIZOUKEN!
大童澄瞳

VOLUME 3
ISBN 978-1-50671-899-6
$12.99

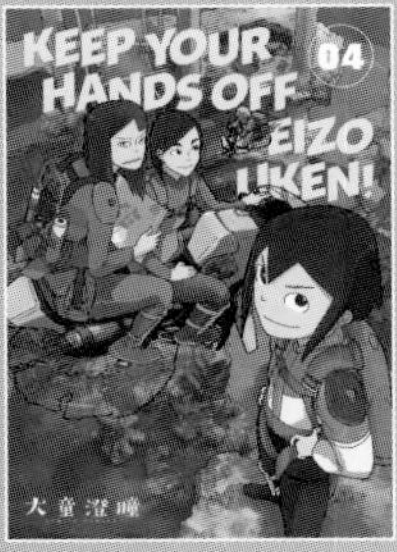
KEEP YOUR HANDS OFF
04
EIZOUKEN!
大童澄瞳

VOLUME 4
ISBN 978-1-50673-149-0
$14.99

AVAILABLE AT YOUR LOCAL COMICS SHOP OR BOOKSTORE

To find a comics shop near you, visit comicshoplocator.com. For more information or to order direct, visit darkhorse.com. *Prices and availability subject to change without notice.

EMANON

FROM KENJI TSURUTA, THE ARTIST OF THE
EISNER-NOMINATED *WANDERING ISLAND*,
AND THE AWARD-WINNING JAPANESE
SCIENCE FICTION AUTHOR SHINJI KAJIO!

Emanon is the eternal stranger who belongs here
more than any of us— a woman possessing a
mind that evolved over the entire history of life
on earth, and who carries within her over three
billion years of memories. Set in 1960s and 70s
Japan, *Emanon* tells of her encounters with the
lives of people who can no more forget her, than
she can forget any person. Drawn in both
Tsuruta's elegant black-and-white linework and
his signature painted color, *Emanon* is a literary
SF manga at the intersection of life, memory,
family, and existence.

VOL. 1 : **MEMORIES OF EMANON**
    ISBN 978-1-50670-981-9 - 192 pages

VOL. 2 : **EMANON WANDERER
    PART ONE**
    ISBN 978-1-50670-982-6 - 216 pages

VOL. 3 : **EMANON WANDERER
    PART TWO**
    ISBN 978-1-50670-983-3 - 240 pages

VOL. 4 : **EMANON WANDERER
    PART THREE**
    ISBN 978-1-50673-383-8 - 240 pages

$14.99 EACH!

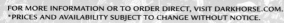

Wandering island

FROM THE ARTIST OF *EMANON*—
AN EISNER-NOMINATED TALE OF EXPLORATION AND ADVENTURE

Mikura Amelia is a free-spirited young woman who operates an air delivery service. When her beloved grandfather passes away suddenly, Mikura discovers he had been obsessed with the legend of an island that seems to appear and disappear in the Pacific. Soon the obsession becomes her own, and Mikura turns explorer . . . but what is she truly searching for?

WANDERING ISLAND
Story and art by Kenji Tsuruta

Vol. 1: ISBN 978-1-50670-079-3 | $14.99
Vol. 2: ISBN 978-1-50671-021-1 | $14.99

Ms. Koizumi loves ramen noodles.

The original manga that inspired the anime series from Crunchyroll!

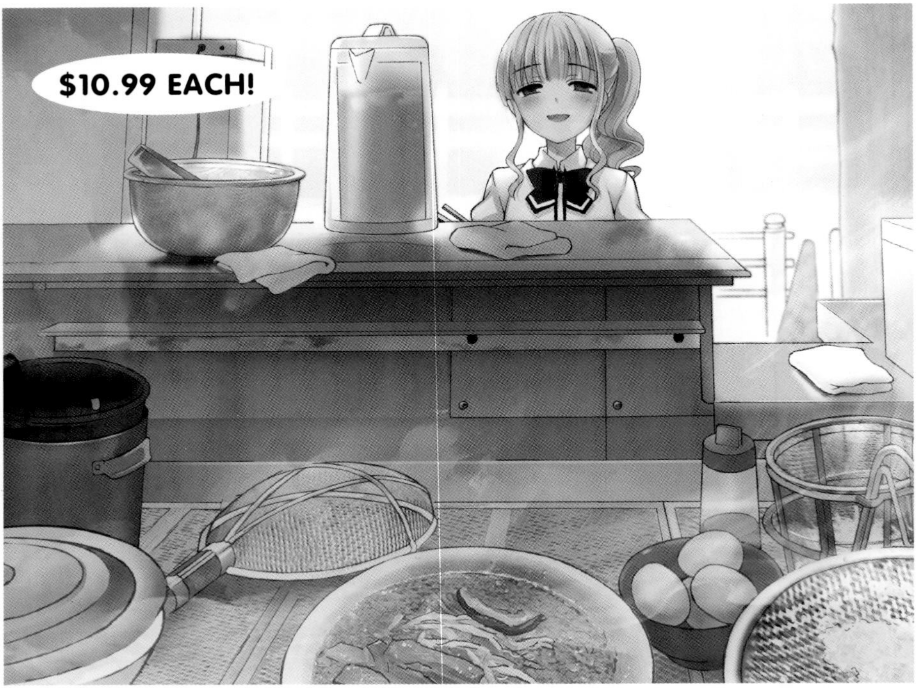
$10.99 EACH!

Ms. Koizumi loves ramen noodles . . . and Yu likes Ms. Koizumi! But she soon discovers that the only way to get closer to this cool, mysterious transfer student is to become her pupil on the path of ramen!

Translated by Japanese chef Ayumi Kato Blystone, *Ms. Koizumi Loves Ramen Noodles* is a fun food manga that shows you all around the authentic ramen culture of everyday Japan, from crazy home-cooked versions to famous restaurants reached by bullet train! Do you know about sauce vs. broth? How to pair sushi with ramen? Or even sweet ramen dishes like chocolate, pineapple, and ice cream? You soon will—and with bonus notes on real ramen shops to visit, this manga will leave you hungry for more!

VOL. 1 | ISBN 978-1-50671-327-4 | 136 pages ♥ **VOL. 2** | ISBN 978-1-50671-328-1 | 136 pages

VOL. 3 | ISBN 978-1-50671-329-8 | 136 pages

AVAILABLE AT YOUR LOCAL COMICS SHOP OR BOOKSTORE

To find a comics shop near you, visit comicshoplocator.com. For more information or to order direct, visit darkhorse.com. *Prices and availability subject to change without notice.

ALSO BY SATOSHI KON

Gifted anime director Satoshi Kon (*Paprika*, *Paranoia Agent*, *Tokyo Godfathers*, *Millennium Actress*, *Perfect Blue*) died tragically young in 2010. But before he directed those unforgettable films, he was a manga artist, and Dark Horse is honored to remember Kon with the release of some of his most significant books.

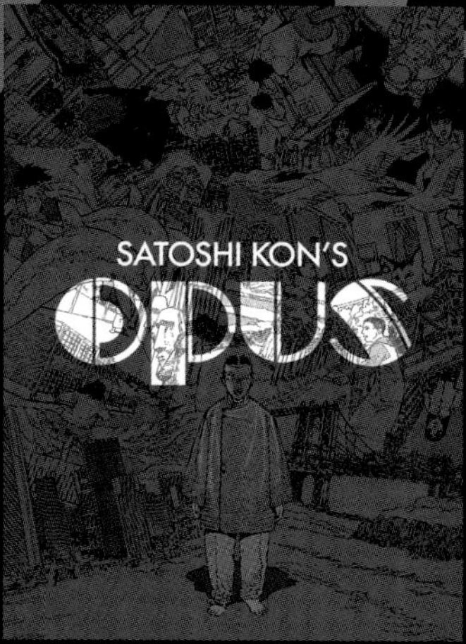
SATOSHI KON'S
OPUS

SATOSHI KON'S OPUS

OPUS contains the mastery of both realism and surrealism that would make Kon famous, as a manga artist planning a shocking surprise ending to his story gets literally pulled into his own work—to face for himself what he had planned for his characters!

ISBN 978-1-61655-606-8

$19.99

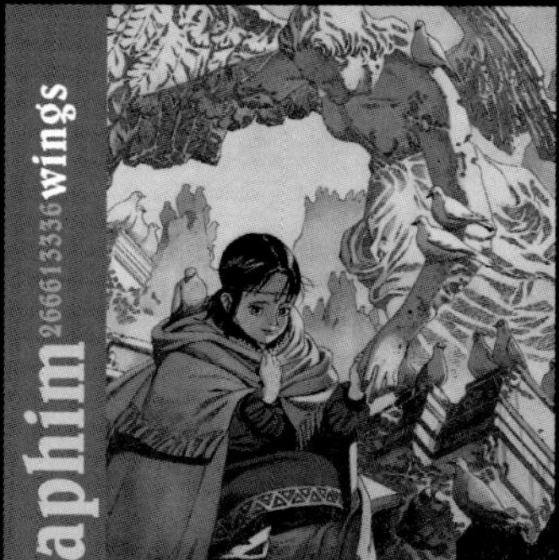
seraphim 266613336 wings
mamoru oshii
satoshi kon

SERAPHIM 266613336 WINGS

With Mamoru Oshii

Two of the most acclaimed anime directors of all time, *Ghost in the Shell*'s Mamoru Oshii and Satoshi Kon, collaborated on a work of manga: *Seraphim 266613336 Wings*. *Seraphim* is the story of a future earth devastated by the "Angel Plague," a pandemic that induces apocalyptic visions in the afflicted even as it ossifies their bodies into hauntingly beautiful seraphic forms . . .

ISBN 978-1-61655-608-2

$19.99

AVAILABLE AT YOUR LOCAL COMICS SHOP OR BOOKSTORE
TO FIND A COMICS SHOP NEAR YOU, VISIT COMICSHOPLOCATOR.COM
For more information or to order direct: •On the web: DarkHorse.com
•E-mail: mailorder@darkhorse.com •Phone: 1-800-862-0052 Mon.–Fri. 9 AM to 5 PM Pacific Time.

DarkHorse.com

GOU TANABE

These moody and evocative manga volumes strike directly at the dark heart of the Cthulhu mythos, with all the fear and wonder for which they have become famous! These graphic adaptations of some of H.P. Lovecraft's most infamous stories of cosmic horror (and the intrepid adventurers who just can't leave well enough alone) will unsettle and delight in equal measure!

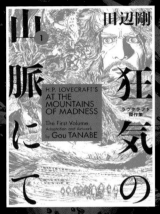

H.P. LOVECRAFT'S
AT THE MOUNTAINS OF MADNESS
VOLUME 1 | ISBN 978-1-50671-022-8 | $19.99
VOLUME 2 | ISBN 978-1-50671-023-5 | $19.99

H.P. LOVECRAFT'S
THE HOUND AND OTHER STORIES
ISBN 978-1-50670-312-1 | $12.99

DARK HORSE MANGA

H.P. Lovecraft's the Hound and Other Stories
2019–2022 © Gou Tanabe
H.P. Lovecraft's At the Mountains of Madness
2019–2022 © Gou Tanabe
First published in Japan by
KADOKAWA CORPORATION ENTERBRAIN
English translation rights arranged with
KADOKAWA CORPORATION ENTERBRAIN
through TOHAN CORPORATION, Tokyo. All rights
reserved. Dark Horse Manga is a trademark of Dark
Horse Comics LLC. All rights reserved. (BL7066)

the KUROSAGI corpse delivery service

黒鷺死体宅配便

OMNIBUS EDITIONS

Five young students at a Buddhist university find there's little call for their job skills in today's Tokyo . . . among the living, that is! But their studies give them a direct line to the dead—the dead who are still trapped in their corpses, and can't move on to the next incarnation! Whether death resulted from suicide, murder, sickness, or madness, the Kurosagi Corpse Delivery Service will carry the body anywhere it needs to go to free its soul!

"Nobody does horror-comedy comics better than Otsuka and Yamazaki"

—Booklist

Each 600+ page omnibus book collects three complete volumes of the series!

Vol. 1:
Contains vols. 1–3, originally published separately.
ISBN 978-1-61655-754-6 $24.99

Vol. 2:
Contains vols. 4–6, originally published separately.
ISBN 978-1-61655-783-6 $24.99

Vol. 3:
Contains vols. 7–9, originally published separately.
ISBN 978-1-61655-887-1 $24.99

Vol. 4:
Contains vols. 10–12, originally published separately.
ISBN 978-1-50670-055-7 $24.99

Vol. 5:
Contains vols. 13 and 14, originally published separately, plus the previously unpublished vol.15.
ISBN 978-1-50671-484-4 $24.99

AVAILABLE AT YOUR LOCAL COMICS SHOP OR BOOKSTORE!
To find a comics shop in your area, visit comicshoplocator.com
For more information or to order direct, visit DarkHorse.com

DARK HORSE MANGA
DarkHorse.com

Corpse Delivery Service © 2002–2022 EIJI OTSUKA OFFICE © HOUSUI YAMAZAKI. First published in Japan by KDAOKAWA SHOTEN Publishing Co., Ltd.,Tokyo. English translation rights arranged with KADOKAWA SHOTEN Publishing Co., Ltd., Tokyo, through TOHAN CORPORATION, Tokyo. Dark Horse Manga is a trademark of Dark Horse Comics LLC. All rights reserved. (BL 7001)

STOP!

THIS IS THE BACK OF THE BOOK!

This manga collection is translated into English, but arranged in right-to-left reading format to maintain the artwork's visual orientation as originally drawn and published in Japan. If you've never read comics this way before, take a look at the diagram below to give yourself an idea of how to go about it. Basically, you'll be starting in the upper right-hand corner, and will read each word balloon and panel moving right to left. It may take a little getting used to, but you should get the hang of it very quickly. Have fun! If this is the millionth manga you've read this way, never mind. ^_^

1
ONEE-CHAN? RIN...?
ALL OUT
2
Y-YOU WERE RIGHT...
3
...WHY DID I EVEN BOTHER COMING HERE?
sob sob
4
WELL...
5
...MAYBE SO YOU COULD GET THIS...?
6
IS IT BECAUSE YOU FEEL OBLIGED TO...?
7
NO, SILLY. IT'S BECAUSE VALENTINE'S IS A DAY FOR GIVING CHOCOLATES TO SOMEONE...
8
...YOU LOVE.

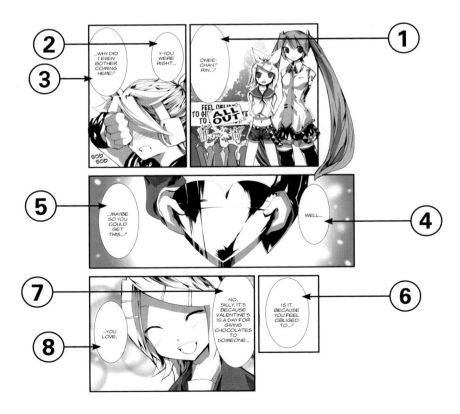